Communications in Computer and Information Science   1026

Commenced Publication in 2007
Founding and Former Series Editors:
Phoebe Chen, Alfredo Cuzzocrea, Xiaoyong Du, Orhun Kara, Ting Liu,
Krishna M. Sivalingam, Dominik Ślęzak, Takashi Washio, and Xiaokang Yang

More information about this series at http://www.springer.com/series/7899

Fisseha Mekuria · Ethiopia Nigussie ·
Tesfa Tegegne (Eds.)

Information and Communication Technology for Development for Africa

Second International Conference, ICT4DA 2019
Bahir Dar, Ethiopia, May 28–30, 2019
Revised Selected Papers

 Springer

Editors
Fisseha Mekuria
Council for Scientific and Industrial
Research
Meraka ICT Institute
Pretoria, South Africa

Ethiopia Nigussie ⓘ
Department of Future Technologies
University of Turku
Turku, Finland

Tesfa Tegegne
ICT4D Research Center
Bahir Dar University
Bahir Dar, Ethiopia

ISSN 1865-0929   ISSN 1865-0937 (electronic)
Communications in Computer and Information Science
ISBN 978-3-030-26629-5   ISBN 978-3-030-26630-1 (eBook)
https://doi.org/10.1007/978-3-030-26630-1

This Springer imprint is published by the registered company Springer Nature Switzerland AG
The registered company address is: Gewerbestrasse 11, 6330 Cham, Switzerland

Preface

The proceedings of the second edition of the International Conference on ICT for Development for Africa (ICT4DA), which was organized by the Bahir Dar Institute of Technology in Ethiopia, is hereby presented. The proceedings of ICT4DA 2019 conference was compiled in collaboration with international experts. The conference brings together researchers, developers, and practitioners of ICT for development from around the world. The theme of this year's ICT4DA was "Enabling Sustained & Inclusive Economic Development through ICT Innovations."

The conference program consisted of oral presentations of 29 technical papers. These technical papers were accepted out of the 69 papers received during a paper submission period. The papers were accepted after a technical peer review process. The technical papers were categorized into three tracks, Track 1: Intelligent Systems and Data Science; Track 2: Wireless Communication and Emerging Networking; and Track 3: Natural Language Processing. Besides the technical paper presentations, the technical program also featured three keynote speeches. The three keynote speakers along with the title of the talks were, Keynote 1: "Internet-of-Things for Development in Africa: opportunities and challenges," Adj. Prof. Ethiopia Nigussie from University of Turku, Finland; Keynote 2: "Impact of Noise on Big Data Analytics," Prof. Bhekisipho Twala from University of Johannesburg, South Africa; and Keynote 3: "International collaboration in ICT4D research and development: opportunities, challenges and best practices for sustainability," Prof. Judy van Biljon from University of South Africa. In addition, two panel discussions under the following themes were included, Panel 1: "The role of Emerging ICT Technologies as a Solutions Revolution for the UN-SDGs," chaired by Prof. Fisseha Mekuria and Dr. N. Bekele-Thomas; and Panel 2: "Emerging ICT technologies in Support of Sustainable Bilateral & Institutional Collaboration in Africa," chaired by Dr. Ethiopia Nigussie.

The coordination of the ICT4DA 2019 conference was led by the General Chair of ICT4DA, Dr. Tesfa Tegegne, and the contribution of the Organizing Committee was instrumental for the success of the conference. It was also a great pleasure to work with such an excellent Organizing Committee, and we thank them for their hard work in organizing and supporting the conference. In particular, the Technical Program Committee (TPC) members, led by the TPC chair, Prof. Fisseha Mekuria (CSIR, South Africa), and co-chair, Adj. Prof. Ethiopia Nigussie (University of Turku), who completed the peer-review process of the technical papers and created a high-quality technical program relevant to the conference's theme. We are also grateful to all the authors who submitted their papers, contributing to the success of the ICT4DA 2019 conference. We strongly believe that the ICT4DA 2019 conference provided a good forum for all involved researchers, developers, practitioners, and public/private industry players to discuss ICT technology trends and research aspects that are relevant for socioeconomic development. We also expect that future ICT4DA conferences will be as successful and stimulating, as the conference series continues to develop and deliver relevant and innovative contributions to the global knowledge in ICT4D as presented in this volume.

April 2019   Tesfa Tegegne
                                                                  Fisseha Mekuria
                                                              Ethiopia Nigussie

Organization

Organizing Committee

Proceedings Chair

Tesfa Tegegne   ICT4D Research Center, BiT, Bahir Dar University, Ethiopia

Program Chairs

Fisseha Mekuria   CSIR, South Africa
Ethiopia Nigussie   University of Turku, Finland

Program Committee

Surafel Lemma Abebe	Ababa Institute of Technology, AAU, Ethiopia
Habtamu Abie	Norwegian Computing Centre, Norway
Esubalew Alemneh	Bahir Dar Institute of Technology, Bahir Dar University, Ethiopia
Andres Arcia Moret	University of Cambridge, UK
Dereje Yohannes Ashenafi	Addis Ababa Science and Technology University, Ethiopia
Yaregal Assabie	Addis Ababa University, Ethiopia
Hailu Beshada Balcha	ICT4D Research Center, BiT, Bahir Dar University, Ethiopia
Elefelious Getachew Belay	University of Milan, Italy
Imed Ben Dhaou	University of Monadtir, Tunisia
Desta Berihu	Bahir Dar Institute of Technology, Bahir Dar University, Ethiopia
Mekuanint Agegnehu Bitew	Bahir Dar Institute of Technology, Bahir Dar University, Ethiopia
Taye Girma Debelee	Addis Ababa Science and Technology University, Ethiopia
Sigurd Eskeland	Norwegian Computing Centre, Norway
Ali Farooq	University of Turku, Finland
Gebeyehu Belay Gebremeskel	Bahir Dar Institute of Technology, Bahir Dar University, Ethiopia
Samson Gejibo	University of Bergen, Norway
Fekade Getahun	Addis Ababa University, Ethiopia
Liang Guang	Huawei Technologies, China
Antti Hakkala	University of Turku, Finland
Mesfin Kifle	Addis Ababa University, Ethiopia
Swaib Kyanda Kaawaase	Makerere University, Uganda
Khalid Latif Dentsu	Aegis Network, Finland

Adane Mamuye	University of Gondar, Ethiopia
Fisseha Mekuria	CSIR, South Africa
Fikreselam Gared Mengistu	Bahir Dar Institute of Technology, Bahir Dar University, Ethiopia
Luzango Mfupe	CSIR, South Africa
Drake Patrick Mirembe	Uganda Technology and Management University (UTAMU), Uganda
George Musumba Dedan	Kimathi University of Technology, Kenya
Edward Mutafungwa	Aalto University, Finland
Behailu Shiferaw Negash	University of Turku, Finland
Ethiopia Nigussie	University of Turku, Finland
Petri Sainio	University of Turku, Finland
Hussien Seid	Addis Ababa Science and Technology University, Ethiopia
Zelalem Sintayehu Shibeshi	University of Fort Hare, South Africa
Abiot Sinamo	Mekelle University, Ethiopia
Tesfa Tegegne	ICT4D Research Center, BiT, Bahir Dar University, Ethiopia
Woubishet Zewdu Taffese	Aalto University, Finland
Mesfin Belachew Tefera	Agricultural Transformation Agency, Ethiopia
Dereje Teferi	Addis Ababa University, Ethiopia
Nanda Kumar Thanigaivelan	University of Turku, Finland
Mthulisi Velempini	University of Limpopo, South Africa
Ruth Wario	University of the Free State, South Africa
Hlabishi Kobo	CSIR, South Africa
Kula Kekeba	Addis Ababa Science and Technology University, Ethiopia
Mebiratu Beyene	ICT4D Research Center, BiT, Bahir Dar University, Ethiopia

Web Chair

| Mebiratu Beyene | ICT4D Research Center, BiT, Bahir Dar University, Ethiopia |

Publicity Chairs

| Abinew Ali | Bahir Dar Institute of Technology, Bahir Dar University, Ethiopia |
| Elias Wondemagen | Bahir Dar Institute of Technology, Bahir Dar University, Ethiopia |

Organized by

ICT4D Research center, Bahir Dar Institute of Technology, Bahir Dar University, Bahir Dar

Hosted by

Bahir Dar University

Sponsoring Institutions

Contents

Wireless and Mobile Computing Track

Natural Language Processing Track

Artificial Intelligence and Data Science Track

A Novel Method of Pre-processing Using Dental X-Ray Images by Adaptive Morpho Histo Wavelet Denoising (AMHW) Method

S. G. Saju Simon[1]($\boxtimes$), X. Felix Joseph[2], Ararso Taye Waktola[2], and Derera Senay[2]

[1] Department of Biomedical Engineering, Noorul Islam University, Kumaracoil, India
sajusimon.nta@gmail.com
[2] Department of Electrical and Computer Engineering, Bule Hora University, Hagere Mariam, Ethiopia
felixjoseph75@gmail.com, arasotaye@yahoo.com, derjan06@gmail.com

Abstract. Dental X-ray imaging is one of the medical imaging techniques used by the dental practitioners. This method uses dental X-ray diagnostic file. This has been found to be very helpful to dental doctors to get more information on the oral disease in patients. X-ray radiation is used for wide range of medical imaging applications. Once the technique becomes a success, it produces good quality X-ray images. The X-ray image is very essential for the treatment planning and procedure for the patients. The X-ray image has lot of artifacts which can be removed through various preprocessing methods. In this paper a novel method for preprocessing is introduced through the fusion of adaptive histogram, morphological enhancement and wavelet de-noising (AWHM). The input X-ray image is initially checked with various other existing preprocessing methods such as adaptive histogram equalization, un sharp masking, Gaussian low pass and high pass methods, high pass adaptation, morphological enhancement, contrast enhancement and wavelet de-noising. AWHM is giving better result than all the other methods. The existing method and novel method is compared with various non-reference parameters and the reference parameter. The result of the novel method is better than all other existing methods. The Contrast Per Pixel technique is used for analyzing the pixel brightness in a more better way. Since the CPP value is higher in AMHW method it indicates AMHW method is the best among the pre-existing methods.

Keywords: Adaptive histogram equalization · Un sharp masking · Gaussian low pass and high pass methods · High pass adaptation · Morphological enhancement · Contrast enhancement and wavelet de-noising · AMHW method

1 Introduction

Dental X-ray imaging is a very useful diagnostic method in dentistry. Dental X-ray imaging is only possible on dental lesions. The dental diseases are characterized by variations in the trabecular pattern. These alterations involve depth of the trabecular

© Springer Nature Switzerland AG 2019
F. Mekuria et al. (Eds.): ICT4DA 2019, CCIS 1026, pp. 3–10, 2019.
https://doi.org/10.1007/978-3-030-26630-1_1

pattern, shape and the X-ray absorption amount in the lesion caused by dental tissues. The output from dental X-ray devices, provides high resolution X-ray images. It produces confused trabecular pattern structure and contrasts difference in the region of interest of dental lesions by human observers. Many researches have shown that minute dental lesion in the dental X-ray image cannot be detected by a dentist. The important applications in X-ray diagnosis in dentistry is periodontal bone loss. Periodontitis is one of the most common diseases present and also gingivitis is caused by plaque accumulation. Gingiva inflammation leads the destruction of soft and hard dental tissues. The limitations of X-ray diagnosis in dental diseases is already mentioned above. Image processing using computer is used to detect variations in contrasts; the dentist provides creativity and intelligence to make sense of the findings for the recognition process.

2 Proposed Work

In this paper a novel method for preprocessing is introduced. The existing preprocessing methods are adaptive histogram equalization filtering, unsharp masking filtering, Gaussian low pass filtering, Gaussian high pass filtering, high pass adaptation filtering, morphological enhancement filtering, contrast enhancement filtering and wavelet de-noising filtering.

Adaptive histogram equalization (AHE) is a medical image pre-processing techniques which is used to improve the pixel contrast in images. The AHE differs from normal histogram equalization which uses adaptive technique. The AHE redistributes the lightness value of the images and it is used to improve the normal contrast of the pixels and enhances the edges in each region. The adaptive step function performs Contrast Limited Adaptive Histogram Equalization (CLAHE). The enhancement method is better than regular histogram equalization for dental X-ray images.

Unsharp masking is an image sharpening preprocessing method which is found in digital image processing software such as Matlab. The name Unsharp is derived from the technique which uses a negative or blurred image to create a mask of the input image. Unsharp mask is combined with the input image and creates a new image which is less blurred than the input X-ray image. The function qspecial produces various predefined filters in the form of correlation kernels. This filter has the effect of masking edges and the fine details in the dental X-ray images.

```
A = imread('orginalimage.jpg');
b = qspecial('unsharp');
A2 = imfilter(A, b);
Imshow(A), ('Original Image')
Figure, imshow(A2), title('Filtered Image')
```

Gaussian filter is one of the preprocessing filters whose impulse function is Gaussian function. Such filters have the property of having no overshoot for step function input and minimizes the rise- fall time. They are based on frequency filter and time domain filter. Gaussian filter modifies the input X-ray images by mathematical convolution with Gaussian function and is called as weierstrass transforms. The Gaussian low pass and high pass helps minimizes the problem in the ideal low pass and high pass filter. The ringing effect which appears at the point because of some point transmission between one colour to another cannot be defined precisely (Fig. 1).

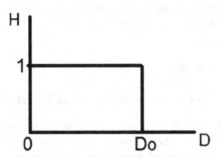

Fig. 1. Graphical representation of ideal low pass filter

The above graph represents an ideal low pass filter. The point Do does not tell whether the value would be 0 or 1. In order to reduce the effect, an ideal low and high pass filter followed by Gaussian low pass and high pass filter is introduced. The filtering concept in Gaussian low pass filter remains same but the transitions become different and smoother. The filtered output from the input dental X-ray image is represented graphically. From the smooth curve, the value of Do can be defined accurately y The Gaussian high pass filter and the ideal high pass filter are similar concepts, but the conversion is smoother in the former case (Fig. 2).

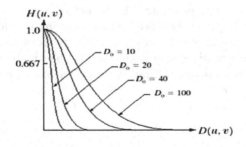

Fig. 2. Contrast enhancement denoising

Morphological enhancement is a non – linear operation in image processing. This operation is related to the shape and features of the dental X-ray image. These pre-processing operations are not based on numerical values but are based on their pixel values. This preprocessing is relative ordering of pixel values of dental X-ray images. This morphological enhancement can be used for gray scale images because the unknown light transfer function and minor interest on the proper pixel value.

The contrast enhancement is an image preprocessing techniques. It is a suitable method for X-ray dental image preprocessing. It helps to improve the details in X-ray images that are under study.

The wavelet – De-noising preprocessing method is used for removing artifacts from X-ray dental images. Artifacts can be white noise or random noise with no coherent noise produced by the algorithms or imaging machines.

3 Result and Discussion

3.1 Adaptive Morpho – Histo Wavelet Denoising (AMHW)

The AMHW is a novel method of preprocessing technique used for medical image processing from the fusion of adaptive morphological histogram wavelet de-noising. The algorithm of AMHW produces better result than any other method which was discussed earlier. The result is checked with various non – reference parameters such as Histogram graphical representation, Contrast per Pixel matrix, Blur Matrix and Anisotropic Quality Measure, Average Information.

The non – reference parameters provide more clarification from the end result. From the histogram graphical representation the novel method provides more information from the input medical dental X-ray image. The AMHW method provides more information than all other existing methods through the graphical representation as shown in the figures (Table 1).

Contrast Per Pixel or CPP which is used to quantify the quality of dental X-ray images. CPP is the average intensity difference between a pixel and the neighboring pixel. Contrast is the difference in color that makes them distinguishable. Contrast is determined by the difference in the brightness and color of the X-ray image. In case of blur matrix, it is the comparing of variations between the adjacent pixels before and after preprocessing with low pass filters. In the initial step, the computation of the intensity variations between adjacent pixels of the input image is to be done (Fig. 3).

Then apply a low pass filter and compute the variations between the adjacent pixels. Finally these intensity variations help to calculate the blur in the input dental X-ray image. If the change between dental X-ray image and the blurred image is more, it can

Table 1. Compression result of AMHW method and various other methods

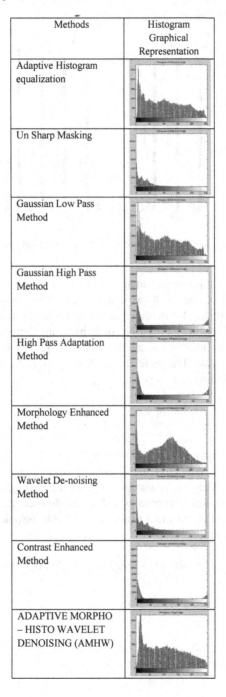

Methods	Histogram Graphical Representation
Adaptive Histogram equalization	
Un Sharp Masking	
Gaussian Low Pass Method	
Gaussian High Pass Method	
High Pass Adaptation Method	
Morphology Enhanced Method	
Wavelet De-noising Method	
Contrast Enhanced Method	
ADAPTIVE MORPHO – HISTO WAVELET DENOISING (AMHW)	

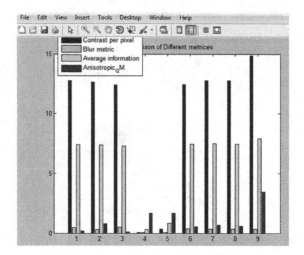

Fig. 3. Graphical representation of various matrix results

be concluded that the preprocessed image is sharp or if the variation between the blurred image and the input dental X-ray image is less, it means that the pre-processed image was already blurred. From the average information matrix, the amount of information from the X-ray image must be coded by using compression algorithm. The less entropy dental X-ray images having lot of black sky, very less contrast and large runs of pixels with the same. The perfectly flat X-ray images have entropy value zero. The entropy is calculated by the formula

$$\text{Entropy} = - \sum_i P_j \text{Log}_2 P_j$$

From the above equation, the probability (P_i) is the difference between two neighbouring pixels and is equal to I, and $\log_2$ is the base 2 logarithms. The anisotropic 'Q' matrix is a no reference quality matrix. Here the input image is compared with its flipped, angle shifted version. The process is done for different angles. In each step the renyi entropy is taken between them (Table 2). The Anisotropic Quality measure is calculated using the formula

$$Q = (1/1 - \text{alpha})) * \log2 \,(\text{sum of renyi entropy})$$

Table 2. Final results of novel method (AMHW) and other existing methods

Methods	Pre Processed Image
Adaptive Histogram equalization	
Un Sharp Masking	
Gaussian Low Pass Method	
Gaussian High Pass Method	
High Pass Adaptation Method	
Morphology Enhanced Method	
Wavelet De-noising Method	
Contrast Enhanced Method	
Adaptive Morpho – Histo Wavelet Denoising (AMHW)	

4   Conclusion

Based on the above said preprocessing methods AMHW, Adaptive morpho histo wavelet de-noising makes a better quality result image after removing artifacts. The image from AMHW produces high pixel brightness than all other existing methods. Therefor the further processing of this dental image produces more information and it will be useful for analysis and diagnosis. Thus the novel AMHW method is a better method for preprocessing to get better result than any other existing method. This image which is obtained is very helpful for the further segmentation.

References

1. Yaroslavsky, L.P.: Local adaptive image restoration and enhancement with the use of DFT and DCT in a running window. In: Proceedings of SPIE, Bellingham, vol. 2825, pp. 2–13 (1996)
2. Mehdizadeh, M., Dolatyar, S.: Study of effect of adaptive histogram equalization on image quality in digital preapical image in pre apex area. Res. J. Biol. Sci. **4**(8), 922–924 (2009)
3. Regezi, J.A.: Periapical disease: spectrum and differentiating features. J. Calif. Dent. Assoc. **27**, 285–289 (1999)
4. Langland, O.E., Langlais, R.P. Preece, J.W.: Principles of Dental Imaging. Lippincott Williams & Wilkins (2002)
5. Noor, M., Khalid, N.E.A., Ali, M.H., Numpang, A.D.A.: Enhancement of soft tissue lateral neck radiograph with fish bone impaction using adaptive histogram equalization (AHE). In: The 2nd International Conference on Computer Research and Development (2010)
6. Khalid, N.E.A., Manaf, M., Aziz, M.E., Ali, M.H.:CR images of metacarpal cortical edge detection-bone profile histogram approximation method. In: Intelligent and Advanced Systems, 2007, ICIAS 2007, pp. 702–708, 25–28 Nov 2007
7. Sakata, M., Ogawapp, K.: Noise reduction and contrast enhancement for small-dose x-ray images in wavelet domain. In: Presented at the Nuclear Science Symposium Conference record (NSS/MIC) (2009)
8. Aufrichtig, R., Xue, P.L.: Dose efficiency and low-contrast detectability of an amorphous silicon X-ray detector for digital radiography. Phys. Med. Biol. **45**, 2653–2669 (2000)
9. Tiwari, R.B.: Dental X-ray image enhancement based on human visual system and local Image statistic. In: Proceeding of the International Conference of Image Processing, Computer Vision and Pattern Recognition, vol. I&II, pp. 100–106 (2006)
10. Gonzales, R.C., Woods, R.E.: Digital Image Processing, 2nd edn. Prentice Hall, Upper Saddle River (2002)
11. Thangavel, K., Manavalan, R., Aroquiaraj, I.L.: Removal of speckle noise from ultrasound medical image based on special filters: comparative study. ICGST-GVIP J. **9**(III), 25–32 (2009)
12. Pisano, E.D.: Contrast limits adaptive histogram equalization image processing to improve the detection of simulated speculations in dense mammograms. J. Digital Imag. **11**, 193–200 (1998)
13. Mahmoud, T.A., Marshall, S.: Medical image enhancement using threshold decomposition driven adaptive morphological filter. In: Presented at the 16th European Signal Processing Conference (EUSIPCO), Laussane, Swizerland (2008)
14. Foi, A.: Noise estimation and removal in MR imaging: the variance-stabilization approach. In: 2011 IEEE International Symposium on Biomedical Imaging: From Nano to Macro, pp. 1809–1814 (2011)
15. Grundland, M., Dodgson, N.A.: Decolorize: fast, contrast enhancing, color to gray scale on version. Pattern Recogn. **40**(11), 891–2896 (2007)

Knowledge Based System for Diagnosis and Treatment of Mango Diseases

Waltengus Birhanie[1(✉)] and Tesfa Tegegne[2]

[1] Assosa University, Assosa, Ethiopia
`walteharamaya@gmail.com`
[2] Bahirdar University, Bahirdar, Ethiopia

Abstract. Mango is one of the world's most important fruits of the tropical and subtropical countries and cultivated extensively as a commercial fruit crop. The mango fruit crop is also cultivated in all parts of Ethiopia. Mango trees in most parts of Ethiopia are developed from seedlings and are inferior in productivity and in fruit quality. Mango tree is attacked by different insects and diseases. With an end goal to address such issues and problems it is very essential to develop knowledge-based system that can provide advice for agriculture professionals and farmers to make possible diagnosis and treatment of mango diseases.

The aim of this study was developing knowledge based system for diagnosis and treatment of mango disease. Ambo Plant Protection Research Center and Assosa plant health clinic were selected area for data collection. Purposive sampling technique was utilized to choose domain experts for knowledge acquisition. In this way, in order to develop the proposed knowledge based system an implicit and explicit knowledge utilized and acquired through interview and document analysis respectively. The knowledge acquired through document analysis and interview is modeled using decision tree. The researchers used experimental research design to developed prototype system. The experiment was conducted using rule based technique. Finally, performance testing and user acceptance evaluation were performed. The performance according to the domain expert's evaluation is scored total of 81.8% and the user acceptance testing scored 86.29% performance. The overall performance of the system is 84.05%. The prototype system meets the objectives of the study. Updating the rules in the knowledge base of the system automatically, developing the system in local language with well designed user interface and applying other techniques are the future works of the study.

Keywords: Knowledge based system · Mango disease · Rule based system

1 Introduction

Agriculture is the corner stone of the development policy of the Government of Ethiopia. The country's economic development will depend, in large part on sustainable improvements in agriculture. Agriculture is the most critical sector in the Ethiopian economy since it straightforwardly bolsters around 85% of the population regarding business and occupation; it contributes around half of the nation's gross

F. Mekuria et al. (Eds.): ICT4DA 2019, CCIS 1026, pp. 11–23, 2019.
https://doi.org/10.1007/978-3-030-26630-1_2

domestic product (GDP) and it produces around 90% of the export earnings [1]. Agriculture is also the major source of food for the population and hence the prime contributing sector to food security [1, 2]. Ethiopia is characterized by having different agro-ecological zones and it accounts about a total area of 1.13 million km^2 [4]. A variety of fruit crops has been growing in different agro ecological Zones by small farmers, for subsistence and income generation. Mango is the most important fruit and it is the second in area coverage after banana in southern region and southwest of Ethiopia [5].

The area of mango production in the different regions is about 3789.47 ha in Oromia, 3375.89 ha in SNNPR, 652.56 ha in Benishangul Gumz, 246.85 ha in Amahara, 180.41 ha in Gambella, 44.5 ha in Dire Dawa, 33.52 ha in Somali, 118.20 in Tigray and 367.24 ha in Harari. The total area allotted for mango is about 8808.64 ha and the country annual production of mango from all mango grower regions is about 697,507 quintals [7]. Agriculture and plantation is an important and interesting research area everywhere in the world and Ethiopia is no exception. Nowadays available land area for a plantation is becoming scarce. This scarce resource is frequently wasted through our bad practices and improper management. Cultivation is a more economical but complex process. Diagnosis and treatment of mango fruit diseases for the maximum profit involves a sequence of tasks. These tasks and the whole process need a lot of expert knowledge and experience. But unfortunately, people having this type of knowledge are very limited. Their assistance is not available when the person who is going to cultivate needs it.

Knowledge based System is one of the important application-oriented branches of Artificial intelligence. The knowledge based systems approach attempts to model the domain knowledge of experts in their respective areas of specialization, for example, diagnosis, planning, forecasting etc. Expert System is based on the knowledge including not only models and data, but more emphasizing on experiences of domain experts [8].

A knowledge based expert System is an intelligent computer program that employs knowledge and inference procedures to address problems that are not easy enough to need human expertise for their solution. The knowledge necessary to perform at such level plus the inference procedures used can be thought of as a model of the expertise or the best practitioners in the field [9]. A knowledge based expert system is based on an extensive body of knowledge about a specific problem area. Knowledge is represented as data or rules that appear in syntax as physical patterns in electronic form in the knowledge base. The knowledge is represented as production rules in the form of condition-action pairs of IF—THEN format [10]. Knowledge engineers gather knowledge from domain experts and put it in such a form that system can use for inferring and reasoning using a knowledge representation technique. Marwaha [9] described as "the need of expert systems for technical information transfer in agriculture can be identified by recognizing the problems in using the traditional system for technical information transfer, and by proving that expert systems can help to overcome the problems addressed, and are feasible to be developed".

Farmers and agronomy expert require timely, accurate and location specific information in relation with different aspects of farming like the pests, diseases, weeds and fertilizer management, etc. for their crops from agricultural experts [12]. On the other hand, the complexity of a whole farming process is growing because it is constrained by many factors such as requirements, goals, regulations, etc. that farmer must satisfy or consider. To provide such information and to achieve an optimal crop plan, the automation is provided by computer-based systems termed as advisory systems. Knowledge based advisory system supports the farmers and experts in getting advices on many activities in farming process [11]. In this study, the researcher proposed knowledge based system to diagnosis and treat mango disease. It is an expert system that recommends farmers and agronomy experts about mango disease diagnosis and treatment.

2 Statement of the Problem

Fruit crops play an important role in the national food security of people around the world. They are generally delicious and highly nutritious, mainly of vitamins and minerals that can balance cereal-based diets. Fruits supply raw materials for local industries and could be sources of foreign currency. The mango fruit crop is cultivated in all parts of Ethiopia and while in southwest Ethiopia, mango is the first fruit crop grown [6]. The total area allotted for mango is about 8808.64 ha and the country annual production of mango from all mango grower regions is about 697,507 quintals [7]. But Mango tree is attacked by different insects and diseases such as, Anthracnose, Bacterial Black spot, Fruit fly, mango gall flies, Mango leaf coating, Mites, Mango seed weevil, Mealy bug, Powdery mildew, Scale, Spider mites, Mango tip borer, Stem-end rot, Termite, Thrips and White flies. Plant diseases are one of the most important reasons that lead to the destruction of plants and crops.

The major production constraints indicated by Bezu [13] were water shortage or erratic rainfall (79%) followed by disease and pest (75.7%) problems. Lack of knowledge and recommended production practices (nutrition, pruning, pest management etc.) and post-harvest losses were also noted as major problems of the mango growers. It is in agreement with CSA [3] report that stated mango production in Ethiopia fluctuates because of occurrence of diseases and lack of proper management [3]. Problems of pests and plant diseases are the main obstacles in increasing agricultural production. Damage occurs, both on the field during the cultivation process and warehouse storage. These conditions will significantly affect the income of farmers and the world's food supply. "Pests and plant diseases are still a complicated issue for owners of the plants, especially for those who do not have the basic knowledge of crop cultivation. The problem becomes more complex due to many types of pests and plant diseases. Identifying the plant diseases is not easy task; it needs experience and knowledge of plant and their diseases. Moreover, it requires accuracy in describing the symptoms of plant diseases [18]. To differentiate the cause of damage to crops, long enough experience are needed so there is no error in concluding the cause in order to take the right decision in an effort to control" [14]. In many countries today, farming has become technologically advanced and expert systems are widely used in the field of agriculture. In this way farmers can get experts opinion on their specific problems like selection of most suitable crop variety, diagnosis or identification of crop/livestock disorder, suggestion, and tactical decisions throughout production cycle from the expert system [15].

Although many applications have been developed for crop production; disease and pest management abroad, in Ethiopia there are very few works done to design knowledge base system for agricultural sector. However, to the best of the researchers' knowledge, no research has been done to apply knowledge based system for diagnosis and treatment of mango disease particularly in Ethiopia. Therefore, the researchers have been developed knowledge based system in mango fruit in order to diagnosis various disease and taking management decisions for the benefit of farmers and experts. Identifying, diagnosis and treating the mango diseases for the maximum yield production involves a sequence of tasks. These tasks and the whole process need a lot of expert knowledge and experience. But unfortunately, people having this type of knowledge are very limited. Their assistance is not available when the person who is going to cultivate needs it.

As a result, the aim of the study is to develop knowledge based system for diagnosis and treatment of mango disease. At the end this study will response the following research questions:

- What suitable domain knowledge exists in an explicit and tacit form for diagnosis and treatment of mango diseases?
- What are the appropriate trends or techniques taken by experts to diagnosis mango disease?
- How to model and represent the acquired knowledge for developing the knowledge-based systems?

3   Objective of the Study

3.1   General Objective

The general objective of this study is to develop a knowledge based system for mango diseases diagnosis and treatment using rule based reasoning approach.

3.2   Specific Objectives

- To acquire knowledge from domain experts and codified sources required for developing the system
- To model and represent the acquired knowledge using appropriate knowledge representation technique.
- To develop prototype knowledge based system for mango diseases diagnosis and treatment.
- To evaluate the overall performance of the prototype knowledge based system.

4 Scope of the Study

The scope of this study was limited to develop a prototype system for diagnosis and treatment of mango diseases and providing possible suggestions for decision making. The activity concerned in conducting this work includes literature review, problem identification, knowledge acquisition, modeling, representation and implementation or encoding. The prototype consists of knowledge base, inference engine, user interface, explanation facility and rule based reasoning mechanism. Even though the prototype includes all these components this system has limitation in automatic updating of the knowledge base by the user when the new factors are introduced.

5 Significance of the Study

The system developed enables to reduce the problem of the limited numbers of experts in giving preliminary diagnosis and treatment of Mango diseases and motivate further researches to be conducted in the area of agricultural expert system. The immediate beneficiaries of the study are primary agriculture workers and agriculture professionals or agronomist. Particularly, the prototype will have great significance to teach primary agriculture extension workers, general agronomy experts in order to have well understanding about mango diseases. As a result, those agriculture workers can use the system in diagnosing mango diseases on primary agriculture sectors where highly qualified mental professionals are unavailable. Additionally, the prototype can be used for agriculture professionals as a guide.

6 Methodology of the Study

6.1 Research Design

Dipanwita [16] used experimental research design to develop intelligent medical system for diagnosis of common disease by acquiring tacit and explicit knowledge from domain knowledge expert. The domain knowledge was acquired and then represented. The acquired and represented knowledge was inserted into the knowledge base. Based on the result of evaluation of inserted knowledge it changed again and again. In addition, during prototype development stages the sequence of the facts and rules were changes again and again until it fitted the best sequence. Moreover, the way to test and evaluate the performance of the prototype system by feeding the cases and records the result to compare it against with the decision made by domain experts in similar settings. Therefore, experimental research design and methodology is used in this study.

6.2 Sources of Data and Data Collection Methods

The researchers used primary and secondary data as source of information. In this study explicit and tacit knowledge is acquired from both codified (documented) sources and non-codified (non-documented) sources respectively. Non-codified sources of knowledge are acquired from agronomy experts (agronomists) who work in the Ambo Plant Protection Research Center and Assosa plant clinic research center by using interview and critique knowledge elicitation methods to filter the acquired knowledge. Similarly, codified sources of knowledge such as agricultural books, training manuals and journal agriculture articles are acquired by using document analysis technique.

6.3   Knowledge Modeling and Representation Method

Knowledge modeling is a cross disciplinary approach to capture and model knowledge. In this study the acquired knowledge was modeled using decision tree and represented using production rule which is one of the knowledge representation techniques. The prototype system uses backward chaining also called goal-driven chaining which begins with possible solutions or goals and tries to gather information that verifies the solution. The knowledge engineer collects Mango disease symptoms or cases and models it by using decision tree structure. For this research the knowledge representation method, rule based is chosen because it clearly demonstrates the domain knowledge. In a rule based system much of the knowledge is represented as a rule that is as conditional sentences relating statements of facts with one another. The following sample rules in the knowledge base of the prototype are expressed with natural language rules IF … THEN …

Rule 1:

If the symptom of mango diseases is Leaf spots
And there is flower, twig, and blossom blight
And Fruit rot
And "Tear staining" is that develops when spore-laden water droplets from infected twigs and panicles wash over and infects the fruit.
And the panicles (flower clusters) start to show as a small black or dark-brown spots
Then Anthracnose is diagnosis

Rule 2:

If the symptom of mango diseases is Leaf spots
And there is flower, twig, and blossom blight
And there is a profusion of rust-colored microscopic "spores" on the leaf surface
And Rust-red "spore" masses will also develop on infected stems
And Altitude is high
Then the Alga Spot (Red Rust, Green Scurf) is diagnosis

Rule 3:

If the symptom of mango diseases is Leaf spots
And there is flower, twig, and blossom blight
And Fruit rot
And "Tear staining" is that develops when spore-laden water droplets from infected twigs and panicles wash over and infects the fruit.
And the panicles (flower clusters) start to show as a small black or dark-brown spots

And the rot produces dark streaking of the water-conducting tissue
Then stem-end rot is diagnosis

Rule 4:

If the symptom of mango diseases is Leaf spots
And there is flower, twig, and blossom blight
And Bacterial leaf spot is noticed on the leaves as angular water soaked spots or lesions, surrounded by clear holes.
And longitudinal cracks also develop on the petioles.
And Cankerous lesions appear on petioles, twigs and young fruits.
Then the Bacterial Canker is diagnosis

These rules are added to the knowledge base using prolog programming language. These rules capture common evidence of problems associated with the symptoms for mango disease diagnosis. The detail is presented in the knowledge base.

6.4   KBS Implementation Tool

To develop the knowledge-based system, Prolog programming language was used. Specifically, SWI-Prolog editor has been chosen for this study. SWI-Prolog editor has debugging tool and it is flexible. It is portable to many platforms, including UNIX/Linux platforms and Windows. Additionally, it is non-commercial version of Prolog.

7   Implementation and Experimentations

This section presents the process of the knowledge based system development. The section also addresses coding and evaluation of the system. The represented knowledge is encoded and implemented using appropriate programming tool.

7.1   Architecture of the Proposed Prototype

Architecture defines how the system is constructed, describes what the critical components are and how they fit together. Architecture design is done in this section as well, which incorporates the knowledge base (facts and rules), explanation facility, inference mechanism, the knowledge base editor and the user interface. This proposed KBS has knowledge acquisition subsystem, knowledge base that contains facts and rules, backward inferencing, user interface and explanation facilities components as shown in the Fig. 1.

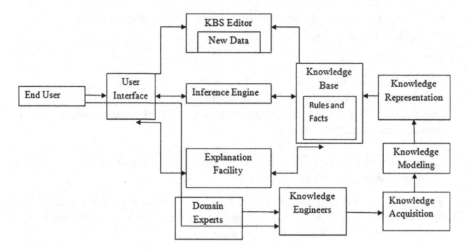

Fig. 1. Architecture of the developed prototype system

The knowledge acquisition subsystem that performs the eliciting and structuring of knowledge from the pathologist and relevant document is presented in the previous section. The core components of the developed KBS system are shown in Fig. 1. The main program that contains the inferencing, requests user to load the knowledge base and starts the identification process. The backward inferencing mechanism identifies disease through asking the characteristics features or symptom of each mango disease. The user interacts with the knowledge base system via user interface. Knowledge base is a set of rules or the encoded knowledge about diagnosis and treatment of mango disease. The validated knowledge is represented in the form of rules by rule-based representation technique and the rules are codified to the knowledge base of the prototype system using Prolog programming language. An inference mechanism consists of search and reasoning methods that enable the system to find solutions and if necessary, provide justification for its answers.

In addition, the system is capable of proving explanation for sign and symptoms of diseases of mango. But, the KBS does not learns and update its fact base when new facts were generated during reasoning.

The following Fig. 2 shows sample of how the prototype system accepts user response and provide the final advice as a solution for diagnosis and treatment. To interact with this system first the users must start the system by typing fruit followed by full stop (fruit).

```
            WELCOME TO KNOWLEDGE BASED MANGO DIAGNOSIS AND TREATMENT SYSTEM
                          PREPARED BY: WALTANIGUS B.
========================================================================================

Do you want to get diagnosis and treatment of mango disease? >>yes.
Please respond the questions by using yes or no, write <yes> for yes or <no> for no:
========================================================================================

Have you seen Leaf spots and black spot at panicles and fruit?>>|: yes.

Is there flower, twig, and blossom blight? >>|: yes.

Is there "Tear staining" that develops when spore laden water droplets from in-
fected twigs and panicles wash over and infects the fruit? >>|: no.

profusion of rust-colored microscopic |spores| on the leaf surface and Rust-red
|spore| masses will also develop on infected stems? >>|: yes.

Cankerous lesions appear on petioles, twigs and young fruits and longitudinal-
cracks also develop on the petioles? >>|: no.

Is white superficial powdery fungal growth on leaves, stalks of panicles, flowers
and young fruits and affected flowers and fruits drop pre-maturely? >>|: no.

Drying of twigs and branches followed by complete defoliation, which gives the tree
an appearance of scorching  by fire and Internal browning in wood tissue is observ-
ed? >>|: no.

The mango plant is infected by Alga Spot (Red Rust, Green Scurf)
If you want to see more about Alga Spot enter 1 from the key board:
If you want to see treatment enter 2 from the key board:
If you donot want to -see anything enter 0 from the key board:
|: 1.
=> A parasitic alga, Cephaleuros virescens, incites this relatively minor disease of mango
=> Leaf spots start as circular green-gray areas that eventually turn rust red as the alga
 rust-colored microscopic |spores| on the leaf surface.
do you want to see the next>>>>>>>>??|: █
```

Fig. 2. How the prototype system accepts user response and provide diagnosis

One of the interesting features of knowledge based systems is their ability to explain themselves. Given that the system knows which rules were used during the inference process, it is possible for the system to provide those rules to the user as a means for explaining the results. In this study, explanation facilities such as; What, Why and Why-Not are incorporated [17]. A prototype system can provide facility of what signs and symptoms mean which is used during diagnosis and why it is selected as the signs and symptoms of mango diseases for diagnosis and treatments. Figure 4 show how a prototype system provides explanation facility for the signs and symptoms.

Researchers used backward chaining reasoning strategy. The explanation facility helps the Knowledge Based System to clarify and justify why such a digression might be needed [19].

```
          WELCOME TO KNOWLEDGE BASED SYSTEM FOR MANGO DISEASE DIAGNOSIS AND TREATMENT
                           PREPARED BY: WALTANIGUS B.
==============================================================================================

Do you want to get diagnosis and treatment of mango disease? >>no.

WELL COME TO KNOWLEDGE BASED RECOMMENDER SYSTEM FOR MANGO DISEASE

press 1 to know History of Mango and Major Mango Diseases in Ethiopia.
----------------------------------------------------------------------------
press 2 to know Major Symptoms of Each Disease of Mango Plant.
----------------------------------------------------------------------------
press 3 to know Insects and Pests those Negatively Affect the Production of Mango.
----------------------------------------------------------------------------
press 4 to know How Prevent Insects and Pests
----------------------------------------------------------------------------
press 5 to know What Cultural management practices are used by Ethiopian Farmers.
----------------------------------------------------------------------------
press 0 to exit from the keyboard
|: 5.
Grower farmers were opted to use variety of cultural practices in efforts to stop/mitigate
the effect of the pest in mango production.

The cultural practices used by Farmers are:

 -Pruning | to inhibit the transmission of the pest

 -Removing the infected trees- not to contaminate other normal tree or part of the tree

 -Smoking of mango tree for chess out the pest from the tree

 -Washing with soluble ash and soap

 -Thinning | for spacing among the planted trees through removing the tree,

 -Burning

 -Keeping the sanitary of soil under the tree

Please insert your choice number from the list>>>>>>>>??|: █
```

Fig. 3. Sample dialogues which shows how prototype system provides information about cultural management practices

```
        WELCOME TO KNOWLEDGE BASED MANGO DIAGNOSIS AND TREATMENT SYSTEM

                        PREPARED BY: WALTANIGUS B.

=================================================================================== >

Do you want to get diagnosis and treatment of mango disease? >>yes.
Please respond the questions by using yes or no, write <yes> for yes or <no> for no:

=================================================================================== >

Please give (yes.) or (no.) answer to the following questions and
If the questions are unclear you can ask by entering (what.) and (why.)

Have you seen Leaf spots and black spot at panicles and fruit?(yes/no/what): |:what.

This is to mean have you seen a small round or roundish mark, holes which appears on the leaves

of the plant. ?(yes/no/why): |: why.

Because leaf spot is the most important symptom of mango disease. So! have seen spots?(yes/no):
|: yes.
```

Fig. 4. Sample dialogues that shows how prototype system gives explanation facility

8   Testing and Evaluation of the Prototype System

To evaluate the performance of the system, two set of testing was conducted. In the first case, the system is tested for its performance on how diagnosis and providing treatment of mango diseases. In the second cases, the evaluation was conducted to evaluate the system's acceptance level by the users through directly interacting with the system. To test the performance of the system we have employed confusion matrix and the performance of the system was computed using recall, precision and F measure for measuring effectiveness. The accuracy of the prototype system is calculated as 81.8% based on the test cases which indicate that the prototype has a very good performance and the average evaluation result filled by the domain experts in the domain area is 86.29%, respectively. The overall performance of the prototype system is 84.05%. The users of the system had given a promising feedback. In general, the testing and evaluation result of the prototype system has achieved the objectives of the study. However, additional study is needed to bring complete implementation and use of knowledge-based system for diagnosis and treatment of mango diseases.

9   Conclusion and Recommendation

9.1   Conclusion

In Ethiopia most of the peoples are farmers, it's believed that more than 80% of the population depends on agriculture and it looks many challenges like plant diseases. Mango diseases are problematic plant diseases all over the word. It causes the destruction of mango plant in many countries especially in tropical area and developing countries where there is scarcity of agronomy experts (pathologist) and tools for diagnosis and treatments. Therefore it's logical to develop a knowledge based expert system to emulate the knowledge of agricultural experts. It gets attention on diagnosis and treatment of diseases. So, Rule based reasoning was used for the development of a prototype KBS and the developed prototype correctly assists agricultural professionals and farmers. However, in order to make the system applicable in the domain area, some adjustments like automatically updating the rules in the knowledge base of the system and incorporating a well designed user interface are needed.

9.2   Recommendation

The following recommendations were given based on the observed opportunities and uncover areas by this research.

- Integrating the application of data mining techniques with knowledge-based systems
- Developing the system in local language, like in Amharic, Afan Oromo and Tigrigna are recommended as future work.
- Last of all, this knowledge base system is not self learning, in the future learning component should be integrated

References

1. ICARDA: Ethiopia and ICARDA. Ties that Bind, no. 29. ICARDA, Aleppo, Syria, iv +20 pp. En (2010). ISBN 92-9127-245-0
2. Mellor, J., Dorosh, P.: Agriculture and the economic transformation of Ethiopia development strategy and governance division: Ethiopia strategy support program 2. In: International Food Policy Research Institute (2010)
3. CSA: Area and Production of Major Crops. Sample Enumeration Survey. Addis Ababa, Ethiopia (2009)
4. Berhe, K., Dessalegn, Y., Baredo, Y., Teka, W., Tegegne, A.: Smallholder-based fruit seedling supply system for sustainable fruit production in Ethiopia. Improving Productivity and Market Success (IPMS) of Ethiopia Farmers Project, Addis Ababa, Ethiopia (2007)
5. Central Intelligence Agency (CIA): Banana in Southern Region of Ethiopia, pp. 119–134 (2010)
6. Etisa, E., Ayele, L., Tadesse, D.: Review on the status of some tropical fruits in Ethiopia. In: Proceeding of the Inaugural and First Ethiopian Horticultural Society Conference, Addis Ababa, Ethiopia, pp. 39–44 (2006)
7. C.S.A (Central Statistics Authority), Addis Ababa, Ethiopia (2012/2013)
8. Dubey, S., Pandey, R., Gautam, S.: Literature review on fuzzy expert system in agriculture. Int. J. Soft Comput. Eng. (IJSCE) **2**, 289–290 (2013)
9. Marwaha, S.: AGRIdaksh—a tool for developing online expert system. Division of Computer Applications, Indian Agricultural Statistics Research Institute, p. 17 (2012)
10. Turban, E., Aronson, J.E.: Decision Support and Intelligent Systems. Prentice Hall International Inc., New Jersey (1990)

11. Ranjan, Y.: Farm advisory system for farmers of Northeastern States of India. Int. J. Innov. Eng. Technol. (IJIET) **5**, 169–172 (2015)
12. Islam, S.N.: Expert System on Wheat Crop Management. Development of Expert System through AGRIdaksh, New Delhi (2004)
13. Bezu, T.: Production Scenarios of Mango (Mangifera indica L.) in Harari Regional State, Eastern Ethiopia. Science, Technology and Arts Research Journal, Haramaya University, Dire Dawa, Ethiopia (2014)
14. Dewanto, S., Lukas, J.: Experet system for diagnosis pest and disease in fruit plants. In: EPJ Web of Conferences, Universitas Bina Nusantara, Computer Engineering Department, Jakarta, Indonesia (2014)
15. Mercy, P., Rani, N.: Expert systems in agriculture: a review. J. Comput. Sci. Appl. **3**(1), 59–71 (2011)
16. Dipanwita, B., Bairagi, S., Panse, N., Shinde, N.: Disease diagnosis system. J. Comput. Sci. Inform. **1**(2), 48–51 (2011)
17. Dagnew, G.: Designing a knowledge based system for blood transfusion (2012)
18. Ambisa, B.: Develop a knowledge based system for coffee diseases and pests' diagnosis and treatment, vol. 1, no. A thesis submitted in partial fulfillment of the requirements for the degree of Master of Information science (2012)
19. Gebremariam, S.: A Self-Learning Knowledge Based System for Diagnosis and Treatment of Diabetes (2013)

A Genetic Algorithm-Based Approach for Test Case Prioritization

Getachew Mekuria Habtemariam and Sudhir Kumar Mohapatra[✉]

Addis Ababa Science and Technology University, Addis Ababa, Ethiopia
getachewmekuria19@gmail.com,
sudhirmohapatra@hotmail.com

Abstract. Software maintenance is the most important and expensive activity in the process of Software Development Life Cycle (SDLC). In the maintenance stage, after modification, the software goes through verification and validation. Regression testing is performed at the maintenance stage of SDLC to ensure that the old functionalities are working perfectly. Test case prioritization, which is about making a sequence of the test case, is one of the important parts of regression testing. Test case prioritization(TCP), which is a class of NP-hard problem, can have a better solution using soft computing approach as per no-free-lunch theorem [1]. The same no-free-lunch theorem states that a soft computing approach yields a case-specific result. In this article, we propose a novel genetic algorithm approach to solve the TCP problem. The proposed algorithm is experimentally compared with random technique. For the experiment three-benchmark program from the software artifact infrastructure repository is selected. From the experiment, it was found that the Average Percentage of Fault Detection (APFD) of the GA technique gives a better result than random technique. Also, an experiment was conducted to record the execution time with different numbers of generations. The results confirm that the result is not directly dependent on the number of generation.

Keywords: Software maintenance · Regression testing ·
Test case prioritization · Soft computing · Genetic algorithm

1 Introduction

The effective application of ICT depends not only on the efficiency of the computer but also robustness of the software that programs the computer. Accuracy and security of software are two important features, which must be ensured, for robustness of the software. Thus, every software has to undergo the process of testing before it is subjected to use. Needless to say, that if a software is inefficient or lacks security then the very purpose behind its development is not only defeated, the economy of the organization is also adversely impacted. The software with high functionality needs stringent testing methodology [2, 3]. The growing size and complexity of the software make regression testing very important in the maintenance stage of SDLC. Test suite prioritization, an important part of regression testing is used to find an ordering of test cases. Test case prioritization promises to detect the faults early in the re-testing process. Thus, finding an optimal order of execution of the selected regression test cases

© Springer Nature Switzerland AG 2019
F. Mekuria et al. (Eds.): ICT4DA 2019, CCIS 1026, pp. 24–37, 2019.
https://doi.org/10.1007/978-3-030-26630-1_3

will maximize the error detection rates at less time and cost. Early detection of error helps us in concluding the testing process in case of time constraints.

A substantial part of the project cost is incurred in testing, which is around 30–50% [4]. As exhaustive testing is practically impossible, early detection of error helps to circumvent the testing process without going for the method of retest all [4]. Looking into the round the clock use of the software, the tester has the responsibility to make the software fault-free [5, 6]. Rather than using retest all approach, it would be better to partially test the software with those test cases, which have the possibility of revealing the maximum number of faults [7]. While the partial selection of the test case will not be always effective, in a resource-constrained environment it is implicit. The strategy of test case prioritization encompasses the execution of the test cases with the highest priority, consistent with some fitness metric and thereby leading to their eventual ordering [8–10]. Rothermel et al. outlined the test case prioritization problem and propounded numerous solutions [9].

The test case prioritization problem, defined (by Rothermel et al.) is stated underneath:

The Test Case Prioritization (TCP) Problem:
Given: T, a test suite; PT, the set of permutations of T; f, a function from PT to the real numbers.
Problem: Find $T' \in PT$ such that $(\forall T'' (T'' \in PT) (T'' \neq T') [f(T'') \geq (T'')])$
The PT represents all permutation of the test case set T and f is a function used to generate an ordering.

Solution to combinatorial problem with minimum cost is best possible using soft computing techniques [11]. Evolutionary algorithms, of which genetic algorithms (GAs) are a subclass, rely on search. GAs use Darwin's "Survival of fittest" theory. In the case of scheduling problems, of which regression test case prioritization is an example, the application of GAs has been shown to be effective [12]. Thus, prioritization techniques based on fault exposing potential of the test case is essentially heuristic [9]. The TCP, which is a class of knapsack-problem belongs to NP-hard [13]. In this research-article, we have tried to probe into the use of fault exposing potential of the test case for test case prioritization.

The organization of this paper is as follows. In Sect. 2 we have specified existing test case prioritization technique. In Sect. 3 an algorithm based on the genetic algorithm for test case reduction is proposed and discussed. The detail execution of the testing process is discussed in Sect. 4 followed by experiment and result discussion in Sect. 5. In the last section, the findings of the paper were summarized.

2 Related Work

Yadev et al. proposed a prioritization technique based fuzzy logic taking multiple factors into consideration [14]. The factors used are fault detection rate of program, execution time and requirement coverage. Khatibsyarbini et al. review the published article on TCP and the review document gives an insight of test case prioritization research [15]. Elbaum et al. and Rothermel et al. used different criteria for test case prioritization in [9, 16]. The authors' used code coverage, branch coverage and calculable ability to reveal faults. These algorithms are the greedy based algorithm. Srivastava and Thiagarajan, using the change created by the program as a basic criterion, proposed TCP [17]. They assumed that for quick detection of error the test case should be ordered in terms of their high potential to cover the affected elements of the program. A model-based prioritization was proposed by Panigrahi and Mall [18, 19]. They made use of UML diagram to propose two TCP techniques, viz., S-RTP and H-RTP. The proposed method considered the affected nodes in the ESDG (Extended System Dependency Graph) model. The number of affected nodes exercised by a test case was used as the base to derive the sequence of the test case. The authors propose a white-box test case prioritization, selection, and minimization considering the reuse context [20]. In order to prioritize regression test cases, Li et al. further proposed other greedy strategies including the 2-optimal strategy [21].

The coverage of the relevant slice of a test case was used as a criterion for TCP by Jeffrey and Gupta [22]. They presented a greedy algorithm where the relevant slice was implemented. Relevant slice is a measure of the statements that influence or could influence the output of a program when executed on a regression test case [22]. Mohapatra et al. proposed a genetic algorithm-based TCP [24]. The multi objective prioritization they proposed was based on code coverage and severity of the test case. Smith et al. used call tree for TCP [23] while Mohapatra et al. used chemical reaction optimization [25] and ant colony optimization [26] for the purpose. A new test case prioritization algorithm is proposed to get better the rate of fault detection and cost reduction using Simulated Annealing (SA) [27]. Noguchi et al. proposed a framework using Ant Colony Optimization [28]. The proposed framework is prioritized test cases for black box testing on a new product using the test execution history collected from a similar prior product.

Various researchers have perused the pros and cons of numerous approaches to test case prioritization. As exemplary evidence, the influence of the greedy algorithm on test case prioritization was scrutinized by Rothermel et al. and conducted a thorough empirical study on the available greedy methods for TCP and found that the greedy strategy is always not suitable [9]. In the study, the authors experimentally proved that these greedy algorithms sometimes consume more time without producing an optimal result. This creates practical snag for the sole use of the greedy algorithm for TCP. In the backdrop of the above, the delving of the plausibility of applying soft computing approach for TCP by scrutiny of its NP-hard nature is an interesting proposition [13].

3   Proposed Algorithm

The algorithm creates a sequence of minimum test cases, capable of exposing all the faults in concert. Initially, the algorithm creates a chromosome of length two (*Chromolen* = 2). On this population, all the genetic operators are applied. If at any generation (epoch) any chromosome is able to expose all the faults then the algorithm stops and returns the sequence. Otherwise, the GA process starts for chromosome length three. The chromosome-length shifts to the $(l + 1)$ level in each iteration until a sequence with 100% fault exposing potential is detected. Once the algorithm generates a sequence the rest of the test cases (which are not in the sequence) may be added in any order.

Input:
1. T={Set of test case}
2. Test case fault detection details as a traceability matrix
3. P_c =Crossover probability
4. P_m =Mutation probability
5. maxGen= Maximum GA generation

Output:
Sequence of minimized test case dis-covering maximum faults(ρmin)

Abbreviations used:
cp: Crossover point
mp: Mutation point

Prio_GA(T, TR, maxGen, P_c, P_m)
```
Begin
1←2
Popsize←20
loop
InitialPopulation(Popsize,l)
g ← 1
loop
CalculateFitness(P,TR)
   Crossover($P_c$,P,l)
   Mutation($P_m$,P,l)
    If  (Any order of test suit dis-cover 100% fault)
      ρmin ← FindMax(P)
else
    g← g+1
until g<=maxGen
l← l+1
until l<= Chromolen
return ρmin
end
```

InitialPopulation(Popsize,Chromolen)
```
Begin
a←1
repeat
Pa ←{∅};
repeat
Pa ← Pa U { Randomly from T which was not in the chromosome}
until | Pa |<= Chromolen
```

```
i←i+1
until i<=Popsize
end
```

CalculateFitness(P,TR)

```
begin
i←1
loop
```

$$P_i = \frac{|\bigcup_{i=1}^{n} Ti \subseteq F|}{|F|}$$

```
i←i+1
until i<Popsize
end
```

Crossover(P_c, P, l)

```
begin
for P_c percentage of chromosome
generate cp ∴1<=sp<=l
at point cp exchange chromosome
end
```

Mutation(P_m, P, l)

```
begin
for P_m percentage of chromosome
generate mp ∴1<=sp<=l
replace a duplicate test case
with a test case which is not
present in that chromosome
end
```

FindMax(P)

```
begin
sort the population in
ascending order of their
fitness value.
end
```

3.1   Initial Population

The function *InitialPopulation (Popsize, Chromolen)* is responsible to generate the initial population. It will consider the population size and chromosome length as the parameters. Permutation encoding was used in our algorithm. The function created a single chromosome at a time (in one iteration of the loop), with the length same as *Chromolen* value. The method is employed with utmost care in order to avoid the duplication of the test cases in a chromosome. A typical case of chromosome <T6, T7, T9, T71, T23, T12, T21>, with *Chromolen = 7*, is represented in Fig. 1.

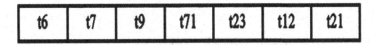

Fig. 1.   Example of chromosome generated using permutation encoding

3.2   Selection

Rank selection method was used to select the chromosome to move to the next epoch. The function *FindMax(P)* was used for this, it sorts the individual chromosome based on their fitness value in ascending order. After sorting it select the best chromosome.

3.3   Crossover

Single point crossover is used in the algorithm. The crossover probability, $P_c = 0.6$ was used. *Crossover (P_c, P, l)* function performed the crossover activity. It could randomly select a point between one and the length of the chromosome. This served as the crossover point. Chromosomal-exchanges at the cross over points generated new off springs, as exemplified in Fig. 2.

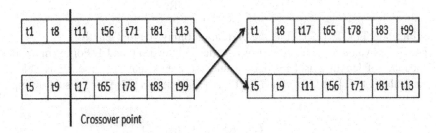

Fig. 2.   Single point crossover applied to the parent to generate children

3.4   Mutation

The *Mutation (P_m, P, l)* method was used to perform the mutation operation of GA. The role of this operator in the algorithm is to remove duplicate test case from the chromosome. Sometimes we get a duplicate test case in a chromosome after crossover. *Mutation (P_m, P, l)* checks a chromosome and if there is any duplicate test case identified, replaces it with a new test case. The number of chromosomes for which mutation is applied will be decided by the parameter P_m *i.e.*, the mutation probability. In the present work, we take *P_m = 0.4*. The mutation process we followed is depicted in Fig. 3.

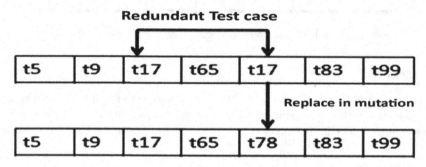

Fig. 3. Mutation operation applied to replace duplicate test case from chromosome

3.5   Fitness Function

This is the most important function, which decides the fitness of the chromosome to go to the next generation. The fitness function, used in the paper, relies on the Eq. (1)

$$\text{Fitness function} = \frac{|U_{i=1}^{n} Ti \subseteq R|}{|R|} \tag{1}$$

Subjects to $Ti \in T$, where T is the current chromosome of l length

The fitness value of each chromosome varies in between 0 and 1. For example, if a chromosome of length 2 is {T3, T5}. Table 1 presents that test case T3 is able to expose faults {f1, f3} and test case T5, {f3, f6}. The fitness value for the said example is

$$\textit{Fitness value} = \frac{|\{f1, f3\} \cup \{f3, f6\}|}{6} = \frac{4}{6} = 0.67$$

The Eq. (1) was applied using the logical OR operator. The TR matrix was used for the fitness calculation of each chromosome. To understand, let us take a chromosome of length two i.e. $T = \{t2, t4\}$ fitness value of T will be (based on TR matrix of Table 1)

$$t2 = \{011110\}$$
$$t4 = \{001001\}$$
$$\overline{\text{OR} \{0\,1\,1\,1\,1\,1\}}$$

Chromosome T reveals five faults and the total number of faults present in the program is six, the fitness value of the $T = \frac{\{011110\} \cup \{001001\}}{6} = \frac{\{011111\}}{6} = \frac{5}{6} = 0.83$

4 Proposed Model

The execution-details of the GA are shown in Fig. 4. Let F represents total faults, total test case represented by T and program to be tested is P. The execution-details of test case T for the previous version are collected from its test oracle. The test oracle is used to create the traceability matrix (TR). This TR matrix is a 0-1 matrix. The row of the matrix represents a test case and a column represents a fault. Table 1 presents an example of the relation between the test case and fault and how TR matrix is generated from Table 1.

Table 1. Traceability(TR) matrix generated from the table representing the test case and fault expose by them.

Test case	Fault expose by the test case					
	F1	F2	F3	F4	F5	F6
T1	1	1	1	0	0	0
T2	0	1	1	1	1	0
T3	1	0	0	0	0	1
T4	0	0	1	0	0	1
T5	0	1	1	0	0	0
T6	1	1	0	0	0	1
T7	0	0	0	1	0	1

$$TR = \begin{pmatrix} 1 & 1 & 1 & 0 & 0 & 0 \\ 0 & 1 & 1 & 1 & 1 & 0 \\ 1 & 0 & 0 & 0 & 0 & 1 \\ 0 & 0 & 1 & 0 & 0 & 1 \\ 0 & 1 & 1 & 0 & 0 & 0 \\ 1 & 1 & 0 & 0 & 0 & 1 \\ 0 & 0 & 0 & 1 & 0 & 1 \end{pmatrix}$$

In the above example, there are seven test cases and six faults. The entry in the cell TR_{ij} represents

$$TR_{ij} = \begin{cases} 1 & if\,testcase\,i\,expose\,fault\,j \\ 0 & otherwise \end{cases}$$

The TR matrix is used by GA to generate prioritised test case T'. The whole methodology of the model is presented in Fig. 4.

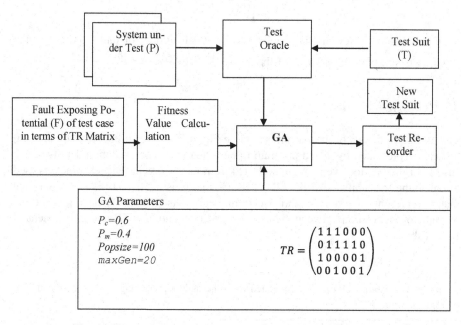

Fig. 4. The methodology applied to generate TCP order using GA

5 Experiment and Results

An empirical study was performed to find out the effectiveness of the technique. The major focus of the experiment was to measure the average percentage of fault detection (APFD) of the different subject program [22, 29]. The proposed model was compared to the much-used random technique. The experiment was carried out on three benchmark subject program from Software-artifact Infrastructure Repository (SIR) repository[1]. SIR is a repository of software-related artifacts meant to support rigorous controlled experimentation with program analysis and software testing techniques, and education in controlled experimentation. The details of the subject program are shown in Table 2.

---

[1] Software-artifact Infrastructure Repository, https://sir.csc.ncsu.edu/portal/index.php (Accessed 5th September 2018).

In order to carry out the experiment, we seeded fault on the benchmark program using Jumble[2]. The test cases were Junit[3] test cases, executed using Eclipse IDE[4]. The GA was implemented on MATLAB R2017a. It was executed on a PC with an Intel Pentium 3.2 GHz CPU and 1 GB memory running the Windows 10 operating system.

Table 2. Summary of programs used in experimentation

Program	Source file (LOC)	Test suite pool (T × R)	Mutation fault
Account	66	25 × 12	20
BST	130	57 × 22	21
Groovy	361	102 × 92	77

5.1 Research Questions

The execution of the experiments was dictated by the following two queries:

Q1: Does our GA increase early detection of fault more significantly than random technique?

Q2: Is GA based TCP efficient in terms of time and chromosome length?

5.2 Experiment to Evaluate APDF of the Different Subject Program Using Random and GA Based Technique

The experiments on the subject program were carried out to calculate APFD value for our GA based technique and random technique. The results are presented in Fig. 5.

Analysis of the APFD value of account program evinced that it could achieve 100% fault exposing potential after execution of 50% test case using GA prioritization. On the contrary, for groovy and BST, 100% achievement was noted after the execution of 67% of the test cases. In the case of random prioritization, 100% FEP was achieved only after execution of all the test cases (like retest all) for BST and account, whereas, in the case of groovy, it was achieved after 83% test case execution. The GA TCP detected all the faults much earlier than random prioritization.

5.3 Experiment to Evaluate the Execution Time (Time Complexity) with Different Chromosome Length and Number of Generations

This experiment was conducted to assess the efficiency of the algorithm in terms of execution time. In order to perform this experiment, we considered variation in number of generations (*maxGen*). The three-subject program was tested for this parameter and their individual execution time was recorded (Fig. 6).

---

[2] Jumble home page http://jumble.sourceforge.net (Accessed 7th September 2018).

[3] JUnit's official website, http://www.junit.org/ (Accessed 7th September 2018).

[4] The Eclipse Foundation website, http://www.eclipse.org/ (Accessed 7th September 2018).

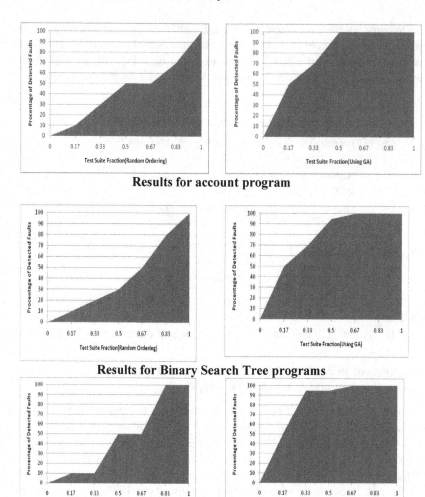

Results for account program

Results for Binary Search Tree programs

Results for groovy programs

Fig. 5. Details of the APFD results of the subject program for GA and random TCP.

GA TCP generates quick result if a number of generations are less. The increase in the number of generations not always gives early result rather it increases execution time. The algorithm could efficiently generate the TCP order with less number of the epoch (generation).

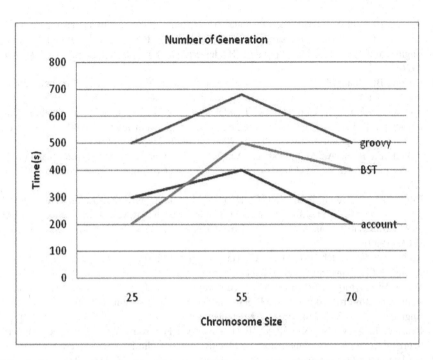

Fig. 6. Execution time results of the three-subject program with different chromosome size.

6 Conclusion

This paper presents a successful design of a GA algorithm to prioritize test cases. The efficiency of the algorithm was assessed with respect to random prioritization. APFD measure was used for the calculation of the efficiency. Analysis of the APFD measure for three-benchmark program gave early fault detection by GA with respect to random technique. GA TCP execution was faster as vouched by the exposition of 100% fault with less number of generations. Future research may be directed towards the improvement of the performance for some higher LOC benchmark programs. It would also be an interesting proposition to investigate whether prioritization technique modified using parallel GA could decrease the execution time with same or better APFD value.

References

1. Koppen, M., Wolpert, D.H., Macready, W.G.: Remarks on a recent paper on the "no free lunch" theorems. IEEE Trans. Evol. Comput. 5(3), 295–296 (2001)
2. Ostrand, T.J., Weyuker, E.J., Bell, R.M.: Where the bugs are. In: ACM SIGSOFT Software Engineering Notes 2004 Jul 11, vol. 29, no. 4, pp. 86–96. ACM (2004)
3. Ahmed, A.: Software Testing as a Service. Auerbach Publications, Boca Raton (2009)

4. Ramler, R., Biffl, S., Grünbacher, P.: Value-based management of software testing. In: Biffl, S., Aurum, A., Boehm, B., Erdogmus, H., Grünbacher, P. (eds.) Value-Based Software Engineering, pp. 225–244. Springer, Heidelberg (2006). https://doi.org/10.1007/3-540-29263-2_11

5. Boehm, B., Huang, L.G.: Value-based software engineering: a case study. Computer **36**(3), 33–41 (2003)

6. Zhang, L., Hou, S.S., Guo, C., Xie, T., Mei, H.: Time-aware test-case prioritization using integer linear programming. In: Proceedings of the Eighteenth International Symposium on Software Testing and Analysis, 19 July 2009, pp. 213–224. ACM (2009)

7. Ashraf, E., Rauf, A., Mahmood, K.: Value based regression test case prioritization. In: Proceedings of the World Congress on Engineering and Computer Science, vol. 1, pp. 24–26 (2012)

8. Rothermel, G., Untch, R.H., Chu, C., Harrold, M.J.: Test case prioritization: An empirical study. In: Proceedings IEEE International Conference on Software Maintenance - (ICSM 1999). Software Maintenance for Business Change (Cat. No. 99CB36360), pp. 179–188. IEEE (1999)

9. Rothermel, G., Untch, R.H., Chu, C., Harrold, M.J.: Prioritizing test cases for regression testing. IEEE Trans. Softw. Eng. **27**(10), 929–948 (2001)

10. Wong, W.E., Horgan, J.R., London, S., Agrawal, H.: A study of effective regression testing in practice. In: Proceedings of the Eighth International Symposium On Software Reliability Engineering, pp. 264–274. IEEE, 2 November 1997

11. Beasley, J., Dowsland, K., Glover, F., Laguna, M., Peterson, C., Reeves, C.R.: Modern heuristic techniques for combinatorial problems, p. 320. Colin R. Reeves, New York (1993)

12. Husbands, P.: Genetic algorithms for scheduling. AISB Q. **89**, 38–45 (1994)

13. Gary, M.R., Johnson, D.S.: Computers and Intractability: A Guide to the Theory of NP-Completeness. WH Freeman, New York (2002)

14. Yadav, D.K., Dutta, S.: Test case prioritization technique based on early fault detection using fuzzy logic. In: 2016 3rd International Conference on Computing for Sustainable Global Development (INDIACom), pp. 1033–1036. IEEE, 16 March 2016

15. Khatibsyarbini, M., Isa, M.A., Jawawi, D.N., Tumeng, R.: Test case prioritization approaches in regression testing: a systematic literature review. Inf. Softw. Technol. **1** (93), 74–93 (2018)

16. Elbaum, S., Malishevsky, A.G., Rothermel, G.: Test case prioritization: a family of empirical studies. IEEE Trans. Softw. Eng. **28**(2), 159–182 (2002)

17. Srivastava, A., Thiagarajan, J.: Effectively prioritizing tests in development environment. In: ACM SIGSOFT Software Engineering Notes, vol. 27, no. 4, pp. 97–106. ACM, 22 July 2002

18. Panigrahi, C.R., Mall, R.: An approach to prioritize the regression test cases of object-oriented programs. CSI Trans. ICT **1**(2), 159–173 (2013)

19. Panigrahi, C.R., Mall, R.: A heuristic-based regression test case prioritization approach for object-oriented programs. Innov. Syst. Softw. Eng. **10**(3), 155–163 (2014)

20. Miranda, B., Bertolino, A.: Scope-aided test prioritization, selection and minimization for software reuse. J. Syst. Softw. **1**(131), 528–549 (2017)

21. Li, Z., Harman, M., Hierons, R.M.: Search algorithms for regression test case prioritization. IEEE Trans. Softw. Eng. **33**(4), 225–237 (2007)

22. Jeffrey, D., Gupta, N.: Experiments with test case prioritization using relevant slices. J. Syst. Softw. **81**(2), 196–221 (2008)

23. Smith, A.M., Geiger, J., Kapfhammer, G.M., Soffa, M.L.: Test suite reduction and prioritization with call trees. In: Proceedings of the Twenty-Second IEEE/ACM International Conference on Automated Software Engineering, pp. 539–540. ACM, 5 November 2007

24. Mohapatra, S.K., Prasad, S.: Evolutionary search algorithms for test case prioritization. In: 2013 International Conference on Machine Intelligence and Research Advancement, pp. 115–119. IEEE, 21 December 2013
25. Mohapatra, S.K., Prasad, S.: A chemical reaction optimization approach to prioritize the regression test cases of object-oriented programs. J. ICT Res. Appl. **11**(2), 113–130 (2017)
26. Mohapatra, S.K., Srinivas, P.: An ant colony algorithm to prioritize the regression test cases of object-oriented programs. Indian J. Sci. Technol. **9**(19), 1–8 (2016)
27. Maheswari, R.U., Mala, D.J.: Combined genetic and simulated annealing approach for test case prioritization. Indian J. Sci. Technol. **8**(35), 1–5 (2015)
28. Noguchi, T., Washizaki, H., Fukazawa, Y., Sato, A., Ota, K.: History-based test case prioritization for black box testing using ant colony optimization. In: 2015 IEEE 8th International Conference on Software Testing, Verification and Validation (ICST), pp. 1–2. IEEE, 13 April 2015
29. Elbaum, S., Malishevsky, A., Rothermel, G.: Incorporating varying test costs and fault severities into test case prioritization. In: Proceedings of the 23rd International Conference on Software Engineering, pp. 329–338. IEEE Computer Society, 1 July 2001

Stationary Wavelet Transform for Automatic Epileptic Seizure Detection

Gebremichael Shiferaw[1]([✉]), Adane Mamuye[2], and Marco Piangerelli[3]

[1] Department of Information Systems, University of Gondar, Gondar, Ethiopia
gebrsh@gmail.com
[2] Department of Computer Science, University of Gondar, Gondar, Ethiopia
adothebigg@gmail.com
[3] Department of Computer science, University of Camerino, Camerino, Italy
marco.piangerelli@unicam.it

Abstract. Visual detection of epileptic seizure from EEG signal is being inefficient and time consuming. Computational EEG signal analysis techniques were then used in the diagnosis and management of epileptic seizures. In this study, we compared the performance of Discrete Wavelet Transform (DWT) and the Stationary Wavelet Transform (SWT) decomposition techniques with 22 wavelet functions (Coiflets (coif), Daubechies (DB) and Symlets (Sym) families) using support vector machine classifier. We used multichannel EEG dataset of the University of Bon Epilepsy Center. From this dataset, five statistical wavelet features: max, min, average, mean of absolute and standard deviation were extracted. In all of the wavelet functions except three, in the Coiflets family, the experimental result showed that SWT achieved better classification accuracy than DWT. SWT and DWT decomposition techniques registered 99.5% and 97.5% highest classification accuracies, respectively.

Keywords: EEG signal · Discrete wavelet transforms ·
Stationary wavelet transforms · Seizure detection · SVM Classifiers ·
Wavelet functions

1 Introduction

Epilepsy is a common chronic neurological disorder which affects around 50 million people of all ages all over the world. In low and middle-income countries, nearly three fourth of the epilepsy patients do not get the treatment they need (Pellegrino et al. 2014; Shi et al. 2017). The hallmark of epilepsy is recurrent seizures, termed epileptic seizures. A seizure occurs when parts of the brain producing abnormal electrical activity that spread throughout the brain and epilepsy is caused by sudden recurrent and transient disturbances of perception.

Monitoring the electrical activities from the brain through the electroencephalogram (EEG) has become an important data source for identification of epileptic seizure (Zandi et al. 2010). Electroencephalogram (EEG) records the

© Springer Nature Switzerland AG 2019
F. Mekuria et al. (Eds.): ICT4DA 2019, CCIS 1026, pp. 38–45, 2019.
https://doi.org/10.1007/978-3-030-26630-1_4

changes of the electrical activity in term of voltage fluctuations of the brain through multiple electrodes placed in the different location of the brain. EEG signal of epilepsy patients during a seizure shows patterns that are significantly different from the normal state of the brain with respect to space, time and frequency patterns. However, visual detection of epileptic seizure using EEG tool has a serious drawbacks. Visual detection is very time consuming and inefficient, especially in long-term recordings practitioners have to go through huge number of EEG data sheets. Additionally, disagreement among the practitioners on the same recording may possible due to the subjective nature of the EEG analysis. Moreover, the EEG patterns that characterize an epileptic seizure are similar to waves that are part of the background noise and to artefacts such as eye blinks and other eye movements, muscle activity, electrocardiogram and electrical interference. Due to these reasons, automated classification has been forwarded as valuable clinical tools for the scrutiny of EEG data in computationally efficient manner (Pellegrino et al. 2014; Tzallas et al. 2012; Orosco et al. 2013; Akareddy et al. 2013; Chen et al. 2015).

In developing the automated classifier, feature extraction and classification methods based on Wavelet and Fourier transformation were employed. However, previous studies have demonstrated that Discrete Wavelet Transform is among the most promising technique for extracting features from EEG signals (Gajic et al. 2014; Kabir et al. 2016; Tibdewal et al. 2016; Prince et al. 2016; Mahdi et al. 2011; Shete et al. 2014).

On the other hand, due to signal to noise ratio, the presence of noise may affect the recognition and localization of spikes. Thus, Stationary Wavelet Transform (SWT) has been used for EEG signal spike detection (Radmehr et al. 2013). The major advantage of SWT is the preservation of time information of the original signal sequence at each level. However, as the best of the researchers' knowledge there is no study that compares the accuracy of the SWT and the DWT classification techniques on the same EEG signal dataset. Thus, the focus of this study is to compare the DWT and SWT decomposition techniques, on the same signal dataset, using support vector machine (SVM) classifier.

2 Methodology

In this study, we follow four steps to decompose and classify the EEG signals.

2.1 Dataset

We used the EEG time series database from the Epilepsy Centre of the University of Bonn (Andrzejak 2001). This database consists of five EEG datasets (Sets A-E), identified as: O, Z, F, N and S; each set holds 100 segments of EEG signals of 23.6 s. The sampling frequency of each signal was 173.6 Hz, so each segment contains 4,097 samples. O and Z datasets were obtained from healthy subjects with eyes open and closed respectively; Datasets F and N were obtained during interictal states, period between seizures, in different zones of the brain and set

S was obtained from a subject during ictal state, seizure period (Tzallas et al. 2012). For this study, 200 EEG signal segments, 100 each from datasets A and dataset E, were selected, as shown in Figs. 1 and 2.

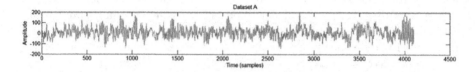

Fig. 1. Sample non-epileptic EEG signal block dataset A.

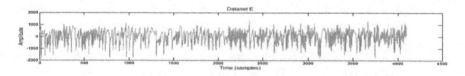

Fig. 2. Sample epileptic EEG signal block dataset E.

2.2 Signal Decomposition

A number of signal analysis techniques are available: including time-domain, frequency-domain, wavelet analysis. Linear analysis (time-domain and frequency-domain analysis) techniques might be insufficient approximation of the nonlinear signals (Guo et al. 2010). Since EEG signal has non-linear and non-stationary characteristic, wavelet analysis techniques (DWT and SWT) are more appropriate and reliable for EEG signal analysis. The two wavelet techniques differ in their way of decomposition. In decimation SWT modify the filter coefficients in each filtration level by padding zeros. In DWT after filtration in each stage, coefficients are destroyed by a factor. Due to decimation of coefficients, DWT fails to preserve translational invariance. In both cases, the maximum decomposition level is set to 7 based on the decomposition level computing equation given by (Chen et al. 2015). Three commonly used wavelet families Coiflets (coif), Daubechies (DB), and Symlets (sym) were used for decomposing EEG signals. The DWT decomposition using DB wavelet family is shown in Fig. 3. The DWT decomposition using DB wavelet family is shown in Fig. 3. As shown in Fig. 3, in DWT the filtered output has half the length of the input signal whereas in SWT the filtered output has the same length, as shown in Fig. 4.

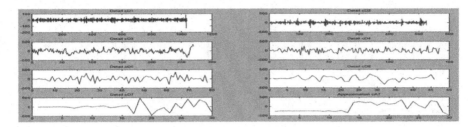

Fig. 3. Sample DWT DB8 detail coefficients of a sample EEG non-epileptic signal block.

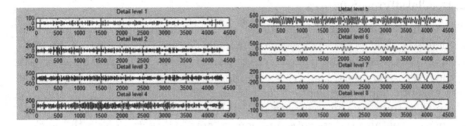

Fig. 4. Sample SWT DB8 detail coefficients of a sample EEG epileptic signal block.

2.3 Feature Extraction

In the signal processing, the low-frequency content (sub-bands) are the most representative part of the original signal. In the general human EEG rhythms (sub-bands) of the EEG signal, the clinical interest is more focused on: delta, theta, alpha, beta and gamma waves that are in the low frequency range (Gajic et al. 2014; Chen et al. 2017). Selecting low frequency sub-bands that best describe the behavior of EEG signals is important to improve seizure detection and classifier performance (Misiti et al. 1996). In this study, using DWT and SWT techniques the EEG raw signals were decomposed into the multi-level low-frequency resolutions.

A single decomposed EEG signal block is represented in the five sub-bands (D4–D7 and A7) frequency resolution spectrum. The 5 detailed low frequency sub-bands then used to extract features from each original raw signal. Each sub-band is divided into windows size called sub-block and each window size overlaps with the half of windows size. A single window size block is computed twice with its adjacent as shown on Fig. 5. Each of the five sub bands separated into 23 windows size and 46 sub-signal blocks. From each sub-block the statistical features, namely: maximum amplitude, minimum amplitude, average, mean and standard deviation are computed.

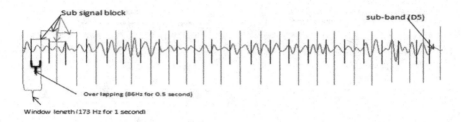

Fig. 5. A single sub-band divide in window size to form sub-signal block

2.4   Classifying Seizures

The ultimate goal of EEG signal detection is classification of signals based on predefined classes. SVM is a supervised machine learning approach that is widely used for data analysis and pattern recognition. Support Vector Machines (SVM) is the most common used supervised learning algorithms to separate EEG signal into epileptic and non-epileptic (Chen et al. 2015, 2017).

In this study, SVM classifier with RBF Kernel function was used. The training matrix contains the epileptic and non-epileptic data sets along with the class labels (class = 1 for epileptic and class = 0 for non-epileptic). The resulting SVM trained classifier, as shown in Fig. 6, contains the optimized parameters that are used to classify the test dataset.

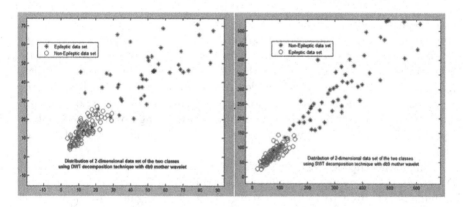

Fig. 6. Distribution of epileptic and non-epileptic signals using DWT and SWT techniques with DB9 wavelet function.

3   Results and Discussion

To compare the performance of the DWT and SWT decomposition techniques, training and testing datasets are randomly generated using 10-fold cross-validation. 200 EEG signals were randomly partitioned into 10 equal size subsamples. From the 10 subsamples, a single subsample (20 EEG signals) was taken as a testing data and the remaining k–1 subsamples (180 EEG datasets) are used as training data. The results from the folds then averaged (or otherwise combined) to produce a single estimation. The advantage of this method is that all observations are used for both training and validation, and each observation is used for validation exactly once. The test result of the DWT and SWT technique with DB9 mother wavelet function is shown on Fig. 7.

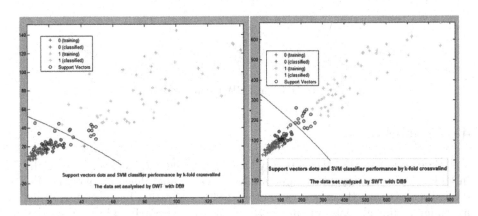

Fig. 7. Seizure prediction using DWT and SWT decomposition techniques

Based on common experimental parameters, the SVM classifier classified the EEG seizure dataset in the range 95% to 97.5% and 96% to 99.5% for DWT and SWT decomposition techniques, respectively. SWT performs better since instead of decimation it decomposes the EEG raw signal by filtering coefficients in each levels by padding them zeros. However, DWT does not implement the translation invariance, the decimation process in each level is eliminated. Due to decimation of coefficients, DWT fails to preserve translational invariance. Thus it suffers from lack of shift invariance. Lack of shift invariance assumes that any small translation in original signal can cause significantly large variations in the distribution of energy between wavelet coefficients. The average accuracy of DWT and SWT are 96.41% and 97.02%, respectively. SWT feature extraction technique scored the highest classification accuracy 99.5% with DB7 mother wavelet function Fig. 8.

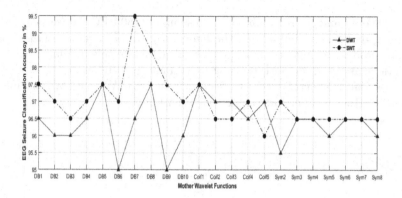

Fig. 8. DWT and SWT comparison

4 Conclusion

Visual detection of EEG signal is very time consuming and inefficient, especially in long-term recordings practitioners have to go through huge number of EEG data sheets. Due to these reasons, automated classification has been forwarded as valuable clinical tools. In this study we compared SWT and DWT decomposition techniques. The experimental result showed SWT mostly achieve high classification accuracy than DWT. The reason why this difference was existed: SWT instead of decimation it modifies the filter coefficients in each levels of stage by padding them zeros. But DWT on the other hand cannot performance translation invariance; hence, decimation process in each level is eliminated. Due to decimation of coefficients, DWT is not as good as SWT to preserve translational invariance.

References

Akareddy, S.M., Kulkarni, P.: EEG signal classification for epilepsy seizure detection using improved approximate entropy. Int. J. Public Health Sci. (IJPHS) **2**, 23–32 (2013)

Andrzejak, R.G., Lehnertz, K., Mormann, F., Rieke, C., David, P., Elger, C.E.: Indications of nonlinear deterministic and finite-dimensional structures in time series of brain electrical activity: dependence on recording region and brain state. Phys. Rev. E **64**, 061907 (2001)

Chen, D., Wan, S., Bao, F.S.: EEG-based seizure detection using discrete wavelet transform through full-level decomposition. In: 2015 IEEE International Conference on Bioinformatics and Biomedicine (BIBM), pp. 1596–1602 (2015)

Chen, D., Wan, S., Xiang, J., Bao, F.S.: A high-performance seizure detection algorithm based on Discrete Wavelet Transform (DWT) and EEG. PLoS ONE **12**, e0173138 (2017)

Gajic, D., Djurovic, Z., Di Gennaro, S., Gustafsson, F.: Classification of EEG signals for detection of epileptic seizures based on wavelets and statistical pattern recognition. Biomed. Eng.: Appl. Basis Commun. **26**, 1450021 (2014)

Guo, L., Rivero, D., Pazos, A.: Epileptic seizure detection using multiwavelet transform based approximate entropy and artificial neural networks. J. Neurosci. Methods **193**, 156–163 (2010)

Juarez-Guerra, E., Alarcon-Aquino, V., Gomez-Gil, P.: Epilepsy seizure detection in EEG signals using wavelet transforms and neural networks. In: Elleithy, K., Sobh, T. (eds.) New Trends in Networking, Computing, E-learning, Systems Sciences, and Engineering. LNCS, vol. 312, pp. 261–269. Springer, Heidelberg (2015). https://doi.org/10.1007/978-3-319-06764-3_33

Kabir, E., Zhang, Y.: Epileptic seizure detection from EEG signals using logistic model trees. Brain Inform. **3**, 93–100 (2016)

Kalbhor, S.D., Harpale, V.K.: The review of detection and classification of epileptic seizures using wavelet transform. In: 2016 International Conference on Computing Communication Control and automation (ICCUBEA), pp. 1–5 (2016)

Mahdi, M.T.O.: A new fast epilepsy detection method using electroencephalogram signal processing. World Appl. Sci. J. **14**, 1119–1124 (2011)

Mallat, S.G.: A theory for multi-resolution signal decomposition: the wavelet representation. IEEE Trans. Pattern Anal. Mach. Intell. **11**, 674–693 (1989)

Orosco, L., Correa, A.G., Laciar, E.: a survey of performance and techniques for automatic epilepsy detection. J. Med. Biol. Eng. **33**, 526–537 (2013)

Pellegrino, G.: Analysis for automatic detection of epileptic seizure from EEG signals. Laurea Specialistica in Bioingegneria (2014). http://tesi.cab.unipd.it/46118/1/ThesisBio.pdf

Prince, P.G.K., Hemamalini, R.R., Kumar, S.: Epileptic seizure detection using EEG signals by means of stationary wavelet transforms. IJCTA, 291–329 (2016). https://healthdocbox.com/Epilepsy/69751917-Epileptic-seizure-detection-using-eeg-signals-by-means-of-stationary-wavelet-transforms.html

Radmehr, M., Anisheh, S.M.: EEG spike detection using stationary wavelet transform and time-varying autoregressive model. Int. J. Comput. Appl. **83**(13) (2013)

Shete, S., Shriram, R.: Comparison of sub-band decomposition and reconstruction of EEG signal by Daubechies9 and Symlet9 wavelet. In: 2014 Fourth International Conference on Communication Systems and Network Technologies (CSNT). IEEE (2014)

Shi, Y., Wang, S., Ying, J., Zhang, M., Liu, P., Zhang, H., et al.: Correlates of perceived stigma for people living with epilepsy: a meta-analysis. Epilepsy Behav. **70**, 198–203 (2017)

Shoeb, A.H.: Application of machine learning to epileptic seizure onset detection and treatment. Massachusetts Institute of Technology, 2 October 2009

Tibdewal, M.N., Dey, H.R., Mahadevappa, M., Ray, A.K., Malokar, M.: Wavelet transform based multiple features extraction for detection of epileptic/non-epileptic multichannel EEG. In: 2016 3rd International Conference on Computing for Sustainable Global Development (INDIACom), pp. 1648–1653 (2016)

Tzallas, A.T., Tsipouras, M.G., Fotiadis, D.I.: Epileptic seizure detection in EEGs using time? Frequency analysis. IEEE Trans. Inf Technol. Biomed. **13**, 703–710 (2009)

Tzallas, A.T., et al.: Automated epileptic seizure detection methods: a review study. In: Epilepsy-Histological, Electroencephalographic and Psychological Aspects. InTech (2012)

Zandi, A.S., Javidan, M., Dumont, G.A., Tafreshi, R.: Automated real-time epileptic seizure detection in scalp EEG recordings using an algorithm based on wavelet packet transform. IEEE Trans. Biomed. Eng. **57**, 1639–1651 (2010)

Misiti, M., Misiti, Y., Oppenheim, G., Michel, J.P.: Wavelet toolbox: for use with MATLAB. citeulike.org (1996)

Classical Machine Learning Algorithms and Shallower Convolutional Neural Networks Towards Computationally Efficient and Accurate Classification of Malaria Parasites

Yaecob Girmay Gezahegn[1,3]([⊠]), Abel Kahsay Gebreslassie[1],
Maarig Aregawi Hagos[1], Achim Ibenthal[2],
and Eneyew Adugna Etsub[3]

[1] Mekelle Institute of Technology, Mekelle University, Mekelle, Ethiopia
yaecob.girmay@gmail.com, abelkahsay10@gmail.com,
maarig2000@gmail.com
[2] HAWK University of Applied Sciences and Arts, Goettingen, Germany
achim.ibenthal@hawk.de
[3] Addis Ababa Instittute of Technology, Addis Ababa University,
Addis Ababa, Ethiopia
eneyew_a@yahoo.com

Abstract. Malaria and its diagnosis methods need significant attention in Ethiopia. Studies show that for 46 laboratory professionals who were given 6 different positive and negative malaria slides, the detection error rates for plasmodium falciparum and vivax were 43.5% and 37%, respectively. Another similar study reports that the overall malaria diagnosis error rate is 40.4%. To circumvent these challenges, there needs to be a system that automatically and instantly analyzes and manipulates data with less bias so as to reduce misdiagnosis error, cost, workload of physicians and experts, and thereby improving the livelihood of the society. In this study, classical machine learning algorithms and shallow Convolutional Neural Networks (CNN) based classification for parasitized and uninfected malaria images are applied. While classical machine learning algorithms are requiring a feature design step for classification, CNNs learn to recognize objects end to end, implicitly without the need for feature engineering. Many machine learning algorithms such as K-Nearest Neighbors, Random Forest, Gradient Boosting, CNNs etc. are compared in this contribution. From our experimental observation, some of the classical models such as Gradient Boost, Random Forest and Stacked ensemble using color, texture and shape features achieved a classification accuracy of 96%, precision of 97%, recall of 97% and f1-score of 97% for the parasitized samples. A model ensemble of two custom CNNs and mini-VGGNet achieved a precision of 99%, recall of 96% and f1-score of 97% for the parasitized. These results of the CNN models are reproducible for each of them. All the approaches have comparable results, however, the classical machine learning models are resource efficient.

Keywords: Classical machine learning · CNN · Ensemble · Classification · Malaria · Automatic diagnosis

© Springer Nature Switzerland AG 2019
F. Mekuria et al. (Eds.): ICT4DA 2019, CCIS 1026, pp. 46–56, 2019.
https://doi.org/10.1007/978-3-030-26630-1_5

1 Introduction

Malaria is an acute infectious disease which is transmitted by Anopheles Mosquitos that carry plasmodium. It has five species which infect humans. Two of these species that are prevalent and have major impacts are plasmodium falciparum and plasmodium vivax. If a person is infected by falciparum, the disease progresses rapidly into cerebral malaria if not treated in time. Therefore, urgent diagnosis is a must [1].

According to a study by the World Health Organization (WHO), nearly half of the world's population is at risk due to malaria. The same study reports that globally there were 212 million cases of malaria and 429,000 deaths in 2015. More than 90% of the cases and deaths are in Africa [2, 3].

Convenient tropical climate for the growth of the parasites, inadequate health facilities, illiteracy, and poor socio-economic conditions made the fight against the disease hard [2]. Even though around 6.8 million lives have been saved from death since 2001, 70% of malaria illness and death happens in children below the age of 5 - still a major killer of children [4]. Hence, The Global Technical Strategy for Malaria has a goal to reduce malaria case incidence & mortality rate by 90% [5]. WHO also envisions to solve healthcare problems through innovative R&D with the theme, "Investing in knowledge for resilient health systems" [6].

A study in the Intensive Care Unit (ICU) of Jima University Specialized Hospital (Ethiopia) shows that the prescription error rate was found to be 52.5% [7]. Another study in the ICU of Tikur Anbessa Specialized Hospital (Addis Ababa, Ethiopia) shows that there is 40.7% of medication prescription error [8]. According to WHO, the main factors for diagnostic errors are low quality and scope of healthcare facilities, lack of competent and sufficient healthcare professionals, low teamwork and low learning and feedback among professionals when errors occur [8]. According to a study in the Tigray region of Ethiopia, out of 46 laboratory professionals who were given 6 different positive and negative malaria slides, their detection rates for plasmodium falciparum and vivax were 56.5% and 63%, respectively [9]. Another similar study reports that the overall malaria diagnosis error rate in Ethiopia is 40.4% and it varies in different parts of the country [10, 11]. Moreover, from our observation on day-to-day experiences of the society, and based on our visit to Tigray Health Research Institute (THRI), we have observed that the diagnosis error is high which is in line with the above reported cases. The main reasons that were identified in the health centers are, (i) few and poor medical facilities (laboratory set-up) with few skilled health professionals, (ii) lack of proper training, and (iii) all the laboratories use manual microscopy diagnosis. Microscopic diagnostics depends on the competencies and skills of laboratory technicians [12]. Manual diagnosis requires careful examination of red blood cells (RBCs) via microscope. A research in 2013 by Johns Hopkins University (USA) discloses that "diagnostic errors - not surgical mistakes or medication overdoses - accounted for the largest fraction of claims, the most severe patient harm, and the highest total of penalty payouts" [13].

To circumvent healthcare challenges, especially, in remote, resource constrained rural areas, automatic diagnosis method could solve the subjective and time consuming nature of manual diagnosis to more reliable and standardized diagnosis [14, 15]. In

[16], automated diagnosis using machine learning based medical image analysis has demonstrated more consistent and objective results compared to manual microscopy. A recent survey on algorithms used for malaria detection on images collected from thick blood smears is presented in [25]. In [26], multilayer perceptron neural networks is used for classification of malaria parasite. The authors of [27] used deep-learning based machine learning approach for detection of malaria from thick blood smear. However, this approach still did not address the problem with identification of the different species and their stages.

In this paper, different classical machine learning algorithms and convolutional neural networks have been employed to classify falciparum parasitized and non-parasitized thin blood smear images.

2   Feature Extraction, Classical Machine Learning Algorithms and Convolutional Neural Networks

Features such as color, texture and shape are widely used in order to efficiently characterize objects in images. Conventionally, there are different techniques which help us understand the semantics by appropriate representation of images. These methods are commonly known as feature extraction techniques, which however need to be designed by experts. As a result, performance of classifying, detecting or recognizing an object depends on how good the representation is and the representation in turn relies on how well the features are extracted. Following feature extraction, the next step is training using machine learning classifiers, in order to categorize the input images into their respective classes. Some of the classifiers include, K-Nearest Neighbors (KNN), Support Vector Machine (SVM), Logistic Regression (logit), Decision Trees (DT), Naïve Bayes (NB) etc. These techniques have been widely used even with images that have complex features; for instance, SVMs can learn nonlinear classification boundaries. Even though conventional techniques have been widely used they have their own limitations [17].

To mitigate the limitations of the individual classifiers mentioned above, ensemble methods can be applied. Some of the ensemble techniques that are widely used are Random Forest (RF), AdaBoost (ABC) and Gradient Boost (GB). However, the approach is different from how we humans learn and perceive objects. So, deep-learning tries to bridge the gap, integrates extraction and classification as one module and learns intuitively as we humans do; learning via example and through experience [18]. The two important parameters, which make learning of objects as accurate as possible in CNNs, are large data sets for training purposes and a model with large learning capacity. CNNs employ prior knowledge learnt from neighboring pixels to compensate data which are missed [19]. Even though there are many techniques on natural images, the challenge of applying CNN techniques to the medical domain often lies in customizing existing architectures [20]. Figure 1 depicts a comparison of classical and CNN based classification of images.

By using classical machine learning algorithms, it is possible to detect and classify malaria infected blood smear images [1]. However, CNNs do end to end tasks without explicitly extracting features first, followed by classification [16, 17]. The main investigations reported subsequently can be categorized into (i) applying different classical techniques to extract features from infected and uninfected malaria datasets in combination with training via different classifiers, (ii) training CNN models on infected and uninfected malaria datasets and performance testing of classification results on a test set, and (iii) using ensemble methods for both classical machine learning algorithms and CNNs.

2.1   Ensemble Models

In ensemble methods, each model looks at slightly different features of the image to make its predictions, getting some fraction of the whole feature [21]. Decision of ensemble methods is based on gathering of information from multiple models, reducing generalization error, and improving overall performance while predicting. There are different types of ensemble learning. Here we have used AdaBoost, Gradient Boost, Stacking etc. for classical machine learning methods, and CNN based model ensembling for neural networks based machine learning techniques [22].

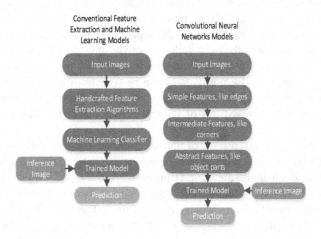

Fig. 1. Comparison of classical machine learning and CNN models.

Ensemble methods have two categories: sequential and parallel; in the first category we have AdaBoost that exploits the dependency between base learners, where the base learners are generated in sequence. In the second category, on the other hand, we have Random Forest, which exploits independence between base learners by generating parallel base learners.

Another Ensemble method is Bagging that stands for bootstrap aggregation which generates multiple versions of a predictor. One way to reduce the variance of an estimate is to take the average of multiple model estimates in case of regression and majority vote for classification. For the training of the base learners it uses bootstrap sampling [23].

Ensemble methods have numerous advantages. Most state-of-the-art academic benchmarks with a single model cannot be compared with these ensemble models. They are useful in weight transferring to other smaller models. However, increased training time and computational cost are disadvantages that should be noted [22].

3   Results, Discussion and Analysis

Different types of machine learning algorithms are applied as can be seen in the Tables 1, 2, 3, 4, 5, 6 and Figs. 2, 3, 4, 5 and 6. The two classes of malaria in the dataset (plasmodium falciparum infected and uninfected) used for training were taken from [24]. The classifiers are evaluated using accuracy, precession, recall and f1-score. However, using only accuracy as a performance measure does not always give correct result. Hence, to have a good knowledge about performance of a classifier used, the other mentioned metrics are also employed in tandem. Precision tells fraction of positive predictions that are actually positive whereas recall shows fraction of positive data predicted to be positive. If the recall is large, precision is small, few infected images are recognized, but includes no false positives (uninfected images). There is a tradeoff between precession and recall; high precision means low recall and vice versa. What is more, precision and recall are usually represented in a single number known as F-score (a harmonic mean of the two). In line with this, precise algorithms in this work, for example, found large positive (malaria images of falciparum) infected images. However, it includes few false positives as can be seen from the Tables and Figures. The confusion matrix shown in Fig. 4 clearly shows that 3% of the test data is false positive; the classifier confused 3% of the test data for non-parasitized (uninfected) with parasitized.

Tables 1 and 2 present results of the different algorithms for parasitized and uninfected cells respectively. Global feature extractors such as color channel statistics (mean and standard deviation) are used. Using just a color feature, Logistic Regression, Support Vector Machine, Random Forest, Gradient Boost, Linear Discriminant Analysis and Stacking Classifiers achieved an Accuracy, Precision, Recall and f1-score greater than 70%. Furthermore, Fig. 2 shows the performance of each classifier mentioned in Tables 1 and 2. As can be noted from the graphs, Gradient Boost, Random Forest and Stacking of classifiers got the highest classification accuracy. Different types of ensemble methods were also used in order to increase the performance of the classifiers as shown in Figs. 2, 3, 4 and Tables 1 and 4. Stacking ensemble is illustrated in Fig. 2. It consists of many of the classical machine learning algorithms mentioned in the table where kNN, RF, NB, GB, etc are base classifiers whose predictions are combined by logit. It can be depicted from Figs. 2, 3, 4, 5 and 6 that stacking achieves higher accuracy than individual classifiers.

Table 1. Classification result of different classical machine learning models using just the color feature for extraction of parasitized plasmodium falciparum.

	Type of classifier	Accuracy	Precision	Recall	f1-score
1	Naïve Bayes (NB)	0.63	0.63	0.61	0.62
2	Multinomial Naïve Bayes (MNV)	0.61	0.60	0.69	0.64
3	Bernoulli Naïve Bayes (BNB)	0.49	0.50	1.00	0.67
4	K-Nearest Neighbors (KNN)	0.66	0.67	0.65	0.66
5	Logistic Regression (Logit)	0.74	0.74	0.78	0.76
6	Decision Tree (DT)	0.67	0.67	0.68	0.67
7	Random Forest (RF)	0.71	0.73	0.70	0.72
8	Support Vector Machine (SVM)	0.74	0.75	0.77	0.76
9	Adaptive Boosting (ABC)	0.64	0.65	0.60	0.63
10	Gradient Boost (GB)	0.71	0.73	0.72	0.72
11	Linear Discriminant Analysis (LDA)	0.73	0.73	0.77	0.75
12	Stacking Classifiers	0.75	0.77	0.79	0.78

Table 2. Classification result of different classical machine learning models using just the color feature for extraction of uninfected RBC.

	Type of classifier	Accuracy	Precision	Recall	f1-score
1	Naïve Bayes (NB)	0.63	0.62	0.65	0.63
2	Multinomial Naïve Bayes (MNV)	0.61	0.63	0.54	0.58
3	Bernoulli Naïve Bayes (BNB)	0.49	0.00	0.00	0.00
4	K-Nearest Neighbors (KNN)	0.66	0.66	0.68	0.67
5	Logistic Regression (logit)	0.74	0.77	0.73	0.75
6	Decision Tree (DT)	0.67	0.67	0.67	0.67
7	Random Forest (RF)	0.71	0.71	0.74	0.73
8	Support Vector Machine (SVM)	0.74	0.77	0.74	0.76
9	AdaBoost (ABC)	0.64	0.63	0.68	0.65
10	Gradient Boost (GB)	0.71	0.72	0.73	0.73
11	Linear Discriminant Analysis (LDA)	0.73	0.76	0.71	0.73
12	Stacking Ensemble (SC)	0.75	0.78	0.76	0.77

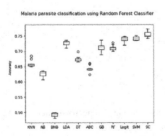
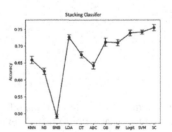

Fig. 2. Performance of different classifiers on the dataset (left), performance of stacked classifiers on the dataset (right) [using color features only].

Tables 3 and 4 present results of the different classical machine learning algorithms applied to classification of parasitized and uninfected cells along with ensemble methods, respectively, with more feature extraction techniques added. A combination of 'Hu-Moments' for shape extraction, color channels for color extraction and 'Haralick' for texture extraction were used. Furthermore, color channel statistics (mean, standard deviation and color histogram) were used to extract the color information of the images. As can be seen in the Tables and Figures, the additional features help improve the performance of the classifiers, even in the ensemble methods. The accuracy, precision, recall and f1-score jumped from around 70% to greater than 96% for the ensemble methods; an increment of greater than 20%. Figure 4, shows confusion matrix of random forest where the classifier is confused infected with non-infected malaria images for less than 3% of the test data while classifying.

Table 3. Classification result of different classical machine learning models using color, texture and shape features for extraction of parasitized plasmodium falciparum.

	Type of classifier	Accuracy	Precision	Recall	f1-score
1	Naïve Bayes (NB)	0.70	0.70	0.74	0.72
2	Bernoulli Naïve Bayes (BNB)	0.90	0.91	0.91	0.91
3	K-Nearest Neighbors (KNN)	0.58	0.58	0.57	0.58
4	Logit (Logistic Regression)	0.72	0.66	0.71	0.68
5	Decision Tree (DT)	0.95	0.95	0.97	0.96
6	Random Forest (RF)	0.96	0.97	0.97	0.97
7	Linear Discriminant Analysis (lda)	0.89	0.88	0.93	0.90
8	Support Vector Machine (svm)	0.75	0.75	0.80	0.77
9	Adaptive Boosting (AdaBoost, ABC)	0.92	0.91	0.97	0.94
10	Gradient Boost (GB)	0.96	0.97	0.97	0.97
11	Stacked Ensemble (SC)	0.96	0.97	0.97	0.97

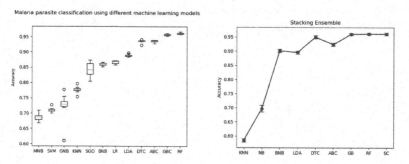

Fig. 3. Performance of different classifiers on the dataset (left), performance of stacked classifiers on the dataset (right) [using color, texture and shape features].

Table 4. Classification result of different classical machine learning models using color, texture and shape features for extraction of uninfected RBC

	Type of classifier	Accuracy	Precision	Recall	f1-score
1	Naïve Bayes (NB)	0.70	0.72	0.68	0.70
2	Bernoulli Naïve Bayes (BNB)	0.90	0.91	0.91	0.91
3	K-Nearest Neighbors (KNN)	0.58	0.58	0.59	0.59
4	Logistic Regression (logit)	0.72	0.69	0.63	0.66
5	Decision Tree (DTC)	0.95	0.97	0.95	0.96
6	Random Forest (RF)	0.96	0.97	0.97	0.97
7	Linear Discriminant Analysis (LDA)	0.89	0.92	0.87	0.90
8	Support Vector Machine (SVM)	0.75	0.79	0.73	0.76
9	Adaptive Boosting (AdaBoost, ABC)	0.92	0.97	0.90	0.93
10	Gradient Boost (GB)	0.96	0.97	0.97	0.97
11	Stacked Classifier (SC)	0.96	0.97	0.97	0.97

Tables 5 and 6, and Figs. 5 and 6, present customized convolutional neural networks, multilayer perceptron, mini-VGGNet and mini-GoogleNet. It is also depicted that ensemble methods were also used for the 3-layered, 4-layered CNN architectures and mini-VGGNet. We have ensembled three CNN architectures, Mini-VggNet, 3-layered and 4-layered customized CNN architectures. The training test split is 0.75/0.25 with total images of 27, 558.

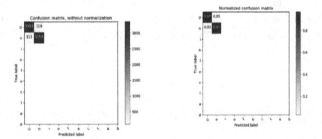

Fig. 4. Normalized and non-normalized confusion matrix for Random Forest classifier.

The overall performance is a little bit better than the classical feature extraction techniques. However, it is at the cost of computational time. Figures 6 and 7 depict the performance of our models during training and validation on the parasitized and uninfected malaria dataset. This is necessary because a model first needs to perform well in the training set in order to predict accurately on unseen images. Validation accuracy is necessary to make sure the models aren't overfitting. After completing training, performance for the two networks was evaluated on 6890 images, 3445 images from each class, that were held out for test time. The ensemble method

(Ensemble of 3 & 4 layer CNNs and mini-VGGNet) has highest performance with a precision, recall and f1-score of 0.99, 0.96 and 0.97, respectively, for the parasitized case, and 0.96, 0.99 and 0.97 for the uninfected cell images.

Table 5. Classification result of CNN models for parasitized plasmodium falciparum

	Type of classifier	Precision	Recall	f1-score
1	3-layered CNN	0.98	0.95	0.96
2	4-layered CNN	0.98	0.96	0.97
3	Multi-layer perceptron	0.84	0.49	0.62
4	Mini-GoogleNet (with 8-layers)	0.96	0.96	0.96
5	Mini-VGG (with 6-layers)	0.97	0.95	0.96
6	Ensemble of 3 and 4 layered CNNs	0.98	0.96	0.97
7	Ensemble of 3 and 4 layer CNNs and mini-VGGNet	0.99	0.96	0.97

Table 6. Classification result of CNN models for uninfected RBC

	Type of classifier	Precision	Recall	f1-score
1	3-layered CNN	0.95	0.98	0.96
2	4-layered CNN	0.96	0.98	0.97
3	Multi-layer perceptron	0.63	0.91	0.74
4	Mini-GoogleNet (with 8-layers)	0.96	0.96	0.96
5	Mini-VGG (with 6-layers)	0.95	0.97	0.96
6	Ensemble of 3 and 4 layered CNNs	0.96	0.98	0.97
7	Ensemble of 3 and 4 layer CNNs and mini-VGGNet	096	0.99	0.97

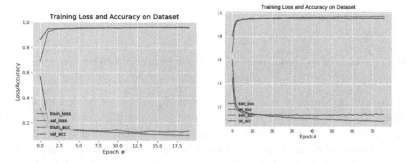

Fig. 5. Performance curves of 3-layers and 4-layers CNN models, from left to right.

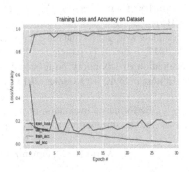
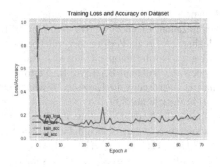

Fig. 6. Performance curves of Mini-GoogleNet and Mini-VGGNet, from left to right

4 Conclusion

The classification of parasitized and uninfected malaria was carried out using classical machine learning techniques and CNN architectures consisting of 3 and 4 layers, mini-VGGNet and mini GoogleNet. Ensemble methods have also been used for both, the classical machine learning and CNN models. The overall performance of the models, individually or using model ensemble, is good considering the number of layers used. What is more, the classical machine learning techniques have comparable result to the state-of-the-art CNN algorithms. The classical techniques don't require high performance computers or GPUs; they can easily be deployed into mobile devices. Furthermore, the shallow model with three CNN layers has comparable performance to the mini-VGG and mini-GoogleNet models. In order to get a better result, ensemble methods are employed in both cases, in the classical and in the CNN architectures. Some of the classical models such as Gradient Boost, Random Forest and Stacked ensemble using color, texture and shape features got a classification accuracy of 96%, precision of 97%, recall of 97% and f1-score of 97% for the parasitized. Similarly, model ensemble of two custom CNNs and mini-VGGNet got precision of 99%, recall of 96% and f1-score of 97% for the parasitized.

References

1. Poostchi, M., et al.: Image analysis and machine learning for detecting malaria. Transl. Res. **194**, 36–55 (2017)
2. Gallup, J., Sachs, J.: The economic burden of malaria. J. Trop. Med. **64**, 85–96 (2001)
3. Korenromp, E., et al.: World malaria report 2005, World Health Organization. Geneva, Technical report (2005)
4. http://www.who.int/mediacentre/factsheets/fs094/en/. Accessed 16 Sep 2017
5. Global Health Issues (2019). http://globalhealthstrategies.com/our-work/. Accessed 04 Jan 2019
6. World Health Organization: Investing in knowledge for resilient health systems: strategic plan 2016–2020 (2016)
7. Agalu, A., et al.: Medication prescribing errors in the intensive care unit of Jimma University specialized hospital, Southwest Ethiopia. J. Multidiscip. Healthc. **4**, 377–382 (2011)

8. Diagnostic Errors: Technical Series on Safer Primary Care. Geneva. World Heal Organization; Licence: CC BY-NC-SA 3.0 IGO (2016)
9. Megbaru, A., et al.: Performance of laboratory professionals working on malaria microscopy in Tigray, North Ethiopia. Hindawi J. Parasitol. Res. **2017**, 1–6 (2017). Article no. 9064917
10. Ayalew, F., Tilahun, B., Taye, B.: Performance evaluation of laboratory professionals on malaria microscopy in Hawassa Town, Southern Ethiopia. BMC Res. Notes **2014**, 1–8 (2014). Article no. 839
11. Yitbarek, T., Nega, D., Tasew, G., Taye, B., Desta, K.: Performance evaluation of malaria microscopists at defense health facilities in Addis Ababa and its surrounding areas. Ethiopia. PLoS ONE **11**(11), e0166170 (2016)
12. WHO. Malaria microscopy quality assurance manual - version 2. World Health Organization (2016)
13. David, E., Newman-Toker, M.D.: Diagnostic Errors More Common, Costly And Harmful Than Treatment Mistakes (2013). https://www.hopkinsmedicine.org/news/media/releases/diagnostic_errors_more_common_costly_and_harmful_than_treatment_mistakes. Accessed 07 Jan 2019
14. Reisenwitz, C.: How deep learning is changing healthcare part 1: diagnosis (2017). https://blog.capterra.com/how-deep-learning-is-changing-healthcare-part-1-diagnosis/. Accessed 04 Jan 2019
15. Bhatia, R.: Understanding The Deep Learning Advantage in Medical Imaging And How Tech Giants Are Rushing to Capitalize On It (2017). https://www.analyticsindiamag.com/understanding-deep-learning-advantage-medical-imaging-tech-giants-rushing-capitalize/. Accessed 05 Jan (2019)
16. Rajaraman, et al.: Pre-trained convolutional neural networks as feature extractors toward improved malaria parasite detection in thin blood smear images. PeerJ **6**, e4568 (2018). https://doi.org/10.7717/peerj.4568
17. Razzak, M.I., Naz, S., Zaib, A.: Deep learning for medical image processing: overview, challenges and future. Computer Vision and Pattern Recognition, Cornell University, 22 April 2017
18. http://cv-tricks.com/cnn/understand-resnet-alexnet-vgg-inception/. Accessed online 07 Feb 2019
19. LeCun, Y., Kavukcuoglu, K., Farabet, C.: Convolutional networks and applications in vision. In: Proceedings of 2010 IEEE International Symposium on Circuits and Systems (ISCAS), pp. 253–256 (2010)
20. Esteva, A., Kuprel, B., et al.: Dermatologist-Level Classification of Skin Cancer with Deep Neural Networks. Macmillan Publishers Limited, London (2017). Part of Springer Nature
21. Chollet, F.: Deep Learning with Python. Manning Publications Co., Shelter Island (2018)
22. https://blog.statsbot.co/ensemble-learning-d1dcd548e936. Accessed 07 Feb 2019
23. Breiman, L.: Bagging predictors. Department of Statistics University of California Berkeley, California 94720, Technical report no. 421, September 1994
24. https://ceb.nlm.nih.gov/repositories/malaria-datasets/. Accessed 10 Dec 2018
25. Jan, Z., Khan, A., Sajjad, M., et al.: A review on automated diagnosis of malaria parasite in microscopic blood smears images. Multimed. Tools Appl. **77**, 9801 (2018)
26. Días, G., González, F.A., Romero, E.: A semi-automatic method for quantification and classification of erythrocytes infected with malaria parasites in microscopic images. J. Biomed. Inform. **42**(2), 296–307 (2009)
27. Quinn, J.A., et al: Deep convolutional neural networks for microscopy-based point of care diagnostics, arXiv: 1608.02989v1 [cs.CV], August 2016 and Sanchez, C.S.: Deep learning for identifying malaria parasites in images. Masters thesis, Artificial Intelligence School of Informatics, University of Edinburgh (2015)

Knowledge Based Decision Support System for Detecting and Diagnosis of Acute Abdomen Using Hybrid Approach

Alemu Workneh[1(✉)], Dereje Teferi[2], and Alemu Kumilachew[3]

[1] Debre Tabor University, Debre Tabor, Ethiopia
a.workneh2005@gmail.com
[2] School of Information Science,
Addis Ababa University, Addis Ababa, Ethiopia
dereji.teferi@aau.edu.et
[3] Institute of Technology, Bahir Dar University, Bahir Dar, Ethiopia
alemupilatose@gmail.com

Abstract. Acute abdomen is one of the emergency diseases which is difficult for follow-up treatment. In developing countries, the mortality and morbidity rate are increasing due to misdiagnosis, delay, lack of knowledge and shortage of skilled manpower. These factors affect the quality of health care service in hospitals and reduce the quality of decisions made by physicians. This research attempts to investigate the applicability KBDSS using integration of rule based and case-based reasoning approach so as to improve the quality of decision made by domain experts, to provide effective and efficient services to the patients and to improve shortage of human expert in specific domain area. Domain knowledge is acquired using semi-structured interview technique. Domain experts are selected from Felege hiwot referral hospital in Bahir-Dar. In addition, secondary data is acquired from different sources following DSR methodology. The conceptual model of the knowledge-based system used a decision tree structure which is easy to understand and interpret the procedures involved in patient diagnoses. Based on the conceptual model, the prototype is developed with SWI prolog and java software tools. Beyond the domain expert, the result shows the system has accuracy of 99% for acute abdominal cause classification, and 66% for severity level identification. Whereas, the accuracy value of physicians has 84% for acute abdominal cause classification, and 50% for severity level identification with regard to the final result. Therefore, the KBDSS can diagnose patients with highest accuracy. We were taking the final observed value as pivoting point to test the KBDSS. In the evaluation of the system that classified the stored attribute according to the target problem is 71.33% accuracy. As the result shows, the three reasoning approaches: hybrid, case-based, and rule-based has an accuracy of 87.66%, 70%, and 60% respectively to retrieve target attributes for the target problem. This shows that hybrid reasoning approach is recommended to health care decision support system. Automation of KBDSS has a high contribution to establish truthful decision-making process in patient's acute abdomen treatment.

Keywords: Prolog · Java · Acute abdomen · KBDSS · Case-based · Rule-based · Hybrid

© Springer Nature Switzerland AG 2019
F. Mekuria et al. (Eds.): ICT4DA 2019, CCIS 1026, pp. 57–67, 2019.
https://doi.org/10.1007/978-3-030-26630-1_6

1 Introduction

Abdominal pain is the feeling of discomfort in abdominal cavity. The abdomen is the area surrounded by the lower margin of ribs, the upper part of diaphragm pelvic bone below and each side flanks. Pain arises from the tissues that surrounds the abdominal cavity which is muscles and skin. The term abdominal pain means sense of discomfort originating form organs in the abdominal cavity such us stomach, spleen, small intestine, large intestine, liver, gallbladder and pancreas (Jay et al. 2017). Abdominal pain is the current common problem which is chronic or acute (acute abdomen). Acute abdomen is the common emergency illness in developed and developing countries. Mortality and morbidity rate of the patients in developing countries due to acute abdomen is 18% and 20% respectively (Nyundo et al. 2013). This is because of misdiagnosis and delayed treatment. One of reasons for the prevalence of the problem is due to lack accurate computer aided supportive systems such as expert system, MYCIN, DSS and others are highly recommended to support the physician in making decisions. They support the physician early to know the disease and then decide the appropriate treatment immediately, since such disease are acute in nature and may lead to death or complications.

Artificial intelligence (AI) supports the human cognitive function. It is the paradigm shift in health care that increases the availability of patient data as well as it improves the diagnosis and treatment of the patient. For this purpose, it uses different algorisms and technique, such as knowledge-based reasoning techniques, NLP and ML (Fei et al. 2017).

A knowledge-based system (KBS) is a computer system which generates and utilizes knowledge from different sources. It supports experts in solving problems, especially complex ones, by utilizing artificial intelligence concepts and are mostly used in problem-solving procedures and to support human learning, decision making and actions. KBS is symbolic, heuristic, transparent and flexible. Knowledge-based systems are applicable in many areas such as health care, business (e-commerce), web information, agriculture (Leondes 2005). Knowledge based reasoning technique are the most common techniques for problem solving in artificial intelligence. Rule based reasoning, case-based reasoning, model-based reasoning and hybrid reasoning approaches are used for problem solving and decision making in different areas. The researchers used hybrid approach to minimize the drawback of individual reasoning approaches. The system was designed for health care to facilitates diagnosis and decision making in short time and with reduced cost, reduced mortality and morbidity rate using a knowledge base as recommended by (Zaraté and Shaofeng 2016).

Decision support system is a software which can replace the thinking process of a human and make logical decisions accordingly and could reduce the diagnostic errors as well as unwanted practice variation between physicians and improve the patient treatments in terms of time and cost (Prasath et al. 2013).

2 Problem Statement

Physicians are needed to provide the diagnostic knowledge to know the disease cause and provide appropriate measures such as extra diagnosis, further investigation and treatment of the disease. Most of the time, the traditional disease diagnosis takes extra time. Moreover, misdiagnosis happens due to different factors such as tiredness of the physician, similarity of cases and symptoms (Ray et al. 2016) (Ashley et al. 2013). This also forces the diagnosis to take more time. This length of time has a side-effect on patients especially for acute diseases. Most people think that the pain is like other chronic disease and take pain remedies, anti-acids, laxatives, or heating pads, which may complicate the problem. Therefore, acute abdomen needs special care, and require immediate diagnosis by a physician, otherwise it may lead to death. Studies conducted in Rwanda (Nyundo et al. 2013) revealed that the mortality and morbidity rate of patients in acute abdomen reach 18% and 20% respectively due to misdiagnosis and delayed treatment.

Furthermore, studies conducted in Nigeria (Adamu et al. 2010) on the waiting time of patients with abdominal pain in emergency department also asserted that 81.6% of the patients had surgical intervention more than 6 h later in developing countries. This waiting time is one hour in developed countries. The mean waiting time in Nigeria Ahmadu Bello University teaching hospital, were 22.3 ± 10.0 h with different factors. They conclude that the patient is waiting too long for emergency of acute abdomen, which resulted in increased mortality and morbidity rate of patients. In Ethiopia the mortality and morbidity rate were very high in case of acute abdomen. Regional health officials and health care providers discuss the way to reduce the acute abdomen mortality and morbidity rate and recommends good patient referral linkage and a quality surgical service in order to reduce its associated impacts and the case could be timely handled by training surgeons and physicians properly (Addisu et al. 2016). However, despite these efforts, the problem still persists. One of reasons for the prevalence of the problem is due to lack of accurate computer aided supportive systems. Expert systems such as MYCIN, DSS and others are highly recommended to support the physician in making better and faster decisions (Thomas et al. 2012). They support the physician to identify the disease early and then provide the necessary treatments immediately since such disease are acute in nature and may lead to death or complications unless treated in time.

The objective of this study is therefore to design and develop a Knowledge Based Decision Support System (KBDSS) for diagnosis and detection of acute abdomen.

To achieve this objective, the following activities are performed:

- Acquire tacit and explicit knowledge from domain experts for acute abdomen
- Analyze and model/design the KBDSS for AA using suitable technique, and
- Classify and identify the severity level of the acute abdominal pain

The output of this research:

- Benefit patients by providing easy and timely identification and diagnosis of acute abdomen which helps them to get quick treatment

- Helps physicians to apply better decision-making mechanism using information from the patients' history, ultrasound, X-ray, and white blood cells count.
- Reduces time and cost wasted due to misdiagnosis and unnecessary practice, and
- Reduces cost by using combinative knowledge, and increased.

3 Methodology of the Study

This research has developed a KBDSS for detecting and diagnosing of acute abdominal diseases. A design science research (DSR) methodology is followed in this research which is appropriate for design and development KBDSS. DSR is a research procedure for producing innovative construction intended to solve problems faced in the real world and to make a contribution to the theory of the discipline in which it is applied (Hamid 2014). The design science research methodology presented here incorporates principles, practices, and procedures required to carry out such research and meets three objectives: it is consistent with prior literature, it provides a nominal process model for doing DSR, and it provides a mental model for presenting and evaluating DSR (Ken and Tuure 2007).

3.1 Data Collection Method

In this research, both primary and secondary sources of knowledge are used to acquire the desired knowledge for the KBS. Primary knowledge is gathered from physicians and patients in Bahir Dar Felege-hiwot referral hospital using interview and observation. Secondary source of knowledge was collected by using document analysis. Acquiring knowledge from domain experts and professionals as well as organizing the collected knowledge in the knowledge base is one of the most important tasks of developing decision support system. One of the problems that professionals face is explaining their implicit knowledge. This makes knowledge acquisition the most difficult steps in the development of the model. Once the knowledge is gathered from the available sources, it is encoded in to the knowledge base.

3.2 Knowledge Representation

The knowledge acquired is represented using hybrid (integration of rule-based and case-based reasoning approaches) representation technique. Knowledge based system is a form of artificial intelligence that aims to capture the knowledge of human expert to support decision making. Knowledge base is the major component of the decision support system, since the quality of this unit determines how the user will deal with the system. The reason to use hybrid reasoning approach for the study was because it can alleviate the limitation of the single reasoning approaches and have better performance to represent knowledge for diagnosing acute abdomen.

3.3   Development Tools

Different tools are used for designing and developing KBDSS for acute abdomen.

Prolog: is a programming tool used in this study for designing and developing KBDSS. Prolog is a widely used programming language for artificial intelligence research. Prolog is used because it is easy to represent knowledge. As (Karde and Stefan 1986) stated, prolog programming answers the questions by logically following facts or rules.

Java: is the programming language used in this study to develop the interface. It was also used to provide a temporary storage for facts and cases in order to minimize the drawback of prolog programming language. Since patient history needs privacy and security, java programming language was recommended for developing the prototype of KBDSS (Tejinder and Jhunjhunu 2013).

MSQL: is used in the development of the prototype. Case-based reasoning approach needs a storage to store cases and other knowledge of domain experts. Therefore, MSQL database is used to develop case-library.

4   Model Development and Prototype Evaluation

Knowledge modeling is a cross disciplinary approach to capture and model knowledge of the domain experts into a knowledge-based system for purpose of preserving, improving, sharing, substituting, aggregating and diagnosing patients. Accordingly, in this research, it is used to simulate intelligence.

4.1   The Processes and Approaches of Decision-Making in KBDSS

The clinical decision support system passes different process stages in giving a decision to a problem. The processes include activities starting from collecting facts form domain experts about the given case to determination of final treatment. In healthcare system, different processes are applied before a final decision is reached for specific problem.

The aim of this research is developing a DSS for detecting and diagnosis of acute abdomen. Knowledge engineering research design was used to develop prototype system.

There are three common integration of rule-based and case-based reasoning approaches. These are rule dominant, case dominant and balanced approach.

4.1.1   Rule Dominant Integration

This is the way of integrating of rule-based and case-based reasoning in which rule-based reasoning is more applicable and case-based reasoning can be the supportive of rule-based reasoning.

4.1.2   Case Dominant Integration

Case-based reasoning is dominated to involve for solving a given problem and the rule-based reasoning can solve the problem when if case-based reasoning is not capable of solving a particular problem.

4.1.3 Balanced Approach

In this approach, the two-individual reasoning (rule-based and case-based) approaches have equal status for problem solving. The final result of individual reasoning's is combined to solve the target problem. The result that have been accessed from this type of reasoning approach is better than that can accessed by using the other two reasoning approach by using the same patient cases. According to (Jim and Ioannis 2009), balanced integration approach is best to be applied to health care. Since the two reasoning approaches have equally participated decision making. Due to this, balanced integration approach has been selected for the process of designing and developing an integrated approach for detecting and diagnosis of acute abdomen.

4.2 Architecture of the Prototype

Figure 1 shows the architecture of the proposed system. The inference engine is between the rule base and the working memory. Retrieving, reuse, revise and retain are included in case-based life cycle. Revising and retaining are done after integrating the two reasoning approaches.

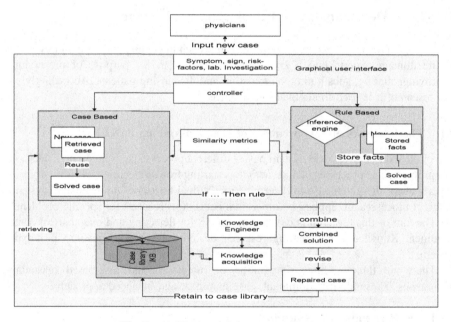

Fig. 1. Architecture of the proposed system

4.3 The Inference Engine

To achieve the goal of decision support system, inference engine helps to determine the order of testing the knowledge base rule, determine a Boolean (true, false uncertainty factor) application rules, and justifies user process of reasoning and generating the result in quantification form. The inference engine can calculate the probability of truth value and made decisions accordingly.

In prolog programming, one of the symptoms, sign, risk-factor or laboratory investigation is false, the inference engine draws, the investigation shows unknown result. It does not create approximate decision.

To solve this problem, temporary storage was created on java NetBeans 8.2 and retrieve facts which are stored in SWI-prolog 7.7.14 tools using prolog programming language to calculate the probability of the occurrence of truth value which helps to decide the severity level of the pain.

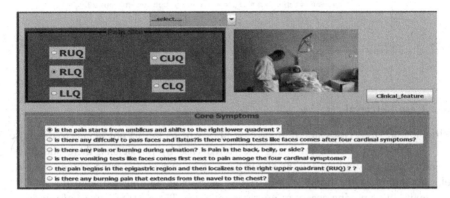

Fig. 2. Retrieving facts from fact base to temporary storage

Figure 2 shows, retrieving facts to store in java temporary storage. Which helps to improve effectiveness of the system. Since inference engine in prolog is difficult to infer from only few satisfied conditions. Therefore, in this system to infer a few satisfied conditions, first the system creates the temporary storage in java programming language. This can simplify the inference engine to draw the appropriate decision by calculating the truth value. After all, in this temporary storage, the system can verify the severity level of the pain using cosine similarity shown in Fig. 3.

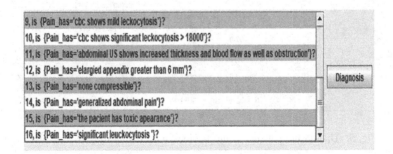

Fig. 3. Diagnosing patients using stored facts

Secondly the system uses case-based reasoning approach which compares the target problem with previously successfully diagnosed cases using cosine similarity metrics. If case-based response does not satisfy any of the condition, the inference engine gives a general recommendation as indicated below in Fig. 4.

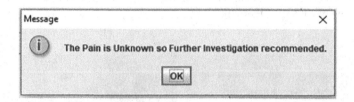

Fig. 4. Recommendation wizard

4.4   Case Retrieval

Retrieving previous cases stored in the case library helps for the physicians to diagnose new similar cases. Before retrieving the stored case by physicians, there should be similarity comparison between the stored cases to be retrieved and the new case which helps to minimize the number of retrieved cases and minimize diagnostic analysis complexity by removing access of unimportant cases. There are two ways of retrieving the stored cases: by directly retrieving the stored case using the result of rule-based reasoning as an attribute and by using the site of pain for retrieval attribute.

Previously successful diagnosed cases for acute abdomen are retrieved in the order of accuracy of clinical investigation. Retrieval of the cases in case library by pain site is shown in Fig. 5.

		ID	date	cause	accouracy	level	treatment	suggestion
		T-61	2018-05-07	appendicitis	0.97	complicaed	surgical	immediate...
		T-30	2018-08-07	appendicitis	0.96	complicated	surgical	interval ap...
		T-45	2018-06-05	appendicitis	0.94	complicated	surgical	immediate...
		T-1	2018-09-04	appendicitis	0.93	complicated	surgical	don't eat m...
RLQ	▼	T-33	2018-05-08	appendicitis	0.93	complicated	surgical	Further stu...
		T-6	2018-09-04	appendicitis	0.9	complicated	surgical	eat vegeta...
		T-26	2018-07-02	appendicitis	0.87	complicated	surgical	interval ap...
appendicitis	▼	T-89	2013-09-05	appendicitis	0.78	likely acute	surgical	immediate...
		T-2	2018-12-02	appendicitis	0.75	likely acute	antibiotics	Antibiotics ...
		T-2	2018-12-02	appendicitis	0.75	likely acute	antibiotics	Antibiotics ...
...select....	▼	T-37	2018-02-06	appendicitis	0.75	likely acute	surgical	immediate...
		T-304	2018-02-01	appendicitis	0.75	likely acute	antibiotics	Antibiotic t...

Fig. 5. Diagnosing patients using previous successfully diagnosed cases

4.5   Similarity Assessment

The similarity of each stored case to the target problem, typically represented as a real number in the range from 0 to 1, is computed using cosine similarity measure.

$$\text{Cos } \theta = \frac{A.B}{||A|| \, ||B||}$$

Where A is the previously diagnosed case or the facts and B is the new patient case.

$$A = [a_1, a_2, a_3, \ldots a_n]$$

$$B = [b_1, b_2, b_3, \ldots b_n]$$

$$\text{Cosine}(A, B) = \frac{\sum_{i=1}^{n} aibi}{\sqrt{\sum_{i=1}^{n} ai} \sqrt{\sum_{i=1}^{n} bi}}$$

4.6   Cause Identification and Leveling Mechanism

In clinical decision-making, cause identification is an initial condition to take appropriate action for the particular cause of acute abdomen.

In this research, cause of acute abdomen was identified by using pain site (abdominal quadrants) and core symptoms. Once the quadrant is known, the pain can be identified using the cosine similarity value. To identify the severity level of the pain, threshold value was put as a pivoting point. Angle of difference between the stored knowledge and the target problem is computed to identify the cases that are very similar, similar and less similar. If the similarity value is greater than cosine of 30 then the pain is complicated, if the similarity value is between cosine of 45 and 30 the problem is likely acute whereas if the similarity is less than cosine of 45 the problem is less likely acute. The threshold value was set by discussion with domain experts.

4.7   Integrating Approach of Rule-Based and Case-Based Reasoning

Integration approach increases the confidence of physicians to diagnose acute abdomen. First the physician diagnoses the patients using rule-based and case-based reasoning and draws appropriate decision in parallel. Then the results of the two decisions can be integrated. For this integration, the mean value of the cosine similarity values of the two reasoning approaches is taken.

5   Conclusion and Recommendation

5.1   Conclusion

Acute abdomen is a type of sudden abdominal pain. In Ethiopia, 90% of surgical emergency is acute abdomen. It needed immediate, accurate and appropriate treatment.

Otherwise, it causes complication or death. KBDSS help physicians in decision making when diagnosing the patients within a short period of time. Knowledge sharing for domain experts in diagnosing patient is the main task of the system. The performance of the system shows promising acceptance by the system evaluators.

According to the system evaluators, the accuracy of the system 99% for acute abdominal cause classification and 66% for severity level identification whereas the accuracy value of physicians with related to the final result were 84% abdominal cause classification and 50% for severity level identification. Therefore, the KBDSS can diagnose patients with highest accuracy. We were taking the final observed value as pivoting point to test the KBDSS. The average result of each reasoning approach from the evaluator or domain experts, rule-based was 60% accuracy, case-based reasoning approach was 70% accuracy and hybrid reasoning approach were 87.66% accuracy. Therefore, hybrid approach was recommended for health care DSS with having the highest accuracy value compared with rule-based and case-based reasoning approaches. The average value of the system classifies attribute which stored in case library and fact base according to the target problem were 71.33% of accuracy. The evaluators and six patients were selected purposively. From this, the system can minimize delay during diagnosis, waste of resources for extra diagnosis and increase knowledge sharing between the domain experts. In addition to this automation of KBDSS has a high contribution for establishment of truthful decision making in acute abdomen patient's treatment.

5.2   Recommendation

Developing a decision support system for clinical diagnosis process is important to facilitate the process of diagnosis of a patient.

Acute abdomen is an emergency disease that cannot give the chance of follow up diagnosis and treatment. Therefore, it is recommended to use this developed KBDSS for diagnosing acute abdomen in health care system.

Integration of different reasoning approach reduces the limitation of individual reasoning. Therefore, it is recommended the researchers use the integration of more than one reasoning approaches and ML algorisms to study knowledge-based systems.

References

Adamu, A., Maigatari, M., Lawal, K., Iliyasu, M.: Waiting time for emergency abdominal surgery in Zaria, Nigeria. Afr. Health Sci. **10**(1), 46–53 (2010). https://www.researchgate.net/publication/46111242

Addisu, M., Tadess, A., Eyobe, T.: Pattern of acute abdomen in Dil Chora referral hospital, Eastern Ethiopia. Int. J. Collab. Res. Internal Med. Publ. Health **8**(11), 607–615 (2016)

Ashley, H., Bennet, B., Marie, C.: The evaluation of the acute abdomen. In: Moore, L., Todd, S. (eds.) Common Problems in Acute Care Surgery, pp. 19–31. Springer, New York (2013). https://doi.org/10.1007/978-1-4614-6123-4_2

Fei, J., et al.: Artificial intelligence in healthcare: past, present and future. Stroke Vasc. **2**, 1–14 (2017)

Hamid, M.: Design science research as an approach to develop conceptual solutions for improving cost management in construction (2014)

Jay, W.M., Charles, P.D., Anand, B.S.: Abdominal Pain (causes, remedies, treatment). (Medicine Net.com) (2017). https://www.medicinenet.com/abdominal_pain_causes_remedies_treatment/article.htm. Accessed 24 Nov 2017

Jim, P., Ioannis, H.: Integration of rule-based and case based reasoning. Hybrid Intell. Syst. **6**(4), 189–209 (2009)

Karde, E., Stefan, J.: Prolog Programming in Artificial Intelligence. Addison-Wesley Publishing Company, Boston (1986)

Ken, P., Tuure, T.: A design science research methodology for information system researches. J. Manag. Inf. Syst. **24**, 45–77 (2007)

Leondes, C.T.: Intelligent Knowledge Based Systems. University of California, Los Angeles, Kluwer Academic Publishers, Los Angeles (2005)

Nyundo, M., Rugwizangoga, E., Ntakiyirutal, G., Kakande, I.: Outcome of emergency abdominal surgery at Kigali university teaching hospital: a review of 229 cases. East Cent. Afr. J. Surg. **18**(1), 31–39 (2013). Retrieved 27 Nov 2017

Prasath, V., Lakshmi, N., Nathiya, M., Bharathan, N., Neetha, P.: A survey on the applications of fuzzy logic in medical diagnosis. Int. J. Sci. Eng. Res. **4**(4), 1199–1203 (2013). http://www.ijser.org

Ray, S., Patel, M., Parmar, H.: Management of acute abdomen: study of 110 cases, **3**(2), 18–24 (2016). http://iaimjournal.com/. Accessed 24 Nov 2017

Tejinder, S., Jhunjhunu, R.: New software development methodology for student of Java programming language. Int. J. Comput. Commun. Eng. **2**(2), 194–196 (2013)

Thomas, M., Fabrizio, C., Shantale, C.: Decision support systems in medicine - anesthesia, critical care and intensive care medicine. McGill University, Intact (2012)

Zaraté, P., Shaofeng, L.: A new trend for knowledge-based decision support system design. Int. J. Inf. Decis. Sci. **8**(3), 305–324 (2016)

Modern CNNs for IoT Based Farms

Patrick Kinyua Gikunda[1,2(✉)] and Nicolas Jouandeau[2]

[1] Department of Information Technology,
Dedan Kimathi University of Technology, Nyeri, Kenya
`patrick.gikunda@dkut.ac.ke`
[2] Le Laboratoire d'Informatique Avancée de Saint-Denis (LIASD),
University of Paris 8, Saint-Denis, France
`n@ai.univ-paris8.fr`

Abstract. Recent introduction of ICT in agriculture has brought a number of changes in the way farming is done. This means use of Internet of Things(IoT), Cloud Computing(CC), Big Data (BD) and automation to gain better control over the process of farming. As the use of these technologies in farms has grown exponentially with massive data production, there is need to develop and use state-of-the-art tools in order to gain more insight from the data within reasonable time. In this paper, we present an initial understanding of Convolutional Neural Network (CNN), the recent architectures of state-of-the-art CNN and their underlying complexities. Then we propose a classification taxonomy tailored for agricultural application of CNN. Finally, we present a comprehensive review of research dedicated to applications of state-of-the-art CNNs in agricultural production systems. Our contribution is in two-fold. First, for end users of agricultural deep learning tools, our benchmarking finding can serve as a guide to selecting appropriate architecture to use. Second, for agricultural software developers of deep learning tools, our in-depth analysis explains the state-of-the-art CNN complexities and points out possible future directions to further optimize the running performance.

Keywords: Convolutional Neural Network · Farming ·
Internet of Things

1   Introduction

The global population is set to touch 9.6 billion mark by year 2050 [4]. The continuous population growth means increase in demand for food to feed the population [5]. Agriculture is the practice of cultivation of land and breeding of animals & plants to provide food and other products in order to sustain and enhance life [6]. Due to the extreme weather conditions, rising climate change and environmental impact resulting from intensive farming practices [8], farmers are now forced to change their farming practices. To cope with the new farming challenges, farmers are forced to practice smart farming [9], which offers solutions of farming management and environment management for better production.

© Springer Nature Switzerland AG 2019
F. Mekuria et al. (Eds.): ICT4DA 2019, CCIS 1026, pp. 68–79, 2019.
https://doi.org/10.1007/978-3-030-26630-1_7

Smart farming focuses on the use of information and communication technology (ICT) in the cyber-physical farm management cycle for efficient farming [10].

Current ICT technologies relevant for use in smart farming include IoT [11], remote sensing [12], CC [13] and BD [14]. Remote sensing is the science of gathering information about objects or areas from a distance without having physical contact with objects or areas being investigated. Data collected through remote sensing and distributed devices is managed by cloud computing technology, which offers the tools for pre-processing and modelling of huge amounts of data coming from various heterogeneous sources [15]. These four technologies could create applications to provide solutions to todays's agricultural challenges. The solutions include real time analytics required to carry out agile actions especially in case of suddenly changed operational or environmental condition (e.g. weather or disease alert). The continuous monitoring, measuring, storing and analysing of various physical aspects has led to a phenomena of big data [16]. To get insight for practical action from this large type of data requires tools and methods that can process multidimensional data from different sources while leveraging on the processing time.

One of the successful data processing tool applied in this kind of large dataset is the biologically inspired Convolutional Neural Networks (CNNs), which have achieved state-of-the-art results [17] in computer vision [18] and data mining [19]. As deep learning has been successfully applied in various domains, it has recently entered in the domain of agriculture [10]. CNN is a subset method of Deep Learning (DL) [20], defined as deep, feed-forward Artificial Neural Network (ANN) [21]. The CNN covolutions allow data representations in a hierarchical way [22]. The common characteristics of CNN models is that they follow the same general design principles of successive applying convolutional layers to the input, periodically downsampling the spatial dimensions while increasing the number of feature maps. These architectures serve as rich feature extractors which can be used for image classification, object detection, image segmentation and many more other advanced tasks. This study investigates the agricultural problems that employ the major state-of-the-art CNN architectures that have participated in the ImageNet Large Scale Visual Recognition Challenge (ILSVRC) [23] with highest accuracy in a multi-class classification problem. ImageNet [26] classification challenge has played a critical role in advancing the CNN state-of-the-art [17]. The motivation for carrying out the study include: (a) CNNs has better precision compared to other popular image-processing techniques in the large majority of problems [27]. (b) CNN has entered in the agricultural domain with promising potential [28]. (c) all the CNN models that have achieved the top-5 error are successful when applied in other computer vision domain with remarkable results [27]. This review aims to provide insight on use of state-of-the-art CNN models in relation to smart farming and to identify smart farming research and development challenges related to computer vision. Therefore the analysis will primarily focus on the success on use of state-of-the-art CNN models in smart farms with a intention to provide this relevant information to the future researchers. From that perspective the research questions to be addressed in the study are:

(a) What is the role of CNN in smart farming?
(b) What type of the state-of-the-art CNN architecture should be used?
(c) What are the benefits of using state-of-the-art CNN in IoT based agricultural systems?

The rest of the paper is organized as follows: in Sect. 2, we present an overview of existing state-of-the-art CNNs architectures including their recent updates. Then we propose a taxonomy to provide a systematic classification of agricultural issues for CNN application. In Sect. 3, we present the existing state-of-the-art CNNs and their scope of application in agri-systems. We conclude the paper in Sect. 4.

2   Methodology

In order to address the research questions a bibliographic analysis in the domain under study was done between 2012 and 2018, it involved two steps: (a) collection of related works and, (b) detailed review and analysis of the works. The choice of the period is from the fact that CNN is rather a recent phenomenon. In the first step, a keyword-based search using all combinations of two groups of keywords of which the first group addresses CNN models (LeNet, AlexNet, NIN, ENet, GoogLeNet, ResNet, DenseNet, VGG, Inception) and the second group refers to farming (i.e. agriculture, farming, smart farming). The analysis was done while considering the following research questions: (a) smart farm problem they addressed, (b) dataset used, (c) accuracy based on author's performance metric, (d) state-of-the-art CNN model used. Its important to note that use of state-of-the-art deep learning has great potential, and there have been recent small comparative studies to analyse and compare the most efficient archtecture to use in agricultural systems. They include: Comparison between LeNet, AlexNet, and VGGNet on automatic identification of center pivot irrigation [29] and comparison between VGG-16, Inception-V4, Resnet and DenseNet for plant disease identification [30].

3   State-of-the-Art CNN: An Overview

CNNs typically perform best when they are large, meaning when they have more deeper and highly interconnected layers [31]. The primary drawback of these architectures is the computational cost, thus large CNNs are typically impractically slow especially for embedded IoT devices [32]. There are recent research efforts on how to reduce the computation cost of deep learning networks for everyday application while maintaining the prediction accuracy [33]. In order to understand the application of the state-of-the-art CNN architectures in agricultural systems, we reviewed the accuracy and computational requirements from relevant literature including recent updates of networks as shown in

Fig. 1. The classical state-of-the-art deep network architectures include; LeNet [34], AlexNet [35], NIN [36], ENet [37], ZFNet [38], GoogLeNet [39] and VGG 16 [40]. Modern architectures include; Inception [41], ResNet [42], and DenseNet [43].

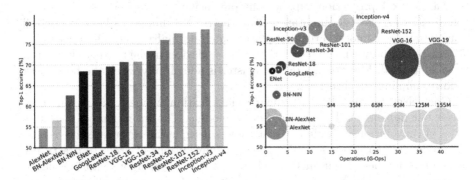

Fig. 1. Top-1 accuracy vs the computational cost. The size of the circles is proportional to number of parameters. Legend; the grey circles at the bottom right represents number of parameters in millions [32].

LeNet-5 is a 7-layer pioneer convolutional network by LeCun et al. [34] to classify digits, used to recognise hand-written numbers digitized in 32×32 pixel greyscale input images. High resolution images require more convolutional layers, so the model is constrained by the availability of the computing resources.

AlexNet is a 5-layer network similar to LeNet-5 but with more filters [35]. It outperformed Lenet-5 and won the LSVRC challenge by reducing the top-5 error from 26.2% to 15.3%. Use Rectified Linear Unit (Relu) [1] instead of Hyperbolic Tangent (Tanh) [2] to add non-linearity and accelerates the speed by 6 times. Droupout was employed to reduce over-fitting in the fully-connected layers. Overlap pooling was used to reduce the size of the network while reducing top-1 error by 0.4% and top-5 error by 0.3%.

Lin et al. [36] created a Network in Network (NIN) which inspired the inception architecture of googlenet. In their paper, they replaced the linear filters with nonlinear multi linear perceptrons that had better feature extraction and accuracy. They also replaced the fully connected layers with activation maps and global average pooling. This move helped reduce the parameters and network complexity.

In their article Paszke et al. [37] introduced an Efficient Neural Network (ENet) for running on low-power mobile devices while achieving state-of-the-art results. ENet architecture is largely based on ResNets. The structure has one master and several branches that separate from the master but concatenate back.

In their work Zeiler and Fergus [38] created ZFNet which won a ILSVRC 2013 [25] image classification. It was able to achieve a top-5 rate of 14.8% an improvement of the AlexNet. They were able to do this by tweaking the hyper-parameters of AlexNet while maintaining the same structure with additional deep learning elements. There is no record observed of use of ZFNet in agricultural systems despite the accuracy improvement. Each branch consists of three convolutional layers. The 'first' 1×1 projection reduces the dimensionality while the latter 1×1 projection expands the dimensionality. In between these convolutions, a regular (no annotation/asymmetric X), dilated (dilated X) or full convolution (no annotation) takes place. Batch normalization [60] and PReLU [61] are placed between all convolutions. As regularizer in the bottleneck, Spatial Dropout is used. MaxPooling on the master is added only when the bottleneck is downsampling which is true.

GoogleNet, a 2014 ILSVRC image classification winner, was inspired by LeNet but implemented a novel inception module. The Inception cell performs series of convolutions at different scales and subsequently aggregate the results. This module is based on several very small convolutions in order to drastically reduce the number of parameters. There has been tremendous efforts done to improve the performance of the architecture: (a) Inception v1 [39] which performs convolution on an input, with 3 different sizes of filters (1×1, 3×3, 5×5). Additionally, max pooling is also performed. The outputs are concatenated and sent to the next inception module. (b) Inception v2 and Inception v3 [41] factorize 5×5 convolution to two 3×3 convolution operations to improve computational speed. Although this may seem counterintuitive, a 5×5 convolution is 2.78 times more expensive than a 3×3 convolution. So stacking two 3×3 convolutions infact leads to a boost in performance. (c) In Inception v4 and Inception-ResNet [44] the initial set of operations were modified before introducing the Inception blocks.

Simonyan and Zisserman created VGGNet while doing investigation on the effect of convolutional network depth on its accuracy in the large-scale image recognition setting. The VGGNet took the second place after GoogLeNet in the competition. The model is made up of 16 convolutional layers which is similar to [35] but with many filters. There have been a number of update to the VGGNet archtecture starting with pioneer VGG-11(11 layers) which obtained 10.4% error rate [40]. VGG-13 (13 layers) obtains 9.9% error rate, which means the additional convolutional layers helps the classification accuracy. VGG-16(16 layers) obtained a 9.4% error rate, which means the additional $3 \times 1 \times 1$ conv layers help the classification accuracy. 1×1 convolution helps increase non-linearity of the decision function, without changing the dimensions of input and output, 1×1 convolution is able to do the projection mapping in the same high dimensionality. This approach is used in NIN [36] GoogLeNet [39] and ResNet [42]. After updating to VGG-16 it obtained 8.8% error rate which means the deep learning network was still improving by adding number of layers. VGG-19 (19 layers) was developed to further improve the performance but it obtained 9.0% showing no improvement even after adding more layers.

When deeper networks starts converging, a degradation problem is exposed: with the network depth increasing, accuracy gets saturated and then degrades rapidly. Deep Residual Neural Network(ResNet) created by He al. [42] introduced a norvel architecture with insert shortcut connections which turn the network into its counterpart residual version. This was a breakthrough which enabled the development of much deeper networks. The residual function is a refinement step in which the network learn how to adjust the input feature map for higher quality features. Following this intuition, the network residual block was refined and proposed a pre-activation variant of residual block [45], in which the gradients can flow through the shortcut connections to any other earlier layer unimpeded. Each ResNet block is either 2 layer deep (used in small networks like ResNet 18, 34) or 3 layer deep (ResNet 50, 101, 152). This technique is able to train a network with 152 layers while still having lower complexity than VGGNet. It achieves a top-5 error rate of 3.57% which beats human-level performance on this dataset. Although the original ResNet paper focused on creating a network architecture to enable deeper structures by alleviating the degradation problem, other researchers have since pointed out that increasing the network's width (channel depth) can be a more efficient way of expanding the overall capacity of the network.

In DenseNet which is a logical extension of ResNet, there is improved efficiency by concatenating each layer feature map to every successive layer within a dense block [43]. This allows later layers within the network to directly leverage the features from earlier layers, encouraging feature reuse within the network. For each layer, the feature-maps of all preceding layers are used as inputs, and its own feature-maps are used as inputs into all subsequent layers, this helps alleviate the vanishing-gradient problem, feature reuse and reduce number of parameters.

3.1 Proposed Agricultural Issues Classification Taxonomy

Many agricultural CNN solutions have been developed depending on specific agriculture issues. For the study purpose, a classification taxonomy tailored to CNN application in the smart farming was developed as shown Fig. 2. In this section, we categorize use of state-of-the-art CNN based on the agricultural issue they solve:

(a) Plant management includes solutions geared towards crop welfare and production. This includes classification (species), detection (disease and pest) and prediction (yield production).
(b) Livestock management address solutions for livestock production (prediction and quality management) and animal welfare (animal identification, species detection and disease and pest control).
(c) Environment management addresses solutions for land and water management.

3.2 Use of State-of-the-Art CNN in Smart Farms

The Table 1, shows use of state-of-the-art CNN in agriculture and in particular the areas of plant and leaf disease detection, animal face identification, plant recognition, land cover classification, fruit counting and identification of weeds.

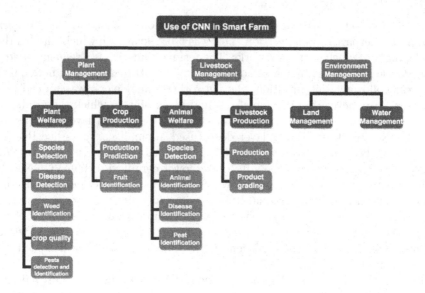

Fig. 2. Proposed classification taxonomy for CNN use in smart farm

It consist of 5 columns to show: the problem description, size of data used, accuracy according to the metrics used, the state-of-the-art CNN used and reference literature.

In their paper, Amara et al. [54] use the LeNet architecture to classify the banana leaves diseases. The model was able to effectively classify the leaves after several experiments. The approach was able to classify leaves images with different illumination, complex background, resolution, size, pose, and orientation. We also reviewed use of CaffeNet archtecture [59] in agricultural application, which is a 1-GPU version of AlexNet. The success of this model at LSVRC 2012 [24] encourage many computer vision community to explore more on the application of deep learning in computer vision. Mohanty et al. [7] combined both AlexNet and GoogLeNet to identify 14 crop species and 26 diseases(or absence thereof) from a dataset of 54,305 images. The approach records an impressive accuracy of 99.35% demonstrating the feasibility of the state-of-the-art CNN architectures. Other areas AlexNet has been used with high accuracy record include; identify plants using different plant views [49], identify plant species [48], identify obstacles in the farm [50] and leaf disease detection [3]. Because of its achievement to improve utilization of the computing resources GoogLeNet has been used in fruit count [53] and plant species classification [7]. VGGNet has been used in classifying weed [56], detect obstacles in the farm [51], fruit detection [47] and animal face recognition [55]. Like ResNet, DenseNet is a recent model that explains why it has not been employed significantly in farming, nevertheless it has been used in thistle identification in winter wheat and spring barley [52]. Since ResNet is a such a recent model, it have only been used by one author in fruit counting [53]. Many of the CNN developed for agricultural use depend on the problem or challenge they solve.

Table 1. Use of state-of-the-art CNN in Smart Farm

No.	Smartfarm problem description	Data used	Accuracy	CNN framework used	Article
1	Fruit detection	Images of three fruit varieties: apples (726), almonds (385) and mangoes (1154)	F1 (precision score) of 0.904 (apples) 0.908 (mango) 0.775 (almonds)	VGGNet	[46]
2	Detection of sweet pepper and rock melon fruits	122 images	0.838 (F1)	VGGNet	[47]
3	Recognize different plant species	Data set of 44 classes	99.60% (CA - correct prediction)	AlexNet	[48]
4	Recognize different plant	91 759 images	48.60% (LC-correct species classification)	AlexNet	[49]
5	Identify obstacles in row crops and grass mowing	437 images	99.9% in row crops and 90.8% in grass mowing (CA)	AlexNet	[50]
6	Identify crop species and diseases	54 306 images	0.9935 (F1)	AlexNet + GoogLeNet	[7]
7	Detect obstacles that are distant, heavily occluded and unknown	48 images	0.72 (F1)	AlexNet + VGG	[51]
8	Leaf disease detection	4483 images	96.30% (CA)	CaffeNet	[3]
9	Identify thistle in winter wheat and spring barley images	4500 images	97.00% (CA)	DenseNet	[52]
10	Predict number of tomatoes in images	24 000 images	91% (RFC-Ratio of total fruits counted) on real images, 93% (RFC) on synthetic images	GoogLeNet + ResNet	[53]
11	Classify banana leaf diseases	3700 images	96% (CA), 0.968 (F1)	LeNet	[54]
12	Identify pig face	1553 images	96.7% (CA)	VGGNet	[55]
13	Classify weed from crop species based on 22 different species in total	10413 images	86.20% (CA)	VGGNet	[56]
14	Detecting and categorizing the criticalness of Fusarium wilt of radish based on thresholding a range of color features	1500 images		GoogLeNet	[57]
15	Fruit counting	24 000 images	91% accuracy	Inception-ResNet	[53]
16	Automatic Plant disease diagnosis for early disease symptoms	8178 images	Overall improvement of the balanced accuracy from 0.78 to 0.87 from previous 2017 study	Deep ResNet	[58]

4   Conclusions and Recommendations

Despite remarkable achievement in use state-of-the-art CNN in agriculture in general, there exist grey areas in relation to smart farm that future researchers may look at. These areas may include; real-time image classification, interactive image classification and interactive object detection. State-of-the-art CNN is relatively a new technology that explain why the finding of the study about their use in smart farm is relatively small. However, its is important to note that models built from state-of-the-art architectures have a impressive record of better precision performance. In this paper, we aimed at establishing the potential of state-of-the-art CNN in IoT based smart farms. In particular we first discussed the architectures of state-of-the-art CNNs and their respective prediction accuracy at the ILSVRC challenge. Then a survey on application of the identified CNNs in Agriculture was performed; to examine the particular application in a smart farm, listed technical details of the architecture employed and overall prediction accuracy achieved according to the author precision metrics. From the study its evident of continuous accuracy improvement of the state-of-the-art CNN architectures as computer vision community put effort to perfect the methods. The findings indicate that state-of-the-art CNN has achieved better precision in all the cases applied in the agricultural domain, scoring higher accuracy in majority of the problem as compared to other image-processing techniques. Considering that the state-of-the-art CNN has achieved state-of-the-art results in prediction in general and high precision in the few farming cases observed, there is great potential that can be achieved in using the methods in smart farming. It has been observed that many authors apply more than one architecture in order to optimize the performance of the network without compromising the expected accuracy. This approach is very efficient in the observed cases, and we recommend similar hybrid approach when building robust IoT based networks which are computationally fair to the mobile devices. This study aims to motivate researchers to experiment and apply the state-of-the-art methods in smart farms problems related to computer vision and data analysis in general.

References

1. Xu, B., Wang, N., Chen, T., Li, M.: Empirical evaluation of rectified activations in convolutional network. CoRR, abs/1505.00853 (2015)
2. Luo, P., Li, H.: Research on quantum neural network and its applications based on tanh activation function. Comput. Digit. Eng. **16**, 33–39 (2016)
3. Sladojevic, S., Arsenovic, M., Anderla, A., Culibrk, D., Stefanovic, D.: Deep neural networks based recognition of plant diseases by leaf image classification. Comp. Int. Neurosci. (2016)
4. Godfray, H.C., et al.: Food security: the challenge of feeding 9 billion people. Science **327**(5967), 812–818 (2010)
5. Lutz, W.L., Sanderson, W.C., Scherbov, S.: The coming acceleration of global population ageing. Nature **451**, 716–719 (2008)
6. Bruinsma, J. (ed.): World Agriculture: Towards 2015/2030. An FAO Perspective. Earthscan, London (2003)
7. Mohanty, S.P., Hughes, D.P., Salathé, M.: Using deep learning for image-based plant disease detection. Front. Plant Sci. **7**, 1419 (2016)
8. Gebbers, R., Adamchuk, V.I.: Precision agriculture and food security. Science **327**(5967), 828–831 (2010)
9. Krintz, C., et al.: SmartFarm: improving agriculture sustainability using modern information technology (2016)
10. Kamilaris, A., Prenafeta Boldú, F.: A review of the use of convolutional neural networks in agriculture. J. Agric. Sci. **156**, 312–322 (2018). https://doi.org/10.1017/S0021859618000436

11. Weber, R.H., Weber, R.: Internet of Things: Legal Perspectives. Springer, Heidelberg (2010). https://doi.org/10.1007/978-3-642-11710-7
12. Ray, A.S.: Remote sensing in agriculture. Int. J. Environ. Agric. Biotechnol. (IJEAB) 1(3) (2016)
13. Jinbo, C., Xiangliang, C., Han-Chi, F., et al.: Clust. Comput. https://doi.org/10.1007/s10586-018-2022-5
14. Chi, M., Plaza, A., Benediktsson, J.A., Sun, Z., Shen, J., Zhu, Y.: Big data for remote sensing: challenges and opportunities. Proc. IEEE 104, 2207–2219 (2016)
15. Waga, D., Rabah, K.: Environmental conditions' big data management and cloud computing analytics for sustainable agriculture. World J. Comput. Appl. Technol. 2, 73–81 (2017)
16. Chen, M., Mao, S., Liu, Y.: Big data: a survey. MONET 19, 171–209 (2014)
17. Russakovsky, O., et al.: ImageNet large scale visual recognition challenge. Int. J. Comput. Vis. 115, 211–252 (2015)
18. Liang, M., Hu, X.: Recurrent convolutional neural network for object recognition. In: IEEE Conference on Computer Vision and Pattern Recognition (CVPR), pp. 3367–3375 (2015)
19. Poria, S., Cambria, E., Gelbukh, A.F.: Aspect extraction for opinion mining with a deep convolutional neural network. Knowl.-Based Syst. 108, 42–49 (2016)
20. Goodfellow, I.J., Bengio, Y., Courville, A.C.: Deep learning. Nature 521, 436–444 (2015)
21. Bhandare, A., Bhide, M., Gokhale, P., Chandavarkar, R. Applications of convolutional neural networks (2016)
22. Schmidhuber, J.: Deep learning in neural networks: an overview. Neural Netw. 61, 85–117 (2015)
23. http://image-net.org/challenges/LSVRC/2017. Accessed 02 Sept 2018
24. http://image-net.org/challenges/LSVRC/2012/. Accessed 02 Sept 2018
25. http://image-net.org/challenges/LSVRC/2013/. Accessed 02 Sept 2018
26. ImageNet. http://image-net.org. Accessed 21 Oct 2018
27. Zahangir, M.A., et al.: The history began from AlexNet: a comprehensive survey on deep learning approaches. https://arxiv.org/pdf/1803.01164
28. Kamilaris, A., Prenafeta-Boldu, F.X.: Deep learning in agriculture: a survey. Comput. Electron. Agric. 147, 70–90 (2018)
29. Zhang, C., Yue, P., Liping, D., Zhaoyan, W.: Automatic identification of center pivot irrigation systems from landsat images using convolutional neural networks. Agriculture 8, 147 (2018)
30. Chebet, E., Yujian, L., Njuki, S., Yingchun, L.: A comparative study of fine-tuning deep learning models for plant disease identification. Comput. Electron. Agric. https://doi.org/10.1016/j.compag.2018.03.032
31. Andri, R., Cavigelli, L., Rossi, D., Benini, L.: Hyperdrive: a systolically scalable binary-weight CNN inference engine for mW IoT end-nodes. In: 2018 IEEE Computer Society Annual Symposium on VLSI (ISVLSI), pp. 509–515 (2018)
32. Canziani, A., Paszke, A., Culurciello, E.: An analysis of deep neural network models for practical applications. CoRR, abs/1605.07678 (2016)
33. HasanPour, S.H., Rouhani, M., Fayyaz, M., Sabokrou, M., Adeli, E.: Towards principled design of deep convolutional networks: introducing SimpNet. CoRR, abs/1802.06205 (2018)
34. LeCun, Y., Bottou, L., Bengio, Y.: Gradient-based learning applied to document recognition. Proc. IEEE 86(11), 2278–2324 (1998)
35. Krizhevsky, A., Sutskever, I., Hinton, G.E.: ImageNet classification with deep convolutional neural networks. Commun. ACM 60, 84–90 (2012)

36. Lin, M., Chen, Q., Yan, S.: Network in network. CoRR, abs/1312.4400 (2013)
37. Paszke, A., Chaurasia, A., Kim, S., Culurciello, E.: ENet: a deep neural network architecture for real-time semantic segmentation. CoRR, abs/1606.02147 (2016)
38. Zeiler, M.D., Fergus, R.: Visualizing and understanding convolutional networks. In: Fleet, D., Pajdla, T., Schiele, B., Tuytelaars, T. (eds.) ECCV 2014. LNCS, vol. 8689, pp. 818–833. Springer, Cham (2014). https://doi.org/10.1007/978-3-319-10590-1_53
39. Szegedy, C., et al.: Going deeper with convolutions. In: IEEE Conference on Computer Vision and Pattern Recognition (CVPR), pp. 1–9 (2015)
40. Simonyan, K., Zisserman, A.: Very deep convolutional networks for large-scale image recognition. CoRR, abs/1409.1556 (2014)
41. Szegedy, C., Vanhoucke, V., Ioffe, S., Shlens, J., Wojna, Z.: Rethinking the inception architecture for computer vision. In: IEEE Conference on Computer Vision and Pattern Recognition (CVPR), pp. 2818–2826 (2016)
42. He, K., Zhang, X., Ren, S., Sun, J.: Deep residual learning for image recognition. In: 2016 IEEE Conference on Computer Vision and Pattern Recognition (CVPR), pp. 770–778 (2015)
43. Huang, G., Liu, Z., Maaten, L.V., Weinberger, K.Q.: Densely connected convolutional networks. In: 2017 IEEE Conference on Computer Vision and Pattern Recognition (CVPR), pp. 2261–2269 (2017)
44. Szegedy, C., Ioffe, S., Vanhoucke, V.: Inception-v4. In: Inception-ResNet and the Impact of Residual Connections on Learning. AAAI (2017)
45. He, K., Zhang, X., Ren, S., Sun, J.: Identity mappings in deep residual networks. In: Leibe, B., Matas, J., Sebe, N., Welling, M. (eds.) ECCV 2016. LNCS, vol. 9908, pp. 630–645. Springer, Cham (2016). https://doi.org/10.1007/978-3-319-46493-0_38
46. Bargoti, S., Underwood, J.P.: Deep fruit detection in orchards. In: 2017 IEEE International Conference on Robotics and Automation (ICRA), pp. 3626–3633 (2017)
47. Sa, I., Ge, Z., Dayoub, F., Upcroft, B., Perez, T., McCool, C.: DeepFruits: a fruit detection system using deep neural networks. Sensors 16, 1222 (2016)
48. Lee, S.H., Chan, C.S., Wilkin, P., Remagnino, P.: Deep-plant: plant identification with convolutional neural networks. In: 2015 IEEE International Conference on Image Processing (ICIP), pp. 452–456 (2015)
49. Reyes, A.K., Caicedo, J.C., Camargo, J.E.: Fine-tuning deep convolutional networks for plant recognition. In: CLEF (2015)
50. Steen, K.A., Christiansen, P., Karstoft, H., Jørgensen, R.N.: Using deep learning to challenge safety standard for highly autonomous machines in agriculture. J. Imaging 2, 6 (2016)
51. Christiansen, P., Nielsen, L.N., Steen, K.A., Jørgensen, R.N., Karstoft, H.: Deep-Anomaly: combining background subtraction and deep learning for detecting obstacles and anomalies in an agricultural field. Sensors 16, 1904 (2016)
52. Sørensen, R.A., Rasmussen, J., Nielsen, J., Jørgensen, R.N.: Thistle detection using convolutional neural networks. In: EFITA WCCA 2017 Conference, Montpellier Supagro, Montpellier, France, 2–6 July 2017
53. Rahnemoonfar, M., Sheppard, C.: Deep count: fruit counting based on deep simulated learning. Sensors 17, 905 (2017)
54. Amara, J., Bouaziz, B., Algergawy, A.: A deep learning-based approach for banana leaf diseases classification. In: BTW (2017)
55. Hansen, M.F., et al.: Towards on-farm pig face recognition using convolutional neural networks. Comput. Ind. 98, 145–152 (2018)

56. Dyrmann, M., Karstoft, H., Midtiby, H.: Plant species classification using deep convolutional neural network. Biosyst. Eng. **151**, 72–80 (2016)
57. Hyun, J., Ibrahim. H., Irfan, M., Minh, L., Suhyeon, I.: UAV based wilt detection system via convolutional neural networks. Sustain. Comput. Inform. Syst. https://doi.org/10.1016/j.suscom.2018.05.010
58. Picona, A., Alvarez, A., Seitz, M., Ortiz, O., Echazarra, J., Johannes, A.: Deep convolutional neural networks for mobile capture device-based crop disease classification in the wild. Comput. Electron. Agric. https://doi.org/10.1016/j.compag.2018.04.002
59. Jia, Y., et al.: Convolutional architecture for fast feature embedding. In: ACM Multimedia (2014)
60. Ioffe, S., Szegedy, C.: Batch normalization: accelerating deep network training by reducing internal covariate shift. In: ICML (2015)
61. He, K., Zhang, X., Ren, S., Sun, J.: Delving deep into rectifiers: surpassing human-level performance on ImageNet classification. In: 2015 IEEE International Conference on Computer Vision (ICCV), pp. 1026–1034 (2015)

A Collaborative Approach to Build a KBS for Crop Selection: Combining Experts Knowledge and Machine Learning Knowledge Discovery

Mulualem Bitew Anley[1][(✉)] and Tibebe Beshah Tesema[2]

[1] Faculty of Informatics, University of Gondar, Gondar, Ethiopia
mulerkal@gmail.com, mulualem.bitew@uog.edu.et
[2] School of Information Science, Addis Ababa University,
Addis Ababa, Ethiopia
tibebe.beshah@gmail.com, tibebe.beshah@aau.edu.et

Abstract. This study proposed designing knowledge based solution through the collaboration of experts' knowledge with the machine learning knowledge base to recommending suitable agricultural crops for a farm land. To design the collaborative approach the knowledge was acquired from document analysis, domain experts' interview and hidden knowledge were extracted from Ethiopia national meteorology agency weather dataset and from central statistics agency crop production dataset by using machine learning algorithms. The study follows the design science research methodology, with CommonKADS and HYBRID models; and WEKA, SWI-Prolog 7.32 and Java NetBeans tools for the whole process of extracting knowledge, develop the knowledge base and for developing graphical user interface respectively.

Based on the objective measurement PART rule induction have the highest classifier algorithm which classified correctly 82.6087% among 9867 instances. The designed collaborative approach of experts' knowledge with the knowledge discovery for agricultural crop selections based on the domain expert, farmers and agriculture extension evaluation 95.23%, 82.2% and 88.5% overall performance respectively.

Keywords: Crop selection · Collaborative approach ·
Knowledge based system · Machine learning · Expertise knowledge

1 Introduction

Crop selection is a process of picking suitable crops for a farm unit based on the physical, economical, climatic and socio-political factors associated with the farm unit [1]. Those parameters are affecting the production yield of the crop. Farmers are facing a challenge during their cropping plan [1]. Taking a correct selection at suited time is directly affecting the whole product of the crop. Taking a selection is a very complex process as there are various factors affecting whole farming process. In order to enhance the decision, it needs to consider rainfall parameters, atmospheric condition, humidity, type of soil and many other factors [2].

© Springer Nature Switzerland AG 2019
F. Mekuria et al. (Eds.): ICT4DA 2019, CCIS 1026, pp. 80–92, 2019.
https://doi.org/10.1007/978-3-030-26630-1_8

Land evaluators and crop experts help farmers to choose the most productive crop that is best suited for a farm unit by assessing its land characters. But not all farmers get such advice and information, especially farmers living in developing country Ethiopia also no exception [3, 4]. On the other hand, agriculture is the main source of economy and the means of employment for nearly 85% of the population, meals supply of the home market and methods for outside cash acquiring. Beside of these, agricultural specialist assistance is not always available when the farmer needs it. In order to alleviate this problem a collaborative approach for combining experts' knowledge with results of knowledge discovery is a suitable solution that can overcome the scarcity of experts [3, 5]. Knowledge can be acquired from different sources such as making interview with the domain experts, document analysis, observation and automatic by using machine learning. Since tacit knowledge is personal and the knowledge expert may not tell all the knowledge she or he knows during the interview, there is hidden knowledge about the problem. Machine learning more general knowledge discovery techniques proposed for extracting hidden and previously unknown knowledge from datasets by different researchers [6].

2 Related Works

A study by Joshi [7] attempted to examine the fuzzy based intelligent system to predict most suitable crop. The fundamental goal of the work is to outline, improvement and organization of a fuzzy based agricultural decision support system which help farmers to make wise decisions regarding selection of a crop. They used a rule based system fuzzy decision support system (DSS) in light of MATLAB and they considered 15 parameters which are greatest among contemporary works and 22 different fuzzy rules.

Another study conducted by Ponnusamy [3] conducted on the design and development of a prototype knowledge based spatial decision support system. The investigation concentrates on assessing land assets and choosing suitable agricultural crops for a farm unit. The researcher considers the land evaluation process by including many experts from varied scientific domains. They at long last create a crop advisor expert system takes land information and recommend in consultation with the farmer a gathering of appropriate harvest decisions that are best as far as physical, monetary, social and political elements related with a farm unit.

A study by Abdulkerim [8] has conducted research on integrating data mining with knowledge based system on the network intrusion detection area and general objectives of his study was to construct a prototype knowledge base system which can update its knowledge base using the hidden knowledge extracted from the intrusion dataset by using data mining techniques. The researcher used knowledge discovery in database (KDD) model for the data mining task, rule based knowledge representation approach to represent knowledge, prototyping approach to develop the knowledge based system, WEKA 3.8.1 to mine hidden knowledge and compare the performance of classifiers, Java NetBeans IDE 7.3 with JDK 6 to develop an integrator application, PROLOG to represent rules in knowledge base, Precision, Recall, F-measure and True Positive rate to evaluate accuracy of the models and test cases to evaluate the performance of the KBS. The system was aimed at utilizing hidden knowledge extracted by employing an induction algorithm of data mining, specifically JRip from sampled KDDcup'99 intrusion dataset. They recommended applying integration of machine learning with a knowledge based system in other domain areas than intrusion detection specially the area that scarce of domain expert.

However, most of the research that has been conducted in the area of KBS their knowledge base was dependent on either domain expert knowledge only or on machine learning techniques which will limit the performance of the recommender. As pointed by [9, 10] each approach has its own limitation on the DSS. In the domain expert only knowledge acquisition experts do often provide a mixture of relevant, irrelevant and erroneous information. On the other side the machine learning approach has a limitation of the too dependent on the data that is provided from outside. According to [11] that have a problem of discovering knowledge might not be the needs of the real world and also has a problem of the rules surplus in depth and in quantity. Due to these problems the user of the rule is needed to decide many times during the use of the rule. Another problem the algorithm produces so many rules that are confused to choose the best rule to make a decision and the rules have too far from the facts so decision maker doesn't believe that rule to make a decision in real world decision making process. A study conducted by [12] stated that collaborating experts with a machine learning approaches was higher benefit to increase the accuracy of the developed knowledge base.

3 Methodology of the Study

3.1 General Research Approach

This study followed the design science research approach as suggested by [13] to design the collaborative approach based KBS that combine experts' knowledge with machine learning knowledge for agricultural extensions and farmers to crop selection decision support system with GUI. According to [13] the design science research process have six basic steps those are problem identification and motivation, definition of objectives for a solution, design and development, demonstration and evaluation lastly communication.

3.2 Data Source

For this study, we used crop production and land information data sourced from the central statics agency agricultural dataset from year 2009 up to year 2015 G.C and climatic dataset obtained from Ethiopian national meteorology agency covering from years 1952 to 2016. After, filtering by the crop type we have get 9867 among 64,327 instances. On the other hand, the NMA data are in Excel for each station by different sheets and monthly data are collected.

3.3   Knowledge Modeling and Representation

The researcher used by adopting the knowledge discovery process model to acquire knowledge from the central statistical agency (CSA) agricultural dataset and climate condition data from the national meteorology agency (NMA) for machine learning knowledge discovery. Machine learning (ML) methods build models based on previous observations which can then be used to predict new data. The model built as a result of a learning process that extracts useful information about the data generation process of the system using the previous observations. Machine learning methods take a set of data corresponding to the process and construct a model of that process in a variety of ways to predict that process. The resulting model can be applied to future data to attempt to predict the crop selection of the knowledge base. We used classification methods J48, PART and JRip decision trees and rule induction classification algorithms.

Expert knowledge base design approach for the development of the knowledge based system we used the CommonKADS knowledge based design model. CommonKADS gives handy documentation for framework configuration transform furthermore energize more awesome modularity and reusability of the model. Arranged with help knowledge engineers in selection knowledge representations and programming techniques with a specific end goal to create a decent outline of a KBS framework. Expects to do this in a way which is both nonspecific platform independent for as long as possible thus opening up possibilities for reusability and economical it encourages preservation of the structures within the expertise model. Nowadays CommonKADS are the primary methodology to support KBS engineering. It helps to perform a detailed analysis of knowledge tasks and processes [14].

3.4   Implementation Procedures and Tools

In order to mine the hidden knowledge from the preprocessed dataset and compare the performance of classifiers the researcher would use WEKA data mining tool. In order to process the data that was collected from the CSA we have used SPSS and Microsoft Excel software. To represent rules in the knowledge base and construct the prototype of crop selection knowledge based system, the researcher used SWI-Prolog. We have used JPL jar file for incorporating the SWI-prolog knowledge base into GUI and java NetBeans for developing the prototype of GUI system.

3.5   Validation and Evaluation Approaches

The performance of the model developed using machine learning techniques are evaluated based on accuracy of classifiers, Precision, Recall, F-measure and True Positive rate. The prototype of KBS is evaluated using system performance testing by preparing test cases. Moreover it is also tested by domain experts and users to ensure user acceptance and check the extent to which the system meets user requirements.

4   Experiment and Result Findings

4.1   Knowledge Modeling

The researchers have used expert knowledge and knowledge from machine learning knowledge elicitation. The expert knowledge are modeled by CommonKADS knowledge modeling. We represented the knowledge model with a unified modeling language (UML) class diagram. In the knowledge modeling stage UML was proposed as a standard notation for CommonKADS methodology for this research.

4.2   Knowledge Discovery

(I) **Data Preprocessing.** This research used weather and crop production sample survey datasets. CSA dataset was available in the SPSS software format in the CSA of Ethiopia database. Then, the researchers export those datasets into MS-excel for deciding on the usefulness of the data used as input for the stated machine learning methodology accordingly.

(II) **Missing Value Handling Method.** The researchers use mean imputation method for the meteorology agency dataset. This method is an effective method to fill missing values in the case of time series where the missed value is strongly related to its previous and next values. For NMA data total 11 attributes of the original dataset collected from since 1952 from different district and zonal stations. Among that dataset we use the data that are collected 2009–2015 G.C because of integrating with the CSA agricultural data and the remaining year data have high missing values from station to station. For the remaining NMA data attributes the researchers' uses to handles the missed attribute, the attribute mean to fill in the missing value. For this research CSA agricultural data have total 43 attributes of the original data set, 9 attributes were ignored because of their high missing values and 15 attributes that have no relation to the research goals have been removed. For the remaining attributes the researchers uses to handles the missed attribute values a global constant to fill in the missing value.

(III) **Data Integration.** The integration was done by being able to identify attributes which match in both data sets and integrating the data based on those variables. In this case the basis for my integrating was the district, season and year where these variables were the same. Other points to consider during data integration on the time unit chosen as a basis for recording time of the data.

(IV) **Data Transformation and Data Conversion.** The process of converting an attributes values from numeric to nominal and vice versa. Since, for the purpose of this research work, the researchers employed to attribute values convert depicted on Table 1.

(V) **Attribute Selection.** The attributes used for conducting this research were selected using domain experts investigation and information gain attribute evaluator and ranker search method which are relevant to the proposed study. Descriptions of the selected attributes that have been taken from the original dataset for experimentation are shown in Table 2.

Table 1. Converted attributes value

S. no.	Attributes	Previous values	Values after conversion
1	Field type	Numeric {1, 2, 3}	1 = Pure Stand, 2 = Mixed Crops 3 = Other Land Use
2	Percent of field in use	Numeric {0, 100}	0 = Land Use Only, 100 = Single Crop
3	Seed type	Numeric {1, 2}	1 = Improved Seed, 2 = Non Improved Seed,
4	Irrigation used	Numeric {1, 2}	1 = YES, 2 = NO
5	Irrigation source	Numeric {1, 2, 3, 4, 5}	1 = River, 2 = Lake, 3 = Pond, 4 = Harvested Water, 5 = Others
6	Fertilizer used	Numeric {1, 2}	1 = YES, 2 = NO
7	Fertilizer type	Numeric {1, 2, 3}	1 = Natural, 2 = Chemical, 3 = Both
8	Chemical fertilizer type	Numeric {1, 2, 3, 9}	1 = UREA, 2 = DAP, 3 = BOTH, 9 = NOT STATED
9	Crop damage	Numeric {1, 2}	1 = YES, 2 = NO
10	Prevention measure taken	Numeric {1, 2}	1 = YES, 2 = NO
11	Damage prevention	Numeric {1, 2, 3}	1 = Chemical, 2 = Non Chemical, 3 = Both
12	Extension program	Numeric {1, 2}	1 = YES, 2 = NO
13	Crop type	Numeric {1, 2, 7}	1 = BARLEY, 2 = MAIZE, 7 = TEFF

Table 2. Attributes used for experiment with description

S. no.	Attribute name	Representation type	Value	Description
1	Elevation	Nominal	High, medium, low	The elevation/Altitude of the district
2	Temperature	Nominal	Low, medium, high	Average temperature of each district
3	Fertilizer type	Nominal	Natural, chemical, Both	Type of fertilizer the farmers used
4	Rain fall	Nominal	High, medium, low	Annual rainfall in different stations
5	Field type	Nominal	Pure stand, mixed crop	A plot of land which is used to produce same or mixed crops
6	Seed type	Nominal	Improved, non-Improved	Varieties of seeds
7	Ownership	Nominal	Private, leased	Describes the owner of the farm land
8	Fertilizer used	Nominal	YES, NO	Fertilizer used for harvesting
9	Main season	Nominal	Belg, meher	Seasons for crop cultivation
10	Crop yield	Numeric	Low, medium, high	The total amount of crops produce
11	Irrigation used	Nominal	YES, NO	Farmers used irrigation for cropping or not
12	Percent of field in use	Numeric	Single crop, Land use only	The field in which used to weather cropping or for land use
13	Crop type	Nominal	Barley, Maize, Teff,	Describes most common cereal crops on north Gondar

4.3 Experimental Settings

After data preparation task completed and suitable for WEKA data miner software, we continue the experiment for building a classification model that can support a decision for farmers to choice crops based on their farmland. In order to do these the researchers conduct twelve different experimentations in four models from each three classification algorithms on integrated field information dataset and meteorology datasets to select the best model. In all experiment we have using 9867 instances were taken for training and model building. These experiments were done by using J48 decision tree classifier, PART rule based classifier and JRip rule based classifier algorithms. In the experimentation test set, cross-validation (10 folds) and percentage split (66%) training options employed and WEKA 3.8.0 data mining tool was used. The experiments conducted using confidence factor it ranges from 0.5–0.4 and minnumobj from 1–35 for every classifier algorithm since it permits accomplishing better precision compared with changing the default parameter values.

Experiment One Using J48 Decision Tree. The J48 algorithm is used for building the decision tree model. This experiment were conducted with two scenarios, J48 with pruned and J48 with unpruned tree. In addition the researchers used a test set, cross-validation and percentage split testing options. As a result pruned tree has been simple to interpret and understand the rules generated from the datasets and it makes the decision making easier. The pruned tree J48 model has 286 tree size and 172 numbers of leaves. The algorithm has correctly classified 8139 instances in other word 82.4871% among 9867 instances and 1728 instances in other word 17.5129% classified incorrectly and time taken to build model 0.74 s.

Experiment Two Using PART Rule Based Classifier. This experiment is done by using PART rule based classifier. This experiment was done by using testing set, cross-validation and percentage split test option belongs to the WEKA data mining software. Cross validation was better classified correctly for training the classification model. The model generates 108 rules. The algorithm has correctly classified 8151 (82.6087%) among 9867 instances and 1716 (17.3913%) classified incorrectly and time taken to build model 0.32 s.

Experiment Three Using JRip. This experiment was done by testing set, cross-validation and percentage split test option belongs to the WEKA data mining software. The algorithm generates a model with 32 rules and correctly classified instances are 7666 (77.6933%) and incorrectly classified instances are 2201 (22.3067%) from total number of instances of 9867. The algorithm takes 0.16 s to develop the model.

In algorithms evaluation, from above experiment, it is clearly observed that PART algorithm with the cross-validation test option accuracy and TP rate is better than other algorithms. As a result, it is reasonable to conclude that PART algorithm is better than J48 and JRip method for this study. Therefore, the model which is developed with the PART rule with cross-validation test option classification techniques is considered as the selected working model for the next use in the development of machine learning knowledge base of the KBS and some of the rules generated from the selected model are presented here below:

Rules

```
Rule 1:  If temperature = Low AND elevation = high AND
rainfall = Medium AND Irrigation_used = No AND Crop_Yield
= High: then crop type = BARLEY (1008.0/21.0)
Rule 2: If temperature = Low AND Crop_Yield = Low AND
Main_Season = Belg AND Field_Type = Pure: then crop type=
BARLEY (837.0/96.0)
Rule 3: if Fertilizer_Used = Yes AND Fertilizer_Type =
Both AND temperature = Medium AND Irrigation_used = No
AND Crop_Yield = High AND Field_Type = Pure: then crop
type= TEFF (11.0)
Rule 4: if Fertilizer_Used = Yes AND Fertilizer_Type =
Both AND rainfall = high AND Crop_Yield = Low: then crop
type= MAIZE (12.0/3.0)
```

4.4   The Proposed Solution Architecture

As depicted below on Fig. 1 the design of knowledge based system through the collaboration of expert's with the knowledge discovery to crop selection was begun from document analysis, interview the domain expert understanding the domain area and problem as a whole acquiring knowledge from the experts' and from dataset using machine learning approaches. This research proposed to use dual knowledge base the first knowledge base contained in the machine learning rules which was extracted from the dataset by using a PART rule induction algorithm. The other knowledge base was contained the experts knowledge in the rule representation format. The inference engine inferred from those dual knowledge base for the user input parameters.

The contribution of this study is design an approach that collaborate the experts knowledge with the knowledge extracted by machine learning. The knowledge based system of this research, domain experts, knowledge collaboratively works with machine learning rule. Other contribution of this study, we have developed a java based GUI in Amharic language. Here below is the discussion of the above architecture through the collaboration of expert's with the knowledge discovery for agricultural crop selection using GUI general collaborative approach.

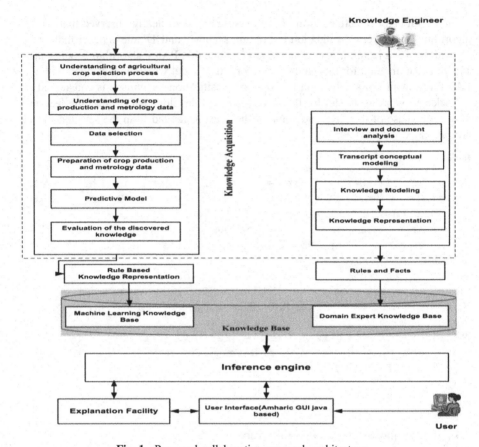

Fig. 1. Proposed collaborative approach architecture

(i) Inference Engine. After accessing the user interface the user feed the major land properties and climatic conditions parameter then the inference engine matches these with the existing rules in the knowledge bases and suggest most suited crop to that precise farming unit. It acts as an interpreter between the knowledge bases and the user interface here below the inference algorithms are discussed using flowchart depicted in Fig. 2.

(ii) User Interface. These studies is contributing to solve the gap that are rising on language barriers by designing and developing Amharic language GUI interface. Here below depicts on Fig. 3 the interface that the crop selection process pages.

As depicted in Fig. 3 shows the user means agricultural extension and farmers properly select the options, then based on the given input the system return barley (ገብስ) as a recommended crop for the given input parameters.

Proposed Algorithm for Collaborative Inference

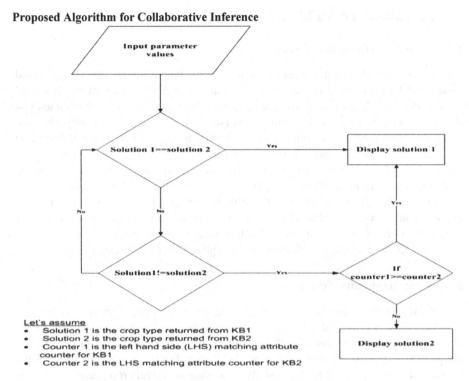

Let's assume
- Solution 1 is the crop type returned from KB1
- Solution 2 is the crop type returned from KB2
- Counter 1 is the left hand side (LHS) matching attribute counter for KB1
- Counter 2 is the LHS matching attribute counter for KB2

Fig. 2. Collaborative approach inference engine flow chart

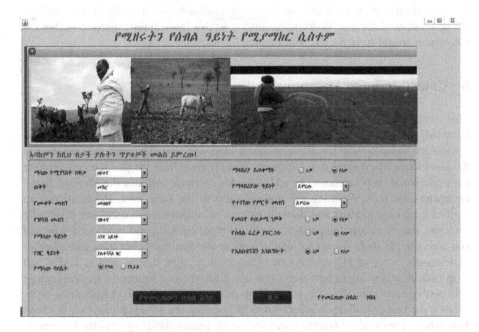

Fig. 3. Crop selection recommendation interface.

5 Evaluation and Validation

5.1 System Performance Testing

To evaluate the designed collaborative approach and prototype knowledge based system we have prepared test cases for evaluating the performance of the proposed system. Purposively the researchers prepared a total of 21 test cases and distributed to 4 domain experts. For each of the three crops type's seven test cases are prepared. The domain expert expected to recommend crops based on the farm land area suitability and the estimated weather condition of the area for each test case. For comparing the performance of the experts and the KBS system confusion matrix is used. Based on the collected results from the domain experts evaluation of the total of 21 test cases the system classified 20 instances correctly to their corresponding classes and 1 instance classified incorrectly to other classes to the expected three crops. This means the proposed system's agricultural crop selection recommendation has 95.23% accuracy according to the evaluation performed by the agriculture domain experts.

5.2 User Acceptance Testing

To accomplish the objectives of evaluation the researchers select evaluators by convenience sampling method 10 farmers and 10 agricultural extension workers in the study area. After the discussion of the system, in order to assess the user acceptance of the proposed system, questionnaires were distributed. For this study the format of the questionnaire was adapted from [4] study conducted on cereal crop disease diagnosis prototype KBS. Accordingly, to the farmers' evaluation the system would have the 82.2% performance on the accuracy. The same evaluation questions were forwarded to the agricultural extension workers. According to the agricultural extension evaluation the system would have 88.5% performance for accuracy.

6 Conclusion and Recommendation

This study designed a collaborative approach to combine the domain experts' knowledge with the knowledge discovery result and implemented a prototype knowledge based system for the agricultural crop selection. The approach we used in the knowledge based system development was different from the previous research on the agricultural crop selection. In addition, this research includes the climatic factor parameters for recommending the optimal crop to the farm land. Information gain attributes ranking method and domain experts' evaluation were used and this study finds out that elevation, temperature, fertilizer type, rainfall, field type, seed type and soil type are the main factors to select crops to the farm land. We have done twelve experiments by using J48 decision tree classification algorithm as well as PART and JRip rule induction algorithms using test set, 10-fold cross validation and percentage split test options then after the experiment shows that the PART classification algorithm is the best classification algorithm to recommend the optimum crops for the farm land which classified 82.6087% correctly which means 8151 are classified correctly among 9867 instances. According to the selected farmers' evaluation the developed prototype succeeds 82.2% performance by the domain experts' evaluations have 95.23% accuracy and by the agricultural extensions evaluation the proposed solution succeed 88.5% performance.

We conclude that the collaborative approach based KBS we designed and developed prototype have the potential to increase the accuracy of knowledge based system and a way to collaboration of expertise with machine learning for decision support, at last for increasing the production of crops.

The machine learning knowledge base for this study was done by the knowledge engineer after the PART algorithm generated, further a researcher can also done to be automatically the machine learning rule read with the knowledge based system. In addition, automatic machine translation for extracting rules in different local language also recommended for further study.

Acknowledgment. We would like thank to all Gondar agricultural research center cereal crop research teams for their expert knowledge and guidance in developing the domain expert knowledge base, farmers and agricultural extensions for willing to evaluate the designed collaborative approach and developed prototype. We thank to the central statics agency and Ethiopian national meteorology agency staffs for providing the necessary data and their support regarding to the nature of the data to select relevant features used for conducting this research.

References

1. Rossiter, D.G.: ALES: a framework for land evaluation using a microcomputer. Soil Use Manag. **6**(1), 7–20 (1990)
2. Beed, D.: Software engineering decision support system for agriculture domain, vol. 431602, pp. 1–5
3. Ponnusamy, T.: Knowledge-based expert system for agricultural land use planning, February 2007
4. Tefera, E.: Developing knowledge based system for cereal crop diagnosis and treatment: the case of Kulumsa agriculture research center (2012)
5. Prasad, G., Babu, A.V.: A study on expert systems in agriculture. In: Extension of Technologies: From Labs to Farms, p. 297 (2008)
6. Heines, J.M.: Basic concepts in knowledge-based systems. Mach. Learn. **1**(1), 65–95 (1983)
7. Joshi, R., Fadewar, H., Bhalchandra, P.: Fuzzy based intelligent system to predict most suitable crop (2017)
8. Abdulkerim, M.: Towards integrating data mining with knowledge based system: the case of network intrusion detection. M.Sc. thesis, Addis Ababa University (2013)
9. Gaines, B.R., Shaw, M.L.G.: Integrated knowledge acquisition architectures. J. Intell. Inf. Syst. **1**(1), 9–34 (1992)
10. Webb, G.I., Wells, J.: Recent progress in machine-expert collaboration for knowledge acquisition. In: AI-CONFERENCE, pp. 291–298 (1995)
11. Huang, A., Zhang, L., Zhu, Z., Shi, Y.: Data mining integrated with domain knowledge. In: Shi, Y., Wang, S., Peng, Y., Li, J., Zeng, Y. (eds.) MCDM 2009. CCIS, vol. 35, pp. 184–187. Springer, Heidelberg (2009). https://doi.org/10.1007/978-3-642-02298-2_28

12. Webb, G.I., Wells, J., Zheng, Z.: An experimental evaluation of integrating machine learning with knowledge acquisition. Mach. Learn. **35**(1), 5–23 (1999)
13. Peffers, K., Tuunanen, T., Rothenberger, M.A., Chatterjee, S.: A design science research methodology for information systems research. J. Manag. Inf. Syst. **24**(3), 45–77 (2007)
14. Schreiber, G., Wielinga, B., de Hoog, R., Akkermans, H., de Velde, W.: CommonKADS: a comprehensive methodology for KBS development. IEEE Expert **9**(6), 28–37 (1994)

Towards Fuzzy Analytical Hierarchy Process Model for Performance Evaluation of Healthcare Sector Services

George Wamamu Musumba$^{(\boxtimes)}$ and Ruth Diko Wario

Department of Computer Science and Informatics, University of Free State,
Private Bag X13, Kestell 9866, South Africa
musumbaggw@gmail.com, wariord@ufs.ac.za

Abstract. All service providers strive to attain superior service quality (SQ), since the demand for provision of high quality customer focused services is constantly rising. In the healthcare sector, it becomes of utmost importance to understand consumer expectations and their needs to effectively remain competitive in the market. Increase in the per capita income of clients has made them increase their aspiration level to demand enhanced quality services. Currently, hospitals in Nairobi City County (NCC) in Kenya, do not offer services to patients based on their aspirations and in the process, they lose clients. There is need for hospital administrators to determine how patients perceive healthcare quality service, and employ techniques that match their expectations. This is probable by using patients to evaluate their services based on identified criteria. Human evaluations are normally imprecise thus uncertainty aspects should be integrated in the evaluation process. Techniques employed should be able to handle the subjective nature of human evaluators. Fuzzy analytic hierarchy process (FAHP) model has been designed to analyze the service quality in the healthcare sector based on SERVQUAL dimensions. The model is capable of handling the uncertainty and vagueness involved in the mapping of one's preference to an exact number or ratio. It has been used to measure the SQ of four hospitals from NCC by computing the priority of each of the dimensions of healthcare SQ attributes. The priority is then used for ranking the best hospital from the patient's perspective. Hospital managers can use the results of this assessment as a basis of employing strategies that would ensure they provide quality services to patients.

Keywords: Fuzzy analytical hierarchy process · SERVQUAL · Service quality · Performance · Healthcare

1 Introduction

All nations regard healthcare as a key component to their sustainable growth. The healthcare sector imparts directly to a nation's medical, social, political, ethical, business, and financial wellbeing. Creation of counties in Kenya when the new constitution was promulgated in 2010 [1], saw the healthcare services getting devolved and primarily became under the management of county governments. The national

© Springer Nature Switzerland AG 2019
F. Mekuria et al. (Eds.): ICT4DA 2019, CCIS 1026, pp. 93–118, 2019.
https://doi.org/10.1007/978-3-030-26630-1_9

government has recently restructured hospitals into five levels i.e. level one to five, and converting all former provincial hospitals into referral ones. The restructuring of the healthcare system, calls for better services for patients. There are numerous opportunities to improve services if business enterprise models are adopted in managing these healthcare facilities. Seemingly, it is evident that healthcare facilities are becoming autonomous while they strive to pursue targeted service outcomes, amidst budget constraints.

In most business enterprises, the more the clients, the more financially sound they are likely to be. This is also true for healthcare providers. Clients prefer to visit where they perceive to be getting quality services. Some works has defined healthcare quality as being able to use legitimate means to achieve desirable objectives implying a better state health-wise [2]. At the same time quality in healthcare can be thought of as achieving an improved healthcare service level for consumers [3]. It cannot be overemphasized that while striving to improve the quality of healthcare, use of the right technology, treatment in a timely manner, and depending on the demand, provision of adequate service, as well as ability of the practitioners to guarantee acceptable medical practice standards, are indeed necessary [4]. In a corporate point of view, better quality in healthcare can lead to the provider extending the client base and gaining a competitive edge in the market. This is admirable as it assures economic viability and profitability in the long run [5–7].

Healthcare quality is multifaceted. Some authors viewed it also as a multi-dimensional entity. The entities and actors that interactively affect it include, financier organizations and healthcare professionals who tend to the needs of the patients. Additionally, there is a category of healthcare consumers who also value the service level provided in terms of hospital staff relationship with patients, hospitality, privacy and patients' dignity considerations. This constitutes what they perceive as better clinical experience and outcomes.

Some service quality aspects as perceived by patients include how accessible, how responsive and how hospitable the healthcare facility is to the consumers. Researchers suggests that these aspects directly influence the perception of consumers on the facility's value and image. Additionally, patients' perception on quality also impacts indirectly on how they behave in regard to how they rank the facility. Depending on the rank, they may choose to visit the facility or seek medical services elsewhere. If patients are satisfied with the level of service, they are more likely to recommend the facility to others [8, 9]. It is for the same reasons that in today's healthcare context, it is necessary to have in place a systematic way of carrying out evaluation of patients' satisfaction [10].

In a number of research works in the healthcare domain, there exist many techniques that have been employed to determine satisfaction of stakeholders. These techniques are: Methods of Stated Importance (MSIs), Methods of Derived Importance (MDIs) and Multi-Criteria Decision-Making (MCDM). In MSIs [11–13], participants fill out a questionnaire that is well detailed which relates to the fundamental service quality aspects that are based on consumer expectations and perceptions. On the other hand, in MDIs [14, 15], participants fill a non-detailed simplified questionnaire. Participants are only required to provide their assessment on the perceptions on service quality aspects. Furthermore, they are also supposed to synthesize their perceived quality of service and then indicate their overall degree of satisfaction. Statistical derivation of the quality expectations are done in phase two, following the survey in the first phase. As stated in a benchmarking work by LuPo [16], *"derivation is on the basis of relations among the collected perceptions and the overall satisfaction degree"*.

The third category, MCDM base its' working on the principle that considers customers' attitudes toward a specific service. Consumers in this case, give their assessment based on how they perceive the importance of the service aspect when they compare it with another service aspect [17]. For instance, the importance of "responsiveness" compared to "empathy" when they are assessed on their contribution to service quality in hospitals. The importance relationship is normally between two aspects of the service. In this regard, MCDM techniques like (1) Analytical Hierarchy Process (AHP) [18], (2) VIsekriterijumska optimizacija I KOmpromisnoResenje (VIKOR) [19], (3) Technique for Order Preference by Similarity to Ideal Solution (TOPSIS) [20] among others, become strong candidates that can be employed in the design and development of models that can be used to assess service quality criteria. Recent application of the above methods in healthcare domain can be found in [16, 21, 22].

Use of the above methods in development of applications can result in imprecise or unreliable outcomes. The length of the questionnaire in SIM, may encourage unreliable results from participants who may want to save on time but still want to please the questionnaire administrators [23]. Authors of this study, are of the opinion that there could be a high tendency of users to rate highly the importance of all service aspects whenever they are requested to directly rate them, potentially leading to overestimation of quality expectations in addition to lower discriminatory power characterization. These methods use linguistic variables in determining preferences of service quality aspects. Research works have stated that using linguistic variables to assess the dimensions of service quality, is plagued with uncertainty, subjectivity and vagueness [24, 25].

To overcome the aforementioned weaknesses, a model should be designed to help healthcare team assess the healthcare service quality. This study proposes a technique based on the ServQual model [26]. ServQual model has been extensively used in literature in assessing service quality in other domains. The proposed model also incorporates the AHP technique to reliably estimate expectations aspects of service quality [27, 28]. AHP is regarded as the most established MCDM method used in various decision situations [29]. It is possible to integrate both quantitative and qualitative techniques in AHP. The ease with which AHP is able to acquire the required data enables it overcome some of the issues that are critical to the decision making process. Some of these critical issues as quoted from Lupo [16] are, *"existence of well documented respondents' tendency to select the central category of the evaluation scale to express their judgments [30], the influence in the evaluation process of the categories number of the evaluation scale, and the form and the type of related linguistic variables"* [31, 32].

Stakeholders while providing their judgments on the service quality aspects, just like it happens in expression of evaluation judgments in other domains, inherently exhibit uncertainty, subjectivity and vagueness [33–35]. This study considers integration of fuzzy set theory (FST) to MCDM techniques. FST was proposed by Zadeh [36]. The result of this integration has been applied in management science, in the decision-making [37] processes, service performance evaluations [38, 39] and information retrievals [40, 41]. The proposed model will provide support to decision makers and administrators in the healthcare sector at the time they need to make choices on the strategies they deem efficient to improve service quality.

2 Literature Review

There exists different interpretations and implementations of service quality as shown in literature. Selecting the best solution for a particular problem is usually the main objective of decision makers. Some decision makers (DMs) consider a single criterion for making decisions. However, a majority of DMs take into account a number of inconsistent and non-commensurable objectives with multiple criteria as it is insufficient to make decisions based on a single criterion. To make decisions based on multiple criteria, some papers propose application of multiple criteria decision making (MCDM) techniques. In essence, this happens in situations where decision criteria are contradictory in nature. In these cases, individuals are facilitated to make decisions based on their preferences [42]. In MCDM approach to decision making, a problem is hierarchically structured with several levels. In level one objective is defined, while level two consists of the set criteria used by individuals to select the best alternative for the decision situation. Sub criteria, sub sub-criteria can be in level three and four respectively. If there is no further division of sub sub-criteria then the list of alternatives to be considered takes the last level of the hierarchy.

The hierarchical structure effectively divides a complex problem into smaller portions and the problem is tackled using both top down and bottom up approaches. Decision makers analyze the criteria, sub criteria to the lowest level in the hierarchy using top down approach and the computation of the analysis is done using bottom up approach. After making the decisions, based on the hierarchical analysis, that have in essence considered issues related to the problem sub divisions, the next step involve the reconstruction of these sub divisions representing an inclusive view of the decision makers (DMs) [43].

Assessment of the service quality, which is the focus of this study, can be done using different qualitative and quantitative criteria that can be structured hierarchically. This effectively suggest the appropriateness of employing the MCDM techniques to address the evaluation of the aspects of quality of service. Literature has also reported several ways that have been used to measure the service quality. They include among others, those based on statistical analysis, analytical hierarchy process (AHP), fuzzy AHP (FAHP), VIsekriterijumska optimizacija i KOmpromisno Resenje (VIKOR), Preference Ranking Organization Method for Enrichment Evaluation (PROMETHEE), and Technique for Order Preference by Similarity to Ideal Solution (TOPSIS) [44].

In many works where MCDM methods have been used in decision situations, the majority of the problems have multiple, conflicting, and incommensurate criteria and/or objectives. There are two categories proposed by Hwang and Yoon [45] to classify the MCDM methods. First, MCDM methods are classified as multi-attribute decision-making (MADM) where emphasis is on the human participation and judgments. The second category is the multi-objective decision-making (MODM) where human participation is seldom emphasized. There is vast amount of research on human judgments and decision making that have continually depicted the human brain as being incapable of holding or consider unlimited amount of information at the same time [46]. These assertions points to its unreliability in taking decisions to solve problems in complex situations. Furthermore, human judgments, in such situations are imprecise which complicates the matter even more. This call for techniques that can simplify this uncertainty aspects in complex decision making environments.

As quoted from Musumba and Wario [47], *"AHP is a MCDM technique that derive weights of importance by using pairwise comparisons (PCMs) of alternatives from a multi-level hierarchical structure. The structure depends on the problem but can have the objective of the problem at the top of the hierarchy and the healthcare facilities as alternatives whose service quality is to be evaluated at the bottom level and the set evaluation criteria in the middle level. Sometimes the comparisons are not consistent. In that case, AHP uses the eigenvalue and consistency checking methods to improve their consistency as described in [48]"*.

AHP is also one of the most applied MADM technique. It has the ability to impartially and logically grade the decision making attributes by reducing the personal biases and allowing for comparison of disparate alternatives. In addition, its flexibility to be integrated with various techniques like Linear Programming (LP), Quality Function Deployment (QFD), Fuzzy Logic (FL) among others [49, 50] made it a good candidate for consideration is this work.

AHP has a number of weaknesses, including its inability to synthesize values that are not crisp in form. As quoted from the works by Musumba and Wario [47], it is stated, *"in order to overcome AHP weaknesses, Mikhailov [51] integrated fuzzy logic [52] into AHP forming fuzzy AHP (FAHP). Fuzzy logic [52] changes the crisp values of AHP into a continuum thus making it able to deal with uncertainty and vagueness characterizing input variables. Therefore, FAHP can be used to make rational decisions under such conditions. Fuzzy logic is considered the best method compared to deterministic approaches, algorithmic approaches, probabilistic approaches and machine learning [53] for problems that users are not certain of the value of parameters to use."*

2.1 MCDM Application in Service Quality

Each industry's success is hinged on the main players' ability to deliver, build, understand and maintain high standards of their service quality. In this regard, in [54], description of service predictions was based on service quality expectations. The key driving forces behind evaluating the service quality are measurement of service performance, diagnosis of service problems, management of the delivery of service and optimal service provision to all customers [55]. It is noted that there exists methods that can be used in the evaluation of the service quality. These methods include MCDM techniques which have been applied in evaluating service quality in airline and other transport industries, websites and Internet services, tourism and the hospitality industry, the healthcare industry, the manufacturing industry, the banking sector, the education sector and service organizations.

2.2 MCDM for Service Quality in Healthcare Industry

Quality service is a key driver in as far as consumer satisfaction is concerned. There is increasing competition due to influx of healthcare providers globally. With increased competition, healthcare consumers have many options of healthcare providers they can consider whenever they need to seek medical attention. With this reality, many healthcare providers know that their continued success going into the future depends on their ability to competitively provide good healthcare service quality [56]. Many patients are concerned with service quality while seeking medical attention. Non satisfaction with the service offered to patients, have higher bearing on them not to return but opting to seek the same in other healthcare facilities. The onus remains with healthcare providers to enhance their healthcare quality if they have to maintain and grow their clientele [57]. Indeed, healthcare providers have very limited options in paying attention to consumers' expectation of service quality if they have to successfully deal with existing globalization challenges and intensive competition. Some of the critical challenges faced by hospital management are, how to meet patients' needs and how to determine the expected service quality [58].

In Shieh et al. [59], hospitals have been classified as service industries because their activities include, direct contact with people, frequent communication with people, provision of customized and professional medical services. Research outputs have shown that development of the service quality of hospitals has existed for many years. However, it is vital to evaluate the consumer service quality expectation to determine with certainty if indeed hospitals' administrators understand the importance attached to quality of service they offer. Furthermore, previous works have shown that the service quality of a hospital can be measured according to different qualitative and quantitative criteria. Consequently, the MCDM approach becomes a suitable choice to evaluate these consumers' expectations of the quality of service healthcare providers' offer. According to findings of a systematic review by Abbas [44], several works have employed the use of MCDM techniques to evaluate the service quality in the healthcare sector.

In the state of the art survey conducted by Kubler et al. [60], it is reported that FAHP evaluation has been applied to the healthcare service sector, where managers need to demonstrate how efficient and customer focused their services are. Büyüközkan et al. [61] developed an evaluation framework for evaluating the performance of service quality among hospitals. The criteria used in the framework include, the level of facilities/equipment, physical appearance of the hospital, its hygiene, responsiveness to consumer issues, degree of reliability, assurance level, empathy and the degree of professionalism exhibited by staff. They concluded that the two most important factors were empathy and professionalism. The study was extended by Büyüközkan and Cifci [50], focusing on the service quality of e-services offered through the hospital's website. They added a sensitivity analysis step to the framework.

As stated earlier, in AHP, the priorities assigned to alternatives depends on the decision makers' highly imprecise judgments, which are subjective in nature. This may lead to instability of the final ranking if there are small variations on the principal weights. It is a common occurrence of people witnessing frequent emergency situations in healthcare facilities which should be tackled in a proper manner. As a result, Ju et al.

[62] has proposed an evaluation index system of the emergency response capability based on FAHP. Their system use 2-tuple linguistic variables which has simplified the understanding of the computed scores by decision makers. In [50, 62], it is pointed out that motivation and skills of human resources significantly affects the hospitals' service quality.

2.3   The SERVQUAL Tool and the Service Quality

According to literature in the business domain as discussed in the works by Shahin and Janatyan [63] and Zaim et al. [64], service quality is defined as the comparison of service expectations with actual performance. Also, service quality as defined by both Parasuraman et al. [65] and Bitner and Hubbert [66] is the impression the consumer creates of the degree of superiority or inferiority of a service provider and its services. Prakash et al. [67] analyzed Grönroos's [68] and Parasuraman et al.'s [26] views on the perceptions of service quality and stated that service quality perceptions are based on multiple dimensions. They neither had any idea about nature nor content of those dimensions.

SERVQUAL tool as presented in [26, 69–73] has been used for a long time to measure healthcare service quality. The tool has the following dimensions, reliability, responsiveness, assurance, empathy and tangibles. When patients receive the appropriate treatment, the healthcare provided is considered to be reliable. Similarly, as discussed in [70], when the healthcare personnel promptly and politely attends to a patient, responsiveness dimension is fulfilled. Regarding the assurance dimension, it is highly rated if patients exude confidence in the qualifications and competence of the healthcare practitioners. Personalized attention to patients from the facility, resulting in better experiences relates to empathy. Lastly, aspects of cleanliness, the physical appearance of the equipment used and the healthcare facility [74] relates to tangibles. In other words, tangible dimension refers to features that are visually visible.

In the Unites Arabs Emirates, Jabnoun and Chacker [75] investigated how patients perceived quality of healthcare service from both private and public hospitals. In addition to reliability, responsiveness, empathy and tangibles dimensions, they also found out that supporting skills was another dimension of the service offered. In Sohail's [73] work to assess the quality of services from Malaysian private hospitals, it is indicated that patients prefer if all aspects of service exceeded expectations in all dimensions. In a study on a hospital in South Africa, it is reported that Boshoff and Gray [76] used communication, tangibles, empathy of nursing staff, assurance, responsiveness of administrative staff, security and physician responsiveness in their evaluations.

A study by Ramsaran-Fowdar [77] on private hospitals in the Mauritian healthcare services, indicated reliability dimension as one of the most important service quality aspect. In Indian hospitals, the SERVQUAL instrument was used by Padma et al. [78] to determine the dimensions of service quality. Patients and their family members/friends perspectives were put into consideration which were eventually proposed to measure the quality dimensions. Attendants' perspectives were also suggested to be part of the aspects of service quality evaluation.

In summary, the preceding literature review has revealed that SERVQUAL instrument can be used to measure the service quality in the healthcare sector. The instrument measures gaps in the service quality based on five dimensions. It is not easy to obtain information on customer expectations. Despite this reality, the "gap model" has continually been used by many studies to address the challenge. With the model, the strengths and weaknesses in specific quality attributes can be identified [79, 80]. This study proposes the use of the SERVQUAL instrument scale [76] to assess patients' perceptions of service quality for healthcare providers. Hospital environment is used. Fuzzy AHP is also used to deal with the subjective nature of human evaluators' perception of service quality where linguistic variables are used.

3 Methodology

3.1 Fuzzy Analytical Hierarchical Process (FAHP)

This study has proposed to use SERVQUAL dimensions for assessing service quality. These dimensions become subjective when human assign to them values of importance. It is needed to define meaning of every word used as labels where boundaries of their values become undefined, fuzzy or uncertain. Furthermore, based on individual evaluators' subjective perception on the level of importance of service quality aspects, the judgment of events by people may be significantly different [81]. Therefore, the study introduces fuzzy numbers for expressing linguistic variables appropriately. Fuzzy numbers are introduced on AHP hence fuzzy AHP (FAHP).

3.2 Fuzzy Set and Triangular Fuzzy Number

As pointed out earlier, while attempting to address the weaknesses in AHP, Mikhailov [51] introduced fuzzy logic [82] in AHP. It is noted from research works that the main focus of fuzzy set theory is on rationalization of uncertainty. Representation of vague data has been synonymous with fuzzy sets. Figure 1 shows a fuzzy number, which is characterized by a membership function. It differs from traditional set which defines an element as either belongs or does not belong to a set (i.e. 0 and 1). It implements grouping of data with boundaries that are not sharply defined (i.e. not crisp).

Methods or theories that implement 'crisp' definitions, for instance, the classical set theory, could be 'fuzzified'. This is possible if the crisp set idea, is generalized to a fuzzy set with blurred boundaries. Extension of crisp theory and analysis methods to fuzzy techniques is beneficial. This can be demonstrated as with the ease it becomes in solving real-world problems. Inevitably, these problems entail some degree of imprecision in the variables and parameters measured and processed for the application. A triangular fuzzy number (TFN) is the special class of fuzzy numbers whose membership is defined by three real numbers, expressed as (a, b, c). The fuzzy triangular membership function gives the foundation for defining other types of membership functions such as general triangular function, right-angled triangular function and trapezoidal function. For example when $a = b$ for a right-angled triangular membership function such as $(1, 1, 3)$.

In this study, TFN has been used to decide the priority of one decision variable over other. A TFN has been given as a $\leq$ b $\leq$ c where b, a, and c are the most likely, the lower bounds and upper bounds decision values, respectively. The TFN, is a linear piece-wise membership function, $\mu_n(x)$ of the form;

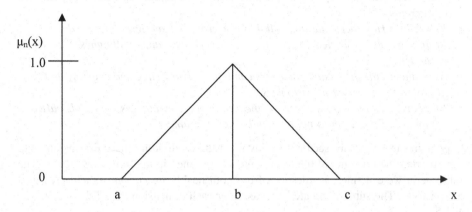

Fig. 1. Fuzzy triangular numbers membership

$$\mu_A = \begin{cases} (x-a)/(b-a), & a \leq x \leq b \\ (c-x)/(c-b), & b \leq x \leq c \\ 0, & \text{otherwise} \end{cases}$$

Where $\infty < a \leq b \leq x \leq c < \infty$

4   Fuzzy AHP Model

Involvement of experts in the healthcare played a bigger role in the design and development of hospital services performance model. The fuzzy AHP model, which is the result of this process adopted a group consensus method, informed by an initial focus group discussions with healthcare domain experts actively involved in the operations of healthcare facilities. The following steps resulted in the model:

(a) Definition of the service quality evaluation criteria and sub-criteria.
(b) Creation of the hierarchical structure based on AHP approach.
(c) Fuzzifying the evaluation criteria and sub-criteria.
(d) Using pair-wise comparison of fuzzified values to estimate the relative weights of elements.
(e) Performance assessment of the estimated elements relative weights.
(f) Defuzzification and performance measurement of the hospitals/healthcare facilities.
(g) Selection of the best healthcare facility based on the determined level of service quality.

4.1 Definition of the Service Quality Evaluation Criteria and Sub-Criteria

This study adopted the five SERVQUAL scale dimensions as the evaluation criteria as described in the following section.

- *Tangibles: Include the physical amenities, available equipment and the appearance of personnel.*
- *Reliability: How accurate and reliable are promised services performed.*
- *Responsiveness: Service performance promptness and willingness to assist customers.*
- *Assurance: This dimension considers employees' knowledge and courtesy and their ability to inspire trust in customers.*
- *Empathy: This dimension considers the ability of the employees to provide care and personalized attention to patients and other consumers.*

Experts in the healthcare sector were involved in sub-dividing these dimensions into sub-criteria. The outcome of the discussions are outlined in the following section. The sub-criteria were defined as questions from both healthcare consumers and providers perspectives. The sub-criteria are indicated after each dimension (See Tables 1, 2, 3, 4 and 5).

Table 1. Reliability

- What is the average time the doctor takes in assessing and treating the patient?
- How long does it take before patients return to hospital for treatment of similar ailment (Reoccurrence rate)?
- Are tests that are prescribed to patients relevant?
- Are tests conducted following in a defined set procedure?

Table 2. Responsiveness

- Do doctors respond to the patients' requests?
- Are there doctor's on-call at night?
- Do nurses respond to patients' requests?
- How quick and convenient is the process of medical care?
- Are emergency cases dealt with promptly by staff?
- Are administrative staff cooperative and helpful?
- How prompt is the ambulance service?

Table 3. Assurance

- Does the hospital physical organization provide safety and convenience to patients?
- Do doctors give confidence to patients?
- What is the extent of confidentiality between doctor and patient?
- Is the hospital reputable among peers?
- Do all staff give confidence to patients?

Table 4. Tangibles

• How clean is the hospital physical environment?
• What is the quality of equipment used for treating patients?
• How are staff organized in terms of appearance (including first-line)?
• How clean are wards in the hospital?
• How excellent is the food in the canteen?
• How excellent is the patients' food?
• How clean/hygienic is the canteen?
• Is water available all the time?
• Is electricity available all the time?
• Does the hospital provide an organized comfortable seating area?
• Is the estimated bill accurate?
• Is there a procedure for paying the final bill?
• Is the hospital well secured?
• Is there a counter for inquiry in the hospital?
• Does the hospital provide for movements of patients and persons with physical disabilities?
• Are beds provided to patients in good condition?
• How patient are doctors in hearing patient details?
• Are nurses patient with patients?
• Do pharmacy staff provide adequate instructions to patients?
• Are service staff (cleaners and ward boys) polite?
• Are patient conditions explained by doctors well to both patients and guardians?
• Do nurses give clear instructions to patients?
• How efficient are doctors when handling emergencies?
• How efficient are other staff when handling the emergency?
• How timely are the scheduled procedures handled?
• Are there exhibitions and displays for directions on living healthy?
• Does the hospital engage in the community training?

Table 5. Empathy

• Does the facility furnish patients with medical information related to their ailments?
• What is the average time patients take to register and / or get admitted?
• What is the average time patients take to be given medicine?
• What is the average time patients take to see a doctor?
• Is there a process in place for reserving a specific service e.g. doctor's consultation?
• How are the schedules for visitors and the duration of the visit?
• Are there facilities for families and visitors and in what state?
• Is the hospital able to respond to patients' requests appropriately?
• Does special requests by patients acceptable?
• When patients' relatives or families make requests, are they attended to?

4.2 Creation of the Hierarchical Structure Based on AHP Approach

The MCDM hierarchical structure created in based on AHP approach. As shown in Fig. 2, it consists of the SERVQUAL dimensions which are the evaluation criteria. Each criteria have sub-criteria that have been defined.

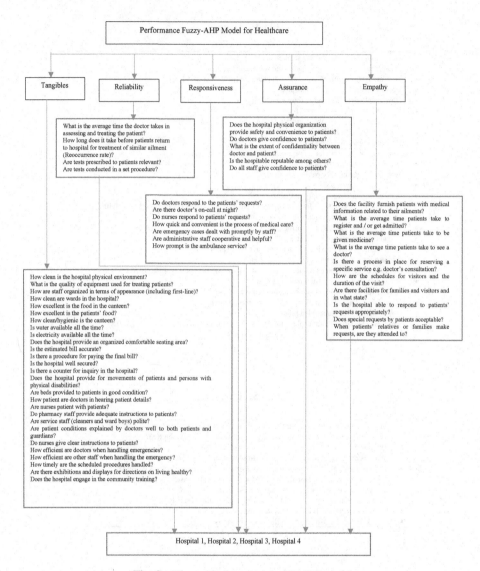

Fig. 2. Hierarchical structure of FAHP model

4.3   Fuzzifying the Evaluation Criteria and Sub-criteria

Using Table 6, the alphabets that have been used to represent linguistic scale, are assigned appropriate crisp values. The SERQUAL scale dimensions are represented using symbols (A, B, C, D, E) with matching nominal scales (equal importance, moderate importance over another, essential or strong importance, very strong or demonstrated importance and absolute importance) as suggested by Sinimole [83]. They are converted to crisp scale and then to fuzzy scale (see Table 6). It should be noted that linguistic symbols can still be converted directly to TFNs.

Table 6. Linguistic scale for importance (adapted from Sinimole [83] and modified)

Linguistic variables	Alphabets	Crisp no.	TFN	Reciprocal of TFN
Equal importance	A	1	(1, 1, 3)	(1/3, 1, 1)
Moderate importance over one another	B	3	(1, 3, 5)	(1/5, 1/3, 1)
Essential or strong importance	C	5	(3, 5, 7)	(1/7, 1/5, 1/3)
Very strong or demonstrated importance	D	7	(5, 7, 9)	(1/9, 1/7, 1/5)
Absolute importance	E	9	(7, 9, 9)	(1/9, 1/9, 1/7)

4.4 Using Pair-Wise Comparison of Fuzzified Values to Estimate the Relative Weights of Elements

The hierarchy was established with the main objective at the top, selection criteria (SERVQUAL dimensions) at second level and the considered healthcare facilities (hospitals) at the last level. In explaining how evaluation of the criteria, assuming the hierarchical structure has s alternatives with respect to a specific objective, which must be evaluated using t criteria, denoted $C_i(i = 1, 2, ...t)$. Let the weight of criterion C_i with respect to the objective be W_{Ci}.

Let the relative weight of alternative r ($1 \leq r \leq s$) with respect to criterion C_i be W_{RCi}. The overall weights, denoted P_i ($1 \leq r \leq s$) of s alternatives with respect to the objective are given by Eq. 1.

$$P_{WI} = AC \times (CO)^T \tag{1}$$

Where: P_{WI}: Overall weight of alternative r, AC: Relative weights of the criteria with respect to the objective, and CO: Relative weight of the alternatives with respect to criteria. Finally, the alternative with the highest weight value is selected. It is important to note that W_{Ci} ($1 \leq i \leq t$) are the relative weights of criteria C_i while W_{RCi} are relative weights of alternatives, in this case, the hospitals. These relative weights are computed for elements at level 2 (for dimensions) of the hierarchical structure, then at levels 3 (for hospitals).

To compute the relative weights of the elements in the hierarchy, first, relative weights (weights at a specific level) of alternatives at each level of the hierarchy are calculated. The higher the weight, the better (or preferable) the alternative is. Assessment of relative weights is performed through pairwise comparison of the alternatives (alternatives in this case refers to elements for comparison at each level e.g. hospitals and dimensions), using the Saaty scale. The values of alternatives to be compared are assigned by evaluators (patients) using some chosen method. This results in so called, pairwise comparison matrices (PCM) of alternatives at a level in the hierarchy. For example, considering Fig. 1, relative weights of criteria C_i with respect to the objective are computed at level 2 because the criteria are at level 2 of the hierarchy.

Secondly, at level 3, relative weights of alternatives (hospitals) with respect to criteria C_i are computed. This is because evaluators compare and assign evaluation values to alternatives according to how they satisfy criteria C_i. Saaty [84] suggested that alternatives can be assigned a crisp (exact) value to show how important the alternative is vis-a-vis others according to how evaluators rate them. The exact/crisp values are fuzzified using the triangular fuzzy number approach. For example alternative 1 weighed against alternative 2 may have numerical value 9 (which means alternative 1 is absolutely important than 2), the numerical value of alternative 1 weighed against alternative 3 can be 5 (alternative 1 is strongly or essentially important than 3) while the numerical value of alternative 2 weighed against alternative 3 may be 7 (alternative 2 has very strong or demonstrated importance than 3). Saaty [84] proposes the eigenvalue method to compute pairwise comparison matrices. Each alternative weighed against itself is of equal importance (1). At any level of the hierarchy the comparisons form a square matrix.

Pair-wise comparisons (PCMs) for all criteria at a level in the hierarchy are done. As has been shown earlier, once crisp values are fuzzified, PCM of the same is then performed using the scale given in Table 6. For this study, pair-wise comparisons are done to assess the relative importance between two dimensions by assigning values to them as per the individual evaluators' perception. The PCM is defined as:

$$\bar{A} = \begin{bmatrix} 1 & \bar{a}_{12} & \dots & \bar{a}_{1n} \\ \bar{a}_{21} & 1 & \dots & \bar{a}_{2n} \\ \dots & \bar{a}_n & m-1 & 1 \end{bmatrix} \tag{2}$$

where $\bar{a} = (A_{jk}, B_{jk}, C_{jk})$ is the relative importance of each dimension in pair-wise comparison and A_{jk}, B_{jk}, C_{jk} are the lower bound value, most likely value and upper bound value of the TFN. There exist various techniques for estimating the fuzzy priorities W_i, where $W_i = (W_i^a, W_i^b, W_i^c)$ and $i = 1, 2, \dots, n$, from the judgment matrix. Logarithmic least-squares technique has been employed in this study due to its effectiveness and reasonableness [81]. Triangular fuzzy weights are computed to represent the relative importance of the criteria according to the values assigned by individuals. The computation of the triangular fuzzy weights using the logarithmic least-squares method, is done using the following equation:

$$W_p = (W_P^a, W_P^b, W_P^c), \quad k = 1, 2, 3, \dots N \tag{3}$$

where,

$$W_P^s = \frac{\left(\prod_{k=1}^{K} a_{jk}^s \right)^{\frac{1}{n}}}{\sum_{i=1}^{n} \left(\prod_{k=1}^{K} a_{jk}^s \right)^{\frac{1}{n}}} \quad s \in \{a, b, c\}$$

Afterwards, computation of the normalized priorities to give the overall weight of each criterion is done.

4.5 Computation of Relative Weights to Rate Hospitals

Patients give feedback on their perception of each service quality by hospitals by rating each hospital based on each dimension. Triangular fuzzy numbers' weighting is used in measuring the patients' evaluations (feedback). The linguistic scales are converted to TFN (see Table 6) to assess the hospitals' performance in its quality of service. Let $PS_j^k = (a_{jk}, b_{jk}, c_{jk})$ denote the normalized triangular fuzzy number used to measure the performance of the jth hospital with respect to the kth criteria ($k = 1, 2, ..., N$; $j = 1, 2, ..., S$, where S = number of hospitals being compared).

4.6 Computation of Group Decisions

The evaluations are carried out by several individual evaluators. It is cumbersome to use individual evaluators hence the need for aggregation of the group evaluation. Geometric mean can satisfactorily deliver fuzzy group weightings. It has been applied in the fuzzy values (a_{jk}, b_{jk}, c_{jk}) from each individual evaluators. Literature show that geometric mean operations have been used for aggregating group decisions [85], especially where AHP is applied:

$$a_{jk} = \left(\prod_{s=1}^{S} a_{jks}\right)^{\frac{1}{s}}, \; b_{jk} = \left(\prod_{s=1}^{S} b_{jks}\right)^{\frac{1}{s}} c_{jk} = \left(\prod_{s=1}^{S} c_{jks}\right)^{\frac{1}{s}} \quad (4)$$

where ($a_{jks}, b_{jks}, c_{jks}$) is the fuzzy values obtained after evaluation hospitals' service aspects s ($s = 1, 2, ..., S$).

4.7 Computation of Overall Aggregated Score

The study use the computed fuzzy assessments PM_j^k with the relative importance W_p to calculate the overall aggregated weight of one hospital in relation to an overall aggregated weight of another. In essence, the weighted mean operator is used to calculate overall aggregated score (OAS) for each alternative as indicated in Eq. 5.

$$OAS_j = \left[\frac{1}{\sum W_j}\right] \times \left[(PM_j^1 \times W^1) + (PM_j^2 \times W^2) + ... + (PM_j^k \times W^p)\right] \quad (5)$$

where OAS_j denotes the fuzzy number indicating the overall aggregated score (or performance) of the jth hospital. Zadeh's extension principle [82] is used to compute the membership function of these fuzzy numbers. However, it is noted that the form of OAS_j does not conform to TFNs, in as much as it is possible to approximate it as one, taking the form (U_j, V_j, W_j).

4.8 Using Center of Gravity to Defuzzify the Aggregated Fuzzy Set

Centre of gravity (COG) is used to defuzzify the OAS, which is a triangular fuzzy number. Defuzzification process results in crisp weight values. COG is preferred in this study because it is easy to use as opposed to other methods like maximum-membership principle, centre of area, weighted average and smallest of maximum. The overall hospital performance (OHP), is then calculated using the following equation:

$$OHP_j = \left[\frac{(C_j - A_j) + (B_j - A_j)}{3} + A_j \right] \tag{6}$$

where OHP_j is the overall hospital performance of the jth hospital, C_j is the upper limit of the TFN, A_j is the lower limit of the TFN and B_j is the average of the TFN. With this outcome, the best healthcare facility (hospital) is selected.

5   Case Study

5.1   Hospitals' Data

This study considered a case of Nairobi city county, Kenya. Four large hospitals were selected to be evaluated based on the quality of their service. This sample was not representative of hospitals in the county but it was good for demonstration purposes. These hospitals included two public or government hospitals and two private hospitals. Patients who had made visits to these hospitals for a minimum of four times were invited to participate. Hospitals used in the study have been given anonymous names at the request of hospital administrators due to the sensitivity of the possible research findings. Use of site locations from the central business district has been employed to name the hospitals. The location does not necessarily indicate where the hospital are located. These hospitals include:

- Nairobi West Hospital (NW).
- Nairobi East Hospital (NE).
- Nairobi North Hospital (NN).
- Nairobi South Hospital (NS).

5.2   Design of the Evaluation Tool

To develop a reliable evaluation tool, to be used by stakeholders in the evaluation of service quality, the study employed the five dimensions (criteria) in the SERVQUAL instrument, namely tangibility, reliability, responsiveness, assurance and empathy. Researchers engaged experienced healthcare practitioners to examine the tool and used their recommendations to make necessary modifications to the tool. Domain expert opinions were used to obtain the weights associated with these criteria. Twenty (20) practitioners gave their opinions on how they rated the four hospitals in each dimension (criterion). In addition 20 patients gave their perceptions on the importance of each dimension when compared with each other in regard to how each contributed to the quality of service as witnessed in each of the four hospitals. All chronbach's alpha (a tool used to check reliability of the evaluation tool) values exceeded 0.8 and the consistency ratio (CR) was less than 0.1, hence ensuring reliability and confirming the appropriateness of the sub-criteria used for each dimension.

Lecture Notes in Computer Science 11675

More information about this series at http://www.springer.com/series/7409

Thomas Hildebrandt · Boudewijn F. van Dongen ·
Maximilian Röglinger · Jan Mendling (Eds.)

Business Process Management

17th International Conference, BPM 2019
Vienna, Austria, September 1–6, 2019
Proceedings

 Springer

Editors
Thomas Hildebrandt (iD)
University of Copenhagen
Copenhagen, Denmark

Maximilian Röglinger (iD)
University of Bayreuth
Bayreuth, Germany

Boudewijn F. van Dongen (iD)
Eindhoven University of Technology
Eindhoven, The Netherlands

Jan Mendling (iD)
Vienna University of Economics
and Business
Vienna, Austria

ISSN 0302-9743   ISSN 1611-3349 (electronic)
Lecture Notes in Computer Science
ISBN 978-3-030-26618-9   ISBN 978-3-030-26619-6 (eBook)
https://doi.org/10.1007/978-3-030-26619-6

LNCS Sublibrary: SL3 – Information Systems and Applications, incl. Internet/Web, and HCI

This Springer imprint is published by the registered company Springer Nature Switzerland AG
The registered company address is: Gewerbestrasse 11, 6330 Cham, Switzerland

Preface

The 17th International Conference on Business Process Management provided a forum for researchers and practitioners in the broad and diverse field of business process management (BPM). To accommodate for the diversity of the field, the BPM conference hosted tracks for foundations, engineering, and management. These tracks cover not only different phenomena of interest and research methods, but also ask for different evaluation criteria. Each track had a dedicated track chair and Program Committee. The track chairs, together with a consolidation chair, were responsible for the scientific program.

BPM 2019 was organized by Jan Mendling, Vienna University of Economics and Business (WU Vienna), and Stefanie Rinderle-Ma, University of Vienna. The conference was held in Vienna, Austria, on the WU Campus during September 1–6, 2019.

The conference received 157 full paper submissions, well-distributed over the tracks, from which 115 went for review. Each paper was reviewed by at least three Program Committee members and a senior Program Committee member who initiated and moderated scientific discussions and reflected these in an additional meta-review. We accepted 23 excellent papers in the main conference (acceptance rate 20%). Moreover, 13 submissions appeared in the BPM Forum, published in a separate volume of the Springer LNBIP series.

In the foundations track chaired by Thomas Hildebrandt, core BPM topics including process verification and formal analysis were presented. The engineering track was chaired by Boudewijn van Dongen. This track featured topics such as process mining and machine learning. The management track was chaired by Maximilian Röglinger. Many papers in this track focused on matters related to process design and improvement as well as organizational challenges such as trusted processes, the alignment of employee rewards with processes, BPM skill configurations, and the adoption of process mining in practice.

Moreover, we had one keynote per track as well as for the Industry Track and the Blockchain Forum. Pat Geary from BluePrism shared his latest insights into robotic process automation, Monika Henzinger from the University of Vienna informed us about the state of the art in dynamic graph algorithms, and Kalle Lyytinen from Case Western University offered a digitalization and organizational routines perspective on BPM. Moreover, Petr Novotny from IBM Research shared a technical perspective on Hyperledger Fabric and its applications, while Max Pucher from Papyrus talked about adaptive case management with Converse. Finally, Stefan Schulte from TU Vienna shared insights on the interoperability of blockchains.

Organizing a scientific conference is a complex process, involving many roles and many more interactions. We thank all our colleagues involved for their excellent work. The workshop chairs attracted 15 innovative workshops, the industry chairs organized a top-level industry program, and the demo chairs attracted many excellent demos. The panel chairs compiled an exciting panel, which opened doors to future research challenges. Without the publicity chairs, we could not have attracted such an excellent number of submissions. Younger researchers benefited from excellent tutorials; doctoral students received feedback about their work from experts in the field at the Doctoral Consortium. The mini-sabbatical program helped to bring additional colleagues to Austria. The proceedings chair, Claudio Di Ciccio, professionally interacted with Springer and with the authors to prepare excellent LNCS and LNBIP.

The members of the track Program Committees and senior Program Committees deserve particular acknowledgment for their dedication and commitment. We are grateful for the help and expertise of the additional reviewers, who provided valuable feedback during the reviewing process and engaged in deep discussions at times. BPM 2019 had a dedicated process to consolidate paper acceptance across tracks. During the very intensive weeks of this phase, many senior Program Committee members evaluated additional papers and were engaged in additional discussions. Special thanks goes to these colleagues, who were instrumental during this decisive phase of the reviewing process.

We cordially thank the colleagues involved in the organization of the conference, especially the members of the Program and Organizing Committees. We thank the Platinum Sponsor Signavio, the Gold Sponsors Austrian Center for Digital Production, Bizagi, Camunda, Celonis, FireStart, Process4.biz, the Silver Sponsors Heflo, JIT, Minit, Papyrus Software, Phactum, and the Bronze Sponsors ConSense, DCR, and TIM Solutions, as well as Springer and Gesellschaft für Prozessmanagement for their support. We also thank WU Vienna and the University of Vienna for its enormous and high-quality support. Finally, we thank the Organizing Committee and the local Organizing Committee, namely, Martin Beno, Katharina Distelbacher-Kollmann, Ilse Kondert, Roman Franz, Alexandra Hager, Prabh Jit, and Doris Wyk.

September 2019
Thomas Hildebrandt
Boudewijn van Dongen
Maximilian Röglinger
Jan Mendling

Organization

The 17th International Conference on Business Process Management (BPM 2019) was organized by the Vienna University of Economics and Business (WU Vienna) and the University of Vienna, and took place in Vienna, Austria.

Steering Committee

Mathias Weske (Chair)   HPI, University of Potsdam, Germany
Boualem Benatallah   University of New South Wales, Australia
Jörg Desel   Fernuniversität in Hagen, Germany
Schahram Dustdar   TU Wien, Austria (until 2018)
Marlon Dumas   University of Tartu, Estonia
Wil van der Aalst   RWTH Aachen University, Germany
Michael zur Muehlen   Stevens Institute of Technology, USA (until 2018)
Barbara Weber   University of St. Gallen, Switzerland
Stefanie Rinderle-Ma   University of Vienna, Austria
Manfred Reichert   University of Ulm, Germany
Jan Mendling   WU Vienna, Austria

Executive Committee

General Chairs

Jan Mendling   WU Vienna, Austria
Stefanie Rinderle-Ma   University of Vienna, Austria

Main Conference Program Chairs

Thomas Hildebrandt   University of Copenhagen, Denmark (Track I)
Boudewijn van Dongen   Eindhoven University of Technology, The Netherlands
                               (Track II)
Maximilian Röglinger   University of Bayreuth, Germany (Track III)
Jan Mendling   WU Vienna, Austria (Consolidation)

Blockchain Forum Chairs

Claudio Di Ciccio   WU Vienna, Austria
Luciano García-Bañuelos   Tecnológico de Monterrey, Mexico
Richard Hull   IBM Research, USA
Mark Staples   Data61, CSIRO, Australia

Central Eastern European Forum Chairs

Renata Gabryelczyk   University of Warsaw, Poland
Andrea Kő   Corvinus University of Budapest, Hungary

Tomislav Hernaus   University of Zagreb, Croatia
Mojca Indihar Štemberger   University of Ljubljana, Slovenia

Industry Track Chairs

Jan vom Brocke   University of Liechtenstein, Liechtenstein
Jan Mendling   WU Vienna, Austria
Michael Rosemann   Queensland University of Technology, Australia

Workshop Chairs

Remco Dijkman   Eindhoven University of Technology, The Netherlands
Chiara Di Francescomarino   Fondazione Bruno Kessler-IRST, Italy
Uwe Zdun   University of Vienna, Austria

Demonstration Chairs

Benoît Depaire   Hasselt University, Belgium
Stefan Schulte   TU Wien, Austria
Johannes de Smedt   University of Edinburgh, UK

Tutorial Chairs

Akhil Kumar   Penn State University, USA
Manfred Reichert   University of Ulm, Germany
Pnina Soffer   University of Haifa, Israel

Panel Chairs

Jan Recker   University of Cologne, Germany
Hajo A. Reijers   Utrecht University, The Netherlands

BPM Dissertation Award Chair

Stefanie Rinderle-Ma   University of Vienna, Austria

Event Organization Chair

Monika Hofer-Mozelt   University of Vienna, Austria

Local Organization Chairs

Katharina   WU Vienna, Austria
  Disselbacher-Kollmann
Roman Franz   WU Vienna, Austria
Ilse Dietlinde Kondert   WU Vienna, Austria

Publicity Chair

Cristina Cabanillas   WU Vienna, Austria

Web and Social Media Chair

Philipp Waibel   WU Vienna, Austria

Proceedings Chair

Claudio Di Ciccio   WU Vienna, Austria

Track I – Foundations

Senior Program Committee

Florian Daniel	Politecnico di Milano, Italy
Jörg Desel	Fernuniversität in Hagen, Germany
Chiara Di Francescomarino	Fondazione Bruno Kessler-IRST, Italy
Dirk Fahland	Eindhoven University of Technology, The Netherlands
Marcello La Rosa	The University of Melbourne, Australia
Fabrizio Maria Maggi	University of Tartu, Estonia
Marco Montali	Free University of Bozen-Bolzano, Italy
John Mylopoulos	University of Toronto, Canada
Manfred Reichert	University of Ulm, Germany
Victor Vianu	University of California San Diego, USA
Hagen Völzer	IBM Research – Zurich, Switzerland
Mathias Weske	HPI, University of Potsdam, Germany

Program Committee

Ahmed Awad	University of Tartu, Estonia
Jan Claes	Ghent University, Belgium
Søren Debois	IT University of Copenhagen, Denmark
Claudio Di Ciccio	WU Vienna, Austria
Rik Eshuis	Eindhoven University of Technology, The Netherlands
Hans-Georg Fill	University of Fribourg, Switzerland
Guido Governatori	Data61, CSIRO, Australia
Gianluigi Greco	University of Calabria, Italy
Richard Hull	IBM Research, USA
Irina Lomazova	National Research University Higher School of Economics, Russia
Andrea Marrella	Sapienza University of Rome, Italy
Oscar Pastor Lopez	Universitat Politècnica de València, Spain
Artem Polyvyanyy	The University of Melbourne, Australia
Wolfgang Reisig	Humboldt-Universität zu Berlin, Germany
Arik Senderovich	University of Toronto, Canada
Tijs Slaats	University of Copenhagen, Denmark
Ernest Teniente	Universitat Politècnica de Catalunya, Spain
Daniele Theseider Dupré	Università del Piemonte Orientale, Italy

Track II – Engineering

Senior Program Committee

Boualem Benatallah	The University of New South Wales, Australia
Josep Carmona	Universitat Politècnica de Catalunya, Spain
Cesare Pautasso	University of Lugano, Switzerland
Hajo A. Reijers	Utrecht University, The Netherlands
Pnina Soffer	University of Haifa, Israel
Wil van der Aalst	RWTH Aachen University, Germany
Ingo Weber	Data61, CSIRO, Australia
Barbara Weber	University of St. Gallen, Switzerland
Matthias Weidlich	Humboldt-Universität zu Berlin, Germany
Lijie Wen	Tsinghua University, China

Program Committee

Marco Aiello	University of Stuttgart, Germany
Amin Beheshti	Macquarie University, Australia
Andrea Burattin	Technical University of Denmark, Denmark
Cristina Cabanillas	WU Vienna, Austria
Fabio Casati	University of Trento, Italy
Massimiliano de Leoni	University of Padua, Italy
Jochen De Weerdt	KU Leuven, Belgium
Remco Dijkman	Eindhoven University of Technology, The Netherlands
Marlon Dumas	University of Tartu, Estonia
Schahram Dustdar	TU Wien, Austria
Gregor Engels	Paderborn University, Germany
Joerg Evermann	Memorial University of Newfoundland, Canada
Walid Gaaloul	Télécom SudParis, France
Avigdor Gal	Technion, Israel
Luciano García-Bañuelos	Tecnológico de Monterrey, Mexico
Chiara Ghidini	Fondazione Bruno Kessler (FBK), Italy
Daniela Grigori	Laboratoire LAMSADE, University of Paris-Dauphine, France
Dimka Karastoyanova	University of Groningen, The Netherlands
Christopher Klinkmüller	Data61, CSIRO, Australia
Agnes Koschmider	Karlsruhe Institute of Technology, Germany
Jochen Kuester	FH Bielefeld, Germany
Henrik Leopold	Kühne Logistics University, Germany
Raimundas Matulevičius	University of Tartu, Estonia
Massimo Mecella	Sapienza University of Rome, Italy
Hamid Motahari	Ernst & Young (EY), USA
Jorge Munoz-Gama	Pontificia Universidad Católica de Chile, Chile
Hye-Young Paik	The University of New South Wales, Australia
Luise Pufahl	Hasso Plattner Institute, University of Potsdam, Germany

Manuel Resinas	University of Seville, Spain
Minseok Song	POSTECH (Pohang University of Science and Technology), South Korea
Arthur ter Hofstede	Queensland University of Technology, Australia
Farouk Toumani	Limos, Blaise Pascal University, Clermont-Ferrand, France
Eric Verbeek	Eindhoven University of Technology, The Netherlands
Moe Wynn	Queensland University of Technology, Australia
Bas van Zelst	Fraunhofer Gesellschaft Aachen, Germany

Track III – Management

Senior Program Committee

Jörg Becker	University of Münster, ERCIS, Germany
Adela Del Río Ortega	University of Seville, Spain
Marta Indulska	The University of Queensland, Australia
Susanne Leist	University of Regensburg, Germany
Mikael Lind	Research Institutes of Sweden (RISE)/Chalmers University of Technology, Sweden
Peter Loos	IWi at DFKI, Saarland University, Germany
Jan Recker	University of Cologne, Germany
Michael Rosemann	Queensland University of Technology, Australia
Flavia Santoro	University of the State of Rio de Janeiro, Brazil
Peter Trkman	University of Ljubljana, Slovenia
Amy Van Looy	Ghent University, Belgium
Robert Winter	University of St. Gallen, Switzerland

Program Committee

Wasana Bandara	Queensland University of Technology, Australia
Daniel Beimborn	University of Bamberg, Germany
Daniel Beverungen	Paderborn University, Germany
Alessio Maria Braccini	University of Tuscia, Italy
Michael Fellmann	University of Rostock, Institute for Computer Science, Germany
Peter Fettke	German Research Center for Artificial Intelligence (DFKI) and Saarland University, Germany
Kathrin Figl	University of Innsbruck, Austria
Andreas Gadatsch	Hochschule Bonn-Rhein-Sieg, Germany
Paul Grefen	Eindhoven University of Technology, The Netherlands
Thomas Grisold	University of Liechtenstein, Liechtenstein
Bernd Heinrich	Universität Regensburg, Germany
Mojca Indihar Štemberger	University of Ljubljana, Slovenia
Christian Janiesch	TU Dresden, Germany
Florian Johannsen	University of Applied Sciences Schmalkalden, Germany

John Krogstie	Norwegian University of Science and Technology, Norway
Michael Leyer	University of Rostock, Germany
Alexander Mädche	Karlsruhe Institute of Technology, Germany
Monika Malinova	WU Vienna, Austria
Juergen Moormann	Frankfurt School of Finance & Management, Germany
Michael zur Muehlen	Stevens Institute of Technology, USA
Markus Nüttgens	University of Hamburg, Germany
Sven Overhage	University of Bamberg, Germany
Geert Poels	Ghent University, Belgium
Jens Poeppelbuss	Ruhr-Universität Bochum, Germany
Michael Räckers	University of Münster, ERCIS, Germany
Shazia Sadiq	The University of Queensland, Australia
Bernd Schenk	University of Liechtenstein, Liechtenstein
Werner Schmidt	Technische Hochschule Ingolstadt (THI Business School), Germany
Theresa Schmiedel	University of Applied Sciences and Arts Northwestern Switzerland, Switzerland
Anna Sidorova	University of North Texas, USA
Oktay Türetken	Eindhoven University of Technology, The Netherlands
Irene Vanderfeesten	Eindhoven University of Technology, The Netherlands
Jan Vanthienen	KU Leuven, Belgium
Axel Winkelmann	University of Würzburg, Germany

Additional Reviewers

Abasi-Amefon Affia	Christian Fleig	Michael Poppe
Simone Agostinelli	Lukas-Valentin Herm	Raphael Schilling
Ivo Benke	Mubashar Iqbal	Roee Shraga
Sabrina Blaukopf	Samuel Kießling	Ludwig Stage
Djordje Djurica	Fabienne Lambusch	Peyman Toreini
Montserrat Estañol	Xavier Oriol	Jonas Wanner
Florian Fahrenbach	Baris Ozkan	Bastian Wurm

Abstracts of Keynotes

Digitalization and Routines - Another Look at Business Process Management

Kalle Lyytinen

Case Western Reserve University, Cleveland, OH 44106, USA
kalle@case.edu

Abstract. This key note examines the changing role of business process management from a broader perspective of organizational change routines. It seeks to integrate and contextualize business process management with recent advances in theorizing about routines and their change in the context of deep digitalization of firm operations. While business process management emerges from the internal, computational view of business process management advocated by computer science community since the 80's where the driving concern has been for semantically correct computational processes and their efficient enactment, the research on organizational routines provides an external view of this focal phenomenon. Studies of organizational routines have emerged from evolutionary economics and organizational theory as scholars have sought to examine and explain the structuring, evolution and effects of business routines and their enactment in evolving organizational and industrial contexts. The main focus of these inquiries been to account for economic or organizational effectiveness of coordination and collaboration tasks enabled by varying routine constellations. In the process management stream the key concerns have been efficient process execution, its semantic correctness, consistent state maintenance, exception handling and possibility for process mining and discovery. In the latter the dominant issues have been environmental fit and change, adaptability, maintenance of organizational memory, performativity and learning from and for process execution. The talk will review both research streams and look for their strengths and weaknesses. We call also for better integration and receptivity of organizational theory concepts to process management and execution and the need for routine theory to recognize the relevance of computational perspectives in accounting for process change and execution. The need for integration has become increasingly relevant and intra and inter-organizational business processes are increasingly automated and engulfed with intelligence. Several examples of using routines as a framing device to study organizational change are offered to demonstrate the value and relevance of such view on process management scholarship.

Keywords: Business process management · Routines · Routine theory · Coordination · Collaboration · Process analysis · Sequence analysis · Process mining · Evolutionary economics

Understanding the Potential of "Real RPA"

Pat Geary

Blue Prism, 338 Euston Road, London NW1 3BG, UK
pat.geary@blueprism.com

Abstract. Since the RPA software category was created over 17 years ago, it now successfully operates in large-scale, demanding, enterprise environments. RPA enables business teams to orchestrate easy-to-control, automated, digital workers to drive tactical change at large organizations - so they keep up with ever-changing demand. This potential to drive digital transformation across the world's workplace operations has created a rapidly expanding market – with over 40 vendors offering some sort of RPA - or intelligent automation capabilities.

This category is now entering its next evolutionary phase – 'connected-RPA' – which is an even more intelligent form of business automation that enables collaborative, technology innovation – and it's also widely acknowledged as providing the foundation for the AI revolution. Ultimately, the future of work is being driven by connected-RPA, and this is already occurring with the creation of entire communities, consisting of teams of humans – working in tandem with thinking, digital workers.

However, connected-RPA is complex and relatively misunderstood, so without a definitive reference point, organizations risk choosing the wrong automation options for enterprise environments. I'll provide insight gained from more than a decade of working with the pioneers of connected-RPA technology, discuss why it's more important than ever to re-define what this technology is – and what it isn't – and where it sits within its industry.

I'll also explain why connected-RPA is the becoming the true standard for collaboration, securely, at scale for global organizations and how it can deliver sustainable, digital transformation. Finally, I'll highlight how connected-RPA will play a key role in shaping the future of work and what outcomes are being achieved now.

Keywords: Robotic process automation · Digital transformation · Collaborative technology innovation

The State of the Art in Dynamic Graph Algorithms

Monika Henzinger

University of Vienna, Währinger Straße 29, 1090 Wien, Austria
monika.henzinger@univie.ac.at

Abstract. A dynamic graph algorithm is a data structure that maintains information about a graph that is being modified by edge and vertex insertions and deletions. Due to the recent increase of dynamically changing huge graphs (such as social network graphs) there is a rising demand for such data structures.

More formally, a dynamic graph algorithm is given an initial graph for which it builds a representation. With this representation it then supports two types of operations, namely (a) update operations and (b) queries. Each update operation modifies the representations to reflect the insertion or deletion of the edge or (isolated) vertex given as parameter to the update operation. Each query operation returns information about a graph property in the current graph. The challenge is to design a data structure for which each update operation is much faster than running the corresponding static algorithm, i.e., recomputation from scratch while keeping the query time small (usually constant or polylogarithmic in the size of the graph). Surprisingly, such data structures exist for certain basic graph properties such as connected components, minimum spanning forest, and maximal matching. Recent conditional lower bounds show, however, that for many other graph properties, such as single-source reachability and single-source shortest paths, no dynamic data structure can exist that is more efficient that the corresponding static algorithm.

We will survey some of the upper and lower bound techniques in this talk.

Keyword: Dynamic graph algorithms

Contents

Tutorials

Everything You Always Wanted to Know About Petri Nets, but Were Afraid to Ask

Wil M. P. van der Aalst[1,2](✉) ⓘ

[1] Process and Data Science (PADS), RWTH Aachen University, Aachen, Germany
[2] Fraunhofer Institute for Applied Information Technology,
Sankt Augustin, Germany
`wvdaalst@pads.rwth-aachen.de`

Abstract. Business Process Management (BPM), Process Mining (PM), Workflow Management (WFM), and other approaches aimed at improving processes depend on process models. Business Process Model and Notation (BPMN), Event-driven Process Chains (EPCs), and UML activity diagrams all build on Petri nets and have semantics involving 'playing the token game'. In addition, process analysis approaches ranging from verification and simulation to process discovery and compliance checking often depend on Petri net theory. For the casual user, there is no need to understand the underlying foundations. However, BPM/PM/WFM researchers and 'process experts' working in industry need to understand these foundational results. Unfortunately, the results of 50 years of Petri net research are not easy to digest. This tutorial paper provides, therefore, an entry point into the wonderful world of Petri nets.

Keywords: Petri nets · Business Process Management · Process Mining

1 Petri Nets and Business Process Management

Since their inception in 1962, Petri nets have been used in a wide variety of application domains. A more recent development is the foundational role of Petri nets in Business Process Management (BPM) [8] and related fields such as Process Mining (PM) [2] and Workflow Management (WFM) [3]. Many WFM systems are based on Petri nets. In fact, the first prototypes developed in the late 1970-ties (e.g., Officetalk and SCOOP) already used Petri nets [1]. In today's BPM/WFM systems, this is less visible. However, popular modeling languages such as Business Process Model and Notation (BPMN), Event-driven Process Chains (EPCs), and UML activity diagrams all borrow ideas from Petri nets (e.g., the 'token game' to describe semantics and to implement BPM/WFM engines and simulation tools) [5].

Petri nets also play a major role in the analysis of processes and event data. Many simulation tools are based on Petri nets [5]. Petri nets are also used for

T. Hildebrandt et al. (Eds.): BPM 2019, LNCS 11675, pp. 3–9, 2019.
https://doi.org/10.1007/978-3-030-26619-6_1

the verification of processes in WFM/BPM systems, e.g., to check soundness
[4]. However, this possibility is not used much in practice. Conversely, Process
Mining (PM) is much more widely used than simulation and verification. Petri
nets are the most widely used representation in PM [2]. There are dozens of
techniques that can discover a Petri net from event data. Moreover, almost all
conformance checking techniques use Petri nets internally.

This short paper is based on a tutorial with the same name presented at the
17th International Conference on Business Process Management (BPM 2019) in
Vienna in September 2019. Here, we can only show a few of the 'gems in Petri
nets' relevant for BPM, PM, and WFM.

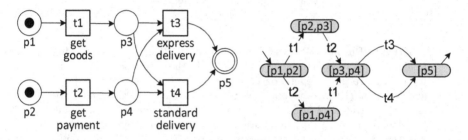

Fig. 1. An accepting petri net N_1 (left) with transitions $T_1 = \{t1, t2, t3, t4\}$, places
$P_1 = \{p1, p2, p3, p4, p5\}$, initial marking $[p1, p2]$, and final marking $[p5]$. N_1 allows
for traces $traces(N_1) = \{\langle t1, t2, t3\rangle, \langle t2, t1, t3\rangle, \langle t1, t2, t4\rangle, \langle t2, t1, t4\rangle\}$. The reachability graph (right) shows the reachable markings $states(N_1) = \{[p1, p2], [p1, p4],$
$[p2, p3], [p3, p4], [p5]\}$.

2   Accepting Petri Nets

Figures 1 and 2 show two so-called *accepting Petri nets*. These Petri nets have
an initial state and a final state. States in Petri nets are called *markings* that
mark certain *places* (represented by circles) with *tokens* (represented by black
dots). The accepting Petri net N_1 in Fig. 1 has five places. In the initial marking,
$[p1, p2]$ two places are marked. Since a place may have multiple tokens, markings
are represented by multisets. *Transitions* (represented by squares) are the active
components able to move the Petri nets from one marking to another marking.
N_1 has four transitions. A transition is called *enabled* if each of the input places
has a token. An enabled transition may *fire* (i.e., *occur*) thereby consuming a
token from each input place and producing a token for each output places. In
the marking showing in Fig. 1, both $t1$ and $t2$ are enabled. Firing $t1$ removes a
token from $p1$ and adds a token to $p3$. Firing $t2$ removes a token from $p2$ and
adds a token to $p4$. In the resulting marking $[p3, p4]$ both $t3$ and $t4$ are enabled.
Note that both transitions require both input places to be marked. However,
only one of them can fire. Firing $t3$ (or $t4$) removes a token from both $p3$ and $p4$
and adds one token to $p5$. Transitions may be labeled, e.g., transitions $t1$, $t2$, $t3$,

and $t4$ represent the activities "get goods", "get payment", "express delivery", and "normal delivery" respectively. For simplicity, we ignore the transition labels and only use the short transition names.

The *behavior* of an accepting Petri net is described by all *traces* starting in the initial marking and ending in the final marking. $\langle t1, t2, t3 \rangle$ is one of the four traces of accepting Petri net N_1. Figure 1 also shows the reachability graph of N_1. The reachability graph shows all reachable markings and their connections. N_1 has five reachable states.

Accepting Petri net N_2 depicted in Fig. 2 also has five reachable states, but allows for infinitely many traces (due to the loop involving $t1$ and $t2$).

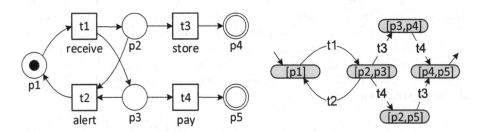

Fig. 2. An accepting petri net N_2 (left) with initial marking $[p1]$ and final marking $[p4, p5]$. N_2 allows for infinitely many traces $traces(N_2) = \{\langle t1, t3, t4 \rangle, \langle t1, t4, t3 \rangle, \langle t1, t2, t1, t3, t4 \rangle, \langle t1, t2, t1, t4, t3 \rangle, \langle t1, t2, t1, t2, t1, t3, t4 \rangle, \ldots\}$. The reachability graph (right) shows the reachable markings $states(N_2) = \{[p1], [p2, p3], [p2, p5], [p3, p4], [p4, p5]\}$.

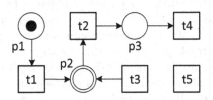

Fig. 3. An accepting petri net N_3 with initial marking $[p1]$ and final marking $[p2]$ showing the declarative nature of Petri nets.

3   Petri Nets Are More Declarative Than You Think

Petri nets are typically considered 'procedural' (like an imperative program) and not 'declarative'. However, an accepting Petri net *without* places allows for any trace involving the transitions in the net. Each place corresponds to a *constraint*. Consider for example the accepting Petri net N_3 in Fig. 3. Place $p1$ models the constraint that $t1$ should occur precisely once. Place $p2$ models the constraint that $t2$ can only occur after $t1$ or $t3$. Each occurrence of $t2$ requires an earlier occurrence of $t1$ or $t3$ and, at the end, the number of occurrences of $t2$ is one less than the sum of $t1$ and $t3$. Place $p3$ models the constraint that each $t4$ occurrence should be preceded by a $t2$ occurrence and, at the end, the number of occurrences of both $t2$ and $t4$ need to be the same. Note that transition $t5$ is not constrained by one of the places and can occur at any point in time and an arbitrary number of times. Removing a place can only enable more traces, thus illustrating the declarative nature of Petri nets (anything is possible unless specified otherwise).

4   Structure Theory and the Marking Equation

Structure theory focuses on behavioral properties that can be derived from the structural properties of a Petri net [6,7,9]. It is impossible to go into details. Therefore, we restrict ourselves to the *marking equation* which nicely shows how linear algebra can be used to exploit the structure of a Petri net. To start, we represent the first two Petri nets as a matrix with a row for each place and a column for each transition. The so-called incidence matrix shows the 'net effect' of firing a transition (column) on each place (row).

$$
\mathbf{N_1} = \begin{array}{c} \\ p1 \\ p2 \\ p3 \\ p4 \\ p5 \end{array}
\begin{array}{cccc} t1 & t2 & t3 & t4 \\ \left(\begin{array}{cccc} -1 & 0 & 0 & 0 \\ 0 & -1 & 0 & 0 \\ 1 & 0 & -1 & -1 \\ 0 & 1 & -1 & -1 \\ 0 & 0 & 1 & 1 \end{array}\right) \end{array}
\qquad
\mathbf{N_2} = \begin{array}{c} \\ p1 \\ p2 \\ p3 \\ p4 \\ p5 \end{array}
\begin{array}{cccc} t1 & t2 & t3 & t4 \\ \left(\begin{array}{cccc} -1 & 1 & 0 & 0 \\ 1 & -1 & -1 & 0 \\ 1 & -1 & 0 & -1 \\ 0 & 0 & 1 & 0 \\ 0 & 0 & 0 & 1 \end{array}\right) \end{array}
$$

The incidence matrix imposes an order on places (rows) and transitions (columns). For N_1 and N_2, the order is $p1, p2, p3, p4, p5$ and $t1, t2, t3, t4$. $\mathbf{t} = (1, 1, 1, 0)^T$ is an example of a transition column vector assigning value 1 to $t1$, $t2$, and $t3$ and value 0 to $t4$. $\mathbf{p} = (1, 1, 0, 0, 0)^T$ is an example of a place column vector assigning value 1 to $p1$ and $p2$, and value 0 to $p3$, $p4$, and $p5$. Assume that $\mathbf{p}'$ and $\mathbf{p}''$ are two place column vectors representing the initial marking $\mathbf{p}'$ and a target marking $\mathbf{p}''$. If $\mathbf{p}''$ is reachable from $\mathbf{p}'$ in some Petri net having incidence matrix $\mathbf{N}$, then the so-called marking equation

$$\mathbf{p}' + \mathbf{N} \cdot \mathbf{t} = \mathbf{p}''$$

has a solution for some transition column vector $\mathbf{t}$ with non-negative values.

Consider N_1 in Fig. 1. We are interested in the different ways to get from the initial marking $[p1, p2]$ to the final marking $[p5]$. Hence, $\mathbf{p}' = (1, 1, 0, 0, 0)^T$ and $\mathbf{p}'' = (0, 0, 0, 0, 1)^T$, resulting in the following marking equation:

$$
\mathbf{p}' + \mathbf{N} \cdot \mathbf{t} = \begin{pmatrix} 1 \\ 1 \\ 0 \\ 0 \\ 0 \end{pmatrix} + \begin{pmatrix} -1 & 0 & 0 & 0 \\ 0 & -1 & 0 & 0 \\ 1 & 0 & -1 & -1 \\ 0 & 1 & -1 & -1 \\ 0 & 0 & 1 & 1 \end{pmatrix} \cdot \begin{pmatrix} t1 \\ t2 \\ t3 \\ t4 \end{pmatrix} = \begin{pmatrix} 0 \\ 0 \\ 0 \\ 0 \\ 1 \end{pmatrix} = \mathbf{p}''
$$

Hence, we can infer from the marking equation that $t1 = 1$, $t2 = 1$, and $t3 + t4 = 1$. Since N_1 allows for trace $\langle t1, t2, t3 \rangle$, we know that $t1 = t2 = t3 = 1$ and $t4 = 0$ should be a solution. Suppose we would like to know whether N_1 allows for trace $\langle t1, t3, t4 \rangle$. Since $t1 = t3 = t4 = 1$ and $t2 = 0$ is not solution of the marking equation, we know that $\langle t1, t3, t4 \rangle$ is impossible *without* replaying the trace. For such a small example, this may seem insignificant. However, the marking equation provides a powerful 'algebraic overapproximation' of all possible traces. Note that the marking equation provides a necessary but not a sufficient condition. The algebraic overapproximation can be used to quickly prune search spaces in verification and conformance checking. For example, the marking equation can be used to guide the search for so-called optimal alignments in conformance checking [2].

The marking equation is related to place and transitions invariants. Any solution of the equation $\mathbf{p} \cdot \mathbf{N} = \mathbf{0}$ is a *place invariant*. For net N_1:

$$\mathbf{p} \cdot \mathbf{N} = (p1, p2, p3, p4, p5) \cdot \begin{pmatrix} -1 & 0 & 0 & 0 \\ 0 & -1 & 0 & 0 \\ 1 & 0 & -1 & -1 \\ 0 & 1 & -1 & -1 \\ 0 & 0 & 1 & 1 \end{pmatrix} = (0, 0, 0, 0) = \mathbf{0}$$

For example, $\mathbf{p} = (p1, p2, p3, p4, p5) = (1, 0, 1, 0, 1)$ is the place invariant showing that the number of tokens in the places $p1$, $p3$, and $p5$ is constant. The so-called 'weighted token sum' is constant for any initial marking. Given the initial marking $[p1, p2]$, the weighted token sum is 1. If the initial marking is $[p1^2, p3, p4^3, p5]$, the weighted token sum is $(2 \times 1) + (0 \times 0) + (1 \times 1) + (3 \times 0) + (1 \times 1) = 4$ and will not change. $\mathbf{p} = (0, 1, 0, 1, 1)$, $\mathbf{p} = (1, 1, 1, 1, 2)$, and $\mathbf{p} = (1, -1, 1, -1, 0)$ are other place invariants since $\mathbf{p} \cdot \mathbf{N_1} = \mathbf{0}$.

Any solution of the equation $\mathbf{N} \cdot \mathbf{t} = \mathbf{0}^T$ is a *transition invariant*. For net N_2:

$$\mathbf{N} \cdot \mathbf{t} = \begin{pmatrix} -1 & 1 & 0 & 0 \\ 1 & -1 & -1 & 0 \\ 1 & -1 & 0 & -1 \\ 0 & 0 & 1 & 0 \\ 0 & 0 & 0 & 1 \end{pmatrix} \cdot \begin{pmatrix} t1 \\ t2 \\ t3 \\ t4 \end{pmatrix} = \begin{pmatrix} 0 \\ 0 \\ 0 \\ 0 \\ 0 \end{pmatrix} = \mathbf{0}^T$$

Any non-negative solution points to firing sequences returning to the same state. For example, $\mathbf{t} = (t1, t2, t3, t4)^T = (3, 3, 0, 0)^T$ is the transition invariant showing that if we are able to execute $t1$ and $t2$ three times, we return to the initial state. Again this property is independent of the initial marking. Trace invariants can again be seen as an 'algebraic overapproximation' of all possible traces returning to the same state.

5 A Beautiful Subclass: Free-Choice Petri Nets

The three models shown in Figs. 1, 2 and 3 are all *free-choice Petri nets*. These nets satisfy the constraint that any two transitions having the same place as input place should have identical sets of input places. Formally, for any two transitions $t1, t2 \in T$ such that $\bullet t1 \cap \bullet t2 \neq \emptyset$: $\bullet t1 = \bullet t2$. In Fig. 1, $\bullet t3 \cap \bullet t4 \neq \emptyset$, but $\bullet t3 = \bullet t4 = \{p3, p4\}$. The free-choice requirement implies that choice and synchronization are 'separable', i.e., choices are 'free' and not controlled by places that are not shared by all transitions involved in the choice. Free-choice Petri nets are very relevant for BPM, PM, and WFM, because most modeling languages have constructs (e.g., gateways in BPMN, control nodes in UML activity diagrams, and connectors in EPCs) modeling AND/XOR-splits/joins. As a result, choice (XOR-split) and synchronization (AND-join) are separated.

To exploit the properties of free-choice Petri nets, we often 'short-circuit' the accepting Petri net, i.e., we add a transition consuming tokens from the places in the final marking and producing tokens for the places in the initial marking. This implies that when reaching the final marking, it is possible to do a 'reset' and start again from the initial state.

We refer to [7] for the many results known for free-choice Petri nets, e.g., Commoner's Theorem, the two Coverability Theorems, the Rank Theorem, the Synthesis Theorem, the Home Marking Theorem, the two Confluence Theorems, the Shortest Sequence Theorem, and the Blocking Marking Theorem.

6   Conclusion

This short paper should be considered as a 'teaser' for researchers and experts working on BPM, PM, and WFM. Although often not directly visible, many techniques and tools depend on Petri nets. See [5–7,9] to learn more about the Petri net theory. For the use of Petri nets in BPM, PM, and WFM, see [1–4].

Acknowledgments. We thank the Alexander von Humboldt (AvH) Stiftung for supporting our research.

References

1. van der Aalst, W.M.P.: Business process management: a comprehensive survey. ISRN Softw. Eng. 1–37 (2013). https://doi.org/10.1155/2013/507984
2. van der Aalst, W.M.P.: Process Mining: Data Science in Action. Springer, Berlin (2016). https://doi.org/10.1007/978-3-662-49851-4
3. van der Aalst, W.M.P., van Hee, K.M.: Workflow Management: Models, Methods, and Systems. MIT Press, Cambridge (2004)
4. van der Aalst, W.M.P., et al.: Soundness of workflow nets: classification, decidability, and analysis. Formal Aspects Comput. **23**(3), 333–363 (2011)
5. van der Aalst, W.M.P., Stahl, C.: Modeling Business Processes: A Petri Net Oriented Approach. MIT Press, Cambridge (2011)
6. Best, E., Wimmel, H.: Structure theory of petri nets. In: Jensen, K., van der Aalst, W.M.P., Balbo, G., Koutny, M., Wolf, K. (eds.) Transactions on Petri Nets and Other Models of Concurrency VII. LNCS, vol. 7480, pp. 162–224. Springer, Heidelberg (2013). https://doi.org/10.1007/978-3-642-38143-0_5

7. Desel, J., Esparza, J.: Free Choice Petri Nets. Cambridge Tracts in Theoretical Computer Science, vol. 40. Cambridge University Press, Cambridge (1995)
8. Dumas, M., La Rosa, M., Mendling, J., Reijers, H.: Fundamentals of Business Process Management. Springer, Berlin (2013). https://doi.org/10.1007/978-3-642-33143-5
9. Reisig, W., Rozenberg, G. (eds.): ACPN 1996. LNCS, vol. 1491. Springer, Heidelberg (1998). https://doi.org/10.1007/3-540-65306-6

Responsible Process Mining - A Data Quality Perspective

Moe Thandar Wynn[1]([⊠]) and Shazia Sadiq[2]

[1] Queensland University of Technology, Brisbane, Australia
m.wynn@qut.edu.au
[2] The University of Queensland, Brisbane, Australia
shazia@itee.uq.edu.au

Abstract. Modern organisations consider data to be their lifeblood. The potential benefits of data-driven analyses include a better understanding of business performance and more-informed decision making for business growth. A key road block to this vision is the lack of transparency surrounding the quality of data. A process mining study that utilises low-quality, unrepresentative data as input has little or no value for the organisation and becomes a catalyst for erroneous conclusions ('Garbage-in-Garbage-out'). Many process mining techniques do not take into account inherent inaccuracies in the data, or how the data might have been manipulated or pre-processed. It is thus impossible to ascertain the degree to which analysis outcomes can be relied upon. This tutorial paper outlines foundational concepts of data quality with a special focus on typical data quality issues found in event data used for process mining analyses. Key challenges and possible approaches to tackle these data quality problems are elaborated on.

Keywords: Process mining · Data quality

1 Introduction

Process Mining is a specialised form of data-driven process analytics where data about process executions, collated from the different IT systems typically available in organisations, is analysed to uncover *the real behaviour and performance* of business operations [2]. Without question, the extent to which the outcomes from process mining analyses can be relied upon for insights is directly related to the quality of the input data. The onus is usually on a process analyst to identify, assess and appropriately remedy data quality issues so as to avoid inadvertently introducing errors into the data while minimising information loss. It is widely acknowledged that eighty percent of the work of data scientists is taken up by data preparation and handling data quality issues[1]. The case of the process analyst is no different [17].

---

[1] https://www.forbes.com/sites/gilpress/2016/03/23/data-preparation-most-time-consuming-least-enjoyable-data-science-task-survey-says/#58f51e5d6f63.

© Springer Nature Switzerland AG 2019
T. Hildebrandt et al. (Eds.): BPM 2019, LNCS 11675, pp. 10–15, 2019.
https://doi.org/10.1007/978-3-030-26619-6_2

There has been an increased interest in research investigating the issues of responsible data science [3,15]. Key dimensions in the notion of responsible data science (such as fairness, accuracy, transparency, and confidentiality [3]) are being explored and also for different domains (e.g., healthcare). In order to take steps towards responsible process mining, there is the dual need to increase the importance of data quality awareness and mitigate the opportunity to make erroneous conclusions, while helping process analysts overcome the burden of managing data quality.

In this tutorial paper, we focus on event logs as the primary form of input into process mining. Accordingly, we first present a brief summary of existing work on understanding data quality requirements for event logs. In the words of Edward Demming, the father of quality management, you can't manage what you can't measure. Hence, our next section outlines key techniques for measuring data quality in event logs. Finally, we provide a synopsis of current contributions and future needs of data quality awareness in process mining.

2   Understanding Data Quality Requirements for Event Logs

An event log used for process mining contains a collection of cases whereby each case can be seen as a sequence of events [2]. Each event refers to a case, an activity being undertaken, a point in time and a transaction type. An event may also refer to a resource or an organisational role and other data attributes (e.g., customer details and case outcomes).

The process mining manifesto [1] highlighted the need for high-quality event logs for process mining. The manifesto describes five levels of maturity ranging from one star to five stars. At the lowest level of maturity (*) where events are recorded manually, one may find that events that are incorrectly entered (e.g., incorrect timestamps or activity labels) or events may be missing. At the highest level of maturity (*****), event logs are considered to be complete and accurate as events are recorded automatically by a system (e.g., a process-aware information system). Most real-life event logs are found to be in-between these two extremes of the scale with many quality issues [6,17].

As most process mining techniques make use of key event data, namely, case identifiers, activity labels, and timestamps, missing, inaccurate or erroneous values (e.g., only a date is recorded but no time, incorrect spellings or variations in how activities are labeled) for any of this data may mean that a case or an event has to be filtered out or an erroneous value may need to be replaced, or a missing value may need to be inferred.

Given the diversity of data quality problems, it is important to understand the key requirements. While Juran and Godfrey [10] provide the fundamental "fitness for use" principle, decades of data quality research has proliferated various understandings of data quality requirements through its underlying dimensions [8,14,16,20]. Over the course of time, many of the definitions for different data quality dimensions have overlapped, and the same definitions for the same dimensions have developed conflicting interpretations, resulting in a level of disparity that does not support a shared understanding. Recent work offers an empirically validated consolidation of these dimensions covering both academic and practitioner perspectives [9], and provides 33 dimensions clustered into eight categories, namely Completeness, Accuracy, Validity, Consistency, Currency, Availability and Accessibility, Reliability and Credibility, and Usability and Interpretability. These studies indicate that data quality requirements cover both objective (e.g. uniqueness and format consistency) as well as subjective (e.g. relevance and freshness) dimensions.

There have been efforts by process mining researchers to classify data quality issues typically found in event logs [6,12,17,18] with a view to take steps towards addressing these issues and thus to increase the reliability of analysis results.

Bose et al. [6] identify four broad categories of issues affecting event log quality: missing data (where data items are not recorded in an event log), incorrect data (where data items are incorrectly recorded in an event log), imprecise data (where recorded values are considered too coarse to be useful) and irrelevant data (where data items contains irrelevant information). The authors also identify 27 classes of event log quality issues (e.g., problems related to timestamps in event logs, imprecise activity names, and missing events) depending on where they occur such as cases, events, activity labels, timestamps, resources. Their intention is to "encourage systematic logging approaches (to prevent event log issues), repair techniques (to alleviate event log issues) and analysis techniques (to deal with the manifestation of process characteristics in event logs)" [6]. These issues were illustrated from the analysis of five real-life event logs from different application domains.

Suriadi et al. [17] identify eleven event log imperfection patterns based on their experience with over 20 Australian industry data sets which confirm the severity of data quality issues in process data and their potential impact on process mining analyses. The eleven patterns include form-based event capture, inadvertent time travel, unanchored event, scattered event, elusive case, scattered case, collateral event, polluted label, distorted label, synonymous labels and homonymous label. Each pattern is described using the following components: description of the pattern, real-life example of the pattern, affect which captures the consequence of the occurrence of the pattern on process mining outcomes, the type of data event and event log entities affected by the pattern, strategy to detect the presence of a pattern, potential remedies and side-effects of these remedies, and indicative rules for detection.

Lu and Fahland [12] propose a conceptual framework to better understand event data quality for process mining analysis. The framework categorises event data into three entities: quality of events, quality of ordering of events and quality of labels of event. These three entities are then evaluated based on two dimensions: individual trustworthiness and global conclusiveness whereby individual trustworthiness focuses on the intrinsic qualities of event data (e.g., accuracy or correctness dimensions) while the global conclusiveness indicates if a significant pattern is being observed.

3   Measuring Data Quality of Event Logs

Data quality requirements continue to be dictated by the fitness for use principle [10], thus making them highly dependent on the use context. Further a plethora of diversified requirements (i.e. dimensions) exist, which are in turn deeply bound to use context making them complicated to model, analyse, and re-use, resulting in a prohibitive capacity to have a common set of measures for detecting and quantifying data quality.

Batini et al. [4] provide a comprehensive analysis of existing approaches for data quality assessment. We note that most, if not all, of these approaches follow a user centric approach where requirements are solicited from users before the data is explored (see e.g. [5,11,19]).

However, in the process mining context, access to the creators of data that constitutes event-logs cannot be relied on. This is mostly the case for publicly available event logs. Furthermore a process analyst cannot typically influence data capture practices and hence expectation of cleaning of the source data may be misplaced. Thus it is imperative to measure the quality of an event log respective to the particular type of analysis intended such as process discovery, performance analysis or conformance checking. For instance, the missing values metric assesses the fraction of the log for which a particular log attribute is populated which contributes to quantifying the Completeness dimension. In a log where the majority of events only have "complete" (rather than "start" and "complete") timestamps, i.e. have a high degree of missing values, the suitability of that log for performance analysis is low while the suitability for process discovery may not be negatively affected. On the other hand, if recorded timestamps do not accurately reflect when an activity occurred, process discovery will be compromised.

In [18], the authors propose an extensible framework to measure event data quality based on twelve dimensions collated from prior literature and to quantify the prevalence of data quality issues in event data. They include completeness, uniqueness, timeliness, validity, accuracy/correctness, consistency, believability, credibility, relevancy, security/confidentiality, complexity, coherence, representation/format.

Another early advocate of detecting data quality issues in event logs is Anna Rozinat, the co-founder of Disco Process Mining Tool. Through a number of blog posts which have now been collated into a book on process mining in practice[2], various data quality issues in event logs and ways to detect and (potentially) repair them were discussed. The quality issues mentioned in the book include formatting errors, missing data (event, attribute values, case IDs, activities, timestamps, attribute history, timestamps for activity repetition) as well as zero timestamps, wrong timestamps, same timestamps for multiple activities and different timestamp granularity.

---

[2] http://processminingbook.com.

4   Data Quality Awareness in Process Mining

Keeping a detailed record of the origins of data and how data is transformed along the way will increase its traceability and trustworthiness. Where such information is unavailable, the extent and effect of changes on the data will be opaque to the analyst who, may view the data as 'ground truth', i.e. direct observations as opposed to already modified data. Such a view can result in inaccurate or misleading analysis results or inappropriate further transformations. For instance, where the analyst is unaware that a data set extracted from a hospital's emergency department has been modified through time-shifting in order to de-identify patients (as in the case of MIMIIC critical care data set[3]), using this data for performance analysis will lead to incorrect results.

There has been some work to detect and repair quality issues associated with event logs. For example, Dixit et al. [7] presents a user-guided technique to detect event ordering imperfection patterns in a log associated with timestamps and then repairing identified issues using user input. The timestamp related quality issues such as different granularities, order anomaly and statistical anomaly are detected and repaired. Similarly, Lu et al. [13] presents an interactive way to assist users explore data quality patterns of interest using the context information contained in an event log. Five measures to quantify the pervasiveness of a pattern in an event log are also proposed. They include the pattern support, pattern confidence, case support, case confidence and case coverage.

To date there has been little research aimed at developing a comprehensive framework to address the issue of incorrect analysis results from inadequate data quality of event logs. Lessons from prior work in quality awareness for database (e.g., [21]) indicate that there are at least three essential components of such frameworks, each of which presents a number of research challenges, namely (1) data quality profiling that builds on shared understanding of data quality dimensions and associated metrics, (2) user preference modelling that allows users analytic needs to be captured, and (3) visibility of quality profiles together with analysis (process mining) results to improve understanding of the impact of inadequate data quality. We invite process mining researchers to tackle these challenges to move towards responsible process mining with the aim to improve the credibility and trust of stakeholders in process mining results.

Acknowledgements. The authors would like to acknowledge the input from QUT researchers (Professor ter Hofstede, Dr Andrews, Dr Suriadi and Dr Poppe) who work on this topic. This work is partly supported by ARC Discovery Project DP190102141 on Building Crowd Sourced Data Curation Processes.

References

1. van der Aalst, W., et al.: Process mining manifesto. In: Daniel, F., Barkaoui, K., Dustdar, S. (eds.) BPM 2011. LNBIP, vol. 99, pp. 169–194. Springer, Heidelberg (2012). https://doi.org/10.1007/978-3-642-28108-2_19

---

[3] https://mimic.physionet.org/.

2. Van der Aalst, W.M.P.: Process Mining: Data Science in Action, 2nd edn. Springer, Heidelberg (2016). https://doi.org/10.1007/978-3-662-49851-4d
3. van der Aalst, W.M.P., Bichler, M., Heinzl, A.: Responsible data science. Bus. Inf. Syst. Eng. 59(5), 311–313 (2017)
4. Batini, C., Cappiello, C., Francalanci, C., Maurino, A.: Methodologies for data quality assessment and improvement. ACM Comput. Surv. 41(3), 16 (2009)
5. Batini, C., Scannapieco, M.: Data Quality: Concepts, Methodologies and Techniques. Springer, Heidelberg (2006). https://doi.org/10.1007/3-540-33173-5
6. Bose, J.C., Mans, R., van der Aalst, W.M.P.: Wanna improve process mining results - it's high time we consider data quality issues seriously. In: IEEE Symposium on Computational Intelligence and Data Mining, pp. 127–134 (2013)
7. Dixit, P.M., et al.: Detection and interactive repair of event ordering imperfection in process logs. In: Krogstie, J., Reijers, H.A. (eds.) CAiSE 2018. LNCS, vol. 10816, pp. 274–290. Springer, Cham (2018). https://doi.org/10.1007/978-3-319-91563-0_17
8. Eppler, M.J.: Managing Information Quality: Increasing the Value of Information in Knowledge-intensive Products and Processes. Springer, Heidelberg (2006). https://doi.org/10.1007/3-540-32225-6
9. Jayawardene, V., Sadiq, S., Indulska, M.: The curse of dimensionality in data quality. In: 24th Australasian Conference on Information Systems (ACIS), pp. 1–12. RMIT University (2013)
10. Juran, J., Godfrey, A.: Quality Handbook. Republished McGraw-Hill, New York (1999)
11. Lee, Y.W., Strong, D.M., Kahn, B.K., Wang, R.Y.: AIMQ: a methodology for information quality assessment. Inf. Manag. 40(2), 133–146 (2002)
12. Lu, X., Fahland, D.: A conceptual framework for understanding event data quality for behavior analysis. In: Kopp, O., Lenhard, J., Pautasso, C. (eds.) Central European Workshop on Services and their Composition ZEUS. CEUR Workshop Proceeedings, vol. 1826, pp. 11–14 (2017)
13. Lu, X., et al.: Semi-supervised log pattern detection and exploration using event concurrence and contextual information. In: Panetto, H., et al. (eds.) OTM 2017. LNCS, vol. 10573, pp. 154–174. Springer, Cham (2017). https://doi.org/10.1007/978-3-319-69462-7_11
14. Scannapieco, M., Catarci, T.: Data quality under a computer science perspective. Arch. Comput. 2, 1–15 (2002)
15. Srivastava, D., Scannapieco, M., Redman, T.C.: Ensuring high-quality private data for responsible data science: vision and challenges. J. Data Inf. Qual. 11(1), 1:1–1:9 (2019)
16. Stvilia, B., Gasser, L., Twidale, M.B., Smith, L.C.: A framework for information quality assessment. J. Am. Soc. Inform. Sci. Technol. 58(12), 1720–1733 (2007)
17. Suriadi, S., Andrews, R., ter Hofstede, A.H.M., Wynn, M.T.: Event log imperfection patterns for process mining: towards a systematic approach to cleaning event logs. Inf. Syst. 64, 132–150 (2017)
18. Verhulst, R.: Evaluating quality of event data within event logs: an extensible framework. Master's thesis, Technische Universiteit Eindhoven, August 2016
19. Wang, R.Y.: A product perspective on total data quality management. Commun. ACM 41(2), 58–65 (1998)
20. Wang, R.Y., Strong, D.M.: Beyond accuracy: what data quality means to data consumers. J. Manag. Inf. Syst. 12(4), 5–33 (1996)
21. Yeganeh, N.K., Sadiq, S., Sharaf, M.A.: A framework for data quality aware query systems. Inf. Syst. 46, 24–44 (2014)

IoT for BPMers. Challenges, Case Studies and Successful Applications

Francesco Leotta, Andrea Marrella, and Massimo Mecella$^{(\boxtimes)}$

Sapienza Università di Roma, Rome, Italy
{leotta,marrella,mecella}@diag.uniroma1.it

Abstract. The Internet-of-Things (IoT) refers to a network of connected and interacting devices (e.g., sensors, actuators) collecting and exchanging data over the Internet. In the last years, we have witnessed an increasing presence of IoT devices in scenarios of the Business Process Management (BPM) domain, which can strongly influence the coordination of the real-world entities (e.g., humans, robots) that execute specific tasks or entire business processes in such environments. While, on the one hand, the IoT can provide many opportunities for improving BPM initiatives, on the other hand, it poses challenges that require enhancements and extensions of the current state-of-the-art in BPM. This paper discusses how BPM can benefit from IoT, *(i)* showing which emerging challenges have to be tackled to integrate the IoT technology in a BPM project, and *(ii)* presenting concrete case studies on process adaptation and habit mining exploiting IoT and addressing the specific challenges posed by IoT itself.

Keywords: IoT · Business process · Habit mining · Process adaptation

1 Introduction

Business Process Management (BPM) is an active area of research based on the observation that each product and/or service that an organization offers, is the outcome of a number of performed activities. Business processes (BPs) are the key instrument for organizing such activities and improving the understanding of their interrelationships. Nowadays, BPs are enacted in many complex industrial (e.g., manufacturing, logistics, retail) and non-industrial (e.g., emergency management, healthcare, smart environments) domains [10]. In all these domains, we have witnessed an increasing presence of Internet-of-Things (IoT) devices (e.g., sensors, RFIDs, video cameras, actuators) that operate over the existing network infrastructure, including the Internet, to collect data from the physical environment, monitor in detail the evolution of several real-world objects of interest, and actuate concrete feedbacks (e.g., in the form of suggestions or alerts) in response to the observed information. From a BPM perspective, the knowledge extracted from the physical environment by IoT devices allows to

© Springer Nature Switzerland AG 2019
T. Hildebrandt et al. (Eds.): BPM 2019, LNCS 11675, pp. 16–22, 2019.
https://doi.org/10.1007/978-3-030-26619-6_3

depict the contingencies and the context in which BPs are carried out, providing a fine-grained monitoring, mining, and decision support for them.

The interplay of IoT devices with BPM can provide many opportunities for improving the enactment of BPs. For example, among the main benefits, the execution of BPs can be driven by event data detected at real-time, enabling BPs to become more *adaptive* and *reactive* to what is happening in the real world. However, on the other hand, there is a conflict between the stability and meaningfulness of the services at work in a BP as opposed to the dynamic and changing environment that IoT is able to offer. This poses several challenges to concretely interconnect the two worlds and make them interact, which require enhancements and extensions to the current state-of-the-art in BPM.

According to the BPM-Meet-IoT manifesto [4], sixteen challenges have been identified to make this vision a reality. In this contribution, we focus on two specific areas from the BPM literature where it is strongly required to tackle these challenges, namely *habit mining* and *process adaptation*.

In Sect. 2, we show how data collected by IoT devices (a.k.a. IoT data) should be properly abstracted and managed when willing to employ BP discovery techniques [1] to model human habits as "personal processes". Secondly, in Sect. 3, we present a reference conceptual architecture to build a BPM engine that is able to reason over the discrete counterpart of the "continuous" IoT data for achieving automated adaptation of running BPs in case of unanticipated exceptions. Finally, in Sect. 4, we conclude the paper.

2   Visual Process Maps for Habit Mining

A smart space (e.g., a smart house) represents a typical example of IoT environment. The aim of a smart space is providing people with automatic or semi-automatic services realizing the concept of ambient intelligence (AmI). To this aim, a set of both software and hardware networked artefacts, acting as sensors (e.g, presence, temperature sensors) or actuators (e.g., ovens, rolling shutters), are coordinated according to a previously acquired knowledge expressed in the form of models representing human preferences and environmental dynamics.

Models in smart spaces are usually classified as *specification-based*, which are hand-made by experts, or *learning-based*, which are instead obtained by applying machine learning and data mining. In the first case, models are usually based on logic formalisms, relatively easy to read and validate (once the formalism is known to the reader), but their creation requires a major cost in terms of expert time and effort. In the latter case, the model is automatically learned from a training set (whose labeling cost may vary according to the proposed solution) but employed formalisms are usually not "explanaible" due to the statistic techniques they are based on, making them less immediate to understand.

Authors in [5] suggested that applying methods originally taken from BPM to human habits may represent a compromise between specification-based and learning-based methods, provided that the gap between raw sensor measurements and human actions can be filled in by performing a log-preprocessing

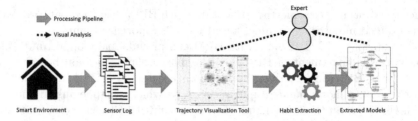

Fig. 1. The conceptual architecture of the Visual Process Maps (VPM) system.

step. Such a step may consist of simple inferences on data, or complex machine learning algorithms. On the line of this argument, [2,6] propose the Visual Process Maps (VPM) system, consisting of a complete pipeline formed by *(i)* a tool for the visual analysis of sensor logs, *(ii)* a method to transform raw movement measurements into actions, and *(iii)* a method to identify and visually analyze precedence relationships between human actions through the employment of fuzzy mining [3].

Figure 1 shows the conceptual architecture of VPM. A smart space produces, during runtime, a *sensor log* containing raw measurements from available sensors. Measurements can be produced by a sensor on a periodic base (e.g., temperature) or whenever a particular event is detected (e.g., a door opening). The current version of VPM focuses on sensor logs produced by a grid of Passive InfraRed (PIR) sensors triggering upon the detection of an object entering their field of view and automatically reset after a fixed amount of time since the last detected movement. The detection area of a PIR can be usually tuned to cover different area sizes ranging from a tile on the floor to an entire room.

The first step of VPM consists in a visual analysis tool, named Trajectory Visualization Tool, able to "play" specific portions of a log, perform automatic analysis tasks and visualize the result. Here, playing means to animate the sensor log showing the trajectory followed by a person in the house. The tool also allows to produce an *event log* obtained from the sensor log by aggregating simple PIR sensor measurements into sub-trajectories representing movement actions belonging to the following categories: *(a)* moving between areas of the house, *(b)* staying still under a PIR, or *(c)* moving in a specific area of the house.

Such an event log can be used as input for fuzzy mining. The rationale here is that, if we know the location of devices that humans can interact with inside the space, we can associate to each of these movement actions, the physical actions performed by humans (e.g., using the oven). As an example, if the model contains a precedence relation between the action "moving inside the bathroom" and "stay under the PIR sensor corresponding to the bed", we have a clear idea of the human actions determined by the movement actions.

The process extracted by fuzzy mining depends on how the sensor log fed into VPM is labeled. If no label is available, the mined process model will represent the daily habit of a person. If instead, labels corresponding to the beginning and the end of daily routines are available, it is possible to obtain specialized process models for them.

3   A Conceptual Architecture for Process Adaptation

During the enactment of BPs in IoT-based environments, variations or divergence from structured reference models are common due to exceptional circumstances arising in form of *exogenous events*, thus requiring the ability to properly *adapt* the process behavior. *Process adaptation* can be seen as the ability of a BP to react to exceptional circumstances (that may or may not be anticipated) and to adapt/modify its structure accordingly.

Since in IoT-based environments the number of possible anticipated exceptions is often too large, manual implementation of exception handlers at design-time is not feasible, since it is required to anticipate all potential problems and ways to overcome them in advance directly in the BP [10]. Furthermore, in such environments, many unanticipated exogenous events may arise during the BP execution, and the needed knowledge to tackle such events at the outset is often missing. Finally, a BPM engine can only reason over a discrete knowledge of the world, thus requiring to convert the continuous raw data collected by the IoT technology into discrete information.

To tackle this issue, we summarize the main ideas discussed in [8,9] and we introduce our architectural solution to build a BPM engine that is able to automatically adapt BPs at run-time when *unanticipated exceptions* occur in IoT-based environments, thus requiring no specification of recovery policies at design-time. The general idea builds on the dualism between an *expected reality* and a *physical reality*: process execution steps and exogenous events have an impact on the physical reality and any deviation from the expected reality results in a mismatch to be removed to allow process progression. As shown in Fig. 2, we identified 5 main architectural layers that we present in a bottom-up fashion.

The *cyber-physical layer* consists mainly of two classes of physical components: *(i)* sensors (such as GPS receivers, RFIDs, 3D scanners, cameras, etc.) that collect data from the physical environment by monitoring real-world objects and *(ii)* actuators (robotic arms, 3D printers, electric pistons, etc.), whose effects affect the state of the physical environment. The cyber-physical layer is also in charge of providing a physical-to-digital interface, which is used to transform *raw* data collected by the sensors into machine-readable events, and to convert *high-level* commands sent by the upper layers into *raw* instructions readable by the actuators. The cyber-physical layer does not provide any intelligent mechanism neither to clean, analyse or correlate data, nor to compose high-level commands into more complex ones; such tasks are in charge of the uppers layer.

On top of the cyber-physical layer lies the *service layer*, which contains the set of services offered by the real-world entities (software, robots, agents, humans, etc.) to perform specific BP activities. In the service layer, available data can be aggregated and correlated, and high-level commands can be orchestrated to provide higher abstractions to the upper layers. For example, a smartphone

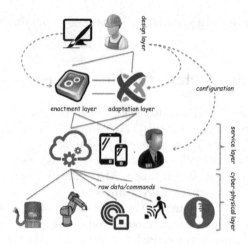

Fig. 2. A conceptual architecture for BPs enacted in IoT-based environments.

equipped with an application allowing to sense the position and the posture of a user is at this layer, as it collects the raw GPS, accellerometer and motion sensor data and correlates them to provide discrete and meaningful information.

On top of the service layer, there are two further layers interacting with each other. The *enactment layer* is in charge of *(i)* enacting complex BPs by deciding which activities are enabled for execution, *(ii)* orchestrating the different available services to perform those activities and *(iii)* providing an execution monitor to detect the anomalous situations that can possibly prevent the correct execution of BP instances. The execution monitor is responsible for deciding if process adaptation is required. If this is the case, the *adaptation layer* will provide the required algorithms to *(i)* reason over the available BP activities and contextual data and to *(ii)* find a recovery procedure for adapting the BP instance under consideration, i.e., to re-align the BP to its expected behaviour. Once a recovery procedure has been synthesized, it is passed back to the enactment layer for being executed.

Finally, the *design layer* provides a GUI-based tool to define new BP specifications. A BP designer must be allowed not only to build the BP control flow, but also to explicitly formalize the data reflecting the contextual knowledge of the IoT-based environment under study. It is important to underline that data formalization must be performed without any knowledge of the internal working of the physical components that collect/affect data in the cyber-physical layer. To link activities to contextual data, which are the main driver for triggering process adaptation, the GUI-based tool must go beyond the classical "activity model" as known in the literature, by allowing the BP designer to explicitly state what data may constrain an activity execution or may be affected after an activity completion or an exogenous event. Finally, besides specifying the BP, configuration files should also be produced to properly configure the enactment, the services and the sensors/actuators in the bottom layers.

The SMARTPM system presented in [7] is a concrete instantiation of the above reference architecture.

4   Concluding Remarks

This paper provides an introduction to the IoT with the eyes of a BPM researcher. The focus is on identifying and presenting those IoT features that directly impact BPM, i.e., *data, quality* and *granularity of such data, events, identification of process instances*, etc. In particular, we have focused on the issue of dealing with continuous and frequent data readings, and on the low level of abstraction provided by IoT measurements wrt. the traditional concept of "events" and "traces" in the BPM literature. Through two specific outcomes of our research activities, we have exemplified the above concepts in order to provide insights for further research.

Acknowledgments. The multi-year research work has been partly supported by the "Dipartimento di Eccellenza" grant, the H2020 RISE project FIRST (grant #734599), the H2020 ERC project NOTAE (grant #786572), the Sapienza grants IT-SHIRT, ROCKET and METRICS, the Lazio regional initiative "Centro di eccellenza DTC Lazio" and the projectARCA.

References

1. Augusto, A., et al.: Automated discovery of process models from event logs: review and benchmark. TKDE **31**(4), 686–705 (2019)
2. Dimaggio, M., Leotta, F., Mecella, M., Sora, D.: Process-based habit mining: experiments and techniques. In: 2016 International IEEE Conferences on Ubiquitous Intelligence and Computing (UIC), pp. 145–152. IEEE (2016)
3. Günther, C.W., van der Aalst, W.M.P.: Fuzzy mining – adaptive process simplification based on multi-perspective metrics. In: Alonso, G., Dadam, P., Rosemann, M. (eds.) BPM 2007. LNCS, vol. 4714, pp. 328–343. Springer, Heidelberg (2007). https://doi.org/10.1007/978-3-540-75183-0_24
4. Janiesch, C., et al.: The internet-of-things meets business process management: mutual benefits and challenges. arXiv preprint arXiv:1709.03628 (2017)
5. Leotta, F., Mecella, M., Mendling, J.: Applying process mining to smart spaces: perspectives and research challenges. In: Persson, A., Stirna, J. (eds.) CAiSE 2015. LNBIP, vol. 215, pp. 298–304. Springer, Cham (2015). https://doi.org/10.1007/978-3-319-19243-7_28
6. Leotta, F., Mecella, M., Sora, D.: Visual process maps: a visualization tool for discovering habits in smart homes. J. Ambient Intell. Humaniz. Comput. 1–29 (2019). https://link.springer.com/article/10.1007/s12652-019-01211-7
7. Marrella, A., Halapuu, P., Mecella, M., Sardiña, S.: SmartPM: an adaptive process management system for executing processes in cyber-physical domains. In: BPM Demo Track 2015. CEUR-WS.org (2015). http://ceur-ws.org/Vol-1418/paper24.pdf
8. Marrella, A., Mecella, M., Sardina, S.: Intelligent process adaptation in the SmartPM system. ACM Trans. Intell. Syst. Technol. **8**(2), 1–43 (2016)

 9. Marrella, A., Mecella, M., Sardiña, S.: Supporting adaptiveness of cyber-physical processes through action-based formalisms. AI Commun. **31**(1), 47–74 (2018)
10. Reichert, M., Weber, B.: Enabling Flexibility in Process-Aware Information Systems - Challenges, Methods, Technologies. Springer, Heidelberg (2012). https://doi.org/10.1007/978-3-642-30409-5

Exploring Explorative BPM - Setting the Ground for Future Research

Thomas Grisold[2(✉)], Steven Gross[3(✉)], Maximilian Röglinger[1(✉)],
Katharina Stelzl[1(✉)], and Jan vom Brocke[2(✉)]

[1] University of Bayreuth, 95444 Bayreuth, Germany
{maximilian.roeglinger,
katharina.stelzl}@uni-bayreuth.de
[2] University of Liechtenstein, 9490 Vaduz, Liechtenstein
{thomas.grisold,jan.vom.brocke}@uni.li
[3] Vienna University of Economics and Business, 1020 Vienna, Austria
steven.gross@wu.ac.at

Abstract. Recent claims in the literature highlight that BPM should become more explorative and opportunity-driven. The underlying argument is that BPM has been mainly concerned with exploitation activities – i.e., analysis and improvement of existing business processes – but it has neglected the role of innovation. In this conceptual article, we aim to establish a systematic understanding of what explorative BPM is and how it can be brought about. We pursue three goals. First, we derive an overarching definition of explorative BPM. Second, we propose the "triple diamond model" as a means to integrate explorative BPM activities in business process work. Third, we point to future research opportunities in the context of explorative BPM.

Keywords: Explorative BPM · Process innovation · Opportunity identification

1 Introduction

Recent claims highlight that BPM should become more innovation-driven [15, 29, 30]. Underlying these claims is the observation that BPM has made considerable progress to increase efficiency and effectiveness of business process work but has neglected the question of how organizations can facilitate innovation. That said, it is remarkable that Michael Hammer, founder of the Business Process Reengineering discipline and perhaps the most influential promoter of the process paradigm, prominently stated in one of his last articles that BPM has two primary intellectual antecedents: the quality movement and business process engineering. The first focusing on improving existing processes and the second focusing on rethinking processes using new technology aiming at innovation [11]. To some extent, this element of innovation, which has been at the core of BPM, seems to have faded into the background over the past decade. Moreover, digital technology today drives innovation at such speed and scale [3] that it provides new opportunities and challenges for BPM. What is subsumed under the term *explorative BPM* suggests that process-oriented organizations should be able to develop new capabilities and competences to detect emerging opportunities in terms of

© Springer Nature Switzerland AG 2019
T. Hildebrandt et al. (Eds.): BPM 2019, LNCS 11675, pp. 23–31, 2019.
https://doi.org/10.1007/978-3-030-26619-6_4

new technologies and business models [22]. In light of today's highly dynamic business environment, this is considered essential to ensure customer satisfaction and foster inter- and intra-organizational collaboration [8]. Research on explorative BPM is still a new frontier and innovation and opportunity-driven process redesign are, to some extent, contradictory to the logics of what has been researched and practiced referred to as BPM in the recent past. Following Benner and Tushman [1], BPM helps organizations to achieve error reduction and variance control but, due to increasing standardization, it decreases an organization's capability to sense, seize, and transform ground-breaking innovations. How can exploration be integrated into business process work? This is a question that should deserve more attention in the literature [8, 15, 22].

Within the tutorial presented at BPM 2019, we aim to approach explorative BPM in a systematic way and develop the grounds for future research agendas. In particular, we will (1) point to related (management) disciplines, (2) review the most important features of explorative BPM, (3) introduce an integrated framework to realize explorative BPM in organizations, and (4) derive a research agenda.

2   Related Fields and Agendas

Following Rosemann's call to "mix up relevant communities" when studying explorative BPM [17, p. 637], we draw on a number of related fields and research agendas in the domains of management and organizational science. We draw on research on organizational ambidexterity (OA) and innovation management (IM) as both fields seem promising to extend our understanding of explorative BPM.

OA has been a buzzword in the management literature for more than twenty years, promising organizations long-term survival in turbulent environments [24, 27]. In essence, OA is an organization's dual capability to develop management capabilities for both exploitation, i.e., incremental innovation leading to short-term efficiency gains, and exploration, i.e., radical long-term innovation activities [12, 20, 24]. In detail, *exploration* is characterized as a consistent opportunity-seeking approach with a focus on long-term growth through the development and introduction of radical innovation in line with external demands [12, 21]. It requires organizations to develop adaptive processes and structures that can be (re-) configured on demand [20] and a culture marked as risk-taking, flexible, and fast, supported by a visionary leadership style. Moreover, OA research investigates how to put OA into practice, e.g. by systematically developing OA capabilities based on an OA maturity model or by using a decision model that assists organizations in selecting and scheduling exploration and exploitation projects to become ambidextrous in an economically reasonable manner [18, 23].

IM encourages the development and introduction of new products, services, business models, and processes by frequently following an outside-in approach that is guided by customers' needs [28]. Specifically, process innovation describes the "implementation of a new or significantly improved production or delivery method [i.e., process]. This includes significant changes in techniques, equipment and/or software" (OECD 2005, p. 49). Hence, process innovation comprises the effective redesign (and efficiency or effectiveness improvement) of existing processes but also the development of new ones by following a structured procedure [6, 14]. Process innovation can further be split into 'technological process innovation' and 'organizational process innovation' [9, 11], ranging from single process elements (e.g. activities) to whole process chains [14], and it can be described as incremental or radical [25, 28]. Triggers for (process) innovation can be push and pull factors, where the former is based on the demand of internal or external customers while the latter is brought about by new technologies [28]. Besides the definition of IM, researchers and practitioners have developed a large set of methods and tools to generate new ideas for innovation, and have brought them into practice for an organizational competitive advantage [25]. All in all, descriptive and prescriptive knowledge on OA and IM appears to be a promising theoretical lens for closing the theoretical and methodological gap in explorative BPM.

3 Conceptualizing Explorative BPM

While there is no explicit definition of explorative BPM, authors highlight a number of features that are commonly associated with it.

First and foremost, explorative BPM emerged as a complementary view to established understandings of BPM. Over the past decades, the main focus of BPM has shifted towards an exploitative management discipline that pursues "reaction-based" improvements when negative deviance and changes occur. From this perspective, BPM has been driven by an "inside-out" logic, ensuring the efficiency and effectiveness of processes. Innovation, on this view, occurs when organizations face a pressure to do so. This implies that innovation is incremental as it relies on existing resources and capabilities to detect and correct for undesired deviance [2].

Explorative BPM, in contrast, calls for an "outside-in" logic that applies "environmental scanning capabilities" to identify new opportunities in dynamic business environments [22, p. 3]. It is transformational in the sense that it develops new capabilities, identifies new business opportunities, and capitalizes on emerging technologies [19]. While new opportunities and emerging technologies might be novel and unfamiliar, organizations should be able to recognize and evaluate them in terms of their affordances and underlying potentials [3, 17]. Even if organizations do not face any threat or crisis, they are able to rethink or unlearn their established practices and approaches [16] to integrate innovations into their business process work.

When organizations capitalize on new business opportunities such as emerging technologies or new customer expectations, explorative BPM can transform business processes in three different ways leading to different value propositions for customers. For a better overview, Fig. 1 differentiates between three dimensions of process innovation and its typical combinations for explorative and exploitative BPM. Focusing on explorative BPM, in the first and second case, new opportunities can lead to a reengineering of existing processes that, in turn, entail the same or an enhanced value proposition for customers [4]. For example, leveraging artificial intelligence for detecting fraudulent insurance claims innovates the process from the company's internal perspective, while the value proposition for the consumer remains the same. An enhanced value proposition may result from the integration of customers' connected devices into the insurance premium calculation, especially for cost-conscious customers. In the third case, new opportunities may enable the creation of entirely new

Three dimensions of BPM			
Trigger	Problem-driven		Opportunity-driven
Action	Improve existing process	Reengineer existing process	Create new process
Value proposition	Same value proposition	Enhanced value proposition	New value proposition

Typical combinations for explorative and exploitative BPM	
Exploration	Opportunity + Reengineer existing process + Same value proposition
	Opportunity + Reengineer existing process + Enhanced value proposition
	Opportunity + Create new process + New value proposition
Exploitation	Problem + Improve existing process + Same value proposition
	Problem + Reengineer existing process + Same value proposition
	Problem + Improve existing process + Enhanced value proposition
	Problem + Reengineer existing process + Enhanced value proposition

Fig. 1. The three dimensions of process innovation and its typical combinations for explorative and exploitative BPM

processes resulting in a new value proposition for customers [4]. For example, building on smart contracts enables insurances to provide a flight delay coverage without the required customer trust, as the involved parties may even remain anonymous and the contract executes itself. This clearly differs from traditional insurance contracting where the insurance payout depends on and is initiated by the insurance company.

A third important feature is that explorative BPM activities must not to be understood as selective and single interventions but require continuity [32]. Explorative BPM needs ongoing visioning [22] and experimenting [8] to develop new resources and capabilities [19]. Establishing continuity in terms of exploration is a challenge for process-oriented organizations. According to [1, 2], BPM, while reducing errors and variation, leads to inertia in the long run. Organizations become path-dependent in the sense that they draw on existing capabilities, resources, and best practices; those practices that helped organizations to achieve efficiency in the first place can now "impede an organization's adaptation to major technological transitions" [2, p. 323]. In order to ensure continuity in terms of explorative BPM, organizations can, for example, implement "opportunity points" in business processes to integrate new technologies, or establish teams and units that are concerned with identifying new trends and opportunities and mapping them to organizational work [2, 22]. Central to these interventions is that explorative BPM is contingent on capabilities to continuously sense, seize and transform opportunities into innovations.

To summarize, based on the features commonly associated with explorative BPM, we understand it as *the continuous process of questioning underlying business logics – i.e. the established understanding how value is generated – and integrating innovation opportunities (both in terms of business and technology) into business process work, even if there is no perceived pressure to do so. Explorative BPM refers to the offering of the same, enhanced, or new value propositions through the reengineering of existing processes or the creation of new processes.*

4 Realizing Explorative BPM: Towards an Integrated Model

Having outlined the features and characteristics of explorative BPM, we now introduce an integrated framework to realize explorative BPM in organizations. Figure 2 depicts the so-called *Triple Diamond Model*. This model builds on the concept of divergent and convergent thinking [5] to integrate innovation opportunities. Within divergent thinking, novelty is created through a creative process. Taking the information at hand, multiple alternative solutions are created through unexpected combinations, a transformation of information into unexpected forms and other techniques [5]. Convergent thinking evaluates a solution according to criteria such as speed, accuracy, or logic [5].

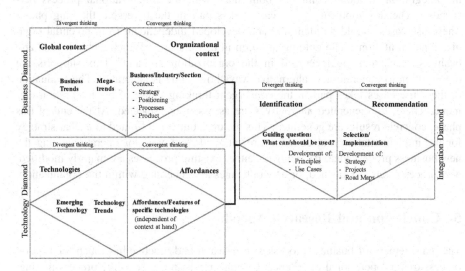

Fig. 2. The "Triple Diamond Model" to foster explorative BPM

This process of divergent exploration and convergent evaluation is the core of the three diamonds. These diamonds represent the business perspective, the technology perspective, and the integration perspective. It is not meant to be understood as a rigid method, but rather as a blueprint which forms the explorative BPM process. This also means that there is no strict order within its elements. The model is context-aware, i.e. it takes into consideration the specific situation of the organization at hand [7, 31].

In the business diamond, current local and global trends are identified. This may be a shift of consumer expectations towards higher data control, greater personalization of products and services, or an orientation towards subscription-based models, to name a few examples. The identification and exploration of these trends is part of the divergent thinking phase, in which new ideas are generated regardless of their feasibility or limitations given. Subsequently, in the convergent thinking phase, the context of the organization is considered. This includes the industry, its strategy, positioning, current products and processes. The previously identified and generated alternatives are thereby evaluated regarding criteria like applicability, feasibility, and fit to the current strategy.

The technology diamond identifies current technological trends and innovations. Emerging technical solutions have been found to be a promising source of business process innovation [8, 13]. In the divergent thinking phase, it is first explored which technological trends are available and how these technologies can potentially influence future process interactions and executions [3]. This boundless exploration of emerging technologies is followed by the convergent thinking phase. In this stadium, the identified opportunities are evaluated regarding their associated risks, technological affordances, and features of the specific technologies. In this phase, the evaluation of the technology is yet context-independent of a specific application scenario.

Once both business and technological trends have been identified and evaluated, the integration diamond combines both sides with the organizational process perspective. The development of use cases takes part in the divergent thinking phase. These use cases should be identified and developed independent from potential organizational limitations. The guiding question in this phase is: Which technological and business trends can be leveraged in the organization at hand? This supports the organization to generate new alternative ways how value is generated. The evaluation of these use cases takes part in the convergent thinking phase of the integration diamond. There, the generated alternatives are assessed and selected. At the end of this phase, concrete results are generated. This includes but is not limited to a clear strategy for the implementation and concrete projects and roadmaps for operationalizing the new business process idea. By doing so, either existing processes are majorly modified, new processes are established, or new outcomes are generated within the organization.

5   Conclusion and Research Agenda

The management of business processes in research and practice has much focused on process-driven operational excellence. Current trends in the area like process mining, which has received great attention beyond the BPM community, emphasize this course by targeting and analyzing existing processes for identifying operational weaknesses. This paper aims at expanding this exploitative view on BPM by an integration of innovation opportunities into organizational business processes – called explorative BPM.

In the course of this paper, we defined explorative BPM and its characteristics. While radically re-thinking existing business processes has been aimed for over three decades, it is only a part of what we describe as explorative BPM. Compared to the traditional exploitative perspective, it is opportunity-driven and includes the creation of new processes offering new value propositions. Thus, rather than focusing solely on existing processes, explorative BPM also takes into consideration novel ways to extend the organizations' existing process landscape. The exploration of new opportunities is also a continuous endeavor rather than a one-time process. We also proposed an integrated model, which incorporates the different dimensions of explorative BPM into one consistent framework.

We see explorative BPM as a promising research stream which has the potential to reshape existing paradigms and self-perceptions in BPM research and practice. We acknowledge that, despite existing research which aims to define and characterize explorative BPM, more research is needed to understand its nature and integration into organizational practices. Hence, we want to point to the following future research streams.

1. *Defining and evaluating methods which put explorative BPM into practice.* A plethora of methods and management approaches exist which aim to incrementally improve existing processes [7, 10]. However, more research is needed to design procedures that help implement explorative BPM in a step-wise manner [29]. To evaluate these methods, appropriate criteria have to be defined to ensure the applicability of these methods of the validity of their results.
2. *Investigating which organizational capabilities foster explorative BPM.* Despite the methodological view on the topic, other organizational capabilities such as culture and governance are likely to affect the successful integration of explorative BPM into practice. We see explorative BPM as a holistic approach [30], within the organizational context, thus investigating required capabilities that affect the successful integration of the approach is of high interest [15].
3. *Expanding the theoretical foundation by other research streams.* Although explorative BPM specifically targets business processes within organizations, relevant insights from the IM, OA, and organization science discipline and related fields should be used to complement the theoretical foundation by integrating relevant concepts and theories. For practical and historical reasons, research has often been conducted within separate communities. However, explorative BPM should build on and integrate innovation research from different disciplines like innovation-, design-, and organizational research, to name but a few.

We believe the BPM community has the chance to complement its existing mature understanding of methods, techniques, and tools for operational excellence by an explorative perspective. We want to emphasize that these are two sides of the same coin. It is not a shift but an expansion of the current understanding of BPM and thus beneficial for the community as a whole.

References

1. Benner, M.J., Tushman, M.L.: Exploitation, exploration, and process management: the productivity dilemma revisited. Acad. Manag. Rev. **28**(2), 238–256 (2003)
2. Benner, M.J., Tushman, M.L.: Process management, technological innovation, and organizational adaptation. In: Grover, V., Markus, M.L. (eds.) Business Process Transformation, pp. 317–326. M.E. Sharpe, Irvine (2007)

3. Berger, S., Denner, M.S., Röglinger, M.: The nature of digital technologies: development of a multi-layer taxonomy. In: 26th European Conference on Information Systems (ECIS), Portsmouth, UK, 2018, p. 96 (2018)
4. Christensen, C.M., Hall, T., Dillon, K., Duncan, D.S.: Know your customers' "jobs to be done". Harvard Bus. Rev. **94**, 54–62 (2016)
5. Cropley, A.: In praise of convergent thinking. Creat. Res. J. **18**(3), 391–404 (2006)
6. Davenport, T.H.: Process Innovation: Reengineering Work through Information Technology. Harvard Business School Press, Bosten (1992)
7. Denner, M.-S., Röglinger, M., Schmiedel, T., Stelzl, K., Wehking, C.: How context-aware are extant BPM methods? - development of an assessment scheme. In: Weske, M., Montali, M., Weber, I., vom Brocke, J. (eds.) BPM 2018. LNCS, vol. 11080, pp. 480–495. Springer, Cham (2018). https://doi.org/10.1007/978-3-319-98648-7_28
8. Dezi, L., Santoro, G., Gabteni, H., Pellicelli, A.C.: The role of big data in shaping ambidextrous business process management: case studies from the service industry. Bus. Process. Manag. J. **24**(5), 1163–1175 (2018)
9. Edquist, C., Hommen, L., McKelvey, M.: Innovation and Employment: Process Versus Product Innovation. Edward Elgar Publishing, Cheltenham (2001)
10. Gross, S., Malinova, M., Mendling, J.: Navigating through the maze of business process change methods. In: Proceedings of the 52nd Hawaii International Conference on System Sciences, pp. 6270–6279 (2019)
11. Hammer, M., Champy, J.: Reengineering the Corporation: A Manifesto for Business Revolution. Harper Business Books, New York (1993)
12. He, Z.-L., Wong, P.-K.: Exploration vs. exploitation: an empirical test of the ambidexterity hypothesis. Organ. Sci. **15**(4), 481–494 (2004)
13. Kemsley, S.: Emerging technologies in BPM. In: vom Brocke, J., Schmiedel, T. (eds.) BPM - Driving Innovation in a Digital World. MP, pp. 51–58. Springer, Cham (2015). https://doi.org/10.1007/978-3-319-14430-6_4
14. Kern, E.-M., Röser, T., Ulrich, S.: Prozessmanagement: Trigger Und Befähiger Für Prozessinnovation? In: Mieke, C. (ed.) Prozessinnovation Und Prozessmanagement. Zwei Managementfelder Zur Stärkung Der Prozessleistung in Unternehmen, pp. 1–26. Logos, Berlin (2013)
15. Kerpedzhiev, G., König, U., Röglinger, M., Rosemann, M.: Business process management in the digital age. BPT Trends (2017)
16. Klammer, A., Grisold. T., Güldenberg, S.: Introducing a 'stop-doing' culture: how to free your organization from rigidity. Business Horizons (in press)
17. Kohlborn, T., Mueller, O., Poeppelbuss, J., Roeglinger, M.: Interview with Michael Rosemann on ambidextrous business process management. Bus. Process. Manag. J. **20**(4), 634–663 (2014)
18. Linhart, A., Röglinger, M., Stelzl, K.: A project portfolio management approach to tackling the exploration/exploitation trade-off. Bus. Inf. Syst. Eng. 1–17 (2018)
19. Ohlsson, J., Han, S., Bouwman, H.: The prioritization and categorization method (PCM) process evaluation at Ericsson: a case study. Bus. Process. Manag. J. **23**(2), 377–398 (2017)
20. O'Reilly, C.A., Tushman, M.L.: The ambidextrous organization. Harvard Bus. Rev. **82**(4), 74–81 (2004)
21. O'Reilly, C.A., Tushman, M.L.: Organizational ambidexterity: past, present, and future. Acad. Manag. Perspect. **27**(4), 324–338 (2013)
22. Rosemann, M.: Proposals for future BPM research directions. In: Ouyang, C., Jung, J.-Y. (eds.) AP-BPM 2014. LNBIP, vol. 181, pp. 1–15. Springer, Cham (2014). https://doi.org/10.1007/978-3-319-08222-6_1

23. Röglinger, M., Schwindenhammer, L., Stelzl, K.: How to put organizational ambidexterity into practice – towards a maturity model. In: Weske, M., Montali, M., Weber, I., vom Brocke, J. (eds.) BPM 2018. LNBIP, vol. 329, pp. 194–210. Springer, Cham (2018). https:// doi.org/10.1007/978-3-319-98651-7_12

24. Teece, D.J.: Explicating dynamic capabilities: the nature and microfoundations of (sustainable) enterprise performance. Strateg. Manag. J. **28**(13), 1319–1350 (2007)

25. Tidd, J., Bessant, J.: Managing Innovation: Integrating Technological, Market and Organizational Change, 5th edn. Wiley, Chichester (2013)

26. Tumbas, S., Berente, N., vom Brocke, J.: Three types of chief digital officers and the reasons organizations adopt the role. MISQ Exec. **16**(2), 121–134 (2017)

27. Tushman, M.L., O'Reilly, C.A.: Ambidextrous organizations: managing evolutionary and revolutionary change. Calif. Manag. Rev. **38**(4), 8–30 (1996)

28. Vahs, D., Brem, A.: Innovationsmanagement: Von Der Idee Zur Erfolgreichen Vermarktung, 4th edn. Schäffer-Poeschel, Stuttgart (2013)

29. vom Brocke, J., Mendling, J.: Frameworks for business process management: a taxonomy for business process management cases. In: vom Brocke, J., Mendling, J. (eds.) Business Process Management Cases. MP, pp. 1–17. Springer, Cham (2018). https://doi.org/10.1007/ 978-3-319-58307-5_1

30. vom Brocke, J., Rosemann, M. (eds.): Handbook on Business Process Management 2: Strategic Alignment, Governance, People and Culture. Springer, Heidelberg (2014). https:// doi.org/10.1007/978-3-642-01982-1

31. vom Brocke, J., Zelt, S., Schmiedel, T.: On the role of context in business process management. Int. J. Inf. Manag. **36**, 486–495 (2016)

32. vom Brocke, J., Schmiedel, T., Recker, J., Trkman, P., Mertens, W., Viaene, S.: Ten principles of good business process management. Bus. Process. Manag. J. **20**(4), 530–548 (2014)

Foundations

Dynamic Reconfiguration of Business Processes

Leandro Nahabedian[1]($\boxtimes$), Victor Braberman[1], Nicolás D'ippolito[1],
Jeff Kramer[2], and Sebastián Uchitel[1,2]

[1] Universidad de Buenos Aires/CONICET, Buenos Aires, Argentina
{lnahabedian,vbraber,ndippolito,suchitel}@dc.uba.ar
[2] Department of Computing, Imperial College, London, UK
j.kramer@imperial.ac.uk

Abstract. Organisations require that their business processes reflect their evolving practices by maintaining compliance with their policies, strategies and regulations. Designing workflows which satisfy these requirements is complex and error-prone. Business process reconfiguration is even more challenging as not only a new workflow must be devised but also an understanding of how the transition between the old and new workflow must be managed. Transition requirements can include both domain independent, such as delayed and immediate change, or user-defined domain specific requirements. In this paper we present a fully automated technique which uses control synthesis to not only produce correct-by-construction workflows from business process requirements but also to compute a reconfiguration process that guarantees the evolution from an old workflow to a new one while satisfying any user-defined transition requirements. The approach is validated using three examples from the BPM Academic Initiative described as Dynamic Condition Response Graphs which we reconfigured for a variety of transitions requirements.

Keywords: Dynamic reconfiguration · Controller synthesis ·
DCR graph

1 Introduction

Business processes are invaluable for ensuring that task and activity execution achieves business objectives. Workflows, operational representations of business processes, are typically derived from requirements in a manual process that is complex and error-prone. Organisations require that their business processes reflect their evolving practices maintaining compliance with their policies, strategies and regulations (e.g., [27]). Workflows must be evolved accordingly too. *Business process reconfiguration* involves not only devising the new workflow but also dynamically changing the old workflow with the new one.

Key to reconfiguration is understanding how the transition between the old and new workflow should be managed. Domain independent transition requirements have been studied extensively. For instance, [9] discusses "immediate"

© Springer Nature Switzerland AG 2019
T. Hildebrandt et al. (Eds.): BPM 2019, LNCS 11675, pp. 35–51, 2019.
https://doi.org/10.1007/978-3-030-26619-6_5

reconfiguration requirements that assert that reconfiguration must occur as soon as possible but only at a state in which the new workflow prescribes behaviour consistent with the old one. "Delayed" reconfiguration asserts that living instances must finish using the old workflow, while fresh instances are created using the new one. In some cases, *domain specific transition requirements* are required. For instance, reconfiguration may be required as soon as possible yet for some live instances in particular states an exceptional treatment may be required, including repeating or roll-backing an activity.

Indeed, business process reconfiguration can be extremely challenging and can greatly benefit from automated techniques that support *(i)* analysing business process requirements and transition requirements, and *(ii)* constructing workflows and reconfiguration strategies satisfying these requirements.

One approach to automation is *build and verify*, in which formal verification techniques provide a sound basis for workflow analysis and can be used to ensure workflow requirement satisfaction. However, post-hoc verification requires prior construction of the workflow, and modification entails re-verification. An alternative approach is to automatically produce *correct-by-construction* workflows and reconfiguration strategies directly from requirements.

Although automatic construction of workflows from requirements has been studied (e.g., [11,20]), the *synthesis of reconfiguration strategies* for domain specific user defined transition requirements has not received attention so far.

In this paper we present a fully automated technique for business process reconfiguration based on discrete event controller synthesis. We use synthesis to not only produce correct-by-construction workflows from business process requirements but also to compute a reconfiguration strategy that guarantees progress from an old workflow towards the a new one while satisfying any user-defined transition requirements. We discuss a translation of Dynamic Condition Response (DCR) graphs [11], a declarative language for business process requirements, into a formalism based on Labelled Transition Systems and Linear Temporal Logic [21] which is suitable for controller synthesis [7] and build upon recent work on dynamic controller update [19]. We validate the approach using three examples from the BPM Academic Initiative [1] described as DCR graphs which we reconfigured for a variety of transitions requirements.

The rest of the paper is structured as follows. Section 2 presents an illustrative example. Formal definitions are presented in Sect. 3. In Sect. 4 we present problems setting out how to frame it as a synthesis problem. An analysis of our technique is presented in Sect. 5. Finally, we present a discussion on related work.

2   Motivating Example

Consider a hospital process taken from a real-life study on a oncology workflow at Danish hospitals [11]. This workflow has *prescribe medicine* and *sign* activities, representing a doctor adding and signing a prescription to the patient record. In addition, a nurse, is capable of doing *give medicine* in response to the

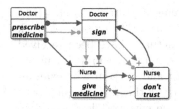

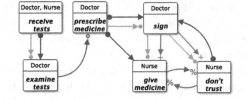

Fig. 1. DCR graph for a hospital process

Fig. 2. DCR graph model for new hospital process.

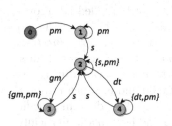

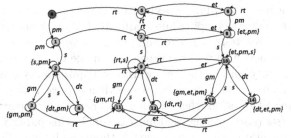

Fig. 3. Workflow for a hospital process

Fig. 4. Workflow for new hospital process.

doctor prescription, or, in contrast, the nurse may indicate that they do not trust the prescription or signature by performing the *don't trust* activity. Workflow requirements include that *(i)* the doctor must perform *prescribe medicine* to a patient before *sign*, *(ii)* the nurse can not do *give medicine* nor *don't trust* if the doctor has not done *sign*, and *(iii)* the nurse can not perform both *give medicine* and *don't trust*, only one is allowed.

Figure 1 shows these requirements modelled using Dynamic Condition Response (DCR) graphs as originally presented in [11]. A workflow that satisfies these requirements is depicted in Fig. 3 where *pm*, *s*, *gm* and *dt* labels refer to activities *prescribe medicine*, *sign*, *give medicine* and *don't trust*, respectively. The workflow is the underlying semantics of the model in Fig. 1 and can be constructed automatically using controller synthesis as described in Sect. 4.

Consider a scenario in which while patients are being treated the workflow must be changed (taken from [18]). For instance, suppose that a new internal regulation is to be put in place stating that doctors must not do *prescribe medicine* if new tests have arrived (*receive tests*) but have not been examined (*examine tests*). Also, as expected, *receive tests* must happen before *examine tests*. This change involves two new activities and extra rules as depicted in Fig. 2 which describes a significantly more complicated workflow (Fig. 4 where *rt* and *et* labels refer to *receive tests* and *examine tests*) that can be automatically synthesised.

A crucial decision to make is how to reconfigure a live instance running the old workflow to the new one. A naive approach would be to require an immediate [9] reconfiguration regardless of the living instance's state. Thus, if the living instance is in state 2 of Fig. 3 it should evolve to being in state 2 of Fig. 4 (i.e., $2 \rightsquigarrow 2$). However, this puts the patient at risk: The old workflow does not track the occurrence of *receive tests*, yet new tests may actually have been received and new prescriptions should not be done without examining them. It is safer to assume, at reconfiguration time, that tests may exist and to require be examining them (should they be available) rather than ignoring them. Consequently, it is more appropriate to update the old workflow to the new workflow according to the following mapping: $(0 \rightsquigarrow 5), (1 \rightsquigarrow 7), (2 \rightsquigarrow 9), (3 \rightsquigarrow 11), (4 \rightsquigarrow 12)$.

The provision of a mapping between workflow states ensuring that a transition requirement holds can be very difficult for complex workflows. An alternative is to allow a declarative description of transition requirements and to compute a mapping automatically. For our example, what is needed is to force *examine tests* when reconfiguring. Note that is inconsistent with both the old and new workflow requirements. In the old workflow, there is no *examine tests* activity and in the new workflow requirements *examine tests* is required after *receive tests*. Thus, what we need to express is that there is a period during the reconfiguration where neither workflow requirements hold and in which *examine tests* (and nothing else) must occur. In this paper we show how domain specific transition requirements such as these can be modelled and how to automatically build a strategy for taking a live instance running a workflow to a new workflow guaranteeing all transition requirements.

3   Preliminaries

In this work we use Dynamic Condition Response Graphs [12] to specify business processes. To simplify presentation we use a reduced version that does not include nesting, roles, principals and roles assignments.

Definition 1 (Dynamic Condition Response Graph). *A Dynamic Condition Response Graph (DCR Graph) is a tuple $DG = (A, R, M)$ where A is a finite set of activities, the nodes of the graph. R is a set of graph edges. Edges are partitioned into five kinds, named and drawn as follows: conditions ($\rightarrow\bullet$), responses ($\bullet\rightarrow$), inclusions ($\rightarrow_+$), exclusions ($\rightarrow_\%$) and milestones ($\rightarrow_\Diamond$). M is the marking of the graph. This is a triple of sets of activities (Ex, Re, In), where Ex are the previously executed, Re the currently pending and In the currently included. For all $(e, e') \in E \times E$, $e \rightarrow_+ e'$ or $e \rightarrow_\% e'$ or neither of them. We denote $(\bullet\rightarrow e) = \{e' \in A \mid e'\bullet\rightarrow e\}$, $(e\bullet\rightarrow) = \{e' \in A \mid e\bullet\rightarrow e'\}$, and similarly for $\rightarrow\bullet$, $\rightarrow_+$, $\rightarrow_\%$ and $\rightarrow_\Diamond$.*

Definition 2 (Enable activity of a DCR Graph). *Let $DG = (A, R, M)$ be a DCR graph, with $M = (Ex, Re, In)$. An activity $e \in A$ is enabled if and only if (a) $e \in In$, (b) $(In \cap (\rightarrow\bullet e)) \subseteq Ex$, and (c) $Re \cap In \cap (\rightarrow\Diamond e) = \emptyset$.*

Definition 3 (Executing DCR Graph). *Let $DG = (A, R, M)$ be a DCR graph, with marking $M = (Ex, Re, In)$ and e is enabled. The result of executing e is a DCR Graph $DG' = (A, R, M')$ with $M' = (Ex', Re', In')$ such that (a) $Ex' = $*

$Ex \cup \{e\}$, (b) $Re' = (Re \setminus \{e\}) \cup (e\bullet\!\!\rightarrow)$, and (c) $In' = (In \cup (e\rightarrow_+)) \setminus (e\rightarrow_\%)$. We assume that initially $In = A$ and $Re = Ex = \emptyset$.

To capture the underlying semantics of DCR graphs we use Labelled Transition Systems [14]. They are a canonical, compositional, representation of events structures ideally suited to model checking of business processes and synthesis of discrete event controllers.

Definition 4 (Labelled Transition System). *A Labelled Transition System (LTS) E is a tuple $(S_E, L_E, \Delta_E, e_0)$, where S_E is a finite set of states, $L_E \subseteq \mathcal{L}$ is its communicating alphabet, $\mathcal{L}$ is the universe of all observable events, $\Delta_E \subseteq (S_E \times L_E \times S_E)$ is a transition relation, and $s_0 \in S_E$ is the initial state. A path of E is a sequence $\pi = s_0, \ell_0, s_1, \ell_1, s_2, \ldots$ where for every $i \geq 0$ we have $(s_i, \ell_i, s_{i+1}) \in \Delta_E$. A trace w is a sequence obtained by removing states from π.*

Definition 5 (Parallel Composition). *The parallel composition $E \| C$ of LTS $E = (S_E, L_E, \Delta_E, e_0)$ and $C = (S_C, L_C, \Delta_C, c_0)$ is an LTS $(S_E \times S_C, L_E \cup A_C, \Delta_\|, (e_0, c_0))$ such that $\Delta_\|$ is the smallest relation that satisfies the rules:*

$$\frac{(e, \ell, e') \in \Delta_E \wedge \ell \notin L_C}{((e,c), \ell, (e',c)) \in \Delta_\|} \quad \frac{(c, \ell, c') \in \Delta_C \wedge \ell \notin L_E}{((e,c), \ell, (e,c')) \in \Delta_\|} \quad \frac{(e, \ell, e') \in \Delta_E \wedge (c, \ell, c') \in \Delta_C \quad \ell \in L_E \cap L_C}{((e,c), \ell, (e',c')) \in \Delta_\|}$$

We use a linear temporal logic of fluents to provide a uniform framework for specifying state-based temporal properties in event-based models [10]. FLTL [10] is a linear-time temporal logic for reasoning about fluents. A *fluent* is defined by a pair of sets and a Boolean value: $f = \langle I, T, Init \rangle$, where $f.I$ is the set of initiating events, $f.T$ is a set of terminating events and $f.I \cap f.T = \emptyset$. A fluent may be initially *true* or *false* as indicated by $f.Init$.

Let $\mathcal{F}$ be the set of all possible fluents. An FLTL formula is defined inductively using the standard Boolean connectives and temporal operators $\mathbf{X}$ (next), $\mathbf{U}$ (strong until) as follows: $\varphi ::= f \mid \neg\varphi \mid \varphi \vee \psi \mid \mathbf{X}\varphi \mid \varphi\mathbf{U}\psi$, where $f \in \mathcal{F}$. We define $\varphi \wedge \psi$ as $\neg\varphi \vee \neg\psi$, $\Diamond\varphi$ (eventually) as $\top\mathbf{U}\varphi$, $\Box\varphi$ (always) as $\neg\Diamond\neg\varphi$, and $\varphi\mathbf{W}\psi$ (weak until) as $\varphi\mathbf{U}\psi \vee \Box\varphi$.

The trace $\pi = \ell_0, \ell_1, \ldots$ satisfies a fluent f at position i, denoted $\pi, i \models f$, if and only if, one of the following conditions holds: (a) $f.Init \wedge (\forall j \in \mathbb{N} \cdot 0 \leq j \leq i \Rightarrow \ell_j \notin f.T)$, and (b) $\exists j \in \mathbb{N} \cdot (j \leq i \wedge \ell_j \in f.I) \wedge (\forall k \in \mathbb{N} \cdot j < k \leq i \Rightarrow \ell_k \notin f.T)$ In other words, a fluent holds at position i if and only if it holds initially or some initiating event has occurred, but no terminating event has yet occurred.

We say φ is a safety formula if there is a finite trace π such that:

$$\begin{aligned}
\pi, i &\models \neg\varphi \quad \triangleq \neg(\pi, i \models \varphi) \\
\pi, i &\models \varphi \vee \psi \triangleq (\pi, i \models \varphi) \vee (\pi, i \models \psi) \\
\pi, i &\models \mathbf{X}\varphi \quad \triangleq \pi, i+1 \models \varphi \\
\pi, i &\models \varphi\mathbf{U}\psi \triangleq \exists j \geq i \cdot \pi, j \models \psi \ \wedge \ \forall i \leq k < j \cdot \pi, k \models \varphi
\end{aligned}$$

We use $\pi \models \varphi$, instead of $\pi, 0 \models \varphi$.

Control problems aim to build an LTS that satisfies a given set of declarative requirements under certain environment conditions by having control of only a subset of the events of the environment.

Definition 6 (LTS Control [7]). *Let $E = (S_E, L_E, \Delta_E, e_0)$ be an environment model in the form of an LTS, $L_c \subseteq L_E$ be a set of controllable events, and G be a controller goal in the form of an FLTL property. A solution for the LTS control problem with specification $\mathcal{E} = (E, G, L_c)$ is an LTS C such that C only blocks events in L_c, $E \| C$ is deadlock free, and $E \| C \models G$.*

Definition 7 (DCU Problem [19]). *Let $\mathcal{E} = (E, G, L_c)$ be an old specification, $\mathcal{E}' = (E', G', L_c')$ be a new specification, T be a safety FLTL formula, $R \subseteq (S_E \times S_{E'})$ be a mapping relation of states and, stopOldReq and startNewReq are special events denoting the ending of old and start of new requirements, respectively. A solution for the DCU Synthesis Problem is a controller C_u such that: (a) $C_u \models G$ **W** stopOldReq, (b) $C_u \models T$, (c) $C_u \models \Box(startNewReq \rightarrow G')$, and (d) $C_u \models \Box$ (beginReconf $\rightarrow (\Diamond stopOldReq \wedge \Diamond startNewReq))$*

The output of a DCU problem is an LTS C_u where every trace satisfies that (a) the old requirements hold G until *stopOldReq* is triggered, (b) the transition requirements hold, (c) the new specification G' must be valid from *startNewReq* is onwards, and (d) the update eventually happens.

4   Dynamic Reconfiguration of Business Processes

In this section we first show how to synthesize a workflow from a DCR graph using controller synthesis (Definition 6) and then show how to use dynamic controller update (Definition 7) for workflow reconfiguration.

4.1   Workflow Synthesis as a Control Problem

We now show how to extract from a DCR graph a set of controllable events L_C, an LTS E, and a FLTL formula G such that controller synthesis (Definition 6) results in a controller that enables and disables activities in such a way that its environment, as long as it only executes enabled activities, satisfies the business process requirements as described in the DCR graph. Thus L_C will contain activity enabling and disabling events, while events modelling the execution of activities will be monitorable but not controllable. The LTS E will model the assumptions the controller can rely upon to guarantee workflow requirements. Finally, the formula G encodes the domain specific aspects of the DCR graph, namely the arrows that establish dependencies between activities.

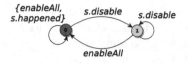

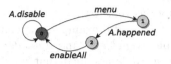

Fig. 5. *Happens*(*s*) LTS constraining the occurrence of *s.happened*.

Fig. 6. *Turns* LTS constraining controller and environment turns.

Controllable and Monitorable Events. The set of events that describe the control problem are defined by the activities that appear in the DCR graph (i.e., the set A). We introduce two events for each activity $a \in A$: $a.disable$ and $a.happened$. The first is an event controlled by the controller. The second, is an event that will be selected by the environment (e.g., the nurse and the doctor) to indicate that the activity was executed. We say that $a.happened$ is monitorable or uncontrolled. Note that we do not introduce $a.enabled$, rather we assume an event *enableAll* to reduce the number of events and states of the control problem. The controller will *enableAll* activities then select which ones to disable in such a way that if the environment executes an enabled activity, it will be consistent with the business process requirements.

We introduce one extra event, *menu*, to model the turn based interaction where the controller offers to its environment a menu of activities to perform. First, the controller will select what activities to disable then it indicates using *menu* that it is the environment's turn to decide what activity to execute.

In conclusion, the set of controllable and uncontrollable events are $L_C = \{a.disable \,|\, a \in A\} \cup \{menu, enableAll\}$ and $\overline{L_C} = \{a.happened \,|\, a \in A\}$

Environment Model. The LTS E models the two assumptions that the controller can rely upon to guarantee workflow requirements.

The first assumption is that activities can only happen when they are enabled. This can be modelled using one LTS model for each activity and composing them all in parallel. In Fig. 5 we show an LTS, $Happens(s)$, modelling the assumption for activity *sign*. State 0 models that *sign* is enabled (thus, the outgoing transition *s.happened*) while state 1 models that the activity is disabled (i.e., there is no outgoing *s.happened* transition). Events *enableAll* and *s.disable* toggle between state 0 and 1. We assume the activity is initially enabled.

The second assumption is that the environment will play in turns with the controller. The controller chooses what activities may be executed without violating workflow requirements, and then, the environment picks which of the enabled activities is to be executed. We use only one LTS, *Turns* depicted in Fig. 6, to model this assumption. The initial state (0) models the turn of the controller where any activity in A can be disabled. Event *menu* models when the controller relinquishes its turn offering a menu of activities to perform. State 1 is the environment's turn in which it can select only one activity in A to be executed, going to state 2. Here, all activities are enabled with *enableAll* event to start again with controller's turn at state 0.

The assumptions reflect the operation of the workflow engine that will be controlled. In the hospital example, the controller first decides which activities should be enabled (*enableAll* and *a.disabled*) and then presents them to hospital staff (*menu*). It is assumed that nurses and doctor will only perform an activity if the activity is displayed by the engine, and that once performed they will report back through the engine (*a.happened*). At this point, the controller will decide again what activities to enable and update the engine display. Obviously, the *menu* event must only occur when the controller has enabled exactly all activities that if executed would not violate workflow requirements. This controller behaviour is synthesised automatically based on the formalisation of goals described next. In conclusion the LTS environment E is defined as follows $E = Turns \parallel Happens(a_1) \parallel \ldots \parallel Happens(a_n)$ with $A = \{a_1, \ldots, a_n\}$.

Controller Goals. Goal G must model the constraints between activities that are expressed in DCR Graphs with arrows between activities. Our encoding resembles that of [20] where LTL formulas are used to formalise activity constraints of similar nature to those of DCR graphs.

We introduce three fluents for each activity $a \in A$ modelling if a belongs to sets Ex, Re, and In according to Definition 3. For simplicity, we assume that the initial marking of the DCR graph is such that $In = A$ and $Re = Ex = \emptyset$.

- $a.Executed$ models if $a \in Ex$ and is defined as $\langle\{a.happened\}, \emptyset, \bot\rangle$. In other words, initially no activity is in Ex and once in Ex it is never removed (see Definition 3a).
- $a.Required$ models if $a \in Re$ and is defined as $\langle\{a'.happened \mid a' \in (\bullet \to a)\}, a.happened, \bot\rangle$. That is, all activities are initially not required and the execution of a activity makes it no longer required, and any activity in a response relation with a makes it a required (see Definition 3b). In the hospital example, fluent $s.Required$ is defined as $\langle\{pm.happened, dt.happened\}, s.happened, \bot\rangle$ because activity *sign* is a response to *don't trust* and *prescribe medicine* according to Fig. 1. Note that for cases where $a\bullet \to a$, we define $a.Required$ as $\langle\{a'.happened \mid a' \in (\bullet \to a)\}, \emptyset, \bot\rangle$ because the execution of a does not turn false the fluent.
- $a.In$ models if $a \in In$ and is defined as $a.In = \langle\{a'.happened \mid a' \in (\to_+ a)\}, \{a'.happened \mid a' \in (\to_\% a)\}, \top\rangle$, which mimics Definition 3c. Based on the relations modelled in Fig. 1, the fluent $gm.In$ is defined as $\langle\{s.happened\}, \{dt.happened\}, \top\rangle$.

We introduce FLTL formulas to preserve the rules that govern when an activity can be executed (i.e., is enabled) according to Definition 2. In other words, the formulas will relate the occurrence of *a.happened* with fluents $a'.Executed$, $a'.Required$, and $a'.In$ for all $a' \in A$.

- For rule (a) of Definition 2 we introduce for every activity $a \in A$ a formula $\alpha_a = \Box(a.happened \to a.In)$.

- For rule (b) of Definition 2 we introduce for all $a \in A$: $\beta_a = \Box(a.happened \rightarrow \bigwedge_{a' \in (\rightarrow \bullet a)}(a'.In \rightarrow a'.Executed))$. For instance, for $sign$, according to Fig. 1 we have $\beta_s = \Box(s.happened \rightarrow (pm.In \rightarrow pm.Executed))$.
- For rule (c) of Definition 2 we introduce for each $a \in A$: $\kappa_a = \Box(a.happened \rightarrow \bigwedge_{a' \in (\rightarrow \diamond a)}(\neg a'.Required \vee \neg a'.In))$. For instance, $\kappa_{pm} = \Box(pm.happened \rightarrow (\neg et.Required \vee \neg et.In))$ for Fig. 2.

In summary, G is defined as $\bigwedge_{a \in A} \alpha_a \wedge \beta_a \wedge \kappa_a$.

Workflow Synthesis. Above we have described how to build from a DCR graph model D, the set of controllable events L_c, the LTS environment E, and the FLTL formula G that can be used to define a control problem $\mathcal{E} = (E, G, L_c)$. A solution to this problem is a controller LTS C that decides when to enable and disable activities (which correspond to events in L_c) such that when running with an environment that plays in turns and only executes enabled activities (as described in E) satisfies all business process requirements (as captured in G). In other words: $E \| C \models G$ (Definition 6).

Note that $E \| C \models G$ is not enough. We need the controller to be maximal in the sense of that at any *menu*, the maximal set of activities should be enabled that do not violate G. Consider a workflow for the hospital in which after *sign* only *give medicine* is enabled. The sequence *sign, give medicine* does not violate G, but *sign* followed by *don't trust* should also be possible. To ensure maximality we exploit a characteristic of the synthesis algorithm implemented in the MTSA tool [6] that we use for synthesis: MTSA builds eager components in the sense that they take the shortest route to satisfying their requirements. As the controller is forced to do *enableAll*, the synthesis algorithm will try to do as few disable actions as possible while still ensuring G, thus a maximal number of activities will always be enabled.

The controllers for the DCR graphs depicted in Figs. 1 and 2 have 188 and 2291 states respectively and are too large to depict in this paper. Instead we show abstract versions of these controllers (Figs. 3 and 4) in which *enableAll*, disable and *menu* events are hidden. This provides a view similar to what the Nurse and Doctor would see, only the activities that are enabled and not the controllers incremental decisions of enabling and disabling activities. Note that the abstract controllers are built automatically by MTSA tool using a hiding operator and weak bisimilarity minimisation [17].

4.2 Workflow Reconfiguration as a Dynamic Controller Update

This section is organised as follows. We first discuss how domain specific transition requirements for a workflow reconfiguration can be described using FLTL. This involves introducing two new events. We then discuss what a solution to a reconfiguration problem may look like and finally how such solutions can be built automatically solving a Dynamic Controller Update problem.

Specification of Transition Requirements. Recall the Hospital workflow example discussed in Sect. 2 where a transition requirement stating that activity *examine tests* should be forced when reconfiguring. More precisely, just before the moment the new business process requirements should be enforced, *examine tests* is required. The reason for requiring "just before" is that executing *examine tests* without a previous *receive tests* is not allowed in the new business process.

To formalise this transition requirement we need to refer to the moment in which the old business requirements are to be dropped (*stopOldReq*) and the moment in which the new business requirements come into force (*startNewReq*). With these two new events the transition requirement can be formulated as follows $T_h = \Box(stopOldReq \rightarrow ((\bigwedge_{a \in A \setminus \{et\}} \neg a.happened)$ **W** $(et.Executed \land startNewReq)))$. Note that guaranteeing this formula requires enabling and disabling activities such that the uncontrolled events $a.happened$ occur or not as required by T_h. A standard domain independent transition requirement that states that at any point one of the two business process must be adhered to (i.e., there is no transition period) can be stated as follows: $T_\emptyset = \Box((StopOldReq \land \neg StartNewReq) \rightarrow \bigwedge_{a \in A} \neg a.happened)$.

Reconfiguration Workflows. Returning to T_h, what would a solution to this reconfiguration problem be? Assume the workflow in Fig. 3 is in state 2, a solution to the reconfiguration is to deploy a workflow that does forces *examine tests* and then reaches a state 10 in Fig. 4. In other words, we need to build a workflow that manages the transition from the old to the new workflow, we call this workflow the *reconfiguration workflow*.

This reconfiguration workflow that assumes that the old workflow is in state 2 is inadequate as, before it takes control, a new activity (e.g., *give medicine*) may be executed taking the old workflow (Fig. 3) in state 2 to state 3. Should this happen then the reconfiguration should force *examine tests* and then move to state 13 in Fig. 4 instead of 10. Thus, the goal is to build a reconfiguration workflow that can manage the transition from any state in the old workflow.

Conceptually, our solution builds one reconfiguration workflow that consists of three phases. The first is structurally equivalent to the old workflow (modulo a new event *beginReconf*). This allows hot-swapping the old workflow with the reconfiguration workflow, and setting the initial state of the latter according to the current state of the former. The second phase is triggered by an event *beginReconf*. At this point, the reconfiguration workflow may start to deviate from the behaviour of the old workflow to ensure transition requirements. At the point it does so, it must first signal *stopOldReq*. The third phase is one in which the new workflow requirements are satisfied. Entering this third phase is signalled with *startNewReq*.

In Fig. 7 we depict an abstract reconfiguration workflow (enabling, disabling and *menu* events are hidden) that implements the reconfiguration from business process requirements of Fig. 1 to those of Fig. 2 under transition requirement T_h. The blue rectangle on the left represents the first phase of the reconfiguration workflow. Note that the structure of states and transitions is that of the workflow

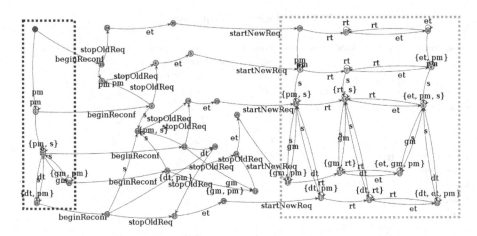

Fig. 7. Reconfiguration workflow with transition requirement T_h.

to be replaced (Fig. 3), thus hotswapping this workflow in is trivial. Note that all states in the blue region have an outgoing transition labelled *beginReconf*. When *beginReconf* is triggered, no matter what the current state is, there is a path to the yellow region on the right. The yellow region represents the new workflow as in Fig. 4. The transition from the old requirements to new ones, while satisfying the transition requirements is represented by between both rectangles. Is noteworthy that there are no loops during the transition phase which guarantees that eventually the new business process requirements will be enforced.

Automatic Construction of Reconfiguration Workflows. Summarising, Fig. 7 represents a solution to the problem of reconfiguring business process requirements in Fig. 1 to those of Fig. 2 under transition requirement T_h. We now discuss how such solution can be built by solving a DCU problem Definition 7. The DCU problem requires two control problems $\mathcal{E} = (E, G, L_c)$ and $\mathcal{E}' = (E', G', L'_c)$ which represent in this case the old and new business process synthesis problems as described in Sect. 4.1. DCU also requires a transition requirement T and a state mapping R from the states of E to those of E'. We have discussed T, we now discuss R.

The purpose of relation R is to explain the relationship between the assumptions modelled in each control problem. The issue is that E tracks assumptions for a controller synthesised from C, when a reconfiguration is deployed it is not possible to know what the state of the assumption E' is. R must be provided by a user to address this problem. In this setting, the mapping can be trivially defined as the only differences between E and E' are the LTSs (like the one in Fig. 5) representing activities that are present in one business process and not the other. Furthermore, we know that for any new activity, this one can never have been enabled by the controller of the old workflow. In consequence, R can be defined as the state

Table 1. Case study summary

Case study	# Activities	# Arrows	Transition requirement	Reconfiguration workflow (# States)	Minimised reconf. workflow (# States)
Oncology hospital	6	13	$T_\top$	18667	54
			$T_\emptyset$	9817	34
			T_h	11155	39
			T_h'	15094	54
Doctor assessment process	10	25	$T_\emptyset$	22448	39
			T_D	27512	42
Insurance process	11	25	$T_\emptyset$	15484	51
			T_I	14233	48
Computer repair process	18	26	$T_\emptyset$	43307	59
			T_C	52652	63

identity relation for all LTS that are in E and E' and as the constant relation 0 (i.e., the initial state) for LTSs representing new activities.

Thus, given two DCR graphs D and D' describing the old and new business process requirements and a transition requirement T we can automatically build control problems $\mathcal{E} = (E, G, L_c)$ and $\mathcal{E}' = (E', G', L_c')$ as described in Sect. 4.1 and R to describe and solve a DCU problem. An abstraction of the solution to the DCU problem for the Hospital reconfiguration problem with T_h described above is depicted in Fig. 7 and was built automatically using MTSA.

An important methodological note is that not every DCU problem has a solution. It is possible to provide two control problems $\mathcal{E}$ and $\mathcal{E}'$ that are individually realisable yet for certain transition requirements, the update is impossible. In terms of business process reconfiguration this means that it is possible to start with two sets of business process requirements that are consistent yet to propose a transition requirement that is too stringent to allow for a correct reconfiguration. An example of this, for the Hospital example, is to require $T = \Box(startNewReq \rightarrow \neg pm.Executed)$. There is no reconfiguration strategy that can guarantee that the new business process requirements will be put in force *independently of the current state* of the live instances of the old workflow: There is no reconfiguration strategy for a live instance in which activity *prescribe medicine* has been executed.

5   Validation

The purpose of this section is to show applicability of the approach by using, in addition to motivational example, three business processes taken from BPM Academic Initiative [1] that were also modelled in the DCR Graph Tool [15]. We chose these to avoid bias in producing our own DCR graphs from workflows.

Each case study requires two DCR graphs, a source and a target for reconfiguration. We manually produced variants for each case study and used domain independent transition requirement such as $T_\emptyset$ (see Sect. 4.2) in addition to domain specific ones. All examples were run using an extension of the MTSA tool [6] and can be found at [2]. Overall, 10 reconfigurations were defined and solved, corresponding to different choices of transition requirements for each case study. In Table 1 we report on examples, the number of distinct activities and constraints they involve, the size of the resulting reconfiguration workflow and of its minimised version (this involves hiding all enable, disable, and *menu* events).

5.1 Oncology Hospital

This case study already discussed above is the only one for which both reconfiguration source and target DCR graphs existed. Both were taken from [18]. We modelled various alternative transition requirements and built business process reconfiguration for each of them.

We first used a trivial transition requirement ($T_\top = \top$) to confirm that a reconfiguration strategy exists but it allows undesired behaviour. Indeed the reconfiguration process allowed: *beginReconf, stopOldReq, give medicine, start-NewReq* ... The trace is one in which a live instance for which no activities have occurred start to be reconfigured, the old business process requirements are dropped and before the new ones are enforced the patient is given medicine (without a signed prescription by a doctor!). This problem arises because $T_\top$ allows any activity during reconfiguration. Using a stronger domain independent transition requirement, $T_\emptyset$, the reconfiguration behaviour obtained is exactly that of an immediate reconfiguration es defined by [9].

We considered two domain specific transition requirements, T_h as discussed in Sect. 4.2 and one that delays reconfiguration when a nurse has indicated distrust regarding a patient's record: $T_h' = T_\emptyset \wedge \Box((dt.Executed \wedge \neg gm.Executed) \rightarrow \neg stopOldReq)$. As expected the resulting reconfiguration behaviour is like that of $T_\emptyset$ except that *stopOldReq* is delayed when between *don't trust* and *give medicine*.

5.2 Doctor Assessment Process

An assessment process for doctors in a hospital involves a manager asking an expert to evaluate each doctor. We used the original DCR graph as the target for reconfiguration and removed one activity to produce the source DCR graph. We considered a process that initially does not pay experts for their evaluation and that is to be reconfigured to support paying expert revision fees.

Using the transition requirement $T_\emptyset$ we obtain a reconfiguration that can be performed immediately at any point of the execution of the first process. This is because the activity of paying experts simply adds to the end of the current process an additional activity. However, immediate reconfiguration may result in paying experts that had agreed to do a review for free in the old process. to avoid this scenario we specified the transition requirement T_D stating that if reconfiguration is requested after receiving expert review, the expert must not be paid: $T_D = T_\emptyset \land (\Box(startNewReq \land recExp.Executed) \to \Box\neg pay.Executed)$ where $recExp$ is the activity representing the reception of expert review.

5.3 Insurance Process

The business process for an insurance company includes two roles: agents and clerks. Originally, the clerk must, upon receiving a *new customer claim*, *call the agent* to check the claim and *create a new customer case*. The new requirement to be put in place states that *create a new case* must happen before *call the agent* (this corresponds to the classic parallel to sequential reconfiguration [27]). We solved the reconfiguration for two different transition requirements.

We used $T_\emptyset$ to compute a reconfiguration workflow which delays reconfiguration when *call the agent* has been executed but *create a new case* has not. For all other scenarios, the reconfiguration workflow do an immediate change. An alternative is to modify the target DCR graph with a *kill* activity that excludes all other activities, modelling the killing of an instance. Then a transition requirement that forces *kill* when *call the agent* has been executed before *create a new case* can be specified as $T_I = T_\emptyset \land \Box((call.Executed \land \neg create.Executed \land startNewReq) \to (\neg ED \textbf{ W } kill.Executed))$, where ED is the disjunction of disable events for all activities except *kill* plus *enableAll*.

5.4 Computer Repair Process

A computer repair service starts when a customer brings a defective computer. If service provider and customer agree on a budget, then hardware and software repair activities are performed. We added a new role, that of a supervisor, that must approve a budget before it is sent to the customer. We used three activities for this: *send to supervisor*, *approve*, and *reject*.

Initially, we solved this reconfiguration problem with the transition requirement $T_\emptyset$. As expected, executions in which the reconfiguration is requested after the budget is sent to the customer, the reconfiguration is delayed so as to not contradict the requirement of supervisor approval.

An alternative we modelled is one in which we force asking for approval for any instance in which the customer has received the budget but repair has not started. If the supervisor rejects the budget, then the customer must be contacted and apologies must be offered. The following formula (where *sup* is the activity *send to supervisor*) captures this reconfiguration requirement: $T_C = \Box((stopOldReq \land \neg RepairStart) \to (\neg Happens \textbf{ W } (sup.Executed \land startNewReq)))$ where $Happens$ is the disjunction of disable events for all activities except *yes*, *no*, and *sup* plus *enableAll*.

6 Discussion and Related Work

The problem of business process reconfiguration has been studied extensively for some time [9]. [27] provides a classification of potential errors resulting from process changes. A survey of correctness criteria guaranteed by dynamic change techniques is presented in [24]. A taxonomy of reasons for reconfiguration is presented in [25] Methodological and automated support for reconfiguration has also been studied previously. Work such as [3,4,9] approach reconfiguration as a problem of defining dynamic transitions from one state of current workflow to another one in the new one. Without transition periods, changes can be partitioned into immediate or delayed [9]. A different take on reconfiguration is workflow versioning (e.g., [13,29]) where multiple workflow versions such are running simultaneously. In all cases, and in contrast to our work, the notion of a transition period in which remedial activities need to be implemented that are not compliant with the current and new workflow is not considered. The notion of reconfiguration is related to that of dynamic software updates. These have also been studied in terms of the different properties that may be expected during the update (e.g. [28]).

To reason about reconfiguration, our approach assumes a declarative specification of business process requirements (rather than an operational description in the form of a workflow). Declarative modelling approaches for business processes have been studied before. The ConDec [20] language was introduced for modelling business process based on linear temporal logic (LTL [21]). In [11], an operational semantics for a declarative graph based language is proposed and a tool [15] for enacting the underlying workflow is available. Rule based descriptions of business process requirements have also been proposed (e.g., [16,26]). Such descriptions are naturally executable. Both support changing rules during the execution of a workflow, however there is no support for understanding or guaranteeing properties of the reconfiguration. Thus, understanding if a delayed or a immediate change is needed must be done before introducing a new rule. Our approach requires a declarative description of business process requirements in a rather general language (FLTL) and provides guarantees over the reconfiguration process. The choice of DCR graphs as a starting point is accidental, we could apply a similar translation for other declarative languages.

Automatic construction of operational or executable models from declarative requirements has also been studies extensively, including work on supervisory control [23], synthesis of reactive designs [22] and automated planning [5]. This paper builds on the synthesis of discrete event controllers and in particular the work presented in [8] that uses LTS and FLTL as the input for synthesis. We strongly build on the result presented in [19] where a general technique for updating at runtime a controller. In this paper we adapt and apply this technique in the context of business process reconfiguration for DCR graph specifications.

7   Conclusions

We address the problem of business process reconfiguration by providing an automatic technique that builds a reconfiguration workflow that is guaranteed to preserve any reconfiguration transition requirements provided by a user. The technique requires a declarative description of the current and new business process requirements: in this paper we start from DCR graphs, and an LTL property that describes the properties that must hold during the reconfiguration. The approach allows immediate and delayed changes, and also reconfigurations in which there is a period between business processes in which additional domain specific preparatory or remedial activities can be executed. The result is a workflow that can be hotswapped with the current one and actively manages the transition to the new business process requirements ensuring correctness.

Acknowledgement. This project has received funding from the European Union's Horizon 2020 research, innovation programme under the Marie Skłodowska-Curie grant agreement No. 778233, PPL CAIS-0204-11, Pict 2014 No. 1656, Pict 2015 No. 3638 and Ubacyt 2018-0297BA.

References

1. Business process management academic initiative. https://bpmai.org/
2. MTSA synthesis tool and examples. http://mtsa.dc.uba.ar
3. van der Aalst, W.M.: Exterminating the dynamic change bug: a concrete approach to support workflow change. Inf. Syst. Front. **3**(3), 297–317 (2001)
4. Badouel, E., Oliver, J.: Reconfigurable nets, a class of high level Petri nets supporting dynamic changes within workflow systems. Ph.D. thesis, Inria (1998)
5. Cimatti, A., Pistore, M., Roveri, M., Traverso, P.: Weak, strong, and strong cyclic planning via symbolic model checking. Artif. Intell. **147**, 35–84 (2003)
6. D'Ippolito, N., Fischbein, D., Chechik, M., Uchitel, S.: MTSA: the modal transition system analyser. In: ASE 2008, pp. 475–476 (2008)
7. D'Ippolito, N., Braberman, V., Piterman, N., Uchitel, S.: Synthesising non-anomalous event-based controllers for liveness goals. ACM TOSEM **22**(1) (2013)
8. D'Ippolito, N.R., Braberman, V., Piterman, N., Uchitel, S.: Synthesis of live behaviour models. In: FSE 2010, pp. 77–86. ACM, New York (2010)
9. Ellis, C., Keddara, K., Rozenberg, G.: Dynamic change within workflow systems. In: COOCS 1995, pp. 10–21. ACM (1995)
10. Giannakopoulou, D., Magee, J.: Fluent model checking for event-based systems. In: ESEC/SIGSOFT FSE 2003, pp. 257–266. ACM, New York (2003)
11. Hildebrandt, T., Mukkamala, R.R.: Declarative event-based workflow as distributed dynamic condition response graphs. In: PLACES 2010, vol. 69, pp. 59–73 (2010)
12. Hildebrandt, T., Mukkamala, R.R., Slaats, T.: Nested dynamic condition response graphs. In: Arbab, F., Sirjani, M. (eds.) FSEN 2011. LNCS, vol. 7141, pp. 343–350. Springer, Heidelberg (2012). https://doi.org/10.1007/978-3-642-29320-7_23
13. Kradolfer, M., Geppert, A.: Dynamic workflow schema evolution based on workflow type versioning and workflow migration. Int. J. Coop. Info. Syst. (1999)
14. Magee, J., Kramer, J.: State Models and Java Programs. Wiley, Hoboken (1999)
15. Marquard, M., Shahzad, M., Slaats, T.: Web-based modelling and collaborative simulation of declarative processes. In: Motahari-Nezhad, H.R., Recker, J., Weidlich, M. (eds.) BPM 2015. LNCS, vol. 9253, pp. 209–225. Springer, Cham (2015). https://doi.org/10.1007/978-3-319-23063-4_15
16. Mejia Bernal, J.F., Falcarin, P., Morisio, M., Dai, J.: Dynamic context-aware business process: a rule-based approach supported by pattern identification. In: SAC 2010, pp. 470–474 (2010)

17. Milner, R. (ed.): A Calculus of Communicating Systems. LNCS, vol. 92. Springer, Heidelberg (1980). https://doi.org/10.1007/3-540-10235-3
18. Mukkamala, R.R.: A formal model for declarative workflows. Ph.D. thesis, IT University of Copenhagen (2012)
19. Nahabedian, L., et al.: Dynamic update of discrete event controllers. IEEE TSE 1 (2018, early access)
20. Pesic, M., van der Aalst, W.M.P.: A declarative approach for flexible business processes management. In: Eder, J., Dustdar, S. (eds.) BPM 2006. LNCS, vol. 4103, pp. 169–180. Springer, Heidelberg (2006). https://doi.org/10.1007/11837862_18
21. Pnueli, A.: The temporal logic of programs. In: FOCS 1977, pp. 46–57 (1977)
22. Pnueli, A., Rosner, R.: On the synthesis of a reactive module. In: POPL 1989 (1989)
23. Ramadge, P.J., Wonham, W.M.: The control of discrete event systems. Proc. IEEE **77**(1), 81–98 (1989)
24. Rinderle, S., Reichert, M., Dadam, P.: Correctness criteria for dynamic changes in workflow systems–a survey. Data Knowl. Eng. **50**(1), 9–34 (2004)
25. Schonenberg, H., Mans, R., Russell, N., Mulyar, N., van der Aalst, W.M.: Towards a taxonomy of process flexibility. In: CAiSE 2008, vol. 344, pp. 81–84 (2008)
26. Vasilecas, O., Kalibatiene, D., Lavbič, D.: Rule-and context-based dynamic business process modelling and simulation. J. Syst. Softw. **122**, 1–5 (2016)
27. Van Der Aalst, W.M., Stefan, J.: Dealing with workflow change: identification of issues and solutions. CSSE **15**(5), 267–276 (2000)
28. Zhang, J., Cheng, B.H.: Model-based development of dynamically adaptive software. In: ICSE 2006, pp. 371–380 (2006)
29. Zhao, X., Liu, C.: Version management in the business process change context. In: Alonso, G., Dadam, P., Rosemann, M. (eds.) BPM 2007. LNCS, vol. 4714, pp. 198–213. Springer, Heidelberg (2007). https://doi.org/10.1007/978-3-540-75183-0_15

A First-Order Logic Semantics for Communication-Parametric BPMN Collaborations

Sara Houhou[1,2], Souheib Baarir[1,3], Pascal Poizat[1,3(✉)], and Philippe Quéinnec[4]

[1] Sorbonne Université, CNRS, LIP6, 75005 Paris, France
{sara.houhou,souheib.baarir,pascal.poizat}@lip6.fr
[2] LINFI Laboratory, Biskra University, Biskra, Algeria
[3] Université Paris Lumières, Université Paris Nanterre, 92000 Nanterre, France
[4] IRIT - Université de Toulouse, 31000 Toulouse, France
philippe.queinnec@irit.fr

Abstract. BPMN is suitable to model not only intra-organization work-flows but also inter-organization collaborations. There has been a great effort in providing a formal semantics for BPMN, and then in building verification tools on top of this semantics. However, communication aspects are often discarded in the literature. This is an issue since BPMN has gained interest outside its original scope, e.g., for the IoT, where the configuration of communication modes plays an important role. In this paper, we propose a formal semantics for a subset of BPMN, taking into account inter-process communication and parametric verification with reference to communication modes. As opposed to transformational approaches, that map BPMN into some formal model such as transition systems or Petri nets, we give a direct formalization in First-Order Logic that is then implemented in TLA$^+$ to enable formal verification. Our approach is tool supported. The tool, as well as the TLA$^+$ theories, and experiment models are available online.

Keywords: BPMN · Formal semantics · Collaboration ·
Communication · Verification · TLA$^+$ · Tool

1 Introduction

BPMN collaboration diagrams [1] provide an efficient way to describe how several business entities, each one with its own internal process, can interact with one another to reach objectives. The BPMN standard defines an execution semantics using natural language, that could be qualified as semi-formal. This leaves room for interpretation and hampers formal analysis of the models. This issue has been addressed in the last decade in different proposals for a formalization of the BPMN execution semantics (see Sect. 4), some of them with available tools. But

This work was supported by project PARDI ANR-16-CE25-0006.

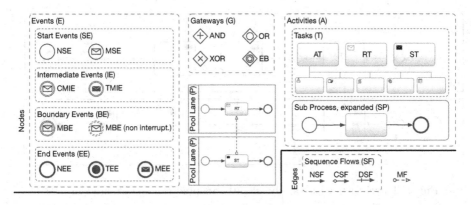

Fig. 1. BPMN subset being supported, with types used in the formalization (*e.g.*, MSE stands for Message Start Events and SE for Start Events). Due to lack of space, the support for boundary events is presented in [13].

these proposals often leave apart features related to communication. Meanwhile, BPMN is gaining interest as a modeling language for the Internet of Things (IoT) [4,18], There, the communication between the nodes of the system, and the configuration of different communication modes, is an issue.

Contribution. The contribution of this paper is twofold. First, (1) we provide a formalization of a subset of BPMN execution semantics that *supports interaction* and that is *parametric with reference to the properties of the communication* between participants, and (2) we support this formalization with *tools that automatically perform the verification of correctness properties* for BPMN collaboration models.

As far as (1) is concerned, we chose to define a direct First-Order Logic (FOL) semantics for BPMN. Instead of using an intermediary formal model, *e.g.*, Petri nets or process algebra, this choice of a simple yet expressive framework enables one to get a formal semantics that is amenable to implementation in different formal frameworks while still being close to the semi-formal semantics of the standard (hence it can be related to it). We implement our FOL semantics in TLA$^+$ [17] as a set of TLA$^+$ theories. This corresponds to a pure syntactic transformation of FOL into the corresponding TLA$^+$ fragment. Our semantics supports the six point-to-point communication models that exist when considering local and global message ordering, and it is easily extensible. As far as the subset of BPMN is concerned, we have first based our choice on the analysis of the 825 BPMN processes available in the BIT process library, release 2009 [12], given in [15]. We have then taken more constructs into account, mainly relative to our focus on communication: creation and termination of processes using messages, message-related tasks and intermediary events, and event-based gateways. The whole subset of the notation that we support is given in Fig. 1.

With respect to (2), our approach relies on two steps. First, one uses the fbpmn tool that we have developed to get a TLA$^+$ representation of the model

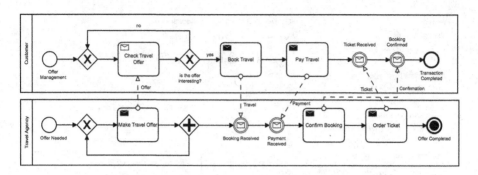

Fig. 2. Travel agency case study (slightly adapted from an example in [7]).

to verify. Then, one uses the TLC model-checker from the TLA$^+$ tool-suite to perform the verification. The properties of interest are encoded in the TLA$^+$ theories we have implemented. They include usual correctness properties for workflows as well as ones (proposed more recently [7]) that are more specific to BPMN. Both tools are open source and freely available online. Furthermore, the models we have used for evaluation in Sect. 3 are also available online. To get the tools and the models, see the fbpmn repository [3].

Due to space considerations, we assume the reader has a basic knowledge of the BPMN notation. We refer to [1] if this is not the case.

Case Study. Figure 2 presents the case study we use to illustrate some definitions and to perform verification. The outcomes of verification on more examples, including ones from the literature, are synthesized in Sect. 3.

The collaboration involves two participants: a customer and a travel agency. The agency sends offers to the client. The client may accept or decline the offers (loop using two exclusive gateways). Once it has accepted an offer, the client will not be ready to receive another one and it proceeds to the exchange part relative to the offer of interest. On the other side, the agency (through the use of a parallel gateway) is able both to send other offers and begin the exchange part: at the parallel gateway a token is generated both to get back to offer sending and to wait for the booking. This case study is interesting for several reasons. First, due to the agency behavior, the collaboration is possibly unsafe: one can have an unbounded number of tokens on the right of the parallel gateway. Second, observe that the partners do not agree on the order of confirmation *wrt.* ticket reception. Depending on the communication model, this may cause a deadlock.

Overview. The formal part of the paper is developed in Sect. 2, with Subsects. 2.1 and 2.2, respectively addressing the presentation of the model underlying the semantics, and then the semantics itself. The implementation of the semantics in TLA$^+$, verification, and evaluation are then presented in Sect. 3. This section also includes a short introduction to the TLA$^+$ language and verification framework. Related work is given in Sect. 4, and we end with conclusions and perspectives in Sect. 5.

2   Formal Semantics

In this section, we first present the model on which we base the definition of the communication-parametric semantics for BPMN collaborations. This model is used to represent collaborations as typed graphs. In a second step, we present the semantic itself. It follows the "token game" of the standard [1, Ch. 13], with a notion of state that evolves with activation and completion of graph nodes.

2.1   A Typed Graph Representation of BPMN Collaborations

In our work, a BPMN model is seen as a typed graph (Definition 1), where nodes and edges are associated to types corresponding to the BPMN syntax (see Fig. 1): $T_{Nodes} = \{AT, RT, ST, SP, NSE, MSE, CMIE, TMIE, NEE, TEE, MEE, AND, OR, XOR, EB, P\}$ and $T_{Edges} = \{NSF, CSF, DSF, MF\}$. The hierarchical structure of collaborations, with processes and sub-processes is dealt with by using specific types for nodes, P and SP, and a relation denoting containment, R. From our example, Fig. 2, we would then have two nodes of type P (say n_1 for Customer, n_2 for Travel Agency) with their respective contents related by R, e.g., a node n_3 for Make Travel Offer of type ST with $n_3 \in R(n_2)$.

Definition 1 (BPMN Graph). *A BPMN graph is a tuple $\widehat{G} = (N, E, \mathbb{M}, cat_N, cat_E, source, target, R, msg_t)$ where N is the set of nodes, E ($N \cap E = \emptyset$) is the set of edges, $\mathbb{M}$ is the set of message types, $cat_N : N \to T_{Nodes}$ gives the type of a node, $cat_E : E \to T_{Edges}$ gives the type of an edge, $source/target : E \to N$ give the source/target of an edge, $R : N^{\{SP,P\}} \to 2^{N \cup E}$ gives the set of nodes and edges which are directly contained in a container (process or sub-process), and $msg_t : E^{MF} \to \mathbb{M}$ gives the message associated to a message flow.*

Notation. We use N^T (resp. E^T) to denote the subset of nodes (resp. edges) of type T, e.g., $N^T = \{n \in N \mid cat_N(n) \in T\}$. By abuse of notation, we may write N^t instead of $N^{\{t\}}$, e.g., N^{NSE} instead of $N^{\{NSE\}}$. We use for cat_E the same simplified notations as for cat_N.

We then define some auxiliary functions that will be used in the semantics.

Auxiliary Functions. For a graph $\widehat{G} = (N, E, \mathbb{M}, cat_N, cat_E, source, target, R, msg_t)$, we introduce the following auxiliary functions:

- $in/out : N \to 2^E$ give the incoming/outgoing edges of a node, $in(n) = \{e \in E \mid target(e) = n\}$ and $out(n) = \{e \in E \mid source(e) = n\}$.
- a family of functions in^T (resp. out^T) $: N \to 2^E$ is used to combine in (resp. out) with E^T, $in^T(n) = in(n) \cap E^T$ and $out^T(n) = out(n) \cap E^T$.
- $procOf : N \to N^P$ gives the container process of a given node, $procOf(n) = p$ if and only if $n \in R^+(p)$, with R^+ being the transitive closure of R.

It is desirable to enforce that models respect some well-formedness rules before performing verification. Due to a lack of space, we give the rules that we impose (most coming from [1]) for a BPMN graph to be well-formed in [13].

2.2   A FOL Semantics for BPMN Collaborations

In order to maintain traceability with the standard, we use a token-based approach. The movement of tokens is based on node types. We define an execution model based on two predicates (St, Ct) for each node type which correspond to, respectively, the enabling of the node to start its execution, and the enabling of the node to complete its execution. Some nodes only have a start transition (*e.g.*, end events), and others only have a completion transition (*e.g.*, gateways). The definition of these predicates relies a notion of *state* of the BPMN Graph.

Definition 2 (State). *The state of a BPMN graph is given by a couple of functions* $s = (m_n, m_e)$, $m_n : N \to \mathbb{N}$ *and* $m_e : E \to \mathbb{N}$, *that associate a number of tokens to nodes (gateways are always 0) and edges, respectively. The set of all states of a BPMN graph is denoted by States.*

Definition 3 (Initial state). *The initial state of a BPMN graph, denoted by* $s_o = (m_{n0}, m_{e0})$, *associates a token to the NSE nodes of the processes, all the other nodes and edges being unmarked:* $\forall e \in E, m_{e0}(e) = 0$, *and* $\forall n \in N, m_{n0}(n) = 1$ *if* $\exists p \in N^P, n \in N^{NSE} \cap R(p)$, *and 0 otherwise.*

The properties of communication between two participants (process nodes) for a given type of message are abstracted with two predicates, *send* and *receive*. These predicates specify when a communication action is enabled and the effect of this communication. For instance, with FIFO asynchronous communication (`NetworkFifo`, Sect. 3.3), messages must be delivered in the order they were sent. Thus $send(p_1, p_2, m)$ is always enabled and $receive(p_1, p_2, m)$ is true only if m is the oldest message and thus the next one to be delivered. Observe that the value of these predicates evolve as the processes send and receive messages.

Definition 4 (Communication Model). *The communication model is characterized by two predicates send/receive* $: N^P \times N^P \times \mathbb{M} \to Bool$.

The formal execution semantics is given in Tables 1 and 2. We consider that m_n and m_n' (resp. m_e and m_e') denote two successive markings of a node (resp. edge) in the execution semantics. $\triangle$ is a predicate that denotes marking equality but for nodes and edges given as parameter, $\triangle(X)$ means "*nothing changes but for X*": $\triangle(X) \stackrel{def}{\equiv} \forall n \in N \setminus X, m_n'(n) = m_n(n) \wedge \forall e \in E \setminus X, m_e'(e) = m_e(n)$.

Starting and Terminating. The behavior of an NSE node is defined only through completion: it consumes one token and generates one token on all its outgoing sequence flow edges. If it is the initial node of a process p, it activates it by generating a token on p. For a sub-process, it is the SP starting predicate that will perform activation (see below). The behavior of an NEE node is defined only through a starting predicate: it is enabled if it has at least one token on one of its incoming edges, that is added to the node. A TEE node is also defined only through a starting predicate: it is enabled if it has at least one token on one of its incoming edges, then it drops down all the remaining tokens of the process or sub-processes to which it belongs. The behavior of an activity node

Table 1. FOL semantics (part 1 – events)

Events

$n \in N^{NSE}$	$Ct(n) \stackrel{def}{=} (m_n(n) \geq 1) \wedge (m'_n(n) = m_n(n) - 1)$ $\wedge (\forall e \in out^{SF}(n), (m'_e(e) = m_e(e) + 1))$ $\wedge ((\exists p \in N^P, n \in R(p) \wedge (m_n(p) = 0) \wedge (m'_n(p) = 1)$ $\wedge \triangle (\{n,p\} \cup out^{SF}(n)))$ $\vee (\exists p \in N^{SP}, n \in R(p) \wedge \triangle(\{n\} \cup out^{SF}(n))))$
$n \in N^{MSE}$	$St(n) \stackrel{def}{=} (m_n(n) = 0) \wedge (m'_n(n) = 1)$ $\wedge (\exists e \in in^{MF}(n), (m_e(e) \geq 1) \wedge (m'_e(e) = m_e(e) - 1)$ $\wedge\, receive(procOf(source(e)), procOf(n), msg_t(e))$ $\wedge \triangle (\{n,e\}))$
	$Ct(n) \stackrel{def}{=} (m_n(n) = 1) \wedge (m'_n(n) = m_n(n) - 1)$ $\wedge (\exists p \in N^P, n \in R(p) \wedge (m_n(p) = 0) \wedge (m'_n(p) = 1)$ $\wedge (\forall e \in out^{SF}(n), (m'_e(e) = m_e(e) + 1))$ $\wedge \triangle (\{n,p\} \cup out^{SF}(n)))$
$n \in N^{TMIE}$	$St(n) \stackrel{def}{=} (\exists e \in in^{SF}(n), (m_e(e) \geq 1) \wedge (m'_e(e) = m_e(e) - 1)$ $\wedge (\exists e' \in out^{MF}(n), (m'_e(e') = m_e(e') + 1)$ $\wedge\, send(procOf(n), procOf(target(e')), msg_t(e'))$ $\wedge\, \forall e" \in out^{SF}(n), (m'_e(e") = m_e(e") + 1)$ $\wedge \triangle (\{e,e'\} \cup out^{SF}(n))))$
$n \in N^{CMIE}$	$St(n) \stackrel{def}{=} (\exists e \in in^{SF}(n), (m_e(e) \geq 1) \wedge (m'_e(e) = m_e(e) - 1)$ $\wedge (\exists e' \in in^{MF}(n), (m_e(e') \geq 1) \wedge (m'_e(e') = m_e(e') - 1)$ $\wedge\, receive(procOf(source(e)), procOf(n), msg_t(e'))$ $\wedge (\forall e" \in out^{SF}(n), (m'_e(e") = m_e(e") + 1))$ $\wedge \triangle (\{e,e'\} \cup out^{SF}(n))))$
$n \in N^{NEE}$	$St(n) \stackrel{def}{=} (\exists e \in in^{SF}(n), (m_e(e) \geq 1) \wedge (m'_e(e) = m_e(e) - 1)$ $\wedge (m'_n(n) = m_n(n) + 1) \wedge \triangle(\{n,e\}))$
$\forall n \in N^{TEE}$	$St(n) \stackrel{def}{=} (m'_n(n) = 1)$ $\wedge (\exists e \in in^{SF}(n), (m_e(e) \geq 1))$ $\wedge (\exists p \in N^{\{P,SP\}}, n \in R(p)$ $\wedge (\forall nn \in ((R^+(p) \cap N) \setminus \{n\}), m'_n(nn) = 0)$ $\wedge (\forall ee \in (R^+(p) \cap E), m'_e(ee) = 0)$ $\wedge \triangle (R^+(p)))$
$n \in N^{MEE}$	$St(n) \stackrel{def}{=} (\exists e \in in^{SF}(n), (m_e(e) \geq 1) \wedge (m'_e(e) = m_e(e) - 1)$ $\wedge (\exists e' \in out^{MF}(n), send(procOf(n), procOf(target(e')), msg_t(e'))$ $\wedge (m'_e(e') = m_e(e') + 1)$ $\wedge (m'_n(n) = m_n(n) + 1) \wedge \triangle(\{n,e,e'\})))$

AT is defined by a starting and a completion predicate. The node is started by the arrival of at least one token on one of its incoming edges. Completion is realized by adding one token on each of its outgoing edges. The behavior of a SP node extends the one of an AT node with additional conditions: when enabled, a sub-process adds a token to the start event it contains. It completes when at least one end event it contains has some tokens and neither one of its edges nor one of its non end event nodes is still active (*i.e.*, owning a token).

Table 2. FOL Semantics (part 2 – gateways and activities)

Gateways	$n \in N^{XOR}$	$Ct(n) \stackrel{def}{=} (\exists e \in in^{SF}(n), (m_e(e) \geq 1) \wedge (m'_e(e) = m_e(e) - 1)$ $\wedge (\exists e' \in out^{SF}(n), (m'_e(e') = m_e(e') + 1))$ $\wedge \triangle(\{e, e'\}))$
	$n \in N^{AND}$	$Ct(n) \stackrel{def}{=} (\forall e \in in^{SF}(n), (m_e(e) \geq 1) \wedge (m'_e(e) = m_e(e) - 1)$ $\wedge (\forall e' \in out^{SF}(n), (m'_e(e') = m_e(e') + 1))$ $\wedge \triangle(in^{SF}(n) \cup out^{SF}(n))$
	$n \in N^{OR}$	$Ct(n) \stackrel{def}{=} (In^+(n) \neq \emptyset) \wedge (\forall e \in In^+(n), (m'_e(e) = m_e(e) - 1)$ $\wedge (\forall ez \in In^-(n), \forall ee \in (Pre_E(n, ez) \setminus ignore_E(n)), (m_e(ee) = 0)$ $\wedge (\forall nn \in (Pre_N(n, ez) \setminus ignore_N(n)), (m_n(nn) = 0)))$ $\wedge ((\exists Outs \subset (out^{SF}(n) \cap E^{\{NSF, CSF\}}), (Outs \neq \emptyset)$ $\wedge (\forall e \in Outs, (m'_e(e) = m_e(e) + 1) \wedge \triangle(In^+(n) \cup Outs))$ $\vee (\exists e \in out^{DSF}(n), (m'_e(e) = m_e(e) + 1) \wedge \triangle(In^+(n) \cup \{e\}))))$
	$n \in N^{EB}$	$Ct(n) \stackrel{def}{=} (\exists e \in in^{SF}(n), (m_e(e) \geq 1) \wedge (m'_e(e) = m_e(e) - 1$ $\wedge (\exists e' \in out^{SF}(n), \exists e'' \in in^{MF}(target(e')), (m_e(e'') \geq 1)$ $\wedge (m'_e(e') = m_e(e') + 1) \wedge \triangle(e, e')))$
Activities	$n \in N^{AT}$	$St(n) \stackrel{def}{=} (\exists e \in in^{SF}(n), (m_e(e) \geq 1) \wedge (m'_e(e) = m_e(e) - 1$ $\wedge (m'_n(n) = m_n(n) + 1) \wedge \triangle(\{n, e\}))$
		$Ct(n) \stackrel{def}{=} (m_n(n) \geq 1) \wedge (m'_n(n) = m_n(n) - 1)$ $\wedge (\forall e \in out^{SF}(n), (m'_e(e) = m_e(e) + 1)) \wedge \triangle(\{n\} \cup out^{SF}(n))$
	$n \in N^{ST}$	$St(n) \stackrel{def}{=} (\exists e \in in^{SF}(n), (m_e(e) \geq 1) \wedge (m'_e(e) = m_e(e) - 1$ $\wedge (m'_n(n) = m_n(n) + 1) \wedge \triangle(\{n, e\}))$
		$Ct(n) \stackrel{def}{=} (m_n(n) \geq 1) \wedge (m'_n(n) = m_n(n) - 1)$ $\wedge (\forall e \in out^{SF}(n), (m'_e(e) = m_e(e) + 1))$ $\wedge (\exists e' \in out^{MF}(n), send(procOf(n), procOf(target(e')), msg_t(e'))$ $\wedge (m'_e(e') = m_e(e') + 1) \wedge \triangle(\{n, e'\} \cup out^{SF}(n)))$
	$n \in N^{RT}$	$St(n) \stackrel{def}{=} (\exists e \in in^{SF}(n), (m_e(e) \geq 1) \wedge (m'_e(e) = m_e(e) - 1$ $\wedge (m'_n(n) = m_n(n) + 1) \wedge \triangle(\{n, e\}))$
		$Ct(n) \stackrel{def}{=} (m_n(n) \geq 1) \wedge (m'_n(n) = m_n(n) - 1)$ $\wedge (\forall e \in out^{SF}(n), (m'_e(e) = m_e(e) + 1))$ $\wedge (\exists e' \in in^{MF}(n), (m_e(e') \geq 1) \wedge (m'_e(e') = m_e(e') - 1)$ $\wedge receive(procOf(source(e')), procOf(n), msg_t(e'))$ $\wedge \triangle(\{n, e'\} \cup out^{SF}(n)))$
	$n \in N^{SP}$	$St(n) \stackrel{def}{=} (\exists e \in in^{SF}(n), (m_e(e) \geq 1) \wedge (m'_e(e) = m_e(e) - 1)$ $\wedge (m'_n(n) = m_n(n) + 1)$ $\wedge (\forall n_{se} \in (N^{SE} \cap R(n)), (m'_n(n_{se}) = m_n(n_{se}) + 1))$ $\wedge \triangle(\{e, n\} \cup (N^{SE} \cap R(n))))$
		$Ct(n) \stackrel{def}{=} (m_n(n) \geq 1) \wedge (m'_n(n) = 0)$ $\wedge (\forall e \in R(n) \cap E, (m_e(e) = 0))$ $\wedge (\exists n_{ee} \in (N^{EE} \cap R(n)), (m_n(n_{ee}) \geq 1))$ $\wedge (\forall nn \in R(n) \cap N, (m_n(nn) \geq 1 \Rightarrow nn \in N^{EE}))$ $\wedge (\forall nn \in (R(n) \cap N^{EE}), (m'_n(nn) = 0))$ $\wedge (\forall e \in out^{SF}(n), (m'_e(e) = m_e(e) + 1))$ $\wedge \triangle(\{n\} \cup (R(n) \cap N^{EE}) \cup out^{SF}(n))$

Communication. The communication elements (MSE, $TMIE$, $CMIE$, MEE, ST, RT) require additional conditions for starting and completing due to the presence of sending/reception behaviors. When enabled by a token on one of their incoming edges, $TMIE$, MEE, and ST send a message on their outgoing message flow and a token on all their outgoing sequence flows. MSE, $CMIE$, and RT require a message offer on one of their incoming message flows. They receive the message and produce tokens on their outgoing edges. MSE and RT have both starting and completion transitions while $CMIE$ is an instantaneous event with only a starting transition.

Gateways. Gateways are atomic and define only the completion behavior. An AND gateway is ready to complete if it has at least one token on all its incoming edges. It completes by removing one token on each of these edges, and producing one on all its outgoing edges. An XOR gateway is ready to complete if it has at least one token on one of its incoming edges. It completes by removing this token, and producing one on one of its outgoing edges, depending on conditions. Since we abstract from data, we proceed choosing non-deterministically the concerned edge. An EB gateway behaves as an XOR gateway in that it consumes and produces a token from and to only one edge. However, its completion relies on the presence of external message triggers. The outgoing edge activation depends on the enabledness of the $CMIE$ or RT which is the target of this edge. The activation of an OR gateway g is more complex [1, Chap. 13]. It is activated if (1) it has at least one token on one of its incoming edges, and (2) for each node or edge x such that there is a path – that does not pass through g – from x to an unmarked incoming edge of g, there must be also a path – that does not pass through g – from x to a marked incoming edge of g. This is illustrated in Fig. 3 where gateway g cannot be activated since there is a path from marked e^{pre} to unmarked e^- and no path from e^{pre} to some marked e^+. The OR gateway completes by adding a token either to all its outgoing edges whose condition it true, or else to its default sequence flow edge. Again, since we abstract from data, we chose non-deterministically to add a token either to a combination (1 or more) of the outgoing non default edges, or to the default edge.

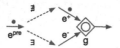

Fig. 3. Non activable inclusive gateway. It has to wait for the token on e^{pre}.

To formalize the semantics of an OR gateway we use several functions:

- $Pre_N : N \times E \to 2^N$ gives the predecessor nodes of an edge such that n^{pre} is in $Pre_N(n, e)$ if there is a path from n^{pre} to e that never visits n. Accordingly, $Pre_E : N \times E \to 2^E$ gives predecessor edges.
- $In^- : N \to E$ gives the unmarked incoming edges of a node, $In^-(n) = \{e^- \in in^{SF}(n) \mid m_e(e^-) = 0\}$.

- $In^+ : N \rightarrow E$ gives the marked incoming edges of a node, $In^+(n) = \{e^+ \in in^{SF}(n) \mid m_e(e^+) \geq 1\}$.
- $ignore_E : N \rightarrow 2^E$ gives the predecessor edges of the marked incoming edges of a given node: $ignore_E(n) \overset{def}{=} \underset{e^+ \in In^+(n)}{\bigcup} Pre_E(n, e^+)$.
- $ignore_N : N \rightarrow 2^N$ gives the predecessor nodes of the marked incoming edges of a given node: $ignore_N(n) = \underset{e^+ \in In^+(n)}{\bigcup} Pre_N(n, e^+)$.

3 Implementation and Verification

In this section, we present our encoding of the FOL semantics in TLA$^+$. This allows one to easily parameter the properties of the communication, and to benefit from the efficient TLC model checker to automatically verify collaborations.

3.1 The TLA$^+$ Specification Language and Verification Framework

TLA$^+$ [17] is a formal specification language based on untyped Zermelo-Fraenkel set theory for specifying data structures, and on the temporal logic of actions (TLA) for specifying dynamic behaviors. TLA$^+$ allows one to specify symbolic transition systems with variables and *actions*. An action is a transition predicate between a state and a successor state. It is an arbitrary first-order predicate with quantifiers, set and arithmetic operators, and functions. In an action, x denotes the value of a variable x in the origin state, and x' denotes its value in the next state. Functions are primitive objects in TLA$^+$. The application of function f to an expression e is written as $f[e]$. The expression $[x \in X \mapsto e]$ denotes the function with domain X that maps any $x \in X$ to e. The expression $[f \text{ EXCEPT } ![e_1] = e_2]$ is a function that is equal to the function f except at point e_1, where its value is e_2. A system specification is usually a disjunction of actions. Fairness, usually expressed as a conjunction of weak or strong fairness on actions, or more generally as an LTL (Linear Temporal Logic) property, ensures progression. The TLA$^+$ toolbox, freely available at http://lamport.azurewebsites.net/tla/tla.html, contains the TLC model checker, the TLAPS proof assistant, and various other tools.

3.2 Encoding of FOL Semantics in TLA$^+$

The expression and action fragment of TLA$^+$ contains FOL, and the encoding of the semantics in TLA$^+$ is straightforward (459 lines of TLA$^+$ formulae). The resulting theories are available in the fbpmn repository [3] under `theories/tla`.

Module PWSTypes defines the abstract constants that correspond to the node and edge types. Module PWSDefs specifies the constants that describe a BPMN graph (Definition 1): Node (for N), Edge (for E), Message (for $\mathbb{M}$), CatN (for cat_N), CatE (for cat_E), ContainRel (for R)... This module also defines auxiliary functions such as in^T. Module PWSWellFormed encodes the well-formedness predicates for BPMN graphs. Last, module PWSSemantics contains the semantics. It defines the variables for the marking: nodemarks ($\in [Node \rightarrow Nat]$) and edgemarks ($\in [Edge \rightarrow Nat]$). Then it contains a translation of the FOL formulas given in Tables 1 and 2. Each rule yields one TLA$^+$ action. For instance, the St predicate of the SP nodes becomes:

$$
\begin{aligned}
&subprocess\_start(n) \triangleq \\
&\quad CatN[n] = SubProcess \\
&\quad \wedge\ \exists e \in intype(SeqFlowType, n) : edgemarks[e] \geq 1 \\
&\qquad \wedge\ edgemarks' = [edgemarks \text{ EXCEPT } ![e] = edgemarks[e] - 1] \\
&\quad \wedge\ nodemarks' = [nn \in \text{DOMAIN } nodemarks \mapsto \\
&\qquad \text{IF } nn = n \text{ THEN } nodemarks[nn] + 1 \\
&\qquad \text{ELSE IF } CatN[nn] \in StartEventType \wedge nn \in ContainRel[n] \\
&\qquad\quad \text{THEN } nodemarks[nn] + 1 \\
&\qquad \text{ELSE } nodemarks[nn]] \\
&\quad \wedge\ Network!unchanged
\end{aligned}
$$

The $Next$ predicate specifies a possible transition between a starting state and a successor state. It is a disjunction of all the actions. The full specification is then, as usual in TLA$^+$, $Init \wedge \Box[Next]_{vars} \wedge Fairness$, where $Init$ specifies the initial state (Definition 3), and $\Box[Next]$ specifies that $Next$ (or stuttering) is verified along all the execution steps. In our case, $Fairness$ is a temporal property that ensures that any permanently enabled transition eventually occurs. This means that no process may progress forever while others are never allowed to do so if they can. Moreover, we include in the fairness that no choice is infinitely often ignored: if a XOR, OR, or EB gateway is included in a loop, the fairness forbids the infinite executions that never use some output edges.

3.3 Communication as a Parameter

One of the objectives of our FOL semantics is to be able to specify the communication behavior as a parameter of the verification. To achieve this, all operations related to communication are isolated in a Network module. This module is a proxy for several implementations that correspond to communication models with different properties, such as their delivery order.

We provide six communication models which differ in the order messages can be sent or received, and are all the possible point-to-point models when considering local ordering (per process) and global ordering (absolute time). They are formally defined in [5] and informally are: unordered (modelled by a bag of message), first-in-first-out between each couple of processes (modelled by an array of queues), fifo inbox (each process has an input queue where senders add their messages), fifo outbox (each process has an output queue from where receivers fetch messages), global fifo (a unique shared queue), and RSC (realizable with synchronous communication, modelled as a unique message slot that forces alternation of send and receive tasks). If the collaboration is sound, no message is left in transit, and RSC and synchronous communication yield the same behaviors.

The state of the communication model is specified with a variable **net**, whose content depends on the communication model. The communication actions are two transition predicates **send** and **receive** which are true when the action is enabled. These actions take three parameters, the sender process, the destination process and the message. Their specification depends on the communication model. For instance, **NetworkFifo** specifies a communication model where the delivery order is globally first-in first-out: messages are delivered in the order they have been sent. Its realization is a queue and the two predicates are:

$$send(from, to, m) \triangleq net' = Append(net, \langle from, to, m \rangle)$$
$$receive(from, to, m) \triangleq net \neq \langle \rangle \wedge \langle from, to, m \rangle = Head(net) \wedge net' = Tail(net)$$

3.4   Mechanized Verification

A specific BPMN diagram is described by instantiating the constants in **PWSDefs** (**Node**, **Edge**...) from the BPMN collaboration. This is automated using our fbpmn tool. Regarding the well-formedness of the BPMN diagram, the predicates from **PWSWellFormed** are *assumed* in the model. Before checking a model, The TLA$^+$ model checker checks these assumptions with the instantiated constants that describe the diagram, and reports an error if an assumption is violated. Otherwise, this proves that the diagram is well-formed.

The TLA$^+$ model checker, TLC, is an explicit-state model checker that checks both safety and liveness properties specified in LTL. This logic includes operators $\Box$ and $\Diamond$ that respectively denote that, in all executions, a property F must always hold ($\Box F$) or that it must hold at some instant in the future ($\Diamond F$). TLC builds and explores the full state space of the diagram to verify if the given properties are verified. These properties are generic properties related to any Business Process diagram, or specific properties for a given diagram. Some of the generic properties are safe collaboration, sound collaboration and message-relaxed sound collaboration [7]. A collaboration is safe if no sequence flow holds more than one token:

$$\Box(\forall e \in E^{SF}, m_e(e) \leq 1) \tag{1}$$

A collaboration is sound if all processes are sound and there are no undelivered messages. A process is sound if there are no token on its inside edges, and one token only on its end events.

$$SoundProc(p) \stackrel{def}{=} \forall e \in R(p) \cap E^{SF}, m_e(e) = 0$$
$$\land \forall n \in R(p) \cap N, (m_n(n) = 0 \lor (m_n(n) = 1 \land n \in N^{EE}))$$
$$Soundness \stackrel{def}{=} \Diamond(\forall p \in N^P, SoundProc(p) \land \forall e \in E^{MF}, m_e(e) = 0) \qquad (2)$$

A collaboration is message-relaxed sound (3) if it is sound when ignoring messages in transit, *i.e.*, when ignoring the Message Flow edges. This is the same as (2) without the second conjunction.

Other generic properties are available, such as the absence of undelivered message or the possible activation which states there does not exist a task node (Abstract Task, Send Task, Receive Task) that is never activated in any execution. From a business process point of view, it means that there are no tasks in the diagram that are never used. This is expressed as $\forall n \in N^T : \mathbf{EF}(m_n(n) \neq 0)$ (TLC can check for the invalidity of the negation of this CTL formula).

Last, the user can also define business model properties concerning a specific diagram. For instance, one can check that the marking of a given node is bounded by a constant (*i.e.*, $\Box(nodemarks["Confirm\ Booking"]) \leq 1$), or that the activation of one node necessarily leads to the activation of another node $(\Box(nodemarks["Book\ Travel"] \neq 0 \Rightarrow \Diamond(nodemarks["Offer\ Completed"] \neq 0))$.

When the model checker finds that a property is invalid, it outputs a counter-example trace that we animate on the BPM graphical model to help the user understand it. As TLC uses a breadth-first algorithm, this trace is minimal for safety properties.

3.5 Experiments

Experiments were conducted on a laptop with a 2.1 GHz Intel Core i7 processor (quad core) with 8 GB of memory. Results are presented in Table 3. The first column is the reference of the example in our archive. The characteristics of a model are: number of participants, number of nodes (incl. gateways), number of flow edges (sequence or message flows), whether the model is well-balanced (for each gateway with n diverging branches we have a corresponding gateway with n converging branches) and whether it includes a loop. The communication model is asynchronous (bag), fifo-ordered between each couple of processes (fifo pair), globally fifo (fifo all), or synchronous-like (RSC). The results of the verification then follow. First, data on the resulting transition system are given: number of states, number of transitions, and depth (length of the longest sequence of transitions that the model checker had to explore). For each of the three correctness properties presented above, we indicate if the model satisfies it. Lastly, the accumulated time for the verification of the three properties is given. Our tool supports more verifications (see Table 4) and can be easily extended with new properties. We selected these three ones since they are more BPMN specific [7].

Table 3. Experimental Results.

ref.	Characteristics					Com.	LTS size			validity			total
	proc.	nodes (gw.)	SF/MF	B	L	model	states	trans.	depth	(1)	(2)	(3)	time
001	2	17 (2)	14/3	✓	×	bag	93	173	25	✓	✓	✓	5.17s
						fifo pair	85	161	21	✓	×	×	5.19s
						RSC	77	147	19	✓	×	×	5.09s
002	2	16 (2)	13/3	✓	×	bag	83	154	24	✓	✓	✓	4.93s
						fifo pair	75	142	20	✓	×	×	4.74s
						RSC	67	128	18	✓	×	×	4.48s
003	1	14 (6)	16/0	×	✓	none	41	59	15	✓	✓	✓	2.89s
006	2	20 (4)	18/5	×	✓	bag	470	966	43	×	×	✓	8.98s
						fifo all	522	932	40	×	×	×	8.58s
						RSC	247	420	38	×	×	×	6.58s
007	1	8 (2)	7/0	×	×	none	44	73	15	×	×	×	2.52s
008	1	11 (2)	9/0	×	×	none	48	77	19	×	✓	✓	2.60s
009	2	12 (2)	9/1	×	×	bag	170	395	19	×	×	×	4.86s
010	2	15 (2)	11/1	×	×	bag	186	423	23	×	×	✓	5.32s
011	2	15 (2)	11/1	×	×	bag	100	209	21	×	✓	✓	4.73s
012	1	15 (8)	17/0	✓	✓	none	71	137	15	✓	✓	✓	3.16s
013	1	17 (8)	21/0	✓	✓	none	407	1049	15	✓	✓	✓	5.93s
018	1	19 (8)	25/0	✓	✓	none	4631	15513	18	✓	✓	✓	28.46s
015	2	14 (2)	10/2	×	×	bag	68	117	11	✓	×	×	4.67s
016	2	14 (2)	10/2	×	×	bag	36	53	11	✓	✓	✓	4.25s
017	1	32 (12)	36/0	×	×	none	93	141	37	✓	✓	✓	4.03s
020	4	39 (6)	34/8	×	✓	bag	4648	14691	54	✓	✓	✓	53.05s
020						fifo all	2564	6872	54	✓	✓	✓	28.25s
020						RSC	1224	3271	54	✓	×	×	18.77s

Table 3 presents the results for a selection from our repository [3] for a variety of gateways and activities. These illustrative examples include realistic business process models (001 and 002 two client-supplier models, 006 from Fig. 2, 017 from [15], and 020 from [9]), and models dedicated to specific concerns: termination end events and sub processes (007–011 from [7]), inclusive gateways (003, 012, 013 and 018), exclusive and event-based gateways (015 and 016).

A first conclusion is that verification is rather fast: the verification of one property generally takes just a few seconds per model, the longest being for model 020 that takes up to 53s of accumulated time for the three properties (5s for the construction of the state space). Experiments also show the effect of the communication model on property satisfaction (models 1, 2, 6, 20), the use of TLA$^+$ fairness to avoid infinite loops (12, 13, 18, 20), and the use of terminate end events combined with user given constraints [3] to deal with unsafety (6).

Table 4. Comparison of tool-supported approaches for the analysis of communication in BPMN.

		transformation						direct				
approach												
reference		[10]	[14]	[20]	[21]	[22]	[11]	[9]	[7]	[8]	[16]	ours
year		2018	2017	2013	2011	2008	2008		2018	2018	2012	2019
formalism		CPN	ECATNets	In-Place Graph	CSP	YAWL Nets	RDP		LTS	LTS	LTL	FOL
tool		not avail. CP4PBMN	not avail. BPMNChecker	GrGen	OWorkflow	BPMN2YAWL	transformer	MIDA	–	BProVe	prototype	fBPMN
		not avail.	not avail.	yes	yes	yes	yes	yes	–	yes	not avail.	yes
supported elements	*AND* gateway	•	•	•	•	•	•	•	•	•	•	•
	XOR gateway	•	•	•	•	•	•	•	•	•	•	•
	OR gateway	•	–	•	•	•	•	•	•	•	•	•
	EB gateway	•	•	•	–	•	•	•	•	•	•	•
	ST	•	•	•	•	•	•	•	•	•	•	•
	RT	•	•	•	•	•	•	•	•	•	•	•
	MSE	•	•	•	–	•	•	•	•	•	•	•
	TMIE	•	–	•	–	–	•	•	•	•	•	•
	CMIE	•	•	•	–	–	–	•	•	•	•	•
	MEE	•	–	•	–	–	–	•	•	•	•	•
	TEE	–	•	•	•	•	•	•	•	–	•	•
	sub-processes	•	•	•	–	–	–	–	–	–	–	–
	data	•	•	•	–	–	–	–	–	–	–	–
	multi instance (pools)	–	–	•	–	•	•	–	–	–	–	–
	multi instance (activities)	•	•	•	•	•	•	–	–	–	–	–
verification	option to compl.	–	•	–	–	•	•	–	–	•	–	•
	proper compl.	–	–	–	–	•	•	–	–	•	–	•
	no dead activity	–	–	–	•	–	•	–	•	•	•	•
	safety	–	–	–	–	–	–	–	•	•	–	•
	collaboration soundness	–	–	–	–	–	–	–	•	–	–	•
	msg relaxed soundness	–	–	–	–	–	–	–	–	–	–	•
	undelivered msg	–	–	–	–	–	–	–	•	–	•	•
	general-purpose	•	•	•	•	•	•	–	–	•	–	•
	communication models	–	–	–	–	–	–	–	–	–	–	•

4   Related Work

The formalization of the BPMN execution semantics, and on a wider scale the formal study of business processes, is a very active field of research. We here focus on recent work that provides tool support for the verification of collaboration diagrams and communication features in BPMN [7–10,14,16,20]. We add [11] due to its role as a seminal paper and [21,22] as recent representatives for the formal model they use. Table 4 gives a synthetic presentation of a comparison between these proposals and ours.

Some works are based on transformations, while others provide a direct semantics. The former rely on an intermediary model, while the later have the benefit to provide a direct link between BPMN constructs and the verification formalism. Our work is in this line. Further, the choice of FOL lets one implement the semantics in different tools, *e.g.*, TLA$^+$ as here or SMT solvers.

As far as the BPMN coverage criteria is concerned, we can observe that we are among the approaches with a high coverage. To make verification tractable, we have abstracted from the data and the multi-instance constructs, that are often related to data. Works taking data into account in verification either require to bound domains or operate on the basis of configurations (a state and a substitution from variables to closed terms). The former is still subject to state-space explosion, while the later is closer to animation than to full-fledged verification, and makes it impossible to verify a model for any possible initial value of the data. A perspective of our work is to rely on symbolic techniques instead [19].

The work in [9] provides a very rich formal semantics with animation capacities but does not enable verification in the large. Most of the work, still, support the verification of BP correctness properties or, at least, all-purpose formal properties (reachability, deadlock). The use of FOL to define the semantics, and its implementation in TLA$^+$, made it possible for us to implement quite easily these correctness checks as temporal logic properties to be checked against the model.

5   Conclusion and Future Work

In this work we have proposed a formalization of a subset of the BPMN execution semantics. It supports interaction and is parametric with reference to the properties of the communication between participants. We have seen in Table 3 that these properties can have an effect on the satisfaction of correctness properties by the collaboration model. Communication-parametric verification techniques for BPMN are therefore helpful when it comes to use this standard in contexts such as the IoT [4,18] where communication may vary. Our proposal is equipped with open source tools that are freely available and automatically perform the transformations and verification steps. A direct perspective of this work is the integration of our proposal as a plug-in of a platform for business processes that goes beyond modeling, namely ProM [2].

An on-going work is to replace the network theories that specify the communication model with a more general and versatile solution based on a communication framework we have developed [6]. This framework allows a large variety of configurations for the communication model, including which ordering policies are to be applied per participant, per couples of communicating participants, using priorities, or bounds on the number of messages in transit.

Some BPMN features that play a role in full-fledged executable collaboration have been discarded, in a first step, when selecting a relevant BPMN subset. This is the case of the support for data and the multi-instances activity, that are supported for example in [9] to provide the business process designers with model animation. However, to keep verification tractable, we had to abstract from these features. Our main perspective goes in this direction, using techniques from symbolic execution and symbolic transition systems [19] while keeping a direct semantics, *i.e.*, relatable to the parts of the BPMN informal semantics.

References

1. Business Process Modeling Notation. http://www.omg.org/spec/BPMN/2.0.2/
2. ProM Framework. http://www.processmining.org/prom
3. fbpmn repository. https://github.com/pascalpoizat/fbpmn, v0.3.0 (c389b6d)
4. Casati, F., et al.: Towards business processes orchestrating the physical enterprise with wireless sensor networks. In: Proceedings of ICSE (2012)
5. Chevrou, F., Hurault, A., Quéinnec, P.: On the diversity of asynchronous communication. Form. Asp. Comput. **28**(5), 847–879 (2016)
6. Chevrou, F., Hurault, A., Quéinnec, P.: A Modular Framework for Verifying Versatile Distributed Systems. Journal of Logical and Algebraic Methods in Programming (to appear)
7. Corradini, F., et al.: A classification of BPMN collaborations based on safeness and soundness notions. In: Proceedings of EXPRESS/SOS (2018)
8. Corradini, F., et al.: A formal approach to modeling and verification of business process collaborations. Sci. Comput. Program. **166**, 35–70 (2018)
9. Corradini, F., Muzi, C., Re, B., Rossi, L., Tiezzi, F.: Animating multiple instances in BPMN collaborations: from formal semantics to tool support. In: Weske, M., Montali, M., Weber, I., vom Brocke, J. (eds.) BPM 2018. LNCS, vol. 11080, pp. 83–101. Springer, Cham (2018). https://doi.org/10.1007/978-3-319-98648-7_6
10. Dechsupa, C., Vatanawood, W., Thongtak, A.: Transformation of the BPMN design model into a colored Petri net using the partitioning approach. IEEE Access **6**, 38421–38436 (2018)
11. Dijkman, R.M., Dumas, M., Ouyang, C.: Semantics and analysis of business process models in BPMN. Inf. Softw. Technol. **50**(12), 1281–1294 (2008)
12. Fahland, D., et al.: Instantaneous soundness checking of industrial business process models. In: Dayal, U., Eder, J., Koehler, J., Reijers, H.A. (eds.) BPM 2009. LNCS, vol. 5701, pp. 278–293. Springer, Heidelberg (2009). https://doi.org/10.1007/978-3-642-03848-8_19
13. Houhou, S., et al.: A first-order logic semantics for communication-parametric BPMN collaborations (extended version). http://pardi.enseeiht.fr/BPM19
14. Kheldoun, A., Barkaoui, K., Ioualalen, M.: Formal verification of complex business processes based on high-level Petri nets. Inf. Sci. **385**, 39–54 (2017)
15. Krishna, A., Poizat, P., Salaün, G.: Checking business process evolution. Sci. Comput. Program. **170**, 1–26 (2019)
16. Lam, V.S.: A precise execution semantics for BPMN. Int. J. Comput. Sci. **39**(1), 20–33 (2012)

17. Lamport, L.: Specifying Systems: The TLA+ Language and Tools for Hardware and Software Engineers. Addison Wesley, Boston (2002)
18. Meyer, S., Ruppen, A., Hilty, L.: The things of the internet of things in BPMN. In: Persson, A., Stirna, J. (eds.) CAiSE 2015. LNBIP, vol. 215, pp. 285–297. Springer, Cham (2015). https://doi.org/10.1007/978-3-319-19243-7_27
19. Nguyen, H.N., Poizat, P., Zaïdi, F.: A symbolic framework for the conformance checking of value-passing choreographies. In: Liu, C., Ludwig, H., Toumani, F., Yu, Q. (eds.) ICSOC 2012. LNCS, vol. 7636, pp. 525–532. Springer, Heidelberg (2012). https://doi.org/10.1007/978-3-642-34321-6_36
20. Van Gorp, P., Dijkman, R.: A visual token-based formalization of BPMN 2.0 based on in-place transformations. Inf. Softw. Technol. **55**(2), 365–394 (2013)
21. Wong, P.Y., Gibbons, J.: Formalisations and applications of BPMN. Sci. Comput. Program. **76**(8), 633–650 (2011)
22. Ye, J., Sun, S., Song, W., Wen, L.: Formal semantics of BPMN process models using YAWL. In: Proceedings of IITA (2008)

Modeling and Enforcing Blockchain-Based Choreographies

Jan Ladleif[1(✉)], Mathias Weske[1], and Ingo Weber[2]

[1] Hasso Plattner Institute, University of Potsdam, Potsdam, Germany
{jan.ladleif,mathias.weske}@hpi.de
[2] Technische Universität Berlin, Berlin, Germany
ingo.weber@tu-berlin.de

Abstract. Distributed Ledger Technology (DLT) and blockchains in particular have been identified as promising foundations to realize inter-organizational business processes. Capabilities such as shared data and decision logic defined as smart contracts open up entirely new ways to implement process choreographies. However, current choreography modeling languages solely focus on direct interactions between organizations; they do not take into account the conceptually new features of blockchains, like shared data and smart contracts. To bridge the gap between choreography modeling and implementation, this paper critically analyzes the assumptions of choreography languages. We propose new language concepts specifically targeting blockchain capabilities, and we define their operational semantics. Our work is evaluated with a proof-of-concept implementation and an analysis of three real-world case studies from the private and the corporate sectors.

Keywords: Choreography · Blockchain · Interacting processes · BPMN

1 Introduction

Recent developments in blockchain technology promise to fundamentally impact various domains. Business Process Management (BPM) is no exception. It has been shown that decision management [4], model design [15] or process execution [6,16] can be facilitated using smart contracts, a type of user-defined program running on a blockchain system. Especially when mutually distrustful participants want to cooperate, the trustless architecture of blockchains unfolds its potential. This has made the blockchain a central piece of interest for inter-organizational processes, which can be modeled as choreographies. Issues such as enactment, enforcement and monitoring that have largely been solved for the intra-organizational case [18] could now be solved for choreographies as well [17].

A number of challenges towards that goal have been identified [9]. Most notably, there is no consensus on the level of abstraction required for the design of blockchain-based choreographies. Established and widely used standards like

© Springer Nature Switzerland AG 2019
T. Hildebrandt et al. (Eds.): BPM 2019, LNCS 11675, pp. 69–85, 2019.
https://doi.org/10.1007/978-3-030-26619-6_7

Business Process Model and Notation (BPMN) 2.0 collaboration diagrams are not well equipped to express choreographies in a succinct fashion. A more promising solution is provided by Business Process Model and Notation (BPMN) 2.0 choreography diagrams [13]. Abstracting from internal orchestration details, choreography diagrams represent business contracts on a purely interaction-centric level. As such, they are emerging as a prime contender for modeling processes in a way befitting the blockchain [9].

However, choreography diagrams are widely regarded to be of a purely descriptive nature. Lacking a central orchestrator, they also lack the executable character that model-driven process enactment approaches aim for. Further, they do not reflect important blockchain capabilities such as on-chain data storage, or shared logic. Local observability and vague ownership assumptions make it hard to properly represent a participant's responsibilities. These limitations are obstacles in establishing choreography diagrams as the standard for blockchain-based choreography design.

In this paper, we critically analyze and question the limitations and decisions in the BPMN 2.0 choreography standard against the possibilities given by blockchain technology. We provide suggestions to refine and extend the standard where suitable, so as to elevate choreography diagrams to be enforceable artifacts using execution semantics founded in blockchain technology. We developed a proof-of-concept implementation, and use it to test the expressiveness, practical feasibility, and a number of properties of our proposal.

The paper is structured as follows: We start by establishing the basic concepts of BPMN 2.0 choreography diagrams, how they pertain to the blockchain, and discuss prior work in Sect. 2. Our approach is introduced in Sect. 3. We evaluate and discuss our contribution in Sect. 4 before concluding in Sect. 5.

2   Background and Motivation

In this section, we will introduce the necessary background information in choreography modeling and how blockchain and smart contract technology ultimately motivates our approach. We will also give an overview of relevant related work on choreography modeling and enactment.

2.1   Choreography Modeling

BPMN 2.0 choreography diagrams model the interactions between two or more individual parties to reach a common business goal [13]. The interfaces and communication between the participants are in focus rather than the work done within them. In that sense, choreography diagrams represent business contracts specifying the expected behavior of each participant.

For the remainder of this paper, we will use the running example given in Fig. 1. The choreography models a part of the rental process for private residences, specifically the interactions around bond refund that follow the termination of a tenancy. A rental bond is a deposit of the tenant to cover any damage

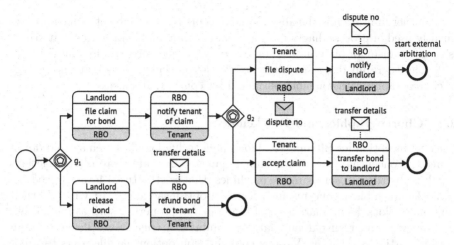

Fig. 1. A BPMN 2.0 choreography diagram of the interactions between a landlord, a tenant and a rental bond agency for rental bond handling after tenancy termination

to the property, and the process is modeled based on guidelines by the state of New South Wales, Australia.[1] A government service called Rental Bond Online (RBO) lodges the bond at the start of the tenancy. After the termination, the landlord may either release the bond and trigger its refund to the tenant, or file a claim for the bond in which case the tenant gets notified. The latter case is further subdivided: the tenant may file a dispute, which starts an external arbitration process; otherwise the bond is transferred to the landlord.

The example shows the main components of BPMN 2.0 choreography diagrams. Each choreography task (rounded rectangles) represents an interaction between an initiator and a respondent (shaded background). An initiating message exchange from the initiator to the respondent is always implied and may be refined by an attached envelope. A response message may be indicated with a shaded envelope. Choreography tasks are connected via sequence flows which incorporate gateways and events similar to BPMN 2.0 collaboration diagrams [13].

When modeling choreographies, two limiting criteria have to be kept in mind: ownership (who enforces which element) and observability (who knows what). Since "there is no central controller, responsible entity, or observer" [13, p. 23] in standard BPMN 2.0 choreography diagrams, all elements need to be owned by one specific participant. In the running example (see Fig. 1), for instance, the event-based gateways are implicitly owned by the landlord (g_1) and the tenant (g_2), respectively, based on a set of rules defined by the standard. The modeler must make sure that a participant responsible for a diagram element has sufficient information to correctly enforce it by being included in all relevant previous interactions.

---

[1] https://www.fairtrading.nsw.gov.au/housing-and-property/renting/rental-bonds-online, accessed 2019-03-14.

Another limitation is the absence of concepts like data objects which are frequently used in process diagrams. The standard pragmatically states that "there is no mechanism for maintaining any central process (choreography) data" [13, p. 319]. Choreography diagrams follow an interaction-centric paradigm, and storage of choreography data was not considered for conceptual reasons.

2.2   Choreographies and Blockchain

Since its inception for Bitcoin [12], blockchain technology has seen a rapid development. Conceptually, "a blockchain is [an append-only store of transactions which is distributed across many machines] that is structured into a linked list of blocks. Each block contains an ordered set of transactions." [19, Ch. 1] In their core, most blockchains share a set of fundamental properties such as immutability, integrity and transparency, largely eliminating trust issues between cooperating parties [19, Ch. 3]. Various configuration options enable users to tailor blockchains to their needs, e.g., incorporating access permissions or off-chain data storage. Second-generation blockchains like Ethereum expand on the core idea and cater for expressive smart contracts, which are deterministic "programs deployed as data in the blockchain ledger and executed in transactions on the blockchain." [19, Ch. 1] Since it is ledger data, smart contract code is immutable once deployed.

As such, a blockchain architecture may provide the crucial components needed to eventually facilitate secure and trustless inter-organizational process enactment. This is highlighted by Mendling et al. in their discussion of opportunities and challenges for BPM with blockchains [9]. They state that the "whole area of choreographies may be re-vitalized by [blockchain] technology." While BPMN 2.0 choreography diagrams have not found wide-spread industry adoption, Mendling et al. still consider them one of the promising approaches for designing inter-organizational business processes. The limitations in expressiveness regarding ownership and observability mentioned in the previous section still present a major obstacle, even though they can be mostly lifted when using a blockchain as a decentralized entity driving the choreography execution: In a sense, a choreography can be regarded as a smart contract itself. The smart contract may store and manipulate data, own decisions and their logic and keep track of the overall execution state. Interactions within the choreography become transactions. Observability broadens considerably as each participant has access to the whole distributed ledger of transactions attached to the choreography.

The aim of this paper is to tackle the challenges mentioned and extend and refine BPMN 2.0 choreography diagrams to these changes in assumptions. Models should be expressive enough to deduce interfaces for each participant and enforce the order of all message exchanges. It should be obvious which elements of the choreography and which data is stored and executed on the blockchain. The approach should not impose technical restrictions on the participants' internal orchestration processes and should not introduce additional trust to the interactions. On the other hand, the approach should reflect the set of capabilities common to second-generation blockchains, rather than specific implementations, to remain as platform-independent as possible. This strategy aims at minimizing barriers to the adoption of blockchain-based choreography diagrams.

2.3   Prior Work on Choreographies

Utilizing blockchains to monitor and enforce business processes is a relatively new development in BPM. Research has been focused on exploring whether blockchains can extend or even replace traditional Business Process Management Systems (BPMS). On a modeling basis, these approaches use interpretations of BPMN 2.0 process diagrams [16], collaboration diagrams [6] or other automata [15]. In the declarative space, contract formalizations [3] as well as Dynamic Condition Response (DCR) graphs [8] are employed. To the best of our knowledge, there have been no systematic efforts to adapt BPMN 2.0 choreography diagrams to suit the needs of blockchain-based process execution.

There has been some work on a more conceptual level. Weber et al. [17] discuss the general impact of blockchain on collaborative processes, such as conflict resolution, monitoring and auditing. They use choreography diagrams for their argumentation, but do not challenge the standard's underlying assumptions regarding ownership and observability. In this respect, this paper takes the next step towards using blockchains for choreography execution.

Establishing a shared understanding of data in choreographies has been the subject of previous work by Meyer et al. [10,11]. The authors extend BPMN 2.0 collaboration diagrams with an explicit data perspective, introducing the notion of a global data model which establishes the concrete structure of all message exchanges. Participants then use the global data model to implement or generate adapters to their local data model. Since Meyer et al. assume that there is no central management entity, messages remain transient and there is no shared choreography data, which makes this approach inapplicable to blockchains.

A different approach to collaborative process modeling for the blockchain is presented by López-Pintado et al. [7]. Their idea is that if participants share the same execution infrastructure, i.e., the blockchain, they may act as if they were located within the same organization. The choreography is thus modeled like an intra-organizational orchestration process which uses a traditional BPMS. There are no explicit choreography concepts such as message exchange. While this approach has the advantage of using modeling elements familiar to most process modelers, it is also prone to issues that sparked the development of choreography modeling in the first place, namely an insufficient level of abstraction.

Lastly, Breu et al. introduce the concept of living inter-organizational processes [1]. Taking into account developments in cloud infrastructure, such processes are enacted by multiple organizations sharing control and power. The authors identify perspectives of distribution of power, behavior, data and resources, but do not provide a concrete solution for modeling or enacting them. The extension proposed in this paper could be motivated as a concrete realization of living inter-organizational processes powered by the blockchain.

Table 1. Categories of modeling elements in blockchain-based choreography diagrams

Category	BPMN 2.0 model elements	Ownership	Status
Interaction	Choreography tasks with message flow	Participants	Adapted
Decomposition	Sub-choreographies, call choreographies	Smart contract	Adapted
Data	Data objects, data input, data output	Smart contract	Introduced
Logic	Script tasks	Smart contract	Introduced
Control flow	Sequence flow, gateways	Smart contract	Adapted
Events	Start, intermediate, and end events	Smart contract	Adapted

3   Blockchain-Based Choreographies

We propose an extension and refinement of BPMN 2.0 choreography diagrams with a specific focus on the capabilities of blockchain technology. In particular, blockchain allows us to store choreography data and evaluate logic in a shared environment that is not controlled by a single participant. This presents a major shift in the understanding of choreographies. Following the approach of the BPMN standard, we describe the intended semantics of our proposal textually.

3.1   Modeling Elements and Their Ownership

We avoided introducing entirely new modeling elements in the extensions. Instead, we opted to reuse as many familiar BPMN 2.0 concepts as possible to facilitate the adoption of the proposal. The proposal is backward-compatible: all valid choreography diagrams are still valid in our extended notation. Table 1 lists the six categories of modeling elements that we considered in this paper and whether they were changed. These include previously available elements and elements from other BPMN 2.0 diagrams, e.g., script tasks or data objects.

Ownership is a central issue in choreography diagrams. The owner of an element is responsible for all managerial tasks that need to be completed for triggering and enforcing that element in an actual execution. Whereas in standard choreography diagrams only participants could be owners, the smart contract now represents another entity capable of that. Most notably, only the interaction group contains elements that are owned by or require any input from participants, namely choreography tasks. All other elements are entirely managed by the smart contract, eliminating most of the confusion and ambiguities regarding element ownership present in the standard (see Sect. 2.1).

Figure 2 shows an example of a blockchain-based choreography diagram modeled using our approach. It extends the running example from Sect. 2.1 with additional elements covering the whole duration of the tenancy. While the syntax looks very similar to the diagram shown before, there are fundamental differences. For example, the event-based gateway e_2 is followed by two choreography tasks that can be initiated by a tenant who was not involved in the task immediately preceding the gateway. In standard choreographies, this would not be

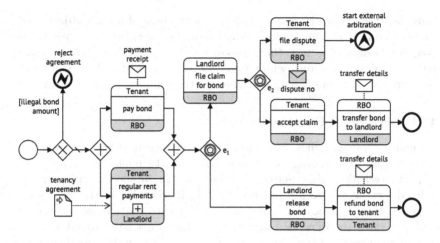

Fig. 2. Extended choreography for the interactions between a landlord, a tenant and an online rental bond agency during the entire duration of a tenancy

realizable because of observability issues. Furthermore, the 'regular rent payments' sub-choreography does not have an initiating participant. Instead, it is implicitly owned by the smart contract, which is not displayed in a band but manages the sub-choreography. These and other changes will be explained in the following sections.

3.2   Shared Data Model and Storage

Introducing shared data in choreographies comes with multiple challenges. For one, a shared data model is essential [11]. Participants need to have a common understanding of which data is stored and how it is mapped to properly connect their local data model and assess security and privacy concerns. This means that all data in the model, including messages, needs to be refined with concrete data structures provided by the modeler. Implementations of blockchain-based choreographies may require specific data mappings based on their underlying technology. Secondly, data needs to be suitably represented in the model itself, in our case with messages and data objects. The union of all messages and data objects with their associated structures constitutes the shared data model.

Messages are a peculiar instance of data in that they used to be an inherently transient concept. Message flows were defined as a bilateral interaction between two participants, with no provision to store or share specific message content. This situation changes in blockchain-based choreographies as message exchanges become transactions, which are automatically logged and permanently saved in the blockchain. All participants can observe these transactions, and interpret the payload according to the shared message structure.

In addition to messages, we chose to adopt the notion of data objects as specified for BPMN 2.0 process diagrams. Data objects can be regarded as variables in a concrete choreography instance, and their values are exclusively stored within the smart contract. Figure 2 shows an example of a data object used to store the details of a tenancy agreement. The main conceptual difference between messages and data objects is that messages are owned and triggered by participants through transactions, while data objects are owned and managed by the smart contract. The blockchain guarantees a consistent view on all data.

3.3 Observability Constraints

In standard choreographies, observability as introduced in Sect. 2.1 was purely local and based on message exchanges. Each participant could only see the details of interactions they were directly involved in, implicitly capturing a very restricted view of the overall process state. In blockchain-based choreographies this assumption does not hold true anymore as each participant has complete visibility of the state. In certain scenarios, this might not be a satisfying solution. For example, some messages and data objects might contain sensitive information that should only be visible to a subset of participants.

We propose using sub-choreographies and call choreographies as a means of decomposition and to restrict observability. As they have similar semantics, we will focus on the former in the following. Every level of decomposition opens a new scope, and all the participants referenced by the sub-choreography through its bands are part of it. This allows modelers to partition a choreography into different areas with different sets of participants. Data objects can be passed to and from sub-choreographies with data inputs and data outputs, special kinds of data objects marked with a stroked and filled arrow, respectively.

Figure 2 shows an example: the tenancy agreement data input is passed to the 'regular rent payments' sub-choreography using a dotted data association. Because RBO is not attached to the sub-choreography, they are not able to participate in its execution. Neither can they observe its current state, nor can they inspect the content of messages or data objects contained in it. The instantiation of the sub-choreography and management of data inputs and outputs is handled by the smart contract. The implementation of observability constraints depends on the concrete blockchain chosen, and is discussed further in Sect. 4.3.

3.4 Control Flow and Embedded Logic

The handling of control flow and of gateways in particular presents a major shift from the standard. As mentioned above, there is no need to have overlapping sets of participants in tasks anymore; this also applies to pairs of tasks with a gateway between one another. In our approach, gateways are not manifested through the internal orchestrations of one or more controlling participants, but through the smart contract directly. The strict sequencing rules in the standard (ensuring that involved participants have a common knowledge of all relevant data and the choreography state) are no longer needed given the shared data storage and global observability. Instead, *data-based exclusive gateways* are transparently evaluated using formal condition expressions attached to the model. For *event-based gateways*, the smart contract ensures that only one outgoing sequence flow is activated. It also keeps track of *parallel* execution branches and enforces correct join behavior. The execution semantics of control flow logic elements will be discussed in Sect. 3.5.

These mechanisms are based on one of the main novelties of smart contracts, the decentralized execution of shared logic in the form of smart contract code. The shared logic is used to enforce and manage all elements owned by the smart contract. Modelers may also directly exploit these capabilities in two ways: through condition expressions attached to data-based exclusive gateways as mentioned above, and script tasks. Both script tasks and conditions can be embedded in our extended choreography diagrams by refining the respective elements with concrete code which can be evaluated in the smart contract. They may access all data that is available in the scope at the time of encountering the specific element. For example, the conditions of the exclusive data-based gateway in Fig. 2 may only access the values of the 'tenancy agreement' data object; no other data object or message exists at this point.

3.5 Transaction-Driven Semantics

When choreography diagrams were initially designed, they were intended to be primarily descriptive, hence no specific execution semantics were defined. Instead, a mapping to equivalent collaboration diagrams was given that distributes power and trust to participants based on the implicit ownership of elements (see Sect. 2.1). That definition-by-mapping fails for blockchain-based choreographies as there is no way to model shared data or logic in collaboration diagrams.

For that reason, we introduce the notion of transaction-driven semantics for blockchain-based choreographies. Because of the nature of current blockchain technology, smart contracts are never invoked outside the context of a transaction. The smart contract can only advance the state of a choreography within a transaction from some participant or the call of another smart contract, never just by itself. In the context of enacting a choreography, there are two types of

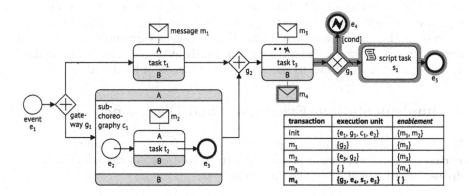

Fig. 3. Execution units of a sample blockchain-based choreography

transactions: one transaction for initiating the smart contract, and one for each message exchange. We use these transactions to bundle choreography elements into so-called execution units, which contain all elements that may possibly be executed within the respective transaction. The extent of an execution unit is delimited by elements necessitating another transaction, i.e., choreography tasks.

Figure 3 shows an example for a simple blockchain-based choreography with all execution units. For instance, the execution unit of the transaction belonging to message exchange m_4 is $\{g_3, e_4, s_1, e_5\}$ (see the shaded highlights). This means that when participant B sends message m_4, g_3 is executed by evaluating the outgoing sequence flows' conditions. If cond evaluates to true, the end event e_4 is executed. Otherwise, the script task s_1 is executed, followed by e_5. The order of evaluation and execution is based on the constraints defined by sequence flow. The example also illustrates that not all elements in the execution units necessarily have to be executed. Rather, the execution unit contains all elements that could possibly be executed as a part of that transaction subject to sequence flow. Elements can be in multiple execution units, e.g., when the order of the transactions determines which one will be able to execute a parallel join gateway (see m_1 and m_2 in the example).

Naturally, there is an ordering to messages. Message m_3 will only be accepted after both m_1 and m_2 have been sent. We express this with the notion of enablement which can be visualized as a kind of token system. Within a transaction, tokens are consumed and propagated through the model based on the execution units. A message attached to a task t is only enabled and can be sent when t is in possession of a token and, for response messages, the initiating message has been sent. A transaction may consume multiple tokens, for example if it directly follows an event-based gateway. In that case, the transaction also consumes the tokens of all the other "competing" elements following the gateway. Race conditions are automatically resolved by the blockchain's ordering consensus: blocks and the transactions they contain are totally ordered. Figure 3 shows the potential enablement after each transaction, as per the sequence flow.

These semantics have some direct conceptual consequences. The initiating and response message of a choreography task do not form an atomic unit anymore as postulated in the BPMN 2.0 standard. Instead, both messages constitute separate transactions, with separate execution units. Further, data objects will never delay the execution of an element. Transactions are executed in an isolated environment in which blockchain data is instantly available, while external data sources cannot be used due to the closed-world nature of blockchain.

4   Implementation, Evaluation, and Discussion

We show the feasibility of our approach by a proof-of-concept implementation. Furthermore, we implement and analyze three concrete use cases and critically discuss our proposed solution's properties.

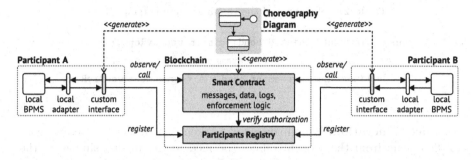

Fig. 4. Architecture for executing choreographies as smart contracts (based on [17])

4.1 Proof-Of-Concept Implementation

The proof-of-concept implements our approach for the Ethereum blockchain and smart contracts written in the Solidity language.

Execution Architecture. One of the requirements for our choreography modeling approach was to not impose any restrictions on the internal software landscape of any of the participants. The architecture of the proof-of-concept as shown in Fig. 4 reflects this goal, and is generally based on the layout proposed by Weber et al. [17]. The main artifact is the choreography model. It is used to generate several components, most prominently the smart contract encapsulating the enforcement logic and storing messages, data and logs. Additionally, a custom interface component can be deduced for each participant. This interface component hides the complexity of the blockchain and can connect to local adapters, which in turn communicate with the local BPMS. Another smart contract is used as a registry for the participants. Before executing the choreography, participants register for specific roles with their addresses. The choreography smart contract can then authorize actions which are to be taken by certain roles only.

Refinement. The choreography models need to be expressive enough to generate concrete smart contract code. BPMN 2.0 already provides model attributes to refine certain model elements to an implementation level, namely the concept of item definitions attached to messages and data objects, scripts attached to script tasks, as well as formal expressions attached to sequence flows. We use these attributes to specify conditions and data structures within the model.

For the proof-of-concept, data structures are expected to be a flat list of variables using Solidity data types. Expressions must be given as Solidity expressions evaluating to a boolean value. Script tasks must contain a valid block of Solidity code. A snippet of the refinement for the running example (see Fig. 2) is given in Table 2. For example, the tenancy agreement contains the bond amount as well as the weekly rent, and the bond may only be at most four times the weekly rent (as per official guidelines in New South Wales, Australia).

Table 2. Refinement of the running example (snippet)

Tenancy agreement	`uint16 bond; uint16 weeklyRent;`
Transfer details	`int32 timestamp; uint32 transferID;`
[illegal bond amount]	`agreement_bond > 4 * agreement_weeklyRent`

Contract Generation. We implemented a token system which generates control flow logic from the sequence flows specified in the model, similar to the Petri net-approach presented by García-Bañuelos et al. [2]. Each sequence flow can potentially possess a token that is used to enable the target element. Tokens are propagated through the model whenever a valid transaction arrives (initially deploying/starting the choreography or sending a message). The smart contract propagates the tokens as far as possible until a participant-owned element is encountered, which emulates the execution units described in Sect. 3.5.

```
1  pragma solidity ^0.4.23;
2  interface Choreography { [...]
3      function start() external;
4      function sendRequest(uint8 task, bytes message) external;
5      function sendResponse(uint8 task, bytes message) external;
6  }
```

Listing 1. Common interface (excerpt) of all choreography smart contracts

We opted for a minimal common interface shared by all choreography contracts partly shown in Listing 1. The **start** function executes the initial token propagation from the start events. **sendRequest** and **sendResponse** correspond to the request and response messages of specific tasks, respectively. Tasks are assigned an ID and all message data is encoded in a single byte array. This simple interface facilitates inter-contract communication, e.g., between sub-choreographies and their parents. It also enables the use of generic oracles sending data through requests without requiring specific code for each choreography.

4.2   Case Studies

We have modeled, executed, and analyzed three case studies that cover all the elements discussed in this paper. Apart from the rental bond example already discussed in the course of this paper we discuss two corporate case studies.

The **grain delivery** case study describes the interactions between a producer and a seller of grain, including payment using an escrow agent and analysis of the grain by a silo and laboratory. The general use-case is modeled after an example by AgriDigital[2] enriched with legal details obtained from Grain Trade Australia (GTA). A distinctive feature of this choreography is that script tasks are used to communicate with an external smart contract representing the grain

---

[2] https://www.agridigital.io/, accessed 2019-03-11.

Table 3. Number of elements in each use case

Element	Rental agreement	Grain delivery	Interline agreement
Roles	3	5	2
Choreography tasks	7	9	11
Sub/call choreographies	1/0	1/3	0/2
Data objects	1	9	5
Script tasks	0	6	4
Gateways	5	7	12
Events	5	13	11

title, allowing secure transfer of titles. In case of conflicts, an external arbitration entity is assigned. This shows how our approach can be integrated with other smart contracts running on the same blockchain, and can be used to implement applications that go beyond what can be achieved with choreography models alone. For example, external oracles could be introduced using this technique.

The **bilateral interline traffic agreement** case study describes a contract between two airlines when booking passengers for flights with the other airline, e.g., in case of a cancellation. Prices are tallied and a monthly settlement is performed. The use case is modeled after guidelines of the International Air Transport Association (IATA) and is an example for a long-running contract which can only be canceled via mutual agreement. The interline agreement case study especially showcases the degree of parallelism that can be achieved. Multiple branches of the choreography are active at the same time, sharing data through data objects. The case study also showcases an example of timing constraints in that the gap between two settlements needs to be at least 30 days.

The case studies and derived artifacts can be found in an online appendix.[3] All examples were fully modeled, refined and successfully executed with our proof-of-concept implementation. Table 3 shows the numbers of elements in the case studies as indicators of their complexity. We can represent sophisticated processes and sequences with relatively few elements, which supports the claim

Table 4. Cost metrics of a sample trace for each case study

Case study	Factory deployment	Root deployment	Transactions		
			Count	Avg. cost	
Rental agreement	1,195,765 gas	2,022,705 gas	8	151,794 gas	(64% deploym.)
Grain delivery	4,933,814 gas	2,191,847 gas	15	278,368 gas	(78% deploym.)
Interline agreement	2,825,324 gas	2,093,638 gas	13	368,792 gas	(80% deploym.)

---

[3] https://github.com/jan-ladleif/bpm19-blockchain-based-choreographies.

that choreography diagrams are a suitable means of modeling diverse inter-organizational processes. Also, the newly introduced elements such as script tasks and data objects are heavily used and fit well into the overall diagram structure.

Furthermore, we investigated the cost of our approach. Cost in Ethereum is measured in gas, which is determined based on the computational complexity and memory intensity of a transaction. Table 4 shows the preliminary results for one sample trace of each case study (more detailed data is available in the online appendix). There are three relevant stages. In a first stage, factory contracts for sub and call choreographies are deployed. This has to be done once and factories can be reused for multiple instances. Second, the root contract and a participant registry contract need to be deployed for each instance of the choreography. Third, based on the concrete conversation, a variable number of transactions, i.e., initializations and message exchanges, are performed. These transactions potentially involve deploying new contract instances of sub or call choreographies, which largely dominates the cost of the average transaction (see the share in Table 4). As yet, there are no provisions to evenly distribute costs between participants. Presumably, realizations of blockchain-based choreographies in production would rely on permissioned blockchains for their access controls. For those types of blockchains, transaction cost is more relevant regarding throughput and usually not directly equated to fiat currency.

4.3 Discussion

Our proof-of-concept implementation shows the feasibility of our approach in practice, while the case studies show its conceptual expressiveness. While there still is space for further extensions and a broader empirical analysis of the impact of blockchain-based choreography modeling, we present a first step into the direction laid out by Mendling et al. [9].

Our approach was partly motivated by previous work posing challenges in inter-organizational process modeling. Breu et al. postulate four challenges: flexibility, correctness, traceability and scalability [1]. Our blockchain-based solution performs well regarding correctness and traceability. The smart contract already provides runtime verification with an explicit data perspective, and known static verification techniques could be applied to our extended choreography diagrams. The blockchain's log makes choreography executions traceable and auditable.

Flexibility is not the strong suit of the proposed approach. In general, blockchains focus on immutable storage and dynamically changing or evolving smart contracts do not fit well into that paradigm. For business contracts, however, this might even be the desired behavior as a deal is usually fixed once negotiated. Explicit upgrade mechanisms may technically still be incorporated in smart contracts, though, and general architectural patterns and paradigms could be adapted to the specifics of choreographies [19]. Regarding scalability, our solution is dependent on the underlying blockchain's performance.

Not all elements are currently supported by our implementation or blockchains in general. For example, the monthly settlement in the interline agreement case study cannot be triggered by the smart contract itself through timer events due to current limitations in the underlying technology. Until that changes, we have to rely on a workaround where either of the airlines requests payment, with the smart contract checking the time conditions when that occurs. It also became apparent that choreography models cannot capture all the intricacies of a contractual agreement, signified by the external arbitration and litigation pattern used in the rental agreement as well as the grain delivery case studies. The degree to which business contracts can be formalized with smart contracts is a topic of ongoing discussion [5]. Given that smart contracts and legal contracts are different types of "things" [14], this is unlikely to be fully resolvable.

Privacy and confidentiality pose further challenges. While the transparency of a blockchain is a requirement for some use cases, and a feature for others, many organizations would hesitate to give up confidentiality of their business contracts and associated data. While we model observability constraints using sub and call choreographies, the proof-of-concept implementation on Ethereum cannot yet realize these restrictions. Techniques like symmetric encryption or zero-knowledge proofs may be incorporated for trade-offs in cost, transparency or performance. Other blockchain platforms, like Quorum or Hyperledger Fabric, have native support for confidentiality. They provide private contracts which could be used to shield instances of sub-choreographies from certain participants as specified in the model. At a loss of trustlessness, such permissioned blockchains might be a promising solution to these issues.

Lastly, in all of the case studies, payments between participants need to be tracked. This is done through escrow agents (grain delivery), transfer receipts (rental agreement) or simple counting (interline agreement). Payments in cryptocurrencies are an inherent capability of blockchains. As blockchain-based choreographies are realized using smart contracts, they could technically hold cryptocurrency as well. As suggested by Weber et al., the choreography itself could be the escrow account, cutting out middlemen and allowing payment processing directly in the choreography [17]. However, Weber et al. handled this by custom parameter extensions. Ideally, the concept should be implemented with dedicated modeling elements and techniques to prevent locking or losing funds.

5   Conclusion

In this paper, we critically assessed capabilities and limitations of current choreography modeling approaches. We discussed how these limitations restrict the expressiveness of choreographies, and how they can be lifted using blockchain technology. To do so, we gave a backward-compatible extension and refinement of BPMN 2.0 choreography diagrams and provided operational semantics based on blockchain concepts. We implemented a proof of concept based on the Ethereum blockchain and Solidity smart contracts to show the practical feasibility of our approach. Three case studies allowed us to examine different aspects of the approach, while highlighting its versatility and remaining limitations. We see this paper as an initial step towards re-vitalizing the area of choreography modeling and adapting for new technologies such as blockchain.

In future work, we plan to address the current limitations, including model elements for payments and escrow, and how to implement observability constraints. Preliminary investigations using Quorum showed that the latter is not a straightforward task, and deserves significant additional attention.

References

1. Breu, R., et al.: Towards living inter-organizational processes. In: IEEE Conference on Business Informatics (CBI) (2013)
2. García-Bañuelos, L., Ponomarev, A., Dumas, M., Weber, I.: Optimized execution of business processes on blockchain. In: Carmona, J., Engels, G., Kumar, A. (eds.) BPM 2017. LNCS, vol. 10445, pp. 130–146. Springer, Cham (2017). https://doi. org/10.1007/978-3-319-65000-5_8
3. Governatori, G., Idelberger, F., Milosevic, Z., Riveret, R., Sartor, G., Xu, X.: On legal contracts, imperative and declarative smart contracts, and blockchain systems. Artif. Intell. Law **26**(4), 377–409 (2018). https://doi.org/10.1007/s10506-018-9223-3. ISSN 1572-8382
4. Haarmann, S., Batoulis, K., Nikaj, A., Weske, M.: DMN decision execution on the ethereum blockchain. In: Krogstie, J., Reijers, H.A. (eds.) CAiSE 2018. LNCS, vol. 10816, pp. 327–341. Springer, Cham (2018). https://doi.org/10.1007/978-3-319-91563-0_20
5. Kõlvart, M., Poola, M., Rull, A.: Smart contracts. In: Kerikmäe, T., Rull, A. (eds.) The Future of Law and eTechnologies, pp. 133–147. Springer, Cham (2016). https://doi.org/10.1007/978-3-319-26896-5_7
6. López-Pintado, O., García-Bañuelos, L., Dumas, M., Weber, I.: Caterpillar: a blockchain-based business process management system. In: International Conference on Business Process Management (BPM), Demo Track (2017)
7. López-Pintado, O., García-Bañuelos, L., Dumas, M., Weber, I., Ponomarev, A.: Caterpillar: a business process execution engine on the Ethereum blockchain. CoRR abs/1808.03517 (2018)
8. Madsen, M.F., Gaub, M., Høgnason, T., Kirkbro, M.E., Slaats, T., Debois, S.: Collaboration among adversaries: distributed workflow execution on a blockchain. In: Symposium on Foundations and Applications of Blockchain (2018)
9. Mendling, J., Weber, I., et al.: Blockchains for business process management - challenges and opportunities. ACM Trans. Manag. Inf. Syst. (TMIS) **9**(1), 41–416 (2018). https://doi.org/10.1145/3183367. ISSN 2158-656X
10. Meyer, A., Pufahl, L., Batoulis, K., Fahland, D., Weske, M.: Automating data exchange in process choreographies. Inf. Sys. **53**, 296–329 (2015)
11. Meyer, A., et al.: Data perspective in process choreographies: modeling and execution. Technical report BPM-13-29, BPMcenter.org (2013)
12. Nakamoto, S.: Bitcoin: a peer-to-peer electronic cash system (2008)
13. OMG: Business Process Model and Notation (BPMN), Version 2.0.2, December 2013. http://www.omg.org/spec/BPMN/2.0.2/
14. Staples, M., et al.: Risks and opportunities for systems using blockchain and smart contracts. Technical report, Data61 (CSIRO) (2017)
15. Sturm, C., Szalanczi, J., Schönig, S., Jablonski, S.: A lean architecture for blockchain based decentralized process execution. In: Daniel, F., Sheng, Q.Z., Motahari, H. (eds.) BPM 2018. LNBIP, vol. 342, pp. 361–373. Springer, Cham (2019). https://doi.org/10.1007/978-3-030-11641-5_29

16. Tran, A.B., Lu, Q., Weber, I.: Lorikeet: a model-driven engineering tool for blockchain-based business process execution and asset management. In: International Conference on Business Process Management (BPM), Demo Track (2018)
17. Weber, I., Xu, X., Riveret, R., Governatori, G., Ponomarev, A., Mendling, J.: Untrusted business process monitoring and execution using blockchain. In: La Rosa, M., Loos, P., Pastor, O. (eds.) BPM 2016. LNCS, vol. 9850, pp. 329–347. Springer, Cham (2016). https://doi.org/10.1007/978-3-319-45348-4_19
18. Weske, M.: Business Process Management, 2nd edn. Springer, Heidelberg (2012). https://doi.org/10.1007/978-3-642-28616-2
19. Xu, X., Weber, I., Staples, M.: Architecture for Blockchain Applications. Springer, Cham (2019). https://doi.org/10.1007/978-3-030-03035-3

Formal Reasoning on Natural Language Descriptions of Processes

Josep Sànchez-Ferreres[1]([⊠]), Andrea Burattin[2], Josep Carmona[1], Marco Montali[3], and Lluís Padró[1]

[1] Universitat Politècnica de Catalunya, Barcelona, Spain
{jsanchezf,jcarmona,padro}@cs.upc.edu
[2] Technical University of Denmark, Kongens Lyngby, Denmark
andbur@dtu.dk
[3] Free University of Bozen-Bolzano, Bolzano, Italy
montali@inf.unibz.it

Abstract. The existence of unstructured information that describes processes represents a challenge in organizations, mainly because this data cannot be directly referred into process-aware ecosystems due to ambiguities. Still, this information is important, since it encompasses aspects of a process that are left out when formalizing it on a particular modelling notation. This paper picks up this challenge and faces the problem of ambiguities by acknowledging its existence and mitigating it. Specifically, we propose a framework to partially automate the elicitation of a formal representation of a textual process description, via text annotation techniques on top of natural language processing. The result is the ATDP language, whose syntax and semantics are described in this paper. ATDP allows to explicitly cope with several interpretations of the same textual description of a process model. Moreover, we link the ATDP language to a formal reasoning engine and show several use cases. A prototype tool enabling the complete methodology has been implemented, and several examples using the tool are provided.

1 Introduction

Organizing business processes in an efficient and effective manner is the overarching objective of *Business Process Management* (BPM). Classically, BPM has been mainly concerned with the quantitative analysis of key performance dimensions such as time, cost, quality, and flexibility [10] without considering in depth the analysis of textual data that talks about processes.

Hence, textual descriptions of processes in organizations are a vast and rather unexploited resource. Not neglecting the information that is present in natural language texts in a organization brings opportunities to complement or correct process information in conceptual models. In spite of this, only very recently *Natural Language Processing* (NLP)-based analysis has been proposed in the BPM context, as reported in [12,14,15,22].

© Springer Nature Switzerland AG 2019
T. Hildebrandt et al. (Eds.): BPM 2019, LNCS 11675, pp. 86–101, 2019.
https://doi.org/10.1007/978-3-030-26619-6_8

This paper is a first step towards the challenge of unleashing formal reasoning on top of textual descriptions of processes. By relying on *textual annotations*, we propose ATDP, a multi-perspective language that can be connected to a reasoner so that a formal analysis is possible. From a raw textual description, annotations can be introduced manually, or selected from those inferred by NLP analysis (e.g., from libraries like [16]), thus alleviating considerably the annotation effort. Remarkably, our perspective differs from the usual trend in conceptual modelling, i.e., ATDP specifications can contain several interpretations, so ambiguity is not forced to be ruled out when modelling, for those cases when the process is under-specified, or when several interpretations are equally valid.

We formalize ATDP, and describe its semantics using linear temporal logic (LTL), with relations defined at two different levels, thanks to the notion of *scopes*. Then we show how to cast reasoning on such a specification as a model checking instance, and provide use cases for BPM, such as model consistency, compliance checking and conformance checking. Notably, such reasoning tasks can be carried out by adopting the standard infinite-trace semantics of LTL, or by considering instead finite traces only, in line with the semantics adopted in declarative process modeling notations like Declare [17]. Finally, a tool to convert ATDP specifications into a model checking instance is reported.

The paper is organized as follows: in the next section we provide the work related to the contributions of this paper. Then Sect. 3 contains the preliminaries needed for the understanding of the paper content. Section 4 describes a methodology to use ATDP in organizations. In Sect. 5 we provide intuition, syntax and semantics behind the ATDP language. Then in Sect. 6 it is shown how reasoning on ATDP specification can be done through model checking and finally Sect. 7 concludes the paper.

2 Related Work

In order to automatically reason over a natural language process description, it is necessary to construct a formal representation of the actual process. Such generation of a formal process model starting from a natural language description of a process has been investigated from several angles in the literature. We can project these techniques into a spectrum of support possibilities to automation: from fully manual to automatic.

The first available option consists in converting a textual description into a process model by manually modeling the process. This approach, widely discussed (e.g., [9,10]), has been thoroughly studied also from a psychological point of view, in order to understand which are the challenges involved in such process of process modeling [4,18]. These techniques, however, do not provide any automatic support and the possibility for automatic reasoning is completely depending on the result of the manual modeling. Therefore, ambiguities in the textual description are subjectively resolved.

On the opposite side of the spectrum, there are approaches that autonomously convert a textual description of a process model into a formal representation [13]. Such representation can be a final process model (e.g., as BPMN) [7] and, in this case, it might be possible to automatically extract information. The limit of these techniques, however, is that they need to resolve ambiguities in the textual description, resulting in "hard-coded" interpretations.

In the middle of the spectrum, we have approaches that automatically process the natural language text but they generate an intermediate artifact, useful to support the manual modeling by providing intermediate diagnostics [8,20]. The problem of having a single interpretation for ambiguities is a bit mitigated in this case since a human modeler is still in charge of the actual modeling. However, it is important to note that the system is biasing the modeler towards a single interpretation.

The approach presented in this paper drops the assumption of resolving all ambiguities in natural language texts. Therefore, if the text is clear and no ambiguities are manifested, then the precise process can be modeled. However, if this is not the case, instead of selecting one possible ambiguity resolution, our solution copes with the presence of several interpretations for the same textual description.

3   A Recap on Linear Temporal Logics

In this paper, we use Linear Temporal Logic (LTL) [19] to define the semantics of the ATDP language. In particular, we use the standard interpretation of temporal logic formulae over *infinite traces*.

LTL formulae are built from a set $\mathcal{P}$ of propositional symbols and are closed under the boolean connectives, the unary temporal operator O (*next-time*) and the binary temporal operator U (*until*):

$$\varphi ::= a \mid \neg\varphi \mid \varphi_1 \wedge \varphi_2 \mid O\varphi \mid \varphi_1 \, U \, \varphi_2 \text{ with } a \in \mathcal{P}$$

Intuitively, $O\varphi$ says that φ holds at the *next* instant, $\varphi_1 \, U \, \varphi_2$ says that at some future instant φ_2 will hold and *until* that point φ_1 always holds. Common abbreviations used in LTL include the ones listed below:

- Standard boolean abbreviations, such as $\top$, $\bot$, $\vee$, $\rightarrow$.
- $\Diamond\varphi = \top \, U \, \varphi$ says that φ will *eventually* hold at some future instant.
- $\Box\varphi = \neg\Diamond\neg\varphi$ says that from the current instant φ will *always* hold.
- $\varphi_1 \, W \, \varphi_2 = (\varphi_1 \, U \, \varphi_2 \vee \Box\varphi_1)$ is interpreted as a *weak until*, and means that either φ_1 holds until φ_2 or forever.

Recall that the same syntax can also be used to construct formulae of LTL interpreted over *finite traces* [6]. Later on in the paper we show how our approach can also accommodate this interpretation. Recall however that the intended meaning of an LTL formula may radically change when moving from infinite to finite traces [5].

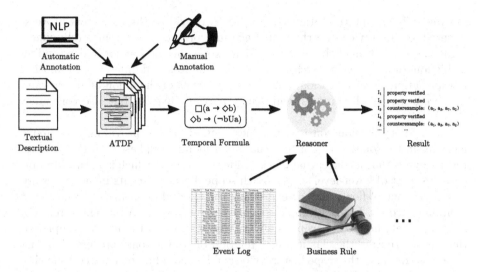

Fig. 1. Annotation framework overview

4 A Framework for Semantic Reasoning of Natural Language Descriptions of Processes

We briefly describe our envisioned framework for process modelling and management based on natural language. Figure 1 overviews the framework. Given a textual description of a process, automatic or manual annotation (or a combination of both) is used to obtain an Annotated Textual Description of a Process (ATDP), which contains all the interpretations of the original text. This specification can then be automatically transformed into temporal formula that encompasses the semantics of the process. The temporal formula can then be queried with the help of a reasoner (e.g., a model checker). Typical use cases may require the encoding of additional inputs, e.g., traces of an event log, compliance rules, among others. The result of the reasoner is the satisfaction or rebuttal (with the corresponding counterexample) of the query. Notice that query results may not hold in all possible interpretations of the text.

5 Processes as Annotated Textual Descriptions

We now propose ATDP, a language for annotated textual descriptions of processes starting with a gentle introduction relying on a real-world example. Specifically, we use the textual description of the examination process of a Hospital extracted from [21]. Figure 2 shows the full text, while Fig. 3 contains a fragment of the visualization for an ATDP specification of the description.

One of the key features of the ATDP approach is the ability to capture *ambiguity*. In our example, we can see this at the topmost level: the text is associated to three different interpretations I_1, I_2 and I_3, providing three different process-oriented semantic views on the text. Each interpretation is a completely unambiguous specification of the process, which fixes a specific way for understanding ambiguous/unclear parts. Such parts could be understood differently in another interpretation. A specification in ATDP then consists of the union of all the valid interpretations of the process, which may partially overlap but also contradict each other.

Each interpretation consists of a hierarchy of *scopes*, providing a recursive mechanism to isolate parts of text that correspond to "phases" in the process. Each scope is thus a conceptual block inside the process, which is in turn decomposed as a set of lower-level scopes. Each scope dictates how its inner scopes are linked via control-flow relations expressing the allowed orderings of execution of such inner scopes. In our example, I_1 contains two scopes. A sequential relation indicates that the second scope is always executed when the first is completed, thus reconstructing the classical flow relation of conventional process modeling notation. All in all, the scope hierarchy resembles that of a process tree, following the variant used in [1].

Inside leaf scopes, *text fragments* are highlighted. There are different types of fragments, distinguished by color in our visual front-end. Some fragments (shown in red) describe the atomic units of behavior in the text, that is, activities and events, while others (shown in blue) provide additional perspectives beyond control flow. For example, outpatient physician is labelled as a *role* at the beginning of the text, while informs is labelled as an *activity*. Depending on their types, fragments can be linked by means of *fragment relations*. Among such relations, we find:

- Fragment relations that capture background knowledge induced from the text, such as for example the fact that the outpatient physician is the role responsible for performing (i.e., is the Agent of) the informs activity.
- Temporal constraints linking activities so as to declaratively capture the acceptable courses of execution in the resulting process, such as for example the fact that informs and signs an informed consent are in succession (i.e., informs is executed if and only if signs an informed consent is executed afterwards).

As for temporal relations, we consider a relevant subset of the well-known patterns supported by the Declare declarative process modeling language [17]. In this light, ATDP can be seen as a multi-perspective variant of a process tree where the control-flow of leaf scopes is specified using declarative constraints over the activities and events contained therein. Depending on the adopted constraints, this allows the modeler to cope with a variety of texts, ranging from loosely specified to more procedural ones. At one extreme, the modeler can choose to nest scopes in a fine-grained way, so that each leaf scope just contains a single activity fragment; with this approach, a pure process tree is obtained. At the other extreme, the modeler can choose to introduce a single scope containing all activity fragments of the text, and then add temporal constraints relating

> *The process starts when the female patient is examined by an outpatient physician, who decides whether she is healthy or needs to undertake an additional examination. In the former case, the physician fills out the examination form and the patient can leave. In the latter case, an examination and follow-up treatment order is placed by the physician, who additionally fills out a request form. Furthermore, the outpatient physician informs the patient about potential risks. If the patient signs an informed consent and agrees to continue with the procedure, a delegate of the physician arranges an appointment of the patient with one of the wards. Before the appointment, the required examination and sampling is prepared by a nurse of the ward based on the information provided by the outpatient section. Then, a ward physician takes the sample requested. He further sends it to the lab indicated in the request form and conducts the follow-up treatment of the patient. After receiving the sample, a physician of the lab validates its state and decides whether the sample can be used for analysis or whether it is contaminated and a new sample is required. After the analysis is performed by a medical technical assistant of the lab, a lab physician validates the results. Finally, a physician from the outpatient department makes the diagnosis and prescribes the therapy for the patient.*

Fig. 2. Textual description of a patient examination process.

arbitrary activity fragments from all the text; with this approach, a pure declarative process model is obtained.

5.1   ATDP Models

ATDP models are defined starting from an input text, which is separated into *typed text fragments*. We now go step by step through the different components of our approach, finally combining them into a coherent model. We then move into the semantics of the model, focusing on its temporal/dynamic parts and formalizing them using LTL.

Fragment Types. Fragments have no formal semantics associated by themselves. They are used as basic building blocks for defining ATDP models. We distinguish fragments through the following types.

Activity. This fragment type is used to represent the atomic units of work within the business process described by the text. Usually, these fragments are associated with verbs. An example activity fragment would be `validates` (from `validates the sample state`). Activity fragments may also be used to annotate other occurrences in the process that are relevant from the point of view of the control flow, but are exogenous to the organization responsible for the execution of the process. For instance, `(the sample) is contaminated` is also an activity fragment in our running example.

Role. The role fragment type is used to represent types of autonomous actors involved in the process, and consequently responsible for the execution of activities contained therein. An example is `outpatient physician`.

Business Object. This type is used to mark all the relevant elements of the process that do not take an active part in it, but that are used/manipulated by activities contained in the process. An example is the (medical) `sample` obtained and analyzed by physicians within the patient examination process.

When the distinction is not relevant, we may refer to fragments as the entities they represent (e.g. *activity* instead of *activity fragment*).

Given a set F of text fragments, we assume that the set is partitioned into three subsets that reflect the types defined above. We also use the following dot notation to refer to such subsets: (i) F.activities for activities; (ii) F.roles for roles; (iii) F.objects for business objects.

Fragment Relations. Text fragments can be related to each other by means of different non-temporal relations, used to express multi-perspective properties of the process emerging from the text. We consider the following relations over a set F of fragments.

Agent. An *agent relation* over F is a partial function

$$agent_F : F.\text{activities} \rightarrow F.\text{roles}$$

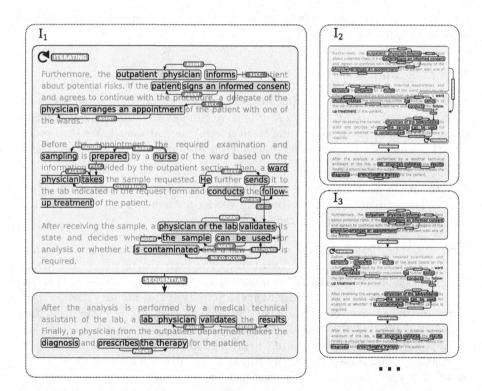

Fig. 3. Example annotation of a textual process description with multiple ambiguous interpretations. Some relations are omitted for brevity. (Color figure online)

indicating the role responsible for the execution of an activity. For instance, in our running example we have $agent(\texttt{informs}) = \texttt{physician}$, witnessing that informing someone is under the responsibility of a physician.

Patient. A *patient relation* over F is a partial function

$$patient_F : F.\text{activities} \rightarrow F.\text{roles} \cup F.\text{objects}$$

indicating the role or business object constituting the main recipient of an activity. For instance, in our running example we have $patient(\texttt{prepare}) = \texttt{sample}$, witnessing that the $\texttt{prepare}$ activity operates over a $\texttt{sample}$.

Coreference. A *coreference relation* over F is a (symmetric) relation

$$coref_F \subseteq F.\text{roles} \times F.\text{roles} \cup F.\text{objects} \times F.\text{objects}$$

that connects pairs of roles and pairs of business objects when they represent different ways to refer to the same entity. It consequently induces a coreference graph where each connected component denotes a distinct process entity. In our running example, all text fragments pointing to the $\texttt{patient}$ role corefer to the same entity, whereas there are three different physicians involved in the text: the $\texttt{outpatient physician}$, the $\texttt{ward physician}$ and the $\texttt{physician of the lab}$. These form disconnected coreference subgraphs.

Text Scopes. To map the text into a process structure, we suitably adjust the notion of process tree used in [1]. In our approach, the blocks of the process tree are actually *text scopes*, where each scope is either a *leaf scope*, or a *branching scope* containing a one or an ordered pair[1] of (leaf or branching) sub-scopes.

Each activity is associated to one and only one leaf scope, whereas each leaf scope contains one or more activities, so as to non-ambiguously link activities to their corresponding process phases.

Branching scopes, instead, are associated to a corresponding control-flow operator, which dictates how the sub-scopes are composed when executing the process. At execution time, each scope is enacted possibly multiple times, each time taking a certain amount of time (marked by a punctual scope start, and a later completion). We consider in particular the following scope relation types:

Sequential ($\rightarrow$) A sequential branching scope s with children $\langle s_1, s_2 \rangle$ indicates that each execution of s amounts to the sequential execution of its sub-scopes, in the order they appear in the tuple. Specifically: *(i)* when s is started then s_1 starts; *(ii)* whenever s_1 completes, s_2 starts; *(iii)* the completion of s_2 induces the completion of s.

Conflicting ($\times$) A conflicting branching scope s with children $\langle s_1, s_2 \rangle$ indicates that each execution of s amounts to the execution of one and only one of its children, thus capturing a choice. Specifically: *(i)* when s is started, then one among s_1 and s_2 starts; *(ii)* the completion of the selected sub-scope induces the completion of s.

---

[1] We keep a pair for simplicity of presentation, but all definitions carry over to n-ary tuples of sub-blocks.

Inclusive ($\vee$) An inclusive branching scope s with children $\langle s_1, s_2 \rangle$ indicates that each execution of s amounts to the execution of at least one of s_1 and s_2, but possibly both.

Interleaving ($\wedge$) An interleaving branching scope s with children $\langle s_1, s_2 \rangle$ indicates that each execution of s amounts to the interleaved, parallel execution of its sub-scopes, without ordering constraints among them. Specifically: *(i)* when s is started, then s_1 and s_2 start; *(ii)* the latest, consequent completion of s_1 and s_2 induces the completion of s.

Iterating ($\circlearrowleft$) An iterating branching scope s with child s_1 indicates that each execution of s amounts to the iterative execution of s_1, with one or more iterations. Specifically: *(i)* when s is started, then s_1 starts; *(ii)* upon the consequent completion of s_1, then there is a non-deterministic choice on whether s completes, or s_1 is started again.

All in all, a *scope tree* T_F over the set F of fragments is a binary tree whose leaf nodes S_l are called *leaf scopes* and whose intermediate/root nodes S_b are called *branch nodes*, and which comes with two functions:

- a total *scope assignment* function *parent* : F.activities $\rightarrow S_l$ mapping each activity in F to a corresponding leaf scope, such that each leaf scope in S_l has at least one activity associated to it;
- a total *branching type* function *btype* : $S_b \rightarrow \{\rightarrow, \times, \vee, \wedge, \circlearrowleft\}$ mapping each branching scope in S_b to its control-flow operator.

Temporal Constraints Among Activities. Activities belonging to the same leaf scope can be linked to each other by means of temporal relations, inspired by the Declare notation [17]. These can be used to declaratively specify constraints on the execution of different activities within the same leaf scope. Due to the interaction between scopes and such constraints, we follow here the approach in [11], where, differently from [17], constraints are in fact scoped.[2]

We consider in particular the following constraints:

Scoped Precedence Given activities $a_1, \ldots, a_n, b$, Precedence($\{a_1, \ldots, a_n\}, b$) indicates that b can be executed only if, within the same instance of its parent scope, at least one among $a_1, \ldots, a_n$ have been executed *before*.

Scoped Response Given activities $a, b_1, \ldots, b_n$, Response($a, \{b_1, \ldots, b_n\}$) indicates that whenever a is executed within an instance of its parent scope, then at least one among $b_1, \ldots, b_n$ has to be executed *afterwards*, within the same scope instance.

Scoped Non-Co-Occurrence Given activities a, b, NonCoOccurrence(a, b) indicates that whenever a is executed within an instance of its parent scope, then b *cannot* be executed within the same scope instance (and vice-versa).

Scoped Alternate Response Given activities $a, b_1, \ldots, b_n$, AlternateResp $-$ onse($a, \{b_1, \ldots, b_n\}$) indicates that whenever a is executed within an instance of its parent scope, then a *cannot be executed again* until, within the same scope, at least one among $b_1, \ldots, b_n$ is *eventually* executed.

---

[2] It is interesting to notice that Declare itself was defined by relying on the patterns originally introduced in [11].

Terminating Given activity a, Terminating(a) indicates that the execution of a within an instance of its parent scope terminates that instance.

Mandatory Given activity a, Mandatory(a) indicates that the execution of a must occur at least once for each execution of its scope.

Interpretations and Models. We are now ready to combine the components defined before into an integrated notion of text interpretation. An *ATDP inter-pretation* I_X over text X is a tuple $\langle F, agent_F, patient_F, coref_F, T_F, C_F, \rangle$, where: *(i)* F is a set of *text fragments* over X; *(ii)* $agent_F$ is an *agent function* over F; *(iii)* $patient_F$ is a *patient function* over F; *(iv)* $coref_F$ is a *coreference relation* over F; *(v)* T_F is a *scope tree* over the activities in F; *(vi)* C_F is a set of *temporal constraints* over the activities in F, such that if two activities are related by a constraint in, then they have to belong to the same leaf scope according to T_F.

An *ATDP model* M_X over text X is then simply a finite set of ATDP interpretations over X.

5.2   ATDP Semantics

We now describe the execution semantics of ATDP interpretations, in particular formalizing the three key notions of scopes, scope types (depending on their corresponding control-flow operators), and temporal constraints over activities. This is done by using LTL, consequently declaratively characterizing those execution traces that conform to what is prescribed by an ATDP interpretation. We consider execution traces as finite sequences of atomic activity executions over interleaving semantics.

Scope Semantics. To define the notion of scope execution, for each scope s, we introduce a pair of artificial activities st_s and en_s which do not belong to F.activities. The execution of s starts with the execution of st_s, and ends with the execution of en_s. The next three axioms define the semantics of scopes:

A1.   An activity a inside a scope s can only be executed between st_s and en_s:

$$\neg a \, W \, st_s \wedge \Box(en_s \rightarrow \neg a \, W \, st_s)$$

A2.   A scope s can only be started and ended inside of its parent s':

$$\neg(st_s \vee en_s) \, W \, st_{s'} \wedge \Box(en_{s'} \rightarrow \neg(st_s \vee en_s) \, W \, st_{s'})$$

A3.   Executions of the same scope cannot overlap in time. That is, for each execution of a scope s's start there is a unique corresponding end:

$$\Diamond en_s \rightarrow (\neg en_s \, U \, st_s) \wedge \Box(st_s \rightarrow \Diamond en_s) \wedge$$

$$\Box(st_s \rightarrow \bigcirc(\Diamond st_s \rightarrow (\neg st_s \, U \, en_s))) \wedge$$

$$\Box(en_s \rightarrow \bigcirc(\Diamond en_s \rightarrow (\neg en_s \, U \, st_s)))$$

Temporal Constraint Semantics. In this section, we define the semantics of temporal constraints between activities. Note that, in all definitions we will use the subindex s to refer to the scope of the constraint.

$$\text{Precedence}_s(\{a_1, .., a_K\}, b) := \bigvee_{i=1}^{N} \Box(st_s \rightarrow (\neg b\, U(a_i \vee en_s)))$$

$$\text{Response}_s(a, \{b_1, .., b_N\}) := \bigvee_{i=1}^{N} \Box(st_s \rightarrow (a \rightarrow (\neg en_s\, U\, b_i))\, U\, en_s)$$

$$\text{NonCoOccurrence}_p(a, b) := \Box(st_s \rightarrow (a \rightarrow (\neg b\, U\, en_s))\, U\, en_s) \wedge$$

$$\Box(st_s \rightarrow (b \rightarrow (\neg a\, U\, en_s))\, U\, en_s)$$

$$\text{AlternateResponse}_p(a, b) := \text{Response}_p(a, b) \wedge$$

$$\Box(st_s \rightarrow (a \rightarrow O(\neg a\, U(b \vee en_s)))\, U\, en_s)$$

$$\text{Terminating}_p(a) := \Box(a \rightarrow O\, en_s)$$

$$\text{Mandatory}_p(a) := \Box(st_s \rightarrow (\neg en_s\, U\, a))$$

Scope Relation Semantics. In all our definitions, let $\langle s_1, s_2 \rangle$ denote the children of a branching scope s, associated to the control-flow operator being defined. Note that by $\text{Sequence}(a, b)$ we refer to the formula $\text{Precedence}(\{a\}, b) \wedge \text{Response}(a, \{b\})$.

Sequential $(\rightarrow)$: $\text{Sequence}_s(en_{s_1}, st_{s_2}) \wedge \text{Mandatory}_s(st_{s_1}) \wedge \text{Mandatory}_s(st_{s_2})$

Conflicting $(\times)$: $\text{Mandatory}_s(st_{s_1}) \oplus \text{Mandatory}_s(st_{s_2})$

Inclusive $(\vee)$: $\text{Mandatory}_s(st_{s_1}) \vee \text{Mandatory}_s(st_{s_2})$

Interleaving $(\wedge)$: $\text{Mandatory}_s(st_{s_1}) \wedge \text{Mandatory}_s(st_{s_2})$

Iterating $(\circlearrowleft)$: This relation is defined by negation, with any non-iterating scope s, child of s', fulfilling the property:

$$(st_{s'} \rightarrow (\neg en_{s'}\, U\, st_s \wedge (st_s \rightarrow O(\neg st_s\, U\, en_{s'}))\, U\, en_{s'}))$$

Additionally, iterating scopes may be affected by the presence of terminating activities, as defined by the following property: A terminating activity a_t inside an iterating scope s, child of s', stops the iteration. That is, its execution cannot be repeated anymore inside its parent:

A4. $\Box(st_{s'} \rightarrow ((a_t \rightarrow (\neg st_s\, U\, en_{s'}))\, U\, en_{s'}))$

6   Reasoning on ATDP Specifications

A specification in ATDP is the starting point for reasoning over the described process. This section shows how to encode the reasoning as a model checking instance, so that a formal analysis can be applied on the set of interpretations of the model. Furthermore, we present three use cases in the scope of business process management: *checking model consistency, compliance checking* and *conformance checking*.

6.1   Casting Reasoning as Model Checking

Reasoning on ATDP specifications can be encoded as an instance of model checking, which allows performing arbitrary queries on the model. The overall system can be defined by the following formula

$$(A \wedge C_F \wedge C_{T_F}) \implies Q \tag{1}$$

where A is the conjunction of all LTL formulas defined by the axioms, C_F is the conjunction of the activity temporal constraints, C_{T_F} is the conjunction of all LTL formulas defined by the semantics of the process tree, and Q is an arbitrary query expressed in LTL (cf. Sect. 5.2).

In this paper, we present an encoding of the ATDP's semantics into NuSMV, a well-known software for model-checking [3]. First, the notion of process execution is defined using an *activity* variable, with a domain of all the activities in the ATDP. At any given step, the system may choose a single value for this variable, meaning that this activity has been executed. This ensures that simultaneous execution of activities will not happen.

The system definition for an ATDP is then split into two parts: a transition system and an LTL property specification. The transition system is a graph defining the next possible values for the *activity* variable given its current value. In our proposed encoding the transition system is specified as a complete graph, since all the behavioural constraints are specified in A, C_F and C_{T_F} as parts of the property specification, as seen in Eq. (1). This property specification is directly encoded as a single LTL formula.

We can adapt NuSMV, which performs model checking on infinite traces, to check properties on finite traces when necessary. In order to do that, we add a special activity value STOP. In the transition system, an edge is added from any possible activity to STOP. Additionally, the constraint $\Diamond$STOP is added to the antecedent of the LTL property specification. This enforces that all traces accepted by the model end in an infinite loop repeating the (only) execution of the STOP activity, which is equivalent to terminating execution.

Non-temporal information can be introduced in the queries without increasing the problem complexity, since the information is statically defined. For example, when the text mentions that several activities are performed by a certain role, this information remains invariant during the whole model-checking phase. Thus, queries concerning roles can be translated directly into queries about the set of activities performed by that role. A possible encoding of this into a model checker consists of adding additional variables during the system definition.

When dealing with multiple interpretations, the above framework is extended with two types of queries:

Existential: Is the proposition true in any interpretation of the process?
$$\exists I \in \text{ATDP} : (A_I \wedge C_{F_I} \wedge C_{T_{F_I}}) \implies Q$$
Complete: Is the proposition true in all interpretations of the process?
$$\forall I \in \text{ATDP} : (A_I \wedge C_{F_I} \wedge C_{T_{F_I}}) \implies Q$$

Existential and complete queries can be used to reason in uncertain or incomplete specifications of processes.

An application of complete queries would be finding invariant properties of the process. That is, a property that holds in all possible process interpretations. Existential queries, in turn, fulfill a similar role when the proposition being checked is an undesired property of the process. By proving invariant properties, it is possible to extract information from processes even if these are not completely specified or in case of contradictions. A negative result for this type of query would also contain the non-compliant interpretations of the process, which can help the process owner in gaining some insights about which are the assumptions needed to comply with some business rule.

Tool Support. The encoding technique described in Sect. 6.1 has been implemented in a prototype tool, `ATDP2NuSMV`. The tool can be used to convert an ATDP specification into a `NuSMV`instance.

`ATDP2NuSMV` is distributed as a standalone tool, that can be used in any system with a modern Java installation, and without further dependencies. A compiled version as well as the source code can be found in the following repository: https://github.com/setzer22/atdp2nusmv.

In the next subsection, we present use cases that have been tested with `ATDP2NuSMV` and `NuSMV`. The `ATDP` specifications as well as the exact query encodings can be found in the repository. The use case examples are based on a full version of the specification presented in Fig. 3.

Use Case 1: Model Consistency. An ATDP specification can be checked for consistency using proof by contradiction. Specifically, if we set $Q = \bot$, the reasoner will try to prove that $A \wedge C_F \wedge C_{T_F} \rightarrow \bot$, that is, whether a false conclusion can be derived from the axioms and constraints describing our model. Since this implication only holds in the case $\bot \rightarrow \bot$, if the proof succeeds we will have proven that $A \wedge C_F \wedge C_{T_F} \equiv \bot$, i.e. that our model is not consistent. On the contrary, if the proof fails we can be sure that our model does not contain any contradiction.

To illustrate this use case, we use interpretations `hosp-1` and `hosp-1-bad`, available in our repository. The first interpretation consists of a complete version of the specification in Fig. 3, where F.activities includes $a_1 =$ takes (the sample) and $a_2 =$ validates (sample state), and constraints in C_F include: Mandatory(a_1), Precedence($\{a_1\}, a_2$) and Response($a_1, \{a_2\}$).

NuSMVfalsifies the query in interpretation `hosp-1` with a counter-example. When the model is consistent, the property is false, and the resulting counter example can be any valid trace in the model.

The second specification, `hosp-1-bad` adds Precedence($\{a_2\}, a_1$) to the set of relations R. This relation contradicts the previously existing Precedence($\{a_1\}, a_2$), thus resulting in an inconsistent model. Consequently, NuSMVcannot find a counter-example for the query in interpretation `hosp-1-bad`. This result can be interpreted as the model being impossible to fulfill by any possible trace, and thus inconsistent.

Use Case 2: Compliance Checking. Business rules, as those arising from regulations or SLAs, impose further restrictions that any process model may need to satisfy. On this regard, compliance checking methods assess the adherence of a process specification to a particular set of predefined rules.

The presented reasoning framework can be used to perform compliance checking on ATDP specifications. An example rule for our running example might be: "An invalid sample can never be used for diagnosis". The relevant activities for this property are annotated in the text: a_3 = (the sample) can be used, a_4 = (the sample) is contaminated, a_5 = makes the diagnosis, and the property can be written in LTL as: $Q = \Box(a_4 \rightarrow (\neg a_5 \, U \, a_3))$.

In the examples from our repository, interpretations `hosp-2-i`, with i=$\{1,2,3\}$, correspond to the three interpretations of the process shown in Fig. 3. Particularly, the ambiguity between the three interpretations is the scope of the repetition when the taken sample is contaminated. The three returning points correspond to: `sign an informed consent`, `sampling is prepared` and `take the sample`. NuSMVfinds the property true for all three interpretations, meaning that we can prove the property $\Box(a_4 \rightarrow (\neg a_5 \, U \, a_3))$ without resolving the main ambiguity in the text.

Use Case 3: Conformance Checking. Conformance checking techniques put process specifications next to event data, to detect and visualize deviations between modeled and observed behavior [2]. On its core, conformance checking relies on the ability to find out whereas an observed trace can be reproduced by a process model.

A decisional version of conformance checking can be performed, by encoding traces inside Q as an LTL formulation. Given a trace $t = \langle a_1, a_2, \cdots, a_N \rangle$, we can test conformance against an ATDP interpretation with the following query[3]:

$$Q = \neg(a_1 \wedge O(a_2 \wedge O(... \wedge O(a_N \wedge \text{OSTOP}))))$$

This query encodes the proposition "Trace t is not possible in this model". This proposition will be false whenever the trace is accepted by the model.

---

[3] The proposed query does not account for the start and end activities of scopes, which are not present in the original trace. A slightly more complex version can be crafted that accounts for any invisible activity to be present between the visible activities of the trace. We do not show it here for the sake of simplicity.

Other variants of this formulation allow for testing trace patterns: partial traces or projections of a trace to a set of activities. In this case, the counter-example produced will be a complete trace which fits the model and the queried pattern.

As an example of this use-case, we provide the example ATDP interpretation hosp-3 in our repository. We project the set of relevant activities to the set a_6 = informs (the patient), a_7 = signs (informed consent) a_8 = arranges (an appointment). Two trace patterns are tested, the first: $t_1 = \langle \cdots a_6, a_7, a_8, \cdots \rangle$ and $t_2 = \langle \cdots a_7, a_6, a_8, \cdots \rangle$. NuSMVfinds the trace pattern t_1 fitting the model, and produces a full execution trace containing it. On the other hand, t_2 does not fit the model, which is successfully proven by NuSMV.

7   Conclusions and Future Work

This paper proposes ATDP, a novel multi-perspective language for the representation of processes based on textual annotation. On the control-flow dimension, ATDP is a mixture of imperative constructs at general level via scopes, and declarative constructs inside each scope. In a way, the language generalizes process trees, allowing declarative relations instead of atomic activities in the leaf nodes. The paper also shows how to translate ATDP specifications into temporal formulas that are amenable for reasoning. Three use cases in the context of BPM are shown, illustrating the potential of the ideas in this paper.

Several avenues for future work are under consideration. First, to explore alternatives or refinements of the encoding in Eq. (1) to make it more suitable in a model-checking context. Second, to validate the proposed language against more examples and use cases, specifically by testing how the ATDP primitives accommodate to different document styles. Finally, studying the connection between ATDP and other process model notations may serve as a bridge between textual descriptions and their operationalization within an organization.

Acknowledgments. This work has been supported by MINECO and FEDER funds under grant TIN2017-86727-C2-1-R and by Innovation Fund Denmark project EcoKnow.org (7050-00034A).

References

1. Buijs, J.C.A.M., van Dongen, B.F., van der Aalst, W.M.P.: A genetic algorithm for discovering process trees. In: Proceedings of the IEEE Congress on Evolutionary Computation (CEC), pp. 1–8 (2012)
2. Carmona, J., van Dongen, B., Solti, A., Weidlich, M.: Conformance Checking - Relating Processes and Models. Springer, Cham (2018). https://doi.org/10.1007/978-3-319-99414-7
3. Cimatti, A., Clarke, E.M., Giunchiglia, F., Roveri, M.: NUSMV: a new symbolic model checker. STTT **2**(4), 410–425 (2000)
4. Claes, J., Vanderfeesten, I., Pinggera, J., Reijers, H.A., Weber, B., Poels, G.: A visual analysis of the process of process modeling. Inf. Syst. e-Bus. Manag. **13**(1), 147–190 (2015)

5. De Giacomo, G., De Masellis, R., Montali, M.: Reasoning on LTL on finite traces: insensitivity to infiniteness. In: Proceedings of the 28th AAAI Conference on Artificial Intelligence, pp. 1027–1033. AAAI Press (2014)
6. De Giacomo, G., Vardi, M.Y.: Linear temporal logic and linear dynamic logic on finite traces. In: Proceedings of the 23rd International Joint Conference on Artificial Intelligence (IJCAI), pp. 854–860. IJCAI/AAAI (2013)
7. Delicado, L., Sanchez-Ferreres, J., Carmona, J., Padró, L.: NLP4BPM - natural language processing tools for business process management. In: BPM Demo Track (2017)
8. Delicado, L., Sanchez-Ferreres, J., Carmona, J., Padró, L.: The model judge - a tool for supporting novices in learning process modeling. In: BPM 2018 Demonstration Track (2018)
9. Dijkman, R., Vanderfeesten, I., Reijers, H.A.: Business process architectures: overview, comparison and framework. Enterp. Inf. Syst. **10**(2), 129–158 (2016)
10. Dumas, M., La Rosa, M., Mendling, J., Reijers, H.: Fundamentals of Business Process Management, 2nd edn. Springer, Heidelberg (2018). https://doi.org/10.1007/978-3-662-56509-4
11. Dwyer, M.B., Avrunin, G.S., Corbett, J.C.: Patterns in property specifications for finite-state verification. In: Proceedings of the 1999 International Conference on Software Engineering (ICSE), pp. 411–420. ACM (1999)
12. Leopold, H.: Natural Language in Business Process Models. Springer, Cham (2013). https://doi.org/10.1007/978-3-319-04175-9. Ph.D. thesis
13. Maqbool, B., et al.: A comprehensive investigation of BPMN models generation from textual requirements—techniques, tools and trends. In: Kim, K.J., Baek, N. (eds.) ICISA 2018. LNEE, vol. 514, pp. 543–557. Springer, Singapore (2019). https://doi.org/10.1007/978-981-13-1056-0_54
14. Mendling, J., Baesens, B., Bernstein, A., Fellmann, M.: Challenges of smart business process management: an introduction to the special issue. Decis. Support Syst. **100**, 1–5 (2017)
15. Mendling, J., Leopold, H., Pittke, F.: 25 challenges of semantic process modeling. Int. J. Inf. Syst. Softw. Eng. Big Co. **1**(1), 78–94 (2015)
16. Padró, L., Stanilovsky, E.: Freeling 3.0: towards wider multilinguality. In: Proceedings of the Eighth International Conference on Language Resources and Evaluation (LREC), pp. 2473–2479 (2012)
17. Pesic, M., Schonenberg, H., van der Aalst, W.M.P.: DECLARE: full support for loosely-structured processes. In: Proceedings of the Eleventh IEEE International Enterprise Distributed Object Computing Conference (EDOC 2007), pp. 287–298. IEEE Computer Society (2007)
18. Pinggera, J.: The process of process modeling. Ph.D. thesis, University of Innsbruck, Department of Computer Science (2014)
19. Pnueli, A.: The temporal logic of programs, pp. 46–57. IEEE (1977)
20. Sànchez-Ferreres, J., Carmona, J., Padró, L.: Aligning textual and graphical descriptions of processes through ILP techniques. In: Dubois, E., Pohl, K. (eds.) CAiSE 2017. LNCS, vol. 10253, pp. 413–427. Springer, Cham (2017). https://doi.org/10.1007/978-3-319-59536-8_26
21. Semmelrodt, F.: Modellierung klinischer prozesse und compliance regeln mittels BPMN 2.0 und eCRG. Master's thesis, University of Ulm (2013)
22. van der Aa, H., Carmona, J., Leopold, H., Mendling, J., Padró, L.: Challenges and opportunities of applying natural language processing in business process management. In: Proceedings of the 27th International Conference on Computational Linguistics (COLING), pp. 2791–2801 (2018)

Goal-oriented Process Enhancement and Discovery

Mahdi Ghasemi$^{(\boxtimes)}$ ⓘ and Daniel Amyot ⓘ

EECS, University of Ottawa, Ottawa, Canada
{mghasemi,damyot}@uottawa.ca

Abstract. Process mining practices are mainly activity-oriented and they seldom consider the (often conflicting) goals of stakeholders. Involving goal-related factors, as often done in requirements engineering, can improve the rationality and interpretability of mined models and lead to better opportunities to satisfy stakeholders. This paper proposes a new Goal-oriented Process Enhancement and Discovery (GoPED) method to align discovered models with stakeholders' goals. GoPED first adds goal-related attributes to traditional event characteristics (case identifier, activities, and timestamps), selects a subset of cases with respect to a goal-related criterion, and finally discovers a process model from that subset. We define three types of criteria that suggest desired satisfaction levels from a (i) case perspective, (ii) goal perspective, and (iii) organization perspective. For each criterion, an algorithm is proposed to enable selecting the best subset of cases were the criterion holds. The resulting process models are expected to reproduce the desired level of satisfaction. A synthetic event log is used to illustrate the proposed algorithms and to discuss their results.

Keywords: Business process management · Process mining · Goal modeling · Requirements engineering · Event logs · Performance indicators

1 Introduction

The process mining community has developed various algorithms and tools to enable the analysis of event logs to discover process models and improve their underlying processes. Process mining activities involve: (1) *Discovery*, where a model is being created from event logs; (2) *Conformance checking*, where differences between the model and reality are detected; and (3) *Enhancement*, where an existing process model is improved or extended using some additional desired data from different aspects [16].

Event logs, resulting from the execution of processes, are the main input of process discovery activities. However, process mining approaches usually do not consider specific goals that individual cases pursue and satisfaction levels that traces yielded for different stakeholders' goals [7]. This situation not only threatens the *rationality* behind the discovered models, but also often results in unstructured *"spaghetti-like"* process models. Although such models reflect reality, they cover many exceptions and many traces misaligned with goals [12]. Process mining practitioners have to deal with such problems especially in flexible environments that allow multiple alternatives within process execution.

© Springer Nature Switzerland AG 2019
T. Hildebrandt et al. (Eds.): BPM 2019, LNCS 11675, pp. 102–118, 2019.
https://doi.org/10.1007/978-3-030-26619-6_9

There are currently some strategies that deal with unstructured discovered processes often taking into account the *frequency* of activities and transitions. For example, keeping the activities that occur at least for 20% of cases is a way to simplify the model. In contrast to strategies that change logs, abstraction techniques such as fuzzy mining [16] are applied to the resulting process graphs. Also, current *declarative* approaches, e.g., based on linear temporal logic, exist to enforce some constraints (e.g., on sequencing) and discover complying models at the *activity level* [12].

Goal modeling, a requirements engineering approach that enables the description of the interrelated (and often conflicting) goals of systems and stakeholders, can be leveraged for addressing the aforementioned problems. Goal modeling is used to support heuristic, qualitative, or formal reasoning about goals, and ultimately trade-off analysis, what-if analysis, and decision making. In contrast to process mining where *"how"*, *"what"*, *"where"*, *"who"*, and especially *"when"* questions are answered, goal modeling focuses mainly on complementary *"why"* questions [2].

We hypothesize that a goal-oriented approach combined to process mining enables leveraging goals to improve process models and their realization. Process models that are discovered with respect to different goals are aligned with such goals and hence more likely to produce high levels of satisfaction.

The objective in this paper is to offer a process mining method concerned not only with the sequencing of activities, but also with processes' goals and satisfaction indicators. To this end, we propose a *goal-oriented process enhancement and discovery* (GoPED) method that adds satisfaction levels of different goals to event logs and considers traces of activities beside their contribution to predefined goals. Goal satisfaction levels are derived from a model capturing goals, stakeholders, and their relationships. Note that the "enhancement" part of GoPED is about enhancing logs with goal information to produce higher-quality and simpler process models, and not about improving processes after their discovery.

As an example, a trace of activities in a healthcare process may take a very short time (i.e., it satisfies the goal "to decrease process time") but may end up with a wrong diagnosis (i.e., it violates the goal "to diagnose correctly"). Inversely, a trace may take a long time and impose an unaffordable cost but may end up with a correct diagnosis. GoPED takes advantage of goal models to manage such conflicting goals and to support trade-off analysis. With GoPED, good historical experiences will be found within the whole event log to be used as a basis for inferring good models and bad experiences will be found to be avoided. The *goodness* of traces and models is defined with regards to three categories of goal-related criteria: satisfaction of individual cases in terms of some goals (*case perspective*), overall satisfaction of some goals rather than individual cases (*goal perspective*), and a comprehensive satisfaction level for all goals over all cases (*organization perspective*). GoPED is expected to guide process discovery approaches towards specific goal-related properties of interest.

The paper is structured as follows. Section 2 explains the fundamentals of GoPED and highlights its contribution to current process mining approaches. Section 3 explicitly describes three algorithms for selecting traces according to the three categories of criteria discussed in the previous paragraph. Then, in Sect. 4, the GoPED method is applied to an illustrative example of a healthcare process, with a discussion of the results. Related work at the intersection of process mining and goal modeling is briefly discussed in Sect. 5. Finally, a summary and conclusions are provided in Sect. 6.

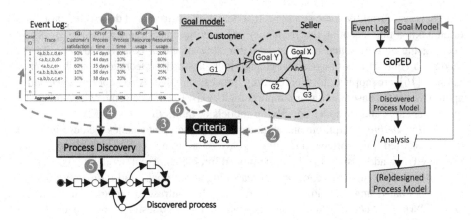

Fig. 1. Overview of goal-oriented process enhancement and discovery (GoPED)

2   GoPED Method

Figure 1 gives an overview of the proposed method through an example that exploits the Goal-oriented Requirement Language (GRL) standard [2]. Let us assume that there are three leaf goals (G1, G2 and G3), with G1 contributing to Goal Y and Goal X being AND-decomposed by G2 and G3. Each goal may be fed by its Key Performance Indicators (KPIs), allowing to quantify its satisfaction level. Let us also assume that the event logs store the value of each goal-related KPI, e.g., **"process time"** associated to the goal G2 **"to take a short process time"**. Such KPIs and how they contribute to goal satisfaction (e.g., by providing a function that converts a current, observable value to an abstract satisfaction value between 0/violated and 100/satisfied) are also defined in the goal model (see [1] for details). Based on this scheme, the satisfaction level of the leaf goals in Fig. 1 are computed from corresponding KPIs (arrows ❶). We define the satisfaction level of Goal i as Sat (G_i). The satisfaction of actors (dashed circles in Fig. 1) and of the whole models can be computed in a similar fashion [1].

After finding the current satisfaction of considered goals, GoPED defines some criteria related to the goals (arrow ❷). The main objective is to design a process model that fulfills one or many such criteria. The goal-related criteria are defined from three perspectives as follows:

- The resulting process model achieves (based on current evidence) a minimum satisfaction level for every single case in terms of one or multiple goals (*row* or *case perspective*). For example, in Fig. 1, $Sat(G_2)$ should be more than 60 for all cases.
- The resulting process model achieves a threshold for the *aggregated* satisfaction level of one or multiple goals rather than the level for individual cases (overall *column* or *goal perspective*). For example, in Fig. 1, the aggregated satisfaction level of G2 (where the aggregation function is defined as the *average* here) should be higher than 70 (but is currently 45).
- The resulting process model achieves a threshold for the comprehensive satisfaction level of many goals over all cases (*table* or *organization perspective*, arrow ❻).

This may be computed through the goal model (e.g., in GRL) or through a function derived from that model. For example, according to the structure of the model in Fig. 1, the satisfaction of the stakeholder "Seller" is the average of Goal Y (computed from G1) and Goal X (the minimum of G1 and G2).

The basis of process mining is generally to use historical event logs and infer valuable insights. Following this general approach, GoPED selects a *subset* of the input traces that have already fulfilled the given criteria and uses them to find process models of interest (arrow ❹). For example, if the objective is to secure at least 50 as a satisfaction level for G2 for all the customers, the cases #1 and #3 will be selected because they have a satisfaction level over 50 for goal G2. After such a selection, a process model is mined through the selected traces using a process discovery algorithm (arrows ❹ and ❺). The discovered model does not represent all existing behaviours, but rather represents the desired behaviours towards the goals. Different model mined through different goal-related criteria can shed some light on different aspects and alternatives involved in the real or the discovered model. Such criteria are purposely defined by a domain expert in collaboration with a modeller. Moreover, an analyst can compare the model discovered from the whole log with the model discovered by GoPED. Such a comparison can also reveal some valuable insights from potential discrepancies. Goal-oriented conformance checking approaches [5, 6] can also suggest some way of reconsidering the goal model with respect to misalignments between the process and goal perspectives, as shown in the right graph of Fig. 1.

The process model resulting from GoPED is inferred from cases selected based on their goals. Therefore, irrelevant cases (that likely pursue goals different from the expected goals) are filtered out. The discovered model will be more likely well-structured as GoPED intentionally decreases the number of variations of traces and, in turn, decreases the chance of producing a spaghetti-like process model.

Another benefit of GoPED relates to the quality dimensions considered in usual process mining activities. In addition to the *fitness*, *precision*, *generalization*, and *simplicity* dimensions [16], GoPED brings into consideration a new *intention* dimension, formalized by the goal model.

3   Algorithms to Select Cases

In process mining, the three attributes (columns) that must minimally exist in an event table are *case identifier*, *activity* and *timestamp*. There might be some other event attributes stored in such a table that can be used for the analysis of discovered models (e.g., *resource*). Similarly, there might be some attributes about the case (e.g., age) or about a case's trace (e.g., total process time). In GoPED, we add some new case attributes related to goals, which are usually absent in process mining practice. Table 1 shows the architecture of event logs enhanced with goal-related attributes, used as input of GoPED.

Table 1. Event log enhanced with n goal-related attributes (*EnhancedLog*)

Case	Trace	Goal 1	Goal 2	...	Goal n	Overall
c_1	t_1	$s_{1,1}$	$s_{1,2}$	...	$s_{1,n}$	$s_{1.Ove}$
c_2	...	$s_{2,1}$	$s_{2,2}$	...	$s_{2,n}$	$s_{2.Ove}$
...	...					...
c_m	t_m	$s_{m,1}$	$s_{m,2}$	...	$s_{m,n}$	$s_{m.Ove}$
Aggregated satisfaction:		$s_{Agg.1}$	$s_{Agg.2}$	...	$s_{Agg.n}$	s_{Comp}

3.1 Preliminaries

The notations that are used through this paper are defined as follows:

Definition 1. Basic concepts (*activity, trace, case, event log*).

- A is the set of all experienced *activities* labelled a_i.
- A *trace* is a finite sequence of activities $t = \langle a_1, \cdots, a_k \rangle$, where $k \in \mathbb{N}^+$ is the trace length. T is the set of all observed traces.
- A *case* $c = \langle id, t \rangle$ has a case identifier $id \in \mathbb{N}^+$ and contains a trace $t \in T$.
- $trace(c) = t$ is a shorthand to indicate that the trace of the case c is $t \in T$.
- $L = \langle c_1, \cdots, c_m \rangle$ is an *event log* consisting of a finite sequence of cases of size m.
- C is the set of all possible cases (with traces) represented in the log L.

Definition 2. *EnhancedLog* structure.

To select the best subset of cases in a log through GoPED's algorithms, an event log enhanced with additional goal-related attributes is needed. The structure of such log, shown in Table 1, and the elements of that structure are defined as follows:

- *EnhancedLog* is the event log L enhanced with goal-related attributes. This log is a table of all cases $c \in C$ beside their traces $t \in T$. The satisfaction levels of all considered goals (including KPIs and actors) are stored in the next columns. $\mathbb{G}$ is the set of all considered goals, i.e., $\mathbb{G} = \{G_1, G_2, \cdots, G_n\}$. We assume that *EnhancedLog* consists of m cases and n considered goals.
- $s_{i,j}$ in *EnhancedLog* shows the level of satisfaction of $case_i$ in terms of $Goal_j$.
- $s_{i.Ove}$, found in the last column of the table *EnhancedLog*, is the overall satisfaction level for $case_i$. This represents the satisfaction level of the whole goal model. The satisfaction level of the goal model is evaluated through bottom-up analysis as elaborated in the goal-oriented modeling literature [1]. This evaluation is based on AND/OR refinements, contribution links, the importance level of a goal to its actor, and the actor importance in the whole model.
- Function g is derived from the goal model to compute the overall satisfaction level based on satisfaction levels of all sub-goals in $\mathbb{G}$ [4]. Therefore, as $s_{i,j}$ is the satisfaction level of $Goal_j$ for $case_i$, we have $s_{i.Ove} = g(s_{i.1}, s_{i.2}, \cdots, s_{i.n})$.
- $s_{Agg.i}$, in the last row of *EnhancedLog*, show the aggregated satisfaction level of each goal based on the satisfaction level of all cases in terms of that goal. $s_{Agg.i}$ is a function (e.g., average, median, etc.) of satisfaction levels of all m cases for $Goal_j$.

- Function f_j is the aggregation function of $Goal_j$. For each goal $G_j \in \mathbb{G}$ we have $s_{Agg,j} = f_j(s_{1,j}, s_{2,j}, \cdots, s_{m,j})$. F is a tuple of functions $(f_1, f_2, \ldots, f_n)$ that keeps aggregation functions of all goals.
- s_{Comp} is the comprehensive satisfaction level that the process has yielded. This factor can be defined either by composing the aggregated satisfactions (last row) or by aggregating the overall satisfaction levels (last column) using some function.

Definition 3. GoPED offers three types of goal-related criteria, discussed in Sect. 3.1:

- $\boldsymbol{Q_{case}}$ is a set of criteria q_j. Each q_j is a tuple composed of one goal $G_j \in \mathbb{G}$ and a threshold, sl_j, for the satisfaction level of that goal, $Q_{case} = \{q_j = (G_j, \overline{sl}_j) | G_j \in \mathbb{G} \wedge 0 \leq \overline{sl}_j \leq 100\}$. A confidence level, $0 \leq conf \leq 1$, together with Q_{case}, constitute the whole criteria. Such criteria represent that (with a confidence $conf$) the satisfaction level of every single case in terms of the considered goals G_j will be at least $\overline{sl}_j$. It is noteworthy that all goals in $\mathbb{G}$ are not necessarily considered by Q_{case}. For example, when $\mathbb{G} = \{G_1, G_2, G_3\}$ and $Q_{case} = \{(G_2, 90), (G_3, 75)\}$ and $conf = 0.8$, GoPED is looking for a process model that will yield minimum satisfaction levels of 90 for G2 and 75 for G3, for at least 80% of the cases (i.e., confidence of 0.8).
- $\boldsymbol{Q_{goal}}$ refers to the second type of goal-related criteria. Q_{goal} consists of a set of criteria q_j composed of one goal $G_j \in \mathbb{G}$ and a satisfaction level for that goal. $Q_{goal} = \{q_j = (G_j, \overline{sl}_j) | G_j \in \mathbb{G} \wedge 0 \leq \overline{sl}_j \leq 100\}$. Q_{goal} is looking for a process model that can deliver an *aggregated* satisfaction level for the considered $G_j \in \mathbb{G}$ of at least $\overline{sl}_j$. Again, all goals in $\mathbb{G}$ are not necessarily considered by Q_{goal}. For example, when $\mathbb{G} = \{G_1, G_2, G_3\}$ and $Q_{goal} = \{(G_2, 90), (G_3, 75)\}$, Q_{goal} is looking for a process model that will yield minimum *aggregated* satisfaction levels of 90 for G2 and 75 for G3.
- $\boldsymbol{Q_{Comp}}$ consists of one value between 0 and 100 called $\overline{sl}_{Comp}$. This criterion looks for a process model that can yield a *comprehensive* satisfaction of at least $\overline{sl}_{Comp}$.

Definition 4. *SelectedCases* $\subseteq C$ is the main output of GoPED algorithms and the set of selected cases that satisfy one of the aforementioned criteria.

3.2   GoPED Algorithms

As the goal-related criteria are based on three different viewpoints of *EnhancedLog*, three different algorithms for trace selection are required. The main idea in all three algorithms is to select the largest subset of cases that satisfy the selected criterion.

Searching for the *largest* subset of cases is needed because if one simply selects very few cases that meet the desired criteria, the discovered model will be based on an event log suffering from potential *incompleteness* problems. When the event log consists of too few events, the discovered model is less realistic and risks becoming overfitted.

Another feature of our search approach is that we look over the *cases* $\in C$ rather than the *traces* $\in T$. This is because many cases might have a same trace but different levels of satisfaction for the goals. Moreover, the frequency of each trace contains very important knowledge about real-world behaviors. Therefore, we need to end up with a subset that consists of variations of traces together with their frequencies.

Algorithm 1 Selecting a subset of an event log to infer a process model that guarantees a minimum satisfaction level for one or multiple goals in each selected case

---

Input: *EnhancedLog*: An enhanced structured event log ▷ explained in Definition 2
Q_{case}: A set of criteria; ▷ explained in Definition 3
conf: a confidence level ▷ explained in Definition 3
Output: *SelectedCases* ▷ a subset of cases selected according to the criteria and the all-or-none rule

1   sort_by_trace(*EnhancedLog*) ▷ sort the cases based on their traces
2    $trace(case_0) \leftarrow \langle\rangle$ ▷ $\langle\rangle$ is an empty trace, which cannot happen in reality
3    $trace(cases_{NumberOfCases+1}) \leftarrow \langle\rangle$ ▷ also flag the end of the log
4   *SelectedCases* $\leftarrow \emptyset$
5   index $\leftarrow 1$
6   **while** index $\leq$ NumberOfCases ▷ NumberOfCases is m in Table 1
7   SameTraceCases $\leftarrow \emptyset$ ▷ a set of cases whose traces are the same
8   NumberOfSatisfiedCasesOfTrace $\leftarrow 0$ ▷ counts the satisfied cases of a trace
9   **do**
10   SameTraceCases $\leftarrow$ SameTraceCases $\cup \{case_{index}\}$
11   **if** $case_{index}$ meets all criteria of Q_{case} **then**
12   NumberOfSatisfiedCasesOfTrace $++$
13   **end if**
14   index $++$
15   **while** $trace(case_{index}) = trace(case_{index-1})$
16   **if** NumberOfSatisfiedCasesOfTrace / size(SameTraceCases) $\geq$ *conf* **then**
17   *SelectedCases* = *SelectedCases* $\cup$ SameTraceCases
18   **end if**
19   **end while**
20   **return** *SelectedCases* ▷ the resulting subset of cases

---

One consequence of searching within cases is that there might be some cases with trace t_k that are eligible to be selected and, simultaneously, some cases with the same trace that are not. Although including the former cases and excluding the latter ones appears to be a simple solution, it would not be correct. The reason is that a discovered model either allows a trace (and all its cases) or avoids it. We respect an "*all-or-none*" rule, i.e., the *SelectedCases* should have either all cases of a same trace or none of them. Based on the above explanation, we define the three algorithms for selecting the best subset of cases regarding the three types of goal criteria and the *all-or-none* rule.

Algorithm 1: Guaranteeing One or Multiple Goals for All Cases. This type of goal-related criterion is looking for a model that guarantees (with a given confidence level) a predefined satisfaction level for one or multiple goals for all cases. This criterion considers every single case in a row viewpoint, therefore each case will be assessed against all goals considered in the criterion. There might be cases with trace t_k that meets all $q_i \in Q_{case}$ and some cases with the same trace that do not. Algorithm 1 checks all cases of one trace against Q_{case} (line 11). If the proportion of complying cases is not inferior to the given confidence level *conf*, all the cases with that trace will be selected, otherwise all of them will be filtered out (lines 16–17). For example, assume *conf* is 0.8 and the event log has 100 cases with trace $\langle a, b, c, g \rangle$, including 83 cases that meet Q_{case} and 17 cases that do not. As 83% of these cases comply with the criterion, which is above the confidence level of 80%, all 100 cases are selected. Algorithm 1 first sorts all cases according to their trace (line 1). Searching within all cases of a trace and checking them against the criteria is hence efficient (lines 9–15).

Algorithm 2 Selecting a subset of an event log to infer a process model that guarantees the overall satisfaction level(s) of one or multiple goals

---

Input: *EnhancedLog*: An enhanced structured event log ▷ explained in Definition 2
Q_{goal}: A set of criteria (some goals and thresholds for their satisfaction level) ▷ Definition 3
g: A function computing the satisfaction of the whole goal model ▷ Definition 3
Output: *SelectedCases* ▷ a subset of all cases selected regarding the criteria and
the all-or-none rule, *SelectedCases* ⊆ *C*, Definition 4

1 *SelectedCases* ← ∅
2 **Solve the binary optimization below:** (x_i is a flag for either selecting case$_i$ or not)

> $Max\ z = \sum_{i=1}^{m} x_i$ ▷ this is to find the largest subset
> **s.t.**
> $\forall r, t\ \ 1 \le r < t \le m$: if $trace(c_r) = trace(c_t)$ $x_r = x_t$ ▷ all-or-none rule
> $\forall j$ where $G_j \in G$: $\dfrac{\sum_{i=1}^{m} x_i \cdot s_{i,j}}{\sum_{i=1}^{m} x_i} \ge \overline{sl}_j$ ▷ $|Q_{goal}|$ constraints
> $x_i = 0, 1$ ▷ if $x_i = 1$, case i should be selected

3 **end of binary optimization**
4   **for** $i = 1$ to NumberOfCases **do** ▷ NumberOfCases is m in Table 1
5   **if** $x_i = 1$ **then**
6   *SelectedCases* ← *SelectedCases* ∪ $\{c_i\}$
7   **end**
8   **end**
9 **return** *SelectedCases* ▷ the resulting subset of cases that meets the criteria

---

Algorithm 2: Guaranteeing the Aggregated Satisfaction Levels of Goals. Here, in a column perspective, the focus is on the *aggregated* satisfaction level of one or multiple goals. Logically, the largest subset that simultaneously meets all criteria is the intersection of the largest subsets that separately meet all criteria. Therefore, one can focus on all considered goals individually and find the largest subsets for each G_j regarding $\overline{sl}_j$, then use their intersection as *SelectedCases*. However, finding the largest subset is not trivial because the largest subset that satisfies the criterion of one goal might not be unique and different subsets with similar (and largest) sizes may satisfy the condition. This might be the case even when the aggregation function is simple (e.g., *average*). In this situation, a subset that makes the largest intersection of all subsets (generated by all considered goals) should be selected. If this situation happens for several goals, we have to deal with the challenge of selecting one combination that finally makes the largest set.

Addressing such a difficulty, Algorithm 2 generates a binary optimization whose number of variables (x_i) equals the number of cases (m). The binary variable x_i is a flag variable associated to case c_i. If $x_i = 1$, then the case c_i will be selected and, if not, it will be excluded. As we are looking for the largest subset, $\sum x_i$ should be as large as possible. There are two categories of constraints for the optimization problem. The first aims to preserve the *all-or-none* rule, i.e., the selected subset should have either all cases of a same trace or none of them. The second category of constraints takes care of the threshold for the aggregated satisfaction level of each goal, i.e., $\overline{sl_j}$. This category of constraints is based on f_j, i.e., the aggregation function. In Algorithm 2 we assumed that all f_j are the *average* function (but others could be defined).

Algorithm 3 Selecting the largest subset of an event log to infer a process model that guarantees a comprehensive satisfaction level

---

Input: *EnhancedLog*: An enhanced structured event log; ▷ as explained by Definition 2

Q_{Comp} : $\overline{sl}_{Comp}$ ▷ a minimum threshold for comprehensive satisfaction level

F: a tuple of functions $(f_1, f_2, ..., f_n) \mid s_{Agg.j} = f_j (s_{1,j}, s_{2,j}, ..., s_{m,j}), j = 1,...,n$

g: a function derived from the goal model. $s_{i.ove} = g (s_{i,1}, s_{i,2}, ... , s_{i,n})$

Output: *SelectedCases* ▷ a subset of all cases selected regarding the criteria and the all-or-none rule, *SelectedCases* $\subseteq C$

1   *SelectedCases* $\leftarrow \varnothing$
2   **if** $s_{Comp} = f_{n+1}(s_{1.ove}, s_{2.ove}, ... , s_{m.ove})$ **then**
3   use Algorithm 2 and exit.
4   **else**
5   **Solve the binary optimization below:**

> $Max\ z = \sum_{i=1}^{m} x_i$ ▷ this is to find the largest subset.
> **s.t.**
>
> $\forall r, t\ \ 1 \le r < t \le m$: if $trace(c_r) = trace(c_t)$ $x_r = x_t$ ▷ all-or-none rule
>
> $g\left(\dfrac{\sum_{i=1}^{m} x_i.s_{i1}}{\sum_{i=1}^{m} x_i}, \dfrac{\sum_{i=1}^{m} x_i.s_{i2}}{\sum_{i=1}^{m} x_i}, ..., \dfrac{\sum_{i=1}^{m} x_i.s_{in}}{\sum_{i=1}^{m} x_i}\right) \ge \overline{sl}_{Comp}$
>
> $x_i = 0, 1$

6   **end**
7   **for** $i = 1$ to NumberOfCases **do** ▷ NumberOfCases is m in Table 1
8   **if** $x_i = 1$ **then**
9   *SelectedCases* $\leftarrow$ *SelectedCases* $\cup \{c_i\}$
10   **end**
11   **end**
12   **return** *SelectedCases* ▷ the resulting subset of cases that meets the criterion

---

Algorithm 3: Guaranteeing Comprehensive Satisfaction Levels. The two above types of criteria considered the goals from a row perspective and a column perspective. The third type of criteria, however, considers the goals from a *table* perspective.

Here, the overall satisfaction level of all columns is aggregated and represented by one number as a *comprehensive satisfaction level*. Finding the largest subset of cases that guarantees a minimum threshold for comprehensive satisfaction level ($\overline{sl}_{comp}$) is,

Table 2. *EnhancedLog*, event log and satisfaction level of goals for the DGD process

Case	Trace	G_1: To decrease process time	G_2: To decrease cost	G_3: To do a smooth process	G_4: To screen accurately	Overall (To satisfy the patient)
Patient#1	$\langle a, b, c, g \rangle$	100	100	88	100	97
Patient#2	$\langle a, b, c, g \rangle$	94	100	88	100	95
Patient#3	$\langle a, b, c, g \rangle$	94	100	88	0	0
Patient#4	$\langle a, b, c, d, e, c, g \rangle$	61	59	75	100	64
Patient#5	$\langle a, b, c, d, e, c, g \rangle$	72	59	63	100	65
Patient#6	$\langle a, b, c, d, e, c, g \rangle$	67	59	75	100	66
Patient#7	$\langle a, b, c, f, b, c, g \rangle$	78	82	63	100	76
Patient#8	$\langle a, b, c, f, b, c, d, e, c, g \rangle$	41	20	50	100	36
Patient#9	$\langle a, b, c, f, b, c, d, e, c, g \rangle$	43	20	40	100	34
Patient#10	$\langle a, b, c, d, b, c, d, e, c, g \rangle$	9	10	30	100	15
Aggregated satisfaction:		65.9	60.9	66	90	**64.1**

also, not trivial. This is because adding a trace to the subset might increase the aggregated level of one goal and, at the same time, decrease the level of another goal.

As explained in Definition 3, the *comprehensive* level might be calculated in two different ways. It can be the overall satisfaction level of the aggregated levels of all goals, or the aggregated level of the overall satisfaction level of each case. The latter one will work only with the column of the overall satisfaction level (the right column of Table 1), therefore, the problem will be solved in a way similar to that of the second type of criteria (Algorithm 2). Accordingly, Algorithm 3. first checks the definition of *comprehensive*. If it is not like Algorithm 2, then Algorithm 3 generates a new binary optimization problem. Here, the first category of constrains aims to preserve the *all-or-none* rule, whereas the last constraint makes sure that the comprehensive level of the selected subset is not less than the given threshold $\overline{sl}_{comp}$.

4 Illustrative Example

The process of *diagnosis of gestational diabetes* (DGD) will be used to illustrate the proposed methods. To this end, three types of goal-related criteria discussed in Sect. 2 will be taken into consideration. The main assumption here is that the log is realistic but *not real* and is used only to study the GoPED method and its algorithms.

4.1 Event Log of an Illustrative DGD Process

The event log of 10 patients who have used the DGD process is shown in Table 2. We use short names to encode the activities: a = admission, b = regular test, c = check the result, d = request for advanced test, e = advanced test, f = request for repetition, and g = send the result. According to Table 2 and the definitions described in Sect. 3.1, the event log (L) includes five different variants of traces:

$$L = [\langle a,b,c,g \rangle^3, \langle a,b,c,d,e,c,g \rangle^3, \langle a,b,c,f,b,c,g \rangle^1,$$

$$\langle a,b,c,f,b,c,d,e,c,g \rangle^2, \langle a,b,c,d,b,c,d,e,c,d,e,c,g \rangle^1]$$

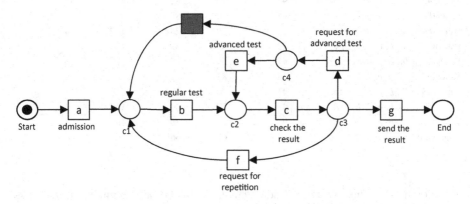

Model 1. Process model discovered from the original event log by the α-algorithm

As shown in Table 2, there are four additional goal-oriented fields related to the DGD process. Due to space limitation, we directly show the satisfaction levels of the goals in the table (without their indicators or actors), which are values in the range [0–100].

An advanced version of the α-algorithm [17] generates Model 1 using the whole event log. The main story of this DGD process is as follows: after admission of a patient, a regular blood test is done. Then, based on the result of the test the patient may need to do an advanced test, the patient may need to repeat the regular test, or the result will be sent to the related department, and then the process ends. A *silent* transition is shown in Model 1 with black color. That is a particular transition not observable in the event log, but needed to make a *sound* Petri-net [16]. Considering the traces, the source of this need is that for Patient#10, after the activity *d*, request for advanced test, the activity *b*, regular test, has executed, while the activity *e*, advanced test, was supposed to execute. Model 1 will be used as a basis for considering the resulting models from GoPED respecting three types of goal-related criteria.

4.2   Example Models Resulting from GoPED

Guaranteeing Satisfaction of One or Multiple Goals for All Cases. This goal-related criterion is looking for a model that guarantees a predefined satisfaction level for all cases in terms of one or multiple goals, with a given confidence level. For example, the condition is as follows:

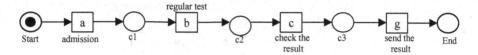

Model 2. To satisfy goal criteria of Q_{case}

- *Case perspective:* generate a model that guarantees (with a confidence of 90%) that the satisfaction level for all patients in terms of goal "To decrease process time" will be at least 75 and that in terms of goal "To do a smooth process" will be at least 80.

In this case, we have $Q_{case} = \{(G_1, 75), (G_3, 80)\}$ and $conf = 0.9$. Using Algorithm 1, only all the cases of trace $\langle a, b, c, g \rangle$ are returned, i.e., Patients #1, #2 and #3. All cases of this trace meet $Q_{case.}$, so the fraction of eligible cases of this trace is 100%, which is more than the required 90% confidence level. Such a parameter for the four remaining traces is zero, which is less than 90% by far. Therefore, we have *SelectedCases* = {Patient#1, Patient#2, Patient#3}, resulting in the log $\{\langle a, b, c, g \rangle^3\}$. The α-algorithm [17] produces Model 2 from this log. This is the process to be encouraged in the organization to meet these goals.

Guaranteeing the Aggregated Satisfaction Levels of Goals. Here, from a column perspective, the focus is on the aggregated satisfaction level of one or multiple goals rather than on the satisfaction of every single case.

- *Goal perspective:* Generate a model that results in an *aggregated* satisfaction levels of the goal "To decrease time process" higher than 80 and of the goal "To do a smooth process" higher than 78, simultaneously.

In this case, we have $Q_{goal} = \{(G_1, 80), (G_3, 78)\}$. Here the functions f showing how to calculate the aggregation of each column is required. Let us assume that for all goals in the DGD process, the function is the *average*. Therefore, the optimization problem of Algorithm 2 can be formalized as follows:

$$Max\ z = \sum_{i=1}^{10} x_i$$

s.t.

$$x_1 = x_2 = x_3, \quad x_4 = x_5 = x_6, \quad x_8 = x_9 \quad \leftarrow (\textit{all-or-none}\ \text{rule})$$

$$\frac{100x_1+94x_2+94x_3+61x_4+72x_5+67x_6+78x_7+41x_8+43x_9+9x_{10}}{\sum_{i=1}^{m} x_i} \geq 80$$

$$\frac{88x_1+88x_2+88x_3+75x_4+63x_5+75x_6+63x_7+50x_8+40x_9+30x_{10}}{\sum_{i=1}^{m} x_i} \geq 78$$

$$x_i = 0, 1$$

The answer of the above problem is unique: $x_1 = x_2 = x_3 = x_4 = x_5 = x_6 = 1$ and $x_7 = x_8 = x_9 = x_{10} = 0$. Therefore, *SelectedCases* = {Patient#1, Patient#2, Patient#3, Patient#4, Patient#5, Patient#6}, leading to the log $\{\langle a, b, c, g \rangle^3, \langle a, b, c, d, e, c, g \rangle^3\}$. For this subset of cases, the aggregation satisfaction level for G1 and G3 will be 81.3 and 79.5, respectively. The α-algorithm produces Model 3 from this log.

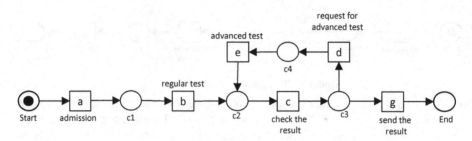

Model 3. To satisfy goal criteria of Q_{goal}

Guaranteeing Comprehensive Satisfaction Levels. Here, from a table perspective, the focus is on the *comprehensive* satisfaction level, which we assume to be the *overall* satisfaction level of the *aggregated* levels of all goals. Therefore, the goal model should be used to evaluate s_{Comp} based on the satisfaction levels of all sub goals. Figure 2 shows the goals model related to the DGD process using the GRL language. In the graph, the root is the main goal and the sub goals are the leaves. Based on the goal model and its AND/OR refinements and the weight of contributions, the s_{Comp} is defined as follows:

$$s_{Comp} = Sat(G_6) = \text{Minimum}(s_{Agg.4}, 0.4 \times s_{Agg.1} + 0.35 \times s_{Agg.2} + 0.25 \times s_{Agg.3})$$

This kind of evaluation is known as *forward propagation* in GRL. The jUCMNav tool is an Eclipse-based graphical editor that can be used for evaluating GRL models [9].

- *Organization perspective*: Generate a model where the comprehensive satisfaction level is no less than 75.

The above criterion leads to $Q_{Comp} = 75$. Recall that $s_{Agg.j}$ is the aggregated satisfaction of goal j, in our case the *average* of column of $Goal_j$ in Table 2. According to the function derived from the goal model of Fig. 2, Algorithm 3 generates the optimization problem as follows:

$$Max\ z = \sum_{i=1}^{10} x_i$$

s.t.

$$x_1 = x_2 = x_3, \quad x_4 = x_5 = x_6, \quad x_8 = x_9 \quad \leftarrow (all\text{-}or\text{-}none\ \text{rule})$$

$$\text{Minimum}\left(\frac{\sum_{i=1}^{m} x_i \cdot s_{i,4}}{\sum_{i=1}^{m} x_i}, \ 0.4 \times \frac{\sum_{i=1}^{m} x_i \cdot s_{i,1}}{\sum_{i=1}^{m} x_i} + 0.35 \times \frac{\sum_{i=1}^{m} x_i \cdot s_{i,2}}{\sum_{i=1}^{m} x_i} + 0.25 \times \frac{\sum_{i=1}^{m} x_i \cdot s_{i,3}}{\sum_{i=1}^{m} x_i}\right) \geq 75$$

$$x_i = 0, 1$$

($s_{i,j}$ refers to the cells of Table 2, e.g., $s_{2,1} = 94$).

The answer of the above problem is, also, unique: $x_1 = x_2 = x_3 = x_4 = x_5 = x_6 = x_7 = 1$ and $x_8 = x_9 = x_{10} = 0$. Therefore, *SelectedCases* = {Patient#1, Patient#2, Patient#3, Patient#4, Patient#5, Patient#6, Patient#7}, resulting in the log {$\langle a, b, c, g \rangle^3$, $\langle a, b, c, d, e, c, g \rangle^3$, $\langle a, b, c, f, b, c, g \rangle$}. For this subset, the *comprehensive satisfaction level* is 79.5. The α-algorithm produces Model 4 from this log.

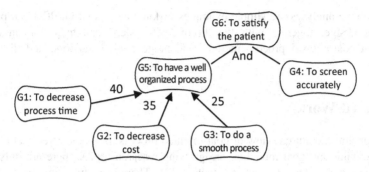

Fig. 2. Goal model showing the relations between the goals pursued by the DGD process

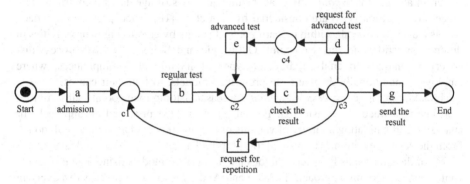

Model 4. To satisfy goal criteria of Q_{Comp}

4.3 Discussion

We generated three models using three types of goal-related criteria. Comparing the models, we find that the main difference between Model 2 and the other models relates to the loops. Model 2 does not allow repeating the regular test or to do an advanced test. Here, the decision point "check the result" is spurious as it will not actually make any decision. According to the goals considered in the generation of such a model, i.e., G1 and G3, one can hypothesize that doing advanced blood test or repeating the regular test are not aligned with the goals of having short process time and of providing all patients with a smooth process. Considering the trace $\langle a, b, c, g \rangle$ that Model 2 can generate, we find that there are three patients who experienced this trace. One of these patients has been diagnosed wrongly ($s_{3,4} = 0$). The goal model shown in Fig. 2 implies that the goal "To screen accurately" participates to an AND refinement; therefore, when this goal is denied, regardless of the other goals in the refinement, the main goal of the process gets denied. Using the goal model, the overall satisfaction level of those three patients are 97, 95 and 0, respectively. This suggests that although Model 2 highly satisfies all cases in terms of process time and smoothness of the process, it will end up with a third of the patients who will be dissatisfied.

The above analyses are simple examples of knowledge that GoPED can provide. Such knowledge, together with the discovered models, can help domain experts (re)design goal-aligned process models, encourage good behaviors, and discourage bad ones.

5   Related Work

Our systematic literature review of goal-oriented process mining showed that although process mining and goal modeling are growing research topics, there are only a few rare studies conducted at their intersection [7]. Therefore, this suggests that goal-oriented processes discovery can still be considered a gap to be filled between the process mining and requirements engineering communities.

From an *agent viewpoint*, the goals behind activities of agents who contribute in a process (e.g., employees) are considered by Yan et al. [18]. Their proposed approach adopts a decision tree algorithm to learn goals of agents by classifying their activities in different situations. In this viewpoint, Outmazgin and Soffer [11] used process discovery techniques to analyze different types of intentional incompliances, where employees intentionally deviate from prescribed models, to find their causes.

In addition, in a *process viewpoint* (or case/customer viewpoint) all activities constituting a trace are considered. Ponnalagu et al. [13] proposed an approach for analyzing and validating a family of variants of a single process based on a goal model. From the same view point, Horita et al. [8] proposed a method to detect and analyze the effects of disagreements between real logs and prescribed models using a goal-oriented conformance checking approach. Bernard and Andritsos [3] used process discovery in conjunction with customers' journeys and developed a tool that facilitates navigation through many different journeys in a goal-oriented fashion.

An *organization viewpoint* considers the overall goals that should be achieved by performing business processes. Santiputri et al. [14] considered the sequence of events in multi-layered event logs and proposed an approach to discover goal refinement patterns of the goal models.

Trace clustering is a solution proposed by the process mining community to improve interpretability of discovered process models by splitting different behaviors on different process perspectives into multiple sub-logs. Similar to our approach, the main idea in the existing clustering approaches is to discover models from subsets of logs. However, the clustering approach yet considers the log at an activity-level and does not bring the satisfaction of competing goals of stakeholders into account [10, 15].

6   Conclusion

This paper proposed a new method that exploits the capabilities of goal modeling and performs process discovery in a goal-oriented fashion. This method first enhances an event log by adding new goal-related information to all traces. Then, it quantifies the satisfaction level of goals using a goal model. Such a goal model shows correlations between (often conflicting) goals of different stakeholders and allows what-if analysis and balancing trade-offs between confliction goals. Three types of goal-related criteria were introduced as the basis for generating goal-oriented models promising to achieve predefined goals. The real behaviors that are aligned with the goals and achieve desired satisfaction levels are selected. Three algorithms for such a selection were explicitly explained. The selected subset becomes the basis for conventional process discovery. The resulting model can be compared to a model discovered from the original event log to reveal new insights about the ability of different forms of process models to satisfy the goals. Learning from *good* behaviors that satisfy goals and detecting *bad* behaviors that hurt them is an opportunity to redesign models so they are better aligned with goals.

Acknowledgment. This work was supported by Natural Sciences and Engineering Research Council of Canada (NSERC, Discovery and CGS-D).

References

1. Amyot, D., Ghanavati, S., Horkoff, J., Mussbacher, G., Peyton, L., Yu, E.: Evaluating goal models within the goal-oriented requirement language. Int. J. Intell. Syst. **25**(8), 841–877 (2010). https://doi.org/10.1002/int.20433
2. Amyot, D., Mussbacher, G.: User requirements notation: the first ten years, the next ten years. J. Softw. **6**(5), 747–768 (2011)
3. Bernard, B., Andritsos, P.: CJM-ex: goal-oriented exploration of customer journey maps using event logs and data analytics. In: BPM Demo Track and BPM Dissertation Award (BPMD&DA), vol. 1920. EUR-WS (2017)
4. Fan, Y., Anda, A.A., Amyot, D.: An arithmetic semantics for GRL goal models with function generation. In: Khendek, F., Gotzhein, R. (eds.) SAM 2018. LNCS, vol. 11150, pp. 144–162. Springer, Cham (2018). https://doi.org/10.1007/978-3-030-01042-3_9
5. Ghasemi, M.: Towards goal-oriented process mining. In: 2018 IEEE 26th International Requirements Engineering Conference (RE), pp. 484–489. IEEE CS (2018). https://doi.org/10.1109/re.2018.00066
6. Ghasemi, M.: What requirements engineering can learn from process mining. In: 2018 1st International Workshop on Learning from other Disciplines for Requirements Engineering (D4RE), pp. 8–11. IEEE (2018). https://doi.org/10.1109/d4re.2018.00008
7. Ghasemi, M., Amyot, D.: From event logs to goals: a systematic literature review of goal-oriented process mining. Requir. Eng. 1–27 (2019). https://doi.org/10.1007/s00766-018-00308-3
8. Horita, H., Hirayama, H., Tahara, Y., Ohsuga, A.: Towards goal-oriented conformance checking. In: Proceedings of the International Conference on Software Engineering and Knowledge Engineering SEKE, pp. 722–724 (2015)
9. jUCMNav (2016). http://softwareengineering.ca/jucmnav
10. Mannhardt, F., de Leoni, M., Reijers, H., van der Aalst, W., Toussaint, P.: Guided process discovery – a pattern-based approach. Inf. Syst. **76**, 1–18 (2018). https://doi.org/10.1016/j.is.2018.01.009
11. Outmazgin, N., Soffer, P.: A process mining-based analysis of business process work-arounds. Softw. Syst. Model. **15**(2), 309–323 (2016)

12. Pesic, M., van der Aalst, W.M.P.: A declarative approach for flexible business processes management. In: Eder, J., Dustdar, S. (eds.) BPM 2006. LNCS, vol. 4103, pp. 169–180. Springer, Heidelberg (2006). https://doi.org/10.1007/11837862_18

13. Ponnalagu, K., Ghose, A., Narendra, Nanjangud C., Dam, H.K.: Goal-aligned categorization of instance variants in knowledge-intensive processes. In: Motahari-Nezhad, H.R., Recker, J., Weidlich, M. (eds.) BPM 2015. LNCS, vol. 9253, pp. 350–364. Springer, Cham (2015). https://doi.org/10.1007/978-3-319-23063-4_24

14. Santiputri, M., Deb, N., Khan, M.A., Ghose, A., Dam, H., Chaki, N.: Mining goal refinement patterns: distilling know-how from data. In: Mayr, H.C., Guizzardi, G., Ma, H., Pastor, O. (eds.) ER 2017. LNCS, vol. 10650, pp. 69–76. Springer, Cham (2017). https://doi.org/10.1007/978-3-319-69904-2_6

15. Seeliger, A., Nolle, T., Mühlhäuser, M.: Finding structure in the unstructured: hybrid feature set clustering for process discovery. In: Weske, M., Montali, M., Weber, I., vom Brocke, J. (eds.) BPM 2018. LNCS, vol. 11080, pp. 288–304. Springer, Cham (2018). https://doi.org/10.1007/978-3-319-98648-7_17

16. van der Aalst, W.: Process Mining Data Science in Action, 2nd edn. Springer, Heidelberg (2016). https://doi.org/10.1007/978-3-662-49851-4

17. Wen, L., van der Aalst, W., Wang, J., Sun, J.: Mining process models with non-free-choice constructs. Data Min. Knowl. Disc. 15(2), 145–180 (2007)

18. Yan, J., Hu, D., Liao, S., Wang, H.: Mining agents' goals in agent-oriented business processes. ACM Trans. Manag. Inf. Syst. 5(4), 1–22 (2014)

Checking Regulatory Compliance: Will We Live to See It?

Silvano Colombo Tosatto, Guido Governatori, and Nick van Beest[✉]

Data61, CSIRO, Dutton Park, Queensland, Australia
{silvano.colombo,guido.governatori,nick.vanbeest}@data61.csiro.au,
colombotosatto.silvano@gmail.com

Abstract. Checking regulatory compliance of business processes prior to deployment is common practice and numerous approaches have been developed over the last decade. However, the computational complexity of the problem itself has never received any major attention. Although it is known that the complexity of the problem is generally in **NP**-complete, many existing approaches ignore the issue using the excuse that current problems are small enough to be solved anyway. However, due to the current race towards digitalisation and automatisation, the size and complexity of the problems is bound to increase. As such, this paper investigates the computational complexity of all sub-classes of the problem and categorises some of the existing approaches, providing a detailed overview of the issues that require to be tackled in order for current compliance checking solutions to remain feasible in future scenarios.

Keywords: Business process modelling · Regulatory compliance · Computational complexity

1 Introduction

Recently more and more effort is put into digitalising and automatising businesses and services in various sectors. Considering both the importance and complexity of proving regulatory compliance of such automated business models, studying and understanding the details about the computational complexity of such problems becomes of paramount importance.

Current approaches aiming at proving regulatory compliance of business process models (i.e. verifying whether their executions follow the required regulations) already exist. However, due to the limited size and complexity of the models currently used, the computational complexity of these problems has not yet been an insurmountable issue. Nevertheless, due to the increase in automation and digitalisation, the size of the problems and their complexity are also bound to increase. This, in turn, will lead the computational complexity to be an issue in the future.

With this in mind, we study the computational complexity of some variants of the problem identified by considering some properties, namely the number of

© Springer Nature Switzerland AG 2019
T. Hildebrandt et al. (Eds.): BPM 2019, LNCS 11675, pp. 119–138, 2019.
https://doi.org/10.1007/978-3-030-26619-6_10

regulations to be verified, their expressivity and whether they affect the process partially or entirely. Given these properties, we identify 8 variants. The computational complexity for some of these variants has already been studied by Colombo Tosatto et al. [22,23], showing that the upper bound complexity of the variants of the problem considered in the present paper is **NP**-complete, while the lower bound is in **P**.

While being aware that the regulatory framework is not the only source of computational complexity in the regulatory compliance problem, we have decided to explore and study the variants of the problem obtainable by considering a relatively simple business process model, acyclic structured business processes, and varying the properties of the regulatory framework. Although the computational complexity study provided in this paper does not investigate the whole problem, it still provides an analysis of many variants of the problem. As such, it can be used in the future to start a further computational complexity analysis, such as for instance how the properties of a business process model contribute to the computational complexity of the problem.

Additionally, we analyse some of the existing solutions, and assign them to the variants of the problem identified in this paper. Our goal is to show in this way, which of the currently available solutions are bound to hit the computational complexity wall as automatising compliance proving gains popularity.

The remainder of this paper is structured as follows. Section 2 introduces the problem of proving regulatory compliance of business process model and its semantics. Subsequently, Sect. 3 introduces the classification and acronyms of the variants of the problem studied in this paper, and discusses some of the existing computational complexity results. Next, Sect. 4 extends the computational complexity results and provides additional ones for some of the variants. Section 5 shows how some of the existing approaches aiming at solving the regulatory compliance problem can be assigned to the problem's variants identified and studied. Finally, Sect. 6 concludes the paper. In order to preserve the readability of the paper, we have collected the computational complexity proofs in the Appendix.

2   Proving Regulatory Compliance

In this section, we introduce the problem of proving regulatory compliance of business process models analysed in this paper. The problem consists of two components: (i) the business process model compactly describing a set of possible executions, and (ii) a regulatory framework, describing the compliance requirements.

2.1   Structured Business Processes

We limit our study to structured process models, as the soundness[1] of such models can be verified in polynomial time with respect to their size, and allows

---

[1] A process is sound, as defined by van der Aalst [1,24], if it avoids livelocks and deadlocks.

us to reuse some existing results to prove our claims. These processes are similar to structured workflows defined by Kiepuszewski et al. [15].

Definition 1 (Process Block). *A process block B is a directed graph: the nodes are called* elements *and the directed edges are called* arcs. *The set of elements of a process block are identified by the function $V(B)$ and the set of arcs by the function $E(B)$. The set of elements is composed of tasks and coordinators. There are 4 types of coordinators:* and_split, and_join, xor_split *and* xor_join. *Each process block B has two distinguished nodes called the* initial *and* final *element. The initial element has no incoming arc from other elements in B and is denoted by $b(B)$. Similarly the final element has no outgoing arcs to other elements in B and is denoted by $f(B)$.*

A directed graph composing a process block is defined inductively as follows:

- *A single task constitutes a process block. The task is both initial and final element of the block.*
- *Let $B_1, \ldots, B_n$ be distinct process blocks with $n > 1$:*
  - SEQ$(B_1, \ldots, B_n)$ *denotes the process block with node set $\bigcup_{i=0}^{n} V(B_i)$ and edge set $\bigcup_{i=0}^{n} (E(B_i) \cup \{(f(B_i), b(B_{i+1})) : 1 \le i < n\})$. The initial element of* SEQ$(B_1, \ldots, B_n)$ *is $b(B_1)$ and its final element is $f(B_n)$.*
  - XOR$(B_1, \ldots, B_n)$ *denotes the block with vertex set $\bigcup_{i=0}^{n} V(B_i) \cup \{$xsplit, xjoin$\}$ and edge set $\bigcup_{i=0}^{n} (E(B_i) \cup \{($xsplit$, b(B_i)), (f(B_i),$xjoin$) : 1 \le i \le n\})$ where* xsplit *and* xjoin *respectively denote an* xor_split *coordinator and an* xor_join *coordinator, respectively. The initial element of* XOR$(B_1, \ldots, B_n)$ *is* xsplit *and its final element is* xjoin.
  - AND$(B_1, \ldots, B_n)$ *denotes the block with vertex set $\bigcup_{i=0}^{n} V(B_i) \cup \{$asplit, ajoin$\}$ and edge set $\bigcup_{i=0}^{n} (E(B_i) \cup \{($asplit$, b(B_i)), (f(B_i),$ajoin$) : 1 \le i \le n\})$ where* asplit *and* ajoin *denote an* and_split *and an* and_join *coordinator, respectively. The initial element of* AND$(B_1, \ldots, B_n)$ *is* asplit *and its final element is* ajoin.

By enclosing a process block as defined in Definition 1 along with a start and end task in a sequence block, we obtain a *structured process model*. The effects of executing the tasks contained in a business process model are described using annotations as shown in Definition 2.

Definition 2 (Annotated process). *Let P be a structured process and T be the set of tasks contained in P. An annotated process is a pair: (P, ann), where* ann *is a function associating a consistent set of literals to each task in T:* ann $: T \mapsto 2^{\mathcal{L}}$. *The function* ann *is constrained to the consistent literals sets in $2^{\mathcal{L}}$.*

The update between the states of a process during its execution is inspired by the AGM[2] belief revision operator [2] and is used in the context of business

---

[2] The operator is named after the initials of the authors introducing it: Alchourrón, Gärdenfors, and Makinson.

processes to define the transitions between states, which in turn are used to define the *traces*.

Definition 3 (State update). *Given two consistent sets of literals L_1 and L_2, representing the process state and the annotation of a task being executed, the update of L_1 with L_2, denoted by $L_1 \oplus L_2$ is a set of literals defined as follows:*

$$L_1 \oplus L_2 = L_1 \setminus \{\neg l \mid l \in L_2\} \cup L_2$$

Definition 4 (Executions and Traces). *Given a structured process model identified by a process block B, the set of its executions, written $\Sigma(B) = \{\epsilon | \epsilon$ is a sequence and is an execution of $B\}$. The function $\Sigma(B)$ is defined as follows:*

1. *If B is a task t, then $\Sigma(B) = \{(\{t\}, \emptyset)\}$*
2. *if B is a composite block with sub-blocks $B_1, \ldots, B_n$:*
   (a) *If $B = \mathsf{SEQ}(B_1, \ldots, B_n)$, then $\Sigma(B) = \{\epsilon_1 +_{\mathcal{E}} \cdots +_{\mathcal{E}} \epsilon_n | \epsilon_i \in \Sigma(B_i)\}$ and $+_{\mathcal{E}}$ the operator concatenating two executions.*
   (b) *If $B = \mathsf{XOR}(B_1, \ldots, B_n)$, then $\Sigma(B) = \Sigma(B_1) \cup \cdots \cup \Sigma(B_n)$*
   (c) *If $B = \mathsf{AND}(B_1, \ldots, B_n)$, then $\Sigma(B) = \{$the union of the interleavings of: $\epsilon_1, \ldots, \epsilon_n | \epsilon_i \in \Sigma(B_i)\}$*

Given an annotated process (B, ann) and an execution $\epsilon = (t_1, \ldots, t_n)$ such that $\epsilon \in \Sigma(B)$, a trace θ is a finite sequence of states: $(\sigma_1, \ldots, \sigma_n)$. Each state of $\sigma_i \in \theta$ is a pair: (t_i, L_i) capturing what holds after the execution of a task t_i, expressed by a set of literals L_i. A set L_i is constructed as follows:

1. $L_0 = \emptyset$
2. $L_{i+1} = L_i \oplus \mathsf{ann}(t_{i+1})$, *for* $1 \leq i < n$.

To denote the set of possible traces resulting from a process model (B, ann), we use $\Theta(B, \mathsf{ann})$.

Example 1. Annotated Process Model.
Figure 1 shows a structured process containing four tasks labelled t_1, t_2, t_3 and t_4 and their annotations. The process contains an AND block followed by a task and an XOR block nested within the AND block. The annotations indicate what has to hold after a task is executed. If t_1 is executed, then the literal a has to hold in that state of the process (Table 1).

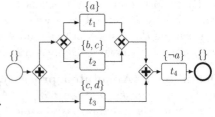

Fig. 1. An annotated process

Table 1. Executions and Traces of the annotated process in Fig. 1.

$\Sigma(B)$	$\Theta(B, \text{ann})$
$(\text{start}, t_1, t_3, t_4, \text{end})$	$((\text{start}, \emptyset), (t_1, \{a\}), (t_3, \{a, c, d\}), (t_4, \{\neg a, c, d\}), (\text{end}, \{\neg a, c, d\}))$
$(\text{start}, t_2, t_3, t_4 \text{end})$	$((\text{start}, \emptyset), (t_2, \{b, c\}), (t_3, \{b, c, d\}), (t_4, \{\neg a, b, c, d\}), (\text{end}, \{\neg a, b, c, d\}))$
$(\text{start}, t_3, t_1, t_4 \text{end})$	$((\text{start}, \emptyset), (t_3, \{c, d\}), (t_1, \{a, c, d\}), (t_4, \{\neg a, c, d\}), (\text{end}, \{\neg a, c, d\}))$
$(\text{start}, t_3, t_2, t_4 \text{end})$	$((\text{start}, \emptyset), (t_3, \{c, d\}), (t_2, \{b, c, d\}), (t_4. \{\neg a, b, c, d\}), (\text{end}, \{\neg a, b, c, d\}))$

2.2 Regulatory Framework

We hereby introduce the regulatory framework through the use of obligations, which are the conditions that a process model needs to fulfil in order to be considered compliant. As such, we use a subset of Process Compliance Logic (PCL), introduced by Governatori and Rotolo [9]. Obligations can be either *global* or *local*. A global obligation is in force for the entire duration of an execution, while the in force interval of a local obligation is determined by its trigger and deadline conditions. Additionally, an obligation can be either an achievement or a maintenance obligation and it determines how such an obligation is fulfilled by an execution when in force.

Definition 5 (Global and Local Obligations).

Global *A global obligation $\mathcal{O}^o\langle c \rangle$, where $o \in \{a, m\}$ represents whether the obligation is achievement or maintenance. The element c represents the condition of the obligation.*

Local *A local obligation $\mathcal{O}^o\langle c, t, d \rangle$, where $o \in \{a, m\}$ represents whether the obligation is achievement or maintenance. The element c represents the condition of the obligation, the element t the trigger, and the element d the deadline.*

While the in force interval of a global obligation spans the entire duration of a trace, the in force interval of a local obligation is determined as a sub-trace where the first state of such a sub-trace satisfies the trigger, and the last state satisfies the deadline. Generally the trigger, deadline and condition of an obligation are defined as propositional formulae. Assuming the literals from $\mathcal{L}$ contained in a state to be true, then a propositional formula can then be evaluated when that state implies it.

Evaluating the Obligations. Whether an in force obligation is fulfilled or violated is determined by the states of the trace included in the in force interval of the obligation. Moreover, whether an in force obligation is fulfilled depends on the type of an obligation, as described in Definition 6.

Definition 6 (Achievement and Maintenance Obligations).

Achievement *If this type of obligation is in force in an interval, then the ful-*
filment condition specified by the regulation must be satisfied by
the execution in at least one point in the interval before the dead-
line is satisfied. If this is the case then the obligation in force is
considered to be satisfied, otherwise it is violated.

Maintenance *If this type of obligation is in force in an interval then the ful-*
filment condition must be satisfied continuously in all points of
the interval until the deadline is satisfied. If this is the case then
the obligation in force is satisfied, otherwise it is violated.

Process Compliance. The procedure of proving whether a process is compliant
with a regulatory framework can return different answers. A process is said to
be *fully compliant* if every trace of the process is compliant with the regulatory
framework. A process is *partially compliant* if there exists at least one trace that
is compliant with the regulatory framework, and *not* compliant if there is no
trace complying with the framework.

Definition 7 (Process Compliance). *Given a process (P, ann) and a regu-*
latory framework composed by a set of obligations $\mathbb{O}$, the compliance of (P, ann)
with respect to $\mathbb{O}$ is determined as follows:

- *Full compliance* $(P, \text{ann}) \vdash^{F} \mathbb{O}$ *if and only if*
  $\forall \theta \in \Theta(P, \text{ann}), \theta \vdash \mathbb{O}$.
- *Partial compliance* $(P, \text{ann}) \vdash^{P} \mathbb{O}$ *if and only if*
  $\exists \theta \in \Theta(P, \text{ann}), \theta \vdash \mathbb{O}$.
- *Not compliant* $(P, \text{ann}) \nvdash \mathbb{O}$ *if and only if*
  $\neg \exists \theta \in \Theta(P, \text{ann}), \theta \vdash \mathbb{O}$.

Note that we consider a trace to be compliant with a regulatory framework
if it satisfies every obligation belonging to the set composing the framework.

3   Existing Complexity Results

In this section, we introduce some of the existing computational complexity
results related variants of the problem discussed in this paper. In particular, we
use such results as a starting point from which we analyse the elements bringing
the computational complexity of the problem into the class of **NP** problems.

3.1   Problem Acronyms

Before discussing the existing results, we first introduce a compact system to
refer to different variants of the problem through acronyms representing their
properties.

Definition 8 (Compact Acronyms). *The variants of the problem we refer to in this paper constantly aim to check regulatory compliance of a structured process model. The acronym system refers to the properties of the obligations being checked against the process model.*

1/n *Whether the structured process is checked against a single (1) or a set of (n) obligations.*

G/L *Whether the in force interval of the obligations is **G**lobal, meaning that it spans the entirety of an execution of the model, or it is **L**ocal, meaning that the in force interval is determined by the trigger and deadline elements of an obligation.*

−/+ *Whether the elements of the obligation being checked on the structured process model are composed by literals (−) or propositional formulae (+).*

For instance, the variant **1G−** consists of verifying whether a structured process model is compliant with a single obligation, whose condition is expressed as a propositional literal and its in force interval spans the entire execution of the process model. Note that in the binary properties of the problems considered in this paper, the leftmost, i.e. 1 in **1/n** represents a subset of the right side. Intuitively, the case on the right side is at least as complex as the left case. For instance, a solution for a problem including a set of regulations requires also to solve the case where the set of regulations is composed of exactly 1 regulation.

3.2 Complexity Results

Table 2 outlines the existing complexity results. Note that, even if Colombo Tosatto et al. provide a reduction showing how the Hamiltonian Path problem can be reduced to **nL−**, the same reduction can also be used to show that the more expressive **nL+** is in **NP**-complete.

Table 2. Regulatory compliance complexity

Problem	Source	Compliance	Complexity Class
1G−	Colombo Tosatto et al. [23]	Full and partial	**P**
nL−	Colombo Tosatto et al. [22]	Partial	**NP**-complete
1L+	Colombo Tosatto et al. [22]	Full	co**NP**-complete
nL+	Colombo Tosatto et al. [22]	Partial	**NP**-complete

From the existing results, it can be noticed that the computational complexity of the variants of the problem jumps from **P** to **NP** as soon as the obligations become **L**ocal, and either the number of obligations is more than one or the elements describing them can be represented by propositional formulae.

Partial Compliance for 1L+ is in NP-complete. Colombo Tosatto et al. [22] show that proving full compliance in **1L+** is co**NP**-complete by providing a reduction from the *tautology* problem. We extend the existing result by showing that verifying whether a structured process model is *partially compliant* with a single local obligation whose elements are expressed using formulae is in **NP**-complete.

We show that proving partial compliance in **1L+** is in **NP**-complete by exploiting the relation between *Tautology* and *Satisfiability* problems. The relation is that in a tautology problem, it is required that every interpretation satisfies the formula, while in a satisfiability problem it is required that there exists one. This relation is the same as the one between *full* and *partial* compliance, where the former checks whether every execution satisfies the regulatory framework, while the latter checks whether there is one. Thus, through the relation mentioned above, and by reusing some elements in the reduction used for the proof showing that proving full compliance of **1L+** is in co**NP**-complete, we prove that checking whether **1L+** is partial compliant is in **NP**-complete.

4   Further Complexity Results

Starting from the existing computational complexity results, we analyse their relations and provide some additional results and insights on the matter.

4.1   From Global to Local Obligations

From Table 2 it might seem that the feature of the problems increasing the computational complexity to the **NP** class is changing the regulations from being global to local, as this very feature is the common one between the variants **nL−** and **1L+**. However, we argue that such a property is not the main cause of the computational complexity jump from **P** to **NP**.

Considering now the variant **nG−**, where each obligation contains a single literal in its condition, we can reduce it to **2G+**, which is a special case of **nG+**, where the set of regulatory requirements contain exactly 2 regulations. This is effectively the simplest case of **nG+**.

Reduction 1. *Consider a set of regulations $\mathbb{R}$, where each regulation r_i contains a fulfilment condition c_i. Consider now the complementary subsets of $\mathbb{R}$: $\mathbb{R}^a$ and $\mathbb{R}^m$, which respectively contain the obligations of type achievement and of type maintenance originally in $\mathbb{R}$.*

The variant $nG-$ can be reduced to $nG+$ with an obligation set containing 2 obligations, by collapsing each obligation belonging to one of the subsets into a single one. The obligation resulting from the reduction contains a condition constructed as follows: $\bigwedge_{i=0}^{n} c_i$. This results in a problem containing two obligations, one achievement and one maintenance, which are in force for the entire execution of the process model and whose conditions are represented by conjunctions of literals.

Proof. The correctness of the reduction follows directly from Definition 6.

The reduction allows us to claim that from a computational complexity perspective **nG−** $\leq$ **nG+**, when proving partial compliance of business process models. This result does not look too surprising initially as the second problem is clearly more complex than the first, due to stepping from − to +, while seemingly maintaining the other properties. However, for the sake of precision, the reduction does reduce **nG−** to **2G+**, as the reduced problem contains exactly two obligations, one for each of the possible types. In the next step of the analysis, we focus on the computational complexity of **1G+**.

Partial Compliance of 1G+ is in NP-complete. We prove now that **1G+**, aiming at proving whether a business process model is partially compliant with a single global obligation, whose condition is represented by a formula, is in **NP**-complete. We use a similar approach to the one used to prove the computational complexity class of **1L+**. The difference between the problems is that the current one is limited to use a global obligation.

Despite the differences, we can still reduce *satisfiability* to **1G+**, showing that it indeed belongs to the **NP**-complete complexity class. Considering **1G−** as a starting variant, this also shows that stepping from the simplest elements of the regulation being verified (whose elements are composed of literals) to the more complex variant (where formulae are allowed) brings it into **NP**. Thus, despite the first impression that moving from global to local obligations could have been the main cause of the computational complexity increase, we have shown here that the expressivity of the elements of the obligations indeed contributes to the computational complexity.

Partial Compliance of nG− is in NP-complete. We prove now that **nG−** (aiming at proving whether a business process model is partially compliant with a set of global obligations, whose condition is represented by a single literal) is in **NP**-complete.

When considering a satisfiability problem like 3-SAT, consisting of deciding whether a formula composed of a conjunction of clauses, where each clause is composed of a disjunction of at least 3 literals, is satisfiable. This problem is computationally hard, as illustrated by Karp [14]. Differently, if the number of disjoint literals is lower than 3, then the problem is solvable in polynomial time, as Krom illustrates [17].

Intuitively, when considering **nG−** and knowing that **1G−** is in **P**, then similarly to a satisfiability problem where multiple clauses are involved in the formula being verified mirrored in a compliance problem by the number of obligations, the computational complexity of proving partial compliance in **nG−** should also be in **NP**. We prove that **nG−** is in **NP** by reducing *3-SAT* to it.

4.2   Computational Complexity Recap

Table 3 provides an overview of the computational complexity results introduced in this paper for the problem of proving partial compliance of business process models with respect to a set of obligations with varying features. We can immediately see that the variants of the problem analysed in this paper have been proven to be **NP**-complete.

Table 3. Additional regulatory compliance complexity

Problem	Compliance	Complexity class
nG−	Partial	**NP**-complete
1G+	Partial	**NP**-complete
1L+	Partial	**NP**-complete

A variant having difficult features that are a superset of another, is at least as difficult as the other. For instance, the variant **nG+** is at least as difficult as both **nG−** or **1G+**. Furthermore, following the same reasoning, it can also be said that **nL+** is at least as difficult as **nG+**. Thus the following computational complexity relations are true: **nG− ≤ nG+ ≤ nL+** and **1G+ ≤ nG+ ≤ nL+**.

Consider now Tables 2 and 3. Note that we are missing a computational complexity result for **nG+**. However, it can be seen in the computational complexity relations that **nG+** is at most as difficult as **1G+** and at most as difficult as **nL+**. Knowing that both **1G+** and **nL+** are in **NP**-complete, we can conclude that **nG+** is also in **NP**-complete.

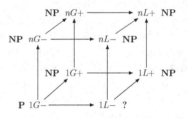

Fig. 2. Partial compliance complexity lattice.

Additionally, aggregating the existing results from Table 2 with the newly obtained results in Table 3, we obtain the computational complexity map for proving partial compliance shown in Fig. 2. Finally, note that Fig. 2 assigns a complexity class to each problem with the exception of **1L−**. We conclude this section by proposing a conjecture regarding the computational complexity of **1L−**.

Conjecture 1 (1L− is in P). We currently have no information about the computational complexity of **1L−**. That is, we cannot infer its belonging to a computational complexity class in a similar way as for **nG+**, as in this case the simpler variant (**1G−**) is in **P**.

Our conjecture is that the computational complexity of **1L−** is in **P**. We have proven that moving from − to +, or from **1** to **n**, definitely brings the complexity into **NP**. In general, solutions tackling such variants have to explore the entire set of possible executions in the worst case scenarios, which precludes efficient solutions. Despite moving from **G** to **L** seems to definitely increase the complexity, we strongly believe that it does not influence the computational complexity of the problem enough to move it into **NP**, and polynomial solutions are still possible.

5   Existing Approaches and Their Complexity

Compliance checking in itself is a generic term, and it is used in different ways in various approaches and the type of rules and regulations that are supported (along with the properties supported) differ for each approach. As a result, each approach may correspond to a different problem class as defined in this paper.

For example, approaches such as [3,18] that are merely checking the control-flow of a process using temporal logic or other logic are typically $\mathbf{nG}-$. However, control-flow constraints may be conditional and apply therefore only locally, e.g. when using CTL* such as in [10]. In these cases, the enforcing part of the rules can be conditional and the problem belongs to the variant $\mathbf{nL}-$. Similarly, when variables (i.e. literals) are included in the approach in temporal logic [5], the problem can immediately be classified as the variant $\mathbf{nL}-$ as well. Approaches based on classical logic where propositional formulae are supported in addition to literals [7,8,11,13,16,20] can be classified as $\mathbf{nL}+$.

As a result of the inherent computational complexity of such approaches, several methods describe a state-space reduction to limit state explosion in concurrent processes. However, these approaches either generate large amounts of overhead (e.g. [19]), or lose information on concurrency and local activity orders in concurrent branches due to linearisation (e.g., [4,6,12,21]). The reduction approach described in [10] does reduce the state space while preserving all concurrency information, but provides only a practical optimisation and the theoretical complexity $(\mathbf{nL}-)$ remains the same.

As such, each of the approaches discussed above is **NP**-complete, hence they are bound to be come infeasible, due to the current race towards digitalisation and automatisation.

6   Conclusion

In this paper, we discussed and analysed the computational complexity of some variants of the problem of proving partial compliance of structured business process models. Despite lacking a computational complexity proof for $\mathbf{1L}-$, the results provided along with the classifications of some existing approaches tackling the problem, shows that many solutions belong to the **NP**-complete computational complexity class.

While this was not unexpected, we claim that the current focus on optimisation is bound to lead to many complications in the future, as it is disregarding the worst case scenarios due to the limited size of current practical problems. Digitalisation and automatisation is leading towards bigger and more complex automated processes, which current approaches would miserably fail to solve due to the, largely ignored, computational complexity of the problem. While optimising approaches tailored to current problems is still useful, dealing with the *elephant in the room* becomes more and more crucial, and will soon be impossible to ignore.

As future work to complete the computational complexity picture of the variants covered by the umbrella of **nL+**, we plan to prove the computational complexity of the problem **1L−**. Moreover, we also plan to switch the computational complexity analysis focus from the regulatory framework to the business process model, and studying how different variants of the business process model (i.e. including loops) influence the computational complexity of the problem.

Acknowledgments. This research is supported by the Science and Industry Endowment Fund.

A Proofs

A.1 Proving NP-completenes in General

Definition 9 (NP-complete). *A decision problem is **NP**-complete if it is in the set of **NP** problems and if every problem in **NP** is reducible to it in polynomial-time.*

To prove membership in **NP** of a variant of the problem of proving partial compliance, we show that a process is partially compliant with a set of obligations if and only if there is a certificate whose size is at most polynomial in terms of the length of the input (comprising the business process model and the set of obligations) with which we can check whether it fulfils the regulatory framework in polynomial time. As a certificate we use a trace of the model and we check whether it satisfies the regulatory framework.

NP Membership. The following algorithm allows to verify whether a trace of a business process model satisfies a set of obligations in polynomial time with respect to the length of the execution.

Algorithm 1 *Given a set of obligations $\mathbb{O}$ and a trace $\theta = (\sigma_{start}, \sigma_1, \ldots, \sigma_n, \sigma_{end})$ such that $\sigma_{start} = (\mathsf{start}, L_0)$ and $\theta \in \Theta(P, \mathsf{ann})$, the algorithm $A_1(\theta, \mathbb{O})$ is defined as follows:*

Certificate Checking Algorithm

```
Let Ob = ∅ be the set of in force obligations
for each σ in θ do
    for each ω = O°⟨c, t, d⟩ in O do
        if σ ⊨ t then
            Ob = Ob ∪ ω
        end if
    end for each
    for each ω = O°⟨c, t, d⟩ in Ob do
        if o = a then
            if σ ⊨ c then
                Ob = Ob \ ω
            else
                if σ ⊨ d then
                    return θ ⊭ O
                end if
            end if
        else
            if t = m then
```

```
        if σ ⊭ c then
            return  θ ⊬ O
        end if
        if σ ⊨ d then
            Ob = Ob \ ω
        end if
    end if
  end if
end for each
end for each

return  θ ⊢ O;
```

*Notice that in case of **Global** obligations, whose in force interval spans the entirety of the execution, the set* Ob *is pre-loaded with each obligation of such type.*

Algorithm 1 identifies whether a trace fulfils a set of obligations. If this is the case, then following from Definition 7 it is a sufficient condition to say that the process model is partially compliant with the regulatory framework defined by such obligations.

Complexity: the complexity of checking whether a trace is compliant with the set of obligations using Algorithm 1 is at most polynomial in time $O(n \times o)$ where n is the number of tasks in the process and o is the number of obligations. Since checking whether the interpretation provided in a state satisfies a formula φ can be done in constant time, it does not affects the complexity of the algorithm. The above asymptotic time bound is at most polynomial in the length of the input (which includes the size of both the process and the set of obligations). Therefore, we can conclude that verifying Partial Compliance is indeed in **NP**.

Note that Algorithm 1 allows to check whether a trace is compliant with a regulatory framework where the class of the problem is **nL+**. With **nL+** being the most generic of the problem classes discussed in the paper, the same algorithm can be used to verify traces for every other problem. This allows to prove **NP**-completeness of various classes of the problems by just showing their **NP**-hardness, as their membership is taken care of by Algorithm 1. In the remainder of the appendix, we prove **NP** hardness of some of the problem classes by reducing existing **NP**-complete problems to the problem of proving partial regulatory compliance of a process.

A.2 NP Hardness of 1L+

We reduce the satisfiability problem to **1L+**.

Definition 10 (Satisfiability Problem). *The satisfiability problem is the problem of determining if there exists an interpretation that satisfies a given propositional formula. In other words, it asks whether there exists an interpretation of the propositions in such a way that the formula evaluates to* **true**. *If this is the case, the formula is satisfiable.*

Reduction. Let φ be a propositional formula for which we want to verify whether it is satisfiable or not, as described in Definition 10, and let L be the set of propositions contained in φ.

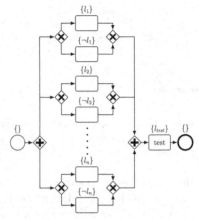

For each proposition belonging to L, we construct an XOR block containing two tasks, one labelled and containing in its annotation the positive proposition (i.e. l) and the other the negative counterpart (i.e. $\neg l$). Notice that we have not explicitly labeled the task, as they can be distinguished by their annotations. All the XOR blocks constructed from L are then included within a single AND block. This AND block is in turn followed by a task

Fig. 3. Process for **1L+** reduction.

labelled "test" and containing a single literal in its annotation: l_{test}. The sequence containing the AND block and the task *test* is then enclosed within a start and an end, composing the annotated business process model (P, ann), as graphically represented in Fig. 3.

The set of obligations, to which the constructed business process has to be verified to be fully compliant with, is composed of a single obligation constructed as follows from the propositional formula φ: $\langle \mathcal{O}^a l_{test}, \varphi, \bot \rangle$. We claim that there exists a trace $\theta \in \Theta(P, \mathsf{ann})$ such that $\theta \vdash \mathbb{O}$ if and only if φ is satisfiable.

Reduction Complexity: The process P and the obligation $\langle \mathcal{O}^a l_{test}, \varphi, \bot \rangle$ can be constructed in time proportional to $|L| + |\varphi|$ where $|\varphi|$ denotes the length of formula φ. Since $|L| \leq |\varphi|$ by construction, the time is at most polynomial in the length of the formula φ.

Correctness. Here we prove the soundness $((P, \mathsf{ann}) \vdash^{\mathrm{P}} \mathbb{O} \Rightarrow \varphi$ is satisfiable) and the completeness (φ is satisfiable $\Rightarrow (P, \mathsf{ann}) \vdash^{\mathrm{P}} \mathbb{O}$) of our reduction.

Proof. **Soundness:** $(P, \mathsf{ann}) \vdash^{\mathrm{P}} \mathbb{O} \Rightarrow \varphi$ is satisfiable.

From the hypothesis and Definition 7, we know that there exists a trace of the business process model (P, ann) that fulfils the obligation in $\mathbb{O}$. Following from the construction of the reduction, we know that the only obligation belonging to $\mathbb{O}$ is $\langle \mathcal{O}^a l_{test}, \varphi, \bot \rangle$.

From Definition 4 and the construction of the reduction we know that each trace of P contains the task l_{test}. Therefore, according to Definition 6, in order for the obligation $\langle \mathcal{O}^a l_{test}, \varphi, \bot \rangle$ to be fulfilled each trace contains a state following the one where l_{test} appears.

From Definition 4 and the construction of the reduction, in particular how (P, ann) is constructed, we have that in the only state following the one where l_{test} appears the first time, the set of literals associated to that state corresponds to an interpretation of the propositions contained in φ. Moreover, again from dimensions. Hospital managers can use the results of this assessment as a basis of employing strategies that would ensure quality of service in terms of giving care and general experience while patients are using their facilities. Customer satisfaction is easily achieved with higher service quality.

Each region has different social, cultural, economic and political settings which has effects on the operations of the hospital in service delivery. Hospital service delivery in itself is complex. Due to these differences, there are bound to be differences on how various factors play out in different hospital settings. Eventually trade-offs between decision criteria are inevitable. These were evident in this study, making FAHP the most appropriate tool that could be successfully applied to evaluate the service quality. This was because there were multiple dimensions to be used in decision-making by patients.

Use of FAHP to measure performance of hospitals had the following merits:

(a) The service at each hospital was multi-dimensional and while the dimensions were subjective in nature, FAHP could easily be used to model the measurement of performance of such systems.

(b) There exists fuzzy group decision making techniques that employ AHP approach. Use of multiple evaluators for the service quality performance measurement, makes the process, a group decision-making one.

(c) It is easy to identify inefficient aspects of service quality measurements by examining the specific hospital dimensions by use of this hierarchical analysis.

There is a paradigm shift in performance measurement in hospitals. Patients assess overall organizational performance of the hospital as opposed to assessing the individual staff performance. It is therefore necessary to have in place tools/techniques that can be used to evaluate the performance level of the organization's the systems and processes. To address this requirement, FAHP model for healthcare sector has been developed as a tool that can be applied to evaluate the level of service quality in hospitals in Nairobi City County. Hospital administrators can use the results of model to form the basis for employing strategies that ensures desirable service quality that satisfy patients. They can do this by improving the hospitals' operational performance.

The most sensitive task in the model entails, metric development whose weight matrix may be subjective. However, the subjective nature of the matrix weight has been reduced by the use of fuzzy linguistic variables. Researchers propose more exhaustive and substantial work with more data to improve performance of the model. It is also proposed that hospital facilities should be considered as one of the evaluation factor.

In conclusion, this study analyzed the service quality performance of the healthcare sector of the Nairobi City County using the FAHP model. The SERVQUAL instruments dimensions were used as evaluation criteria. The fuzzy nature of evaluators in expressing their judgments on service quality was handled using FST integrated in AHP. Service quality expectations were obtained using the AHP component of FAHP. Finally, the results show that healthcare service quality can be assessed and depending on the outcome, administrators can adjust their strategies to achieve desirable results.

References

1. The Constitution of Kenya (2010). https://www.wipo.int/edocs/lexdocs/laws/en/ke/ke019en. pdf. Accessed Aug 2018
2. Donabedian, A.: Quality assessment and assurance: unity of purpose, diversity of means. Inquiry **25**(1), 175–192 (1988)
3. Marshall, G.N., Ron, D.H., Rebecca, M.: Health status and satisfaction with healthcare: results from the medical outcomes study. J. Consult. Clin. Psychol. **64**(2), 380–390 (1996)
4. Li, L., Benton, W.C.: Hospital capacity management decisions: emphasis on cost control and quality enhancement. Eur. J. Oper. Res. **146**(3), 596–614 (2003)
5. Headley, D.E., Miller, S.J.: Measuring service quality and its relationship to future consumer behaviour. Mark. Health Serv. **13**(4), 32–42 (1993)
6. Sgroi, F., Di Trapani, A.M., Testa, R., Tudisca, S.: Strategy to increase the farm competitiveness. Am. J. Agric. Biol. Sci. **9**, 394–400 (2014)
7. Squatrito, R., Sgroi, F., Tudisca, S., Di Trapani, A.M., Testa, R.: Post feed-in scheme photovoltaic system feasibility evaluation in Italy: sicilian case studies. Energies **7**, 7147–7165 (2014)
8. Choi, K.S., Cho, W.H., Lee, S., Lee, H., Kim, C.: The relationships among quality, value, satisfaction and behavioral intention in health care provider choice: a South Korean study. J. Bus. Res. **57**(8), 913–921 (2004)
9. Lee, M.A., Yom, Y.H.: A comparative study of patients' and nurses' perceptions of the quality of nursing services, satisfaction and intent to revisit the hospital: a questionnaire survey. Int. J. Nurs. Stud. **44**, 545–555 (2007)
10. Hulton, L.A., Matthews, Z., Stones, R.W.: Applying a framework for assessing the quality of maternal health services in urban India. Soc. Sci. Med. **64**(10), 2083–2095 (2007)
11. Brown, T.J., Churchill, G.A.: Peter, J: Improving the measurement of service quality. J. Retail. **69**(1), 127–139 (1993)
12. Kaplan, R.S., Norton, D.P.: The balanced scorecard: measures that drive performance. Harv. Bus. Rev. 71–79 (1992)
13. Schvaneveldt, S.J., Enkawa, T., Miyakawa, M.: Consumer evaluation perspectives of service quality: evaluation factors and two-way model of quality. Total Qual. Manag. **2**, 149–161 (1991)
14. Kucukarslan, S.N., Nadkarni, A.: Evaluating medication-related services in a hospital setting using the disconfirmation of expectations model of satisfaction. Res. Soc. Adm. Pharm. **4**(1), 12–22 (2008)
15. Laschinger, H.S., Hall, L.M., Pedersen, C., Almost, J.: A psychometric analysis of the patient satisfaction ith nursing care quality questionnaire: an actionable approach to measuring patient satisfaction. J. Nurs. Care Qual. **20**(3), 220–230 (2005)
16. Lupo, T.: Benchmarking of airports service quality by a new fuzzy MCDM approach. Eur. Transp. Trasporti Europei **57** (2015)
17. Fishbein, M., Ajzen, I.: Belief, Attitude, Intention and Behavior: An Introduction to Theory and Research. Addion-Wesley, Reading (1975)
18. Saaty, T.L.: Decision making with the analytic hierarchy process. Int. J. Serv. Sci. **1**(1), 83–98 (2008)
19. Opricovic, S., Tzeng, G.H.: Compromise solution by MCDM methods: a comparative analysis of VIKOR and TOPSIS. Eur. J. Oper. Res. **156**(2), 445–455 (2004)
20. Hwang, C.L., Yoon, K.: Multiple Attribute Decision Making: Methods and Applications. Springer, New York (1981). https://doi.org/10.1007/978-3-642-48318-9

21. Li, Y., Hu, Y., Zhang, X., Deng, Y., Mahadevan, S.: An evidential DEMATEL method to identify critical success factors in emergency management. Appl. Soft Comput. J. **22**, 504–510 (2014)
22. Chang, T.H.: Fuzzy VIKOR method: a case study of the hospital service evaluation in Taiwan. Inf. Sci. **271**, 196–212 (2014)
23. Chou, C.C., Liu, L.J., Huang, S.F., Yih, J.M., Han, T.C.: An evaluation of airline service quality using the fuzzy weighted ServQual method. Appl. Soft Comput. **11**, 2117–2128 (2011)
24. De Battisti, F., Nicolini, G., Salini, S.: The Rasch model in customer satisfaction survey data. Qual. Technol. Quant. Manag. **7**(1), 15–34 (2010)
25. Hu, H.Y., Lee, Y.C., Yen, T.M.: Service quality gaps analysis based on fuzzy linguistic SERVQUAL with a case study in hospital out-patient services. TQM J. **22**(5), 499–515 (2010)
26. Parasuraman, A., Zeithaml, V.A., Berry, L.L.: A conceptual model of service quality and its implications for future research. J. Mark. **49**, 41–50 (1985)
27. Aktas, A., Cebi, S., Temiz, I.: A new evaluation model for service quality of healthcare systems based on AHP and information axiom. J. Intell. Fuzzy Syst. **28**, 1009–1021 (2015)
28. Baki, B., Peker, I.: An integrated evaluation model for service quality of hospitals: a case study from Turkey. J. Mult. Valued Logic Soft Comput. **24**(5–6), 453–474 (2015)
29. Lee, G., Lin, H.: Customer perceptions of e-service quality in online shopping. Int. J. Retail Distrib. Manag. **33**(2), 161–176 (2005)
30. Mardani, A., Jusoh, A., Zavadskas, E.K.: Fuzzy multiple criteria decision-making techniques and applications: two decades review from 1994 to 2014. Expert Syst. Appl. **42**(8), 4126–4148 (2015)
31. Calabrese, A.: Service productivity and service quality: a necessary trade-off? Prod. Int. J. Econ. **135**(2), 800–812 (2012)
32. Babakus, E., Boller, G.W.: An empirical assessment of the SERVQUAL scale. J. Bus. Res. **24**(3), 253–268 (1992)
33. Wasserman, G.S.: On how to prioritize design requirements during the QFD planning process. IIE Trans. **25**(3), 59–65 (1993)
34. Sgroi, F., Tudisca, S., Di Trapani, A.M., Testa, R.: Economic evaluation of aquaculture investments under conditions of risk and uncertainty in the Mediterranean Sea. Am. J. Appl. Sci. **11**, 1727–1734 (2014)
35. Sgroi, F., Tudisca, S., Di Trapani, A.M., Testa, R., Squatrito, R.: Efficacy and efficiency of Italian energy policy: the case of PV systems in greenhouse farms. Energies **7**(6), 3985–4001 (2014)
36. Zadeh, L.: Fuzzy sets. Inf. Control **8**, 338–353 (1965)
37. Certa, A., Enea, M., Galante, G.M., La Fata, C.M.: A multistep methodology for the evaluation of human resources using the evidence theory. Int. J. Intell. Syst. **28**(11), 1072–1088 (2013)
38. Montes, R., Sánchez, A.M., Villar, P., Herrera, F.: A web tool to support decision making in the housing market using hesitant fuzzy linguistic termsets. Appl. Soft Comput. **35**, 949–957 (2015)
39. Heradio, R., Cabrerizo, F.J., Fernandez-Amoros, D., Herrera, M., Herrera-Viedma, E.: A fuzzy linguistic model to evaluate the quality of library 2.0 functionalities. Int. J. Inf. Manag. **33**(4), 642–654 (2013)

40. Cabrerizo, F.J., Martínez, M.A., López-Gijón, J., Esteban, B., Herrera-Viedma, E.: Anew quality evaluation model generating recommendations to improve the digital services provided by the academic digital libraries. In: 2011 International Fuzzy Systems Association World Congress and the 2011 Asian Fuzzy Systems Society (IFSA 2011), Surabaya and Bali Island (Indonesia), pp. RW 202 1–RW 202 6 (2011)

41. López-Herrera, A.G., Herrera-Viedma, E., Herrera, F.: Applying multi-objective evolutionary algorithms to the automatic learning of extended boolean queries in fuzzy ordinal linguistic information retrieval systems. Fuzzy Sets Syst. **160**, 2192–2205 (2009)

42. Bogetoft, P., Pruzan, P.: Planning with multiple criteria: investigation, communication and choice. J. Multi-Criteria Decis. Anal. **8**(2), 112 (1997)

43. Dodgson, J., Spackman, M., Pearman, A., Phillips, L.: Multi-criteria analysis: a manual. Department for Communities and Local Government, London (2009). http://eprints.lse.ac.uk/12761/

44. Abbas, M., Ahmad, J., Edmundas, K.Z., Zainab, K., Khalil, M.D.N.: Application of multiple-criteria decision-making techniques and approaches to evaluating of service quality: a systematic review of the literature. J. Bus. Econ. Manag. **16**(5), 1034–1068 (2015)

45. Hwang, C.L., Yoon, K.: Multiple Attribute Decision-Making Methods and Applications. Springer, Heidelberg (1981). https://doi.org/10.1007/978-3-642-48318-9

46. Simpson, L.: Do decision makers know what they prefer?: MAVT and ELECTRE II. J. Oper. Res. Soc. **47**(7), 919–929 (1996)

47. Musumba, G.W., Wario, R.D.: Towards group fuzzy analytical hierarchy process. In: Mekuria, F., Nigussie, E.E., Dargie, W., Edward, M., Tegegne, T. (eds.) ICT4DA 2017. LNICST, vol. 244, pp. 283–307. Springer, Cham (2018). https://doi.org/10.1007/978-3-319-95153-9_27

48. Saaty, T.L.: The Analytic Hierarchy Process. McGraw-Hill, New York (1980)

49. Saaty, T.L., Vargas, L.G.: Models, methods, concepts & applications of the analytic hierarchy process, vol. 175. Springer, New York (2001). https://doi.org/10.1007/978-1-4614-3597-6

50. Vaidya, O., Kumar, S.: Analytic hierarchy process: an overview of applications. Eur. J. Oper. Res. **169**(1), 1–29 (2006)

51. Mikhailov, L.: Deriving priorities from fuzzy pairwise comparison judgements. Fuzzy Sets Syst. **134**(3), 365–385 (2003)

52. van Laarhoven, P., van Pedrycz, W.: A fuzzy extension of Saaty's priority theory. Fuzzy Sets Syst. **11**(1), 199–227 (1983)

53. Ahmad, A., Basir, O., Hassanein, K.: Adaptive user interfaces for intelligent e-learning: issues and trends. In: Proceedings of the Fourth International Conference on Electronic Business (ICEB 2004), Beijing, pp. 925–934 (2004)

54. Tseng, M.L.: A causal and effect decision making model of service quality expectation using grey-fuzzy DEMATEL approach. Expert Syst. Appl. **36**(4), 7738–7748 (2009)

55. Li, L.X.: Relationships between determinants of hospital quality management and service quality performance – a path analytic model. Omega **25**(5), 535–545 (1997)

56. Min, H., Mitra, A., Oswald, S.: Competitive benchmarking of health care quality using the analytic hierarchy process: an example from Korean cancer clinics. Soc.-Econ. Plan. Sci. **31**(2), 147–159 (1997)

57. Chang, S.J., Hsiao, H.C., Huang, L.H., Chang, H.: Taiwan quality indicator project and hospital productivity growth. Omega **39**(1), 14–22 (2011)

58. Teng, C.I., Ing, C.K., Chang, H.Y., Chung, K.P.: Development of service quality scale for surgical hospitalization. J. Formos. Med. Assoc. **106**(6), 475–484 (2007)

59. Shieh, J.I., Wu, H.-H., Huang, K.K.: A DEMATEL method in identifying key success factors of hospital service quality. Knowl.-Based Syst. **23**(3), 277–282 (2010)

60. Kubler, S., Robert, J., Derigent, W., Voisin, A., Le Traon, Y.: A state-of the-art survey & testbed of Fuzzy AHP (FAHP) applications. Expert Syst. Appl. **65**, 398–422 (2016)
61. Büyüközkan, G., Cifci, G., Güleryüz, S.: Strategic analysis of healthcare service quality using fuzzy AHP methodology. Expert Syst. Appl. **38**(8), 9407–9424 (2011)
62. Ju, Y., Wang, A., Liu, X.: Evaluating emergency response capacity by Fuzzy AHP: and 2-tuple fuzzy linguistic approach. Expert Syst. Appl. **39**(8), 6972–6981 (2012)
63. Shahin, A., Janatyan, N.: Estimation of customer dissatisfaction based on service quality gaps by correlation and regression analysis in a travel agency. Int. J. Bus. Manag. **6**(3), 99–108 (2011)
64. Zaim, H., Bayyurt, N., Zaim, S.: Service quality and determinants of customer satisfaction in hospitals: Turkish experience. Int. Bus. Econ. Res. J. **9**(5), 51 (2010)
65. Parasuraman, A., Zeithaml, V.A., Berry, L.L.: An empirical test of the extended gaps model of service quality. In: Marketing Science Institute Working Paper, pp. 90–122 (1990)
66. Bitner, M.J., Hubbert, A.R.: Encounter satisfaction versus overall satisfaction versus service quality: the consumer's voice. In: Rust, R.T., Oliver, R.L. (eds.) Service Quality: New Directions in Theory and Practice, pp. 72–94. Sage Publications, Thousand Oaks (1994)
67. Prakash, A., Mohanty, R.P., Kallurkar, S.P.: Service quality modelling for life insurance business using neural networks. Int. J. Prod. Qual. Manag. **7**(3), 263–286 (2011)
68. Grönroos, C.: Strategic Management and Marketing in the Service Sector. Swedish School of Economics and Business Administration, Helsingfors (1982)
69. Akter, S., Hani, U., Upal, M.: Service quality perception and satisfaction: a study in suburban public hospitals in Bangladesh. Int. J. Serv. Res. February (Special Issue), 125–145 (2008)
70. Jager, D.J., Plooy, D.T.: Are public hospitals responding to tangible and reliable service related needs of patients in the new South Africa? J. Manag. Policy Pract. **12**(2), 105–119 (2011)
71. Kuo, H.P.: Fuzzy comprehensive evaluation applied in the performance assessment of service quality of insurance companies in Taiwan. J. Am. Acad. Bus. **16**(1), 84–92 (2010)
72. Priporas, C.V., Laspa, C., Kamenidou, I.: Patient satisfaction measurement for in hospital services: a pilot study in Greece. J. Med. Mark. **8**(4), 325–340 (2008)
73. Sohail, M.: Service quality in hospitals, more favourable than you might think. Manag. Serv. Qual. **13**(2), 197–206 (2003)
74. Sajid, M.S., Baig, M.K.: Quality of health care, an absolute necessity for public satisfaction. Int. J. Health Care Qual. Assur. **20**(6), 545–548 (2007)
75. Jabnoun, N., Chacker, M.: Comparing the quality of private and public hospitals. Manag. Serv. Qual. **13**(4), 290–299 (2003)
76. Boshoff, C., Gray, B.: The relationships between service quality, customer satisfaction and buying intentions in the private hospital industry. South Afr. J. Bus. Manag. **35**(4), 27–38 (2004)
77. Ramsaran-Fowdar, R.R.: The relative importance of service dimensions in a healthcare setting. Int. J. Health Care Qual. Assur. **21**(1), 104–124 (2008)
78. Padma, P., Rajendran, C., Sai, L.P.: A conceptual framework of service quality in healthcare perspectives of Indian patients and their attendants. Benchmark. Int. J. **16**(2), 157–191 (2009)
79. Aagja, J.P., Garg, R.: Measuring perceived service quality for public hospitals (PubHosQual) in the Indian context. Int. J. Pharm. Healthc. Mark. **4**(1), 60–83 (2010)
80. Ladhari, R.: Alternative measure of service quality: a review. J. Manag. Serv. Qual. **18**(1), 65–86 (2008)
81. Chen, M.F., Tzeng, G.H., Tang, T.: Fuzzy MCDM approach for evaluation of expatriate assignments. Int. J. Inf. Technol. Decis. Mak. **4**(2), 277–296 (2005)

82. Zadeh, L.A.: The concept of a linguistic variable and its application to approximate reasoning: parts 1, 2 and 3. Inf. Sci. **8**, 199–249 (1975)
83. Sinimole, K.R.: Performance evaluation of the hospital services–a fuzzy analytic hierarchy process model. Int. J. Prod. Qual. Manag. **101**, 112–130 (2012)
84. Saaty, T.L.: Multicriteria Decision Making: The Analytic Hierarchy Process. RWS Publications, Pittsburgh (1990)
85. Davis, M.A.P.: A multi-criteria decision model application for managing group decisions. J. Oper. Res. Soc. **45**(1), 47–58 (1994)

Design of Hybrid Neuro-Fuzzy Controller for Magnetic Levitation Train Systems

Yakob Kiros Teklehaimanot[1]([⊠]), Dereje Shiferaw Negash[2,3],
and Endrias Alemayehu Workiye[3]

[1] Mekelle University, Mekelle, Ethiopia
yakobkiros81@gmail.com
[2] Addis Abeba University, Addis Abeba, Ethiopia
dnderejesh@gmail.com
[3] Adama Science and Technology, Adama, Ethiopia
endrias1873@gmail.com

Abstract. Maglev is a system in which the train runs levitated from the guideway by using electromagnetic forces between superconducting magnets (ferromagnetic materials) on board of the train and coils on the ground. The magnetic levitation train system are based on two types, electrodynamics suspension (EDS) and electromagnetic suspension (EMS). EDS is based on repulsive forces acting on a magnet and is inherently stable system and even has well robustness in many cases with open loop control. In this paper, we have assumed the EMS based train system. The electromagnetic suspension system is based on attractive forces acting on a magnet and is complex, unstable and the model is strongly nonlinear. In addition, due to the external disturbances like wind, the unbalanced magnetic forces between the guideway and the train, and parameter perturbation, the system model has greater uncertainty. This paper presents a hybrid neuro-fuzzy controllers for the magnetic levitation train system. The controllers are designed to bring the magnetic levitation system in a stable region by keeping the train suspended in the air in the required position in the presence of uncertainties. PID controller is used to generate the data which requires to train the hybrid controllers. The performance and robustness of the controllers have been compared by simulating the system with disturbances. After implementing and validating, the Matlab simulation results show that the performance of the system (overshoot, settling time, rise time and peak response) have improved and the controller have good robustness and adaptability.

Keywords: Magnetic levitation · EDS · EMS · Fuzzy controller ·
Hybrid neuro-fuzzy controller · Taylor's series linearization ·
Robustness · Adaptability

1 Introduction

Maglev train is a system which uses magnetic fields to levitate so there is no physical contact between the train and the track (guideways). The motion of

© Springer Nature Switzerland AG 2019
F. Mekuria et al. (Eds.): ICT4DA 2019, CCIS 1026, pp. 119–133, 2019.
https://doi.org/10.1007/978-3-030-26630-1_10

the maglev train is based on electromagnetism and magnetic fields. Electromagnetism is magnetism produced by an electric current [1,2]. So the basic idea behind electromagnets are that you can create a magnetic field by running an electric current through a conductor (wire). So the maglev train can levitate above it track or guideway, and propel forward using this magnetic field. There are two types of levitation s namely, EMS (Electromagnetic suspension) and EDS (Electrodynamics suspension). The electromagnetic suspension EMS uses attractive force system to levitate where as EDS uses repulsive forces to levitate [3,4].

The main advantage of EDS Maglev systems is that they are naturally stable minor narrowing in distance between the track and the magnets, which creates the strong forces to repel the magnets back to their original position. But, EMS maglev train system is inherently unstable. At high speed, it becomes difficult to maintain the correct distance between train and guideway. If this distance cannot be kept, the train will fail to levitate and come grinding to a halt. To protect this, EMS needs a complex feedback control system to ensure the train is always stable [3,5].

Additionally in EMS system, the air gap between the guide ways and train magnets is very small (8–10) mm, whereas the air gap in the EDS system may be as large as (100–150) mm. The small air gap of the EMS system implies much more stringent controls to maintain this small gap. So, the EMS magnetic levitation based train system is not stable because of this and different disturbances like wind and other factors. In this paper, a hybrid neuro-fuzzy controller is designed to control the levitation distance which is around 8–10 mm. The controller is designed in order to keep stable the suspension gab between the electromagnet and electromagnet rail (levitation gab) [4].

2   Mathematical Modeling

Mathematical modeling of the maglev train system is developed by considering different assumption. Since the train is levitated on the air, there is drag force which affects the stability of the train like wind.later on the simulation, the response is simulated by adding different disturbance to the system modeling and shown the results by comparing with and without disturbances.

Consider the transrapid maglev train system, which is simplified as single mass system on a rigid guide-way as shown in Fig. 1:

Where, mg is train weight (including the electromagnets), S_M is vertical gab between the guideway and the train, S_0 is vertical gab between the guideway and the equilibrium position of the train, $L(S_M)$ is coil inductance, R is coil resistance and U_M is input voltage.

2.1   Non-linear Modeling

The electromagnetic force produced by current is given by the Kirchhoff's voltage law [7,8]

$$u(t) = V_R + V_L = i_M R + \frac{d}{dt}(L(s_M)i_M) \tag{1}$$

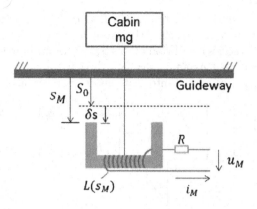

Fig. 1. Simplified Model of train levitation system [6]

The Net force is given by Newton's 3rd law of motion while neglecting drag force of the air on the train [1]

$$f_{net} = f_g - f_m \tag{2}$$

Where,

$$f_m = \frac{\mu_0 N^2 A}{2} \left(\frac{i_M}{s_M}\right)^2 = C \left(\frac{i_M}{s_M}\right)^2 \tag{3}$$

and the net force is,

$$f_{net} = f_g - f_m = mg - C \left(\frac{i_M}{s_M}\right)^2 \tag{4}$$

The non-linear system model will be

$$
\begin{aligned}
m\ddot{s}_M &= mg - C \left(\frac{i_M}{s_M}\right)^2 \\
\dot{i}_M &= \frac{i_M}{s_M}\dot{s}_M - \frac{R i_M s_M}{C} + \frac{U s_M}{C} \\
\dot{s}_M &= v
\end{aligned} \tag{5}
$$

State Space form of the non-linear model
Let $x_1 = $ Current (i_M), $x_2 = $ Velocity (v) and $x_3 = $ Position (s_M)

$$
\begin{aligned}
\dot{x}_1 &= \frac{x_1 x_2}{x_3} + \frac{x_3}{C}(U - R x_1) \\
\dot{x}_2 &= -\frac{C x_1^2}{m x_3^2} + g \\
\dot{x}_3 &= x_2
\end{aligned} \tag{6}
$$

2.2 Linear Modeling

To carryout controller design and analysis of maglev train system, the obtained non-linear model has to be linearized. Such linearization is done in the equilibrium point which can be calculated from,
$f_g = f(s_M, i_M)$ at S_0, I_0

At equilibrium, the force due to gravity f_g and the magnetic force are equal and opposite to each other so that the train levitates. We can linearize the model using Taylor's series expansion at $f(s_M, i_M)$ around the equilibrium point (S_0, I_0), where $s_M = S_0 + \delta s$ and $i_M = I_0 + \delta i$ [7,9,10].

Putting the linearized model into state space representation,

$$
\begin{bmatrix} \dot{x}_1 \\ \dot{x}_2 \\ \dot{x}_3 \end{bmatrix} = \begin{bmatrix} -\frac{RS_0}{C} & \frac{I_0}{S_0} & 0 \\ -\frac{CI_0}{mS_0^2} & 0 & \frac{CI_0^2}{mS_0^3} \\ 0 & 1 & 0 \end{bmatrix} \begin{bmatrix} x_1 \\ x_2 \\ x_3 \end{bmatrix} + \begin{bmatrix} \frac{S_0}{C} \\ 0 \\ 0 \end{bmatrix} [U],
$$

$$
y = \begin{bmatrix} 0 & 0 & 1 \end{bmatrix} \begin{bmatrix} x_1 \\ x_2 \\ x_3 \end{bmatrix}
$$

(7)

The values of the System parameters which are used in simulation is shown in Table 1.

Table 1. System parameter values [6]

$m(kg)$	N	$A(mm^2)$	$S_0(mm)$	$L_0(h)$	$R(\Omega)$	$U(V)$	$I_0(A)$
10000	1000	80	10	0.1	1	140	140

Initial conditions, $S_0 = 10\,\text{mm}$ and $I_0 = 140\,\text{A}$. Substituting all the values, state space model of the system will be

$$
\dot{x} = \begin{bmatrix} -10 & 14 & 0 \\ -0.00014 & 0 & 0.00196 \\ 0 & 1 & 0 \end{bmatrix} \begin{bmatrix} x_1 \\ x_2 \\ x_3 \end{bmatrix} + \begin{bmatrix} 10 \\ 0 \\ 0 \end{bmatrix} U,
$$

$$
y = \begin{bmatrix} 0 & 0 & 1 \end{bmatrix} \begin{bmatrix} x_1 \\ x_2 \\ x_3 \end{bmatrix}
$$

(8)

3   Controller Design

The controller simulation is implemented via four types of Adaptive Neuro-Fuzzy Inference System (ANFIS) control strategies. The control problem is to design a controller which computes the control signal (u) to magnetic levitation train system so as to keep the train stable at the required levitation position.

3.1   Hybrid Neuro-Fuzzy System

Fuzzy systems are popular in industrial application, but the development of a fuzzy system with good performance is not an easy task. The problem of finding membership functions and appropriate rules is frequently a tiring process of attempt and error. This lead to the idea of applying learning algorithms to the fuzzy systems. The neural networks, that have efficient learning algorithms, had been presented to automate or to support the development of tuning fuzzy systems. Neural networks and fuzzy systems can be combined to join its advantages and to cure its individual luck [11,12].

While neural networks are low-level computational structures that perform well when dealing with raw data, fuzzy logic deals with reasoning on a higher level, using linguistic information acquired from domain experts. However, fuzzy systems lack the ability to learn and cannot adjust themselves to a new environment [11]. On the other hand, although neural networks can learn, they are opaque to the user. Integrated neuro-fuzzy systems can combine the parallel computation and learning abilities of neural networks with the human-like knowledge representation and explanation abilities of fuzzy systems. As a result, neural networks become more transparent, while fuzzy systems become capable of learning [13–15].

3.2 ANFIS Controller

Adaptive Neuro-Fuzzy Inference System (ANFIS) is one of the most successful schemes which combine the benefits of these two powerful paradigms into a single capsule. An ANFIS works by applying neural learning rules to identify and tune the parameters and structure of a Fuzzy Inference System (FIS) [16]. According to the neuro-fuzzy approach, a neural network is proposed to implement the fuzzy system, so that structure and parameter identification of the fuzzy rule base are accomplished by defining, adapting and optimizing the topology and the parameters of the corresponding neuro-fuzzy network, based only on the available data. The network can be regarded both as an adaptive fuzzy inference system with the capability of learning fuzzy rules from data, and as a connectionist architecture provided with linguistic meaning [11,17].

3.3 Architecture of ANFIS

ANFIS is an adaptive network which is a multilayer feed-forward network composed of nodes connected by directed links, in which each node performs a particular function on its incoming signals to generate a single node output. Each link in an adaptive network specifies the direction of signal flow from one node to another; no weights is associated with the link. More specifically, the configuration of an adaptive network performs a static node function on its incoming signals to generate a single node output and each node function is a parameterized function with modifiable parameters; by changing these parameters, the node functions as well as the overall behavior of the adaptive network, are changed [18,19]. Figure 2 shows entire system architecture. With input/output data for given set of parameters, the ANFIS method models a fuzzy inference system (FIS) whose membership function parameters are tuned (adjusted) using either a back-propagation algorithm alone, or with a least squares type of method. The main objective of the ANFIS is to determine the optimum values of the equivalent fuzzy inference system parameters by applying a learning algorithm. The parameter optimization is done in such a way during the training session that the error between the target and the actual output is minimized [19].

The parameters to be optimized in ANFIS are the premise parameters and consequent parameters. In order to reduce the error measure, any of several optimization routines can be applied after constituting membership functions. The parameter set of an adaptive network allows fuzzy systems to learn from the data they have been trained. This thesis assumes that adaptive system under consideration has two inputs V_1 and V_2 and one output f. Let us scrutinize a first order Takagi, Sugeno and Kang (TSK) fuzzy inference system containing two rules [14].

Rule 1:If(v is V_1) and (d is D_1) then $f_1 = p_1 v + q_1 d + r_1$
Rule 2:If(v is V_2) and (d is D_2) then $f_2 = p_2 v + q_2 d + r_2$

Where p_1, p_2, q_1, q_2, r_1 and r_2 are linear parameters and V_1, V_2, D_1 and D_2 are non linear parameters, in which V_1 and D_1 are the membership functions of ANFIS (antecedent). p_1, q_1 and r_1 are the consequent parameters. To reflect adaptive capabilities, we use both circle and square. A circle indicates fixed node whereas square indicates adaptive node i.e. the parameter can be changed during adapting or training [14,18].

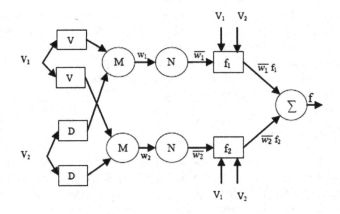

Fig. 2. Basic architecture of ANFIS [14]

It can be observed that ANFIS architecture consists of two adaptive layers, namely the first layer and the fourth layer. The three modifiable parameters a_i, b_i, c_i are so-called premise parameter in first layer and in the fourth layer, there are also three modifiable parameters p_i, q_i, r_i pertaining to the first order polynomial. These parameters are so-called consequent parameters [16].

3.4 Learning Algorithm of ANFIS

The basic idea of Neuro-fuzzy adaptive learning techniques is to provide a method for the fuzzy modeling procedure to learn information about a data set, in order to automatically compute the membership function parameters that best allow the associated fuzzy inference system (FIS) to track the given input/output data [14, 16].

The membership function parameters are tuned using a combination of least squares estimation and back-propagation algorithm for membership function parameter estimation. These parameters associated with the membership functions will change through the learning process similar to that of a neural network. Their adjustment is facilitated by a gradient vector, which provides a measure of how well the FIS is modeling the input/output data for a given set of parameters. Once the gradient vector is obtained, any of several optimization routines could be applied in order to adjust the parameters so as to reduce error between the actual and desired outputs. This allows the fuzzy system to learn from the data it is modeling. The approach has the advantage over the pure fuzzy paradigm that the need for the human operator to tune the system by adjusting the bounds of the membership functions [18–20]. To design ANFIS controller, first it has to be trained using input/output data. So, here data is generated using PID controller.

3.5 Controller Design Objectives

Since maglev train system is very nonlinear and unstable system, a controller is designed to stabilize it despite of any disturbances which affects the system. In this paper, the Adaptive NeuroFuzzy Inference System (ANFIS) which is a hybrid neuro-fuzzy controller is designed. ANFIS is a controller which has the ability to learn and adapt. The suspension control is always the technical difficulty of EMS Maglev train. ANFIS controller algorithm should meet the following requirements:

– Good adaptability for the uncertainty suspension system model
– Good robustness for the interference of the external system.

3.6 Sample Generated Data

We have used ANFIS controller with two inputs and one output. The data is generated error, error derivative (change of error) and the control signal using PID controller.

Training vector has two input parameters that of error E and the rate of change of error EC. In this simulation, the PID controller is applied to the magnetic levitation train system to get input and output data. The sampling time is set to 0.1 s. 1000 sample data is selected as the ANFIS controller training data as shown in Table 2 The simulink structure of magnetic levitation train controller based on adaptive neural network simulation is shown in Fig. 3.

Table 2. Generated data using PID

error	errorderiv	control signal	error	errorderiv	control signal
1	0	-72000	-0.07492	0.015649376	-10.28232534
0.988756	-0.209415116	-36081.04789	-0.07339	0.015283181	-9.561249632
0.937753	-0.618734304	-16120.37842	-0.0719	0.014928116	-8.88659933
0.850472	-0.979919494	-4296.599869	-0.07044	0.014583474	-8.253612715
0.741668	-1.088047024	2745.402569	-0.06902	0.014248605	-7.657588295
0.624763	-1.169045816	6742.562558	-0.06763	0.01392292	-7.094116474
0.509366	-1.153971941	8744.148387	-0.06627	0.013605896	-6.559203626
0.401517	-1.078490552	9446.172708	-0.06494	0.013297067	-6.049323878
0.304538	-0.969785574	9327.959348	-0.06364	0.012996025	-5.561424108
0.21985	-0.846884786	8721.653212	-0.06237	0.012702408	-5.092900299
0.147616	-0.722333785	7854.811132	-0.06112	0.0124159	-4.641557863
0.087227	-0.603893431	6879.724237	-0.05991	0.012136221	-4.205564516
0.037633	-0.495938463	5894.721591	-0.05872	0.011863121	-3.783401301
-0.00242	-0.400528291	4959.923811	-0.05756	0.011596376	-3.373815293
-0.03424	-0.318197331	4108.897101	-0.05643	0.011335786	-2.975775999
-0.05909	-0.248523865	3357.208366	-0.05532	0.011081167	-2.588436481
-0.07814	-0.190530246	2708.629869	-0.05424	0.010832351	-2.211099555
-0.09244	-0.142957455	2159.570329	-0.05318	0.010589181	-1.843188989
-0.10289	-0.104447641	1702.17989	-0.05215	0.010351512	-1.484225363
-0.11025	-0.073660437	1326.474761	-0.05113	0.010119206	-1.133806128
-0.11519	-0.049342475	1021.746651	-0.05014	0.009892131	-0.791589343
-0.11822	-0.030364566	777.4584003	-0.04918	0.009670164	-0.457280567
-0.1198	-0.015737167	583.7771224	-0.04823	0.009453185	-0.130622394
-0.12026	-0.004611794	431.8572424	-0.04731	0.009241078	0.188613801
-0.11988	0.003726162	313.9557979	-0.0464	0.009033732	0.500634325
-0.1189	0.009869415	223.4394926	-0.04552	0.008831037	0.805628168
-0.11747	0.014302997	154.7257311	-0.04466	0.00863289	1.103770847
-0.11573	0.017419012	103.1869965	-0.04381	0.008439188	1.39522733
-0.11377	0.019530868	65.03845638	-0.04299	0.00824983	1.680154231
-0.11168	0.020886397	37.22180792	-0.04218	0.008064719	1.958701458
-0.10952	0.021679543	17.29346262	-0.04139	0.00788376	2.231013426
-0.10731	0.022060519	3.3217344	-0.04062	0.007706861	2.497229948
-0.1051	0.022144453	-6.204655785	-0.03987	0.007533929	2.757486881
-0.10289	0.022018632	-12.45600116	-0.03913	0.007364877	3.011916586
-0.10072	0.02174848	-16.32918516	-0.03841	0.007199617	3.260648266
-0.09858	0.021382429	-18.50422601	-0.03771	0.007038064	3.503808196
-0.09648	0.020955833	-19.49091202	-0.03702	0.006880136	3.741519891
-0.09444	0.020494099	-19.66677227	-0.03635	0.006725751	3.973904225
-0.09243	0.020015138	-19.3076312	-0.03569	0.00657483	4.201079519
-0.09048	0.019531289	-18.61192642	-0.03505	0.006427296	4.423161604
-0.08858	0.019050799	-17.71986014	-0.03442	0.006283071	4.640263872
-0.08672	0.018578951	-16.72832737	-0.03381	0.006142083	4.852497319
-0.08491	0.018118923	-15.70243345	-0.03321	0.006004258	5.059970584
-0.08314	0.01767242	-14.68428761	-0.03262	0.005869526	5.262789982
-0.08141	0.017240155	-13.69964439	-0.03205	0.005737817	5.461059542
-0.07973	0.016822181	-12.76286173	-0.03148	0.005609064	5.654881041
-0.07809	0.016418142	-11.88055636	-0.03094	0.005483199	5.844354041
-0.07649	0.016027444	-11.05426104	-0.0304	0.005360159	6.029575924

After training data, next step is establishment of ANFIS network structure. For ANFIS model, first step is to determine the output and input variables membership functions. The system uses triangular and gaussian shaped memberships function to represent the first input membership function.

In next step, for adjusting the parameters of ANFIS fuzzy model the hybrid learning algorithm is chosen. ANFIS learning methods integrated use of gradient descent learning method and least square method (LSE).

After selecting initial membership function, Sugeno fuzzy model identification methods and hybrid learning algorithm are selected. By using the grid partition method fuzzy rules and modified membership function are identified. Closing value of the error (Error Tolerance) is set to 0 and the training times (epoch) is set to 100.

In final step, the FIS output can be exported to workspace for the ANFIS controller to make its rules The ANFIS controller is attached to the plant and simulated.

If the operating input-output data are outside their training data range, estimator will not operate accurately. As a result, the training data set should possess sufficient operational range including the maximum and minimum values for input output variables.

3.7 Design of ANFIS Controller

The ANFIS controller is designed using Matlab/Simulink software. In this Paper, ANFIS with two input and one output is used. Inputs to the ANFIS controller are error and change in error which are defined as follow:

$$e(s) = X_{ref} - X_{act}$$
$$\nabla e(s) = \frac{d}{dt}e(s)$$

(9)

Where,

X_{ref} is the reference position (levitation) of the train system
X_{act} is the actual position (levitation) of the train system

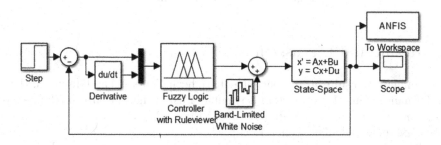

Fig. 3. Simulation Model of Magnetic levitation train system based on ANFIS

As shown in Fig. 3, Band-Limited White Noise is used as input disturbance to test the robustness and adaptability of the controllers.

In this paper, four types of ANFIS controllers have designed as shown in Table 3.

Table 3. Input-output membership functions

Controller type	Input membership function	Output membership function
ANFIS1	Triangular	Constant
ANFIS2	Triangular	Linear
ANFIS3	Gaussian	Constant
ANFIS4	Gaussian	Linear

All types of member function of error and change of error are automatically generated base on the data trained and the current value of the input signals. Membership function of the error and change of error are shown in Figs. 4 and 5 respectively for ANFIS1 and ANFIS2. And membership function of the error and change of error are shown in Figs. 6 and 7 respectively for ANFIS3 and ANFIS4.

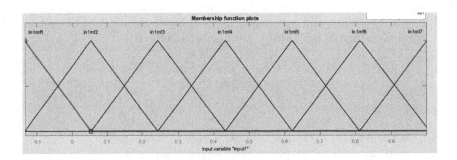

Fig. 4. Error membership function

4   Result and Discussion

The simulation results of the controllers have been compared and discussed their performance. The Maglev system is simulated using the Matlab/Simulink environment. The dynamic performance of ANFIS and PID controllers have been discussed under different scenarios.

The graph in Fig. 8 shows the overall step response of the magnetic levitation train system for controllers considering no disturbance and Fig. 9 shows step response when there is an input disturbance. From Fig. 8 and Table 4, it can

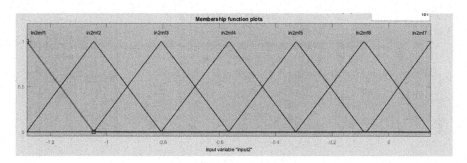

Fig. 5. Membership function for change of error

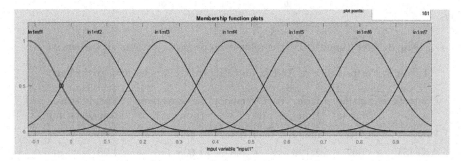

Fig. 6. Gaussian error membership function

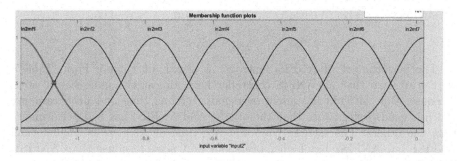

Fig. 7. Gaussian membership function for change of error

observe that ANFIS1 and ANFIS3 have small settling time, overshoot, and peak response but they have rise time which is greater than ANFIS2 and ANFIS4. This means that the response of ANFIS1 and ANFIS3 is slower than ANFIS2 and ANFIS4 until it reaches 90% but it settles to the desired state with in short settling time. Comparing ANFIS1 and ANFIS3, ANFIS3 has small overshoot, settling time and peak response and it has good performance than ANFIS1. Comparing ANFIS2 and ANFIS4, they have almost the same response as shown in Fig. 8 except ANFIS2 has smaller settling time than ANFIS4.

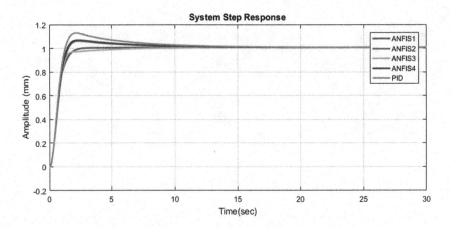

Fig. 8. ANFIS and PID controllers step response without disturbance

Table 4. Performance of ANFIS and PID controllers without disturbance

Controllers	Setting time (s)	Rise time (s)	Overshoot (%)	Peak response (mm)	Steady state response (mm)
PID	6.784	0.830	11.798	1.130	1.00
ANFIS1	1.667	1.127	0.268	1.008	1.00
ANFIS2	3.621	0.958	5.851	1.012	1.00
ANFIS3	1.552	1.014	−0.737	1.007	1.00
ANFIS4	4.4425	0.936	5.851	1.010	1.00

The performance of ANFIS controller is shown in Table 5. From Table 5, we can observe that all ANFIS controller have almost the same steady state response. But ANFIS3 has small overshoot, settling time and peak response which is good performance than the others. And ANFIS4 has bad performance than the others. The settling time and rise time of ANFIS2 is smaller than ANFIS1 but ANFIS2 has higher overshoot and peak response than ANFIS1. Since the overshoot measures how much the response exceeds the target point and if the response has large overshoot, it is bad performance which bring system instability. This implies ANFIS1 has better performance than ANFIS2 with large disturbance is added to maglev train system as load disturbance.

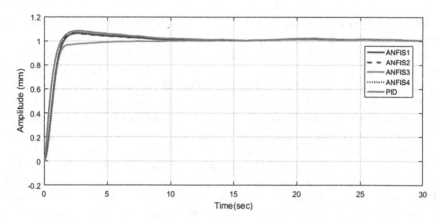

Fig. 9. ANFIS and PID controllers step response with White Noise input disturbance

Table 5. Performance of ANFIS and PID controllers with white noise disturbance

Controllers	Setting time (s)	Rise time (s)	Overshoot (%)	Peak response (mm)	Steady state response (mm)
PID	7.780	1.078	13.068	1.148	1
ANFIS1	4.08	0.988	4.737	1.062	1
ANFIS2	3.851	0.958	5.851	1.064	1
ANFIS3	1.552	1.035	−0.817	1.008	1
ANFIS4	4.77	0.957	5.851	1.075	1

5 Conclusion

ANFIS controllers have been designed with different types of input/output membership functions. Based on the input/output types of membership functions, four types of ANFIS controllers have designed and compared their performance with PID controller.

When there no disturbance which affect the train system, from Fig. 8 and Table 4 shows that All ANFIS controllers have better performance than PID. Comparing between ANFIS controllers, ANFIS3 has better performance than the other ANFIS controllers. ANFIS3 has designed with Gaussian input membership function and constant output function. This shows that Gaussian membership function has better representation of the input data than triangular and constant type membership function has better representation of output data than linear. When there is input disturbance which is considered as load variation only in this paper and modeled as band limited white noise, as shown in Fig. 9 and Table 5, ANFIS3 has better performance than the others. And ANFIS4 has bad performance than the other ANFIS controllers.

When there is process disturbance which brings system parameter perturbation and this disturbance is modeled as random number in this paper, from matlab simulation results shows that ANFIS3 has better performance than the other ANFIS controllers.

The overall performance of the controllers under input disturbance, process disturbance and without disturbance, it has been observed that ANFIS controllers have better performance than PID. One of the main advantages of the ANFIS scheme is that, it is computationally efficient, increases the dynamic performance and provides good stabilization when there is a sudden fluctuation in the levitation of the train. This shows the excellent response of the proposed control scheme as it has the learning capability using the neural networks.

When we have compared ANFIS controllers with PID, we have shown that ANFIS has minimum settling time, Overshoot and the peak response than PID controller. From this observation, the speed of convergence of the response increased and Superior performance, robustness, and efficiency of the proposed method have been proved through extensive simulation results. The proposed ANFIS controller is a powerful approach to retrieve the deceptiveness of a maglev system. The results show that this approach is robustness and suitable for optimizing various control problems if the controller is trained well. Finally, The simulation results show that the designed ANFIS controllers meets the requirements for the robust stability and adaptability performance. And among ANFIS controllers, we have shown that ANFIS3 controller has good robustness and adaptability than the other ANFIS controllers.

References

1. Sharkawy, A.B., Abo-Ismail, A.A.: Intelligent control of magnetic levitation system. J. Eng. Sci. Assiut Univ. **37**(4), 909–924 (2009)
2. Liu, Z., Long, Z., Li, X.: Maglev train overview. In: Liu, Z., Long, Z., Li, X. (eds.) Maglev Trains, pp. 1–28. Springer, Heidelberg (2015). https://doi.org/10.1007/978-3-662-45673-6_1
3. Tandan, G.K., Sen, P.K., Sahu, G., Sharma, R., Bohidar, S.: A review on development and analysis of maglev train. Int. J. Res. Advent Technol. **3**(12), 14–17 (2015)
4. Bajuri, M.F.: Modelling magnetic levitation (maglev) train. Ph.D. thesis, UMP (2012)
5. Magnetic levitation train system. http://techdatacare.blogspot.com/2011/12/magnetic-levitation.html. Accessed 1 Sept 2017
6. Cabral, T., Chavarette, F.: Dynamics and control design via LQR and SDRE methods for a maglev system. Int. J. Pure Appl. Math. **101**(2), 289–300 (2015)
7. Choudhary, S.K.: Robust feedback control analysis of magnetic levitation system. WSEAS Trans. Syst. **13**(27), 285–291 (2014)
8. Pati, A., Pal, V.C., Negi, R.: Design of a 2-DoF control and disturbance estimator for a magnetic levitation system. Eng. Technol. Appl. Sci. Res. **7**(1), 1369 (2016)
9. Ahmad, I., Javaid, M.A.: Nonlinear model & controller design for magnetic levitation system. In: Recent Advances in Signal Processing, Robotics and Automation, pp. 324–328 (2010)
10. Sun, Y., Qiang, H., Lin, G., Ren, J., Li, W.: Dynamic modeling and control of nonlinear electromagnetic suspension systems. Chem. Eng. Trans. **46**, 1039–1044 (2015)

11. Al-Hmouz, A., Shen, J., Al-Hmouz, R., Yan, J.: Modeling and simulation of an adaptive neuro-fuzzy inference system (ANFIS) for mobile learning. IEEE Trans. Learn. Technol. **5**(3), 226–237 (2012)
12. Panda, G., Panda, S., Ardil, C.: Hybrid neuro fuzzy approach for automatic generation control of two-area interconnected power system. Int. J. Comput. Intell. **5**(1), 80–84 (2009)
13. Kaur, A., Kaur, A.: Comparison of fuzzy logic and neuro-fuzzy algorithms for air conditioning system. Int. J. Soft Comput. Eng. **2**(1), 417–420 (2012)
14. Walia, N., Singh, H., Sharma, A.: ANFIS: adaptive neuro-fuzzy inference system - a survey. Int. J. Comput. Appl. **123**(13), 32–38 (2015)
15. Vieira, J., Dias, F.M., Mota, A.: Neuro-fuzzy systems: a survey. In: 5th WSEAS NNA International Conference on Neural Networks and Applications, Udine, Italia (2004)
16. Allaoua, B., Laoufi, A., Gasbaoui, B., Abderrahmani, A.: Neuro-fuzzy DC motor speed control using particle swarm optimization. Leonardo Electron. J. Pract. Technol. **15**, 1–18 (2009)
17. Kusagur, A., Kodad, S., Ram, B.V.S.: Modeling, design & simulation of an adaptive neuro-fuzzy inference system (ANFIS) for speed control of induction motor. Int. J. Comput. Appl. **6**(12), 29–44 (2010)
18. Sivakumar, R., Sahana, C., Savitha, P.: Design of ANFIS based estimation and control for mimo systems. Int. J. Eng. Res. Appl. **2**(3), 2803–2809 (2012)
19. Yousef, H.A., Khalfan, A.K., Albadi, M.H., Hosseinzadeh, N.: Load frequency control of a multi-area power system: an adaptive fuzzy logic approach. IEEE Trans. Power Syst. **29**(4), 1822–1830 (2014)
20. Rashid, U., Jamil, M., Gilani, S.O., Niazi, I.K.: LQR based training of adaptive neuro-fuzzy controller. In: Bassis, S., Esposito, A., Morabito, F.C., Pasero, E. (eds.) Advances in Neural Networks. SIST, vol. 54, pp. 311–322. Springer, Cham (2016). https://doi.org/10.1007/978-3-319-33747-0_31

Wireless and Mobile Computing Track

Optimization of Electrical Tilt for Addis Ababa LTE Deployment Scenario

Taddege Assefa Beyene[1]([⌂]) and Beneyam Berehanu Haile[2]([⌂])

[1] Ethio Telecom, Addis Ababa, Ethiopia
taddege.assefa@ethiotelecom.et
[2] Addis Ababa Institute of Technology, Addis Ababa University,
Addis Ababa, Ethiopia
beneyamb.haile@aait.edu.et

Abstract. Demand for mobile broadband connectivity is significantly increasing and mobile network operators are continuously improving their network by introducing new technologies to accommodate the demand. After mobile network is operational for the first time, to maximize network performance, it is common to perform further optimization of initially planned and configured network parameters. One important category of such network parameters that incur significant network performance impact is antenna parameters including antenna tilt. Optimization of antenna tilt plays a major role in improving network coverage, capacity, load balancing and mitigating interference of mobile networks. To deliver mobile data services with better quality of experience, long term evolution (LTE) network has been operational in Addis Ababa, Ethiopia since 2015. In this paper, we evaluate performance of this Addis Ababa LTE network from antenna tilt perspective. Based on the evaluation, we also perform optimization of the antenna tilt by applying educated trial and error optimization approach that is focused to address worst performance areas. The performance evaluation and optimization of the network are undertaken using WinProp simulation tool. Results show that there is still a room to optimize antenna tilt further for better performance.

Keywords: LTE · Electrical tilt · SINR · Throughput · Network simulation · Addis Ababa · Ethiopia

1 Introduction

To address mainly better mobile data rate and network capacity demand, standardization of long term evolution (LTE) has been launched in November 2004 by the third generation partnership project (3GPP) [1]. Specific goals include improving efficiency, lowering costs, improving services, making use of new spectrum opportunities, and better integration with other open standards. LTE is selected as the next generation broadband wireless technology for 3GPP and 3GPP2. The LTE standard supports both frequency division duplex (FDD) and time division duplex (TDD). After Rel 8, Rel 9 was a relatively small update on top of Rel 8, and Rel 10, also known as LTE-Advanced, provided a major step in terms of data rates and capacity with carrier

© Springer Nature Switzerland AG 2019
F. Mekuria et al. (Eds.): ICT4DA 2019, CCIS 1026, pp. 137–145, 2019.
https://doi.org/10.1007/978-3-030-26630-1_11

aggregation, support for heterogeneous network (HetNet), higher-order Multi-Input-Multi-Output (MIMO) up to eight antennas in downlink and four antennas in uplink.

LTE air interface uses orthogonal frequency division multiple access (OFDMA) for downlink transmission to achieve high peak data rates in high spectrum bandwidth and single carrier frequency division multiple access (SC-FDMA) for uplink transmission, a technology that provides advantages in power efficiency. LTE supports advanced adaptive MIMO, balance average/peak throughput, and coverage/cell-edge bit rate. Compared to 3G, significant reduction in delay over air interface can be supported in LTE, and it is suitable for real-time applications.

LTE Rel 8 was frozen in December 2008 and it has been the basis for first wave of LTE equipment. Since then several operators have been planning and deploying LTE network to satisfy data demands of their mobile users that use various innovative mobile data services. As a result, global number of LTE commercial networks and subscriptions has reached 681 and 3.2 billion, respectively by the end of quarter 1 of 2018 [2]. The number of subscriptions accounts for 38.5% of total mobile subscriptions. It has also been forecasted that LTE will account for more than 50% of all global mobile subscriptions by 2020 and more than 60% by 2022.

Ethiopian incumbent operator ethio telecom has also deployed and provided LTE based data service since 2015 but the service is limited in the Ethiopian capital, Addis Ababa. Thus, LTE has only a small share not more than a few hundred thousand out of ethio telecom mobile subscribers that has reached 39.54 million mobile subscribers as of February 2019 [3]. Due to increasing penetration of social media, video streaming and other innovative data services in the Ethiopian mobile market, mobile data demand has been significantly increasing [4]. As a result, beside optimizing existing limited LTE network in Addis Ababa, it is important to expand it to meet demands of data customers in major cities and other parts of the country.

In mobile radio network planning and optimization tasks, antenna parameters including tilt, azimuth and height are very important parameters to meet target network capacity, coverage and quality of service [5–7]. Various researchers analyze impacts of antenna tilt and its optimization to achieve quality LTE network, for instance authors of [8–11]. Authors in [8] have performed comparative analysis of mechanical and electrical down tilt on performance of LTE using a snapshot LTE simulator with 3D antenna modeling and they show that electrical down tilt has significant LTE performance impact, mainly in case of interference limited system. In [9] and [10], they have expanded the analysis including other antenna parameters and from perspective of self-optimization network. In [11], antenna tilt impact on performance of LTE network has also been evaluated considering realistic antenna radiation patterns.

In this paper, we present performance evaluation of existing Addis Ababa LTE network and then perform antenna tilt optimization work by applying educated trial and error optimization approach. For the work, we select a hotspot LTE network scenario and perform network simulation using WinProp software [14, 15]. Signal-to-interference-plus-noise-ratio (SINR) and throughput metrics are used for performance comparison. Results reveal that there is still room to improve existing LTE network performance by reconfiguring antenna tilt parameters. For instance, signal–to-interference-plus-noise-ratio (SINR) and throughput results show that we are able to achieve 12.5% and 4.4% peak SINR and throughput gains, respectively, with further optimization of existing electrical tilt configuration of the LTE network. We also believe that this work presents contribution to LTE optimization and expansion efforts of ethio telecom.

Remaining parts of the paper are organized as follows. Section 2 presents Addis Ababa LTE deployment scenario, network modelling and assumptions. Section 3 discusses antenna tilt optimization approach. In Sect. 4, results and performance comparison are presented. Finally, Sect. 5 provides concluding remarks and future works.

2 Deployment Scenario, Network Modeling and Assumptions

2.1 Addis Ababa LTE Deployment Scenario

Currently, there are 331 three-sector LTE evolved node Bs (eNBs) that are deployed in Addis Ababa to provide LTE data services. All sectors configuration is single carrier and apply 1800 MHz frequency band that is shared with existing 2G system.

Two types of antenna solutions are adopted in Addis Ababa LTE network: green-field and rooftop. In the green-field solution, antennas are mounted on towers and operate on dual mode within a frequency range of 1710–2200 MHz. One mode is for 1800 MHz band where LTE and 2G operate and the other one is for 2100 MHz band where 3G operates. In the rooftop solution where the antennas are installed on top of buildings and can operate in frequency ranges of 790–960 MHz and 1710–2180 MHz. The former is used for 2G while the latter is used for both LTE and 3G.

For this study, we select hotspot Bole area (Addis Ababa, Ethiopia) covered by 34 eNBs (102 cells). The selected area is shown in Fig. 1.

Fig. 1. Selected Bole area

Other configuration of the LTE radio network including antenna tilt are used for our work but all not directly presented here for confidentiality purpose. Only important parameters for completeness of this work are discussed.

2.2 Network Modelling and Assumption

One of the most useful performance metric of the LTE network is the SINR and is defined as

$$SINR = \frac{Pr}{\Sigma P' + N}$$

Where Pr is signal power, P' is interference power and N is noise power. Another performance metric is throughput. The SINR metric is mapped to the throughput. The network performance evaluation and comparison is depicted using these metrics.

The simulation tool used for this study is the WinProp simulation tool. This tool is commercial and has been used in different research activities by senior researchers and academicians [12, 13]. The mapping in SINR to throughput is assumed in the WinProp simulation tool. The details about the tool is found in [14, 15]. Summary of basic network parameters and assumptions is depicted in Table 1. It has various modules such as the AMan (Antenna Manager) tool used for developing the antenna pattern of a practical antenna. In this study the antenna pattern is developed using AMan software module for each tilt of the antenna in both the horizontal and vertical planes and then convert them to a 3D pattern by extrapolating the pattern in both planes.

The propagation model adopted for the network simulation is the dominant path loss model. This model is used for modeling the propagation because it can be applied for urban scenario while majorly it concentrates only on the dominant paths and does not calculate the paths with small energy contributions. Hence, it doesn't consider all the details of the database, requiring less time to pre-process it. The accuracy of the model in very complex environments (with high shadowing of the direct ray) is higher than other models like ray tracing.

Table 1. Basic simulation parameters/assumptions

Parameters	Values
Number of eNBs	34 (102 cells)
Air interface	LTE FDD
Carrier frequency/bandwidth	1800/20 MHz
Simulation	System level simulator (WinProp)
Propagation model	Dominant path loss
Transmitter power	43 dBm
Antenna type	Aggison ADU451819 & ATR451704v01
UE distribution	Uniform

3   Tilt Optimization Approach

The selected Bole area existing network parameters configuration are used to simulate the network. Keeping other parameters setting, electrical antenna tilt parameter of the cells with worst SINR and throughput performance are altered and then simulated iteratively. The simulation iteration is done until optimal performance is achieved. Here, optimal value is to mean the best value obtained by this work. There could be other better possible values in other iterations. Figure 2 shows the steps of the optimization approach. The adjustment as in Table 2 shows the tilt setting to obtain best network performance improvement.

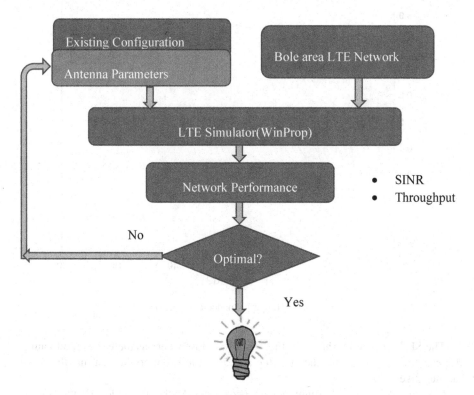

Fig. 2. Optimization approach

Table 2. Electrical down tilt adjustment

Site	34			4			6			8			5		
Antenna	Ant 1	Ant 2	Ant 3	Ant 1	Ant 2	Ant 3	Ant 1	Ant 2	Ant 3	Ant 1	Ant 2	Ant 3	Ant 1	Ant 2	Ant 3
Existing EDT	2	2	0	5	5	7	3	7	0	1	2	4	2	4	3
New EDT	2	4	1	4	5	5	4	5	0	3	2	1	3	5	3

4   Results and Performance Comparison

The SINR performance plot shown in Fig. 3 compares the performance for both the existing network configuration and after electrical tilt has been adjusted. The maximum achievable SINR for the existing network configuration is 16 dB and it is 18 dB after the electrical tilt adjustment as stated in Table 2. The highest SINR performance gain is observed at 70%.

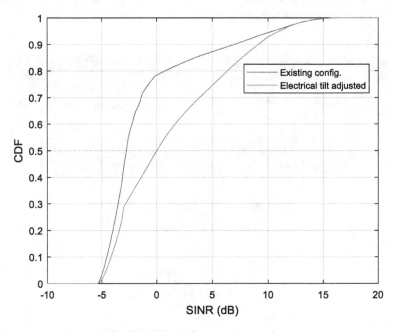

Fig. 3. SINR performance comparison

The SINR percentile shown in Fig. 4 shows a loss where as there is a good gain at 90 percentiles. The loss for the 10 %tile and 50 %tile is due to the fact that the SINR had negative values.

Figure 5 shows the throughput gain percentile. At the 10 %tile (1), there is no significant improvement. It shows better improvement at the 50th %tile (2) whereas there is best throughput gain at 90 percentiles (3) compared to 10 and 50 percentiles.

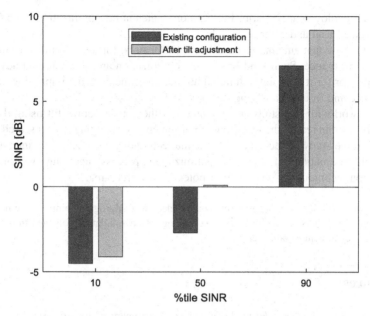

Fig. 4. SINR percentile; 10%, 50% and 90%

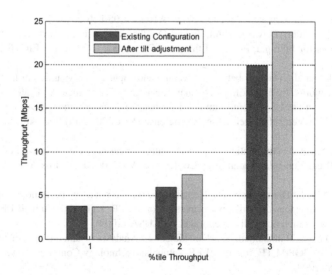

Fig. 5. Throughput percentile; 10%, 50% and 90%

5   Conclusions

In this paper, we have reviewed Addis Ababa LTE network and deployed antenna solutions. Moreover, antenna electrical down tilt parameter has been studied to investigate their impact on LTE network performance, particularly for an Addis

Ababa LTE deployment scenario. Furthermore, antenna tilt optimization is performed using educated trial and error approach.

Results show that antenna electrical down tilt can be further optimized to improve network performance. Such kind of antenna optimization are of paramount advantage for the operator for it does not require additional investments while improving network performance and in turn satisfying customers.

Future works for this study include study of the antenna down tilt using dynamic simulators since in reality the traffic and environment are changing. The research can be extended to the study of the future of antenna technology such as active antenna. Full or partial automation of antenna optimization process applying various self-optimization techniques is also another potential research area.

Acknowledgment. This work is performed under telecom MSc program jointly implemented by ethio telecom and Addis Ababa Institute of Technology. Network data is collected from staffs of engineering department of ethio telecom.

References

1. 3gpp. http://www.3gpp.org/technologies/keywords-acronyms/98-lte. Accessed 18 Sept 2018
2. GSA Report: Status of the LTE Ecosystem, Global Mobile Suppliers Association, August 2018
3. Ethio telecom. http://www.ethiotelecom.et/. Accessed 05 Feb 2019
4. Haile, B.B., Bulti, D.A., Zerihun, B.M.: On the relevance of capacity enhancing 5G technologies for Ethiopia. In: 10th Ethiopian ICT Annual Conference (EICTC-2017), June 2017
5. Hampel, G., et al.: Tradeoff between coverage and capacity in dynamic optimization of 3G cellular networks. In: 58th IEEE Vehicular Technology Conference (VTC 2003-Fall) (2003)
6. Lozano, M., et al.: UMTS optimum cell load balancing for inhomogeneous traffic patterns. In: 60th IEEE Vehicular Technology Conference (VTC2004-Fall), Los Angeles, CA, USA (2004)
7. Pettersen, M., et al.: Automatic antenna tilt control for capacity enhancement in UMTS FDD. In: 60th IEEE Vehicular Technology Conference (VTC2004-Fall), Los Angeles, CA, USA (2004)
8. Yilmaz, O.N.C., Hämäläinen, S., Hämäläinen, J.: Comparison of remote electrical and mechanical antenna downtilt performance for 3GPP LTE. In: 70th IEEE Vehicular Technology Conference Fall, Anchorage, AK, USA (2009)
9. Yilmaz, O.N.C., Hämäläinen, S., Hämäläinen, J.: Analysis of antenna parameter optimization space for 3GPP LTE. In: 70th IEEE Vehicular Technology Conference Fall, Anchorage, AK, USA (2009)
10. Yilmaz, O.N.C., Hämäläinen, S., Hämäläinen, J.: Self-optimization of remote electrical tilt. In: 21st Annual IEEE International Symposium on Personal, Indoor and Mobile Radio Communications, Istanbul, Turkey (2010)
11. Ruise,A.C.: LTE Mobile network performance with antenna tilt considering real radiation patterns. M.Sc. thesis, KTH Royal Institute of Technology, May 2015
12. Haile, B.B., Mutafungwa, E., Hämäläinen, J.: LTE-advanced enhancements for self-backhauled LTE-U small cells: an addis Ababa case study. In: IEEE AFRICON 2015, 14–17 September 2015, Addis Ababa, Ethiopia (2015)

13. Haile, B.B., Mutafungwa, E., Hämäläinen, J.: Coordinated multi-point transmission for relaxation of self-backhauling bottlenecks in heterogeneous networks. EURASIP J. Wirel. Commun. Netw. **2015**, 78 (2015)
14. Altair Engineering: WinProp-Propagation Modeling. https://altairhyperworks.com/product/FEKO/WinProp-Propagation-Modeling
15. https://www.slideshare.net/ProjectENhANCE/winprop-propagation-modeling-and-network-planning-tool. Accessed 06 Aug 2018

Low Complexity Radio Mobile Speed Estimation Using Count of Received Envelop Peaks and Troughs

Atli Lemma[(✉)]

Haramaya University, P.O. Box 138, Dire Dawa, Ethiopia
atli.lemma@outlook.com

Abstract. Low complexity mobile speed estimation is required for power control, mobility and resource management, effective handoff, and outage probability computation of cellular mobile communication systems. It is also useful for mobility determination and energy-efficient packet routing in wireless sensor and mobile ad-hoc networks. In this paper, we present a low complexity mobile speed estimation model using count of peaks and troughs of the received signal envelop. Our simulation result shows that the model has a maximum error of 0.25 m/s. The model has two advantages. First, it does not require measurement of the received signal power; it only counts envelop peaks and troughs. Second, the model is independent of dc offset inherent in the radio receivers. However, the model has one limitation- it does not give the crossing component of a mobile's velocity.

Keywords: Mobile speed estimation · Envelop peaks and troughs · Resource management

1 Introduction

Accurate and low complexity mobile speed estimation is required for power control, radio resource and mobility management such as dynamic channel assignment, effective handoff, and outage probability computations in cellular mobile communication systems [1–11]. Specifically, the long term evolution (LTE) network is designed to provide high data rates under various mobility conditions [1]. Thus, low complexity and high accuracy mobile speed estimation is required in these systems. In addition, speed estimation is needed for mobility determination and energy-efficient packet routing in wireless sensor and mobile ad-hoc networks respectively [1, 9]. Moreover, adaptive transmission in mobile systems depends on knowledge of mobile speed [8]. In all these applications, it is sufficient to determine the magnitude of the mobile velocity.

A number of mobile speed estimation techniques can be found in literature. The first is based on the level crossing rate of the received signal envelop. The scheme is efficient and robust to signal variation [5]. However, since it requires envelop power which in turn depends on mobile location and shadowing, it requires dynamic adjustment of the level and hence it is difficult to use this model in practice [5, 8]. The second technique is based on the zero crossing rates of the inphase or quadrature

© Springer Nature Switzerland AG 2019
F. Mekuria et al. (Eds.): ICT4DA 2019, CCIS 1026, pp. 146–153, 2019.
https://doi.org/10.1007/978-3-030-26630-1_12

components of the received radio signal. Like the level crossing technique, this model is efficient and robust [5, 8]. But, it requires mobiles or base stations to use coherent detectors [5, 8]. The third technique employs the auto-covariance of the received signal envelop [5, 8]. This technique requires measurement of envelop power, which is difficult in cellular systems [5, 8]. The fourth method is based on diversity combiner and has high complexity [5]. The fifth technique uses the rate of maxima of the received signal envelop [1]. We have found that this method does not require measurement of mean envelop power [5]. Nevertheless, its performance degrades with prevalence of shadowing [5]. In addition, when compared with our technique, it has higher complexity. Finally, a mobile speed estimation technique is given in [11] that is based on average slope duration of the received signal envelop. The technique does not require measurement of mean envelop power [11]. Also, since it does not require variable observation window, it is convenient to implement in practice [11]. However, the model has high complexity. In our work, we have developed a mobile speed estimation model that has all the advantages of the previous models plus it has low complexity. This paper is organized as follows. In Sect. 2, the received envelop model is given. Here, we presented a modified form of Jake's the sum-of-sinusoids model. In Sect. 3, we derived the speed estimation model using the count of received envelop peaks and troughs. In Sect. 4, we presented our simulation results and discussions. Finally, in Sect. 5, we give important conclusions.

2 Received Envelop Model

2.1 Modified Sum of Sinusoids

In a multipath radio environment, there is no scenario specific information and obstacles are not uniformly spaced as often assumed [13, 14]. Moreover, multipath has different fading distributions for different scenarios [14]. Let us consider a frequency selective channel characterized by multipath fading. A mobile node receives multiple attenuated versions of the transmitted signal, $s(t)$. For the sake of simplicity, let us neglect noise; for a fairly big signal-to-noise ratio (SNR), the model is independent of the noise. Thus, the received signal can be written as [12–14]:

$$r(t) = A_t e^{-j\omega_t t} \sum_{n=1}^{N} c_n e^{j(\omega_{rm} t \cos[\theta_n] + \varphi_n)} \tag{1}$$

Here, A_t is the transmit signal strength, ω_t is the transmit frequency, c_n is the multipath attenuation coefficient, ω_{rm} is the received maximum frequency with respect to the transmit frequency, θ_n is the angle of arrival of the nth path and is the angle between the velocity vector and the radial direction between the mobile node and the base station, and φ_n is the phase of nth path received signal.

The inphase and quadrature components of the received signal envelop in (1) are given by

$$
\left.
\begin{aligned}
r_i(t) &= A_t cos(\omega_t t) \sum_{n=1}^{N} c_n cos[\omega_{rm} t cos(\theta_n) + \varphi_n] \\
r_q(t) &= A_t sin(\omega_t t) \sum_{n=1}^{N} c_n sin[\omega_{rm} t cos(\theta_n) + \varphi_n]
\end{aligned}
\right\}
\tag{2}
$$

The maximum radian frequency of the received signal can be found by applying Doppler equation given by [12, 14]:

$$
\omega_{rm} = \omega_t \left(1 \pm \frac{v}{c}\right)
\tag{3}
$$

2.2 Phase of Arrival

For multipath and Doppler fading mobile communication channel, the propagation delay of each path can be chosen from an exponentially distributed delay variable [16–17]. The probability density function (PDF) of such a variable, τ, is given by [19–20]:

$$
f_\tau(\tau) = \frac{1}{T_{av}} e^{-\frac{\tau}{T_{av}}}
\tag{4}
$$

Here, T_{av} is a constant that can be determined as follows. First, the minimum average propagation delay can be estimated, for example, with a 3 m minimum separation of the mobile from the base station. So, for free space τ_{min} = 10 ns. Then, the maximum delay, on the other hand, can be estimated from a cell diameter D and microwave propagation speed c = 3e+8 m/s using:

$$
\tau_{max} = \frac{D}{2c}
\tag{5}
$$

The probability distribution function over all possibilities of the propagation delay is unity. That is:

$$
\int_{\tau_{min}}^{\tau_{max}} \frac{1}{T_{av}} e^{-\frac{\tau}{T_{av}}} d\tau = 1
\tag{6}
$$

Carrying out the integration, we get the following:

$$
e^{-\frac{\tau_{min}}{T_{av}}} - e^{-\frac{\tau_{max}}{T_{av}}} = 1
\tag{7}
$$

The equation above is transcendental and we resorted to numerical methods to obtain T_{av}. For a known value of the average propagation delay, the cumulative distribution function (CDF) of τ is [14]:

$$F_\tau(\tau) = \int\limits_{-\infty}^{\tau} f_\tau(\delta)d\delta \tag{8}$$

After computing the integral and simplifying it further in the interval $\tau_{min} < \tau < \tau_{max}$ we get:

$$F_\tau(\tau) = 1 - e^{-\frac{\tau}{T_{av}}} \tag{9}$$

Thus, the delay can be obtained from the CDF in (9) and the phase of the received radio signal can be found from:

$$\varphi = 2\pi n\tau \tag{10}$$

3 Speed Estimation Model

Studies showed that the count of envelop peaks and troughs contains rich information about the speed of a mobile. Also, empirical measurements show that the adjacent envelop peaks are half wavelength apart. That is, as the mobile moves faster, the number of envelop peaks and troughs per unit time increases. We have simulated the envelop at two different speeds as shown in Fig. 1. Thus, the count of envelop peaks and troughs are a function of the mobile's radial speed. Thus, it should be possible to estimate the mobile speed from count of the envelop peaks and troughs. If we take the time derivative of the signal envelop, then the zeros of this rate will indicate the locations of envelop peaks and troughs. So, the counts of the zeros of this derivative is equal to the count of the envelop peaks and troughs. The signal envelop is Rayleigh distributed and the count of the envelop peak and trough is given by [12, 13]:

$$R_r(t) = 2 \int\limits_{-\infty}^{+\infty} |r'(t)| f_{rr'}(r = 0, r')dr' \tag{11}$$

Where the received signal envelop is a random process with a probability density function $f_r(r, r')$. Now, making the transformation $W(t) = r^2(t)$, we get:

$$W'(t) = 2r(t)r'(t) \tag{12}$$

Therefore, the count of the envelop peak and trough can be written as [9, 11]:

$$R_{W'}(t) = 2 \int\limits_{-\infty}^{+\infty} |W''(t)| f_{rr'}\left(W' = 0, W''(t)\right)dW'' \tag{13}$$

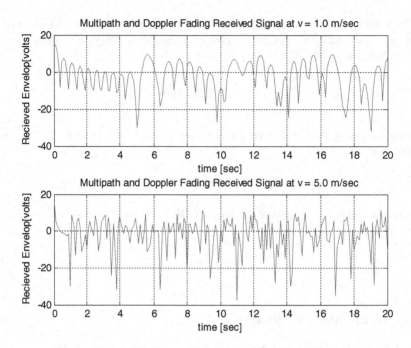

Fig. 1. Rayleigh fading envelop at two different mobile speeds

Thus, the count of zeros of the time derivative of the envelop $R_{r'}(t)$ and the count of zeros of the time derivative of the envelop squared $R_{W'}(t)$ are equal [11]. That is:

$$R_{r'}(t) = R_{W'}(t) \tag{14}$$

The average number of envelop peaks and troughs per second can be found from (13) and (14) to be [11]:

$$R_{W''}(t) = \frac{1}{2\pi} \sqrt{\frac{b_2}{b_0}} I_W \tag{15}$$

I_W is the indefinite integral of (13) and is numerically computed to be 4.2757 [8]. On the other hand, the field moments are given by [12, 13]:

$$b_2 = 2b_0 [f_{max}(t)]^2 \tag{16}$$

The maximum frequency of the received signal is given by the Doppler equation [11–15]:

$$f_{max}(t) = f_t \frac{v(t)}{c} \tag{17}$$

Now, from (15), (16), and (17), we obtain:

$$R_{W'}(t) = \frac{v(t)}{c\sqrt{2}} f_t l_W \tag{18}$$

Finally, from (14) and (18), we get the estimate of the radial speed of the mobile to be:

$$\hat{v}(t) = 1.323 \frac{c}{f_t} R_{r'}(t) \tag{19}$$

The Algorithm:
Step 1: Generate the reference mobile speed which is to be estimated. We have generated the reference mobile speed using $v = \sqrt{t}$.
Step 2: Generate large samples of the received signal envelop for a speed estimation interval using (2) and the reference speed obtained in step 1.
Step 3: Compute the count of the received envelop peaks and troughs from the sample set.
Step 4: Find the estimate of the mobile speed using (19), increment the time.

4   Results and Discussions

In our work, we simulated the signal envelop by implementing the modified form of Jakes Sum-of-Sinusoids presented in Sect. 2. The simulation parameters are given in Table 1. The distance dependent path loss does not affect the performance of this model and hence it is neglected. We have used envelop averages and neglected the effect of noise on the model.

Table 1. Simulation parameter.

Parameter	Value	Description
c	3.00e + 8 m/s	Speed of propagation
f_t	5.00e + 9 Hz	Transmit frequency
D	5.00e + 3 m	Diameter of cell site
τ_{min}	1.00e − 8 s	Minimum envelop delay
τ_{max}	4.30e − 7 s	Maximum envelop delay

We have given the reference and estimated mobile speeds as shown in Fig. 2. The estimated speed is close to the reference speed with a maximum error of 0.25 m/s. However, the moving average of the estimated speed is very close to the reference speed. This signifies that better speed estimates can be obtained by slightly increasing the complexity with the use of a moving average filter. For example, the worst error for the peak and tough count model is 0.25 m/s (at v = 2.5 m/s). Furthermore, the error range is from 0 m/s to 0.25 m/s for the peak and trough count model.

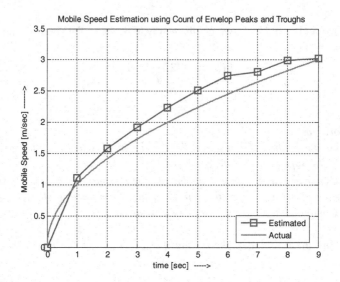

Fig. 2. Speed estimates using count of envelop peaks and troughs

5 Conclusions

Accurate and low complexity mobile speed estimation is required in wireless communications systems. We have developed a simple and practical mobile speed estimation model that has two advantages. First, it does not require measurement of the received signal power. Second, the model is independent of dc offset inherent in the radio receivers. However, our model has one limitation- it does not give the crossing component of a mobile's velocity. The model is developed to estimate the radial speed of a mobile with respect to another node which may or may not be mobile. The model has high accuracy and low complexity that makes it attractive for time sensitive speed estimation, such as mobile handoff.

References

1. Osfiko, M.O., Okubanjo, A.A., Abolade, O.R., Oyetola, O.K., Oyedeji, A.O., Sanusi, O.I.: Evaluating the effect of mobility speed on the performance of three handover algorithms in long term evolution networks. J. Appl. Sci. Environ. Mang. **22**(4), 503–506 (2018)
2. Merwadey, A., Guvenc, I.: Handover Count Based Velocity Estimation and Mobility State Detection in Dense HetNets (2016)
3. Zheng, Y.R., Xiao, C.: Mobile speed estimation for broadband wireless communications over Rician fading channels. IEEE Trans. Wirel. Commun. **8**(1), 1–5 (2009)

4. Abdi, A.: A New Velocity Estimator for Cellular Systems Based on Higher Order Crossings
5. Patachaianand, R., Sandrasegaran, K.: User speed estimation techniques for UMTS. Electron. Lett. **43**(19), 1036–1037 (2007)
6. Iera, A., Molinaro, A., Marano, S.: Handoff management with mobility estimation in hierarchical systems. IEEE Trans. Veh. Technol. **51**(5), 915–934 (2002)
7. Abdi, A., Kaveh, M.: Level crossing rate in terms of the characteristic functions: a new approach for calculating the fading rate in diversity systems. IEEE Trans. Commun. **50**(9), 1397–1400 (2002)
8. Abdi, A., Zhang, H., Tepedelenlioglu, C.: A unified approach to the performance analysis of speed estimation techniques in mobile communication. IEEE Trans. Commun. **56**(1), 126–135 (2008)
9. Li, Z., Sun, L., Ifeachor, E.C.: Rang-based relative velocity estimations for networked mobile devices. IEEE Trans. Veh. Technol. **58**(4), 2095–2099 (2009)
10. Juncker, C., Toft, P., Morch, N.: Speed Estimation for WCDMA on the Channel Envelop Derivative
11. Zhao, L., Mark, J.W.: Mobile speed estimation based on average slope duration. IEEE Trans. Commun. **52**(12), 2066–2069 (2004)
12. Stuber, G.L.: Principle of Mobile Communications, 4th edn. Springer, Atlanta (2017)
13. Jakes, W.C.: Microwave Mobile Communications, 2nd edn. CRC/IEEE Press (1995)
14. Jeruchim, M.C., Balaban, P., Shanmugan, K.: Simulations of Communication Systems: Modeling, Methodology, and Techniques, 2nd edn. (2000)
15. Xiao, C., Rosa, Y., Beaulieu, N.C.: Novel sum-of-sinusoids simulation model for Rayleigh and Rician fading channels. IEEE Trans. Wirel. Commun. **5**(12), 3667–3679 (2006)

Performance Analysis of Vertical Sectorization for LTE Realistic Deployment Scenario

Seifu Girma Zeleke$^{(\boxtimes)}$ and Beneyam Berehanu Haile

Addis Ababa Institute of Technology, Addis Ababa University,
Addis Ababa, Ethiopia
{seifu.girma, beneyamb.haile}@aait.edu.et

Abstract. Mobile network capacity demand has been continuous increasing due to increasing penetration of data intensive services. To meet the increasing capacity demand, vertical sectorization has been considered one important capacity enhancing technology through vertical cell splitting into inner and outer cells by applying active antenna system. Planning vertically sectorized network is a new concept and need to be investigated well in order to characterize its impact on cell edge performance and capacity. Although this method presented by different authors, still various issues needs to be further investigated. Analyzing this method in realistic network environment, vendor antenna pattern and effect of spacing between vertical pattern with considering cell edge performance are rarely reported. In this paper, impact of this technology with performance metrics of 5% tile, 50% tile and 90% of CDF of SINR and their modified shannon mapping in realistic environment are examined. Propagation computation is performed using deterministic path loss model and network simulation is made using matlab. According to simulation results the identified 3×2 configuration out performs others 3×2 studied scenarios. And this configurations can enhance system performance up to 51.8% compared to the existing 3×1 network.

Keywords: Vertical sectorization · Active antenna system · Antenna pattern

1 Introduction

The introduction of new application, new devices and services has driven the network demand growth at an exponential rate. Forecasts also indicate that global mobile data and internet traffic will show an increase from the current 11,183 PB/month to 48,270 PB/month by 2021 [1]. Similarly, significant mobile traffic growth has also been seen in emerging market like Ethiopia due to significant growth of mobile internet penetration and the increasing social media and other multimedia service usage, particularly in the major cities like Addis Ababa, Ethiopia [2]. This increase of traffic demand has motivated the development of different solutions for increasing network capacity. Network densification technique using vertically sectorized cells has been recently considered due to its capability enhancing system performance without introducing additional sites unlike small cell densification. This is done by splitting the cell vertically, creating inner and outer layouts by active antenna system. Both beams

© Springer Nature Switzerland AG 2019
F. Mekuria et al. (Eds.): ICT4DA 2019, CCIS 1026, pp. 154–163, 2019.
https://doi.org/10.1007/978-3-030-26630-1_13

use the same communication resources [3–6]. A graphical representation of vertical sectorization is shown in Fig. 1 where the outer and the inner beams forms the outer and the inner sectors respectively. The inner cell is closed to the BS and typically covers a small portion of the cell surface.

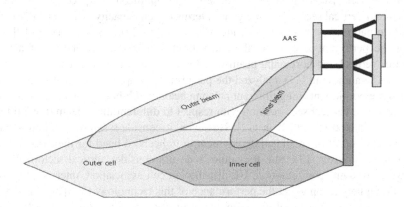

Fig. 1. Sector layout of vertical sectorization system [3].

Mobile operators like Ethio telecom are expected to optimize their mobile networks with these emerging technologies to accommodate the continuous data demand growth. However optimizing network with vertical sectorization is a new concept and needs further investigation to characterize its impact for different antenna configuration. Figure 2 shows a traffic data collected around bole, Addis Ababa and covers an area of about 1.62 km^2.

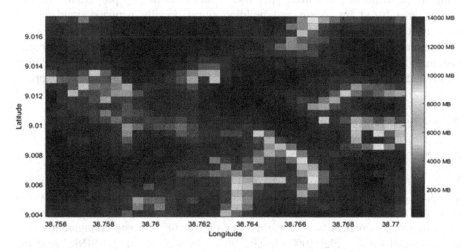

Fig. 2. Traffic data collected during June, 10, 2018 around bole, Addis Ababa

Researchers have shown the effectiveness of vertical sectorization on system performance [5–12]. Performance of vertical sectorization in LTE system for single user is tested in [4]. Simulation results indicated that the co-channel interference between the inner and outer cells is the main source of throughput impact. [5] and [6] investigate the performance impact of this technology for various vertical half-power beam widths (HBPW) and electrical tilt angles to observe the optimization space of the overlap between two vertical sectors and the gain in terms of cell capacity. They use 3GPP case simulation parameters and antenna pattern proposed by [7]. The authors [8–10] optimizing the performance of vertical sectorization with site configuration of antenna down tilt, vertical and horizontal beam width and transmit power in LTE-A downlink systems. The authors in [11] analyzed the performance impact of vertical sectorization in realistic environment using different antenna beam width but for super cell case. The performance of vertical sectorization with respect to different inner beam down tilt and power ratio is also examined in [12]. However, it considers synthetic environments. Performance impact of small cell deployment in unlicensed band for the case of Addis Ababa is analyzed in [13]. But, the author's do not consider vertical sectorization in their work. Antenna configuration, UE distribution cell association, inters site distance and building height can affect the performance of this technology [3–6] and [12]. Most of the above work carried out their simulation in unrealistic environment and antenna pattern. This results in neglecting the influence of side lobes. Furthermore, investigation of this technology for varying vertical beams bore sights angle difference considering both cell edge performance and capacity is rarely reported.

The purpose of this study is to analyze the performance impact of vertical sectorization for different site configuration and to compare with the existing 3×1 network in realistic network environment and vendor antenna pattern by varying outer beams electrical tilt angle.

To do this, first we identified the studied antenna configuration. Then we model user distribution based on traffic data. The received power of each user is obtained using the deterministic dominant path loss model in win prop propagation tool of studied area based on terrain and building maps. Finally network simulation is implemented using Matlab.

The remaining part is organized as follows. Section 2 provides deployment scenario, system model and assumptions used in the paper for simulation purpose. Simulation results and discussions are described in Sect. 3. Finally, Sect. 4 concludes the work.

2   System Model, Deployment Scenario, and Assumptions

2.1   System Model

In this work we consider a down link LTE mobile network 6 macro cells in the studied area. Cell association is made based on user's received power. The received power is computed using deterministic dominant path loss model based on building and terrain maps of the deployment area. Performances of the different site configurations are studied based on 5% tile, 50% tile and 90% tile of CDF of the SINR. And the performance of the identified site configuration is compared with the existing network by corresponding modified Shannon mapping of CDF of SINR and throughput. Throughput is expressed using modified Shannon formula [14] as:

$$TP = BW_{eff}N_{PRB}B_{PRB} \log_2(1 + \frac{SINR}{SINR_{eff}}) \qquad (1)$$

Where N_{PRB} is the number of PRBs, B_{PRB} is the bandwidth per PRB, BW_{eff} is the adjusted bandwidth to fit with LTE the system bandwidth efficiency and $SINR_{eff}$ is the adjusted $SINR$ implementation efficiency.

Antenna Models: In this paper we used huawei antenna patterns of the following models: ADU451819 for the existing 3 × 1 reference network, ADU451900 for 3 × 2 the outer cell with different remote electrical tilt and A19451800 for 3 × 2 inner cell. Sample antenna pattern used is shown in Fig. 3 below.

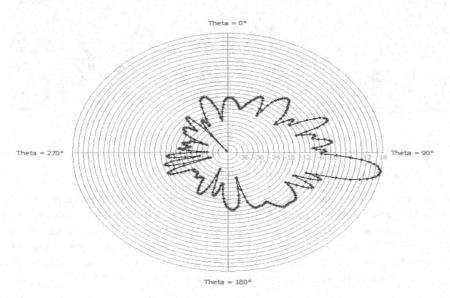

Fig. 3. Sample vertical antenna patteren used in simulation (RET 10 and V.HPBW 7.5 Deg.)

2.2 Deployment Scenario

To study the performance impact of vertical sectorization, a realistic network environment in Addis Ababa Ethiopia that exemplifies an urban scenario with dense hotspots is selected. It is specifically found at around Dembele, a place where high data traffic is recorded. It covers an area of 1.1 km × 1.0 km, building of various heights up to 70 m and terrain with topography range from 2000–3000 m. The area consists of trisector of 6 macro sites with real location of eNodeBs for existing Addis Ababa LTE network. For vertical sectorization study purpose those 3 × 1 sectors are replaced by 3 × 2 vertically sectorized cells. The location of macro sites are shown in Fig. 4 below.

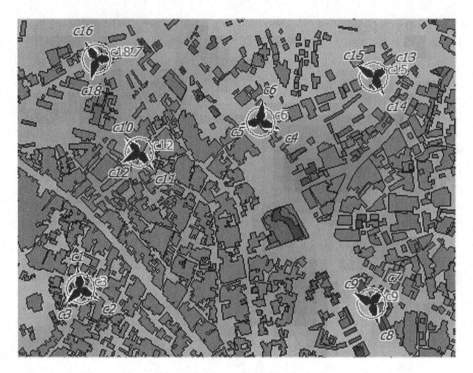

Fig. 4. Performance studied area

2.3 Simulation Parameters and Assumptions

In this work we have studied antenna configurations and simulation parameters shown in Tables 1 and 2 below respectively. The existing 3 × 1 configuration comprises of 3 sectors in each macro sites and antenna pattern describes in Sect. 2.1. For the case of 3 × 2 vertically sectorized cells we considered 10° RET for all inner beams and different RET for outer beams. The studied configurations are selected to observe the optimization space between the inner and the outer cells.

Table 1. Studied antenna configuration

Scenarios/ configuration (3 × 2)	V.HPBW out. beam (Deg.)	V.HPBW inn. beam (Deg.)	RET inn. beam (Deg.)	RET out. beam (Deg.)	Mech. tilt (Deg.)	Antenna height (m)	RET angle difference (Deg.)
1	4.5	7.5	10	0	10	40	10
2	4.5	4.5	10	2	10	40	8
3	4.5	4.5	10	4	10	40	6
4	4.5	4.5	10	6	10	40	4
5	4.5	4.5	Same as existing 3 × 1 configuration				

Most of system simulation parameters are taken from 3GPP case 3 except network layout and traffic distribution. Real building and terrain maps is used as network layout and modeled user distribution based on recorded traffic is used in place of traffic distribution.

Table 2. Simulation parameters and assumptions

Parameters	Values/Assumptions
Downlink transmit power	46 dBm
System frequency	1800 MHz
Antenna technique	2 × 2 MIMO
Frequency reuse factor	1
Base station height	40 m
Horizontal HPBW	63°
Number of UEs/Vertical sector	10
UE height	1.5 m
Simulation area	1.1×1.0 km^2
Receive antenna gain	0 dBi
BW$_{eff}$	0.60
SINR$_{eff}$	1.8
Thermal floor	−174 dBm/Hz
Traffic distribution	Hotspot
Cell association	RSRP

3 Results and Discussions

In this section, the impact of vertical sectorization in LTE downlink cellular networks is evaluated. CDF of SINR and throughput performance are analyzed for different antenna configuration in realistic network environment. Simulations are carried out to select antenna configuration that can give the best performance among the selected site configuration. Then throughput performance of the identified configuration is compared with the exsting LTE network configuartion. The performance matrices and antenna configurations used in the simulation are described in Sect. 2.3.

Performances of the outer and inner beams with respect to CDF of SINR and the associated UE load distribution are shown in Fig. 5 and Table 3. From Fig. 5(a), CDF of SINR increasing with increasing spacing between RET tilt except for the exsting site configuration. Among the studied configuration, RET of 10 and 0° (configuration 1) out performs the other configurations. For example, SINR at 50% tile, configuration 1 has 4 dB performance difference with that of Configuration 4. And also, this configuration has a 2 dB and 2.2 dB performance difference with that of angle difrence of 4 (configuration 2) configuration 3 at 50% tile of CDF. For inner cells case as shown in Fig. 5(b), angle difference of 8° (configuration 2) gives the best performance. However in both cases the exsting 3 × 1 configuration outperforms all the studied configurations interms of SINR with the corresponding load distribution as shown in Table 3.

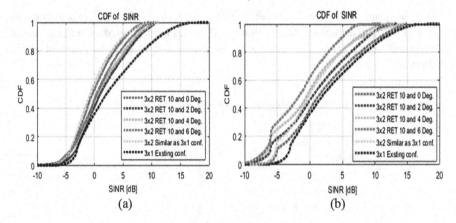

Fig. 5. Comparisions of CDF of SINR, (a) Outer cells users (b) Inner cells users

Table 3. User load distribution for inner and outer cell for different configuration

Scenarios/ configuration	RET tilt (Deg.)		Mechanical tilt. (Deg.)	UE-load distribution outer cell (%)
	Inner cell	Outer cell		
1	10	0	10	79.8
2	10	2	10	79.2
3	10	4	10	83.2
4	10	6	10	88.8
5	Same as the exsting 3 × 2 configuration		10	71%

The combined effect of both inner and outer beams users CDF of SINR are compared using the exsting 3 × 1 network as reference configuration as shown in Fig. 6. From Fig. 6, configuration 1 having angle difference 10° (scenario 1) gives the best SINR results compared to other 3 × 2 scenaros with respect to all the three performance metrices. In all cases, CDF of SINR of the exsting 3 × 1 configuration outperforms other studied configuration. This is mainly because when vertical sectorization is activated additional co-channel interferences are introduced beside vertical sectorization doubling the resource elements.

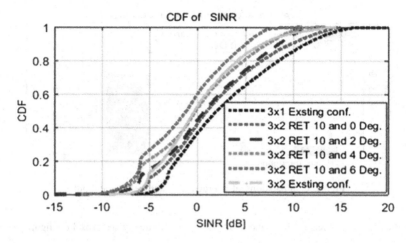

Fig. 6. Comparisions of CDF of SINR for diffrent cells configuration

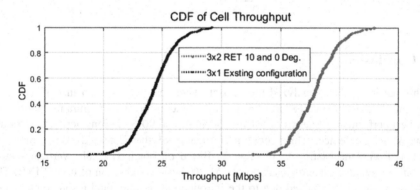

Fig. 7. CDF of cell throughput

Figure 7 show CDF throughput comparisons of the exsting 3×1 and the identified 3×2 vertically sectorized cells configuration. As it can be seen in Fig. 7 although vertical sectorization reduce the SINR performance of each user as shown in the Fig. 6 above, it improves CDF of cell throughput. This is because of vertical sectorization doubling the resource elements.

Figure 8 show performances of average cell and user throughput of the exsting 3×1 configuration and the identified 3×2 configuration. As we can see from the figure both average user and cell throughput of vertically sectorized cells out performs the exsting configuration. For example there is 1.36 Mbps incremental in average user throughput and 51.8% Mbps performance gain compared to the exsting network with and without vertical sectorization (Table 4).

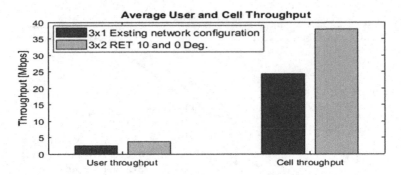

Fig. 8 Comparisions of average user and cell throughput

Table 4. Performance gain of the identified 3×2 vertically sectorized configuration

Down link average cell throughput with out vertical sectorization	Down link average cell throughput with vertical sectorization	Capacity gain by vertical sectorization
24.89 Mbps	37.78 Mbps	51.8%

4   Conclusion

In this paper, we have analyzed the impact of vertical sectorization in realistic environment of Addis Ababa, for diffrent scenarios to identify site configuration which can give best performance interms of 5% tile, 50% tile and 90% tile considering the exsting network as a refernce. Throughput performance of the identified configuration is compared with the exsting LTE network. Based on obtained results vertical sectorization can inhance system capacity upto 51.8% besides reduction of users SINR. The performance gain is obtained due to the introduction of additional resource elements. We also note that, when the angle separation between the inner and outer beams become narrow and narrow a high performance degradation is observed on both the capacity and cell edge performance. Increasing spacing between vertical RET keeping other parameters constant enhance both capacity and cell edge performance. Effect of vertical sectorization in high rise building, multi objective optimization and cell association in vertical sectorization can be an important future work.

References

1. Cisco white paper, Cisco Visual Networking Index: Forecast and Methodology, 2016–2021. Cisco Public (2017)
2. Adam, L.: Understanding what is happening in ICT in Ethiopia. A supply and demand side analysis of the ICT sector, Evidence for ICT Policy, Action Policy Paper (2012)
3. Weiliang, X., Qimei, C., Fengyi, Y., Qi, B., Yifei, Y.: Experimental investigation on a vertical sectorization system with active antenna. IEEE Commun. Mag. **54**, 89–97 (2016)

4. Fengyi, Y., Jianmin, Z., Weiliang, X., Xuetian, Z.: Field trial results for vertical sectorization in LTE network using active antenna system. In: IEEE International Conference on Communications (ICC), pp. 2508–2512. IEEE, Sydney (2014)
5. Osman, N., Yilmaz, S., Jyri, H.: System level analysis of vertical sectorization for 3GPP LTE. In: 6th International Symposium on Wireless Communication Systems, pp. 453–457. IEEE, Tuscany (2009)
6. Youqi, F., Jian, W., Zhuyan, Z., Liyun, D., Hongwen, Y.: Analysis of vertical sectorization for HSPA on a system level: capacity and coverage. In: IEEE Vehicular Technology Conference (VTC Fall), pp. 1–5. IEEE, Quebec (2012)
7. Derege, K., Wegmann, B., Viering, I., Klein, A.: Mathematical model for vertical sectorization (VS) in AAS based LTE deployment. In: 11th International Symposium on Wireless Communication Systems, pp. 100–105. IEEE, Barcelona (2014)
8. Joydeep, A., Salam, A.: Optimizing vertical sectorization for high-rises. In: International Conference on Computing, Networking and Communications (ICNC), pp. 1–5. IEEE, Garden Grove (2015)
9. Siew, N., Zhong, L., Sai, W., Yong, C.: Optimizing radio network parameters for vertical sectorization via Taguchi's method. IEEE Trans. Veh. Technol. **65**, 860–869 (2015)
10. Jinping, N., Geoffrey, Y., Li, F., Wei, W., Weike, N., Xun, L.: Downtilts optimization and power allocation for vertical sectorization in AAS-based LTE-A downlink systems. In: IEEE 86th Vehicular Technology Conference (VTC-Fall), pp. 1–5. IEEE, Toronto (2017)
11. Muhammad, H., Usman, S., Jukka, L.: Analysis of vertical and horizontal sectorization in suburban environment using 3D ray tracing. In: 23rd International Conference on Telecommunications (ICT), pp. 1–6. IEEE, Thessaloniki (2016)
12. Fangchao, Z., et al.: A system level evaluation of vertical sectorization for active antenna system. In: 2015 IEEE/CIC International Conference on Communications, pp. 126–131. IEEE, China (2015)
13. Beneyam, B., Biruk, E., Bekele, M.: Planning of small cells in unlicensed band for Addis Ababa deployment scenario, Wireless World Research Forum Meeting, Durban (2018)
14. Preben, M., et al.: LTE system capacity compared to Shannon bounds. In: IEEE VTC Spring 2007, pp. 1234–1238. IEEE, Dublin (2007)

Quality Evaluation for Indoor Mobile Data Customers in Addis Ababa Business Area Using Data from Network Management System, Walk Test, Crowdsourcing and Subjective Survey

Abera Reesom Bisrat[1]([⊠]), Beneyam Berehanu Haile[2],
Edward Mutafungwa[3], and Jyri Hämäläinen[3]

[1] Ethio telecom, Addis Ababa, Ethiopia
abera.reesom@ethiotelecom.et
[2] Addis Ababa Institute of Technology,
Addis Ababa University, Addis Ababa, Ethiopia
beneyamb.haile@aait.edu.et
[3] Department of Communications and Networks,
Aalto University, Espoo, Finland
{edward.mutafungwa,jyri.hamalainen}@aalto.fi

Abstract. Introduction and penetration of high-speed and innovative mobile data services including social media and video services have been increasing significantly across the globe. This growth is driven by deployment and availability of capable and affordable mobile networks and smartphones. These trends have also been observed in Ethiopia as the country's sole incumbent operator ethio telecom has expanded coverage and capacity of its mobile data network, especially for universal mobile telecommunications system (UMTS) network. The successful provision of these innovative services requires mobile operators to have continuous monitoring of the quality of their networks and customer satisfaction. To that end, this monitoring allows the operator to make timely network optimization, marketing and other relevant decisions that enhance service quality. Traditionally measurement and analysis of network quality of service (QoS) is performed using data from network management system (NMS) and drive/walk test (DT/WT). In recent times, the usage QoS data from crowdsourcing (CS) is also emerging as useful monitoring tool. However, all these methods do not fully capture users' quality of experience (QoE), which is a function of not only network QoS but also other factors including subjective users' technical literacy and opinion. As a result, operators have recently provided attention not only for QoS but also QoE. Yet, most quality related analyses are performed using data from only subjective survey, NMS, DT/WT, or CS. It is not straightforward to find quality investigation based on data from all the methods. More importantly, such quality investigation has not been made in the context of Ethiopia's mobile market. In this paper, we perform QoS and QoE evaluation for UMTS mobile data service based on quality data from all NMS, WT, CS and subjective survey for a business area in Addis Ababa. The evaluation is made using downlink user throughput and mean opinion score (MOS) metrics. The obtained 50th percentile throughput results from NMS, WT and CS are good enough for web browsing and offline video streaming but not

© Springer Nature Switzerland AG 2019
F. Mekuria et al. (Eds.): ICT4DA 2019, CCIS 1026, pp. 164–175, 2019.
https://doi.org/10.1007/978-3-030-26630-1_14

for high definition (HD) video calls and live HD video streaming. Furthermore, CS provides optimistic results compared to NMS and WT and its 90th percentile throughput is very good even for live HD video streaming. Moreover, the obtained MOS results from subjective survey almost fit to the QoS results, thus indicating that the network QoS is a significant contributor to users' perceived QoE.

Keywords: Quality of experience · Quality of service · UMTS · Throughput · Mobile operators · Data service · Customer satisfaction · Mean opinion score · Network management system · Walk test · Crowdsourcing · Subjective survey

1   Introduction

Because of advancement of mobile networks, mobile device technologies and innovative data services, it has been observed that mobile data usage and traffic are significantly increasing [1, 2]. As a result, mobile operators are being challenged to successfully serve the increasing diverse mobile data services with satisfactory users' quality of experience (QoE). To meet the increasing demand, they are expected to continuously monitor and optimize their network and operations while expanding network capacity and coverage on a need basis.

Seeing Ethiopian mobile market, the country's incumbent operator ethio telecom with its Long Term Evolution (LTE) network in Addis Ababa and Universal Mobile Telecommunications System (UMTS) network in all urban areas of the country has been serving increasing number of active mobile data subscriptions that reach around 20 million as of the beginning of 2019 [3]. Due to the increased penetration of users, social media and video services, mobile data traffic has also been challenging the mobile networks. As Ethiopian mobile data market is not yet saturated in terms of data subscription, data price has recently seen up to 50% reduction and people income is expected to increase, mobile data demand is expected to continue increasing significantly. For instance, Addis Ababa mobile data demand is predicted to be around 20 petabytes per month in 2021, see Fig. 1 from [4].

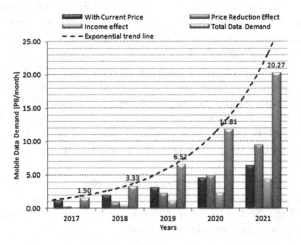

Fig. 1. Mobile data demand forecast for Addis Ababa [4]

To achieve and maintain successful operational business, mobile operators need to continuously meet QoE for their users [5]. User QoE for a given service is a function of quality of service (QoS), terminal capability, subscription, technical literacy, subjective opinion and other factors. To monitor and quantify QoS, operators traditionally collect and analyze data from their network management system (NMS) and drive/walk test (DT/WT) and recently from crowdsourcing (CS) systems complementing each other having their own pros and cons [6–8]. On the other hand, QoE is measured using mean opinion square (MOS) results from subjective surveys [2, 9]. For instance, ethio telecom continuously analyzes quality related key performance indicators (KPIs) and key quality indicators (KQIs) from its NMSs such as Huawei Nastar and undertakes DT/WT quality checks based on relevant user complaints but has not yet applied CS approach. Furthermore, to understand its customers' QoE, it has been performing subjective survey interviewing its individual and enterprise customers across the main cities of the nation twice a year. These quality related tasks are done by marketing departments of ethio telecom in collaboration with other stakeholders. We have noted that there is a need to reinforce quality handling process of departments under network and customer service divisions in ethio telecom while enhancing quality monitoring, quantifying and analyzing mechanisms so that significant number of customers' complaints, particularly for UMTS data users are successfully addressed [10].

Most QoE related researches are based on data from either NMS, DT/WT, CS or subjective survey or a combination of them. For instance, authors in [6] and [11] analyze QoE based on data from NMS and feedback survey while [7] presents QoE analysis based on quality data from DT, CS and subjective survey. Only subjective survey based quality analysis is also conducted in [2, 12, 13]. Thus, it is difficult to find QoE study using data from all NMS, DT/WT, CS and Subjective Survey. Furthermore, such a study has not been undertaken considering the Ethiopian mobile data market context. Yet, [14] presents QoS analysis for UMTS voice service in Addis Ababa using NMS and DT data while [15] compares DT and CS techniques based on collected data from Addis Ababa LTE networks.

In this work, we present QoE/QoS evaluation for UMTS data users based on data from all NMS, WT, CS and subjective survey. The evaluation is performed for a business area in Addis Ababa using downlink user throughput and MOS metrics. Furthermore, obtained throughput results are compared to required minimum throughput for browsing, offline video streaming, high definition (HD) video call and live HD video streaming, adapted from [16]. Results show that NMS, WT and CS provide 50th percentile throughput values that is good enough for browsing and offline video streaming but not for HD video call and live video streaming. For live HD video streaming, only the result from CS is optimum at the 90th percentile. Furthermore, we see that obtained MOS results from subjective survey aligned well with the QoS results. This shows that unsatisfied QoS is the main contributors to mobile users' dissatisfactions.

The remaining parts of the paper are organized as follows. Sections 2 and 3 provide description of quality measurement methods and data collection mechanism for target business area. Then Sect. 4 presents obtained results and interpretations. Finally, Sect. 5 presents concluding remarks of the work.

2 Quality Measurement Methods

2.1 Network Management System

QoS is measured from the network side using various KPIs and KQIs that are computed based on counters collected from mobile network elements and measurement reports from user equipment and application server [17]. Such quality measurement is operationally efficient to easily gather 24/7 quality data with low cost but its data spatial resolution is limited to cell-level.

For this work, geographic throughput data is collected from ethio telecom NMS called Nastar. Nastar is a comprehensive Huawei network monitoring and analysis platform that provides various UMTS quality analysis based on counters from base stations and reports from users [18, 19]. Besides data service quality data, Nastar also provides voice related quality data. The author in [14] presents voice QoS to evaluate voice quality of service in Addis Ababa using the Nastar platform and position of the Nastar is shown in Fig. 2.

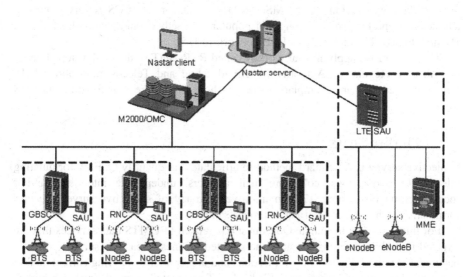

Fig. 2. Position of the Nastar in the network [14]

2.2 Drive/Walk Test

QoS can also be measured from user side and traditionally it is performed using DT where a team of experts with specialized and/or standard terminal devices in a car drives around target test area within coverage of network [7]. If target area is indoor, rather than driving the team performs WT moving around target indoor environment. Usually, target area for DT or WT is preplanned based on customer complaints and other network quality problems. Although DT or WT is providing very localized user side quality understanding, it is spatially and temporally limited and operationally costly due to required experts, devices and vehicle for DT, mainly when there is a need to cover large area.

For our study, we perform indoor WT for the target business area using most popular WT tool used by mobile operators called Nemo Handy [20]. We recall that there are quality related researches based on data from Nemo Handy based tests, see [14, 20–22].

2.3 Crowdsourcing

CS is another recently emerging user side QoS measurement method where mobile users report their QoS measured using a client application to a centralized server at which further overall QoS analysis is made [23]. The client application designed and developed for QoS measurement purpose is expected to be installed and used by users who might get various incentives for doing so. CS provides relatively inexpensive approach while its spatial and temporal coverage is limited by distribution of users who use the client application. Like NMS and DT/WT, accuracy of CS is very important and accuracy performance of couple of popular CS methods and Nemo Handy based DT are studied for Addis Ababa LTE network in [15].

The CS tool we apply for our work is called RTR-NetTest that is developed under the Austrian Regulatory Authority for Broadcasting and Telecommunications [24]. References [24–26] are exemplary works on how to use the tool for different QoS analysis.

2.4 Subjective Survey

Subjective survey is a standard method to articulate and quantify QoE by formulating relevant QoE questions, collecting their answers, undertaking interviews and/or focused group discussion [17]. To improve accuracy of subjective survey, besides formulating right questions, it needs proper sampling.

For this work, we formulate QoE questions related to UMTS data services that are targeted to mobile data customers in the selected business area. The survey questionnaire consists of 15 quality related questions and is prepared by filtering current quality issues and learning experience from [2, 12, 13]. To collect answers, the questionnaire is distributed to the target participants using hard copies and Google Form. Of the 15 quality related questions, the following four questions are sorted out for analysis.

- *How satisfied or dissatisfied are you with the overall quality of 3G data service?*
- *How satisfied or dissatisfied are you when you download files or video/music?*
- *How satisfied or dissatisfied are you when you access social media networks?*
- *How satisfied or dissatisfied are you with the quality of videos (in YouTube or video chatting)?*

3   Data Collection for Business Area of Addis Ababa

The indoor quality evaluation is performed for 20 enterprise buildings including ethio telecom headquarter within one of the business areas of Addis Ababa that is depicted in Fig. 3. The throughput data from the NMS, WT and CS are collected daily within office hours (9 am – 4 pm) in a study period of June and July months of 2018. Furthermore, answers of quality questionnaire from mobile data customers in the selected business area are also collected within the study period.

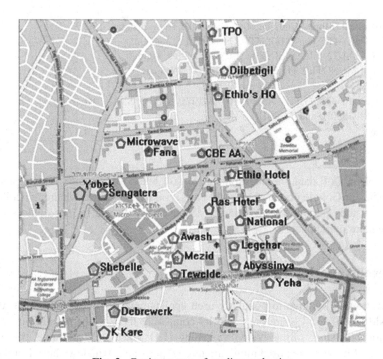

Fig. 3. Business area of quality evaluation

The NMS provides a 50 m geographic resolution for the downlink throughput and other metrics data for the whole Addis Ababa. Then we do data processing to localize this data to the buildings of the business area for further quality analysis. Accuracy of the localization effort has been validated by cross checking geographic coordinates of the buildings from the NMS with independently collected coordinates.

The indoor WT throughput data is collected with Nemo Handy on floors of the buildings within office hours of the study period. The applied Nemo Handy is configured well to generate required downlink throughput data.

The throughput data using the CS RTR is collected with the help of mobile data customers within the buildings to download and install RTR client in their smart phones and perform measurement test during office hours within the study period. The measurements are undertaken by 31 participants within and around their offices by locking their smartphones to 3G only. They use 21 unique smart phone models that are listed in Table 1 with their capabilities of supporting a maximum download speed for the UMTS network. Correct collections of the data from the RTR–NetTest server is made using technology type, the device model and timestamp on the screenshots of the tests that has been shared to us.

Table 1. List of mobile devices

Mobile devices	Maximum download speed (Mbps)
Max Download (Mbps), Che2-UL00, Galaxy S4 LTE-A, Galaxy S5, HTC One (HTC One_M8), HTC One E9PLUS dual sim, Huawei G620-L72, HUAWEI P8max, iPhone 6 Plus, Lenovo PB2-650M, MI NOTE LTE, SM-G965F, SM-J320W8 and TECNO-W5	42.2
Galaxy Grand DuoS, Galaxy Note 3, HUAWEI TIT-AL00, SM-C710F, SM-G530H, and T1-701u	21.1
iPhone 4s	14.4

To collect QoE data, the questionnaire is distributed to 129 staffs of enterprises in hard copies or Google doc on their need basis. Answers to questionnaire are collected within the study period. The WT and NMS data are collected near the offices of the questionnaire participants.

4   Results and Interpretations

To measure QoS relative to popularly used applications, obtained throughput results from NMS, WT and CS are presented by comparing them to the required minimum value for browsing, offline video streaming, HD video call and live HD video streaming. We use the required minimum throughput values which we have learnt from [16] for the aforementioned popular services and the values are listed in Table 2. The comparison is made by dividing obtained throughput results by the required minimum throughput.

Table 2. Minimum required download throughput [16]

Service type	Minimum requirement download speed (Mbps)
Web browsing	0.3
Offline video streaming (e.g. YouTube videos)	0.5
HD video calls (e.g. Skype)	1.5
Live HD video streaming (e.g. iPlayer)	3.2

4.1   QoS Results Compared to Browsing and Offline Video Streaming

Figures 4 and 5 show 10%-ile, 50%-ile and 90%-ile throughput results of NMS, WT and CS compared to web browsing and offline video streaming, respectively. As can be seen in the figures for both services, the 50%-ile and 90%-ile throughput ratio results are more than 1 indicating the majority and peak users achieve a very good QoS. On the other hand, the 10%-ile ratio results are below 1 indicating unsatisfactory QoS is experienced by at least 10% of unfavorable indoor users.

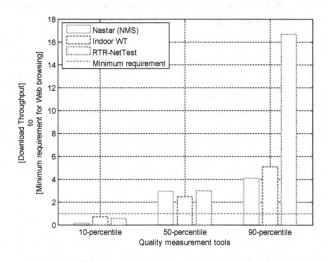

Fig. 4. Throughput results of NMS, WT & CS relative to browsing service

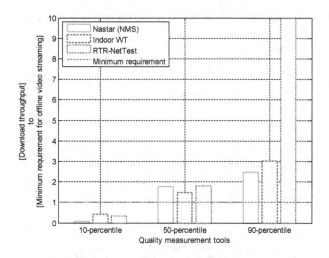

Fig. 5. Throughput results of NMS, WT & CS relative to offline video streaming

4.2   QoS Results Compared to HD Video Call and Live Streaming

The 10%-ile, 50%-ile and 90%-ile throughput ratio results of NMS, WT and CS compared to HD video calls and live HD video streaming are shown in Figs. 6 and 7, respectively. As can be seen from the figures, only the 90%-ile throughput ratio results from CS and WT are more than 1 for the video call while only the former is greater than 1 for the live video streaming. On the other hand, for both services, the 10%-ile and 50%-ile ratio results are far below 1. Thus, only the most optimistic CS results indicate only peak users can have satisfactory QoS for HD video call and live video streaming while majority of users cannot achieve satisfactory services according to any of the QoS measurement methods.

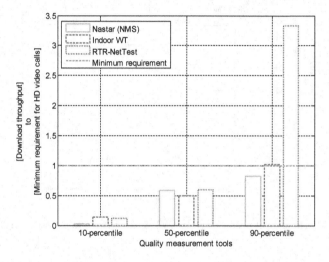

Fig. 6. Throughput results of NMS, WT & CS relative to HD video call

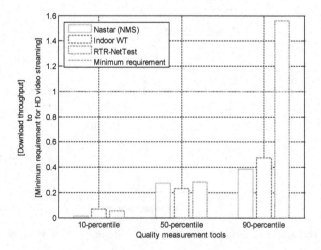

Fig. 7. Throughput results of NMS, WT & CS relative to live HD video streaming

4.3   Subjective Survey: Perception of Participants

MOS results of quality perceptions of survey participants on download speed, social media usage, video streaming usage and overall data usage are depicted in Fig. 8. The download speed, social media and video streaming perception questions are selected as they are the most popular use cases among staffs of the enterprises and related with the four services used for QoE comparison in the previous subsections.

In [9], it is mentioned that MOS value of greater than 3.5 is recommended to obtain a fair user experience for downlink bandwidth, uplink bandwidth and network delays. In addition to this, it is described in [27] that a perceived video quality is achieved when the MOS value is in the range of 3.5 and 4.0. In our case, we have taken a MOS value of 3.5 as a reference.

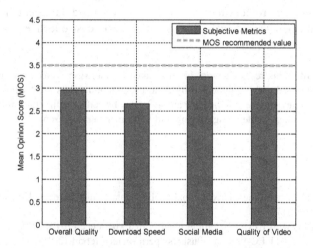

Fig. 8. MOS results of the perception survey

As can be seen in Fig. 8, the MOS values for download speed, social media, video streaming and overall data quality are 2.65, 3.25, 3.00 and 2.96, respectively. All MOS values are less than 3.5 which is the minimum value to claim that users have customer satisfaction, according to [9] and [27]. Thus, users on average are not satisfied with the quality of the overall UMTS data service and also specifically for the download speed, social media and video streaming usages.

5   Conclusion

To achieve successful operational business, mobile operators should meet quality of experience (QoE) expected by their customers. QoE is a function of network quality of service, users' literacy, terminal capability, subscription, opinion and other factors. To meet the required QoE, operators need to monitor, quantify and analyze QoE and QoS that are achieved by users. To that end, they undertake QoS and QoE analysis based on quality data measured and collected from network management system, drive/walk test, crowdsourcing and subjective survey, each with its pros and cons. Although various literature presents QoE and QoS analysis based on one or more of the quality measurement methods for various data usage context, it is not common to find indoor quality analysis based on data from all four measurement methods.

In this paper, we have presented QoS and QoE analysis for UMTS indoor data users for an Addis Ababa business area considering 20 enterprise buildings based on quality data from all the four methods. QoS is measured in terms of download speed and obtained results indicate that achieved quality for majority users is good enough for web browsing and offline video streaming (e.g. YouTube) but not for high definition video calls and live streaming services. The QoE results also show that users are not satisfied with UMTS download speed, social media and video streaming services. This indicates QoS has significant contribution for unsatisfied UMTS data users. Furthermore, crowdsourcing provides the most optimistic download throughput results that its accuracy should be checked well although it presents cost effective 24/7 QoS measurement methods for operators.

Acknowledgment. This research work is undertaken by the MSc. Telecom Engineering program jointly developed and implemented by ethio telecom and Addis Ababa Institute of Technology. To attain relevant research data, we are supported by staffs of ethio telecom (Departments of Service Management Center, Engineering and Customer Service Front Office).

References

1. Cisco: Visual Networking Index: Global Mobile Data Traffic Forecast Update, 2016–2021, White Paper (2017)
2. HOT TELECOM: 4 Keys to Shaping Quality of Experience (2015)
3. Ethio telecom: 2011 EC first half business performance report (2019)
4. Haile, B.B., Bulti, D.A., Zerihun. B.M.: On the relevance of capacity enhancing 5G technologies for Ethiopia. In: CONFERENCE 2017, EICTC, Addis Ababa (2017)
5. Lakhtaria, K.I.: Enhancing QoS and QoE in IMS enabled next generation networks. Int. J. Appl. Graph Theor. Wirel. Ad Hoc Netw. Sens. Netw. **2**(2), 61–71 (2010)
6. Schatz, R., Egger, S.: Vienna surfing – assessing mobile broadband quality in the field. In: Proceedings of the First ACM SIGCOMM Workshop on Measurements Up the Stack, Toronto, pp. 19–24 (2011)
7. Lin, H.Y., Hsieh, S.H., Chen, K.H., Wu, T.C.: Large-scale mobile internet performance measurement in Taiwan. In: 2014 6th International Conference on Ubiquitous and Future Networks, Shanghai, pp. 516–519 (2014)
8. Streijl, R.C., Winkler, S., Hands, D.S.: Mean Opinion Score (MOS) revisited: methods and applications, limitations and alternatives. Multimed. Syst. **22**, 213–227 (2016)
9. Pedro, C., Raimund, S.: Quality of experience in cloud services: survey and measurements. Comput. Netw. **68**, 149–165 (2018)
10. Universal Mobile Telecommunications System (UMTS): 3G Telecom Management: Principles and high level requirements, ETSI TS 132 101 V3.4.0 (2001)
11. Casas, P., Gardlo, B., Seufert, M., Wamser, F., Schatz R.: Taming QoE in cellular networks: from subjective lab studies to measurements in the Field. In: 2015 11th International Conference on Network and Service Management, Barcelona, pp. 237–245 (2015)

12. Reason to Complain Research, Ofcom Fieldwork (2016)
13. Customer Satisfaction Survey – Mobile Results, CICRA 16/10 (2016)
14. Ayele, J.: Quality of service evaluation of voice over UMTS network: the case of Addis Ababa. M.Sc. dissertation, Department of Electrical and Computer Engineering, Addis Ababa Institute of Technology, Addis Ababa (2017)
15. Alemayehu, B.: Evaluation of user side quality of service measurement techniques for Addis Ababa LTE data service. M.Sc. dissertation, Department of Electrical and Computer Engineering, Addis Ababa Institute of Technology, Addis Ababa (2018)
16. Ken's Tech Tips. https://kenstechtips.com/index.php/download-speeds-2g-3g-and-4g-actual-meaning. Accessed 01 Aug 2018
17. Rodriguez, D.Z., Rosa, R., Nunes, R.D., Affonso, E.T.: Assessment of quality-of-experience in telecommunication services. Int. J. Dig. Inf. Wirel. Commun. **6**(4), 241–259 (2016)
18. Wang, Y., Zhou, W., Zhang, P.: QoE Management in Wireless Networks. Springer, Heidelberg (2017)
19. Massam, P.: Intelligent CEM Making the NPS Connection, A Huawei White Paper, Huawei (2015)
20. Gupta, S., Garg, R.: Taxonomy of tools and techniques for network monitoring and quality assurance in 3G networks. Int. J. Comput. Appl. **120**(21), 34–41 (2015)
21. Afroz, F., Subramanian, R., Heidary, R., Sandrasegaran, K., Ahmed, S.: SINR, RSRP, RSSI and RSRQ measurements in long term evolution networks. Int. J. Wirel. Mob. Netw. **7**(4), 113–123 (2015)
22. Palazon, J.A., Sepulcre, M., Gozalvez, J., Orozco, J., Lopez, O.: Heterogeneous wireless connectivity for fixed and mobile sensing applications in industrial environments. In: Proceedings of the 16th IEEE International Conference on Emerging Technologies and Factory Automation, Toulouse, pp. 1–8 (2011)
23. BEREC Preliminary report in view of a common position on monitoring mobile coverage. BEREC BoR (17), 186 (2017)
24. Lipenbergs, E., Bobrovs, V., Ivanovs, G.: Investigation of service quality of measurement reference points for the internet services on mobile networks. Latvian J. Phys. Tech. Sci. **5**, 64–73 (2016)
25. Kousias, K., Lutu, A., Midoglu, C., Argyriou, A., Alay, O., Riegler, M.: The same, only different: contrasting mobile operator behavior from crowdsourced dataset. In: IEEE 28th Annual International Symposium on Personal, Indoor, and Mobile Radio Communications, Montreal, pp. 1–6 (2017)
26. Khatouni, A.S., et al.: Speedtest-like measurements in 3G/4G networks: the MONROE experience. In: IEEE 2017 29th International Teletraffic Congress (ITC 29), Genoa, pp. 169–177 (2017)
27. Elkotob, M., Grandlund, D., Andersson, K., Ahlund, C.: Multimedia QoE optimized management using prediction and statistical learning. In: 35th Annual IEEE Conference on Local Computer Networks, Denver, pp. 324–327 (2010)

Performance Evaluation of 6-Sector Site and Small Cell for Addis Ababa UMTS Network

Tirufire Aberra Fulle[1]($\boxtimes$) and Beneyam Berehanu Haile[2]($\boxtimes$)

[1] Ethiotelecom, Addis Ababa, Ethiopia
tirufire.aberra@ethiotelecom.et
[2] Addis Ababa Institute of Technology, Addis Ababa University,
Addis Ababa, Ethiopia
beneyamb.haile@aait.edu.et

Abstract. The demand for high mobile data rate has been increasing due to introduction of various innovative mobile data services to improve our life. To accommodate the increasing data demand with satisfactory quality of service operators must continuously improve their network capacity. To that end, besides deploying fourth generation network, already operational third generation (3G) network capacity can be improved by applying some capacity improvement techniques including six-sectorization, densification, multiple input multiple output and using multiple carriers. Although these capacity improving techniques have been well investigated theoretically and practically, their performance is not studied well to address capacity challenges of most widely used 3G data network in Ethiopia. In this paper, we select six-sectorization and small cell based on relevance and device availability trends and investigate their performance in addressing capacity challenges of selected Addis Ababa 3G deployment scenario considering realistic capacity demand, propagation environment and legacy network topology. Propagation computation and network simulation are made using WinProp and dominant path model based on building and topography maps are used for propagation computation. Performance results show that deployment of six-sector or/and small cells provide significant performance gain compared to already existing full 3 sector cells. For instance, six-sector deployment provides a 284.23% average downlink throughput gain. Furthermore, deployment of small cells with 5% penetration presents a 114.67%, average throughput gains over the existing full 3-sector.

Keywords: UMTS · 3G · Capacity challenges ·
Capacity enhancement techniques · Six sectorization · Small cell · Addis Ababa

1 Introduction

Universal Mobile Telecommunication System (UMTS) is the most widely deployed 3G mobile system that presents a range of data, voice, text, and multimedia-based mobile services [1]. To improve quality of data services the first UMTS standard Release 99 (R99) packet domain has been evolved to High-Speed Packet Access (HSPA) and

© Springer Nature Switzerland AG 2019
F. Mekuria et al. (Eds.): ICT4DA 2019, CCIS 1026, pp. 176–187, 2019.
https://doi.org/10.1007/978-3-030-26630-1_15

HSPA+ in the consecutive Third-Generation Partnership Project (3GPP) releases applying various advanced enhancements including multiple carriers, higher order modulation, higher order, Multiple Input Multiple Output (MIMO) and other features. To accommodate demand of Third Generation (3G) data users, most mobile operators across the globe have already deployed HSPA/HSPA+ network and Ethiopian incumbent ethio telecom has also deployed them in almost all cities and other parts of the country (Ethiopian Telecommunications Corporation [2]: click to the Ethiopian Millennium: special issue, September 2009).

The 3G technology share in 2017 and forecasted 3G share in 2025 both across the globe and in Sub-Saharan countries is shown in Fig. 1 (GSM Association [3]: The Mobile Economy 2018). As can be seen from the figure, 3G has been and will be significantly contributing to accommodating mobile services. Its role is more significant in Sub-Sahara countries including Ethiopia.

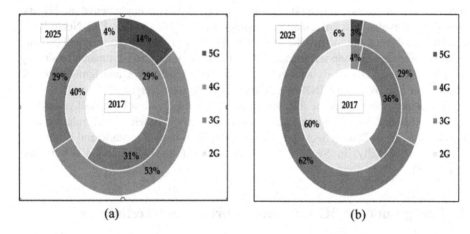

Fig. 1. Technology share in the (a) world and (b) Sub-Saharan Africa [13]

As quality mobile data demand continuously increasing due of innovative data services, besides preparing and deploying 4G network, mobile operators shall continuously optimize their existing 3G network. Currently, there is a growing demand for data services and the adoption of mobile data service is increasing rapidly ([4]). Expanding mobile network to support these increasing data demand and introducing new relevant technologies is an important work for mobile operators even before it creates capacity limitations.

There has been some progress in recent years to meet the increasing data demand in Addis Ababa [5]. Nonetheless, several challenges remain in terms of how to enhance and expand these networks to meet the growing demands of an increasingly digital economy and society. To improve capacity of UMTS network without rework, proper selection, study and evaluation of capacity improvement techniques is important.

The paper presented in [6] show that before the deployment of a network or before expansion work, different options should be evaluated using different metrics. Yet, these techniques are not evaluated well in the context of Ethiopia considering existing network topology, realistic capacity demand and accurate propagation environment so that viable technics can be selected and implemented.

In this paper, first analyzed network traffic and connection failures data of existing Addis Ababa 3G network from network management system and we have seen that there is considerable amount of capacity challenges that need to be addressed. Secondly, six-sectorization and small cell technologies are selected based on relevance in terms of user device availability trend and then their performances are investigated for selected Addis Ababa deployment scenario. Note that currently only 20% of user devices support MIMO or multicarrier operations [7].

Propagation computation are made using deterministic dominant path model based on building and terrain map information of the selected Addis Ababa deployment scenario [8]. Network simulation are made using WinProp implementation [9] and performance evaluations are undertaken using Carrier-to-Interference-Plus-Noise-Ratio (CINR) and throughput metrics. Results show that both six sectorization, small cell and their hybrid usage provide significant CINR and throughput gains compared to already existing 3-sector macro only network. For instance, full 6 sector and femto with 5% penetration improved the CINR by 2.9 and 0.3 dB respectively.

The paper is organized as follows. In Sect. 2, we provide a brief background on selected capacity improvement techniques and Sect. 3, baseline and enhancement scenarios are described. In Sect. 4, we describe the deployment scenario and simulation assumptions. Finally, in Sect. 5 and 6, we present detail simulation results and conclusion.

2 Background on 3G Capacity Improvement Techniques

To address UMTS network capacity challenges, there are some capacity improvement techniques including six sectorization, small cell, and advanced MIMO that are not yet implemented in existing WCDMA/HSPA/HSPA+ network. These capacity enhancement techniques are studied well from theoretical and practical perspectives [10–12]. Capacity enhancement techniques such as adding a new site or spectrum are challenging for operators since new site acquisition is becoming difficult and a spectrum is scarce resources. Moreover, in Ethiopia, user devices availability which supports multiple frequency bands for UMTS is another challenge. As a result, upgrading to 6-sector and using small cells are more feasible enhancement options.

2.1 Six Sector

Sectorization is one important capacity enhancing method by using multiple directional antennas unlike Omni directional antenna case. Six-sector site can be implemented using 6 directional antennas or nowadays applying dual beam technology with only three antennas. The latter is advantageous in terms of reducing load on the tower and interference leakage [13].

Different research has showed that six-sector site can be used to improve network capacity, coverage, and quality [13–19]. In [14], a case study of hotspots 6-sectored with maximum DL power of 20 W, showed that there was a 23% increase in coverage and 1.8x capacity increase. In paper [15], further demonstrated simultaneous users increase when the number of sectors increases for 384 kbps. For example, for bit energy to noise ratio (Eb/No) value of 4 dB, 88 users are simultaneously connected in 6-sectors but for 3-sectors, 45 users are simultaneously connected. Furthermore, a study in [16] showed that not only higher order sectorization but also the beam width of the antenna affects capacity and coverage. The sectorization gain can vary from 1 for Omni to 5.07 for 6-sector with 33-degree orientation in DL.

Moreover, a study conducted in central London area of Telefonica UK's network with 51 sites is presented in [17]. For inter-site distances of 500 m, 6-sector with 34-degree beamwidth has 1.82x capacity gain over 3-sector at 62-degree beamwidth. The research also shows that the gain increases as the number of users increases. For example, network simulation showed that 6-sector has 1.41x, 1.71x, 1.85x and 1.87x capacity gain over 3-sector with 500, 1000, 2000 and uniform traffic. Additionally, it is shown that six-sectorization with dual-beam increases site capacity by 50% to 85% and improves the coverage performance by 3 dB [13]. For instances, AIS has progressively used different method to improve the service but it is 6-sector cell with dual beam technology that showed remarkable performance up to 70% capacity gain [18]. Similarly, Globe's 2100 MHz UMTS network downlink data traffic increase by 50%, uplink data traffic by 74.73% and voice traffic by 31.69% [19].

2.2 Introduction of Small Cells

The second technique selected that can improve the capacity of UMTS network is deploying small cells. Small cells are low-power radio access nodes which can be used in densely populated areas and indoor hotspots where adding spectrums or macro base stations may not visible. Small cell has easy site acquisition and flexible deployment to improve the user experience [20].

Femtocells bring benefits such as increasing cell density at realistic costs, enhancing indoors coverage, improving spectrum usage efficiency, reducing the load from the macro layer, improving service for outdoor users and giving a better SINR distribution (MIMO works better). Some femtocell deployment challenges have already been overcome. For example, the interference issues have now been resolved by introducing interference mitigation techniques which enable co-channel operation between the femtocell and macrocell. Study done in [21], shows that the use of adaptive UL attenuation for the uplink and downlink transmit power calibration of femtocell to limit interference to the macro layer has shown both capacity and coverage performance gains. Another challenge of small cells is backhaul availability. Backhaul network provides connectivity between the core network, and the small cells to deliver the service with the desired QoS level [22–24]. Currently, there are different options to choose from like using self-backhauling using LTE macrocell ([25]).

3 Baseline and Enhancement Scenarios

3.1 Baseline Scenarios

Four Carrier per Cell Full 3-Sector: It has been deployed according to real network configure position, antenna azimuths, tilt and a total of 4 carriers are used except two NodeBs which has 3 and 2 carriers per cell and named as four-carrier per cell full 3-sector (4-SC full 3-sector) (Fig. 2).

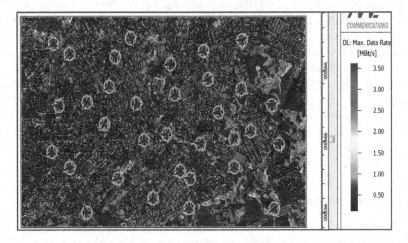

Fig. 2. Data rate plot of full 3-sector with four single carriers per cell

One Carrier per Cell Full 3 Sector: In this scenario, macrocells have been deployed according to real network configured positions, antenna azimuths and tilt but one carrier per cell is used named as one carrier per cell full 3-sector (1-SC full 3-sector) and four carriers are reused.

3.2 Enhancement Scenarios

Full Six Sector: All Node Bs are 6-sector with same positions as the baseline scenario but with different antenna azimuth and tilt (5-degree). One carrier per cell is used and a total of 4 carriers are reused (Fig. 3).

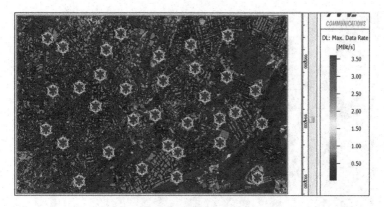

Fig. 3. Data rate plot of full 6-sector

Hybrid: Containing both 3 and 6-sectored Node Bs with same site positions as the first scenario but with different antenna azimuth and tilt. The placement of 6-sector Node Bs is based on data rate from experiment 1(1-SC full 3-sector). 3-sector Node Bs are upgraded to 6-sectored if have low data rate or are within a layer of worst cells. One carrier per cell is used and a total of 4 carriers are reused (Fig. 4).

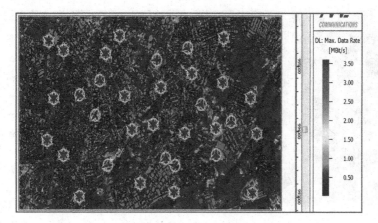

Fig. 4. Data rate plot of hybrid

Three Sectors with 0.05 Femto Penetration: Three sectors with 0.05 femto penetration using orthogonal deployment between macrocells and femtocells. The placement of femtocell is based on data rate values from the first experiment which is 1-SC full 3-sector (circle marked by orange are Omni directional small cells) (Fig. 5).

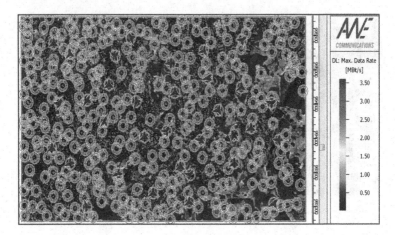

Fig. 5. Data rate plot of three sectors with 0.05 femto penetration (Color figure online)

Hybrid with 0.005 Femto Penetration: Hybrid with 0.005 femto penetration using orthogonal deployment. The placement of femtocell is based on data rate values from the third experiment that is hybrid. Specific parameters related to each scenario is shown in Table 1 (Fig. 6).

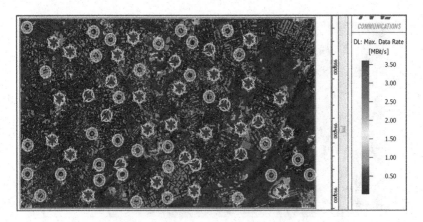

Fig. 6. Data rate plot of hybrid with 0.005 femto penetration

Table 1. Parameters for baseline and enhancement scenarios

Scenarios	Number of macrocells	Number of Femtocells
Single carrier per cell Full 3-Sector	99	–
Four carrier per cell Full 3-Sector	396	–
Full 6-Sector	198	–
Hybrid (both 3 and 6-sectored)	165	–
Femto with 5% penetration	99	308
Hybrid with 0.55% femto penetration	165	31

4   Deployment Scenario and Simulation Assumptions

4.1   Deployment Scenario

Addis Ababa is the capital city of Ethiopia that shares most urban population [26]. World Bank study shows, in Ethiopia, an increase in urban population as % of total population from 18.6% in 2013 to 20.4% in 2017. For this study, 15Sq Km is used in bole area which has 2,694.1 population density per sq. m and also densely populated buildings [27]. In this regard, network deployment in this area will have higher propagation losses which presents the worst-case scenario. Currently, 33 macro sites with 3 sector per site are deployed in the specified location. Figure 7 shows topographic with building databases.

Fig. 7. Topographic database with building data on it

4.2   Simulation Parameters and Assumptions

General simulation assumptions and parameters are shown in Table 2.

Table 2. General simulation assumptions and parameters

Parameter	Values/Assumptions
Air interface	Five 5 MHz carrier, 3.84 Mchips/s, Duplexing scheme FDD
Prediction height	1.5 m
Propagation	Dominant Path Model
Macro Node B (MNB)	Power 43 dBm, antenna gain 17.5 dBi, 4 dB noise figure, cable loss 2 dB/100 m, Coupling loss 10, Radiating cable loss 2 dB
Antenna	Aggison ADU451819 for 3-sector MNB [28]

(continued)

Table 2. (*continued*)

Parameter	Values/Assumptions
Femto	Omnidirectional antenna with a power of 23 dBm
UE	Omnidirectional 1 dB body losses, 6 dB noise figure
Femtocell height	From 2–7 m
User distribution	Uniform
Buildings	Heights 3–56 m, penetration loss: 10 dB

5 Simulation Results and Discussions

The CDF of different deployment scenarios is presented Figs. 8 and 9. As it can be seen, full 6-sectored deployment significantly improves the CINR by delivering 2.9 dB, 2.2 dB and 0.5 dB gains at 10, 50 and 90-percentile respectively compared to 1-SC full 3-sector. Further, full 6-sector deployment gives 2.8 dB, 2.1 dB and 0.4 dB gains compared to 4-SC full 3-sector at 10, 50 and 90-percentiles respectively which indicates 4-SC full 3-sector has 0.1 dB gain compares to 1-SC full 3-sector. Hybrid deployment has also shown remarkable performances at 10, 50 and 90-percentiles with 2.2 dB, 2.1 dB, and 0.5 dB gains correspondingly. With the addition of femto at 0.55% penetration to hybrid, the CINR increases by 0.4 dB at 10-percentile compared to hybrid. Moreover, femto with 5% penetration improved the performance by 0.3 dB, 0.3 dB and 0.2 dB relative to 1-SC 3-sector case at 10, 50 and 90-percentile.

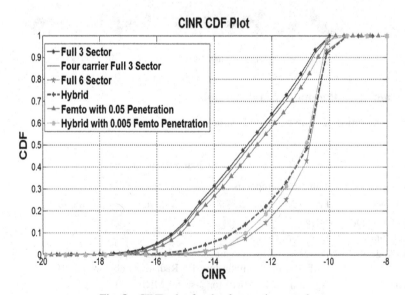

Fig. 8. CINR plot for the 6 scenarios tested

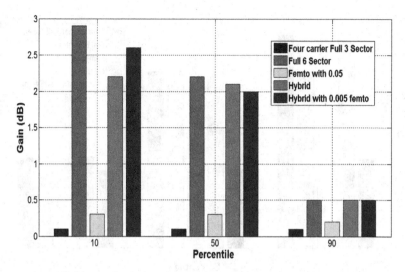

Fig. 9. Performance compared to one carrier full three-sector

CDF of DL maximum throughputs are presented in Fig. 10 and performance gains when compared to full 3-sector deployments at 10, 50 and 90-percentiles are shown in Fig. 11. The results show that full 6-sectored deployment delivers 284.23%, 280.00%, and 118.81% gain at 10, 50 and 90-percentile respectively when compared to 1-SC full three-sector. Moreover, full 6-sector compared with 4-SC Full 3-sector, improves the throughput by 2.44x, 2.72x and 1.17x at 10, 50 and 90-percentile respectively. In addition, femto 0.05 penetration, hybrid, and hybrid with 0.005 femto improved the DL throughput by 114.67%, 231.05%, and 278.73% compared to 1-SC full 3-sector respectively at 10-percentile. While in at 50-percentile hybrid, femto with 0.05 penetration and hybrid with 0.005 femto deliver 232.26%, 104.86%, and 230.02% gains compared to 1-SC full 3-sector.

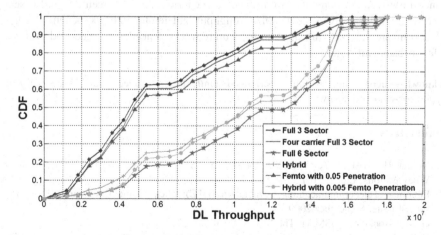

Fig. 10. CDF of DL throughput (Mbps)

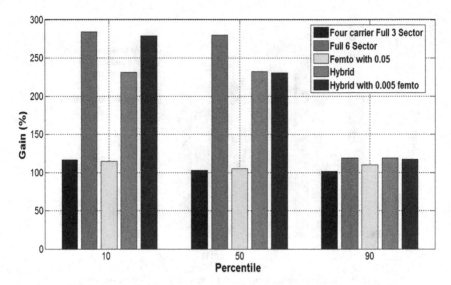

Fig. 11. DL throughput percentile compared to one carrier full 3-sector

6 Conclusions and Future Work

This paper has first studied network challenges from network management system data. We observed that, there is significant amount of network failures to due to limited channel element and power resources. To overcome these resource challenges, we have evaluated various different improvement techniques namely MIMO, carrier aggregation, adding another band, macro densification, six sector cell and small cell. Then due to their practicability and relevance six sector site and small cell technologies are selected.

The Simulation study highlighted the potential benefits of using 6-sectorization and Femtocells. Two different deployment strategies for 6 sectors, full and hybrid, have been studied and potential benefits are shown. Full 6 sector has a remarkable performance improvement compared to all studied scenarios. At 10-percentile, Full 6 sectored deployment delivers 2.84x DL throughput and femto with 5% penetration has 1.14x compared to 1-SC full three sector. Future works is needed to select and evaluate different backhaul options.

Acknowledgment. The research is performed jointly by ethio telecom and AAiT with the support of Aalto University.

References

1. Holma, H., Toskala, A.: WCDMA for UMTS HSPA Evolution and LTE, 5th edn. John Wiley & Sons, Ltd. (2010)
2. Ethiopian Telecommunications Corporation (ETC): click to the Ethiopian Millennium: special issue, September 2009
3. GSM Association (GSMA): The Mobile Economy 2018
4. Haile, B.B., Bulti, D.A., Zerihun, B.M.: On the relevance of capacity enhancing 5G technologies for Ethiopia. In: 10th Ethiopian ICT Annual Conference (EICTC-2017) (2017)

5. Ministry of Finance and Economic Development: Growth and Transformation Plan Annual Progress Report for F.Y. 2012/13, Ministry of Finance and Economic Development, Addis Ababa, February 2014

6. Real wireless: Techniques for increasing the capacity of wireless broadband networks: UK, 2012–2030, April 2012

7. Altair: WinProp - Propagation Modeling. https://altairhyperworks.com/product/FEKO/ WinProp-Propagation-Modeling, Accessed 29 Aug 2018

8. Altair: About. https://altair.com/about/. Accessed 5 Aug 2018

9. Huawei: Service & experience quality analyst. Software

10. Holma, H., Toskala, A., Tapia, P.: HSPA + Evolution To Release 12 Performance and Optimization. John Wiley & Sons (2014)

11. Holma, H., Toskala, A.: HSDPA/HSUPA for UMTS, 5th edn. John Wiley & Sons, Ltd. (2010)

12. Chapman, T., Larsson, E., von Wrycza, P., Dahlman, E., Parkvall, S., Skold, J.: HSPA Evolution the Fundamentals for Mobile Broadband. Elsevier Ltd (2015)

13. Sorrells, P.: Twin beam technology adds immediate capacity without additional antennas, White Paper, CommScope (2013)

14. Hagerman, B., Imbeni, D., Barta, J., Pollard, A., Wohlmuth, R., Cosimini, P.: WCDMA 6-sector deployment-case study of a real installed UMTS-FDD network. In: IEEE 63rd Vehicular Technology, Melbourne, Australia (2006)

15. Fazlul, A., Mohammad, M., Baitul, M., Ka, M., Fokhray, M.: Performance analysis of UMTS cellular network using sectorization based on capacity and coverage. Int. J. Adv. Comput. Sci. Appl. 2(6), 48–55 (2011)

16. Wacker, A., Laiho-Steffens, J., Sipila, K., Heiska, K.: The impact of the base station sectorization on WCDMA radio network performance. In: IEEE 50th Vehicular Technology, Amsterdam, Netherlands (1999)

17. Joyce, R., Morris, D., Brown, S., Vyas, D., Zhang, L.: Higher order horizontal sectorization gains for 6, 9, 12 and 15 sectored cell sites in a 3GPP/HSPA + network. IEEE Trans. Veh. Technol. 65(5), 3440–3449 (2016)

18. Ashish, P.: HOW TO OPERATE: Philippines Globe: New network configuration, new MBB gains, ISSUE 80, Globe, October 2016

19. Huawei: Thailand AIS: A Shift from Embarrassing to Wonderful. http://carrier.huawei.com/en/ success-stories/wireless-network/03-ubiquitious-mbb/thailand%20ais. Accessed 14 July 2018

20. Small Cell Forum: Small cells - what's the big idea? White Paper, UK, February 2012

21. Yavuz, M., et al.: Interference management and performance analysis of UMTS/HSPA + femtocells. IEEE Commun. Mag. 47, 102–109 (2009)

22. Ericson: It all comes back to Backhaul, White Paper, February 2012

23. Zhang, J., la Roche, G.D.: Femtocells: Technologies and Deployment. John Wiley & Sons (2010)

24. Next Generation Mobile Networks (NGMN): Small Cell Backhaul Requirements, White Paper, NGMN Alliance, June 2012

25. Amin, P., Kibret, N.S., Mutafungwa, E., Haile, B.B., Hamalainen, J., Nurminen, J.K.: Performance study for off-grid selfbackhauled small cells in dense informal settlements. In: Proceedings of the 25th IEEE Annual International Symposium on Personal, Indoor, and Mobile Radio Communication (IEEE PIMRC 2014), pp. 1652–1657, September 2014

26. The World Bank: World Development Indicators. http://databank.worldbank.org/data/ reports.aspx?source=2&series=SP.URB.TOTL.IN.ZS&country=#selectedDimension_WDI_ Ctry. Accessed 03 Mar 2018

27. Addis Ababa city government, population. http://www.addisababa.gov.et/es/web/guest/bole-sub-city. Accessed 03 Mar 2018

28. Huawei Technologies Co., Ltd.: Antenna Specification, ADU451819 datasheet (2014)

Techno-Economic Investigation of LTE-Advanced Deployment for Africa: Case of Addis Ababa City

Gizachew Hailegebriel Mako[1]([⊠]) (iD), Beneyam Berehanu Haile[2]([⊠]),
and Edward Mutafungwa[3]([⊠])

[1] Ethio Telecom, Addis Ababa, Ethiopia
gizachew.hgebriel@ethiotelecom.et
[2] Addis Ababa Institute of Technology, Addis Ababa, Ethiopia
beneyamb.haile@aait.edu.et
[3] Department of Communications and Networks, Aalto University,
Espoo, Finland
edward.mutafungwa@aalto.fi

Abstract. The proliferation of innovative data services and subsequent increase in mobile data traffic continues to be a prevailing trend across the globe. For instance, according to Ericsson, mobile data traffic is forecast to reach 71 Exabyte per month in 2022 from 8.8 Exabyte per month in 2016. Moreover, it is noted that Sub-Saharan Africa region including Ethiopia exhibit fastest growth rates in terms of mobile data demand. To accommodate this increasing demand, beside Long Term Evolution (LTE), mobile operators are optimizing their network and deploying LTE-Advanced (LTE-A) and LTE-A Pro technologies. Having operational LTE network in capital Addis Ababa, the Ethiopian incumbent sole operator ethio telecom is still at the early preparation phase of upgrading their network to include LTE-A capabilities. To that end, there is a need of understanding techno-economically viable LTE-A deployment scenarios to meet the local demand. In this paper, relevant LTE-A deployment scenarios are developed for Addis Ababa using the scenario-planning method considering the local context. To observe viability of the developed scenarios, we also perform techno-economic analysis using modified TERA model assuming 6 years study period and 10% discount rate. The findings of our study note that the net present value and payback period results show that LTE-A scenario that applies Progressive Deployment with Out-of-band small cells is the most viable scenario for Addis Ababa.

Keywords: LTE · LTE-Advanced · Scenario planning · Carrier Aggregation · Small cell · Techno-economics · TEA · TERA · Addis Ababa · Africa

1 Introduction

Mobile data demand and corresponding traffic due to introduction of various data services have been significantly increasing across the globe [28]. Various sources have also forecasted that the growth continue exponentially mainly due to emerging data

© Springer Nature Switzerland AG 2019
F. Mekuria et al. (Eds.): ICT4DA 2019, CCIS 1026, pp. 188–202, 2019.
https://doi.org/10.1007/978-3-030-26630-1_16

intensive quality video services including augmented reality, virtual reality and ultra-high definition live video streaming. For instance, Ericsson report has forecasted that in 2022 global mobile traffic generated by mobile data users will reach 71 Exabyte per month from 8.8 Exabyte per month in 2016 [28]. Same report also indicated that similar significant data traffic growth will be seen in Sub-Saharan Africa with largest growth rate. Mainly due to increasing new data users, mobile based social media and video service penetrations. The Ethiopian market also experiencing significant mobile data traffic growth, mainly in the capital Addis Ababa [3, 29, 30].

To successfully deliver the increasing mobile data demand with satisfactory quality of service, mobile operators expanding their network capacity by deploying LTE-A and LTE-A Pro technologies [24]. These technologies enhance network capacity by exploiting different sub-technologies such as Carrier Aggregation (CA), enhanced Multiple Input Multiple Output (eMIMO) and Heterogeneous Networks (HetNet).

Ethio telecom, has partially deployed LTE in some parts of Addis Ababa. To meet the increasing capacity demand, besides expanding the LTE network coverage, there is a need in ethio telecom to deploy LTE-A in Addis Ababa to provide further capacity enhancements [3]. However, there is no concrete understanding on which LTE-A scenario is most viable for the Addis Ababa context, from both technical and eco-nomical perspectives. Addis Ababa has its own context in terms of existing network, user demand distribution, spectrum availability and other factors.

The aim of this paper is to identify most likely LTE-A deployment scenarios for Addis Ababa and perform techno-economic analysis on them to analyze their viability, assuming a six year study period and 10% discount rate. Scenario planning method is applied to identify suitable LTE-A scenarios while modified TERA model is used to analyze techno-economic viability of the scenarios [27]. Based on two main uncer-tainties, full or progressive deployment and out-of-band or in-band small cells, four potential scenarios are devolved: *Full LTE-A Deployment with Out-of-band Small Cells (SC1), Progressive LTE-A Deployment with Out-of-band Small Cells (SC2), Full LTE-A Deployment with In-band Small Cells (SC3)* and *Progressive LTE-A Deployment with In-band Small Cells (SC4)*. Techno-economic evaluation results, i.e. Net Present Value (NPV) and Payback Period (PP), show that the LTE-A scenario with *Progressive LTE-A Deployment with Out-of-band Small Cells* is the most viable option for Addis Ababa.

The remaining part of the paper is organized as follows. Background on LTE-A technologies is provided in Sect. 2 and identification of potential LTE-A scenarios for Addis Ababa is discussed in Sect. 3. Then description of methodology, assumptions and parameter values for the techno-economic analysis are presented in Sect. 4 which is followed by presentation of results of the techno-economic analysis in Sect. 5. Finally, concluding remarks are provided in Sect. 6.

2   Background on LTE-A Technologies

Base line LTE is evolved to LTE-A that is standardized in 3rd Generation Partnership Project (3GPP) since Release 10 and it presents further enhancements to LTE in terms of network capacity, spectral efficiency, energy efficiency, interference mitigation for dense network, as well as, cost-per-bit [1, 2]. To achieve the enhancements LTE-A exploits four key technology components: CA, eMIMO, densification and Coordinated Multipoint (CoMP) transmission & reception.

2.1 Carrier Aggregation (CA)

CA is one important LTE-A technology component that enhance network capacity by increasing system bandwidth by combining component carriers (CCs) from same or different frequency bands [1]. The CCs can have any of LTE Release 8 bandwidths: 1.4, 3, 5, 10, 15, 20 MHz and in principle a maximum of five CCs can be aggregated to achieve a maximum of 100 MHz, as can be seen in Fig. 1 [7–9]. For practical usages considering bandwidth availability for operators, various CA configurations are standardized in 3GPP Release 10 and beyond within intra-band and inter-band aggregation types [7–9]. In Frequency Division Duplexing (FDD) mode, aggregated CCs in downlink and uplink can be different and UL CCs ca be less than or equal to number of DL CCs [5, 8]. In case of Time Division Duplexing (TDD), number of CCs as well as the bandwidths of each CC shall normally be same [8].

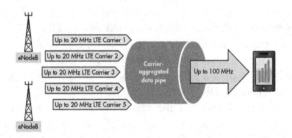

Fig. 1. Aggregation of LTE CCs to get higher bandwidth [11]

2.2 Enhanced MIMO (eMIMO)

To improve network spectral efficiency, one key technology of LTE-A is eMIMO that enables LTE-A to apply up to 8×8 MIMO in 3GPP Release 10 to enjoy more MIMO multiplexing, diversity and array gains compared to LTE Release 8 that uses up to 4×4 MIMO [6]. Of course, an achieved gain depends on radio environment and applied transmission mode [6]. Different transmission models are defined for LTE-A eMIMO in Release 10 (and beyond) that could be for single user MIMO, multi user MIMO and dynamic hybrid of the two.

2.3 Heterogonous Network (HetNet)

It has been well noted even before LTE-A that traditional macro cell only deployment is not effective to meet the increasing spatiotemporally heterogeneous data demand, that emanates mostly form indoor [10]. One important technology to meet the heterogeneous data demand is densification where low-power nodes (such as Pico cells, femto cells, relays) are deployed under umbrella macro network, resulting HetNet [27].

This brings considerable architectural change that affects network efficiencies in terms of capacity, coverage, energy, cost and other factors [10, 15, 16]. The low-power nodes can be planned and deployed to enhance data capacity, coverage, cost efficiency and energy efficiency while meeting the heterogeneous demand considering its spatiotemporal distribution.

Although densification has already started even before 3GPP LTE release 8, the LTE-A Release 10 and beyond incorporate efficient interference management techniques between cells. This enables LTE-A to enjoy much better spectral efficient densification.

2.4 Coordinated Multi Point (CoMP)

To address inconsistent quality of experience across mobile network challenge, LTE-A can use a technology called CoMP that mitigate inter-cell interference (main reason of inconsistent experience) by coordinating neighboring cells in various levels. CoMP can be performed among macro cells and between macro and small cells and both in uplink and downlink [6].

3 Scenario Planning for Addis Ababa

3.1 Scenario Planning Method

To formulate potential LTE-A scenarios for Addis Ababa, we adopt scenario-planning method that is described in [4, 12]. The method consists of four important steps: *Trend analysis, Uncertainty identification, Forming correlation matrix* and *Formulating scenario matrix.* Accordingly, we first perform trend analysis for LTE-A considering the technology, best experiences, expert opinions, vendor reports and Addis Ababa demands. The resulted trend is then compiled using PESTLE (*Political, Economic, Social, Technological, Legal and Environmental*) [25] and summarized as presented in Table 1.

Table 1. Summary of trends (PESTLE [25])

PESTLE analysis	Trends
Political (P)	Unutilized/free bands are available in 2G, 3G and LTE networks. Also acquiring new bands is possible
Economical (E)	Possible to deploy LTE-A on the existing mobile sites, mobile tariff reduction performed, less trend on CAPEX and OPEX cost vs. energy consumption analysis, high cost of LTE-A capable devices, mobile services takes high share from ethio telecom revenue
Social (S)	User awareness on new technologies, less effort on local content creation, digital growth helps to boost social capital, customization of phones
Technological (T)	Availability of LTE-A capable devices, mobile penetration rate increasing, underutilized backhaul and spectrum, indoor traffic, data traffic increasing
Legal (L)	Placement of macro and small sites
Environmental (En)	Alternative energy sources used for remote BSs, possible technological solutions to promote Green ICT

Then, from the key trends, several uncertainties including *deployment strategy* and *band usage of small cells* compared to macro cells are identified and their correlation is analyzed in the correlation matrix forming step, see [27] for details. Finally, we select the aforementioned two uncertainties and develop a scenario matrix that provides four potential LTE-A deployment scenarios for Addis Ababa. Other uncertainties are used for further definition of the selected scenarios.

3.2   Potential LTE-A Deployment Scenarios for Addis Ababa

The formulated LTE-A scenario matrix based on the two uncertainties is shown in Fig. 2. The obtained four potential scenarios are defined further based on other uncertainties including suitability of LTE-A features for local context, national spectrum status and small cell backhauling. The potential scenarios are briefly defined as follows for the Addis Ababa demography's, i.e. Dense Urban (DU), Urban (U) and Sub-Urban (SU):

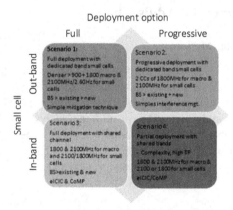

Fig. 2.   LTE-A scenario matrix

SC1: This is a scenario that applies *Full deployment of LTE-A with Out-of-band small cells*. For the U areas non-contiguous CCs, intra-band CA, of *900* and *1800* MHz with 30 MHz aggregated bandwidth (BW_{agg}). For DU, contiguous CCs, i.e. inter-band CA, of *1800* MHz for macro cells allocated to get an BW_{agg} of 30 MHz. Regarding small cells, bands different from the macro cell are allocated. Based on these, *2100* MHz for *small scale* and 2.6 GHz *large scale* small cells assigned. For SU, *1800* MHz used for macro coverage and *2100* MHz for *hotspot* areas that helps to obtain enhanced experience for the UEs on the overlapping areas. **SC2**: This is a scenario that applies *Progressive deployment of LTE-A with Out-of-band small cells* for DU and U areas. For these scenario contiguous CCs of *1800* MHz used for macro cells that can provide 30 MHz BW_{agg}. Whereas, CCs of *2100* MHz for *small scale* and/or *2.6 GHz* for *large scale* small cells used.

SC3: This is a scenario that applies *Full deployment of LTE-A with In-band small cells*. Similar bands will be used for the macro and small cells. For the possible interference, these scenario necessities interference management techniques such as eICIC and CoMP. Contiguous CCs of *1800* MHz for macro and small cells in DU areas whereas non-contiguous CCs from *1800* and *2100* MHz allocated for macro cells and *2100* MHz for small cells in U areas. In SU, *1800* MHz for macro coverage and other CCs of *1800* MHz for hot spot areas to provide increased bandwidth for users in the overlapping areas.

SC4: This is a scenario that applies Progressive deployments of LTE-A with In-band small cells for DU and U areas. Similar to SC3 the allocated bands shared between macro and small cells and requires interference management techniques. For these, CCs of *1800* MHz used for macro cell and available CCs of *1800* MHz for *small scale* and/or *2.6* GHz for *large scale* assigned for small cells.

Due to availability of significant unused bands in Addis Ababa even in the most popularly used *1800* MHz, *2100* MHz and *900* MHz bands, see Fig. 3, we select SC1 and SC2 for further techno-economic investigation.

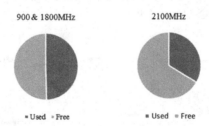

Fig. 3. Ethio telecom band usage [3]

For the selected LTE-A deployment scenarios, the network layout designated in Figs. 4 and 5 relying on the applied bands propagation characteristics.

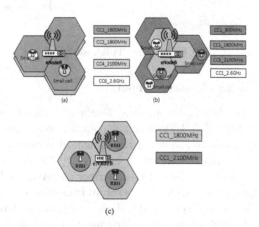

Fig. 4. Full LTE-A deployment with Out-of-band small cells: (a & b) DU/U and (c) SU

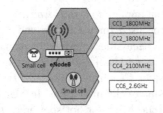

Fig. 5. Progressive LTE-A deployment with Out-of-band small cells

4 Techno-Economic Methodology and Assumptions

For the techno-economic analysis, we adopt techno-economic models from TERA framework that is described in [20, 21] and tune it to suit our study. The modification is to include important input parameters for the study and resulted modified TERA model is show in Fig. 6. The most essential parts of the TERA model are described briefly in the remainder of Sect. 4. In the tool market analysis, dimensioning, value of network elements and spectrum are taken as major parameters together with economic inputs, discussed in the following sub-section.

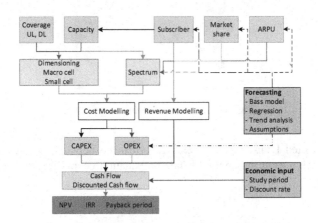

Fig. 6. Modified TERA model

4.1 Market Analysis and Economic Input

For the market analysis, data driven analysis, forecasting, reports and other relevant assumptions are considered [27]. LTE-A data plan/dimensioning performed taking the existing LTE monthly data plan and taking recommended minimum data requirements for intensive apps and services. Regarding LTE-A capable device penetration, we relied on reports taken from [3]. Candidate subscriber and Average Revenue per User (ARPU) estimated, taking ten years back data record from ethio telecom and forecasted for the study period. While market share of LTE-A are determined based on [27–30]. In addition, study period and discount rate defined for the economic input.

4.2   LTE-A Radio Network Dimensioning

LTE-A planning differs from other wireless network planning is mainly in the allocation of Physical Resource Block (PRB) and bandwidth gain because of CA and MIMO [15]. Different parameters are taken in to consideration for dimensioning process [3, 24, 27].

Macro Cell Dimensioning. Depending on adaptive modulation scheme, coding, available bandwidth and required data plan per user capacity driven eNodeBs determined [14]. Whereas, Allowed Propagation Loss (APL) produced using path loss to estimate the coverage radius of eNodeB regarding coverage dimensioning [14, 27]. Separate selected link budget calculations are performed for DU, U and SU for the selected scenarios. For this, excel based link budget tool used for coverage dimensioning while COST-231 Hata applied as a propagation model, Eq. (1), [14].

$$PL = -46.3 -33.9Log (f) -13.82Log (hBS) -a (hUE) -[44.9 -6.55Log(hBS)]Log(d) -C_0 \qquad (1)$$

In (1), the *blue* and *red* colors represent the path loss constant and path loss exponent, respectively, and *a(hUE)* is UE antenna gain function and defined for urban (Eq. (2)) and sub-urban (Eq. (3)) areas as the following:

$$a(hUE) = 3.2(log11.75hUE)^2 - 4.97, f \geq 400\,\text{MHz} \qquad (2)$$

$$a(hUE) = 1.1(logf - 0.7)hUE - (1.56logf - 0.8) \qquad (3)$$

whereby, f = carrier aggregation in MHz, hBS BS antenna height in meters, hUE UE antenna height in meters, d is the cell radius in km and the term Co (0 dB for SU and 3 dB for DU/U) are used to account for different trains [24]. The obtained number of eNodeBs in the LTE-A radio network dimensioning are summarized in Table 2.

Table 2. Summary of results of coverage and capacity dimensioning

Scenario	Capacity	Coverage
SC1	701	420
SC2	580	328

Small Cell Dimensioning. In this study, hot spot areas are identified and organized in clusters for indoor SCs based on the geographic area [27]. To select the area, existing LTE KPI report and building density of Addis Ababa are used as a key dimensioning parameter for indoor small cells [4, 27]. While for the outdoor SCs, beside LTE KPI report, building density, optimal placement of cells among concentrated traffic hotspots analyzed, Table 3 [17, 27, 3GPP TR 36.932].

Table 3. Impact of placement on effectiveness of metro cells [17]

MeBS distance from MaBS	% gain in median user throughput
200 m	2%
400 m	70%
700 m	467%

Based on the above points, assumptions and recommendations the small cell dimensioning result summarized in the following table for the selected scenarios, Table 4.

Table 4. SCs for full and progressive deployments

Scenario	Outdoor SC	Indoor SC
SC1	200	1240
SC2	100	709

Spectrum Dimensioning. The methodology adopted from ITU to predict future spectrum requirement for ethio telecom for the macro and small cells [27]. To check whether the existing spectrum support LTE-A or not, i.e. the amount of spectrum required, Eq. (4) [18, 19] is used taking the forecasted number of end-users for the study period, required bandwidth for the macro and small cells and other market analysis and dimensioning results [27].

$$BW_R = Cell_C(Mbps)/\eta \left(\frac{\frac{bps}{Hz}}{cell} \right) \tag{4}$$

Whereby, BW_R is required bandwidth, $Cell_C$ is cell capacity (calculated based on Eqs. (5) and (6)) and η is spectral efficiency, Eq. (7).

$$Cell_C = S * \left(8192 \left(\frac{Mb}{GB} \right) \right) * \frac{D_P \left(\frac{GB}{\frac{sub}{month}} \right)}{\left(S_T * S_C * 3600 \left(\frac{s}{hr} \right) * 30 \left(\frac{day}{month} \right) \right)} * D \tag{5}$$

$$D = \frac{9\%(BH\ share)}{50\%(Maxlaod)} * \frac{50\%}{15\%} \tag{6}$$

Whereby, S is the subscriber assumed in scenario one and two, S_T is no. of sites, S_C is sector per BS, D_P data plan and D is the distribution. D is based on BH share, maximum load in which 50% of the traffic is carried by 15% of the cells.

$$\eta = P \cdot R_{av} \cdot \frac{G}{BW} \tag{7}$$

Whereby, η is spectral efficiency in bps/Hz/cell, P = 600 Mbps is peak data rate, R_{av} = 64QAM $\rightarrow$ 2/3 is average modulation and coding scheme, G = 2 is gain by MIMO and CA and BW = 40 MHz.

The required bandwidth for the deployment of LTE-A in either *full* or *progressive deployment* with out-of-band small cells predicted for the study period. The result show that SC1 requires 72.22 MHz while it is 72.21 MHz for SC2. Compared to the existing unutilized bandwidth, i.e. S_{UN} = 89 MHz is sufficient for the study period.

4.3 Modeling

After the required number of eNodeBs, indoor and outdoor small cells are determined from the dimensioning process, the related Capital Expenditure (CapEx) and Operational Expenditure (OpEx) cost driven based on [13, 22, 23, 26] to be used as an input for the *Cost* and *Revenue Modelling*. In [13], CapEx cost for deploying multicarrier BS for LTE-A with existing 4G LTE site and site with no LTE network is assumed. Furthermore, in [23] the total CapEx cost to deploy LTE-A, both for macro cell and small cells, is given. Similarly, in [13, 22], the operational cost related to Operations, Administration and Management (OA&M) given. In [23], OpEx cost for 3 CCs with erosion factor of 5% per year considered for upgrading and new site. For this study average value assumed for new and upgrading existing LTE site [27]. For outdoor and indoor small cells, 20 and 10% of the macro cell CapEx and OpEx cost assumed for the TEA based on respectively [23].

Cost Modeling. Costs can be generally split between CapEx and OpEx and broadly categorized as top-down and bottom-up approaches [20, 26]. In this study, a hybrid approach modelled [27]. Accordingly, the cost model is illustrated as in Eq. (8).

$$C_T = N_M C_M + N_S C_S + C_{Spectrum} + C_{BH} + C_{Core} + OPEX \tag{8}$$

Whereby, C_T is total cost, N_M and N_S are number of macro and small cells, C_M, C_S, $C_{Spectrum}$, C_{BH} and C_{core} are the CapEx cost related to macro, small cell, spectrum, backhaul and core network respectively and *OPEX* cost to run the network.

Revenue Modelling. The number of subscribers, ARPU and market share are the main inputs for calculating the revenues. Together with indirect revenues stemmed from, for example, roaming and advertising [20]. Equation (9) shows the revenue modelling used in the study.

$$R_T = ARPU * S_P * PM_S + I_R \tag{9}$$

Whereby, R_T is the generated revenue, S_P is predicted number of subscribers, PM_S is predicted market share of LTE-A and I_R is indirect revenue from for example roaming, sale of SIM.

4.4   TEA Evaluation

For the TEA evaluation, Cash Flow (CF), Discounted CF (DCF), NPV and PP are used.

CF and DCF. Cash flow is the net amount of cash that is received and disbursed during the study period. Based on cash and revenue model, the CF model is represented as

$$CF = \sum_{i=1}^{6} (R_T - C_T)i \tag{10}$$

Whereby, CF is the cash flow, R_T and C_T revenue and cost models and i is the study period.

Whereas, DCF analysis, in Eq. (11), is the process of calculating the present value of an investment's future cash flows in order to arrive at a current fair value estimate for the investment i.e., time value of money [20].

$$DCF = \frac{CF_1}{(1+r)^1} + \frac{CF_2}{(1+r)^2} + \cdots + \frac{CF_i}{(1+r)^i} \tag{11}$$

Whereby, CF is cash flow, r is discount rate and i the study period.

NPV and PP. These parameters are used to evaluate the viability of the investment. NPV calculated, as indicated in Eq. (12) [20]. Whereas, PP calculated as in Eq. (13).

$$NPV = CAPEX - DCF = CAPEX - \sum_{i=1}^{6} CF_i/(1+r)^i \tag{12}$$

$$PP = LA + [\frac{Abs(CCF)}{TCF}] \tag{13}$$

Whereby, LA is last period of negative cumulative CF, CCF = value of cumulative CF at the end of LA, TCF = Total CF i.e. the period after LA.

5   Result and Discussion

5.1   Techno-Economic Evaluation Result

The existing 329 LTE BSs upgraded and new sites added relying on BS requirement, see [27]. In terms of spectrum, no cost for additional band is assumed since the unutilized bandwidth from the existing network is used. Then the output of techno-economic evaluation is performed for the two scenarios, as discussed below, using key TE evaluation parameters like NPV, CF, DCF and PP.

Full LTE-A Deployment with Out-band Small Cells: Figure 7 shows results of cash flow analysis for coverage and capacity for SC1. The output indicates positive NPV for DU, U and SU with payback period in the range of 3 to 5 years in terms of coverage,

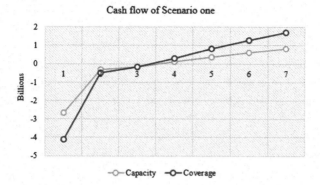

Fig. 7. Cash flow analysis for scenario one

Table 5. Whereas, in the case of capacity the result shows negative NPV with extended PP or more time period than the predefined study period.

Table 5. Summary of TEA for SC1

Deployment	Dimensioning	NPV	Payback period
DU and U	Coverage	1,162.47	4.13
SU		1,975.89	3.19
DU, U and SU		565.52	4.68
DU, U and SU	Capacity	(1,277.80)	-

Progressive LTE-A Deployment with Out-band Small Cells: Techno-economic evolution result for both coverage and capacity point of view shows positive NPV with payback period in the range of 3 to 5 years, Table 6. Cash flow for coverage and capacity analysis illustrated in Fig. 8.

Table 6. Summary of TEA for SC2

Deployment	Dimensioning	NPV	Payback period
DU and U	Coverage	2,290.55	3.29
DU and U	Capacity	644.02	4.70

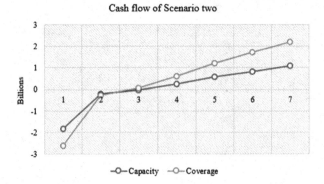

Fig. 8. Cash flow analysis of scenario two

5.2 Discussion

There is always a tradeoff between QoS and cost. In such scenario, efficient planning helps to properly manage resources and save unnecessary wastage. In scenario-planning approach presented in this study, the list of possible LTE-A deployment options are proposed and two of them identified as viable deployment scenarios and evaluated techno-economically. Subsequently, market analysis and dimensioning processes performed by applying the modified TERA framework and developed TEA tool.

In SC1, the NPV and PP indicated that LTE-A is feasible in DU, U and SU areas from coverage perspective with 4.13 and 3.19 PP for DU/U and SU respectively. However, SC1 is capacity limited and the NPV and PP results indicated that it is not feasible in the defined study period. While in SC2, the NPV and PP indicated that LTE-A is feasible in DU and U areas both in coverage and capacity perspective with PP 3.29 and 4.70 respectively.

In general, the TE evaluation result showed that progressive deployment of LTE-A is practical and feasible deployment option of LTE-A for Addis Ababa.

6 Conclusion

The study themed with describing the cellular technology evolution giving focus on LTE-A and the ever-growing end-user demand. The analysis indicates that the current infrastructure cannot cope with demand and requirement of an efficient network. Employing systematic literature reviews, standards, reports, expert opinions and state-of-the-art surveys, a scenario is planned to pinpoint realistic LTE-A deployment options for Addis Ababa. For these PESTLE analysis method is used to study the possible trends and uncertainties for the local context. Positioning on the result macro, small cell and spectrum dimensioning performed to drive needful NE for CapEx and OpEx analysis. In the study, the status and applicability of existing resources, such as spectrum, base station and backhaul for LTE-A are identified. It is then concluded that the backhaul has the capacity to handle LTE-A while LTE base stations can be upgraded and new sites added depending on the scenarios. Concerning spectrum, a six year demand forecasted and the possibility of reusing the unutilized bandwidth verified.

Furthermore, a suitable TEA framework was identified to evaluate the selected deployment scenarios techno-economically. The framework is modified to enclose parameters that will reduce cost and escalate revenue. Based on the modified framework, the results indicated that SC1 is not feasible within the defined study period while SC2 is a viable LTE-A deployment option for Addis Ababa. In general, it is an inevitable that mobile data demand and traffic volumes will continue to increase in the coming years in Ethiopia, specifically in Addis Ababa. Therefore, a technology that can handle this demand is required. It is then important to identify proper planning and scientific analysis method and evaluate technology viability in technical and economic measures.

References

1. Cox, C.: An Introduction to LTE: LTE, LTE-A, SAE, VoLTE and 4G Mobile Communications, 2nd edn. Wiley, Hoboken (2014)
2. Holma, H., Toskala, A.: LTE for UMTS, Evolution to LTE-Advanced, 2nd edn. Wiley, Hoboken (2010)
3. Ethio Telecom: Ethio Telecom company profile, documents and reports 2013–2018
4. Haile, B.B., et al.: Development of the Wi-Fi offloading business concept within the African Market Context. Aalto University, Finland, October 2012
5. 3GPP TS 36.300: Evolved universal terrestrial radio access (E-UTRA) and evolved universal terrestrial radio access network (E-UTRAN); overall description; Stage 2, Release 15, 3GPP, V15.2.0, June 2018
6. Khasdev, B., Hirwe, A.: Overview of MIMO technology in LTE, LTE-A & LTE-A-Pro. Int. J. Eng. Comput. Sci. 5(11), 19227–19229 (2016)
7. Kiwoli, L., et al.: Performance analysis of carrier aggregation for various mobile network implementation scenarios based on spectrum allocated. IJWMN 9(5) (2017)
8. Wannstrom, J.: Carrier aggregation explained. www.3gpp.org/technologies. Accessed 14 Jan 2019
9. 4G Americas: LTE carrier aggregation technology development and deployment world wide, October 2014
10. Sánchez, S.B., Pocovi Gerardino, G.A.: LTE-advanced HetNet investigations under realistic conditions. MSc thesis, Aalborg University, Denmark, May 2014
11. Electronic Design: Carrier aggregation: implications for mobile-device RF front-ends, 19 February 2016
12. Schoemaker, P.J.H.: Scenario planning: a tool for strategic thinking. Sloan Manag. Rev. 36, 25–40 (1995)
13. Duan, L.: Economic analysis of 4G upgrade timing. IEEE Trans. Mob. Comput. 14, 975–989 (2015)
14. ElNashar, A.: Design, Deployment and Performance of 4G Networks: A Practical Approach. Wiley, Hoboken (2014)
15. Acharya, J.: Heterogeneous Networks in LTE-Advanced. Wiley, Hoboken (2014)
16. Ek, P.: Deployment of indoor small cells for 4G mobile broad band. MSc thesis, October 2013
17. Buddiket, M., Soni, R.: Small cell technology overview, Alcatel, 13 March 2013

18. Riaz, A.: Spectrum forecasting for future use: methods and techniques. ITU Regional Workshop, Bangkok, Thailand, 3–4 May 2017
19. Chung, W.G.: Calculation of spectral efficiency for estimating spectrum requirements of IMT-advanced in Korean mobile communication environment. ETRI J. **29**, 153–161 (2007)
20. Smura, T.: Techno-economic modelling of wireless network and industry architecture. Ph.D. dissertation, Aalto University, Finland (2012)
21. METIS II: Quantitative techno-economic feasibility assessment. Deliverable D1.2, 15 June 2017
22. Nikolikj, V., Janevski, T.: Applicable cost modeling of LTE-advanced and IEEE 802.11ac based heterogeneous wireless access networks. In: 10th Advanced International Conference on Telecommunications (2014)
23. Oughton, E.J., Frias, Z.: Exploring the cost, coverage and rollout implications of 5G in Britain. MSc thesis, Madrid, Spain (2016)
24. Skinner, T.: 30% of operators investing in LTE-A, VoLTE rollouts grow, 23 July 2015 report. http://telecoms.com. Accessed 14 Jan 2019
25. Stork, C.: Strategic analysis of the telecommunication sector. Research ICT Africa, 9 August 2012
26. Zareen, U.: LTE Advanced: techno economic perspective. Univ. J. Commun. Netw. **2**, 93–100 (2014)
27. Hailegebriel, G.: Techno-economic investigation of LTE-advanced deployment for Addis Ababa, Ethiopia. MSc thesis. Addis Ababa University, AAiT, November 2018
28. Heuveldop, N.: Ericsson mobility report. Ericson, June 2017
29. Ericsson mobility report-interim update, Sweden, February 2018
30. Haile, B.B., Aga, D., Mulu, B.: On the relevance of capacity enhancing 5G technologies for Ethiopia. In: 10th Ethiopian ICT Annual Conference, Addis Ababa, Ethiopia, June 2017

Peak-to-Average Power Ratio Reduction of OFDM Signals Using Selected Mapping

Workineh Gebeye Abera[✉] and Yihenew Wondie Marye[✉]

School of Electrical and Computer Engineering,
Addis Ababa Institute of Technology, Addis Ababa University,
Addis Ababa, Ethiopia
Workinehgebeye@gmail.com, yiheneww@gmail.com
{workineh.gebeye,yihenew.wondie}@aait.edu.et

Abstract. Orthogonal Frequency Division Multiplexing (OFDM) signaling is highly applicable in wireless communications, like 4G cellular networks, as it has better performance in a fading environment. However, OFDM signal has large Peak-to-Average Power Ratio (PAPR) which leads to signal distortion in the electronic components of the OFDM system transmitter. As a result, PAPR reduction techniques are used in OFDM systems. Selected Mapping (SLM) scheme is one method of reducing PAPR of OFDM signals. In this paper, we have demonstrated the PAPR reduction capability of SLM through simulation on MATLAB. In addition, we have shown the computational complexity incurred in using SLM to reduce PAPR. It is shown that the PAPR reduction capability of OFDM increases with increase in the number of candidate OFDM symbols. However, this is achieved at the cost of increased computational complexity, where the complexity also linearly with the number of candidate OFDM symbols.

Keywords: Orthogonal Frequency Division Multiplexing · Peak-to-Average Power Ratio · Selected Mapping

1 Introduction

OFDM is a multicarrier signaling scheme which subdivides an available frequency-selective wideband channel into a number of narrowband subchannels (subcarriers) which are non-frequency-selective. Hence, OFDM signaling has high immunity to frequency selective fading. The subcarriers are overlapping but orthogonal, which avoids the need to separate the carriers by means of guard-bands, and therefore makes OFDM highly spectrally efficient. Furthermore, the arrangement of the subcarriers makes receiver implementation simple as the subcarriers can be perfectly separated. For its good properties, OFDM, in its multiple access version, OFDMA, has been adopted for downlink transmission in long term evolution-advanced (LTE-A) network [1, 2]. In addition, it is used in wireless systems, which use multimedia service applications, like, digital audio broadcasting systems, digital video broadcasting terrestrial TV (DVB-T) systems, asymmetric digital subscriber line (ADSL) systems, IEEE 802.11a/g/n wireless local area network (WLAN), IEEE 802.16 worldwide interoperability for

© Springer Nature Switzerland AG 2019
F. Mekuria et al. (Eds.): ICT4DA 2019, CCIS 1026, pp. 203–212, 2019.
https://doi.org/10.1007/978-3-030-26630-1_17

microwave access (WiMAX) systems, and ultra-wideband (UWB) multiband-OFDM systems [3].

However, the required features of OFDM are obtained at the expense of large envelope variation, which is a major drawback of OFDM and is usually quantified through the Peak-to-Average Power Ratio (PAPR). Such signal envelope variations can be difficult for practical High Power Amplifiers (HPAs) and Digital to Analog Convertors (DACs)/Analog to Digital Converters (ADCs) of the OFDM system to accommodate, resulting in either low power efficiency or signal distortion, including signal clips [4]. Consequently, the signal distortion results in Bit Error Rate (BER) increase and Power Spectral Density (PSD) degradation. These effects can be avoided by making the HPA to work in its linear region with large back-off however, this results in poor power efficiency. Similarly, the DAC/ADC can be designed to accommodate the large dynamic range of the OFDM signal but, this results in a reduced Signal to Noise Ratio (SNR), as the DAC/ADC already has significant amount of quantization noise. Hence, a better solution is to reduce the PAPR of the OFDM signal with some manipulation of the OFDM signal itself [4].

As a result, a number of researches have been done on the development of PAPR reduction schemes for OFDM signals. The first class of schemes reduce PAPR with signal distortion, which include amplitude clipping [5], clipping and filtering [6]; but the schemes have in-band distortion and out-of-band spectral regrowth limitations. Distortionless schemes such as coding [7], Selected Mapping (SLM) [8], Partial Transmit Sequence (PTS) [9], etc. are the second class of PAPR reduction schemes. An overview of the various PAPR reduction schemes can also be found in [4].

In this paper, we will show SLM's, one of the distortionless PAPR reduction schemes, PAPR reduction capability and the associated computational cost incurred in using the scheme. In SLM, for every OFDM symbol intended for transmission, D candidate OFDM symbols are generated (by rotating the phase of every data symbol within an OFDM symbol with D distinct phase rotation vectors $\mathbf{P}^{(d)}$) by the transmitter, among which the one with the least PAPR will be selected for transmission. To recover the original OFDM symbol, the receiver has to know the phase vector $\mathbf{P}^{\bar{d}}$ (or the index $\bar{d}$) that gives the least PAPR OFDM symbol. To this end, side information (SI) (with $\log_2 D$ bits) has to be transmitted along with the OFDM symbol, which reduces the information throughput.

Hence, the Author in [8] has proposed a novel technique that helps to recover the transmitted OFDM symbol from the received OFDM symbol itself; i.e. blindly. In the technique, the parameter $\bar{d}$ is made to be linked with a set of distinct amplitude functions. The Author has shown through simulation that the proposed method gives the same PAPR reduction performance as the original SLM (with SI) method.

However, the paper would have been more comprehensive, had it shown the PAPR reduction performance of SLM as the number of candidate OFDM symbols increase. In addition, the paper doesn't show the computational cost incurred in using SLM to reduce PAPR.

As a result, in our paper we have shown the PAPR reduction performance of the scheme with the number of candidate OFDM symbols. We have also analyzed the computational complexity of the scheme. Furthermore, we have shown the optimum condition for the choice of phase rotation factors so that the best PAPR reduction capability of SLM can be enjoyed.

The remaining part of the paper is organized as follows. Section 2 discusses about the OFDM signal model used in the paper. The Scheme's system model is presented in Sect. 3. The computational complexity of the scheme is analyzed in Sect. 4. Section 5 presents simulation results and discussions. Finally, the concluding remarks are made in Sect. 6.

2 OFDM Signal Model

For a given data vector $\mathbf{S}^\mu = [S_0^\mu S_1^\mu \cdots S_{N-1}^\mu]^T$, a sequence of complex numbers drawn from a finite constellation (MPSK or MQAM) in the μth signaling interval, the baseband OFDM symbol $\left\{ s_{n/L}^\mu \right\}_{n=0}^{LN-1}$ is an oversampled IFFT output of $\mathbf{S}^\mu$. That is [10, 11]

$$s_{n/L}^\mu = \frac{1}{\sqrt{N}} \sum_{k=0}^{N-1} S_k^\mu e^{j\frac{2\pi}{LN}kn}, n = 0, 1, \cdots, LN - 1$$

$$s_{n/L}^\mu = \frac{1}{\sqrt{N}} \left\{ \sum_{k=0}^{N/2-1} S_k^\mu e^{j\frac{2\pi}{LN}kn} + \sum_{k=LN-\frac{N}{2}}^{LN-1} S_{k-N(L-1)}^\mu e^{j\frac{2\pi}{LN}kn} \right\}$$

$$s_{n/L}^\mu = IFFT\left\{ \sqrt{L}S_L^\mu \right\} \tag{1}$$

where N is the number of subcarriers, $L \geq 1$ is an integer and it is the oversampling factor, $IFFT\{\cdot\}$ is NL-point oversampled IFFT indexed by n/L, and $\mathbf{S}_L^\mu = \left[S_0^\mu \cdots S_{\frac{N}{2}-1}^\mu 0 \cdots 0 S_{\frac{N}{2}}^\mu \cdots S_{N-1}^\mu \right]^T$ is the L times oversampled equivalent data vector generated by zero padding $\mathbf{S}^\mu$ with $N(L-1)$ zeros at its middle [10, 11].

The baseband PAPR is defined as [10, 11]

$$PAPR\left\{ s_{n/L}^\mu \right\} = \frac{\max_{n\in[0,LN)} \left| s_{n/L}^\mu \right|^2}{E\left\{ \left| s_{n/L}^\mu \right|^2 \right\}} \tag{2}$$

which is a random variable.

As the passband PAPR is roughly twice (3 dB higher than) the baseband PAPR, it is sufficient to consider only the PAPR of the baseband OFDM signal [10], pp. 22–23. In addition, the cyclic prefix of duration T_g, which is a repetition of part of the OFDM symbol, attached to the OFDM symbol to combat Inter-Symbol Interference (ISI) can be neglected for the purposes of PAPR analysis as the prefix will not produce a peak which is not already present in the OFDM symbol $s^\mu_{n/L}$. Theoretically, $\text{PAPR}\{s^\mu_{n/L}\}$ approaches $\text{PAPR}\{s^\mu(t)\}$ as L becomes sufficiently large. However, it is has been shown in [11, 12] that when $L \geq 4$ the PAPR of $s^\mu_{n/L}$ approximates the PAPR of $s^\mu(t)$ and hence $L = 4$ is used in the simulation results of this paper.

3 Selected Mapping System Model

SLM is a distortionless PAPR reduction scheme [8, 13]. In the SLM scheme, the transmitter generates a set of sufficiently different candidate data vectors, all representing the same information as the original data vector, for each data vector intended for transmission by rotating the phase of each data symbol and then selects the candidate data vector with the lowest PAPR for transmission [8, 13].

A set of D markedly different, distinct, pseudorandom but fixed phase rotation vectors [11, 13]

$$\mathbf{P}^{(d)} = [P_0^{(d)} P_1^{(d)} \cdots P_{N-1}^{(d)}]^T, \tag{3}$$

with $P_k^{(d)} = e^{j\phi_k^{(d)}}$, $\phi_k^{(d)} \in [0, 2\pi)$, $k = 0, 1, \cdots, N-1$, $d = 1, 2, \cdots, D$ must be defined and available both at the transmitter and receiver. The data vector $\mathbf{S}^\mu$ is multiplied element-wise with each one of the D phase rotation vectors $\mathbf{P}^{(d)}$, resulting in a set of D different phase rotated data vectors $\mathbf{S}^{(\mu,d)}$ given by [11, 13]

$$\mathbf{S}^{(\mu,d)} = \mathbf{S}^\mu \circ \mathbf{P}^{(d)}. \tag{4}$$

Then, all the D data vectors are transformed into time domain to get D candidate OFDM symbols by using D length-LN IFFTs [11, 13]

$$s_{n/L}^{(\mu,d)} = \frac{1}{\sqrt{N}} \sum_{k=0}^{N-1} S_k^\mu P_k^{(d)} e^{j\frac{2\pi}{LN}kn}, \, n = 0, 1, \cdots, LN-1$$

$$s_{n/L}^{(\mu,d)} = IFFT\left\{\sqrt{L} S_L^{(\mu,d)}\right\} \tag{5}$$

Among the D candidate OFDM symbols, the transmitter selects one, $s_{n/L}^{(\mu,\bar{d})}$, with the lowest PAPR, for transmission where [11, 13]

$$\bar{d} = arg \min_{1 \leq d \leq D} PAPR\left\{s_{n/L}^{(\mu,d)}\right\} \tag{6}$$

Therefore, the SLM-OFDM transmitter is as shown in Fig. 1.

In our work, it is expected that the transmitter and the receiver have the D phase rotation vectors $\mathbf{P}^{(d)}$. But, so as to recover an OFDM symbol, the receiver has to know the phase rotation vector $\mathbf{P}^{(\bar{d})}$ which has been used by the transmitter in generating the least PAPR transmit OFDM symbol. The easiest approach can be to transmit $\bar{d}$ as side information (SI), which requires $\log_2 D$. As SI transmission decreases the information throughput, another scheme to determine $\bar{d}$ is the blind technique [8], where it is determined based only on the received OFDM symbol and the known phase rotation vectors.

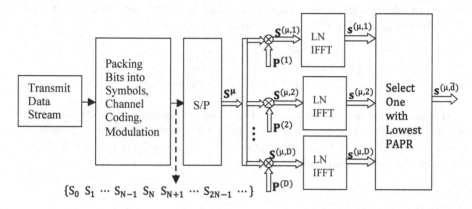

Fig. 1. SLM-OFDM transmitter block diagram.

Then, the original data vector $\mathbf{S}^\mu$ is recovered by multiplying the received data vector $\tilde{\mathbf{S}}^\mu$ element-wise by $\mathbf{P}^{(\bar{d})} = \left[e^{-j\phi_0^{(d)}} e^{-j\phi_1^{(d)}} \cdots e^{-j\phi_{N-1}^{(d)}} \right]$. In the paper, we have assumed that the blind technique is used.

We have shown through simulation in Fig. 3 that for a given D, choosing $P_k^{(d)}$ such that the corresponding $\phi_k^{(d)}$ are uniformly distributed in $[0, 2\pi)$, then the PAPR reduction capability of SLM is the same whether $P_k^{(d)}$ are chosen from set $\{\pm 1\}$ or $\{\pm 1, \pm j\}$.

4 SLM Scheme Computational Complexity Analysis

As it is shown in (4), ND complex multiplications are required to generate $S^{(\mu,d)}, d = 1, 2, \ldots, D$. Then, D length LN IFFTs are required to generate $s_{n/L}^{(\mu,d)}$. Each LN-point IFFT needs $(LN/2)\log_2(LN)$ complex multiplications and $LN \log_2(LN)$ complex additions [14, 15]. Finally, $\left| s_{n/L}^\mu \right|^2 = Re\left\{ s_{n/L}^\mu \right\}^2 + Im\left\{ s_{n/L}^\mu \right\}^2$ need to be calculated for each n in determining the PAPR, which requires 2DLN real multiplications and DLN additions.

Four real multiplications and two real additions are required for a complex multiplication. On the other hand, a complex addition requires two real additions. Therefore, the total number of real additions A and multiplications M required for the scheme can be summarized as

$$A_{SLM} = DLN(3\log_2(LN) + 1) + 2ND \tag{7}$$

$$M_{SLM} = 2DLN(\log_2(LN) + 1) + 4ND \tag{8}$$

To quantify the computational complexity of SLM, a parameter f, which is the number of addition instructions required for each multiplication operation, is used. Thus, the overall computational complexity of the scheme for $f = 4$ is

$$C_{SLM} = A_{SLM} + fM_{SLM}$$

$$C_{SLM} = [11LN\log_2(LN) + 9N(L + 2)]D \tag{9}$$

The receiver of the scheme uses one FFT, which is the same as the OFDM system without any PAPR reduction scheme, to detect the transmitted OFDM symbol from the received OFDM symbol. Hence, the additional system complexity in using the PAPR reduction scheme is found in the transmitter.

5 Simulation Results

This section presents the simulation results that show the PAPR reduction capability of SLM and the computational complexity of the scheme. The simulations are done using MATLAB.

For every Complementary Cumulative Distribution Function (CCDF) curve, 10^5 OFDM symbols, each containing $N = 256$ data symbols from QPSK modulation constellation, are randomly generated. The oversampling factor used in the simulations is L = 4. The elements of every phase rotation vector $\mathbf{P}^{(d)}, d = 1, 2, \cdots, D$, are chosen from the set $\{\pm1\}$ with equal probability or from the set $\{\pm1, \pm j\}$ with equal probability and hence the candidate OFDM symbols are mutually independent.

Figure 2 shows the CCDF of PAPR of SLM-OFDM signal for different number of candidate OFDM symbols **D** along with the CCDF of PAPR of OFDM signal. The elements of every phase rotation vector are chosen from the set $\{\pm1, \pm j\}$ with equal probability. In fact, the phase rotation vectors are obtained from a randomly generated binary data mapped onto QPSK symbols and hence the number of bits per symbol m = 2 and the number of constellation points $Q = 2^m = 4$. Thus, the number of elements of the phase rotation factor set is Q = 4.

The plot shows that for D = 1, the CCDF curve overlaps with the CCDF curve of the OFDM signal. For D = 1, the candidate OFDM symbol is the original OFDM symbol itself and hence the plot illustrates that there is no PAPR reduction. Whereas, for D = 2 and above, the PAPR reduces significantly. As an example, for the original OFDM signal the probability that the PAPR is greater than around 10.2 dB is 10^{-2}, i.e.

one in 100 OFDM symbols will have a PAPR greater than 10.2 dB. But, for the SLM-OFDM signal with D = 2, to get the same CCDF value, 10^{-2}, the PAPR reduces to around 9 dB. This shows a reduction of around 1.2 dB. For the same CCDF value, the PAPR reduction is even much greater than 1.2 dB as D increases. In summary, the plot illustrates that the PAPR reduction capability of SLM increases with the number of candidate OFDM symbols D. But, this is at the cost of increased computational complexity as shown in Fig. 4.

Figure 3. shows the CCDF of PAPR of SLM-OFDM and OFDM signals. For each D, two CCDF curves are shown where one of the curves is for an SLM-OFDM signal with the elements of every $\mathbf{P}^{(d)}$ chosen from the set $\{\pm 1\}$ with equal probability and the other one is for the same SLM-OFDM signal but the elements of every $\mathbf{P}^{(d)}$ chosen from the set $\{\pm 1, \pm j\}$ with equal probability. The simulation is done to illustrate the PAPR reduction capability of SLM with these two phase rotation factor sets.

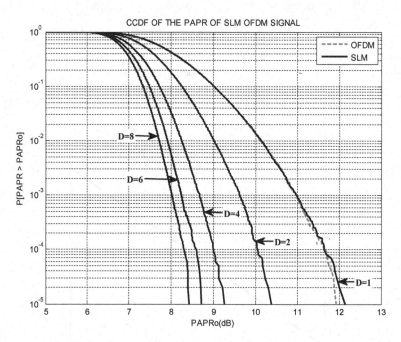

Fig. 2. CCDF of PAPR of SLM and OFDM signals for the elements of $\mathbf{P}^{(d)}$ chosen from the set $\{\pm 1, \pm j\}$.

The phase rotation vectors with elements from the set $\{\pm 1\}$ are actually obtained from a randomly generated binary data mapped onto BPSK symbols, i.e. m = 1 and hence $Q = 2^m = 2$.

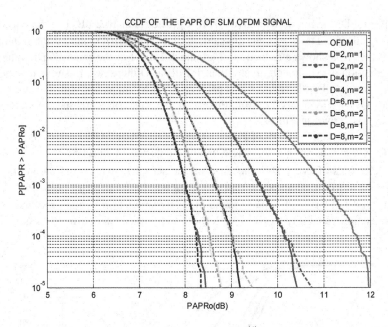

Fig. 3. CCDF of PAPR of SLM and OFDM signals for $P_k^{(d)}$ chosen from $\{\pm 1\}$ and $\{\pm 1, \pm j\}$.

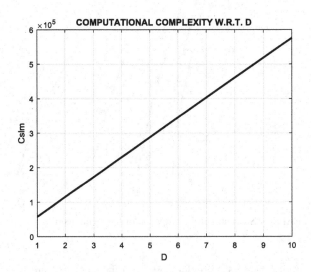

Fig. 4. Computational complexity of SLM with respect to (w.r.t.) D.

The plot illustrates that for a given number of candidate OFDM symbols D, the PAPR reduction capability of SLM is the same whether the elements of the phase rotation vectors are chosen from the set $\{\pm 1\}$ or $\{\pm 1, \pm j\}$. Hence, irrespective of the phase rotation factor set from which we choose the elements of the phase rotation vectors, the PAPR reduction capability of SLM is the same, if the corresponding phase rotation angles $\phi_k^{(d)}$ are uniformly distributed in $[0, 2\pi)$.

We have shown above that the PAPR reduction capability of SLM increases with increase in D, number of candidate OFDM symbols generated per OFDM symbol for transmission. The plot in Fig. 4 illustrates the computational cost incurred with increase in D. The plot shows that the computational complexity increases linearly with D. As a result, a compromise has to be made between the required PAPR reduction level and the accompanying increase in computational cost.

6 Conclusion

Though OFDM signaling is preferable in a multipath fading environment for its better performance, its large PAPR leads to signal distortion and hence BER degradation in the electronic devices like ADC, DAC, & high power amplifiers. Hence, schemes that can reduce the PAPR of OFDM signal have been introduced.

In this paper, we have shown that the PAPR reduction capability of SLM scheme. In the scheme, for a given OFDM symbol intended for transmission, D length LN candidate OFDM symbols are generated and then the one with the least PAPR is chosen for transmission. The D candidate OFDM symbols are generated using D parallel LN-point IFFTs.

Our simulation results show that the PAPR reduction capability of SLM is the same irrespective of the number of elements of the phase rotation factor set, as far as the phase rotation angles are uniformly distributed in $[0, 2\pi)$.

The simulation results also show that the SLM scheme can reduce the PAPR of OFDM signal to a required level. The PAPR reduction capability of SLM increases with increase in the number of candidate OFDM symbols D, but at the cost of linear increase in computational complexity with D. Hence, we can make a compromise between the required PAPR reduction level and the associated increase in computational complexity.

References

1. Mahmoud, E., Abdelmohsen, A., Walaa, H.: Cellular LTE-A technologies for the future Internet-of-Things: physical layer features and challenges. IEEE Commun. Surv. Tutorials **19**(4), 2544–2572 (2017)
2. Haitham, S.B.A., Warip, M.N.M., Ong, B.L., Naimah, Y.: An efficient scheduling scheme for heterogeneous services in OFDMA based 5G LTE-Advanced network with carrier aggregation, pp. 275–280. IEEE (2018)
3. Hwang, T., Yang, C., Wu, G., Li, S., Li, Y.: OFDM and its wireless applications: a survey. IEEE Trans. Veh. Technol. **58**(4), 1673–1694 (2009)
4. Jiang, T., Wu, Y.: An overview: peak-to-average power ratio reduction techniques for OFDM signals. IEEE Trans. Broadcast. **54**(2), 257–268 (2008)

5. O'Neil, R., Lopes, L.B.: Envelope variations and spectral splatter in clipped multicarrier signals. In: The 6th IEEE International Symposium on Personal, Indoor and Mobile Radio Communications, vol. 1, pp. 71–75 (1995)
6. Armstrong, J.: Peak-to-average power reduction for OFDM by repeated clipping and frequency domain filtering. Electron. Lett. **38**(5), 246–247 (2002)
7. Paterson, K.G., Paterson, V.: On the existence and construction of good codes with low peak-to-average power ratios. IEEE Trans. Inf. Theory **46**(6), 1974–1987 (2000)
8. Tong, G.: Peak-to-average power ratio reduction in OFDM: blind selected mapping for PSK inputs. In: IEEE ICASSP, pp. 293–296 (2006)
9. Reisi, N., Attari, M.A., Navid, R.: Embedded SI partial transmit sequence with improved bit error rate. In: IEEE 2nd International Conference on Electrical Engineering, March 2008
10. Jose, T.: Multicarrier Modulation with Low PAR: Applications to DSL and Wireless. Kluwer Academic Publishers, Dordrecht (2002). Norwell
11. Abera, W.G.: Comparative study of the performances of peak-to-average power ratio (PAPR) reduction techniques for orthogonal frequency division multiplexing (OFDM) signals. Master of Science thesis, Addis Ababa University, Faculty of Technology (2010)
12. Ochiai, H., Imai, H.: On the distribution of the peak-to-average power ratio in OFDM signals. IEEE Trans. Commun. **49**, 282–289 (2001)
13. Bäuml, R.W., Fisher, R.F.H., Huber, J.B.: Reducing the peak-to-average power ratio of multicarrier modulation by selected mapping. IEEE Electron. Lett. **32**(22), 2056–2057 (1996)
14. Kang, S.G., Kim, J.G., Joo, E.K.: A novel subblock partition scheme for partial transmit sequence OFDM. IEEE Trans. Broadcast. **45**(3), 333–338 (1999)
15. Cochran, W.T., et al.: What is the fast Fourier transform? IEEE Trans. Audio Electroacoust. **AU-15**(2), 45–55 (1967)

Techno-Economic Analysis of LTE Deployment Scenarios for Emerging City in Africa: A Case of Adama, Ethiopia

Dechasa Negash Fekadu[1][✉] and Beneyam Berehanu Haile[2][✉]

[1] Ethio Telecom, Addis Ababa, Ethiopia
dechasa.negash@ethiotelecom.et
[2] Addis Ababa Institute of Technology, Addis Ababa, Ethiopia
beneyamb.haile@aait.edu.et

Abstract. The exponential growth of mobile broadband demand in emerging cities has been pushing deployment of long-term evolution (LTE) mobile technology. LTE can have various deployment scenarios in terms of various factors including enabled features, bandwidth usage, transmission frequency, requirements and other factors. To plan and deploy comprehensively effective LTE network for a given city, undertaking techno-economic analysis (TEA) is a very important task for mobile operators. Various literature also presents TEA for LTE deployment for different network requirements and deployment environment. Yet, such LTE study is rare for African emerging cities and it has not been done for Ethiopian ones. In this paper, we first formulate potential LTE deployment scenarios for one of the emerging cities in Ethiopia called Adama. Then to thoroughly understand viability of the formulated deployment scenarios, we present TEA assuming 7 years study period and continuation of current monopoly telecom market in the city. For the analysis, we apply modified TERA model that is implemented in MATLAB. The payback period results show that deployment of LTE in the emerging city using 1800 MHz band under high and low capacity demand and using 2100 MHz band under only high capacity demand are economically viable as they have payback periods less than 3.5 years.

Keywords: LTE · Radio access network · Scenario planning · TERA · Techno-economic analysis · Adama · Ethiopia · Africa

1 Introduction

Mobile networks of most operators have been witnessing an unprecedented rise in data traffic globally [1]. This has been happening due to an increase in mobile user demand to access bandwidth-intensive content and increasing penetration of capable mobile devices such as smartphones and tablets. This data demand rise trend has been challenging mobile operators and their networks. Similar data demand growth trend has also been seen in Africa including Ethiopia [2].

To continuously meet the increasing data demand with satisfactory user experience, operators have been expanding their network infrastructure to include contemporary

© Springer Nature Switzerland AG 2019
F. Mekuria et al. (Eds.): ICT4DA 2019, CCIS 1026, pp. 213–226, 2019.
https://doi.org/10.1007/978-3-030-26630-1_18

mobile technology including long term evolution (LTE). LTE represents an important evolutionary step in the development of mobile technology while providing significant improvement in spectral efficiency, cost-per-bit, user data rate and an overall network capacity [3]. This is proved in its penetration rate and as of August 2018, there are around 712 and more than 102 commercial LTE networks globally and in Africa, respectively [4]. Most of the LTE networks in Africa are deployed in capital cities and in the coming years it is expected emerging cities of Africa other than the capitals get LTE services, following the increasing data demand in those cities. For instance, Ethiopia already has LTE in its capital Addis Ababa but not in other emerging cities including Adama, Bahir Dar, Mekelle and Hawassa.

Deployment of mobile technologies in Africa is commonly vendor driven and not supported by localized techno-economic analysis (TEA) that is very important to make viable decisions both technically and economically, very key for developing countries [5, 6, 12]. Yet, it is seldom to find techno-economic study of mobile technologies in African context. We believe related study for Africa is exemplary and important. Therefore, in this paper, we present TEA for potential LTE deployment scenarios for one of Ethiopian emerging cities, Adama using modified TERA model that is implemented in Matlab. The potential LTE deployment scenarios are also formulated using a scenario planning method that is presented in [8]. The TEA is undertaken considering 7 years study period and forecasting Adama's future mobile network environment. The TEA results show that deployment of LTE in Adama using 1800 MHz band under high and low capacity demand and using 2100 MHz band under only high capacity demand are economically viable with payback periods less than 3.5 years.

Remaining parts of the paper are organized as follows. Section 2 presents background on LTE and formulation of deployment scenarios for Adama. Section 3 provides modelling, assumptions and parameter values for the TEA. Then Sect. 4 presents TEA results and discussion which is followed by concluding remarks in Sect. 5.

2 LTE and Deployment Scenarios for Adama

2.1 Background on LTE

To insure high speed demand, 3GPP introduces its new radio access technology called LTE in 2004 to support extensively high throughput and low latency system with improved coverage and capacity performance compared to UMTS 3G systems [8]. LTE developed to satisfy a set of high-level requirements such as reduced cost per bit, simple architecture and open interfaces, flexibility usage of existed and future frequency band and enhanced user experience-more services with lower cost and high speed. LTE's network architecture is introduced to be all - internet Protocol based on simplified network architecture with open interfaces. Its architecture consists of the evolved Node B (eNodeB), evolved packet core (EPC) and user equipment (UE) as shown in Fig. 1. The eNodeB provides the evolved UMTS terrestrial radio access network (E-UTRA) user plane (UP) and control plane (CP) protocol terminations towards the UE. The eNodeB's are interconnected with each other by means of the

X2 - interface. The eNodeB's are connected by means of the S1 - interface to the EPC. The S1 - interface supports a many-to-many relation between eNodeB's and mobility management entity/serving-gateway (MME/SGWs).

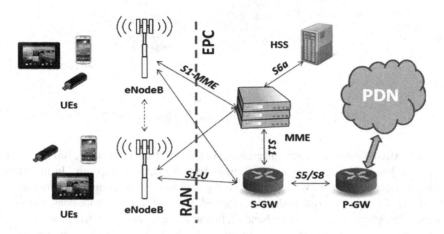

Fig. 1. LTE architecture [5, 7]

LTE is composed of several new technologies when compared to the previous cellular systems (2G/3G) such as multiple-input and multiple-output (MIMO), orthogonal frequency-division multiplexing (OFDM) and single carrier - frequency division multiple access (SC-FDMA). They enable LTE to be able to operate more efficiently with respect to the use of spectrum, and to provide the much higher data rates. LTE offers increased performance attributes, such as high peak data rates, low latency, and greater efficiencies in using the wireless spectrum over other wireless technologies [3].

2.2   LTE Deployment Scenarios for Adama

Adama city is one of emerging city in Ethiopia where potential customers revolve, hosts of many governmental and non-governmental conferences and center of trade next to capital city. In this city; high data rate capable technology such as LTE is vital for the development of the city and enhancement of quality of life in this era. Before proceeding to techno-economic analysis of LTE for Adama, we first need to formulate potential LTE deployment scenarios for the city using scenario planning method presented in [9, 10]. In this method, five important steps depicted in Fig. 2 are undertaken. Following scenario planning method; first the scope, time frame and actors are identified and defined for deployment of LTE in Adama city. Then, factors affecting LTE deployment in Adama city collected and analyzed using political, economic, social and technology (PEST) framework to find uncertain factors and events to deploy LTE in the city. Then, we formulate four potential LTE deployment scenarios using the two most important uncertainties and result is shown in Fig. 3.

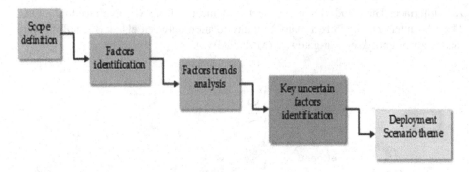

Fig. 2. General scenario planning in five phases [9]

The extrema value of each uncertain event defined as 1800 and 2100 MHz for frequency band, and high and low customers base for demand capacity. In uncertain events extrema value definition; global LTE popular band, handset operating frequency and status of currently existing devices (capability to support LTE) are considered. In addition, in-service spectrum extra bandwidth and its associated cost, trends of existing technology users and ethio telecom marketing plan into account for uncertain extrema definition. Threshold to say high and low demand capacity is defined based on 3G network capacity plan in the city (which is around 168,000 number of users). Then the scenarios defined further based on the other uncertainties and Adama context:

Deployment Scenario 1: Deployment of LTE in 1800 MHz under high demand capacity
Deployment Scenario 2: Deployment of LTE in 2100 MHz under high demand capacity
Deployment Scenario 3: Deployment of LTE in 1800 MHz under low demand capacity
Deployment Scenario 4: Deployment of LTE in 2100 MHz under low demand capacity.

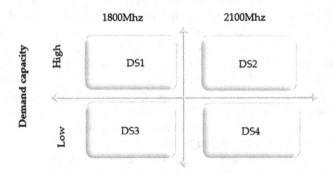

Fig. 3. Formulated LTE deployment scenarios

3 Techno-Economic Modeling and Assumptions

To analyze techno-economic viability of the potential deployment scenarios presented in Subsect. 2.2, we use modified TERA model that is shown in Fig. 4. TERA model is selected for this study as baseline model and widely used techno-economic model in wireless technology and industry [5–7]. We undertake minor modification of TERA model to improve the quality of inputs to suit our study. As shown in Fig. 4, the first part of model investigates marketing analysis which encompasses number of service users, the service user's penetration rate and revenue modeling parameters. The second component is the technology dimensioning which contains capacity and coverage dimensioning parameters. Capacity dimensioning requires input from two sides; from marketing section and the technology characteristics as per formulated deployment scenarios. Whereas, coverage analysis takes inputs of environmental condition and technology parameters to measure pathloss, system gain and loss. In the model, site number attained from both approaches are compared and taken as input to roll out plan to tune number of network elements inline to number of users forecasted within the study period. The third component is the economic part, this block modeled into two capital expenditure (CAPEX) and operational expenditures (OPEX) cost structures. The network dimensioning output, rollout plan and the associated network elements price is determined for CAPEX and OPEX cost modeling. Lastly, based on discount cash flow analysis, economic indicators like net present value (NPV), payback period (PP) and internal rate of return (IRR) are measured for each formulated deployment scenario.

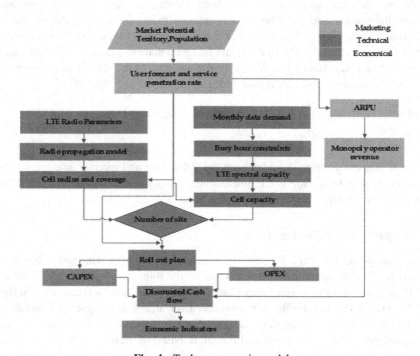

Fig. 4. Techno-economic model

3.1 Market Forecast

Understanding market segmentation, service profile and existing revenue collection is always the starting point for marketing forecasting as noted from different operators experience and literatures [5]. To forecast new technology service users', researchers frequently use the Bass-model. Bass model equation used in this study is stated below [11]. The coefficients determined in this paper in considering in-service technology service users' trends of past five years. Likewise, service penetration rate and operator revenue are projected in considering users forecast, service consumption level (monthly) and charging policy stated by operator. In this paper, market potential expressed with respect to current population of the city.

$$Y(t) = M\left[1 - e^{-t(P+Q)}\right] / [1 + [\frac{Q}{P}] e^{-t(P+Q)}] \tag{1}$$

Where, M is the market potential, P is innovation coefficient, Q is the imitation coefficient and Y(t) is the number of subscribers at a time t.

3.2 LTE Radio Link Budget Model

The target of the radio access network (RAN) dimensioning is to estimate the required site density and site configurations information. Dimension inputs can be broadly divided into three categories; quality, coverage and capacity-related inputs. Radio link budget has central importance to coverage planning in LTE [5–7]. The link budget calculations estimate the maximum allowed signal attenuation, called path loss, between the mobile and the base station antenna based on the required Signal-to-Interference-Noise Ratio (SINR) level at the receiver and by putting interference ad shadow into consideration. Detail radio link budget parameters assumptions considered in this study are summarized in Annex 1. We selected COST-231 Hata radio propagation model for coverage calculation and it is expressed as follow [8, 9].

$$PL(dB) = 46.3 + 33.9(f) - 13.82 \log(h_{BS}) + [44.9 - 6.55 \log(h_{BS})] \log(d) \\ - a(h_{UE})(c_m) \tag{2}$$

Where d is the distance (Km) between the transmitter and receiver antenna, f is the frequency used in MHz, h_{UE} is UE antenna height(m), h_{BS} is BTS antenna height(m), c_m is 0 dB for suburban and 3 dB for urban areas.

3.3 Capacity Dimensioning

To dimension the cell capacity, first it is essential to model data traffic based on monthly user's data consumption level. Accordingly, three user's categories (5, 10 and 15 GB) defined based on service usage ratio of 60, 30 and 10%, respectively. Further, 70/30% downlink/uplink traffic ratio considered for all users' categories. From these, average throughput per subscriber in busy hour is calculated using Eq. (3). Peak throughput per site in both uplink and downlink based on frame structure and coding rate is obtained using Eq. (4) [5, 11, 13]. The maximum number of users per site is calculated in considering users forecast, average throughput per subscribers and peak cell throughput for each formulated deployment scenarios. Hence, total number of sites obtained, in taking maximum number of subscribers from uplink and downlink.

$$\Omega(\text{Kbps}) = \rho * \alpha * \left(8\text{bit} * 10^6/30\,\text{day} * 24 * 60 * 60\right)$$
$$* \text{ Usage ratio of the services } * \frac{\text{UL}}{\text{DL}}\text{traffic ratio} \qquad (3)$$

$$\delta(\text{Mbps}) = \text{data RE/sec} * \text{bits per RE} * \text{MIMO effect} * \text{coding rate}$$
$$* \frac{\text{UL}}{\text{DL}}\text{Traffic ratio} \qquad (4)$$

Where Ω (Kbps) is average throughput per subscriber in busy hour (UL and DL), α is traffic ratio of busy hour to whole day traffic, ρ the traffic usage in Month/User. δ (Mbps) is the peak throughput per site per modulation, data RE/s is the data in resource element per second, coding rate indicates the volume coding rate of the channel code.

3.4 Cost and Revenue Modeling

The network cost generally splits into investments (CAPEX) and operational costs (OPEX). In techno-economic modelling, usually bottom-up approach is preferable and typically used when calculating investments cost. Whereas, operational costs are often modelled using a combination of the two approaches. CAPEX and OPEX cost modelled using Eqs. (5) and (6) [12, 13]. The cost of each parameter in CAPEX estimation was vendor specific. In this study, already deployed LTE network in Addis Ababa and industry standard per unit cost database considered for CAPEX cost estimation. Similarly, OPEX cost related to a certain project are often more difficult to predict. Therefore, the data for OPEX cost estimation mainly taken from annual OPEX report of currently in-service LTE network in Addis Ababa. In parallel, operator revenue also projected in consideration of number of service users forecasted, monthly data consumption level of each user and stated operator pricing policy (in this paper only service charging and connection fee parameters are considered).

$$CAPEX^{(i)} = \sum M_j^{(i)} C_j^{capex} \left(1 + P_j^{capex}\right)^{i-1} \qquad (5)$$

$$\text{OPEX}^{(i)} = \sum N_j^{(i)} C_j^{opex} \left(1 + P_j^{opex}\right)^{i-1} \qquad (6)$$

Where, $j \in$ (key components of CAPEX), $M_j^{(i)}$ is the number of items of type j purchased in year i, c_j^{capex} are the per-unit investment for each asset j in the 1st year, P_j^{capex} its yearly price trends and CAPEX$^{(i)}$ the investment in year I, $j \in$ (network driven and customer driven costs category parameters), $N_j^{(i)}$ is the number of items of type j operated during year i, $C_j^{(opex)}$ is Per unit operating cost for each asset j, P_j^{opex} j its yearly price trends.

3.5   Discounted Cash Flow Analysis

Commonly, if the return on investment is greater than total cost of ownership it is believed that the investment can make money. However, this approach is not enough to determine the feasibility of each formulated LTE deployment scenarios (DSs) as it only shows gross profit. Thus, we considered the economic feasibility indicators like net present value (NPV), internal rate of return (IRR), and payback period (PP) to maximize the decision indicators [5, 6]. All aforementioned economic indicators are calculated based on projected cash flow with in study period. In this paper, 13% discount rate considered for NPV calculation as it is a common value in most of literatures. From NPV rule, If NPV is positive, the formulated LTE DSs are economically feasible.

$$NPV = \sum_{t=0}^{T} \frac{CF_t}{(1+r)^t} \tag{7}$$

Where, t – the length of the study period, CFt – cash flow occurring in time period t and r – discount rate (industry average).

The IRR is the discount rate at which the present value of all future cash flow is equal to the initial investment. It is discount rate that makes NPV = 0. Whereas, PP is the number of years in which deployed LTE deployment scenarios takes before the cumulative incomes equal the initial investments.

4   Results and Discussion

The data service users forecast results for each formulated deployment scenario with in seven years period based on defined market potential depicted in Fig. 5(a). For user forecast, past five years existing technology service users' trends in Adama city considered. Consequently, 2% innovation and 40% imitation coefficients values attained to forecast LTE data service users in Adama city. Users forecast under deployment scenario 1 and 2 (DS1 and 2), and deployment scenario 3 and 4 (DS3 and 4) basis on the market potential (MP) of 100% and 50% respectively. In addition, $DS1_1$&$DS2_1$ and $DS3_1$&$DS4_1$ are specially considered formulated deployment scenarios based on 80% and 30% MP respectively. The service user's penetration rate result with respect to defined MP and projected population of the city depicted in Fig. 5(b). The service users' penetration rate is less than 10% at the starting period of the deployment and after 7 years it is estimated to reach 75% with respect to defined MP for all explicit deployment considered due to the network externality effect.

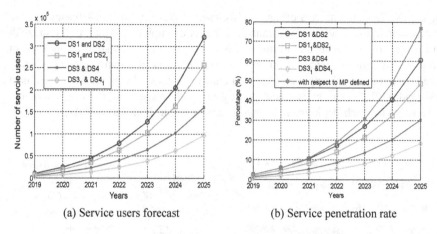

(a) Service users forecast   (b) Service penetration rate

Fig. 5. Service users forecast (a) and penetration rate (b)

Based on cell edge data rate target definition (i.e. 2 Mbps and 1 Mbps for downlink and uplink respectively), projected SINR at the cell edge are 1.06 and 1.55 dB for both downlink and uplink respectively. Estimated cell radius in both considered environmental model and center frequency via COST-231 propagation model was depicted in Fig. 6(a). Further, to comprise the effect of multipath, average cell radius taken for number of site calculation based on geographical information and environmental model defined. From obtained cell radius and defined area, urban environmental conditions required a high number of evolved Node B's to mitigate the loss due to a multipath effect of transmission system compared to suburban areas.

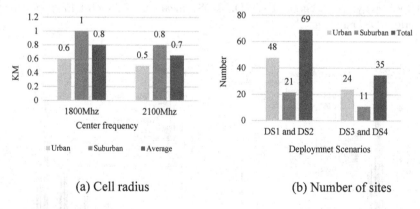

(a) Cell radius   (b) Number of sites

Fig. 6. Cell radius (a) and number of sites via capacity dimensioning (b)

To dimension network capacity, number of users at the end of the study period considered as input. Number of evolved Node B's via traffic model are depicted in Fig. 6(b). In result, average downlink throughput per subscriber is almost twice that of the uplink due to the natures of data service users. Likewise, downlink throughput was greater than uplink due to slower transmission mode in uplink. Further, to minimize the cost of network elements and to use existing resource wisely, existing technology site number and setup considered through overlay network deployment strategy. Also, 70/30 rollout approach applied for chosen number of sites. The initial year investments cost and OPEX cost breakdown percentage with respect to its key component parameters for each deployment scenarios are shown in Fig. 7(a) and (b).

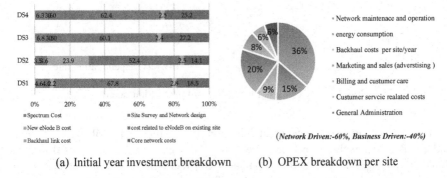

(a) Initial year investment breakdown   (b) OPEX breakdown per site

Fig. 7. Initial year investment cost and annual OPEX breakdown

Yearly CAPEX and OPEX cost trends within the study period is calculated in consideration of 5% yearly equipment price trends as shown in Fig. 8(a). In view of ethio telecom pricing policy and monthly users data consumption survey (1 GB for residential and 10 GB for enterprise user's category), operator revenue is projected in a monopoly telecom market as shown in Fig. 8(b). In Fig. 8(a), "O-DS1 means OPEX cost for deployment scenario 1 (DS1), C-DS1 means CAPEX cost for deployment scenario 1(DS1) and etc...".

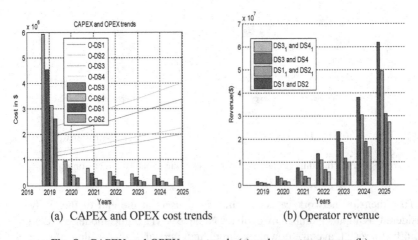

(a) CAPEX and OPEX cost trends   (b) Operator revenue

Fig. 8. CAPEX and OPEX cost trends (a) and operator revenue (b)

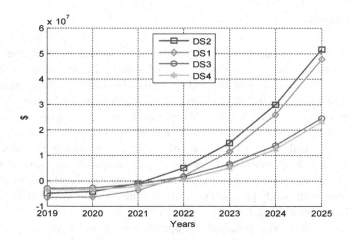

Fig. 9. Net present value (NPV)

As shown in Fig. 9, NPV is negative in the first three years and after the third year of the deployment, it is increases exponentially to high positive value. This exponential incremental arises due to the service user's behavior. Moreover, in all formulated deployment scenarios positive net present value recorded at the end of study period which indicates the economic feasibility of all formulated deployment scenarios. Similarly, as shown in Table 1, the obtained internal rate of return for all considered deployment scenarios are greater than 13% (value defined initially to calculate cash flow). Higher IRR values (greater than discount rate defined) indicates the economic feasibility of formulated deployment scenarios.

Table 1. Economic feasibility indicators value for each DS

	Deployment scenarios			
	DS1	DS2	DS3	DS4
Internal rate of return (IRR) (%)	82.1	68.4	72.7	65.3
Payback period (PP) (in years)	2.79	3.1	3.3	3.72

Moreover, the formulated LTE deployment scenarios are profitable and feasible if the payback period was in between 3 and 4 years (less than 3.5 years) in span 7 years as noted from several literatures. Hence, the payback period recorded for DS1, DS2, DS3 and DS4 are 2.79, 3.1, 3.3 and 3.72 years respectively. That means, the time (year) required to return the investment for deployment of LTE in an emerging city under DS1 is 2.79 years. Whereas, for the rest of LTE deployment scenarios the return on investments (ROI) achieved in 3.1, 3.3 and 3.72 years for DS2, DS3 and DS4 respectively.

5 Conclusion

Significantly increasing demand of innovative data service in emerging cities of developing countries is pushing deployment of state-of-the art mobile technologies including LTE. Yet, to be technically and economically viable, decisions on moving to LTE should be made after techno-economic study which is rare in the context of Africa mainly due to the common vendor driven mobile network deployment approach. Aiming to contribute in addressing this challenge, in this work we have presented techno-economic analysis of LTE for one of the emerging cities in Ethiopia, Adama. The analysis has been performed for formulated potential deployment scenarios (DSs) for the city assuming 7 years study period and continuation of existing monopoly telecom market in the study period. The analysis is made using modified TERA model that is implemented in Matlab.

From the results, market potential and operating frequency have a great impact on network capacity, coverage and number of evolved Node B which in turn influences the rate of return on investments in all formulated LTE deployment scenarios. In most of the explicit deployment, the system is coverage limited. And, for all formulated deployment scenarios, LTE data service users increases exponentially with slow start rate within the first three years of operation period. Likewise, total OPEX cost is greater than twice of CAPEX cost and high share of CAPEX cost taken by evolved Node B related cost due to chosen network deployment strategy (60–67%). Deployment of LTE in 1800 MHz band under high and low demand capacity and in 2100 MHz band under high demand capacity are feasible technically and economically for an emerging city with the payback period of less than 3.5 years within the span of 7 years operation duration. Additional, from specially considered formulated deployment scenarios, the optimistic and coverage favored deployment scenarios (in 1800 MHz band under high and low demand capacity) are the most feasible LTE DSs for an emerging city with payback period range of 3–3.25 years.

Annex 1

Detail radio link parameters assumptions.

Parameters	Variable for both UL and DL
Duplex Mode	FDD
Operating frequency	1800/2100
System Bandwidth (MHz)	20
Number of PRB per assigned BW	100 for 20
MIMO Scheme (MS)	1×2 UL, 2×2 DL
Cell Edge Rate (Mbps)	1 for UL, 2 for DL
Allocated RB at cell edge (10%)	10 for 20BW

(*continued*)

(continued)

Parameters	Variable for both UL and DL
Factor A	0.42 X2 for 2 × 2 MIMO, 0.42 for 1 × 2 MIMO
Factor B	0.85 for 2 × 2MIMO
PRB bandwidth (Mbps)	180 kHz
Rate per PRB (Mbit/s)	Cell edge/Allocated PRB
Required Spectral efficiency (bits/s/Hz)	Rate per PRB/PRB
SINR (LINEAR)	Factor B * (2^ (SE/Factor A)-1)
SINR (dB)	10 * log SINR(Linear)
eNodeB - UE	
Number of PRBs (10%)	10
Downlink data rate (Mbps)	1 for UL, 2 for DL
eNodeB TX power (dBm)	46
eNodeB antenna gain (dBi)	∼18
eNodeB antenna cable loss (dB)	1–2
EIRP (dB)	=gains − losses
UE receiver characteristics	
UE noise figure (dB)	∼7 dB
Thermal noise	B * T * PRB * BW
Receiver noise floor (dBm)	NF + B * T * PRB * BW
Required SINR (dB)	10 * log SINR(Factor B * (2^ (SE/Factor A) − 1))
Receiver sensitivity	Required SINR+ Receiver Noise
Control channel overhead (dB)	5%–25% (1 dB–4 dB overhead)
Rx antenna gain	0 for handset
Body loss	3–5 dB
Environmental characteristics	
Indoor Penetration Loss (dB)	12–16 dB
Cell Edge Coverage Probability (%)	90–95%
Shadowing Margin (dB)	9.25–10.5
Interference margin (dB)	5–8
Maximum Allowed propagation loss (MAPL) (dB)	=gains − losses

References

1. Cisco: Global mobile data traffic forecast update 2016–2021 (2017). https://www.cisco.com/c/en/us/solutions/collateral/service-provider/visual-networking-index-vni/mobile-white-paper-c11-520862.html. Accessed 10 Oct 2018
2. Haile, B.B., Bulti, D.A., Zerihun, B.M.: On the relevance of capacity enhancing 5G technologies for Ethiopia. In: ICT Annual Conference (EICTC-2017), Addis Ababa, Ethiopia. https://www.researchgate.net/publication/320730399_On_the_Relevance_of_Capacity_Enhancing_5G_Technologies_for_Ethiopia. Accesses 10 Oct 2018

3. Knoll, T.: LTE network design from a techno-economic perspective. LTE-business-model, pp. 1–68 (2012)
4. Global Mobile Suppliers Association (GSA): Evolution from LTE to 5G: global market status, January 2019. https://gsacom.com/paper/evolution-lte-5g-2/. Accessed 02 Feb 2019
5. Fekadu, D.N.: Techno-economic analysis of LTE deployment scenarios for emerging city: a case of Adama, Ethiopia. Master's thesis. AAiT, Addis Ababa, Ethiopia 2018 (2014)
6. Smura, T.: Techno-economic modelling of wireless network and industry architectures. Doctoral dissertations. Aalto University School Electrical Engineering, Helsinki (2012)
7. Frias, Z., Pérez, J.: Techno-economic analysis of femtocell deployment in long-term evolution networks. EURASIP J. Wirel. Commun. Netw. **2012**, 1–15 (2012)
8. GPP Website: 3GPP technologies. http://www.3gpp.org/techneologies. Accessed 23 Feb 2018
9. Schoemaker, P.: Scenario planning: a tool for strategic thinking. Sloan Manag. Rev. **36**, 36–40 (1995)
10. Haile, B.B.: Development of the Wi-Fi offloading business concept within the African market context, Addis Ababa, Ethiopia (2012)
11. Sokele, M.: Analytical method for forecasting of telecommunications service life-cycle quantitative factors. Doctoral dissertations. University of Zagreb, Croatia (2009)
12. Vidal, J., Pérez, J., Agustín, A., Marina, N., Høst-Madsen, A.: Technoeconomic evaluation of cooperative relaying transmission techniques in OFDM cellular networks. EURASIP J. Adv. Signal Process. **60** (2012)
13. Arif, M., Yameen, M., Matin, A.: Femtocell suburban deployment in LTE networks. Int. J. Inf. Electron. Eng. **3**(2), 208 (2013)

SAMoC: Self-aware Access Monitoring and Controlling Framework for Android

Nanda Kumar Thanigaivelan, Ethiopia Nigussie$^{(\boxtimes)}$, Seppo Virtanen, and Jouni Isoaho

Department of Future Technologies, University of Turku, Turku, Finland
{nakuth,ethnig,seppo.virtanen,jisoaho}@utu.fi

Abstract. We present the concept and specification of a self-aware access monitoring and controlling framework for Android. The lack of users' security awareness, Android operating system's security limitations and the widespread use of Android for personal and organizational activities emphasizes the importance of improving its security. The proposed SAMoC framework strengthens the security of Android through learning based operation refinements. The introduction of a monitoring agent on each resource and a self-aware layer in the Android software stack allows to detect unexpected events and perform fine-grained access control over the resources. The self-aware layer can automatically refine the policies or provide suggestions depending on its configuration. The SAMoC framework enforces specific restrictions on an individual user basis and allows the users to play a role in the system operation optimization due to its transparent nature.

Keywords: Self-aware security · Mobile security · Access control

1 Introduction

Mobile devices are becoming the dominant devices for communication and online service consumption among individual users and organizations. The exponential growth in the number and diversity of the available applications is the main reason for widespread popularity of mobile devices. The increase in popularity of mobile devices along with users' limited security awareness, and operating system vulnerabilities make these devices easy target for security attacks. An increasing number of organizations is allowing employees to access the enterprise's resources through mobile devices and even encouraging to use their own devices (Bring Your own Devices (BYoD)). In addition to enterprise apps, a number of other apps from various channels may also be installed in the same device, exposing the enterprise to numerous security threats and attack vectors.

This work focuses on access control for Android based mobile devices to ensure their security. Android is an open-source operating system developed based on the Linux kernel [1]. The Android operating system deploys mechanisms such as application sandboxing and the Android permission model. The

© Springer Nature Switzerland AG 2019
F. Mekuria et al. (Eds.): ICT4DA 2019, CCIS 1026, pp. 227–238, 2019.
https://doi.org/10.1007/978-3-030-26630-1_19

sandboxing provides application isolation and containment using Linux access control and process protection mechanisms. The permission model restricts an application's capabilities by regulating sensitive API calls that access protected resources. Permissions to access certain resources are granted during first access request. Users tend to approve all requested permissions since the users may not understand fully the consequences. Though runtime permission revocation is introduced in Android 6.0. it still fails to allow fine grained permission control. Third-party libraries (for example, advertisement and analytics) cannot be prevented from abusing the granted permissions of their host apps because of the unavailability of separation mechanisms. In other words, Android lacks runtime configurable access control for preventing an application from accessing any open interfaces of another application and abusing its granted permissions.

The future mobile devices will be part of the internet-of-things (IoT) and they can operate as sensing, actuating, and intermediate gateway devices in IoT. Intercommunication among mobile devices is highly likely in future IoT applications. These activities will enhance the roles and usage of mobile devices which makes them an attractive target for attacks since the impact of attacks can be higher. Therefore, it is necessary to come up with a system which is able to reconfigure and adapt its operation to ever evolving threat. To counter such circumstances, the system has to be self-aware.

In this work, we present the concept and specification of a self-aware access monitoring and controlling framework for Android. The main working principle of the framework is to monitor, to learn and then to refine existing policies or defining new ones at runtime. A self-aware layer is introduced in the Android software stack with the sole intention of learning from the monitored information and implementing appropriate controlling measures. The contributions of this work are as follows:

- Introduction and adaptation of self-awareness in Android Mandatory Access Control (MAC): to detect and/or prevent unexpected events including the current and future intentional or unintentional malicious activities and resource abuses.
- Self-optimization of operations: through continuous monitoring and learning, the framework defines new access policies or refines existing policies which in turn optimizes the operation and resource usage.
- Multiuser environment support: to allow enforcing different restriction policies and customizing them accordingly for each user account in a single device.

The rest of the paper is structured as follows. Android and its security limitations are presented in Sect. 2. The key features of the proposed self-aware access monitoring and controlling (SAMoC) framework are discussed in Sect. 3. The concept of self-awareness in general and its importance in Android security context are explained in Sect. 4. The detailed specification of the SAMoC framework is presented in Sect. 5. Finally, discussion and conclusion are presented in Sects. 6 and 7, respectively.

2   Android and Its Security Limitations

Android is a Linux-based open source mobile operating system, developed by Open Handset Alliance led by Google. The Linux kernel is customized for Android to provide features such as Binder, asynchronous shared memory, process memory allocator and power management. The kernel layer acts as a hardware abstraction layer and provides various services such as networking, file system and device drivers. The middleware layer consists of Android framework, native and runtime libraries including Android Runtime (ART). It is responsible for handling application life cycle management and other system services along with the access restrictions on application resource accessibility. The application layer hosts the core/system applications and other applications written by Android developers. In addition to Java, developers can use C/C++ through the Java Native Interface (JNI). The Android application architecture is unique in such a way that it is designed to provide application compatibility, portability and security.

2.1   Android Security Model

Since Android is Linux-based operating system, it inherits user resource isolation and process isolation from Linux. Android extends the user resource isolation feature by extending to application level. Under this modification, each application is assigned with unique ID (UID) upon installation and executes it as a dedicated process using the same UID. Also, dedicated data directory for its resources is given and restricts to access other files unless explicitly permitted. The system resources such as daemons and system applications are owned either by system or root user and executed under pre-defined UID. Thus, it achieves isolation in terms of both process level as well as file level.

Due to the isolation, application cannot access any resources other than their own resources. In order to provide access to the resources such as internet connectivity, data and hardware features, Android introduced access rights in the form of permissions. Application required to access those features need to obtain appropriate permission and the developer must declare the required permission in the AndroidManifest. Android offers 130 permissions and also allow developers to define their own permissions to enforce access restrictions on their application's critical application resources [7]. Android framework enforces access verification during runtime to ensure applications has appropriate access rights. There are few permissions which are not monitored by the Android framework since they are mapped to the low level operating system control.

2.2   Limitations

Isolation of applications and their resource accessibility is contained through application sandboxing. Android also caters permission to access other resources in order to capitalize their features for enhancing user experiences. Due to its popularity and continuous increase in user base, it has attracted the attention of research community to identify the vulnerabilities and possible solutions [2–5,8–10]. Also, it has gained the attention of adversaries, who aim to exploit the vulnerabilities for their own benefits. To enhance the security through the enforcement of MAC at kernel layer, SE Linux is introduced into the Android platform since version 4.3 (as SEAndroid). The implementation of SE Linux is still evolving in Android from permissive mode in version 4.3 to full enforcement mode in version 5.0. SEAndroid provides huge advantage in protecting the device, for example, it has the capability to prevent application installation based on its signatures [6]. However, it is not possible to define the certificates for all available applications in the policy. Extending SE Linux to cover the Android's middleware is challenging mainly because of implementations complexity as well as requiring an invasive and costly set of changes [6]. Due to these constraints the middleware is loosely protected by Android's default security model. SE Linux also requires specialized skills for implementing and enforcing policies.

From version 6.0 onwards, several enhancements are introduced and one example is runtime permission revocation. It allows users to change (grant or revoke) the status of the applications' permissions as needed. This is one important step in improving security but it fails to provide fine granularity for controlling the resources. In this work, we are presenting a framework which provide fine granular access control, and more controllable system features.

3   Key Features of SAMoC Framework

A self-aware system is capable of knowing its environment, the on-going activities and implementing appropriate corrective measures at run-time in order to achieve and maintain the required performance. By introducing a self-aware concept in mobile MAC, we are aiming to achieve the following main goals:

- Self-awareness: to reduce user intervention in security policy enforcement and maintenance by creating self-aware components. These components can access logs, learn, able to predict unexpected behaviors/events, and refine/define new policies accordingly.
- Highly refined policies: to attain higher granularity in policy refinement, access restriction enforcement based on the resource features rather than the enforcement on application level or resource level will be introduced. For example, in the proposed framework, instead of blocking entire internet access resource, it is possible to allow certain protocol on particular port(s) and deny the rest of the protocol for an application.
- BYOD and parental solutions: The system will provide multi-user support and it is tightly coupled with device users. This allows enforcement of different sets of control policies and customization of each policy set for individual user account in a device.
- Improved system resilience: The integration of five subsystems into the framework (application installation and monitor, device resource controller, communication controller, self-aware subsystem, and SAMoC user interface)

enhances the system's resiliency by allowing to run atleast one subsystem continuously. The user can decided to enable/disable the certain subsystem(s)/policies and keep the rest active all the time.

- Easy to use: since there is no predefined structure/syntax for writing most of the policies, the personal users can easily adopt to the system.
- Transparency: Allowing device users to access the system logs and the enforced policies enables the users to understand behind-the-scene operations either fully or partially depending on their knowledge.

4   Adaptation of Self-awareness in Security Context

A number of researches have been conducted and many solutions have been proposed to thwart the threats in the Android but most of them are concentrated on either providing resource access restriction or prevention of identified threats and few works target both cases [5,6]. The existing research on mobile security fail to recognize the assimilation of mobile devices in IoT and the resulting change in the mobile usage landscape. Mobile device are part of IoT and play an important role in IoT as a sensing, actuating, and/or intermediate gateway. The interoperability of mobile in IoT is facilitated due to the introduction of 6lowPAN based wireless sensor networks. There is also on-going effort to connect IP networks through bluetooth low energy [11,12]. One potential example of this integration is the possibility of gathering information through crowd sensing by using the sensors available in the mobile devices along with other sensor networks [13,14]. Intercommunication between the mobile devices is highly likely in future IoT applications. In these circumstances, it is difficult to know the security threats beforehand. In order to protect the device resources, we need to develop a system which is capable of self-reconfiguration and self-adaptation. To realize this objective, we have to make the system self-aware.

Any system which has the capability to learn and adapt itself through monitoring its own operations and environment is termed as self-aware system. Implementation of self-aware systems is not an easy task but they can offer numerous benefits upon proper employment.

4.1   Self-awareness in Security Context

The advantages of self-awareness especially detection and prevention of malicious activities through monitoring and learning are critical to the security of the systems since threats or threat sources are dynamic and evolving. To capitalize on these benefits, we have adapted the self-awareness into the security context. The customized self-aware agent is shown the Fig. 1.

The self-aware agent comprises of five components and the tasks of each component are described as follows.

Self-configure: the purpose of self-configuration is to update the settings of the self-aware agent components by considering the previous and current circumstances to ensure the required objectives are fulfilled with minimal overheads.

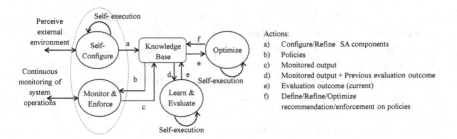

Fig. 1. Customized self-aware agent for security context

The self-configure component is also responsible for guiding the rest of self-aware agent components execution for efficient power and device usability. It will oversee the internal and external factors such as peek device usage, active and idle duration, and then define/refine execution period for itself, *Learn and Evaluate* and *Optimize* components.

Monitor and Enforce: it engages in continuous observation and enforcement of the policies on the systems activities. It ensures that the applications behavior and system resources accessibility conform with the provided policies. It is also responsible for transferring the observation to the *Knowledge Base (KB)*. The information observed by this component will be used as a basis for the *Learn and Evaluate* component.

Learn and Evaluate: this component has two operating phases. In the learning phase, information gathered by *Monitor and Enforce* component are analyzed in order to derive the common system behavior patterns. On successive execution of this phase, it will generate a new pattern if there is a change in the systems application behavior, otherwise the same common pattern will be generated. In the evaluate phase, the identified pattern is compared against the common patterns. Upon on detection of deviation, it will construct appropriate changes and submit the recommended changes to the *KB*.

Optimize: this component examines the recommendations provided by the *Learn and Evaluate* component and change the policies accordingly or provide them as suggestions to the user depending on the chosen configuration. It is also responsible for restoring the policies to the previous states if the applied changes fails to fullfill the requirement.

Knowledge Base: is used as a storage space for all activities. It contains the policies, system activities as logs, derived patterns, and policy recommendations, along with the setting configuration of the self-aware agent. As can be seen from Fig. 1, all the inputs and outputs for the other four components of self-aware agent are from and to the *KB*.

5   SAMoC Framework Specification

The primary objective of the proposed framework is to achieve higher degree of security by inhibiting malicious or unintended activities through highly refined policy enforcement, self-learning, and self-reconfiguration. The system which is developed by incorporating the SAMoC framework will reduce the requirement for human involvement in making more appropriate decisions which in turn improve the security of the mobile device as well as system usability. The framework engages in continuous monitoring of the resources and communication channels to ensure that all apps are working appropriately according to the defined policies. It also performs periodic assessment of monitored information as this is necessary for policies and processes refinement. Since the framework will be ingrained into the Android platform, it will start functioning upon device boot. The framework operates along with Android's default security implementation.

5.1 Assumptions

As in other system developments, we have defined certain assumptions to ensure proper functioning of the system. The users and administrators who are configuring the polices are fully trusted and they required to posses knowledge on system functionality principles. We assume that no application is granted root permission and the device will not be rooted in any circumstances as this may result in applications to abuse system resources intentionally or unintentionally. The Android operating system and the components that we are introducing are fully trusted.

5.2 SAMoC Mobile

The mobile part consists of the following components: handlers, self-aware components and synchronization components. The architecture of the SAMoC mobile is shown in Fig. 2.

Handlers: The handlers consist of two major components: policy handlers and event-log handlers. They play a crucial role in the framework since all the communication towards logs and policies are directed by them. Policy handlers are responsible for providing appropriate policy to the monitoring and enforcing component to act upon the resources. Event-log handlers perform log maintenance by allowing other SAMoC mobile components to read or write the logs as and when they needed.

Self-aware Component: Self-aware component is the core of the framework. It comprises of self-configuration, monitoring and enforcing components, evaluation and optimization components. The self-configuration component is responsible for guiding the rest of self-aware components by updating their execution settings. Monitoring and enforcing enhances the normal Android execution flow by placing appropriate hooks in the Android components which are responsible for handling applications and their device services accessing capabilities. The evaluation component is responsible for making policy recommendations by accessing the logs, identifying the correlation and establishing relationship among the correlated information. The optimization component will refine the existing policies, define new policies or recommend changes to the user based on the recommendations provided by the evaluation component.

Synchronization Components: Synchronization component is responsible for handling request access to the policies by the SAMoC UI. In addition, it will also handle compression, decompression and purging old logs from the repository.

Repository is a storage component which contains the policies and logs generated by the framework components. It will also acts as knowledge base for self-aware components by storing and retrieving the settings required for their self-execution, behavioural patterns and policy recommendations.

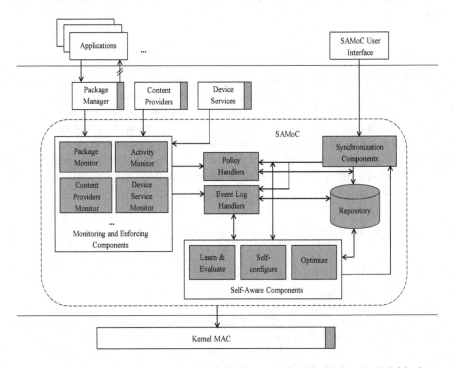

Fig. 2. Mobile software stack with SAMoC framework. The fully shaded blocks are the proposed new modules of the framework and the partially shaded blocks consist of framework module extensions in Android.

5.3 SAMoC Mobile Subsystems

One of the goals of the framework is to guarantee the existence of least degree of security at any time in order to maintain system resiliency. In order to achieve this goal, SAMoC mobile is classified into five subsystems: application installation and monitor, device resource controller, communication controller, self-aware subsystem and SAMoC user interface. The subsystems relies on different components and in certain cases, they can share the same components for the fulfilment their operations.

Application installation and monitor subsystem is responsible for handling the applications related activities including installation restriction and inter-communication between the applications.

Device resource controller functions are responsible to oversee the resource accessibility by the applications and enforce appropriate policies to restrict the access.

Communication controller will regulate the applications communication with external networks. It is in charge for allowing or refusing the outside connections based on the protocols and networks.

Self-aware subsystem observes the external environment and configure its own operations accordingly. It will also access logs, learn, create and test the established patterns, construct and apply/revoke suggestions to improve the framework operations.

SAMoC user interface is the interface application for SAMoC mobile which provides appropriate user interfaces for different subsystems. The user is able to control the subsystems or access logs through the interface.

5.4   SAMoC Mobile Software Architecture

In order to reduce development complexity as well as future enhancement and maintenance, we have adopted layered architecture for the implementation. The layered architecture allows to have complete control over the SAMoC mobile components individually and it is easier to add additional components in future. The architecture also helps in restricting the visibility of the implementations. The SAMoC mobile software architecture is shown in Fig. 3.

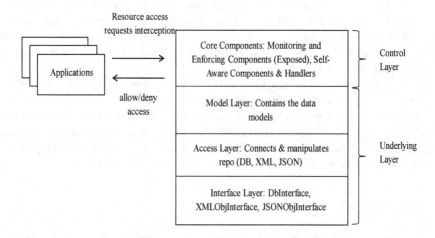

Fig. 3. SAMoC mobile software architecture

The entire architecture is grouped into two layers: control layer and underlying layer. The control layer contains all the implementation of the SAMoC mobile components (handlers, self-aware component and synchronization). The visibility of the handlers and self-aware component except the monitoring and enforcing tasks are hidden. The monitoring and enforcing components are visible and hooked into the Android's system service implementations while synchronization component provides interface to SAMoC application (SAMoC user interface). Using SAMoC user interface, users are able to perform administration tasks, such as writing policies and reviewing logs. It will be installed by default as system application in Android operating system.

The underlying layer comprises of three sublayers (Model, Access and Interface Layers) which contains the basic classes required to manipulate the repository. The model layer represents the data models of the database tables and XML structures. The access layer will manipulate the repository objects whose references will be provided by the interface layer. The Control layer components use the models to store/retrieve the information by calling the Access layer methods which in turn get the appropriate reference on the information objects from the Interface layer.

5.5 SAMoC Mobile Policy

SAMoC mobile policies are highly refined which restrict access to resources using its very own features. The efficiency of the framework depends on the policies available in the repository which will be defined by the users. The defined policies play a crucial role in determining the system efficiency during initial phase of its operations. There are certain control policies which will be delivered as settings to control the self-aware agent behaviors such as automatic enforcement of learned changes or provide them as recommendation to the user.

There are no pre-defined profiles/profile names in the SAMoC framework but pre-defined policies are available. SAMoC framework has default policies which will be enforced upon device boot for example denial of non-market application installation and denial of adb install command. Policies are created and enforced on individual account basis.

SAMoC framework does not force users to learn/develop special skills before using the system since most of the policies do not have any syntax or pre-defined structure. One of the goals of SAMoC is to make the system easy to use even for the user who has limited knowledge. To realize this, most of the policies will configured through the SAMoC user interface application. It will provide appropriate user interface in the form of settings for policy writing.

6 Challenges

At the current development stage, self-awareness including self-configuration of the self-aware agent is adopted. The self-configuration allows to configure and adapt the learn and evaluate processes, and to optimize the components of the

the construction of the reduction, we know that in all the traces of (P, ann), all the possible combinations of interpreting the propositions belonging to φ are considered.

Therefore, since the obligation $\langle \mathcal{O}^a l_{test}, \varphi, \perp \rangle$ is fulfilled by at least a trace and each trace corresponds to an interpretation, it follows from Definition 10 that φ is indeed satisfiable by the interpretation corresponding to the execution satisfying the obligation.

Proof. **Completeness:** φ is satisfiable $\Rightarrow (P, \mathsf{ann}) \not\vdash^P \mathbb{O}$.

From the construction of the reduction we know that the condition of the only obligation contained in $\mathbb{O}$ is constituted by φ. However, from the hypothesis we know that φ is satisfiable. Hence, according to Definition 6 such obligation is fulfilled by at least an interpretation of its proposition. Therefore, as by construction the process contains every possible interpretation for the formulae being analysed, and from Definition 7 it follows that if φ is satisfiable, then the compliance problem constructed using the reduction results in partial compliance, as one execution must fulfil the obligation.

A.3   NP Hardness of 1G+

We reduce the satisfiability problem to proving partial regulatory compliance for **1G+**.

Reduction. Let φ be a propositional formula for which we want to verify whether it is satisfiable, and let L be the set of propositions in φ. For each proposition l belonging to L, we construct an XOR block containing two tasks, one labelled and containing in its annotation the positive proposition (i.e. l) and the other the negative counterpart (i.e. $\neg l$). All the XOR blocks constructed from L are then included within a single AND block.

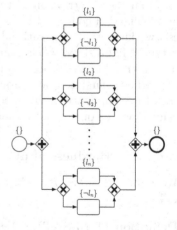

The set of obligations, to which the constructed process has to be verified to be fully compliant with, is composed of a single obligation constructed as follows from the propositional formula φ: $\langle \mathcal{O}^a \varphi \rangle$. We claim that there exists a trace $\theta \in \Theta(P, \mathsf{ann})$ such that $\theta \vdash \mathbb{O}$ if and only if φ is satisfiable.

Fig. 4. Process for **1G+** reduction.

Note that differently from the construction shown in Fig. 3, we do not need to include a *test* task to trigger the verification, as the obligation being global means that it is always in force and its condition is required to be achieved by the end of the execution.

Reduction Complexity: As the reduction is similar to the one used for **1L+**, the translation complexity is the same, which is in time polynomial with respect to the size of the formula φ.

Correctness. Here we prove the soundness $((P, \mathsf{ann}) \vdash^{\mathsf{P}} \mathbb{O} \Rightarrow \varphi$ is satisfiable) and the completeness (φ is satisfiable $\Rightarrow (P, \mathsf{ann}) \vdash^{\mathsf{P}} \mathbb{O}$) of our reduction.

Proof. **Soundness:** $(P, \mathsf{ann}) \vdash^{\mathsf{P}} \mathbb{O} \Rightarrow \varphi$ is satisfiable.

From the hypothesis and Definition 7, we know that there exists a trace of the business process model (P, ann) that fulfils the obligation in $\mathbb{O}$. Following from the construction of the reduction we know that the only obligation belonging to $\mathbb{O}$ is $\langle \mathcal{O}^a \varphi \rangle$.

From Definition 4 and the construction of the reduction we know that each trace of P contains a task related to the truth value for each literal appearing in φ. Moreover, again from the construction of the reduction, we know that in all the traces of (P, ann) all the possible combinations of interpreting the propositions belonging to φ are considered.

Therefore, since the obligation $\langle \mathcal{O}^a \varphi \rangle$ is fulfilled by at least a trace and each trace corresponds to an interpretation, it follows from Definition 10 that φ is indeed satisfiable by the interpretation corresponding to the execution satisfying the obligation.

Proof. **Completeness:** φ is satisfiable $\Rightarrow (P, \mathsf{ann}) \vdash^{\mathsf{P}} \mathbb{O}$.

From the construction of the reduction we know that the condition of the only obligation contained in $\mathbb{O}$ is constituted by φ. However, from the hypothesis we know that φ is satisfiable. Hence, according to Definition 6, such obligation is fulfilled by at least an interpretation of its proposition. Therefore, as by construction the process contains every possible interpretation for the formulae being analysed, and from Definition 7, it follows that if φ is satisfiable, then the compliance problem constructed using the reduction results in partial compliance, as one execution must fulfil the obligation.

A.4   NP Hardness of nG-

We reduce the *3-SAT* problem to proving partial regulatory compliance for nG−.

Definition 11 (3-SAT). *A propositional formula is in 3-CNF (Conjunctive Normal Form) if it is of the form $\alpha_1 \wedge \alpha_2 \wedge ... \wedge \alpha_k$ where each α_i is a disjunction of three or less literals. A propositional formula is in 3-SAT if it is in 3-CNF form and is also satisfiable.*

Reduction. Let 3-CNF : $\alpha_1 \wedge \alpha_2 \wedge ... \wedge \alpha_k$ be a propositional formula in 3-CNF, as shown in Fig. 5, for which we want to verify whether it is satisfiable or not, as described in Definition 11.

For each proposition l_i belonging to 3-CNF, we construct an XOR block containing two tasks, one labelled and containing in its annotation the positive proposition (i.e. a literal l_i) and the other the negative counterpart (i.e. its negation $\neg l_i$). All the XOR blocks constructed from L are then included within a single AND block. This

$$\underbrace{\{l_1 \vee l_2 \vee l_3\}}_{\alpha_1} \wedge \underbrace{\{\ldots\}}_{\alpha_2} \wedge \cdots$$

Fig. 5. 3-SAT formula

results in the same process model construction used in the computational complexity proof for **1G+** as graphically represented in Fig. 4.

For each clause α_i in 3-CNF, a global achievement obligation is created and its condition is set to the literal l_{α_i}, referring to the identifier of the clause. For each literal l_j in a clause α_i a *count as* rule is created as follows: $l_j \Rightarrow l_{\alpha_i}$.

Definition 12 (Count As Rule). *Consider a count as rule:* $\alpha \Rightarrow \beta$, *where* α *and* β *are literals. If* α *is true in the process' state, then the process' state is considered to contain* β.

Notice that the introduction of *count as* in such atomic version (meaning a literal to literal interpretation) does not increase the computational complexity of the problem **nG−**, as such interpretation can be computed in polynomial time while using Algorithm 1 to verify a trace in the reduced problem **nG−**.

Reduction Complexity: The construction of the process model in the reduction is the same as the one used for **1G+**. Differently, the regulatory framework is built by creating a set of obligations and count as rules. Still, constructing the regulatory framework is in time polynomial with respect to the size of 3-CNF. Therefore, the entire reduction is polynomial.

Correctness. Here we prove the soundness $((P, \text{ann}) \vdash^P \mathbb{O} \Rightarrow$ 3-CNF is satisfiable) and the completeness (φ is satisfiable $\Rightarrow (P, \text{ann}) \vdash^P \mathbb{O}$) of our reduction.

Proof. **Soundness:** $(P, \text{ann}) \vdash^P \mathbb{O} \Rightarrow$ 3-CNF is satisfiable.

From the hypothesis and Definition 7 we know that there exists a trace of the business process model (P, ann) that fulfils the obligation in $\mathbb{O}$. Following from the construction of the reduction we know that each obligation in $\mathbb{O}$ is in the form of $\langle \mathcal{O}^a C_i \rangle$.

Moreover, from the construction of the reduction, we know that for each literal in a clause of the 3-CNF formula, a count as rule is created having the literal in its condition and the clause identifier in the conclusion. As each of the obligations in $\mathbb{O}$ is satisfied and the literals used in the condition of the elements of the obligations cannot directly appear in the process' execution state, the condition of at least one of the count as rules associated to a clause must be true in a execution state of the process.

From Definition 4 and the construction of the reduction we know that each trace of P contains a task related to the truth value for each literal appearing in the 3-CNF formula. Moreover, again from the construction of the reduction, we know that in all the traces of (P, ann), all the possible combinations of interpreting the propositions belonging to the 3-CNF formula are considered. Additionally, we also know that: let $\mathcal{I}$ be the final interpretation holding at the end of an execution and let $\mathcal{I}_i$ be an intermediate interpretation, then the following is true $\mathcal{I} \models \mathcal{I}_{i+1} \models \mathcal{I}_i$ for any i.

Therefore, as the interpretation holding at $\mathcal{I}$ is a possible interpretation of the literals in the 3-CNF formula, and the partial interpretation are not in contradiction with the final one, it follows from Definition 11 that the 3-CNF formula is indeed satisfiable by the interpretation corresponding to the execution satisfying the obligations since the obligations $\langle \mathcal{O}^a l_{\alpha_i} \rangle$ are all fulfilled by at least a trace and each trace corresponds to an interpretation, where at least one of the literals in each of the clauses is true.

Proof. **Completeness:** 3-CNF is satisfiable $\Rightarrow (P, \text{ann}) \models^P \mathbb{O}$

From the construction of the reduction we know that the obligations contained in $\mathbb{O}$ are constituted by $\langle \mathcal{O}^a l_{\alpha_i} \rangle$. However, from the hypothesis we know that $\alpha_1 \wedge \alpha_2 \wedge \ldots \wedge \alpha_k$ is satisfiable. Hence, according to Definition 6, such obligation is fulfilled by at least an interpretation of its proposition. Moreover, from the construction of the reduction, we know that each literal in a clause forms the condition of a count as rule having the condition of one of the global obligations in its conclusion.

Therefore, as by construction the process contains every possible interpretation for the formulae being analysed, and from the hypothesis we know that $\alpha_1 \wedge \alpha_2 \wedge \ldots \wedge \alpha_k$ is satisfiable, then each clause α_i is satisfied, meaning that one of the disjunct propositions in α_i must be true in the interpretation.

From the construction, and given that there exists an interpretation satisfying the condition of at least a count as rule for each clause, then it follows that each obligation $\langle \mathcal{O}^a l_{\alpha_i} \rangle$ is satisfied. Thus, from Definition 7 it follows that if the 3-CNF is satisfiable then the compliance problem constructed using the reduction results in partial compliance, as one execution must fulfil the obligations.

References

1. Aalst, W.M.P.: Verification of workflow nets. In: Azéma, P., Balbo, G. (eds.) ICATPN 1997. LNCS, vol. 1248, pp. 407–426. Springer, Heidelberg (1997). https://doi.org/10.1007/3-540-63139-9_48
2. Alchourrón, C.E., Gärdenfors, P., Makinson, D.: On the logic of theory change: partial meet contraction and revision functions. J. Symbolic Logic **50**(2), 510–530 (1985)
3. Awad, A., Decker, G., Weske, M.: Efficient compliance checking using BPMN-Q and temporal logic. In: Dumas, M., Reichert, M., Shan, M.-C. (eds.) BPM 2008. LNCS, vol. 5240, pp. 326–341. Springer, Heidelberg (2008). https://doi.org/10.1007/978-3-540-85758-7_24
4. Choi, Y., Zhao, J.L.: Decomposition-based verification of cyclic workflows. In: Peled, D.A., Tsay, Y.-K. (eds.) ATVA 2005. LNCS, vol. 3707, pp. 84–98. Springer, Heidelberg (2005). https://doi.org/10.1007/11562948_9

5. Elgammal, A., Turetken, O., van den Heuvel, W.-J., Papazoglou, M.: Formalizing and appling compliance patterns for business process compliance. Softw. Syst. Model. **15**(1), 119–146 (2016)
6. Feja, S., Speck, A., Pulvermüller, E.: Business process verification. In: GI Jahrestagung, pp. 4037–4051 (2009)
7. Ghose, A., Koliadis, G.: Auditing business process compliance. In: Krämer, B.J., Lin, K.-J., Narasimhan, P. (eds.) ICSOC 2007. LNCS, vol. 4749, pp. 169–180. Springer, Heidelberg (2007). https://doi.org/10.1007/978-3-540-74974-5_14
8. Governatori, G.: The regorous approach to process compliance. In: 2015 IEEE 19th International Enterprise Distributed Object Computing Workshop, pp. 33–40. IEEE (2015)
9. Governatori, G., Rotolo, A.: Norm compliance in business process modeling. In: Dean, M., Hall, J., Rotolo, A., Tabet, S. (eds.) RuleML 2010. LNCS, vol. 6403, pp. 194–209. Springer, Heidelberg (2010). https://doi.org/10.1007/978-3-642-16289-3_17
10. Groefsema, H., van Beest, N.R.T.P., Aiello, M.: A formal model for compliance verification of service compositions. IEEE Trans. Serv. Comput. **11**(3), 466–479 (2018)
11. Haarmann, S., Batoulis, K., Weske, M.: Compliance checking for decision-aware process models. In: Daniel, F., Sheng, Q.Z., Motahari, H. (eds.) BPM 2018. LNBIP, vol. 342, pp. 494–506. Springer, Cham (2019). https://doi.org/10.1007/978-3-030-11641-5_39
12. Hoffmann, J., Weber, I., Governatori, G.: On compliance checking for clausal constraints in annotated process models. Inf. Syst. Frontiers **14**(2), 155–177 (2012)
13. Indiono, C., Fdhila, W., Rinderle-Ma, S.: Evolution of instance-spanning constraints in process aware information systems. In: Panetto, H., Debruyne, C., Proper, H., Ardagna, C., Roman, D., Meersman, R. (eds.) OTM 2018. LNCS, vol. 11229. Springer, Cham (2018). https://doi.org/10.1007/978-3-030-02610-3_17
14. Karp, R.M.: Reducibility among combinatorial problems. In: Miller, R.E., Thatcher, J.W. (eds.) Complexity of Computer Computations, pp. 85–103. Plenum Press, New York (1972)
15. Kiepuszewski, B., ter Hofstede, A.H.M., Bussler, C.J.: On structured workflow modelling. In: Wangler, B., Bergman, L. (eds.) CAiSE 2000. LNCS, vol. 1789, pp. 431–445. Springer, Heidelberg (2000). https://doi.org/10.1007/3-540-45140-4_29
16. Knuplesch, D., Ly, L.T., Rinderle-Ma, S., Pfeifer, H., Dadam, P.: On enabling data-aware compliance checking of business process models. In: Parsons, J., Saeki, M., Shoval, P., Woo, C., Wand, Y. (eds.) ER 2010. LNCS, vol. 6412, pp. 332–346. Springer, Heidelberg (2010). https://doi.org/10.1007/978-3-642-16373-9_24
17. Krom, M.R.: The decision problem for a class of first-order formulas in which all disjunctions are binary. Math. Logic Q. **13**(1–2), 15–20 (1967)
18. Lu, R., Sadiq, S., Governatori, G.: Compliance aware business process design. In: ter Hofstede, A., Benatallah, B., Paik, H.-Y. (eds.) BPM 2007. LNCS, vol. 4928, pp. 120–131. Springer, Heidelberg (2008). https://doi.org/10.1007/978-3-540-78238-4_14
19. Nakajima, S.: Verification of web service flows with model-checking techniques. In: Proceedings of International Symposium on Cyber Worlds, pp. 378–385 (2002)
20. Sadiq, S., Governatori, G., Namiri, K.: Modeling control objectives for business process compliance. In: Alonso, G., Dadam, P., Rosemann, M. (eds.) BPM 2007. LNCS, vol. 4714, pp. 149–164. Springer, Heidelberg (2007). https://doi.org/10.1007/978-3-540-75183-0_12

21. Sadiq, S., Orlowska, M.E., Sadiq, W.: Specification and validation of process constraints for flexible workflows. Inf. Syst. **30**(5), 349–378 (2005)
22. Colombo Tosatto, S., Governatori, G., Kelsen, P.: Business process regulatory compliance is hard. IEEE Trans. Serv. Comput. **8**(6), 958–970 (2015)
23. Colombo Tosatto, S., Kelsen, P., Ma, Q., El Kharbili, M., Governatori, G., van der Torre, L.W.N.: Algorithms for tractable compliance problems. Frontiers Comput. Sci. **9**(1), 55–74 (2015)
24. van der Aalst, W.M.P.: The application of petri nets to workflow management. J. Circuits Syst. Comput. **8**(1), 21–66 (1998)

Modeling and Reasoning over Declarative Data-Aware Processes with Object-Centric Behavioral Constraints

Alessandro Artale[1], Alisa Kovtunova[1], Marco Montali[1(⊠)],
and Wil M. P. van der Aalst[2]

[1] Free University of Bozen-Bolzano, Bolzano, Italy
{artale,kovtunova,montali}@inf.unibz.it
[2] Process and Data Science, RWTH Aachen University, Aachen, Germany
wvdaalst@pads.rwth-aachen.de

Abstract. Existing process modeling notations ranging from Petri nets to BPMN have difficulties capturing the data manipulated by processes. Process models often focus on the control flow, lacking an explicit, conceptually well-founded integration with real data models, such as ER diagrams or UML class diagrams. To overcome this limitation, *Object-Centric Behavioral Constraints* (OCBC) models were recently proposed as a new notation that combines full-fledged data models with control-flow constraints inspired by declarative process modeling notations such as DECLARE and DCR Graphs. We propose a formalization of the OCBC model using temporal description logics. The obtained formalization allows us to lift all reasoning services defined for constraint-based process modeling notations without data, to the much more sophisticated scenario of OCBC. Furthermore, we show how reasoning over OCBC models can be reformulated into decidable, standard reasoning tasks over the corresponding temporal description logic knowledge base.

1 Introduction

Despite the plethora of notations available to model business processes, process modelers struggle to capture real-life processes using mainstream notations such as Business Process Model and Notation (BPMN), Event-driven Process Chains (EPC), and UML activity diagrams. All such notations require the simplifying assumption that each process model focuses on a single, explicitly defined *case* notion (also referred to as *process instance*). The discrepancy between the single case view and reality becomes evident when using process mining techniques to reconstruct processes based on the available data [2]. Process mining starts from the available data and, unless one is using a Business Process Management (BPM) or Workflow Management (WFM) system for process execution, explicit case information is typically missing. Process-centric diagrams using BPMN, EPCs, or UML describe the life-cycle of individual cases. When formal languages like Petri nets, automata, and process algebras are used to describe business

© Springer Nature Switzerland AG 2019
T. Hildebrandt et al. (Eds.): BPM 2019, LNCS 11675, pp. 139–156, 2019.
https://doi.org/10.1007/978-3-030-26619-6_11

processes, they tend to model cases in isolation, and the data perspective is secondary or missing completely. Languages like BPMN allow modelers to attach data to processes, but without the possibility to express complex constraints over such data (e.g., cardinality constraints, is-a links, disjointness, covering, etc. as in ER/UML/ORM data models). Mainstream business process modeling notations describe the *lifecycle of one type of process instance* at a time missing the opportunity to capture the co-evolution of multiple, interacting instances. In particular, complex constraints over data attached to processes *must* influence the behavior of the process itself—e.g., consider the management of different orders, where the evolution of one order impacts on the possible evolutions of the related orders.

Object-Centric Behavioral Constraint (OCBC) [3,21,22] models have been proposed as a modeling language that combines ideas from declarative, constraint-based languages like *DECLARE* [1], and from data modeling languages. OCBC allows to: *(i)* describe the temporal interaction between activities in a given process and to attach (structured) data to processes in a *unified framework*; *(ii)* model the *interactions between multiple process instances*, specifically when there is a *one-to-many* or *many-to-many* relationship between them. Figure 1 illustrates the way in which OCBC models tackle the above two issues. `Register Email` and `Send Invite` are two activities related to object classes `Person` and `Meeting`, respectively. A meeting is organized by many persons, each of which can in turn organize many meetings. The double-headed arrow connecting `Register Email` and `Send Invite` expresses the constraint that an invitation for a meeting can be sent only if at least one organizer of *that* meeting has previously registered her e-mail. Assuming that the object targeted by each activity is indeed a case for that activity, this simple example already contains two distinct case notions (`Person` and `Meeting`) that are intertwined. In conventional notations, this can only be modeled from the viewpoint of one of the two instances: the registration process of a person or the invitation process for a meeting. Taking the latter viewpoint using conventional notations such as BPMN would require to explicitly introduce a loop to handle the registration of one or more persons organizing a meeting. However, this is incorrect because one registration may be followed by many meetings. One-to-many and many-to-many relationships lead to convergence and divergence problems that cannot be handled in notations describing isolated cases.

OCBC models are related to artifact- and data-centric approaches [12,16,19] aiming to integrate data and processes. However, this is not done in a single diagram representing different types of process instances and their interactions. In addition, these approaches usually assume complete knowledge over the data, and require to fully spell out data

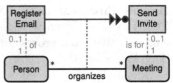

Fig. 1. An OCBC constraint

updates when specifying the activities [14,26]. The few proposals dealing with artifact-centric models with incomplete knowledge [10] do not come with a fully

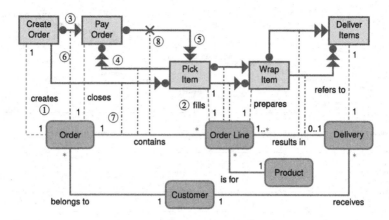

Fig. 2. Example of an OCBC model

integrated, declarative semantics as done here, but follow instead the Levesque functional approach [20] to separate the evolution of the system from the inspection of (incomplete) knowledge in each state.

This paper provides a complete characterization of the formal semantics of the OCBC approach, unambiguously defining the logical *meaning* of OCBC constraints. We provide a visual and textual syntax for OCBC, then defining the semantics of the different modeling constructs in terms of *temporal description logics*, i.e., a temporal extension of (fragments of) the well-known OWL language. The obtained formalization, in turn, allows us to lift all reasoning services defined for constraint-based process modeling notations without data, to the much more sophisticated setting of OCBC. In particular, we show how reasoning over OCBC models can be reformulated into decidable, standard reasoning tasks over the corresponding temporal description logic knowledge base, giving solid foundations to the boundaries of decidability and complexity of reasoning over processes and their manipulated data.

The paper is organized as follows. We present a running example in Sect. 2. Section 3 briefly illustrates the temporal DL that will be used to encode and reason over OCBC models. Section 4 shows the syntax for OCBC models and their semantics via the temporal DL encoding. Reasoning and verification tasks for OCBC models are tackled in Sect. 5. We present our remarks and future work in Sect. 6.

2 Running Example

The driving assumption underlying our proposal is that processes are modeled as a mirror of their manipulated data. Such data is structured according to complex data modeling constraints (see the lower part of Fig. 2). Data can be attached to activities (see the dotted lines of Fig. 2) and ad-hoc *co-reference* constraints can be expressed on those manipulated data (see the dash-dotted lines of Fig. 2) describing how activities can share/reuse the same data objects.

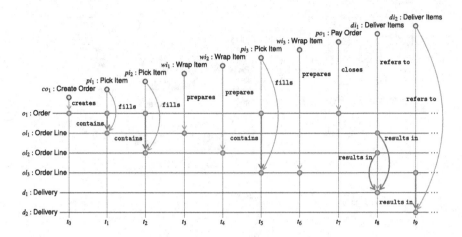

Fig. 3. Trace fragment for the OCBC model in Fig. 2

Example 1. Figure 2 shows an OCBC model for a process composed by five activities (`CreateOrder`, `PickItem`, `WrapItem`, `PayOrder` and `DeliverItems`) and five object classes in the data model (`Order`, `OrderLine`, `Delivery`, `Product` and `Customer`). The top part describes the temporal ordering of activities and the bottom part how objects relevant for the process execution are structured (read the lower part as a standard UML class diagram). The middle layer (dotted lines) relates activities and data. We now informally describe the constructs highlighted in Fig. 2. ① There is a one-to-one correspondence between a `CreateOrder` activity and an `Order`, i.e., the execution of a `CreateOrder` activity creates a unique `Order` and, vice-versa, due to the 1 on the `CreateOrder` side, each `Order` has been *generated* by a single execution of a `CreateOrder` activity. ② Every execution of the `PickItem` activity refers to a unique `OrderLine` and each `OrderLine` has been *generated by* an execution of a `PickItem` activity (and not by a `WrapItem` activity). ③ Each `CreateOrder` activity is followed by exactly one (single arrow) `PayOrder` activity related to the same order. ④ Each `PayOrder` activity is preceded by possibly many (double arrow) `PickItem` activities. ⑤ Whenever we execute `PayOrder` we will never execute `PickItem` on the same paid order. ⑥ The dash-dotted line denotes a *co-reference constraint* over an object class, imposes that when the `CreateOrder` creates an order instance, *that* order instance will eventually be paid by executing a `PayOrder` activity. ⑦ The dash-dotted line is, in this case, a *co-reference constraint* now over a relationship which imposes that when we fill an order line it must have been contained in exactly one order created by executing a `CreateOrder` activity. Since an order line instance could not exist at the same time we create an order instance and relationships are instantiated by co-existing objects, the UML model correctly specifies that, at each point in time, each order participates zero or more times in the `contains` relation. On the other hand, the co-reference constraint together with the mandatory cardinalities constraints and the temporal constraints between `CreateOrder`, `PayOrder` and `PickItem` imply the *eventual* existence of *at least one* order line contained in any given order. ⑧ The dash-dotted line starting with a × denotes a *negative co-reference constraint* that forbids filling with further order lines an order that has been closed by a `PayOrder` activity.

A possible execution of an OCBC process, called in the following *trace fragment*, records at once events, with their execution time, and the objects they operate on. In addition, it also captures facts that are known to hold over such objects in a given timestamp, in particular, the classes to which objects belong to at that time, as well as how objects are related to each other. In addition, the trace fragment captures, as customary in a standard first-order logic setting, *incomplete knowledge* about a process execution, and OCBC constraints are hence interpreted under the *open-world semantics*. This means that a trace fragment conforms to an OCBC model if it can be extended towards a full trace that satisfies all the constraints contained therein. A trace fragment conforming to the OCBC model of Fig. 2 is depicted in Fig. 3 and shown in the following first-order logic notation (but also as a DL ABox after a small transformation). We abbreviate activity names with their initials. Instances of activities, classes and relationships are timestamped denoting the execution time of the activity, and the time point when the described fact holds (timestamps respect the time ordering starting from t_0).

$CO(co_1, t_0), PI(pi_1, t_1), PI(pi_2, t_2), WI(wi_1, t_3), WI(wi_2, t_4), PI(pi_3, t_5), WI(wi_3, t_6), PO(po_1, t_7),$
$DI(di_1, t_8), DI(di_2, t_9), \text{creates}(co_1, o_1, t_0), \text{fills}(pi_1, ol_1, t_1), \text{contains}(o_1, ol_1, t_1), \text{fills}(pi_2, ol_2, t_2),$
$\text{contains}(o_1, ol_2, t_2), \text{prepares}(wi_1, ol_1, t_3), \text{prepares}(wi_2, ol_2, t_4), \text{fills}(pi_3, ol_3, t_5),$
$\text{contains}(o_1, ol_3, t_5), \text{prepares}(wi_3, ol_3, t_6), \text{closes}(po_1, o_1, t_7), \text{refers to}(di_1, d_1, t_8),$
$\text{results in}(ol_1, d_1, t_8), \text{results in}(ol_2, d_1, t_8), \text{refers to}(di_2, d_2, t_9), \text{results in}(ol_3, d_2, t_9),$

The process described in the example cannot be modeled using conventional process modeling languages, because (a) three different types of instances (of activities, classes and also relationships instances) are intertwined in a uniform framework so that no further coding or annotations are needed, and (b) cardinality and structural constraints in the object class model influence the allowed behavior of activities, and vice-versa. Take, e.g., the fact that in the example we have three different `OrderLine` instances (ol_1, ol_2, ol_3), then, together with the co-reference constraints on `OrderLine`, we implicitly enforce the occurrence of three different `PickItem` and `WrapItem` activities.

3   A Gentle Introduction to Temporal DLs

Since description logics (DLs) are able to capture data models [4,11,17] and are the logical formalism underpinning ontologies expressed in the standard Web Ontology Language OWL (www.w3.org/2007/OWL), while the linear temporal logic (LTL) is able to formalize the temporal interweaving of the activities in a process [1], we propose here to use temporal description logics based on $T_{US}\mathcal{ALCQI}$ and its fragments [8,18,27] to formally describe the semantics of

OCBC models and to capture in a uniform formalism both the processes and their attached data.

$\mathcal{T}_{US}\mathcal{ALCQI}$ is one of the most expressive and still decidable temporal description logics. The language alphabet contains *object names* $a_0, a_1, \ldots$, *concept names* $A_0, A_1, \ldots$ and *role names* $P_0, P_1, \ldots$. Then, *roles* R and *concepts* C are given by the following grammar:

$$R ::= P_i \mid R^- \qquad C ::= \top \mid A_i \mid (\geq q\, R\, C) \mid \neg C \mid C_1 \sqcap C_2 \mid C_1 \mathcal{U} C_2 \mid C_1 \mathcal{S} C_2$$

where R^- denotes the *inverse* of the role R (obtained by reversing the relation R) and q is a positive integer. We use the standard abbreviations: $C_1 \sqcup C_2 = \neg(\neg C_1 \sqcap \neg C_2)$, $\bot = \neg\top$, $\exists R = (\geq 1\, R\, \top)$, $\exists R.\, C = (\geq 1\, R\, C)$, $(\leq q\, R\, C) = \neg(\geq (q+1)\, R\, C)$. Furthermore, all the temporal operators used in LTL can be expressed via $\mathcal{S}$ 'since' and $\mathcal{U}$ 'until' [18]. Operators $\Diamond_F$ and $\Diamond_P$ ('sometime in the future/past') can be expressed as $\Diamond_F G = \top \mathcal{U} C$ and $\Diamond_P C = \top \mathcal{S} C$; operators $\Box_F$ ('always in the future') and $\Box_P$ ('always in the past') are defined as dual to $\Diamond_F$ and $\Diamond_P$, i.e., $\Box_F C = \neg\Diamond_F\neg C$ and $\Box_P C = \neg\Diamond_P\neg C$. The non-strict operators (including the current evaluation time), denoted as $\Diamond_P^+$ and $\Diamond_F^+$, can be captured as $\Diamond_P^+ C = C \sqcap \Diamond_P C$ and $\Diamond_F^+ C = C \sqcap \Diamond_F C$ (similarly, $\Box_P^+$ and $\Box_F^+$ are defined as the dual operators of $\Diamond_P^+$ and $\Diamond_F^+$, respectively). The 'always' operator $\boxdot$ can be expressed as $\boxdot C = \Box_F \Box_P C$, while the dual 'sometime' is defined as $\Diamond C = \neg \boxdot \neg C$. Finally, the temporal operators $\bigcirc_F$ ('next time') and $\bigcirc_P$ ('previous time') can be defined as $\bigcirc_F C = \bot \mathcal{U} C$ and $\bigcirc_P C = \bot \mathcal{S} C$.

A $\mathcal{T}_{US}\mathcal{ALCQI}$ *TBox* $\mathcal{T}$ is a finite set of *concept* and *role inclusion* axioms of the form $C_1 \sqsubseteq C_2$ and $R_1 \sqsubseteq R_2$, respectively. An *ABox*, $\mathcal{A}$, consists of assertions of the form $\bigcirc^n A_k(a_i)$, $\bigcirc^n P_k(a_i, a_j)$, where A_k is a concept name, P_k a role name, a_i, a_j object names and, for $n \in \mathbb{Z}$,

$$\bigcirc^n = \underbrace{\bigcirc_F \cdots \bigcirc_F}_{n \text{ times}}, \text{ if } n \geq 0, \text{ and } \bigcirc^n = \underbrace{\bigcirc_P \cdots \bigcirc_P}_{-n \text{ times}}, \text{ if } n < 0.$$

Taken together, the TBox $\mathcal{T}$ and ABox $\mathcal{A}$ form the *knowledge base* (KB) $\mathcal{K} = (\mathcal{T}, \mathcal{A})$. In this paper, OCBC models will be encoded using TBoxes (see Sect. 4.4), while single process executions (i.e., trace fragments as shown in Example 1) are encoded as ABoxes (e.g., $\mathtt{CO}(co_1, t_0)$ is encoded as $\bigcirc^{t_0} \mathtt{CO}(co_1)$).

A *temporal interpretation* is a structure of the form $\mathcal{I} = ((\mathbb{Z}, <), \Delta^{\mathcal{I}}, \{\cdot^{\mathcal{I}} \mid n \in \mathbb{Z}\})$, where $(\mathbb{Z}, <)$ is the linear model of time, $\Delta^{\mathcal{I}}$ is a non-empty interpretation domain and $\mathcal{I}(n)$ gives a standard DL interpretation for each time instant $n \in \mathbb{Z}$: $\mathcal{I}(n) = (\Delta^{\mathcal{I}}, a_0^{\mathcal{I}(n)}, A_0^{\mathcal{I}(n)}, \ldots, P_0^{\mathcal{I}(n)}, \ldots)$, assigning to each concept name A_i a unary predicate $A_i^{\mathcal{I}(n)} \subseteq \Delta^{\mathcal{I}}$ and to each role name P_i a binary relation $P_i^{\mathcal{I}(n)} \subseteq \Delta^{\mathcal{I}} \times \Delta^{\mathcal{I}}$. We assume that the domain $\Delta^{\mathcal{I}}$ and the interpretations $a_i^{\mathcal{I}} \in \Delta^{\mathcal{I}}$ of object names are the same for all $n \in \mathbb{Z}$, i.e., we adopt the *constant domain assumption* and *rigid designators* (consult [18] for more details on these assumptions). At each time instant $n \in \mathbb{Z}$, role and concept constructs are interpreted as follows

$$(R^-)^{\mathcal{I}(n)} = \{(y,x) \in \Delta^{\mathcal{I}} \times \Delta^{\mathcal{I}} \mid (x,y) \in R^{\mathcal{I}(n)}\},$$

$$(\geq q\,R\,C)^{\mathcal{I}(n)} = \{x \in \Delta^{\mathcal{I}} \mid \sharp\{y \in C^{\mathcal{I}(n)} \mid (x,y) \in R^{\mathcal{I}(n)}\} \geq q\},$$

$$(\neg C)^{\mathcal{I}(n)} = \Delta^{\mathcal{I}} \setminus C^{\mathcal{I}(n)}, \quad \top^{\mathcal{I}} = \Delta^{\mathcal{I}}, \quad (C_1 \sqcap C_2)^{\mathcal{I}(n)} = C_1^{\mathcal{I}(n)} \cap C_2^{\mathcal{I}(n)},$$

$$(C_1\,\mathcal{U}\,C_2)^{\mathcal{I}(n)} = \bigcup_{k>n}\left(C_2^{\mathcal{I}(k)} \cap \bigcap_{n<m<k} C_1^{\mathcal{I}(m)}\right),$$

$$(C_1\,\mathcal{S}\,C_2)^{\mathcal{I}(n)} = \bigcup_{k<n}\left(C_2^{\mathcal{I}(k)} \cap \bigcap_{n>m>k} C_1^{\mathcal{I}(m)}\right),$$

where $\sharp X$ denotes the cardinality of X. Thus, for example, $x \in (C_1\,\mathcal{U}\,C_2)^{\mathcal{I}(n)}$ iff there is a moment $k > n$ such that $x \in C_2^{\mathcal{I}(k)}$ and $x \in C_1^{\mathcal{I}(m)}$, for all moments m between n and k. Note that the operators $\mathcal{S}$ and $\mathcal{U}$ are 'strict' in the sense that their semantics does not include the current moment of time.

Concept and role inclusion axioms (TBox) are interpreted in $\mathcal{I}$ *globally*:

$$\mathcal{I} \models C_1 \sqsubseteq C_2 \quad \text{iff} \quad C_1^{\mathcal{I}(n)} \subseteq C_2^{\mathcal{I}(n)} \quad \text{for all } n \in \mathbb{Z},$$

$$\mathcal{I} \models R_1 \sqsubseteq R_2 \quad \text{iff} \quad R_1^{\mathcal{I}(n)} \subseteq R_2^{\mathcal{I}(n)} \quad \text{for all } n \in \mathbb{Z}.$$

ABox assertions are interpreted relatively to the *initial moment*, 0:

$$\mathcal{I} \models \bigcirc^n A_k(a_i) \quad \text{iff} \quad a_i^{\mathcal{I}} \in A_k^{\mathcal{I}(n)},$$

$$\mathcal{I} \models \bigcirc^n P_k(a_i, a_j) \quad \text{iff} \quad (a_i^{\mathcal{I}}, a_j^{\mathcal{I}}) \in P_k^{\mathcal{I}(n)}.$$

We call $\mathcal{I}$ a *model* of a KB $\mathcal{K} = (\mathcal{T}, \mathcal{A})$ and write $\mathcal{I} \models \mathcal{K}$ if $\mathcal{I}$ satisfies all inclusions in $\mathcal{T}$ and all assertions in $\mathcal{A}$. A KB $\mathcal{K}$ is *satisfiable* if it has a model. A concept C (role R) is *satisfiable* with respect to $\mathcal{K}$ if there are a model $\mathcal{I}$ of $\mathcal{K}$ and $n \in \mathbb{Z}$ such that $C^{\mathcal{I}(n)} \neq \emptyset$ (respectively, $R^{\mathcal{I}(n)} \neq \emptyset$). It is readily seen that the concept and role satisfiability problems are equivalent to KB satisfiability.

Reasoning in $\mathcal{T}_{\mathcal{US}}\mathcal{ALCQI}$ w.r.t. to a KB is a problem which has been proven to be ExpTime-complete [18,27]. To achieve better complexity results fragments of $\mathcal{ALCQI}$ must be considered. Nice results have been gained when temporalizing *DL-Lite* logics [6,13]—see, e.g., the temporal *DL-Lite* called $\mathcal{T}_{\mathcal{US}}DL\text{-}Lite_{bool}^{(\mathcal{HN})}$ where reasoning has the same complexity of LTL reasoning, i.e., PSpace-complete [8].

4   The OCBC Model

We now present the syntax and graphical appearance of OCBC models, together with their formal semantics. The original proposal of the OCBC model is the way activities and data are related. In particular, an OCBC model captures, at once: *(i) Data dependencies*, represented using standard data modeling constructs, i.e., *classes*, *relationships* and *constraints* between them; *(ii) Activities*, accounting for units of work within a process; *(iii) Mutual relationships between activities and classes*, linking the execution of activities in a given process with the data objects they manipulate; *(iv) Temporal constraints* between activities; *(v) Co-reference constraints* that enforce the application of temporal constraints, and in particular limit their application to those activities that indirectly co-refer thanks to the objects and relationships they point to.

4.1   The Data Model – ClaM

Data used by the activities of an OCBC model is structured according to a standard modeling language, i.e., ER/UML/ORM. While $\mathcal{ALCQI}$ is able to fully capture the semantics of such data models (see [4,11,17] and references therein) in the following, just for the sake of simplicity and lack of space, we present only a subset of the complete set of modeling constructs allowed in those standard data modeling languages and denote such set of modeling constructs as the ClaM data model (which stands for *CLAss data Model*). In particular, the following syntax limits ClaM to capture object classes that can be organized along ISA hierarchies (with possibly disjoint sub-classes and covering constraints), binary relationships between object classes and cardinalities expressing participation constraints of object classes in relationships.

Definition 1 (ClaM Syntax). *A conceptual schema Σ in the Class Model, ClaM, is a tuple $\Sigma = (\mathcal{U}_C, \mathcal{U}_R, \tau, \#_{dom}, \#_{ran}, \mathsf{ISA}, \mathrm{DISJ}, \mathrm{COV})$, where:*

- *$\mathcal{U}_C$ is the universe of object classes. We denote object classes as $O_1, O_2, \ldots$;*
- *$\mathcal{U}_R$ is the universe of binary relationships among object classes. We denote relationships as $R_1, R_2, \ldots$;*
- *$\tau : \mathcal{U}_R \to \mathcal{U}_C \times \mathcal{U}_C$ is a total function associating a signature to each binary relationship. If $\tau(R) = (O_1, O_2)$ then O_1 is the range and O_2 the domain of the relationship;*
- *$\#_{dom} : \mathcal{U}_R \times \mathcal{U}_C \nrightarrow \mathbb{N} \times (\mathbb{N} \cup \{\infty\})$ is a partial function defining cardinality constraints on the domain of a relationship. $\#_{dom}(R, O)$ is defined only if $\tau(R) = (O, O_1)$;*
- *$\#_{ran} : \mathcal{U}_R \times \mathcal{U}_C \nrightarrow \mathbb{N} \times (\mathbb{N} \cup \{\infty\})$ is a partial function defining cardinality constraints on the range of a relationship. $\#_{ran}(R, O)$ is defined only if $\tau(R) = (O_1, O)$;*
- *$\mathsf{ISA} \subseteq \mathcal{U}_C \times \mathcal{U}_C$ is a binary relation defining the super-class and sub-class hierarchy on object classes. If $\mathsf{ISA}(C_1, C_2)$ then C_1 is said to be a sub-class of C_2 while C_2 is said to be a super-class of C_1;*
- *$\mathrm{DISJ} \subseteq 2^{\mathcal{U}_C} \times \mathcal{U}_C$ is a binary relation defining the set of disjoint sub-classes in an ISA hierarchy;*
- *$\mathrm{COV} \subseteq 2^{\mathcal{U}_C} \times \mathcal{U}_C$ is a binary relation defining the set of sub-classes covering the super-class in an ISA hierarchy.*

As for the full-fledged syntax of ER/UML/ORM, their formal set-theoretic semantics, and their translation as $\mathcal{ALCQI}$ KBs we refer to [4,11,17]. Concerning the semantics of the ClaM constructs, cardinality constraints are interpreted as the number of times each instance of the involved class participates in the given relationship, ISA is interpreted as sub-setting, DISJ and COV are interpreted

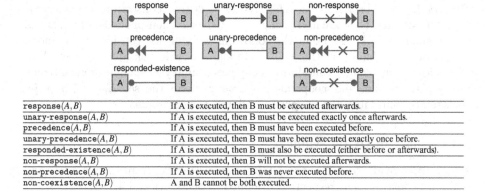

response(A,B)	If A is executed, then B must be executed afterwards.
unary-response(A,B)	If A is executed, then B must be executed exactly once afterwards.
precedence(A,B)	If A is executed, then B must have been executed before.
unary-precedence(A,B)	If A is executed, then B must have been executed exactly once before.
responded-existence(A,B)	If A is executed, then B must also be executed (either before or afterwards).
non-response(A,B)	If A is executed, then B will not be executed afterwards.
non-precedence(A,B)	If A is executed, then B was never executed before.
non-coexistence(A,B)	A and B cannot be both executed.

Fig. 4. Types of temporal constraints between activities and their intuitive semantics

in the obvious way using disjointness/union between classes, relationships are interpreted as binary predicates, while the relationship signature acts as a typing for its arguments.

Example 2. The lower part of the OCBC model shown in Fig. 2 captures the data model as a ClaM diagram with:

$$\mathcal{U}_C = \{\texttt{Order}, \texttt{OrderLine}, \texttt{Product}, \texttt{Customer}, \texttt{Delivery}\};$$

$$\mathcal{U}_R = \{\texttt{contains}, \texttt{belongs to}, \texttt{is for}, \texttt{results in}, \texttt{receives}\};$$

$$\tau(\texttt{contains}) = (\texttt{Order}, \texttt{OrderLine}), \ldots$$

$$\#_{dom}(\texttt{contains}, \texttt{Order}) = (0, \infty); \ \#_{ran}(\texttt{contains}, \texttt{OrderLine}) = (1,1); \ldots$$

Cardinalities are shown in the diagram following the UML reading.

4.2   Temporal Constraints over Activities

Taking inspiration from the DECLARE patterns [1], we present here the temporal constraints between (pairs of) activities that can be expressed in OCBC. Figure 4 graphically renders such constraints together with their intuitive meaning. In the following we present their syntax.

Definition 2 (Temporal constraints). *Let*

- *$\mathcal{U}_A$ be the universe of activities, denoted with capital letters $A_1, A_2, \ldots$;*
- *$\mathcal{U}_{TC}$ be the universe of temporal constraints, i.e., $\mathcal{U}_{TC}$ = {response, unary-response, precedence, unary-precedence, responded-existence, non- response, non-precedence, non-coexistence}, where each $tc \in \mathcal{U}_{TC}$ is a binary relation over activities, i.e., $tc \subseteq \mathcal{U}_A \times \mathcal{U}_A$.*

The set of temporal constraints in a given OCBC model is denoted as Σ_{TC} and is conceived as a set of elements of the form $tc(A_1, A_2)$, where $tc \in \mathcal{U}_{TC}$ and $A_1, A_2 \in \mathcal{U}_A$.

Remark 1. We observe that the *non-precedence* constraint is syntactic sugar, as it can be emulated using *non-response*: non-precedence$(A, B) \equiv$ non-response(B, A). Thus, in the following we will not consider it anymore. When defining later on the OCBC model we will consider the set Σ_{TC}^+ of *positive* constraints containing response, unary-response, precedence, unary-precedence, and responded-existence, and the set Σ_{TC}^- of *negative* constraints containing non-response and non-coexistence.

4.3   Syntax of OCBC Models

We are now ready to define the OCBC model starting from data models and temporal constraints as respectively defined in Sects. 4.1 and 4.2.

Definition 3 (OCBC syntax). *An OCBC model, $\mathcal{M}$, is a tuple:*
$$(ClaM, \Sigma_{TC}, \mathcal{U}_A, \mathcal{U}_{R_{AC}}, \tau_{R_{AC}}, \#_{act}, \#_{obj}, cref, neg\text{-}cref), \ where:$$

- *ClaM is a data model as in Definition 1, and Σ_{TC} a set of temporal constraints as in Definition 2;*
- *$\mathcal{U}_A$ is the universe of activities;*
- *$\mathcal{U}_{R_{AC}}$ is the universe of* activity-object relationships *being a set of binary relationships;*
- *$\tau_{R_{AC}} : \mathcal{U}_{R_{AC}} \rightarrow \mathcal{U}_A \times \mathcal{U}_C$ is a total function associating a signature to each activity-object relationship. If $\tau_{R_{AC}}(R) = (A, O)$ then $A \in \mathcal{U}_A$ and $O \in \mathcal{U}_C$;*
- *$\#_{act} : \mathcal{U}_{R_{AC}} \times \mathcal{U}_A \twoheadrightarrow \mathbb{N} \times (\mathbb{N} \cup \{\infty\})$ is a partial function defining cardinality constraints on the participation of activities in activity-object relationships. $\#_{act}(R, A)$ is defined only if $\tau_{R_{AC}}(R) = (A, O)$;*
- *$\#_{obj} : \mathcal{U}_{R_{AC}} \times \mathcal{U}_C \twoheadrightarrow \{1\}$ is a partial function denoting the activity that generated a given object in O. $\#_{obj}(R, O)$ is defined only if $\tau_{R_{AC}}(R) = (A, O)$;*
- *cref is the partial function of* co-reference constraints *s.t.*
$$cref : \Sigma_{TC}^+ \times \mathcal{U}_{R_{AC}} \times \mathcal{U}_{R_{AC}} \twoheadrightarrow \mathcal{U}_C \cup \mathcal{U}_R;$$
- *neg-cref is the partial function of* negative co-reference constraints *s.t.*
$$neg\text{-}cref : \Sigma_{TC}^- \times \mathcal{U}_{R_{AC}} \times \mathcal{U}_{R_{AC}} \twoheadrightarrow \mathcal{U}_C \cup \mathcal{U}_R.$$

Inverses of activity-object relationships are assumed to be functional capturing the intuition that a single occurrence of an activity can manipulate an object at a given point in time. To clarify the syntax of the OCBC modeling language we illustrate the scenario provided in Example 1.

Example 3. We consider the OCBC model in Fig. 2 where the activities are depicted in the upper part of the figure while the lower part shows the ClaM data model for the data manipulated by the activities of the process. The set $\mathcal{U}_{R_{AC}}$ of the *activity-object relationships* is: $\mathcal{U}_{R_{AC}} = \{create, closes, fills, prepares, refers\ to\}$ connecting an activity with the manipulated objects as an effect of executing the activity itself. For example, the activity CreateOrder creates an instance of the object class Order when it is executed. Cardinality constraints can be added to activity-object relationships to specify participation constraints either on the activity side or on the object class side. For example, each execution of PickItem fills one and only one OrderLine, i.e., $\#_{act}(\texttt{fills}, \texttt{PickItem}) = (1,1)$. On the other hand, any OrderLine must be necessarily filled by executing a PickItem activity, i.e., $\#_{obj}(\texttt{fills}, \texttt{OrderLine}) = 1$. The *co-reference constraints* involving object classes specify constraints on how objects connected to different activities can be shared. For example, the OrderLine instance filled by a PickItem is the same as the one prepared by the corresponding WrapItem. These co-reference constraints can be expressed using the following OCBC syntax:

$$cref\big(\texttt{unary-response}(\texttt{PickItem}, \texttt{WrapItem}), \texttt{fills}, \texttt{prepares}\big) = \texttt{OrderLine},$$
$$cref\big(\texttt{unary-precedence}(\texttt{WrapItem}, \texttt{PickItem}), \texttt{prepares}, \texttt{fills}\big) = \texttt{OrderLine}.$$

The co-reference constraint ⑦, and the negative co-reference constraint ⑧ are expressed as, respectively:

$$cref(\texttt{unary-precedence}(\texttt{PickItem}, \texttt{CreateOrder}), \texttt{fills}, \texttt{creates}) = \texttt{contains};$$
$$neg\text{-}cref(\texttt{non-response}(\texttt{PayOrder}, \texttt{PickItem}), \texttt{closes}, \texttt{fills}) = \texttt{contains}.$$

4.4 Semantics of OCBC Models

We now focus on the semantics of OCBC models. As pointed out in Sect. 2, OCBC models are interpreted using traces that capture the occurrence of events, the relationships between events and objects, and the evolution of objects and relationships over time. Here, we base the OCBC semantics on *infinite* traces (cf. Sect. 6 for a remark on finite traces). The information recorded in an actual execution trace is interpreted under incomplete knowledge, i.e., as a *trace fragment* containing explicit factual knowledge that is known to certainly hold but, in general, only partially capturing what actually occurred. Thus, the notion of trace as used in event log formats such as the XES IEEE standard has to be interpreted, in our setting, as a trace fragment.

Our effort is to reconcile the process flow semantics with the data model semantics. We thus resort to a knowledge base expressed in the temporal DL $T_{\mathcal{US}}\mathcal{ALCQI}$. In particular, we map both activities and object classes to $T_{\mathcal{US}}\mathcal{ALCQI}$ concepts, while activity-object relationships and relationships of the data model are mapped to $T_{\mathcal{US}}\mathcal{ALCQI}$ roles. Such an encoding of OCBC models using KBs in the temporal DL $T_{\mathcal{US}}\mathcal{ALCQI}$ interprets constraints of an OCBC model over infinite traces, while the ABox, that encodes the explicit factual knowledge, i.e., the *trace fragment* at hand, is interpreted as a finite portion of such infinite traces. Here we detail the encoding.

Concerning the semantics of the *ClaM data model*, we interpret it via a mapping to $\mathcal{ALCQI}$ as already discussed in Sect. 4.1. Furthermore, we can add to the data model temporal constraints captured in $T_{\mathcal{US}}\mathcal{ALCQI}$ as shown in [5,7].

As for *activity-object relationships*, let $R \in \mathcal{U}_{R_{AC}}$ so that $\tau_{R_{AC}}(R) = (A, O)$. The following $T_{\mathcal{US}}\mathcal{ALCQI}$ axioms captures *inverse functionality*, and *domain* and *range* restrictions for R:

$$(\geq 2\ R^- \ \top) \sqsubseteq \bot, \qquad \exists R \sqsubseteq A, \quad \exists R^- \sqsubseteq O. \tag{1}$$

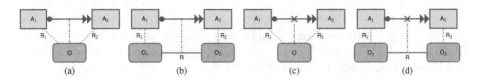

Fig. 5. Co-reference (response) constraints over (a) object classes and (b) relationships, with their negated versions (c-d)

A cardinality constraint of the form $\#_{obj}(R, O) = 1$, denoting the activity that generated an object of class O, is captured as:

$$O \sqsubseteq \Diamond_P^+(O \sqcap \exists R^-).$$

Cardinality constraints for the participation of activities in activity-object relationships ($\#_{act}$) are instead captured as classical cardinalities in data models (see [5, 7, 11]).

Semantics of Co-reference Constraints. Having fixed the semantics for the ClaM data model and the one for the activity-object relationships we are left with the most tricky aspect of OCBC, namely the semantics of *co-reference constraints*. In the following, we consider the different kinds of co-reference constraints which, according to Definition 3, can be either positive or negative, and can range either over object classes (as illustrated in Fig. 5a and c) or over relationships (as illustrated in Fig. 5b and d). Let $R_1, R_2 \in \mathcal{U}_{R_{AC}}$, $A_1, A_2 \in \mathcal{U}_A$ and $O \in \mathcal{U}_C$ s.t. $tc(A_1, A_2) \in \Sigma_{TC}^+$, $\tau_{R_{AC}}(R_1) = (A_1, O)$, $\tau_{R_{AC}}(R_2) = (A_2, O)$ and *cref* be a *co-reference constraint over object classes* of the form: $cref(tc(A_1, A_2), R_1, R_2) = O$ (as in Fig. 5a). Then, *co-reference over object classes* when tc is the **response** temporal constraint is captured by the axiom:

$$\exists R_1^- \sqsubseteq \Diamond_F \exists R_2^- \tag{2}$$

This expresses that *"whenever an object is in the range of R_1 then sometime in the future it must be also in the range of R_2"*. This semantics enforces a temporal constraint over the activities via the co-referenced object, i.e., when the activity A_1 is linked via R_1 to an object in O then it must be followed by an execution of A_2 referencing the *same* object via R_2. Formally, the following logical implication holds:

$$\{(1), (2), A_1 \sqsubseteq \exists R_1\} \models A_1 \sqsubseteq \exists R_1 . \Diamond_F \exists R_2^- . A_2 \tag{3}$$

When tc is the **unary-response** temporal constraint we need to add to formula (2) another formula that guarantees a *unique* occurrence of A_2 over the co-referenced object:

$$\exists R_2^- \sqcap \Diamond_P \exists R_1^- \sqsubseteq \Box_F \neg \exists R_2^- \tag{4}$$

Fig. 6. (a) Trace fragment for (2) but not (4); (b) trace fragment for (8) but not (10)

Figure 6a shows a possible instantiation of the OCBC model in Fig. 5a which, in turn, is not a valid fragment in case the temporal constraint is changed to **unary-response**.

Similar formulas hold when tc is a temporal constraint over the past, i.e., either **precedence** (formula (5)), **unary-precedence** (formulas (5) and (6)) or **responded-existence** (formula (7)).

$$\exists R_1^- \sqsubseteq \lozenge_P \exists R_2^- \tag{5}$$

$$\exists R_2^- \sqcap \lozenge_F \exists R_1^- \sqsubseteq \square_P \neg \exists R_2^- \tag{6}$$

$$\exists R_1^- \sqsubseteq \lozenge \exists R_2^- \tag{7}$$

We now consider *co-reference constraints over relationships*. As in Fig. 5b, let $O_1, O_2 \in \mathcal{U}_C$, $R \in \mathcal{U}_R$, with $\tau(R) = (O_1, O_2)$, $\tau_{R_{AC}}(R_1) = (A_1, O_1)$, $\tau_{R_{AC}}(R_2) = (A_2, O_2)$ and *cref* be a co-reference of the form: $cref(tc(A_1, A_2), R_1, R_2) = R$. Then, the semantics of *co-reference over relationships* when tc is the **response** constraint is captured by:

$$\exists R_1^- \sqsubseteq \lozenge_F \exists R. \exists R_2^- \tag{8}$$

Expressing that "*every object in the range of R_1 sometime in the future should be connected via R to an object in the range of R_2.*" A logical implication similar to (3) holds:

$$\{(1), (8), A_1 \sqsubseteq \exists R_1\} \models A_1 \sqsubseteq \exists R_1. \lozenge_F \exists R. \exists R_2^-. A_2 \tag{9}$$

When tc is **unary-response** we should add to formula (8) another formula that guarantees that activity A_1 is followed by a single occurrence of A_2 via R. The following axiom expresses that "*whenever an object is in the range of R_2 (thus under the occurrence of A_2) and is connected via R^- to an object that before was in the range of R_1 (due to the occurrence of the activity A_1) then, it will never be in the range of R_2.*"

$$\exists R_2^- \sqcap \exists R^-. \lozenge_P \exists R_1^- \sqsubseteq \square_F \neg \exists R_2^- \tag{10}$$

Figure 6b shows an instantiation of the OCBC model in Fig. 5b that, in turn, is not anymore a valid fragment in case the temporal constraint is changed to unary-response (because o_2 is pointed to by two different instances—b_1, b_2—of the activity A_2).

Similar formulas hold when tc is precedence (axiom (11)), unary-precedence (axioms (11) and (12)) and responded-existence (axiom (13))

$$\exists R_1^- \sqsubseteq \exists R. \Diamond_P \exists R_2^- \tag{11}$$

$$\exists R_2^- \sqcap \Diamond_F \exists R^-. \exists R_1^- \sqsubseteq \Box_P \neg \exists R_2^- \tag{12}$$

$$\exists R_1^- \sqsubseteq \Diamond \exists R. \Diamond \exists R_2^- \tag{13}$$

Note that axiom (13) allows for responded-existence to be symmetric—as for axiom (7)—i.e., $\{(13)\} \models \exists R_2^- \sqsubseteq \Diamond \exists R^-. \Diamond \exists R_1^-$.

We now consider co-references in the presence of *negative behavioral constraints* (see Fig. 5c-d). We start with co-reference over object classes. In case tc is non-response (as in Fig. 5c) then the following axiom expresses that *"whenever an object is in the range of R_1 then never in the future it could be in the range of R_2"*:

$$\exists R_1^- \sqsubseteq \Box_F \neg \exists R_2^-. \tag{14}$$

As a consequence of this axiom, and of the fact that the domains of R_1 and R_2 are activities A_1 and A_2, while they both range over the same class O, we can also read this negative co-reference as *"every instance of activity A_1 can never be followed by instances of A_2 sharing the same object in O"*. The right-hand side of the axiom is the negation of the right-hand side of axiom (2). When tc is non-coexistence, we have

$$\exists R_1^- \sqsubseteq \boxdot \neg \exists R_2^- \tag{15}$$

Again, the right-hand side is the negation of the right-hand side of axiom (7).

When negative co-references involve a relationship and tc is non-response (as in Fig. 5d) the following axiom expresses that *"whenever an object is in the range of R_1 then never in the future it could be connected via R to an object in the range of R_2 (thus under the occurrence of A_2)"*:

$$\exists R_1^- \sqsubseteq \Box_F \neg \exists R. \exists R_2^- \tag{16}$$

implying that *"every instance of activity A_1 can never be followed by instances of A_2 sharing the same pair of objects in R"*. Notice again that the right-hand side of the above axiom is the negation of the right-hand side of axiom (8). Finally, by negating the right-hand side of axiom (13) we capture the case when tc is non-coexistence

$$\exists R_1^- \sqsubseteq \boxdot \neg \exists R. \Diamond \exists R_2^- \tag{17}$$

Similar to `responded-existence`, `non-coexistence` over both object classes (15) and relationships (17) is obviously symmetric. Formally, considering the co-reference over a relationship, $\{(17)\} \models \exists R_2^- \sqsubseteq \boxdot \neg \exists R^- . \diamondsuit \exists R_1^-$.

Altogether, an OCBC model can be captured via a TBox in $T_{US}\mathcal{ALCQI}$, and its trace fragments using corresponding ABoxes. Overall, a $T_{US}\mathcal{ALCQI}$ KB is thus able to provide a uniform representation for OCBC, on which we can apply ad hoc reasoning services as described in the following section.

5   Verification and Reasoning over OCBC Models

The main motivation to provide a mapping from OCBC models to a DL Knowledge Base is the possibility of carrying out automated reasoning over them. We discuss how the typical services for verifying declarative, constraint-based process models can be lifted to the more sophisticated setting of OCBC. To do so, we build on the services defined for the well-established DECLARE language [24, 25]. In the following, we show how such services can be reformulated as standard reasoning tasks over $T_{US}\mathcal{ALCQI}$ knowledge bases, in turn inheriting their decidability and worst-case complexity.

Let $\mathcal{M}$ be an OCBC model of interest, and ρ a trace fragment over $\mathcal{M}$. We denote by $T_{\mathcal{M}}$ and $\mathcal{A}_\rho$ the TBox and ABox obtained by encoding $\mathcal{M}$ and ρ in $T_{US}\mathcal{ALCQI}$, and by $\mathcal{K}_{\mathcal{M},\rho}$ the resulting $T_{US}\mathcal{ALCQI}$ KB, i.e., $\mathcal{K}_{\mathcal{M},\rho} = (T_{\mathcal{M}}, \mathcal{A}_\rho)$.

Model Consistency. The most fundamental service is to check whether $\mathcal{M}$ is consistent, that is, supports the empty trace fragment (in turn witnessesing that it supports at least one full trace). This directly reduces to check whether $T_{\mathcal{M}}$ is satisfiable.

Activity Executability. An OCBC model may be consistent, but including so-called *dead activities* [25], i.e., activities that cannot be executed at all. We can show whether an activity A in $\mathcal{M}$ can be executed by verifying whether such an activity is not logically implied to be empty in the corresponding TBox, i.e., $T_{\mathcal{M}} \not\models A \sqsubseteq \bot$.

Implied Properties. Let α be a model property expressible in $T_{US}\mathcal{ALCQI}$. We can check whether $\mathcal{M} \models \alpha$ by checking whether $\mathcal{K}_{\mathcal{M},\rho} \models \alpha$. E.g., (3) is a property implied by $\mathcal{M}$. The presented encoding of OCBC into $T_{US}\mathcal{ALCQI}$ allows us to use its reasoning capabilities to detect so-called *hidden constraints* [24], i.e., constraints that are implicitly present in $\mathcal{M}$ even though they are not shown graphically.

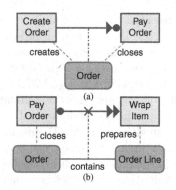

Fig. 7. Implied (a) and non-implied (b) constraints by the OCBC model of Fig. 2

Example 4. Consider again the OCBC model of Fig. 2 and the two constraints in Fig. 7 where Fig. 7a captures that an order can be paid only if it has been created before, and Fig. 7b that no order line of an order can be wrapped after that order is paid. It is easy to verify that the former constraint is indeed implied, while the latter constraint it is not. While it is true that once an order is paid no further items can be picked for it, already picked order lines may still need to be wrapped.

Execution Trace Compliance. This amounts to check whether a trace fragment ρ satisfies the constraints in $\mathcal{M}$. Since ρ is a trace fragment, we require that no explicit violation is contained in ρ and that ρ can be'completed' into a fully specified, infinite trace that satisfies $\mathcal{M}$. This corresponds to the notion of *conditional compliance* recently introduced in [15]. In our setting, this amounts to check whether the ABox $\mathcal{A}_\rho$ encoding ρ is satisfiable w.r.t. the TBox $\mathcal{T}_\mathcal{M}$, i.e., whether the KB $\mathcal{K}_{\mathcal{M},\rho}$ is satisfiable.

Complexity Considerations. Notice that, KB satisfiability and logical implication are mutually reducible in $\mathcal{ALCQI}$ [6] (and thus in $T_{\mathcal{US}}\mathcal{ALCQI}$) and these reasoning problems over $T_{\mathcal{US}}\mathcal{ALCQI}$ are ExpTime-complete [18, 27], which establishes an ExpTime upper bound for verifying properties of OCBC models. The need to use $\mathcal{ALCQI}$ as the base DL is due to co-reference constraints over relationships, which requires the power of qualified existential ($\exists R.\,C$) and its dual. If we renounce such constraints (i.e., only consider OCBC constraints co-referring on classes), we could use a temporalized version of a *DL-Lite* dialect. In particular, the temporal *DL-Lite* fragment $T_{\mathcal{US}}DL\text{-}Lite_{bool}^{(\mathcal{HN})}$, showed to be PSpace-complete in [8], is able to capture OCBC models with the exception of co-reference constraints over relationships while, at the level of the data model, $T_{\mathcal{US}}DL\text{-}Lite_{bool}^{(\mathcal{HN})}$ captures the main constructs of UML—with the exception of ISA between relationships and n-ary relationships (cf. [4, 7] for details).

6   Conclusions

We presented the first, complete formalization of *object-centric behavioral constraints* (OCBC): a new approach to business process modeling where data models and declarative constraints over activities are seamlessly integrated. Our approach comes with a logic-based semantics for OCBC in terms of an encoding into the temporal DL $T_{\mathcal{US}}\mathcal{ALCQI}$. This unambiguously defines the meaning of OCBC models, and lays the foundations for reasoning over them, allowing us to understand the (decidability and) complexity boundaries of reasoning tasks over OCBC models. $T_{\mathcal{US}}\mathcal{ALCQI}$ interprets time as a linear, infinite structure, which contrasts with the finite-trace semantics adopted in other declarative process modeling languages such as Declare. The study of temporal description logics with finite-time semantics is rather novel [9], and may constitute the basis for reasoning over OCBC models on finite traces.

We have considered here standard data models to capture the structural aspects of OCBC. Variants of OCBC with non-conventional temporalized cardinality constraints over relationships have been used [21,22]. We intend to study whether such constraints may impact on the decidability and complexity of reasoning over OCBC models.

In our research agenda, we are interested not only in design-time reasoning of OCBC models, but also in enactment, monitoring, and runtime verification. This poses two major challenges. On the one hand, a monitored trace has to be considered under a "partially closed" semantics, that is, by interpreting it as a complete record of what happened so far, while missing information about the future. On the other hand, a more fine-grained analysis, in the style of [23], regarding if and how a monitored trace conforms to an OCBC model is needed. We intend to attack this problem by combining finite and infinite reasoning over a partially closed knowledge base.

Acknowledgments. This research has been partially supported by the UNIBZ CRC projects PWORM and REKAP.

References

1. van der Aalst, W., Pesic, M., Schonenberg, H.: Declarative workflows: balancing between flexibility and support. Comput. Sci.-Res. Dev. **23**(2), 99–113 (2009)
2. van der Aalst, W.M.P.: Process Mining: Data Science in Action. Springer, Heidelberg (2016). https://doi.org/10.1007/978-3-662-49851-4
3. van der Aalst, W.M.P., Li, G., Montali, M.: Object-centric behavioral constraints. CoRR Technical report, CoRR (2017). http://arxiv.org/abs/1703.05740
4. Artale, A., Calvanese, D., Kontchakov, R., Ryzhikov, V., Zakharyaschev, M.: Reasoning over extended ER models. In: Parent, C., Schewe, K.-D., Storey, V.C., Thalheim, B. (eds.) ER 2007. LNCS, vol. 4801, pp. 277–292. Springer, Heidelberg (2007). https://doi.org/10.1007/978-3-540-75563-0_20
5. Artale, A., Parent, C., Spaccapietra, S.: Evolving objects in temporal information systems. Ann. Math. Artif. Intell. **50**(1–2), 5–38 (2007)
6. Artale, A., Calvanese, D., Kontchakov, R., Zakharyaschev, M.: The DL-Lite family and relations. JAIR **36**, 1–69 (2009)
7. Artale, A., Kontchakov, R., Ryzhikov, V., Zakharyaschev, M.: Complexity of reasoning over temporal data models. In: Proceedings of the 29th International Conference on Conceptual Modeling (ER). LNCS, vol. 4801, pp. 277–292. Springer, Heidelberg (2010)
8. Artale, A., Kontchakov, R., Ryzhikov, V., Zakharyaschev, M.: A cookbook for temporal conceptual data modeling with description logics. ACM Transactivity Comput. Logic (TOCL) **15**(3), 25 (2014)
9. Artale, A., Mazzullo, A., Ozaki, A.: Do you need infinite time? In: Proceedings of the 28th International Joint Conference on Artificial Intelligence (IJCAI) (2019, to appear)
10. Bagheri Hariri, B., Calvanese, D., Montali, M., De Giacomo, G., De Masellis, R., Felli, P.: Description logic knowledge and action bases. JAIR **46**, 651–686 (2013)
11. Berardi, D., Calvanese, D., De Giacomo, G.: Reasoning on UML class diagrams. Artif. Intell. J. **168**(1–2), 70–118 (2005)

12. Bhattacharya, K., Gerede, C., Hull, R., Liu, R., Su, J.: Towards formal analysis of artifact-centric business process models. In: Alonso, G., Dadam, P., Rosemann, M. (eds.) BPM 2007. LNCS, vol. 4714, pp. 288–304. Springer, Heidelberg (2007). https://doi.org/10.1007/978-3-540-75183-0_21

13. Calvanese, D., De Giacomo, G., Lembo, D., Lenzerini, M., Rosati, R.: Tractable reasoning and efficient query answering in description logics: the DL-Lite family. J. Autom. Reasoning 39(3), 385–429 (2007)

14. Calvanese, D., De Giacomo, G., Montali, M.: Foundations of data-aware process analysis: a database theory perspective. In: Proceedings of 32nd PODS. ACM (2013)

15. Chesani, F., et al.: Compliance in business processes with incomplete information and time constraints: a general framework based on abductive reasoning. Fundamenta Informaticae 159(3), 1–37 (2018)

16. Cohn, D., Hull, R.: Business artifacts: a data-centric approach to modeling business operations and processes. IEEE Data Eng. Bull. 32(3), 3–9 (2009)

17. Franconi, E., Mosca, A., Solomakhin, D.: ORM2: formalisation and encoding in OWL2. In: Herrero, P., Panetto, H., Meersman, R., Dillon, T. (eds.) OTM 2012. LNCS, vol. 7567, pp. 368–378. Springer, Heidelberg (2012). https://doi.org/10.1007/978-3-642-33618-8_51

18. Gabbay, D., Kurucz, A., Wolter, F., Zakharyaschev, M.: Many-Dimensional Modal Logics: Theory and Applications. Studies in Logic. Elsevier, Amsterdam (2003)

19. Gonzalez, P., Griesmayer, A., Lomuscio, A.: Verification of GSM-based artifact-centric systems by predicate abstraction. In: Barros, A., Grigori, D., Narendra, N.C., Dam, H.K. (eds.) ICSOC 2015. LNCS, vol. 9435, pp. 253–268. Springer, Heidelberg (2015). https://doi.org/10.1007/978-3-662-48616-0_16

20. Levesque, H.J.: Foundations of a functional approach to knowledge representation. Artif. Intell. J. 23, 155–212 (1984)

21. Li, G., de Carvalho, R.M., van der Aalst, W.M.P.: Automatic discovery of object-centric behavioral constraint models. In: Abramowicz, W. (ed.) BIS 2017. LNBIP, vol. 288, pp. 43–58. Springer, Cham (2017). https://doi.org/10.1007/978-3-319-59336-4_4

22. Li, G., de Murillas, E.G.L., de Carvalho, R.M., van der Aalst, W.M.P.: Extracting object-centric event logs to support process mining on databases. In: Mendling, J., Mouratidis, H. (eds.) CAiSE 2018. LNBIP, vol. 317, pp. 182–199. Springer, Cham (2018). https://doi.org/10.1007/978-3-319-92901-9_16

23. Maggi, F.M., Westergaard, M., Montali, M., van der Aalst, W.M.P.: Runtime verification of LTL-based declarative process models. In: Khurshid, S., Sen, K. (eds.) RV 2011. LNCS, vol. 7186, pp. 131–146. Springer, Heidelberg (2012). https://doi.org/10.1007/978-3-642-29860-8_11

24. Montali, M., Pesic, M., van der Aalst, W.M.P., Chesani, F., Mello, P., Storari, S.: Declarative specification and verification of service choreographies. ACM Trans. TWEB 4(1), 3 (2010)

25. Pesic, M., Schonenberg, H., van der Aalst, W.M.: DECLARE: Full support for loosely-structured processes. In: Proceedings of the Eleventh IEEE International Enterprise Distributed Object Computing Conference (EDOC 2007), pp. 287–298. IEEE Computer Society (2007)

26. Vianu, V.: Automatic verification of database-driven systems: a new frontier. In: Proceedings of the 12th International Conference on Database Theory (ICDT), pp. 1–13 (2009)

27. Wolter, F., Zakharyaschev, M.: Temporalizing description logics. In: Frontiers of Combining Systems, pp. 379–401. Research Studies Press-Wiley (2000)

Formal Modeling and SMT-Based Parameterized Verification of Data-Aware BPMN

Diego Calvanese[1], Silvio Ghilardi[2], Alessandro Gianola[1(✉)], Marco Montali[1], and Andrey Rivkin[1]

[1] Faculty of Computer Science, Free University of Bozen-Bolzano, Bolzano, Italy
`gianola@inf.unibz.it`
[2] Dipartimento di Matematica, Università degli Studi di Milano, Milan, Italy

Abstract. We propose DAB – a data-aware extension of BPMN where the process operates over case and persistent data (partitioned into a read-only database called catalog and a read-write database called repository). The model trades off between expressiveness and the possibility of supporting parameterized verification of safety properties on top of it. Specifically, taking inspiration from the literature on verification of artifact systems, we study verification problems where safety properties are checked irrespectively of the content of the read-only catalog, and accepting the potential presence of unboundedly many tuples in the catalog and repository. We tackle such problems using an array-based backward reachability procedure fully implemented in MCMT – a state-of-the-art array-based SMT model checker. Notably, we prove that the procedure is sound and complete for checking safety of DABs, and single out additional conditions that guarantee its termination and, in turn, show decidability of checking safety.

1   Introduction

In recent years, increasing attention has been given to multi-perspective models of business processes that strive to capture the interplay between the process and data dimensions [21]. Conventional finite-state verification techniques only work in this setting if data are abstractly represented, e.g., as finite sate machines [20] or process annotations [23]. If data are instead tackled in their full generality, verifying whether a process meets desired temporal properties (e.g., is safe) becomes highly undecidable, and cannot be directly attacked using conventional finite-state model checking techniques [1]. This triggered a flourishing research on the formalization and the boundaries of verifiability of data-aware processes, focusing mainly on data- and artifact-centric models [1,10]. Recent results in this stream of research [4,11] come with two strong advantages. First, they consider the relevant setting where the running process evolves a set of relations (henceforth called a data *repository*) containing data objects that may have been injected from the external environment (e.g., due to user interaction),

© Springer Nature Switzerland AG 2019
T. Hildebrandt et al. (Eds.): BPM 2019, LNCS 11675, pp. 157–175, 2019.
https://doi.org/10.1007/978-3-030-26619-6_12

or borrowed from a read-only relational database with constraints (henceforth called *catalog*). The repository acts as a working memory and a log for the process. Notably, it may accumulate unboundedly many tuples resulting from complex constructs in the process, such as while loops whose repeated activities insert new tuples in the repository (e.g., the applications sent by candidates in response to a job offer). The catalog stores background, contextual facts that do not change during the process execution, such as the catalog of product types, the usernames and passwords of registered customers in an order-to-cash process. In this setting, verification is studied parametrically to the catalog, so as to ensure that the process works as desired irrespectively of the specific read-only data stored therein. This is crucial to verify the process under robust conditions, also considering that actual data may not yet be available at modeling time. The second advantage of these techniques is that they tame the infinity of the state space to be verified with a symbolic approach, paving the way for the development of feasible implementations [17] or the usage of mature symbolic model checkers for infinite-state systems [4, 15].

In a parallel research line more conventional, activity-centric approaches, such as the de-facto standard BPMN, have been extended towards data support, mainly focusing on modeling and enactment [6,7,18], but not on verification. At the same time, several formalisms have been brought forward to capture multi-perspective processes based on Petri nets enriched with various forms of data: from data items carried by tokens [16,22], to case data with different datatypes [8], and persistent relational data manipulated with the full power of FOL/SQL [9,19]. While these formalisms qualify well to directly capture data-aware extensions of BPMN (e.g., [7,18]), they suffer of two main limitations. On the foundational side, they require to specify the data present in the read-only storage, and only allow boundedly many tuples (with an a-priori known bound) to be stored in the read-write ones. On the applied side, they have not yet led to the development of actual verifiers.

This leads us to the main question tackled by this paper: *how to extend BPMN towards data support, guaranteeing the applicability of the existing parameterized verification techniques and the corresponding actual verifiers, so far studied only in the artifact-centric setting?* We answer this question by considering the framework of [4] and the verification of safety properties (i.e., properties that must hold in every state of the analyzed system). Our *first contribution* is a data-aware extension of BPMN called DAB, which supports case data, as well as persistent relational data partitioned into a read-only catalog and a read-write repository. Case and persistent data are used to express conditions in the process as well as task preconditions; tasks, in turn, change the values of the case variables and insert/update/delete tuples into/from the repository. The resulting framework is similar, in spirit, to the BAUML approach [12], which relies on UML and OCL instead of BPMN as we do here. While [12] approaches verification via a translation to first-order logic with time, we follow a different route, by encoding DABs into the array-based artifact system framework from [4]. Thanks to this encoding, we can effectively verify safety properties of

DABs using the MCMT (*Model Checker Modulo Theories*) model checker [13,14]. MCMT implements a backward reachability procedure that relies on state-of-the-art Satisfiability Modulo Theories (SMT) solvers, and that has been widely used to verify infinite-state *array-based systems*.

Using the encoding above, we provide our *second contribution*: we show that this backward reachability procedure is sound and complete when it comes to checking safety of DABs. In this context, soundness means that whenever the procedure terminates the returned answer is correct, whereas completeness means that if the process is unsafe then the procedure will always discover it.

The fact that the procedure is sound and complete does not guarantee that it will always terminate. This brings us to the *third and last contribution* of this paper: we introduce further conditions that, by carefully controlling the interplay between the process and data components, guarantee the termination of the procedure. Such conditions are expressed as syntactic restrictions over the DAB under study, thus providing a concrete, BPMN-grounded counterpart of the conditions imposed in [4,17]. By exploiting the encoding from DABs to array-based artifact systems, and the soundness and completeness of backward reachability, we derive that checking safety for the class of DABs satisfying these conditions is decidable.

To show that our approach goes end-to-end from theory to actual verification, we finally report some preliminary experiments demonstrating how MCMT checks safety of DABs. An extended version of this paper is available in [2]. Full proofs of our technical results and the files of the experiments with MCMT can be found in [3].

2   Data-Aware BPMN

We start by describing our formal model of data-aware BPMN processes (DABs). We focus here on private, single-pool processes, analyzed considering a single case, similarly to soudness analysis in workflow nets [24].[1] Incoming messages are therefore handled as pure nondeterministic events. The model combines a wide range of (block-structured) BPMN control-flow constructs with task, event-reaction, and condition logic that inspect and modify persistent as well as case data.

First, some preliminary notation. We consider a set $\mathcal{S} = \mathcal{S}_v \uplus \mathcal{S}_{id}$ of (semantic) *types*, consisting of *primitive types* $\mathcal{S}_v$ accounting for data objects, and *id types* $\mathcal{S}_{id}$ accounting for identifiers. We assume that each type $S \in \mathcal{S}$ comes with a (possibly infinite) domain $\mathbb{D}_S$, a special constant $\mathtt{undef}_S \in \mathbb{D}_S$ to denote an undefined value in that domain, and a type-wise equality operator $=_S$. We omit the type and simply write $\mathtt{undef}$ and $=$ when clear from the context. We do not consider here additional type-specific predicates (such as comparison and arithmetic operators for numerical primitive types); these will be added in future

---

[1] The interplay among multiple cases is also crucial. The technical report [3] already contains an extension of the framework presented here, in which multiple cases are modeled and verified.

work. In the following, we simply use *typed* as a shortcut for *S-typed*. We also denote by $\mathbb{D}$ the overall domain of objects and identifiers (i.e., the union of all domains in $\mathcal{S}$). We consider a countably infinite set $\mathcal{V}$ of typed variables. Given a variable or object x, we may explicitly indicate that x has type S by writing $x : S$. We omit types whenever clear. We indicate a possibly empty tuple $\langle x_1, \ldots, x_n \rangle$ of variables as $\vec{x}$, and write $\vec{x} \subseteq \vec{y}$ if all variables in $\vec{x}$ also appear in $\vec{y}$.

2.1   The Data Schema

Consistently with BPMN, we consider two main forms of data: *case data*[2], instantiated and manipulated on a per-case basis; *persistent data* (cf. *data store references* in BPMN), accounting for global data that are accessed by all cases. For simplicity, case data are defined at the whole process level, and are directly visible by all tasks and subprocesses (without requiring the specification of input-output bindings and the like).

To account for persistent data, we consider relational databases. We describe relation schemas by using the *named perspective*, i.e., by assigning a dedicated typed attribute to each component (i.e., column) of a relation schema. Also for an attribute, we use the notation $a : S$ to explicitly indicate its type.

Definition 1. *A relation schema is a pair* $R = \langle N, A \rangle$*, where: (i)* $N = R.\mathsf{name}$ *is the relation name; (ii)* $A = R.\mathsf{attrs}$ *is a nonempty tuple of attributes.*   ◁

We call $|A|$ the *arity* of R. We assume that distinct relation schemas use distinct names, blurring the distinction between the two notions (i.e., $R.\mathsf{name} = R$). We also use the predicate notation $R(A)$ to represent a relation schema $\langle R, A \rangle$. A sample relation schema is $User(Uid{:}\mathsf{Int}, Name{:}\mathsf{String})$, where the first component represents the id-number of a user, and the second component is the string of her name.

Data Schema. First of all, we define the *catalog*, i.e., a read-only, persistent storage of data that is not modified during the execution of the process. Examples of the cat-relations are product types and registered customers in an order-to-cash scenario.

Definition 2. *A* catalog *Cat is a set of relation schemas equipped with* single-column primary key *and* foreign key *constraints. We assume that the primary key of relation schema R is always its first attribute, and denote it by $R.\mathsf{id}$. The type of $R.\mathsf{id}$ is a dedicated id type from $\mathcal{S}_{id}$ (i.e., no two relation schemas from Cat have the same id type). If another attribute a of R has as type an id-type $S \in \mathcal{S}_{id}$, then a is a foreign key referencing the relation schema whose primary key has type S.*   ◁

Example 1. Consider a simplified example of a job hiring process. To store background information related to the process we use the catalog with relation schemas:

---

[2] These are called *data objects* in BPMN, but we prefer to use the term *case data* to avoid name clashes with the formal notions.

- *JobCategory*(*Jcid*:jobcatID) - storing the (ids of the) job categories available in the company (e.g., programmer, analyst);
- *User*(*Uid*:userID, *Name*:StringName, *Age*:NumAge) - storing data about users registered to the company website, who may apply to positions offered by the company.

Each case of the process is about a job. Jobs are identified by the type jobcatID.

◁

The full data schema of a BPMN process combines a catalog with: (i) a persistent data *repository*, consisting of updatable relation schemas possibly referring to the catalog; (ii) a set of *case variables*, constituting local data carried by each process case.

Definition 3. *A* data schema $\mathcal{D}$ *is a tuple* $\langle Cat, Repo, X \rangle$, *where (i)* $Cat = \mathcal{D}$.cat *is a* catalog, *(ii)* $Repo = \mathcal{D}$.repo *is a set of relation schemas called* repository, *and (iii)* $X = \mathcal{D}$.cvars $\subset \mathcal{V}$ *is a finite set of typed variables called* case variables.

We use bold-face to distinguish case and normal variables. We call repo-relation (resp., cat-relation) a relation whose schema is in the repository (resp., catalog).

Relation schemas in the repository are not equipped with an explicit primary key, and thus they cannot reference each other, but may contain foreign keys pointing to the catalog or the case identifiers. In particular, similarly to foreign keys in the catalog, every attribute in *Repo* and case variable in X whose type is an id-type $S \in \mathcal{S}_{id}$ references a corresponding cat-relation whose primary key has type S. It will be clear how tuples can be inserted and removed from the repository once we introduce updates.

Example 2. To manage key information about the applications submitted for the job hiring, the company employs a repository that consists of one relation schema:

$$Application(Jcid:\text{jobcatID}, Uid:\text{userID}, Score:\text{NumScore}, Eligible:\text{Bool})$$

NumScore is a finite-domain type containing 100 scores in the range $[1, 100]$. For readability, we use the usual comparison predicates for variables of type NumScore: this is syntactic sugar and does not require to introduce datatype predicates in our framework. Since each posted job is created using a dedicated portal, its corresponding data do not have to be stored persistently and thus can be maintained just for a given case. At the same time, some specific values have to be moved from a specific case to the repository and vice-versa. This is done by resorting to the following case variables $\mathcal{D}$.cvars: *(i)* **jcid** : jobcatID references a job type from the catalog, matching the type of job associated to the case; *(ii)* **uid** : userID references the identifier of a user who is applying for the job associated to the case; *(iii)* **result** : Bool indicates whether the user identified by **uid** is eligible for winning the position or not; *(iv)* **qualif** : Bool indicates whether the user identified by **uid** qualifies for directly getting the job (without the need of carrying out a comparative evaluation of all applicants); *(v)* **winner** : userID contains the identifier of the applicant winning the position.

◁

At runtime, a *data snapshot* of a data schema consists of three components:

- An immutable *catalog instance*, i.e., a fixed set of tuples for each relation schema contained therein, so that the primary and foreign keys are satisfied.
- An assignment mapping case variables to corresponding data objects.
- A *repository instance*, i.e., a set of tuples forming a relation for each schema contained therein, so that the foreign key constraints pointing to the catalog are satisfied. Each tuple is associated to a distinct primary key that is not explicitly accessible.

Querying the Data Schema. To inspect the data contained in a snapshot, we need suitable query languages operating over the data schema of that snapshot. We start by considering boolean *conditions* over (case) variables, to express choices in the process.

Definition 4. *A condition is a formula of the form* $\varphi ::= (x = y) \mid \neg\varphi \mid \varphi_1 \wedge \varphi_2$, *where x and y are variables from* $\mathcal{V}$ *or constant objects from* $\mathbb{D}$. ◁

We make use of the standard abbreviation $\varphi_1 \vee \varphi_2 = \neg(\neg\varphi_1 \wedge \neg\varphi_2)$.

We now extend conditions to also access the data stored in the catalog and repository, and to ask for data objects subject to constraints. We consider the well-known language of unions of conjunctive queries with atomic negation, which correspond to unions of select-project-join SQL queries with table filters.

Definition 5. *A conjunctive query with filters over a data component* $\mathcal{D}$ *is a formula of the form* $Q ::= \varphi \mid R(x_1, \ldots, x_n) \mid \neg R(x_1, \ldots, x_n) \mid Q_1 \wedge Q_2$, *where* φ *is a condition with only* atomic *negation,* $R \in \mathcal{D}.\mathsf{cat} \cup \mathcal{D}.\mathsf{repo}$ *is a relation schema of arity n, and* $x_1, \ldots, x_n$ *are variables from* $\mathcal{V}$ *(including* $\mathcal{D}.\mathsf{cvars}$*) or constant objects from* $\mathbb{D}$*. We denote by free(Q) the set of variables occurring in Q that are* not *case variables in* $\mathcal{D}.\mathsf{cvars}$*.* ◁

For example, a conjunctive query $JobCategory(c) \wedge c \neq \mathsf{HR}$ lists all the job categories available in the company, apart from HR.

Definition 6. *A guard G over a data component* $\mathcal{D}$ *is an expression of the form* $q(\vec{x}) \leftarrow \bigvee_{i=1}^{n} Q_i$*, where: (i)* $q(\vec{x})$ *is the head of the guard with* answer variables $\vec{x}$*; (ii) each* Q_i *is a conjunctive query with filters over* $\mathcal{D}$*; (iii) for some* $i \in \{1, \ldots, n\}$*,* $\vec{x} \subseteq free(Q_i)$*. We denote by casevars(G) ⊆* $\mathcal{D}.\mathsf{cvars}$ *the set of* case variables used in G*, and by* $normvars(G) = \bigcup_{i \in \{1,\ldots,n\}} free(Q_i)$ *the other variables used in G.* ◁

To distinguish guard heads from relations, we write the former in camel case, while the latter shall always begin with capital letters.

Definition 7. *A guard G over a data component* $\mathcal{D}$ *is repo-free if none of its atoms queries a relation schema from* $\mathcal{D}.\mathsf{repo}$*.* ◁

As anticipated before, this language can be seen as a query language to retrieve data from a snapshot, or as a mechanism to constrain the combinations of data objects that can be injected into the process. E.g., guard $input(y\text{:string}, z\text{:string}) \rightarrow y \neq z$ returns all pairs of strings that are different from each other. Picking an answer in this (infinite) set of pairs can be seen as a (constrained) user input for y and z.

Going beyond this guard query language (e.g., by introducing universal quantification) would hamper the soundness and completeness of SMT-based verification over the resulting DABs. We will come back to this important aspect in the conclusion.

2.2 Tasks, Events, and Impact on Data

We now formalize how the process can access and update the data component when executing a task or reacting to the trigger of an external event.

The Update Logic. We start by discussing how data maintained in a snapshot can be subject to change while executing the process.

Definition 8. *Given a data schema $\mathcal{D}$, an update specification α is a pair $\langle G, E \rangle$, where: (i) $G = \alpha.\mathsf{pre}$ is a guard over $\mathcal{D}$ of the form $q(\vec{x}) \leftarrow Q$, called precondition; (ii) $E = \alpha.\mathsf{eff}$ is an effect rule that changes the snapshot of $\mathcal{D}$, as described next. Each effect rule has one of the following forms:*

(Insert&Set) *INSERT $\vec{u}$ INTO R AND SET $\mathbf{x}_1 = v_1, \ldots, \mathbf{x}_n = v_n$, where: (i) $\vec{u}, \vec{v}$ are variables in $\vec{x}$ or constant objects from $\mathbb{D}$; (ii) $\vec{\mathbf{x}} \in \mathcal{D}.\mathsf{cvars}$ are distinct case variables; (iii) R is a relation schema from $\mathcal{D}.\mathsf{repo}$ whose arity (and types) match $\vec{u}$. Either the INSERT or SET parts may be omitted, obtaining a pure* **Insert** *rule or* **Set** *rule.*

(Delete&Set) *DEL $\vec{u}$ FROM R AND SET $\mathbf{x}_1 = v_1, \ldots, \mathbf{x}_n = v_n$, where: (i) $\vec{u}, \vec{v}$ are variables in $\vec{x}$ or constant objects from $\mathbb{D}$; (ii) $\vec{\mathbf{x}} \in \mathcal{D}.\mathsf{cvars}$; (iii) R is a relation schema from $\mathcal{D}.\mathsf{repo}$ whose arity (and types) match $\vec{u}$. As in the previous rule type, the AND SET part may be omitted, obtaining a pure (repository)* **Delete** *rule.*

(Conditional update) *UPDATE $R(\vec{v})$ IF $\psi(\vec{u}, \vec{v})$ THEN η_1 ELSE η_2, where: (i) $\vec{u}$ is a tuple containing variables in $\vec{x}$ or constant objects from $\mathbb{D}$; (ii) ψ is a repo-free guard (called* filter*); (iii) R is a repo-relation schema; (iv) $\vec{v}$ is a tuple of new variables, i.e., such that $\vec{v} \cap (\vec{u} \cup \mathcal{D}.\mathsf{cvars}) = \emptyset$; (v) η_i is either an atomic formula of the form $R(\vec{u}')$ with $\vec{u}'$ a tuple of elements from $\vec{x} \cup \mathbb{D} \cup \vec{v}$, or a nested IF $\ldots$ THEN $\ldots$ ELSE.*   ◁

We now comment on the semantics of update specifications. An update specification α is executable in a given data snapshot if there is at least one answer to $\alpha.\mathsf{pre}$ in that snapshot. If so, the process executor(s) nondeterministically pick an answer, *binding* the answer variables of $\alpha.\mathsf{pre}$ to corresponding data objects in $\mathbb{D}$. This confirms the interpretation of $\alpha.\mathsf{pre}$ as a *constrained user input* when multiple bindings are available. Once a binding for the answer variables is picked, the effect rule α.eff is instantiated with that binding and issued. How this affects the current data snapshot depends on which effect rule is adopted.

If α.eff is an insert&set rule, the binding is used to *simultaneously* insert a tuple in one of the repo-relations, and update some of the case variables – with the implicit assumption that those not explicitly mentioned in the SET part maintain their current values. Since repo-relations do not have an explicit primary key, upon insertion of a tuple $\vec{u}$ in the instance of a repo-relation R, a fresh primary key is generated and attached to $\vec{u}$. Two insertion semantics can then be used to characterize the insertion. Under the first semantics of *multiset insertion*, the update always succeeds in inserting $\vec{u}$ into R. Under the *set insertion* semantics, instead, R comes not only with its implicit primary key, but also with a key constraint defined over a subset $K \subseteq R$.attrs of its attributes (by default, coinciding with R.attrs itself); the update is then committed only if such a key constraint is satisfied. In the case of $K = R$.attrs, this implies that the update succeeds only if $\vec{u}$ is not already present in R, thus treating R as a proper set.

Example 3. We continue the job hiring example, by considering update specifications of type insert&set. When a new case is created, the update specification InsJobCat indicates what is the job category associated to the case. Specifically, InsJobCat.pre selects a job category from the corresponding cat-relation, while InsJobCat.eff assigns the selected job category to the case variable **jcid**:

$$\text{InsJobCat.pre} \triangleq getJobType(c) \leftarrow JobCategory(c) \quad \text{InsJobCat.eff} \triangleq \text{SET jcid} = c$$

When the case receives an application, the user id is picked from the corresponding *User* via the update specification InsUser, where:

$$\text{InsUser.pre} \triangleq getUser(u) \leftarrow User(u, n, a) \quad \text{InsUser.eff} \triangleq \text{SET uid} = u$$

A different usage of precondition, resembling a pure external choice, is the update specification CheckQual to handle a quick evaluation of the candidate and check whether she has such a high profile qualifying her to directly get an offer:

$$\text{CheckQual.pre} \triangleq isQualified(q : \text{Bool}) \leftarrow \text{true} \quad \text{CheckQual.eff} \triangleq \text{SET qualif} = q$$

As an example of insertion rule, we consider the situation where the candidate whose id is currently stored in the case variable **uid** has not been directly judged as qualified. She is then subject to a more fine-grained evaluation via the EvalApp specification, resulting in a score that is then registered in the repository.

$$\text{EvalApp.pre} \triangleq getScore(s : \text{NumScore}) \leftarrow 1 \leq s \wedge s \leq 100$$
$$\text{EvalApp.eff} \triangleq \text{INSERT } \langle \text{jcid}, \text{uid}, s, \text{undef} \rangle \text{ INTO } Application$$

Here, the insertion indicates an **undef** eligibility, since it will be assessed in a consequent step of the process. Notice that with the *multiset insertion semantics*, the same user may apply multiple times for the same job (resulting multiple times as applicant). With the *set insertion semantics*, we could instead enforce the uniqueness of the application by declaring the second component (i.e., the user id) of *Application* as a key.   ◁

If α.eff is a delete&set rule, then the executability of the update is subject to the fact that the tuple $\vec{u}$ selected by the binding and to be removed from R, is actually present in the current instance of R. If so, the binding is used to *simultaneously* delete $\vec{u}$ from R and update some of the case variables – with the implicit assumption that those not explicitly mentioned in the SET part maintain their current values.

Finally, a conditional update rule applies, tuple by tuple, a bulk operation over the content of R. Each tuple in R is reviewed. If the tuple passes the filter associated to the rule, it is updated according to the THEN part, otherwise according to the ELSE part.

Example 4. Continuing with our running example, we now consider the update specification MarkE handling the situation where no candidate has been directly considered as qualified, and so the eligibility of all received (and evaluated) applications has to be assessed. Here we consider that each application is eligible if and only if its evaluation resulted in a score greater than 80. Technically, MarkE.pre is a true precondition, and:

MarkE.eff $\triangleq$ UPDATE $Application(c, u, s, e)$
    IF $s > 80$ THEN $Application(c, u, s, \mathbf{true})$ ELSE $Application(c, u, s, \mathbf{false})$

If there is at least one eligible candidate, she can be selected as a winner using the SelWinner update specification, which deletes the selected winner tuple from *Application*, and transfers its content to the corresponding case variables (also ensuring that the **winner** case variable is set to the applicant id). Technically:

SelWinner.pre $\triangleq$ $getWinner(c, u, s, e) \leftarrow Application(c, u, s, e) \wedge e = \mathbf{true}$
SelWinner.eff $\triangleq$ DEL $\langle c, u, s, e \rangle$ FROM *Application*
    AND SET $\mathbf{jcid} = c, \mathbf{uid} = u, \mathbf{winner} = u, \mathbf{result} = e, \mathbf{qualif} = \mathbf{false}$

Deleting the tuple is useful when the selected winner may refuse the job, and hence should not be considered again if a new winner selection is done. To keep such tuple in the repository, one would just need to remove the DEL part from SelWinner.eff. ◁

The Task/Event Logic. We now substantiate how the update logic is used to specify the task/event logic within a DAB process. The first important observation, not related to our specific approach, but inherently present whenever the process control flow is enriched with relational data, is that update effects manipulating the repository must be executed in an atomic, non-interruptible way. This is essential to ensure that insertions/deletions into/from the repository are applied on the same data snapshot where the precondition is checked. Breaking simultaneity would lead to nondeterministic interleaving with other update specifications potentially operating over the same portion of the repository. This is why we consider two types of task: *atomic* and *nonatomic*.

Each atomic task/catching event is associated to a corresponding update specification. In the case of tasks, the specification precondition indicates under which circumstances the task can be enacted, and the specification effect how enacting the task impacts on the underlying data snapshot. In the case of events, the specification precondition constrains the data payload that comes with the event (possibly depending on the data snapshot, which is global and therefore accessible also by an external event trigger). The effect dictates how reacting to a triggered event impacts on the data snapshot.

This is realized according to the following lifecycle. The task/event is initially idle, i.e., quiescent. When the progression of a case reaches an idle task/event, such a task/event becomes enabled. An enabled task/event may nondeterministically fire depending on the choice of the process executor(s). Upon firing, a binding satisfying the precondition of the update specification associated to the task/event is selected, consequently grounding and applying the corresponding effect. At the same time, the lifecycle moves from enabled to compl. Finally, a compl task/event triggers the progression of its case depending on the process-control flow, simultaneously bringing the task/event back to the idle state (which would then make it possible for the task to be executed again later, if the process control-flow dictates so).

The lifecycle of a nonatomic task diverges in two crucial respects. First, upon firing it moves from enabled to active, and later on nondeterministically from active to compl (thus having a duration). The precondition of its update specification is checked and bound to one of the available answers when the task becomes active, while the corresponding effect is applied when the task becomes compl. Since these two transitions occur asynchronously, to avoid the aforementioned transactional issues we assume that the task effect operates only on case variables (and not on the repository).

2.3 Process Schema

A process schema consists of a block-structured BPMN diagram, enriched with conditions and update effects expressed over a given data schema, according to what described in the previous sections. As for the control flow, we consider a wide range of block-structured patterns compliant with the standard. We focus on private BPMN processes, thereby handling incoming messages in a pure nondeterministic way. So we do for timer events, nondeterministically accounting for their expiration without entering into their metric temporal semantics. Focusing on block-structured components helps us in obtaining a direct, execution semantics, and a consequent modular and clean translation of various BPMN constructs (including boundary events and exception handling). However, it is important to stress that our approach would seamlessly work also for non-structured processes where each case introduces boundedly many tokens.

As usual, blocks are recursively decomposed into sub-blocks, the leaves being task or empty blocks. Depending on its type, a block may come with one or more nested blocks, and be associated with other elements, such as conditions, types of the involved events, and the like. We consider a wide range of blocks, covering the basic, flow, and exception handling patterns in [2]. Figure 1 gives an idea about what is covered by our approach. With these blocks at hand, we finally obtain the full definition of a DAB.

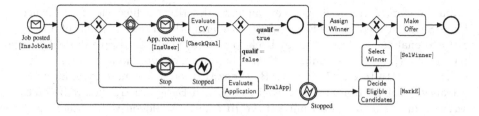

Fig. 1. The job hiring process. Elements in squared brackets attach the update specifications in Examples 3 and 4 to corresponding tasks/events.

Definition 9. *A DAB $\mathcal{M}$ is a pair $\langle \mathcal{D}, \mathcal{P} \rangle$ where $\mathcal{D}$ is a data schema, and $\mathcal{P}$ is a root process block such that all conditions and update effects attached to $\mathcal{P}$ and its descendant blocks are expressed over $\mathcal{D}$.* ◁

Example 5. The full hiring job process is shown in Fig. 1, using the update effects described in Examples 3 and 4. Intuitively, the process works as follows. A case is created when a job is posted, and enters into a looping subprocess where it expects candidates to apply. Specifically, the case waits for an incoming application, or for an external message signalling that the hiring has to be stopped (e.g., because too much time has passed from the posting). Whenever an application is received, the CV of the candidate is evaluated, with two possible outcomes. The first outcome indicates that the candidate directly qualifies for the position, hence no further applications should be considered. In this case, the process continues by declaring the candidate as winner, and making an offer to her. The second outcome of the CV evaluation is instead that the candidate does not directly qualify. A more detailed evaluation is then carried out, assigning a score to the application and storing the outcome into the process repository, then waiting for additional applications to come. When the application management subprocess is stopped (which we model through an error so as to test various types of blocks in the experiments reported in Sect. 3.3), the applications present in the repository are all processed in parallel, declaring which candidates are eligible and which not depending on their scores. Among the eligible ones, a winner is then selected, making an offer to her. We implicitly assume here that at least one applicant is eligible, but we can easily extend the DAB to account also for the case where no application is eligible. ◁

As customary, each block has a lifecycle indicating its current state, and how the state may evolve depending on the specific semantics of the block, and the evolution of its inner blocks. In Sect. 2.2 we have already characterized the lifecycle of tasks and catch events. For the other blocks, we continue to use the standard states `idle`, `enabled`, `active`, and `compl`. We use the very same rules of execution described in the BPMN standard to regulate the progression of blocks through such states, taking advantage from the fact that, being the process block-structured, only one instance of a block can be enabled/active at a given time for a given case. As an example, we describe the lifecycle of a sequence block S with nested blocks B_1 and B_2 (considering that the transitions of S from idle to enabled and from compl back to idle are inductively regulated by its parent block): *(i)* if S is enabled, then it becomes active, inducing a transition of B_1 from idle to enabled; *(ii)* if B_1 is compl, then it becomes idle, inducing a transition of B_2 from idle to enabled; *(iii)* if B_2 is compl, then it becomes idle, inducing S to move from active to compl. Analogously for other block types.

2.4   Execution Semantics

We intuitively describe the execution semantics of a case over DAB $\mathcal{M} = \langle \mathcal{D}, \mathcal{P} \rangle$, using the update/task logic and progression rules of blocks as a basis. Upon execution, each state of $\mathcal{M}$ is characterized by an $\mathcal{M}$-*snapshot*, which consists of a data snapshot of $\mathcal{D}$ (cf. Sect. 2.1) and an assignment mapping each block in $\mathcal{P}$ to its current lifecycle state. Initially, the data snapshot fixes the immutable content of the catalog $\mathcal{D}$.cat, while the repository instance is empty, the case assignment is initialized to all undef, and the control assignment assigns to all blocks in $\mathcal{P}$ the idle state, with the exception of $\mathcal{P}$ itself, which is enabled. At each moment in time, the $\mathcal{M}$-snapshot is then evolved by nondeterministically evolving the case through one of the executable steps in the process, depending on the current $\mathcal{M}$-snapshot. If the execution step is about the progression of the case inside the process control-flow, then the control assignment is updated. If instead the execution step is about the application of some update effect, the new $\mathcal{M}$-snapshot is obtained according to Sect. 2.2.

3   Parameterized Verification of Safety Properties

We now focus on parameterized verification of DABs using the framework of array-based artifact systems of [4], which bridges the gap between SMT-based model checking of array-based systems [13,14], and data- and artifact-centric processes [10,11].

3.1   Array-Based Artifact Systems and Safety Checking

In general terms, an array-based system describes the evolution of array data structures of unbounded size. The logical representation of an array relies on a theory with two types of sorts: one for the array indexes, and the other for the elements stored in the array cells. Since the content of an array changes

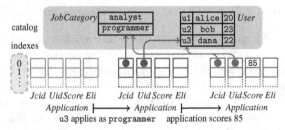

Fig. 2. Array-based representation of the *Application* repo-relation of Example 2, and manipulation of a job application. Empty cells contain undef.

over time, it is represented by a *function* variable, called *array state variable*, which defines for each index what is the value stored in the corresponding cell. Its interpretation changes when moving from one state to another, reflecting the intended manipulation of the array. Hence, an array-based system working over array a is defined through: *(i)* a state formula $I(a)$ describing the *initial configuration(s)* of a; *(ii)* a formula $\tau(a, a')$ describing the *transitions* that transforms the content of the array from a to a'. By suitably using logical operators, τ can express in a single formula a set of different updates over a. One of the most studied verification problems is that of *unsafety verification*: it checks whether the evolution induced by τ over a starting from a configuration in $I(a)$ eventually *reaches* an *unsafe* configuration described by a state formula $K(a)$. Several mature model checkers exist to ascertain (un)safety of these type of systems. In our work, we rely on MCMT [15].

In [4], we have extended array-based systems towards an array-based version of the artifact-centric approach, considering in particular the sophisticated model in [17]. In the resulting formalism, called RAS, a *relational* artifact system accesses a read-only database with keys and foreign keys (cf. our DAB catalog). In addition, the RAS operates over a set of relations possibly containing unboundedly many updatable entries (cf. our DAB repository). Figure 2 gives an intuitive idea of how this type of system looks like, using the catalog and repository from Example 2. The catalog is treated as a rich, background theory, which can be considered as a more sophisticated version of the element sort in basic array systems. Each repo-relation is treated as a set of arrays, where each array accounts for one component of the corresponding repo-relation. A tuple in the relation is reconstructed by accessing all such arrays with the same index.

Verification of RAS is also tamed in [4], checking whether there exists an instance of the read-only database so that the RAS can reach an unsafe configuration. This is approached by extending the original symbolic *backward reachability* procedure for unsafety verification of array-based systems to the case of RAS. The procedure starts from the undesired states captured by $K(a)$, and iteratively computes so-called *preimages*, i.e., logical formulae symbolically describing those states that, through consecutive applications of τ, directly or indirectly reach configurations satisfying $K(a)$. A preimage formula may contain existentially quantified variables referring to data objects in the catalog. MCMT employs novel quantifier elimination techniques [4,5] to suitably remove such variables, and obtain a state formula that describes the predecessor states. A fixpoint check is delegated to a state-of-the-art SMT solver, so as to check whether the computed predecessors all coincide with already iteratively computed states. If no new state has been produced, the procedure stops by emitting *safe*. Otherwise, the preimage formula is conjoined with $I(a)$ and sent to the SMT solver to check for satisfiability: if so, then the computed preimage states intersect the initial ones, and the procedure stops by emitting *unsafe* as a verdict; if not, new preimages are iteratively computed and the steps above are repeated. This procedure is shown to be sound and complete for checking unsafety of RAS in [4], where we also single out subclasses of RAS with decidable unsafety, and for which MCMT is ensured to terminate. One class is that of RAS operating over arrays whose maximum size is bounded a-priori. This type of RAS is called SAS (for *simple artifact system*). All in all, this framework provides a natural foundational and practical basis to formally analyze DABs, which we tackle next.

3.2   Verification Problems for DABs

First, we need a language to express unsafety properties over a DAB $\mathcal{M} = \langle \mathcal{D}, \mathcal{P} \rangle$. Properties are expressed in a fragment of the *guard* language of Definition 6 that queries repo-relations and case variables as well as the cat-relations that tuples from repo-relations or case variables refer to. Properties also query the control state of $\mathcal{P}$. This is done by implicitly extending $\mathcal{D}$ with additional, special case *control variables* that refer to the lifecycle states of the blocks in $\mathcal{P}$ (where a block named B gets variable **Blifecycle**). Given a snapshot, each such variable is assigned to the lifecycle state of the corresponding block (i.e., idle, enabled, and the like).

Definition 10. *A* property *over* $\mathcal{M} = \langle \mathcal{D}, \mathcal{P} \rangle$ *is a guard* G *over* $\mathcal{D}$ *and the control variables of* $\mathcal{P}$, *such that every non-case variable in* G *also appears in a relational atom* $R(y_1, \ldots, y_n)$, *where either* R *is a repo-relation, or* R *is a cat-relation and* $y_1 \in \mathcal{D}.\text{cvars}$.

Example 6. By naming HP the root process block of Fig. 1, the property (**HPlifecycle** = completed) checks whether some case of the process can terminate. This property is *unsafe* for our hiring process, since there is at least one way to evolve the process from the start to the end. Since DAB processes are block-structured, this is enough to ascertain that the hiring process is *sound*. Property **EvalApplifecycle** = completed $\land$ *Application*$(j, u, s, \text{true}) \land s > 100$ (the **5th safe** in Sect. 3.3) describes instead the undesired situation where, after the evaluation of an application, there exists an applicant with score greater than 100. The hiring process is *safe* w.r.t. this property.   ◁

We study unsafety of these properties by considering the general case, and also the one where the repository can store only boundedly many tuples, with a fixed bound. In the latter case, we call the DAB *repo-bounded*.

Translating DABs into Array-Based Artifact Systems. Given an unsafety verification problem over a DAB $\mathcal{M} = \langle \mathcal{D}, \mathcal{P} \rangle$, we encode it as a corresponding unsafety verification problem over a RAS that reconstructs the execution semantics of $\mathcal{M}$. We only provide here the main intuitions behind the translation, which is fully addressed in [3]. In the translation, $\mathcal{D}.\text{cat}$ and $\mathcal{D}.\text{cvars}$ are mapped into their corresponding abstractions in RAS (namely, the RAS read-only database and artifact variables, respectively). $\mathcal{D}.\text{repo}$ is instead encoded using the intuition of Fig. 2: for each $R \in \mathcal{D}.\text{repo}$ and each attribute $a \in R.\text{attrs}$, a dedicated array is introduced. Array indexes represent (implicit) identifiers of tuples in R, in line with our repository model. To retrieve a tuple from R, one just needs to access the arrays corresponding to the different attributes of R with the same index. Finally, case variables are represented using (bounded) arrays of size 1. On top of these data structures, $\mathcal{P}$ is translated into a RAS transition formula that exactly reconstructs the execution semantics of the blocks in $\mathcal{P}$.

With this translation in place, we define BackReach as the backward reachability procedure that: (1) takes as input *(i)* a DAB $\mathcal{M}$, *(ii)* a property φ to be verified, *(iii)* a boolean indicating whether $\mathcal{M}$ is repo-bounded or not (in the first case, also providing the value of the bound), and *(iv)* a boolean indicating whether the semantics for insertion is set or multiset; (2) translates $\mathcal{M}$ into a corresponding RAS $\mathcal{M}'$, and φ into a corresponding property φ' over $\mathcal{M}'$ (Definition 10 ensures that φ' is indeed a RAS state formula); (3) returns the result produced by the MCMT backward reachability procedure (cf. Sect. 3.1) on $\mathcal{M}'$ and φ'.

3.3 Verification Results

Using the DAB-to-RAS translation and the results in [4], we provide now our main technical contributions. First: DABs can be correctly verified using BackReach.

Theorem 1. BackReach *is sound and complete for checking unsafety of DABs that use the multiset or set insertion semantics.*   ◁

Soundness tell us that when BackReach terminates, it produces a correct answer, while completeness guarantees that whenever a DAB is unsafe with respect to a property, then BackReach detects this. Hence, BackReach is a semi-decision procedure for unsafety.

We study additional conditions on the input DAB to guarantee termination of BackReach, then becoming a full decision procedure for unsafety. The first, unavoidable condition, in line with [4,17], is that the catalog must be *acyclic*: its foreign keys cannot form referential cycles (where a table directly or indirectly refers to itself).

Theorem 2. BackReach *terminates when verifying properties over repo-bounded and acyclic DABs using the multiset or set insertion semantics.*   ◁

If the input DAB is not repo-bounded, acyclicity of the catalog is not enough: termination requires to carefully control the interplay between the different components of the DAB. While the conditions required by the technical proofs are quite difficult to grasp at the syntactic level, they can be intuitively understood using the following *locality principle*: whenever the progression of the DAB depends on the repository, it does so only via a single entry in one of its relations. Hence, direct/indirect comparisons and joins of distinct tuples within the same or different repo-relations cannot be used. To avoid indirect comparisons/joins, queries cannot mix case variables and repo-relations.

Thus, set insertions cannot be supported, since by definition they require to compare tuples in the same relation. The next definition is instrumental to enforce locality.

Definition 11. *A guard $G \triangleq q(\vec{x}) \leftarrow \bigvee_{i=1}^{n} Q_i$ over data component $\mathcal{D}$ is separated if $normvars(Q_i) \cap normvars(Q_j) = \emptyset$ for every $i \neq j$, and each Q_i is of the form $\chi \wedge R(\vec{y}) \wedge \xi$ (with χ, $R(\vec{y})$, and ξ optional), where: (i) χ is a conjunctive query with filters only over $\mathcal{D}$.cat, and that can employ case variables; (ii) $R \in \mathcal{D}$.repo is a repo-relation schema; (iii) $\vec{y}$ is a tuple of variables and/or constant objects in $\mathbb{D}$, such that $\vec{y} \cap \mathcal{D}$.cvars $= \emptyset$, and $normvars(\chi) \cap \vec{y} = \emptyset$; (iv) ξ is a conjunctive query with filters over $\mathcal{D}$.cat only, that possibly mentions variables in $\vec{y}$ but does not include any case variable, and such that $normvars(\chi) \cap normvars(\xi) = \emptyset$. A property is separated if it is so as a guard.* ◁*

A separated guard is made of two isolated parts: a part χ inspecting case variables and their relationship with the catalog, and a part $R(\vec{y}) \wedge \xi$ retrieving a single tuple $\vec{y}$ from some repo-relation R, possibly filtering it through inspection of the catalog via ξ.

Example 7. Consider the refinement `EvalApp.pre` $\triangleq$ *GetScore*(s : Num Score) $\leftarrow \xi \wedge \chi$ of the guard `EvalApp.pre` from Example 3, where χ := *User*(**uid**, *name*, *age*) checks if the variables $\langle$**uid**, *name*, *age*$\rangle$ form a tuple in *User*, and ξ := $1 \leq s \wedge s \leq 100$. This guard is separated since χ and ξ match the requirements of the previous definition. ◁

Theorem 3. *Let $\mathcal{M}$ be an acyclic DAB that uses the multiset insertion semantics, and is such that for each update specification u of $\mathcal{M}$, the following holds: 1. If u.eff is an insert&set rule (with explicit INSERT part), u.pre is repo-free; 2. If u.eff is a set rule (with no INSERT part), then either (i) u.pre is repo-free, or (ii) u.pre is separated and all case variables appear in the SET part of u.eff; 3. If u.eff is a delete&set rule, then u.pre is separated and all case variables appear in the SET part of u.eff; 4. If u.eff is a conditional update rule, then u.pre is repo-free and boolean, so that u.eff only makes use of the new variables introduced in its UPDATE part (as well as constant objects in $\mathbb{D}$). Then, BackReach terminates when verifying separated properties over $\mathcal{M}$.*

The conditions of Theorem 3 represent a concrete, BPMN-like counterpart of the abstract ones used in [17] and [4] towards decidability.

Specifically, Theorem 3 employs: *(i)* repo-freedom, and *(ii)* separation with the manipulation of *all* case variables at once. We intuitively explain how these conditions substantiate the locality principle. Overall, the main difficulty is that case variables may be loaded with data objects extracted from the repository. Hence, the usage of a case variable may mask an underlying reference to a tuple component stored in some repo-relation. Given this, locality demands that no two case variables can simultaneously hold data objects coming from different tuples in the repository. At the beginning, this is trivially true, since all case variables are undefined. A safe snapshot guaranteeing this condition continues to stay so after an insertion of the form mentioned in point 1 of Theorem 3: a repo-free precondition ensures that the repository is not queried at all, and hence trivially preserves locality. Locality may be easily destroyed by arbitrary set or delete&set rules whose precondition accesses the repository. Three aspects have to be considered to avoid this. First, we have to guarantee that the precondition does not mix case variables and repo-relations: Theorem 3 does so thanks to separation. Second, we have to avoid that when the precondition retrieves objects from the repository, it extracts them from different tuples therein: this is again guaranteed by separation, since only one tuple is extracted. A third, subtle situation that would destroy locality is the one in which the objects retrieved from (the same tuple in) the repository are only used to assign *a proper subset* of the case variables: the other case variables could in fact still hold objects previously retrieved from a *different* tuple in the repository. Theorem 3 guarantees that this never happens by imposing that, upon a set or delete&set operation, *all* case variables are involved in the assignment. Those case variables that get objects extracted from the repository are then guaranteed to all implicitly point to the same repository tuple retrieved by the separated precondition.

Example 8. The hiring DAB obeys to all conditions in Theorem 3, ensuring termination of BackReach. E.g., EvalApp in Example 3 matches point 1: its precondition is repo-free. SelWinner from the same example matches point 3: SelWinner.pre is trivially separated and *all* case variables appear in the SET part of SelWinner.eff.   ◁

First mcmt Experiments. We have encoded the job hiring DAB in MCMT, systematically applying the translation rules recalled in Sect. 3.2, and fully spelled out in [3] when proving the main theorems of Sect. 3.3. We have then checked the DAB for process termination (which took 0.43 s), and against five safe and five unsafe properties. E.g., the 1st **unsafe** property describes the desired situation in which, after having evaluated an application (i.e., EvalApp is completed), there exists at least an applicant with a score greater than 0. Formally: **EvalApplifecycle** = $\texttt{completed} \land Application(j, u, s, e) \land s > 0$. The 4th **safe** property represents the situation where a winner has been selected after the deadline (i.e., SelWin is completed),

prop.	time(s)
safe 1	0.20
2	5.85
3	3.56
4	0.03
5	0.27
unsafe 1	0.18
2	1.17
3	4.45
4	1.43
5	1.14

but the case variable **result** indicates that the winner is not eligible. Formally: **SelWinlifecycle** = $\texttt{completed} \land \textbf{result} = \texttt{false}$. MCMT returns SAFE, witnessing that this configuration is not reachable from the initial one. The table on the right summarizes the obtained, encouraging results (time in seconds). The MCMT specifications with all the checked properties (and their intuitive interpretation) are available in [3]. All tests are directly reproducible.

4 Conclusion

We have introduced a data-aware extension of BPMN, called DAB, balancing between expressiveness and verifiability. We have shown that parameterized safety problems over DABs can be tackled by array-based SMT techniques, and in particular the backward reachability procedure of the MCMT model checker. We have then identified classes of DABs with conditions that control how the process operates over data and ensure termination of backward reachability. Methodologically, such conditions can be seen as modeling principles for data-aware process designers who aim at making their processes verifiable. Whether these conditions apply to real-life processes is an open question that calls for novel research in their empirical validation on real-world scenarios, and in the definition of guidelines to refactor arbitrary DABs into verifiable ones.

From the foundational perspective we want to equip DABs with datatypes and arithmetic operators, widely supported by SMT solvers. We also want to attack the main limitation of our approach, namely that guards and conditions are existential formulae, and the only (restricted) form of universal quantification in the update language is that of conditional updates. From the experimental point of view, the initial results obtained in this paper and [4] indicate that the approach is promising. We intend to fully automate the translation from DABs to array-based systems, and benchmark the performance of verifiers for data-aware processes, starting from the examples in [17]: they are inspired by reference BPMN processes, and consequently should be easily encoded as DABs.

References

1. Calvanese, D., De Giacomo, G., Montali, M.: Foundations of data aware process analysis: a database theory perspective. In: Proceedings of the PODS, pp. 1–12 (2013)
2. Calvanese, D., Ghilardi, S., Gianola, A., Montali, M., Rivkin, A.: Formal modeling and SMT-based parameterized verification of data-aware BPMN (extended version). Technical report arXiv:1906.07811 (2019)
3. Calvanese, D., Ghilardi, S., Gianola, A., Montali, M., Rivkin, A.: Formal modeling and SMT-based parameterized verification of multi-case data-aware BPMN. Technical report arXiv:1905.12991 (2019)
4. Calvanese, D., Ghilardi, S., Gianola, A., Montali, M., Rivkin, A.: From model completeness to verification of data aware processes. In: Lutz, C., Sattler, U., Tinelli, C., Turhan, A.Y., Wolter, F. (eds.) Description Logic, Theory Combination, and All That. LNCS, vol. 11560, pp. 212–239. Springer, Cham (2019). https://doi.org/10.1007/978-3-030-22102-7_10
5. Calvanese, D., Ghilardi, S., Gianola, A., Montali, M., Rivkin, A.: Model completeness, covers and superposition. In: Automated Deduction - CADE 27, LNCS (LNAI), vol. 11716. Springer, Cham (2019)
6. Combi, C., Oliboni, B., Weske, M., Zerbato, F.: Conceptual modeling of processes and data: connecting different perspectives. In: Trujillo, J., et al. (eds.) ER 2018. LNCS, vol. 11157, pp. 236–250. Springer, Cham (2018). https://doi.org/10.1007/978-3-030-00847-5_18
7. De Giacomo, G., Oriol, X., Estañol, M., Teniente, E.: Linking data and BPMN processes to achieve executable models. In: Dubois, E., Pohl, K. (eds.) CAiSE 2017. LNCS, vol. 10253, pp. 612–628. Springer, Cham (2017). https://doi.org/10.1007/978-3-319-59536-8_38

8. de Leoni, M., Felli, P., Montali, M.: A holistic approach for soundness verification of decision-aware process models. In: Trujillo, J., et al. (eds.) ER 2018. LNCS, vol. 11157, pp. 219–235. Springer, Cham (2018). https://doi.org/10.1007/978-3-030-00847-5_17

9. De Masellis, R., Di Francescomarino, C., Ghidini, C., Montali, M., Tessaris, S.: Add data into business process verification: bridging the gap between theory and practice. In: Proceedings of AAAI, pp. 1091–1099. AAAI Press (2017)

10. Deutsch, A., Hull, R., Li, Y., Vianu, V.: Automatic verification of database-centric systems. SIGLOG News 5(2), 37–56 (2018)

11. Deutsch, A., Li, Y., Vianu, V.: Verification of hierarchical artifact systems. In: Proceedings of the PODS, pp. 179–194 (2016)

12. Estañol, M., Sancho, M.-R., Teniente, E.: Verification and validation of UML artifact-centric business process models. In: Zdravkovic, J., Kirikova, M., Johannesson, P. (eds.) CAiSE 2015. LNCS, vol. 9097, pp. 434–449. Springer, Cham (2015). https://doi.org/10.1007/978-3-319-19069-3_27

13. Ghilardi, S., Nicolini, E., Ranise, S., Zucchelli, D.: Towards SMT model checking of array-based systems. In: Armando, A., Baumgartner, P., Dowek, G. (eds.) IJCAR 2008. LNCS (LNAI), vol. 5195, pp. 67–82. Springer, Heidelberg (2008). https://doi.org/10.1007/978-3-540-71070-7_6

14. Ghilardi, S., Ranise, S.: Backward reachability of array-based systems by SMT solving: termination and invariant synthesis. Log. Methods Comput. Sci. 6(4), 1–48 (2010)

15. Ghilardi, S., Ranise, S.: MCMT: a model checker modulo theories. In: Giesl, J., Hähnle, R. (eds.) IJCAR 2010. LNCS (LNAI), vol. 6173, pp. 22–29. Springer, Heidelberg (2010). https://doi.org/10.1007/978-3-642-14203-1_3

16. Lasota, S.: Decidability border for Petri nets with data: WQO dichotomy conjecture. In: Kordon, F., Moldt, D. (eds.) PETRI NETS 2016. LNCS, vol. 9698, pp. 20–36. Springer, Cham (2016). https://doi.org/10.1007/978-3-319-39086-4_3

17. Li, Y., Deutsch, A., Vianu, V.: VERIFAS: a practical verifier for artifact systems. PVLDB 11(3), 283–296 (2017)

18. Meyer, A., Pufahl, L., Fahland, D., Weske, M.: Modeling and enacting complex data dependencies in business processes. In: Daniel, F., Wang, J., Weber, B. (eds.) BPM 2013. LNCS, vol. 8094, pp. 171–186. Springer, Heidelberg (2013). https://doi.org/10.1007/978-3-642-40176-3_14

19. Montali, M., Rivkin, A.: DB-Nets: on the marriage of colored Petri Nets and relational databases. ToPNoC 28(4), 91–118 (2017)

20. Müller, D., Reichert, M., Herbst, J.: Data-driven modeling and coordination of large process structures. In: Meersman, R., Tari, Z. (eds.) OTM 2007. LNCS, vol. 4803, pp. 131–149. Springer, Heidelberg (2007). https://doi.org/10.1007/978-3-540-76848-7_10

21. Reichert, M.: Process and data: two sides of the same coin? In: Meersman, R., et al. (eds.) OTM 2012. LNCS, vol. 7565, pp. 2–19. Springer, Heidelberg (2012). https://doi.org/10.1007/978-3-642-33606-5_2

22. Rosa-Velardo, F., de Frutos-Escrig, D.: Decidability and complexity of Petri nets with unordered data. Theor. Comput. Sci. 412(34), 4439–4451 (2011)

23. Sidorova, N., Stahl, C., Trcka, N.: Soundness verification for conceptual workflow nets with data: early detection of errors with the most precision possible. Inf. Syst. 36(7), 1026–1043 (2011)

24. Aalst, W.M.P.: Verification of workflow nets. In: Azéma, P., Balbo, G. (eds.) ICATPN 1997. LNCS, vol. 1248, pp. 407–426. Springer, Heidelberg (1997). https://doi.org/10.1007/3-540-63139-9_48

Engineering

Estimating Process Conformance by Trace Sampling and Result Approximation

Martin Bauer, Han van der Aa$^{(\boxtimes)}$, and Matthias Weidlich

Department of Computer Science, Humboldt-Universität zu Berlin, Berlin, Germany
{martin.bauer,han.van.der.aa,matthias.weidlich}@hu-berlin.de

Abstract. The increasing volume of event data that is recorded by information systems during the execution of business processes creates manifold opportunities for process analytics. Specifically, conformance checking compares the behaviour as recorded by an information system to a model of desired behaviour. Unfortunately, state-of-the-art conformance checking algorithms scale exponentially in the size of both the event data and the model used as input. At the same time, event data used for analysis typically relates only to a certain interval of process execution, not the entire history. Given this inherent data incompleteness, we argue that an understanding of the overall conformance of process execution may be obtained by considering only a small fraction of a log. In this paper, we therefore present a statistical approach to ground conformance checking in trace sampling and conformance approximation. This approach reduces the runtime significantly, while still providing guarantees on the accuracy of the estimated conformance result. Comprehensive experiments with real-world and synthetic datasets illustrate that our approach speeds up state-of-the-art conformance checking algorithms by up to three orders of magnitude, while largely maintaining the analysis accuracy.

1 Introduction

Process-oriented information systems coordinate the execution of a set of actions to reach a business goal [15]. The behaviour of such systems is commonly described by process models that define a set of activities along with execution dependencies. However, once event data is recorded during runtime, the question of conformance emerges [9]: how do the modelled behaviour of a system and its recorded behaviour relate to each other? Answering this question is required to detect, interpret, and compensate deviations between a model of a process-oriented information system and its actual execution.

Driven by trends such as process automation, data sensing, and large-scale instrumentation of process-related resources, the volume of event data and the frequency at which it is generated is increasing in today's world: Event logs comprise up to billions of events [2]. Also, information systems are subject to

T. Hildebrandt et al. (Eds.): BPM 2019, LNCS 11675, pp. 179–197, 2019.
https://doi.org/10.1007/978-3-030-26619-6_13

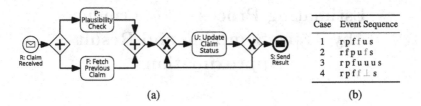

(a)   (b)

Fig. 1. (a) Model of a claim handling process; (b) events of four process executions.

frequent changes [34], so that analysis is often a continuous process, repeated when new event data becomes available.

Acknowledging the resulting need for efficient analysis, various angles have been followed to improve the runtime performance of state-of-the-art, alignment-based conformance checking algorithms [4], which suffer from an exponential worst-case complexity. Efficiency improvements have been obtained through the use of search-based methods [13,25], planning algorithms [21], and distributed computing [16,22]. Furthermore, several authors suggested to compromise correctness and approximate conformance results to gain efficiency, e.g., by employing approximate alignments [29] or applying divide-and-conquer schemes in the computation of conformance results [3,12,20,23]. However, these approaches primarily target the applied algorithms. Fundamentally, they still require the consideration of *all*, possibly billions, of recorded events.

In practice, an event log is recorded for a certain interval of process execution, not the entire history. Given this inherent incompleteness of event data, which is widely acknowledged [1,17,26], analysis often strives for a general understanding of the conformance of process execution. This may relate, e.g., to the overall fitness of recorded and modelled behaviour [4] or the activities that denote hotspots of non-conformance [3].

In this paper, we argue that for a general understanding of the overall conformance, it is sufficient to compute conformance results for only a small fraction of an event log. Since the latter per se provides an incomplete view, minor differences in the conformance results obtained for the whole log and a partial log may be attributed to the inherent uncertainty of the conformance checking setting. We illustrate this idea with a claim handling process in Fig. 1. Here, the events recorded for the first case indicate non-conformance, as a previous claim is fetched twice (f). Considering also the second case, the average amount of non-conformance (one deviation) and the set of non-conforming activities ({F}) are the same, though, despite the different sequence of events. Considering also the third and fourth case, new information on the overall conformance of process execution is obtained. Yet, the fourth case resembles the first one. Hence, its conformance (two deviations w.r.t. the model) may be approximated based on the result of the first case (one deviation) and the difference between both event sequences (one event differs).

To realise the above ideas, we follow two complimentary angles to avoid computation of conformance results for all available data. First, we contribute an incremental approach based on trace sampling, which, for each trace, assesses whether it yields new information on the overall conformance. Assuming the view of a series of binomial experiments, we establish bounds on the error of the conformance result derived from a partial event log. Second, we show how trace sampling is combined with result approximation that, instead of computing a conformance result for a trace at hand, relies on a worst-case approximation of its implications on the overall conformance. This way, we further reduce the amount of data for which conformance results are actually computed. We instantiate this framework for two types of conformance results as mentioned above, a numerical fitness measure and a distribution of conformance issues over all activities.

In the remainder, we first give preliminaries in Sect. 2. We then introduce our approach to sample-based (Sect. 3) and approximation-based (Sect. 4) conformance checking. Experimental results using real-world and synthetic event logs are presented in Sect. 5. We review related work in Sect. 6, before we conclude in Sect. 7.

2   Preliminaries

Events and Event Logs. We adopt an event model that builds upon a set of activities $\mathcal{A}$. An event recorded by an information system is assumed to be related to the execution of one of these activities. By $\mathcal{E}$, we denote the universe of all events. A single execution of a process, called a *trace*, is modelled as a sequence of events $\xi \in \mathcal{E}^*$, such that no event can occur in more than one trace. An event log is a set of traces, $L \subseteq 2^{\mathcal{E}^*}$. Our example in Fig. 1b defines four traces. While each event is unique, we represent them with small letters $\{r, p, f, u, s\}$, that indicate for which activity of the process model, denoted by respective capital letters $\{R, P, F, U, S\}$, the execution is signalled. Two distinct traces that indicate the same sequence of activity executions are of the same *trace variant*.

Process Models. A process model defines the execution dependencies between the activities of a process. For our purposes, it is sufficient to abstract from specific process modelling languages and focus on the behaviour defined by a model. That is, a process model defines a set of execution sequences, $M \subseteq \mathcal{A}^*$, that capture sequences of activity executions that lead the process to its final state. For instance, the model in Fig. 1a defines the execution sequences $\langle R, P, F, U, S \rangle$ and $\langle R, F, P, U, S \rangle$, potentially including additional repetitions of U. We write $\mathcal{M}$ for the set of all process models.

Alignments. State-of-the-art techniques for conformance checking construct *alignments* between traces and execution sequences of a model to detect deviations [4,23]. An alignment between a trace ξ and a model M, denoted by $\sigma(\xi, M)$ in the remainder, is a sequence of steps, each step comprising a pair of an event and an activity, or a *skip* symbol $\perp$, if an event or activity is without counterpart. For instance, for the non-conforming trace ξ_1 (case 1 from Fig. 1b), an alignment is constructed as follows:

Trace ξ_1	r	p	f	f	u	s
Execution sequence	R	P	F	$\perp$	U	S

Assigning costs to skip steps, a cost-optimal alignment (not necessarily unique) is constructed for a trace in relation to all execution sequences of a model [4]. An optimal alignment then enables the quantification of non-conformance. Specifically, the *fitness* of a log with respect to a given model is computed as follows:

$$\text{fitness}(L, M) = 1 - \frac{\sum_{\xi \in L} c(\xi, M)}{\sum_{\xi \in L} c(\xi, \emptyset) + |L| \times \min_{x \in M} c(\langle\rangle, \{x\})} \tag{1}$$

Here, $c(\xi, M)$ is the aggregated cost of an optimal alignment $\sigma(\xi, M)$. The denominator captures the maximum possible cost per trace, i.e., the sum of the costs of aligning a trace with an empty model, $c(\xi, \emptyset)$, and the minimal costs of aligning an empty trace with the model, $\min_{x \in M} c(\langle\rangle, \{x\})$. Using a standard cost function (all skip steps have equal costs), the fitness value of the example log $\{\xi_1, \xi_2, \xi_3, \xi_4\}$ in Fig. 1b is 0.9. Alignments further enable the detection of hotspots of non-conformance. To this end, the conformance result can be defined in terms of a *deviation distribution* that captures the relative frequency with which an activity (not to be confused with a task of a process model) is part of a conformance violation. For a log L and a model M, this distribution follows from skip steps in the optimal alignments of all traces. It is formalised based on a bag of activities, $dev(L, M) : \mathcal{A} \to \mathbb{N}_0$ (note that multiple skip steps may relate to a single activity even in the alignment of one trace). The relative deviation frequency of an activity $a \in \mathcal{A}$ is then obtained by dividing the number of occurrences of a in the bag of deviations by the total number of deviations, i.e., $f_{dev(L,M)}(a) = dev(L, M)(a)/|dev(L, M)|$.

For our example in Fig. 1, assuming that skip steps relate to the highlighted trace positions, it holds that $dev(\{\xi_1, \xi_2, \xi_3, \xi_4\}, M) = [F^3, U]$ and $f_{dev(\{\xi_1,...,\xi_4\},M)}(F) = 3/4$, so that the fetching of a previous claim (F) is identified as a hotspot of non-conformance.

3   Sample-Based Conformance Checking

This section describes how trace sampling can be used to improve the efficiency of conformance checking. The general idea is that it often suffices to only compute alignments for a subset of all trace variants to gain insights into the overall conformance of a log to a model. However, we randomly sample an event log trace-by-trace, not by trace variant, which avoids to load the entire log and step-wise reveals the distribution of traces among the variants. At some point, though, the sampled traces then do not provide new information on the overall conformance of the process.

In the remainder of this section, we first describe a general framework for sample-based conformance checking (Sect. 3.1), which we then instantiate for two types of conformance results: fitness (Sect. 3.2) and deviation distribution (Sect. 3.3).

3.1 Statistical Sampling Framework

To operationalise sample-based conformance checking, we regard it as a series of binomial experiments. In this, we follow a log sampling technique introduced in the context of process discovery [5,7] and lift it to the setting of conformance checking.

Information Novelty. When parsing a log trace-by-trace, some traces may turn out to provide information on the conformance of a log to a model that is similar or equivalent to the information provided by previously encountered traces. To assess whether this is the case, we capture the conformance information associated with a log by a *conformance function* $\psi : 2^{\mathcal{E}^*} \times \mathcal{M} \to \mathcal{X}$. That is, $\psi(L, M)$ is the conformance result (of some domain $\mathcal{X}$) between a log L and a model M. If we are interested in the distribution of deviations, ψ provides information on the model activities for which deviations are observed, whereas for fitness, it would return the fitness value.

Based thereon, we define a random Boolean predicate $\gamma(L', \xi, M)$ that captures whether a trace $\xi \in \mathcal{E}^*$ provides new information on the conformance with model M, i.e., whether it changes the result obtained already for a set of previously observed traces $L' \subseteq 2^{\mathcal{E}^*}$. Assuming that the distance between conformance results can be quantified by a function $d : \mathcal{X} \times \mathcal{X} \to \mathbb{R}_0^+$, we define a *new information predicate* as:

$$\gamma(L', \xi, M) \Leftrightarrow d(\psi(L', M), \psi(\{\xi\} \cup L', M)) > \epsilon. \tag{2}$$

Here, $\epsilon \in \mathbb{R}_0^+$ is a relaxation parameter. If incorporating trace ξ changes the conformance result by more than ϵ, then it adds new information over L'.

Framework. We exploit the notion of information novelty for hypothesis testing when sampling traces from an event log L. We determine when *enough* sampled traces have been included in a log $L' \subseteq L$ to derive an understanding of its overall conformance to a model M. Following the interpretation of log sampling as a series of binomial experiments [5], L' is regarded as sufficient if the algorithm consecutively draws a certain number of traces that did not contain new information. Specifically, with δ as a measure that bounds the probability of a newly sampled trace to provide new information over L', at a significance level α, a minimum sample size N is computed. Based on the normal approximation to the binomial distribution, the latter is given as $N \geq 1/2\delta \left(-2\delta^2 + z^2 + \sqrt{z} \right)$, where z corresponds to the realisation of a standardised normal random variable for $1 - \alpha$ (one-sided hypothesis test). As such, N is calculated given values for δ and α for the desired levels of similarity and significance, respectively.

Consider $\alpha = 0.01$ and $\delta = 0.05$, so that $N \geq 128$. Hence, after observing 128 traces without new information, sampling can be stopped knowing with 0.99 confidence that the probability of finding new information in the remaining log is less than 0.05.

Using the above formulation, our framework for sample-based conformance checking is presented in Algorithm 1. The algorithm takes as input an event log L, a process model M, the number of trials that need to fail N, a predicate γ

to determine whether a trace provides new information, and a conformance function ψ. Going through L trace-by-trace (lines 3–12), the algorithm conducts a series of binomial experiments that check, if a newly sampled trace provides new information according to the predicate γ (line 5). Once N consecutive traces without new information have been selected, the procedure stops and the conformance result is derived based on the sampled log L'.

Result Re-use. Note that the algorithm provides a conceptual view, in the sense that checking the new information predicate $\gamma(L', \xi, M)$ in line 5 according to Eq. 2, requires the computation of $\psi(L', M)$ and $\psi(\{\xi\} \cup L', M)$ in each iteration. A technical realisation of this algorithm, of course, shall exploit that most types of conformance results can be computed incrementally. For instance, considering fitness and the deviation distribution, an alignment is computed only once per *trace variant*, i.e., per unique sequence of activity executions, and reused in the iterations of the algorithm. Also, the value of $\psi(L', M)$ for $\gamma(L', \xi, M)$ in line 5 is always known from the previous iteration, while the conformance result in line 13 is not actually computed at this stage, as the respective result is known from the last evaluation of $\gamma(L', \xi, M)$.

In the next sections, we discuss how to define γ when the conformance function assesses the fitness of a log to a model, or the observed deviation distribution.

3.2 Sample-Based Fitness

The overall conformance of a log to a model may be assessed by considering the log fitness (see Sect. 2) as a conformance function, $\psi_{fit}(L, M) = \text{fitness}(L, M)$. Then, determining whether a trace ξ provides new information over a log sample L' requires us to assess, if incorporating ξ leads to a difference in the overall fitness for the sampled log. Following Eq. 2, we capture this by computing the absolute difference between the fitness value for traces in the sample L' and the value of the sample plus the new trace:

$$d_{fit}(\psi_{fit}(L', M), \psi_{fit}(\{\xi\} \cup L', M)) = |\text{fitness}(L', M) - \text{fitness}(\{\xi\} \cup L', M)|. \tag{3}$$

If this distance is smaller than the relaxation parameter ϵ, the change in the overall fitness value induced by trace ξ is considered to be negligible.

To illustrate this, consider a scenario with $\epsilon = 0.03$ and a sample consisting of the traces ξ_1 and ξ_3 of our running example (Fig. 1). Then, the log fitness for $\{\xi_1, \xi_3\}$ is 0.95. In this situation, if the next sampled trace is ξ_2, the distance function yields $|\text{fitness}(\{\xi_1, \xi_3\}, M) - \text{fitness}(\{\xi_1, \xi_2, \xi_3\}, M)| = 0.95 - 0.93 = 0.02$. In this case, since the distance is smaller than ϵ, we would conclude that the additional consideration of ξ_2 does not provide new information. By contrast, considering trace ξ_4 would yield a distance of $0.95 - 0.89 = 0.06$. This indicates that trace ξ_4 would imply a considerable change in the overall fitness value, i.e., it provides new information.

Algorithm 1. Framework for Sample-Based Conformance Checking

---

   input : L, an event log; M, a process model; N, a number of failed trials to observe;
           γ, a predicate that holds true, if a trace provides new information;
           ψ, a conformance function.
   output: $\psi(L')$, the conformance results for sampled traces.

1 $L', \hat{L} \leftarrow \emptyset$; /* The sampled logs, overall and for current experiment series */
2 $i \leftarrow 0$;   /* The number of current iterations without new information */
3 **repeat**   /* Repeat until N traces without new information have been seen */
4     $\xi \leftarrow select(L \setminus \hat{L})$;   /* Sample a single trace */
      /* Check if ξ provides new information. Re-uses alignments of traces of
          the same variant and the previous conformance result $\psi(L', M)$.   */
5   **if** $\gamma(L', \xi, M)$ **then**
6        $i \leftarrow 0$;   /* Reset the counter */
7        $\hat{L} \leftarrow \emptyset$;   /* Reset log for current experiment series */
8   **else**
9        $i \leftarrow i + 1$;   /* Increment the counter */
10      $\hat{L} \leftarrow \hat{L} \cup \{\xi\}$;   /* Add trace to log for current experiment series */
11    $L' \leftarrow L' \cup \{\xi\}$;   /* Add trace to overall sampled log */
12 **until** $i \geq N \vee L' = L$;
13 **return** $\psi(L')$;   /* Return results based on the overall sampled log */

3.3   Sample-Based Deviation Distributions

Next, we instantiate the above framework for conformance checking based on the deviation distribution. As detailed in Sect. 2, this distribution captures the relative frequency with which activities are related to conformance issues.

To decide whether a trace ξ provides new information over a log sample L', we assess if the deviations obtained for ξ lead to a considerable difference in the overall deviation distribution. As such, the distance function for the predicate γ needs to quantify the difference between two discrete frequency distributions. This suggests to employ the L1-distance, also known as the *Manhattan distance*, as a measure:

$$d_{dev}(\psi_{dev}(L', M), \psi_{dev}(\{\xi\} \cup L', M)) = \sum_{a \in \mathcal{A}} \left| f_{dev(L',M)}(a) - f_{dev(\{\xi\} \cup L', M)}(a) \right| \quad (4)$$

Taking up our example from Fig. 1, processing only the trace ξ_1, all deviations are related to the activity of fetching an earlier claim, i.e., $f_{dev(\{\xi_1\}, M)}(F) = 1$. Notably, this does not change when incorporating traces ξ_2 and ξ_3, i.e., $f_{dev(\{\xi_1, \xi_2, \xi_3\}, M)}(F) = 1$, as they do not provide new information in terms of the deviation distribution. If, after processing trace ξ_1, however, we sample ξ_4, we do observe such a difference: based on $f_{dev(\{\xi_1, \xi_4\}, M)}(F) = 2/3$ and $f_{dev(\{\xi_1, \xi_4\}, M)}(U) = 1/3$, we compute a Manhattan distance of $2/3$. With a relaxation parameter ϵ that is smaller than this value, we conclude that ξ_4 provides novel information.

Given the distance functions based on trace fitness and deviation distribution, it is interesting to note that these behave differently, as illustrated in our example: If the log is $\{\xi_1, \xi_2\}$ and trace ξ_3 is sampled next, the overall fitness changes. Yet, since ξ_3 is a conforming trace, it does not provide new information on the distribution of deviations.

4   Approximation-Based Conformance Checking

This section shows how conformance results can be approximated, further avoiding the need to compute a conformance result for certain traces. Our idea is to derive a worst-case approximation for traces that are similar to variants for which results have previously been derived. Approximation complements the sampling method of Sect. 3: Even when a trace of a yet unseen variant is sampled, we decide whether to compute an actual conformance result or whether to approximate it. As such, the decision on whether a trace provides new information may be taken either based on a computed or an approximated result.

Against this background, our technique for approximation-based conformance checking, formalised in Algorithm 2, extends our procedure given in Algorithm 1. In fact, it primarily provides a realisation of checking the new information predicate $\gamma(L', \xi, M)$, as done in line 5 of Algorithm 1. That is, whether the sampled trace ξ, of an unseen variant, provides new information is potentially decided based on the approximated, rather than computed impact of it on the overall conformance result. At the same time, however, the algorithm also needs to keep track of all sampled traces $L'' \subseteq L'$, for which the approximated results shall be used whenever a conformance result is computed. This leads to an adaptation of the conformance function ψ, i.e., we consider a *partially approximating conformance* function $\hat{\psi} : 2^{\mathcal{E}^*} \times 2^{\mathcal{E}^*} \times \mathcal{M} \to \mathcal{X}$. Given a log L' and a subset $L'' \subseteq L'$, this function approximates the conformance result $\psi(L', M)$ by computing solely $\psi(L' \setminus L'', M)$, i.e., the impact of traces L'' is not precisely computed. In the same way, to use the approximation technique as part of sample-based conformance checking, the use of the conformance function ψ in Algorithm 1 also has to be adapted accordingly.

Turning to the details of Algorithm 2, its input includes a log sample L', a sampled trace $\xi \notin L'$, and a process model M, i.e., the arguments of γ in line 5 of Algorithm 1, as well as a distance function d and relaxation parameter ϵ from the definition of γ (Eq. 2). Moreover, there is a similarity threshold k to determine which traces may be used for approximation. Finally, the aforementioned set of traces L'' for which results shall be approximated and the respective adapted conformance function $\hat{\psi}$ are given as input.

From the sampled traces for which approximation is not applied (i.e., $L' \setminus L''$), the algorithm first selects the trace that is most similar to ξ, referred to as the reference trace ξ_r (line 1). Then, we assess whether this similarity is above the threshold k (line 2). If not, we check the trace for new information as done before, just using the adapted conformance function (lines 9–10). If ξ_r is sufficiently similar, however, we perform a worst-case approximation of the impact of ξ on the overall conformance result based on ξ_r (line 3). As part of that, we may obtain several different approximations Φ, each of which is checked whether it

---

Algorithm 2. Framework for Approximation-Based Conformance Checking

---

input : L', a log sample; M, a process model; ξ, a trace sampled of a yet unseen variant with $\xi \notin L'$; d, a distance function; ϵ, a relaxation parameter; k, a similarity threshold; $\hat{\psi}$, a partially approximating conformance function; $L'' \subseteq L'$, traces for which approximated results are used.

output: (v, L''), where $v \in \{true, false\}$ indicates whether ξ provides new information; L'' is the updated set of traces, for which approximated results are used.

```
1   ξr ← argminξ'∈L'\L'' sim(ξ, ξ');              /* Select most similar trace */
2   if sim(ξ, ξr) ≤ k then                        /* Check if ξ and ξr are k-similar */
3   |   Φ ← approx(ξ, ξr, L', M) ;                 /* Derive all possible approximations */
4   |   if ∃ φ ∈ Φ : d(ψ̂(L', L'', M), φ) > ε then
        |   |   /* Approx. indicates new information, use actual result          */
5   |   |   return (true, L'');
6   |   else   /* Approx. does not indicate new information, use approx. result */
7   |   |   return (false, L'' ∪ {ξ});
8   else                   /* No k-similar trace available, check for new information */
9   |   v ← d(ψ̂(L', L'', M), ψ̂({ξ} ∪ L', L'', M)) > ε;
10  |   return (v, L'');
```

---

indicates new information over the current sample L' (line 4). Only if this is not the case, we conclude that ξ indeed does not provide new information and, by adding it to L'' make sure that its impact on the overall conformance will always only be approximated, but never precisely computed (line 7).

Next, we give details on the assessment of trace similarity (function sim, Sect. 4.1) and the conformance result approximation (function $approx$, Sect. 4.2).

4.1 Trace Similarity

Given a trace ξ and the part of the sample log for which approximation did not apply ($L' \setminus L''$), Algorithm 2 requires us to identify a reference trace ξ_r that is most similar according to some function $sim : \mathcal{E}^* \times \mathcal{E}^* \to [0, 1]$. As we consider conformance results that are based on alignments, we define this similarity function based on the alignment cost of two traces. To this end, we consider a function c_t, which, in the spirit of function c discussed in Sect. 2, is the sum of the costs assigned to skip steps in an optimal alignment of two traces. To obtain a similarity measure, we normalise this aggregated cost by a maximal cost, which is obtained by aligning each trace with an empty trace. This normalisation resembles the one discussed for the fitness measure in Sect. 2. We define the similarity function for traces as $sim(\xi, \xi') = 1 - c_t(\xi, \xi')/(c_t(\xi, \langle \rangle) + c_t(\xi', \langle \rangle))$.

Considering trace $\xi_4 = \langle r, p, f, f, s \rangle$ of our running example, the most similar trace (assuming equal costs for all skip steps) is $\xi_1 = \langle r, p, f, f, u, s \rangle$, with $c_t(\xi_1, \xi_4) = 1$ and, thus, $sim(\xi_1, \xi_4) = 10/11$.

4.2   Conformance Result Approximation

In the approximation step of Algorithm 2, we derive a set of worst-case approximations of the impact of the trace ξ on the overall conformance result, using the reference trace ξ_r (which is at least k-similar). Based thereon, it is decided whether ξ provides new information. The approximation, however, depends on the type of conformance result.

Fitness Approximation. To approximate the impact of trace ξ on the overall fitness, we compute a single value, i.e., $approx(\xi, \xi_r, L', M)$ in line 3 of Algorithm 2 yields a singleton set. This value is derived by reformulating Eq. 3, which captures the change in fitness induced by a sample trace. That is, we assess the difference between the current fitness, $fitness(L', M)$, and an approximation of the fitness when incorporating ξ, i.e., $fitness(\{\xi\} \cup L', M)$. This approximation, denoted by $\widehat{fit}(\xi, \xi_r, L', M)$, is derived from (i) the change in fitness induced by the reference trace ξ_r, and (ii) the differences between ξ and ξ_r. The former is assessed using the aggregated alignment cost $c(\xi_r, M)$, whereas the latter leverages the aggregated cost of aligning the traces, $c_t(\xi, \xi_r)$. Normalising these costs, function $approx_{fit}(\xi, \xi_r, L', M)$ yields a worst-case approximation for the change in overall fitness imposed by ξ, as follows:

$$approx_{fit}(\xi, \xi_r, L', M) = \left\{ \left| fitness(L', M) - \widehat{fit}(\xi, \xi_r, L', M) \right| \right\} \tag{5}$$

$$\widehat{fit}(\xi, \xi_r, L', M) = 1 - \frac{\sum\limits_{\xi' \in L'} c(\xi', M) + c(\xi_r, M) + c_t(\xi, \xi_r)}{\sum\limits_{\xi' \in L'} c(\xi', \emptyset) + \max\limits_{\xi' \in \{\xi, \xi_r\}} c(\xi', \emptyset) + (|L'| + 1) \min\limits_{x \in M} c(\langle\rangle, \{x\})}$$

Turning to our running example, assume that we have sampled $\{\xi_1, \xi_2\}$ and computed the precise fitness value based on both traces, which is $1 - 2/(12 + 10) \approx 0.909$ using a standard cost function. If trace ξ_4 is sampled next, we approximate its impact using the similar trace ξ_1. To this end, we consider $c(\xi_1, M) = 1$ and $c_t(\xi_1, \xi_4) = 1$, which yields an approximated fitness value of $1 - (2 + 1 + 1)/(12 + 6 + 15) = 1 - 4/33 \approx 0.879$. This is close to the actual fitness value for $\{\xi_1, \xi_2, \xi_4\}$, which is $1 - 4/(17 + 15) \approx 0.875$. The minor difference stems from ξ_1 being slightly longer than ξ_4.

Deviation Distribution Approximation. To approximate the impact of trace ξ on the deviation distribution, we follow a similar approach as for fitness approximation. However, we note that the approximation function here yields a set of possible values, as there are multiple different distributions to be considered when measuring the Manhattan distance to the current distribution. The reason being that the difference between ξ and the reference trace ξ_r induces a set of possible changes of the distribution.

Specifically, we denote by $ed(\xi, \xi_r)$ the edit distance of the two traces, i.e., the pure number of skip steps in their alignment. This number gives an upper bound for the number of conformance issues that need to be incorporated in addition to those stemming from the alignment of the reference trace and the model, i.e., $dev(\{\xi_r\}, M)$. Yet, the exact activities are not known, so that we need to consider all bags of activities of size $ed(\xi, \xi_r)$, the set of which is denoted by $[\mathcal{A}]^{ed(\xi, \xi_r)}$.

Each of these bags leads to a different approximation $\widehat{f_{dev}}(\beta, \xi_r, L', M)$ of the distribution $f_{dev(\{\xi\} \cup L', M)}$ that we are actually interested in. We compute those as follows:

$$approx_{dev}(\xi, \xi_r, L', M) = \bigcup_{\beta \in [\mathcal{A}]^{ed(\xi, \xi_r)}} \left\{ \sum_{a \in \mathcal{A}} \left| f_{dev(L', M)}(a) - \widehat{f_{dev}}(\beta, \xi_r, L', M)(a) \right| \right\}$$

(6)

$$\widehat{f_{dev}}(\beta, \xi_r, L', M)(a) = \frac{dev(L', M)(a) + dev(\{\xi_r\}, M)(a) + \beta(a)}{|dev(L', M)| + |dev(\{\xi_r\}, M)| + |\beta|}$$

Consider our example again: Based on $\{\xi_1, \xi_2\}$, we determine that $dev(\{\xi_1, \xi_2\}, M) = [F^2]$ and $f_{dev(\{\xi_1, \xi_2\}, M)}(F) = 1$. If ξ_4 is then sampled, we obtain an approximation based on $dev(\{\xi_1\}, M) = [F]$ and $ed(\xi_4, \xi_1) = 1$. We therefore consider the change in the distribution incurred by approximating the deviations of ξ_4 as $[F] \uplus \beta$ with $\beta \in \{[R], [P], [F], [U], [S]\}$. For instance, $\widehat{f_{dev}}([R], \xi_4, \{\xi_1, \xi_2\}, M)$ yields a distribution assigning relative frequencies of $3/4$ and $1/4$ to activities F and R, respectively.

The above approximation may be tuned heuristically by narrowing the set of activities that are considered for β, i.e., the possible deviations incurred by the difference between ξ and ξ_r. While this means that $\widehat{f_{dev}}$ is no longer a worst-case approximation, it may steer the approximation in practice, hinting at which activities shall be considered for possible deviations. Such an approach is also beneficial for performance reasons: Since β may be any bag built of the respective activities, the exponential blow-up limits the applicability of the approximation to traces that are rather similar, i.e., for which $ed(\xi, \xi_r)$ is small.

Here, we describe one specific heuristic. First, we determine the overlap between ξ and ξ_r in terms of their maximal shared prefix and suffix of activities, for which the execution is signalled by their events. Next, we determine the events that are *not* part of the shared prefix and suffix, and derive the activities referenced by these events. Only these activities are then considered for the construction of β.

In our example, traces ξ_1 and ξ_4 share the prefix $\langle r, p, f, f \rangle$ and suffix $\langle s \rangle$. Thus, ξ_1 contains one event between the shared prefix and suffix, u, while there is none for ξ_4. Hence, we consider a single bag of deviations, $\beta = [U]$, and $\widehat{f_{dev}}([U], \xi_4, \{\xi_1, \xi_2\}, M)$ is the only distribution considered in the approximation.

5   Evaluation

This section reports on an experimental evaluation of the proposed techniques for sample-based and approximation-based conformance checking. Section 5.1 describes the three real-world and seven synthetic event logs used in the experimental setup, described in Sect. 5.2. The evaluation results demonstrate that our techniques achieve considerable efficiency gains, while still providing highly accurate conformance results (Sect. 5.3).

5.1 Datasets

We conducted our experiments based on three real-world and seven synthetic event logs, which are all publicly available.

Real-World Data. The three real-world event logs differ considerably in terms of the number of unique traces they contain, as well as their average trace lengths, which represent key characteristics for our approach.

- *BPI-12* [31] is a log of a process for loan or overdraft applications at a Dutch financial institute that was part of the Business Process Intelligence (BPI) Challenge. The log contains 13,087 traces (4,366 variants), with 20.0 events per case (avg.).
- *BPI-14* [32] is the log of an ICT incident management process used in the BPI Challenge. For the experiments, we employed the event log of incidence activities, containing 46,616 traces (31,725 variants), with 7.3 events per case (avg.).
- *Traffic Fines* [11] is a log of an information system managing road traffic fines. The log contains 150,370 traces (231 variants), with 3.7 events per case (avg.).

We obtained accompanying process models for these logs using the inductive miner infrequent [19] with its default parameter settings (i.e., 20% noise filtering).

Synthetic Data. To analyse the scalability of our techniques, we considered a synthetic dataset designed to stress-test conformance checking techniques [24]. It consists of seven process models and accompanying event logs. The models are considerably large and complex, as characterised in Table 1, which impacts the computation of alignments. Furthermore, the included event logs consist of a high number of variants (compared to the number of traces), which may affect the effectiveness of log sampling.

5.2 Experimental Setup

We employed the following measures and experimental setup to conduct the evaluation.

Measures. We measure the *efficiency* of our techniques by the fraction of traces from a log required to obtain our conformance results. This fraction indicates for how many traces the conformance computation was not needed due to the trace not being sampled, or the result being approximated. Simultaneously, we consider the fraction of the total trace variants for which our techniques actually had to establish alignments. As these fractions provide us with analytical measures of efficiency, we also assess the *runtime* of our techniques, based on a prototypical implementation. Again, this is compared to the runtime of the conformance checking over the complete log. Finally, we assess the impact of sampling and

Table 1. Characteristics of the synthetic model-log pairs

Characteristic	PrA	PrB	PrC	PrD	PrE	PrF	PrG
Activities	363	317	317	429	275	299	335
Traces	1,200	1,200	500	1,200	1,200	1,200	1,200
Variants	1,049	1,126	500	1,200	1,200	1,200	1,200
Events per trace (avg.)	31.6	41.5	42.9	248.6	98.8	240.8	143.1

approximation on the *accuracy* of conformance results. We determine the accuracy by comparing the results, i.e., the fitness value or the deviation distribution, obtained using sampling and approximation, to the results for the total log.

All presented results are determined based on 20 experimental runs (i.e., replications) of which we report on the mean value, along with the 10th and 90th percentiles.

Environment. Our approach has been implemented as a plugin in ProM [33], which is publicly available.[1] For the computation of alignments, we rely on the ProM implementation of the search-based technique recently proposed in [13]. Runtime measurements have been obtained on a PC (Dual-Core, 2.5 GHz, 8 GB RAM) running Oracle Java 1.8.

5.3 Evaluation Results

This section first considers the overall efficiency and accuracy of our approach on the real-world event logs, using default parameter values ($\delta = 0.01$, $\alpha = 0.99$, $\epsilon = 0.01$, and $k = 1/3$), before conducting a sensitivity analysis in which these values are varied. Lastly, we demonstrate the scalability of our approaches by showing that their performance also applies to complex, synthetic datasets.

Efficiency. We first explore the efficiency of our approach in terms of sample size and runtime for four configurations: conformance in terms of fitness, without (f) and with approximation (fa), as well as for the deviation distribution without (d) and with approximation (da). Figure 2 reveals that all configurations only need to consider a tiny fraction of the complete log. For instance, for BPI-14, the sample-based fitness computation (f) requires only 685 traces (on average) out of the total of 46,616 traces (i.e., 1.5% of the log). This sample included traces from 144 out of the total 31,725 variants (less than 0.5%), which means that the approach established just 144 alignments. As expected, these gains are propagated to the runtime of our approach, as shown in Fig. 3.

When looking at the overall efficiency results, we observe that the additional use of approximation generally does not lead to considerable improvements in comparison to just sampling. However, this is notably different for the deviation distribution of the Traffic Fines dataset. Here, without approximation, the

---

[1] https://github.com/Martin-Bauer/Conformance_Sketching.

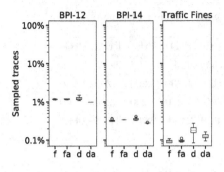

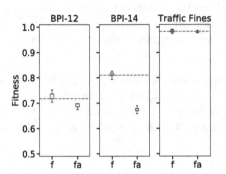

Fig. 2. Sample size efficiency

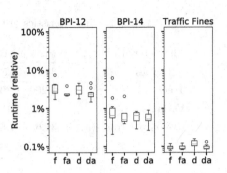

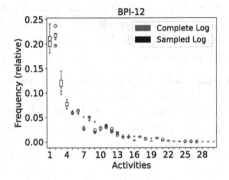

Fig. 3. Runtime efficiency

Fig. 4. Accuracy (fitness)

Fig. 5. Accuracy (deviation distribution)

sample size is 1323 on average (0.88%), whereas the sample size drops to 713 traces (0.47%) with approximation (da). Hence, approximation appears to be more important if sampling alone is not as effective.

Accuracy. The drastic gains in efficiency are obtained while maintaining highly accurate conformance results. According to Fig. 4, the fitness computed using sample-based conformance checking differs by less than 0.1% from the original fitness (indicated by the dashed line). Since the accuracy in terms of deviation distribution is harder to capture in a single value, we use Fig. 5 to demonstrate that the deviation distribution obtained by our sample-based technique closely follows the distribution for the complete log. In decreasing order, Fig. 5 depicts the activities with their numbers of deviations observed in the complete log and in the sampled log. As shown, our technique clearly identifies which activities are most often affected by deviations, i.e., our technique correctly identifies the main hotspots of non-conformance. Although, for clarity, not depicted, our approach including approximation achieved comparable results.

Parameter Sensitivity. We performed a parameter sensitivity analysis using sample-based conformance checking on the BPI-12 dataset. We explored how parameters δ (probability bound), α (significance value), and ϵ (relaxedness

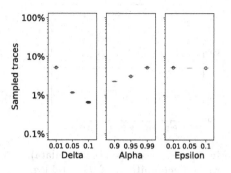

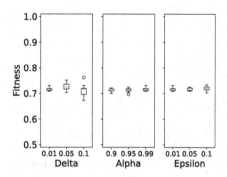

Fig. 6. Sample size sensitivity   **Fig. 7.** Fitness sensitivity

value), affect the performance of our approach in terms of efficiency (number of traces) and accuracy (fitness).[2] Figure 6 shows that selection of δ and α have a considerable impact on the sample required for conformance checking. For instance, for $\delta = 0.01$ we require an average sample size of 684.9, whereas when we relax the bound to $\delta = 0.10$, the average size is reduced to 85.8 traces. For α, i.e., the confidence, we observe a range from 296.5 to 684.9 traces. By contrast, varying epsilon is shown to result in only marginal differences (ranging between 659.0 and 684.9). Still, for all these results, it should be considered that even the largest sample sizes represent only 5% of the traces in the original log.

Notably, as shown in Fig. 7, the average accuracy of our approach remains highly stable throughout this sensitivity analysis, ranging from 0.711 to 0.726. However, we do observe that the variance across replications differs for the parameter settings using smaller sample sizes, specifically for $\delta = 0.1$. Here, the obtained fitness values range between 0.67 and 0.76. This indicates that for such sample sizes, the selection of the particular sample may impact the obtained conformance result in some replications.

Scalability. The results obtained for the synthetic datasets confirm that our approaches are able to provide highly accurate conformance checking results in a small fraction of the runtime. Here, we reflect on experiments performed using our fitness-based sampling approach with $\delta = 0.05$, $\alpha = 0.99$, and $\epsilon = 0.01$. Figure 8 shows that, for six out of seven cases, runtime is reduced to 21.2% to 25.5% of the time needed for the total log (sample sizes range from 10.7% to 12.2%). At the same time, for all cases, the obtained fitness results are virtually equivalent to those of the total log, see Fig. 9, where the fitness values of the total logs are given by the crosses. When comparing these results to those of the real-world datasets, it should be noted that the synthetic logs hardly have any re-occurring trace variants, which makes it harder to generalize over the sampled results. This is particularly pronounced for process PrC: There is virtually no difference between the fitness obtained for the total log and the samples. Yet,

---

[2] While keeping the other parameter values stable at their respective defaults.

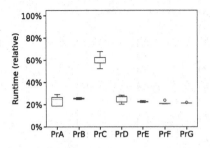

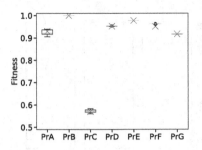

Fig. 8. Runtime efficiency, sample-based fitness computation (synthetic data)

Fig. 9. Fitness (synthetic data). Crosses denote fitness of the total log.

the relatively low fitness value of 0.57 along with a comparatively small number of traces in the log (500 vs. 1,200) lead to a runtime of 59% with sampling. Still, overall, the results on the synthetic data demonstrate that our approach is beneficial in highly complex scenarios.

6   Related Work

Conformance checking can be grounded in various notions. Non-conformance may be detected based on a comparison of sets of binary relations defined over events of a log and activities of a model, respectively [35]. Other work suggests to 'replay' traces in a process model, thereby identifying whether events denote valid activity executions [27]. However, both of these streams have limitations with respect to completeness [9]. Therefore, alignment-based conformance checking techniques [4,23], on which we focus in this work, are widely recognized as the state-of-the-art.

Acknowledging the complexity associated with the establishment of alignments, various approaches [13,16,25,28], discussed in Sect. 1, have been developed to improve runtime efficiency. Other work also aims to achieve efficiency gains by approximating alignments, cf., [14,30]. While these approaches can lead to efficiency gains, all of them fundamentally depend on the consideration of an entire event log. Moreover, our angle for approximation is different: We do not approximate alignments, but estimate a conformance result (fitness, deviation distribution) based on the distance between traces.

The sampling technique that we employ to avoid this is based on sampling used in sequence databases, i.e., datasets that contain traces. Sampling techniques for event logs have been previously applied for specification mining [10], for mining of Markov Chains [6], and for process discovery [5,8]. However, we are the first to apply these sampling techniques to conformance checking, a use case in which computational efficiency is arguably even more important than in discovery scenarios.

7 Conclusion

In this paper, we argued that insights into the overall conformance of an event log with respect to a process model can be obtained without computing conformance results for *all* traces. Specifically, we presented two angles to achieve efficient conformance checking: First, through trace sampling, we achieve that only a small share of the traces of a log are considered in the first place. By phrasing this sampling as a series of random experiments, we are able to give guarantees on the introduced error in terms of a potential difference of the overall conformance result. Second, we introduced result approximation as a means to avoid the computation of conformance results even for some of the sampled traces. Exploiting similarities of two traces, we derive an upper bound for the conformance of one trace based on the conformance of another trace. Both techniques, trace sampling and result approximation, have been instantiated for two notions of conformance results, fitness as a numerical measure of overall conformance and the deviation distribution that highlights hotspots of non-conformance in terms of individual activities.

Our experiments highlight dramatic improvements in terms of conformance checking efficiency: Only 0.1% to 1% of the traces of real-world event logs (12% for synthetic data) need to be considered, which leads to corresponding speed-ups of the observed runtimes. At the same time, the obtained conformance results, whether defined as fitness or the deviation distribution, are virtually equivalent to those obtained for the total log.

In future work, we intend to lift our ideas to conformance checking that incorporates branching conditions in a process model or temporal deadlines. Moreover, we strive for an integration of divide-and-conquer schemes [18] in our approximation approach.

References

1. Van der Aalst, W.M.P.: Process Mining - Discovery, Conformance and Enhancement of Business Processes. Springer, Heidelberg (2011). https://doi.org/10.1007/978-3-642-19345-3
2. Aalst, W.M.P.: Data scientist: the engineer of the future. In: Mertins, K., Bénaben, F., Poler, R., Bourrières, J.-P. (eds.) Enterprise Interoperability VI. PIC, vol. 7, pp. 13–26. Springer, Cham (2014). https://doi.org/10.1007/978-3-319-04948-9_2
3. der Aalst, W.M.P.V., Verbeek, H.M.W.: Process discovery and conformance checking using passages. Fundam. Inform. **131**(1), 103–138 (2014)
4. Adriansyah, A., van Dongen, B., Van der Aalst, W.M.P.: Conformance checking using cost-based fitness analysis. In: EDOC, pp. 55–64 (2011)
5. Bauer, M., Senderovich, A., Gal, A., Grunske, L., Weidlich, M.: How much event data is enough? A statistical framework for process discovery. In: CAiSE, pp. 239–256 (2018)
6. Biermann, A.W., Feldman, J.A.: On the synthesis of finite-state machines from samples of their behavior. IEEE Trans. Comput. **100**(6), 592–597 (1972)
7. Busany, N., Maoz, S.: Behavioral log analysis with statistical guarantees. In: ICSE, pp. 877–887. ACM (2016)

8. Carmona, J., Cortadella, J.: Process mining meets abstract interpretation. In: Balcázar, J.L., Bonchi, F., Gionis, A., Sebag, M. (eds.) ECML PKDD 2010. LNCS (LNAI), vol. 6321, pp. 184–199. Springer, Heidelberg (2010). https://doi.org/10. 1007/978-3-642-15880-3_18

9. Carmona, J., van Dongen, B., Solti, A., Weidlich, M.: Conformance Checking - Relating Processes and Models. Springer, Cham (2018). https://doi.org/10.1007/ 978-3-319-99414-7

10. Cohen, H., Maoz, S.: Have we seen enough traces? In: ASE, pp. 93–103. IEEE (2015)

11. De Leoni, M.M., Mannhardt, F.F.: Road traffic fine management process (2015). https://doi.org/10.4121/uuid:270fd440-1057-4fb9-89a9-b699b47990f5

12. Dixit, P.M., Buijs, J.C.A.M., Verbeek, H.M.W., van der Aalst, W.M.P.: Fast incremental conformance analysis for interactive process discovery. In: Abramowicz, W., Paschke, A. (eds.) BIS 2018. LNBIP, vol. 320, pp. 163–175. Springer, Cham (2018). https://doi.org/10.1007/978-3-319-93931-5_12

13. Dongen, B.F.: Efficiently computing alignments - using the extended marking equation. In: Weske, M., Montali, M., Weber, I., vom Brocke, J. (eds.) BPM 2018. LNCS, vol. 11080, pp. 197–214. Springer, Cham (2018). https://doi.org/10.1007/ 978-3-319-98648-7_12

14. van Dongen, B., Carmona, J., Chatain, T., Taymouri, F.: Aligning modeled and observed behavior: a compromise between computation complexity and quality. In: Dubois, E., Pohl, K. (eds.) CAiSE 2017. LNCS, vol. 10253, pp. 94–109. Springer, Cham (2017). https://doi.org/10.1007/978-3-319-59536-8_7

15. Dumas, M., Rosa, M.L., Mendling, J., Reijers, H.A.: Fundamentals of Business Process Management, 2nd edn. Springer, Heidelberg (2018). https://doi.org/10. 1007/978-3-662-56509-4

16. Evermann, J.: Scalable process discovery using map-reduce. IEEE TSC **9**(3), 469–481 (2016)

17. van Hee, K.M., Liu, Z., Sidorova, N.: Is my event log complete? - a probabilistic approach to process mining. In: International Conference on Research Challenges in Information Science, pp. 1–7 (2011)

18. Lee, W.L.J., Verbeek, H.M.W., Munoz-Gama, J., der Aalst, W.M.P.V., Sepúlveda, M.: Recomposing conformance: closing the circle on decomposed alignment-based conformance checking in process mining. Inf. Sci. **466**, 55–91 (2018)

19. Leemans, S.J.J., Fahland, D., van der Aalst, W.M.P.: Discovering block-structured process models from event logs containing infrequent behaviour. In: Lohmann, N., Song, M., Wohed, P. (eds.) BPM 2013. LNBIP, vol. 171, pp. 66–78. Springer, Cham (2014). https://doi.org/10.1007/978-3-319-06257-0_6

20. Leemans, S.J.J., Fahland, D., der Aalst, W.M.P.V.: Scalable process discovery and conformance checking. Softw. Syst. Model. **2**, 599–631 (2018)

21. de Leoni, M., Marrella, A.: How planning techniques can help process mining: the conformance-checking case. In: Italian Symposium on Advanced Database Systems, p. 283 (2017)

22. Luo, C., He, F., Ghezzi, C.: Inferring software behavioral models with MapReduce. Sci. Comput. Program. **145**, 13–36 (2017)

23. Munoz-Gama, J., Carmona, J., van der Aalst, W.: Single-entry single-exit decomposed conformance checking. Inf. Syst. **46**, 102–122 (2014)

24. (Jorge) Munoz-Gama, J.: Conformance checking in the large (dataset) (2013). https://data.4tu.nl/repository/uuid:44c32783-15d0-4dbd-af8a-78b97be3de49

25. Reißner, D., Conforti, R., Dumas, M., Rosa, M.L., Armas-Cervantes, A.: Scalable conformance checking of business processes. In: Panetto, H., et al. (eds.) OTM 2017. LNCS, vol. 10573, pp. 607–627. Springer, Cham (2017). https://doi.org/10.1007/978-3-319-69462-7_38

26. Rogge-Solti, A., Senderovich, A., Weidlich, M., Mendling, J., Gal, A.: In log and model we trust? A generalized conformance checking framework. In: La Rosa, M., Loos, P., Pastor, O. (eds.) BPM 2016. LNCS, vol. 9850, pp. 179–196. Springer, Cham (2016). https://doi.org/10.1007/978-3-319-45348-4_11

27. Rozinat, A., Van der Aalst, W.M.P.: Conformance checking of processes based on monitoring real behavior. Inf. Syst. **33**(1), 64–95 (2008)

28. Taymouri, F., Carmona, J.: Model and event log reductions to boost the computation of alignments. In: Ceravolo, P., Guetl, C., Rinderle-Ma, S. (eds.) SIMPDA 2016. LNBIP, vol. 307, pp. 1–21. Springer, Cham (2018). https://doi.org/10.1007/978-3-319-74161-1_1

29. Taymouri, F., Carmona, J.: A recursive paradigm for aligning observed behavior of large structured process models. In: La Rosa, M., Loos, P., Pastor, O. (eds.) BPM 2016. LNCS, vol. 9850, pp. 197–214. Springer, Cham (2016). https://doi.org/10.1007/978-3-319-45348-4_12

30. Taymouri, F., Carmona, J.: An evolutionary technique to approximate multiple optimal alignments. In: Weske, M., Montali, M., Weber, I., vom Brocke, J. (eds.) BPM 2018. LNCS, vol. 11080, pp. 215–232. Springer, Cham (2018). https://doi.org/10.1007/978-3-319-98648-7_13

31. Van Dongen, B.: BPI Challenge 2012 (2012). https://doi.org/10.4121/uuid:3926db30-f712-4394-aebc-75976070e91f

32. Van Dongen, B.: BPI Challenge 2014 (2014). https://doi.org/10.4121/uuid:c3e5d162-0cfd-4bb0-bd82-af5268819c35

33. Verbeek, E., Buijs, J.C.A.M., van Dongen, B.F., der Aalst, W.M.P.V.: ProM 6: the process mining toolkit. In: Business Process Management (Demonstration Track) (2010)

34. Weber, B., Reichert, M., Rinderle-Ma, S.: Change patterns and change support features - enhancing flexibility in process-aware information systems. DKE **66**(3), 438–466 (2008)

35. Weidlich, M., Polyvyanyy, A., Desai, N., Mendling, J., Weske, M.: Process compliance analysis based on behavioural profiles. Inf. Syst. **36**(7), 1009–1025 (2011)

Trace Clustering on Very Large Event Data in Healthcare Using Frequent Sequence Patterns

Xixi Lu[1]([✉]), Seyed Amin Tabatabaei[2], Mark Hoogendoorn[2],
and Hajo A. Reijers[1]

[1] Department of Information and Computing Sciences,
Utrecht University, Utrecht, The Netherlands
{x.lu,h.a.reijers}@uu.nl
[2] Department of Computer Science, Vrije Universiteit Amsterdam,
Amsterdam, The Netherlands
{s.tabatabaei,m.hoogendoorn}@vu.nl

Abstract. Trace clustering has increasingly been applied to find homogenous process executions. However, current techniques have difficulties in finding a meaningful and insightful clustering of patients on the basis of healthcare data. The resulting clusters are often not in line with those of medical experts, nor do the clusters guarantee to help return meaningful process maps of patients' clinical pathways. After all, a single hospital may conduct thousands of distinct activities and generate millions of events per year. In this paper, we propose a novel trace clustering approach by using sample sets of patients provided by medical experts. More specifically, we learn frequent sequence patterns on a sample set, rank each patient based on the patterns, and use an automated approach to determine the corresponding cluster. We find each cluster separately, while the frequent sequence patterns are used to discover a process map. The approach is implemented in ProM and evaluated using a large data set obtained from a university medical center. The evaluation shows F1-scores of 0.7 for grouping kidney injury, 0.9 for diabetes, and 0.64 for head/neck tumor, while the process maps show meaningful behavioral patterns of the clinical pathways of these groups, according to the domain experts.

Keywords: Trace clustering · Frequent sequential patterns ·
Process mining · Machine learning

1 Introduction

Clinical pathways are known to be enormously complex and flexible. Process mining techniques are often applied to analyze event data related to clinical pathways, in order to obtain valuable insights [1]. The resulting findings can help to improve process quality, patient outcomes and satisfaction, and optimizing resource planning, usages, and reallocation [2]. Finding coherent, relatively

© Springer Nature Switzerland AG 2019
T. Hildebrandt et al. (Eds.): BPM 2019, LNCS 11675, pp. 198–215, 2019.
https://doi.org/10.1007/978-3-030-26619-6_14

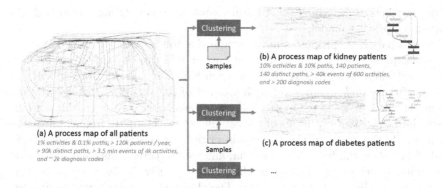

Fig. 1. An example of the partial trace clustering problem and an overview of our approach using sample sets and frequent sequence patterns.

homogenous patient groups helps process mining techniques to obtain accurate insights [3–5].

Many existing systems have tried to classify patients and provide such a well-defined group, known as Patient classification systems (PCSs). PCSs provide a categorization of patients based on clinical data (i.e. diagnoses, procedures), demographic data (i.e. age, gender), and resource consumption data (i.e. costs, length of stay) [6]. While useful, such systems often do not align well with the patient groups as clinicians would define them. Patients who have received the same diagnosis (codes) may be treated for different purposes. For example, patients who get reconstructive breast surgery caused by breast cancer or by gender change can be assigned to the same group, while they have different characteristics and should be assigned to different groups, according to medical experts [7]. Consequently, the process models derived for such a patient group is often also inaccurate and not aligned with the pathways which clinicians would have in their mind. As a result, much manual work involving medical experts is needed to obtain meaningful patient groups.

Emerged from the process mining discipline, trace clustering techniques aim to help finding such homogenous groups of process instances (in our case the patients) [3–5,8]. These techniques cluster the process instances based on the similarity between the sequences of executed activities. However, when applied on hospital data, these approaches face several challenges. Firstly, they have difficulties in scaling-up to handle such large data sets, which may contain hundreds of thousands of patients and millions of events per year. Secondly, they assume that the cases within a group show more homogenous behavior than the cases of different groups, whereas in healthcare, patients treated for the same purpose could have disjoint paths and vice versa. Thirdly, feature vectors (or other intermediate models) are often used to represent the cases and to compute similarity measures; the resulting clusters are often based on an average of the measures and, therefore, may not have clear criteria and may be difficult to explain. Finally, a resulting cluster of patients could still have thousands of distinct activities, which prevents any process discovery algorithm to find a reasonable process model.

In this paper, we propose a novel perspective to the trace clustering problem. We use sample sets to find one patient cluster at a time by exploiting frequent sequential pattern mining techniques, exemplified in Fig. 1. More specifically, *we assume for each group a small sample set of patients (i.e., patient ids) that belongs to the group is made available by medical experts*. Using the available event data of patient pathways of the sample set, we compute frequent sequence patterns (FSPs) to learn the behavioral criteria of the group. All patients are ranked based on the behavioral criteria, and we use thresholds to automatically determine whether they belong to the group (see Fig. 2, discussed in Sect. 4). Each group is clustered independently. The obtained sequence patterns are used to discover simple process maps.

The approach is implemented in the Process Mining toolkit ProM[1] and evaluated using three real-life cases obtained from a large academic hospital in the Netherlands. The results are validated with a semi-medical expert and a data analyst of the hospital, both of them work closely with medical experts; the semi-medical expert is a manager who has acquired relevant medical knowledge regarding the patient pathways.

The contribution of this work is that it gives a concrete method to identify patient clusters from a wealth of data and high variety of pathways with relatively little input from experts. Moreover, this clustering will lead to simple process maps of frequent behavioral patterns in the clinical pathways that can be used in the communication with medical experts. Such a method may be useful to reason about clinical pathways within hospitals for the sake of process improvement or quality control.

In the remainder, we first discuss related work in Sect. 2. We recall the concepts and define the research problem in Sect. 3. The proposed approach is described in Sect. 4. The evaluation results are presented in Sect. 5, and Sect. 6 concludes the paper.

2   Related Work

In this section, we discuss three streams of trace clustering techniques, categorizing them by their similarity measures.

Feature-Vector-Based Similarity. Early work in trace clustering has followed the ideas in traditional data clustering. Each trace is transformed into a vector of features based on, for example, the frequency of activities, the frequency of *directly-followed* relations, the resources involved, etc. Between these feature vectors, various distance metrics in data mining are reused to estimate the similarity between the traces. Subsequently, distance-based clustering algorithms are deployed, such as k-means or agglomerative hierarchical clustering algorithms [3,4,8].

---

[1] http://www.promtools.org/, in the *TraceClusteringFSM* package (see source code).

In line with feature-vector based trace clustering techniques, the work of Greco et al. [3] was one of the first approaches that incorporated trace clustering into process discovery algorithms. Their work uses frequent (sub)sequences of activities to constitute feature vectors that represent traces. Hierarchical clusters are then built using a top-down approach which iteratively refines the most imprecise process model (represented as disjunctive workflow schemas). Song et al. [4] present a technique that generalizes the *feature space* by considering data attributes in other dimensions than solely focusing on the control-flow. Features of traces in one dimension are grouped into a so-called *trace-profile*, e.g., resource, performance, case attribute profiles, etc. Furthermore, a multitude of vector-based distance metrics and clustering techniques (both partitioning and hierarchical) are deployed. In [8], Bose and van der Aalst compute reoccurring sequences of activities, known as *tandem arrays,* and used these patterns as features in the feature space model in order to improve the way the control-flow information is taken into account in trace clustering.

Trace-Sequence Based Clustering. The second category proposes that the similarity can be measured by the syntax similarity between two trace sequences. A trace can be edited into another trace by adding and removing events. The similarity between two traces is measured by the number of the edit operations needed. An example of this category of measure is the Levenshtein Edit Distance (LED). Bose and van der Aalst [9] propose a trace-sequence distance by generalizing the LED and use the agglomerative clustering technique. Chatain et al. [10] assume that a normative process model is available and align the traces with the runs of the model. In essence, the traces that are close to the same run (in terms of sequence distance) are clustered into the same group.

Model-Based Trace Clustering. Recently, the aim of trace clustering to discover better models has become more prominent. Consequently, the definition of the similarity between traces has shifted from the traces themselves to the quality of the models discovered from those traces. In essence, it is proposed that a trace is more similar to a cluster of traces, if a more fitting, precise, and simple model can be discovered from the cluster [5,11,12].

Early work in sequence clustering used first-order Markov models as the intermediate models to represent the clusters. In 2003, Cadez et al. [11] proposed to learn a mixture of first-order Markov models from user behavior by applying the Expectation Maximization problem. The approach is evaluated on a web navigation data set. Later, Ferreira et al. [12] followed the same idea and qualitatively evaluated the clustering algorithm in a process mining setting using two additional data sets.

De Weerdt et al. [5] use Petri nets as intermediate models and optimize a F-measure of the models discovered from the clusters. The algorithm, called ActiTraC, first samples distinct traces, based on frequency or distance, as initial clusters. The traces that "fit" into the intermediate-model of a cluster are assigned to the cluster. The remaining noisy traces either are distributed over the clusters or returned as a garbage cluster. More recently, De Koninck et al. [13] proposed to incorporate domain knowledge by assuming that a complete clustering solution is provided by experts. The proposed technique then aims to improve the quality of such a complete expert-driven clustering in terms of the model qualities.

Discussion. Regarding the feature-based techniques, the number of possible features can be immense, especially in process mining [4]. For example, for n activities, we could have n^2 number of *directly-followed* relations and n^3 if we consider three activities. With thousands of distinct activities, it can be computationally expensive if we consider the full feature space. Moreover, as the clusters are calculated based on the average distances between feature vectors, it is often difficult to explain the reason of a particular clustering. In many cases, the feature-based techniques have difficulties in finding clusters that are in line with those of domain experts [13]. Sequence-based trace clustering faces similar limitations as the feature-based. Furthermore, patients who have disjoint sets of activities and diagnosis (codes) may belong to the same group. Both feature-based and sequence-based would have difficulties finding those. For model-based trace clustering techniques, it would be difficult to handle the complexity of the intermediate models. The clinical pathway of a well-defined patient group could still be extremely complex with thousands distinct activities being executed and each patient following a unique path tailored towards their conditions (see Sect. 5.1). Assuming that a complete expert-driven clustering is available would put too much effort on medical experts and is not feasible for this reason. Our approach, therefore, needs to be scalable and able to deal with this complexity. The approach should also put more emphasis on the abundant domain knowledge available and find clear behavioral criteria of the clusters such that the behavioral criteria are meaningful for domain or medical experts.

3   Research Problem

In this section, we first recall the preliminary concepts such as event logs, traces, and activities. Using these concepts, we define our research problem.

3.1   Preliminaries

A *process* describes a set of *activities* executed in a certain order. For example, each patient in a hospital follows a certain *process* to treat a certain diagnosis of a disease, also known as *clinical pathway*. An *event log* is a set of *traces*, each describing a sequence of *events* through the process. Each *event* records additional information regarding the executed *activity*. For example, Table 1 shows a snippet of an event log of a healthcare process. Each row records an executed event, which contains information such as the event id, the patient id, the activity, the timestamps, the diagnosis code (also known as diagnosis-related group (DRG) [6], or DBC in Dutch), and potentially some additional attributes regarding the event.

Table 1. An example of an event log of a healthcare process

Event	PID	Activity	Time stamps	DBC	Attr.
1	1001	Registration (Reg)	22-10-2018	DBC1	...
2	1001	Doctor appointment (Doc)	23-10-2018	DBC1	...
3	1001	Lab test (Lab)	24-10-2018	DBC1	...
4	1001	Surgery (Srg)	30-10-2017	DBC2	...
5	1001	Doctor appointment (Doc)	01-11-2017	DBC2	...
21	1002	Registration (Reg)	23-10-2017	DBC3	...
22	1002	Lab test (Lab)	25-10-2017	DBC3	...
23	1002	Surgery (Srg)	26-10-2017	DBC4	...
31	1003	Registration (Reg)	25-10-2017	DBC1	...
32	1003	Surgery (Srg)	26-10-2017	DBC1	...
...	...	...	...	...	...

Definition 1 (Universes). *We write the following notations for universes: $\mathcal{E}$ denotes the universe of unique events, i.e., the set of all possible event identifiers. U denotes the set of all possible attribute names. Val denotes the set of all possible attribute values. $Act \subset Val$ denotes the set of all possible activity names. $PI \subset Val$ denotes the set of all possible process instance identifiers.*

Definition 2 (Event, Attribute, Label). *For each event $e \in \mathcal{E}$, for each attribute name $d \in U$, the attribute function $\pi_d(e)$ returns the value of attribute d of event e. A labeling function $\pi_l : \mathcal{E} \to Val$ is a function that assigns the label to each event $e \in \mathcal{E}$.*

If the value is undefined, $\pi_d(e) = \perp$. Examples of attribute names used in this paper are listed as follows: $\pi_{pi}(e) \in PI$ denotes the process instance identifier of e; $\pi_{act}(e) \in Act$ is the activity associated with e; $\pi_{time}(e)$ denotes the timestamp of e; $\pi_{dbc}(e)$ denotes the diagnosis code of e. For example, given the log listed in Table 1, $\pi_{pi}(e_1) = 1001$, $\pi_{act}(e_1) = $ Registeration, $\pi_{dbc}(e_1) = $ DBC1.

The labeling function $\pi_l(e)$ returns the activity label of event e in the process (also known as an *event classifier*). In this paper, we combine both the activities and the diagnosis codes and use them as labels, i.e., $\pi_l(e) := \pi_{act}(e) + \pi_{dbc}(e)$, because the data analyst from the hospital indicated that both are important for the clinical pathway. For example, given the log listed in Table 1, the label of event 1 is $\pi_l(e_1) := \pi_{act}(e_1) + \pi_{dbc}(e_1) = $ "*Reg-DBC1*"; the label of event 23 is $\pi_l(e_{23}) = $ "*Srg-DBC4*".

A *trace* $\sigma = \langle e_1, e_2, \cdots, e_n \rangle \in \mathcal{E}^*$ is a sequence of events, where for $1 \leq i < n$, $\pi_{time}(e_i) \leq \pi_{time}(e_{i+1})$ and $\pi_{pi}(e_i) = \pi_{pi}(e_{i+1})$. An *event log* $L = \{\sigma_1, \cdots, \sigma_{|L|}\} \subseteq \mathcal{E}^*$ is a set of traces.

Definition 3 (Simplified Trace, Simplified Log). *Let π_l be the labeling function. Let $L = \{\sigma_1, \cdots, \sigma_{|L|}\}$ be a log and $\sigma = \langle e_1, e_2, \cdots, e_{|\sigma|} \rangle$ a trace. We*

overload the labeling function such that, given σ, the labeling function returns the sequence of labels of the events in σ, i.e., $\pi_l(\sigma) = \langle \pi_l(e_1), \pi_l(e_2), \cdots, \pi_l(e_{|\sigma|}) \rangle \in$ Val*. Furthermore, given the log L, the labeling function returns the multi-set of the sequences of the labels of the traces in L, i.e., $\pi_l(L) = [\pi_l(\sigma_1), \cdots, \pi_l(\sigma_{|L|})]$.

Let $\sigma = \langle e_1, \cdots, e_n \rangle \in L$ be a trace. For $1 \le i < n$, we say event e_i is *directly-followed* by e_{i+1}. For $1 \le i < j \le n$, we say event e_i is *eventually-followed* by e_j. For the sake of brevity, we write $L^l = \pi_l(L)$ and $\sigma^l = \pi_l(\sigma)$. For instance, the simplified trace of patient 1001 listed in Table 1 is $\pi_l(\sigma_{1001}) = \sigma_{1001}^{act,dbc} = \langle$"Reg-DBC1", "Doc-DBC1", "Lab-DBC1", "Srg-DBC2", "Doc-DBC2"$\rangle$. Note that a patient (an activity) could be associated with multiple diagnosis codes [6], e.g., patient 1001 (activity *Doc*).

3.2   Research Problem - Grouping Patients

Traditional trace clustering aims to divide the traces of a log into clusters, such that the traces of the same cluster show more homogenous behavior than the traces of different clusters. In the healthcare domain, we are facing a very large, complex data set and abundant domain knowledge. As discussed at the end of Sect. 2, we would like to (1) handle such a large data set, to (2) incorporate, leverage, and put more emphasis on the domain knowledge, in order to obtain clusters that are more in line with those of medical experts, while requiring little effort from such experts, and to (3) be able to find the clusters accurately and validate clusters quality, we propose the following.

We assume that medical experts can provide a small sample set P of the patients that belong to a patient group $\hat{C}$ of interest. Giving a sample requires little effort from their side. We assume that $\hat{C}$ is unknown (because when $\hat{C}$ gets large, it would require too much effort for medical experts to exhaustively list all patients that belong to $\hat{C}$ and to repeat this process). We use the available traces of all patients in the sample P, and the objective is to find a cluster C in such a way that C is as close to the group $\hat{C}$ as possible (i.e., the highest recall and precision possible). We do this separately for each group $\hat{C}_i$ where the sample set P_i is available. To generalize, we define the partial trace clustering formally as follows.

Definition 4 (Partial Trace Clustering). *Let $L = \{\sigma_1, \cdots, \sigma_n\}$ be the event log, and $PI = \{\pi_{pi}(\sigma_1), \cdots, \pi_{pi}(\sigma_n)\}$ the set of case ids of L. Let $P_1, P_2, \cdots, P_x \subset PI$ be the sets of samples that respectively belong to clusters $\hat{C}_1, \hat{C}_2, \cdots, \hat{C}_x$, provided by experts (e.g., a doctor), with $x \in \mathbb{N}$. We would like to find the clusters $C_1, C_2, \cdots, C_x \subset PI$, such that the set difference between C_i and $\hat{C}_i$ is minimized.*

Note that clusters $C_1, \cdots, C_x$ can be non-overlapping or form an incomplete clustering of PI (i.e., $C_1 \cup \cdots \cup C_x \subseteq PI$), and x could be 1. Based on these properties, we do not have to find all clusters or to compute a complete clustering of all traces. It allows us to mine, cluster, and validate each cluster independently.

4 Approach

As explained above, we assume that for each cluster C to be found we have a small sample P of the cases that belongs to the true-but-unknown cluster $\hat{C}$. For all other cases it is unknown whether they belong to the cluster or not. By exploiting the available sample set P and the event log L of all cases, the objective is to find *behavioral criteria* for determining the cluster. To find the behavioral criteria and to handle the large number of features, we compute frequent *behavioral patterns*. In Sect. 4.1, we first explain the use of sequence pattern mining to learn the frequent sequence patterns (FSPs) of the sample set. In Sect. 4.2, we then match the FSPs to the other cases in the sample to train our parameters. Finally, we match all cases to the clustering criteria to return the computed cluster in Sect. 4.3. Figure 2 shows an overview of the approach.

4.1 Finding Frequent Sequence Patterns

The first step of the approach is to find frequent sequence patterns repeated among the samples. A *frequent sequence pattern* is a sequence that occurs in the traces with a frequency no less than a specified threshold. We adapt the definition of sequence patterns in our context as follows.

Definition 5 (Sequence Pattern). *A sequence pattern* $s = \langle a_1, \cdots, a_m \rangle \in Val^*$ *is a sequence of labels in which* a_i *is said to be eventually followed by* a_{i+1} *for* $1 \leq i < m$.

When a trace *matches* a sequence pattern, it means that the trace contains a sub sequence where the labels occur in the same order.

Definition 6 (Support of Sequence Pattern). *Let* L *be an event log and* π_l *the labeling function. Let* $\sigma \in L$ *be a trace, with* $\pi_l(\sigma) = \langle a_1, a_2, \cdots, a_n \rangle$. *Let* $s = \langle s_1, \cdots, s_m \rangle \in Val^*$ *be a sequence pattern. We say* σ *matches* s *if and only if there exist integers* $i_1, i_2, \cdots, i_m$ *such that* $1 \leq i_1 < i_2 < \cdots < i_m \leq n$ *and* $s_1 = a_{i_1}, s_2 = a_{i_2}, ..., s_m = a_{i_m}$. *We write* $s \sqsubseteq \pi_l(\sigma)$.

The support *of sequence* s *in* L *is the number of traces in* L *that matches* s, *i.e.,*

$$supp(s, L) = \frac{| \{ s \sqsubseteq \pi_l(\sigma) \mid \sigma \in L \} |}{| L |}$$

Let ϕ_s denote the minimum support threshold. A sequence pattern s is said to be *frequent* if and only if $supp(s, L) \geq \phi_s$. We write $SP(L, \phi_s)$ to denote the set of all sequence patterns in L with a support of at least ϕ_s, i.e.,

$$SP(L, \phi_s) = \{ s \in Val^* \mid supp(s, L) \geq \phi_s \}$$

Step 1 in Fig. 2 exemplifies mining frequent sequence patterns, with the minimum support $\phi_s = 0.8$. Let $L' = \{\sigma_1, \sigma_2, \sigma_3\}$, as shown in Fig. 2. We have $SP(L', 0.8) = \{\langle A \rangle, \langle C \rangle, \langle D \rangle, \langle E \rangle, \langle F \rangle, \langle A, C \rangle, \langle A, D \rangle, \langle A, E \rangle, \cdots, \langle A, C, D, F \rangle\}$.

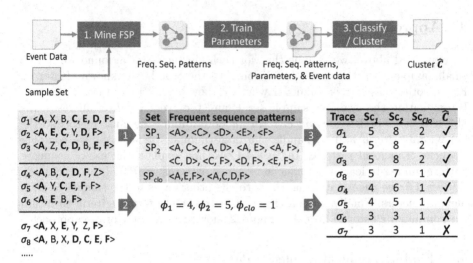

Fig. 2. An example of our approach applied on the event log (on the left), with the FSPs mined (in the middle), and the scores of the traces (on the right).

There are several well-known algorithms to compute frequent sequence patterns. In this paper, we use the CloFAST algorithm [14] and its SPMF implementation [15] due to its fast run-time, which is also used in [16] for next activity prediction.

4.2 Trace Ranking by Sequence Pattern Matching

To automatically find behavioral criteria for determining the cluster C, we divide the sample set P into a training set P_{tr} and use the entire P as our test set. On the training set P_{tr}, we compute the set of frequent sequence patterns (FSPs).

The FSPs mined on the training set P_{tr} could still be very large. Therefore, we select a subset of the FSPs. We use the FSPs of length 1, 2, and the closed sequence patterns as our behavioral criteria. Note that this step can be generalized with ease and any other subset of the FSPs can be selected as behavioral criteria. We select these three subsets because of the following. The FSPs of length 1 represent the frequent activity labels occurred in the training set; the FSPs of length 2 represent the frequent *eventually-followed* relations occurred. The *closed sequence patterns* $s \in SP(L, \phi_s)$ are the sequence patterns s such that for all other patterns which s satisfies have a lower support. Thus, these three provide a good coverage of all FSPs with less redundancy.

Definition 7 (Closed Sequence Pattern). *Let $SP(L, \phi_s)$ denote all frequent sequence patterns in L with a support of at least ϕ_s. A sequence pattern $s \in SP(L, \phi_s)$ is a closed sequence pattern if and only if for all $s' \in SP(L, \phi_s)$, $s \sqsubseteq s' \Leftrightarrow (s = s' \vee supp(s, L) > supp(s', L))$.*

Next, using these subsets of these patterns, we rank each trace in P based on the number of patterns it satisfies. Let $SP(P, \phi_s) = \{s_1, s_2, \cdots s_n\}$ be the set of frequent sequence patterns of P above support threshold ϕ_s. Let $SP_1, SP_2, SP_{clo} \subseteq SP(P, \phi_s)$ be the set of patterns of size 1, size 2, and closed sequence patterns, respectively. We give each case a score based on the number of patterns in SP_1, SP_2, and SP_{clo} the trace satisfies and rank the cases based on their score. Thus,

$$score_k(\sigma) = |\{s \in SP_k | s \sqsubseteq \pi_l(\sigma)\}|$$

For example, see Fig. 2, step 1 shows SP_1 of five sequence patterns, SP_2 of eight, and SP_{clo} of two, which are mined on the $P_{tr} = \{\sigma_1, \sigma_2, \sigma_3\}$ using a minimum support of 0.8. Given trace $\sigma_4 \notin P_{tr}$, it matches to $\langle A \rangle$, $\langle C \rangle$, $\langle D \rangle$, and $\langle E \rangle$ in SP_1, to $\langle A, C \rangle$, $\langle A, D \rangle$, $\langle A, F \rangle$, $\langle C, D \rangle$, $\langle C, F \rangle$, and $\langle D, F \rangle$ in SP_2, and to $\langle A, C, D, F \rangle$ in SP_{clo}. Thus, $score_1(\sigma_4) = 4$, $score_2(\sigma_4) = 6$, $score_{clo}(\sigma_4) = 1$.

4.3   Computing Criteria Threshold

For each case, we have now computed $score_1$, $score_2$, and $score_{clo}$, as explained above. For the three scores, we respectively introduce three thresholds, $\phi_1 \in \mathbb{N}$, $\phi_2 \in \mathbb{N}_0$, and $\phi_{clo} \in \mathbb{N}_0$. We decide on whether a case belongs to cluster C based on whether the scores of the trace are above the corresponding thresholds, i.e.,

$$C_{\phi_1, \phi_2, \phi_{clo}} = \{\pi_{pi}(\sigma) | \sigma \in L \wedge score_1(\sigma) \geq \phi_1 \wedge score_2(\sigma) \geq \phi_2 \wedge score_{clo}(\sigma) \geq \phi_{clo}\}$$

To estimate the quality of $C_{\phi_1, \phi_2, \phi_{clo}}$, we then compute the estimated recall with respect to P, i.e., $\overline{recall}_{\phi_1, \phi_2, \phi_{clo}} = \frac{|C_{\phi_1, \phi_2, \phi_{clo}} \cap P|}{|P|}$. When the sample set P gets closer to the ideal cluster $\hat{C}$, the estimated $\overline{recall}$ gets closer to the true recall. When we decrease ϕ_1, ϕ_2, and ϕ_{clo}, more cases are included in C. After a certain point, the increase of $\overline{recall}$ starts to flatten, which suggests that further lowering the thresholds does not help to retrieve a large number of true positive cases, which is likely to result in a low precision. To approximate such a point, we use $max_{\phi_1, \phi_2, \phi_{clo}} \frac{\overline{recall}^2_{\phi_1, \phi_2, \phi_{clo}}}{|C_{\phi_1, \phi_2, \phi_{clo}}|}$ [17], but only consider the thresholds when $\overline{recall} \geq 0.8$. The number of iterations to find such a maximum depends on the maximal values of $score_1$, $score_2$, and $score_{clo}$.

5   Evaluation

We implemented the described approach in the process mining toolkit ProM. We used a real-life data set to evaluate our approach with respect to the following three objectives:

(EO1) How accurate (in terms of F1-scores) are the clusters returned by our automated approach, compared to the optimal scores?

Table 2. General information of the real-life data set and the ground truth clusters.

Data	#cases	#dpi	#avg. c/dpi	#events	#avg. e/c	#max. e/c	#acts	#dbcs	#dst. labels	Perc. of all
All17	128,505	97,771	1.3	$3.70 * 10^6$	28.8	2,924	4,666	1,915	150,244	-
$\hat{C}$_Kidney17	140	140	1.0	40,071	286.2	2,167	676	237	4,777	0.11%
$\hat{C}$_Diabetes17	1,521	1,520	1.0	139,454	91.7	2,861	1,414	646	16,496	1.18%
$\hat{C}$_HNTumor17	1,050	1,048	1.0	105,613	100.6	905	1,001	380	9,211	0.82%
All13	133,438	99,196	1.3	$4.32 * 10^6$	32.4	2,558	4,871	1,813	168,096	-
$\hat{C}$_Kidney13	81	81	1.0	26,949	332.7	1,577	651	159	3,601	0.06%
$\hat{C}$_Diabetes13	1,573	1,573	1.0	142,737	90.7	1,057	1,427	663	16,966	1.18%
$\hat{C}$_HNTumor13	1,350	1,334	1.0	147,491	109.3	2,227	1,237	437	12,678	1.01%

(EO2) How accurate can we find the clusters using our approach, compared to a related approach that uses frequent item sets (FIS) [7]?

(EO3) Can we discover a simple and insightful behavioral criteria for each patient group such that the criteria can be used to communicate with medical experts?

In the following, we first discuss the data set in Sect. 5.1 and then report our results Sect. 5.2 with respect to these three objectives. All experiments are run on an Intel Core i7- 8550U 1.80 GHZ with a processing unit of 16 GB running Windows 10 Enterprise. The maximal queue size of CloFAST algorithm [14,15] is set to 10^5. The obtained results were discussed with the semi-medical expert and the data expert in the hospital who cooperate closely with medical experts in their daily work.

5.1 Experimental Setup

For the evaluation, we used anonymized patient records provided by the VU University Medical Center Amsterdam, a large academic hospital in the Netherlands. All patients that have a diagnosis code registered between 2013 and 2017 are selected. The administrative and dummy activities are filtered out. As a result, we have in total 328,256 patients over the five years. There are 7,426 unique activities and 2,251 unique diagnosis codes registered. In total more than 15.5 million events are recorded in the logs.

In addition, lists of patients of three groups divided over the five years are provided by the analyst, patients with kidney failure, with diabetes, or with head/neck-tumor. We use $\hat{C}_{KidneyYY}$, $\hat{C}_{DiabetesYY}$, and $\hat{C}_{HNTumorYY}$ to refer to them, respectively, where YY denotes the particular year. Table 2 lists the number of cases (c), distinct process instances (dpi), events (e), activities (acts), and other statistical information related to the event logs of 2013 and 2017 as examples. For instance, in Table 2 row 2, 3, and 4 show an overview of $\hat{C}_{Kidney17}$, $\hat{C}_{Diabetes17}$, and $\hat{C}_{HNTumor17}$, respectively. These 15 clusters are used as the ground truth. For each cluster, 30 patient ids are provided by medical experts as the sample set (i.e., $|P| = 30$), the same as a previous study [7]. For finding the clusters, we use all the patient records of the same year and the provided P to compute our cluster C. The quality of C is evaluated against the corresponding ground truth cluster $\hat{C}$ by calculating the recall, precision, and F1-score, i.e., $recall(C, \hat{C}) = \frac{|C \cap \hat{C}|}{|\hat{C}|}$, $precision(C, \hat{C}) = \frac{|C \cap \hat{C}|}{|C|}$, and $F1\_measure(C, \hat{C}) = 2 \cdot \frac{precision(C,\hat{C}) \cdot recall(C,\hat{C})}{precision(C,\hat{C}) + recall(C,\hat{C})}$.

It is worthwhile to mention that the data analyst stated that it took a lot of time and effort to obtain each of these ground truth clusters. Multiple intensive discussion sessions were scheduled with different groups of medical experts to come to the definitions and criteria for each of these clusters. This suggests that if our algorithmic approach can identify the behavioral criteria and the clusters with a reasonable accuracy using only a small sample set, it would help reducing the workload of both the analysts and the medial experts and making this process feasible to be repeated for other patient clusters or in other hospitals. Another important remark is that the ground-truth clusters which we are trying to find are very small and unbalanced compared to the full event logs, making this trace clustering problem a very challenging task. For instance, the $\hat{C}\_Kidney17$ ($\hat{C}\_Diabetes17$) contains only 140 (1521) patients, about 0.1% (1.2%) of the 128,505 patients in the log of 2017.

5.2   Results

(EO1) F1 Scores of Automated Approach Compared To Maximum. To determine the support threshold ϕ_s, we started with 1.0 and decreased the value by 0.1 until a reasonable large amount of patterns are found and the F1 scores stopped increasing. For the C_Kidney groups, ϕ_s ranges from 1.0 down-to 0.6, for $C\_Diabetes$, 0.4 down-to 0.2, and for $C\_HNTumor$, 0.5 down-to 0.2. We used either 10 or 15 (of the 30 in the sample) as the training set to learn the frequent sequential patterns, i.e., $k = |P_{tr}| \in \{10, 15\}$. We write TC-FSMa for our approach with the automatically determined ϕ_1, ϕ_2, and ϕ_{clo}; TC-FSM* for the maximum F1 score using the same ϕ_s and k but based on the optimal ϕ_1, ϕ_2, and ϕ_{clo}.

Figure 3 shows the difference in F1-scores between TC-FSMa (dotted lines) and TC-FSM* (filled lines). We observe that in most cases the F1-scores of the automated TC-FSMa (dotted line) are very close to the ones of the optimal TC-FSM* (filled line). For some clusters, for example Diabetes16&17 and HNTumor15&17, TC-FSMa returns the exact same F1-scores as the maximum for all ϕ_s and k. Only in a few cases, for example, for Diabetes13 when k is 15 and the support ϕ_s is 0.2, TC-FSMa scores considerably lower than TC-FSM* with a difference of 0.26. Nevertheless, for the same ϕ_s when k is set to 10, this difference is immediately decreased to 0.01. Taking into account that we only have a sample set of 30 patients and the number of activities ranges in the thousands, the TC-FSMa is able to approximate the optimal F1-scores very well.

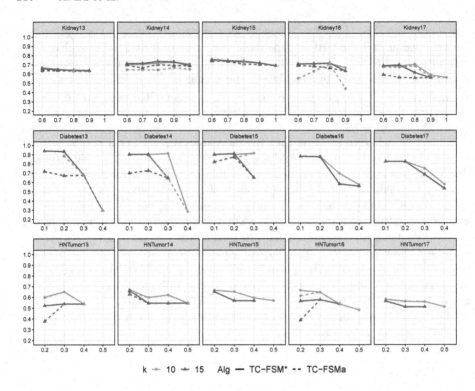

Fig. 3. The differences in the F1-scores of the automated approach (TC-FSMa) shown in dotted lines and the maximum scores achieved (TC-FSM*) shown in filled lines, using various support threshold (on the x-axis) and training sample size k (Color figure online).

For the support threshold ϕ_s, we observe overall a slight increase in the F1-scores for the Kidney and HNTumor groups when we decrease ϕ_s. For the Diabetes groups, there is a considerable increase in F1-scores during the beginning (when ϕ_s is decreased from 0.4 to 0.2), but this improvement also fades out. One reason for this is because when the support threshold is low, more patterns are found and used as criteria; thus, more patients are included in the cluster including false positives. While the recall increases, the precision becomes lower, which led to a small increase in the F1-scores. For the diabetes group, when the support ϕ_s is 0.4, the number of sequence patterns is extremely small (1 or 3). When the support decreases, it allowed the algorithm to find a consider number of defining patterns that is significant to retrieve the patients of the ground truth clusters. This increases the recall dramatically without a significant decrease in precision. Furthermore, Fig. 3 also shows that using fewer training samples ($k = 10$, denoted using light blue), our approach can achieve the same scores as when using a larger training sample set ($k = 15$, denoted using darker blue). In many cases, the former (i.e., $k = 10$) even achieved a better result. This may be due to that the training test set $P \backslash P_{tr}$ is larger.

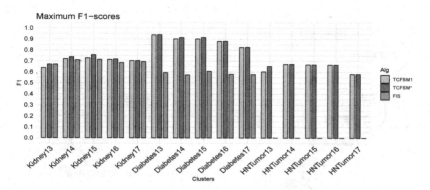

Fig. 4. F1-measures achieved by our approaches TC-FSM1 and TC-FCM* for the three groups, compared to the ones achieved by the previous approach FIS [7].

(EO2) Comparing the F1-Scores Achieved. We write TC-FSM* to refer to the maximum score of our approach using the above settings. We write TC-FSM1 to denote our approach with a single setting (0.8 for kidney, 0.2 for diabetes, and 0.2 for NH-tumor, with sample size 30 and $k_{tr} = 10$), to compare our results to the previous work [7]. The parameters are selected on the results of EO1. We write FIS for referring to the previous approach that uses frequent item sets [7].

Figure 4 shows the maximum F1-scores of TC-FSM*, TC-FSM1, and FIS on the 15 clusters over 5 years and three groups. For the diabetes group, we achieved a considerable improvement of 0.2–0.3 in the F1-scores, compared to the FIS approach [7]. Overall, our approach achieved a better result. One reason for this improvement is with the use of sequential patterns (instead of frequent item sets), our approach is able to decrease the number of false positives and find the clusters with a higher precision.

(EO3) Frequent Sequence Patterns to Simple Process Maps. We used the closed sequence patterns mined on the samples as the traces that represent the frequent behavior shared by the group. Using these sequence patterns, the discovered process maps overall seem to be simple and insightful, representing only the crucial behavioral criteria of the patient groups. We show three process maps in Figs. 5, 6 and 7, for $C_{kidney17}$, $C_{HNTumor16}$, and $C_{Diabetes16}$ to illustrate our results. All the process maps contain all activities and paths (thus no filters applied). As can be seen in Fig. 5, the number of activity labels in the process is reduced from about 4,700 to 11. The number of distinct variants is reduced from 140 to 8.

The process maps are shown to the semi-medical expert and the data analyst. The semi-medical expert observes and confirms that the activities shown (e.g., *"kalium"* (potassium), *"kreatinine"* (creatinine), *"calcium"* (calcium), *"fosfaat"* (phosphate), *"albumine"* (albumin), *"natrium"* (sodium), *"ureum bloed"* (ureum blood), etc.) are important activities (e.g., lab activities) in the clinical pathway of the kidney groups (patients with renal insufficiency). The data analyst

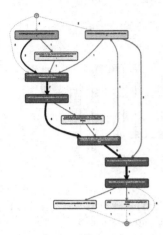

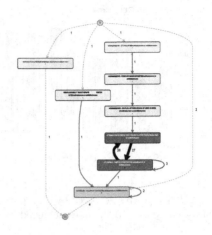

Fig. 5. The full process map based on the closed FSPs of the kidney group; 600 activities are reduced to 11 labels.

Fig. 6. The full process map based on the closed FSPs of the HNTumor group.

confirms that the diagnosis code "Chronic renal failure eGFR < 30 ml/min" associated with these activities is a crucial criteria for defining the kidney groups.

In Figs. 6 and 7, we also observe that multiple distinct diagnosis codes are used for the HNTumor and diabetes group, respectively. In the process map for $C_{Diabetes16}$, we found the process map being divided into three sub processes based on the diagnosis codes: [SG1] "*diabetes mellitus without secondary complications*", [SG2] "*diabetes mellitus with secondary complications*", and [SG3] "*diabetes mellitus chronic pump therapy*" (see Fig. 7, highlighted in red).

The semi-medical expert also observes and confirms that some of these activities are important indicators for different groups. For example, "*creatinine*" is important for both the kidney and diabetes groups. Nevertheless, because our approach is able to combine and handle the activities with their diagnosis codes as activity labels (in terms of the large variety of distinct labels and process variants), it enabled us to accurately distinguish the "*creatinine*" for the kidney group (i.e., "creatinine||*Chronic renal failure eGFR < 30 ml/min*") versus the same "*creatinine*" but for the diabetes group (i.e., "creatinine||*SG1*" and "creatinine||*SG3*", see Fig. 7, highlighted in blue).

5.3   Discussion

The results have shown that our approach using the discovered and selected frequent sequence patterns can help to cluster the patient groups with a reasonably high accuracy (e.g., a maximum of 0.75 for the Kidney group, 0.94 for Diabetes, and 0.67 for HNTumor), despite the very large data sets (on average, about 130,000 of patients and 3.9 millions of events per year) and the relatively

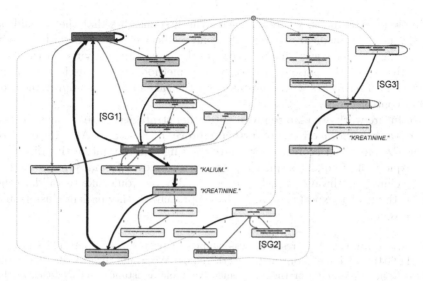

Fig. 7. The full process map based on the closed FSPs of the diabetes group; three distinct subgroups SG1, SG2, and SG3 are found (Color figure online).

very small and unbalanced clusters. Moreover, the proposed approach that automatically determines the parameters achieved F1-scores that are very close to the optimal scores. This means after setting the support ϕ_s and with no further input, we can find the clusters with a reasonable quality as well. Using the process maps, we show the meaningful and insightful behavioral patterns and criteria in the clinical pathways of the patient groups. According to the semi-medical expert, the maps can be a useful tool in the communication with the domain experts regarding the pathways. Note that we do not have any prior knowledge of the specific activities or diagnosis codes of the patient groups.

A remark is that these process maps of FSPs have a different semantics than the formal process models discovered using the traces. For example, an edge from A to B in the map, in essence, means that such an *eventually-followed* relation is frequent. To obtain formal models, we may project the patterns on the traces and use the instances of the patterns in the traces to discover models [18].

6   Conclusion and Future Work

In this paper, we investigated the trace clustering problem in healthcare and proposed an approach that can handle the characteristics of healthcare data. Using a small sample set of patients, the proposed approach finds frequent sequence patterns and uses these as behavioral criteria for determining a cluster. The results of the evaluations show that the approach is able to identify patient clusters with a very reasonable quality on the basis of very limited input from medical experts, despite the very large data sets and the small, unbalanced clusters (ground-truth). The obtained behavioral criteria also led to the generation of simple process maps, where we have some first insights that these could be actually used by medical experts. The semi-medical expert who works closely with medical experts was able to recognize the important activities in the clinical pathways of the patient groups. Such a method may be useful to reason about clinical pathways within hospitals for the sake of process improvement or quality control.

For future work, we plan to investigate other strategies for selecting sequence patterns as behavioral criteria to further improve the F1-scores. Also, the effect of sample size on the F1-scores is worth investigating. Another interesting direction is to exploit the frequent sequence patterns to discover formal process models for the clinical pathways of each cluster. Finally, we would like to validate the maps with medical experts and apply our approach to other patient clusters and other hospitals.

Acknowledgments. This research was supported by the NWO TACTICS project (628.011.004) and Lunet Zorg in the Netherlands. We would also like to thank the experts from the VUMC for their extremely valuable assistance and feedback in the evaluation.

References

1. Rojas, E., Munoz-Gama, J., Sepúlveda, M., Capurro, D.: Process mining in healthcare: a literature review. J. Biomed. Inform. **61**, 224–236 (2016)
2. Caron, F., Vanthienen, J., Vanhaecht, K., van Limbergen, E., De Weerdt, J., Baesens, B.: Monitoring care processes in the gynecologic oncology department. Comput. Biol. Med. **44**, 88–96 (2014)
3. Greco, G., Guzzo, A., Pontieri, L., Saccà, D.: Discovering expressive process models by clustering log traces. IEEE Trans. Knowl. Data Eng. **18**(8), 1010–1027 (2006)
4. Song, M., Günther, C.W., van der Aalst, W.M.P.: Trace clustering in process mining. In: Ardagna, D., Mecella, M., Yang, J. (eds.) BPM 2008. LNBIP, vol. 17, pp. 109–120. Springer, Heidelberg (2009). https://doi.org/10.1007/978-3-642-00328-8_11
5. De Weerdt, J., vanden Broucke, S.K.L.M., Vanthienen, J., Baesens, B.: Active trace clustering for improved process discovery. IEEE Trans. Knowl. Data Eng. **25**(12), 2708–2720 (2013)
6. Schreyögg, J., Stargardt, T., Tiemann, O., Busse, R.: Methods to determine reimbursement rates for diagnosis related groups (DRG): a comparison of nine european countries. Health Care Manag. Sci. **9**(3), 215–223 (2006)
7. Tabatabaei, S.A., Lu, X., Hoogendoorn, M., Reijers, H.A.: Identifying patient groups based on frequent patterns of patient samples. CoRR abs/1904.01863 (2019)
8. Bose, R.P.J.C., van der Aalst, W.M.P.: Trace clustering based on conserved patterns: towards achieving better process models. In: Rinderle-Ma, S., Sadiq, S., Leymann, F. (eds.) BPM 2009. LNBIP, vol. 43, pp. 170–181. Springer, Heidelberg (2010). https://doi.org/10.1007/978-3-642-12186-9_16
9. Bose, R.P.J.C., van der Aalst, W.M.P.: Context aware trace clustering: towards improving process mining results. In: Proceedings of the SDM 2009, pp. 401–412 (2009)
10. Chatain, T., Carmona, J., van Dongen, B.: Alignment-based trace clustering. In: Mayr, H.C., Guizzardi, G., Ma, H., Pastor, O. (eds.) ER 2017. LNCS, vol. 10650, pp. 295–308. Springer, Cham (2017). https://doi.org/10.1007/978-3-319-69904-2_24

11. Cadez, I.V., Heckerman, D., Meek, C., Smyth, P., White, S.: Model-based clustering and visualization of navigation patterns on a web site. Data Min. Knowl. Discov. **7**(4), 399–424 (2003)
12. Ferreira, D., Zacarias, M., Malheiros, M., Ferreira, P.: Approaching process mining with sequence clustering: experiments and findings. In: Alonso, G., Dadam, P., Rosemann, M. (eds.) BPM 2007. LNCS, vol. 4714, pp. 360–374. Springer, Heidelberg (2007). https://doi.org/10.1007/978-3-540-75183-0_26
13. De Koninck, P., Nelissen, K., Baesens, B., vanden Broucke, S., Snoeck, M., De Weerdt, J.: An approach for incorporating expert knowledge in trace clustering. In: Dubois, E., Pohl, K. (eds.) CAiSE 2017. LNCS, vol. 10253, pp. 561–576. Springer, Cham (2017). https://doi.org/10.1007/978-3-319-59536-8_35
14. Fumarola, F., Lanotte, P.F., Ceci, M., Malerba, D.: CloFAST: closed sequential pattern mining using sparse and vertical id-lists. Knowl. Inf. Syst. **48**(2), 429–463 (2016)
15. Fournier-Viger, P., Gomariz, A., Gueniche, T., Soltani, A., Wu, C., Tseng, V.S.: SPMF: a Java open-source pattern mining library. J. Mach. Learn. Res. **15**(1), 3389–3393 (2014)
16. Ceci, M., Spagnoletta, M., Lanotte, P.F., Malerba, D.: Distributed learning of process models for next activity prediction. In: IDEAS, pp. 278–282. ACM (2018)
17. Lee, W.S., Liu, B.: Learning with positive and unlabeled examples using weighted logistic regression. In: ICML, vol. 3, pp. 448–455 (2003)
18. Lu, X., et al.: Semi-supervised log pattern detection and exploration using event concurrence and contextual information. In: Panetto, H., et al. (eds.) OTM 2017. LNCS, vol. 10573, pp. 154–174. Springer, Cham (2017). https://doi.org/10.1007/978-3-319-69462-7_11

ProcessExplorer: Intelligent Process Mining Guidance

Alexander Seeliger[✉][ID], Alejandro Sánchez Guinea, Timo Nolle[ID],
and Max Mühlhäuser

Telecooperation Lab, Technische Universität Darmstadt, Darmstadt, Germany
{seeliger,sanchez,nolle,max}@tk.tu-darmstadt.de

Abstract. Large amount of data is collected in event logs from information systems, reflecting the actual execution of business processes. Due
to the highly competitive pressure in the market, organizations are particularly interested in optimizing their processes. Process mining enables
the extraction of valuable knowledge from event logs, such as deviations,
bottlenecks, and anomalies. Due to the increase of process complexity in
flexible environments, visual exploration is increasingly becoming more
challenging. In this paper, we propose ProcessExplorer, an interactive
process mining approach to enable fast data analysis and exploration.
ProcessExplorer takes an event log as input to automatically suggest
subsets of similar process behavior, evaluate each subset, generate interesting insights, and suggest the subsets with the most interesting characteristics. We implemented our approach into an interactive visual exploration system, which we use as part of a user study conducted to evaluate
our approach. Our results show that ProcessExplorer can be successfully
applied to analyze and explore real-life data sets efficiently.

Keywords: Process mining · Interactive data exploration ·
Data analytics · Business intelligence · Recommender system

1 Introduction

Information systems in organizations support and automate the processing of
business transactions. Typically, these systems are highly integrated into companies' business processes. Each executed activity in an information system is
recorded in an event log, storing information about what activity was executed
at a certain point in time. Due to the highly competitive pressure in the market, organizations are strongly interested in analyzing these event logs to optimize their business processes. Process mining provides an accurate view on how
processes are actually executed. Specifically, process discovery helps analysts to
visually understand the underlying relationship between activities, find potential
bottlenecks, and compare the actual execution with the desired one.

Due to the growth of available event data and the increase of process complexity, finding interesting insights is more challenging. Often extensive domain

© Springer Nature Switzerland AG 2019
T. Hildebrandt et al. (Eds.): BPM 2019, LNCS 11675, pp. 216–231, 2019.
https://doi.org/10.1007/978-3-030-26619-6_15

knowledge is required to analyze highly complex process models (e.g., spaghetti-like models) to obtain valuable insights [16]. Efforts, such as the PM^2 or the L^* methodology, have been made to systematize the workflow of analysts to guide the planning and execution of process mining projects. Despite the increasing number of available tools that incorporate process mining capabilities, existing tools lack proper computer-assisted support. In practice, the work of analysts is characterized as largely manual, leading to many ad-hoc tasks.

Let us consider the following scenario, which exemplifies a common situation an analyst may encounter today. *Julia is an analyst who is interested in the process performance of the BPIC 2019 event log. The process discovery returns a spaghetti-like process model which reflects the actual behavior of the process. To simplify the view, Julia manually filters cases based on domain knowledge. For instance, she selects cases that start with a requisition and are of item type "subcontracting". Afterwards, she computes the case duration of the subset and compares it with the case duration over all cases. For this particular selection, the case duration turns out to be significantly lower with 31.8d compared to 71.5d. Next, Julia considers a different selection and computes the case duration again.* As we can see, this repetitive work is time-consuming and error-prone, hampering efficient exploration and analysis.

In this paper, we present ProcessExplorer, a novel approach that provides automatic guidance during process discovery. Our work is inspired by the typical workflow of analysts, intended to obtain a general overview of the different process behaviors and their performance observed in the event log. ProcessExplorer recommends subsets of interesting cases that follow a certain behavior pattern. Based on the identified subsets, ProcessExplorer recommends insightful process performance indicators (PPIs) that characterize each subset. As part of our work, we developed an interactive visual exploration system that implements the underlying techniques of our approach. Our system does not make any assumptions about the process or the event log, which makes it specifically useful for exploring unknown processes. We evaluated the usefulness of our system by conducting a user study with process analysts (Sect. 6). The results show that both types of recommendations are valuable and useful for analysts, specifically for event logs with a large set of events.

In summary, our contributions are:

1. A novel approach to automatically compute recommendations that guide process analysts during the analysis of large event logs (Sect. 4). Specifically, we introduce a number of innovative techniques:
   - An adapted version of trace clustering capable of automatically generating subset recommendations of cases with interesting process behavior, related to the control-flow and data perspectives (Sect. 4.1).
   - A mechanism, based on statistical significance analysis, that identifies the most deviating PPIs that are relevant and insightful for the analyst to explore (Sect. 4.2).
   - A diversifying top-k ranking approach that generates a ranked list of subset and insights recommendations (Sect. 4.3).

2. An interactive visual exploration system that enhances analytic support to quickly explore large event logs (Sect. 5).

The rest of the paper is organized as follows. In Sect. 2 we provide an overview of the related work, followed in Sect. 3 by some preliminaries used throughout the paper. In Sect. 4 we describe the details of our approach. Then, in Sect. 5 an implementation system of our approach is presented, which is used for evaluating the usefulness of our approach, as described in Sect. 6. In Sect. 7 we present a brief discussion on the validity of our evaluation and limitations of our approach. Finally, in Sect. 8 we conclude the paper with a discussion and future work.

2   Related Work

Exploratory Data Analysis. Our work is highly related to exploratory data analysis (EDA), which deal with the issue that users do not know beforehand the characteristics of the data set. One direction to support is to provide the user with automatic visualization recommendations during the analysis. SEEDB [24] evaluates the interestingness of columns from relational data to obtain such recommendations. Voyager [26] suggests data charts according to statistical and perceptual measures, and provides faceted browsing. Both approaches focus on the selection of data attributes and aggregations. DeepEye [14] suggests which type of visualization yields the best data representation. VizRec [18] additionally provides personalized visualizations based on the user's perception. Our approach supports the visual exploration of process executions in event data.

Data Insights. Another direction of exploratory data analysis is to automatically provide interesting insights rather than exploring data dimensions or encodings. Foresight [7] recommends visual insights by analyzing the statistical properties (e.g., correlations between data attributes). DBExplorer [22] aims to improve the understanding of the characteristics of the data attributes and querying of hidden attributes by using conditional attribute dependency views. In [11] a smart interactive drill-down approach is presented which discovers and summarizes interesting data groups. Milo and Somech [17] introduce a next step recommendation engine which suggests follow-up analysis actions based on prior action recordings. In process mining, a similar analysis is applicable to case attributes and PPIs. Our approach investigates how to extract interesting case attributes and PPIs from event logs automatically.

Interactive Browsing in Process Mining. Process mining tools such as ProM, Fluxicon Disco or Celonis are highly exploratory, enabling the user to interactively inspect and analyze event logs. P-OLAP [3] enables to analyze and summarize big process graphs as well as it provides multiple views at different granularity. VIT-PLA [27] summarizes traces and automatically creates data explanations from trace attributes using regression analysis. A linguistic summary approach is presented in [8]. In [2] the authors evaluate PPIs to identify the key differences between process variants. Similarly, Bolt et al. [4] use annotated transition systems to obtain the differences between process variants. Business rules on decision points are generated from the case attributes, revealing the influence of data values to the control-flow. However, different from our approach, existing tools lack of explicit analysis guidance.

Complexity Reduction of Event Logs. Many different approaches have been investigated to reduce the complexity of event logs such as trace or activity clustering. Smaller sub-logs that are obtained by grouping similar process behavior together tend to be less complex and easier to analyze. Clustering can be divided into alignment based [5,25] and model-based [21,23] approaches. An artifact-centric approach is presented in [9] where complex models are split into smaller and simpler ones with fewer states and transitions using statistical significance testing. In our approach, we build on the existing trace clustering technique to extract subsets with similar process behavior to reduce analytic complexity.

3   Preliminaries

We first provide some formal definitions, derived from [1], which are used in the exposition of our approach.

Let $\mathcal{E}$ be the set of all possible event identifiers, $\mathcal{A}$ be the set of attributes, and $\mathcal{V}_a$ the set of all possible values of attribute $a \in \mathcal{A}$. For an event $e \in \mathcal{E}$ and an attribute $a \in \mathcal{A}$: $\#_a(e)$ is the value of attribute a for event e.

Let $\mathcal{C}$ be the set of all possible case identifiers. For a case $c \in \mathcal{C}$ and an attribute $a \in \mathcal{A}$: $\#_a(c)$ is the value of attribute a for case c. Each case contains a mandatory attribute *trace*: $\#_{trace}(c) \in \mathcal{E}^*$, denoted as $\hat{c} = \#_{trace}(c)$.

A *trace* is a finite sequence of events $\sigma \in \mathcal{E}^*$ such that each event only occurs once: $1 \leq i < j \leq |\sigma| : \sigma(i) \neq \sigma(j)$. Finally, an *event log* is a set of cases $L \subseteq \mathcal{C}$ such that each event only occurs at most once in the log.

4   ProcessExplorer Approach

ProcessExplorer follows three main steps to provide intelligent guidance for event log exploration:

1. *Discovery of Subset Recommendations.* Our approach automatically discovers subsets that contain process cases of similar behavior using trace clustering based on the control-flow and the data perspective. These subsets are computed by splitting the event log into smaller and relevant subsets that are much more structured and easier to understand for analysts.
2. *Discovery of Insights Recommendations.* Our approach automatically discovers relevant PPIs and identifies the most interesting ones. The criteria to decide on the interestingness of PPIs is based on how much the subset deviates from a given reference.
3. *Ranking of Recommendations.* We rank the recommendations based on the analysis goals by applying diversifying top-k ranking. This ensures that our approach highlights most diversifying recommendations instead of showing very similar subsets or PPIs.

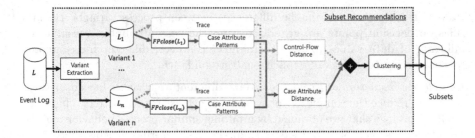

Fig. 1. Architecture of the subset recommendation generation.

Next, we provide a detailed description of each step.

4.1 Discovery of Subset Recommendations

In this step, our approach automatically finds interesting process behaviors based on a modified version of trace clustering. The event log is split into cases of similar behavior, which are then used as the basis for the subset recommendations. Subset recommendations are similar to filters typically found in existing tools, but they are generated automatically from the event log.

We adapt the trace clustering algorithm introduced in [21], which incorporates the control-flow and data perspective to generate clusters of cases. It defines a combined similarity function that balances the two perspectives. Let L be an event log, and let $L_1, L_2, ..., L_n \subseteq L$ be the variants of L solely based on the control-flow. Furthermore, let $L_i \cap L_j = \emptyset$ for all $i, j \in [1, ..., n]$ and $i \neq j$, i.e., cases are assigned to exactly one variant. For computing the similarity between cases, the two process perspectives are inspected separately before they are combined (see Fig. 1):

– For the *control-flow perspective*, we compute the Levenshtein edit distance $lev((\hat{x}), (\hat{y}))$ between two cases $x, y \in L$. The Levenshtein edit distance is defined as the minimum edit operation costs to modify the trace of a case to another by insertion, deletion, or substitution of activities. For comparing traces of different length we use the normalized edit distance, which is the edit costs divided by the sum of the lengths of both traces. We compute the control-flow similarity between two sets of cases using the normalized Levenshtein edit distance for all variants, where $X, Y \subseteq L$:

$$sim_C(X, Y) = \sum_{x \in X} \sum_{y \in Y} lev((\hat{x}), (\hat{y}))/(|X| \cdot |Y|) \tag{1}$$

– For the *data perspective*, we explore the relationships between case attributes. We are particularly interested in values of case attributes that co-occur with other values. We extract the case attribute relationships by applying frequent pattern mining, which is an unsupervised data mining technique that searches for recurring patterns or relationships among itemsets. In particular, we use the FPclose algorithm [10] on case attributes (as itemsets) to find co-occurring case attribute values. The application of the FPclose algorithm is denoted as

$$\mathcal{I}_{L_i} = \{FPclose(X, s) : X \in L_i\} \tag{2}$$

where s is the *minimum support threshold* in the range $0 \leq s \leq 1$, and $\mathcal{I}_{L_i}$ is the set of all case attribute value patterns in L_i. The support threshold s determines the percentage of how often a pattern must be observed in the event log to be considered frequent. The FPclose algorithm only returns closed patterns, reducing thus the number of patterns considered. A pattern I is closed if there exists no proper superset J that has the same support as I. Case attribute value patterns are calculated for each variant L_i separately and mapped to the corresponding cases. We denote all case attribute patterns as $\mathcal{I} = \mathcal{I}_{L_1} \cup ... \cup \mathcal{I}_{L_n}$. Extracted case attribute value patterns are compared with the following formula, which returns the proportion of case attribute values that are contained in both sets:

$$sim_D(I_i, I_j) = \frac{2 \cdot |I_i \cap I_j|}{|I_i| + |I_j|} \tag{3}$$

where $I_i, I_j \subseteq \mathcal{I}$.

For calculating the clusters, the two similarity functions are combined such that the influence of the control flow and the data perspective can be controlled by a weighting factor w, with $0 \leq w \leq 1$. We define a similarity matrix over the case attribute value patterns instead of cases:

$$M = (m_{ij}) = w \cdot sim_C(cases(I_i), cases(I_j)) \\ + (1 - w) \cdot sim_D(I_i, I_j) \tag{4}$$

where *cases* is the mapping function $\mathcal{I} \to \mathcal{C}$ that returns the set of cases of the case attribute value pattern. We use *Hierarchical Agglomerative Clustering* with ward linkage to compute the clusters for the similarity matrix M. Because we cluster case attribute value patterns, we need to obtain the corresponding cases to generate the subsets. These subsets may contain overlapping cases because similar case attribute value patterns may be shared among different clusters which may come from the same case. This issue is resolved by assigning the cases to the cluster with the minimum distance concerning the control flow.

Finally, our method automatically determines the optimal number of clusters k, the minimum support threshold s, and the weighting factor w. We formulate an optimization problem that maximizes the fitness of the underlying process models of each cluster, maximizes the silhouette coefficient of the clusters, and minimizes the number of clusters to obtain k, s, and w. The optimization problem is solved by Particle Swarm Optimization [12], which is a genetic optimization algorithm inspired by the group dynamics of bird swarms. For each identified subset, we discover a C-Net using the Data-Aware Heuristics Miner [15] and compute the replay fitness.

Table 1. Case- and subset-based process performance indicators (PPIs).

PPI		Description
Case	Control-flow	Directly/eventually followed by Loops
	Resource	Number/distribution of resources
	Data	Case/event attribute value
	Time	Duration of events/trace
	Function	Number/(Co-) Occurence of events
Subset	Control-flow	Start/End event distribution
	Resource	Attribute resources
	Data	Distribution of case/event attribute values

4.2 Discovery of Insights Recommendations

In this step, our approach automatically obtains relevant process performance indicators (PPIs) yielding only the most interesting insights for each of the subset recommendations. PPIs, which are visually prepared for analysis, measure potential process bottlenecks, inefficiencies, and compliance violations. Our approach helps alleviating the abundant manual and repetitive work caused by the wide range of different PPIs that need to be evaluated.

We adapt the idea introduced in SEEDB [24] where the interestingness of visualizations is judged by how large the deviation of the visualized data is from a reference (e.g., a different event log, historical data, or other subsets). Similarly, we calculate PPIs from the selected subset and compare them to a reference to assess interestingness. Although there are other criteria that may make PPIs interesting, process analysts are particularly interested in deviations as these are indicators for process inefficiencies or anomalies. We propose a set of basic PPIs which distinguishes between case- and subset-based PPIs (see Table 1). Case-based PPIs describe a case-specific characteristic, and subset-based PPIs are defined as aggregations over all cases within a subset. The set of PPIs does not necessarily consider all existing aspects of a process, but our approach is largely agnostic to the particular definition of the PPI.

We gather interesting insights from the event log by performing statistical significance testing on the selected PPIs. These tests determine whether the PPI values of the subset and the reference set are drawn from different distributions. Specifically, the null hypothesis of the statistical significance test is that the two PPI value sets are drawn from the same distribution. For each test, a significance level is set beforehand which is the accepted probability that the null hypothesis is true, but wrongly rejected. Based on the p-value and the significance level, we decide to reject the null hypothesis or not. If the null hypothesis is rejected, the corresponding PPI is considered as an insight recommendation. We apply two different statistical significance test based on the type of the PPI: For case-based PPIs, we use the Kolmogorov-Smirnov test, and for subset-based PPIs, we use the Jensen-Shannon divergence.

We additionally calculate Cohen's d effect size because the significance value does not necessarily indicate how large or small such a deviation is. For two measurement series x_1, x_2, it is defined as follows:

$$d = \frac{\bar{x}_1 - \bar{x}_2}{\sqrt{(s_1^2 + s_2^2)/2}} \quad \text{with} \quad s_i^2 = \frac{1}{n_i - 1} \sum_{j=1}^{n_i} (x_{j,i} - \bar{x}_i)^2$$

The effect size illustrates the amount of deviation in a comprehensive and understandable scale. Cohen introduces ranges that determine how large or small the deviation is: $0.2 < d \leq 0.5$ indicates a small effect, $0.5 < d \leq 0.8$ a medium effect, and $d > 0.8$ a large effect.

In our experiments, we found that some PPIs have a strong correlation between each other which leads to additional redundant insights. We summarize correlating insights by grouping them together using clustering. The pairwise Spearman correlation matrix is computed over all relevant PPIs, and it is used as the input for the clustering. The optimal number of clusters is determined by the elbow method.

4.3 Ranking of Recommendations

In this step, our approach ranks subset recommendations based on their relevance, yielding a ranked top-k recommendation list. The score given to each subset is the average score of the identified insights within, as defined by the product of effect size and coverage. The coverage is the proportion of cases in a subset that fulfill the specific insight. This criterion ensures that subsets with high representative insights are ranked higher.

In addition, we apply diversifying top-k ranking [20] over the list of relevant subsets, which returns a list of k items based on the score and diversity. We do this to avoid the typical issue of top-k lists, which tend to have very similar items on top of the list. Users tend to pay more attention to items on top of the list which can cause low selection diversity and the filter bubble effect [19]. We define diversity as the combination of trace and case attribute similarity of the cases within each subset. We use the same similarity function that was used for generating the subset recommendations to identify most diversifying subsets. Based on the similarities of the subsets and the calculated relevance score, we return a ranked top-K list of subset recommendations.

5   ProcessExplorer Implementation System

We implemented our approach into an interactive exploration system to illustrate and evaluate its usefulness. Our system allows analysts to interactively explore event logs with the automatic guidance provided by the ranked subset and insights recommendations. We describe our system using the publicly available event log of the BPI Challenge 2019[1] as a use case example. This event

---

[1] van Dongen, B.F., Dataset BPI Challenge 2019. 4TU.Centre for Research Data.

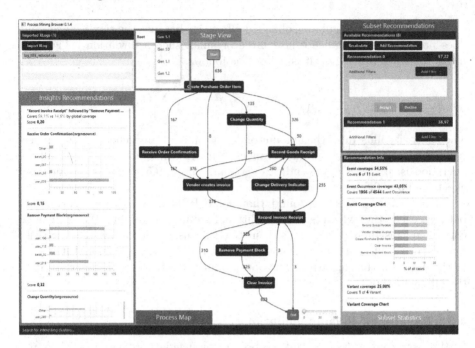

Fig. 2. User interface of ProcessExplorer showing the subset and insights recommendations, the process map of the selected subset, the stage view, and the subset statistics.

log contains data of the purchase order handling process collected from a multinational company in the Netherlands that deals with coatings and paints. The event log consists of 1,595,923 events relating to 42 activities in 251,734 cases. The events are executed by 627 different users (607 human users and 20 batch users). The overall user interface of our system is depicted in Fig. 2 and consists of the subset recommendations, the insights recommendations, the process map, the stage view, and the subset statistics. A detailed view of the components is presented in Fig. 3.

Process Map. Similar to other process mining tools, the process map visually shows the underlying process with navigation and visualization features found in existing process mining tools. This is depicted in Fig. 2. The user can hide activities and transitions using the relative occurrence slider at the bottom right of the process map. The figure presents the process map of an applied subset recommendation.

Subset Recommendations. The list of subset recommendations shown in Fig. 3 top-right are obtained from the event log. Subset recommendations are presented to the user as a list sorted by their assigned score. The user can modify subset recommendations by adding additional filters, such as the variant filter, the start and end activity filter, or happy path filter. Subset recommendations

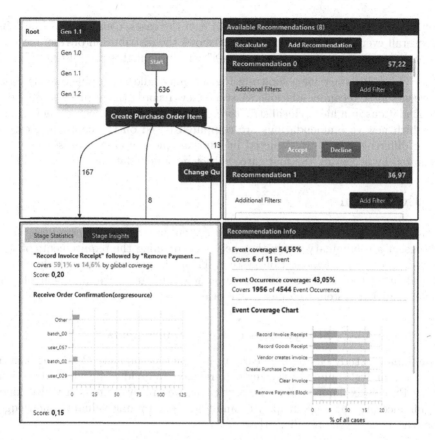

Fig. 3. Detailed overview of the stage view, the subset recommendations, the insights recommendations, and the subset statistics (from top-left to bottom-right).

can be applied or deleted by the user. For the use case event log, 10 subset recommendations are returned.

Subset Statistics. The subset statistics depicted in Fig. 3 bottom-right give an overview of the activity distribution, variants, traces, and transitions of the containing cases. The subset statistic of our example use case shows that the selected subset only contains 6 out of 11 events, covers 1956 event occurrences, and shows the distribution of events compared to the previous stage.

Insights Recommendations. The insights recommendations depicted in Fig. 2 are the insights of the subset that the user decided to apply. Trace-based PPIs are rendered as text, describing the identified deviations. Cluster-based PPIs are rendered as bar charts, showing the distribution of values. Specifically for our running example, Fig. 3 bottom-left shows 2 out of 6 insights recommendations. In the example, subset PPIs were compared to all cases in the event log. The first indicates that the "Record Invoice Receipt" activity is directly followed by

"Remove Payment Block" activity in 59.1% of the cases, compared to 14.6% in the overall event log. The second insight shows the distribution of resources for the activity "Receive Order Confirmation" which highlights the "user_029".

Stage View. The stage view shown in Fig. 3 top-left allows simplified navigation between subset recommendations. A stage view records the applied subset recommendations in a hierarchical structure. Applying a subset creates a new stage for which new recommendations are computed based on the containing cases. Three different stages are depicted in our example use case. The stages were generated by accepting the first three subset recommendations.

6   Evaluation

In this section, we evaluate our proposed system in two different studies. First, we present a preliminary study that helped us defining the requirements of our ProcessExplorer implementation system. Then, we present a user study aimed at evaluating the usefulness of our approach through the application of our implementation system to a particular case.

6.1   Preliminary Study: Identify Key Requirements

A preliminary study based on an early prototype was conducted to define, based on expert analysts opinions, the key requirements to build a fully-fledged version of the ProcessExplorer system. In particular, we are interested on which kind of guidance may be more helpful to analysts for obtaining valuable knowledge from the event log more efficiently.

Setup. The prototype was shown to five process mining consultants (1 female) which are all familiar with state-of-the-art tools, such as Fluxicon Disco, PAFnow Process Mining (all participants), QPR Process Analyzer (4), Celonis and ProM (2). For the user study, we used the publicly available real-life event log from the BPI Challenge 2017. The interface was compared in three different modes. In the first mode, we consider only manual filtering with no guidance being provided. In the second mode, we introduce the stage view functionality allowing the analyst to focus on specific parts. In the third mode, we further introduce the subset recommendation feature which enables to analyze certain parts of the process in a semi-automatically fashion. All participants were asked to get familiar with the provided guidance and explore the given event logs. After exploring the event log with a specific mode, the participants were asked to fill out a post-stage questionnaire to rate their explicit experience and preference with the interfaces. Finally, we asked the participants to fill out the *User Experience Questionnaire* (UEQ) [13]. The UEQ consists of 5 scales: *Attractiveness* which reflects the overall impression, *perspicuity*, *efficiency*, *dependability* (pragmatic quality), *stimulation* and *novelty* (hedonic quality).

Results. According to the responses we obtained from the post-stage questionnaire, participants rated the stage view with the ability to navigate between the

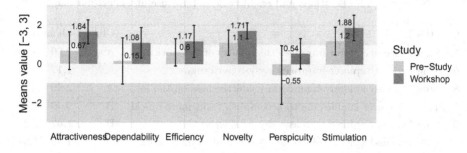

Fig. 4. Results of the UEQ for the preliminary study and for the final prototype. Range from −3 (horribly bad) to 3 (extremely good).

different subsets as beneficial and useful for the systematic exploration of large event logs. However, two participants took longer to analyze the event log due to the increased navigation capabilities. The participants rated negatively the need to navigate between the different views to change the selection. The subset recommendation feature received positive comments, but the information presented was not sufficient to let users directly see what the subset is all about. Furthermore, one participant criticized the top-down approach which makes it difficult to find the really important parts of the process. He suggested recommending potential interesting subsets of groups which can be inspected one-by-one.

In Fig. 4 we present the results of the UEQ. We observed that stimulation and novelty got the highest score, attractiveness, efficiency, and dependability only an average score and perspicuity a negative score. Furthermore, our study shows that participants consider the idea of a systematic analysis innovative and promising. However, our results do not offer conclusive evidence that the analysis experience is improved with our preliminary prototype's user interface. The detailed comments from the participants show a steep learning curve for the preliminary prototype implementation, indicating that more guidance support was required.

6.2   User Study: Evaluation of Usefulness

A user study with the ProcessExplorer system was conducted to evaluate the usefulness of the system and the underlying concepts. Particularly, we are interested in how useful the subset and insights recommendations are for exploring large event logs.

Setup. The system was shown to six, different from the pre-study, process mining experts in a user study workshop. The workshop took 60 min and was divided into two parts. In the first part, ProcessExplorer was presented to the participants, and we introduced the implemented guidance features. We used BPI Challenge 2019 event log which was known to all study participants, so that little or no explanation was required about the inspected process. Participants

Table 2. The questions and results of the TAM usefulness estimation.

Question	Cluster	Mean	SD
1. Using ProcessExplorer improves the quality of the work I do	A	2.60	0.49
6. Using ProcessExplorer improves my job performance	A	1.17	2.11
8. Using ProcessExplorer enhances my effectiveness on the job	A	2.40	0.80
3. ProcessExplorer enables me to accomplish tasks more quickly	B	2.40	0.80
5. Using ProcessExplorer increases my productivity	B	1.67	2.21
7. Using ProcessExplorer allows me to accomplish more work than would otherwise be possible	B	1.80	1.94
4. ProcessExplorer supports critical aspects of my job	C	1.33	2.21
9. Using ProcessExplorer makes it easier to do my job	C	2.60	0.49
2. Using ProcessExplorer gives me greater control over my work	D	2.20	0.75
10. Overall. I find the ProcessExplorer system useful in my job	NA	2.80	0.4

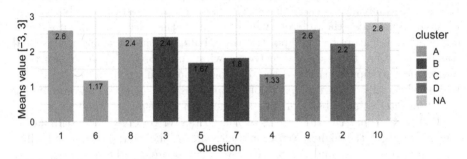

Fig. 5. Overview of the TAM usefulness estimation for ProcessExplorer according to the question clusters which scales from −3 (strong disagree) to 3 (strong agree).

were asked to express their explicit opinion about the system. In the second part of the workshop, the participants were able to explore the implemented guidance features to see how ProcessExplorer guides their analysis work.

For the evaluation of ProcessExplorer, we applied the *Technology Acceptance Model* (TAM) [6], which is a quantitative method to evaluate the potential acceptance of a given technology by end users. The standard evaluation form of the TAM consists of 10 statements (see Table 2) each assigned to a specific cluster related to the usefulness aspects (A = job effectiveness, B = productivity and time savings, C = importance of the system to the users' job, D = control over the job). The statements were rated by the study participants to what extent they agree on a scale of −3 "*Strongly disagree*" to 3 "*Strongly agree*".

Results. Our results in Fig. 5 show that the ProcessExplorer system received a positive overall usefulness mean score of 2.8 ($SD \doteq 0.4$). For each of the specific cluster of the TAM, our system obtained a positive mean score. Statement 1 in cluster A received a high positive rate with a mean of 2.6 ($SD = 0.49$).

This can be explained by the fact that the ProcessExplorer system provides analysts a more in-depth view into the event log. Analysts can quickly explore the different process behaviors. In spite of this, we observed that the job performance (statement 6) did not improve, showing a lower score of 1.17 ($SD = 2.11$), suggesting that not all participants share the same positive opinion about the system. This might be caused by the short period of exploration time. Most study participants agreed that productivity and time savings can be achieved through the system (cluster B). The participants agreed on the importance of the system to their job (cluster C) because our system improves the exploration of the different process behaviors.

We also asked the participants to fill out the UEQ (see Fig. 4). In comparison to the preliminary study, all values improved. *Attractiveness, novelty,* and *stimulation* are now in the above average range.

Lastly, we report on some individual feedback we received from the workshop participants. Most of the participants liked the idea of getting additional guidance during the analysis, instead of beginning without any hints. The idea of generating sub logs and presenting them as subset recommendations was described as *"very innovative"* (P1) and *"super interesting"* (P4). One participant wrote, that *"It's a very useful tool to gain quick control over unknown data"* (P5). However, one participant (P6) does not think that the insights recommendations are useful. One could argue that the visual representation of these insights need to be clarified. Still, the subset recommendation was seen *"as the real added value to process mining."* (P6). Two participants found the user interface (P2, P4) too overloaded with all the information shown at the same time.

7   Discussion

Validity. While our evaluation on the usefulness of ProcessExporer provided relevant observations, other aspects specific to our approach deserve further analysis. For instance, the effectiveness of the subset recommendation approach was discussed in the prior paper [21] which introduced the multi-perspective trace clustering. However, we did not conduct an effectiveness analysis of the insights proposed by ProcessExplorer for practical use. In terms of our evaluation methodology, we consider that a larger number of study participants could help finding more insights on the practicality of our approach.

Limitations. We consider that our approach exhibits mainly two limitations. One is related to the user interface, which is based on other process discovery tools and extended the process model view with recommendations. A non-static dashboard-like interface with customization capabilities could further improve our system. The second limitation we consider is that we score the interestingness of insights based on deviations. This may limit our approach to only work with PPIs that follow this behavior pattern. However, related work [24] has shown the efficacy of this deviation-based metric.

8   Conclusion and Future Work

In this paper, we presented ProcessExplorer, a novel interactive process mining guidance approach. It automatically generates ranked subsets of interesting cases based on control flow and data attributes, similar to the workflow of analysts who manually select certain cases. ProcessExplorer also evaluates a range of relevant PPIs and suggests those with the most significant deviation. We implemented our approach into an interactive exploration system, which we built based on requirements of expert analysts gathered during a preliminary study. To evaluate the usefulness of our approach we conducted a user study with business process analysts. Our results show that our approach can be successfully applied to analyze and explore real-life data sets efficiently.

As future work, we plan to extend our subset recommendation mechanism by applying activity clustering, which will allow to further narrow the analysis to specific parts of the process. It may also be of high interest to investigate different interestingness measures. We also plan to extend the user study to consider a longer period of time and larger number of participants. It may also be of interest to investigate in the ranking as well as the negative implications of automatic guidance to experts' analysis performance.

Acknowledgements. This work is funded by the German Federal Ministry of Education and Research (BMBF) Software Campus project "AI-PM" [01IS17050] and the research project "KI.RPA" [01IS18022D].

References

1. van der Aalst, W.M.P.: Process Mining: Discovery, Conformance and Enhancement of Business Processes. Springer, Heidelberg (2011). https://doi.org/10.1007/978-3-642-19345-3
2. Ballambettu, N.P., Suresh, M.A., Bose, R.P.J.C.: Analyzing process variants to understand differences in key performance indices. In: Dubois, E., Pohl, K. (eds.) CAiSE 2017. LNCS, vol. 10253, pp. 298–313. Springer, Cham (2017). https://doi.org/10.1007/978-3-319-59536-8_19
3. Beheshti, S.M.R., Benatallah, B., Motahari-Nezhad, H.R.: Scalable graph-based OLAP analytics over process execution data. Distrib. Parallel Databases **34**(3), 379–423 (2015)
4. Bolt, A., de Leoni, M., van der Aalst, W.M.P.: Process variant comparison: using event logs to detect differences in behavior and business rules. Inf. Syst. **74**, 53–66 (2018)
5. Chatain, T., Carmona, J., van Dongen, B.: Alignment-based trace clustering. In: Mayr, H.C., Guizzardi, G., Ma, H., Pastor, O. (eds.) ER 2017. LNCS, vol. 10650, pp. 295–308. Springer, Cham (2017). https://doi.org/10.1007/978-3-319-69904-2_24
6. Davis, F.D.: A technology acceptance model for empirically testing new end-user information systems: theory and results. Ph.D. thesis, MIT (1985)
7. Demiralp, Ç., Haas, P.J., Parthasarathy, S., Pedapati, T.: Foresight: recommending visual insights. Proc. VLDB **10**, 1937–1940 (2017)

8. Dijkman, R., Wilbik, A.: Linguistic summarization of event logs – a practical approach. Inf. Syst. **67**, 114–125 (2017)
9. van Eck, M.L., Sidorova, N., van der Aalst, W.M.P.: Guided interaction exploration and performance analysis in artifact-centric process models. Bus. Inf. Syst. Eng. 1–15 (2018)
10. Grahne, G., Zhu, J.: Fast algorithms for frequent itemset mining using FP-trees. IEEE Trans. Knowl. Data Eng. **17**(10), 1347–1362 (2005)
11. Joglekar, M., Garcia-Molina, H., Parameswaran, A.: Interactive data exploration with smart drill-down. In: Proceedings of the 32nd ICDE. IEEE (2016)
12. Kennedy, J., Eberhart, R.: Particle swarm optimization. In: Proceedings of ICNN 1995 - International Conference on Neural Networks. IEEE (1995)
13. Laugwitz, B., Held, T., Schrepp, M.: Construction and evaluation of a user experience questionnaire. In: Holzinger, A. (ed.) USAB 2008. LNCS, vol. 5298, pp. 63–76. Springer, Heidelberg (2008). https://doi.org/10.1007/978-3-540-89350-9_6
14. Luo, Y., Qin, X., Tang, N., Li, G.: DeepEye: towards automatic data visualization. In: Proceedings of the 34th ICDE (2018)
15. Mannhardt, F., De Leoni, M., Reijers, H.A.: Heuristic mining revamped: an interactive, data-aware, and conformance-aware miner. In: BPM Demos, vol. 1920 (2017)
16. Mendling, J., Reijers, H.A., Cardoso, J.: What makes process models understandable? In: Alonso, G., Dadam, P., Rosemann, M. (eds.) BPM 2007. LNCS, vol. 4714, pp. 48–63. Springer, Heidelberg (2007). https://doi.org/10.1007/978-3-540-75183-0_4
17. Milo, T., Somech, A.: Next-step suggestions for modern interactive data analysis platforms. In: Proceedings of the 24th SIGKDD. ACM Press (2018)
18. Mutlu, B., Veas, E., Trattner, C.: VizRec: recommending personalized visualizations. ACM Trans. Interact. Intell. Syst. **6**, 1–39 (2016)
19. Nguyen, T.T., Hui, P.M., Harper, F.M., Terveen, L., Konstan, J.A.: Exploring the filter bubble: the effect of using recommender systems on content diversity. In: Proceedings of the 23rd WWW. ACM Press (2014)
20. Qin, L., Yu, J.X., Chang, L.: Diversifying top-k results. Proc. VLDB **5**, 1124–1135 (2012)
21. Seeliger, A., Nolle, T., Mühlhäuser, M.: Finding structure in the unstructured: hybrid feature set clustering for process discovery. In: Weske, M., Montali, M., Weber, I., vom Brocke, J. (eds.) BPM 2018. LNCS, vol. 11080, pp. 288–304. Springer, Cham (2018). https://doi.org/10.1007/978-3-319-98648-7_17
22. Singh, M., Cafarella, M.J., Jagadish, H.V.: DBExplorer: exploratory search in databases. In: EDBT, pp. 89–100 (2016)
23. Sun, Y., Bauer, B., Weidlich, M.: Compound trace clustering to generate accurate and simple sub-process models. In: Maximilien, M., Vallecillo, A., Wang, J., Oriol, M. (eds.) ICSOC 2017. LNCS, vol. 10601, pp. 175–190. Springer, Cham (2017). https://doi.org/10.1007/978-3-319-69035-3_12
24. Vartak, M., Madden, S., Parameswaran, A., Polyzotis, N.: SeeDB. Proc. VLDB **7**, 1581–1584 (2014)
25. Wang, P., Tan, W., Tang, A., Hu, K.: A Novel trace clustering technique based on constrained trace alignment. In: Zu, Q., Hu, B. (eds.) HCC 2017. LNCS, vol. 10745, pp. 53–63. Springer, Cham (2018). https://doi.org/10.1007/978-3-319-74521-3_7
26. Wongsuphasawat, K., Moritz, D., Anand, A., Mackinlay, J., Howe, B., Heer, J.: Voyager: exploratory analysis via faceted browsing of visualization recommendations. IEEE Trans. Vis. Comput. Graph. **22**(1), 649–658 (2016)
27. Yang, S., et al.: VIT-PLA: visual interactive tool for process log analysis. In: KDD IDEA Workshop, vol. 5, pp. 130–137 (2016)

Machine Learning-Based Framework for Log-Lifting in Business Process Mining Applications

Ghalia Tello[1]([✉]), Gabriele Gianini[2,3]([✉]), Rabeb Mizouni[1]([✉]), and Ernesto Damiani[1,2]([✉])

[1] Khalifa University of Science and Technology, Abu Dhabi, UAE
{ghalia.tello,rabeb.mizouni,ernesto.damiani}@ku.ac.ae
[2] Etisalat British Telecom Innovation Center (EBTIC), Abu Dhabi, UAE
gabriele.gianini@ku.ac.ae
[3] Computer Science Department, Università degli Studi di Milano, Milan, Italy

Abstract. Real-life event logs are typically much less structured and more complex than the predefined business activities they refer to. Most of the existing process mining techniques assume that there is a one-to-one mapping between process model activities and events recorded during process execution. Unfortunately, event logs and process model activities are defined at different levels of granularity. The challenges posed by this discrepancy can be addressed by means of log-lifting. In this work we develop a machine-learning-based framework aimed at bridging the abstraction level gap between logs and process models. The proposed framework operates of two main phases: *log segmentation* and *machine-learning-based classification*. The purpose of the segmentation phase is to identify the potential segment separators in a flow of low-level events, in which each segment corresponds to an unknown high-level activity. For this, we propose a segmentation algorithm based on maximum likelihood with n-gram analysis. In the second phase, event segments are mapped into their corresponding high-level activities using a supervised machine learning technique. Several machine learning classification methods are explored including ANNs, SVMs, and random forest. We demonstrate the applicability of our framework using a real-life event log provided by the SAP company. The results obtained show that a machine learning approach based on the random forest algorithm outperforms the other methods with an accuracy of 96.4%. The testing time was found to be around 0.01s, which makes the algorithm a good candidate for real-time deployment scenarios.

Keywords: Process mining · Segmentation · Log lifting · Machine learning

1 Introduction

With the evolution of Information Technology (IT), companies and organizations increasingly rely on IT services to support their business processes in different

© Springer Nature Switzerland AG 2019
T. Hildebrandt et al. (Eds.): BPM 2019, LNCS 11675, pp. 232–249, 2019.
https://doi.org/10.1007/978-3-030-26619-6_16

forms. Managing business processes in an accurate, efficient, and well-organized way has an important influence on the organization output and on its success [12]. Today, a number of existing process mining methods can automatically discover process models, check the conformance of process execution to model specification, and even propose enhancement to the currently used model itself [2]. Most of those process mining methods, however, assume that there is a one-to-one mapping between events in the log and the process model activities. Whereas, in real-life scenarios, event logs and process model activities are at different level of granularity [13].

The common praxis of obtaining an activity sequence simply by means of a one-to-one mapping from one events to an activity (e.g. by simple string substitution of the event names with activities names) is ineffective and produces models, less meaningful, difficult to mine and to interpret [24]. Indeed, events in the log are finer grained than activities in process models with $n:m$ relationship [22]. In other words, a high-level activity typically consists of multiple low-level events, also, one type of low-level event might be related to multiple high-level activities. For example, activity *notify the request's outcome* might contain multiple low-level events such as *make a phone call* and *send an email*. On the other hand, *send an email* event might be as well part of *notify the request's outcome* and of *file a complaint*. Therefore, in order to cover all the possible cases, a mapping approach that can support $n:m$ relationship between events and activities is required. One way around this is to map a "sequence" of low-level events to the corresponding activity. However, generating such sequences is also a challenge.

Existing techniques focus on grouping similar events to form higher level activities, which are then used to discover simpler process models of the underlying behavior. A critical assumption in such techniques is that the discovered event clusters correspond to occurrences of meaningful business activities. In such case, the abstracted log might support model discovery, however, it is not very useful for detecting violations and deviations from the expected business process model. Accordingly, a mapping approach that can map flow of low-level events to predefined business model activities is needed. Besides, it is important that the manual work required by such approach should be minimal, in order to provide fast and feasible performance.

In line with these challenges, in this paper, we design and implement a Machine Learning (ML) framework that is able to learn the mapping between low-level event logs and process model activities. Our framework operates in two main phases: *log segmentation* and ML-based classification. The purpose of the former phase is to identify the potential segment separators in a flow of low-level events: each segment corresponds to an unknown high-level activity. The purpose of the second phase is to map each segment to a corresponding high-level activity, using a supervised machine learning algorithm. We show that this approach can automatically and accurately bridge the abstraction level gap.

The paper is structured as follows. We start summarizing the related work in Sect. 2. Section 3 provides preliminary definitions and presents the proposed framework. Section 4 describes the implementation of this framework and demonstrates its applicability using the case study of a real-life event log (from the software company SAP). Section 5 concludes the paper.

2   Related Work

Most of the existing approaches focus on clustering techniques to group coherent low-level events and then map them to high-level activities. For example, Günther and van der Aalst [16] developed a clustering approach to group event instances to high-level activities according to their closeness to other events in their trace. In this approach an event class can exist in multiple high-level activities. However, this approach has serious performance issues such as high memory consumption and a run-time complexity exponential with the log size [17]. In line with this, Günther et al. [17] proposed a new approach based on global trace segmentation that can cluster the events based on the class level. It is a bottom up technique that starts with low-level events in a trace. Then, it tries to find coherent event sub-sequences and successively combine them into clusters. The correlation among events is found from the co-occurrence of events in the log. From correlation, a hierarchy of event classes is inferred. Although their approach provides better performance with linear complexity, it doesn't support $n : m$ relations between events and activities, since event classes can only belong to one activity. Moreover, they provide no clear guidance regarding when to stop clustering low-level events into higher level of abstraction.

Pérez-Castillo et al. [23] proposed an approach to study the correlation between events using event attributes. Again, this approach only considers $1 : 1$ mapping between events and activities. Li et al. [20] proposed an approach to identify semantically related patterns of events. This approach can handle $n : m$ relations. However, it doesn't allow more than two events to occur between the events of the same activity instance.

Bose et al. [5] introduced an approach to discover abstractions (high-level activities). It consisted in recognizing frequent event patterns in the event log. After that, each frequent pattern is considered as one high-level activity. Then, the abstracted log is created replacing the frequent patterns. Finally, the abstracted log can be used to discover process models using discovery techniques such as the α-algorithm [1], the genetic miner [10], or the heuristics miner [25]. The drawback of this approach is that there is no guarantee that the discovered frequent event patterns actually correspond to meaningful activities in the business process.

Mannhardt et al. [22] proposed an event abstraction method based on behavioral activity patterns. It basically aims at developing an abstracted log by aligning low-level event logs with activity patterns. An activity pattern is a low-level process model of a certain activity. An integrated model is built by combining the activity patterns in one model. After that, the integrated model is aligned with the event log using existing alignment techniques in order to create the aligned log. Although this approach seems easy to follow, however it has some disadvantages. First, it seems unreasonable to expect the user to create a low-level model (e.g. petri nets) for each high-level activity. Moreover, the formalized pattern of the user might miss important patterns that occur in reality.

Several works have addressed the use of taxonomies and ontologies to operate at different levels of abstractions [6,15,19]. They try to relate elements in the logs to concepts they represent in ontologies [8,9]. For example, in [18] the authors use company-specific ontologies and databases to get multiple abstraction levels. However, not all organizations have taxonomies and ontologies. It is important to mention that our work target the case when taxonomies and ontologies are not available. Therefore, these works are only loosely related to our contribution.

To the best of our knowledge, in the field of process mining, our approach is the first to utilize and compare different machine learning techniques to fill the gap between low-level event logs and high-level activities defined in the process model. Moreover, our approach overcomes the limitations of the existing works as it can map the event logs into meaningful and predefined activities, does not require ontologies, supports $n : m$ relationships, and operates with minimal human intervention.

3   Overview of the Proposed Framework

Figure 1 shows an overview of the overall log-lifting framework. First, a segmentation algorithm is needed to locate the segment separators in a flow of low-level events where each segment corresponds to an unknown high-level activity that is yet to be discovered. For this, a supervised machine learning-based algorithm is used in order to classify a real-time flow of event segments (testing-set). However, in order to apply a supervised algorithm, a number of labeled examples are needed to train the classifier. In fact, labeled logs are usually unavailable, and manual labeling might be infeasible, time consuming or too expensive. To cope up with this challenge, a clustering-based labelling approach is introduced to label a set of event sequences which will then be used to train the classifier. After training, only the decision boundaries are kept as mathematical formulas in order to classify future real-time flow of low-level event sequences.

The proposed framework can be seen as a two-phase approach. The first phase is log-segmentation, followed by a machine learning-based classification phase. In the following sections, we will discuss each phase separately.

3.1   Log Segmentation

The flow of low-level events has to undergo a segmentation process: the segments yielded by such a process would represent estimated high level activities. Conceptually it is analogous to taking a long text provided without separating spaces and breaking down the text into words (adding spaces). It is analogous to a decoding problem, where one has to guess which pairs of low level symbols/letters need to be decoded by adding a space symbol. At the end of this

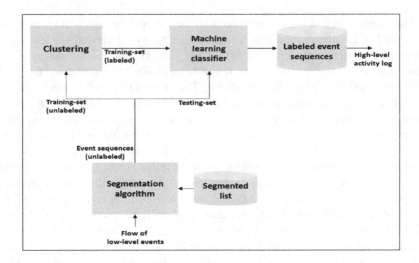

Fig. 1. Schematic description of the log-lifting framework

step, each segment contains a number of low-level events and corresponds to an activity; we call it low-level sequence, or event sequence.

This kind of segmentation is very sensitive to the assumptions about the potential segment separators. The presence of common prefixes is a critical challenge that needs to be addressed. In other words, one activity could be the prefix of another. For example, given four activities A, B, C and D with the corresponding low-level event sequences: $\{\alpha, \beta, gamma\}$, $\{\alpha, \beta\}$, $\{\delta, \psi\}$ and $\{\rho, \delta, \psi\}$, respectively. In such case, there is an ambiguity in selecting the potential segment separators for the flow: $\{\alpha, \beta, \gamma, \delta, \psi\}$, as two possible mappings might be generated: $A + C$ or $B + D$. Starting the mapping by both activities A or B is a good start. However, in the long term perspective, one mapping (i. e. $A + C$) might be better than the other with respect to the subsequent flow of events. Because segmenting the flow as $A + C$ has a perfect match between the low-level events and high-level activities. However, the second mapping option, i.e. $B + D$, has less similarity as D in fact map to $\{\rho, \delta, \psi\}$ rather than $\{\gamma, \delta, \psi\}$.

In line with this, we propose an optimization approach based on maximum likelihood technique to address the segmentation problem. The segmentation requires a relatively small set of examples, provided by the data owner (e.g. SAP) annotated with the correct separation between one activity and the next, we call it "segmented list". In fact, the same agent naturally sets a break between sequences of high level activities. The break can correspond to the end of a working session or to a pause within a working session. Alternatively, the separation between two sentences can be realized using time gaps. Since activities in organizations are usually repetitive, the segmented list is relatively small and concise.

3.1.1   Walkthrough

For the sake of clarity hereafter we will use mostly the English text analogy terms as follows:

- Low level events correspond to letters/symbols: e.g. "e", "d", "i", "t".
- Low level event sequences correspond to words: e.g. "edit".
- In the decoded text one word is separated from the next by a space: e.g. "open edit save close".
- The non-decoded text is analogous to a sequence without spaces where all the words are attached one after the other: e.g. "openeditsaveclose".
- The words form sentences (i.e. high level sequences of activities), that we distinguish from the time gap between one and the next, analogous to the period: e.g. "open edit save edit save edit save close".
- Some sentences are normal and highly probable in a log/text, some others are anomalous: e.g. "open save close open save close open save close".

The segmented list allowed to run a standard n-gram analysis. For example, counting digrams allowed creating a prefix-suffix table with one letter as a prefix and one as suffix. The frequencies of each row would provide an estimate of the likelihood of a given digram actually occurring. The choice of n for n-gram matrix depends on the dataset. For this, we plot a histogram with a bar for each segment length in the segmented list. The length corresponds to the highest bar is chosen as n.

Given an un-decoded sequence and given the n-gram matrix one can compute the likelihood of any candidate decoding. By standard optimization techniques one could find the optimal decoding, but a satisfactory decoding can also be accepted to limit the run time of the procedure. The output of this phase is sequence of words representing high-level activities.

3.1.2   Running Example

We demonstrate steps taken by the algorithm using a simple example. Assume we have the following segmented list: {{A}, {AB}, {BC}, {CG}, {DE}, {F}, {DBCA}}, and we want to segment the following flow of events: {D E F D B C A C G}:

1. Build a digram matrix. For this, we have to create a unique events vector in order to construct a dictionary with event-index values. Then, we construct the digram matrix by looping over the segmented list and incrementing the corresponding digrams in the matrix. Accordingly, each cell in the matrix table will be representing the frequency of occurrence for the corresponding event digram. Initially, the digram matrix looks as follows:

–	A	B	C	G	D	E	F
–	0	2	1	1	0	2	0	1
A	2	0	1	0	0	0	0	0
B	1	0	0	2	0	0	0	0
C	1	1	0	0	1	0	0	0
G	1	0	0	0	0	0	0	0
D	0	0	1	0	0	0	1	0
E	1	0	0	0	0	0	0	0
F	1	0	0	0	0	0	0	0

2. The likelihood of each digram is calculated by dividing its frequency by the total sum of its row. In order to allow for unobserved combinations a small value (e.g. 0.01) can be added to all matrix values. The resulted matrix is as follows:

–	A	B	C	G	D	E	F
–	0.0014	0.2838	0.1426	0.1426	0.00141	0.2838	0.0014	0.1426
A	0.6525	0.0032	0.3279	0.0032	0.00324	0.0032	0.0032	0.0032
B	0.3279	0.0032	0.0032	0.6525	0.00324	0.0032	0.0032	0.0032
C	0.3279	0.3279	0.0032	0.0032	0.32792	0.0032	0.0032	0.0032
G	0.9351	0.0092	0.0092	0.0092	0.00925	0.0092	0.0092	0.0092
D	0.0048	0.0048	0.4855	0.0048	0.0048	0.0048	0.4855	0.0048
E	0.9351	0.0092	0.0092	0.0092	0.00925	0.0092	0.0092	0.0092
F	0.9351	0.0092	0.0092	0.0092	0.00925	0.0092	0.0092	0.0092

3. Compute the likelihood of the given flow using the following equation, which is inspired by the Markov chain Monte Carlo algorithm [11]. Given a matrix $M(x; y)$, the likelihood of the flow with n events $\{e_1, e_2, \ldots, e_n\}$ is:

$$\mathcal{L} = \prod_i M(e_i, e_{i+1}) \tag{1}$$

Alternatively:

$$\mathcal{L} = \sum \log M(e_i, e_{i+1}) \tag{2}$$

4. Scan the flow and insert a separator in a random position within a window. The total likelihood is then calculated again to check whether there is an improvement in the segmentation likelihood. If it is the case, then we insert the separator and update the flow, otherwise, we skip and shift the window and repeat same steps again until we reach the end of the flow.

5. Keep scanning the flow and randomly update the position of the separator until reaching a convergence in segmentation likelihood.

The resulted final positions of the separators: {D E _ F _ D B C A _ C G}.

3.2 Machine Learning-Based Classification

After segmentation, each segment contains a number of low-level events that corresponds to an unknown activity, namely low-level sequence. These sequences have to undergo a mapping approach in order to map them to the corresponding high-level activity. As shown in Fig. 2, a two-stage approach is proposed. The first stage consists of a clustering-based labeling approach. As high-level target labels should be available to learn the mapping between low-level events and high-level activities, manual labeling should be performed, which is time consuming and could be even unfeasible. Therefore, a clustering-based labeling approach is proposed to create sample of labeled examples. For every activity, a cluster of low-level event sequences should be formed. And then, all samples will be labeled with same labels as their corresponding clusters. After that, these labeled examples are refined by taking only subset of examples that contribute to the goodness of the labeling task. In the second phase, the labeled examples are used to train a machine learning classifier. The classifier will learn the mapping between low-level event sequences and high-level activities and map a new set of unlabeled low-level sequences of events to the corresponding high-level activities. Hence, a high-level activity log can be created.

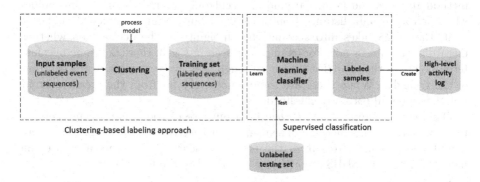

Fig. 2. Overview of the proposed mapping approach

3.2.1 Stage 1: Clustering-Based Labeling

The goal of this phase is to create labeled examples to feed the supervised machine learning classifier of the next phase. The input samples of this phase are unlabeled event sequences. Each sample is a set of low-level events. In order to provide labels for these samples, we will cluster them into different clusters representing high-level activities. Different clustering algorithms can be used to achieve this task. For example, k-prototypes can be utilized to cluster multivariate time series log sequences with numerical and categorical attributes, while k-medoids is applied to cluster samples with categorical attributes. Furthermore, the number of high-level activities can be known from the high-level process model, which accordingly represents the number of clusters k that should be formed. Each sample within one cluster will be labeled with its cluster label. In fact, in order to label the clusters, the domain expert should label only the cluster centers, and then each cluster label will be the same as the label of its center.

In the process mining field, the execution of processes is reflected by event logs. The eXtensible Event Stream (XES) defines a standard for recording information system's events. Typically, an event in the log is defined as $e = (n, c, r, s, t)$, representing the occurrence of an event n, in a case c, using the resource r, having a status $s \in \{start, complete\}$, at time-stamp t [7]. Additional attributes for the events can be included such as price, originator, location, etc.

It is worth to mention that clustering is an unsupervised approach with high level of ambiguity that will probably result in a number of mislabeled examples. These mislabeled examples will degrade the clustering accuracy and hence will affect the quality of the training set in the next phase. Therefore, in order to enhance the accuracy of clustering approach, cluster members should be prioritized. Cluster members are refined by taking only the subset that contributes more to the goodness of the clustering process. For this, we adopt a variant of the silhouette cutting method, called hereafter Second Best Based Selection (SBBS), and based on distance comparison. Whereas the standard silhouette method removes the points around the centroids, and risks discarding points which fall at a high distance from a centroid but are unambiguously assigned to it, the SBBS takes into account the ambiguity in the decision on whether discarding a point or not. For example, as seen in Fig. 3, there are some misclustered points in the triangles cluster although they are very close to the centroid of the triangles. While there are some points very far from the green centroid but they are still correctly classified.

This is more appropriate to the final purpose of the operation in the current context, i.e. classification of sequences into activities: in principle, the more unambiguous points are left to the upcoming learner, the more accurate the model will be. The SBBS algorithm is described in the following steps:

1. At the last iteration of the clustering algorithm, for each object store in a table its distance/dissimilarity to all the centers (each object is assigned to the cluster-center with minimal distance, i.e. the first best center)
2. For each object compute the difference between the distance to the first best and the distance to the second best cluster-center. Call this discrepancy D.
3. For each cluster, sort the objects by increasing D.
4. Start deletion, using the predefined distance based criterion: e.g. delete a fixed percentage of the elements in order of increasing D, or delete a fixed percentage of the elements of each cluster in order of increasing D.

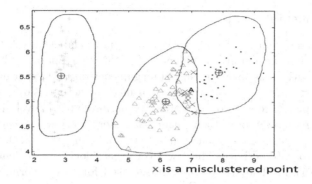

x is a misclustered point

Fig. 3. Ambiguity in overlapped clusters

At this point the dataset L* is ready to be used as a training dataset for classification algorithms.

3.2.2   Stage 2: Classification

After preparing the training set via the previous clustering-based labeling module, machine learning techniques is used in order to classify event segments to the corresponding high-level activities. To do this, several machine learning classification methods have been explored including Random Forest (RF), Artificial Neural Network (ANN), and Support Vector Machine (SVM). Results of the classification will be detailed in the next section.

4   Case Study

To evaluate the proposed framework, a log provided by SAP company[1] has been used. The event log contains around 12 weeks of activities collected from SAP systems deployed in a test environment. The following features of the dataset samples has been considered: "subobject", "User", "Time", "Date", "Role", and "Action". Below is description of each feature with its possible values:

- *subObject*: which describes the operation being performed on the object. Its possible values are: IOBJ_SAVE, IOBJ_DEL, IOBJ_ACC (related to infocubes, kind of analytic objects meta-data), SDL (for personal/sensitive data operation), and TCD (for maintenance).
- *User*: which represents the name of the user performing the action.
- *Role*: which represents the role of the user. Its possible values are: ADMIN, CREATOR, LAMBDA, and CLEARED.
- *Action*: is the operation name. Its possible values are: CHANGE, DELETE, READ, and ADMIN.
- *Time*: is the start time of the performed action.
- *Date*: is the start date of the performed action.

---

[1] SAP dataset https://doi.org/10.5281/zenodo.2566022.

4.1 Experimental Setup

In order to validate our research hypotheses, we had to label the SAP dataset by direct observation (i.e. empirical evidence). For this, the separation between two sentences/activities was realized using time gaps determined experimentally. By considering a specific range of dates, we identified the activities of a specific user which has a specific role. In other words, we performed two level ordering: the log was first ordered by 'user' then within each user we ordered events by 'time'. Accordingly, the ground truth was generated by labeling each block of low-level events as a separate activity. The low-level event blocks were identified using time gap of 15 min. The size of the dataset used for this experiment is 1,730 low-level event instances with 20 classes of high-level activities.

4.2 Log Segmentation Phase Results

As mentioned before, the first phase of the proposed framework is log segmentation. For this step, we applied the maximum likelihood-based segmentation (introduced in Sect. 3.1). A relatively small set of examples annotated with the correct separation between one activity and the next are taken to form the segmented list. The resulting segmented list used contains 50 sequences, where each sequence contains a series of low-level events.

4.2.1 n-gram Analysis

Following the first step of the segmentation algorithm, a standard n-gram analysis is run on the segmented list. The choice of n in n-gram analysis is specified based on the segment lengths existed in the segmented list. For this, we plot a histogram with a bar for each segment length found in the segmented list. In this example, the segment length correspond to the highest bar is $n = 3$. Hence, we performed trigram analysis.

Accordingly, we constructed a likelihood 3D data structure by counting the number of occurrences for each trigram in the segmented list as follows:

```c
for (int i = 0; i < segmentedListSize; ++i)
    {
        int segmentedListSequenceSize = (int)segmentedList[i].size();

        for (int j = 1; j < segmentedListSequenceSize-1; ++j)
        {
            x = eventIndecis[segmentedList[i][j - 1]];
            y = eventIndecis[segmentedList[i][j]];
            z = eventIndecis[segmentedList[i][j + 1]];

            ++trigramsMatrix[x][y][z];
        }
    }
```

In the above C code excerpt, *"eventIndecis"* is a dictionary constructed using the map standard implementation. It contains key-value pairs, where the keys are unique and used to find the associated values. In our case, the key is the unique event and the values is the associated index in the trigram matrix. Using this idea of dictionary is more efficient as it reduces the time needed to locate an event in a trigram matrix.

After that, the likelihood of trigrams is calculated by dividing its frequency by the total sum of the row.

4.2.2 Maximum Likelihood Analysis

After that, a flow of 243 low-level events is fed to the segmentation module and the initial likelihood of the flow is calculated. Then, a window of size 3 scans the flow and tries to insert a separator in a random position within the window. The total likelihood is then calculated again to check whether there is an improvement in the likelihood value after inserting the separator. We keep scanning the flow again and update the position of the separator within the window until reaching a convergence in the likelihood value. The output of this phase is segmented low-level sequences that can be fed to the next phase (machine learning phase). We utilized the ground-truth that was constructed using time gap procedure in order to validate our approach, the resulted number of miss-segmented sequences is 11 out of 130 (total number of flow segments). Thus, the percent error of the estimated segments to the actual amount is 0.084, which corresponds to segmentation accuracy of 91.54%.

4.3 Mapping Phase Results

After the segmentation phase, each segment contains a number of low-level events, which corresponds to an unknown activity. These sequences have to undergo a classification approach in order to classify/map each sequence to the corresponding high-level activity. For this, the dataset samples of 1,730 low-level events have been split into training and testing sets. The total number of the sequences/segments is 466. Accordingly, 70% of the data, i.e., 326 sequences have been used for training and the remaining for testing. Before starting with the classification, the training samples are fed into clustering-based labeling module in order to automatically label them and form the training set, which will be then used to learn the classifier. Below we describe the result of each stage.

4.3.1 Clustering-Based Labelling

The clustering analysis is an unsupervised learning, thus, we aim to find similarities between the underlying sequences according to their characteristics and to properly group similar sequences into clusters. We deployed the k-medoids algorithm to group similar low-level events into different 20 clusters ($k = 20$), where each cluster represents a high-level activity.

Table 1 shows an excerpt of the constructed distance matrix containing the distance between each point and another (for all points in dataset). With this matrix, we can directly access the distance between the desired points instead of re-computing it each time we need to update the centroids or members.

The output of k-medoids on a collection of sequences U is a labeling of the sequences by the cluster identifier (i.e. a labeled dataset L). To evaluate the

Table 1. Excerpt of the distance matrix

	p1	p2	p3	p4	p5	p6	p7
p1	0	0.8	0.75	0.2	0.4	1	0.666
p2	0.8	0	0.4	0.6	0.75	0.2	0.4
p3	0.75	0.4	0	0.8	0.8	0.3	0.55
p4	0.2	0.6	0.8	0	0.333	1	0.75
p5	0.4	0.75	0.8	0.333	0	0.75	0.666
p6	1	0.2	0.3	1	0.75	0	0.333
p7	0.666	0.4	0.55	0.75	0.666	0.333	0

accuracy of the k-medoids, we compare the labels obtained by the clustering approach against the ground-truth labels. The resulted clustering accuracy is 80.06%.

After that, we reduced each cluster based on the similarity of objects to the centroids, by a variant of the silhouette method (SBBS), yielding a reduced dataset L*, fit to be used by a supervised algorithm. Accordingly, the accuracy increased to 91.15%

4.3.2   Machine Learning-Based Classification

In this section, we explore and compare the performance of different machine learning classifiers namely: Support Vector Machines (SVMs), Artificial Neuron Network (ANN), and Random Forest (RF).

A. Support Vector Machines (SVMs):
Since this dataset is non-separable, SVM utilizes a method called soft margin to maximize the margin by allowing some objects to be miss-classified so that a linear separability is still possible. In fact, a slack variable is added to lead to a margin called *"soft"*. As increasing a penalty variable C, more weights are imposed on the slack variables. Whereas, reducing C towards 0 makes the margin softer. Consequently, this has an affect on overfitting and underfitting the dataset. The penalty variable C is also called *"BoxConstraint"*, as it sets bounds on Lagrange multipliers.

Regarding the type of the separator (kernel), we verified the SVM performance using the most popular kernel types: linear, polynomial and Gaussian. The best testing accuracy is achieved using the Gaussian kernel function. However, the sigma value of the Gaussian kernel, a.k.a, *"kernelScale"* needs to be tuned. In fact, tuning both the penalty variable C and sigma is very important as they collectively manage the tradeoff between underfitting and overfitting. For this, we utilized the *"OptimizeHyperparameters"* option for SVM, where a cross validation approach is followed to find the best values for sigma, C, coding design, etc.

In order to apply a multiclass SVM, the problem should be transformed into a series of binary problems. To achieve this, there are two possible coding designs one-versus-all and one-versus-one. In one-versus-all, each binary learner has to consider only one class as positive and the rest as negative. Accordingly, for k number of classes, k binary learners have be trained. Whereas in one-versus-one coding design, one class is considered as a positive class and one as negative while the remaining classes are ignored. This leads to $k(k-1)/2$ binary learners. In this case study, the best coding design turned out to be *"one-versus-all"*.

After training the model, we tested it on a separate testing set sequences and it achieved an accuracy of 93.57%. It worth mentioning that SVM might be computationally expensive for large datasets, as it depends on the square root of the number of examples when finding the maximum margin. Moreover, SVM needs to store all support vectors.

B. Artificial Neural Networks

In this section we verify the performance of a feed forward multi-layer perceptrons (MLP). In this case study, the network is trained with training goal as 0.001 and learning rate as 0.01. Moreover, Levenberg-Marquardt optimization algorithm is utilized to update weights and bias values of the MLP network.

The transfer function used in output layer is the sigmoidal function since the activation in output units ranges between 0 and 1. In fact, the output coding in this experiment is based on a binary conversion of the class labels. As mentioned earlier, this dataset contains 20 possible class labels (activities). Therefore, we used a 5-digit binary number to represent each class (e.g. 00001 for activity1, 00010 for activity 2, 00011 for activity 3, and so on), resulting in 5 output units in the output layer.

Figure 4 shows the accuracy of ANN model using different number of units in the hidden layer. Empirically, ANN achieved an accuracy of 95.71% using 35 hidden units, increasing the number of units further did not add a significant improvement in the accuracy. Thus, we chose 35 units as the optimal number of hidden units for this model.

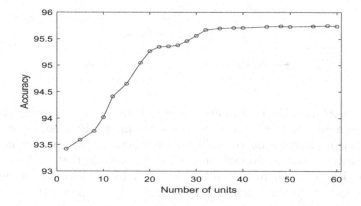

Fig. 4. ANN accuracy vs number of units

C. Random Forest (RF)

Training a single tree is known to be very easy and straightforward. However, decision trees lack stability as a minor change in input might change the tree structure drastically. Accordingly, we employed the rationale of combining learning models (i.e. bagging). With bagging we can reduce the variance of the base learner. Hence, we utilized a large collection of decorrelated decision trees (i.e. random forest).

During the training phase, we constructed the forest which includes n-trees. Each tree contains random event sequences from the training set with replacement. With all of these trees we create different variations of the main activity classification. After building the forest, we tested the random forest model with a separate testing set sequences, where each tree gives an activity class (vote). The final activity decision is the class with the most votes in the forest. Indeed, the more trees in the forest the more robust is the model, and thus the higher the accuracy. As seen in Fig. 5, the classification accuracy of RF is 96.42% with 100 trees, then it stabilizes. Hence, adding more than 100 trees will unnecessarily require additional memory and computation cost for learning these additional trees.

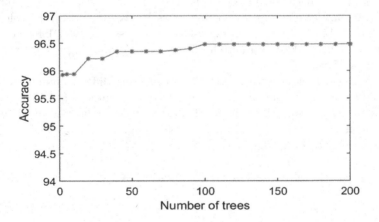

Fig. 5. RF accuracy vs number of trees

Table 2 compares the performance results of the machine learning classifiers in terms of accuracy, ROC, and time to test the model. Random forest outperforms other machine learning classifiers in terms of all performance measures. RF achieved accuracy of 96.48%. It is worth to mention that, as found in the literature, RF is known to be a robust classifier to label-noise in several classification and prediction studies [3,4,14,21,26]. Accordingly, RF was able to maintain a good classification result even with the presence of some label-noise in the training set, which was generated by the previous phase (clustering-based labeling).

Table 2. Performance comparison of different ML-models

Model	Accuracy (%)	ROC	Time to test model (s)
ANN (MLP)	95.71	0.983	0.02
SVM	93.57	0.978	0.01
Random Forest	96.42	0.984	0.01

5 Conclusions

With our proposed machine learning based log-lifting framework we are able to bridge the gap between low-level event logs and high-level model activities, as commonly found in real business scenarios. The proposed framework overcomes the limitations of the existing work as it can map the event logs into meaningful and predefined activities, does not require ontologies, supports n:m relations, and operates with minimal human intervention.

The proposed log-lifting module consists of two main phases: log segmentation and machine learning-based classification. The purpose of the segmentation phase is to identify the potential segment separators in a flow of low-level events, in which each segment corresponds to an unknown high-level activity. For this, we adopt our proposed segmentation algorithm based on maximum likelihood with n-gram analysis. In the second phase, the event sequences are mapped into their corresponding high-level activities using a supervised machine learning algorithm. Several machine learning classification methods are explored including artificial neural networks, support vector machine, and random forest. We demonstrate the applicability of our approach by conducting a case study using a real-life event log provided by SAP company. Results obtained show that a machine learning approach based on random forest method outperforms the other methods with an accuracy of 96.4%. The testing time was found to be around 0.01 s, which verifies that the adopted algorithm is a successful candidate for real-time deployment scenarios.

References

1. Van der Aalst, W., Weijters, T., Maruster, L.: Workflow mining: discovering process models from event logs. IEEE Trans. Knowl. Data Eng. **16**(9), 1128–1142 (2004)
2. Van der Aalst, W.M.: Process Mining - Discovery, Conformance and Enhancement of Business Processes. Springer, Heidelberg (2011). https://doi.org/10.1007/978-3-642-19345-3
3. Altendrof, J., Brende, P., Lessard, L.: Fraud detection for online retail using random forests. Technical report (2005)
4. Boinee, P., De Angelis, A., Foresti, G.L.: Ensembling classifiers-an application to image data classification from Cherenkov telescope experiment. In: IEC (Prague), pp. 394–398 (2005)

5. Bose, R.P.J.C., Verbeek, E.H.M.W., van der Aalst, W.M.P.: Discovering hierarchical process models using ProM. In: Nurcan, S. (ed.) CAiSE Forum 2011. LNBIP, vol. 107, pp. 33–48. Springer, Heidelberg (2012). https://doi.org/10.1007/978-3-642-29749-6_3
6. Casati, F., Shan, M.-C.: Semantic analysis of business process executions. In: Jensen, C.S., et al. (eds.) EDBT 2002. LNCS, vol. 2287, pp. 287–296. Springer, Heidelberg (2002). https://doi.org/10.1007/3-540-45876-X_19
7. Ceravolo, P., Damiani, E., Torabi, M., Barbon, S.: Toward a new generation of log pre-processing methods for process mining. In: Carmona, J., Engels, G., Kumar, A. (eds.) BPM 2017. LNBIP, vol. 297, pp. 55–70. Springer, Cham (2017). https://doi.org/10.1007/978-3-319-65015-9_4
8. Alves de Medeiros, A.K., van der Aalst, W.M.P.: Process mining towards semantics. In: Dillon, T.S., Chang, E., Meersman, R., Sycara, K. (eds.) Advances in Web Semantics I. LNCS, vol. 4891, pp. 35–80. Springer, Heidelberg (2008). https://doi.org/10.1007/978-3-540-89784-2_3
9. de Medeiros, A.K.A., et al.: An outlook on semantic business process mining and monitoring. In: Meersman, R., Tari, Z., Herrero, P. (eds.) OTM 2007. LNCS, vol. 4806, pp. 1244–1255. Springer, Heidelberg (2007). https://doi.org/10.1007/978-3-540-76890-6_52
10. van der Aalst, W.M.P., de Medeiros, A.K.A., Weijters, A.J.M.M.: Genetic process mining. In: Ciardo, G., Darondeau, P. (eds.) ICATPN 2005. LNCS, vol. 3536, pp. 48–69. Springer, Heidelberg (2005). https://doi.org/10.1007/11494744_5
11. Diaconis, P.: The Markov chain Monte Carlo revolution. Bull. Am. Math. Soc. **46**(2), 179–205 (2009)
12. Dumas, M., Van der Aalst, W.M., Ter Hofstede, A.H.: Process-Aware Information Systems: Bridging People and Software Through Process Technology. Wiley, New York (2005)
13. Fazzinga, B., Flesca, S., Furfaro, F., Masciari, E., Pontieri, L.: Efficiently interpreting traces of low level events in business process logs. Inf. Syst. **73**, 1–24 (2018)
14. Folleco, A., Khoshgoftaar, T.M., Van Hulse, J., Bullard, L.: Software quality modeling: the impact of class noise on the random forest classifier. In: 2008 IEEE Congress on Evolutionary Computation (IEEE World Congress on Computational Intelligence), CEC 2008, pp. 3853–3859. IEEE (2008)
15. Grando, M.A., Schonenberg, M., van der Aalst, W.M.: Semantic process mining for the verification of medical recommendations. In: HEALTHINF, pp. 5–16 (2011)
16. Günther, C.W., van der Aalst, W.M.: Mining activity clusters from low-level event logs. Beta, Research School for Operations Management and Logistics (2006)
17. Günther, C.W., Rozinat, A., van der Aalst, W.M.P.: Activity mining by global trace segmentation. In: Rinderle-Ma, S., Sadiq, S., Leymann, F. (eds.) BPM 2009. LNBIP, vol. 43, pp. 128–139. Springer, Heidelberg (2010). https://doi.org/10.1007/978-3-642-12186-9_13
18. Jareevongpiboon, W., Janecek, P.: Ontological approach to enhance results of business process mining and analysis. Bus. Process. Manag. J. **19**(3), 459–476 (2013)
19. Leonardi, G., Striani, M., Quaglini, S., Cavallini, A., Montani, S.: Towards semantic process mining through knowledge-based trace abstraction. In: Ceravolo, P., van Keulen, M., Stoffel, K. (eds.) SIMPDA 2017. LNBIP, vol. 340, pp. 45–64. Springer, Cham (2019). https://doi.org/10.1007/978-3-030-11638-5_3
20. Li, J., Bose, R.P.J.C., van der Aalst, W.M.P.: Mining context-dependent and interactive business process maps using execution patterns. In: zur Muehlen, M., Su, J. (eds.) BPM 2010. LNBIP, vol. 66, pp. 109–121. Springer, Heidelberg (2011). https://doi.org/10.1007/978-3-642-20511-8_10

21. Ma, Y., Guo, L., Cukic, B.: A statistical framework for the prediction of fault-proneness. In: Advances in Machine Learning Applications in Software Engineering, pp. 237–263. IGI Global (2007)
22. Mannhardt, F., de Leoni, M., Reijers, H.A., van der Aalst, W.M.P., Toussaint, P.J.: From low-level events to activities - a pattern-based approach. In: La Rosa, M., Loos, P., Pastor, O. (eds.) BPM 2016. LNCS, vol. 9850, pp. 125–141. Springer, Cham (2016). https://doi.org/10.1007/978-3-319-45348-4_8
23. Pérez-Castillo, R., Weber, B., de Guzmán, I.G.R., Piattini, M., Pinggera, J.: Assessing event correlation in non-process-aware information systems. Softw. Syst. Model. **13**(3), 1117–1139 (2014)
24. Veiga, G.M., Ferreira, D.R.: Understanding spaghetti models with sequence clustering for ProM. In: Rinderle-Ma, S., Sadiq, S., Leymann, F. (eds.) BPM 2009. LNBIP, vol. 43, pp. 92–103. Springer, Heidelberg (2010). https://doi.org/10.1007/978-3-642-12186-9_10
25. Weijters, A., van der Aalst, W., Alves de Medeiros, A.: Process mining with the heuristics algorithm. Technical report, BETA Working Paper Series 166, TU Eindhoven (2006)
26. Zhang, J., Zulkernine, M.: Network intrusion detection using random forests. In: PST. Citeseer (2005)

Approximate Computation of Alignments of Business Processes Through Relaxation Labelling

Lluís Padró[(✉)] and Josep Carmona

Computer Science Department, Universitat Politècnica de Catalunya,
Barcelona, Spain
{padro,jcarmona}@cs.upc.edu

Abstract. A fundamental problem in conformance checking is aligning
event data with process models. Unfortunately, existing techniques for
this task are either complex, or can only be applicable to restricted classes
of models. This in practice means that for large inputs, current techniques
often fail to produce a result. In this paper we propose a method to
approximate alignments for unconstrained process models, which relies
on the use of relaxation labelling techniques on top of a partial order
representation of the process model. The implementation on the proposed
technique achieves a speed-up of several orders of magnitude with respect
to the approaches in the literature (either optimal or approximate), often
with a reasonable trade-off on the cost of the obtained alignment.

1 Introduction

Conformance checking is expected to be the fastest growing segment in process
mining for the next years[1]. The main reason for this forthcoming industrial
interest is the promise of having event data and process models aligned, thus
increasing the value of process models within organizations [5]. On its core, most
conformance checking techniques rely on the notion of *alignment* [1]: given an
observed trace σ, query the model to obtain the run γ most similar to σ. The
computation of alignments is a computational challenge, since it encompasses the
exploration of the model state space, an object that is worst-case exponential
with respect to the size of the model or the trace.

Consequently, the process mining field is facing the following paradox: whilst
there exist techniques to discover process models arbitrarily large, most of the
existing alignment computation techniques will not be able to handle such models. This hampers the widespread applicability of conformance checking in industrial scenearios.

In some situations, one can live with approximations: For instance, when the
model must be *enhanced* with the information existing in the event log (e.g.,

---

[1] https://www.marketsandmarkets.com/Market-Reports/process-analytics-market-254139591.html.

© Springer Nature Switzerland AG 2019
T. Hildebrandt et al. (Eds.): BPM 2019, LNCS 11675, pp. 250–267, 2019.
https://doi.org/10.1007/978-3-030-26619-6_17

performance, decision point analysis), or when one aims to *animate* the model by replaying the log on top of it (two of the most celebrated functionalities of commercial process mining tools). Examples of approximations are *token-replay* techniques [14], which do not guarantee optimality, or the techniques in [16,17], which do not guarantee replayability in general, but that significantly alleviate the complexity of the alignment computation. The method presented in this paper is of this latter type.

We propose a method that is applied on a partial order representation of the process model [7]. A pre-processing step is then done once on the partial order, to gather information (shortest enabling paths between event activations and computing the behavioral profiles) that is used for aligning traces. We assume this is a plausible scenario in many situations, where the model is well-known and it is admissible to have some pre-processing before of aligning traces. For computing alignments, the method uses *Relaxation Labeling* algorithm to map events in each trace to nodes in the partial order. On a training phase, the weights that guide the relaxation labelling problem are tuned. Once this information is obtained, the approach is ready to be applied in the second phase. It is remarkable that several modes can be considered corresponding to different objectives, e.g., strive for replayability, optimality, or a weighted combination.

Experimental results computed over existing benchmarks show promising speedups in computation time, while still being able to derive reasonable approximations when compared to reference techniques.

The paper is organized as follows: next section provides related work for the problem considered in this paper. Then in Sect. 3 we introduce the background of the paper, necessary for understanding the main content in Sect. 4. Experimental evaluation and tool support is provide in Sect. 5, before concluding the paper.

2 Related Work

The work in [1] proposed the notion of alignment, and developed a technique based on A^* to compute optimal alignments for a particular class of process models. Improvements of this approach have been presented in [20]. Alternatives to A^* have appeared very recently: in the approach presented in [6], the alignment problem is mapped as an *automated planning* instance. Automata-based techniques have also appeared [10,13].

The work in [17] presented the notion of *approximate* alignment to alleviate the computational demands by proposing a recursive paradigm on the basis of structural theory of Petri nets. In spite of resource efficiency, the solution is not guaranteed to be executable. A follow-up work of [17] is presented in [21], which proposes a trade-off between complexity and optimality of solutions, and guarantees executable results. The technique in [16] presents a framework to reduce a process model and the event log accordingly, with the goal to alleviate the computation of alignments. The obtained alignment, called *macro-alignment* since some of the positions are high-level elements, is expanded based on the information gathered during the initial reduction. Techniques using local search have recently been also proposed [15]. Decompositional techniques have been presented [11,19] that instead of computing optimal alignments, they focus on the *decisional problem* of whereas a given trace fits or not a process model.

Recently, two different approaches have appeared: the work in [3] proposes using binary decision diagrams to alleviate the computation of alignments. The work in [4], which has the goal of maximizing the synchronous moves of the computed alignments, uses a pre-processing step on the model.

The method of this paper is an alternative to the methods in the literature, useful when computation time and/or memory requirements hamper their applicability, and suboptimal solutions are acceptable. In such a scenario, our approach produces solutions close to the optimum with a much smaller computational cost.

3 Preliminaries

3.1 Petri Nets, Unfoldings and Process Mining

A Process Model defined by a *labeled Petri net system* (or simply *Petri net*) consists of a tuple $N = \langle P, T, F, m_0, m_f, \Sigma, \lambda \rangle$, where P is the set of places, T is the set of transitions (with $P \cap T = \emptyset$), $F \subseteq (P \times T) \cup (T \times P)$ is the flow relation, m_0 is the initial marking, m_f is the final marking, Σ is an alphabet of actions, and $\lambda : T \rightarrow \Sigma \cup \{\tau\}$ labels every transition with an action or as silent. The semantics of Petri nets is given in terms of *firing sequences*. A *marking* is an assignment of a non-negative integer to each place. A transition t is *enabled* in a marking m when all places in its preset ${}^\bullet t \overset{\text{def}}{=} \{y \in P \cup T \mid (t, y) \in F\}$ are marked. When a transition t is enabled, it can *fire* by removing a token from each place in ${}^\bullet t$ and putting a token to each place in its postset $t^\bullet \overset{\text{def}}{=} \{y \in P \cup T \mid (y, t) \in F\}$. A marking m' is *reachable* from m if there is a sequence of firings $\langle t_1 \ldots t_n \rangle$ that transforms m into m', denoted by $m[t_1 \ldots t_n \rangle m'$. The set of reachable markings from m_0 is denoted by $[m_0\rangle$. A Petri net is *k-bounded* if no marking in $[m_0\rangle$ assigns more than k tokens to any place. A Petri net is *safe* if it is 1-bounded. In this paper we assume safe Petri nets. A firing sequence $u = \langle t_1 \ldots t_n \rangle$ is called a *run* if it can fire from the initial marking: $m_0[u\rangle$; it is called a *full run* if it additionally reaches the final marking: $m_0[u\rangle m_f$. We write $Runs(N)$ for the set of full runs of Petri net N. Given a full run $u = \langle t_1 \ldots t_n \rangle \in Runs(N)$, the sequence of actions $\lambda(u) \overset{\text{def}}{=} \langle \lambda(t_1) \ldots \lambda(t_n) \rangle$ is called a *(model) trace of N.*

A *finite and complete unfolding prefix* π of a Petri net N is a finite acyclic net which implicitly represents all the reachable states of N, together with transitions enabled at those states. It can be obtained through unfolding N by successive firings of transitions, under the following assumptions: (a) for each new firing, a fresh transition (called an *event*) is generated; (b) for each newly produced token a fresh place (called a *condition*) is generated. The unfolding is infinite whenever N has an infinite run; however, if N has finitely many reachable states, then the unfolding eventually starts to repeat itself and can be truncated (by identifying a set of *cut-off* events) without loss of information, yielding a finite and complete prefix. We denote by B, E and $E_{cut} \subseteq E$ the sets of conditions, events and cut-off events of the prefix, respectively. Efficient algorithms exist for building such prefixes [7–9].

In this paper we use *behavioral profiles* [23] to guide the search for alignments.

Definition 1 (Behavioral Profiles [23]). *Let x, y be two transitions of a Petri net N. $x \succ y$ if there exists a run of N where x appears before of y. A pair of transitions (x, y) of a Petri net is in at most one of the following behavioral relation:*

- *The* strict *order relation $x \rightsquigarrow y$, if $x \succ y$ and $y \not\succ x$*
- *The* exclusiveness *order relation $x + y$, if $x \not\succ y$ and $y \not\succ x$*
- *The* interleaving *order relation $x \| y$, if $x \succ y$ and $y \succ x$*

Definition 2 (Log, Alignment). *A log over an alphabet Σ is a finite set of words $\sigma \in \Sigma^*$, called* log traces. *Given a Petri net $N = \langle P, T, F, m_0, m_f, \Sigma, \lambda \rangle$, and a log trace σ, an alignment is a full run of the model $\gamma \in Runs(N)$ with minimal edit distance to σ, i.e., $\forall \gamma' \in Runs(N) : \gamma' \neq \gamma \implies dist(\sigma, \gamma') \geq dist(\sigma, \gamma)$.*

3.2   Relaxation Labelling Algorithm

Relaxation labelling (RL) is a generic name for a family of iterative algorithms which perform function optimization based on local information, from a constraint satisfaction approach. Although other optimization algorithms could have been used (e.g. genetic algorithms, simulated annealing, or even ILP) we found RL to be suitable to our purposes, given its ability to use models based arbitrary context constraints, to deal with partial information, and to provide a solution even when fed with inconsistent information (though the solution will not necessarily be consistent if that is the case).

Given a set of variables $V = \{v_1, \ldots, v_n\}$, the algorithm goal is to assign a value (label) to each of them. Values for each $v_i \in V$ are chosen from a finite discrete set of labels $\mathcal{L}(v_i) = \{t_{i_1}, \ldots, t_{i_{m_i}}\}$. Variable-label assignments are rewarded or penalized by a set of constraints $\mathcal{C}$. Each constraint $r \in \mathcal{C}$ has the form:

$$C_r \quad (v_i : t_{ij}) \quad [(v_{i_1} : t_{i_1 j_1}), \ldots, (v_{i_{d_r}} : t_{i_{d_r} j_{d_r}})]$$

where $(v_i : t_{ij})$ is the *target assignment* of the constraint (i.e the assignment that is rewarded or penalized by the constraint), $[(v_{i_1} : t_{i_1 j_1}), \ldots, (v_{i_{d_r}} : t_{i_{d_r} j_{d_r}})]$ are the constraint *conditions* (i.e. the assignments of other variables required for the constraint to be satisfied), and C_r is a real value expressing *compatibility* (or *incompatibility* if negative) of the target assignment with respect to the conditions.

Algorithm 1 shows the pseudo-code of the used RL variant (a variety of formulas can be used to compute S_{ij} or $p_{ij}(s+1)$. See [18] for a summary), where:

- p_{ij} is the current weight for the assignment $(v_i : t_j)$. Assignment weights are normalized so that $\forall i \sum_{j=1}^{m_i} p_{ij} = 1$.

- $Inf(r) = C_r \times p_{i_1 j_1}(s) \times \ldots \times p_{i_{d_r} j_{d_r}}(s)$, is the *influence* of constraint r on its target assignment, computed as the product of the current weights (at time step s) of the assignments in the constraint *conditions* (representing *how satisfied* the conditions are in the current context) multiplied by the constraint compatibility value C_r (stating *how compatible* is the target assignment with the context).
- $\mathcal{C}_{ij} \subseteq \mathcal{C}$ is the subset of constraints that have the pair $(v_i : t_j)$ as target assignment.
- S_{ij} is the total support received by pair $(v_i : e_j)$ from all constraints targeting it. Since S_{ij} depends on the conditioning pairs, it will change over time.

```
/* Start in a uniformly distributed labelling P              */
P := {{p₁₁ ... p₁ₘ₁}, ..., {pₙ₁ ... pₙₘₙ}};
/* Time step counter                                         */
s := 0;
repeat
    /* Compute the support Sᵢⱼ that each label receives from the
       current weights for the labels of the other variables and the
       constraints contributions                             */
    for each variable vᵢ ∈ V do
        for each label tᵢⱼ ∈ L(vᵢ) do
            Sᵢⱼ :=  ∑   Inf(r)
                   r∈Cᵢⱼ
        end
    end
    /* Compute (and re-normalize) weights for each variable label at
       time step s+1 according to the support they receive   */
    for each variable vᵢ ∈ V do
        for each label tᵢⱼ ∈ L(vᵢ) do
                              pᵢⱼ(s) × (1+Sᵢⱼ)
            pᵢⱼ(s+1) :=  ─────────────────────────
                          mᵢ
                          ∑ pᵢⱼ(s) × (1+Sᵢₖ)
                         k=1
        end
    end
    s := s+1
until no more changes;
```

Algorithm 1. Pseudo code of the RL algorithm.

At each time step, the algorithm updates the weights of each possible labels for each variable. The results are normalized per variable, raising weights for labels with higher support, and reducing them for those with lower support. Advantages of the algorithm are:

- Its expressivity: The problem is stated in terms of assigning *labels* to variables, and a set of constraints between variable-label assignments, allowing to model any discrete combinatorial problem. The algorithm can deal with any kind of constraints encoding any relevant domain information.

- Its highly local character (each variable can update its label weights given only the state at previous time step), which makes the algorithm highly parallelizable.
- Its flexibility: Total consistency or completeness of constraints is not required.
- Its robustness: It can give an answer to problems without an exact solution (incomplete or partially incompatible constraints, insufficient data, etc.)
- Its complexity. Being n the number of variables, v the average number of possible labels per variable, c the average number of constraints per label, and I the average number of iterations until convergence, the average cost is $n \times v \times c \times I$. Note that some of these factors can be made constants: The algorithm can be stopped if convergence is not reached after a maximum number of iterations. In most problems v and c do not depend on n, or if they do, they can be bounded (e.g. generating constraints only for nearby neighbors instead of all variables, or pre-filtering unlikely values). In general, for problems with a large amount of variables, the complexity can be controlled at the price of reducing expressivity and/or result accuracy, obtaining accurate enough models with linear or quadratic asymptotic costs.

Drawbacks of the algorithm are:

- Found optima are local, and convergence is not guaranteed in the general case.
- Constraints must be designed manually, since they encode the domain knowledge about the problem.
- Constraint weights must be assigned manually and/or optimized on tuning data.

4 Framework to Approximate Alignments

Figure 1 presents an overall description of the framework: A preprocessing step, *(a)* inside the gray box, is executed only once per model to compute the model unfolding, its behavioural profile, and the shortest enabling path between each pair of nodes. Then, it is used as many times as needed to align log traces. The alignment algorithm, *(c)* relaxation labeling, uses weighted constraints *(b)*, and although their weights can simply be set manually, better results are obtained if they are tuned using available training data. The algorithm produces partial alignments without model moves, which are added –if needed– by a completion post-process *(d)*. The weight tuning procedure is exactly the same: The system is run on different combinations of constraint weights on a separate section of the dataset, and the combination producing the best results is chosen to be used on test data (or used in production).

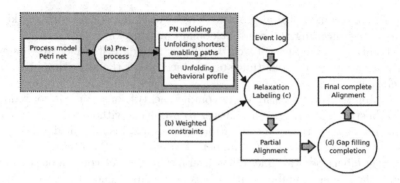

Fig. 1. Overall framework representation.

4.1 Stage 1: Pre-computation of Model Unfolding and Additional Information

We use one of the state-of-the-art techniques to compute an unfolding π of the Petri net [9]. There are two main reasons to use the unfolding instead of the Petri net. First, events in the unfolding correspond to a particular firing of a transition in a Petri net, thus making the correspondence between events in the trace and events in the unfolding meaningful[2]. Second, by being well-structured (e.g., having a clear initial and final node), the computation of alignments is facilitated.

Two types of information between any pair of events in the unfolding are required in our setting: (1) Behavioral relations are used to guide RL in order to reward/penalize particular assignments between events in the trace and unfolding transitions. (2) Shortest enabling paths are necessary for completing the alignment when gaps exist in alignment arising from the solution found by the RL algorithm. Notice that this information is computed only once per model, before aligning each trace in the log.

Behavioral Relations Between Unfolding Events. As it has been pointed out [2,22], not all runs of the Petri net are possible in the complete unfolding, which impacts the behavioral information between events in the unfolding. To amend this, either the unfolding is extended beyond cut-off events so that all relations are visible [2], or the behavioral relations are adapted to consider the discontinuities due to cut-off events [22].

In this paper we opted instead for a pragmatic setting: next to the original unfolding π, a copy π^r where the backward-conflicts branches and loops corresponding to the cut-off events are computed (see Fig. 2). We call π^r *reconnected unfolding*. Notice that, in contrast to the original unfolding, in a reconnected unfolding all the runs of the original Petri net are possible.

---

[2] Notice that a transition can correspond to several different firing modes, that depend on the context, which will be represented as different events in the unfolding.

Next, the behavioral profiles (c.f. Definition 1) for both π and π^r are computed. Apart from obtaining the behavioral relations for events, computing these relations both in π and π^r is useful to elicit loop behavior: for two events e_1, e_2, if $e_1 \nparallel e_2$ in π, but $e_1 \| e_2$ in π^r, then the concurrency of e_1 and e_2 is due to the existence of a loop in the original Petri net[3], while if $e_1 \| e_2$ in π, then e_1 and e_2 are in a parallel section (which may or may not be inside a loop). These behavioral relations (ordering, exclusiveness, interleaving and loop relations) are then used to assign different constraint weights in the created constraint satisfaction problem instance (see next Section).

Shortest Enabling Paths Between Unfolding Events. Given two events e_1, e_2 in π^r, the *shortest enabling path* is the minimal set of events needed to enable e_2 after e_1 fires. Since we pose the problem as choosing an event (transition) in the unfolding for each event in the trace, the RL algorithm will not suggest new events to be inserted in the trace (i.e. *model moves*). To complete the alignment with required model moves, we fill the gaps in the trace with the shortest enabling path between events, which is precomputed off-line, only once per model.

The length of the shortest enabling path between two nodes is also used to modulate the weight of the constraints (see Sect. 4.2).

4.2   Stage 2: Computation of Mapping Through RL

Given π^r and a trace $\sigma = a_1 \ldots a_n \in L$, we post the alignment problem as a *consistent labelling problem* (CLP), which can be solved via suboptimal constraint satisfaction methods, such as RL. We will illustrate how we build our labelling problem, as well as how it is handled by the RL algorithm, with the example M8 model from the dataset described in [12][4], and shown in Fig. 2. Below, to avoid ambiguities, we will refer to events in the unfolding as *transitions*. The CLP is built as follows:

- Each event $a_i \in \sigma$ is a variable v_i for the CLP problem. The set of variables is $\mathcal{V} = \{v_1, \ldots, v_n\}$.
- For each variable $v_i \in \mathcal{V}$, we have a set of labels $\mathcal{L}(v_i) = \{e_{i_1}, \ldots, e_{i_{m_i}}, \texttt{NULL}\}$, containing all transitions e_{i_k} in π^r such that $\lambda(e_{i_k}) = a_i$, plus one $\texttt{NULL}$ label to allow for the option to not align a particular event in the trace (a *log move*). Figure 3 shows the aforementioned encoding for the trace $BCGHEFDA$ and the M8 model in Fig. 2[5]. Notice that selecting the possible labels for each

---

[3] In case models do not have duplicate labels, the detection of loops can alternatively be performed as it was done in [2].

[4] https://data.4tu.nl/repository/uuid:44c32783-15d0-4dbd-af8a-78b97be3de49.

[5] Notice that, for the sake of simplicity, the example in Fig. 2 only contains one unfolding event per label. In general several events in the unfolding can have the same label, and our technique handles that general case.

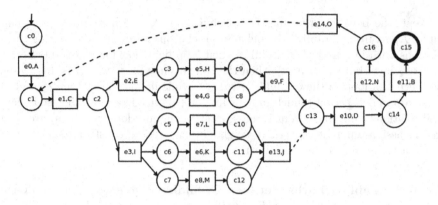

Fig. 2. Reconnected unfolding π^r for model M8. Dashed edges indicate reconnected cut-offs.

variable we can introduce hard constraints (e.g. if an assignment is not possible because of, e.g., data type incompatibility, that value is excluded from $\mathcal{L}(v_i)$, avoiding the need of having to encode this fact as a constraint).

- In this work, we base our constraints on the similarity between the order of the events in the trace and the model, although other kinds of information could be used if available. For instance, a possible constraint for the trace in Fig. 3 and the M8 process model in Fig. 2 could be $+10.0$ $(v_3 : e4)$ $[(v_2 : e1), (v_4 : e5)]$, stating that the assignment of label $e4$ to variable v_3 gets a positive reward of $+10.0$ from a context where v_2 is assigned label $e1$ and v_4 is assigned label $e5$.

Trace events (variables)	v_1 (B)	v_2 (C)	v_3 (G)	v_4 (H)	v_5 (E)	v_6 (F)	v_7 (D)	v_8 (A)
Possible alignments (labels)	e11	e1	e4	e5	e2	e9	e10	e0
	NULL	NULL	NULL	NULL	**NULL**	NULL	NULL	**NULL**

Fig. 3. Mapping of the trace *BCGHEFDA* alignment with model M8 as a consistent labelling problem. Boldface labels indicate the solution selected by the RL algorithm.

To avoid an explosion of the number of constraints, we restricted ourselves to use binary constraints –that is, involving just one target assignment and one condition–, except in the case of the *Deletion* constraint (see below). We now provide a description of the constraints used.

Compatibility Constraints. Each constraint has a *compatibility value* that may be either positive (to reward consistent assignments) or negative (to penalize inconsistent combinations). The weight for each constraint is tuned experimentally.

In what follows, $d(v_i, v_j) \overset{\text{def}}{=} |i - j|$ refers to the distance between events a_i and a_j in σ, and $d(e_i, e_j)$ corresponds to the length of a shortest enabling path between transitions e_i and e_j in π^r.

Constraint Patterns: For each combination of two possible assignments $(v_i : e_p), (v_j : e_q)$, we create the following constraint instances:

$$C_r \quad (v_i : e_p) \quad [(v_j : e_q)]$$
$$C_r \quad (v_j : e_q) \quad [(v_i : e_p)]$$

for each of the following cases that are applicable. The compatibility value C_r depends on each case:

- *Right order.* If v_i precedes v_j in σ (i.e., $i < j$), and $e_p \rightsquigarrow e_q$ in π^r, C_r is positive, and inversely proportional to $|d(v_i, v_j) - d(e_p, e_q)|$, rewarding assignments in the right order, with higher rewards for closer assignments.
- *Wrong order.* If v_i follows v_j in σ (i.e., $i > j$), and $e_p \rightsquigarrow e_q$ in π^r, C_r is negative, penalizing assignments with crossed ordering in the trace with respect to the model.
- *Exclusive.* If v_i and v_j co-occur in the trace but $e_p + e_q$ in π^r, C_r is negative, penalizing assignments that should not happen in the same trace.
- *Parallel.* If v_i and v_j co-occur in the trace, and $e_p \| e_q$ in π, indicating the presence of a parallel section, C_r is positive, and inversely proportional to $|d(v_i, v_j) - d(e_p, e_q)|$, rewarding this combination in any order, with higher rewards for closer assignments.
- *Loop.* If v_i and v_j co-occur in the trace, $e_p \| e_q$ in π^r, and $e_p \nparallel e_q$ in π indicating that the interleaving is due to the presence of a loop, C_r is positive, which allows the repetition and alternation of looped events.

Deletion. Also, for each combination of three possible assignments $(v_{i-1} : e_m), (v_i : e_p), (v_{i+1} : e_q)$ such that $1 < i < n$ (i.e. three consecutive events in the trace) if the shortest enabling path from e_m to e_q via e_p in π^r is longer than the shortest enabling path from e_m to e_q not crossing e_p, we create the constraint instance:

$$C_r \quad (v_i : e_p) \quad [(v_{i-1} : e_m), (v_{i+1} : e_q)]$$

where C_r is negative. This constraint penalizes the alignment of an event if that would require more model moves (and thus a higher cost) than its deletion.

Figure 4 shows examples of how these patterns are instantiated in the M8 example. Note that the high negative weight of the *wrong order* constraints will cause that in every pair, at least one of the variables (that with less positive contribution from others) will end up selecting any other label (which in this case will be the NULL label). Weights for *right order* constraints are inversely proportional to $|d(v_i, v_j) - d(e_p, e_q)|$. The other constraints in the example use a constant value.

It is important to remark that a single constraint does not determine the alignment chosen for a particular event. All constraints affecting the assignment (v_i, e_j) are combined in S_{ij}. The re-normalization of the label weights for each variable ensures that there will always be one value selected: even if all values for a variable had a negative support, the weight for the

Constraint examples

Right order	+8.3 $(v_2 : e1)$	[$(v_3 : e4)$]
	+12.5 $(v_2 : e1)$	[$(v_6 : e9)$]
	+25 $(v_6 : e9)$	[$(v_7 : e10)$]
Wrong Order	-500 $(v_1 : e11)$	[$(v_2 : e1)$]
	-500 $(v_4 : e5)$	[$(v_5 : e2)$]
	-500 $(v_7 : e10)$	[$(v_8 : e0)$]
Parallel	+5 $(v_3 : e4)$	[$(v_4 : e5)$]
Deletion	-200 $(v_5 : e2)$	[$(v_4 : e5), (v_6 : e9)$]

Fig. 4. Some example constraint pattern instantiations for the M8 alignment example.

one with less negative S_{ij} would be increased. In our case, we have the NULL value, which has neither penalization nor reward ($S_{ij} = 0$) causing its weight to be raised when all the other possible values have negative support.

The algorithm stops when convergence is reached –i.e. no more changes in the weight assignment–. Typical solutions consist of weight assignments of 1 for one label in each variable, and zero for the rest. However, if constraints are incomplete or contradictory, the final state may be a uniform distribution among a subset of values for some variables. Also, since the optimized cost function depends on the constraints, convergence is not theoretically guaranteed (since they may be incomplete or contradictory), although empirical results show that –if constraints are properly defined as it is the case of our formalization– the algorithm normally converges.

As described in Sect. 3.2 the complexity of RL is $n \times v \times c \times I$. In our particular trace alignment problem, v is a small constant (about 2 o 3 possible labels per variable). Since we generate constraints for every pair of trace events, the number of constraints per variable c is proportional to n. The number of required iterations I is in the order of a few dozens, though a safety stop is forced after 500 iterations. Thus, in our case, the complexity is $\mathcal{O}(n \times c \times K) = \mathcal{O}(n^2)$ (though it could be reduced to linear limiting the created constraints to only nearby neighbor events).

4.3   Stage 3: Generation of Approximate Alignment

The CLP solved via RL will produce a partial alignment, where some trace events will be assigned to some transitions in the unfolding, and some events will be assigned the NULL label (see Fig. 3). If the solution is consistent, it represents synchronous moves (events in the trace are mapped to a transition in the unfolding) and log moves (events in the trace are assigned to NULL). It may only lack model moves, i.e., necessary transitions in the unfolding to recover a full model run.

The approach used to add the needed model moves is to simulate the partial trace on the Petri net, until a mismatch is found (notice that this is a deterministic procedure, since unfolding transitions are unique). Assuming the RL solution alignments and deletions are correct, the mismatch can only be caused by a missing event in the trace. Thus, the shortest enabling path (previously computed) connecting the transition where the mismatch was detected and the transition corresponding to the next event in the trace is inserted at this point, and the simulation is continued. Note that this completion procedure is also able to re-insert events that were wrongly deleted by the RL algorithm. However, if the RL solution contains crucial errors (i.e. alignment of an event that should have been deleted), the resulting alignment may not be fitting.

To handle the insertions at the beginning or end of the trace, we add two *phantom* events, one at the beginning and one the end of the trace, respectively aligned to the initial and final states. In this way, the simulation will detect if there are missing events before the first trace element or after the last one.

Figure 5 shows an example of the results of the completion process, i.e., the technique computes the run $ACEGHFDB$, which is at edit distance 6 (counted as number of insertions and deletions) for the input trace $BCGHEFDA$.

Variables (trace events)	v_1 (B)		v_2 (C)		v_3 (G)	v_4 (H)	v_5 (E)	v_6 (F)	v_7 (D)	v_8 (A)	
Selected (or inserted) labels	**NULL**	*e0 (A)*	**e1**	*e2 (E)*	**e4**	**e5**	**NULL**	**e9**	**e10**	**NULL**	*e11 (B)*

Fig. 5. Complete alignment for example in Fig. 3, after adding necessary insertions to make the trace fitting. Boldface labels correspond to the alignment produced by RL. Transitions in italics are model moves inserted by the completion postprocess.

5   Experiments and Tool Support

To evaluate the performance of our approach, we resorted to datasets previously used in the state-of-the-art to test the performance of alignment techniques [12, 16,17]. Some of these benchmarks are either very large, and/or contain loops and duplicate activities in the model. We also applied the tool to a real-world case: We used the Inductive Miner [10] (with default parameters) to extract a model for BPIC 2017 loan application data[6], and then we aligned it with the whole set of traces. Source code for our tool is available at https://github.com/lluisp/RL-align.

Since RL results largely depend on the constraint compatibility values, we used part of the data as a development set to tune the constraint weights, and we evaluated on the rest. We compared the solution of our approach with a reference solution: Optimal A* alignment by ProM for the models where it is available, backing off to an approximate method (ILPSDP, see [15]) when ProM failed to process the model trace file due to memory or time limitations. The used partition and some statistics about the models and traces can be found in

---

[6] https://data.4tu.nl/repository/uuid:5f3067df-f10b-45da-b98b-86ae4c7a310b.

Table 1. Statistics about dataset used in the experiments.

	Model	#places	Trace length			#traces	Reference alignment			Preprocess CPU time (s)	
			Avg	Max	Min		Avg. cost	Avg. fitness	Method	Paths	BPs
Tuning	M1	40	13.1	37	8	500	5.8	0.65	ProM	1	2
	M3	108	35.9	217	10	500	8.9	0.79	ProM	4	26
	M5	35	34.0	71	27	500	14.7	0.64	ProM	1	2
	M7	65	37.6	147	20	500	26.3	0.49	IPLSDP	1	5
	M9	47	44.3	216	16	500	21.3	0.61	ProM	1	6
	ML1	27	28.9	123	11	500	17.9	0.51	ProM	1	4
	ML3	45	26.4	194	8	500	22.9	0.35	ProM	1	3
	ML5	159	42.0	595	12	500	30.0	0.55	IPLSDP	12	53
	prAm6	347	31.6	41	19	1,200	4.1	0.90	ProM	133	829
	prCm6	317	42.8	59	15	500	29.3	0.51	IPLSDP	95	394
	prEm6	277	98.7	116	80	1,200	4.0	0.96	IPLSDP	64	153
	prGm6	357	143.0	159	124	1,200	26.3	0.83	IPLSDP	136	134
	TOTAL		*59.3*	*595*	*8*	*8,100*	*16.0*	*0.71*		*447*	*1,611*
Evaluation	M2	34	17.6	52	14	500	10.3	0.56	ProM	1	2
	M4	36	26.8	176	8	500	22.7	0.35	ProM	1	6
	M6	69	53.3	125	42	500	42.3	0.46	IPLSDP	1	5
	M8	17	16.5	109	8	500	7.3	0.65	ProM	1	1
	M10	150	58.2	240	30	500	42.7	0.47	IPLSDP	10	28
	ML2	165	87.4	582	27	500	80.9	0.30	IPLSDP	14	33
	ML4	36	28.1	89	17	500	25.6	0.34	ProM	1	2
	prBm6	317	41.5	59	14	1,200	0.0	1.00	ProM	96	388
	prDm6	529	248.4	271	235	1,200	3.6	0.99	IPLSDP	341	100
	prFm6	362	240.6	245	234	1,200	36.7	0.86	IPLSDP	107	34
	TOTAL		*109,9*	*582*	*8*	*7,100*	*24.0*	*0.70*		*570*	*599*
Total			**83.0**	**595**	**8**	**15,200**	**19.8**	**0.71**		**1,017**	**2,210**
Realistic	BPIC2017	280	38.1	180	10	31,509	38.2	0.10	IPLSDP	27	1,479

Table 1. Cost is computed as edit distance (number of log moves plus number of model moves). Fitness is computed as the ratio of sync moves over the length of the trace. The *average cost* and *average fitness* columns show the average cost/fitness per trace over the whole log. Last two columns show the CPU time required to precompute behavioural profiles and shortest enabling paths.

The tuning procedure consisted on a grid search of weights for each constraint type. Since *Loop* and *Parallel* use the same weight (the former as a constant, the latter in inverse proportion to the distance), we have 5 weights to set. We explored between 6 and 8 possible values for each –totalling over 16,000 combinations– and selected the weight combinations that maximized the desired measure over the tuning dataset.

Tables 2 and 3 show the results for the performed experiments. We report the percentage of cases where a fitting alignment was found, in how many of those

Table 2. Results obtained in scenario 1 (Maximize alignment F_1 score)

	Model	% fitting	% same cost	Obtained alignment				CPU time (sec)		
				Avg. cost	Δ with reference	Avg. fitness	Δ with reference	RL	ILPSDP	ProM
Tuning	M1	99.4	81.9	6.0	0.3	0.64	−0.01	1	23	4
	M3	90.8	75.8	8.9	1.3	0.78	−0.02	5	234	142
	M5	44.4	49.5	14.9	1.7	0.64	−0.01	6	59	587
	M7	45.2	25.2	16.8	−1.7	0.61	0.06	5	103	-
	M9	57.0	62.8	16.1	2.0	0.61	−0.02	10	123	51
	ML1	44.8	47.3	14.9	3.8	0.53	−0.03	7	67	18
	ML3	43.8	13.2	46.3	27.3	0.30	−0.08	7	89	61
	ML5	87.3	51.6	20.3	3.9	0.60	0.01	23	688	-
	prAm6	100.0	91.5	4.3	0.2	0.90	−0.003	5	822	58
	prCm6	89.8	21.6	27.0	−2.5	0.54	0.04	4	476	-
	prEm6	100.0	100.0	4.0	0.0	0.96	0.00	21	3,145	-
	prGm6	0.0	-	-	-	-	-	114	7,757	-
	TOTAL	*66.8*	*71.2*	*11.7*	*1.6*	*0.75*	*−0.001*	*208*	*13,586*	*-*
Test	M2	97.6	55.1	11.0	0.8	0.55	−0.004	1	30	20
	M4	54.8	22.3	31.4	14.6	0.34	−0.05	5	99	29
	M6	4.4	4.5	21.7	−7.0	0.68	0.11	8	165	-
	M8	62.6	70.3	6.5	1.9	0.68	−0.03	2	19	3
	M10	22.4	16.1	32.0	−1.6	0.59	0.08	11	411	-
	ML2	52.2	4.6	54.4	−9.0	0.61	0.26	61	1,743	-
	ML4	28.0	6.4	30.8	11.0	0.33	−0.05	4	63	579
	prBm6	100.0	100.0	0.0	0.0	1.00	0.00	5	856	54
	prDm6	61.0	0.0	42.5	39.1	0.84	−0.15	177	34,653	-
	prFm6	57.2	0.0	9.1	−27.8	0.96	0.10	159	20,631	-
	TOTAL	*59.5*	*42.3*	*18.0*	*3.2*	*0.79*	*0.003*	*433*	*58,670*	*-*
Realistic	BPIC2017	99.9	0.4	43.8	5.6	0.15	0.05	2,091	8,702	-

the solution had the same cost than the reference approach (ProM or ILPSDP), the average cost and fitness of the alignments, and their differences with the cost and fitness achieved by the reference approach. In some cases the cost difference is negative (and/or the fitness difference is positive) showing that RL obtained better solutions than ILPSDP.

We also report the required CPU time to process the trace file for each model. Dashes in CPU time columns for ProM correspond to files were ProM run out of memory (using a 8 GB Java heap) or did not end after 8 h (wall clock time). Reported CPU times exclude time required to preprocess each model computing two behavioural profiles (original and reconnected unfolding) and shortest enabling paths for all event pairs (see Table 1). Note that the preprocessing is performed only once per model, so it is amortized in the long run when the number of aligned traces is large enough.

Scenario 1: Maximize Quality of Obtained Alignments. Our first scenario is selecting weights that get better alignments, even this may cause a lower percentage of cases with a fitting solution. In order to keep a balance between the quality of the alignments and the number of solved cases, we measure *precision* ($P = \#sync/(\#sync + \#log)$, maximized when there are no log moves) and *recall* ($R = \#sync/(\#sync + \#model)$, maximized when there are no model moves), and we aim at maximizing their harmonic mean, or F_1 score ($F_1 = 2PR/(P + R)$). The weight combination obtaining higher F_1 on tuning data is: *Right Order* $= +15$, *Wrong Order* $= -100$, *Exclusive* $= -300$, *Deletion* $= -20$, *Parallel/Loop* $= +5$.

Results of this configuration both on tuning and test data are shown in Table 2.

Scenario 2: Maximize Number of Aligned Traces. A second configuration choice consists of selecting the weights that maximize the number of fitting alignments, even if they have a higher cost. The weight combination obtaining a higher percentage of fitting alignments on tuning data is: *Right Order* $= +5$, *Wrong Order* $= -500$, *Exclusive* $= -400$, *Deletion* $= -300$, *Parallel/Loop* $= +5$.

Results of this configuration both on tuning and test data are shown in Table 3.

Discussion. Selecting constraint weights that maximize the percentage of fitting traces (scenario 2) results on large negative values for constraints penalizing unconsistent assignments (i.e. *Wrong Order*, *Exclusive*, and *Deletion*), which create a larger number of NULL assignments. Thus, the obtained alignments will contain more deletions (including wrong deletions of events that could have been aligned), creating gaps that will be filled by the completion post-process, solving more cases with a fitting alignment, though more likely to differ from the original trace, and thus with a higher cost.

On the other hand, when selecting weights that maximize F_1 score of the obtained solution (scenario 1), milder penalization values are selected. Thus, less events are deleted, causing less alignments to be fitting (a single wrongly aligned event can cause the whole trace to become non-fitting), but for those that are, the cost is closer to the reference (since the alignment does not discard trace events unless there is a strong evidence supporting that decision).

It is interesting to note that the proposed algorithm allows us to choose the desired trade-off between the percentage of fitting alignments and the quality of the obtained solutions. Moreover, it is also worth remarking that we tuned the weights for the dataset as a whole, but that they could be optimized per-model, obtaining configurations best suited for each model, if our use case required so.

Regarding computing time, the polynomial cost of the algorithm offers competitive execution times, making it suitable for real-time conformance checking, and feasible to explore configuration space to customize the weights to specific use cases, even on large models. Specifically, our computation times are about

Table 3. Results obtained in scenario 2 (Maximize number of aligned traces)

	Model	% fitting	% same cost	Obtained alignment				CPU time (sec)		
				Avg. cost	Δ with reference	Avg. fitness	Δ with reference	RL	ILPSDP	ProM
Tuning	M1	100.0	58.8	7.5	1.7	0.59	−0.06	1	23	4
	M3	89.4	62.9	9.9	2.2	0.76	−0.03	5	234	142
	M5	100.0	11.4	21.7	7.0	0.55	−0.10	3	59	587
	M7	99.8	11.8	30.7	4.6	0.49	−0.01	3	103	-
	M9	58.4	18.8	27.4	12.4	0.42	−0.21	5	123	51
	ML1	69.4	19.3	26.2	10.3	0.36	−0.16	3	67	18
	ML3	49.2	8.1	46.5	26.3	0.27	−0.10	2	89	61
	ML5	86.7	13.7	34.1	16.8	0.36	−0.22	24	688	-
	prAm6	100.0	77.1	5.5	1.4	0.88	−0.02	4	822	58
	prCm6	100.0	4.4	61.3	32.0	0.17	−0.33	3	476	-
	prEm6	100.0	100.0	4.0	0.0	0.96	0.00	40	3,145	-
	prGm6	98.9	4.5	35.3	9.1	0.78	−0.05	65	7,757	-
	TOTAL	*90.8*	*42.1*	*22.0*	*7.8*	*0.66*	*−0.05*	*158*	*13,586*	-
Test	M2	100.0	21.4	15.0	4.7	0.44	−0.12	1	30	20
	M4	60.6	11.9	35.0	16.2	0.30	−0.08	2	99	29
	M6	63.6	4.1	37.7	0.5	0.51	0.02	5	165	-
	M8	62.0	59.7	7.0	2.4	0.66	−0.05	1	19	3
	M10	73.2	4.1	57.3	18.0	0.35	−0.13	6	411	-
	ML2	85.4	4.0	65.8	−9.6	0.57	0.26	45	1,743	-
	ML4	54.6	0.4	44.1	20.1	0.14	−0.20	2	63	579
	prBm6	100.0	100.0	0.0	0.0	1.00	0.00	8	856	54
	prDm6	99.6	0.0	57.2	53.6	0.80	−0.19	258	34,653	-
	prFm6	100.0	5.2	35.0	−1.7	0.87	0.01	160	20,631	-
	TOTAL	*85.8*	*26.9*	*33.4*	*12.8*	*0.70*	*−0.05*	*488*	*58,670*	-
Realistic	BPIC2017	100.0	0.0	40.3	2.2	0.06	−0.04	1,576	8,702	-

two orders of magnitude smaller than those offered by ILPSDP and ProM, as presented in Tables 2 and 3.

Our tool also performs well on BPIC 2017 real-world data, achieving results comparable to other state-of-the-art methods, and solving them in a shorter time (although the speed-up is not as large in this case).

We must remark that ProM offers optimal solutions (when computational resources are enough), while relaxation labeling does not. Also, even ILPSDP is also suboptimal, it produces a fitting alignment for all cases, while RL may produce non-fitting solutions for some traces. However, we believe that our approach can be used as fast preprocess to obtain accurate enough suboptimal alignments, before resorting to more complex and computationally expensive approaches. RL solutions, either fitting or not, can also be useful as heuristic information to guide optimal search algorithms such as A*.

6   Conclusions and Future Work

We presented a flexible approach to align log traces with a process model. The used problem representation allows a trade-off between amount of solved cases and quality of the obtained solutions. The behaviour can be customized to particular use cases tuning the weights of the used constraints. Weights can be optimized for a whole dataset (as in presented scenarios 1 and 2), but better results can be obtained if they are optimized for each model, which may be useful for some use cases.

The algorithm requires one-time preprocessing to compute model unfolding, behavioural profile, and shortest enabling paths. Once this is done, any number of traces can be aligned in linear time, with a CPU time orders of magnitude smaller than other state-of-the-art methods. The obtained results show that the method is able to achieve competitive alignments with reasonable costs.

Further research lines include exploring higher-order constraints that allow the algorithm to use more fine-grained context information, and use the results as heuristic information to guide optimal search algorithms.

Acknowledgments. This work has been supported by MINECO and FEDER funds under grant TIN2017-86727-C2-1-R.

References

1. Adriansyah, A.: Aligning observed and modeled behavior. Ph.D. thesis, Technische Universiteit Eindhoven (2014)
2. Armas-Cervantes, A., Baldan, P., Dumas, M., García-Bañuelos, L.: Behavioral comparison of process models based on canonically reduced event structures. In: Sadiq, S., Soffer, P., Völzer, H. (eds.) BPM 2014. LNCS, vol. 8659, pp. 267–282. Springer, Cham (2014). https://doi.org/10.1007/978-3-319-10172-9_17
3. Bloemen, V., van de Pol, J., van der Aalst, W.M.P.: Symbolically aligning observed and modelled behaviour. In: 18th International Conference on Application of Concurrency to System Design, ACSD, Bratislava, Slovakia, 25–29 June, pp. 50–59 (2018)
4. Bloemen, V., van Zelst, S.J., van der Aalst, W.M.P., van Dongen, B.F., van de Pol, J.: Maximizing synchronization for aligning observed and modelled behaviour. In: Weske, M., Montali, M., Weber, I., vom Brocke, J. (eds.) BPM 2018. LNCS, vol. 11080, pp. 233–249. Springer, Cham (2018). https://doi.org/10.1007/978-3-319-98648-7_14
5. Carmona, J., van Dongen, B., Solti, A., Weidlich, M.: Conformance Checking - Relating Processes and Models. Springer, Cham (2018). https://doi.org/10.1007/978-3-319-99414-7
6. de Leoni, M., Marrella, A.: Aligning real process executions and prescriptive process models through automated planning. Expert Syst. Appl. **82**, 162–183 (2017)
7. Esparza, J., Römer, S., Vogler, W.: An improvement of McMillan's unfolding algorithm. Form. Methods Syst. Des. **20**(3), 285–310 (2002)
8. Khomenko, V., Koutny, M.: Towards an efficient algorithm for unfolding Petri nets. In: Larsen, K.G., Nielsen, M. (eds.) CONCUR 2001. LNCS, vol. 2154, pp. 366–380. Springer, Heidelberg (2001). https://doi.org/10.1007/3-540-44685-0_25
9. Khomenko, V., Koutny, M., Vogler, W.: Canonical prefixes of Petri net unfoldings. Acta Inf. **40**(2), 95–118 (2003)
10. Leemans, S.J.J., Fahland, D., van der Aalst, W.M.P.: Scalable process discovery and conformance checking. Softw. Syst. Model. **17**(2), 599–631 (2018)

11. Munoz-Gama, J., Carmona, J., Van Der Aalst, W.M.P.: Single-entry single-exit decomposed conformance checking. Inf. Syst. **46**, 102–122 (2014)
12. (Jorge) Munoz-Gama, J.: Conformance checking in the large (BPM 2013) (2013)
13. Reißner, D., Conforti, R., Dumas, M., La Rosa, M., Armas-Cervantes, A.: Scalable conformance checking of business processes. In: Panetto, H., et al. (eds.) OTM 2017. LNCS, vol. 10573, pp. 607–627. Springer, Cham (2017). https://doi.org/10.1007/978-3-319-69462-7_38
14. Rozinat, A., van der Aalst, W.M.P.: Conformance checking of processes based on monitoring real behavior. Inf. Syst. **33**(1), 64–95 (2008)
15. Taymouri, F.: Light methods for conformance checking of business processes. Ph.D. thesis, Universitat Politècnica de Catalunya (2018)
16. Taymouri, F., Carmona, J.: Model and event log reductions to boost the computation of alignments. In: Ceravolo, P., Guetl, C., Rinderle-Ma, S. (eds.) SIMPDA 2016. LNBIP, vol. 307, pp. 1–21. Springer, Cham (2018). https://doi.org/10.1007/978-3-319-74161-1_1
17. Taymouri, F., Carmona, J.: A recursive paradigm for aligning observed behavior of large structured process models. In: La Rosa, M., Loos, P., Pastor, O. (eds.) BPM 2016. LNCS, vol. 9850, pp. 197–214. Springer, Cham (2016). https://doi.org/10.1007/978-3-319-45348-4_12
18. Torras, C.: Relaxation and neural learning: points of convergence and divergence. J. Parallel Distrib. Comput. **6**, 217–244 (1989)
19. van der Aalst, W.M.P.: Decomposing Petri nets for process mining: a generic approach. Distrib. Parallel Databases **31**(4), 471–507 (2013)
20. Dongen, B.F.: Efficiently computing alignments. In: Weske, M., Montali, M., Weber, I., vom Brocke, J. (eds.) BPM 2018. LNCS, vol. 11080, pp. 197–214. Springer, Cham (2018). https://doi.org/10.1007/978-3-319-98648-7_12
21. van Dongen, B., Carmona, J., Chatain, T., Taymouri, F.: Aligning modeled and observed behavior: a compromise between computation complexity and quality. In: Dubois, E., Pohl, K. (eds.) CAiSE 2017. LNCS, vol. 10253, pp. 94–109. Springer, Cham (2017). https://doi.org/10.1007/978-3-319-59536-8_7
22. Weidlich, M., Elliger, F., Weske, M.: Generalised computation of behavioural profiles based on Petri-net unfoldings. In: Bravetti, M., Bultan, T. (eds.) WS-FM 2010. LNCS, vol. 6551, pp. 101–115. Springer, Heidelberg (2011). https://doi.org/10.1007/978-3-642-19589-1_7
23. Weidlich, M., Mendling, J., Weske, M.: Efficient consistency measurement based on behavioral profiles of process models. IEEE Trans. Softw. Eng. **37**(3), 410–429 (2011)

Metaheuristic Optimization for Automated Business Process Discovery

Adriano Augusto[1,2(✉)], Marlon Dumas[2], and Marcello La Rosa[1]

[1] University of Melbourne, Melbourne, Australia
{a.augusto,marcello.larosa}@unimelb.edu.au
[2] University of Tartu, Tartu, Estonia
marlon.dumas@ut.ee

Abstract. The problem of automated discovery of process models from event logs has been intensely investigated in the past two decades, leading to a range of approaches that strike various trade-offs between accuracy, model complexity, and execution time. A few studies have suggested that the accuracy of automated process discovery approaches can be enhanced by using metaheuristic optimization. However, these studies have remained at the level of proposals without validation on real-life logs or they have only considered one metaheuristics in isolation. In this setting, this paper studies the following question: To what extent can the accuracy of automated process discovery approaches be improved by applying different optimization metaheuristics? To address this question, the paper proposes an approach to enhance automated process discovery approaches with metaheuristic optimization. The approach is instantiated to define an extension of a state-of-the-art automated process discovery approach, namely Split Miner. The paper compares the accuracy gains yielded by four optimization metaheuristics relative to each other and relative to state-of-the-art baselines, on a benchmark comprising 20 real-life logs. The results show that metaheuristic optimization improves the accuracy of Split Miner in a majority of cases, at the cost of execution times in the order of minutes, versus seconds for the base algorithm.

1 Introduction

The problem of automatically discovering business process models from event logs has been intensely studied in the past two decades. Research in this field has led to a wide range of Automated Process Discovery Approaches (APDAs) that strike various trade-offs between accuracy, model complexity, and execution time [7].

A few studies have suggested that the accuracy of APDAs can be enhanced by applying optimization metaheuristics. Early studies in this direction considered population-based metaheuristics, chiefly genetic algorithms [10,14]. These heuristics are computationally heavy, requiring execution times in the order of

© Springer Nature Switzerland AG 2019
T. Hildebrandt et al. (Eds.): BPM 2019, LNCS 11675, pp. 268–285, 2019.
https://doi.org/10.1007/978-3-030-26619-6_18

hours to converge when applied to real-life logs [7]. Another work has considered single-solution-based metaheuristics such as simulated annealing [15,21], which are less computationally demanding. However, these latter studies have remained at the level of proposals without validation on real-life logs and comparison of trade-offs between alternative heuristics.

In this setting, this paper studies the following question: *to what extent can the accuracy of APDAs be improved by applying single-solution-based meta-heuristics?* To address this question, we propose a flexible approach to enhance APDAs by applying different optimization metaheuristics. The core idea is to perturb the intermediate representation of event logs used by the majority of the available APDAs, namely the Directly-follows Graph (DFG). The paper specifically considers perturbations that add or remove edges with the aim of improving fitness or precision, and in a way that allows the underlying APDA to discover a process model from the perturbed DFG. An instantiation of our approach is defined for a state-of-the-art APDA, namely Split Miner.

Using a benchmark of 20 real-life logs, the paper compares the accuracy gains yielded by four optimization metaheuristics relative to each other and relative to state-of-the-art APDAs. The experimental evaluation also considers the impact of metaheuristic optimization on model complexity measures as well as on execution times.

The next section gives an overview of APDAs and optimization metaheuristics. Section 3 presents the proposed metaheristic optimization approach. Section 4 reports on the empirical evaluation and Sect. 5 draws conclusions and future work directions.

2 Background and Related Work

In this section, we give an overview of existing approaches to automated process discovery, followed by an introduction to optimization metaheuristics in general, and their application to automated process discovery in particular.

2.1 Automated Process Discovery

The execution of business processes is often recorded in the form of *event logs*. An event log is a collection of event records produced by individual instances (i.e. cases) of the process. The goal of automated process discovery is to generate a process model that captures the behavior observed in or implied by an *event log*. To assess the goodness of a discovered process model, four quality dimensions are used [23]: fitness, precision, generalization, and complexity. *Fitness* (a.k.a. recall) measures the amount of behavior observed in the log that is captured by the model. A perfectly fitting process model is one that recognizes every trace in the log. *Precision* measures the amount of behavior captured in the process model that is observed in the log. A perfectly precise model is one that recognizes only traces that are observed in the log. *Generalization* measures to what extent the process model captures behavior that, despite not being observed in the log, is implied by it. Finally, *complexity* measures the understandability of a process model, and it is typically measured via size and structural measures. In this paper, we focus on fitness, precision, and F-score (the harmonic mean of fitness and precision).

A recent comparison of state-of-the-art APDAs [7] showed that an approach capable of consistently discovering models with the best fitness-precision trade-off is currently missing. The same study showed, however, that we can obtain consistently good trade-offs by hyperparameter-optimizing some of the existing APDAs based on DFGs – Inductive Miner [19], Structured Heuristics Miner [6], Fodina [24], and Split Miner [8]. These algorithms have a hyperparameter to tune the amount of filtering applied when constructing the DFG. Optimizing this and other hyperparameters via greedy search [7], local search strategies [11], or sensitivity analysis techniques [20], can greatly improve the accuracy of the discovered process models. Accordingly, in the evaluation reported later we use a hyperparameter-optimized version of Split Miner as one of the baselines.

2.2 Optimization Metaheuristics

The term *optimization metaheuristics* refers to a parameterized algorithm, which can be instantiated to address a wide range of optimization problems. Meta-heuristics are usually classified into two broad categories [9]: (i) *single-solution-based metaheuristics*, or S-metaheuristics, which explore the solution space one solution at a time starting from a single initial solution of the problem; and (ii) *population-based metaheuristics*, or P-metaheuristics, which explored a population of solutions generated by mutating, combining, and/or improving previously computed solutions. Single-solution based metaheuristics tend to converge faster towards an optimal solution (either local or global) than P-metaheuristics, since the latter by dealing with a set of solutions require more time to assess and improve the quality of each single solution. P-metaheuristics are more computationally heavy but they are more likely to escape local optima. An exhaustive discussion on all available metaheuristics is beyond the scope of this paper, in the following we focus only on the S-metaheuristics that we explore in our approach: iterated local search, tabu search, and simulated annealing.

Iterated Local Search [22] starts from a (random) solution and explores the neighbouring solutions (i.e. solutions obtained by applying a perturbation) in search of a better one. When a better solution cannot be found, it perturbs the current solution and starts again. The perturbation is meant to avoid local optimal solutions. *Tabu Search* [16] is a memory-driven local search. Its initialization includes a (random) solution and three memories. The short-term memory keeps track of recent solutions and prohibits to revisit them. The intermediate-term memory contains criteria driving the search towards the best solutions. The long-term memory contains characteristics that have often been found in many visited solutions, to avoid revisiting similar solutions. Using these memories, the neighbourhood of the initial solution is explored and a new solution is selected accordingly. *Simulated Annealing* [17] is based on the concepts of Temperature (T, a parameter choose arbitrarily) and Energy (E, the objective function to minimize). At each iteration the algorithm explores (some of) the neighbouring solutions and compares their energies with the one of the current solution. This latter is updated if the energy of a neighbour is lower, or with a probability that is function of T and the energies of the current and candidate solutions (usually $e^{-\frac{|E_1-E_2|}{T}}$). The temperature drops over time, thus reducing the chance of updating the current solution with a higher-energy one. The algorithm ends when a criterion is met (e.g. energy below a threshold or $T = 0$).

2.3 Optimization Metaheuristics in Automated Process Discovery

Metaheuristic optimization has been considered in a few previous studies on automated process discovery. An early attempt to apply P-metaheuristics for automated process discovery was the Genetic Miner proposed by De Medeiros [14], subsequently overtaken by the Evolutionary Tree Miner [10]. In this latter approach, an evolutionary algorithm is used on top of process trees (i.e. a block-structured representation of a process model). Other applications of P-metaheuristics to automated process discovery are based on the imperialist competitive algorithms [3] and particle swam optimization [12]. The main limitation P-metaheuristics in this context is that they are computationally heavy due to the cost of constructing a solution (i.e. process model) and evaluating its accuracy. This leads to execution times in the order of hours to converge to a solution, which on the end is comparable to that obtained by state-of-the-art algorithms that do not rely on optimization metaheuristics [7].

Only a handful of studies have considered the use of S-metaheuristics in this setting, specifically simulated annealing [15,21]. However, these latter proposals are preliminary and have not been compared against state-of-the-art approaches on real-life logs.

3 Approach

This section outlines our approach for extending APDAs by means of S-metaheuristics (cf. Sect. 2). First, we give an overview of the approach and its components. Next, we discuss the adaptation of the metaheuristics to the problem of process discovery. Finally, we describe an instantiation of the approach for Split Miner.

3.1 Preliminaries

An APDA takes as input an event log. This log is transformed into an intermediate representation from which a model is derived. In many APDAs, the intermediate representation is the DFG, which is represented as a numerical matrix as formalized below.

Definition 1 [Event Log]. *Given a set of activities $\mathscr{A}$, an event log $\mathscr{L}$ is a multiset of traces where a trace $t \in \mathscr{L}$ is a sequence of activities $t = \langle a_1, a_2, \ldots, a_n \rangle$, with $a_i \in \mathscr{A}, 1 \leq i \leq n$.*

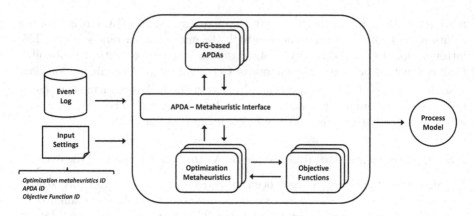

Fig. 1. Overview of our approach.

Definition 2 *[Directly-Follows Graph (DFG)]. Given an event log $\mathscr{L}$, its Directly-Follows Graph (DFG) is a directed graph $\mathscr{G} = (N, E)$, where: N is the set of nodes, $N = \{a \in \mathscr{A} \mid \exists t \in \mathscr{L} \wedge a \in t\}$; and E is the set of edges $E = \{(x, y) \in N \times N \mid \exists t = \langle a_1, a_2, \ldots, a_n \rangle, t \in \mathscr{L} \wedge a_i = x \wedge a_{i+1} = y\, [1 \leq i \leq n - 1]\}$.*

Definition 3 *[DFG-Matrix]. Given a DFG $\mathscr{G} = (N, E)$ and a function $\theta : N \to [1, |N|]$,[1] the DFG-Matrix is a squared matrix $X_{\mathscr{G}} \in [0, 1] \cap \mathbb{N}^{|N| \times |N|}$, where each cell $x_{i,j} = 1 \iff \exists (a_1, a_2) \in E \mid \theta(a_1) = i \wedge \theta(a_2) = j$, otherwise $x_{i,j} = 0$.*

An APDA is said to be *DFG-based* if it first generates the DFG of the event log, then applies an algorithm to filter (e.g. removing activities) from the DFG, and finally converts the processed DFG into a process model.[2] Examples of DFG-based APDAs are Inductive Miner [18], Heuristics Miner [6,25], Fodina [24], and Split Miner [8].

Different DFG-based APDAs may extract different DFGs from the same log. Also, a DFG-based APDA may discover different DFGs from the same log depending on its hyperparameter settings (e.g. the filtering threshold). The algorithm(s) used by a DFG-based APDA to discover the DFG from the event log and convert it into a process model may greatly affect the accuracy of an APDA. Accordingly, our approach focuses on optimizing the discovery of the DFG rather than its conversion into a process model.

3.2 Approach Overview

As shown in Fig. 1, our approach takes three inputs (in addition to the log): (i) the optimization metaheuristics; (ii) the objective function to be optimized (e.g.

---

[1] θ maps each node of the DFG to a natural number.

[2] Herein, when using the term DFG, we refer to the processed DFG (after filtering).

Algorithm 1. Optimization Approach

---

input : Event Log $\mathcal{L}$, Metaheuristic ω, Objective Function $\mathcal{F}$, DFG-based APDA α

1 CurrentDFG $\mathcal{G}_c \leftarrow$ DiscoverDFG(α, $\mathcal{L}$);
2 BestModel $\hat{m} \leftarrow$ ConvertDFGtoProcessModel(α, $\mathcal{G}_c$);
3 CurrentScore $s_c \leftarrow$ AssessQuality($\mathcal{F}$, $\hat{m}$);
4 BestScore $\hat{s} \leftarrow s_c$;

5 **while** *CheckTerminationCriteria() = FALSE* **do**
6 $\quad$ Set $V \leftarrow$ GenerateNeighbours($\mathcal{G}_c$);
7 $\quad$ Map $S \leftarrow \varnothing$;
8 $\quad$ Map $M \leftarrow \varnothing$;
9 $\quad$ **for** $\mathcal{G} \in V$ **do**
10 $\quad\quad$ ProcessModel $m \leftarrow$ ConvertDFGtoProcessModel(α, $\mathcal{G}$);
11 $\quad\quad$ Score $s \leftarrow$ AssessQuality($\mathcal{F}$, m);
12 $\quad\quad$ add ($\mathcal{G}$, s) to S;
13 $\quad\quad$ add ($\mathcal{G}$, m) to M;

14 $\quad$ $\mathcal{G}_c \leftarrow$ UpdateDFG(ω, S, $\mathcal{G}_c$, s_c);
15 $\quad$ $s_c \leftarrow$ GetMapElement(S, $\mathcal{G}_c$);
16 $\quad$ **if** $\hat{s} < s_c$ **then**
17 $\quad\quad$ $\hat{s} \leftarrow s_c$;
18 $\quad\quad$ $\hat{m} \leftarrow$ GetMapElement(M, $\mathcal{G}_c$);

19 **return** $\hat{m}$;

F-score); (iii) and the DFG-based APDA to be used for discovering a process model.

Algorithm 1 describes how our approach operates. First, the input event log is given to the APDA, which returns the discovered DFG and its corresponding process model (lines 1 and 2). This DFG becomes the current DFG and process model becomes the best process model (so far). The model's objective function score (e.g. F-score) is stored as the current score and the best score (lines 3 and 4). The current DFG is then given as input to function *GenerateNeighbours*, which applies changes to the current DFG to generate a set of neighbouring DFGs (line 6). These latter are given as input to the APDA, which returns the corresponding into process models. The process models are assessed by the objective function evaluators (line 9 to 13). When the metaheuristic receives the results from the evaluators (along with the current DFG and score), it chooses the new current DFG and updates the current score (lines 14 and 15). If the new current score is higher than the best score (line 16), it updates the best process model and the best score (lines 17 and 18). After the update, a new iteration starts, unless a termination criterion is met (e.g. a timeout, a maximum number of iterations, or a minimum threshold for the objective function). In this latter case, it outputs the best model found, i.e. the process model scoring the highest value for the objective function.

3.3   Adaptation of the Optimization Metaheuristics

To adapt Iterative Local Search (ILS), Tabu Search (TABU), and Simulated Annealing (SIMA) to the problem of automated process discovery, we need to define the following three concepts: (i) the problem solution space; (ii) a solution neighbourhood; (iii) the objective function. These design choices determine how each of the metaheuristics navigates the solution space and escapes local minima, i.e. how to design the Algorithm 1 functions: *GenerateNeighbours* and *UpdateDFG*, resp. lines 6 and 14.

Solution Space. Being our goal the optimization of APDAs, we are forced to choose a solution space that fits well our context regardless the selected APDA. If we assume that the APDA is DFG-based (that is the case for the majority of the available APDAs), we can define the solution space as the set of all the DFG discoverable from the event log. Indeed, any DFG-based APDA can generate deterministically a process model from a DFG.

Solution Neighbourhood. Having defined the solution space as the set of all the DFG discoverable from the event log, we can refer to any element of this solution space as a DFG-Matrix. Given a DFG-Matrix, we define its neighbourhood as the set of all the matrices having one different cell value (i.e. DFGs having one more/less edge). In the following, every time we refer to DFG we assume it is represented as a DFG-Matrix.

Objective Function. It is possible to define the objective function as any function assessing one of the four quality dimensions for discovered process models (introduced in Sect. 2). However, being interested in optimizing the APDAs to discover the most accurate process model, in the remaining of this paper, we refer to the objective function as the F-score of fitness and precision: $\frac{2 \cdot fit \cdot prec}{fit + prec}$. Nonetheless, we remark that our approach can operate also with objective functions that take into account multiple quality dimensions striving for a trade-off, e.g. F-score and model complexity.

Having defined the solution space, a solution neighbourhood, and the objective function, we can turn our attention on how ILS, TABU, and SIMA navigate the solution space. ILS, TABU, and SIMA share similar traits in solving an optimization problem, especially when it comes to the navigation of the solution space. Given a problem and its solution space, any of these three S-metaheuristics starts from a (random) solution, discovers one or more neighbouring solutions, and assesses them with the objective function to find a solution better than the current. If a better solution is found, it is chosen as the new current solution and the metaheuristic performs a new neighbourhood exploration. If a better solution is not found, e.g. the current solution is locally optimal, the three metaheuristics follow different approaches to escape the local optimum and continue the solution space exploration. Algorithm 1 orchestrates and facilitates the parts of this procedure shared by the three metaheuristics. However, we must define the functions *GenerateNeighbours* (GNF) and *UpdateDFG* (UDF).

The GNF receives in input a solution of the solution space, i.e. a DFG, and it generates a set of neighbouring DFGs. By definition, GNF is independent from the metaheuristic and it can be as simple or as elaborate as we demand. An example of a simple GNF is a function that randomly selects neighbouring DFGs turning one cell of the input DFG-Matrix to 0 or to 1. Whilst, an example of an elaborate GNF is a function that accurately selects neighbouring DFGs relying on the feedback received from the objective function assessing the input DFG, as we show in Sect. 3.4.

The UDF is at the core of our optimization, and it represents the metaheuristic itself. It receives in input the neighbouring DFGs, the current DFG, and the current score, and it selects among the neighbouring DFGs the one that should become the new current DFG. At this point, we can differentiate two cases: (i) among the input neighbouring DFGs there is at least one having a higher objective function score than the current; (ii) none of the input neighbouring DFGs has a higher objective function score than the current. In the first case, UDF always outputs the DFG having the highest score (regardless the selected metaheuristic). In the second case, the current DFG may be a local optimum, and each metaheuristic escapes it with a different strategy.

Iterative Local Search applies the simplest strategy, it perturbs the current DFG. The perturbation is meant to alter the DFG in such a way to escape the local optimum, e.g. randomly adding and removing multiple edges from the current DFG. The perturbed DFG is the output of the UDF.

Tabu Search relies on its three memories to escape a local optimum. The short-term memory (a.k.a. Tabu-list), containing DFG that must not be explored further. The intermediate-term memory, containing DFGs that should lead to better results and, therefore, should be explored in the near future. The long-term memory, containing DFGs (with characteristics) that have been seen multiple times and, therefore, not to explore in the near future. TABU updates the three memories each time the UDF is executed. Given the set of neighbouring DFGs and their respective objective function scores (see Algorithm 1, map S), TABU adds each DFG to a different memory. DFGs worsening the objective function score are added to the Tabu-list. DFGs improving the objective function score, yet less than another neighbouring DFG, are added to the intermediate-term memory. DFGs that do not improve the objective function score are added to the long-term memory. Also, the current DFG is added to the Tabu-list, being it already explored. When TABU does not find a better DFG in the neighbourhood of the current DFG, it returns the latest DFG added to the intermediate-term memory. If the intermediate-term memory is empty, TABU returns the latest DFG added to the long-term memory. If both these memories are empty, TABU requires a new (random) DFG from the APDA, and outputs its DFG.

Simulated Annealing avoids getting stuck in a local optimum by allowing the selection of DFGs worsening the objective function score. In doing so, SIMA explores areas of the solution space that other S-metaheuristics do not. When a better DFG is not found in the neighbourhood of the current DFG, SIMA analyses one neighbouring DFG at a time. If this latter does not worsen the objective function score, SIMA outputs it. Instead, if the neighbouring DFG worsens the objective function score, SIMA outputs it with a probability of $e^{-\frac{|s_n - s_c|}{T}}$, where s_n and s_c are the objective function scores of (respectively) the neighbouring DFG and the current DFG, and the temperature T is an integer that converges to zero as a linear function of the maximum number of iterations.

The temperature is fundamental to avoid updating the current DFG with a worse one if there would be no time to recover from the worsening (i.e. too few iterations left for continuing the exploration of the solution space from the worse DFG).

3.4   Instantiation for Split Miner

To assess our approach, we define an instantiation of it for Split Miner – a DFG-based APDA that performs favourably relative to other state-of-the-art APDAs [7]. To instantiate our approach for a concrete APDA, we need to implement an interface that allows the metaheuristics to interact with the APDA (as discussed above). The interface should provide four functions: *DiscoverDFG* and *ConvertDFGtoProcessModel* (see Algorithm 1), the *Restart Function* (RF) for TABU, and the *Perturbation Function* (PF) for ILS. The first two functions come with the DFG-based APDA, in our case Split Miner. Note that, the output of *DiscoverDFG* of Split Miner varies according to the hyperparameters settings.[3] To discover the initial DFG (Algorithm 1, line 1), Split Miner uses its default parameters. We removed the randomness for discovering the initial DFG because most of the times, the DFG discovered by Split Miner with default parameters is already a good solution [8], and starting the solution space exploration from this latter can reduce the total exploration time.

Function RF is very similar to *DiscoverDFG*, since it requires the APDA to output a DFG, the only difference is that RF must output a different DFG every time it is executed. We adapted the *DiscoverDFG* of Split Miner to output the DFG discovered with default parameters the first time it is executed, and for the following executions a DFG discovered with random parameters.

Finally, function PF can be provided either by the APDA (via the interface) or by the metaheuristic. However, PF can be more effective when not generalised by the metaheuristic, allowing the APDA to apply different perturbations to the DFGs, taking into account how the APDA converts the DFG to a process model. We invoke Split Miner's concurrency oracle to extract the possible parallelism relations in the log using a randomly chosen parallelism threshold. For each new parallel relation discovered (not present in the current solution), two edges are removed from the DFG, whilst, for each deprecated parallel relation, two edges are added to the DFG. Alternatively, it is possible to set PF = RF, so that instead of perturbing the current DFG, a new random DFG is generated. This variant of the ILS is called Repetitive Local Search (RLS). In the evaluation reported below, we use both ILS and its variant RLS.

We use the F-score as the objective function, which is computed from the fitness and precision. Among the existing measures of fitness and precision we selected the Markovian fitness and precision defined in [5] (boolean function variant, order $k = 5$). The rationale for this choice is that these measures of fitness

---

[3] Split Miner has two hyperparameters: the noise filtering threshold, used to drop infrequent edges in the DFG, and the parallelism threshold, used to determine which potential parallel relations between activities are used when discovering the process model from the DFG.

Algorithm 2. Generate Neighbours Function (GNF)

---

input   : CurrentDFG $\mathscr{G}_c$, CurrentMarkovianScore s_c, Integer $size_n$

1 **if** $getFitnessScore(s_c) > getPrecisionScore(s_c)$ **then**
2 | Set $E_m \leftarrow$ getEdgesForImprovingPrecision(s_c);
3 **else**
4 | Set $E_m \leftarrow$ getEdgesForImprovingFitness(s_c);

5 Set $N \leftarrow \varnothing$;
6 **while** $E_m \neq \varnothing \wedge |N| \neq size_n$ **do**
7 | Edge $e \leftarrow$ getRandomElement(E_m);
8 | NeighbouringDFG $\mathscr{G}_n \leftarrow$ copyDFG($\mathscr{G}_c$);
9 | **if** $getFitnessScore(s_c) > getPrecisionScore(s_c)$ **then**
10 | | **if** $canRemoveEdge(\mathscr{G}_n, e)$ **then** add $\mathscr{G}_n$ to N;
11 | **else**
12 | | addEdge($\mathscr{G}_n, e$);
13 | | add $\mathscr{G}_n$ to N;

14 **return** N;

---

and precision are the fastest to compute among state-of-the-art measures [4, 5]. Furthermore, the Markvovian fitness (precision) provides a feedback that tells us what edges could be added to (removed from) the DFG to improve the fitness (precision). This feedback allows us to design an effective GNF. In the instantiation of our approach for Split Miner, the objective function's output is a data structure composed of: the Markovian fitness and precision of the model, the F-score, and the mismatches between the model and the event log identified during the computation of the Markovian fitness and precision, i.e. the sets of the edges that could be added (removed) to improve the fitness (precision).

Given this objective function's output, our GNF is described in Algorithm 2. The function receives as input the current DFG ($\mathscr{G}_c$), its objective function score (the data structure s_c), and the number of neighbours to generate ($size_n$). If fitness is greater than precision, we retrieve (from s_c) the set of edges (E_m) that could be removed from $\mathscr{G}_c$ to improve its precision (line 2). Conversely, if precision is greater than fitness, we retrieve (from s_c) the set of edges (E_m) that could be added to $\mathscr{G}_c$ to improve its fitness (line 4). The reasoning behind this design choice is that, given that our objective function is the F-score, it is preferable to increase the lower of the two measures (precision or fitness). i.e. if the fitness is lower, we increase fitness, and conversely if the precision is lower. Once we have E_m, we select randomly one edge from it, we generate a copy of the current DFG ($\mathscr{G}_n$), and we either remove or add the randomly selected edge according to the accuracy measure we want to improve (precision or fitness), see lines 7 to 13. If the removal of an edge generates a disconnected $\mathscr{G}_n$, we do not add this latter to the neighbours set (N), line 10. We keep iterating over E_m until the set is empty (i.e. no mismatching edges are left) or N reaches its max size (i.e. $size_n$). We then return N.

The algorithm ends when the maximum execution time is reached or and the maximum number of iterations it reached (in the experiments below, we set them by default to 5 min and 50 iterations).

4   Evaluation

We implemented our approach as a Java command-line application[4] using Split Miner as the underlying automated process discovery approach and Markovian accuracy F-score as the objective function (cf. Sect. 3.4). We compared the quality of the models discovered by applying each of the optimization metaheuristics mentioned against those discovered by four baselines: (i) Split Miner; (ii) Split Miner with hyper-parameter optimization; (iii) Evolutionary Tree Miner; and (iv) Inductive Miner.

The experiments were performed on an Intel Core i5-6200U@2.30 GHz with 16 GB RAM running Windows 10 Pro (64-bit) and JVM 8 with 14 GB RAM (10 GB Stack and 4 GB Heap). The approach's implementation, the batch tests, the results, and all the models discovered during the experiments are available for reproducibility purposes at https://doi.org/10.6084/m9.figshare.7824671.v1.

4.1   Dataset

For our evaluation we used the dataset of the benchmark of automated process discovery approaches in [7], which to the best of our knowledge is the most recent benchmark on this topic. This dataset includes twelve public logs and eight private logs. The public logs originate from the 4TU Centre for Research Data, and include the *BPI Challenge* (BPIC) logs (2012-17),[5] the *Road Traffic Fines Management Process* (RTFMP) log[6] and the *SEPSIS* log[7]. These logs record executions of business processes from a variety of domains, e.g. healthcare, finance, government and IT service management. In seven logs (BPIC14, the BPIC15 collection and BPIC17), the filtering technique in [13] was applied to remove infrequent behavior; this step was necessary to maintain consistency with the benchmark dataset. The eight proprietary logs are sourced from several companies in the education, insurance, IT service management and IP management domains.

Table 1 reports the characteristics of the logs. As seen in the table, the dataset comprises simple logs (e.g. BPIC13$_{cp}$) and very complex ones (e.g. SEPSIS, PRT2) in terms of percentage of distinct traces, and both small logs (e.g. BPIC13$_{cp}$ and SEPSIS) and large ones (e.g. BPIC17 and PRT9) in terms of total number of events.

---

[4] Available under the label "Metaheuristically Optimized Split Miner" at http://apromore.org/platform/tools.

[5] https://doi.org/10.4121/uuid:3926db30-f712-4394-aebc-75976070e91f,
https://doi.org/10.4121/uuid:a7ce5c55-03a7-4583-b855-98b86e1a2b07,
https://doi.org/10.4121/uuid:c3e5d162-0cfd-4bb0-bd82-af5268819c35,
https://doi.org/10.4121/uuid:31a308ef-c844-48da-948c-305d167a0ec1,
https://doi.org/10.4121/uuid:5f3067df-f10b-45da-b98b-86ae4c7a310b.

[6] https://doi.org/10.4121/uuid:270fd440-1057-4fb9-89a9-b699b47990f5.

[7] https://doi.org/10.4121/uuid:915d2bfb-7e84-49ad-a286-dc35f063a460.

Table 1. Descriptive statistics of the real-life logs (public and proprietary).

Log		BPIC12	BPIC13$_{cp}$	BPIC13$_{inc}$	BPIC14$_f$	BPIC15$_{1f}$	BPIC15$_{2f}$	BPIC15$_{3f}$	BPIC15$_{4f}$	BPIC15$_{5f}$
Total Traces		13,087	1,487	7,554	41,353	902	681	1,369	860	975
Dist. Traces(%)		33.4	12.3	20	36.1	32.7	61.7	60.3	52.4	45.7
Total Events		262,200	6,660	65,533	369,485	21,656	24,678	43,786	29,403	30,030
Dist. Events		36	7	13	9	70	82	62	65	74
Tr. length	(min)	3	1	1	3	5	4	4	5	4
	(avg)	20	4	9	9	24	36	32	34	31
	(max)	175	35	123	167	50	63	54	54	61

Log		BPIC17$_f$	RTFMP	SEPSIS	PRT1	PRT2	PRT3	PRT4	PRT6	PRT7	PRT9	PRT10
Total Traces		21,861	150,370	1,050	12,720	1,182	1,600	20,000	744	2,000	787,657	43,514
Dist. Traces(%)		40.1	0.2	80.6	8.1	97.5	19.9	29.7	22.4	6.4	0.01	0.01
Total Events		714,198	561,470	15,214	75,353	46,282	13,720	166,282	6,011	16,353	1,808,706	78,864
Dist. Events		41	11	16	9	9	15	11	9	13	8	19
Tr. length	(min)	11	2	3	2	12	6	6	7	8	1	1
	(avg)	33	4	14	5	39	8	8	8	8	2	1
	(max)	113	2	185	64	276	9	36	21	11	58	15

4.2   Experimental Setup

For each log in our dataset, we discovered eight process models: four using the
metaheuristics presented in Sect. 3 (RLS, ILS, TABU and SIMA) and four baselines. The baselines include the Evolutionary Tree Miner (ETM) [10], Inductive
Miner infrequent variant (IM) [18], and Split Miner (SM) [8], all with default
parameters settings. ETM was allowed to run with a 4-h timeout. All comparisons with ETM are meant as comparisons of accuracy (fitness, precision,
F-score) and not as execution time comparisons, as the computational heaviness
of ETM has already been shown in previous work [7,10]. The fourth baseline
(HPO$_{sm}$) is a hyperparameter-optimized version of the SM algorithm, where we
varied the two hyperparameters of SM (noise filtering and parallelism filtering
threshold) across their full range with steps of 0.01 (from 0.01 to 1.00), and
retaining the model with the highest Markovian F-score.

ETM, IM and SM were selected as baselines because they had the highest
accuracy in a recent benchmark comparison of APDAs [7]. We also selected
HPO$_{sm}$ to compare the effects of optimization metaheuristics versus hyperparameter optimization.

For each of the discovered models we measured accuracy, complexity and
discovery time. For the accuracy, we adopted two different sets of measures: one
based on *alignments*, computing fitness and precision with the approaches proposed in [1,2] (alignment-based accuracy); and one based on *Markovian abstractions*, computing fitness and precision with the approaches proposed in [4,5]
(Markovian accuracy). For assessing the complexity of the models we relied
on *size* (number of nodes of the model), Control-Flow Complexity (CFC) (the
amount of branching caused by split gateways in the model), and Structuredness
(the percentage of nodes located directly inside a well-structured single-entry
single-exit fragment).

4.3   Results

Tables 2 and 3 show the results of our comparative evaluation. Each row reports the quality of each discovered process model in terms of accuracy (both alignment-based and Markovian) and complexity, as well as the discovery time.

Due to space, we held out from the tables four logs: $BPIC13_{cp}$, $BPIC13_{inc}$, BPIC17, and PRT9. For these logs, none of the metaheuristics could improve the accuracy of the model already discovered by SM. This is due to the high fitness score achieved by SM in these logs. By design, our metaheuristics try to improve the precision by removing edges, but in these four cases, no edge could be removed without compromising the structure of the model (i.e. the model would become disconnected).

For the remaining 16 logs, all the metaheuristics improved consistently the Markovian F-score w.r.t. SM. Also, all the metaheuristics performed better than HPO_{sm}, except in two cases (BPIC12 and PRT1). Overall, the most effective optimization metaheuristic was ILS, which delivered the highest Markovian F-score nine times out of 16, followed by SIMA (eight times), RLS and TABU (six times each). Compared to ETM, the four metaheuristics achieved better Markovian F-scores in 15 out of 16 cases, and better alignment F-scores 14 times out of 16, while compared to IM, all the optimization metaheuristics achieved better Markovian F-scores in 15 cases out of 16, and better alignment F-scores across the whole dataset.

Despite the fact that the objective function of the metaheuristics was the Markovian F-score, all four metaheuristics optimized in half of the cases the alignment-based F-score. This is due to the fact that any improvement on the Markovian fitness translates into an improvement on the alignment-based fitness, though the same does not hold for the precision. This result highlights the (partial) correlation between the alignment-based and the Markovian accuracies, already reported in previous studies [4,5]. Analysing the complexity of the models, we note that most of the times (nine cases out of 16) the F-score improvement achieved by the metaheuristics comes at the cost of size and CFC. This is expected, since SM tends to discover models with higher precision than fitness [7]. What happens is that to improve the F-score, new behavior is added to the model in the form of new edges (note that new nodes are never added). Adding new edges leads to new gateways and consequently to increasing size and CFC. On the other hand, when the precision is lower than fitness and the metaheuristic aims to increase the value of this measure to improve the overall F-score, the result is the opposite: the model complexity reduces as edges are removed. This is the case of the RTFMP and PRT10 logs. As an example of the two possible scenarios, Fig. 2 shows the models discovered by SIMA and SM from the $BPIC14_f$ log (where the model discovered by SIMA is more complex than that obtained with SM), while Fig. 3 shows the models discovered by SIMA and SM from the RTFMP log (where the model discovered by SIMA is simpler). Comparing the results obtained by the metaheuristics with HPO_{sm}, we can see that our approach allows us to discover models that cannot be discovered simply by tuning the hyperparameters of SM. This relates to the solution space

Table 2. Comparative evaluation results for the public logs.

Event Log	Discovery Approach	Align. Acc.			Markov. Acc. ($k=5$)			Complexity			Exec. Time(s)
		Fitness	Prec.	F-score	Fitness	Prec.	F-score	Size	CFC	Struct.	
BPIC12	ETM	0.440	**0.820**	0.573	0.536	**0.462**	**0.496**	67	16	**1.00**	14,400
	IM	**0.990**	0.502	0.666	0.280	0.002	0.005	59	37	**1.00**	6.6
	SM	0.963	0.520	0.675	**0.818**	0.139	0.238	51	41	0.69	3.2
	HPO_{sm}	0.781	0.796	**0.788**	0.575	0.277	0.374	**40**	17	0.58	4295.8
	RLS_{sm}	0.921	0.671	0.776	0.586	0.247	0.348	49	31	0.90	159.3
	ILS_{sm}	0.921	0.671	0.776	0.586	0.247	0.348	49	31	0.90	159.4
	$TABU_{sm}$	0.921	0.671	0.776	0.586	0.247	0.348	49	31	0.90	140.7
	$SIMA_{sm}$	0.921	0.671	0.776	0.586	0.247	0.348	49	31	0.90	151.1
BPIC14$_f$	ETM	0.610	**1.000**	0.758	0.009	0.313	0.017	23	9	**1.00**	14,400
	IM	0.890	0.646	0.749	0.501	0.346	0.409	31	18	**1.00**	3.4
	SM	0.772	0.881	0.823	0.150	**1.000**	0.262	**20**	14	**1.00**	**0.8**
	HPO_{sm}	0.852	0.857	0.855	0.449	**1.000**	0.619	22	16	0.59	575.8
	RLS_{sm}	**1.000**	0.771	**0.871**	**1.000**	0.985	**0.992**	28	34	0.54	139.0
	ILS_{sm}	**1.000**	0.771	**0.871**	**1.000**	0.985	**0.992**	28	34	0.54	151.3
	$TABU_{sm}$	0.955	0.775	0.855	0.856	0.999	0.922	26	31	0.69	154.7
	$SIMA_{sm}$	**1.000**	0.771	**0.871**	**1.000**	0.985	**0.992**	28	34	0.54	140.3
BPIC15$_{1f}$	ETM	0.560	**0.940**	0.702	0.235	0.284	0.257	67	19	**1.00**	14,400
	IM	**0.970**	0.566	0.715	0.665	0.001	0.002	164	108	**1.00**	1.1
	SM	0.899	0.871	0.885	0.701	0.726	0.713	111	45	0.51	**0.7**
	HPO_{sm}	0.962	0.833	**0.893**	**0.804**	0.670	0.731	117	55	0.45	1242.3
	RLS_{sm}	0.925	0.839	0.880	0.774	0.803	0.788	124	63	0.39	163.6
	ILS_{sm}	0.925	0.839	0.880	0.774	0.803	0.788	124	63	0.39	166.8
	$TABU_{sm}$	0.948	0.843	0.892	0.774	0.805	**0.789**	125	64	0.33	187.2
	$SIMA_{sm}$	0.920	0.839	0.878	0.772	**0.807**	**0.789**	125	63	0.43	160.4
BPIC15$_{2f}$	ETM	0.620	**0.910**	0.738	0.301	0.389	0.339	**95**	**32**	**1.00**	14,400
	IM	**0.948**	0.556	0.701	0.523	0.002	0.004	193	123	**1.00**	1.7
	SM	0.783	0.877	0.828	0.514	0.596	0.552	129	49	0.36	**0.6**
	HPO_{sm}	0.808	0.851	0.829	0.561	0.582	0.572	133	56	0.30	1398.9
	RLS_{sm}	0.870	0.797	**0.832**	0.667	0.670	0.668	156	86	0.20	158.3
	ILS_{sm}	0.869	0.795	0.830	0.663	**0.680**	**0.671**	157	86	0.20	157.6
	$TABU_{sm}$	0.870	0.794	0.830	0.665	0.667	0.666	150	83	0.23	176.8
	$SIMA_{sm}$	0.871	0.775	0.820	**0.677**	0.662	0.669	159	93	0.26	167.4
BPIC15$_{3f}$	ETM	0.680	0.880	0.767	0.238	0.172	0.199	**84**	**29**	**1.00**	14,400
	IM	**0.950**	0.554	0.700	0.480	0.002	0.003	159	108	**1.00**	1.3
	SM	0.774	**0.925**	0.843	0.436	0.764	0.555	96	35	0.49	**0.5**
	HPO_{sm}	0.783	0.910	0.842	0.477	0.691	0.564	99	39	0.56	9230.4
	RLS_{sm}	0.812	0.903	**0.855**	0.504	**0.775**	0.611	110	53	0.35	151.5
	ILS_{sm}	0.833	0.868	0.850	0.533	**0.775**	**0.631**	120	66	0.23	153.8
	$TABU_{sm}$	0.832	0.852	0.842	0.558	0.690	0.617	121	64	0.23	173.4
	$SIMA_{sm}$	0.827	0.839	0.833	**0.565**	0.694	0.623	123	71	0.18	159.4
BPIC15$_{4f}$	ETM	0.650	**0.930**	0.765	0.351	0.292	0.319	**83**	**28**	**1.00**	14,400
	IM	**0.955**	0.585	0.726	0.567	0.001	0.002	162	111	**1.00**	2.4
	SM	0.762	0.886	0.820	0.516	0.615	0.562	101	37	0.27	**0.5**
	HPO_{sm}	0.785	0.860	0.821	0.558	0.578	0.568	103	40	0.27	736.4
	RLS_{sm}	0.825	0.854	**0.839**	0.634	**0.672**	0.652	114	57	0.21	146.9
	ILS_{sm}	0.853	0.807	0.829	**0.649**	0.657	**0.653**	117	64	0.27	147.8
	$TABU_{sm}$	0.811	0.794	0.803	0.642	0.661	0.651	115	61	0.24	161.7
	$SIMA_{sm}$	0.847	0.812	0.829	0.624	0.649	0.636	117	61	0.18	148.2
BPIC15$_{5f}$	ETM	0.570	0.940	0.710	0.365	0.504	0.423	**88**	**18**	**1.00**	14,400
	IM	**0.937**	0.179	0.301	0.242	0.000	0.000	134	95	**1.00**	2.5
	SM	0.806	0.915	0.857	0.555	0.598	0.576	110	38	0.34	**0.6**
	HPO_{sm}	0.789	**0.941**	**0.858**	0.529	0.655	0.585	102	30	0.33	972.3
	RLS_{sm}	0.868	0.813	0.840	0.737	0.731	0.734	137	78	0.14	159.3
	ILS_{sm}	0.868	0.813	0.840	0.737	0.731	0.734	137	78	0.14	153.8
	$TABU_{sm}$	0.885	0.818	0.850	**0.739**	**0.746**	**0.743**	137	79	0.14	173.3
	$SIMA_{sm}$	0.867	0.811	0.838	0.734	0.727	0.731	137	78	0.16	154.3
RTFMP	ETM	0.990	0.920	0.954	0.981	0.010	0.019	57	32	**1.00**	14,400
	IM	0.980	0.700	0.817	0.934	0.046	0.087	34	20	**1.00**	13.9
	SM	**0.996**	0.958	0.977	**0.959**	0.311	0.470	22	17	0.46	**2.9**
	HPO_{sm}	0.887	**1.000**	0.940	0.685	0.696	0.690	**20**	**9**	0.35	2452.7
	RLS_{sm}	0.988	**1.000**	**0.994**	0.899	0.794	0.843	22	14	0.46	142.8
	ILS_{sm}	0.988	**1.000**	**0.994**	0.899	0.794	0.843	22	14	0.46	143.8
	$TABU_{sm}$	0.988	**1.000**	**0.994**	0.899	0.794	0.843	22	14	0.46	114.8
	$SIMA_{sm}$	0.986	**1.000**	0.993	0.875	**0.893**	**0.884**	23	15	0.39	131.0
SEPSIS	ETM	0.830	0.660	**0.735**	0.696	0.096	0.169	108	101	**1.00**	14,400
	IM	**0.991**	0.445	0.614	0.741	0.012	0.024	50	32	**1.00**	1.3
	SM	0.764	**0.706**	0.734	0.349	**0.484**	0.406	**32**	**23**	0.94	**0.4**
	HPO_{sm}	0.925	0.588	0.719	**0.755**	0.293	0.423	33	34	0.39	28,846
	RLS_{sm}	0.839	0.630	0.720	0.508	0.430	0.466	35	29	0.77	145.4
	ILS_{sm}	0.812	0.625	0.706	0.455	0.436	0.445	35	28	0.86	157.1
	$TABU_{sm}$	0.839	0.630	0.720	0.508	0.430	**0.466**	35	29	0.77	137.0
	$SIMA_{sm}$	0.806	0.613	0.696	0.477	0.445	0.460	35	30	0.77	137.2

Table 3. Comparative evaluation results for the proprietary logs.

Event Log	Discovery Method	Align. Acc.			Markov. Acc. ($k = 5$)			Complexity			Exec. Time(s)
		Fitness	Prec.	F-score	Fitness	Prec.	F-score	Size	CFC	Struct.	
PRT1	ETM	0.990	0.811	0.892	0.977	0.213	0.350	23	12	**1.00**	14,400
	IM	0.902	0.673	0.771	0.232	0.051	0.084	20	9	**1.00**	3.8
	SM	0.976	**0.974**	**0.975**	0.730	0.669	0.698	20	14	**1.00**	**0.4**
	HPO$_{sm}$	**0.999**	0.948	0.972	**0.989**	0.620	0.762	**19**	14	0.53	298.3
	RLS$_{sm}$	0.976	**0.974**	**0.975**	0.730	0.669	0.698	20	14	**1.00**	155.3
	ILS$_{sm}$	0.976	**0.974**	**0.975**	0.730	0.669	0.698	20	14	**1.00**	153.2
	TABU$_{sm}$	0.976	**0.974**	**0.975**	0.730	0.669	0.698	20	14	**1.00**	10.3
	SIMA$_{sm}$	0.983	0.964	0.974	0.814	**0.722**	**0.765**	20	15	**1.00**	132.6
PRT2	ETM	0.572	**0.943**	0.712	0.105	0.788	0.186	86	21	**1.00**	14,400
	IM	ex	ex	ex	0.329	0.179	0.232	45	33	**1.00**	2.3
	SM	0.795	0.581	0.671	0.457	**0.913**	0.609	29	23	**1.00**	**0.3**
	HPO$_{sm}$	0.826	0.675	**0.743**	0.501	0.830	0.625	**21**	13	0.67	406.4
	RLS$_{sm}$	0.886	0.421	0.571	0.629	0.751	0.685	29	34	**1.00**	141.4
	ILS$_{sm}$	**0.890**	0.405	0.557	**0.645**	0.736	**0.688**	29	35	**1.00**	172.3
	TABU$_{sm}$	0.866	0.425	0.570	0.600	0.782	0.679	29	33	**1.00**	143.1
	SIMA$_{sm}$	0.886	0.424	0.574	0.629	0.751	0.685	29	34	**1.00**	139.7
PRT3	ETM	**0.979**	0.858	0.915	0.858	0.313	0.459	51	37	**1.00**	14,400
	IM	0.975	0.680	0.801	**0.874**	0.481	**0.621**	37	20	**1.00**	0.9
	SM	0.882	0.887	0.885	0.381	0.189	0.252	31	23	0.58	**0.4**
	HPO$_{sm}$	0.890	0.899	0.895	0.461	0.518	0.488	**26**	14	0.81	290.2
	RLS$_{sm}$	0.945	**0.902**	**0.923**	0.591	0.517	0.551	31	23	0.55	138.4
	ILS$_{sm}$	0.945	**0.902**	**0.923**	0.591	0.517	0.551	31	23	0.55	144.2
	TABU$_{sm}$	0.944	**0.902**	0.922	0.589	**0.519**	0.552	30	20	0.60	134.7
	SIMA$_{sm}$	0.945	**0.902**	**0.923**	0.591	0.517	0.551	31	23	0.55	133.7
PRT4	ETM	0.844	0.851	0.847	0.629	0.950	0.757	64	28	**1.00**	14,400
	IM	0.927	0.753	0.831	0.615	0.952	0.747	27	13	**1.00**	1.1
	SM	0.884	**1.000**	0.938	0.483	**1.000**	0.652	**25**	15	0.96	**0.5**
	HPO$_{sm}$	0.973	0.930	**0.951**	0.929	0.989	0.958	26	24	0.31	867.5
	RLS$_{sm}$	**0.997**	0.903	0.948	**0.993**	0.990	**0.992**	26	28	0.92	140.1
	ILS$_{sm}$	**0.997**	0.903	0.948	**0.993**	0.990	**0.992**	26	28	0.92	152.3
	TABU$_{sm}$	0.955	0.914	0.934	0.883	0.988	0.932	26	26	0.77	138.6
	SIMA$_{sm}$	**0.997**	0.903	0.948	**0.993**	0.990	**0.992**	26	28	0.92	136.9
PRT6	ETM	0.980	0.796	0.878	0.890	0.611	0.725	41	16	**1.00**	14,400
	IM	**0.989**	0.822	0.898	**0.946**	0.444	0.604	23	10	**1.00**	2.9
	SM	0.937	**1.000**	**0.967**	0.542	**1.000**	0.703	**15**	4	**1.00**	**0.3**
	HPO$_{sm}$	0.937	**1.000**	**0.967**	0.542	**1.000**	0.703	**15**	4	**1.00**	105.1
	RLS$_{sm}$	0.984	0.928	0.955	0.840	0.818	**0.829**	22	14	0.41	141.1
	ILS$_{sm}$	0.984	0.928	0.955	0.840	0.818	**0.829**	22	14	0.41	144.2
	TABU$_{sm}$	0.984	0.928	0.955	0.840	0.818	**0.829**	22	14	0.41	124.9
	SIMA$_{sm}$	0.984	0.928	0.955	0.840	0.818	**0.829**	22	14	0.41	131.2
PRT7	ETM	0.900	0.810	0.853	0.969	0.217	0.355	60	29	**1.00**	14,400
	IM	**1.000**	0.726	0.841	**1.000**	0.543	0.704	29	13	**1.00**	1.3
	SM	0.914	0.999	0.954	0.650	**1.000**	0.788	29	10	0.48	**0.6**
	HPO$_{sm}$	0.944	**1.000**	0.971	0.772	**1.000**	0.871	**22**	9	0.64	173.1
	RLS$_{sm}$	0.993	**1.000**	**0.996**	0.933	**1.000**	**0.965**	23	11	0.78	139.2
	ILS$_{sm}$	0.993	**1.000**	**0.996**	0.933	**1.000**	**0.965**	23	11	0.78	142.9
	TABU$_{sm}$	0.993	**1.000**	**0.996**	0.933	**1.000**	**0.965**	23	11	0.78	134.0
	SIMA$_{sm}$	0.993	**1.000**	**0.996**	0.933	**1.000**	**0.965**	23	11	0.78	131.9
PRT10	ETM	**1.000**	0.627	0.771	0.748	0.001	0.003	61	45	**1.00**	14,400
	IM	0.964	0.790	0.868	**0.945**	0.001	0.001	41	29	**1.00**	4.6
	SM	0.970	0.943	**0.956**	0.905	0.206	0.335	45	47	0.84	**0.5**
	HPO$_{sm}$	0.936	0.943	0.939	0.810	0.243	0.374	**30**	22	0.73	1214.3
	RLS$_{sm}$	0.917	**0.989**	0.952	0.741	**0.305**	**0.432**	44	41	0.86	153.0
	ILS$_{sm}$	0.917	**0.989**	0.952	0.741	**0.305**	**0.432**	44	41	0.86	155.4
	TABU$_{sm}$	0.917	**0.989**	0.952	0.741	**0.305**	**0.432**	44	41	0.86	117.6
	SIMA$_{sm}$	0.917	**0.989**	0.952	0.741	**0.305**	**0.432**	44	41	0.86	136.7

exploration. Indeed, while HPO$_{sm}$ can only explore a limited number of solutions (DFGs), i.e. those that can be generated by the underlying APDA, SM in this case, by varying its hyperparameters, the metaheuristics go beyond the solution space of HPO$_{sm}$ by exploring new DFGs in a pseudo-random manner.

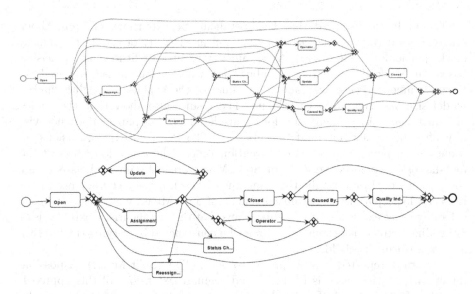

Fig. 2. BPIC14$_f$ models discovered with SIMA (above) and SM (below).

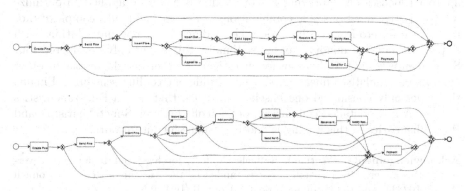

Fig. 3. BPIC14$_f$ models discovered with SIMA (above) and SM (below).

In terms of execution times, the four metaheuristics perform similarly, having an average discovery time close to 150 s. While this is considerably higher than the execution time of SM (~1 s on average), it is much lower than HPO$_{sm}$ and ETM, while consistently achieving higher accuracy.

5   Conclusion

This paper showed that the use of S-metaheuristics is a promising approach to enhance the accuracy of DFG-based APDAs. The outlined approach takes advantage of the DFG's simplicity to define efficient perturbation functions that improve fitness or precision while preserving structural properties required to ensure model correctness.

The evaluation showed that the metaheuristic extensions of Split Miner achieve considerably higher accuracy for a clear majority of logs in the benchmark, particularly when using fine-grained measures of fitness and precision based on Markovian abstractions, but also when using measures based on trace alignment. These accuracy gains come at the expense of slightly higher model size and structural complexity. The results also show that the choice of S-metaheuristics (among the four considered in this paper) does not visibly affect accuracy nor model complexity. The metaheuristic extensions do come with a penalty in terms of execution times. The execution times of the metaheuristic-enhanced versions of Split Miner are ~2–3 min versus ~1 s for the base miner. Interestingly, the S-metaheuristics improve accuracy even with respect a hyperparameter-optimized version of Split Miner, while achieving considerably lower execution times. This means that the metaheuristic extensions of Split Miner explore solutions that cannot be constructed by varying the filtering and parallelism thresholds.

The study reported here is limited to one APDA (Split Miner). A possible direction for future work is to define and evaluate extensions of this approach for other DFG-based APDAs such as Fodina and Inductive Miner. Also, the approach focuses on improving F-score, while it could be applied to optimize other objective functions (e.g. combinations of F-score and model complexity) or to perform Pareto-front optimization, i.e. finding Pareto-optimal solutions with respect to multiple quality measures. Finally, this study only considered four S-metaheuristics. There is room for investigating other metaheuristics or other variants of simulated annealing, e.g. using different cooling schedules. Finally, the paper only considered one baseline approach that uses a P-metaheuristics (ETM). A more detailed comparison of tradeoffs between S-metaheuristics and P-metaheuristics in this setting is another avenue for future work.

Acknowledgements. We thank Raffaele Conforti for his input to an earlier version of this paper. This research is partly funded by the Australian Research Council (DP180102839) and the Estonian Research Council (IUT20-55).

References

1. Adriansyah, A., Munoz-Gama, J., Carmona, J., van Dongen, B., van der Aalst, W.: Measuring precision of modeled behavior. ISeB **13**(1), 37–67 (2015)
2. Adriansyah, A., van Dongen, B., van der Aalst, W.: Conformance checking using cost-based fitness analysis. In: EDOC. IEEE (2011)
3. Alizadeh, S., Norani, A.: ICMA: a new efficient algorithm for process model discovery. Appl. Intell. **48**(11), 4497–4514 (2018)
4. Augusto, A., Armas-Cervantes, A., Conforti, R., Dumas, M., La Rosa, M., Reissner, D.: Abstract-and-compare: a family of scalable precision measures for automated process discovery. In: Weske, M., Montali, M., Weber, I., vom Brocke, J. (eds.) BPM 2018. LNCS, vol. 11080, pp. 158–175. Springer, Cham (2018). https://doi.org/10.1007/978-3-319-98648-7_10

5. Augusto, A., Armas Cervantes, A., Conforti, R., Dumas, M., La Rosa, M., Reissner, D.: Measuring fitness and precision of automatically discovered process models: a principled and scalable approach. Technical report, University of Melbourne (2019)
6. Augusto, A., Conforti, R., Dumas, M., La Rosa, M., Bruno, G.: Automated discovery of structured process models from event logs: the discover-and-structure approach. DKE **117**, 373–392 (2017)
7. Augusto, A., et al.: Automated discovery of process models from event logs: review and benchmark. IEEE TKDE **31**(4), 686–705 (2019)
8. Augusto, A., Conforti, R., Dumas, M., La Rosa, M., Polyvyanyy, A.: Split miner: automated discovery of accurate and simple business process models from event logs. KAIS **59**, 251–284 (2018)
9. Boussaïd, I., Lepagnot, J., Siarry, P.: A survey on optimization metaheuristics. Inf. Sci. **237**, 82–117 (2013)
10. Buijs, J.C.A.M., van Dongen, B.F., van der Aalst, W.M.P.: On the role of fitness, precision, generalization and simplicity in process discovery. In: Meersman, R., et al. (eds.) OTM 2012. LNCS, vol. 7565, pp. 305–322. Springer, Heidelberg (2012). https://doi.org/10.1007/978-3-642-33606-5_19
11. Burattin, A., Sperduti, A.: Automatic determination of parameters' values for heuristics miner++. In: IEEE Congress on Evolutionary Computation (2010)
12. Chifu, V.R., Pop, C.B., Salomie, I., Balla, I., Paven, R.: Hybrid particle swarm optimization method for process mining. In: ICCP. IEEE (2012)
13. Conforti, R., La Rosa, M., ter Hofstede, A.: Filtering out infrequent behavior from business process event logs. IEEE TKDE **29**(2), 300–314 (2017)
14. de Medeiros, A.K.A.: Genetic process mining. Ph.D. thesis, Eindhoven University of Technology (2006)
15. Gao, D., Liu, Q.: An improved simulated annealing algorithm for process mining. In: CSCWD. IEEE (2009)
16. Glover, F.: Future paths for integer programming and links to artificial intelligence. Comput. Oper. Res. **13**(5), 533–549 (1986)
17. Kirkpatrick, S., Gelatt, C.D., Vecchi, M.P.: Optimization by simulated annealing. Science **220**(4598), 671–680 (1983)
18. Leemans, S.J.J., Fahland, D., van der Aalst, W.M.P.: Discovering block-structured process models from event logs containing infrequent behaviour. In: Lohmann, N., Song, M., Wohed, P. (eds.) BPM 2013. LNBIP, vol. 171, pp. 66–78. Springer, Cham (2014). https://doi.org/10.1007/978-3-319-06257-0_6
19. Leemans, S., Fahland, D., van der Aalst, W.: Scalable process discovery and conformance checking. Softw. Syst. Model. **17**, 599–631 (2016)
20. Ribeiro, J., Carmona Vargas, J.: A method for assessing parameter impact on control-flow discovery algorithms. In: Algorithms and Theories for the Analysis of Event Data (2015)
21. Song, W., Liu, S., Liu, Q.: Business process mining based on simulated annealing. In: ICYCS. IEEE (2008)
22. Stützle, T.: Local search algorithms for combinatorial problems. Ph.D. thesis, Darmstadt University of Technology (1998)
23. van der Aalst, W.: Process Mining - Data Science in Action. Springer, Heidelberg (2016). https://doi.org/10.1007/978-3-662-49851-4
24. vanden Broucke, S., De Weerdt, J.: Fodina: a robust and flexible heuristic process discovery technique. DSS **100**, 109–118 (2017)
25. Weijters, A., Ribeiro, J.: Flexible heuristics miner (FHM). In: CIDM. IEEE (2011)

Learning Accurate LSTM Models
of Business Processes

Manuel Camargo[1,2](✉) [iD], Marlon Dumas[1] [iD], and Oscar González-Rojas[2] [iD]

[1] University of Tartu, Tartu, Estonia
{manuel.camargo,marlon.dumas}@ut.ee
[2] Universidad de los Andes, Bogotá, Colombia
o-gonza1@uniandes.edu.co

Abstract. Deep learning techniques have recently found applications in the field of predictive business process monitoring. These techniques allow us to predict, among other things, what will be the next events in a case, when will they occur, and which resources will trigger them. They also allow us to generate entire execution traces of a business process, or even entire event logs, which opens up the possibility of using such models for process simulation. This paper addresses the question of how to use deep learning techniques to train accurate models of business process behavior from event logs. The paper proposes an approach to train recurrent neural networks with Long-Short-Term Memory (LSTM) architecture in order to predict sequences of next events, their timestamp, and their associated resource pools. An experimental evaluation on real-life event logs shows that the proposed approach outperforms previously proposed LSTM architectures targeted at this problem.

Keywords: Process mining · Deep learning ·
Long-Short-Term Memory

1 Introduction

Models of business process behavior trained with deep learning techniques have recently found several applications in the fields of predictive process monitoring [2,7,13]. Such models allow us to move from predicting boolean, categorical, or numerical performance properties, to predicting what will be the next event in a case, when will it occur, and which resource will trigger it. They also allow us to predict the most likely remaining path of an ongoing case and even to generate entire execution traces of a business process (or entire event logs), which opens up the possibility of using such models for process simulation. Yet another application of such models can be found in the field of anomaly detection [8].

This paper addresses the question of how to use deep learning techniques to train accurate models from business process event logs. This question has been previously addressed in the context of predictive process monitoring by using Recurrent Neural Networks (RNNs) with Long-Short-Term Memory (LSTM)

© Springer Nature Switzerland AG 2019
T. Hildebrandt et al. (Eds.): BPM 2019, LNCS 11675, pp. 286–302, 2019.
https://doi.org/10.1007/978-3-030-26619-6_19

architecture. Specifically, Evermann et al. [2] proposed an approach to generate the most likely remaining sequence of events (suffix) starting from a prefix of an ongoing case. However, this architecture cannot handle numerical variables and hence it cannot generate sequences of timestamped events. This inability to predict timestamps and durations is also shared by the approach of Lin et al. [6]. An alternative approach by Tax et al. [13] can predict timestamps but it does not use the embedded dimension of the LSTM network, which forces it to one-hot-encode categorical variables. In particular, it one-hot-encodes the type of each event (i.e. the activity to which the event refers). As a result, its accuracy deteriorates as the number of event types increases. As shown later in this paper, this choice leads to poor accuracy when applied to real-life event logs with a couple of dozen event types.

The paper addresses the limitations of the above approaches by proposing new pre- and post-processing methods and architectures for building and using generative models from event logs using LSTM neural networks. Specifically, the paper proposes an approach to learn models that can generate traces (or suffixes of traces starting from a given prefix) consisting of triplets (event type, role, time-stamp). The proposed approach combines the advantages of Tax et al. [13] and Evermann et al. [2] by making use of the embedded dimension while supporting both categorical and numerical attributes in the event log. The paper considers three architectures corresponding to different combinations of shared and specialized layers in the neural network.

The paper reports on two experimental evaluations. The first one compares alternative instantiations of the proposed approach corresponding to different architectures, pre-processing, and post-processing choices. The goal of this evaluation is to derive guidelines as to which design choices are preferable depending on the characteristics of the log. The second evaluation compares the accuracy of the proposed approach relative to the three baselines mentioned above.

The next section provides an overview of RNNs and LSTMs and discusses related work on the use of deep learning techniques in the field of process mining and predictive process monitoring. Section 3 introduces the proposed approach, while Sect. 4 presents its evaluation. Finally, Sect. 5 summarizes the contributions and findings and outlines future work.

2 Background and Related Work

2.1 RNN and LSTM Networks

Deep Learning is a sub-field of machine learning concerned with the construction and use of networks composed of multiple interconnected layers of neurons (perceptrons), which perform non-linear transformations of data [4]. The main goal of these transformations is train the network to "learn" the behaviors/patterns observed in the data. Theoretically, the more layers of neurons there are in the network, the more it becomes possible to detect higher-level patterns in the data thanks to the composition of complex functions [5].

Recurrent Neural Networks (RNN) contain cyclical connections that have been specially designed for the prediction of sequential data [10]. In this type of data, the state of an observation depends on the state of its predecessor. So the RNNs use a part of the processed output (h) of the preceding unit of processing (a cell) for the processing of a new input (X). Figure 1 presents the basic RNN cell structure. Even though, RNNs have a good performance when predicting sequences with short-term temporary dependencies, they fail to account for long-term dependencies. Long Short-Term Memory (LSTM) networks address this problem. In LSTM networks apart from the use of part of the previous output for a new processing, a long-term memory is implemented. In the long term memory, the information flows from cell to cell with minimal variation, keeping certain aspects constant during the processing of all inputs. This constant input allows to remain the coherence of the predictions in long periods of time.

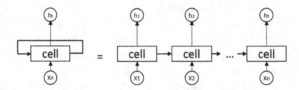

Fig. 1. RNN basic structure

2.2   Related Work

Tax et al. [13] use LSTM networks to predict the type of the next event of an ongoing process case and the time until the next event (its timestamp). In this approach, each event is mapped to a feature vector by encoding the event type using one-hot encoding and supplementing it with features related to the event's occurrence time, such the time of the day, the time since the previous event, and the accumulated duration since the start of the case. The weights in the network are set so as to minimize the cross-entropy between the ground-truth one-hot encoding of the next event and the predicted one-hot encoding as well as the Mean Absolute Error (MAE) between the ground truth time until the next event and the predicted time. The network architecture consists of a shared LSTM layer that feeds two independent LSTM layers specialized in predicting the next event and the other in predicting times. By repeatedly predicting the next event in a case and its timestamp, the authors also use their approach to predict the remaining sequence of events until case completion and the remaining cycle time. The experiments show that the LSTM approach outperforms automata-based approaches for predicting the remaining of sequence of events and the remaining time [1,9]. In this approach the embedded dimension in LSTMs is not used to capture the event type, but instead the event type is one-hot encoded. This design choice is suitable when the number of event types is low, but detrimental for larger numbers of event types as shown later in this paper.

2 IoT in Agriculture

With the continuous development of times and information technology (IT), networking technology provide important input for industry development. The easiest thing to understand IoT is based on Internet, mobile communication, and other communication networks, through intelligent sensors, radio frequency identification, infrared sensors, global positioning systems, laser scanner s, remote sensing, etc. [7]. Agricultural IoT technology is used to combine variety of sensor organizations to form the sensor network, through which we can collect farmland sensor information (field planting, horticulture, livestock and poultry, aquatic product s' site information breeding, agricultural logistics, and other areas) and real- time analysis of the results transmitted to farmers to enable them to make the most profitable decisions.

Most researchers done IoT based agricultural system on different specification and parameters. Currently, IoT applications in agriculture are mainly in the following mature technologies:

1. Agricultural sensor technology. Agricultural products have been covered by many categories of sensors such as soil sensors, water sensors, meteorological sensors, heavy metal detection sensors, biosensors, gas sensors, and so on [7].
2. Radio transmission technology. ZigBee wireless sensor networks can achieve self-organizing wireless data transmission, which has been widely applied in large-scale farming.
3. RFID (Radio-frequency identification) technology. It is widely used in animal identification, which can be performed on animals to achieve intelligent recognizing, positioning, tracking, monitoring, traceability, and management.
4. Technical quality safety of agricultural products. In the agricultural "production circulation sales" industrial chain, recording and monitoring the chain can realize the whole process of regulation [7].
5. Intelligent irrigation technology. Relying on satellite positioning network and "shallow wells underground cables + field + automatic irrigation system pipe" technology, it can collect irrigation water, electricity, irrigation, and time data to achieve automation of farmland irrigation and through a comprehensive analysis of information technology software to guide irrigation.
6. Precision seeding and spraying techniques. Relying on technology combined with GPS navigation technology, variable rate fertilization, and seeding technology, it can achieve uniform implementation of the planting, spraying, and improving the utilization of seeds, pesticides, and so on.

The Table 1 below presents the studies conducted on IOT based agricultural system in different agricultural parameters and potential application areas.

Table 1. Studies conducted on IoT based agricultural system

Authors	Parameters	IoT Technology	Protocol	Application areas
Abd El-kader et al. [8]	Potato crop	Agricultural sensor technology	APTEEN protocol	Plant monitoring (precision farming)
Mohanraj et al. [3]	Plant growth and Irrigation Planner	TI CC3200 Launchpad interconnected sensors and KM-Knowledge base	Not specified	Field Monitoring and Automation
Nikolidakis et al. [9]	Irrigation	Agricultural sensor technology	Equalized Cluster Head Election Routing Protocol	Irrigation control
Li et al. [10]	Apple orchards	Agricultural sensor and GPRS technology	ZigBee	Air monitoring
Chen et al. [11]	Soil temperature and moisture	Agricultural sensor and GPRS technology	ZigBee	Soil monitoring
Yue et al. [12]	pH, oxygen density and turbidity	Wireless sensor network technology	IEEE 802.15.4	Water monitoring
Fourati et al. [13]	Humidity, solar radiation, temperature, and rain	Wireless sensor network technology, GPS and GIS	Zigbee, GSM and RS-232	Plant monitoring
Ehsan et al. [14]	Wildlife tracking	Delay-tolerant networks (DTNs)	Not specified	Animal monitoring
Jain et al. [15]	Behaviour and migration	Wireless sensor network technology and GPS	Zigbee	Animal monitoring
Khriji et al. [16]	Water need for plant	Wireless sensor network technology and GPS	IEEE 802.15.4	Irrigation control
Pahuja et al. [17]	Greenhouse climate	Wireless sensor network technology	ZigBee based on IEEE 802.15.4	Fertilizer and pesticide control
Luvisi et al. [18]	Vineyards	RFID	Not specified	Production monitoring
Vellidis et al. [19]	Cotton	Wireless sensor network technology and Radio Frequency Identification	RFID tags	Production monitoring
Papetti et al. [20]	Cheese	Radio Frequency Identification	Not specified	Sales monitoring and traceability
Wang et al. [21]	Meat	Radio Frequency Identification and GIS system	Not specified	Sales monitoring and traceability
Abad et al. [22]	Fish	Radio Frequency Identification sensors	Not specified	Circulation monitoring
Amador et al. [23]	Pineapples	Radio Frequency Identification	RFID tags	Circulation monitoring
Kim [24]	Crop diseases	Cloud-based and Wireless sensor network technology	Backhaul IPv4	Smart farming

3 Potential Applications of IoT in Agriculture

Internet of Things can be incorporated in different environmental applications in order to help human's day to day activities. To produce dense and real-time maps of air and water pollution, noise level, temperature and harmful radiation among others IoT technology is the important and emerging technology [6]. Now a days, agricultural technology and precision farming have arisen as new scientific fields that use data intensive approaches to drive agricultural productivity while minimizing its environmental impact [25]. IoT has been used in several application areas; one of the dominant domains is agriculture. Zhao et al. [26] stated that IoT is dominant used in greenhouse technology to monitor production environment and control system; temperature, humidity, and soil signals are collected in real-time in the production process using wireless sensor networks through machine-to-machine support system. The application of IoT in Agriculture is versatile. In the subsequent section we present the major areas that IoT can be used in the domain.

(a) **Smart Farming**

Farming is one of the potential application areas of IoT. The adoption of IoT for of smart technology includes using sensors, robots, systems of control, and autonomous vehicles [27, 28]. IoT farming also offers farmers with appropriate pesticides, climate information, soil information (acidity, moisture, nitrogen level etc.), fertilizer information, crop disease management, and weather forecast. Precision farming [28] is one of the most famous applications of IoT in agriculture sector. For example, Crop Metrics is a precision agriculture organization working on the management of precision irrigation to monitor the soil moisture and to increase water use efficiency in order to maximize yields [28].

(b) **Green Housing**

Light, temperature and humidity determine productivity and plant growth [29]. Continuous monitoring of these environmental variables provides valuable information to the farmer to know the effect of each factor and how to increase crop productivity [29]. Adjusting the greenhouse climate enables the farmer to improve productivity. Several studies have been conducted on IoT application to monitor greenhouse environment using wireless sensor technologies.

(c) **Livestock Management/Monitoring**

There are enormous number of publications on animal monitoring using ICT. IoT applications can be used to collect data regarding the location, well-being, and health of their cattle For example, some of the applications of IoT utilized in livestock management monitoring are the study of animal behavior monitoring (ZebraNet in Kenya), the behavior analysis of sheep within vineyards based on IoT technology [30], and the animal posture behavior [31]. Williams et al. [32] studied the grazing behavior of cows using GPS. In their study, they classified the behavior into three states: grazing, walking and resting. Another IoT intervention area is estrus detection [32, 33]. Missed inseminations causes additional feed costs for fertile cows, artificial insemination costs, and reduce production of calves and milk yield. Kim et al., used bio-sensor that measures the body temperature of cows in real time that allows accurate detection of estrus. The biosensor is inserted orally into the cow; and transmit biometric information is forward to data gathering box and the data is transmitted to the server using cellular or WiFi technology for data analysis. The server notifies the status of estrus detection (whether the cow is in estrus cycle or not) to the manager or veterinarian through a mobile application. Several related studies have been conducted to detect estrus [34, 35].

Generally, IoT can be applied in every fields of Agriculture. It has immense potential to increase productivity and in general it is a means to foster socio-economic development.

4   Architecture of IoT in Agriculture

Based on the review of different research work on smart agriculture and its analysis on IoT's critical technologies in smart agriculture. In the general framework of IoT based agriculture, we shall ensure the size of IoT, mobility sensor communication and its data security. The application of IoT is still relatively very less in Ethiopia, and there is no large-scale, systematic development trend, so a scalable and open architecture of IoT should be established in the agricultural industrial chain technology as well as application and formation system in ideal aspects in order to break through the barriers of application in large-scale and promote the IoT industry's transition from the start-up period to the growth period. The overall general architecture of IoT includes data acquisition layer, information exchange layer and application layer. The overall technical architecture of IoT is shown in Fig. 1.

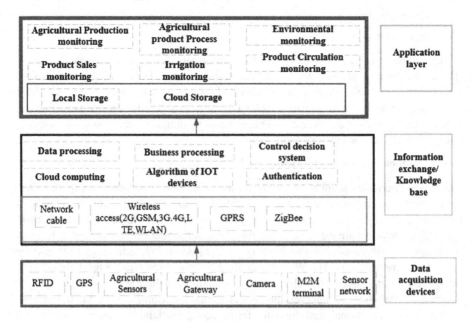

Fig. 1. The general architecture of IoT

4.1   IoT Based Monitoring System in Agriculture

In the process of agricultural production, the most important thing is the real time data collection in terms of data acquisition sensors like temperature, moisture, carbon dioxide content, and soil temperature and soil moisture content and etc. Monitoring System in agricultural based on IoT aims at the target of making information collection towards several indexes in agricultural production, process, sales, environmental monitoring, irrigation and in product circulation and carrying out systematic monitoring towards the plantation area, crop pattern, crop growing, the breaking out and development of agricultural damages, crop output and so on. The monitoring system is composed by the wireless sensor monitoring network and distant monitoring information system. The Fig. 2 describe a typical IoT deployed for agricultural applications.

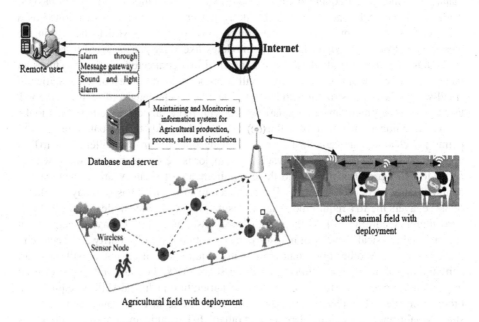

Fig. 2. IOT deployed for agricultural applications

5   Challenges of Using IoT in Agriculture

As we have discussed in section two, IoT is the network of physical objects, devices, vehicles, buildings and other items which are embedded with electronics, software, sensors, and network connectivity, which enables these objects to collect and exchange data. Implementing this concept in agricultural field is not an easy task. These is may be for many reasons including the complex nature of the different components of the ecosystem of IoT. The challenges of IoT in agriculture limit to meet the needs of the future along with efficient use of resources in Ethiopia. There are considerations to adopt IoT technologies in agriculture of Ethiopia. In this regards the popularity of any technology is depends on the ease of its adoption and implementation [36]. According to [37] studied there are some challenges to implement the application of IoT required high cost than expectation that the technology must available at low cost with a large number of objects. Many other challenges are also faced in order to adopt IoT application for developing countries, in these regards for Ethiopia because of different factors. Challenges of IoT like scalability, self-organizing, data volumes, data interpretation, interoperability, automatic discovery, software complexity, fault tolerance, power supply, wireless communication, security and privacy are discussed [37–39] studies. For instance: complexity of software and hardware are some of the challenges associated with the IoT in agriculture for developing countries like Ethiopia. Minimal resources and software infrastructures are needed in smart agriculture. The study by [40] examined that the appropriate programming tools and low-power capabilities are mandatory, since the frequent battery replacement of the stations. This is not easy to deploy in large scale open field. In the study power harvesting was mentioned as a solution to some extent, however, the power consumption has still to be within the power budget of small power harvesting modules like solar panels, wind turbines etc. According to [40, 41] studied the large number of interconnected devices produces an incredibly large amount of data, which will soon be beyond the resource capacities of small-scale server infrastructures to handle. The other is challenges of security, the IoT technology is an interconnected smart device with more devices together. This make the negative impact on smart agriculture because of it provide the decentralized energy points for creating malware. In this regards it become the main challenge of IoT in agricultural sector. Security and privacy is the major issue for the prevention of widely adopt IoT in agriculture [42]. The three requirements of security are authentication, confidentiality and access control. The architecture of security has four layers. Based on these layers the IoT requirements are to insure security in the whole system of smart agriculture. According to [40] the most security issue include information acquisition security and physical security of hardware in perception layer of security architecture in IoT technology. Another important issue is the requirement of technical skill, in smart agricultural sector capacity building is the essential task. For farming and create an impact on the overall performance in field of agriculture technical skill is required. In order to enable IoT applications in agricultural field like in Precision Farming, Livestock Monitoring, Agricultural Drones and others, IoT technician or skilled individuals on different smart devices are required for farmers to maximize yields using minimal resources such as water, fertilizer and seeds.

6 Conclusion and Future Direction

The introduction of IoT technology is featured to be useful for advancing the agricultural process and animal monitoring process by introducing new dimensions. Ethiopia is an agrarian country where 80% of the population are living in rural area and their income is from Agriculture. However, farming in Ethiopia is very traditional and technology intervention is very minimal. Therefore, IoT can support to modernize Ethiopian agriculture System. There is huge amount of farmland; and the environment is very conducive for much of the crop to grow and cultivate. Besides, Ethiopia ranked first in livestock in Africa and fifth in the World [43]. But, the cattle management, disease monitoring, diary, beef, meat production, etc. trends is very traditional and not reliable. Thus, IoT has a huge potential to boost production in livestock sector.

In agriculture sector, IoT technologies appear in different application areas like precision agriculture or smart farming, irrigation monitoring, environmental monitoring, livestock monitoring and in all other fields of agriculture. Through review on the key technologies of IoT, and the applications in monitoring agricultural products during production, processing, circulation, sales of the whole supply chain and traceability, it showed that consumers can acquire agricultural products information for risk management and traceability, and producers can get high quality and yield products with minimum effort in agriculture based on IoT technology. Nowadays, RFID, WSN, sensors, GPS technology and LPWAN (low power wide area network) protocols such as LoRa, SigFox and NBIOT had been widely used in smart farming and greenhouse management and environmental monitoring, irrigation controlling, animal monitoring cold chain monitoring and tracking, and traceability, etc. This technology made the monitoring of agricultural product processing easier, automatic, effective and real-time, which greatly improved agricultural industrialization. Although there exist challenges in IoT applications, it has many benefits and it has some potential in increasing productivity and alleviate poverty. Some of the challenges IoT faces are: scalability, self-organizing, data volumes, data interpretation, interoperability, automatic discovery, software complexity, fault tolerance, power supply, wireless communication, security and privacy. At present, the demand for IoT is increasing rapidly, and its application in agricultural product processing is a new attempt for Ethiopia. The future works mainly focus on the following aspects:

1. Agricultural industrialization is one of the targets for Ethiopian Government and developing IoT-based framework model is the future work for each application in agricultural sectors.
2. Besides, adopting and developing full-fledged IoT based system which support agricultural industrialization in Ethiopia is also another future work.

References

1. Gebre-Selassie, A., Bekele, T.: A review of Ethiopian agriculture: roles, policy and small-scale farming systems. Ethiopia and DR Congo (2010)
2. Ethiopia Institute of Agricultural Research, Agricultural Mechanization Research. http://www.eiar.gov.et/index.php/agricultural-mechanization-research. Accessed 20 Feb 2019
3. Mohanraj, I., Ashokumar, K., Naren, J.: Field monitoring and automation using IOT in agriculture domain. Procedia Comput. Sci. **93**, 931–939 (2016)
4. Harivallabha, V. M., Anithamahalakshmi, I., Senthamizh Selvi, S.: A model to improve the reliability of ICT in agriculture. In: 2016 IEEE Technological Innovations in ICT for Agriculture and Rural Development (TIAR) (2016)
5. World Bank. ICT in Agriculture (Updated Edition): Connecting Smallholders to Knowledge, Networks, and Institutions. The World Bank (2017)
6. Talavera, J.M., et al.: Review of IoT applications in agro-industrial and environmental fields. Comput. Electron. Agric. **142**, 283–297 (2017)

7. Huang, B., Yao, Y.: Proceedings of the 5th International Conference on Electrical Engineering and Automatic Control. Springer, Heidelberg (2016). https://doi.org/10.1007/978-3-662-48768-6
8. Abd El-kader, S.M., Mohammad El-Basioni, B.M.: Precision farming solution in Egypt using the wireless sensor network technology. Egypt. Inform. J **14**(3), 221–233 (2013)
9. Nikolidakis, S.A., Kandris, D., Vergados, D.D., Douligeris, C.: Energy efficient automated control of irrigation in agriculture by using wireless sensor networks. Comput. Electron. Agric **113**, 154–163 (2015)
10. Li, D., Liu, Y., Chen, Y.: Computer and Computing Technologies in Agriculture IV: 4th IFIP TC 12 Conference, CCTA 2010, Nanchang, China, October 22–25, 2010, Selected Papers. Springer, Heidelberg (2011). https://doi.org/10.1007/978-3-642-18333-1
11. Chen, K., Zhang, H., Wu, T., Hu, J., Zhai, C., Wang, D.: Design of monitoring system for multilayer soil temperature and moisture based on WSN. In: 2014 International Conference on Wireless Communication and Sensor Network, pp. 425–430 (2014)
12. Yue, R., Ying, T.: A novel water quality monitoring system based on solar power supply & wireless sensor network. Procedia Environ. Sci. **12**, 265–272 (2012)
13. Fourati, M.A., Chebbi, W., Kamoun, A.: Development of a web-based weather station for irrigation scheduling. In: 2014 Third IEEE International Colloquium in Information Science and Technology (CIST) (2014)
14. Ehsan, S., et al.: Design and analysis of delay-tolerant sensor networks for monitoring and tracking free-roaming animals. IEEE Trans. Wirel. Commun. **11**(3), 1220–1227 (2012)
15. Jain, V.R., Bagree, R., Kumar, A., Ranjan, P.: wildCENSE: GPS based animal tracking system. In: 2008 International Conference on Intelligent Sensors, Sensor Networks and Information Processing (2008)
16. Khriji, S., Kanoun, O., El Houssaini, D., Viehweger, C., Jmal, M.W., Abid, M.: Precision irrigation based on wireless sensor network. IET Sci. Meas. Technol. **8**(3), 98–106 (2014)
17. Pahuja, R., Verma, H.K., Uddin, M.: A wireless sensor network for greenhouse climate control. IEEE Pervasive Comput. **12**(2), 49–58 (2013)
18. Luvisi, A., Triolo, E., Rinaldelli, E., Bandinelli, R., Pagano, M., Gini, B.: Radiofrequency applications in grapevine: from vineyard to web. Comput. Electron. Agric. **70**(1), 256–259 (2010)
19. Vellidis, G., Tucker, M., Perry, C., Kvien, C., Bednarz, C.: A real-time wireless smart sensor array for scheduling irrigation. Comput. Electron. Agric. **61**(1), 44–50 (2008)
20. Papetti, P., Costa, C., Antonucci, F., Figorilli, S., Solaini, S., Menesatti, P.: A RFID web-based infotracing system for the artisanal Italian cheese quality traceability. Food Control **27**(1), 234–241 (2012)
21. Wang, Z., Ye, T., Xiong, A.: Research of food traceability technology based on the internet of things name service. In: 2016 IEEE International Conference on Internet of Things (iThings) and IEEE Green Computing and Communications (GreenCom) and IEEE Cyber, Physical and Social Computing (CPSCom) and IEEE Smart Data (SmartData), pp. 100–106 (2016)
22. Abad, E., et al.: RFID smart tag for traceability and cold chain monitoring of foods: demonstration in an intercontinental fresh fish logistic chain. J. Food Eng. **93**(4), 394–399 (2009)
23. Amador, C., Emond, J.-P., do Nascimento Nunes, M.C.: Application of RFID technologies in the temperature mapping of the pineapple supply chain. Sens. Instrum. Food Qual. Saf. **3**(1), 26–33 (2009)
24. Kim, S., Lee, M., Shin, C.: IoT-based strawberry disease prediction system for smart farming. Sensors **18**(11), 4051 (2018)

25. Liakos, K., Busato, P., Moshou, D., Pearson, S., Bochtis, D.: Machine learning in agriculture: a review. Sensors **18**(8), 2674 (2018)
26. Zhao, J.-C., Zhang, J.-F., Feng, Y., Guo, J.-X.: The study and application of the IOT technology in agriculture. In: 2010 3rd International Conference on Computer Science and Information Technology (2010)
27. Stokes, P.: IoT applications in agriculture: the potential of smart farming on the current stage. Medium, 02 October 2018. https://medium.com/datadriveninvestor/iot-applications-in-agriculture-the-potential-of-smart-farmingon-the-current-stage-275066f946d8. Accessed 05 Feb 2019
28. IoT Applications in Agriculture—IoT For All. IoT For All, 03 January 2018. https://www.iotforall.com/iot-applications-in-agriculture/. Accessed 05 Feb 2019
29. Akkaş, M.A., Sokullu, R.: An IoT-based greenhouse monitoring system with Micaz motes. Procedia Comput. Sci. **113**, 603–608 (2017)
30. Nobrega, L., Tavares, A., Cardoso, A., Goncalves, P.: Animal monitoring based on IoT technologies. In: 2018 IoT Vertical and Topical Summit on Agriculture - Tuscany (IOT Tuscany) (2018)
31. Umstätter, C., Waterhouse, A., Holland, J.P.: An automated sensor-based method of simple behavioural classification of sheep in extensive systems. Comput. Electron. Agric. **64**(1), 19–26 (2008)
32. Williams, M.L., Mac Parthaláin, N., Brewer, P., James, W.P.J., Rose, M.T.: A novel behavioral model of the pasture-based dairy cow from GPS data using data mining and machine learning techniques. J. Dairy Sci. **99**(3), 2063–2075 (2016)
33. Kim, H., Oh, S., Ahn, S., Choi, B.: Real-time temperature monitoring to enhance estrus detection in cattle utilizing ingestible bio-sensors: method & case studies. J. Korean Inst. Inf. Technol. **15**(11), 65–75 (2017)
34. In, K., Lee, J., Xu, Z., Park, D., Chung, Y., Chang, H.-H.: Real-time vocalization aquisition and oestrus detection of Korean native cows. J. Korean Inst. Inf. Technol. **13**(12), 123 (2015)
35. Zubair, M., Hartmann, K., Loffeld, O.: Design and implementation of a wireless geophone sensor node for target detection and classification. In: Automatic Target Recognition XXII (2012)
36. Kaur, K.: The agriculture internet of things: a review of the concepts and implications of implementation. Int. J. Recent Trends Eng. Res. (IJRTER) **2**(04), 2–4 (2016)
37. Zeinab, K.A.M., Elmustafa, S.A.A.: Internet of things applications, challenges and related future technologies. World Sci. News **2**(67), 126–148 (2017)
38. Davies, R.: The Internet of Things opportunities and challenges. European Parliamentary Research Service (2015)
39. Mattern, F., Floerkemeier, C.: From the internet of computers to the internet of things. In: Sachs, K., Petrov, I., Guerrero, P. (eds.) From Active Data Management to Event-Based Systems and More. LNCS, vol. 6462, pp. 242–259. Springer, Heidelberg (2010). https://doi.org/10.1007/978-3-642-17226-7_15
40. Tzounis, A., Katsoulas, N., Bartzanas, T., Kittas, C.: Internet of Things in agriculture, recent advances and future challenges. Biosyst. Eng. **164**, 31–48 (2017)
41. Atzori, L., Iera, A., Morabito, G.: The internet of things: a survey. Comput. Netw. **54**(15), 2787–2805 (2010)
42. Kumar, S.A., Vealey, T., Srivastava, H.: Security in internet of things: challenges, solutions and future directions. In: 2016 49th Hawaii International Conference on System Sciences (HICSS) (2016)
43. Cook, R.: World Cattle Inventory: Ranking of countries (FAO). Drovers. https://www.drovers.com/article/world-cattle-inventory-ranking-countries-fao. Accessed 19 Feb 2019

Improvement of LEACH Protocol for Wireless Sensor Networks

Atallo Kassaw Takele[1(✉)], Towfik Jemal Ali[2],
and Kebebew Ababu Yetayih[2]

[1] Assosa University, Assosa, Ethiopia
atallo2116@gmail.com
[2] Jimma University, Jimma, Ethiopia
towfikjemal@gmail.com, kebebewss2@yahoo.com

Abstract. Wireless sensor networks are aggregates of large number of small, cheap, self-configured and low power sensor nodes. These nodes will sense, and gather various types of information from the environment or system and transmit the data to the base station for monitoring a system or an environment. However, they are characterized by limited resources (like battery, CPU and memory storage) because, they are small in size. Among those battery is a crucial issue, since they are deployed in remote locations. Most battery is consumed when a node sends data and when it routes where to send the data. Hence, energy efficient routing protocols have received significant research attention. This paper focuses on modifying LEACH protocol, which is a well-known energy efficient protocol for minimizing energy and overheads. On the first-round clusters will be formed as in the original LEACH protocol, then nodes will be scheduled for serving as a cluster head on each round turn by turn sequentially. The scheduled node will automatically be cluster head until two-third of its total energy is consumed. After two-third of the total energy has elapsed, re-clustering will be held in order to remove low powered nodes and dead nodes from the schedule. If the scheduled node dies before it serves as a cluster head, the successor scheduled node will serve. The proposed work has been evaluated comparatively using Castalia 3.3 simulator and it out performs the existing LEACH protocol.

Keywords: WSN · LEACH · Cluster-head selection · WSN routing · Scheduling

1 Introduction

In recent advances with micro electro-mechanical systems technology, wireless communications, and digital electronics, the design and development of low-cost, low-power, multi-functional sensor nodes that are small in size and communicate untethered in short distances have become feasible [1]. The ever-increasing capabilities of these tiny sensor nodes, which include sensing, data processing, and communicating, enable the realization of wireless sensor networks (WSNs) based on the collaborative effort of a large number of sensor nodes. Wireless sensor networks (WSN) are a collection of various nodes which consist of sensors, analog to digital converter (ADC),

© Springer Nature Switzerland AG 2019
F. Mekuria et al. (Eds.): ICT4DA 2019, CCIS 1026, pp. 250–259, 2019.
https://doi.org/10.1007/978-3-030-26630-1_21

micro-controller, memory, radio electronics and antenna, battery and dc-to-dc converter [2]. They are distributed embedded system consisting of large collection of short range collectively work together to monitor a system or an environment. These nodes will sense, and gather information from the environment or system and transmit the data to Base Station.

They are commonly used for military reconnaissance, vehicular movements, volcanic earthquake timing, weather forecasting, environment monitoring like temperature, humidity, pressure, motion, health care applications, etc.

As presented above wireless sensor networks are widely applicable in several areas in our lives, but they have limited resource such as battery, processing capacity, bandwidth and memory [8, 9]. Among those energy is an important resource in order to maximize the lifetime of the network. The replacement of batteries in the nodes is infeasible as most of WSN nodes are deployed normally in hostile and remote locations. Therefore, the node's battery energy drain should be considered while designing a routing protocol since routing process between nodes consumes a lot of energy which determines the network's lifetime [3, 4].

More work has been done to design energy efficient routing protocol for wireless sensor networks such as, PEGASIS [11], TEEN [6], LEACH [5], etc. But, still they have to be improved so as to make them more energy optimized and customized in specific application scenarios. This paper focus on the improvement of LEACH protocol. LEACH is a cluster based energy efficient routing protocol in which cluster head is elected and cluster are formed in the first phase and actual data communication is performed in the second phase in each round [5]. In this case selecting cluster heads and forming clusters in each round consumes time and energy. To minimize this overhead this paper applies a scheduling technique. On the first-round clusters will be formed as in the original LEACH protocol, then nodes will be scheduled for serving as a cluster head on each round turn by turn sequentially until two-third of the total energy will be elapsed.

The rest of the paper is organized as follows. Section 2 states about related works. Section 3 describe about the proposed work. Then Sect. 4 talks the simulation and evaluation of the proposed work and the last section concludes the proposed work.

2 Related Work

Low Energy Adaptive Clustering Hierarchy (LEACH) protocol uses hierarchical topology with which the data is aggregated and the same is sent to the BS. It is self-adaptive and self-organized. The nodes are divided into groups or clusters with uniform size, and a CH is elected for every cluster. The nodes collect physical phenomena related data and send the same to their respective CHs using TDMA schedule. If a node continues to remain as a CH, its energy is drained and the node dies sooner. In order to avoid such a situation, the CH role is rotated after each round of operation. A node forwards the data to its CH and the CH gathers the data from each node supported by it and the CH computes the aggregate of the collected data and the same is forwarded to the BS [5].

Much improvement has been done to overcome the drawbacks of LEACH protocol. Some works are done to make it multi-hop by considering the drawbacks of distance from the base station to the cluster-heads and others are done on single-hop as it is by considering other parameters like energy, way of cluster-head election, etc. Some of them are summarized as follows;

Authors in [8], proposed another improvement on LEACH by introducing an energy efficient Cluster Head (CH) selection considering the energy and distance as parameters. The probability function is modified with the energy and distance metrics to choose energy efficient CH for data transmission. In addition to probability function score function is introduced which is calculated from distance between the base station and the sensor nodes and residual energy. This paper tries to consider the two important parameters (distance and residual energy) but sensor nodes will have more overhead in order to calculate and exchange distance and residual energy for each round.

Authors in [9], tries to minimize advertisement packets of LEACH protocol to form the cluster in each round. But in this approach sensor nodes will send or receive the control packets when it changes the state. This approach considers the energy thresh-hold of the cluster-head to inform the cluster-head, it will no longer be used, initial formation of the cluster to elect the cluster-head, joining of sensor nodes through handshaking and sensor node leaving the cluster. But, if much number of cluster-head have frequent thresh-hold messages there will be frequent formation of cluster hence it will consume extra resource.

Authors in [10], proposed IL-LEACH to suppress the correlated data transmission inside the cluster. This approach assumes that we know location of the sensor nodes. The solution focuses to reduce the data transmissions based on grouping of sensor nodes into a virtual correlated cluster (VCC). The grouping is done based on calculation of a threshold sensing coverage (TSC) and Euclidean distance. Then, on the basis of residual energy of each sensor node, one of the nodes is selected to transmit data from the group. In LEACH the nodes send data based on TDMA schedule made by the cluster head. In this method IL-LEACH all the nodes that are selected to be in a same VCC (virtual correlated cluster) are given same TDMA so that only one of them sends their data to the cluster head.

Gambhir and Parul in [7], proposed OE-LEACH that aims to minimize the energy west during idle listening state. There are many situations where the sensor nodes do not have data to send regularly as they may be event driven. In that case, data are available only when they sense the event. So, the sensor nodes need not to listen the channel at all times. Energy is wasted more on idle listening than that dissipated in transmitting and receiving. Slots are not allocated to the nodes which have no data to send and free slots are converted into useful slots. This will reduce the idle listening problem. This method will decrease the waiting time for nodes as now sensor nodes can get more than one slot in a frame which means throughput of the network increases. But it does not consider the residual energy while selecting cluster heads.

Authors in [4], proposed an improved multipath leach protocol which uses at most one intermediate cluster head. LEACH sends data from the Cluster-Head to the sink directly. Thus, the necessary energy for transmitting data is high. Even more, if the sink is too far the transmission is impossible and the data is lost. The aim of this protocol is to extend the lifetime of the network and send more data compared to the original protocol. It uses only one intermediate cluster head hence it is not scalable for large networks.

In this we have reviewed related works that have been done by different scholars on enhancing LEACH protocol, to conserve energy consumption of wireless sensor networks. Some of them considers parameters like residual energy and distance, minimization of advertisement packets, scheduling densely deployed nodes by turning each node on and off alternatively and optimal cluster head selection. Others made an enhancement on shifting from single hop to multiple hop approach. But, none of them consider minimizing overhead by eliminating unnecessary advertisement messages. The proposed work focuses on improving the battery consumption and delays while nodes select cluster heads and form clusters on each round by scheduling cluster heads for avoiding bulk re-clustering advertisement messages.

3 Proposed Approach

In this paper, we have proposed a modified LEACH routing algorithm in order to minimize energy consumption. The new approach tries to minimize the over-head of selecting cluster head and cluster formation on each round. On the first round, clusters will be formed and nodes will be scheduled to become a cluster head for the next rounds. The first cluster head is elected randomly like the original LEACH and non-cluster heads join the cluster head in order to form the cluster. After the cluster is fully formed, the cluster head schedules cluster heads for the next rounds.

Once the first cluster head schedules the next round cluster heads, the scheduled node will automatically be cluster head until two-third of its total energy is consumed. After two-third of the total energy is elapsed, re-clustering will be held in order to remove low powered nodes and remove dead nodes from the schedule. Then, re-clustering will continue after all members serve as cluster head at least once. Re-clustering process helps to regroup alive nodes and to remove dead nodes from the cluster member cache. Before, re-clustering residual energy of individual nodes will be checked, to decide a cluster-head within at least one next group of rounds. Hence, the cluster-head scheduling removes the over-head of cluster-head advertisement message to get members, join request message to the cluster-head and computation for electing cluster-heads. If the scheduled node dies before it serves as a cluster head, the successor scheduled node will serve.

According to the working process of LEACH, there are several communication patterns for nodes. With those patterns, the energy consumption of nodes can be classified into two parts according to their roles, as demonstrated in Table 1 [12]. In this model broadcast CH message, receive join message from non-CH and send acknowledgement message to non-CH will be eliminated after forming cluster within each group of rounds at the cluster-head. Similarly, receive CH advertisement message and send join request message to CH will also be eliminated at the member nodes. Energy consumption of the proposed model after each group of rounds is demonstrated in Table 2.

Table 1. Energy consumption of nodes in leach algorithm [14].

CH energy consumption	Broadcast CH message
	Receive join message from non CH
	Send acknowledgement message to non-CH (TDMA schedule)
	Receive data from non CH
	Send aggregated data to BS
Non CH energy consumption	Receive CH advertisement message
	Send join request message to CH and receive TDMA schedule
	Send data to CH

Table 2. Energy consumption of nodes in modified leach algorithm after each group of round.

CH energy consumption	Send TDMA schedule to member nodes
	Receive data from member nodes
	Send aggregated data to BS
Non CH energy consumption	Receive TDMA schedule from the CH
	Send data to CH

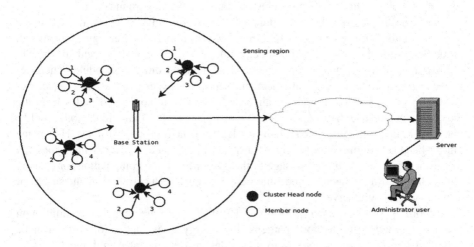

Fig. 1. Topological Architecture of the proposed work

The topology of the proposed work includes member nodes, cluster-head nodes, sink node, server node and an administrator user as shown in the Fig. 1. The sensed data flows from member node to the administrator user. Member nodes send the sensed information to the cluster-head. The cluster-head will aggregate the data that comes from its members, then it will pass to the sink node. Since the sink node is assumed to have enough resource it encapsulates the aggregated data and will send to the main server. The administrator will process the sensed data that comes from the sensor nodes to make a certain useful decision.

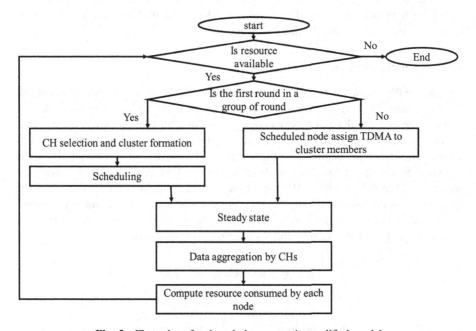

Fig. 2. Flow chart for the whole process in modified model

Figure 2, shows the flow chart of the proposed algorithm. First it checks if enough resource (energy) is available or not. If enough energy is available, it will again check whether it is the first round in a group of round. If it is the first round in a group of round, new cluster will be formed and cluster head scheduling will be held. Group of rounds refers a collection of rounds that all members of the cluster serve as a cluster head at most once and the time from the starting until two third of the total energy consumed is considered as on group of round.

4   Simulation and Evaluation

To evaluate the performance of the proposed model, we have conducted simulation experiment using a simulation tool. Simulator tools are effective tools to evaluate algorithms and protocols at design, development and implementation stages. A number of these tools are available each with different features, characteristics, models and architectures for performance testing in WSNs. Some of these are NS2, OMNeT++ and TOSSIM [13, 14].

Among those we have selected OMNeT++ simulator with Castalia framework for the following reasons. First, Castalia supports networks of low-power embedded devices such as WSNs. Second, it can be utilized to test the distributed algorithms and protocols in realistic radio models and wireless channel. Third, Castalia embraces additional features such as: several popular routing protocols and MAC protocols, a model for temporal variation of path loss, and RSSI calculation, which can provide more convincing and accurate simulation results [13].

4.1 Simulation Result and Discussion

We assume that initial energy for all nodes is identical. All nodes are active as long as they have enough energy to communicate and every node can reach to the sink. We also assume that one third of residual energy is enough for running at least one round. Table 3 presents simulation parameters used in the simulation. In this simulation 100 sensor nodes has been deployed in the surface of 100×100 m^2 for about 100 s. As stated in [5], the optimal number of cluster heads in LEACH protocol is 5% that why we make CH probability 0.05. We have executed the simulation for 10 times and the base station is deployed statically at (1,1). For the first scenario, we made 1 configuration and multiple configurations has been done by varying simulation time and number of nodes for the second and third scenarios respectively.

Table 3. Simulation parameter list

No.	Parameter list	Specified
1	Simulation time	100 s
2	Topology size	100×100 m^2
3	Number of nodes	100
4	CH probability	0.05
5	Number of trials	10
6	Position of base station	(1,1)
7	Number configuration	1
8	Slot length	0.2 s

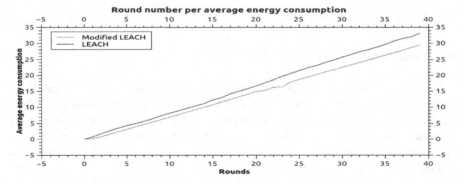

Fig. 3. Energy consumption of the modified and existing protocols on each round

Average consumed energy of the proposed model and the existing model per each round is depicted in Fig. 3. The figure clearly shows that energy consumed per each round in the modified protocol is lower than that of the existing protocol. As we go from the first round to the end the gap between the new and the original protocol increases, which enhances the network life time.

Figure 4, depicts that there is an inclination in average consumed energy with an increase in simulation time in both of the existing and modified protocol. However, the gap between the two graphs increases as the simulation time increases. Hence, as the simulation time increases the average energy consumption of the modified protocol decreases. This will enhance the lifetime of the network.

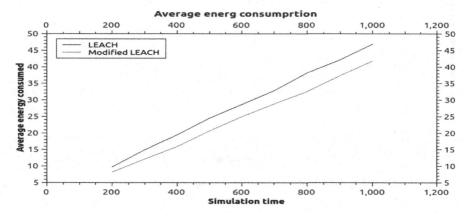

Fig. 4. Simulation result by varying simulation time

Figure 5, shows number of packets received per node to the base station. As the graph shows the proposed model has better performance than the existing model.

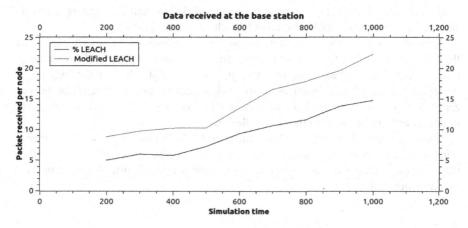

Fig. 5. Packets received per node with varying simulation time

Figure 6, shows the average consumed energy of both the existing and modified protocol as the number of nodes increases. As clearly shown from the graph the average consumed energy of the modified protocol is proportionally lower than that of the existing protocol. Therefore, the proposed protocol is energy efficient within different network sizes.

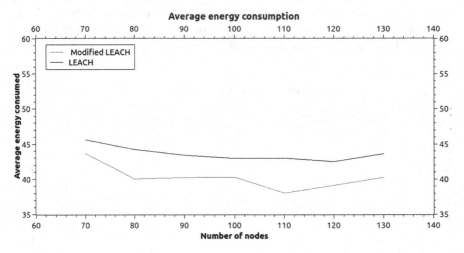

Fig. 6. Simulation result by varying number of nodes

5   Conclusion

Wireless sensor networks are formed from small self-powered devices, consisting of one or more sensors, a microprocessor and one or several radio transceivers. The sensors include an analog-to-digital converter, and the microprocessor can be a micro-controller or a low power processor. The sensor node uses an energy source, usually with very limited capacity. Wireless sensor networks are self-configuring networks since, they are mostly deployed randomly without careful planning.

In wireless sensor networks, energy is an important resource in order to maximize the life time of nodes; they are also characterized by limited CPU and low memory storage. Replacing the battery of the sensor nodes is also difficult since they are mostly deployed in difficult areas such as in forests for sensing fire, in deserts for sensing earthquake, etc. Hence, we have to consider battery consumption while we design protocols and applications to the sensor devices.

This paper puts forward an enhancement on LEACH routing protocol in order to minimize energy consumption and unnecessary over-heads. Modification is applied on the selection of cluster-heads, by scheduling members to be a cluster-head for the next rounds sequentially.

Finally, we have implemented and evaluated the modified protocol using OMNeT++ simulator with Castalia framework. Simulation result shows that the proposed model out performs the existing protocol in terms of energy consumption and the number of packets received by the base station.

References

1. Akyildiz, I.F., Vuran, M.C.: Wireless Sensor Networks. Wiley, Chichester (2010)
2. Kodali, R.K., Kiran A., V.S., Bhandari, S., Boppana, L.: Energy efficient m-level LEACH protocol. IEEE (2015)
3. Sony, C.T., Sangeetha, C.P., Suriyakala, C.D.: Multi-hop LEACH protocol with modified cluster head selection and TDMA schedule for wireless sensor networks. IEEE (2015)
4. Bennani, M., Taj, M., Kbir, M.A.: ICH-LEACH: an enhanced LEACH protocol for wireless sensor network. IEEE (2016)
5. Heinzelman, W.R., Chandrakasan, A., Balakrishnan, H.: Energy-efficient communication protocol for wireless microsensor networks. In: Published in the Proceedings of the Hawaii International Conference on System Sciences, Maui, Hawaii, 4–7 January 2000 (2000)
6. Manjeshwar, A., Agrawal, D.: TEEN: a protocol for enhanced efficiency in wireless sensor networks. In: Proceedings of the 1st International Workshop on Parallel and Distributed Computing Issues in Wireless Networks and Mobile Computing, San Francisco (2001)
7. Gambhir, S., Parul: OE-LEACH: an optimized energy efficient LEACH algorithm for WSNs. IEEE (2016)
8. Amirthalingam, K., Anuratha, D.: Improved LEACH: a modified LEACH for wireless sensor network. IEEE (2016)
9. Bharti, A., Devi, C., Bhatia, D.V.: Enhanced energy efficient LEACH (EEE - LEACH) algorithm using MIMO for wireless sensor network. IEEE (2015)
10. Kandpal, R., Singh, R.: Improving lifetime of wireless sensor networks by mitigating correlated data using LEACH protocol. IEEE (2016)
11. Lindsey, S., Raghavendra, C.: PEGASIS: power efficient gathering in sensor information systems. In: Proceedings of the IEEE Aerospace Conference, Big Sky, Montana (2002)
12. Luo, F., Jiang, C., Zhang, H., Wang, X., Zhang, L., Ren, Y.: Node energy consumption analysis in wireless sensor networks. IEEE (2014)
13. Chhimwal, P., Rai, D.S., Rawat, D.: Comparison between different wireless sensor simulation tools. IOSR-JECE 5, 54–60 (2013)
14. Korkalainen, M., Sallinen, M., Kärkkäinen, N., Tukeva, P.: Survey of wireless sensor networks simulation tools for demanding applications. IEEE (2009)

Towards a Design Research Model for Climate Services: Experiences from a Development Project in Mozambique

Jaakko Helminen[1(✉)], António José Leão[2], Ville Myllynpää[1], Silvia Gaiani[1], Mikko Apiola[1], and Erkki Sutinen[1]

[1] University of Turku, Turku, Finland
{jaakko.a.helminen,ville.myllynpaa,mvapio,
erkki.sutinen}@utu.fi, silviagaiani@yahoo.it
[2] Eduardo Mondlane University, Maputo, Mozambique
ajleao62@gmail.com

Abstract. As one part of our research efforts and exploration in Africa, we have visited the Chokwe Irrigation System area in Mozambique in order to develop hybrid grass-root mobile climate services for and with local farmers to support their cultivation practices. The lessons learned along the explorations inspired us to elaborate an appropriate design research framework for the particular action design research process, which would facilitate us to develop holistic grass-root mobile climate services for local farmers in a developing country. The main outcome of the study was the updated design research framework for the task.

Keywords: Climate Change · Mobile technology · Design Science Research

1 Introduction

With the ongoing climate change and changes in climate variability we encounter quite a variety of climate impacts affecting everyday life, especially in a developing countries. In terms of the design science framework introduced by Hevner et al. [1] as a milestone of the topic we may ask whether we can apply it, when we in a participatory way with local partners co-create climate services appropriate for end-users. Following the design thinking paradigm [2, 3] we started our work with its first stage – empathy within the inspiration space. We acted based on the recommendations of Brown [2], who suggests that the intention during an empathy stage in a project is to experience a problem or opportunity that sets researchers in motion.

We started our project by exploring local climate services and background information in Chókwè District, Mozambique. We had joined a pre-negotiated program, where we had to adjust our tasks to the overall objectives of the program. Still, this arrangement left us with the required freedom to explore pertinent problems as well as opportunities to build an appropriate design research framework.

In the following we briefly describe the situation at the time of our field trip to Chókwè, Mozambique, during August - December 2011. Then we discuss how we processed parts of the interview material and how recent international agreements

© Springer Nature Switzerland AG 2019
F. Mekuria et al. (Eds.): ICT4DA 2019, CCIS 1026, pp. 260–269, 2019.
https://doi.org/10.1007/978-3-030-26630-1_22

[4–8], including agenda for humanity [4], and UN Framework Convention on Climate Change [8], which steered our efforts. Thereafter we show relevant results of the interviews as well as the induced inspirations to tune the Design Science Research framework of Hevner et al. [1] so that we can apply it to develop appropriate hybrid [9] grass-root mobile climate services for local farmers in Chókwè District. In the conclusions we share these inspirations with the readers.

2 Project Consortium

In the context of "Programme of cooperation in Science, Technology and Innovation between Finland and Mozambique" (STIFIMO), we established a joint project "Development of innovative community climate services for agriculture in Chókwè District" (DICCLISEAG) with the Mozambique National Meteorology Institute (INAM) as our local host and together with the District Services of Economic Activities of the Chokwe District Administration (SDAE/CDA), South Zone Center of the Mozambican Institute of Agricultural Research (CZS/IIAM) as well as Instituto Superior Politéchnico de Gaza (ISPG), (Polytechnic Institute of Gaza in English).

3 Trends, Evolutions, and Challenges of the Chókwè Irrigation System and Its Surroundings

The authors of [10–13] discussed the history and present stage of the Chókwè Irrigation System (CIS) and its vicinity. The evolution of events led to a situation, where the government of Mozambique favored large-scale rice cultivation in CIS at the expense of land ownership by local smallholder farmers [11, 12]. In addition, the local historical and social dynamics contributed to gender imbalance towards women. Conflicts between them and the CIS administrator, A Hidráulica do Chokwe, E.P. (HICEP) [10] led to a further weakening of the status of local smallholder farmers.

Chókwè District is a semi-arid region in the flat Limpopo drainage delta area. More upstream there are large elevation differences and also some reservoirs of limited capacity along the route of the Limpopo river. The volume of the reservoirs is not adequate to damp downstream effects of heavy rain episodes in the upper reaches of Limpopo drainage. Hence Chókwè District as part of Limpopo delta area is prone to relatively frequent recurring flash floods, which in the recent past have caused severe disasters, also in CIS.

As climate, its change and the changes in its variability are pertinent factors in the semi-arid region of Chókwè District, it became clear to us that local people, typically smallholder farmers, needed appropriately tailored climate services for actions to improve their baseline and livelihood in a sustainable manner.

In our research, we drew inspiration from the increasing recognition of the social dynamics in climate issues. The World Humanitarian Summit (WHS) 2016 released the Agenda for Humanity (AH) [4] with its five core responsibilities. In his WHS Chief's Summary the then UN Secretary-General Ban Ki-Moon urged the nations to stand up for the humanity and to commit themselves to action [5]. In the context of core responsibility four "Change people's lives – From delivering aid to ending need" its roundtable five discussion under the theme "Natural Disasters and Climate Change: Managing risks and crises differently" [6] led to five core commitments related to climate issues as follows: implement the related strategies, reinforce national and local management, invest in climate services, build community resilience, and ensure regional and global humanitarian assistance.

4 Data and Methods

4.1 Research Question

Based on the community's crucial needs for tailored climate services to improve their livelihood in a sustainable manner, we sought to gain baseline information about current needs, strengths, infrastructure, ICT usage patterns, and climate information sources. We set the research question as follows:

What are the current baselines for crucial information needs, current strengths, infrastructure, skillsets, climate information, and mobile usage patterns in Chókwè District?

In our reflection of the results, we sought to find pertinent additional local issues to environment, IS research and knowledge base columns of the design science research framework of Hevner et al. [1] to tune it for the development of holistic grass-root mobile climate services for local smallholder farmers of Chókwè District.

4.2 Questionnaire and Processing Responses

For the general interviews in Chókwè District we used a questionnaire as our data collection protocol. Group interviews were conducted, thus one response in the questionnaire represented one group. After the interviews had been conducted we scrutinized the responses and took into account the parts we considered to be relevant for the task of our research question. The questionnaire consisted of a general part and specific sections covering agriculture, climate and ICT items. The objective of the interview was to find out both strengths and gaps in baseline items pertinent to the hybrid approach of the project.

Based on recommendations of our partners, we initiated the project by making group interviews and conducting surveys in five communities (acronyms in parentheses); Lionde (**L**), Chókwè (**S**) and Chilembene (**B**), all within the CIS area. The remaining communities Macino (**M**) and Chekelane (**A**) were outside of CIS. In the large farm premises of two foreign agribusiness companies Mozfoods Industrias Alimentares (**MIA**), inside CIS, and EmWest (**EW**), close to the northwestern end of CIS, we surveyed and discussed their automatic weather stations. In the results, one answer represents one community.

5   Results

5.1   Quality of Life

In regard to quality of life the communities responded on a scale of "excellent", "good", "fair" and "bad". One community considered their life to be "Good" (B), two communities "Fair" (S and M) and two communities "Bad" (L and A). Thus, there were two modes (Mo), "Fair" and "Bad".

5.2   Prominent Main Needs

In regard to the main needs of the communities, the following responses were given. All five communities mentioned the need for farm equipments, including ploughs, tractors and water pumps. Four communities mentioned the need for seeds and electricity (L, S, M and A). Two communities mentioned also the need for water and cows (L and A). Individual communities mentioned access to credit, transport, hospital and channel renovation as their main needs. As a secondary need, three communities mentioned local schools.

5.3   Sources of Help

When asked if any organizations were currently addressing their prominent main needs, only two communities had received help in meeting their needs. Community (L) had got an offer from the agribusiness company Mozfoods Industrias Alimentares (MIA) to provide improved maize seeds, but as a part of that deal they would need to sell the yield to them at their price. In addition, community (B) had received two excavators, which were donated by HICEP, but there is still need for additional excavators and other machinery.

5.4   Evaluation of Infrastructure

In regard to evaluation of infrastructure, on a scale of "Good", "Acceptable" and "Not Good" interviewees gave the following responses. In regards of both *irrigation systems,* as well as *marketing services,* all five communities ranked them as "Not good". Four communities (L, S, M and A) ranked *roads, means of transportation,* and *housing* as "Not good", three communities (L, S, and B) ranked *schools* as "Not good". One community (A) ranked *health centers* as "Not good", while three communities (L, S and B) ranked *health centers* as "Acceptable". Two communities ranked (M and A) *schools* as "Acceptable". *Roads* (B), *housing* (B), *availability of electricity* (B) and *means of transportation* (M) where all ranked as acceptable by one (n = 1) community. Only one community (M) ranked one part of infrastructure as "good", which was the *health centers.* Thus, the communities had a relatively negative perception about most infrastructure items in the questionnaire.

5.5   Expectations for the Future

In regard to expectations for the future, communities' responses where mainly related to the *ability to grow various plants and keep livestock*. One community (L) wants to *cultivate maize and vegetables*, while one community (S) wanted to *cultivate rice* and *larger quantities of vegetables,* such as tomatoes, cabbages, beans and onions. Community B wanted to *develop agricultural practices* by cultivating larger areas and keeping livestock, such as cows, pigs and goats. Another community (M) wanted to develop agricultural practices, cultivate potatoes and tomatoes, keep cows and be able to sell various agricultural products including meat. Community A wanted to cultivate peanuts, small beans, cassava, potatoes and pineapples. In additional all communities reported that they would like to have *better machines, knowledge* and *orange plants*. Also, many of the interviewees in community A affirmed that they would like to start cashew nut production and to get a better and bigger storage facility for processing cashew nuts.

5.6   Malnutrition Situation

When asked if their families had run out of money to buy food in the past 30 days, the following answers where received. Representatives from two communities (L and S) replied that it had happened often (=more than 5 days), whereas representatives from three other communities (B, M and A) replied that it had happened only sometimes (=between 1 to 5 days).

5.7   Cultivation Practices

In regard to cultivation responses of the communities brought up following problems. Two communities (L and S) mentioned that the *irrigation system was not functioning well* and there were *not enough available tractors and other machines for seeding, harvesting and transport*. S community also pointed out that *uneven regulation of water channels* could cause issues. Other community (B) pointed out the *lack of fertilizers, poor water quality and the lack of credit* as well as *marketing efforts*, while another community (M) faced *issues with land preparation, plant diseases and problems with wild animals*. One community (A) also complained that *plant diseases were out of control* and there was a *lack of saws to cut trees*.

5.8   Production Constraints

In terms of production constrains, the following responses we given by the communities. Three communities (L, S and A) mentioned *lack of rain*, two of them (L and S) mentioned also *lack of credit*. Two communities (S and M) mentioned *lack of transportation* and *poor market conditions* as well as *very low prices*. Community B referred to their answer for the previous question.

5.9   Suggestions for Changes in Community

In regard to *suggestions for changes in the community*, this was presented as an open-ended question. The responses given by the informants were, in most cases, related to *availability of agriculture inputs, equipment* and *construction of various facilities.* Two communities (L and S) proposed to have better *availability of tractors, fertilizers, seeds* and *finances.* One community (B) suggested to have an *agro-center*, while another (M) proposed to have a *cooling house with needed transportation equipment.* One community (A) proposed to have a *borehole based irrigation system.*

5.10   Past and Present Climate Hazards

When asked how severe the impacts of climate hazards to their crops are, all communities uniformly answered that they are severe. In regard to local responses to climate hazards, all communities again uniformly assessed them to be fair.

5.11   Suggestions to Improve Local Responses

When asked how to improve local responses to climate hazards, communities' responses varied quite much. Two communities (L and S) suggested to *update knowledge on hazards and their occurrence.* One community (B) suggested to *establish their own weather station*, whereas another community (M) proposed that *each community should have its own leader.* Community A anticipated that once their own irrigation system would be established, problems could become more manageable. Another option would be to move farms to more humid areas.

5.12   Access to Climate and Weather Information

In terms of access to seasonal meteorological and agro-meteorological forecasts, three communities (L, S and A) had no idea where to get that information, whereas two communities (B and M) knew that Radio Mozambique broadcasts those information.

This same ignorance applied also to weather and climate services, since all the other communities were unaware of their existence, expect community S, which mentioned radio and TV.

5.13   ICT Ownership

In regard to ownership of ICT technologies, most commonly owned technologies were mobile phones (63 out of 80 responses), radios (9 responses) and TV (7 responses). Both computer and video-TV got one response.

5.14   Most Often Used ICT

Most used technologies in the communities were mobile phones, in addition community S used TV and community S used radio. Community M did not respond to this question.

5.15   Willingness to Contribute to the ICT Development in Your Village

In regard to being interested to contribute to developing/implementing some ICT uses in their village, the following answers were obtained. Community L did not know and community S did not answer. Community M just said "yes", without further elaboration, while community M said that they could help spread the information. Community A said that a local weather station is needed, as well as other equipment's and education.

6   Discussion

In terms of our research question we focus on items pertinent to the tuning of Hevner design research framework [1]. According to the general questions (Sects. 5.1–5.9) the administrative practices of the government steered the small-scale farmers to limit their efforts and co-operation among families, neighbors and, outside of the CIS, also among communities. In these circumstances the smallholder farmers remained poor and underdeveloped, as observed by [14]. The organizations, which addressed these needs to some extent, were MIA and HICEP (Sect. 5.3). For its conditional help in terms of seeds provision MIA kept the right to buy the total crop yield by the price it settled. The farmers of B pointed out their local needs for CIS channel maintenance. The needs for facilities were considerably bigger than the help received from HICEP. Mr. Mugabe of SDAE/CDA said that the whole CIS was in a demand of renovation. The lack of systematic help to smallholder farmers was in line with the preferences of the government to favor large-scale foreign investments and actions. Hence the administrative practices should be included in the environment column of the design research framework.

Another important point inspired by almost all shown responses was the need to establish increasing willingness for open, hybrid, constructive and trans-disciplinary cooperation across the whole society. This aspect should be brought into the environment column of a design model. The surveys and replies in regard to Sects. 5.7–5.9 on farming indicated that the way farming practices had been organized by the big farms (MIA and EW) could give pertinent ideas for the local farmer communities on how to organize their facilities and activities. The answers in Sect. 5.11 spread widely. Regarding Sects. 5.10 and 5.11 one pertinent reaction among farmers was the need to improve their own knowledge of floods and draughts and their occurrence. According to Sect. 5.12 the local smallholder farmers did not know anything about weather and climate services. This indicated lack of knowledge in agricultural practices and in basic climate concepts and led us to replace capacities by capacity building in the environment column.

With the surveyed widespread use of mobile phones it was encouraging to recognize that in communication we could rely on modern devices and networks. In addition (Sect. 5.15) many interviewees indicated their interest to develop and implement ICT uses in their village, although they lacked capacities and know-how.

Many responses indicated that the baseline of livelihood and the abilities to meet impacts of climate hazards were inadequate. To improve the general awareness of the communities we suggest baseline to be included in the knowledge base column. In the context of administrative practices we highly suggest that legislation as well as historical, political and social dynamics are actively kept into consideration.

All in all we could say that the interviewees were aware of the impacts of climate variability in their everyday life in farming issues. However, the awareness of basic climate service concepts and communication skills were inadequate if not non-existent. Hence the lack of knowledge about climate and climate services (Sects. 5.10, 5.11, 5.12) proposes us to emphasize the role of climate knowledge [15] in the context of the baseline in the knowledge base column.

As many of the past flash floods have had severe impacts on the CIS area (Sect. 5.10) proper dimension values e.g. for additional reservoirs upstream from the Limpopo delta area would give a good base for actions to prevent these impacts to occur. Hence also the need of proper dimension values should be emphasized in the context of the baseline in the knowledge base column.

The interviews and assessment of social behavior, like motivation and trust, must be included in the knowledge base column in the design models. With the ongoing climate change and changes in climate variability we used for expert prototype interviews the twelve question set of Critical Systems Heuristics (CSH) [16] and found this approach promising. We suggest heuristics to be part of the knowledge base column.

As we have suggested open, holistic, constructive and trans-disciplinary cooperation across the whole society, we propose synthesis to be added to the justify/evaluate the slot of the IS research column.

With the addition of willingness for an open, hybrid and constructive cooperation, the list of revised and added suggestions to the environment column of the design research framework is as follows:

- capacity building,
- administrative practices as well as
- cooperation.

  and to the foundations of the knowledge base column

- baseline as well as
- heuristics.

7 Conclusions

ISPG together with us submitted a proposal to STIFIMO for the project to prepare and discuss the project at the final DICCLISEAG assembly. Due to lack of open, hybrid and constructive cooperation and misunderstandings between local institutes and ministries the proposal was turned down. We were left with our first lesson. Finally, we come to our lesson learned, which can be put in a nutshell as depicted in Fig. 1.

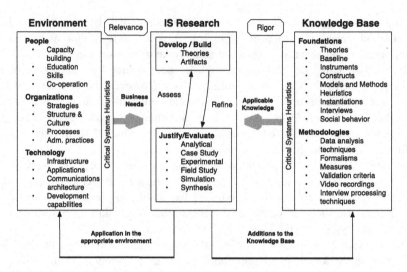

Fig. 1. Elaborated design research framework, based on [1, 16].

Both the environment and knowledge base have in front of them the filter "Critical Systems Heuristics" (CSH) of Ulrich and Reynolds [16]. In essence CSH refers to its twelve question set, through which the suggestions for business needs and applicable knowledge are scrutinized before they enter the IS research column.

Regarding the people in the environment column we have replaced capacities with capacity building not to omit the importance of capacities but to emphasize the needs to replace their lack with capacity building. We have also added co-operation to the essential qualities we expect people to have. As for organizations we found administrative practices to be scrutinized and also followed up.

To the foundations of the knowledge base we added heuristics with the need to take into account increasingly hectic changes in the whole system of systems. We renamed the concept frameworks by baseline in order to widen the scope in system considerations, like climate impacts.

With these updates our first lesson turned out to be quite valuable so that we are now ready to proceed with considerations of our Systems Action Design Research (SADR) in our future projects.

References

1. Hevner, A.R., March, S.T., Park, J., Ram, S.: Design science in information systems research. MIS Q. **28**(1), 75–105 (2004)
2. Brown, T.: Change by Design: How Design Thinking Transforms Organizations and Inspires Innovation. HarperCollins, New York (2009)
3. Both, T.: Design Project Scoping Guide. Hasso Plattner Institute of Design at Stanford, Stanford University, Palo Alto, California, USA (2016). Open Access: https://dschool.stanford.edu/resources/design-project-guide-1

4. Agenda for humanity. Agenda for Humanity Annex to the Report of the Secretary-General for the World Humanitarian Summit (A/70/709, 2 February 2016). United Nations (UN) Office for the Coordination of Humanitarian Affairs, New York, USA (2016). Open Access: https://www.agendaforhumanity.org/agendaforhumanity

5. World Humanitarian Summit. Chair's Summary by the United Nations Secretary-General: Standing up for Humanity: Committing to Action," in World Humanitarian Summit (WHS), Chair's Summary, Istanbul, Turkey (2016a). Open Access: https://www.unocha.org/sites/dms/Documents/Chairs Summary.pdf

6. World Humanitarian Summit. Natural Disasters and Climate Change: Managing Risks & Crises Differently. In: WHS, Key Documents – High-Level Leaders' Round Tables – Core Commitments (2016b). Open Access: http://whsturkey.org/the-summit/key-documents-for-whs

7. United Nations. Transforming our world: the 2030 Agenda for Sustainable Development A/RES/70/1. Resolution adopted by the General Assembly on 25 September 2015 (A/RES/70/1), UN, New York, USA (2015). Open Access: https://sustainabledevelopment.un.org/content/documents/21252030 Agenda for Sustainable Development web.pdf

8. United Nations Framework Convention on Climate Change. Report of the Conference of the Parties on its twenty-first session, held in Paris from 30 November to 13 December 2015. FCCC/CP/2015/10/Add.1, UN, New York, USA (2016). Open Access: https://unfccc.int/process/conferences/pastconferences/paris-climate-change-conference-november-2015/paris-agreement

9. Heeks, R.: Information systems and developing countries: failure, success, and local improvisations. Inf. Soc. **18**(2), 101–112 (2002). https://doi.org/10.1080/01972240290075039

10. Pellizoli, R.: 'Green revolution' for whom? Women's access to and use of land in the Mozambique Chókwè irrigation scheme. Rev. Afr. Polit. Econ. **37**(124), 213–220 (2010)

11. Veldwish, G.J., Beekman, W., Bolding, A.: Smallholder irrigators, water rights and investments in agriculture: three cases from rural Mozambique. Water Altern. **6**(1), 125–141 (2013)

12. van der Struijk, L.F.: Smallholders' strategies in response to contract farming programs in Chokwe, Mozambique – farmers' reactions to the process of relocation of land and water access in the Chokwe Irrigation System. Master thesis, Water Resources Management in International Land and Water Management, Wageningen University, The Netherlands (2013)

13. Veldwisch, G.J.: Contract farming and the reorganization of agricultural production within the Chókwè Irrigation System, Mozambique. J. Peasant Stud. (2015). https://doi.org/10.1080/03066150.2014.991722

14. Kojo, A., Chichava, S.: South-south cooperation, agribusiness, and African agricultural development: Brazil and China in Ghana and Mozambique. World Dev. **81**, 13–23 (2016). https://doi.org/10.1016/j.worlddev.2015.11.021

15. Meinke, H., Nelson, R., Kokic, P., Stone, R., Selvaraju, R., Baethgen, W.: Actionable climate knowledge – from analysis to synthesis. Clim. Res. **33**, 101–110 (2006). www.int-res.com/articles/cr_oa/c033p101.pdf

16. Ulrich, W., Reynolds, M.: Critical systems heuristics. In: Reynolds, M., Holwell, S. (eds.) Systems Approaches to Managing Change: A Practical Guide, pp. 243–292. Springer, London (2010). https://doi.org/10.1007/978-1-84882-809-4_6. Link to the chapter http://oro.open.ac.uk/21299/1/systems-approaches

An Efficient Security Implementation with Power Cane for Visually Challenged

J. Saravanan[1], A. Clement Raj[1(✉)], Raushan Kumar Singh[2], and Ararso Taye[1]

[1] Bule Hora University, Bule Hora, Ethiopia
saravanan.j2k@gmail.com, clementlecturer@gmail.com,
arstay19@gmail.com
[2] Spectrum Solutions, Pondicherry, India
spectrumsolutions.md@gmail.com

Abstract. Eyes considered as the most precious organ of the human body, being blind is considered one of the biggest physical disaster for the human. As per the survey, 39 Million people are blind throughout the world. These blind people go through several challenges throughout their life 24×7. Some of the major critical issues they face are their movement through the lanes especially in dense traffic areas, they are highly vulnerable against robbery, kidnapping, and molestation due to their impairment, and they can't find they are moving through dark or lightened lanes. These are some of the major issues they face which can be mitigated with the efficient use of technology and electronic components. We can enable the walking sticks of the blind person to act as the Stun Gun which produces 20 KV in emergency condition for their protection using Electric Arc Generator and power source. Using Ultrasonic Sensor provides the estimation of the obstacle and vibrates the stick if comes nearby any obstacle below the threshold limit. The major electronic components we use are Ultrasonic Sensor (HC-SR04), Arduino Nano, Electric Arc Generator, LDR, Dry cell, and Vibration Motor. We can design an efficient blend of technology and logic to short out the issues of the blind community which will be our gift to humanity.

Keywords: HC-SR04 · Electric Arc Generator · LDR · Arduino Nano · Vibration motor

1 Introduction

Blind means the disability of vision which reciprocates to the impairment in society too. Visually impaired go through several social and physical traumas. Being impaired and helpless they are not able to defend themselves when finding in a critical scenario like in heavy traffic zone or in case of criminal incidences [2]. There have been many types of research for helping blinds with their proper navigation using several sensors [3, 4, 6]. Especially to find their path and get alert about their navigation path. There

F. Mekuria et al. (Eds.): ICT4DA 2019, CCIS 1026, pp. 270–277, 2019.
https://doi.org/10.1007/978-3-030-26630-1_23

has not been any attempt to enable the physically impaired to find their path in any condition and protect against criminal activities combine. Our proposed system deals with the blinds to help themselves in case of an emergency. To fulfill the requirements we proceed with the brain of our system which is Atmega328 P PU microcontroller based Arduino Nano. It is a small and lightweight yet effective solution which is idle for this scenario due to its tiny size to fit on walking sticks. It is programmed with Embedded C code to perform the task. Then we proceed with our second requirement which has two applications. First to create a sensor based navigation system to alert the blind for any obstacle and second to produce high voltage arc to give a shock to criminals in case of emergency. To perform the first task we use the Ultrasonic Sensor (HC-SR04) which acts with the same fashion as the Bats act using ultrasonic frequency to detect the obstacles. For the second we deal with high voltage arc generator which produces huge power to shock the culprit. For the third we use LDR to make him understand whether he is moving through light or darkened lanes.

1.1   Microcontroller (Brain of the System) Selection

We use Arduino Nano to be used as the logical think-tank to perform our tasks for blind security and navigation system. It has the capability of steady design, smaller form factor and yet powerful analytical ability based on incorporated programming.

1.2   The First, Second and Third Initiative

The first initiative is to solve the issue of obstacle detection and avoidance for blind people. We use ultrasonic sensors for that. The ultrasonic sensor identifies the distance and provides the logic to the microcontroller which activates vibration motor. The vibration motor vibrates the walking stick so the blind person gets alert about the obstacle (Fig. 1).

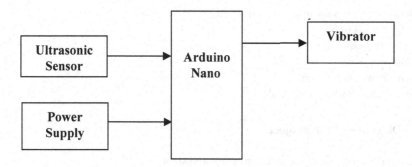

Fig. 1. The obstacle identification and alert scenario

The second initiation is for high voltage current production to provide sufficient shock to the criminals in case of emergency. For that, we use electrical Arc device which can generate a voltage as heavy as 20 kV. This shock does not kill the victim but makes them paralyzed for hours. The device can be operated and energized by just 1.5 V battery itself. It is a lethal weapon if the high voltage battery is used. We have a panic button in the stick itself which activates this feature for the cane. It's so powerful that it can be used for a group of people by producing power from a small battery (Fig. 2).

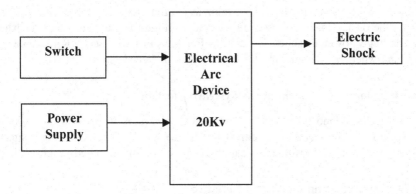

Fig. 2. The electric shock scenario

The system is highly useful and the first of its kind to provide the safety to the blind individual.

1.3   Advantages of the Proposed System

1. Real-Time implementable system
2. Practically Usable
3. Light Weight
4. Compact Size
5. Low Power Consumption
6. Minimum Hardware Possible.

1.4   Objective of the Project

- To make a practically usable lightweight system
- To make a blind stich this actually can be used by a blind person.
- To use a smart-talking system without increasing the hardware and system weight
- To make the system in minimum possible cost.

2 Hardware Components Specifications and Usage

2.1 Ultrasonic Sensor (HC-SR04)

The sensor deals with the process of ultrasonic frequency by transmitting the signal from the transmitter and after reflection from any reflecting body, it gets received by the receiver unit (Fig. 3).

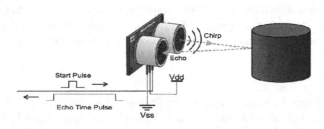

Fig. 3. The working principle of the ultrasonic sensor

2.2 Arduino Nano

It is the think-tank of our system which deals with the C Programming language to provide logic. All the sensor logic is processed and provided to output motor device to vibrate the stick (Fig. 4).

Fig. 4. Arduino Nano

2.3 Electric Arc Device

This device is a powerful shock provider even from a Drycell. The shock is so powerful that it can paralyze a person for hours. This is not deadly but acts as the stun gun in case of emergency (Fig. 5).

Fig. 5. Electric arc working

The combined utilization of the above components can be used to create a powerful supporting and defending cane system for blinds. All necessary information about the combined approach is mentioned below in the form of overall block diagram.

2.4 LDR

It stands for Light Dependent Resistor or Photoresistor, which is passive electronic component, basically a resistor which has a resistance that varies depending of the light intensity. The resistance is very high in darkness, almost high as 1 MΩ but when there is light that falls on LDR, the resistance is falling down to a few KΩ (Fig. 6).

Fig. 6. LDR

2.5 Vibrator Motor

The vibration motor is a special type of motor which produces heavy vibration during obstacle detection. Whenever the vibration is produced in accordance with an obstacle then the user can understand he/she is nearing the obstacle and gets alerted (Fig. 7).

Fig. 7. Vibration motor

3   Design Diagrams and Programming

3.1   Microcontroller Program

```
const int trigPin = 2;
const int echoPin = 4;
#define LEDPin 13 // Onboard
LED
  void setup()
  {
  Serial.println("$bc11");
  Serial.begin(9600);
  pinMode(LEDPin, OUTPUT);
  Serial.println("$bc6");
  Serial.println("Blind navigation
system ");
  Serial.println("*blind navigation
system ");
  delay(2000);
  Serial.println("$ta90");
  Serial.println("$ts40");
  delay(1000);
  }
  void loop()
  {
  Serial.println("$bc12");
  long duration, inches, cm;
  pinMode(trigPin, OUTPUT);
  digitalWrite(trigPin, LOW);
  delayMicroseconds(2);
  digitalWrite(trigPin, HIGH);
  delayMicroseconds(10);
  digitalWrite(trigPin, LOW);
  pinMode(echoPin, INPUT);
  duration   =   pulseIn(echoPin,
HIGH);
  inches = microsecondsToInch-
es(duration);
  cm = microsecondsToCentime-
ters(duration);
  Serial.println("$ts60");
  Serial.print(inches);

  Serial.print(" Inches ");
  Serial.print("      ");
  Serial.print(cm);
  Serial.print(" C.M");
  Serial.println();
  delay(500);
  if (inches <= 2)
  {
  to indicate "out of range" */
  Serial.println("$bc7");
  Serial.println("$ts60");
  Serial.println("*Obstacle is there
");
  delay(1000);
  Serial.println("Obstacle ");
  delay(300);
  Serial.println("$ts40");
  digitalWrite(LEDPin, HIGH);
  delay(300);
  }
  else {
  turn LED OFF to indicate suc-
cessful reading. */
  Serial.println(inches);
  digitalWrite(LEDPin, LOW);
  }
  }
  long microsecondsToInches(long
microseconds)
  {
  return microseconds / 74 / 2;
  }

  long      microsecondsToCentime-
ters(long microseconds)
  {
  return microseconds / 29 / 2;
  }
```

3.2 Overall Block Diagram

See Fig. 8.

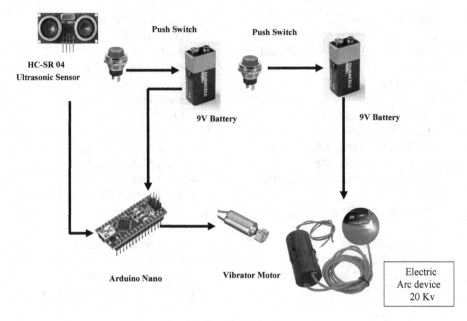

Fig. 8. Overall block diagram

4 Conclusion

Thus we developed a system for visually impaired individuals by a perfect blend of ultrasonic, microcontroller and power generation technology. The efficient utilization of these resources can bring ultimate change in the degrading condition of the blind. It can act as the support system and a helping hand in the case of emergency for physically challenged individuals.

Acknowledgments. This work is the efficient utilization of the perfect technological balance of J. Saravanan, A. Clement Raj, Raushan Kumar and Ararso Taye. The idea of paper and technical implementation is carried out mutually by the authors and brings the perfect implementable concept for social welfare.

References

1. Bernabei, D., Ganovelli, F., Di Benedetto, M., Dellepiane, M., Scopigno, R.: A low-cost time-critical obstacle avoidance system for the visually impaired. In: International Conference on Indoor Positioning and Indoor Navigation (IPIN) (2011)
2. Bach y Rita, P., Kaczmarek, K.A., Tyler, M.E., Garcia-Lara, J.: Form perception with a 49-point electrotactile stimulus array on the tongue: a technical note. J. Rehabil. Res. Dev. **35** (4), 427–430 (1998)
3. Vlaminck, M., Jovanovic, L., Van Hess, P., Goossens, B., Wilfried, P., Aleksa dra, P.: Obstacle detection for pedestrians with a visual impairment based on 3d imaging. In: 2013 International conference on 3D imaging (IC3D), pp. 1–7. IEEE (2013)
4. Sainarayanan, G., Nagarajan, R., Yaacob, S.: Fuzzy image processing scheme for autonomous navigation of human blind. Appl. Softw. Comput. **7**(1), 257–264 (2007)
5. Hersh, M.A., Johnson, M.A.: Assistive Technology for Visually Impaired and Blind People, 1st edn. Springer, London (2008). https://doi.org/10.1007/978-1-84628-867-8
6. Hoang, V.N., Nguyen, T.H., Le, T.L., Tran, T.T.H., Vuong, T.P., Vuillerme, N.: Obstacle detection and warning for visually impaired people based on electrode matrix and mobile Kinect. In: 2nd National Foundation for Science and Technology Development Conference on Information and Computer Science (NICS), pp. 54–59, September 2015
7. Holz, D., Holzer, S., Rusu, R.B., Behnke, S.: Real-time plane segmentation using RGB-D cameras. In: Röfer, T., Mayer, N.M., Savage, J., Saranlı, U. (eds.) RoboCup 2011. LNCS (LNAI), vol. 7416, pp. 306–317. Springer, Heidelberg (2012). https://doi.org/10.1007/978-3-642-32060-6_26
8. Abdullah, S., Noor, N.M., Ghazali, M.Z.: Mobility recognition system for the visually impaired. In: ISTT, Malaysia, pp. 362–367 (2014)
9. Takizawa, H., Yamaguchi, S., Aoyagi, M., Ezaki, N., Mizuno, S.: Kinect cane: object recognition for the visually impaired, Poland, pp. 473–478 (2013)
10. Agarwal, N., Iyer, A., Naidu, S., Rodrigues, S.: Electronic guidance system for the visually impaired—a framework, Mumbai, pp. 1–5 (2015)

Improving Quality of Service of Border Gateway Protocol Multiprotocol Label Switching Virtual Private Network of EthioTelecom Service Level Agreements

Asrat Mulatu Beyene[1]([✉]) and Shimelis Asrat Argaw[2]

[1] Addis Ababa Science and Technology University, Addis Ababa, Ethiopia
asrat.mulatu@aastu.edu.et
[2] St. Mary's University, Addis Ababa, Ethiopia
shimelisas@gmail.com

Abstract. The primary goals of Quality of Service (QoS) are managed bandwidth, controlled jitter, minimized latency, and improved packet loss characteristics to provide satisfactory services for users. Shaping network optimization is crucial for the service provider, too. To implement QoS mechanisms optimizing the current network physical and logical architectures is among the best practices. In this paper, an attempt has been made to investigate the end-to-end QoS parameters of multiprotocol border gateway protocol multiprotocol label switching virtual private network (MP-BGP MPLS VPN) EthioTelecom service level agreement (SLA) customers. That is done using differentiated service (DiffServ) model to manage end-to-end traffic delay, jitter, and packet losses. The traffics are classified and marked depending on their priorities. The proposed network architecture has used weighted fair queueing (WFQ) for congestion management and weighted random early detection (WRED) for congestion avoidance. The Huawei's Enterprise Network Simulation Platform (eNSP) and Wireshark are used to design, demonstrate and evaluate the network architectures. When the results of the existing network are compared with the proposed network architecture its delay, jitter, packet loss and traffic utilization have shown improvements.

Keywords: Quality of Service · Virtual private network ·
Multiprotocol label switching ·
Multiprotocol border gateway protocol · Service level agreement ·
Differentiated service model

1 Introduction

Every day new telecommunication technologies are being developed. Enterprises use these new technologies to upgrade their network services and reduce cost.

© Springer Nature Switzerland AG 2019
F. Mekuria et al. (Eds.): ICT4DA 2019, CCIS 1026, pp. 278–288, 2019.
https://doi.org/10.1007/978-3-030-26630-1_24

Now a day, different kinds of traffic such as voice, video, and data are sent over the same network infrastructure. When transferring different traffic types within the same network infrastructure QoS is one the challenges [1]. MP-BGP MPLS VPN is one alternative solution to private wide area networks (WAN) to assure end-to-end QoS.

In existing networks there is significant problem of meeting consumers QoS demands. This is discussed in [1–3]. Moreover, a preliminary investigation based on data collected from EthioTelecom MP-BGP VPN customers shows there were many verified complaints of end-to-end QoS problems. The primary reasons for this are EthioTelecom uses best effort policy to guarantee QoS demands, first in first out (FIFO) to manage congestion, tail drop to avoid congestion. This can be improved in many different ways. Here, we have implemented the DiffServ QoS model, WFQ for congestion management, WRED for congestion avoidance on EthioTelecom MP-BGP MPLS VPN customers network to better meet QoS expectation based on the SLA. To do that, in this research work, a simplified network architecture is built as shown in Fig. 1. It covers the main steps in designing QoS of MP-BGP MPLS VPN networks. The New Generation Network (NGN) network architecture was chosen according to the requirements of designing networks with service provision and end-to-end QoS implementation.

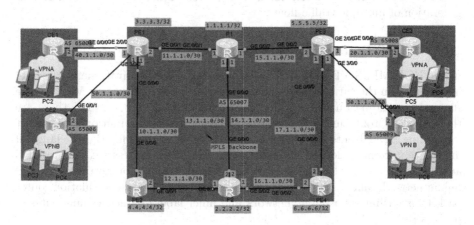

Fig. 1. Simplified MP-BGP MPLS VPN network architecture with end-to-end QoS.

In the proposed network architecture solution there are two provider (P) routers, four provider edge (PE) routers and four customer edge (CE) routers. The P routers are the backbone routers. They provide MPLS label forwarding and maintain public network routing information. PE routers are directly connected with CE routers. The functions of PE routers are maintaining and processing VPN route information, forwarding VPN, running MP-BGP and MPLS. They also do label popping and imposition. CE routers are customer edge routers where the customer's routers or personal computers (PCs) are directly connected.

VPN A and VPN B routers are traffic generators. The two VPN pairs, VPN As and VPN Bs, traffic was evaluated. Both are MPLS based on resource reservation protocol traffic engineering (RSVP-TE) for signaling and tunneling. They use intermediate system to intermediate system (IS-IS) for interior gateway-protocol (IGP) interconnection. Both VPNs use the same networking devices. The P routers in the core network are realized as core routers and route reflectors (RR). These devices are logically divided into two logical systems. These systems are act like separate routers. They have full functional capabilities of two separate hardware devices. The connections between the two logical systems are made with peering the interfaces. The links with the other devices in the networks are recognized with general Gigabit Ethernet interfaces.

The access and aggregation networks are made with secure service routers. They are working in multiprotocol label popping and positioning mode instead of the default packet flow due to the MPLS architecture. The devices are working with Gigabit Ethernet interfaces. The links with the core networks are through Gigabit Ethernet and the links with the end devices are also with full Gigabit Ethernet. The access and aggregation routers apply the QoS to the traffic from the end devices. The two VPN routers are traffic generators. To test the QoS applied in the traffic flow Wireshark and eNSP are used. The two VPNs provide random traffic generation, fixed or non-fixed packet size, and simultaneous generation of multiple traffic flows.

1.1   MP-MP BGP MPLS VPN

In the BGP MPLS VPN, BGP is used to transfer VPN private network route information on the carrier backbone network and MPLS to forward VPN service steams. Depending on the working principles of BGP MPLS VPN there are three aspects: route information advertisement, label distribution and packet forwarding [2,3]. Route information advertisement is used for the exchange of information from the local CE to the ingress PE, from ingress PE to egress PE and egress PE to local CE. Label distribution distributes private network and public network labels. VPN packet forwarding is used for encapsulation, outer packet forwarding on a public network and inner label instructing inner sites of packets [1–3].

1.2   Quality of Service (QoS)

QoS is the mechanism of networks to provide different services to different traffic types [4]. Service providers offer their network service with varying quality levels. To do that they define SLAs. An SLA provides the details of all QoS parameters. It defines the parameters such as end-to-end delay, end-to-end jitter, and packet loss. QoS is not the functionality of a single device and it is an end-to-end mechanism. It provides the intelligence to network devices to treat the different application's traffic as they are defined in the SLA. QoS combines different technologies together such as classifying, marking, scheduling, queuing, allocating and prioritizing bandwidth that are commonly used to provide a scalable end-to-end service [5]. QoS is used to manage the main network performance elements like bandwidth, delay, jitter and packet loss [4,6].

Bandwidth. The amount of data that can be transmitted over the link is bandwidth [4,9]. On the network, IP Packets travel through the best route. The maximum bandwidth of the route is equal to the smallest value of bandwidth on the route. The available bandwidth is the path bandwidth divided by several traffic flows [5,10]. Due to the low bandwidth users experience delay, jitter and packet loss in the communication.

Delay. End-to-end delay is the total time that a packet takes from source to destination [6,7]. End-to-end delay is the sum of processing, queuing, serialization, and propagation delays.

Jitter. Variation in delay is jitter. Packets for the same destination may not arrive at the same rate. Jitter can occur due to different traffic loads on different timings. For voice and video, it is necessary to receive the packets in the same sequence to achieve good quality [10].

Packet Loss. Packet loss occurs due to the low buffer space [8,9]. When the buffer space of interfaces are full packets are dropped. In queue scheduling packet loss occur when the queue is full. Packet loss creates extended delays and jitter. Packet loss can be controlled by applying techniques like tail drop, random early detection, weighted random early detection and traffic shaping and policing [9].

Generally, QoS doesn't depend only on bandwidth, delay, packet loss and delay [10]. It also depends on end-user perception of telecommunication services such as trends, advertising, tariffs and costs which are interrelated with customers' expectation of QoS. Figure 2 shows how end-user perception reaches the QoS satisfaction level.

QoS can be divided into two viewpoints [11,12]. Customer viewpoints and Service provider viewpoints. Customer viewpoints include QoS requirements and perception whereas service provider viewpoints include QoS offered and QoS achieved as shown in Fig. 3.

Generally, if network performance was well optimized, service provider viewpoint reaches the highest level. Moreover, if service provider affords quality services to its customer, customer viewpoint escalates which increases customer quality of experiences.

2   Designed QoS of MP-BGP MPLS VPN

The designed QoS-based network architecture provides different levels of service quality based on end-to-end QoS targets and International Telecommunication Union (ITU) threshold quality requirements for different VPNs. Managing

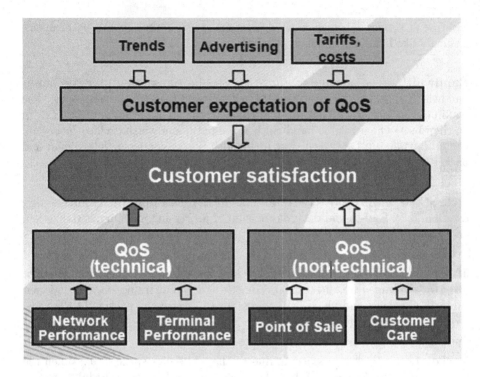

Fig. 2. User perception of end-to-end QoS delivery framework [11,12].

maximum receivable bandwidth, reducing transmission, queueing and processing delay, minimizing jitter and packet loss are the main focus of the design. End-to-end QoS assurance is achieved based on existing resources by using rational scheduling and congestion avoidance methods. DiffServ is used to classify, mark and shape network traffic based on existing SLA agreements. Applying end-to-end QoS using DiffServ can follow the following step by step processes:

- Define access control list (ACL) rules,
- Define traffic classifiers,
- Define traffic classifiers,
- Define traffic behaviors (mark),
- Define traffic policies, and
- Apply traffic policies to interfaces.

2.1 Experimental Resuts

The designed MP-BGP MPLS VPN end-to-end QoS applied on the network architecture depicted in Fig. 1 is fully operational. That means

- All protocols are fully operational,
- Proper implementation of the designed QoS is made,

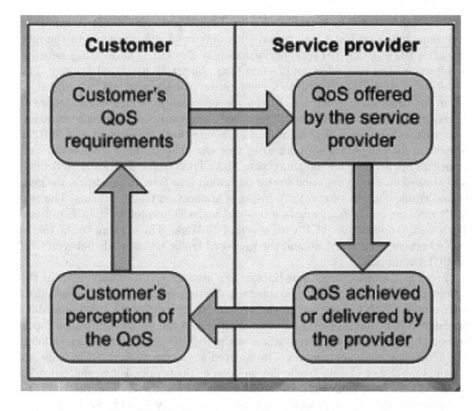

Fig. 3. QoS viewpoints framework [11].

- Provisioning of the required services ensuring MPLS VPN are operational, and
- Redundancy of network resources is made which includes rerouting in case of link or node failure.

The existing and proposed network architectures are the same in devices and physical interconnection. But they have different QoS designs. Table 1 shows the similarities and differences between existing and proposed network architectures.

Table 1. The similarities and differences between existing and proposed network architectures.

Parameters	Existing network architecture	Proposed network architecture
Traffic type	MP-BGP MPLS VPN	MP-BGP MPLS VPN
Service type	MPLS VPN	MPLS VPN
IGP routing protocol	IS-IS	IS-IS
NGN backbone	MPLS	MPLS
QoS model	Best effort model	DiffServ
Congestion management	FIFO	WFQ
Congestion avoidance	Tail drop	WRED

The end-to-end QoS is tested with Wireshark and eNSP tools. A couple of scenarios, based on Fig. 1, are tested with different traffic streams. In the first scenario, the existing network performance is checked. The existing network architecture uses best effort endto- end QoS. All traffic has equal priority. The architecture uses FIFO algorithm for congestion management and tail drop algorithm for congestion avoidance. In the second scenario, which is the proposed network architecture, uses the DiffServ QoS. The traffic has different priorities. The architecture uses WFQ algorithm for congestion management and WRED algorithm for congestion avoidance. In this case, the traffic was classified and prioritized depending on the underlying SLA. Then traffic policies were defined and applied on the aggregation router outbound interface. In this work, the generated traffic consists of two VPN instance application traffic streams. The two VPN instance traffic flows emulate two end nodes connected to the CE routers. Both traffic streams use TCP with speed of 15 Mbps. The existing traffic test is made between CE1 and CE3 and the proposed traffic test is made between CE2 and CE4 routers.

From Fig. 4, one can see that the existing network architecture overturns the bandwidth utilization. This is because the existing network uses the best effort QoS model which cannot isolate the services to guarantee the maximum data transfer. But in the proposed network architecture the bandwidth utilization is respectable. In this case, the network uses the DiffServ QoS model which isolated the network at each aggregation. The isolated aggregate guaranteed to transmit maximum number of data traffic. So, mission critical traffic is transmitted first.

As can be seen from the evaluation testing of Fig. 5, the proposed network architecture, the implementation of DiffServ has many benefits for packet loss compared to the best effort. In the DiffServ model, routers must store traffic and QoS information per aggregation. This creates enough buffer space in the router's queue. A router usually has incoming interface buffers, system buffers, and outgoing interface buffers. In case of congestion, the traffic is remarked and kept in buffer space to avoid the packet loss. But in the case of best effort QoS model, the routers just route packets until they reach the destination. Other packets are dropped causing a higher percentage of packet loss.

DiffServ QoS model minimizes traffic loss. In case of congestion, this model classifies traffic depending on their priority. The classified traffics are marked and shaped depending on the router maximum data transfer rate. Some traffic transmitted, whereas the excess traffics are remarked and transmitted later. This decreases the packet loss ratio.

Latency is the time that a packet waits before being transmitted. As it can be seen from Fig. 6, the proposed network architecture shows lower latency compared to the existing network architecture. The reason for this is that the DiffServ model can guarantee the traffic per aggregation.

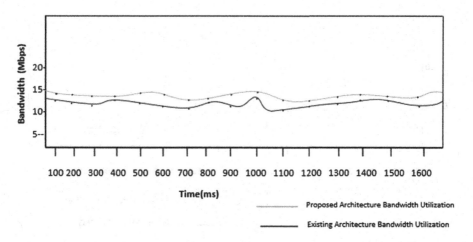

Fig. 4. The bandwidth utilization results of existing and proposed systems.

3 Discussions

The numerical results obtained from the existing and proposed networks are shown in Table 2. Most of the results were as expected. The difference between packet loss and bandwidth in existing and proposed network architecture was visible. But the difference between end-to-end delay and jitter was not that much visible. This happened because we have used ten routers only on both network architectures. This reduces the transmission, serialization, queueing and processing delays. The difference increases as the number of routers (nodes) increases.

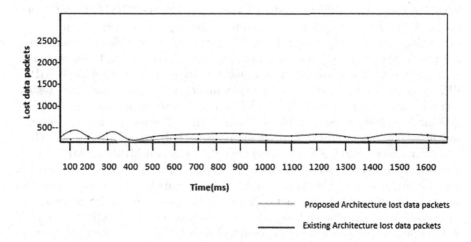

Fig. 5. Packet loss measurement comparison.

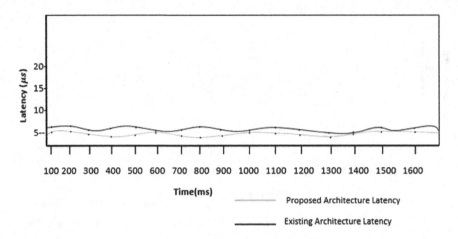

Fig. 6. Latency measurement comparison.

Table 2. Exist and proposed network architecture numerical QoS results.

Parameters	Existing network (Best effort)			Proposed network (DiffServ)		
	Result	SLA targets	ITU threshold	Result	SLA targets	ITU threshold
Packet loss ()	0.169	Within range	Out of range	0.14132	Within range	Within range
Delay (sec)	0.001	Within range	Out of range	0.14132	Within range	Within range
Jitter (sec)	0.001	Within range	Out of range	0.0007747	Within range	Within range
Bandwidth (bps)	15068	Out of range	Out of range	15320	Within range	Out of range

4   Conclusions

In this research, the DiffServ model for the design of MP-BGP MPLS VPN networks with end-to-end QoS was deliberated. This type of networks is suitable for the implementation of QoS for MPLS VPN networks. A simplified network topology was created. Two network architectures were designed, built and evaluated with generic telecommunication equipment. Firstly, the existing BGP MPLS VPN network which used best effort QoS model was implemented and tested. Secondly, the proposed BGP MPLS VPN architecture which uses the DiffServ QoS model was designed and tested. Bandwidth utilization, packet loss, latency and jitter measurements were made for both network models. After the whole evaluations were made, it is observed that the proposed MP-BGP MPLS VPN network architecture has much more benefits than the existing BGP MPLS VPN network architecture. This is due to the opportunity for the class of services and traffic-engineering in the network, which brings better traffic management and provision of suitable end-to-end QoS. The proposed MP-BGP MPLS VPN architecture which uses DiffServ QoS model architecture could be used in many mission-critical applications.

In the proposed DiffServ QoS model better network productivity was achieved. The designed MP-BGP MPLS VPN architecture which uses DiffServ

QoS model network architecture is easy to scale and troubleshoot. The addition of new end devices in the network is simplified and just slight configuration changes are required. In the proposed BGP MPLS VPN architecture, which uses DiffServ QoS model architecture, all services have the required traffic treatment. The designed MP-BGP MPLS VPN network model can easily be used for MPLS VPN services in both centralized and distributed architectures. End-to-end MPLS solutions for the NGN applications are smoothly attended.

Generally, based on the analysis and results gained, it can be concluded that the DiffServ QoS model was more reliable than the best effort QoS model being used by EthioTelecom's MP-BGP MPLS VPN network. The designed QoS uses DiffServ model that can guarantee customers' SLA QoS thresholds. In conclusion, the designed network provides a way of increasing network performance based on the DiffServ QoS model. High network performance indicates better QoS service provision. Better QoS service provision, in turn, creates customer satisfaction and higher quality of experience to customers.

5 Future Works

Based on the scope of this work, the QoS has been guaranteed with respect to SLA QoS targets. But in the future, the network can be extended with more reliability functions. These functions include chassis clustering for access and aggregation devices, implementation of high availability features, implementation of LDP for MPLS label down streaming on demand.

One such future extension is the implementation of self-organizing network architecture, such as self-learning, self-configuration and self-management, self-optimization, prediction of network congestion and traffic loops. To implement advanced extensions there are algorithms for prediction. Algorithms for adaptive training of the network such as the Widrow-Hoff algorithm can be of great use for process predictions in operating networks [13,14]. This way the designed proposed BGP MPLS VPN architecture which uses DiffServ QoS model network architecture can become optimal save operational and maintenance costs. Self-optimization, based on collected data from previous network states and based on predictions can be also be attempted.

References

1. Ahmad, A., Talal, A.: Performance analysis of DiffServ-based quality of service in MPLS networks. Int. J. Sci. Eng. Res. **6**, 15–23 (2015)
2. EthioTelecom. QoS Document on MPLS VPN Services Quality and Customer Experience Related Issues and Complaint Analysis, Version 02 (2017)
3. Huawei technologies. Configuration Guide VPN - Cloud Engine 12800 Series Switches, vol. 6 (2017)
4. Szigeti, T., Hattingh, C.: End-to-End QoS Network Design. Cisco Press, Indianapolis (2005)
5. Lawrence, J.: Designing multiprotocol label switching networks. IEEE Commun. Mag. **39**(7), 134–142 (2001)

6. De Ghein, L.: MPLS Fundamentals epub. Cisco Press, Indianapolis (2016)
7. Pepelnjak, I., Guichard, J.: MPLS and VPN Architectures, vol. 1. Cisco Press, Indianapolis (2002)
8. Mohamed, J.N., Mellachervu, K.R., Ramakrishnan, S.C.: Configuration tool for MPLS virtual private network topologies. Google Patents (2012). (US Patent 8,194,570)
9. Odom, W.: CCNP Route 642–902 Official Certification Guide. Cisco Press, Indianapolis (2010)
10. Grayson, M., Gundavelli, S.: Providing integrated end-to-end architecture that includes quality of service transport for tunneled traffic. U.S Patents (2015). (Patent 9,198,209)
11. Stankiewicz, R., Jajszczyk, A.: A survey of QoE assurance in converged networks. Comput. Netw. **55**(7), 1459–1473 (2011)
12. EthioTelecom. Service Provisioning Manual, July 2014
13. Zhang, G.P.: Time series forecasting using a hybrid ARIMA and neural network model. Neurocomputing **50**, 159–175 (2003)
14. Lee, H., Hwang, J., Kang, B., Jun, K.: End-to-end QoS architecture for VPNs: MPLS VPN deployment in a backbone network. In: 2000 Proceedings of International Workshop on Parallel Processing, pp. 479–483. IEEE (2000)

Natural Language Processing Track

A Scalable Text Classification Using Naive Bayes with Hadoop Framework

Mulualem Mheretu Temesgen[1]([⊠]) and Dereje Teferi Lemma[2]

[1] Collage of Computing and Informatics, Assosa University, Assosa, Ethiopia
mulu2006hu@gmail.com
[2] School of Information Science,
Addis Ababa University, Addis Ababa, Ethiopia
dereje.teferi@aau.edu.et

Abstract. Automated text classification is the labeling of documents to the predefined class label or category using machine learning algorithms. It is one of the important domains in machine learning where the algorithm is applied to classify documents to the appropriate category or genre of the document. For example, the document might be news items and the class/category/genre might be business news, sport news, health news, financial news and social news. Due to the volume of this textual data and its presumed exponential growth, classical data mining techniques may not provide optimal performance in terms of efficiency. To this end, scalable machine learning library apache mahout with hadoop can be used to improve the performance of the algorithm and computation time. In this study Naïve Bayes classification algorithm is implemented on top of hadoop to build automatic document categorizer using Mapreduce programing model. Addis Ababa university institutional repository/Electronic thesis and dissertations text document is used for training and evaluation dataset. The proposed model achieved an accuracy of 79.06%. The result shows that the system can categorize large thesis documents into its predefined class with promising accuracy.

Keywords: Machine learning · Text classification · Naïve Bayes ·
Mapreduce · Hadoop

1 Introduction

Text classification is the task of classifying document by their contents or by the words that they contain [1]. It automates the task of filing documents into pre-defined categories based on a set of example documents [2]. Text document classification is one of important domains in machine learning. It is the application of learning algorithms to classify documents to their appropriate category or genre. Each instance in the dataset represents a document and the instance class represent the document category. For example, the document might be news items and the class might be business news, sport news, health news, financial news and social news. Every document is characterized by words it contains that will be used to predict the class label or category of the document by applying machine learning algorithm.

© Springer Nature Switzerland AG 2019
F. Mekuria et al. (Eds.): ICT4DA 2019, CCIS 1026, pp. 291–300, 2019.
https://doi.org/10.1007/978-3-030-26630-1_25

According to Tiwary [3], text analytics is one of the most used application area of machine learning that is implemented in automatic email filtering, news article clustering and categorization, and sentiment analytics on social media posts. They contend that the estimated size of text data both public and private could be measured in petabytes[1]. They argue that, due to the volume of this textual data and presumed exponential growth, classical data mining techniques may become inadequate to deal with this data. So, they insist that there is huge opportunity to apply a scalable machine learning algorithm to a text document to build a classification application for unstructured digital texts.

Generally, there are three approaches of machine learning: supervised, unsupervised and reinforcement learning. The first two approaches can be applied in text categorization application. In supervised machine learning algorithm, the class label of the document is known and trained to predict the new unseen class label which is referred to as classification. Whereas, unsupervised machine learning algorithm works on the unlabeled documents. This is the class label for each instance is not known and hence one can only work on grouping the data based on some "distance" criteria. Unsupervised learning is also called clustering. Reinforcement learning is a type of machine learning where an agent learns how to behave in an environment by performing actions and seeing the result. This paper uses Addis Ababa University's categorized thesis documents to build the text classifier model. Since thesis documents are found in unstructured format, preprocessing techniques such as tokenization, stop word removal and steaming of text were applied. Moreover, a vector space model is developed after the preprocessing is performed. Sparse vector is the method used in representing the content baring terms as vector.

Several algorithms are used for text classification such as support vector machine (SVM), Decision tree (C4.5), K-NN (a distance weighted K-nearest neighbor), Naïve Bayes and logistic regression using Stochastic Gradient Descent (SGD). Naive Bayes algorithm is easy and fast to implement and best suited for datasets which have one predictor and one target variable like text document and its class/category. Now a days text classification is mostly used in email spam filtering [4], sentiment classification [5, 6]. and news classification [7]. Once the model is developed, its accuracy is evaluated using confusion matrix and several evaluation metrices.

In this paper text document classification model is developed using Naive Bayes and its scalability for large documents is evaluated using mahout with Mapreduce programing model.

2 Background

2.1 Apache Hadoop Framework

Apache hadoop is an open source apache software foundation project written in java. It is distributed software platform for reliable, scalable and distributed processing of large datasets across clusters of commodity hardware using simple programing model [8]. It

---

[1] 1 zetta bytes = 10^{21} bytes or 1000 exabyte = 1 million petabytes = 1billion terabyte.

has a distributed processing framework known as Mapreduce that subdivide problems or jobs to a cluster of computers to process in parallel, hadoop distributed file system (HDFS) for storage and Yet Another Resource Negotiator (YARN) which is used as hadoop cluster resource management. There are many projects that complement hadoop. These ecosystems include apache Pig, HBase, Solr and Lucene, Sqoop, flume, mahout and zookeeper etc.

HDFS is distributed file system that provides reliable, scalable and fault tolerant data storage on commodity hardware. It can store large dataset files by dividing it into blocks (default is 128 MB each) and replicate backs in two or more commodity hardware. HDFS has three daemons to store the data and to make HDFS cluster. These are: Namenode, Datanode and Secondary Namenode. Each of which runs when we start distributed file system.

Mapreduce is a programing model for processing large datasets in cluster nodes using distributed and parallel algorithms in side hadoop. Mapreduce refers to two main tasks, Map and Reduce respectively and executed in three steps: Map, shuffle and Reduce [9]. In map phase, the data is partitioned and each partition is given as input to the worker that execute the Map function and produce the key/value pairs. In shuffle phase, key value pairs are grouped by key and each group is sent to the reducer. The reducer receives key/value pairs from multiple map jobs and aggregate these key/value pairs as a final output.

2.2   Apache Mahout

Apache Mahout is a scalable machine learning library from apache run on hadoop that use Mapreduce as a program execution model or independent of hadoop in single machine to process very large datasets. Classification, clustering and collaborative filtering (recommendation engine) are the machine learning tasks that mahout supports. In each task there are algorithms supported by apache mahout that is executed in parallel (in distributed manner in a cluster of computers using hadoop framework) or Sequential (which is run in a single machine without hadoop).

According to Owen et al. [10], mahout begins to be a good choice when the dataset is between 100,000 to 10 million. However, when the data set is below 100,000, traditional machine learning approaches could work well. Apache mahout on the other hand performs well when the dataset is between 1 million to 10 million. Apache mahout has an advantage on larger data sets because as the input data increases the time or memory requirement for training may not increase linearly in non-scalable system. Figure 1 depicts the advantage of using mahout for large datasets.

Mahout include a number of algorithms used to group document into cluster of similar subject area, for example K-means and classification algorithm used to assign category label to text documents for example Naïve Bayes classification algorithm [11].

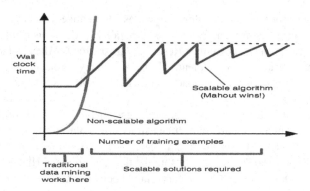

Fig. 1. Advantage of using mahout for large data set and traditional machine learning taken from [10]

3 Naïve Bayes Classifier

Classification is a technique that decides how much a thing/class is or is not a part of some type or category. Naïve Bayes classification algorithm is one of the most widely used supervised algorithm in text classification with mahout. [5] and [12] states that naïve Bayes is proven to be the easy and effective machine learning algorithm for text classification. It is a probabilistic algorithm that build the model based on the relationship between features and categories in training data to predict the category of the class label of the a given new document [13, 14].

Naïve Bayes algorithm is the probabilistic classification algorithm. It uses Bayes theorem on class conditional independence assumption of each features. The training process analyzes the relationship between words in the training documents and categorize and the relationship between categories and the entire training set. Naïve Bayes algorithm doesn't give the absolute probability of the word belonging to a certain class. But it is used to determine that a document containing the word is more likely belonging to a certain category (class label) by comparing the probability assigned to a word for each category [11].

During training the Naïve Bayes algorithm counts the number of times each word appears in a document in the class and divide that by the number of words appearing in that class. This is referred to as conditional probability - that means the probability that a word will appear in particular category which is expressed in Eq. 1.

$$P(word|category) \tag{1}$$

Bayes Theorem
Bayes theorem states that the probability of a category given a document is equal to the probability of document given the category multiplied by the probability of the category divided by the probability of the document. This is expressed mathematically as in Eq. 2 by [11].

$$P(\text{category}|\text{document}) = \frac{P(\text{document}|\text{category} * P(\text{category}))}{P(\text{document})} \qquad (2)$$

4 Related Works

Text classification has been one of the main areas of research to apply machine learning. It has been used for search engine, indexing and blog tagging etc. Several researches have been done on text classification by different researchers.

The use of support vector machine (SVM) for training text classifier has explored by [15]. In this experiment four conventional learning method such as, Naïve Bayes, Rachioo (the most popular learning method in information retrieval), Decision tree (C4.5), K-NN (a distance weighted K-nearest neighbor classifier) and SVM on Routers-21578 compiled by David Lewis and Ohsumed corpus Text dataset. From their theoretical and empirical evidences, it can be seen that SVMs are well suited for text categorization as argued by [16]. Similarly, the application of Support Vector Machine with mixture of kernel (SVM-MK) to design a text classification system has been conducted by [16].

As stated by [17], text classification is playing an important role in information extraction and summarization, text retrieval and question answering. The article described text classification process as depicted in Fig. 2, which is mostly used for automated text categorizer. They identified different machine learning algorithms for text classification, such as decision tree, Naïve Bayes, Rule induction, Neural Network, Nearest Neighbors and Support vector machine.

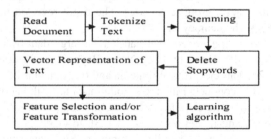

Fig. 2. Text classification process proposed by [17]

Several researches have been done on Amharic news text classification. The use of hierarchical Amharic text classification was explored in [18]. The study presents a comparison of flat and hierarchical Amharic news text classification using SVM and LibSVM multiclass tool. Ethiopian News Agency (ENA) categorized news texts were used to experiment the performance of hierarchical Amharic text classifier. From their research findings, flat news text archive, an accuracy of 68.84% and hierarchical with maximum accuracy of 90.37% is achieved. They have shown that, the performance increases when moving down the hierarchy. Another study has been conducted on the use of machine learning on Amharic news text documents by [19]. The study investigates how to use text classification on Amharic text documents and the effect of stemming or part-of-speech tagging can have on Amharic texts. They have used a corpus of 1065 news documents containing a total of approximately 210,000 word collected form Walta Information Center. They have experimented on their dataset using the RDS system which is rule based machine learning platform. Bagging of decision tree were used as a learning algorithm. Full text representation achieved an accuracy of (69.39%). Artificial Neural network using self-organizing map were used to cluster Amharic texts by using 206 news articles collected from Walta Information Center [20].

Nowadays the size of available data is increasing in volume. Due to the voluminous amount of today's data, it is difficult to use the classical analytics methods and tools for processing. To this end, a number of researches has been conducted to get the best performant classifier. One of the tools developed for this is apache hadoop framework with a scalable machine learning library apache mahout. Mahout includes classification algorithm in its implementation for large datasets [11], described implementation of apache mahout for text classification for large datasets and how it can be integrated using Solr search engine indexing process as document categorizer. Scalable Naïve Bayes algorithm on 1230 news group instances dataset were applied to build the classifier. They produced a classifier that can correctly assign categories with a 79.5% accuracy.

A study conducted by [21], stated that when we have large volume of data, it requires a method such as higher performance parallel computing tools as well as machine learning algorithms. Hadoop is one of distributed file processing and storage and apache mahout for a scalable machine learning algorithm which is run on top of hadoop in parallel. Naïve Bayes classification algorithm were employed to categorize tweets belonging to 3 news group categories. The result revealed that the algorithm classified the tweets with accuracy of 79%.

Robust text classification system that can handle large data by using Mapreduce programing model has developed by [22]. Naïve Bayes classification algorithm have been employed on 2000 articles from Wikipedia and two domains i.e. animal and plant data. The experiment is conducted in single node machine with hadoop configured in pseudo-distributed mode. The classifier achieved an accuracy of 98.8%.

Mapreduce programing model also used in [23], to classify large text documents using multi nominal model using parallel computing. Five categories from 20 newsgroups dataset which has 20,000 texts and 20 categories were used to experiment Naïve Bayes classification algorithm and to test the scalability in five cluster of nodes.

News article classification using Mapreduce programing model with hadoop framework have been used in [24]. They have used Chinese Wikipedia articles for training Naïve Bayes classification algorithm on multimode cluster of computers. The classes are Economy, IT, Health, Sport, Travel, Knowledge, Work, Culture, and Military. Preprocessing of the data by using Chinese word segmentation were applied. Then, features were selected by representing the text as TF-IDF vector. The performance of the classifier was evaluated by precision and recall. Naïve Bayes classifier can also scale up well for large datasets in sentiment analysis [5, 6].

5 Experimental Setup

The proposed algorithm in this research is implemented on the following experimental setup. The type and version of software as well as the hardware used for the experiment is listed in Table 1.

Table 1. Experimental setup

Hadoop version	Hadoop-2.9.2
Programing model	Mapreduce
ML algorithm	Naïve Bayes
File system	HDFS
Operating system	Ubuntu 18.4 which is run on Oracle Virtual box VM
Processor	Intel(R) Core (TM) i5-6200U CPU @ 2.3 GHz
Clustered node	Single node cluster
RAM	4 GB
System type	64 bit operating system
Machine learning library	Mahout -0.12.2
For building mahout code	Maven 3.5.2

6 System Design and Methodology

Hadoop framework is utilized for distributed storage and parallel processing. For the machine learning task, mahout which is a scalable machine learning library that includes classification algorithm in its implementation is used. The dataset for the experiment is gathered from Addis Ababa University[2] digital thesis repository. The total number of thesis documents used for this research are 208. The thesis documents are used as training and test documents to categorize the document based on their genre. Several researchers proposed text classification process model in [7, 17 and 24]. We have proposed text classification process model as shown in Fig. 3. In this study 26.9 MB of size of datasets is used. The documents are first converted into text file and are loaded onto HDFS. Second, the dataset is converted into sequence file by using mahout seqdirectory command on mahout command line interface. This command converts the text file into hadoop SequenceFile by using the file name of the text file as a key and the contents of the text file as a value [25]. Then, to create the TF and TF-IDF vector, one of the mahouts built in utility tool seq2sparse is used. According to Gupta [26], vectors are ordered list of values as defined in two-dimensional space. This TF-IDF vector is used as an input for training the model. The TF-IDF vector dataset is split into training set and testing set with random selection of 60% for training and 40% for testing. Then, training of the Naïve Bayes classification algorithm is performed using HDFS and Mapreduce programing model in single node cluster of computers. After

---

[2] http://etd.aau.edu.et/.

building the classifier, its performance is measured by different metrics. In this study, accuracy, recall and precision are used to measure the performance of the classifier. Figure 3 depicts the proposed process in this study.

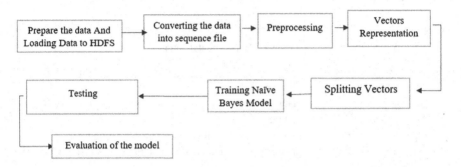

Fig. 3. The proposed process of text categorization

7 Experiment Result and Discussion

In this section, the performance of the automatic thesis document classification to their genre using Naïve Bayes classification algorithm is discussed. Out of the total 208 thesis documents in the dataset, 122 are used for training to build the classifier and 86 are used for testing. Performance is evaluated by using a confusion matrix as shown in Table 2. The model classifies documents with an accuracy of 79.06%. The proposed model also has 85.75% precision and 79.07% of recall. Table 2 discusses the model recall and precision for each class/genre.

Table 2. Confusion matrix

Category		A	B	C	D	E	F	G	H	I	J	K	L	M	N	O	P	Q	Total	Recall(%)
Biomedical Engineering	A	3	0	0	0	0	0	0	0	0	0	0	0	0	0	0	0	0	3	100
Biotechnology	B	0	6	0	0	0	0	0	0	0	0	0	0	0	0	0	0	0	6	100
Chemistry	C	0	0	7	0	0	0	0	0	0	0	0	0	0	0	0	0	0	7	100
Computer_science	D	0	0	0	10	0	1	0	0	0	0	1	0	0	0	0	0	0	12	83.3
Construction_T_managt	E	0	0	0	0	3	0	0	0	0	0	0	0	0	0	0	0	0	3	100
Earth_science	F	0	0	0	0	0	4	0	0	0	0	0	0	0	0	0	0	0	4	100
Enviromental_Science	G	0	2	1	0	0	0	3	0	1	0	0	0	0	1	0	0	0	8	37.5
Food_and_nutriation	H	0	0	2	0	0	0	0	5	1	0	0	0	0	0	0	0	0	8	62.5
General_biology	I	0	2	0	0	0	0	0	0	2	0	0	0	0	0	0	0	0	4	50
Hydrolic_engineering	J	0	0	0	0	0	0	1	0	0	2	0	0	0	0	0	0	0	3	66.6
Information_Science	K	0	0	0	4	0	0	0	0	0	0	4	0	0	1	0	0	0	9	44.4
Mathematics	L	0	0	0	0	0	0	0	0	0	0	0	0	0	0	0	0	0	0	0
Physics	M	0	0	0	0	0	0	0	0	0	0	0	0	2	0	0	0	0	2	100
Sport_science	N	0	0	0	0	0	0	0	0	0	0	0	0	0	5	0	0	0	5	100
Stastistics	O	0	0	0	0	0	0	0	0	0	0	0	0	0	0	6	0	0	6	100
Structural_engineering	P	0	0	0	0	0	0	0	0	0	0	0	0	0	0	0	5	0	5	100
Zoology	Q	0	0	0	0	0	0	0	0	0	0	0	0	0	0	0	0	1	1	100
Precision (%)		100	60	70	71.4	100	80	75	100	50	100	80	0	100	71.4	100	100	100		

As can be seen from the confusion matrix on Table 2, the matrix shows the classifier did an excellent job in classifying biomedical, sport, statistics, earth science, and chemistry text documents accurately. However, the classifier misclassified large number of information science thesis to computer science because the two class labels have almost similar features and unbalanced number of testing data i.e. 12 text documents for computer science and 9 for information science. This indicate that accuracy can be improved by using balanced number of large training datasets.

8 Conclusion and Future Work

In this paper, thesis document repository datasets have been used to build automatic document classification predictive model using a popular machine learning algorithm naïve Bayes on hadoop distributed file system. MapReduce model were employed to process the data in parallel execution mode. We have built the classification model using mahout on top of Hadoop. The classifier gives an accuracy of 79.06%, which is good to classify new documents. The result reveals that, Naïve Bayes algorithm can classify large thesis documents to its category. The experiments were employed on single node cluster of computers, further experiment can be investigated on multi node cluster of computers using large datasets. And also, other classification algorithms can be used to choose highly accurate model on this dataset. Unigram text normalization is used in this paper, it may be effective on bigram and trigrams and accuracy can be improved by taking different parameters.

References

1. Withanawasam, J.: Apache Mahout Essential. Packet, Birmingham (2015)
2. Lucidworks: Text Classification with Mahout and Lucene. https://lucidworks.com/2013/10/30/road-to-revolution-text-classification-powered-by-apache-mahout-and-lucene/. 10 Apr 2019
3. Tiwary, C.: Learning Apache Mahout_Acquire Practical Skills in Big Data Analytics and Explore Data Science with Apache Mahout. Packet, Birmingham (2015)
4. Jiang, E.P.: Content-based spam email classification using machine-learning algorithms. In: Text Mining: Applications and Theory, pp. 37–56. Wiley (2010)
5. Liu, B., Blasch, E., Chen, Y., Shen, D., Chen, G.: Scalable sentiment classification for big data analysis using Naïve Bayes classifier. In: 2013 IEEE International Conference on Big Data, Silicon Valley, CA, pp. 99–104 (2013)
6. Prabhat, A., Khullar, V.: Sentiment classification on big data using Naïve Bayes and logistic regression. In: 2017 International Conference on Computer Communication and Informatics (ICCCI), Coimbatore, pp. 1–5 (2017)
7. Wongso, R., Luwinda, F.A., Trisnajaya, B.C., Rudy, O.R.: News article text classification in Indonesian language. Procedia Comput. Sci. **116**, 137–143 (2017)
8. Ghazi, M.R., Gangodkar, D.: Hadoop, MapReduce and HDFS: a developers perspective. Procedia Comput. Sci. **48**, 45–50 (2015)
9. Kanavos, A., Nodarakis, N., Sioutas, S., Tsakalidis, A., Tsolis, D., Tzimas, G.: Large scale implementations for Twitter sentiment classification. Algorithms **10**, 33 (2017)

10. Owen, S., et al.: Mahout in Action. Manning Publisher, Shelter Island (2012)
11. Ingersoll, G., et al.: Training Naive Bayes using Apache Mahout, pp. 1–10. Mannining Publication, Shelter Island (2015)
12. Kim, S.-B., Rim, H.-C., Yook, D., Lim, H.-S.: Effective methods for improving Naive Bayes text classifiers. In: Ishizuka, M., Sattar, A. (eds.) PRICAI 2002. LNCS (LNAI), vol. 2417, pp. 414–423. Springer, Heidelberg (2002). https://doi.org/10.1007/3-540-45683-X_45
13. Lewis, D.D.: Effective methods for improving Naïve Bayes text classifiers. Mach. Learn. **1398**, 414–423 (2002)
14. Domingos, P., Pazzani, M.: On the optimality of the simple Bayesian classifier under zero one loss. Mach. Learn. **29**, 103–130 (1997)
15. Joachims, T.: Text categorization with support vector machines: learning with many relevant features. In: Nédellec, C., Rouveirol, C. (eds.) ECML 1998. LNCS, vol. 1398, pp. 137–142. Springer, Heidelberg (1998). https://doi.org/10.1007/BFb0026683
16. Wei, L., et al.: Text classification using support vector machine with mixture of Kernel. J. Soft. Eng. Appl. **5**, 55–58 (2012)
17. Ikonomakis, E.K., Kotsiantis, S., Tampakas, V.: Text classification using machine learning techniques. WSEAS Trans. Comput. **4**(8), 966–974 (2005)
18. Tegegnie, A.K., Tarekegn, A.N., Alem, T.A.: A comparative study of flat and hierarchical classification for Amharic news text using SVM. Int. J. Inf. Eng. **9**, 36–42 (2017)
19. Asker, L., Argaw, A.A., Gambäck, B.: Applying machine learning to Amharic text classification. ResearchGate (2014)
20. Eyassu, B., Gamback, B.: Classifying Amharic text using self organizing map. In: Proceedings of the ACL Workshop on Computational Approaches to Semitic Languages, Ann Arbor (2005)
21. Salur, M.U., Tokat, S., Aydilek, İ.B.: Text classification on mahout with Naïve-Bayes machine learning algorithm. In: International Artificial Intelligence and Data Processing Symposium (IDAP), Malatya, pp. 1–5 (2017)
22. Santoso, J., Yuniarno, E.M., Hariadi, M.: Large scale text classification using map reduce and Naive Bayes algorithm for domain specified ontology building. In: 2015 7th International Conference on Intelligent Human-Machine Systems and Cybernetics, pp. 428–432. IEEE Computer Society, Hangzhou (2015)
23. Chen, H., Fu, D.: An improved Naive Bayes classifier for large scale text. In: 2018 2nd International Conference on Artificial Intelligence: Technologies and Applications (ICAITA 2018) (2018)
24. Feng, M., Wu, G.: A distributed Chinese Naive Bayes classifier based on word embedding. In: International Conference on Machinery, Materials and Computing Technologies. Atlantis Press (2016)
25. Gunarathne, T.: Hadoop Mapreduce v2 Cookbook. Packet, Birmingham (2015)
26. Gupta, A.: Learning Apache Mahout Classification. Packet, Birmingham (2015)

Amharic Question Answering for Biography, Definition, and Description Questions

Tilahun Abedissa[1] and Mulugeta Libsie[2(✉)]

[1] Kotebe Metropolitan University, Addis Ababa, Ethiopia
tilaema@gmail.com
[2] Addis Ababa University, Addis Ababa, Ethiopia
mulugeta.libsie@aau.edu.et

Abstract. A broad range of information needs can often be stated as a question. Question Answering (QA) systems attempt to provide users concise answer(s) to natural language questions. The existing Amharic QA systems handle fact-based questions that usually take named entities as an answer. To deal with more complex information needs we developed an Amharic non-factoid QA for biography, definition, and description questions. A hybrid approach has been used for the question classification. For document filtering and answer extraction we have used lexical patterns. On the other hand to answer biography questions we have used a summarizer and the generated summary is validated using a text classifier. Our QA system is evaluated and has shown a promising result.

Keywords: Question Answering

1 Introduction

To successfully operate within an environment, support decisions and solve problems people need precise information. That stimulates a search for information. However, getting precise information from the ocean of electronic information is not simple. QA is proposed to address this problem. In contrast with traditional document retrieval systems/search engines, which return ranked lists of potentially relevant documents that users must then manually browse through, question answering systems try to give users one or more concise answers in the form of sentences or phrases to natural language questions [6].

QA research had a significant boost when it became the subject of interest of the annual Text REtrieval Conferences (TREC), a series of workshops promoted by the US National Institute of Standards (NIST) with the aim of advancing the state-of-the-art in text retrieval [18]. It also attracts a lot of attention due to the availability of public QA datasets such as the Stanford QA dataset [15], WikiQA [22], and the TREC question answering collections [5]. In the earlier days of QA research, non-factoid questions received relatively little attention [16]. [21] have shown that an existing method for factoid question answering is not sufficient for finding answers to non-factoid questions.

© Springer Nature Switzerland AG 2019
F. Mekuria et al. (Eds.): ICT4DA 2019, CCIS 1026, pp. 301–310, 2019.
https://doi.org/10.1007/978-3-030-26630-1_26

Research on Amharic QA focuses on factoid questions, for example [3, 17] answer place, person/organization name, quantity, and date questions, i.e., factoid type questions by extracting entity names for the questions from documents using rule based answer extraction approach. Amharic non-factoid questions like: biographical questions such as "አፄ ቴዎድሮስ ማናቸው?" ("Who is Emperor Tewodros?") compel a system to gather relevant encyclopedic facts about a person/organization from multiple documents; and other complex questions like definition, description, how, or why questions with complex answers oblige reasoning and fusion of multiple "information pieces" from different sources [4].

Even though there are other non-factoid QA systems [10, 14, 26] for other languages, due to the language dependency they only answer their respective language's non-factoid questions. Due to Amharic language morphological complexity [12] and the syntax differences of the question and answer of Amharic non-factoid questions with other languages, other language QA systems cannot answer Amharic non-factoid questions.

Thus, we developed an Amharic QA system (see Sect. 4) that can answer Amharic biography, definition, and description questions. The main contributions of this research are:

- Implement a hybrid approach for automatic question classification.
- Develop lexical patterns that can be used to filter documents and extract candidate answers for definition and description questions.
- Paved a way how Amharic summarizers could be used for non-factoid questions.
- Used text classifier to determine a generated answer for a biography question is actually a biography or not.

The remaining part of this paper is organized as follows. Related works and methodology of the study are given in Sects. 2 and 3 respectively. Section 4 presents a detailed description of our proposed QA model along with its implementation. Section 5 states the evaluation, evaluation criteria, and the empirical results of the proposed system with their discussion. Finally, Sect. 6 concludes the paper with a summary and future works.

2   Related Works

Answering non-factoid questions remains a critical challenge in Web QA. One difficulty is the lexical gap between questions and answers. More knowledge is required to find answers to non-factoid questions [24]. The TREC QA tasks started to incorporate certain categories of non-factoid questions, such as definition questions. One of the first English non-factoid QA system [19] was based on web search using chunks extracted from the original question and ranked the extracted candidate answers using a translation model. Keikha et al. [8] used state-of-the-art passage retrieval method and

Yulianti et al. [25] uses summarization. Recently from the literature we observe that neural networks are widely employed, for example [9, 20, 23]. In addition, using community QA is one way to answer non-factoid questions [16, 22].

3   Methodology

In order to achieve the objective of the study and to understand the state-of-the-art in question answering, books, articles, journals and other publications have been thoroughly reviewed. In addition the following methods are employed.

3.1   Data Collection Methods

To develop an efficient Amharic QA system for biography, definition, and description questions analyzing the characteristics of these question types, their respective answers and the data source used for answering the questions is crucial. Thus, for training and testing the question classifier, questions are prepared from different Amharic documents manually, as well for document retrieval and answer extraction evaluation Amharic documents are collected from different web sites including Amharic Wikipedia[1] using WinHTTrack[2] website copier.

3.2   Performance Evaluation Methods

Evaluation for QA system mainly focuses on the accuracy of the question classifier, document retrieval, and answers returned. Thus, as suggested in [1] our QA system's accuracy is evaluated by comparing the answers returned by the system with human-proposed answers to the same set of questions. Hence, we used precision, recall, and F-score as criteria for measuring the performance.

4   Design and Implementation of the Amharic QA System

As shown in Fig. 1, the QA system consists of document pre-processing, question analysis, document retrieval, and answer extraction components.

4.1   Document Pre-processing

The document pre-processing component performs character normalization, short word expansion, stop word removal, stemming, morphological analysis, and indexing. We used the document pre-processing component that was used by [17], HornMorpho [13] tool for morphological analysis, and Lucene[3] to index the pre processed documents.

---

[1] https://am.wikipedia.org/wiki/ ዋና ው_ ገ ጽ.

[2] HTTrack is a free (GPL, libre/free software) and easy-to-use offline browser utility, http://www. httrack.com.

[3] http://lucene.apache.org/core/.

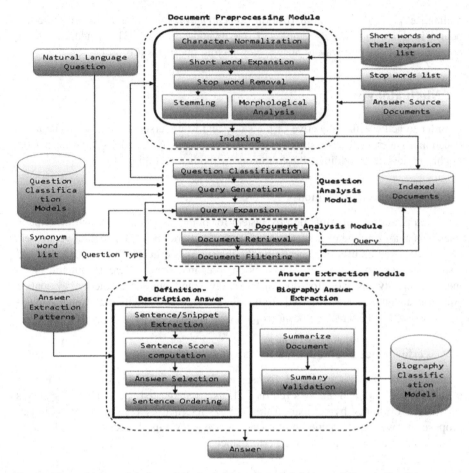

Fig. 1. The architectural design of Amharic biography, definition, and description QA system.

4.2 Question Analysis

This component is dedicated to determine question type, generate query by removing interrogative terms and stop words and expand the query using a synonym list. The question classifier subcomponent determines the type of a question as biography, definition or description. A hybrid approach, i.e., rule based and machine learning techniques are used for the question classification.

A rule based question classifier algorithm determines the question type by using the interrogative terms and question class indicative terms. For example, given the question "በአፍሪካ ውስጥ ድህነትን ለመቅረፍ የትምህርት ጥቅም ምንድን ነው?" ("What is the use of education for eradicating poverty in Africa?") the terms "ጥቅም" (use) and "ምንድን ነው" (what is) indicate that the question is looking for a description. The other approach, machine learning technique predicts the question type of questions based on the training models. The training and classifying tool that we used is Support Vector Machine (SVM) algorithm implementation SVM_light[4] [7]. The svm_learn (learning module) is trained by preparing three question groups (definition versus biography, definition versus description, and description versus biography). Then the svm_classify (classification module) tries to find the class of the question by testing it with the three generated training models for a new question.

4.3 Document Analysis

Once the type of question is identified and the queries have been created and expanded, relevant documents are retrieved from the indexed documents by the document retrieval (implemented using Lucene) sub component. The document retrieval sub-component simply ranks and extracts documents based on word overlap to the query; it does not consider the question type. That means a document ranked to top might be irrelevant to a question. Due to this reason documents should be filtered before passed to the next module. Thus document filtering subcomponent first locates the question target using target extractor. For biography and definition question types the query itself is taken as a target whereas for description types a target is acquired by removing descriptive indicator terms from the query. Then for definition and description questions if a text is extracted by one of their respective rules (formed as regular expressions), the document is kept; otherwise it is removed. On the other hand, for biography question types, the documents that contain all the target terms in the same order as in the query are taken for further analysis.

4.4 Answer Extraction

Answer extraction is the act of extracting text strings constituting the exact answer(s) to a question from the candidate answer-bearing document(s) retrieved by the document analysis module. Based on the question type, the filtered documents are processed by the biography answer extraction or definition-description answer extraction subcomponents.

4.4.1 Definition - Description Answer Extraction

This sub component finds snippets and/or sentences about the current target then ranks, selects, and orders the candidate answers, finally generates an answer for definition and description questions. First every filtered document is tokenized to sentences, and extracts snippets/sentences by using the lexical patterns (we have prepared about 14 rules for definition and 5 rules for description questions). We observed that many documents, while defining a term they usually state the core concepts about the term in the first two or three sentences. Therefore, for definition questions, if the first sentence of a document is extracted by one of the rules, the next two sentences are included to the candidate answer set.

---

[4] http://svmlight.joachims.org/.

To select the appropriate sentences/snippets from the candidate answer set we formulate the sentence scoring function given in Eq. 1, i.e., the score of a sentence S is calculated as the sum of the percentage of the query (Q) terms in the sentence, weight of the pattern that identifies the sentence, the reciprocal of the position of the sentence in the document that contains it, and the Lucene score of the document D that contains S.

$$score(S) = \frac{N_{S \cap Q}}{N_Q} + weight(S, P) + \frac{1}{pos(S)} + luceneScore(D, S) \qquad (1)$$

Since the position of a sentence does not have any impact for description questions, score of sentence S is computed by the formula given in Eq. 2.

$$score(S) = \frac{N_{S \cap Q}}{N_Q} + weight(S, P) + luceneScore(D, S) \qquad (2)$$

At this stage it is likely that some of the snippets or sentences might be redundant and all are not equally important. That is, we have to guarantee that, given sentence A does another sentence B provide any new and relevant information for the purpose of defining or describing a given target? Therefore, one way of determining the similarity of texts is to use word overlap. The more different text fragments share common non-stop words it indicates that they are highly similar [2]. Equation 3 is used to compute the similarity between sentences A and B.

$$sim(A, B) = \frac{|T_A \cap T_B|}{min(|T_A|, |T_B|)} \qquad (3)$$

where *sim(A,B)* is the similarity of the sentences A and B, $|T_A|$ and $|T_B|$ are the number of non-stop tokens in sentences A and B respectively, and $|T_A \cap T_B|$ is the number of common non-stop tokens in A and B.

If the similarity of the sentence S to one of the sentences in the definition/description pool is greater than or equal to 0.7, then skip sentence S; otherwise add it to the definition/description pool. The value of the similarity cut off point is set to 0.7 by doing an experiment. A final answer is generated by selecting 5 top ranked sentences/snippets and then to keep the coherence the candidate answers are ordered in such a way that sentences/snippets beginning with the target term are positioned at the beginning, those that begin with connective terms are in the middle, and sentences which start with other terms are positioned to the end.

4.4.2   Biography Answer Extraction
For biography questions whose focus is a person, important dates in their life (birth, marriage, and death), their major achievements and any other interesting items of note would comprise a 'correct' answer. Otherwise if the focus is an organization, the answer should probably include information about when and by whom it was founded, what it serves/ makes/ sells, who owns it, and other organizations it collaborated with. Therefore, to generate an answer the biography answer extraction component first

merges[5] the filtered documents, summarizes the merged document using the work of [11], and validates the summary. The evaluation task can be considered as a text classification problem. To do so we trained the SVM_Light by using manually prepared biography and non-biography texts and use the model to classify the summary produced by the summarizer. The summary validation subcomponent returns the summarizer result as an answer for the question if the result of the classifier is greater than or equal to 0.5, otherwise no answer will be displayed. We observed that documents that obtain values greater or equal to 0.5 by the classifier contain the basic information that a biography should contain.

5   Results and Discussion

Precision, recall, and F-score are used as criteria for measuring the performance of the document retrieval and answer extraction components. Since the task of the question classifier is identifying question types, its accuracy is evaluated by the percentage of correctly identified question types. The percentage is computed by taking the ratio of correctly identified questions to the total test questions.

Even though there is no standard Amharic QA dataset for performance evaluation, as shown in Table 1 we have prepared 1500 questions. The question classifier is evaluated using 10-fold cross validation approach. The average result of the question classifier is given in Table 2.

As shown in Table 2 both question classifiers have no problem on identifying biography questions. This is due to the reason that either the definition or the description question types do not have any common interrogative term with biography question. The SVM based classifier performance on definition questions is smaller than that of the other. This is because the interrogative word "ምንድን ነው" (what) is shared by definition and description questions.

The document retrieval performance is measured by 60 queries on two corpuses each containing 600 documents. The first corpus contains the documents that are analyzed by the stemmer and the second contains the same documents as the first but analyzed by the morphological analyzer. The result of the experiment is shown in Fig. 2. From the figure we can see that the recall, precision, and F-score of the document retrieval are greater on the data analyzed by the morphological analyzer than the stemmer.

During our experiment we observed that both the stemmer and the morphological analyzer didn't generate the stem and root of every term in the test documents and queries. Moreover, when the morphological analyzer returns root words it gives in Romanized form, for some words in an attempt to transliterate to Amharic the result contains non Amharic characters. For example, the root returned for the term "አይን" (eye) is "'y*" when it is transliterated the result is "አይ**". Thus the performance of the stemmer and the morphological analyzer should be improved.

---

[5] In a biography question an entity may represent different persons/ organizations. To resolve this, our system classifies the filtered documents to different categories and merges the documents in each category separately.

Table 1. Amount of questions used for training and testing.

Type of question	No. of training question set	No. of testing question set	Total
Biography	450	50	500
Definition	450	50	500
Description	450	50	500
Total	1350	150	1500

Table 2. Average performance of the rule based and SVM based question type classifiers on each question type.

Question type	Classification technique	
	SVM based	Rule based
Biography	0.98	0.99
Definition	0.66	0.99
Description	0.86	0.96
Average	0.83	0.98

Biography, definition, and description questions are more difficult to evaluate than factoid questions in that their answers are more complex and can be expressed in different ways. Moreover, answers to these questions can focus on different facets of the concept, entity, person, or organization they are describing. For the evaluation of the answer extraction component a total of 120 questions (40 questions from each type) are prepared. The answers for these questions generated by our system and the answers that are manually constructed are used to compute the precision and recall. The precision, recall, and F-score along with their average value is given in Table 3.

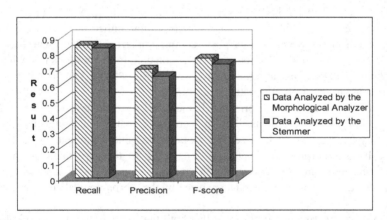

Fig. 2. The recall, precision, and F-score of the document retrieval component on the two data sets.

As shown in Table 3, while conducting the experiment we observed that many documents do not explicitly put the purpose of concepts/entities by using descriptive implication terms rather they put it implicitly. Even in some documents the descriptions are incorporated within their definitions. Due to these reasons the F-score on description questions is less than that of the definition. On the other hand the result that we obtained for the biography questions is highly dependent on the performance of the summarizer.

Table 3. Performance of the answer extraction component

Question type	Recall	Precision	F-score
Biography	0.341	0.895	0.493
Definition	0.725	0.626	0.658
Description	0.762	0.528	0.624
Average	0.609	0.683	0.592

6 Conclusions and Future Works

In this paper we have discussed about an Amharic QA system for biography, definition, and description questions. Question classification, document filtering, and answer extraction patterns are created for their respective purposes. In addition, a machine learning tool has been used for question classification and biography detection. The QA system has been evaluated by preparing a dataset. With minimal amount of tools we were able to achieve a promising result.

Developing co-reference resolution tool, generating lexical patterns automatically, extending this work to more complex question types such as why and how questions, and preparing a standard QA dataset are our future research directions.

References

1. Breck, E., et al.: How to evaluate your question answering system every day and still get real work done. In: Proceedings of the Second International Conference on Language Resources and Evaluation. LREC-2000, Athens, Greece (2000)
2. Manning, C.D., Raghavan, P., Schtze, H.: An Introduction to Information Retrieval. Cambridge University Press, New York (2008)
3. Abebaw, D., Libsie, M.: LETEYEQ (ለጠየቅ)-a web based amharic question answering system for factoid questions using machine learning approach, M.Sc. thesis, Addis Ababa University (2013, Unpublished)
4. Dietz, L., Verma, M., Radlinski, F., Craswell, N.: TREC complex answer retrieval overview. In: TREC 2017 (2017)
5. Voorhees, E.M., et al.: The TREC-8 question answering track report. In: Text Retrieval Conference, vol. 99, pp. 77–82 (1999)
6. Indurkhya, N., Damereau, F.J. (eds.): Handbook of Natural Language Processing, 2nd edn. Chapman & Hall/CRC, Boca Raton (2010)
7. Joachims, T.: Text categorization with support vector machines: learning with many relevant features. In: Nédellec, C., Rouveirol, C. (eds.) ECML 1998. LNCS, vol. 1398, pp. 137–142. Springer, Heidelberg (1998). https://doi.org/10.1007/BFb0026683
8. Keikha, M., Park, J.H., Croft, W.B., Sanderson, M.: Retrieving passages and finding answers. In: Proceedings of the 2014 Australasian Document Computing Symposium, pp. 81–84 (2014)
9. Lee, K., Salant, S., Kwiatkowski, T., Parikh, A., Das, D., Berant, J.: Learning recurrent span representations for extractive question answering. In: International Conference on Learning Representations (2016)

10. Murata, M., Tsukawaki, S., Kanamaru, T., Ma, Q., Isahara, H.: Non-factoid Japanese question answering through passage retrieval that is weighted based on types of answers. In: Proceedings of the third IJCNLP (2008)
11. Tamiru, M., Libsie, M.: Automatic Amharic text summarization using latent semantic analysis, M.Sc. thesis, Addis Ababa University (2009, Unpublished)
12. Abate, M., Assabie, Y.: Development of Amharic morphological analyzer using memory-based learning. In: Przepiórkowski, A., Ogrodniczuk, M. (eds.) NLP 2014. LNCS (LNAI), vol. 8686, pp. 1–13. Springer, Cham (2014). https://doi.org/10.1007/978-3-319-10888-9_1
13. Gasser, M.: HornMorpho: a system for morphological processing of Amharic, Oromo, and Tigrinya. In: Conference on Human Language Technology for Development, Alexandria, Egypt (2011)
14. Trigui, O., Belguith, H.L., Rosso, P.: DefArabicQA: Arabic definition question answering system. In: Workshop on Language Resources and Human Language Technologies for Semitic Languages, 7th LREC, Valletta, Malta (2010)
15. Rajpurkar, P., Zhang, J., Lopyrev, K., Liang, P.: Squad: 100,000 + questions for machine comprehension of text. In: Conference on Empirical Methods in Natural Language Processing, pp. 2383–2392 (2016)
16. Savenkov, D.: Ranking answers and web passages for non-factoid question answering, Emory university at trec liveqa (2015)
17. Muhie, S., Libsie, M.: Amharic question answering (AQA). In: 10th Dutch-Belgian Information Retrieval Workshop (2010)
18. Silvia, Q.: Advanced techniques for personalized, interactive question answering on the web. In: Workshop on Knowledge and Reasoning for Answering Questions, Manchester, pp. 33–40 (2008)
19. Soricut, R., Brill, E.: Automatic question answering using the web: beyond the factoid. Inf. Retrieval 9(2), 191–206 (2006)
20. Wang, W., Yang, N., Wei, F., Chang, B., Zhou, M.: Gated self-matching networks for reading comprehension and question answering. In: 55th Annual Meeting of the Association for Computational Linguistics, pp. 189–198 (2017)
21. Yang, L., et al.: Beyond factoid QA: effective methods for non-factoid answer sentence retrieval. In: Proceedings of the European Conference on Information Retrieval, pp. 115–128 (2016)
22. Yang, Y., Yih, W., Meek, C.: WIKIQA: a challenge dataset for open-domain question answering. In: Proceedings of the 2015 Conference on Empirical Methods in Natural Language Processing, Lisbon, Portugal, pp. 2013–2018 (2015)
23. Yu, Y., Zhang, W., Hasan, K., Yu, M., Xiang, B., Zhou, B.: End-to-end answer chunk extraction and ranking for reading comprehension. In: International Conference on Learning Representations (2016)
24. Yulianti, E., Chen, R.-C., Scholer, F., Sanderson, M.: Using semantic and context features for answer summary extraction. In: Proceedings of the 21st Australasian Document Computing Symposium, pp. 81–84 (2016)
25. Yulianti, E., Chen, R.-C., Scholer, F., Croft, W.B., Sanderson, M.: Document summarization for answering non-factoid queries. IEEE Trans. Knowl. Data Eng. 30(1), 15–28 (2018)
26. Zhang, Z., Zhou, Y., Huang, X., Wu, L.: Answering definition questions using web knowledge bases. In: Dale, R. et al. (eds.) IJCNLP (2005), LNAI, vol. 3651, pp. 498–506. Springer, Heidelberg (2005)

Dictionary Based Amharic Sentiment Lexicon Generation

Girma Neshir Alemneh[1](✉), Andreas Rauber[2], and Solomon Atnafu[3]

[1] IT Doctoral Program, Addis Ababa University, Addis Ababa, Ethiopia
girma1978@gmail.com
[2] Institute of Information Systems Engineering,
Technical University of Vienna, Vienna, Austria
rauber@ifs.tuwien.ac.at
[3] Department of Computer Science,
Addis Ababa University, Addis Ababa, Ethiopia
solomon.atnafu@aau.edu.et

Abstract. Sentiment analysis is a hot research area with several applications including analysis of political opinions, classifying comments, movie reviews, news reviews and product reviews. To employ rule based sentiment analysis, sentiment lexicon is required. However, manual construction of a sentiment lexicon is time consuming and costly for resource-limited languages. To reduce development time and costs, we propose an algorithm for constructing Amharic sentiment lexicons. The proposed approach transfers sentiment labels from a one language (e.g. English) to resource-limited language (e.g. Amharic) relying on Amharic-English dictionary. Using Bilingual/Monolingual dictionaries as a bridge, two Amharic sentiment lexicons are automatically generated the first based on SO-CAL polarity lexicon, the second on SentiWordNet 3.0. For each Amharic word, the algorithm finds the meaning of the corresponding English word(s). For these English words, sentiment information is searched from the aforementioned sentiment lexicon(s). The weighted average of returned sentiment values, part of speech and gloss information is assigned to the Amharic word. Lexicons of 5683 and 13679 words, respectively, are generated automatically and evaluated subsequently.

Keywords: Lexicon generation algorithm · Sentiment analysis ·
Amharic sentiment lexicon · Sentiment lexicon generation

1 Introduction

Sentiment Analysis or opinion mining is the process of detecting subjective or emotional indicators in the text. That is finding the attitude of the author towards a particular topic, event, entity, aspect or issue. Nowadays, due to the advancement of web technology, users are not only consumers of online information but also they are producer of information. Most of these data carry opinions that need further analysis to detect its polarity levels (i.e. negative and positive). For instance, political parties want to gather opinions of voters, or a government wants to collect summarized opinions for improvement towards their new policy or existing public services. Thus, a sentiment lexicon is a

© Springer Nature Switzerland AG 2019
F. Mekuria et al. (Eds.): ICT4DA 2019, CCIS 1026, pp. 311–326, 2019.
https://doi.org/10.1007/978-3-030-26630-1_27

valuable resource that should be readily available for opinion mining tasks. So far, sentiment analysis research works were restricted to dominant languages (mostly English). Currently, opinionated language resources are increasingly generated and used in languages other than English. Amharic is one of these resource-limited languages that has started to get attention. But, still it has no sufficient linguistic resources for sentiment analysis such as part of speech taggers and sentiment lexicons. A sentiment lexicon contains a list of opinion words where each term has been assigned positive and negative values, and sometimes, part of speech and glosses definition are included. This work aims to address the following research questions: (a) how do we develop Amharic sentiment lexicons by employing monolingual and cross-lingual resources automatically? (b) how do we evaluate and validate the quality and accuracy of Amharic polarity lexicon's subjectivity clues? (c) how can we measure the accuracy and the coverage of the generated Amharic Sentiment Lexicons for detecting the subjectivity of Amharic text?

The remaining part of the article is organized as follows: in Sect. 2, we provide an overview of related work. Section 3 describes the data sets and the proposed methods. In Sect. 4, we present results and discussions, followed by a summary of our conclusions in Sect. 5.

2 Related Work

This section briefly presents a few key related works. Gebremeskel [6] manually built Amharic polarity Lexicon of 900 terms. This was, again manually, extended by Tilahun to 1,000 terms [7]. In these works, the polarity value of each term in this Amharic sentiment lexicon was labeled either negative 2 or positive 2 without using numerical value in between or no nominal fine-grained levels of sentiment strength granularities or no part of speech information in the lexicon. The authors used this lexicon for lexicon based (rule based) Amharic opinion mining tasks. However, the effort required to further extend these lexicons manually is prohibitive, calling for automated methods, benefiting from the efforts invested in building such dictionaries in other languages. Taboada et al. [1] propose a semantic orientations calculator (SO-CAL) for lexicon based subjectivity classification. SO-CAL utilizes sentiment dictionaries and also includes intensification and negation to calculate and assign semantic orientation of words in the text. The major strength of this work is that the lexicon performed consistently in any domain to extract word level/sentence level opinion in text and also presented the process of creating and evaluating sentiment dictionaries using Mechanical Turk. SO-CAL performed well in sentiment analysis of user's blog postings. We will use SO-CAL as one of the baseline sentiment lexicons for assigning sentiment values to our translated terms.

Medagoda et al. in [2] built SentiWordNet 3.0 for Sinhala language by mapping English SentiWordNet 3.0 relying on the online English-Sinhala dictionary. The English words in the dictionary were used as search key to generate a lexicon for the corresponding translated Sinhala sentiment lexicon. If the translated Sinhala word is found, then it is inserted with its polarity value and POS tag into the Sinhala sentiment lexicon, otherwise search proceeds for the next English word in the dictionary. The final Sinhala Sentiment Lexicon contains 5973 adjectives and 405 adverbs. This lexicon was evaluated using 2,083 manually classified news article opinions collected from Sinhala online newspaper. Based on the different classification methods using this lexicon, the accuracy achieved was between 56–60%. As this evaluation result is below the baseline, handling negations, multiword with negations and context sensitivity were suggested to be addressed in the forthcoming works to improve the performance of the lexicon generation. We will use a similar approach to generate Amharic Sentiment Lexicon, considering the idiosyncrasies of the Amharic language.

3 Methods

3.1 Data Sets and Lexical Resources

This subsection describes the main data sets and lexical resources used for building and evaluating Amharic Sentiment Lexicons.

(a) **English SentiWordNet 3.0:** SentiWordNet is automatically built based on synsets of wordnet version 3.0 [3]. This lexicon contains 72,092 terms with part of speech, id number, PosScore, NegScore, SynsetTerms and Gloss. The pair (POS, ID) uniquely identifies a WordNet (3.0) synset. The values PosScore and NegScore are the positivity and negativity scores (in the range of 0 to1) assigned to each entry of the synset. The objectivity score is computed as: ObjScore = 1 − (PosScore + NegScore) SynsetTerms column reports the terms, with sense number, belonging to the synset (separated by spaces). We selected to port this lexicon into Amharic because of its extensive coverage.

(b) **SO-CAL Polarity Lexicon:** SO-CAL refers to the Semantic Orientation CALculator, a tool to extract sentiment from text. It has a long history of development. We use this lexicon [1] as a baseline. SO-CAL contains 10126 words with polarity value ranges from −5 to +5. The lexicon is categorized into adjectives, Adverbs, nouns, verbs and intensifier word lists. This lexicon has been extensively tested showing good performance in different domains.

(c) **Amharic-English Dictionary:** This is a dictionary that works in one direction (i.e. Amharic to English). For each Amharic word, it contains part-of-Speech tag(s) and corresponding meanings in English. The English text might be a single word, phrase, or list of synonyms. The total size of this dictionary is more than 31000 terms which are obtained by merging Amharic-English dictionary (12700 Amharic words) [4], Amsalu_Aklilu Amharic-English Dictionary (16231 words) and Amharic-English dictionary by SelamSoft Plc (1,075 words). This dictionary serves as a bridge to propagate sentiment from English sentiment lexicon to Amharic sentiment lexicon.

(d) **Amharic-Amharic Dictionary:** From more than 30 thousand entries of Amharic lexical wordlist in [4], we built 33965 Amharic-Amharic dictionary automatically, where this dictionary is served as gloss source for terms in the generated Amharic Sentiment Lexicon.

(e) **Facebook Comments Data Set:** This dataset consists of 2500 sentence/phrase level sentiment annotated facebook news users' comments collected from the Government Office Affairs Communication (GOAC) between 2008 and 2010. News that received high view counters/frequent comments were selected as "hot topics" and the associated comments labeled by professionals into either positive or negative sentiment.

(f) Amharic Web Corpus: This is an automatically crawled collection of web documents consisting mainly of news, politics and religion documents. It was collected and tokenized, automatically part-of-speech tagged and published under the HaBiT project [5]. The file is a single xml file of size 421 MB. It contains 20 million tokens. We will use this corpus for evaluation of the sentiment annotations.

3.2 Automatic Sentiment Score Calculation

To build an Amharic Sentiment Lexicon relying on bilingual dictionaries, we tried to transfer subjectivity or polarity information from polarity lexicon of resource rich language (i.e. English sentiment lexicon) to resource limited language (i.e. Amharic). Specific to this approach, an algorithm is developed to transfer labels from English SentiWordNet 3.0 and SO-CAL to Amharic Sentiment Lexicon.

As shown in Fig. 1 below, the Amharic-English bilingual dictionary is employed as a bridge between the two languages. The proposed approach of building Amharic Senti-ment Lexicon is similar to Sinhala language in [2]. However, our approach is different at

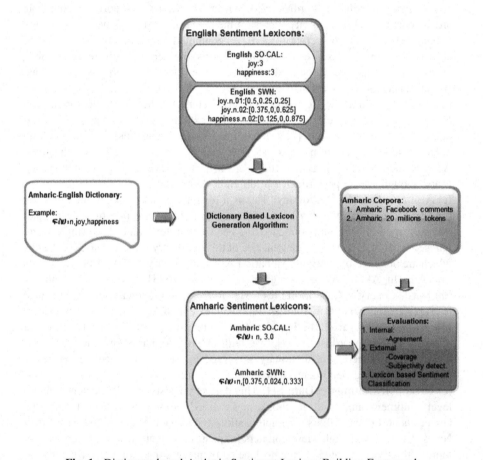

Fig. 1. Dictionary based Amharic Sentiment Lexicon Building Framework

least in three features: (1) algorithm searches for each Amharic word as key rather than English words in the Amharic-English bilingual dictionary. That is why Amharic-English dictionary is used instead of English-Amharic dictionary. (2) our algorithm uses average weighting of synonymous of English to tokens to assign the sentiment score for the corresponding Amharic term in the bilingual Amharic-English dictionary and (3) the approach in this work will also handle negation words that appear in the Amharic text.

Consider Amharic word w_{a_i} in the Amharic-English Dictionary d_{ae} has corresponding meanings in English word(s), $w_{e\_i\_j}$. The Amharic Sentiment Lexicon is denoted by s_a, the English language sentiment lexicon by s_e. As part of preprocessing, we normalized all Amharic words in the Amharic-English dictionary by replacing varied alphabets of the same sound with identical symbols. Moreover, a stemmer is applied during evaluations. Then the algorithm is represented:

BuildAmharicLexicon(s_e)
Input: s_e *(EnglishSentiment Lexicon i.e. either SWN or SO-CAL)*
Output: s_a *(generated Amharic Sentiment Lexicon)*
  Format for s_a is {w_{ai} as key: scores, part of speech, gloss as list} pair.
Initialize: d_{ae}*–load Amharic-English Dictionary from File and initialize other vars*
 1. For each w_{a_i} in the d_{ae}:
   a. Search its {$w_{e\_i\_1}, w_{e\_i\_2,...}, w_{e\_i\_j,...}, w_{e\_i\_n-1}, w_{e\_i\_n}$}
   b. For each synonym word $w_{e\_i\_j}$, search it in s_e
     i. If found, return all the polarity values(+,-,objective) of the synsets
     ii. Keep them in a list L
   c. Find length of +,-, objective list in L
   d. Compute the <u>average weighted</u> polarity in L using equation (1)
   e. Assign the average <u>weighted polarity, part of speech, and gloss</u> to w_{a_i} in s_e. That is,
    $s_a[w_{a\_i}]$=[[Average weighted polarity], part of speech, gloss]

 return s_a

Listing-1. Dictionary based Algorithm

Algorithm Description: In Listing-1, for each Amharic word in the bilingual dictionary, the aggregated sentiment values of corresponding English term(s) in Senti-WordNet 3.0 (or SO-CAL) are assigned to the Amharic word if terms are found in the source lexicon. Finally, the Amharic Sentiment Lexicon contains each Amharic term, its average weighted polarity values, its corresponding part of speech and gloss definitions are assigned [8].

For each Amharic word w_{a_i} in the Amharic-English dictionary, there are list of English words($w_{e\_i\_1}, w_{e\_i\_2,}, w_{e\_i\_j,}, w_{e\_i\_n-1}, w_{e\_i\_n}$) in the dictionary. The assumption is that the first English word $w_{e\_i\_1}$ has more closer in meaning to Amharic word w_{a_i} than the second word $w_{e\_i\_2}$ and in turn $w_{e\_i\_2}$ is more prominent to w_{a_i} than $w_{e\_i\_3}$ and so on. So more weight is given to the first word $w_{e\_i\_1}$ and least weight is given to the last word $w_{e\_i\_n}$. On the basis of this assumption, the weighted average sentiment of English words is computed and then assigned the resulting sentiment value to the corresponding Amharic word w_{a_i}. Then, the sentiment score (w_{a_i}) is given by:

$$= (\text{score}(w_{e\_i\_1})X(n-1+1) + \text{score}(w_{e\_i\_2})X(n-2+1) + .. \text{score}(w_{e\_i\_j})X(n-j+1)..$$
$$+ \text{score}(w_{e\_i\_n})X(n-n+1))/n$$

$$= \frac{\sum_{j=1}^{n} score_{eij}(w_{eij})x(n-j+1)}{n} \tag{1}$$

where n is the number of English words $w_{e\_i\_1}, w_{e\_i\_2}, .., w_{e\_i\_n-1}, w_{e\_i\_n}$ and $score_{eij}$ is in turn refers to:

$$score_{eij} = \left\{ \begin{array}{ll} sentimentScore(w_{eij}), & \textit{if the lexicon} \quad \textit{is} \quad SO - CAL \\ sumOfSentimentScore(Synset(w_{eij})), & \textit{if the lexicon} \quad \textit{is} \quad SWN \end{array} \right\}$$

It should be noted that the gloss definitions are not found in Amharic English dictionary; rather it is propagated from another Amharic–Amharic dictionary. However, there are some terms without gloss definitions as they were not found in the Amharic–Amharic Dictionary [4].

The Amharic sentiment lexicons are generated and used under a few assumptions. (1) The senses of words in the bilingual dictionaries of the two languages are considered to be same. Thus, the sentiment score of an English word in sentiment analysis of English text is assumed to be identical to the sentiment score of an Amharic word in Amharic texts. (2) The parts of speech in both languages in the bilingual dictionary are assumed to be equivalent [2].

From English SentiWordNet 3.0 and SOCAL, two corresponding Amharic Sentiment lexicons are automatically generated. The sizes of these newly built Amharic lexicons are 13679 term entries and 5683 terms, respectively. The experimental results and evaluations are discussed in the subsequent section.

4   Results and Discussion

In this section, the experimental results relying on the generated Amharic sentiment lexicons are discussed. Each of the generated Amharic lexicons is evaluated in two ways using external data as well as intrinsic evaluation and mutual comparison of agreement. Finally the usefulness of the Amharic lexicons is tested in lexicon based sentiment classification of Amharic News Comments. To increase the string matching accuracy in generating the evaluation scores, we apply basic preprocessing: tokenization, stopword removal, punctuation mark removal and stemming.

(i) **Tokenization:** Amharic words are separated by space as delimiter. Thus, Amharic text is tokenized into words if space is found in between tokens.

(ii) **Punctuation mark removal:** Amharic punctuation marks such as ።(full stop), ፤ (double colon), ፡ (single quote), ፥ -(preface colon), « »(double quotes) and so on should be removed.

(iii) **Normalization:** Ethiopic script contains redundant symbols representing the same sound. These symbols are substituted by the symbol on the right. E.g. (ʹህ,ሃ,ሐ,ሓ,ኅ,ኃ,ኻ=>ህ)፤   (ሰ,ሠ=>ሰ)፥ (θ,ጸ=>θ)፥   (0,አ,ኣ,0,ዓ=>0)፥ (ቆ,ቈ,ቖ=>ቆ)፥ (ቄ,ቐ=>ቄ)፥(ኸ,ኈ=>ኸ)፥ (ጎ,ጐ=>ጎ)፥(ኂ,ኺ,ሒ=>ኂ)). Where, the arrow(=>) means "replaced by". That is, if either of the symbols on the left side found in the text, then it is replaced by the symbol right of the arrow(=>).

(iv) **Stopword removal:** For stopword removal, stopwords identified in [5] are used.

(v) **Stemming:** As Amharic is highly morphologically rich language, we develop a shallow stemmer by specifying some conditions to enforce and normalize the morphological variations of Amharic words to a common base form/stem. The stemmer is composed of a set of rules of the regular expressions to remove prefixes and suffixes. During stemming, if Amharic word has a match to one of the patterns of regular expressions, then the word is reduced to its corresponding stem by removing the matched suffix or/and prefix. For example, for the Amharic words such as 'ቆንጆው'/the one who is handsome/masculine/,   'ቆንጆውን' /someone who is handsome/masculine/, object form/, 'ቆንጆዎቹን'/those who are beautiful,   ' ቆንጆዎች/ those who are beautiful, 'ለቆንጆዋ'/to the beautiful one/feminine/and soon. Finally, these Amharic words are reduced to the common stem/root by converting the symbols to corresponding consonant of Amharic/'ቅ-ን-ጅ'/by our stemmer. More sample of Amharic stemmed words are attached in Appendix A of this report.

4.1   External to Lexicon Evaluation

In this research, external evaluation is carried out in two ways.

(a) Subjectivity detection: Each term in the lexicons is counted only if it is present in a particular Amharic news comments. If more terms of the lexicon found in the Amharic comment, then the comment is subjective, otherwise objective. The usefulness of automatically generated lexicons is evaluated by their accuracies in detecting subjectivity in Amharic texts. These lexicons are used to identify subjective (positive or negative) Amharic text from objective (neutral) Amharic text. The accuracy of subjectivity detection increases as we apply stemming along with the sentiment lexicons. As Amharic language is morphologically rich, the variations of words derivations are normalized to the same stem. Usually, the resulting stem will be in root form. This decreases the string mismatches which arise due to morphological variation of Amharic texts.

Table 1. Lexicons' subjectivity detection rate in percent on Facebook comments data

Sentiment Lexicons	Detection with No Stem (%)	Detection With Stem (%)
Amharic Manual (baseline)	43.23	93.56
Amharic SOCAL	31.28	96.65
Amharic SWN	75.83	99.33

Table 1 shows that the generated Amharic Sentiment SentiWord Net Lexicon outperforms the other lexicons, resulting in 99.33% correct subjectivity detection. The rate of detecting the subjectivity of Amharic news comments using Amharic Sentiment SO-CAL is, in turn, outperforming the manual Amharic sentiment lexicon (93.56%). This subjectivity detection result shows that each of the Amharic sentiment lexicons are outperforming above the subjectivity detection result of the baseline lexicon (the manually generated Amharic sentiment lexicon) by 5.77%. One of the reasons for this might be the size of SWN larger than the manual one. Thus, the degree to which the entries of SWN to appear in the Amharic news comment is higher than the other lexicons.

(b) Evaluation of lexicons by its coverage count (or in percent): This way of evaluating the generated lexicons is to measure the size of lexicons in terms of their coverage count in general corpus containing 20 millions tokens and 2500 Amharic facebook news comments.

Table 2. Lexicons' coverage (positive/negative count and in percent) on 2500 Amharic Facebook comments and 20 million tokens of Amharic web corpora

	2500 Amharic comments		20 millions Amharic tokens	
Lexicons	coverage(+,−) count	%	coverage(+,−) count	%
Manual	[4399, 2995]	31.95	[2713167, 2161501]	25.01
SOCAL	[5738, 3953]	41.87	[4169817, 3391213]	38.88
SWN	[9447, 4803]	61.57	[6645592, 4006072]	54.77

Discussion: The results in Table 2 verify that the coverage of the sentiment lexicon based on SWN is larger than the other lexicons on both data corpora. The other aspect that we can verify from this analysis is that the number of positive and negative opinion words are balanced in both SWN and SOCAL. However, the coverage of the Amharic lexicons in both corpuses is below the average benchmark semantic lexical coverage in other languages Welsh (25%) to Arabic (88%) [9], even though, it is very difficult to compare the coverage of Amharic sentiment lexicons with the coverage of these general purpose semantic lexical resources. Moreover, there is difference in languages intrinsic characteristics.

4.2   Internal to Lexicon Evaluation

Internal evaluation of the lexicon is the process of counting common positive and negative opinion terms in the two lexicons. The number of common terms in the two lexicons is expressed in percentage to show the extent of the agreement (overlap) between the generated lexicons and the manual lexicon (baseline). To evaluate the results of the proposed approach, we computed the agreement between lexicons.

Table 3. The Agreement (in percent) between Lexicons

	Amharic Sentiment Lexicons	Agreement (%)
1	SOCAL and Manual Lexicon	70.80
2	SWN and Manual Lexicon	59.49
3	SOCAL and SWN	66.40

Discussion: Table 3 depicts that the Amharic sentiment lexicon from SOCAL generated through dictionary approach has agreement or overlap of 70.80% with manual Amharic sentiment and it overlaps 66.40% with Amharic sentiment generated from SentiWord Net. On the other hand, Amharic Sentiment from SWN agrees for 59.49% of all terms with the manual Amharic Sentiment lexicon. Although the size of Amharic Sentiment from SWN is much larger (more than double) than Amharic Sentiment from SOCAL, the latter is more consistent in its sentiment scores with the other lexicons. The main purpose of finding agreement between lexicons is to know the extent to which the lexicons overlap.

The disagreement level of English Sentiment lexicons are compared in [10]. In this comparison, the agreement level of SWN is better with Harvard General Inquirer (77%) than other English Sentiment lexicons (MPQA, Opinion Lexicon, LIWC). Amharic generated sentiment lexicon is below the agreement levels reported for the English language resources. The reason for this is that it is very difficult to compare Amharic Lexicon with English lexicon as the two languages are very different in morphology apart from difference in cultural connotations. So, as Amharic is morphologically rich where there could be more variations of terms in the lexicons than the terms in English lexicons. This might decrease the extent of agreement of the Amharic sentiment lexicons.

4.3   Lexicon Based Sentiment Classification

Besides the evaluations in the earlier subsections, we will also evaluate the usefulness of the generated lexicons and their combinations for sentiment classification of Amharic facebook news comments. Prior to sentiment aggregations of Amharic texts, we apply basic text preprocessing (tokenization, punctuation mark removal, normalizing Amharic script symbols, stopword removal, spelling corrector, stemming, etc.). The effect of stemming and negation detection technique on Amharic text is investigated to increase the accuracy of lexicon based Amharic sentiment classification.

Table 4. The accuracy (in percent) of Lexicons for Sentiment Classification

Amharic Senti.Lexicons	Accuracies (%)		
	NoStem+NoNeg.	*Stem+NoNeg.*	*Stem+Neg.*
Manual (baseline)	16.7	42.9	52.7
SOCAL	14.6	46.3	50.8
SWN	30.9	50.1	54.7
Manual + SOCAL	37.2	63.4	72
Manual + SWN	49.9	65.9	74.6
SOCAL + SWN	43.7	66.6	73.5
Manual +SOCAL + SWN	53.7	75.8	**86.2**

Discussions: The usefulness of lexicons is evaluated in terms their accuracies of classifying sentiment of Amharic facebook news comments as shown in Table 4. In general, the results in Table 4 also reveal the effect of applying stemming and negation handling on Amharic texts to boost the performance of sentiment classification. The automatically generated lexicon from English SWN outperforms the performance of the manual (baseline) for classifying sentiment of Amharic texts. On the other hand, the manual lexicon (with stemming and negation handling) in turn outperforms the automatically generated lexicon from English SO-CAL. However, Amharic sentiment lexicon (with stemming and without negation handling) from English SO-CAL relatively performs better than the Amharic manual sentiment lexicon in classifying sentiment of Amharic texts. The combination of the automatically generated sentiment lexicon (SWN) with Manual sentiment lexicon (baseline) outperforms (with accuracy of 74.6%) the other combinations of lexicons for sentiment classification of Amharic texts. The automatically generated lexicons (SO-CAL + SWN) perform well (with accuracy of 73.5%) for classification sentiment in Amharic texts. Yet another combinations of the three lexicons(SO-CAL + SWN + Manual) outperform (with accuracy of 86.2%) the other lexicons or their combinations.

4.4   Error Analysis

Unfortunately, it is challenging to trace the sources of errors in the automatically generated lexicons. Let us try to point out some of the causes for the subsets of generated errors in the automatically translated Amharic sentiment lexicons. We present manually identified errors in this subsection:

(a) **On-spot analysis of errors detected in lexicons:** In the automatically generated lexicons, the generated errors in sentiment transfer from source language terms to target language terms are mainly caused by the following issues: (i) We identified mistranslation of Amharic terms in SWN by the bilingual dictionary. For example, in Amharic SWN, the word ሸጋ("SHEGA") is incorrectly translated into target 'hibernation' and it is wrongly assigned with negative sentiment. But, the correct meaning of the word ሸጋ("SHEGA") means "nice" which has positive sentiment value. (ii) We got correctly translated terms which are assigned opposite in polarity to source terms. For example, in Amharic SWN, the word ቆራጥ("QORAT") correctly translated into'courageous decisive in manner'. The translation is correct, but wrong sentiment value (opposite) is assigned. (iii) We discovered few terms are correctly translated, the same sentiment polarity but different sentiment strength. For example, ሰይጣን("SEYTAN") means "devil" in Amharic SWN. It is correctly translated and assigned negative sentiment value but the sentiment strength is small. (iv) We found some terms in SWN which are correctly translated but different sentiment due to cultural connotations. For example, the term እርካሽ("ERKASH") means "cheap" and it is assigned positive sentiment. In English, this might be correct, but in Amharic the word እርካሽ("ERKASH") has negative connotation in that it refers to something which is sinfulness and lower in quality. The level of these type errors can be minimized by incorporating context dependent lexicon generated from Amharic corpus. This leads to another venue of future researches.

(b) Analysis of Incorrectly Detected Amharic News Comments: We identified the associated reasons why the sentiment/subjectivity of Amharic News Comments are wrongly detected. The subsets of reasons which cause wrong subjectivity/sentiment detection include: (i) We discovered some Amharic comments which contains sarcasm and idioms. The nature of these comments is difficult to detect its sentiment relying on ordinary lexicon. For example, 'የራሷ አቃቢት የሰው ታማስላለች/solve your own problem before talking about others/is an Amharic proverb that cannot be translated directly relying on ordinary dictionary. That is why it is wrongly classified by the sentiment lexicons. (ii) Besides handling negation, we discovered that further formulations of linguistic rules (e.g. intensifiers, contrast rules, conjunction rules) are required to handle wrongly detected Amharic news comments. For example, 'ኃይሉ ገ/ስላሴ በሩጫ ነበዝ እንጂ ስለኢትዮጵያዊ መንፈስ ሊሰብክ አይችልም'/H/G/Silasie is the best runner, however, he cannot preach about Ethiopianism/. In this example, the sentiment computation is failed as the semantic orientation of the text is diverted by contrasting word እንጂ /however/. The text next to this contrasting word has dominant sentiment than the phrase before it. (iii) We identified some Amharic comments which are wrongly annotated by human annotator. For example, 'በጣም አሳዛኝ ነው'/it is very tragedy/. The sentiment of this comment is labeled wrongly as positive by the human annotator. Thus, the labeled data should be reviewed for correction. (iv) We also found some Amharic news comments which are detected wrongly as their meanings are implicit where their interpretations are connected to pragmatics. Such context dependent text connotations are difficult to handle by explicitly using our generated lexicons. For example, the Amharic news comments ''ፍትህ ለአማራ''/Justice to Amhara/is assigned negative sentiment by annotator, but lexicon based classifier wrongly detected it as positive. The reason is that the lexicon based classifier is limited in handling the contextual meaning of the comment in place. This comment is primarily connected to the context and implicitly associated to the meaning behind the original news post.

5 Conclusions and Recommendations

Amharic sentiment lexicon is one of the resources required for Amharic sentiment analysis. Yet, extensive lexical resources are expensive to build. To remedy this problem, we propose a dictionary based approach for generating Amharic Sentiment lexicon. It requires a bilingual dictionary to propagate polarity information from sentiment lexicon of source language to target language. This approach can be used to generate large scale sentiment lexicons. However, it generates general sentiment lexicons that may lack accuracy for sentiment analysis. It is unable to handle cultural and language specific connotations in a particular language. So to address these issues, we proposed another approach which is a corpus based approach to be done in the forthcoming work in our project. Then once processed and refined, dictionary based approach generates two Amharic lexicons: Amharic Sentiment Lexicon_SOCAL(5683) and Amharic Sentiment Lexicon SWN(13679).

The lexicons generated using dictionary based approach are evaluated by agreement (internal), coverage (external), subjectivity detection rate (external) and its performance in lexicon based Amharic text sentiment classification. The Amharic sentiment lexicon generated from SWN is not only good in internal evaluation (i.e. it has acceptable agreement rate with both the manual and SOCAL lexicons) but it also has higher coverage in both test corpora than the other two sentiment lexicons. Moreover, the lexicon based sentiment classification of Amharic Sentiment lexicon from SWN outperforms the other Amharic Sentiment lexicon(including the baseline).

This work demonstrates that it is possible to automatically generate sentiment lexicons relying on available bilingual dictionaries to minimize time and labor cost of manual sentiment lexicon preparation. The generated lexicon expected to get sufficient sentiment lexicon size by porting from resource rich language. Some of the contributions of this work are briefly summarized below:

- Being an automatic approach, the algorithm developed reduces cost and time of labeling terms in sentiment lexicon.
- The approach developed is generic enough that it can be adapted to generate sentiment lexicon to other resource limited languages.
- The entries in our lexicons contain part of speech information that can be applied or utilized in other linguistic tasks of interest.
- The approach can also be adapted to other tasks of natural language processing including information extraction, multilingual semantic lexicons, question and answering, just to name a few.
- The combination of all generated lexicons with the manual lexicon achieves best sentiment classification performance on Amharic texts.
- The code and related resources will be available online for research communities.

Yet, the generated sentiment lexicons may lack accuracy for sentiment analysis of a particular language context where the approach potentially does not sufficiently capture the cultural and language specific connotations in a particular language. To address these issues, we may need to consider corpus based approaches that capture and incorporate semantic information on the specific meaning of a term in a given context to provide higher precision in sentiment score assignment for each particular instance.

Appendix A. Sample of Amharic Stemmed Words and Its Variant Word Forms

Three sample words are selected. These are from verb, noun and adjective categories. The base forms of these sample words include ሰበረ/seBeRe/means 'he break something', ቤት/Beet/means 'home' and ቆንጆ/qonJo/means 'beautiful', respectively. Table 5 below shows the different forms of these words and their corresponding stems or roots.

Table 5. Sample of the different variant word forms and their corresponding stems.

Surface Word	SERA form	Stem	Root
'ሰበርኩ'	seBeRku	'ስብር'	'ስብር'
'ሰበርክ'	seBeRk	'ስብር'	'ስብር'
'ሰበርሽ'	seBeRX	'ስብር'	'ስብር'
'ሰበረ'	seBeRe	'ስብር'	'ስብር'
'ሰበረች'	seBeRec	'ስብር'	'ስብር'
'ሰበርን'	seBeRn	'ስብር'	'ስብር'
'ሰበራችሁ'	seBeRachu	'ስብር'	'ስብር'
'ሰበሩ'	seBeRu	'ስብር'	'ስብር'
'ሰበርኩት'	seBeRkut	'ስብር'	'ስብር'
'ሰበርከው'	seBeRkeW	'ስብር'	'ስብር'
'ሰበርሽው'	seBeRXW	'ስብር'	'ስብር'
'ሰበረው'	seBeReW	'ስብር'	'ስብር'
'ሰበረቸው'	seBeRecW	'ስብር'	'ስብር'
'ሰበርነው'	seBeRneW	'ስብር'	'ስብር'
'ሰበራችሁት'	seBeRachut	'ስብር'	'ስብር'
'ሰበሩት'	seBeRut	'ስብር'	'ስብር'
'እስብራለሁ'	IseBRaLehu	'ስብር'	'ስብር'
'ትስብራለህ'	tseBRaLeh	'ስብር'	'ስብር'
'ትስብራለሽ'	tseBRiaLeX	"ትስብሪ'አለ"	'ስብር'
'ይስብራል'	YseBRaL	'ስብር'	'ስብር'
'ትስብራለች'	tseBRaLec	'ስብር'	'ስብር'
'እንስብራለን'	InseBRaLen	'ስብር'	'ስብር'
'ትስብራላችሁ'	tseBRaLachu	'ስብር'	'ስብር'
'ይስብራሉ'	YseBRaLu	'ስብር'	'ስብር'
'አልሰብርም'	aLseBRM	'ስብር'	'ስብር'
'አልሰበርኩም'	aLseBeRkuM	'ስብር'	'ስብር'
'አትሰብርም'	atseBRM	'ስብር'	'ስብር'
'አትስብሪም'	atseBRiM	'ስብር'	'ስብር'
'አንሰብርም'	anseBRM	'ስብር'	'ስብር'

'አትሰብሩም'	atseBRuM	'ስብር'	'ስብር'
'አይሰብርም'	aYseBRM	'ስብር'	'ስብር'
'አልሰበሩም'	aLseBeRuM	'ስብር'	'ስብር'
'አልሰበረችም'	aLseBeRecM	'ስብር'	'ስብር'
'አይሰብሩም'	aYseBRuM	'ስብር'	'ስብር'
'ሰባበሩ'	seBaBeRu	'ስብር'	'ስብር'
'ሰባበርን'	seBaBeRn	'ስብር'	'ስብር'
'ሰባበረች'	seBaBeRec	'ስብር'	'ስብር'
'ሰባበርሽ'	seBaBeRX	'ስብር'	'ስብር'
'ሰባበርህ'	seBaBeRh	'ስብር'	'ስብር'
'ሰባበሩ'	seBaBeRu	'ስብር'	'ስብር'
'ሰባበረ'	seBaBeRe	'ስብር'	'ስብር'
'ሰባበርኩ'	seBaBeRku	'ስብር'	'ስብር'
'አልሰባበሩም'	aLseBaBeRuM	'ስብር'	'ስብር'
'አልሰባበረችም'	aLseBaBeRecM	'ስብር'	'ስብር'
'አልሰባበርንም'	aLseBaBeRnM	'ስብር'	'ስብር'
'አልሰባበረም'	aLseBaBeReM	'ስብር'	'ስብር'
'አልሰባበርከም'	aLseBaBeRkM	'ስብር'	'ስብር'
'አልሰባበርንም'	aLseBaBeRnM	'ስብር'	'ስብር'
'አትሰባብሩትም'	atseBaBRutM	'ስብር'	'ስብር'
'አንሰባብረውም'	anseBaBReW	'ስብር'	'ስብብር'
'አይሰባብሩትም'	aYseBaBRutM	'ስብር'	'ስብር'
'ያልሰበረ'	YaLseBeRe	'ስብር'	'ስብር'
'ያለሰበሩ'	YaLeseBeRu	'አለሰበር'	'ስብር'
'ያለሰበረች'	YaLeseBeRec	'አለሰበረች'	'ስብር'
'ያልሰባበረ'	YaLseBaBeRe	'ስብር'	'ስብር'
'ሳትሰባብረ'	satseBaBRe	'ስብር'	'ስብር'
'ሳንሰብረ'	sanseBRe	'ስብር'	'ስብር'
'ሳንሰባብር'	sanseBaBR	'ስብር'	'ስብር'
'ሳልሰባብር'	saLseBaBR	'ስብር'	'ስብር'

'ሳልሰብር'	saLseBR	'ስብር'	'ስብር'
'ሳይሰበር'	saYseBeR	'ስብር'	'ስብር'
'እየሰባበሩ'	IYeseBaBeRu	'ስብር'	'ስብር'
'ቤቴ'	Beetee	'ቤት'	'ብት'
'ቤትህ'	Beeth	'ቤት'	'ብት'
'ቤታችሁ'	Beetachu	'ቤት'	'ብት'
'ቤታችን'	Beetacn	'ቤት'	'ብት'
'ቤትሽ'	BeetX	'ቤት'	'ብት'
'ቤትሽን'	BeetXn	'ቤት'	'ብት'
'ቤቱ'	Beetu	'ቤት'	'ብት'
'ቤቱን'	Beetun	'ቤት'	'ብት'
'ቤታቸው'	BeetaceW	'ቤት'	'ብት'
'ቤታቸውን'	BeetaceWn	'ቤት'	'ብት'
'ቤታችሁን'	Beetachun	'ቤት'	'ብት'
'ቤታችሁ'	Beetachu	'ቤት'	'ብት'
'ቤትዎ'	BeetWo	'ቤት'	'ብት'
'ቤትዎን'	BeetWon	'ቤት'	'ብት'
'ቤቶች'	Beetoc	'ቤት'	'ብት'
'ቤቱ'	Beetu	'ቤት'	'ብት'
'ቤቱን'	Beetun	'ቤት'	'ብት'
'የቤቱ'	YeBeetu	'ቤት'	'ብት'
'ለቤቱ'	LeBeetu	'ቤት'	'ብት'
'ቤት'	Beet	'ቤት'	'ብት'
'ቤትን'	Beetn	'ቤት'	'ብት'
'የቤት'	YeBeet	'ቤት'	'ብት'
'ለቤት'	LeBeet	'ቤት'	'ብት'
'ቤቶቹ'	Beetocu	'ቤት'	'ብት'
'ቤቶቹን'	Beetocun	'ቤት'	'ብት'
'የቤቶቹ'	YeBeetocu	'ቤት'	'ብት'
'ለቤቶቹ'	LeBeetocu	'ቤት'	'ብት'

'ቤቶች'	Beetoc	'ቤት'	'ብት'
'ቤቶችን'	Beetocn	'ቤት'	'ብት'
'የቤቶች'	YeBeetoc	'ቤት'	'ብት'
'ለቤቶች'	LeBeetoc	'ቤት'	'ብት'
'ቆንጀው'	qonJoW	'ቆንጃ'	'ቅንጅ'
'ቆንጀውን'	qonJoWn	'ቆንጃ'	'ቅንጅ'
'ቆንጀዎቹን'	qonJoWocun	'ቆንጃ'	'ቅንጅ'
'ቆንጀዎች'	qonJoWoc	'ቆንጃ'	'ቅንጅ'
'ለቆንጀዋ'	LeqonJoWa	'ቆንጃ'	'ቅንጅ'

References

1. Taboada, M., Brooke, J., Tofiloski, M., Voll, K., Stede, M.: Lexicon-based methods for sentiment analysis. Comput. Linguist. **37**(2), 267–307 (2011)
2. Medagoda, N., Shanmuganathan, S., Whalley, J.: Sentiment lexicon construction using sentiwordnet 3.0. In: Proceedings of the 11th International Conference on Natural Computation (ICNC), pp. 802–807, IEEE (2015)
3. Baccianella, S., Esuli, A., Sebastiani, F.: Sentiwordnet 3.0: an enhanced lexical resource for sentiment analysis and opinion mining. In: Language Resources and Evaluation (LREC), vol. 10, pp. 2200–2204 (2010)
4. Lexical Data Repository of the Ge'ez Frontier Foundation. https://github.com/geezorg/data. Accessed 15 Feb 2017
5. Project teams from Addis Ababa University, Masarykova univerzita, Norges teknisk-naturvitenskapelige universitet, The University of Oslo, Hawassa University, 7F14047 HaBiT - Harvesting big text data for under-resourced languages. http://habit-project.eu/wiki/HabitSystemFinal. Accessed 05 May 2018
6. Gebremeskel, S.: Sentiment mining model for opinionated Amharic texts, Unpublished Masters thesis, Department of Computer Science, Addis Ababa University, Addis Ababa (2010)
7. Tilahun, T.: Linguistic localization of opinion mining from Amharic blogs. Int. J. Inf. Technol. Comput. Sci. Perspect. **3**(1), 890 (2014)
8. Denecke, K.: Using SentiWordNet for multilingual sentiment analysis. In: Data Engineering Workshop. pp. 507–512, IEEE (2008)
9. Piao, S., Rayson, P.: Lexical coverage evaluation of large-scale multilingual semantic lexicons for twelve languages. In: European Language Resources Association (ELRA), pp. 2614–2619 (2016)
10. Christopher Potts: Sentiment Symposium Tutorial Lexicons, Stanford Linguistics. http://sentiment.christopherpotts.net/lexicons.html. Accessed 10 Jan (2019)

Information Extraction Model
for Afan Oromo News Text

Sisay Abera[1(✉)] and Tesfa Tegegne[2(✉)]

[1] College of Engineering and Technology, Adigrat University,
POBOX 50, Adigrat, Ethiopia
aberasisay79@yahoo.com
[2] Faculty of Computing, Bahir Dar Institute of Technology,
Bahir Dar University, POBOX 26, Bahir Dar, Ethiopia
tesfat@gmail.com

Abstract. Information Extraction (IE) concerned with the automatic extraction of facts from text and stores them in a database for easy use and management of the data. As the first research work on IE from Afan Oromo text, we designed a model that deals with Infrastructure news domains in the Oromo language. The proposed model has document preprocessing, learning and extraction and post processing as its main components. In this work recall, precision and F-measure are used as evaluation metrics for Afan Oromo Text Information Extraction (AOTIE). Being trained and tested for the dataset of size 3169 tokens, AOTIE performed 79.5% precision, 80.5% recall and 80% F-measure. These results are used as a baseline to experiment on AOTIE. We set up two main experimentation scenarios to experiment on AOTIE. The first scenario is conducted by developing a gazetteer. The second scenario is aimed at observing the influence of Afan Oromo grammatical structure. Both scenarios showed that, the performance of AOTIE is mostly dependent on grammatical structure of Afan Oromo.

Keywords: Afan Oromo Text Information Extraction ·
Machine learning approaches to information extraction · Information extraction

1 Introduction

Information Extraction (IE) is an automatic extraction of facts from text [1]. It is based on analyzing natural language in order to extract information. The process takes texts (and sometimes speech) as an input and produces structured data as an output. This data may be used directly by users, or may be stored in a database for later analysis, or may be used for indexing purposes of information retrieval (IR) applications such as web search engines [1–3]. There are more than 80 languages in Ethiopia. Afaan Oromo is one of the language with large number of speakers under Cushitic family [4]. As the Ethiopia's statistical report of 2007 [5] shows there are more than 27 million speakers of Afaan Oromo in Ethiopia and this fact shows that, the language has the largest speaker followed by Amharic language.

F. Mekuria et al. (Eds.): ICT4DA 2019, CCIS 1026, pp. 327–340, 2019.
https://doi.org/10.1007/978-3-030-26630-1_28

There are a number of Media that uses Afaan Oromo as primary language; for instance, Oromia Television and Radio (Web news), Kallacha Oromiyaa, Bariisaa, Yeroo, Voice of America (VOA) (web news), and different academic and recreational medias to mention a few [6]. Those Media present different information (textual) in structured, unstructured and semi-structured forms. Cowie and Wilks [3] noted, manually extracting information from such an often unstructured or semi-structured text is a very tiresome and time consuming job. Thus, getting the right information for decision making from existing abundant of unstructured text is a big challenge. In addition, the unavailability of tools for extracting and exploiting the valuable information, which is effective enough to satisfy the users for Afan Oromo language has also been a major problem. The main objective of this experimental study is to design a model of information extraction system from Afan Oromo news texts (Fig. 1).

Information extraction has three different components regardless of the language and domain on which it is developed for, which are linguistic preprocessing, the learning and application stage and semantic post processing to do the extraction of data from a given text [2]. The linguistic preprocessing uses different tools to make the natural language texts ready for extraction. The learning and the application component learns a model and extracts the required information from the preprocessed text and the last component, which is the semantic post processing assigns the extracted information to their predefined attribute category and manages the normalization and duplication problem with the extracted data [7]. The Afan Oromo Text IE model designed in this work has also linguistic preprocessing, the learning and application stage and semantic post processing components. These three main components of AOTIE also contain different subcomponents which are language specific and general subcomponents that are required in IE. The preprocessing component of AOTIE is responsible for tokenization and parsing of news texts whereas the learning and extraction component extracts candidate texts from the news text and learns a classification model that will be used to predict the category of the candidate text. The post processing component is responsible for the formatting of the extracted data.

2   Methodology

In this paper, we follow an experimental science research methodology. We have conducted three experiments to evaluate the performance of AOTIE. The first experiment is conducted using the dataset that is tagged according to BIO tagging format whereas the second and third experiments are conducted using a gazetteer and a data set tagged based on the Afan Oromo grammatical structure. The information extraction approaches can be divided into two primary categories:

- Knowledge engineering approaches and
- Machine learning approach.

The Knowledge Engineering Approach is characterized by the development of the grammars used by a component of the IE system by a "knowledge engineer," i.e. a person that is familiar with the IE system, and the formalism for expressing rules for that system, who then, either on his own, or in consultation with an expert in the domain of application, writes rules for the IE system component that mark or extract the sought-after information [8]. In this approach, the skill of the knowledge engineers plays a large factor of the level of performance achieved by the overall system. In addition to requiring skill and detailed knowledge of a particular IE system, the knowledge engineering approach usually is laborious (is very intensive) [8]. Therefore, developing an IE system using knowledge engineering approach will be very difficult as there are no experts that know IE and the Afan Oromo language. Additionally, the NLP resources available in Afan Oromo language are almost none.

The Machine Learning approach is quite different. Following this approach, it is not necessary to have someone on hand with detailed knowledge of how the IE system works, or how to write rules for it. It is necessary only to have someone that knows enough about the domain and the task is to take a corpus of texts, and annotate the texts appropriately for information being extracted [8]. The machine learning approach to IE is then focused on the automatic acquisition of the extraction patterns that can be used to extract the information relevant to the particular task from each single document. Rather than focusing on producing rules, the automatic training approach focuses on the training data. Corpus probabilities or rules are then derived automatically from the training data, and used to process novel or unseen data. As long as someone familiar with the domain is available to annotate texts, systems can be customized to a specific domain without intervention from any developers. For this reason, machine learning approaches are used to develop a model for Afan Oromo Text Information Extraction (AOTIE).

3 Design and Implementation of AOTIE System

3.1 Data Source

The data we used to train and test AOTIE system is obtained from Oromia Radio and Television Organization (ORTO). The choice of the organization is the availability of the electronic news items for the Afaan Oromo. The news items from September 2007 to June 2007 E.C. (Ethiopian Calendar) are used as data source for the experiment of this research. One of the challenge is the collected data is not classified. Since, information extraction is domain specific, the news items must be classified into different categories. Therefore, after analyzing the collected news documents, we classify the news items into 11 main categories as presented in the following table (Table 1).

Table 1. News main categories

No.	Category name
1	Infrastructure
2	Sport
3	Economy
4	Social Affairs
5	National Politics
6	Law and Justice
7	Associations
8	Defense and Security
9	Others (Different) Affairs
10	Foreign
11	Governmental organizations

Among the different categories from ORTO news the Infrastructure category is used as a data source for the training and testing for our AOTIE system. The reason for selecting Infrastructure news category, among the other categories is the availability of factual information which can be extracted. During selection of news category as a data source, we consider all the eleven categories and analyze which one of these categories contain facts that can be extracted and stored in the database that can be used by different application and individuals after extraction. Most of the other news categories are more subjective which has less factual data that need to be extracted. The other reason is the importance of the data after extraction. An Infrastructure news contain many vital information that investors, financial organizations or any individuals can use [9] and extracting this information and using them for later stage or by other application will be vital. Due to these reasons and the nature of IE which is very domain specific, the infrastructure category news texts are used as training and testing data set in this research work.

3.2 Components of AOTIE

IE system has three basic components which are: preprocessing, learning and extraction and post processing regardless of the approach, language and domain on which the IE system is developed for [2]. In addition to these three components other subcomponents are also included in each of the main components. The Afan Oromo Text IE model designed in this work has also these three components. These main components also contain different subcomponents, which are language specific and general subcomponents that are required in IE. The main components interact with each other to make information extraction from Afan Oromo news text possible.

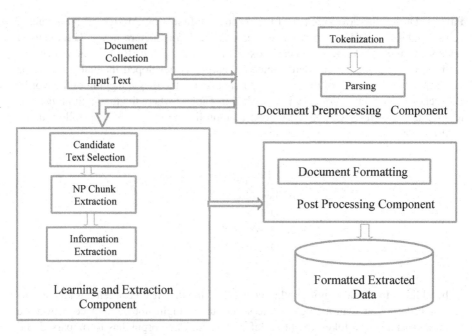

Fig. 1. Afan Oromo Text Information Extraction Model

3.3 Document Preprocessing

The document preprocessing component handles the different language specific issues that are imposed by the nature of the language to make the data ready for remaining phases. The data collected from ORTO requires different preprocessing before it is used by AOTIE system. The document preprocessing component consists of tokenization and parsing.

Tokenization. Tokenization is the task of chopping up the given text into pieces, called tokens [10], which are then used by IE system. Since IE uses tokens and there POS as a candidate text for training and testing classifiers; tokenization is crucial component. Tokenization can occur at a number of different levels: a text could be broken up into paragraphs, sentences or words. For any given level of tokenization, there are many different algorithms for breaking up text depending on the intention of the system and the language under consideration. For example, at the word level, it is not clear how to treat such strings as "can't," "New York," and "so-called". Having these problems, most languages like English, tokenization at the word level is done based on white space.

In Afan Oromo, tokenization is a trivial problem as its writing system looks like English. In fact, there are circumstances in which two words are treated as a single word when they are joined to each other by a hyphen (-) and they are commonly called "*jecha tishoo*". For example "bar-kumee" and "bu'a-qabeessa" are treated as a single word. The tokenizer developed in this research work will treat double words that are connected to each other by a hyphen (-) as a single token.

Parser. During the development of the corpus, we first went through all the obtained news articles and selected those sentences that are Infrastructure news. The obtained sentences are then tokenized and each token was tagged with its BIO tag in accordance with the CoNLL"s 2002 standard. Since the corpus is developed manually it may be vulnerable to errors. One of the errors that may occur is the illegal tagging of the words. BIO scheme's legal tag sequence is described in Table 2 where the first column lists the representation of the tags and the second column lists the tags that may follow them, with the variables ranging over all feature types.

Table 2. BIO legal tag sequence

Tag	Legal following tags
O	O, B-X
B-X	O, I-X, B-Y
I-X	O, I-X, B-Y

In addition to illegal tagging, other errors like: the distance between a token and its tag might be larger than a single white space, there might not be a space between a token and its tag or a token might be left untagged. The corpus has to be parsed and checked against all of the above-mentioned issues. Thus, parsing is a crucial algorithm for checking occurrence of the aforementioned errors and report if errors are found. The parsing algorithm implemented in AOTIE is presented in Fig. 2.

3.4 Learning and Extraction

The main task of learning and extraction component is to extract candidate texts and train and use classifier model for predicting the category of the extracted candidate texts. To train and use the classifier model for learning and extraction component, we use the training and testing phase. The training phase uses the manually annotated news data to train a classifier model which will be used for extraction while testing phase evaluates the performance of the trained model on the unseen news texts.

Training Data Preparation. Training data set preparation to develop an IE system is tedious and time-consuming task. To carry out the experiment of AOTIE system, the infrastructure news category is used. The predefined attributes that we set to extract from infrastructure news are the Infrastructure name, place where the infrastructure is built, the amount of money spent to build the infrastructure, the source of money for the infrastructure development, the number of users that can be benefited from the infrastructure, the person who give the information to the news agency. These six attributes are selected to analyze different infrastructure news and the common facts which exist on most of the infrastructure news and which we thought are relevant facts that should be extracted.

> *For all lines of text in the file*
>   *Read a line*
>   *If not tagged*
>   *If last index is ".O"*
>   *Assign "." To token*
>   *Assign "O" to tag*
>   *Else*
>   *Report illegal line error*
>   *Else*
>   *Assign index of 0 to token*
>   *Assign index of 1 to tag*
>   *End If*
>   *If the space b/n a word & its tag is more than a single space*
>   *Report Error*
>   *If the previous tag is O*
>   *Check if the current tag is one of O & B-X*
>   *Else*
>   *Report error*
>   *If the previous tag is B-X*
>   *Check if the current tag is one of O, I-X, B-Y*
>   *Else*
>   *Report error*
>   *If the previous tag is I-X*
>   *Check if the current tag is one of O, I-X, B-Y*
>   *Else*
>   *Report error*
> *End For*

Fig. 2. AOTIE parsing algorithm

In training data preparation, all the text segments, which are numbers and names are tagged accordingly. If the name is the fact to be extracted, it is tagged according to the tag set for the predefined attribute otherwise it is tagged by other tags.

Paarkiin B-INF Industirii I-INF Adaamaa B-LOC bulchiinsa I-LOC magaalaa I-LOC Adaa-
maatti I-LOC bajata B-FSOUR mootummaa I-FSOUR qarshii B-CAP miliyoona I-CAP 500 I-
CAP oliin O ijaaramaa O jiru O yeroo O xumurametti O lammiilee B-NUS 2000 I-NUS ol O
ta'aniif O carraa O hojii O yeroo O fi O dhaabbataa O kan O uumu O ta'uu O obbo O
Tasfaayee B-REP Abbabaa I-REP beeksisan O.O

The main purpose of tagging all text which is not facts considered for extraction to train classifier is to identify texts that are part of the predefined attributes and those that is not. Attribute tagging is done based on the BIO tagging format as:

- B-INF for infrastructure name
- B-LOC for place where infrastructure is built
- B-CAP for the amount of money spent for the development of the infrastructure
- B-REP for the name of the person that give the information
- B-NUS for the number of users after the infrastructure development
- B-FSOUR for the financial source of the infrastructure development
- O for any attribute found in the document which is not considered as facts.

NP Chunk Extraction. Classifier model generation requires a corpus of chunks. A special type of chunk used in this work is NP chunk which creates noun phrases known as chunks from a sequence of tokens. It is done by NP Chunker. NP Chunk Extraction in AOTIE is implemented in such a way that first the token/tag sequence will be generated based on BIO tagging format. Then tokens are converted into character sequence with each character in the sequence given a position number. Changing the tokens into character sequence helps to compute the range covered by a phrase. Once the input tokens are represented in character sequence, those tokens with BI (Beginning In) tag sequence will be combined to create a chunk. This means from the sequence of tokens, those tokens following each other with tag sequence of the form B-X I-X I-X ... will be combined together to form a chunk of phrases.

Since the extractions are done at phrase level, the task requires deep linguistic analysis. Therefore, developed algorithms are different from an algorithm developed for the same domain but different language. For instance, in Afan Oromo noun phrase formation, nouns come before adjectives which is inverse for English language. For example, in the noun phrase: '*konkolaataa diimaa*' (red car), *konkolaataa* (car) is noun which is succeeded by adjective *diimaa* (red). With regard to our work, NP chunks can be defined as phrases belonging to one of six predefined attribute categories. The obtained chunks will be assigned a tag that was taken from the extension of the constituent BI sequences. The Chunker stores the entity type of the chunk. If a token sequence is not of the form BI sequence, i.e. it has the tag sequence of the form B-X B-Y, then a single token is treated as an NP chunk. Since our concern is extracting NP chunks based on the facts to be extracted, those tokens with tag O are not extracted. The algorithm used to extract NP chunks in AOTIE is presented in Fig. 3.

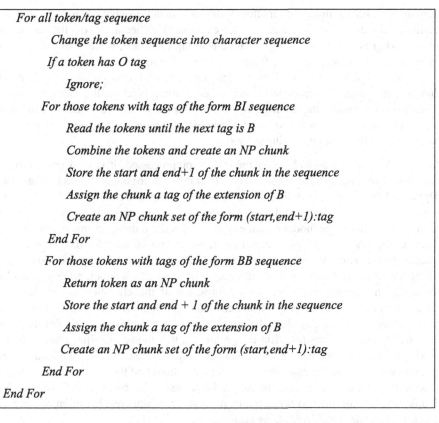

For all token/tag sequence

    Change the token sequence into character sequence

    If a token has O tag

      Ignore;

   For those tokens with tags of the form BI sequence

     Read the tokens until the next tag is B

     Combine the tokens and create an NP chunk

     Store the start and end+1 of the chunk in the sequence

     Assign the chunk a tag of the extension of B

     Create an NP chunk set of the form (start,end+1):tag

   End For

   For those tokens with tags of the form BB sequence

     Return token as an NP chunk

     Store the start and end + 1 of the chunk in the sequence

     Assign the chunk a tag of the extension of B

     Create an NP chunk set of the form (start,end+1):tag

    End For

End For

Fig. 3. Algorithm for NP Chunk Extraction

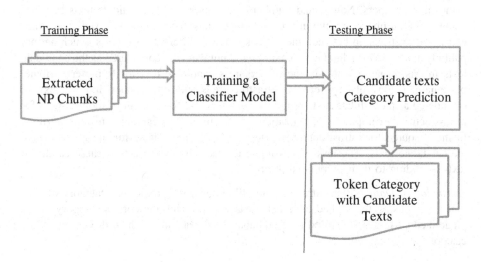

Fig. 4. Information Extraction sub component

Information Extraction. Information Extraction using machine learning approach requires training and test data set to examine the accuracy of the extractor. Since AOTIE is developed using machine learning approach, it has also training and testing phase as presented in the following figure (Fig.4).

In training phase, the classifier model is generated based on the extracted NP chunks. The generated classifier model is used for predicting the category of the candidate texts during the testing phase. The outputs of the information extraction subcomponent are candidate text with their respective predicted category, which is used as an input to the post processing component.

Training A Classifier Model. After the data is preprocessed, it is then passed to the classifier learners in LingPipe. The **Dynamic Language Model Classifier (DynamicLMClassifier)** algorithm is selected among different available machine learning algorithms that LingPipe supports. A DynamicLMClassifier is selected because it is a language model classifier that accepts the training events of categorized character sequences. Training is based on multivariate estimator for the category distribution and dynamic language models for per-category character sequence estimators. It is also used in tag-a-little, learn-a-little supervised learning without retraining epochs. We select this algorithm to see the performance of the classifier and evaluate its efficiency in predicting category for the candidate tokens. Once the classifier model is generated using the training data; the next step is to use the trained classifier model to work on the unseen news text. But the problem is the trained classifier model doesn't directly work for the plain news texts, it rather works on the extracted NP Chunks from the news texts. To use the classifier model for extraction, first the candidate texts should be identified and the NP Chunks of the candidate texts must be extracted using the NP Chunk extractor. In order to achieve this, there is a candidate text selection component which tags all the candidate tokens accordingly.

Candidate Text Selection. The candidate texts for extraction for this research are names and numbers. Names and numbers are considered as candidate texts because, names and numbers are the most important facts for extraction. And also since extracting relationship between the entities requires different NLP tools which are not publicly available for Afan Oromo, names and numbers are considered as the candidate texts in this research work. Name of person is candidate text for Reporter attribute, place name is for a place where the infrastructure is built on, numbers in news text are considered as a candidate text for number of users and for amount of money spent for infrastructure development, organization names are used as candidate texts of attribute financial source for infrastructure development and names used for infrastructure are the candidate texts. The task of candidate text selection is to tag all these candidate texts according to their predefined attributes.

Extraction of Data. After extracting the NP chunks, we predict the category of candidate texts using the trained classifier; texts which match the correct category of the predefined attributes are stored in the database, whereas those which do not match the category are discarded.

4   Post Processing

Different attributes that are extracted from the news texts are finally formatted and stored in the database according to the predefined format of the database slot. The main function of the post processing component is to arrange the format of the extracted data.

5   Results and Discussion

The AOTIE System is trained and tested on the dataset developed by the researchers. The dataset contains 155 news texts which contain a total of 3169 tokens. When trained and tested on the original dataset (dataset which contains 3169 tokens), AOTIE score *Precision* value 79.5%, *Recall* value 80.5% and an **F-measure** value 80% (Table 3).

Table 3. Detailed accuracy by attribute category

Attribute category	Precision	Recall	F-measure
Infrastructure name	65.5%	73.5%	69.2%
Location	79.5%	73.8%	76.5%
Money spent	89.2%	100%	94.3%
Reporter	80%	66.7%	72.7%
Number of users	100%	57.1%	72.7%
Financial source	95.2%	90.9%	93%
Combined cross val.	79.5%	80.5%	80%

These values are used as references to experimentation scenarios to observe effects those scenarios have on the performance of AOTIE.

5.1   Evaluation Scenarios of AOTIE

To evaluate the performance of AOTIE system, we have used two evaluation scenarios: using gazetteer and grammatical structure of Afan Oromo.

Scenario 1: Using Gazetteer In order to examine performance of AOTIE system, we prepared a gazetteer or a set of dictionaries of the six attribute categories. The reason for developing a gazetteer is to reduce the burden of tagging all attributes accordingly. Therefore, the gazetteer which consists of names for different places in Ethiopia, different names that can be used for identification of persons, infrastructure names, and different governmental and nongovernmental organization lists, which are found in Ethiopia are used. We have then trained and tested AOTIE model on the dataset using the gazetteer. The experimental results of scenario 1 is presented in the following table.

Table 4. Detailed accuracy by attribute category for Scenario 1

Attribute category	TP rate	FP rate	Precision	Recall	F-measure
Infrastructure name	70.2%	29.8	70.2%	85.1%	76.9%
Location	62.5%	37.5%	62.5%	78.9%	69.8%
Money spent	91.2%	8.8%	91.2%	100%	95.4%
Reporter	44.4%	55.6%	44.4%	66.7%	53.3%
Number of users	80%	20%	80%	57.1%	66.7%
Financial source	77.3	22.7%	77.3%	89.5%	82.9%
Combined cross val.	72%	28%	72%	85.1%	78%

Table depicts that both precision and F-measure are decreased by 7.5% and 2% respectively while recall increases by 4.6%. From this experiment, we understood that using dictionary reduces the performance of information extraction from Afan Oromo news text.

Scenario 2: Influence of Afan Oromo grammatical structure In order to examine impact of grammatical structure of Afan Oromo writing system on AOTIE system, we prepared a dataset which is tagged based on Afan Oromo grammatical structure. While preparing the dataset, we have also increased the size of our dataset of 3169 tokens to 5187 tokens.

The reason for developing a dataset based on the grammatical structure of the language is that in Afan Oromo writing system a single word (token) can be used as an attribute of different attribute category. For example in the text:

Waarshaan Simintoo Daangootee [1] dureessi Afrikaa Haji Aliko Daangootee [2] godina shawaa kaabaatti ijaaran dargaggoota hoji-dhabeeyyif carraa hojii uumuun ibsame.

Daangootee [1] is in an Infrastructure name category, but depending on the contextual meaning *Daangootee [2]* is in the category of a person who gives a financial support for infrastructural development (Financial Source). The model is then trained and tested on the new dataset. As Table 4 shows the evaluation result increases as the size of the dataset increases depending on grammatical structure of the language (Table 5).

Table 5. Detailed accuracy by attribute category for Scenario 2

Attribute category	TP rate	FP rate	Precision	Recall	F-measure
Infrastructure name	75%	25%	75%	76.6%	75.8%
Location	88.9%	11.1%	88.9%	84.2%	86.5%
Money spent	91.2%	8.8%	91.2%	100%	95.4%
Reporter	80%	20%	80%	66.7%	72.7%
Number of users	100%	0	100%	57.1%	72.7%
Financial source	84.2%	15.8%	84.2%	84.2%	84.2%
Combined cross val.	84.2%	15.8	84.2%	83.1%	83.7%

As it can be seen in the Table – using grammatical structure have improved results of AOTIE. Precision, recall and F-measure have increased by 4.7%, 2.6% and 3.7% respectively.

6 Conclusion

As the growth of unstructured and semi structured documents in an electronic media is increasing from time to time, a tool that can extract relevant data to facilitate decision making is becoming crucial. Information Extraction (IE) is concerned with the automatic extraction of facts from text and stores them in a database for easy use and management of the data. As the first research work on IE from Afan Oromo text, we designed a model that deal with Infrastructure news domains in the Oromo language. The proposed model has document preprocessing, learning and extraction and post processing as its main components. The preprocessing component is responsible for tokenization and parsing of news texts. The learning and extraction component extracts candidate texts from the news text and learns a classification model that are used to predict the category of the candidate text. The post processing component is responsible for the formatting of the extracted data.

In this work Recall, Precision and F-measure are used as evaluation metrics for Afan Oromo Text Information Extraction (AOTIE). Being trained and tested on the dataset of size 3169 tokens, AOTIE performed 79.5% Precision, 80.5% Recall and 80% F-measure. These results are used as a baseline to experiment on AOTIE. We set up two main experimentation scenarios to experiment on AOTIE. The first scenario is conducted by developing a gazetteer. The second scenario is aimed at observing the influence of Afan Oromo grammatical structure. Both scenarios showed that, the performance of AOTIE is mostly dependent on grammatical structure of Afan Oromo.

7 Contribution of the Work

- A model is developed for Afan Oromo text information extraction system using a machine learning approach.
- An algorithm is developed for language specific issues which can handle parsing.
- An algorithm for automatic NP Chunk extractor is developed.

8 Future Work

Information Extraction is a new study for Afan Oromo and also for Ethiopian languages. As IE requires different NLP processing tools for extraction, the task is very complex for such under resourced languages. IE system proposed in this research work is not complete it requires different improvements. The following are our recommendations for future works.

- In this research work names and numbers are the only attributes to be extracted. It does not consider about the relation between attributes. Therefore the inclusion of relation extraction in the further study will be vital for the development of full-fledged information extraction.
- For recognizing names, we try to tag all names in the news which is very complex and time consuming task. Using automatic named entity recognition in later stages might minimize the burden of selecting the named entities.
- Incorporating Afan Oromo spell checkers to minimize the spelling problems which mostly happen in the news text might also have an impact as we manually modify the spelling errors as they have impact for named entity recognition.
- In this work, we used a single algorithm. Interested researchers can use more algorithms and compare the results to obtain best algorithm for AOTIE.
- As we proposed a machine learning approach for the system, interested researchers can develop a rule based approach and compare the performance of the system.

References

1. Corro, L.D.: Methods for open information extraction and sense disambiguation on natural language text, Doktor der Ingenieurwissenschaften (Dr.-Ing.), Naturwissenschaftlich-Technischen, Saarlandes (2015)
2. Fabio Ciravegna, C.G., Kushmerick, N., Lavelli, A., Muslea, I.: Adaptive text extraction and mining (ATEM 2006). In: 11th Conference of the European Chapter of the Association for Computational Linguistics Proceedings of the Workshop, Trento, Italy, 4 April 2006
3. Wilks, J.C.A.Y.: Information extraction, Lecture note on Information extraction
4. Manning, C.D., Raghavan, P., Schütze, H.: Introduction to information retrieval, vol. 1. Cambridge University Press, Cambridge (2008)
5. Ababa, A.: Population Census Commission, Summary and statistical report of the 2007 population and housing census, population size by age and sex (2008)
6. Etnologue: Show Language. http://www.ethnologue.com/web.asp. Accessed 15 Jan 2016
7. Siefkes, C., Siniakov, P.: An overview and classification of adaptive approaches to information extraction. J. Data Semantics IV, 172–212 (2005)
8. Masche, P.: Multilingual information extraction, Master's thesis, University of Helsinki, Faculty of Science, Department of Computer Science (2004)
9. Tsedalu, G.: Information extraction model from Amharic news texts, Addis Ababa University (2010)
10. Stanford tokenization. https://nlp.stanford.edu/IR-book/html/htmledition/tokenization-1.html. Accessed 24 Apr 2017

Design and Development of Sentence Parser for Afan Oromo Language

Hailu Beshada Balcha[1,2(✉)] and Tesfa Tegegne[1,2(✉)]

[1] ICT for Development (ICT4D) Research Center,
Bahir Dar Institute of Technology, Bahir Dar University,
P.O. Box. 26, Bahir Dar, Ethiopia
beshadahailu@yahoo.com, tesfat@gmail.com
[2] Faculty of Computing, Bahir Dar Institute of Technology,
Bahir Dar University, P.O. Box. 26, Bahir Dar, Ethiopia

Abstract. Parser is an efficient and accurate enough to be useful in many natural language processing systems, most notably in machine translation [1]. Previously many sentence parsers are developed for foreign languages such as English, Arabic, etc. as well as for Amharic language from local languages of Ethiopia. However, to the best of the researcher's knowledge concerned, there is no Afan Oromo sentence parser for simple and complex sentences. Thus, we proposed to develop a sentence parser for Afan Oromo language. Parsing Afan Oromo sentence is needed and a necessary mechanism for other natural language processing applications like machine translation, question answering, knowledge extraction and information retrieval, particularly for Afan Oromo language. Rule-based parser using a top-down chart parsing algorithm for Afan Oromo sentences presented in this paper. Context Free Grammar (CFG) is used to represent the grammar. 500 sentences were prepared for sample corpus and CFG rules are extracted manually from sample tagged corpus. We also developed simple algorithm of a lexicon generator to automatically generate the lexical rules. Python programming language and NLTK are used as an implementation tools for this study. From the total of sample dataset 70% is simple sentence type because of we considered four different types of simple sentences (declaratives, interrogatives, imperatives and exclamatory sentences) and the rest 30% is complex sentence type. The parser was trained on 400 sentences of training dataset with the accuracy of 98.25% and tested on 100 sentences of testing dataset with the accuracy of 91%. The experimental results on a parser is an encouraging result since it is the first work for simple and complex sentences of Afan Oromo language.

Keywords: NLP · Parser · Context Free Grammar · Top-down chart parser · Lexicon generator · Lexicon

1 Introduction

One of the fundamental aspects of human behavior is a natural language. Natural language is a language that is spoken by the people. Theoretically motivated range of computational techniques for analyzing and representing naturally occurring texts at

© Springer Nature Switzerland AG 2019
F. Mekuria et al. (Eds.): ICT4DA 2019, CCIS 1026, pp. 341–358, 2019.
https://doi.org/10.1007/978-3-030-26630-1_29

one or more levels of linguistic analysis for the purpose of achieving human like language processing for a range of tasks or applications is natural language processing (NLP) [2]. NLP runs different applications, namely tokenization, lexical analysis, syntactic analysis, semantic analysis, and pragmatic analysis. Among these applications our focus is on parsing (Syntactic analysis), which provides an order and structure of each sentence in the text. According to [3] parsing is the process of assigning structural descriptions to the sequences of words in natural language processing. Mainly two components are used in parsing process: a parser and a grammar. Parser is a procedural component and a computer program, whereas, grammar is a declarative component. Both the parser and grammar depend on the grammar formalism.

Sentence parsing is one of the steps to design a functional NLP application and which can work in cooperation, and as input to other many NLP applications like grammar checker, machine translation, and etc. It is also called syntax analysis [4], which is the process of identifying how words can be put together to form correct sentence and determining what structural role of each word plays in the sentence and what phrases are subparts of what other phrases or what other words modify, which words of the central point of the whole sentence constructed. Parsing has an important role in semantic processing operation on that of sentence constituents. If there is no syntactic parsing step, then the semantics system must decide on its own constituents [5]. If parsing is done, however, it contains the number of constituents that semantic can consider. The present work is a contribution towards designing and developing natural language processing applications for Ethiopian Languages, particularly, for Afan Oromo language. Hence, this study is to develop a sentence parser for Afan Oromo language using top-down chart parsing algorithm and Context Free Grammar (CFG) formalism to represent Afan Oromo grammar rules.

To this end, the researcher has gone through different literatures to find if there is any sentence parser, which can parse simple and complex sentences in Afan Oromo. Thus, to the best of the researcher's knowledge, there is no Afan Oromo sentence parser for simple and complex sentences. However, there is one attempted by [4] on automatic sentence parser for Afan Oromo language using supervised learning technique for simple declarative Afan Oromo sentences. In his study, the chart algorithm has been used. In addition, the unsupervised learning algorithm was designed to guide the parser in predicting unknown and ambiguous words in a sentence. It also adopts an intelligent (Rule-Based learning module) approach to develop a prototype. The result obtained was 95% on the training dataset and 88.5% on the test dataset. The parser was developed purely based on an Intelligent (hybrid of Rule-based and supervised learning) System approach and tagger were not included, which could have been used as a preprocessor to the parser. It was developed only for simple declarative sentences of Afan Oromo language. Due to this fact, we are motivated to develop a parser for simple and complex Afan Oromo sentences. Moreover, as the nature and structure of sentences parsing (syntactic parsing) in Afan Oromo is different from English, Amharic or other languages, sentence parser developed for such languages could not be functional for Afan Oromo language. It (Afan Oromo) has different syntactic and morphological nature, and they have also their own grammatical and word formation technique that is different from other languages. As a result, sentence parser developed for other languages could not be used for Afan Oromo language, which results in the need for the independent sentence parser. So, sentence parser for Afan Oromo language is needed independently.

Even though there are several works on sentence parsing using various approaches, there is only one study for Afan Oromo language regarding sentence parsing. The first parser for an automatic Afan Oromo sentence parser was developed by [4] which was aimed to parse declarative simple sentences. Some works have been done on Amharic sentence parsing. However, it is very few works when compared to the number of works dealing with other foreign natural languages such as Arabic, English, etc. A simple automatic parser for Amharic sentences was developed by [6], to address the problem of developing systems that can automatically process Amharic text. The study was tried to combine probabilistic formalism and rule-based reasoning for developing automatic sentence parser. The total size of sample corpus was 100 Amharic sentences only from simple declarative sentence. The results achieved based on the first set of sample sentences was very high, 100% on the training set and approximately 96% on the test set. As a researcher state in her work, this high accuracy is obtained partly due to the small number of words considered for the experiment. Another reason is that all the sentences have identical constructions, and the highest probability parses were almost always the correct ones. The second attempted was by [7]. The work was the integration of the ideas and outputs of previously attempted by [6], to develop an automatic sentence parser, particularly for complex Amharic sentences. The third work in an Amharic sentence parser was done by [8], which is a hybrid approach to Amharic base phrase chunking and parsing. Its main objective was to extract different types of Amharic phrases by grouping syntactically correlated words, which are found at a different level of the parser using Hidden Markov Model (HMM) model and to transform the chunker to a parser. Another important work and similar approach and parsing strategy that we have been proposed in our study was done by [5]. The researcher was developed top-down chart parser and designed to parse all types of Amharic sentences using a top-down chart parsing algorithm using Context Free Grammar to represent the Amharic grammars. There are also many works of sentence parser systems that have been done globally with different approaches. For an English language sentence parser, the researchers in [9] and [28] are developed a parser. For an Arabic language, some of researchers in [10], [11] and [12] are developed a sentence parser. The researcher in [13] was develop sentence parser for Indian language. The researchers in [14] and [15] are also developed sentence parser for Myanmar language and Chinese language sentences respectively.

2 Research Methodology

Parsing is the step in which a flat input sentence is converted into a hierarchical structure that corresponds to the units of meaning in the sentence. There are two basic approaches in order to parse the sentences efficiently, such as stochastic and rule-based approaches. Stochastic approach is called corpus-based approach, which is based on the use of text corpora. The rules are assigned with probabilities in stochastic sentence parsing approach. On the other hand, rule-based approach is based on a core of solid linguistic knowledge. The advantage of the rule-based approach over the corpus-based approach is for less-resources languages [16]. There are three ways in which this approach can be applied, such as top-down, bottom up, and chart-based approach.

Top-down approach starts with the largest point. It breaks down from the largest into the smaller segments. The advantage of this approach is that the only rules are applied, which can be useful in proving that the sentence is grammatical, and its disadvantage is that the rules are tried blindly without any regard to the lexical material present in the sentence [17]. Unlike top down parsing, the bottom up parser only checks the input sentence once, and only builds each constituent exactly once [18]. This is because a bottom-up parser works from left to right. It has an advantage that the choice of the grammar rules that are applied depends on the words present in the sentence and on analyses for sub-strings of the sentence. Analyses for sub-strings which do not contribute to the overall analysis of the sentence is the disadvantage of bottom-up approach [17]. Chart-based approach combines some of the advantages of top-down and bottom-up approaches. According to [19], in chart parsing approach the process of parsing is an n-word sentence consists of forming a chart with n + 1 vertices and adding edges to the chart one at a time. There is no backtracking, everything that is put in the chart stays there, and chart contains all information needed to create a parse tree. Chart parser is driven by an agenda of completed constituents and the arc extension, which combines active arcs with constituents when they are added to the chart [10]. The technique of extending arcs with constituents can be applied by using both bottom-up and top-down approach. However, the difference is in how new arcs are generated from the grammar. In bottom-up approach, new active arcs are generated whenever a completed constituent is added that could be the first constituent of the right-hand side of the rule, whereas in the top-down approach, new active arcs are generated whenever a new active arc is added to the chart [5, 10]. On the basis of concepts, [5] states that, the number of constituents generated using a top-down chart parser is less than the number of constituents which are generated using bottom-up chart parser. Therefore, [5] suggests the top down chart parser is considerably more efficient for any reasonable grammar. Thus, we are motivated to develop Afan Oromo Sentence Parser by using top-down chart parsing approach.

3   Structures of Afan Oromo Language

Ethiopia is one of the multilingual countries. It constitutes more than 80 ethnic groups with diversified linguistic backgrounds. The country comprises the Afro-Asiatic super family (Cushitic, Semitic, Omotic and Nilotic) [20]. Afan Oromo belongs to an East Cushitic language family of the Afro-Asiatic language super family. It is the most widely spoken language in Ethiopia. Afan Oromo language is the official language of Oromia National Regional State. It is used in offices, schools, colleges, universities and in media. The writing system of this language is nearly phonetic since it is written the way it is spoken, i.e. one letter corresponds to one sound. The language uses Latin alphabet "**Qubee**" which was formally adopted in 1991 G. C [21], and it has its own consonants and vowels sounds. Afan Oromo has thirty- three consonants, of these seven of them are combined consonant letters: **ch, dh, ny, ph, sh, ts** and **zh**. The combined consonant letters are known as '**qubee dachaa**'. Afan Oromo has five short and five long vowels. The Afan Oromo alphabet is characterized by capital and small letters like English alphabet. In Afan Oromo, as in English language, vowels are sound makers and do stand by themselves.

Afan Oromo is morphologically rich language, each root word can combine with multiple morphemes to generate a huge number of word forms [22]. The grammatical system of Afan Oromo is quite complex and exhibits many features common to other Cushitic languages, this means it is an inflected language that uses post-positions more than prepositions [21]. For the purpose of supporting such inflectionally rich languages, the structure of each word has to be identified. Thus, we present about the grammar of Afan Oromo language starting from its word orders, word classes, phrase types and sentence types in the following sections due to their importance for our study.

3.1 Word Order

Words are combined in different orders to form sentences and phrases. One of the primary ways in which languages differ from one another is in the order of constituents or word order. For instance, Afan Oromo and English have differences in their syntactic structure. In Afan Oromo, the sentence structure is subject-object-verb (SOV). SOV is a sentence structure where the subject comes first, then the object and the verb next to the object. For example, if we take Afan Oromo sentence **"Dagaagaan nyaata nyaate"**, "Dagaagaan" is the subject, "nyaata" is the object and "nyaate" is the verb of the sentence. In case of English, the sentence structure is subject-verb-object (SVO). If the above Afan Oromo sentence is translated into English it will be **"Degaga ate food"** where "**Degaga**" is the subject "**ate**" is the verb and "**food**" is the object, however, Afan Oromo follows the Subject-Object-Verb (SOV) format. But nouns change depending on their role within the sentence, word order can be flexible, though verbs always come after their subjects and objects. Typically, indirect objects follow direct objects.

3.2 Word Categories

In Afan Oromo language based on their contextual and formation in the sentences, word classes are categorized into five major groups. These are noun, adjective, verb, adverb and adposition (pre- and post-position). However, this paper adopts the trend that conjunctions and adposition appear in the same category, which is adposition category.

Noun: Nouns are names that are used to name or identify things, people, animals, places or abstract ideas. In Afan Oromo noun, we can have nouns, adjectives and pronouns.

Adjective: An adjective modifies a noun or a pronoun by describing, identifying, or quantifying words. In Afan Oromo, an adjective usually follows the noun or the pronoun which it modifies. Adjectives are also categorized under different categories, like nouns. Afan Oromo adjectives can be either primitive or derived. It comes after the nouns they describe.

Verb: Verb is the most important part of a sentence that says something about the subject to a sentence, expresses an action, events or states of being. In Afan Oromo, verb occurs within the final positions of a sentence. It is not the case that verbs constitute a distinct, open word class in all languages.

Adverb: Adverbs are words, which are used to modify a verb, an adjective, another adverb, or a clause. Adverbs usually precede the verbs they modify or describe in Afan Oromo sentences. An adverb indicates time, manner, place, cause, or degree and answers questions such as, how? when? where? and how much? In the following example, each of the bold words is an adverb.

Adposition: Adpositions are traditionally defined as words that link to other words, phrases, and clauses and express spatial or temporal relations. Adpositions are almost universal part of speech. It is a cover term for prepositions and postpositions. Afan Oromo has both prepositions and postpositions, though postpositions are more common.

Conjunction: A conjunction is the word that is used to connect words, phrases, clauses or sentences. Conjunctions in Afan Oromo are coordinating or subordinating. In this study, conjunction and adpositions are used as the same category.

Numeral: Numerals are words representing numbers, and they can be cardinal or ordinal numbers [2]. Afan Oromo cardinal numbers refer to the counting numbers, because they show quantity. Ordinal numbers, on the other hand, tell the order of things and their rank. In Afan Oromo, the ordinal numbers are formed from the cardinal numbers by suffixing the suffix {–affaa} [2, 4].

3.3   Phrases Categories

A phrase can be defined as a syntactic combination of a word with one or more other words. A phrase is constrained or restricted by two things [4]. These are in terms of the constituents' and the lexical categories like nouns, verbs, etc. Based on the type of lexical categories in Afan Oromo, there are five phrase types in the language [23]. They are briefly presented as following.

Noun Phrase: A noun phrase is made of one noun and one or more other lexical categories, including the noun itself. For example, in the phrase **'mana citaa'** [that-ched house], there are two nouns, which make the noun phrase: **mana** [house] and **citaa** [thatched] [4].

Verbal Phrase: A verb phrase (VP) is composed of a verb as head and other constituents such as complements, modifiers and specifiers. Afan Oromo verb phrases can be captured by dividing verbs into three categories. These are intransitive verbs, strictly transitive verbs and ditransitive verbs [4].

Adverbial Phrase: Adverbial phrase is made up of one adverb as head word and one or more other lexical categories, including adverbs itself as modifiers and specifiers in Afan Oromo. For example, in Afan Oromo it is possible to have two adverbs in an adverb phrase like in a phrase 'kaleessa galgala' [yesterday night]. As indicated above adverbs and their phrases are used to modify verbs. Hence, they precede verbs in a sentence.

Adjectival Phrase: An adjective phrase is a group of words that describe a noun or pronoun in a sentence. In adjectives nouns, can act as adjectives like **'Mana Magarsaa' 'Megersa's house'** or verbs as adjectives like **'farda bite'** 'bought horse'.

Adpositional Phrase: Adpositional phrases are the combination of nouns and adpositions. They usually specify a verb phrase. This phrasal category sometimes is called adpositional objects [4, 23].

4   Design of Afan Oromo Sentence Parser (AOSP)

In this section, the main components of Afan Oromo sentence parser and its proposed architecture is presented.

4.1   Components of Afan Oromo Sentence Parser (AOSP)

Rule-based sentence parser approach has the three basic components such as grammar rule, lexicon and the parsing algorithm. The grammar component is responsible for storing grammar rules written in one of the grammatical formalisms. To learn a set of rules automatically based on the given strings, the parser should enable by grammar rules and then the parser parse sentences based on those rules. The lexicon component is used as a dictionary for the parser by storing lexical rules which are separated from grammar rules. According to [5] states in his work, the rule based parser comprises of the structure of the grammar rules, the lexicon and the parsing algorithm differs from system to system and from one language to the other. Hence, additional components to the basic components such as Sentence Tokenizer and Lexicon Generator are required. Sentence Tokenizer is used to break down or split the input sentence into individual words. whereas, Lexicon Generator is used to avoid the manual preparation of the lexical rules and generate the lexical rules automatically from sample corpus in the form of **tag** → **'word'**. We used the corpus which is manually annotated. However, the POS tagger is not included in our system. Grammar rule component of Afan Oromo sentence parser is required to store Afan Oromo Context Free Grammar rules. The grammar rules are identified in a way that they can represent the structure of Afan Oromo sentences in terms of what phrases and word categories, in case we used Context Free Grammar formalism. The lexicon component stores a list of lexical rules, which specify the possible categories of each word. The parser engine accepts input sentence, by considering the grammar rules of Afan Oromo sentence, and retrieves the POS tag of each word in the sentence from the lexicon and finally returns parsed sentence as an output (Fig. 1).

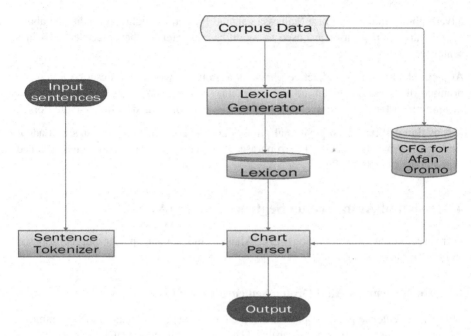

Fig. 1. Architecture of sentence parser for Afan Oromo language

4.2 Context Free Grammar (CFG)

A grammar in human language represents understandable specification of language syntax. The grammar is a collection of words that describes well-informed sentences in a language. An efficient parser can be constructed automatically from a properly designed grammar. The idea of a context-free grammar should be familiar from formal language theory. Furthermore, Context Free Grammar in natural languages represents a formal system which describes a language by specifying how any legal text can be derived from a distinguished symbol called the syntactic symbol [24]. CFG rules for this paper are extracted from sentences collected from Afan Oromo grammar books and previous research papers, which are already tagged manually by researchers. It is used to represent the grammatical structure of valid sentences as much as possible. As we have discussed earlier, there are two main types of sentences in Afan Oromo language, such as simple and complex sentences. Hence, context free grammar rule incorporates both sentences to represent their grammatical structures in this paper.

4.3 Sentence Tokenizer

Tokenization is an early step of processing to divide the input text into units called tokens where each is either a word or something [18]. It also stated in [25] as one of the more basic operations that can be applied to a text to breaking up a stream of characters into words, punctuation marks, numbers and other discrete items. For this reason, we need to have a tokenizer that is responsible to break words of the sentence. The tokenizer spans through the sentence from the beginning to the end and whenever it gets a space gap it considers the text before the space as one word. This process was done by writing python code which is used to split the input sentence into its words.

4.4   Lexicon Generator

A lexicon is the vocabulary of a person, language, or branch of knowledge. It is also thought to include bound morphemes, which cannot stand alone as words, such as most affixes. Because words tend to follow regular morphological patterns, many forms of words are not explicitly included in the lexicon. For example, for the verb 'deem-'(dependent root form), there are different forms of the verb **'deemte, deemuu, deeme, etc.'** [4]. From the sample corpus we have collected, the lexicon was prepared which is a list of words with their POS tag name. Preparing the lexicon manually by typing the word and its word category, especially when there is a large size corpus it is an error prone and time taking. Therefore, it is better to have an automatic lexicon generator that outputs the result correctly and within a short time. We have prepared simple algorithm, then wrote small python code to develop a lexicon generator that output lexical rules from tagged sentences automatically for later used in parsing Afan Oromo sentences. The lexicon generator reads the POS tagged sentence, then generate the result as **(tag name - > 'word').**

4.5   AOSP Chart Parser

This component is the main part of the proposed system. According to Zhu [26], general search(top-down or bottom-up) methods are not best for syntactic parsing, the reason is the same syntactic constituent may be re-derived many times as a part of larger constituents due to the presence of the local ambiguities of the grammar. So, we have considered the idea of chart parsing. A chart is a form of well-formed substring table. Chart parsing is a common context free parsing algorithm which uses dynamic programming techniques to avoid duplication of effort by ignoring differences in derivation where they have no effect [27]. Chart parsing doesn't throw away any information. This means it keeps a record (a chart) of all the structure you have found so far [10]. Chart parsing has two forms: *passive* and *active*. In case of *passive chart parsing*, the chart is simply a record of all constituents that have been recognized. Whereas, *active chart parsing* is to keeping track of a record of complete constituents that we have found, so we record what we are actually looking for and how much of it we have found so far. Such information is recorded in active edges or active arcs. [i.e. **S → NP. VP**]. In this production rules, the arc label as S → NP. VP means: "we are trying to build an S consisting of an NP followed by a VP. So far, we have found an NP arc, and we are still looking for the VP". So, the insignificant looking "." Or *dot* symbol in the middle of the rule is very important, it marks the boundary between what we have found so far, and what we are still looking for, i.e. a boundary between active and passive arcs. Therefore, constituents before the dot are passive edges, whereas active edges can be combined with these passive edges to create new edges. According to [5], the fundamental rule for combining of the passive edges and an active edge can be performed as S → **A. cB.** Suppose that there is the passive edge going from where the active edge ends and has category c on the left side as c $\rightarrow$ **Z.** The dot in the active edge is now moved one category forward (i.e., S $\rightarrow$ **Ac. B**).

Chart parsing has two main approaches to apply the parsing algorithm, such as top-down and bottom-up approach. Bottom-up chart parsing checks the input sentence and builds each constituent exactly once. It can also avoid duplication of effort. However, bottom-up chart parsing may build constituents that cannot be used legally, whereas only grammar rules that can be legally applied will be put on the chart in top-down chart parsing [26]. In addition, the algorithm reads (bottom-up) the rules right-to-left, and starts with the information in passive edges. However, Top-down parsing reads the rules left to right and starts with the information in active edges in the case of top-down chart parsing. Besides, top-down searching will be used to use rules to make active edges. The agenda will have at least one active edge to start the parsing process. The active edge starts at the position zero from the sentence S. Hence, the active edge will be taken from the input sentence. The chart will remain empty until an active edge is added to it. Thus, in our work, we proposed, Context Free Grammar and top-down chart parsing for the grammar rules and for parsing algorithm respectively. The reason why CFG grammar formalism is selected in our work, it is easier to maintain, easy to understand and to add new language features. It also imparts structure to language and builds an efficient parser automatically [24]. On the other hand, the reason we have chosen top-down chart parsing is because it does well if there is useful grammar-driven control [5], and it has the advantage of both top-down and bottom-up parsing.

5 Experiment

In this section the details implementation of Afan Oromo sentence parser is presented.

5.1 Development Environment

We have developed a sentence parser which takes an input sentence from the user and parses the sentence according to the CFG and lexicon based on the parsing method and finally deliver the output for the user. The parser has also automatic lexicon generator as its components. The lexicon generator takes manually tagged sentences from local storage and produces lexical rules automatically. We used python programming language for implementation purpose.

5.2 Corpus Preparation

500 simple and complex sentences have been collected from different sources. Most of the sentences are simple sentences which around 70% and the rest 30% is complex sentences. In this study we have used declarative, exclamatory, interrogative and imperative simple sentence types and complex in Afan Oromo sentences. Some of the sentences are taken from previous research work by [4], some others are taken from Seer-luga Afan Oromo (Afan Oromo grammar) book, and the rests are taken from different Afan Oromo written documents. Sentences are tagged manually using tag set

which was developed by [28] based on Afan Oromo language rule and verified by linguistics of Afan Oromo language.

5.3   Grammar Rules Extraction

CFG rules are used to train the parser with a set of grammar rules and enable it to parse sentences based on rules. In order to extract the grammar rule from manually tagged sentences we have reviewed and identified the morphological property of the language and word order. Then, Context Free Grammar rules are extracted manually from the collected corpus after studying the grammar of Afan Oromo language and verified by the linguists.

Our sample corpus contains manually tagged sentences (POS) in order to identify the word category of each word in the sentence. Sentences (looked at the sentences) are used to construct CFG rule and identify part of speech tag of a phrase (Noun Phrase and Verb Phrase). A number of sentences have similar phrase structure, and some others share common sub-phrases so that a single CFG rule can represent many sentences. Once we have the structure of the sentence, we transformed it into the proper format of the CFG, which is a non-terminal followed by an arrow and then terminal or other non-terminals, which can replace the non-terminal before the arrow, i.e., like S - > NP VP, NP - > NN JJ and VP - > NN VB. The CFG begins from the non-terminal S, which represents sentences, and then phrases, which can form S, most of the time noun phrase (NP) and verb phrase (VP). Each phrase which is on the right side of S will be expanded or expressed by other non-terminals (like NN, JJ, VB, AV, etc.) in next rules. As we have discussed in our previous section in detail there are five phrases in Afan Oromo language (Table 1).

Table 1. Tag name of Afan Oromo phrases

Name phrase	Tag name
Noun phrase	NP
Verb phrase	VP
Adverb phrase	ADP
Adjective phrase	JJP
Adposition phrase	APCP

5.4   Generating Lexical Rules

The same corpus that is used in CFG extraction is used for lexical rules generation. The construction of the lexicon is a one-time process that is done at the very beginning of the parser implementation. However, the result will be needed whenever there is parsing. During the lexicon construction, the lexicon generator reads the corpus from local disk and goes through each sentence. While scanning each sentence, the generator identifies the POS tag name and the word which will be associated with it in lexical rules. The output of the lexicon generator is expected to be formal lexical rules that will be stored in the lexicon in the form of *tag - > "word"*.

Input: Afan Oromo tagged sentences
Read tagged sample corpus from local disk
Scan each sentence of sample corpus
Identify the part of speech (POS) tag name and word that will be associated with it
For each word in each sentence of sample corpus
        Call str2tuple () built-in function from a python library
        If the words and its tags are split in the form of (word, tag)
                Reverse the form into (tag, word)
                Return the reversed value
                generate the result with proper format
                return the result
        End If
End For
Output: lexical rules

Algorithm 1: Lexical Generator Algorithm

5.5   Implementation of Chart Parser

In order to apply a top-down chart parsing algorithm, fundamental rule and other three rules are considered, such as: Top-Down Initialization Rule, Top-Down Expand Rule and Top-Down Match Rule. The main focus of this is to parse the user sentence of Afan Oromo language using top down chart parser. The parser interacts with other components in order to parse the user sentences. Initially, the parser accepts the input sentence resulted from the tokenizer. Before the sentence undergoes through the parsing process, the parser checks the grammar rule and lexical rules of sentence. Then the parser scans through the sentence and asks for the POS tag of each word from the lexicon. Then after, the chart will be initialized by an active edge, which is a grammar rule that has S symbol at the left-hand side. Active chart parsing is to keeping track of a record of complete constituents that have found, so record what actually looking for and how much of it we have found so far. The fundamental rule for combining of the passive edges and an active edge can be performed as $S \rightarrow NP. VP$. Suppose that there is the passive edge going from where the active edge ends and has category VB on the left side as VP $\rightarrow$ VB AV. The dot in the active edge is now moved one category forward (i.e., VP $\rightarrow$ VB. AV, which mean S $\rightarrow$ NP VB. AV). Our intension is working with active chart parser to make use of an agenda. Then the agenda also initialized by a grammar rule that has a non-terminal at its left-hand side. The left-hand side terminal is similar with that of the non-terminal which is immediately after the arrow in a grammar rule in the chart. The grammar rule in the agenda will move to the chart to replace the first non-terminal, in the right-hand side of S, if it can replace unless another grammar rule is added to the agenda till the grammar rule that can replace the non-terminal is found. If there is a terminal that can replace the non-terminal, the parser will replace it and continues to the next non-terminal. However, if the non-terminal in the chart can't be replaced by the terminal, it looks for other non-terminals which can replace it and which can be replaced by terminals later on. This process will continue until all non-terminals in S are replaced by the terminals and the grammar structure of the sentence S is recognized. This means when new edges are created, the parser has to look at them to see whether they can be combined with other edges to create another new edge in any way. It stores them in the agenda to later remember. The agenda contains edges (grammar rules that can replace non-terminals in the chart and creates new active edge or new grammar rule). The parser will then take one edge at a time from the agenda, add it to the chart and then use it to build new edges. The top down chart parsing algorithm we have adopted from [5, 10] with a few modification is shown in Algorithm 2.

Input: Afan Oromo Sentence from the user
Scan and tokenize the input sentence
Check the words of the sentence whether it is in the lexicon or not
If the word of the user sentence in the lexicon
Take the sentence
Make initial the chart and the agenda
Repeat the following until the agenda becomes empty:
    a.   Take the first arc (grammar rule) from the agenda
    b.   Add the arc to chart (if the edge is not already on the chart)
    c.   Combine this arc with arcs from the chart and add the obtained edges to the agenda
    d.   Make a hypothesis about new constituents based on the arc and the rule of the grammar. Add these new arcs to the agenda.
End repeat
See if the chart contains passive edges from the first node to the last node that has labeled S.
    if the chart contains the passive edges that represent all nodes of the sentence then the parsing process succeeds,
    if not, the input sentence has a syntax error with respect to the grammatical production rules in the CFG.
Return the parsed sentence (parse tree).
Output: Parse tree or the sentence is not parsed

Algorithm 2: Top Down Chart Parsing Algorithm for Afan Oromo Sentences

5.6 Evaluations

In this section, the evaluation result of lexicon generator and chart parser is discussed. simple lexicon generator algorithms that constructs lexical rules automatically from a sample tagged sentences of Afan Oromo language was developed. The correctness of the lexical rules was inspected manually by checking whether the words are categorized in their proper word classes or not by comparing with manually tagged sentences. Hence, our lexicon generator generates correct lexical rules from manually tagged sentences as expected. Thus, lexicon generator performed correctly as expected without any error.

The sample result of the lexicon generator for five Afan Oromo Sentences from the sample corpus are as follow: "Tulluun nama gurraacha dha" 'Tullu is a black man', "Inni gara manaa deeme" 'He went to home', "Inni kaleessa galgala dhufe" 'He comes yesterday at evening', "Tolosaan mana guddaa qaba" 'Tolosa has a big house' and "Abdiisaan mana citaa ijaare" 'Abdisa build the thatch house (Fig. 2).'

```
PNS  ->  "Tulluun"
NN   ->  "nama"
JJ   ->  "gurraacha"
CP   ->  "dha"
PPN  ->  "Inni"
APC  ->  "gara"
NN   ->  "manaa"
VB   ->  "deeme"
PPN  ->  "Inni"
AD   ->  "kaleessa"
AD   ->  "galgala"
VB   ->  "dhufe"
PNS  ->  "Tolosaan"
NN   ->  "mana"
JJ   ->  "guddaa"
AV   ->  "qaba"
PNS  ->  "Abdiisaan"
NN   ->  "mana"
NN   ->  "citaa"
VB   ->  "ijaare"
```

Fig. 2. Screenshot of lexical rules generated by the lexicon generator

The input sentence in the parsing process after it is a tokenized word by word, and the word of input sentence is checked whether it exists in the generated a lexicon in the corpus. The sentence tokenizer did not encounter any error in the parser, so it was perfect for tokenize the input sentence into words. Based on this, the system was trained on the training dataset repeatedly and after correcting the man-made error on manually tagged sentences by using CFG rules which manually extracted from sample corpus was obtained the accuracy of 98.25%. In addition, in order to test the effectiveness of the parser, 100 sentences are selected from the corpus as a test set. On average 20 sentences are from each type of the sentences in the corpus. The correctness of the parser is examined by inspecting its result manually. The output can be checked with respect to the right categorization of words in their proper word class, the right identification of sub phrases and main phrases, the right order of sub phrases in building main phrases, and whether all words and phrases are involved during construction of the sentence S. Therefore, before testing, the sentences are parsed manually on paper based on linguist's suggestion and comments, and then compared the results of the chart parser for the same sentences with manually parsed sentences. Any one of the results, which doesn't satisfy one of the criteria is considered as wrong output or if the result or the parse tree doesn't display at all. The result obtained when the parser was trained and run on the same data is shown in Table 2 as follow.

Table 2. Parsing a result on training set before making number of error correction

Dataset	Number of sentences	Number of correctly parsed sentences	Accuracy in %
Training set	400	350	87.5%

The accuracy achieved should be high when a parser is trained and tested on the same data is expected. But, due to man-made errors during the manual tagging of the sentences and manually extracted context free grammar rules from sample sentences the accuracy was not as high as it was expected. To ensure the accuracy of the parser, discussion with linguistics was takes place in order to check the correctness of tagged sentences as well as the extracted grammar rule. Then, the final accuracy obtained on training set after the error were identified and corrected is the result is improved (Table 3).

Table 3. Parsing a result on training set after making most of error correction

Dataset	Number of sentences	Number of correctly parsed sentences	Accuracy in %
Training set	400	393	98.25%

The result obtained when testing the parser on declarative, interrogative, imperative and exclamatory simple sentence type is approximately 95%, 100%, 100% and 90% accuracy respectively and 70% accuracy on complex sentence type. The result obtained from complex sentences was due to man-made errors during the manual parsing process on complex sentences and incorrectly extraction context free grammar rules of the language. These points were identified to be the cause for wrong parse assignments. On average 91% of accuracy was obtained on 100 sentences of test dataset from all type sentences used in sample corpus (Fig. 3).

```
(S
  (NP (PNS Caaltuun))
  (VP
    (ADP (AD ganamaan) (VB kaatee))
    (APCP (APC gara) (NN mana))
    (VP (NN barumsaa) (VB deemte))))
(S
  (NP (PNS Caaltuun))
  (VP
    (ADP (AD ganamaan) (VB kaatee))
    (APCP (APC gara) (NN mana))
    (VP (NN barumsaa) (VP (VB deemte)))))
(S
  (NP (PNS Caaltuun))
  (VP
    (ADP (AD ganamaan) (VB kaatee))
    (APCP (APC gara) (NN mana))
    (VP (NP (NN barumsaa)) (VB deemte))))
(S
  (NP (PNS Caaltuun))
  (VP
    (ADP (AD ganamaan) (VB kaatee))
    (APCP (APC gara))
    (VP (NN mana) (VP (NN barumsaa) (VB deemte)))))
```

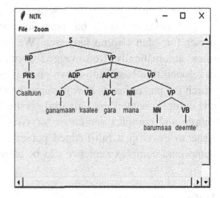

Fig. 3. Screenshot of parsed complex sentence

In general, result shows that the chart parser which is developed to parse Afan Oromo sentence could obtain the accuracy of 98.25% on training set after the correction of errors faced during the first training and 91% on test set, which is an encouraging result.

6 Conclusion

Sentence parsing is one of the steps to design a functional NLP application and which can work in cooperation, and as input to other many NLP applications like grammar checker, machine translation, and etc. Thus, an efficient parsing approach which is top-down chart parsing approaches is developed for Afan Oromo simple and complex sentences is presented in this paper. CFG rule used to represent the grammar of Afan Oromo sentences and simple automatic lexical generator is developed to generate the lexical rules from tagged sample corpus. The total size of 500 Afan Oromo sentences are used and these are collected from previous research works, Afan Oromo grammar book and from other written documents. Developed parser has shown encouraging results in terms of covering simple and complex sentences and automatic construction of the lexical rules from the given sample corpus. An efficient parsing approach which is top-down chart parsing approaches is used in this study rather than using only traditional parsing methods like top-down and bottom-up approaches.

The developed parser is rule-based, so, the parser needs to have components, which are used to enable the system to learn how to parse from grammar rules. This part is composed of lexicon generator, context free grammar rules and lexicon. Lexicon generator is the component used for the automatic construction of the lexical rules. It uses the same POS tagged corpus, which is used for the extraction of context free grammar rules. The parser was trained on 400 sentences of training dataset with the accuracy of 98.25% and tested on 100 sentences of testing dataset with the accuracy of 91%. The experimental results on a parser is an encouraging result since it is the first work for simple and complex sentences of Afan Oromo language.

In general, the study has been designed the general architecture of top-down chart parser for Afan Oromo language. We have been developed how to construct lexical rules automatically from tagged corpus. Another contribution of this study was developed rule-based top-down chart parser, which does not require a tree bank from which the parser learns how to parse through iterative trainings for Afan Oromo simple and complex sentences. This study is the first work in its scope, particularly for parsing simple and complex sentences for Afan Oromo Language, hence, it is still an open issue to develop a full-fledged parser for Afan Oromo language sentence. Besides, compound-complex sentence can be another open research area.

References

1. Katz-Brown, J., et al.: Training a parser for machine translation reordering. In: Proceedings of the 2011 Conference on Empirical Methods in Natural Language Processing (EMNLP 2011), pp. 183–192 (2011)
2. Genemo, A.S.: Afaan Oromo Named Entity Recognition Using Hybrid Approach, M.Sc. thesis, Department of Computer Science, School of Graduate Studies, Addis Ababa University, Addis Ababa (2015)
3. Chomsky, N.: Syntactic Structures, 2nd edn. New York (2002)

4. Megersa, D.: An automatic sentence parser for Oromo language using supervised learning technique, M.Sc.thesis, Department of Information Science, School of Graduate Studies, Addis Ababa University, Addis Ababa (2002)
5. Mohammed, A.D.: A top-down chart parser for Amharic sentences, M.Sc. thesis, Department of Computer Science, School of Graduate Studies, Addis Ababa University, Addis Ababa (2015)
6. Alemu, A.: Automatic sentence parsing for Amharic text an experiment using probabilistic context free grammars, M.Sc. thesis, Department of Information Science, School of Graduate Studies, Addis Ababa University, Addis Ababa (2002)
7. Agonafer, D.G.: An integrated approach to automatic complex sentence parsing for Amharic text, M.Sc. thesis, Department of Information Science, School of Graduate Studies, Addis Ababa University, Addis Ababa (2003)
8. Ibrahim, A.: A hybrid approach to Amharic base phrase chunking and parsing, M.Sc. thesis, Department of Computer Science, School of Graduate Studies, Addis Ababa University, Addis Ababa (2013)
9. Sleator, D.D.K.: Parsing English with a Link Grammar, National Science Foundation under grant CCR-8658139, Oline Corporation. R. R. Donnelley and Sons, New York (1991)
10. Al-Taani, A., Msallam, M., Wedian, S.: A top-down chart parser for analyzing Arabic sentences. Int. Arab. J. Inf. Technol. **9**(3), 109–116 (2012)
11. Khoufi, N., Aloulou, C., Hadrich, L., Anlp, B.: ARSYPAR : a tool for parsing the Arabic language. In: International Arab Conference on Information Technology, ACIT, University of Science & Technology (2013)
12. Bataineh, B.M., Bataineh, E.A.: An efficient recursive transition network parser for Arabic language. In: Proceedings of the World Congress on Engineering 2009, vol. II, pp. 1307–1311 (2009)
13. Hambir, N.: Hindi parser-based on CKY algorithm, vol. 3, no. 2, pp. 851–853 (2012)
14. Thant, W.W., Htwe, T.M., Thein, N.L.: Context free grammar based top-down parsing of Myanmar sentences. International Conference On Information Technology, Pattaya, December 2011, pp. 71–75 (2011)
15. Lian, H.: Chinese language parsing with maximum-entropy-inspired parser maximum-entropy-inspired parser, M.S. thesis, pp. 1–6 (2005)
16. Ouersighni, R.: Robust Rule-based Approach in Arabic processing. Int. J. Comput. Appl. **93** (12), 31–37 (2014)
17. Erbach, G.: A flexible parser for a linguistic development environment. In: Herzog, O., Rollinger, C.-R. (eds.) Text Understanding in LILOG. LNCS, vol. 546, pp. 74–87. Springer, Heidelberg (1991). https://doi.org/10.1007/3-540-54594-8_53
18. Weikum, G.: Foundations of statistical natural language processing. ACM SIGMOD Rec. **31** (3), 37 (2002)
19. Jason: Parsing. https://www.cs.cornell.edu/courses/cs4740/2012sp/lectures/parsing-intro-4pp.pdf. Accessed 03 Feb 2017
20. Thompson, B.I.: Afro Asiatic Language Family (2017). http://aboutworldlanguages.com/afro-asiatic-language-family. Accessed 04 Feb 2017
21. Gamta, T.: The Oromo language and the latin alphabet. J. Oromo Stud. 10–13 (1992). http://www.africa.upenn.edu/Hornet/Afaan_Oromo_19777.html. Accessed 06 Feb 2017
22. Ganfure, G.O., Midekso, D.: Design and implementation of morphology based spell checker, vol. 3, no. 12, pp. 118–125 (2014)
23. Yimam, B.: The phrase structures of ethiopian oromo, Ph.D. Dissertification, Addis Ababa University (1986)
24. Alqrainy, S., Jordan, S., Alkoffash, M.S.: Context-free grammar analysis for Arabic sentences. Int. J. Comput. Appl. **53**(3), 7–11 (2012)

25. Kibble, R.: Introduction to natural language processing undergraduate study in computing and related programmes (2013)
26. Zhu, S.C.: Ch 4 classic parsing algorithms chart parsing in NLP pp. 1–51
27. Fox, H.J.: Lexicalized, edge-based, best-first chart parsing, M.Sc. thesis, Department of Computer Science, Massachusetts Institute of Technology, Brown University (1999)
28. Nedjo, A.T., Huang, D., Liu, X.: Automatic part-of-speech tagging for Oromo language using Maximum Entropy Markov Model (MEMM), vol. 10, pp. 3319–3334 (2014)

Author Index

Printed in the United States
By Bookmasters

Evermann et al. [2] also apply LSTM networks to predict the type of the next event of a case. Unlike [13], this approach uses the embedded dimension of LSTMs to reduce the input's size and to include additional attributes such as the resource associated to each event. The network's architecture comprises two LSTM hidden layers. An empirical evaluation shows that this approach sometimes outperforms the approach of [13] at the task of predicting the next event. However, the approach focuses on predicting event types. It cannot handle numerical variables and hence it cannot predict the next event's timestamp. In this paper, we combine the idea of using the embedded dimension from [2] with the idea of interleaving shared and specialized layers from [13] to design prediction architectures that can handle large numbers of event types.

Lin et al. [6] propose an RNN-based approach, namely MM-Pred, for predicting the next event and the suffix of an ongoing case. This approach uses both the control-flow information (event type) and the case data (event attributes). The proposed architecture is composed of encoders, modulators and decoders. Encoders and decoders use LSTM networks to transform the attributes of each event into and from hidden representations. The modulator component infers a variable-length alignment weight vector, in which each weight represents the relevance of the attribute for predicting the future events and attributes. This work suffers from the same limitation as [2]: It does not support the prediction of attributes with numerical domains, including timestamps and durations.

In [7] the authors propose another approach to predict the next event using a multi-stage deep learning approach. In this approach, each event is first mapped to feature vector. Next, transformations are applied to reduce the input's dimensionality, e.g. by extracting n-grams, applying a hash function, and passing the input through two auto-encoder layers. The transformed input is then processed by a feed-forward neural network responsible for the next-event prediction. Again, this approach suffers from the same limitation as [2], namely that it does not handle numerical variables and hence it cannot predict timestamps or durations.

In [8] the authors propose a neural network architecture called BINet for real-time anomaly detection in business process executions. The core of this approach is a GRU neural network trained to predict the next event and its attributes. The approach is designed to assign a likelihood score to each event in a trace, which is then used to detect anomalies. This approach shows that generative models of process behavior can also be used for anomaly detection. In this paper, we do not consider this possible application. Instead, we focus on training models to produce sequences of timestamped events with associated roles.

In [12], the authors compare the performance of several techniques for predicting the next element in a sequence using real-life datasets. Specifically, the authors consider generative Markov models (including all-k markov models, AKOM), RNN models, and automata-based models, and compare them in terms of precision and interpretability. The results that the AKOM model yields the highest accuracy (outperforming an RNN architecture in some cases) while automata-based models have higher interpretability. This latter study addresses the problem of predicting the next event's type, but it does not consider the problem of simultaneously predicting the next event and its timestamp as we do in this paper.

3   Approach

This section describes the method we propose to build predictive models from business process event logs. This method uses LSTM networks to predict sequences of next events, their timestamp, and their associated resource pools. Three LSTM architectures are proposed that seek to improve the learning of the network in relation to the different events logs characteristics. These architectures can accurately reproduce the behavior observed in the log. Figure 2 summarizes the phases and steps for building predictive models with our method.

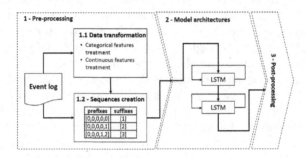

Fig. 2. Phases and steps for building predictive models

3.1   Pre-processing Phase

Data Transformation. According with the attributes nature (i.e. categorical or continuous) specific pre-processing tasks were carried looking for the improvement of the data quality for feeding the LSTM models.

Our main concern in the case of the *categorical attributes* was its transformation into numerical values to be interpreted by the LSTM network without increase the attributes dimensionality. In contrast with approaches that use one-hot encoding (i.e. process flow), which is valid to manage a reduced number of attributes and categories, our model uses activities and resources as categorical attributes. The inclusion of multiple categorical attributes looks for using more information about the process behaviour to improve the prediction accuracy. However, this multiplicity could also increment the number of potential categories exponentially. To deal with this problem, we propose the grouping of resources into roles and the use of embedded dimensions.

On the one hand, the grouping of resources into roles was performed using the algorithm described by Song and Van der Aalst [11]. This algorithm seeks to discover resource pools (called roles in [11]) based on the definition of activity execution profiles for each resource and the creation of a correlation matrix of similarity of those profiles. The use of this algorithm allowed us to reduce the number of categories of this attribute, but keeping enough information to help the LSTM network to make more clear the differences between events.

On the other hand, the use of embedded dimensions helps in the control of the exponential attributes growth while provides more detailed information about the associations between attributes. To exemplify its advantages let's take the event log BPI 2012[1], which has 36 activities and 5 roles. If we use one-hot encoding to represent each unique pair activity-role in the event log, 180 new attributes composed by 179 zeroes are needed. This huge increment in the dimensionality is mostly composed by useless information. In contrast, only 4 dimensions are needed to encode the log if using embedded dimensions to map the categories into a n-dimensional space, in which each coordinate corresponds to a unique category. In this dimensional space the distances between points represents the how close is one activity performed by one role in relation with the same activity performed by other role. This additional information can help the network to understand the associations between events and differentiate them among similar ones. An independent network was trained to coordinate the embedded dimensions. The training network was fed with positive and negative examples of association between attributes, allowing the network to identify and locate near attributes with similar characteristics. The number of embedded dimensions was determined as the fourth root of the number of categories just to avoid a possible collision between them, according to a common recommendation used in the NLP community[2]. The generated values were exported and reused in all the experiments as non-trainable parameters, which allowed not to increase the complexity of the models. The Fig. 3a presents the architecture of the network used for training the embedded layers, and the Fig. 3b shows a representation of the generated 4d space reduced to a 3d space for activities.

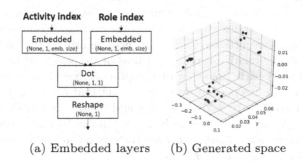

(a) Embedded layers   (b) Generated space

Fig. 3. Embedding network architecture and results

---

[1] https://doi.org/10.4121/uuid:3926db30-f712-4394-aebc-75976070e91f.
[2] https://www.tensorflow.org/guide/feature_columns.

In the case of *continuous attributes*, our major concern was the scaling of the values in a $[0, 1]$ range to be interpreted by the predictive models. Our model uses the relative time between activities as categorical input, calculated as the time elapsed between the complete time of one event and the complete time of the previous one. The relative time is easier to interpret by the models and is useful to calculate the timestamp of the events in a trace. However, due to the nature of each event log the relative time may have a high variability. This high variability can hide useful information about the process behaviour such as time bottlenecks or anomalous behaviours that can be hide if the attribute scaling is performed without care. If the relative times present low variability, the use of log-normalization could also distort the perception of data. Therefore both techniques were evaluated to determine which best fits to the characteristics of the relative times. Figure 4 illustrates the results of scaling the relative times in the event log BPI 2012. In particular, the use of log-normalization makes variations in relative times clearly observable.

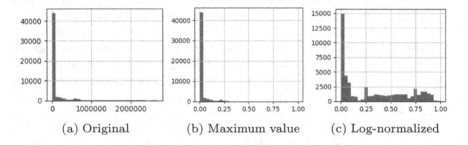

(a) Original   (b) Maximum value   (c) Log-normalized

Fig. 4. Scaling of relative times over the maximum value and log-normalization

Sequences Creation. We decided to extract n-grams of fixed sizes of each event log trace to create the input sequences and expected events to train the predictive network. N-grams allow to control the temporal dimensionality of the input, and bring clear patterns of sub-sequences describing the execution order of activities, roles or relative times, regardless of the length of the traces. One n-gram is extracted each time-step of the process execution, and is done for each attribute on an independent way, this meant that for our models we count with 3 independent inputs: activities, roles and relative times. Table 1 presents five n-grams extracted from the case id 174770 of the BPI 2012 event log. The numbers in the activities, roles, and times correspond to the indexes and scaled values in the data transformation step.

3.2   Model Structure Definition Phase

LSTM networks were used as the core of our predictive models since they are a well-known and proven technology to handle sequences, which are the nature

Table 1. N-grams for case number 174770 of the BPI 2012 event log

Time step	Activities	Roles	Relative times
0	[0 0 0 0 0]	[0 0 0 0 0]	[0. 0. 0. 0. 0.]
1	[0 0 0 0 10]	[0 0 0 0 5]	[0. 0. 0. 0. 0.]
2	[0 0 0 10 7]	[0 0 0 5 5]	[0. 0. 0. 0. 4.73e−05]
3	[0 0 10 7 18]	[0 0 5 5 1]	[0. 0. 0. 4.73e−05 5.51e−01]
4	[0 10 7 18 5]	[0 5 5 1 1]	[0. 0. 4.73e−05 5.51e−01 1]
5	[10 7 18 5 18]	[5 5 1 1 1]	[0. 4.73e−05 5.51e−01 1 7.48e−04]

of a business process event log. Figure 5 illustrates the basic architecture of our network consisted of an input layer for each attribute, two stacked LSTM layers and a dense output layer. The first LSTM layer is in charge of provide a sequence output rather than a single value output to fed the second LSTM layer. Additionally, the categorical attributes have an embedded layer for their coding.

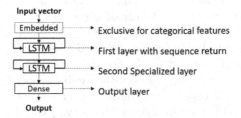

Fig. 5. Baseline architecture

Likewise, three variants of the baseline architecture were tested as is shown in the Fig. 6. The hypothesis behind these approaches is that sharing information between the layers can help to differentiate execution patterns. However, these changes could interfere with the identification of patterns in a log with high variability in relative times or in structure, generating noise in learning.

The specialized architecture (see Fig. 6a) does not share any information, in fact can be understood as three independent models. The shared categorical architecture (see Fig. 6b), concatenates the inputs related with activities and roles, and shares the first LSTM layer. Is expected that this architecture avoids the possible noises introduced by sharing information between attributes of different nature (i.e. categorical or continuous). The full shared architecture (see Fig. 6c), concatenates all the inputs and completely shares the first LSTM layer. In the evaluation section, the possibility of an architecture fits better than other in accordance with the nature of each event log is explored.

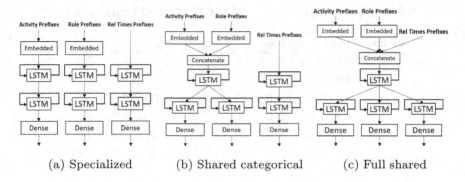

(a) Specialized   (b) Shared categorical   (c) Full shared

Fig. 6. Tested architectures

3.3 Post-processing Phase

Our technique is capable of generate complete traces of business processes starting from a zero prefix size. The way of doing this is by the use of continuous feedback of the model with each new generated event, until the generation of a finalization event (hallucination). This technique has been used by previous approaches, however, we explore the use of arguments of the maxima (arg-max) and random choice as techniques for the category selection of the next predicted event. Arg-max is the technique commonly used to select the next category of a prediction, and consists in selecting the one that has the highest predicted probability. In theory this technique should work well for specific prediction tasks, such as the most likely category of the next event, given an incomplete case. However, if the model is used in a generative way, it could be biased and tends to generate always the same kind of sequences, that is, the most probable ones. To avoid the this, we use the random selection of a new category following the predicted probability distribution. This attribute allows us to generate a greater number of different traces, by not getting stuck in the higher probabilities. This technique also allows us to reveals what the neural network has actually learned from the dynamics observed in the event log. Of course, the introduction of a random element, forces us to perform multiple repetitions of the experiment to find the convergence in the measurements. Both approaches were taken into account in the evaluation of results about the reproduction of the observed current state of business processes.

4 Evaluation

This section describes two experimental evaluations. The first experiment compares different instantiations of the three proposed architectures in terms of pre-processing and post-processing choices. The second experiment compares the proposed approach to the three baselines discussed in Sect. 2.2 for the tasks of next event, suffix, and remaining time prediction.

4.1   Comparison of LSTM Architectures and Processing Options

Datasets. For this experiment, we use nine real-life event logs from different domains and with diverse characteristics:

- The Helpdesk[3] event log contains records from a ticketing management process of the helpdesk of an Italian software company.
- The two event-logs within BPI 2012[4] are related to a loan application process from a German financial institution. This process is composed by three sub-processes from which we used the W sub-process in order to allow the comparison with the existing approaches [2,12].
- The event log within BPI 2013[5] is related to a Volvo's IT incident and problem management. We used the complete cases to learn generative models.
- The five event-logs within BPI 2015[6] contain data on building permit applications provided by five Dutch municipalities during a period of four years. The original event log was subdivided in five parts (one per each municipality). All the event logs were specified at a sub-processes level including more than 345 activities. Therefore, it was pre-processed to be managed at a phases level by following with the steps described in [14].

The sequence flow (SF) of each event log was classified as simple, medium, and complex according with its composition in terms of number of traces, events, activities and length of the sequences. In the same way, the time variability (TV) was classified as stable or variable according with the relation between the mean and max duration of each event log (see Table 2).

Table 2. Event logs description

Event log	Num. traces	Num. events	Num. activities	Avg. activities per trace	Max. activities per trace	Mean duration	Max. duration	SF	TV
Helpdesk	4580	21348	14	4.6	15	40.9 days	59.2 days	Simple	Stedy
BPI 2012	13087	262200	36	20	175	8.6 days	137.5 days	Complex	Stedy
BPI 2012 W	9658	170107	7	17.6	156	8.8 days	137.5 days	Complex	Stedy
BPI 2013	1487	6660	7	4.47	35	179.2 days	6 years, 64 days	Simple	Irregular
BPI 2015-1	1199	27409	38	22.8	61	95.9 days	4 years, 26 days	Medium	Irregular
BPI 2015-2	832	25344	44	30.4	78	160.3 days	2 years, 341 days	Medium	Irregular
BPI 2015-3	1409	31574	40	22.4	69	62.2 days	4 years, 52 days	Medium	Irregular
BPI 2015-4	1053	27679	43	26.2	83	116.9 days	2 years, 196 days	Medium	Irregular
BPI 2015-5	1156	36.234	41	31.3	109	98 days	3 years, 248 days	Medium	Irregular

Experimental Setup. This experiment compares different instantiations of our approach in terms of their ability to learn execution patterns and to reliably

---

[3]   https://doi.org/10.17632/39bp3vv62t.1.

[4]   https://doi.org/10.4121/uuid:3926db30-f712-4394-aebc-75976070e91f.

[5]   https://doi.org/10.4121/uuid:a7ce5c55-03a7-4583-b855-98b86e1a2b07.

[6]   https://doi.org/10.4121/uuid:31a308ef-c844-48da-948c-305d167a0ec1.

reproduce the behavior registered in the event log. Accordingly, we use the LSTM models to generate full event logs starting from size zero prefixes, and we then compare the generated traces against those in the original log.

We used two metrics to assess the similarity of the generated event logs. The Demerau-Levinstain (DL) algorithm measures the distance between sequences in terms of the number of editions necessary for one string character to be equal to another. This algorithm penalizes each time actions such as insertion, deletion, substitution, and transposition are carried out. Their measurements are commonly scaled by using the maximum size between the two sequences that are compared. Therefore, we use its inverse to measure the similarity between a generated sequence of activities or roles and a sequence observed in the actual event log. Then, a higher value implies a higher similarity among the sequences.

We trivially lift the DL measure (which applies to pairs of strings or traces), to measure the difference between two event logs by pairing each generated trace with the most similar trace (w.r.t. DL distance) of the ground-truth log. Once the pairs (generated trace, ground-truth trace) are formed, we calculate the mean DL between them. The Mean Absolute Error (MAE) metric is used to measure the error in predicting time-stamps. This measure is calculated by taking the absolute value of the distance between an observation and the predicted value, and then calculating the average value of these magnitudes. We use this metric to evaluate the distance between the generated relative time and those observed time, for each pair (generated trace, ground-truth trace).

We used cross validation by splitting the event logs into two folds: 70% for training and 30% for validation. The first fold was used as input to train 2000 models (approximately 220 models per event log). These models were configured with different pre-processing techniques and architectures. The configurations' values were selected randomly from the full search space of 972 combinations.

Then, new event logs of complete events are generated with each trained model (cf. techniques for the selection of the next activity described in the Sect. 3). Fifteen logs of each configuration were generated and their results averaged. More than 32000 generated event logs were evaluated.

Results and Interpretation. Table 3 summarizes the similarity results of the event logs generated from different model instantiations. The *Pre-processing, Model definition and Post-processing* columns describe the configuration used in each phase for building the evaluated models. The *DL act* and *DL roles* columns measure the similarity in the predicted categorical attributes. The *MAE* column corresponds to the mean absolute error of the cycle time of the predicted traces.

These results indicate that using this approach it is possible to train models that learn and reliably reproduce the observed behavior patterns of the original logs. Additionally, the results suggest that for the LSTM models is more difficult to learn sequences with a greater vocabulary than longer sequences. To learn these patterns, a greater number of examples is required, as can be seen in the results of BPI2012 and BPI2015. Both logs have more than 30 activities, but there is a great difference in the amount of traces (see Table 2). The high degree of similarity of the BPI2012 also suggests that the use of embedded dimensions

Table 3. Similarity results in event logs for different configurations

Event log	Pre-processing		Model definition	Post-processing	DL act.	DL roles	MAE (days)
	Scaling	N-gram size	Architecture	Selection method			
BPI 2012	Max	15	Specialized	Random	**0.8929**	0.7888	9
	Max	15	Shared cat.	Random	0.885	**0.8998**	9
	Lognorm	15	Concatenated	Random	0.8426	0.856	**4**
BPI 2012 W	Max	15	Specialized	Random	**0.8742**	0.8245	11.8
	Max	15	Concatenated	Random	0.7902	**0.8552**	7.3
	Max	10	Concatenated	Random	0.7855	0.8329	**5.9**
BPI 2013	Lognorm	10	Joint	Arg max	0.5442	0.698	**242.6**
	Max	15	Shared cat.	Random	**0.7209**	0.8139	471.5
	Lognorm	15	Shared cat.	Random	0.4416	**0.8475**	472.5
BPI 2015-1	Max	10	Concatenated	Random	**0.4397**	0.8048	76.6
	Lognorm	10	Specialized	Random	0.4228	**0.8498**	79.3
	Lognorm	10	Concatenated	Arg max	0.3642	0.5922	**40.1**
BPI 2015-2	Lognorm	10	Shared cat.	Arg max	**0.3737**	0.6228	159.4
	Max	15	Concatenated	Random	0.3462	**0.8612**	158.3
	Max	10	Shared cat.	Arg max	0.0431	0.1691	**89**
BPI 2015-3	Lognorm	10	Concatenated	Random	**0.4616**	0.8501	53.2
	Lognorm	5	Concatenated	Random	0.4456	**0.8729**	54.4
	Lognorm	15	Concatenated	Arg max	0.4255	0.7786	**39.6**
BPI 2015-4	Lognorm	5	Concatenated	Arg max	**0.4034**	0.7188	96
	Lognorm	5	Specialized	Random	0.3609	**0.8248**	98.8
	Max	5	Shared cat.	Arg max	0.0581	0.0968	**71.1**
BPI 2015-5	Lognorm	15	Specialized	Random	**0.3633**	0.8653	84.1
	Max	5	Shared cat.	Random	0.3323	**0.9019**	82.5
	Lognorm	10	Concatenated	Arg max	0.3228	0.6547	**49.6**
Helpdesk	Max	5	Shared cat.	Random	**0.9568**	**0.9869**	42.1
	Max	5	Joint	Arg max	0.5773	0.7368	**7.3**

to handle a high number of event types improves the results, so long as the number of examples is enough to learn the underlying patterns.

In relation with the architectural components evaluated in this experiment, we analyze them according to the phases to build generative models: preprocessing, model structure and hyper-parameters selection, and prediction.

Regarding the *pre-processing phase*, Fig. 7a illustrates how logs with little time variability present better results using max value as scaling technique. In contrast, logs that have an irregular structure have lower MAE using lognormalization. Additionally, Fig. 7b presents the results of DL similarity in the use of n-grams of different sizes, in relation to the structure of event logs. We can observe that the use of longer n-grams has better results for logs with longer traces, showing a stable increasing trend. In contrast, it is not clear a trend for the event logs with medium and simple structures. Therefore, the use of long n-grams should be reserved to logs with very long traces.

Regarding the *model structure definition phase*, Fig. 8 illustrates that the concatenated architecture has the lowest overall similarity. In contrast, the model architecture that only shares information between categorical attributes has the median best performance. However, it is not very distant from the specialized architecture, albeit a wider spread. This implies that sharing information

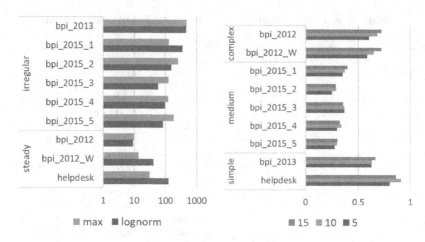

(a) Scaling of relative times results   (b) N-gram size selection

Fig. 7. Preprocessing phase components comparison

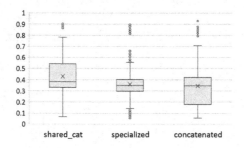

Fig. 8. Shared layers' overall similarity

between attributes of different nature can generate noise in the patterns that the network is processing, thus, hindering the learning process.

Regarding the *prediction phase*, Fig. 9 shows how random choice outperforms arg-max in all the event logs. This behaviour is even more clear in the event logs with longer and complex traces. The results suggest that random choice is advisable for assess the learning process in spite of the event log structure.

4.2   Comparison Against Baselines

Experimental Setup. The aim of this experiment is to assess the relative performance of our approach at the task of predicting the next event, the remaining sequence of events (i.e. suffixes), and the remaining time, for trace prefixes of varying lengths. For *next event prediction*, we feed each model with trace prefixes of increasing length, from 1 up to the length of each trace. For each prefix, we predict the next event and we measure the accuracy (percentage of correct

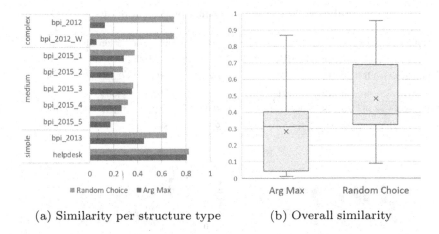

(a) Similarity per structure type   (b) Overall similarity

Fig. 9. Comparison of next-event selection methods

predictions). For suffix and remaining time prediction, we also feed the models with prefixes of increasing lengths. However, this time, we allow the models to hallucinate until the end of the case is reached. The remaining time is then computed by subtracting the timestamp of the last event in the prefix from the timestamp of the last hallucinated event. As in [13], we use DL as a measure of similarity for suffix prediction and MAE for remaining time prediction. For next event and suffix prediction, we use [2,6,13] as baselines while for remaining time prediction, we only use [13], since [2,6] cannot handle this prediction task. We only use the Helpdesk, BPI2012W and BPI2012 event logs, because these are the only logs for which results are reported in [2,6,13]. The results reported for [2] for the Helpdesk and BPI2012 event logs correspond to the re-implementation of this technique reported in [6].

Results and Interpretation. Table 4 summarizes the average accuracy for the next-event prediction task and the average similarity between the predicted suffixes and the actual suffixes. For the task of next-event prediction, our approach performs similar to that of Evermann et al. and Tax et al. while slightly outperforming them for the BPI2012W event log. However, it underperforms the approach by Lin et al. For the task of suffix prediction, our approach outperforms all baselines including that of Lin et al. These results suggest that the measures adopted for the dimensionality control of the categorical attributes, allows our approach to achieve consistently good performance even for long sequences.

Figure 10 presents the MAE for remaining cycle time prediction. Even though the objective of our technique is not to predict the remaining time, it achieves similar performance at this task relative to Tax et al. – slightly underperforming it in one log, and slightly outperforming it for long suffixes in the other log.

Table 4. Next event and suffix prediction results

Implementation	Next event accuracy			Suffix prediction distance		
	Helpdesk	BPI 2012W	BPI 2012	Helpdesk	BPI 2012W	BPI 2012
Our approach	0.789	*0.778*	0.786	*0.917*	*0.525*	*0.632*
Tax et al.	0.712	0.760		0.767	0.353	
Everman et al.	0.798	0.623	0.780	0.742	0.297	0.110
Lin et al.	*0.916*		*0.974*	0.874		0.281

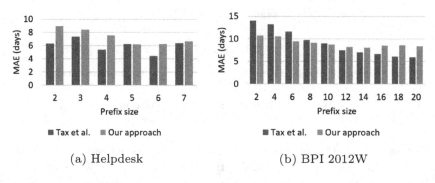

(a) Helpdesk   (b) BPI 2012W

Fig. 10. Results of remaining cycle-time MAE in days

5   Conclusion and Future Work

This paper outlined an approach to train LSTM networks to predict the type of
the next event in a case, its timestamp, and the role associated to the event. By
iteratively predicting the next event, the approach can also predict the remaining
sequence of events of a case (the suffix) and it can also generate entire traces
from scratch. The approach consists of a pre-processing phase (scaling and n-
gram encoding), an LSTM training phase, and a post-processing phase (selection
of the predicted next event among the likely ones). The paper compared several
options for each of these phases with respect to the task of generating full traces
that closely match the traces in the original log. The evaluation shows that
the use of longer n-grams gives higher accuracy, log-normalization is a suitable
scaling method for logs with high variability, and randomly selecting the next
event using the probabilities produced by the LSTM leads to a wider variety
of traces and higher accuracy, relative to always choosing the most likely next
event. The paper also showed that the proposed approach outperforms existing
LSTM-based approaches for predicting the remaining sequence of events and
their timestamps starting from a given prefix of a trace.

We foresee that the proposed approach could be used as a tool for business process simulation. Indeed, in its essence, a process simulator is a generative model that produces sets of traces consisting of event types, resources,
and timestamps, from which it calculates performance measures such as waiting
times, cycle times, and resource utilization. While process simulators rely on

interpretable process models (e.g. BPMN models), any model that can generate traces of events, where each event consists of an event type (activity label), a timestamp, and a resource, can in principle be used to simulate a process. A key challenge to use LSTM networks for process simulation is how to capture "what-if" scenarios (e.g. the effect of removing a task or removing a resource). To this end, we plan to apply techniques to guide the generation of event sequences from LSTM models using constraints along the lines of [3].

Reproducibility. The source code, event logs and example models can be downloaded from https://github.com/AdaptiveBProcess/GenerativeLSTM.git.

Acknowledgments. This research is funded by the Estonian Research Council (IUT20-55) and the European Research Council (Project PIX).

References

1. Breuker, D., Matzner, M., Delfmann, P., Becker, J.: Comprehensible predictive models for business processes. MIS Q. **40**(4), 1009–1034 (2016)
2. Evermann, J., Rehse, J.R., Fettke, P.: Predicting process behaviour using deep learning. Decis. Support Syst. **100**, 129–140 (2017)
3. Di Francescomarino, C., Ghidini, C., Maggi, F.M., Petrucci, G., Yeshchenko, A.: An eye into the future: leveraging a-priori knowledge in predictive business process monitoring. In: Carmona, J., Engels, G., Kumar, A. (eds.) BPM 2017. LNCS, vol. 10445, pp. 252–268. Springer, Cham (2017). https://doi.org/10.1007/978-3-319-65000-5_15
4. Hao, X., Zhang, G., Ma, S.: Deep learning. Int. J. Semant. Comput. **10**(03), 417–439 (2016). https://doi.org/10.1142/S1793351X16500045
5. Lecun, Y., Bengio, Y., Hinton, G.: Deep learning. Nature **521**(7553), 436–444 (2015)
6. Lin, L., Wen, L., Wang, J.: MM-Pred: a deep predictive model for multi-attribute event sequence. In: Proceedings of the 2019 SIAM International Conference on Data Mining, pp. 118–126. Society for Industrial and Applied Mathematics (2019). https://doi.org/10.1137/1.9781611975673.14
7. Mehdiyev, N., Evermann, J., Fettke, P.: A multi-stage deep learning approach for business process event prediction. In: 19th Conference on Business Informatics (CBI), vol. 01, pp. 119–128. IEEE (2017). https://doi.org/10.1109/CBI.2017.46
8. Nolle, T., Seeliger, A., Mühlhäuser, M.: BINet: multivariate business process anomaly detection using deep learning. In: Weske, M., Montali, M., Weber, I., vom Brocke, J. (eds.) BPM 2018. LNCS, vol. 11080, pp. 271–287. Springer, Cham (2018). https://doi.org/10.1007/978-3-319-98648-7_16
9. Polato, M., Sperduti, A., Burattin, A., Leoni, M.D.: Time and activity sequence prediction of business process instances. Computing **100**(9), 1005–1031 (2018)
10. Schmidhuber, J.: Deep Learning in neural networks: an overview. Neural Netw. **61**, 85–117 (2015). https://doi.org/10.1016/j.neunet.2014.09.003
11. Song, M., van der Aalst, W.M.: Towards comprehensive support for organizational mining. Decis. Support Syst. **46**(1), 300–317 (2008). https://doi.org/10.1016/j.dss.2008.07.002
12. Tax, N., Teinemaa, I., van Zelst, S.J.: An interdisciplinary comparison of sequence modeling methods for next-element prediction. CoRR abs/1811.00062 (2018)

13. Tax, N., Verenich, I., La Rosa, M., Dumas, M.: Predictive business process monitoring with LSTM neural networks. In: Dubois, E., Pohl, K. (eds.) CAiSE 2017. LNCS, vol. 10253, pp. 477–492. Springer, Cham (2017). https://doi.org/10.1007/978-3-319-59536-8_30
14. Teinemaa, I., Leontjeva, A., Masing, K.O.: BPIC 2015: diagnostics of building permit application process in Dutch municipalities. BPI Challenge Report 72 (2015)

Management

Trust-Aware Process Design

Michael Rosemann$^{(\boxtimes)}$

Queensland University of Technology, Brisbane, Australia
m.rosemann@qut.edu.au

Abstract. Longitudinal studies point to the global erosion of trust in institutions and their business processes. As a result, the provision of trusted processes has become a new design criterion that exceeds the traditional Business Process Management (BPM) goals of time, cost, and quality, and also goes beyond security and privacy concerns. The notion of trust, however, has rarely been studied in the context of BPM. This paper initiates the conceptualization of trust in BPM by providing two new artefacts, i.e. a four-stage model for the design of trusted processes and a related meta model. Both have been derived from relevant theories and existing, general trust conceptualizations. Two exploratory case studies and secondary data have facilitated the identification of an initial set of application scenarios and trust requirements.

Keywords: Trust management · Uncertainty · Process design · Trustworthiness

1 Introduction

The recent Edelman Trust Barometer reports show a 'world of distrust' in institutions. The trust index for businesses, government, non-government organizations, and media remains low, with countries such as the USA having seen the highest decline in trust ever recorded in 2018 [1, 2]. Business processes are essential institutional artifacts and, as such, are not only severely exposed to this evaporation of trust, but badly managed processes are also a root cause of the drop in institutional trust [3]. Incidents related to organizations such as Facebook, Samsung, or Volkswagen and the spill-over effects into related industries demonstrate the need to make trust an explicit design concern. In addition to reactively dealing with the trust crisis (so called trust repair), there is also evidence that trust managed well has a positive correlation with economic performance and customer loyalty [4].

Trust is required when uncertainty exists within a business process. It is the result of a subjective assessment of this uncertainty (belief), and only if sufficient confidence exists will the process be initiated (action) [5]. For example, a customer might require a process to be completed in a certain timeframe for the decision to order. However, there is only a promised, but no certain, delivery date. Depending on the customer's general propensity to trust [6, 7] and her believe that the process will be completed in the required timeframe, she will take the action and trigger the sales process by placing an order. In order to build the trust required, the organization could: (a) reduce process uncertainties where possible; (b) offer an insurance in case the process will be late;

T. Hildebrandt et al. (Eds.): BPM 2019, LNCS 11675, pp. 305–321, 2019.
https://doi.org/10.1007/978-3-030-26619-6_20

and/or (c) provide additional, trust-building information (e.g., "98% of all processes are completed within 2 days").

Unfortunately, the Business Process Management (BPM) discipline so far has little to offer when it comes to the conceptualization, design, or execution of trust-aware business processes. Trust as an artifact has not made it into process lifecycle models, BPM meta models, or BPM maturity models. There are three reasons for this. First, BPM has emerged in the age of institutional trust. Organizations, and their processes, were largely trusted and competed on economic criteria. This explains why the time–cost–quality triangle still dominates the default set of process goals [8]. As a consequence, a process might be of high transactional excellence (i.e., performs well in terms of time, cost, and quality), but the lack of trust in the process prevents it from being adopted. Second, though substantial BPM research has been invested into compliance and, more recently, the trustworthiness of a process, this research only addresses internal, objective criteria. Trust, however, is an external, subjective assessment. It is a perceptual construct and assessed differently in the context of the same process by different stakeholders depending on their individual tolerance for unpredictability (so called uncertainty avoidance). In other words, BPM research has largely assumed rational behavior and focused on evidence ("the process has a defined Six Sigma score") - not confidence ("the customer believes that the process will deliver in time"). Third, the digital economy has empowered and connected citizens and with it provided new forms of decentralized trust in addition to the previous reliance on institutional trust. This can be seen in platforms and marketplaces where social networks have enabled users to connect quickly with members of their trusted network when executing a process. Trust networks allow access to other users or a group of users as an additional source of trust beyond the typical interaction with an institution only. Furthermore, technological solutions such as Blockchain facilitate trusted processes by providing an infrastructure for secure, local transactions within processes [9]. Embedding these new forms of non-institutional trust into BPM artifacts has rarely been the focus of research so far.

The rising importance of trusted processes, new sources of social and digital trust, and the related gap in the body of BPM knowledge motivated this research and its underlying research question, *"How can trust be embedded in the design of business processes?"* The aim is to provide an additional trust layer to guide process analysts in the design of trusted business processes.

In order to address this research question, relevant trust research and underlying theories (e.g., uncertainty reduction, information asymmetry) were studied and deployed in the context of trusted processes (as opposed to the common focus on trust in organizations or people). The insights gained shaped the methodology proposed here. We derived illustrative processes with trust requirements from two exploratory case studies: a retail bank and a consulate providing services to its nation's citizens. In addition, secondary data has been used to identify exemplary processes with trust requirements.

This paper is structured as follows. Section 2 introduces the relevant trust-related terminology and reflects on its coverage in the context of BPM. Section 3 presents a four-stage model for the design of trusted processes, before Sect. 4 consolidates and interrelates these elements in a meta model. Section 5 summarizes the paper and discusses its limitations and possible future research directions.

2   Trust, Trust Concerns, and Trustworthiness

2.1   Trust

The notion of trust has been comprehensively discussed and researched for decades in a variety of scientific disciplines (e.g., sociology, psychology, economics, game theory). Soellner et al. [10] summarized the status of Information Systems research in the area of trust highlighting the different types of relationships between people, technology and organizations in which trust matters. In comparison, this paper will take a narrow view and not reflect on the diverse connotations of trust in a social context. Instead, it zooms into the requirements of trust in a corporate context, with a new focus on trusted business processes. Other perspectives such as the trust an organization has in its customer (e.g., in the context of a loan application), trust as it relates to the employees involved in a process or trust in the overall purpose or integrity of an organization are out of scope within this paper.

Botsman [11] defines trust as *"a confident relationship with the unknown"*. Therefore, trust only becomes relevant if there is uncertainty. Despite ongoing attempts to create fully automated, compliant, reliable processes, there remains a residual uncertainty within nearly all processes. In fact, 100% process certainty will be in most cases economically or technically impossible and, consequently, trust will nearly always be a success factor for process adoption, unless it is a mandated process (e.g., tax declaration). Botsman's definition allows decomposing trust into the two elements uncertainty and confidence. Uncertainty itself can be further broken down into process uncertainty, i.e. the likelihood that a process does not deliver as promised, and vulnerability, i.e. the uncertainty as it relates to the implications in case a process indeed fails to deliver.

Trust might be needed because of an information overload (e.g., which book to buy?) or a scarcity of information (e.g., will the company deliver the item in time?). Trust is a social construct; that is, different stakeholders trust the expected performance of a process differently depending on their propensity to trust, their previous experiences with the process and contextual factors [6]. A trust judgment might be made intuitively and spontaneously or could be the result of a conscious analytical reflection. Trust can be personalized (e.g., trusting a process case worker) or generalized (e.g., trust in an organization or a specific business process).

In summary, and aligned with McAlister [12], we define trust in a process as the judgment of confident reliance on this process based on positive expectations of its future behavior. A trusted business process gives stakeholders confidence to place their faith into this process in light of an outcome that is uncertain to a degree. Thus, trust consists of a belief (confidence in a future process) and an action (commitment to initiate the process). A business process can be regarded as the trustee, and an external stakeholder who relies on the process is the trustor.

Trust has a close relationship with quality and risk—two artifacts that are intensively discussed in the context of BPM. First, *quality* describes the performance of the process itself and its outcome [13]. Related research and a plethora of widely used BPM methodologies (e.g., Lean Six Sigma) have been dedicated to understanding and improving process qualities. Quality and trust have a close relationship when it comes to reliability as a popular process quality indicator. Quality and trust are also both 'in the eye of the beholder.' However, while quality management is a mature process-aware discipline with engineering-like methods and tools, trust management is far less advanced. Furthermore, quality is often a promise made by an organization to its customer. Whether the customer believes that the company can fulfill this promise (i.e., whether the customer trusts the process) is out of scope. Finally, a process might be of a known sub-quality standard. As there is no uncertainty about it, it would have no trust requirements.

Second, *risk* is the probability or, more broadly, the threat of an occurrence with negative implications for a process [14]. Unlike trust, risk can often be quantified and is not prone to subjective assessments (e.g., its frequency may be derived from log files). Many types of risks along a process, however, are either not relevant to an external customer (e.g., the risk to underestimate the cost of a process) or not known to the customer. Trust materializes in the subjective decision to proceed with a process in light of a risk. This includes perceiving risks where they do not exist (e.g., the inability to assess the quality of a proven technology). Not all risk-taking behavior requires trust.

The dedicated body of knowledge on trust in the context of BPM is very limited. For example, Greenberg et al. [15] studied the role of trust in the governance of outsourcing business processes. In their research the authors integrate transaction cost economy with types of trust as discussed in the Information Systems literature and differentiate contact, contract, and control as the three main stages of a process deserving a trust investigation. Berner et al. [16] discuss the notion of trusted process information in their investigation of 'Process Visibility.' 'Trusted' as an attribute of process visibility is defined here as the degree to which the business process information is perceived to be valid, reliable and objective and a positive attitude is embraced towards the source.

2.2 Trust Concerns

The design of trusted processes requires an understanding of related trust requirements. These are known as *trust concerns,* which capture those issues potentially preventing customers from engaging with a process. Trust concerns can be elicited either directly in the form of interviews or indirectly be derived by experienced process designers [17]. Mohammadi and Heisel [17] provide a comprehensive set of trust concern identification patterns. However, these are rather generic (e.g., "I am concerned about the correct functionality of the services") and not tailored to the elements of a business process.

In our explorative case study work with two organizations (financial service, consulate) we identified a diverse set of trust concerns including issues such as:

- *Quality of a process activity*: Will the forecasted balance of my account be correct?
- *Resource expertise*: Does the person dealing with my case have the specific expertise needed?
- *Resource goal*: Can I trust the organization to incentivize their broker so that they recommend the right product to me?
- *Resource availability*: Will I get my appointment at 9.30 am, or do I have to consider waiting for a while?
- *Data*: Will you respect the privacy of my data that I provide along the process?
- *Process success rate*: Will my application to re-naturalize be successful?

As it can be seen, trust concerns are stated from an end-user perspective. This is different to statements related to risk-aware business processes which are typically made from a process-provider view.

In order to consolidate trust concerns, *trust profiles* can be used to assign users to distinct trust persona [7]. A *trust persona* is a group of users with comparable trust concerns. For example, following the diffusion of innovation model [18], one could differentiate between the very early adopters (innovators) who have a high level of trust in a new process versus skeptical, late movers who only trust a process after they have seen sufficient evidence of its performance.

Note that in addition to trust concerns, it is important to also recognize the existence of *trust opportunities*, i.e. proactively creating customer touchpoints that facilitate the development of trust. Examples for trust opportunities are Amazon re-confirming the desire to order, if a customer orders the same book for the second time or if a telecommunication company proactively downgrades a data plan to appropriately map it to the actual data consumption of its customer [19]. For the purpose of this paper, however, trust opportunities are out of scope.

2.3   Trustworthiness

"Organizations that weave trustworthiness signals into all elements of their [...] processes, over time, earn reputations of trust with their stakeholders" [20]. While trust is in the eye of the customer, organizations have various options to improve the likelihood that their processes will be trusted. They can design trustworthy processes as a response to the articulated trust concerns; that is, processes that deserve to be trusted. Trustworthiness goes beyond security concerns [21] and is discussed in Computer Science as an attribute of technical systems, including characteristics such as privacy, reliability, availability, performance, usability, etc. With regards to the human and organizational capital involved in a process, trustworthiness includes features such as honesty, competence, commitment, benevolence, intentionality, or integrity (for an overview based on a literature review of attributes of trustworthiness see Chong et al. [22]).

Mohammadi and Heisel's [23] work on integrating trustworthiness requirements in business process models using BPMN is an important contribution of relevance for this research. Starting with identified trust concerns of the end user, specific trustworthiness properties are derived, and detailed recommendations are made for how to model these. However, there is no discussion on how to actually build trust.

3 A Four-Stage Model for the Design of a Trusted Process

The BPM discipline has a tradition of developing dedicated perspectives to include emerging requirements and to separate concerns. These optional perspectives are complementing the core scope and methods of established process lifecycle models focused on the control flow and immediate artifacts such as data and resources. This type of research has previously included proposals to support perspectives such as risk-awareness [24], cost-awareness [25], creativity-awareness [26], privacy-awareness [27], or context-awareness [28] of business processes and is summed up in the notion of x-aware BPM [29]. However, to the best of our knowledge, there is no BPM-related research that guides academics and professionals regarding the design of *trust-aware* business processes.

In accordance with the way the previously mentioned additional perspectives have extended BPM approaches, this paper adds a trust layer to the body of BPM knowledge consisting of a methodology and a meta model (Sect. 4) to formalize the integration. The methodology for trust-aware process design comprises four stages. The first stage covers the positioning of trust within the context of business processes whereas the following three stages, inspired by Botsman's trust definition above, address uncertainty, vulnerability and confidence as the core elements of trust.

(1) *Identify moments of trust:* Identify the steps in a process where external stakeholders make a decision that requires trust.
(2) *Reduce uncertainty*: Address operational, behavioral and perceptual issues so that the overall process uncertainty is reduced.
(3) *Reduce vulnerability*: Reduce the vulnerability of the customer in case the process does indeed not perform as expected.
(4) *Build confidence*: Create a positive bias despite uncertainty and vulnerability.

3.1 Identify Moments of Trust

Trust is needed along a process when the external party is about to make a decision and uncertainty exists. For example, a customer might have proceeded in an online sales process to the point where items have been selected, put in the shopping basket, and a decision in the form of hitting the 'order now' button needs to be made. In this moment, the customer will have to trust that the items can be shipped by the desired delivery date, assuming that a late arrival would make these items unusable. This touchpoint when trust matters is called the *moment of trust*.

A conceptualization of moments of trust, therefore, is required to capture the decision point and the uncertainty that the customer is concerned about. Similar to the modeling of risks [24], the latter requires to be selective as there could be a plethora of uncertainties at a moment of trust (e.g., Will my data be protected if I share these? Will the product be of the desired quality? Has the company complied with all standards?).

As a moment of trust locates one or many *trust concerns* within a process, the severity of these concerns can be used as a measure of priority. As trust concerns are assigned to *trust persona*, the relevance of a moment of trust for different external stakeholders can be assessed. The proposed notion for moments of trust is as follows:

```
Name (moment of trust) [Object of uncertainty [process|
activity|resource|data]: Name (trust concern₁), Name (trust
concernₙ)]
```

The following schematic (Fig. 1) shows an example from one of our exploratory case studies of how moments of trust, trust concerns, and related trust persona could be embedded in a process. In this case, applicants for re-naturalized citizenship have two process-related trust concerns at the beginning of the process: (1) Applicants are concerned regarding the success rate of the process (Is it worthwhile to put in all the effort and to pay the application fee?) and (2) Will the process be finished in less than a year? This moment of trust is only relevant for applicants who live outside the country, as there is an awareness that this fact has a negative impact on the success rate and increases the processing time. At the next step, all applicants have a shared data-related trust concern with regards to data security. As this is of relevance for all users, no specific trust persona is associated.

Beyond what has been visualized here, one could envisage that an increased relevance and importance of trust might motivate organizations to assign dedicated *trust owners* (similar to the notion of risk owners) to specific trust concerns or moments of trust as part of their overall trust governance. A translation to specific notations (e.g., BPMN) has not been defined yet but is straightforward.

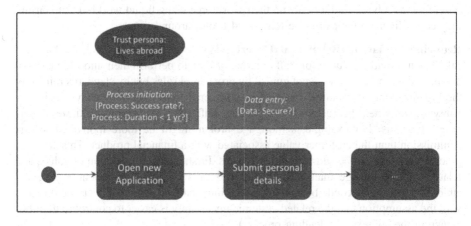

Fig. 1. Example of *moments of trust* and *trust persona* within a business process

3.2 Reduce Process Uncertainty

Trust is only needed when the trustor is uncertain about the performance of the trustee (in this case, the process). If uncertainty is the root cause of a trust concern, reducing this root cause is the most effective way to manage trust. The less uncertainty there is in a process, the higher is the trust in the process.

Process uncertainty comes in three forms, (1) operational uncertainty and (2) behavioral uncertainty which both create actual process *variation,* and (3) perceived uncertainty which is grounded in the lack of process *visibility.*

Reducing Variation (Operational Uncertainty). BPM has a track record of addressing systemic process uncertainty. Uncertainty in a process can be the result of an uncertain activity (e.g., high variation in processing time for this activity), an uncertain resource (e.g., varying levels of qualification), uncertain data (e.g., securing data privacy), or overall process uncertainty (e.g., processing time).

As a common BPM approach, Six Sigma is dedicated to reducing variation; that is, maximizing certainty. The higher the Six Sigma score, the lower the deviation of the outcomes and, as a result, the higher the process certainty. For example, a high Six Sigma score for an airport security process would mean that passengers do not have to rely on a trust-based judgment of the likely processing time, but can expect a predictable throughput time. In the ideal form, uncertainty completely disappears, and a process would show law-like performance. For example, if artificial intelligence (AI)-based interpretations of x-rays reach a level of 100% accuracy for certain types of diagnoses, this process activity converts from an uncertain, human-dependent task to an activity with certainty that equals the predictability of results on a calculator.

Using the case above (Fig. 1), the process-related trust concern regarding the processing time could be addressed by scalable resources. For example, accounting firms providing tax advice tend to scale up their workforce using liquid workforces to ensure they can deliver on their promise (e.g., a 24-h turn-around time).

Reducing Variation (Behavioral Uncertainty). Systems, processes, and business rules often provide freedom for staff in terms of how to perform their allocated tasks in detail. In these cases, staff are not guided by procedural rules but by standards reflecting the organizational commitment to integrity, sincerity, and honesty. Behavioral uncertainty occurs when the customer is unsure if staff will act according to these higher-order standards. For example, a mortgage broker might be more motivated by the commission than the customer value associated with a financial product. This cause of process variation can be addressed in two ways. First, a clear articulation of values and related cultural change management can lead to a higher commitment to relevant ethical standards. Second, behavioral uncertainty can be eliminated via automation with the assumption that the related systemic uncertainty is easier to control (e.g., robo-advice in the context of a lending process).

Increasing Visibility (Perceived Uncertainty). In addition to actual certainty, perceived uncertainty can compromise the trust position of a business process. In this case, a customer does not trust a process, not because the process is in fact uncertain but because the customer believes that the process is uncertain. Perceived uncertainty is grounded in information asymmetry [30] and best addressed by increasing the visibility of a process to overcome this asymmetry. For example, Volkswagen's glass factory makes the final stages of the manufacturing process visible to the future car owner, and open kitchens in restaurants make the cooking process visible to diners. These concepts increase the line of visibility along a process and eliminate perceived uncertainty as a factor for insufficient trust. Similarly, the ability to track delivery processes (open process monitoring), as practiced by many logistics or food delivery companies nowadays, increases the customer's knowledge of the actual arrival time and, as such, reduces uncertainty over time.

In addition to making the actual process status and its progress visible to the customer, tools such as predictive process monitoring and process forecasting can be used to increase the visibility; that is, reduce the uncertainty of future process events. For example, Uber publishes the average estimated time of arrival of its drivers as a real-time data feed at various airports.

3.3 Reduce Vulnerability

Not all forms of uncertainty within a business process can be eliminated. This could be due to technical reasons (e.g., a robotic vision algorithm has only a certain quality to detect items), the impossibility of anticipating all exceptions, reliance on human judgement, external factors (e.g., weather, traffic, suppliers), or other reasons. In this third step of trust-aware process design the focus is on reducing the vulnerability; that is, the negative implication in case the process does not deliver as promised (e.g., a delivery is late). Vulnerability can be seen as the potential cost to a trustor in case the trustee does not perform as expected. The higher this cost, the more trust is required to proceed.

In order to mitigate these costs, different types of vulnerability and corresponding compensations need to be differentiated. Three examples covering time, product, and price vulnerability are provided in the following to clarify this:

(1) *The costs of a process being late.* For example, in 2018 the German Bundesbahn processed 2.7 million claims processes by travelers seeking reimbursements for their late trains. Such an arrangement requires an additional process capability.
(2) *The outcome of a process might not satisfy the customer's expectations.* For example, many online retailers offer a free-of-charge return (e.g., Adidas' change-of-mind returns policy). This requires process-rollback capabilities.
(3) *The value-for-money equation is dissatisfactory.* For example, a consulting company could re-configure its pricing algorithm in its invoicing process so that the fee is based on the value provided as opposed to being time-based. This form of vulnerability management requires a modification of a task within a process.

3.4 Building Confidence

Unfortunately, the bulk of BPM research stops at the design of trustworthy processes (e.g., Mohammadi and Heisel [17]). The conversion of a trustworthy process into a trusted process and the exploration of additional sources of trust, however, has been so far largely out of scope. Trustworthy processes become trusted processes if the customer has confidence that the process will deliver as promised. Das and Teng [31] also show that trust complements control as a confidence builder. The relationship between confidence and trust, and how the latter goes beyond the former, is comprehensively discussed by Mayer et al. [6, p. 713].

Reducing process uncertainty and vulnerability already has an indirect positive effect on confidence. However, there are also ways to directly increase customer confidence in a business process. The fourth and final stage of process-aware trust management therefore deals with mechanisms helping with the emergence of confidence.

Once the moments of trust and related trust concerns have been identified, it needs to be explored how a stakeholder's confidence in the relationship with the identified uncertainty and vulnerability can be increased. For this, it is proposed to identify alternative *sources of trust*. A source of trust provides confidence-building information on which a decision can be made. Depending on the characteristics of the process and the profile of the trust persona—that is, individual preferences and attitudes—certain sources of trust might be more important than others. In the following, six alternative sources of trust will be discussed. For each of these, it will be briefly shown how to use process-aware information systems for these sources of trust.

Democratic Trust: Trust the Majority. A quantitative source of trust is the articulation of confidence-boosting information covering the behavior or experiences of the majority of users at the moment of trust within a process. For example, in our explorative cases we found that some citizens proactively ask questions such as 'how many applications have been successful?' when considering whether to lodge specialized applications such as a request to re-naturalize as a citizen. The provision of such a figure, if high enough, could act as a confidence-boosting piece of information. A similar example of a trust-building piece of information would be a metric stating the (high) number of customers (in percentage) who have not returned products after purchasing a specific product (unseen) online. A variant of democratic trust would be the upfront provision of aggregated process information. For example, Uber uses the average arrival times of their drivers (e.g., 4 min) as a trust-building mechanism for the service latency[1] of their personal mobility process. Thus, democratic trust means trust in numbers and is nurtured via a reference to the positive experiences of the majority of process customers. Democratic trust is popular in platforms using rating systems.

A process-aware information system (PAIS) could embed such sources of trust by consolidating and publishing previous process data (assuming they have confidence-building values). Similar to the idea that data usage is seen as a proxy for data quality, process usage could be seen as an indicator for process quality. This is similar to solutions that are used as part of product recommendation services (e.g., Amazon store).

---

[1] The service latency of a process is the time between the triggering event and the first action of the process.

More advanced systems would be able to consider the trust persona and offer only persona-specific information. For example, process success rates would be offered depending on the applicant's demographic class.

Democratic trust is of relevance in processes with limited decision complexity (limited number of alternatives) and with a high volume of users (so adequate majority scores can be sourced).

Local Trust: Trust in My Personal Network. A user might not trust the process or published frequencies (democratic trust, i.e., wisdom of the crowds). However, there might be trusted people whose (positive) experiences with the process could be confidence-building (i.e., wisdom of friends). This requires finding a way to transfer the trust into these contacts towards trust in the process.

Trust networks capture relationships with trusted people. An existing trusted relationship can be activated as a source of trust in the context of a business process. A trust network can either be explicit—that is, a user expresses in a trust statement (e.g., as a score between 0–1) the extent to which they trust another user—or it can be implicit—that is, trust is inferred from a relationship between two people. Examples of the latter are connections in social networks such as Facebook or LinkedIn. The assumption is that the mutual willingness to create a connection is grounded in mutual trust. If the user can be motivated to share their trust network at the moment of trust in a process, trusted users can be identified. For example, Airbnb Social Connections allow connecting Airbnb with Facebook during the booking process to see if someone from the potential guest's personal network is a personal friend of the host or has reviewed the host. Such a connection could be seen as trust-building for the person using the Airbnb booking process and reduces uncertainties regarding an essential resource in this process; that is, the host.

A concern with this source of trust is that the trust network might reflect a filter bubble; that is, like-minded sources of trust and not objective sources are activated. Unlike democratic trust, this source of trust requires: (1) involvement of the user who has to be incentivized to share their trust network, (2) a track record of members of this trust network who have previously engaged with the process, and (3) the ability to identify these users. The quality of local trust depends on the size and accessibility of the trust network. Thus, local trust is more relevant for community processes (e.g., retail, entertainment, or personal services such as UrbanSitter) with limited privacy concerns as opposed to specialized processes (e.g., health care).

Global Trust: Trust in Respected Users. In more advanced decision-making processes that go beyond simple yes or no decisions, majority statements (of a general population or sourced from a local trust network) might not be sufficient. Instead, what is needed is the confidence that can only be derived from a person with a high commonly accepted reputational value (e.g., intensive user of a specific process). This can be found, for example, in Amazon's book recommendations, Wikipedia's selection of editors, or LinkedIn endorsements.

This source of trust requires access to process users with a high reputational standing. The user could either leave a track of 'endorsed processes' or could be proactively contacted as a source of trust. An example for the former would be the training processes of amateur athletes who follow the training processes of recognized athletes. An example of the latter is the case when during the process of hiring a graduate the recruiting company contacts the academic experts who taught the relevant candidate.

As can be seen, global trust matters for processes when higher levels of expertise are needed to select a process variant (or a resource within a process). In these cases, the reputational standing and the specific expertise matter more than the personal connection (local trust) or the view of the majority of process users (democratic trust).

Specific Trust: Trust in People Like Me. In some cases, trust can only be derived from users who share a number of essential attributes with the user who is about to engage with a process. For example, the platform Patientslikeme.com is a network of more than 600,000 users that allows people with health issues to identify other patients with similar demographics and symptoms who have successfully overcome the identified health problem. A study of the behavior of a specific class of patients (e.g., 90% of them took a certain medication) can be a relevant source of trust for users when deciding about their very own therapy process. In these processes, confidence needs to be built within an individual user who could not derive trust from their trust network (as no member of this network has experience or familiarity with this medical issue). 'People like me' is a trust-building mechanism that, according to the Edelman Trust Barometer, ranks third highest in terms of credibility [2].

In such a scenario, the decision-maker derives the trust required from an endorsement or the process behavior of a person with shared health circumstances or attributes. This type of reasoning underlies predictive process monitoring solutions that identify similar tokens from the process log file. In the context of trust management, this would require: (1) identifying similar tokens, and (2) recommending process paths based on the positivity of the outcome. For example, what therapeutical process did those patients (like me) choose that led to the desired outcome; that is, they overcame the medical issue?

A PAIS will only be able to provide such data if rich insights about the process users do exist. Certain attributes might be derived based on the way the process is executed. Similar to democratic trust, the provider of the process becomes a broker to a new trusted source as opposed to local trust in the form of a trust network where the user has to bring trusted connections to the process.

These previous four forms of trust (democratic, local, global, specific) can be classified as social trust; that is, they derive trust via some form of social interaction. The next two forms of trust are based on forms of organizational trust and grounded in the process provider.

Institutional Trust: Trust in the Organization. This is the traditional source of trust. However, as indicated at the start of this paper, it is also the source of trust most in danger, as institutional trust has been on the decline [1]. Institutional trust in the context of BPM means that there is a flow-on effect of the (dis)trust into the institution to the (dis)trust in a business process provided by this organization.

Building institutional trust is largely grounded in building trustworthy processes by ways of demonstrating compliance, commitment to security and privacy, sufficiently qualified and appropriately incentivized employees, etc. Trust-building beyond these 'hard' process facts could be finding ways of how the trust in the organization spills over to trust in the process. Well-known for this is the capability maturity model. Here an increased organizational maturity score is a proxy for process reliance.

The inclusion of institutional trust in a PAIS could come in the form of proactive statements that highlight the credibility of the various components of the organization (e.g., highlight maturity levels, qualifications of resources involved, ethical standards, etc.). Institutional trust may be the only form of trust for entire new processes in which no historical process data or data for social trust is available yet. Processes that become trusted because of institutional forms of trust are processes that benefit from the additional assurance that the organization can provide assets to the process, especially as a way to mitigate vulnerability (e.g., lending process in a retail bank).

Robotic Trust: Trust in Machines. The sixth and last confidence-building element in a business process is related to reliable technology as a source of trust. Robotic trust becomes relevant when the technology used within the business process has developed a level of maturity that it is commonly trusted. Examples are the use of calculators in invoicing processes or navigation systems in delivery processes. Recent digital technologies (e.g., AI, Blockchain) take robotic trust to new levels and have enabled, for example, decentralized processes such as Powerledger's peer-to-peer energy trading process. It could be easily envisaged that very soon patients will trust an AI algorithm more than the viewpoint of a radiologist within a healthcare process.

Technologies such as robotic process automation are contributing to an increased reliability of a process and thus can be seen as a new form of robotic trust. In such processes, the customer derives the confidence required from the technology used more than from the trust in the corporation providing the process.

4   A Meta Model for Trust-Aware Process Design

In order to formalize the notion of trust-aware process design, a meta model summarizing and interrelating the constructs presented above is provided.

Trust only matters when a *process* has *uncertainties*; that is, the user of the process cannot be sure that the process behaves as promised. Uncertainties in a process can be rooted in *activities*, *resources,* or *data,* matter at a *moment of trust,* and lead to *trust concerns*. The difference in the assessment of process uncertainties by different users is captured in a taxonomy of *trust persona* based on their *trust profiles*.

Organizations have three ways to address these trust concerns: reduce uncertainties, reduce vulnerability, and increase confidence.

First, they need to address process uncertainties which manifest in three alternative forms: (1) they can reduce *actual systemic uncertainties* by addressing and ultimately reducing operational process variations (e.g., via Six Sigma); (2) organizations can address *actual behavioral uncertainties* by ensuring that the staff involved in the process are performing their tasks according to values such as confidentiality, integrity, availability, security, privacy, performance, and others; and (3) organizations need to address *perceived uncertainties* by making the process more visible as a way to overcome this type of uncertainty.

Second, organizations can mitigate uncertainties grounded in the *vulnerability* of an eventually non-performing process. This requires revising processes in a way that the costs of a process not performing to a customer's expectations are mitigated. Here we differentiate mitigating vulnerability as it relates to the *process time,* the *process outcome,* or the *process cost.* Both uncertainty management and vulnerability management lead to a *trustworthy process.*

Third, organizations can provide *sources of trust* in order to further boost the user's confidence in the process. Depending on the process characteristics, the related decisions to be made, and the trust persona, these sources will be of different relevance. As such, we distinguish between *democratic trust, local trust, global trust, specific trust, institutional trust,* and *robotic trust* as sources of trust.

The extent to which a trust persona ends up trusting a process is a result of how well the three elements of trust management address the identified trust concerns. The summarizing meta model, showing the three clusters of user, uncertainty, and trust management, is presented in Fig. 2.

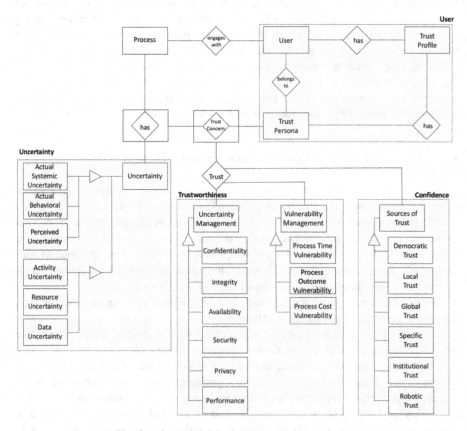

Fig. 2. Meta model for trust-aware process design

5 Conclusions and Future Work

Various cross-sectorial incidents have triggered a significant decline in the trust stakeholders have in institutions and their constituting elements, including their executives, organizational structures, resources, and business processes. At the same time, new forms of social and digital trust (e.g., Blockchain) are emerging and provide new opportunities to increase an organization's trust position. The BPM discipline, however, has not made trust a dedicated concern within its widely used artifacts, such as process lifecycle models, maturity models, or meta models.

Motivated by this demand for and the absence of knowledge in this field, this paper summarized the related body of knowledge before proposing a four-stage model of trust-aware process design. Related literature incl. underlying theories of relevance has been presented, the core trust concepts have been introduced, and ways to identify moments of trust, to reduce process uncertainty and vulnerability and to increase confidence in the process have been discussed. A consolidating meta model formally interrelates these concepts and connects the presented trust constructs as an additional layer of concern to the essential notion of a process. Real-life examples derived from two exploratory cases studies and secondary date have shown the relevance and potential applicability of this model.

This paper is conceptual in nature and, as a result, has to come with a set of *limitations*. First, further trust theories in disciplines such as sociology or economics could have been identified and improved the theoretical foundation of the trust constructs presented here. Second, a more thorough empirical investigation in the tradition of Action Design Research could have led to an iterative, empirically grounded development of the model. Third, and finally, the meta model presented is only a first step towards a more formalized articulation of trust-aware process design (including proposals for trust notations in the context of business process modelling).

As a first contribution to the domain of trust-aware process design, this paper could not cover a number of related topics that need to be addressed in *future research* to arrive at a more complete understanding and conceptualization of trust-aware processes. This includes, among others, rigorously interrelating trust with the known stages of the process lifecycle, addressing issues with regards to the actual measurement of trust and identifying relevant capabilities and including these in BPM maturity models. Substantial empirical work is required to assess the validity, reliability and overall relevance of the proposed model. Future empirical work could also lead to an initial set of trust profiles and typical trust concerns as well as ultimately lead to trust patterns; that is, process building blocks for the design of trust-aware business processes. Each proposed source of trust could attract further work, in particular in terms of its impact on users' trust, their implementation in PAIS and their alignment with process profiles; that is, what type of process requires what source(s) of trust? Researchers with a passion for BPM governance might reflect on the potential roles of trust designers and trust owners or how trust can be embedded in enterprise architectures.

References

1. Edelman Trust Barometer. Global Report. The Battle for Truth (2018). https://www.edelman.com/research/2018-edelman-trust-barometer. Accessed 2 June 2019
2. Edelman Trust Barometer. Global Report: Trust at Work, p. 33 (2019). https://www.edelman.com/trust-barometer. Accessed 2 June 2019
3. Gillespie, N., Siebert, S.: Organizational trust repair. In: Searle, R.H., Nienaber, A.-M.I., Sitkin, S.B. (eds.) The Routledge Companion to Trust, pp. 284–301. Taylor Francis (2018)
4. Kamers, R.: The role of trust in the B2B buying process. In: Proceedings of 6th IBA Bachelor Thesis Conference, Enschede (2015)
5. Sztompka, P.: Trust: A Sociological Theory. Cambridge University Press, Cambridge (2000)
6. Mayer, R.C., Davis, J.H., Schoorman, F.D.: An integrative model of organizational trust. Acad. Manag. Rev. **20**(3), 709–734 (1995)
7. Garbarino, E., Jonson, M.S.: The different roles of satisfaction, trust, and commitment in customer relationships. J. Mark. **63**(2), 70–87 (1999)
8. Dumas, M., La Rosa, M., Mendling, J., Reijers, H.: Fundamentals of Business Process Management, 2nd edn. Springer, Berlin (2018). https://doi.org/10.1007/978-3-662-56509-4
9. Mendling, J., et al.: Blockchains for business process management – challenges and opportunities. ACM Trans. Manag. Inf. Syst. **9**(1) (2018)
10. Soellner, M., Benbasat, I., Gefen, D., Leimeister, M., Pavlou, P.A.: Trust: an MIS quarterly research curation (2016). https://www.misqresearchcurations.org/mis-quarterly-research-curations. Accessed 2 June 2019
11. Botsman, R.: Who Can You Trust? How Technology Brought Us Together and Why It Might Drive Us Apart. Public Affairs, New York (2017)
12. McAllister, D.J.: Affect and cognition-based trust as foundations for interpersonal cooperation in organizations. Acad. Manag. J. **38**(1), 24–59 (1995)
13. Heravizadeh, M.: Quality-aware business process management. Ph.D. thesis, QUT Brisbane, November 2009
14. Suriadi, S., et al.: Current research in risk-aware business process management: overview, comparison, and gap analysis. Commun. AIS **34**(1), 933–984 (2014)
15. Greenberg, P.S., Greenberg, R.H., Antonucci, Y.L.: The role of trust in the governance of business process outsourcing relationships: a transaction cost economics approach. Bus. Process Manag. J. **14**(5), 593–608 (2008)
16. Berner, M., Graupner, E., Maedche, A., Mueller, B.: Process visibility – towards a conceptualization and research themes. In: Proceedings of the 33rd International Conference on Information Systems (ICIS 2012), Orlando (2012)
17. Gol Mohammadi, N., Heisel, M.: Enhancing business process models with trustworthiness requirements. In: Habib, S.M.M., Vassileva, J., Mauw, S., Mühlhäuser, M. (eds.) IFIPTM 2016. IAICT, vol. 473, pp. 33–51. Springer, Cham (2016). https://doi.org/10.1007/978-3-319-41354-9_3
18. Rodgers, E.M.: Diffusion of Innovation, 5th edn. Free Press, NewYork (2003)
19. Peppers, D., Rogers, M.: Extreme Trust. Turning Proactive Honesty and Flawless Execution into Long-Term Profits. Penguin, New York (2016)
20. Hurley, R.F., Gillespie, N., Ferrin, D.L., Dietz, G.: Designing trustworthy organizations. Sloan Manag. Rev. **54**, 74–82 (2013)
21. Kunze, N., Schmidt, A.U., Velikova, Z., Rudolph, C.: Trust in business processes. In: Proceedings of the 9th International Conference for Young Computer Scientists (ICYCS 2008), Zhangjiajie, China (2008)

22. Chong, B., Yang, Z., Wong, M.C.S.: Asymmetrical impact of trustworthiness attributes on trust perceived value and purchase intention: a conceptual framework for cross-cultural study on consumer perception of online auction. In: Proceedings of the 5th International Conference on Electronic Commerce (ICEC 2003), Pittsburgh, Pennsylvania, USA (2003)

23. Mohammadi, N.G., Heisel, M.: Patterns for the identification of trust concerns and specification of trustworthiness requirements. In: Proceedings of the 21st European Conference on Pattern Languages of Programs, p. 31. ACM (2016)

24. Rosemann, M., zur Muehlen, M.: Integrating risks into business process models. In: Proceedings of the 16th Australasian Conference on Information Systems (ACIS 2005), Manly (2005)

25. Wynn, M.T., Low, W.Z., ter Hofstede, A.M., Nauta, W.: A framework for cost-aware process management: cost reporting and cost prediction. J. Univ. Comput. Sci. 20(3), 406–430 (2014)

26. Seidel, S.: Toward a theory of managing creativity-intensive processes: a creative industries study. IseB 9(4), 407–446 (2011)

27. Alhaqbani, B.S., Adams, M.J., Fidge, C.J., ter Hofstede, A.H.M.: Privacy-aware workflow management. In: Glykas, M. (ed.) Business Process Management. SCI, vol. 444, pp. 111–128. Springer, Heidelberg (2013). https://doi.org/10.1007/978-3-642-28409-0_5

28. Rosemann, M., Recker, J.: Context-aware process design: exploring the extrinsic drivers for process flexibility. In: Proceedings of the International Workshop on Business Process Modelling, Development and Support (BPMDS 2006), pp. 149–158 (2006)

29. Rosemann, M.: Proposals for future BPM research directions. In: Ouyang, C., Jung, J.-Y. (eds.) AP-BPM 2014. LNBIP, vol. 181, pp. 1–15. Springer, Cham (2014). https://doi.org/10.1007/978-3-319-08222-6_1

30. Akerlof, G.A.: The market for "lemons": quality uncertainty and the market mechanism. Q. J. Econ. 84(3), 488–500 (1970)

31. Das, T.K., Teng, B.-S.: Between trust and control: developing confidence in partner cooperation in alliances. Acad. Manag. Rev. 23(3), 491–512 (1998)

Mining Process Mining Practices:
An Exploratory Characterization
of Information Needs in Process Analytics

Christopher Klinkmüller[1(✉)], Richard Müller[2], and Ingo Weber[1]

[1] Data61, CSIRO, Eveleigh, NSW, Australia
{christopher.klinkmuller,ingo.weber}@data61.csiro.au
[2] Leipzig University, Leipzig, Germany
rmueller@wifa.uni-leipzig.de

Abstract. Many business process management activities benefit from the investigation of event data. Thus, research, foremost in the field of process mining, has focused on developing appropriate analysis techniques, visual idioms, methodologies, and tools. Despite the enormous effort, the analysis process itself can still be fragmented and inconvenient: analysts often apply various tools and ad-hoc scripts to satisfy information needs. Therefore, our goal is to better understand the specific information needs of process analysts. To this end, we characterize and examine domain problems, data, analysis methods, and visualization techniques associated with visual representations in 71 analysis reports. We focus on the representations, as they are of central importance for understanding and conveying information derived from event data. Our contribution lies in the explication of the current state of practice, enabling the evaluation of existing as well as the creation of new approaches and tools against the background of actual, practical needs.

Keywords: Process mining · Visual analytics ·
Qualitative content analysis

1 Introduction

Many activities in phases of the business process management life-cycle, including process discovery, analysis and monitoring [4], benefit from the investigation of event logs that were generated during the execution of a business process. Such event data can be used to answer questions like "Does the process behave as expected?" or "Are there any bottlenecks that negatively impact process performance?". Commonly, those high-level *domain problems* are too complex to be straightforwardly answered by applying a single analysis technique, and thus analysts divide them into more fine-grain questions, leading to lower-level *information needs* that can be satisfied through the application of analysis techniques. While this divide-and-conquer strategy enables experts to iteratively form a mental picture of the business process, analysts also "[...] often do not know what

© Springer Nature Switzerland AG 2019
T. Hildebrandt et al. (Eds.): BPM 2019, LNCS 11675, pp. 322–337, 2019.
https://doi.org/10.1007/978-3-030-26619-6_21

they do not know" [19, p.43]. Consequently, the information needs are rarely predetermined, but arise from insights gained during the analysis process [7].

Research, predominantly in the field of process mining, has developed a plethora of approaches, e.g. [9,17,18] that enable analysts to satisfy specific types of information needs. Commercial and academic tools (like Apromore, Celonis, Disco, Everflow, Lana, myInvenio, ProM, QPR, TimelinePI, etc.) offer bundles of readily available analysis techniques. Moreover, project methodologies such as [3,21,23] provide universal, problem-independent guidelines for the application of such techniques in process mining projects. Due to the maturity of those research outcomes, they are increasingly adopted in real-world analysis projects, enabling us to examine those projects and elicit insights into the analysts' work practices. So far, reviews of such projects have focused on categorizing re-occurring problems [1,20], but lack insights into strategies that analysts choose to find answers to the domain problems. Yet, such insights would provide a foundation for further refining and enhancing the available approaches and tools.

On this basis, we aim to refine our understanding of the *relationship between the domain problems and the information needs* that arise in analysis projects. To this end, we conduct a systematic study as per [6] and analyze a corpus of 71 project reports that resulted from the problem-driven analysis of real-world event data in the context of the annual business process intelligence challenge (BPIC). While the significance of such studies was in general highlighted in [12,13], our particular contributions to process mining, visual process analytics, and business process management are twofold. First, the schema that we use to examine work practices can serve as a general reference point for assessing existing or for ideating advanced analysis approaches. Second, we take a first step towards a shared and refined understanding of work practices in process mining projects and present a consolidated overview of such practices from a large number of analysis projects. In future work, researchers can rely on these insights to orient the design of techniques towards actual, practical needs. We also hope that our work stimulates further analysis of work practices.

Specific findings from our study show that discovery of control flow is often conducted by analysts to establish a basic understanding of the business process, whereas other problems like the investigation of the time, case or organizational perspectives constitute the actual goal of the project. Moreover, for discovery analysts heavily utilize process mining algorithms to obtain descriptive process models, indicating that the low-level analysis techniques match the domain problem well. By contrast, for other domain problems analysts rely on general-purpose techniques or tables, pointing to situations where the analysis techniques do not match the domain problems. We also derive a set of eight frequent work practice patterns to provide direction for future work.

Following, we describe our methodology including the analyzed material and discuss limitations of our study in Sect. 2. In Sect. 3, we outline the annotation schema used to systematically describe the information needs and domain problems. In Sect. 4 we present the insights from our analysis. We conclude with a summary of related work in Sect. 5 and of our findings in Sect. 6.

2 Research Methodology

In this work, we adopted a qualitative research approach, which is suitable in situations like ours where a deeper understanding of a phenomenon is developed by investigating information material [16]. To this end, we followed guidelines for qualitative content analysis [11] and applied the analysis process depicted in Fig. 1. Following, we outline each of the activities and discuss limitations.

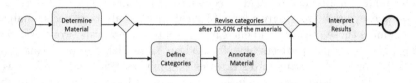

Fig. 1. The qualitative content analysis process (cf. [11])

2.1 Step 1 - *Determine Material*

As source material we used all BPIC reports available to date. The annual BPI Challenge has been organized in conjunction with the international workshop on business process intelligence[1] since 2011. Every year the challenge publishes a dataset containing real-world event logs. The dataset is provided by an organization from industry or government which asked questions related to the underlying business process (except for the first year). Upon publication of the dataset, the organizers invite analysts from academia and industry who are given a few months time to answer the questions by analyzing the dataset and to submit a report. Frequently, the analysts were invited to express any other interesting insights they obtained. Finally, a committee examines the reports and awards the best submissions. At the time of writing, eight BPIC editions were conducted and a total of 71 reports were published with 213 contributors co-authoring at least one report. The reports cover a broad range of scenarios and involve an extensive number of analysts, both from industry and academia, and therefore form a solid basis for obtaining insights into business process analysis practices.

In the study, we focused on analyzing the visual representations from those reports, including amongst others process models, charts, network diagrams, and tables. The reason is that those representations are the major means to convey information related to the underlying business process. Hence, we regard them to be representative of the low-level information needs that arose during the analysis project. Resulting from the application of specific analysis techniques they also provide an overview of those techniques' capabilities. Yet, not all representations were relevant to our study, as some do not reflect a low-level information need. For example, some representations are about the applied methodology, algorithms or tools, or the quality of a prediction model. We thus defined the

---

[1] https://www.win.tue.nl/bpi/, Accessed: 12/02/2019.

following inclusion criterion: *a visual representation must be generated from the provided event data and it must be used for explaining aspects of the underlying business process.* In total, we yielded a set of 2021 visual representations.

2.2 Steps 2 and 3 - *Define Categories* and *Annotate Material*

We next needed to describe the visual representations. As we wanted to analyze the descriptions and derive patterns of work practices from them, it was important that they rely on a consistent vocabulary. Thus, we followed guidelines for qualitative content analysis [11] and determined a set of categories that refer to the dimensions of the representations that we wanted to examine. The dimensions refer to the information need associated with the representations as well as the high-level questions that representations contribute to. Here, we abstract from the applied categories (details are provided in Sect. 3) and focus on the applied methodology. For each category, we then needed to define the set of codes which we used to encode the characteristics that the visual representations show with regard to the respective dimension. These sets must be *exhaustive* and *mutually exclusive* [8], so that (i) the codes cover all relevant aspects, (ii) all visual representations can be annotated appropriately, and (iii) the codes refer to distinct concepts, in order to guarantee that each representation can be described clearly and that there are no two ways of describing a visual representation.

We applied the following procedure to infer the category codes. First, we determined the categories and derived initial code sets from the literature. Then, we began to annotate the visual representations using these categories and codes. While the categories remained unchanged during the study, our code definitions occasionally underwent conceptual changes. That is, when we encountered representations that could not be described appropriately using the code set, we introduced new codes. Additionally, we sometimes experienced that our perception of a certain code changed during the annotation procedure. Due to those conceptual changes, we needed to consolidate the sets of category codes from time to time. Moreover, after a consolidation we revisited previous annotations to ensure consistency with the new schema. These updates occurred during the annotation of the first 50% of the visual representations. After that the schema was mature and could be applied without further changes. Finally, the questions posed in the challenge were annotated as well.

The annotation of visual representations itself was primarily conducted by one author of the paper, and the annotation of the challenge questions was done by another author independently. To ensure high quality of the annotations, we implemented the following procedures. First, the definition of the categories was frequently discussed by all authors. Second, the respective other authors of the paper conducted random sample checks to validate the annotations. Third, annotations that were challenging were discussed among all authors.

2.3 Step 4 - *Interpret Results*

Lastly, we derived descriptions of work practices from the annotations by summarizing and relating them, in order to identify trends in the work practices. In this context, we mostly analyzed the annotations by means of frequency distributions, and pattern mining. The results are presented in Sect. 4.

2.4 Limitations

To any study like ours, a number of limitations and threats to validity are inherent. We discuss the main factors and our approaches to mitigation below.

First, there could be personal bias: the annotation process relies on our subjective perception, and the interpretation was driven by insights relevant to us. We aimed to mitigate this issue as discussed above, but a residual risk remains.

Second, the representativeness of the data and results might be limited. Our source data stems from the BPI Challenge and might differ from process analytics practices in industry. This point is, to a degree, mitigated by the data and challenge questions stemming directly from real-world organizations, as well as by the large numbers of co-authors (>200) and visual representations (>2000).

Finally, the insights into work practices are restricted by the method of sourcing data from the *results* of these practices only. In particular, visual representations in the reports were exclusively two-dimensional and static; in contrast, analysts can interact with tools and data. Also, the reports cannot be assumed to show the full analysis process, e.g., for some information needs the analysts might not have found satisfactory results, and hence did not include any representations in the report. However, in the challenge setting with multiple teams addressing each question, this issue is partly mitigated: as long as *any* team has answered an information need, the data was included in our study. Next, visual representations were annotated based on the respective report's content and structure, which might not cover all influences that a representation had on the analysis process. Further, the choice of visual representations might be based on personal preference or tool access. To mitigate the risk of overemphasizing the visual aspects, we did not only focus on how data was presented, but we also investigated what and why data was analyzed (see Sect. 3).

While some of these limitations and threats could not be mitigated in the chosen study design, we believe the insights gained and described in the following to be of high relevance to advancing the fields of process mining and analytics.

3 The Annotation Schema: Categories and Codes

During the annotation, we focused on describing information needs and domain problems that are associated with the visual representations. According to [13], understanding these two aspects is a prerequisite for the development of data visualization tools. Hence, we defined the categories shown in Fig. 2.

The first category that we considered is the *domain problem*. It refers to the general question that was posed by the dataset provider or that the analysts

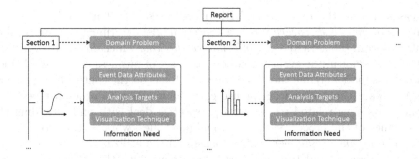

Fig. 2. Categories for the annotation of visual representations

found interesting to explore. The argumentation related to such a question is commonly not backed up by one, but by multiple visual representations. As a consequence, the first step in annotating the representations within a report was to identify the domain problems that this report examined. For each of the questions, we then introduced a conceptual section and assigned all visual representations that are related to the respective problem to that section. We also annotated the sections and thus by extension the representations with the code for the respective domain problem. The resulting conceptual document structure is oriented towards, but does *not* necessarily represent the structure of the report itself, as, e.g., some visual representations were listed in the appendix and referenced in the text, an executive summary outlined basic findings that were presented in more detail in separate sections, or the logical section structure was very fine-grained and divided visual representations by irrelevant aspects. Further, we only assigned representations to one section based on the context in which they were referenced. We hence might ignore their relevance to other sections. Yet, without further inquiry the assignment to other sections reflects our subjective interpretation, but unlikely the representations' actual influence.

We then annotated the visual representations, focusing on the information needs that are linked to them. To this end, we followed the guidelines from [13] that suggest to define a visual representation in terms of what, why, and how data is analyzed. First, we examined what part of the *event data* was used to generate the visual representation. Second, with regard to the why-dimension we focused on the *analysis target*. This category is related to the relationship in the data that is expressed by the visual representation. Finally, we captured how the data was represented by annotating the *visualization technique*. Note that some visual representations might serve multiple information needs; especially tables contained different types of data which needed to be distinguished. Consequently, we obtained 2085 information needs for the 2021 visual representations. In the following, we introduce the specific codes for each of the categories.

Domain Problem. The purpose of this category is to provide an abstract encoding for the specific domain problems that are investigated in the report. In this regard, we derived our initial set of five codes from the process mining use cases [1] and the more general BPM use cases [20]. This set included the problems of *process discovery* where a process model describing the control flow is inferred from the data and of *conformance checking* which deals with verifying that the behavior in the event log adheres to a set of business rules, e.g., defined as a process model. While these two use cases focus on the control-flow perspective, there are three enhancement use cases which refer to other perspectives. Domain problems related to the *time perspective* deal with understanding the performance of the process such as throughput times, working times or waiting times. The *organizational perspective* focuses on the utilization of resources and their dependencies and the *case perspective* deals with the influence of other process attributes, e.g., related to the customer, on the behavior.

During the annotation process, we identified three additional domain problems. First, there are *prediction* problems where analysts aimed to create models that can forecast the development of process instances. This type is strongly related to the case perspective, as it is about comprehending the influences of attributes on the process behavior. However, given its explicit focus on prediction, we decided to capture it separately. Second, *drift detection* aims to recognize points in time at which the underlying behavior of a process changed and to provide details regarding this change. Finally, *familiarization* is an activity that helps experts to understand basic characteristics of the business process and the event data. While not necessarily related to a specific business question, we included it in our study due to its significance for the analysis process.

Event Data Attributes. This category refers to the parts of the data that the visual representation examines and is thus used to capture the attributes in the data that are investigated to satisfy the information need. The codes for this category are not based on a categorization from the literature, but were developed in the context of our study. A first set of codes refers to the entities that are examined in a visual representation. These entities include *cases* representing single process instances and *activity instances* within those cases representing the execution of a certain *activity*. An activity can belong to a *subprocess*. A case often processes an *item*, e.g., a claim, a product, or a diagnosis, and involves *external partners*, e.g., customers or suppliers, as well as *organizational entities* which perform activities or who oversee a case. Types of organizational entities include resources, departments, branches, and locations. Analysts are also interested in relationships between these entities. The *control flow* refers to constraints on the ordering of activities at the process level. The *conformance* to such a control flow definition can be examined at the individual or the aggregated case level. Similarly, *execution patterns* are related to whether a case shows a certain type of behavior or not. With regard to the organizational units, *responsibilities* are often investigated, i.e., the activities that resources work on. Additionally, analysts are interested in the *organizational hierarchy* to identify teams and they evaluate *work practices* which focus on combinations of resources that frequently work on the same cases. The last set of analysis attributes is related to timing. Here, *durations* are examined with regard to the individual or groups of cases as well as to resources and their performance. The data can also be clustered or narrowed down by focusing on certain *time points*, such as years, months, weeks, weekdays, mornings, etc. In this context, the *execution status* of a case at a certain point is a specific derived attribute. Finally, *drift scores* provide information on how well the behavior in a case is aligned with the behavior in cases that were handled in a given time window.

Analysis Targets. There are different ways in which the attributes can be examined. In this regard, we capture the analysis targets. Here, the analysis targets specified in [14] served as a basis for our annotation. There are targets that refer to the entities within the dataset. In this context, *trends* describe overall characteristics of the entities, *outliers* are entities that do not adhere to these characteristics, and *features* are patterns that outline interesting structures within the data. Attribute-specific targets include those that are focused on single attributes: its *distribution* or its *extremes*, i.e., the minimum and maximum values. Relationships between attributes can be quantified based on their *correlation*, i.e., the degree to which their values are related. A *dependency* between attributes exists if the values of one attribute determine values of the other. Additionally, the *similarity* is a quantitative measure that is based on all values of an attribute. Finally, data might be represented as a graph to inspect its *topology*. We also recognized one additional target: *meta-information* is important for analysts to understand the attributes' meaning.

Visualization Technique. The last category refers to the visualization technique that is applied, to make the data interpretable. In this regard, we used the terminology from the data visualization catalogue[2] which specifies general-purpose techniques. The techniques applied in the reports are *bar chart* (including column charts and multi-set versions), *box and whisker plot*, *chloropleth map*, *chord diagram*, *heatmap*, *line graph*, *network diagrams*, *pie chart*, *radar chart*, *scatter plot*, *table*, *tree diagram*, *treemap*, *venn diagram* and *word cloud*. Detailed information on each of these techniques can be found in the catalog.

As can be expected, the source data included process-specific visualization techniques. Following our methodology, we added these to our vocabulary during annotation. Specifically, there are two types of specialized network diagrams. The *process model* depicts the control-flow of a process and the *social network* the relationships between organizational units. The *dotted chart* is a specific scatter plot used to visualize the correlation of attributes of activity instances such as timestamps, activities, resources, and cases. Finally, the *trace alignment* is a table-based technique that shows the sequences of activity instances for a set of cases and how their sequential ordering is aligned with a default ordering.

4 Analysis of Mining Practices

We now evaluate the information needs and domain problems. In particular, we describe patterns of mining practices that we detected based on our annotations. In Sect. 4.1, we provide an overview of all domain problems. We then use the

---

[2] https://datavizcatalogue.com.

Table 1. Distribution of the domain problems per year

	2011	2012	2013	2014	2015	2016	2017	2018	Avg.
Discovery	**55.6%**	**28.4%**	5.5%	4.8%	1.5%	0%	11%	7.3%	14.3%
Conformance	0%	3.4%	32.3%	0.9%	0%	0%	0.6%	0%	4.7%
Time pers.	0%	20.5%	0%	5.1%	19.5%	2.9%	23.5%	0%	8.9%
Org. pers.	8.3%	13.6%	3.1%	4.5%	**37.9%**	0%	8.7%	13%	11.2%
Case pers.	13.9%	6.3%	**54.4%**	**60.7%**	19.9%	**80.3%**	**44.3%**	24.6%	**38.1%**
Prediction	0%	1.1%	0%	3%	0%	0%	0.8%	1.5%	0.8%
Drift detection	0%	0%	0%	6.9%	8.8%	6.6%	0.3%	23.2%	5.7%
Familiarization	22.2%	26.7%	4.7%	14.1%	12.3%	10.2%	10.7%	**30.4%**	16.4%

insights to prioritize the domain problems and present a detailed analysis of the most important problems in Sect. 4.2.

4.1   Holistic View

Our first analysis focuses on the importance of the domain problems to the analysts. As an importance indicator we computed the absolute frequencies of information needs for each combination of domain problem and BPIC edition. For better comparability, we normalized the frequencies per edition, i.e., based on the total number of information needs within an edition. Table 1 shows these frequencies and their averages, per domain problem.

In the first edition in 2011, discovery was the dominating domain problem; it also was the problem that the analysts focused on the most in 2012, although the other domain problems started to receive increased attention. In the remaining editions the case perspective is the most frequently investigated problem. In this regard, 2018 is an exception where many information needs arose during familiarization and the case perspective ranked second. On average, the case perspective was the most important problem. A large share of the information needs also emerged during familiarization and discovery. Moreover, while conformance checking, prediction, and drift detection only played minor roles, the time and organizational perspectives were moderately important.

Next, we compared the importance of the domain problems assigned by the analysts to the importance assigned by the organizations that provided the datasets. To this end, we determined the problem frequencies based on the domain problems that we assigned to these questions. However, about 10% of the questions asked for any interesting insights beyond those addressed by the other questions without providing further direction; for these, we did not assign any problem. Additionally, familiarization was not present as a domain problem, as it is a task that analysts conduct to prepare for the examination of the domain problems. Similar to the reports, in the questions perspective-related problems ranked first, with the case perspective being associated with 29.8% of the questions, the organizational perspective with 14.9% and the time perspective with 10.7%. The group of conformance checking, drift detection and prediction were

Table 2. Correlation between visualization techniques and domain problems

	Discovery	Confor-mance	Time Pers.	Org. Pers.	Case Pers.	Prediction	Drift Detection	Familiar-ization
Bar Chart	6.4%	14.8%	15%	10.3%	14.3%	14.1%	14.2%	13.3%
Chord Diagram	0%	0%	0%	0%	1.7%	0%	0%	0.8%
Line Chart	2%	5.8%	7.7%	5.4%	11.5%	26.9%	6.4%	9%
Network Diagram	0%	0%	0.4%	3.1%	0.5%	0%	2.8%	1%
Pie Chart	0%	0.6%	0.4%	0.4%	2.3%	1.3%	0.7%	1.3%
Scatterplot	0%	0%	1.8%	1.8%	2.6%	10.3%	1.1%	2.1%
Tree	1.5%	0%	0.7%	1.8%	1.4%	0%	1.8%	1.3%
Other	1%	0%	0%	1.8%	1.6%	0%	1.1%	1.1%
General-purpose	10.9%	21.3%	25.9%	24.6%	36%	**52.6%**	28%	29.8%
Heatmap	0.5%	0%	0%	0.4%	1.6%	0%	0.7%	0.9%
Table	20.3%	41.3%	52.2%	41.1%	41.5%	34.6%	55%	42.3%
Tables	20.8%	**41.3%**	**52.2%**	41.5%	43.1%	34.6%	**55.7%**	43.2%
Dotted Chart	5%	0%	0%	6.3%	0.3%	0%	7.1%	2.1%
Process Model	60.4%	34.8%	21.2%	8%	15.6%	12.8%	9.2%	20.1%
Social Network	1%	0.6%	0.7%	19.6%	4.7%	0%	0%	4.3%
Trace Alignment	2%	1.9%	0%	0%	0.2%	0%	0%	0.4%
Process Mining	**68.3%**	37.4%	21.9%	33.9%	20.9%	12.8%	16.3%	27%

the subject of 5.3% to 10.7% of the questions. Interestingly, discovery was only posed as a domain problem by the organizations in three years and hence only 8% of the questions were related to it. We hypothesize that the mismatch between the importance of discovery for organizations and for analysts can be traced backed to the relevance of discovery for establishing a basic understanding of the underlying business process. That is, in accordance with the L* life-cycle model [21] analysts rely on the insights from this activity for the investigation of the other domain problems. Consequently, for analysts discovery often played a role similar to familiarization and supported analysts in their preparation efforts.

To obtain first insights into the analysis process, we next investigated the use of visualization techniques with respect to each domain problem. We focused on the techniques, as we distinguished between general-purpose techniques, tables and those specific to process mining: dotted charts, process models, social networks, and trace alignments. Thus, the techniques provide a rough estimation for the application of process mining-specific analysis techniques. Note however that the general-purpose techniques might display event data attributes and analysis targets that were obtained from the application of process mining techniques. For each combination of domain problem and visualization technique, we computed the absolute frequencies with regard to the information needs, and

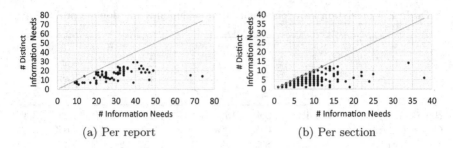

(a) Per report   (b) Per section

Fig. 3. Information needs in total and distinct information needs

normalized the frequencies with respect to the overall number of information needs per domain problem. Table 2 summarizes the results.

The process mining-specific techniques and especially the process models are the most important means for discovery, providing experts with important insights into the control-flow perspective. However, with regard to the other domain problems these techniques are less important. Indeed, process models are used across all problems and satisfy 17.4% of the information needs on average. Moreover, social networks play a key role for the organizational perspective. Yet, the majority of information is represented using general-purpose techniques and tables. Especially tables, as a flexible visualization technique suited for displaying high-dimensional data, are used very frequently and cover 41.6% of all information needs on average across all problems. The general-purpose techniques are applied to 28.6% of the information needs on average, with bar and line charts being the most widely adopted techniques.

The interpretation of these results must be treated with care, as they are insensitive to cases were general-purpose techniques and tables summarize the results of process mining analysis techniques. Nevertheless, the widespread use of general-purpose techniques and tables does indicate a lack of standardized approaches at the domain problem level. That is, while there are invaluable techniques that address issues at the level of information needs, there is limited support for analysts in orchestrating these techniques to understand specific domain problems. For example, discovering process models from logs is indispensable for understanding the control flow; however *discovery at the problem level* is addressed with a broader spectrum of representations than process models.   •

Lastly, we assessed the diversity of the analysts' information needs. To this end, we conducted the following analysis once for each report and once for each section. First, for a given section or report, we counted the information needs contained in it. Among those information needs we also determined the number of distinct information needs, i.e., where the annotations for visualization techniques, event data attributes, and analysis targets are identical. Figure 3 outlines the results. The grey line in the figure marks the equality between both measures, i.e., dots on the line are reports (a) or sections (b) where each information need is unique. The trend in the figure shows that the analysts tend to reuse certain types of visual representations. There are two possible explanations for this observation. First, analysts might be interested in certain aspects and re-apply the same technique to analyze different snapshots of the data. Here, they might benefit from dashboard-like tools, enabling them to configure views that can dynamically be updated with different subsets of the data. Second, analysts might be familiar with only a few analysis techniques. In this case, advanced guidance approaches might help analysts to explore data from various perspectives. Yet, in order to arrive at a final conclusion further experimentation is warranted.

4.2   Details for Frequent Domain Problems

So far, we have looked at the importance of domain problems and general work practices. We now focus on the analysis of specific domain problems and the mining practices associated with them. In particular, we identify and describe frequent information needs. The explication of these needs constitutes important input for assessing and designing analysis techniques. In this regard, we focus on the two most frequent domain problems. First, we examine how analysts familiarize themselves with the data. Here, we also consider discovery problems, as our analysis revealed that discovery is often linked to the familiarization problem. Second, we focus on the case perspective as the most frequent problem.

Familiarization and Discovery. A first result stems directly from our anno-tation process, during which we inductively developed the codes describing the event data attributes. At the level of technique development the data model that is generally applied is a logical data model comprising *log*, *trace*, and *event* entities, relationships between them as well as a set of continuous and discrete

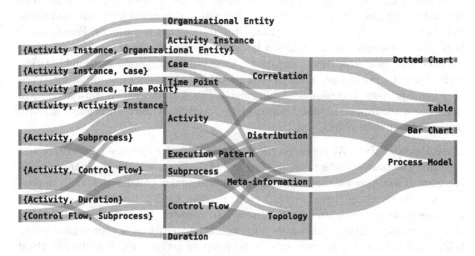

Fig. 4. Frequent analysis patterns related to familiarization and discovery

attributes describing the entities. While this level of abstraction ensures that the developed techniques are reusable, it is also free of semantics. Yet, analysts typically view the data from the conceptual standpoint and think about the data in terms of entities including activities, organizational entities, and items, as well as relationships between them including responsibilities, work practices, or the control flow dependencies. With regard to the development of analysis tools, it might thus be valuable to enable analysts to map the physical data model to a conceptual model and to conduct the analysis based on the conceptual model. Moreover, entities and attributes in this data model might be the result of a specific analysis, e.g., a social network visualization might be used to identify groups of resources within the hierarchy whose performance is later on investigated as well. Thus, tools could also support analysts in incorporating analytical results into the domain model.

To identify analysis patterns specific to familiarization and discovery, we extracted frequent pairs of annotated codes from the information needs associated with these two problems. We only considered pairs and codes that occurred in at least 5% of the information needs. Figure 4 summarizes these pairs using a parallel sets visualization. In this visualization there are four columns of nodes. Starting from the left, sets of event data attributes are depicted in the first column, event data attributes in the second, analysis targets in the third, and visualization techniques in the last. An edge depicts the frequency of a code pair or, in case of the sets of event data attributes, the frequency of attribute containment. Note that the size of the nodes is also proportional to the frequencies of the codes.

The figure shows four main types of analysis. First, process models are used to visualize the topology of the process or the control-flow, respectively. In this regard, the frequency of activities and their connections is displayed as well. Second, meta-information primarily regarding activity and case attributes is captured in tables. Third, the major category of information needs is related to understanding the distribution of cases, activities, execution patterns, and durations, and is visualized using bar charts, tables or other techniques. Fourth, analysts also investigate the correlation between a broad range of attributes including execution patterns, items, durations, time points and organizational entities. This type of information is displayed in tables, dotted charts or other types of general-purpose techniques. Additionally, Fig. 4 shows which data attributes were often examined in combination, e.g., activities and durations, activity instances and time points, etc.

Case Perspective. We repeated the above analysis for the case perspective and obtained the parallel sets visualization in Fig. 5. Here, we identified three main use cases. First, process models including the frequency of activities, their dependencies, or execution times are inspected. Process models are also used to identify execution patterns and to put them into context. Second, the distribution of subprocesses, activity instances, and execution patterns is represented using tables and various other types of general-purpose techniques. Finally, the third and main use case deals with examining the relationships between attributes. In

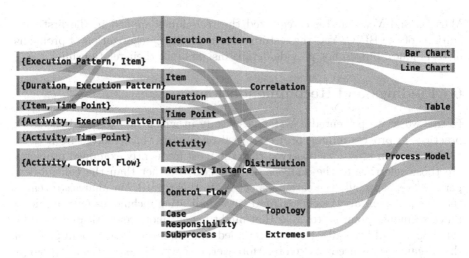

Fig. 5. Frequent analysis patterns related to the case perspective

this context, a large portion of information needs is linked to correlating execution patterns to items, durations, and responsibilities, amongst others. Here, bar charts, line charts, and tables are mainly utilized for visualization.

5   Related Work

There are two streams of research that are relevant to our study. First, there are analysis techniques and visual idioms which support analysts in the analysis of specific sub-questions. The development of visual idioms is subject to the field of *visual process analytics* and examples include the dotted chart which provides an overview of the events in an event log [18]; a technique to replay cases on top of process models [22]; or confusion matrices to compare process variants with respect to different perspectives [15]. The idioms often make use of *process mining* [21] techniques that extract knowledge from event logs, including, amongst others, the process' actual control flow (e.g., [2,9]) and its conformance to the intended behavior (e.g., [5,17]). In this paper, we focused on understanding how these techniques are applied in the context of process mining projects.

More relevant to our work are those works that focus on the work practices of analysts. On the one hand, there are methodologies for systematically approaching analysis projects, e.g., PM² [23], the L* life-cycle model [21], and the Process Diagnostics Method [3]. These methodologies comprise high-level processes including generic activities like data collection, data cleaning, and data analysis. Additionally, they provide anecdotal and exemplary evidence to outline their intended use. In contrast, we focus on explicating and analyzing the actual work practices based on empirical data. In this context, there are a few empirical studies that provide insights into the work practices. This includes catalogs of business process management [20] and process mining use case [1]. Additionally,

Martens and Verheul [10] categorized the techniques applied in the first four editions of the BPIC. Yet, these studies focus on the categorization of problems or techniques, but do not provide details insights into their relationship.

6   Findings and Recommendations

In this work, we presented a systematic study in which we examined the work practices in process mining projects based on reports that resulted from these projects. In our study, we observed that the most frequently examined problems are those referring to the analysis of perspectives other than the control-flow perspective, especially the case perspective. In this regard, our analysis revealed that the problems are largely explored via visualization techniques *not* specific to process mining, pointing to areas that might benefit more sophisticated analytical support. Additionally, the data revealed that discovery is a domain problem that organizations need to explore. Moreover, discovery is also often analyzed as part of the familiarization with the data in order to establish a basic understanding of the underlying process. Finally, we noticed that analysts rely on similar sets of visual representations when addressing different information needs. This indicates that analysts apply a work practice of defining an analysis technique and re-applying it to different data snapshots. We also presented a set of eight work practice patterns that can guide the development of advanced tools.

In future work, it would be interesting to extend the investigation of work practices by assessing the usefulness of a visual representation in the overall analysis process, as well as its contribution towards actually answering a domain question. Doing so would require interviews with analysts and business stakeholders as well as observations in laboratory settings; relying on the reports for these purposes would be too speculative.

References

1. Ailenei, I., Rozinat, A., Eckert, A., van der Aalst, W.M.P.: Definition and validation of process mining use cases. In: Daniel, F., Barkaoui, K., Dustdar, S. (eds.) BPM 2011. LNBIP, vol. 99, pp. 75–86. Springer, Heidelberg (2012). https://doi.org/10.1007/978-3-642-28108-2_7
2. Augusto, A., Conforti, R., Dumas, M., La Rosa, M.: Split miner: discovering accurate and simple business process models from event logs. In: ICDM, pp. 1–10 (2017)
3. Bozkaya, M., Gabriels, J., van der Werf, J.: Process diagnostics: a method based on process mining. In: eKNOW, pp. 22–27 (2009)
4. Dumas, M., La Rosa, M., Mendling, J., Reijers, H.: Fundamentals of Business Process Management. Springer, Heidelberg (2013). https://doi.org/10.1007/978-3-642-33143-5
5. García-Bañuelos, L., van Beest, N., Dumas, M., La Rosa, M., Mertens, W.: Complete and interpretable conformance checking of business processes. IEEE Trans. Softw. Eng. 44, 262–290 (2017)
6. Isenberg, P., Zuk, T., Collins, C., Carpendale, S.: Grounded evaluation of information visualizations. In: Workshop on Beyond Time and Errors: Novel Evaluation Methods for Information Visualization, pp. 6:1–6:8 (2008)

7. Keim, D., Andrienko, G., Fekete, J.-D., Görg, C., Kohlhammer, J., Melançon, G.: Visual analytics: definition, process, and challenges. In: Kerren, A., Stasko, J.T., Fekete, J.-D., North, C. (eds.) Information Visualization. LNCS, vol. 4950, pp. 154–175. Springer, Heidelberg (2008). https://doi.org/10.1007/978-3-540-70956-5_7

8. Krippendorff, K.: Content Analysis: An Introduction to Its Methodology, 2nd edn. Sage Publications, Thousand Oaks (2004)

9. Leemans, S., Fahland, D., van der Aalst, W.: Discovering block-structured process models from event logs - a constructive approach. In: Petri Nets, pp. 311–329 (2013)

10. Martens, J., Verheul, P.: Social performance review of 5 Dutch municipalities: future fit cases for outsourcing? In: BPI (2015)

11. Mayring, P.: Qualitative content analysis. Forum Qual. Soc. Res. 1(2) (2000). Article no. 20

12. Meyer, M., Sedlmair, M., Munzner, T.: The four-level nested model revisited: blocks and guidelines. In: BELIV, pp. 11:1–11:6 (2012)

13. Munzner, T.: A nested model for visualization design and validation. IEEE Trans. Vis. Comput. Graph. 15(6), 921–928 (2009)

14. Munzner, T.: Visualization Analysis and Design. CRC Press, Boca Raton (2014)

15. Nguyen, H., Dumas, M., La Rosa, M., ter Hofstede, A.H.M.: Multi-perspective comparison of business process variants based on event logs. In: Trujillo, J.C., et al. (eds.) ER 2018. LNCS, vol. 11157, pp. 449–459. Springer, Cham (2018). https://doi.org/10.1007/978-3-030-00847-5_32

16. Recker, J.: Scientific Research in Information Systems: A Beginner's Guide. Springer, Berlin (2013). https://doi.org/10.1007/978-3-642-30048-6

17. Rozinat, A., van der Aalst, W.: Conformance checking of processes based on monitoring real behavior. Inf. Syst 33(1), 64–95 (2008)

18. Song, M., van der Aalst, W.: Supporting process mining by showing events at a glance. In: WITS 2007, pp. 139–145 (2007)

19. Spence, R.: Information Visualization - An Introduction. Springer, Cham (2014). https://doi.org/10.1007/978-3-319-07341-5

20. van der Aalst, W.: Business process management: a comprehensive survey. ISRN Softw. Eng. 2013 (2013). Article no. 507984

21. van der Aalst, W.: Process Mining: Data Science in Action. Springer, Berlin (2016). https://doi.org/10.1007/978-3-662-49851-4

22. van der Aalst, W., de Leoni, M., ter Hofstede, A.: Process mining and visual analytics: breathing life into business process models. BPM reports, BPMcenter.org (2011)

23. van Eck, M.L., Lu, X., Leemans, S.J.J., van der Aalst, W.M.P.: PM²: a process mining project methodology. In: Zdravkovic, J., Kirikova, M., Johannesson, P. (eds.) CAiSE 2015. LNCS, vol. 9097, pp. 297–313. Springer, Cham (2015). https://doi.org/10.1007/978-3-319-19069-3_19

Towards a Process Reference Model for Research Management: An Action Design Research Effort at an Australian University

Jeremy Gibson[✉][iD], Kanika Goel[iD], Janne Barnes,
and Wasana Bandara[iD]

Queensland University of Technology, Brisbane, QLD 4000, Australia
{jeremy.gibson,k.goel,janne.barnes,
w.bandara}@qut.edu.au

Abstract. Increasing emphasis in the Higher Education sector for high impact research has generated a proliferation of activities aimed at supporting university research processes, commonly referred to as 'research management'. While there has been considerable growth in this new field, it remains an elusive area, with a lacuna on what comprises good 'research management'. A lack of common terminology and definition of the activities comprised within research management limits the capacity to provide efficient services, properly share learnings and consistently assess the effectiveness of this work.

This paper discusses the development of a research management reference model, through an Action Design Research (ADR) project conducted at a leading Australian university. The model defines 10 core domains (with areas of activities and processes within each) that constitutes the end-to-end research management process. The model was derived and validated across four ADR cycles of a detailed case study – which proved its potential value. Future research is planned to further validate the model in other universities, both within Australia and internationally.

Keywords: Research management · Reference model ·
Action Design Research · Case study

1 Introduction and Background

Research outcomes has become a core indicator of university performance, with its emphasis growing over the last two decades [5]. Many universities across the world have steadily increased their focus on research income and impact [5, 18]. In Australia alone, research income has increased nearly five-fold from 1997 to 2017 [10]. This has initiated an emerging new field of work, designed to support and oversee institutional-wide research activity, commonly referred to as 'research management'. Kirkland et al. [18] defines research management (RM) as institutional activities, separate from the research process itself, that add value to the research activities supporting the relevant stakeholders. Ultimately, research management is about providing services that allow the researchers to do less administration and focus more on research. Research management *does* incur notable cost, which is often built-in to and funded by the research

© Springer Nature Switzerland AG 2019
T. Hildebrandt et al. (Eds.): BPM 2019, LNCS 11675, pp. 338–353, 2019.
https://doi.org/10.1007/978-3-030-26619-6_22

income generated, hence, it is important that the researchers feel the benefit of these services. Recent studies (i.e. [5]) have found that universities with a higher research management index have higher research productivity, in both publications and competitive grants; indicative of the positive impacts it can bring. But the research management domain, in general is in its genesis yet.

Research management practices cover a wide spread of disciplines, including financial management and accounting, contract development, business-relationship management, training and capability building as well as the research specific fields of ethics oversight and research output management. This broad collection of disciplines is then set against the backdrop of ever-changing government legislations, the multitude of funding body requirements and internal strategy and oversight needs, resulting in complex, interdependent processes. While there are societies dedicated to guide and support research managers[1] and some frameworks that provide diverse guidance to research management at different units of analysis and levels of maturity [5, 27], there is still very little direction on what research management "best-practices" are. To date, no resource provides a holistic view on what research management entails, and null resources exist, on how to design, deliver and continuously manage the core services and underlying processes to support institution-wide research management.

Other sectors (such as Health [6], Manufacturing [2] and Finance [31]) have progressed well by applying process-centric approaches to generate efficient and effective service delivery. A process-based approach attempts to change the focus of stakeholders to a single flow of work, resulting in enhanced performance [14]. As stated by Hammer [15] (p. 7), *"Through process management, an enterprise can create high-performance processes, which operate with much lower costs, faster speeds, greater accuracy, reduced assets, and enhanced flexibility."*

For the research management (RM) field, a first crucial (yet missing) step in this journey is to identify and define the involved 'processes', and this is not a trivial task, especially in complex and previously under-examined domains (like RM). While there are many learnings that can be taken from the field of project management, the domain requirements of research management (such as the funding models, legislative and ethical oversight and the segmentation between academic and professional staff) warrant a specific definition of processes. *Reference process models* have been created in diverse domains (e.g. [1, 17, 33]) as a means to address this gap. A reference model presents a synthesis of the most essential/best-practice processes of a domain, ordered in a systematic manner (in logical hierarchies, with standardized sets of actions along with their interdependencies) [7, 16, 24, 25]. A well-developed reference model can be used as a point of reference for diverse process centric purposes; it plays a vital role in the initial 'process discovery' [12] phase, and can be used as a source of guidance for process improvement [13].

Aiming to develop a reference model for research management of a university, this paper addresses the research question: **what are the processes fundamental for research management of a university?** An Action Design Research (ADR) is

---

[1] Two examples are the Society of Research Administrators International (https://www.srainternati onal.org/) and the Australasian Research Management Society (https://researchmanagement.org.au/).

conducted to identify and synthesize research management processes within a multi-tiered hierarchy, forming an evidence-based research management reference model.

2 Methodology

An Action Design Research (ADR) approach is adopted and deployed here, where the aim was to develop an empirically supported research management reference model which would be developed/re-specified and validated through multiple stages. Peterson and Lundberg [22] describe ADR as a means *"to generate prescriptive design knowledge through learning from the intervention of building and evaluating an artefact in an organizational setting to address a problem"*. ADR typically takes place within multiple cycles – each of which follows three-steps [28]: (1) problem formulation; (2) building, intervention and evaluation; and (3) reflection and learning; after which the final step is (4) formalization of learning. The stages are iterated through and built upon over the course of the work. This paper reports on the outcomes resulting after 4 ADR cycles (see Fig. 1), as applied within a single case study at the Queensland University of Technology (QUT), Brisbane, Australia.

2.1 Introducing the Case Study Context

QUT, the selected case study for this work, had undergone rapid growth as a research-intensive university in recent years. It has grown from just under Au $15 million in research income in the year 2000 to over Au $100 million in 2017 [10]. This rapid growth has seen a reciprocated increase in provisioning research support. Through this expansion, processes and systems around research management have proliferated and evolved to various degrees. Overlaps of some services are observed and legacy systems and underlying processes have continued to exist well after their expiry date.

A 'Research Transformation' project was kicked off in 2018, to evaluate the organizational model that would best support QUT's research activity into the future. At the same time the Research Management Systems Upgrade Project, or RMSUP, was underway to replace QUT's core research management system(s), which had been in place for over 20 years. Early phases of these projects raised the lack of a consistent way to speak about the different activities of research management and their interconnected nature. Some of the terminology used was very specific to certain areas and was creating issues and hindering process redesign[2]. It was soon clear that a more holistic frame of reference was needed.

This described context made QUT a very suitable case study candidate for this research. Additionally, the researcher team had ready access to the case with the required support to run an ADR study.

---

[2] One example was between the Research Grants and the Commercial Research team. For the former the term 'project' reflected the entire lifecycle from the development of a grant application, whereas for the latter a 'project' was only considered to exist once a contract had been signed. This simple terminology difference had caused a large deviation between the two in both processes and how systems were used.

2.2 Developing the Research Management Reference Model: ADR Cycles Within the Case Study

Four ADR cycles were conducted, following the guidelines of Sein et al. [28], over a period of 6 months (see Fig. 1). The evolutionary model building efforts are presented here with the final model outlined in Sect. 3. The cycles began first within the ADR team (i.e. the research team members and others from the RMSUP team), where the knowledge of the team's 3 domain experts was drawn on, to obtain the first exploratory model. The next cycles were designed to engage other university-wide stakeholders to further build and evaluate the model. Over the course of these cycles, 15 experts from a variety of domains were engaged (see Table 1), with 5 other experts engaged informally. The primary means of engagement was through detailed structured walkthroughs, as this allowed for both direct feedback from the experts and observation of the effectiveness of the model as a standardized communication tool, a method used effectively in other ADR projects [22, 23]. All up, 10 such walkthroughs were conducted, involving the 15 participants, which were run by the RMSUP team, with researcher observations. They were designed to see how easily understood the reference model was, as well the completeness of the activities it detailed. Some initial framing of the model was delivered in the walkthroughs, but space was allowed to see what the experts' interpretations of terms were, to see if terminology needed to be changed. Each of these cycles are outlined further below.

Table 1. Detailed walkthrough summary

#	Attendees	Domain/Department of origin
1	Director, Office of Research Director, Office of Commercial Services	Strategic Management/Grants & Commercial Research
2	Manager, Research Development Unit	Research Grants
3	Manager, Research Partnerships	Commercial Research
4	Business Manager, Office of Commercial Services	Commercial Research
5	Director of the Office of Research Ethics and Integrity	Ethics & Governance
6	Research Governance and Compliance Coordinator	Ethics & Governance
7	Associate Director, Office of Commercial Services Project Officer, Office of Commercial Services	Commercial Research
8	Manager, Research Finance Unit	Research Finance
9	Research Quality Coordinator Research Information and Systems Support (3 members)	Reporting & Systems Support
10	Senior Research Fellow, School of Psychology	End User Academic

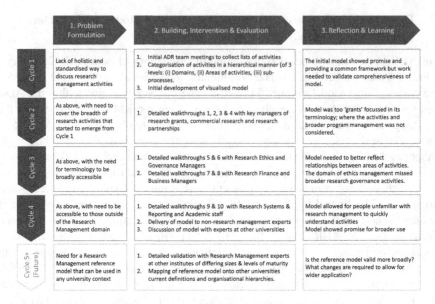

Fig. 1. Overview of ADR cycles

2.2.1   Cycle 1

The first cycle aimed to address the problem of the lack of a holistic framework to discuss research management activities. Initial discovery was synthesized from a variety of QUT corporate documentation, including service catalogues for the Division of Research and Commercialisation, organizational hierarchies as well as artefacts generated by RMSUP, such as business requirements, use cases and business process documentation. The RMSUP, through its market scan process, had been exposed to a wide variety of research management systems and was able to draw on the processes these systems supported and map this to the QUT context. Following this a series of brainstorming sessions were held with the RMSUP team to collate a list of activities that are part of research management. The RMSUP team consisted of 3 process-oriented business analysts, who had all been focused on the research management domain for the prior year and 3 subject matter experts who had worked in a series of roles across the gamut of research management for a decade each. The combination of knowledge and process-oriented thinking provided a solid basis for this initial work.

From this, a categorization of groups of activities and an overall flow (of research management activities) was recognized. This was split into a three-tier hierarchy of *domains*, *areas of activity* and *processes*[3]. Following this session, work was done to create a visual presentation of this hierarchy. This was conducted over the course of two weeks with the research team being embedded within the RMSUP team to allow for immediate feedback and iteration of the model. At the conclusion of this process 9[4]

---

[3] Domains are high level groupings, ordered in a loose logical flow, each consisting of several areas of activity, with their own list of processes.

[4] The final domains are presented in detail in Sect. 3.

key high-level domains were identified, each containing a collection of areas of activity and 153 different processes divided between those areas. At this stage, the model was deemed ready for initial engagement with members outside the research team.

2.2.2   Cycle 2

This engagement was focused on the area of managing research projects[5], as this was the area at QUT with the greatest diversity of processes and terminology, and hence of key importance for validating the model.

The model showed promise in facilitating discussions around processes related to research project-management, but the language was considered by some to be too "research grants" focused. This prompted a rewrite of the activities to better address this. Additionally, the linear presentation of the model caused some people to assume it meant that all research projects must follow this path. To address this, the model was framed as not being prescriptive for every project, but more indicative of the norm.

One major discovery from these walkthroughs was the need for a 10th domain that was all-encapsulating, *program management*. This related to broader activities that the university would undertake to support research more generally. These didn't fit well into the project-oriented process of the model, but instead helped to create a healthy ecosystem for new research projects to emerge.

2.2.3   Cycle 3

In the third cycle, the implementation of the model was expanded to new domains, looking at the areas of research ethics and finance, considering their significance to research management. At this point, the model had a domain entitled *Ethics Approval* but in discussions with the research ethics experts it became clear that there was far more involved that just ethics management. These more broadly went to activities of risk identification, mitigation and incident management. There was a common pattern of governance and compliance processes, of which ethics was just a subset. This domain underwent a name change, to *Governance & Compliance*, and a significant rewrite to accommodate these changes.

2.2.4   Cycle 4

By this cycle the model was becoming more robust and so engagement began to branch broader than active managers of research. Detailed walkthroughs were held with people working in the research system support and research reporting spaces as well as informal discussions with research managers from other institutions. Changes at this point were very minor, limited to process renaming and the addition of more con-nection points between domains. The model began to be used as a communication tool for people unfamiliar with research management and proved to be very effective in providing an initial grounding. This evidenced the completeness and relevance of the model within this case context, ending the cycles within the case. By the end, the total number of processes in the model had grown from 153 to 218.

---

[5] Management of research projects covers activities to support funding application and the subsequent oversight of funding and project obligations. It forms part of most of the domains identified with the exception of research outputs, performance and HDR management.

3   The Research Management Reference Model

The resulting research management reference model was captured and presented across 4 levels of abstraction (following the example of other reference models, such as [4, 21]). It provides a model overview (see Fig. 2), which consists of 10 domains (see Sects. 3.1–3.10) which are ordered as a flow within the model, indicative of common practice, but not necessarily dictating a chronological flow. Each domain captures the core areas of activities that forms the domain, and there are relevant processes underlying each area[6]. While there already exists accepted language and notation to document process hierarchies (such as [8]), the end users of this model are administrators with little to no business process experience, hence a customized approach was needed to be easily comprehensible. For similar reasons the model uses icons and colors to avoid end-users disengaging with the model at first due to cognitive overload [26].

The model overview essentially presents a first high-level overview of the "life-cycle" of research management, reflecting the life of a research project, from initial conception through proposal development and approval, into conducting the project, including financial, ethical and contractual management, then into the outcomes of the project, in research outputs and the reporting around these. Note how the HDR (Higher Degree Research student) Management (domain 9, see Sect. 3.9 below) is kept separate from this, to reflect its individual processes, but a research student's journey bares many similarities to a research project, so color-coding is used to indicate the points of overlap. Each of the domains are outlined briefly below, and the full reference model and descriptions of the areas of activity can be found at https://doi.org/10.6084/m9.figshare.7819424.

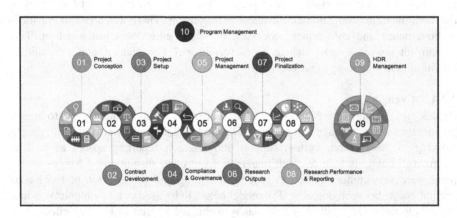

Fig. 2. Research management reference model overview (Color figure online)

---

[6] For example, Domain (1) – *'Project Conception'*, consists of 6 areas (*Project Idea Initiation, Funding Sources Identification ... Review and Revision* - see Sect. 3.1) and each area has a list of clearly identified processes (see Fig. 3).

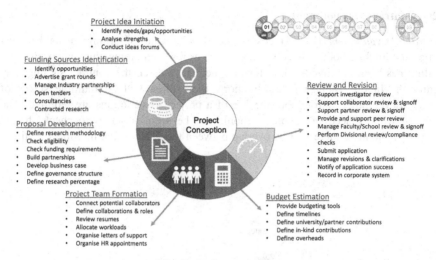

Fig. 3. Project conception

3.1 Project Conception

Project Conception refers to the initial stages of any research, where ideas are spawned, teams are formed, and proposals are developed. This work is often nebulous and difficult to define; hence it will often lack well defined processes or oversight. Within the research management field, this is often described as "pre-award", followed by "post-award" management once the application is successful. Some universities have distinct teams to manage pre and post, with others having the same team follow the project throughout its lifecycle [29].

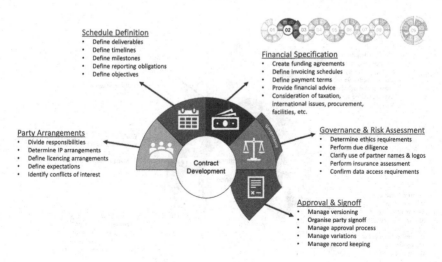

Fig. 4. Contract development

3.2   Contract Development

Contract Development (Fig. 4) covers the development of arrangements between parties and funding bodies. In some cases, such as research grants, this may occur after funding has been approved, while for commercial research the contract signing may signify the funding approval. Furthermore, there often will be multiple stages of contract development throughout the life of a project as variations are required. The domains, while placed in an order, should not be seen as stages to check-off and progress to the next, there will be overlap between them, and often multiple iterations.

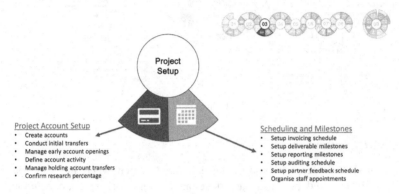

Fig. 5. Project setup

3.3   Project Setup

Project Setup (Fig. 5) refers to the administrative work that supports the project commencement. There are a number of financial administrative tasks as well as scheduling of milestones to ensure that obligations are met by all parties.

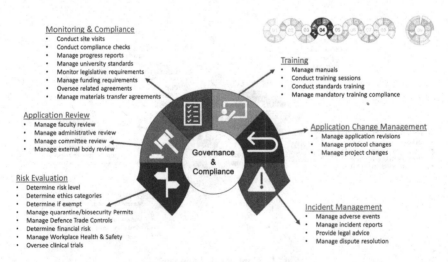

Fig. 6. Governance & compliance

3.4   Governance & Compliance

As mentioned previously, *Governance & Compliance* (Fig. 6) first began as looking at ethical management of the project but there are many other areas of project governance that follow a similar process of risk identification, mitigation strategy development, ongoing monitoring and incident reporting and management. Some of these may be managed by an ethics unit, others by different areas of the research institute and some may be managed by the researchers themselves. Due to the overlapping regulations between universities, governments and other organizations there can often be significant administrative overheads in this space, resulting in slow responsiveness [20].

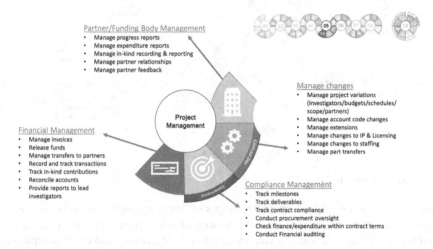

Fig. 7. Project management

3.5   Project Management

Project Management (Fig. 7) outlines the administrative activities that occur during the life of the project. This domain will often cover the longest period, but the degree of administrative engagement may be minimal. However, some universities are starting to provide centralized resources to support the day-to-day management of projects [30]. This domain ensures compliance with the obligations and strategies identified in previously areas, as well as managing any changes to the project that may occur.

3.6   Research Outputs

Research Outputs (Fig. 8) covers the creation and dissemination of all outputs from the research activity. What was previously referred to as publications is increasingly being called research outputs in an effort to broaden the scope beyond standard publishing avenues. In this domain all of the outcomes of research, both tangible and intangible are considered as outputs. This includes traditional publications but also research data, commercial outputs (such as IP, patents or business relationship), media engagements and real-world research impact. All of these items have value to a research institute and can feed into future research, but the standard reporting models of journal articles will fail to consider these.

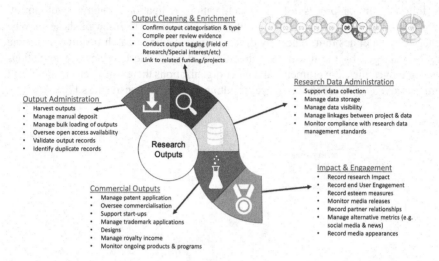

Fig. 8. Research outputs

3.7 Project Finalization

Project Finalization (Fig. 9) covers the stages of "clean-up" that need to occur once a project is completed. This can often be difficult as while certain projects may have a nominal date of completion, the various stages of final delivery and client acceptance, as well as final expenditure of funds, can continue long past this initial date as project timelines slip. Additionally, contracts may be extended or renewed, meaning that what was initially meant to be a 6-month project can continue for many years.

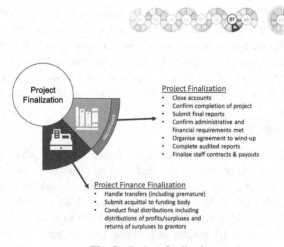

Fig. 9. Project finalization

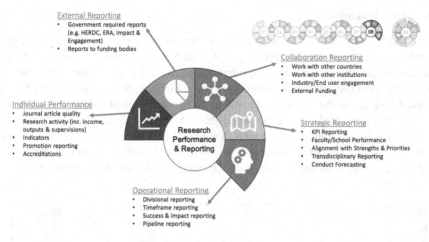

Fig. 10. Research performance

3.8 Research Performance

Research Performance (Fig. 10) details the reporting and analysis applied to research activity. The fruits of the previous stages are collated and presented to give a clear picture of how a research institute is performing. To properly be able to demonstrate performance at this stage, data collection and aggregation needs to underpin all of the previous domains. Also benchmarks and KPI's are used here to indicate expected levels of performance. External metrics, such as journal rankings or citation counts are used to give an indication of the quality of the research activity.

Fig. 11. HDR management

3.9 HDR Management

HDR Management (Fig. 11) refers to the management activities to support higher degree research students. A Higher Degree Research Student follows a similar path to a research project and so there is a large amount of overlap with existing areas already outlined. The color-coded bands surrounding the pie indicate these relationships, but the pie itself focuses on the activities specific to HDR management, which cover the full lifecycle of a student. It should be noted that while research management can be a consideration for undergraduate students, a study by [11] found that less than a quarter of universities have a specific strategy towards this, and of those more than 80% were handled separately from the Deputy Vice Chancellor of Research (or similar role).

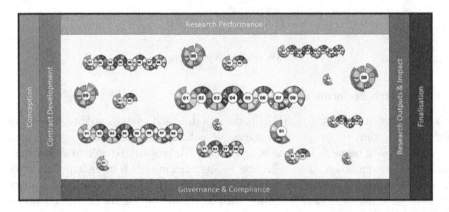

Fig. 12. Program management (Color figure online)

3.10 Program Management

Finally, *Program Management* reflects the broader ecosystem that supports research activity at an institute. This is a higher level of proactive strategic management that looks beyond individual projects and support transformative research initiatives [9]. These programs support the creation of many new projects or students. As Fig. 12 shows, there will be similar analogues to many of the previous stages, with these programs going through the process of conception, contractual setup and governance. Similarly, they will create outputs, including those of the research projects they contain and will have reporting requirements to show the effectiveness of the program.

4 Discussion

Despite the growth of research within universities and the proliferation of support staff, the lack of a holistic framework that describes the activities of research management limits the capacity to provide efficient services, properly share learnings and consistently assess the effectiveness of research. In an endeavor to address this gap, this paper addressed the research question: *what are the processes fundamental for research management of a university?* A preliminary reference model for research management was developed through an ADR effort consisting of 4 cycles. The first cycle aimed at identifying high level activities, the second cycle focused on capturing activities related to research project administration, the third cycle addressed the areas of governance, ethics and research finance with the final cycle confirming the reporting, system and end-user academic dependencies. This ADR effort served the goals of the research well by allowing for constant feedback loops with people well experienced in the research management space.

The findings illustrate the primary components of the reference model. The resulting model is a comprehensive and highly detailed model, which can be used as a point of guidance to identify the processes underlying research management at a higher education or research institute. It takes the form of normative guidelines to guide users to approach research management. It is a multi-disciplinary artefact bridging two communities of researchers, namely from the field of BPM and from the higher education sector. Diverse stakeholders (i.e. research managers, researchers and university leaders) can greatly benefit from the clarity and visibility of research management processes that the resulting reference model provides. It is a useful tool for research process management, investigations and communication [19, 32]. For example, on an anecdotal level, the project manager of RMSUP, who was involved in many of the end-user sessions, commented on the effectiveness of the model to elicit requirements from stakeholders who may not have been used to process-oriented thinking, as it provided a frame of reference for them to consider their daily activities. It also was used to introduce people unfamiliar with research management to the concept, in a simple and easily accessible way.

This research management reference model can be used by a research institute to not just assess what they are presently doing, but what sub-processes of the model they may not be currently addressing. Additionally, it can be used to assess what data is captured about different processes, to ensure that work is visible and can be reported upon. Similarly, it can be used to determine the systems used to support these processes and the adequacy of them. Finally, it can be used to assess service delivery, by examining researchers' experiences and satisfaction with each of the sub-processes. These are just examples of the potential applications of the reference model to a specific research institute context.

While this model has varied applications, we do acknowledge limitations. A reference model by its nature is designed in one specific context, but can be applied to other contexts [3], and as yet this model has not been validated beyond one university. Informal engagement has been conducted and shown promising signs of generalizability, but a rigorous evaluation is required to confirm that the reference model is an accurate representation of research management internationally. Additionally, engagement with research manager's specifically focusing on Higher Degree Research (HDR) was minimal in the current ADR cycles. Hence, more work is needed to confirm the completeness (with the appropriate inclusion of all processes like HDR) of the resulting reference model.

We suggest that the model be tested; re-specified as needed and validated with insights from other universities to consider both its generalizability and its completeness. Future studies should be extended to include other stakeholders (such as research academics, funding bodies and HDR students) to enable the inclusion of diverse viewpoints. Mechanisms to adapt the model (for different institutional contexts and to address dynamic needs) and to allow the model to evolve with changing industry demands also needs to be investigated. As the model matures, work should be done to develop measures that can be used to assess a research institutes maturity in these different domains. Future research in this field can deliver real benefits for research institutes to provide effective services for research management.

References

1. APQC: APQC Process Classification Framework (PCF). APQC (2018)
2. Barber, K.D., et al.: Business-process modelling and simulation for manufacturing management. Bus. Process Manag. J. **9**(4), 527–542 (2003). https://doi.org/10.1108/14637150310484544
3. Becker, J., Delfmann, P., Knackstedt, R.: Adaptive reference modeling: integrating configurative and generic adaptation techniques for information models. In: Becker, J., Delfmann, P. (eds.) Reference Modeling, pp. 27–58. Physica-Verlag HD, Heidelberg (2007). https://doi.org/10.1007/978-3-7908-1966-3_2
4. Becker, J., Schutte, R.: A reference model for retail enterprise. In: Reference Modeling for Business Systems Analysis, pp. 182–205. IGI Global (1)AD. https://doi.org/10.4018/978-1-59904-054-7.ch009
5. Beerkens, M.: Facts and fads in academic research management: the effect of management practices on research productivity in Australia. Res. Policy **42**(9), 1679–1693 (2013). https://doi.org/10.1016/j.respol.2013.07.014
6. Bertolini, M., et al.: Business process re-engineering in healthcare management: a case study. Bus. Process Manag. J. **17**(1), 42–66 (2011). https://doi.org/10.1108/14637151111105571
7. Carpinetti, L.C.R., et al.: Quality management and improvement: a framework and a business-process reference model. Bus. Process Manag. J. **9**(4), 543–554 (2003). https://doi.org/10.1108/14637150310484553
8. Davis, R.: British telecom - six level process hierarchy. In: Process Days Conference, Sydney, 22–24 August 2006 (2006)
9. Demes, K.W., et al.: Catalyzing clusters of research excellence: an institutional case study. J. Res. Adm. **L**(1), 108–122 (2019)
10. Department of Education and Training: Research Income Data (2004–2017). https://docs.education.gov.au/documents/herdc-research-income-time-series
11. Droegemeier, K.K., et al.: The roles of chief research officers at American research universities: a current profile and challenges for the future. J. Res. Adm. **XLVIII**(1), 26–64 (2017)
12. Dumas, M., La Rosa, M., Mendling, J., Reijers, H.A.: Process discovery. In: Dumas, M., La Rosa, M., Mendling, J., Reijers, H.A. (eds.) Fundamentals of Business Process Management, pp. 155–184. Springer, Heidelberg (2013). https://doi.org/10.1007/978-3-642-33143-5_5
13. Fettke, P., Loos, P.: Perspectives on reference modeling. In: Reference Modeling for Business Systems Analysis, pp. 1–21. IGI Global (1)AD. https://doi.org/10.4018/978-1-59904-054-7.ch001
14. Greasley, A.: Using process mapping and business process simulation to support a process-based approach to change in a public sector organisation. Technovation **26**(1), 95–103 (2006). https://doi.org/10.1016/J.TECHNOVATION.2004.07.008

15. Hammer, M.: What is business process management? In: Brocke, J., Rosemann, M. (eds.) Handbook on Business Process Management 1, pp. 3–16. Springer, Heidelberg (2014). https://doi.org/10.1007/978-3-642-00416-2_1

16. Hollingsworth, D.: The Workflow Reference Model. The Workflow Management Coalition Specification, Hampshire, UK (1995)

17. IBM: Align IT with business goals using the IBM Process Reference Model for IT. IBM Corporation (2007)

18. Kirkland, J., et al.: International research management: benchmarking programme. Association of Commonwealth Universities (2006)

19. Lawrence, R.J., Després, C.: Futures of transdisciplinarity. Futures **36**(4), 397–405 (2004). https://doi.org/10.1016/J.FUTURES.2003.10.005

20. Liberale, A.P., Kovach, J.V.: Reducing the time for IRB reviews: a case study. J. Res. Adm. **XLVIII**(2), 37–51 (2018)

21. Mauser, A.: A reference model for savings bank. In: Advances in Banking Technology and Management, pp. 232–242. IGI Global (2008). https://doi.org/10.4018/978-1-59904-675-4.ch014

22. Petersson, A.M., Lundberg, J.: Applying action design research (ADR) to develop concept generation and selection methods. Procedia CIRP **50**, 222–227 (2016). https://doi.org/10.1016/J.PROCIR.2016.05.024

23. Du Preez, J.L., et al.: Developing a methodology for online service failure prevention: reporting on an action design research project-in-progress. In: Australasian Conference on Information Systems (ACIS 2015), Adelaide (2015)

24. Rosemann, M.: Using reference models within the enterprise resource planning lifecycle. Aust. Account. Rev. **10**(22), 19–30 (2000). https://doi.org/10.1111/j.1835-2561.2000.tb00067.x

25. Rosemann, M., van der Aalst, W.M.P.: A configurable reference modelling language. Inf. Syst. **32**(1), 1–23 (2007). https://doi.org/10.1016/J.IS.2005.05.003

26. Saadé, R.G., Otrakji, C.A.: First impressions last a lifetime: effect of interface type on disorientation and cognitive load. Comput. Hum. Behav. **23**(1), 525–535 (2007). https://doi.org/10.1016/j.chb.2004.10.035

27. Schützenmeister, F.: University Research Management: An Exploratory Literature Review. Institute of European Studies, UC Berkeley (2010)

28. Sein, M.K., et al.: Action design research. MIS Q. **35**(1), 37–56 (2011). https://doi.org/10.2307/23043488

29. Squilla, B., et al.: Research shared services: a case study in implementation. J. Res. Adm. **XLVIII**(1), 86–99 (2017)

30. Wedekind, G.K., Philbin, S.P.: Research and grant management: the role of the project management office (PMO) in a European research consortium context. J. Res. Adm. **XLIX**(1), 43–62 (2018)

31. Wei Khong, K., Richardson, S.: Business process re-engineering in Malaysian banks and finance companies. Manag. Serv. Qual. Int. J. **13**(1), 54–71 (2003). https://doi.org/10.1108/09604520310456717

32. Wickson, F., et al.: Transdisciplinary research: characteristics, quandaries and quality. Futures **38**(9), 1046–1059 (2006). https://doi.org/10.1016/J.FUTURES.2006.02.011

33. Zimmermann, H.: OSI reference model-the ISO model of architecture for open systems interconnection. IEEE Trans. Commun. **28**(4), 425–432 (1980). https://doi.org/10.1109/TCOM.1980.1094702

What the Hack? – Towards a Taxonomy of Hackathons

Christoph Kollwitz[(⊠)] and Barbara Dinter

Chemnitz University of Technology, 09126 Chemnitz, Germany
{christoph.kollwitz,
barbara.dinter}@wirtschaft.tu-chemnitz.de

Abstract. In order to master the digital transformation and to survive in global competition, companies face the challenge of improving transformation processes, such as innovation processes. However, the design of these processes poses a challenge, as the related knowledge is still largely in its infancy. A popular trend since the mid-2000s are collaborative development events, so-called hackathons, where people with different professional backgrounds work collaboratively on development projects for a defined period. While hackathons are a widespread phenomenon in practice and many field reports and individual observations exist, there is still a lack of holistic and structured representations of the new phenomenon in literature. The paper at hand aims to develop a taxonomy of hackathons in order to illustrate their nature and underlying characteristics. For this purpose, a systematic literature review is combined with existing taxonomies or taxonomy-like artifacts (e.g. morphological boxes, typologies) from similar research areas in an iterative taxonomy development process. The results contribute to an improved understanding of the phenomenon hackathon and allow the more effective use of hackathons as a new tool in organizational innovation processes. Furthermore, the taxonomy provides guidance on how to apply hackathons for organizational innovation processes.

Keywords: Hackathon · Taxonomy · Digital innovation · Open innovation · Innovation process

1 Introduction

One of the central tasks of business process management (BPM) is to deal with changing environmental conditions [1]. In recent years, such a transformation appears in trends like shorter product life cycles and increasingly heterogeneous customer requirements. In this context, business processes in the field of innovation management are opening up and changing rapidly, which is addressed by BPM, e.g. by new information sources. Companies invest significant sums in R&D to master the challenges of digital transformation and to survive in the global economy. Traditionally, they have innovated almost solely to prevent leaking knowledge, technologies and process know how to unauthorized third parties or competitors [2]. However, companies merely focusing on internal competencies and resources fall behind in a

© Springer Nature Switzerland AG 2019
T. Hildebrandt et al. (Eds.): BPM 2019, LNCS 11675, pp. 354–369, 2019.
https://doi.org/10.1007/978-3-030-26619-6_23

hardening competition. Therefore, since the beginning of the 21st century a paradigm shift towards opening innovation changes the way how innovation processes are designed and how external knowledge contributes to the development of new products and services. As a bottom line of this so-called open innovation (OI) Chesbrough [3 p. XXIV] states that companies "can and should use external ideas as well as internal ideas, and internal and external paths to market" and over time various approaches for its operationalization have been developed. On the one hand, the advent of Web 2.0 technologies has enabled OI tools like online communities and product platforms for OI, while, on the other hand, the involvement of lead users and other stakeholders in (offline) innovation workshops was highlighted. All these approaches have in common that they understand innovation as the result of collaborative processes in (interdisciplinary) teams rather than as the work of individuals [4]. In addition to the paradigm of OI, digitalization has radically changed the nature of innovation. Digital innovation is in particular shaped by emerging (information) technology and the ubiquitous availability of (digital) data, enabling companies to provide "data-enriched offerings" to their customers [5].

Facing the trends towards openness and digitalization, companies need to find new ways to manage innovation processes in the digital age. More precisely, it poses a challenge for business process management to manage creative processes within and outside organizational boundaries [6], especially when organizations have little or no knowledge about their innovation partners [7]. In this paper, we will therefore investigate a phenomenon in which these two trends are manifested - so-called hackathons. Hackathons can be briefly described as events in which participants collaborate intensively on completing projects over a defined period of time [8]. Such projects focus on an IT-related topic, e.g. developing hardware and/or software, analyzing data sets or identifying IT-security issues. Hackathons can help companies, especially in the early stages of innovation, to generate new ideas, develop concepts or test solutions [9]. Although hackathons are becoming more and more popular in practice, related research is still in the fledgling stage. Thus, existing literature often consists of experience reports, white papers or reflections on specific application domains such as healthcare or smart cities. Companies need help for answering the question of how they can support the application of OI tools [10]. Therefore, they need a holistic view on phenomena like hackathons, which is currently not provided by the literature [11]. This leads us to our research question: How can the complex phenomenon of hackathons be systematically conceptualized in order to enable organizations to utilize them for their innovation processes? In order to answer the research question, we build a taxonomy of hackathons, applying the method for taxonomy development according to Nickerson et al. [12]. A taxonomy is a frequently hierarchical and evolutionary classification of empirical entities that can be used by researchers to organize research fields or entities [13, 14] and is frequently used in the Information Systems (IS) research domain.

The paper is organized as follows: In Sect. 2, we discuss hackathons as a manifestation of OI in more detail and clarify in particular which role they can play in OI processes. Afterwards, our research method is explained in Sect. 3, followed by the presentation of the resulting taxonomy in Sect. 4. The results are discussed in Sect. 5 before we draw a conclusion in Sect. 6.

2   A Process-Centric Perspective on Open Innovation and Hackathons

OI represents a challenge for the management of innovation processes, as it is linked to a shift from well-defined and structured processes to more interactive and agile processes [15]. Uncertainties regarding the results, process structures and required resources prevail within creativity-intensive process stages [16], which are particularly important at the beginning of the innovation process. Many different approaches to conceptualize innovation at the process level can be found in the literature (for an overview cf. [17]). In this paper, we follow Hansen and Birkinshaw [18], who make a simple distinction between: (1) idea generation, (2) idea conversion and (3) idea diffusion. Thereby, the innovation process is often described as a "funnel", since at the early stages there are many opportunities for innovation, of which only a few are concretized and realized at the later stages [19]. Based on this basic process model, innovation processes can be opened for different purposes for external knowledge. Gassmann and Enkel [20] distinguish three types of OI: (1) outside-in OI describes the sourcing and acquisition of expertise and ideas for the innovation process, while (2) inside-out OI focuses on the exploitation of ideas and the results of innovation processes. If outside-in and inside-out processes are combined, it is referred to as (3) coupled OI. The different types are in turn associated with different tasks. The outside-in perspective of OI comprises the identification, procurement and integration of innovations as well as the interaction with external partners [21]. The inside-out process, which receives less attention compared to the first perspective in the literature, can in turn be subdivided into the search for technology users and the commercialization phase [10]. In order to operationalize these processes, many different means are discussed in research. Battistella et al. [22] identify a total of 23 practices which were used by companies to implement out-side (e.g. crowdsourcing), inside-out (e.g. out-licensing of intellectual property) or coupled OI (e.g. joint ventures). With a focus on Web 2.0 technologies, Möslein and Bansemir [23] distinguish between innovation contests, innovation markets, innovation communities, innovation toolkits and innovation technologies as OI tool categories. Additionally, various authors emphasize the involvement of stakeholders such as customers/users through innovation workshop [24].

In this context, hackathons are considered as an OI tool, which can hardly be classified into existing tool categories since it combines elements of different tool classes. The term hackathon is a portmanteau from "hack" and "marathon" and was first coined at an OpenBSD developer event in Calgary in 1999. There is a variety of synonyms or similar terms such as hack day or hackfest, however, hackathon is by far the most popular term. Furthermore, hackathons that focus on the collection, analysis and/or visualization of data are also referred to as "datathons". Hackathons are rooted in the open source movement and have often been associated with civic engagement and open data [25]. Thus, there are initiatives from government agencies, which aim to increase the participation of citizens and to foster government transparency [26]. Other hosts of hackathons are organizations from the non-profit sector, such as educational institutions or research institutes or NGOs, which address social problems like environmental protection or poverty reduction [27]. However, since large digital players such as Google and Facebook have regularly conducted hackathons in which also external developers have participated [28], they have become a more and more interesting topic for companies of all industries who aim to complement traditional organizational innovation processes. Although there is a high variance in the activities and routines that take place during hackathons, three phases can be roughly distinguished [11]. In the (1) pre-hackathon phase, the focus lies on planning and design tasks. Besides, team building and initial idea generation can also start in this phase. Subsequently, the (2) hackathon phase includes the execution of the event, i.e. the collaborative work of the participants. In the (3) post-hackathon phase, the decision must be made whether and how the results of the hackathon should be followed up (by the host organization or the participants) or should be dropped. Hackathons aim to harness external knowledge for organizations, which corresponds with the outside-in type of OI. The knowledge is integrated mainly in the phases of idea generation and idea conversion and thus serves the organization primarily for knowledge exploration. However, hackathons can also be used in the later innovation process and enhance the diffusion of innovations [9].

3 Research Approach

3.1 Taxonomy Development

As mentioned in the introduction, our research is motivated by the emerging phenomenon of hackathons - in particular, by the discrepancy between the large number of anecdotal observations and field reports on the one hand and the lack of a holistic and comprehensive view on hackathons on the other hand. We would like to emphasize that there are many (scientific) publications on hackathons, which are also shown by the results of our literature search. However, these describe single instances or potential applications in specific areas and do not provide a consolidated and comprehensive view of the phenomenon. Taxonomies are particularly suitable for structuring and classifying complex research topics and therefore play an important role in various areas of IS research [29]. Especially with regard to emerging digital technologies or the management of novel (open) processes, taxonomies can help to consolidate knowledge and make it usable for practitioners as well as for researchers [30, 31]. For the development of the taxonomy we apply the established method of Nickerson et al. [12], which is guided by best practices from other research disciplines as well as the principles of Design Science Research [e.g. 32].

The first step in taxonomy development is the definition of a (1) meta characteristic, which is intended to support researchers to identify meaningful categories and dimensions that relate to the purpose of the taxonomy. In our case, the taxonomy is supposed to support the integration of hackathons into organizational innovation processes. Therefore, we examine hackathons from an organizational perspective and focus on dimensions and characteristics that cover the broad spectrum of design decisions associated with the design and execution of hackathons. The second step of Nickerson's method involves the determination of objective and subjective (2) ending conditions. Objective ending conditions are achieved when all objects of a population or a statistical sample have been analyzed and the result meets the requirements of a taxonomy (e.g. no redundancies/duplications, mutual exclusivity) [12]. Subjective ending conditions affect the researchers assessment of the resulting taxonomy and describe to what extent the taxonomy is considered to be concise, robust, comprehensive, extendible and explanatory [12]. In the third step, the taxonomy is created. Nickerson suggests an iterative process, which is performed until the previously defined ending conditions are met. In general, this process can be inductive (empirical-to-conceptual) or deductive (conceptual-to-empirical), whereby our approach focuses on the former one. Thus, our taxonomy is mainly based on a systematic literature review, which is described in more detail in Subsect. 3.2. The articles were manually screened and analyzed according to the meta characteristic using open, axial and selective coding [cf. 33]. Three iterations were carried out until the ending conditions were reached:

- Open coding: In the first iteration (empirical-to-conceptual), we examined the articles of the literature base according to the meta characteristic for statements on design, execution and objectives of hackathons and grouped by similar characteristics.
- Axial coding: In the second iteration (conceptual-to-empirical), existing taxonomies or taxonomy-like artifacts (e.g. morphological boxes, typologies) from similar research areas were included [e.g. 34–36] and compared with the attributes identified in the first iteration. In case of similarities, the dimensions and characteristics (partially modified) were included in the taxonomy.
- Selective coding: In the third iteration (empirical-to-conceptual), the characteristics identified in the literature, which could not be assigned to any dimension in the second iteration, were summarized in new dimensions and integrated into the taxonomy. Furthermore, the complete taxonomy was refined based on the objective and subjective ending conditions. In addition, the characteristics and their attributes were checked for correlations and dependencies (cf. Subsect. 4.1).

3.2 Literature Review

In recent years, a growing number of scientific publications in books, journals as well as conference proceedings reflect the increasing complexity of research. In this context, literature reviews can help to consolidate knowledge from different research areas and to gain insights into specific problem areas [37]. We decided to use a systematic literature review for the development of a hackathon taxonomy mainly for two reasons. First, such a meta-analysis allows us to access and investigate a large number of hackathon reports covering a broad spectrum of applications. Second, we can apply established methods for the literature review which facilitate the systematic development of our hackathon taxonomy [38, 39]. Vom Brocke et al. [38] propose a five phase model for literature reviews in IS.

The first step is to define the scope, which can be described using Cooper's literature review taxonomy [37]. Table 1 shows the scope of our literature review. We focus on hackathons described in the literature, whereby analyzing their (A) application and design and only marginally considering the results, the methods and underlying theories presented in the papers. Our goal is to (B) integrate existing knowledge and make it usable, in other words, we aim at a (C) conceptualization of the hackathon phenomenon. Our perspective is (D) neutral to avoid distorting the results of the review. As already mentioned in the introduction, our target (E) audience consists of practitioners on the one hand and general researchers on the other. Our aim is to consider an exhaustive literature basis when developing the taxonomy, whereby we prove the individual dimensions and characteristics of the taxonomy based on selected articles. Therefore, we assign our review in category (F) coverage as exhaustive and selective.

Table 1. Taxonomy of literature reviews [37, 38]

Characteristics	Categories			
(A)Focus	research out-come	research method	theories	applications
(B) Goal	integration	criticism		central issues
(C) Organisation	historical	conceptual		methodological
(D) Perspective	neutral representation		espousal of position	
(E) Audience	specialized scholars	general scholars	practitioners / politicans	general public
(F) Coverage	exhaustive	exhaustive and selective	representa-tive	Central / pivotal

The second step includes a broad conceptualization of the research subject, in our case hackathons, for which we would like to refer to Sect. 2. The third step consists of the literature search, which includes the selection of databases and keywords as well as the forward and backward search for literature [38]. Regarding the keywords, we searched for the terms, which are depicted in Table 2. We have deliberately excluded related terms such as "jam", since they are often used in other contexts. Following the recommendations of vom Brocke et al. [38], we first searched the top journals of IS discipline (Senior Scholars' Basket of Journals) for relevant publications. We did not find any relevant hits, which corresponds to our expectation that hackathons have not yet found their way into the most renowned journals. Then we expanded our search to the scientific databases AIS Electronic Library (AISeL), IEEE Xplore Digital Library (IEEE) as well as the citation database "Web of Science Core Selection" (WoS), where we searched in "titles", "abstracts" and "keywords" for the mentioned terms.

Table 2. Database search results by keywords

		Keywords				
		hackathon / hack-a-ton	hack day	datathon	hackfest	codefest
Data-bases	AISeL	4	1	2	0	0
	IEEE	63	2	0	1	0
	WoS	147	6	6	1	1

We received 234 hits in total. After eliminating duplicates, removing irrelevant papers (by checking titles and abstracts) and a forward and backward search, we ended up with 189 publications, which we included in the literature analysis. These publications are mostly conferences proceedings or practice-oriented journal articles. Some of the papers describe hackathons that have taken place in the context of conferences, teaching in higher education or other events. The third step of a literature review according to vom Brocke et al. [38] contains the analysis and synthesis of literature. For this purpose, we followed the approach proposed by Nickerson et al. [12] as explained in Subsect. 3.1. The final step of the literature review framework is the development of a research agenda. Since our main interest is the taxonomy development for hackathons and we do not primarily aim to identify research gaps, we have decided not to derive a research agenda. However, in Sect. 6 we highlight potentials for further research.

4   A Taxonomy of Hackathons

4.1   Overview of the Taxonomy

In the course of the analysis, it became apparent that the dimensions could be assigned to two categories. Strategic design decisions (SDD) tend to be abstract in character and are derived from the overall goals and business model of organizations, while operational design decisions (ODD) mainly determine the workflow and processes that take place during a hackathon. With regard to the benefits of the taxonomy for organizations, these categories serve different purposes. The SDD support the organization in identifying useful application scenarios for hackathons. They outline the options in terms of which challenges could be addressed for which purposes. The ODD can in turn support organizations in designing specific settings that fit their organizational environment. For example, different dimensions can be adjusted according to the financial, human and spatial resources of an organization. Some SDD dimensions partly have an influence on ODD or determine them. Table 3 gives an overview of our taxonomy of hackathons, while we present the dimensions and characteristics in the Subsects. 4.2 and 4.3.

Table 3. Taxonomy of hackathons

Dimension	Characteristics			
SDD				
OI integration	idea generation	idea conversion	idea diffusion	
Challenge design	technology-centric (API, software, hardware)	topic-centric (social issue, business problem)	data-centric (analysis, visualization, gathering)	
Solution space	open	semi-structured	structured	
Value proposition	focus on challenge output		focus on human interaction	
ODD				
Duration	short (<24 h)	medium (>24h – 72h)	long (>72h)	
Degree of elaboration	ideas and broad concepts	conceptual solutions	functional solutions	finished products / services
Venue	physical	virtual		combined
Incentives	competition		collaboration	
Target audience	domain experts	(semi-) professionals	general public	
Resources	provided	partially provided	not provided	

4.2 Strategic Design Decisions

OI Integration. As already mentioned in Sect. 2, hackathons can be considered as OI tools that are typically applied to the outside-in process. In general, they can be applied in all phases of the innovation process [18], with different objectives being pursued. In the *idea generation* phase, hackathons aim to generate initial innovation impulses from the outside. With regard to the *idea conversion*, promising ideas are to be selected for further development in cooperation with external developers. The phase *idea diffusion* involves testing and presenting products and services that have already been available on the market [9]. For example, software can be provided in order to deduce room for improvement or possible applications from hackathon results. This dimension is of particular importance since it constitutes the interface between OI process management and hackathon design.

Challenge Design. A common characteristic of all investigated hackathons is that they are associated with the handling of a task or the solution of a problem. This dimension represents the focus of the hackathon's task or challenge. The primal form of hackathons, originated in the open source movement, was strongly oriented towards specific *technology* issues, including software, hardware or APIs related tasks [11]. Hackathon challenges can also pursue social or business *topics*, which does not mean that technology does not play a role, rather their purpose is focused on solving a problem by using technologies [27]. In addition to these two characteristics, which are similarly proposed by Briscoe and Mulligan [25], we add *data-centric* as a third characteristic. Thus, the general trend towards "big data" means that challenges aim at generating value from data without having a dedicated technology or a specific business case in mind [40]. Such tasks focus on the processing, analysis or visualization of data sets [41], and in some cases on the collection or generation of data [42].

Solution Space. This dimension refers to specifications made with regard to the execution of the hackathon. We distinguish between *open, semi-structured* and *structured* settings. Open settings are characterized by wide-ranging challenges that leave plenty room for interpretation and own ideas. Requirements and restrictions that could potentially limit creativity are reduced to a minimum. The SPIE Software Hack Day 2014 [43] offers a vivid example of such an open solution space. Participants were invited to "collaborate on innovative solutions to problems of their choice" [43]. The format took place without prior registration, a fixed schedule or formal presentations. Semi-structured settings on the one hand provide certain specifications that limit the solution space, but on the other hand leave room for individual approaches [44]. Either the procedure can be limited by the specification of e.g. technologies, data sets or methods that have to be used [45]; or the expected results are specified by technical and/or functional requirements [46]. Structured settings in turn place strict demands on the procedure and the results, which severely limits the solution space. For example, the JUCE Machine Learning Hackathon [47] was an event in which the technology to be used (a C++ framework focusing on audio applications) as well as the type of solution (application of machine learning) were specified.

Value Proposition. This dimension takes into account that hackathons are not autotelic, but are organized for specific purposes. In reality, there are overlaps, as organizations are likely to pursue different objectives simultaneously. This is contradictory to the principle that the characteristics of a taxonomy should be mutually exclusive [12]. However, we consider this dimension to be important, thus we assume that organizations, even if they pursue different goals, associate a primary value proposition with a hackathon. In our analysis, two primary value propositions with different focuses emerged. On the one hand, value propositions with a *focus on challenge output* aim to harness the results of the participative work in the hackathon. Usually this involves results developed in the hackathon such as ideas, models, prototypes or data visualizations as well as extension, improvement or evaluation of existing entities (e.g. extension of software functionalities or detection of security breaches) [25]. On the other hand, value propositions with a *focus on human interaction* aim to generate benefits with respect to the participants. This includes educational aspects as well as the recruitment of new employees [41]. Furthermore, hackathons can be utilized as a communication platform for stakeholders and marketing purposes [11]. In any case, it is important for organizations to be aware of their own expectations and to establish measures for making the results connectable in their own organization.

4.3   Operational Design Decisions

Duration. Hackathons are events that take place over a short period of time, whereby the concrete timing varies greatly in practice. On one side of the continuum, there are hackathons with *short* duration that last only a few hours as a one-day event, which is particularly likely when they are part of other events (e.g. scientific conferences). Lau and Lei [48], who describe a 30-min hackathon at the "International Microwave Symposium 2017", provide a demonstrative but extreme example of this characteristic. The vast majority of the hackathons discussed in the literature lasted between 24 and 72 h, which we refer to as the *medium* period of time [9]. On the other side of the continuum, there exist *long* duration hackathons that can last from four days up to several weeks [49]. Hackathons with long duration are usually not continuous but consist of multiple events (e.g. kick-off and award ceremony) linked by an intervening development period.

Venue. Hackathons not only deal with technology-related topics. Information technology can also act as a medium for communication and cooperation during the events. While "classic" hackathons take place at *physical* locations [44], there are also formats that are completely organized *virtually* via online platforms or social networks (e.g. Kaggle) and therefore do not require physical presence [42]. Additionally there is the possibility to *combine* physical and virtual venues [49]. Concerning the physical venues, the analyzed articles describe frequently the importance of open and innovation-friendly spaces equipped with tools for collaboration and ideation (e.g. flipcharts or brown paper). Choosing a physical venue also means limiting capacity, while virtual venues allow a literally unlimited number of participants.

Degree of Elaboration. Hackathons are aimed at dealing with technology related issues, but differ greatly in terms of the intended results. We have decided to cluster the different characteristics according to the degree of elaboration, as there is an unlimited variety of resulting artifacts in practice. Artifacts with a relatively low degree of elaboration require only a basic understanding of technologies and operate at a high level of abstraction. The focus is on creativity and the development of *ideas and broad concepts* [50]. A higher degree of elaboration requires a further development of ideas and to *conceptual solutions*. These conceptual prototypes are usually demonstrative paper-based or computer-aided mock-ups that represent a concept resulting from a hackathons, but do not contain any functionalities [51]. The next higher degree of elaboration is obtained when functionalities of the solution are also implemented. Such *functional solutions* include core functions of an e.g. prototype and thus demonstrate the general feasibility of a concept (proof of concept) [8]. The highest degree of elaboration is reached when the hackathon results in *finished products/services*, which are at least mature enough to be launched (minimal viable product) [52]. As the degree of elaboration increases, the demands of the technical and professional skills of the participants usually also increase, while creativity and the ability of abstraction become less important.

Incentives. In general, hackathons are team events, whereby the type of team composition (e.g. before or during the event) and the team sizes can vary. Although hackathons generally emphasize the value of cooperation, they can be designed as *competitions* in which participants compete among each other. Based on a jury decision, audience vote or self-assessment, the winners usually receive a prize which is intended to increase the extrinsic motivation of the participants [9, 53]. The alternative concept relies entirely on *collaboration* rather than any competition between participants [54].

Target Audience. Although hackathons are traditionally open events, there could be various restrictions concerning the participation. We identified various types of hard restrictions in the literature. For example, in-house hackathons which can only be visited by employees of an organization or hackathons that target socio-demographic characteristics of the participants, such as age, gender or profession [11]. Furthermore, tasks can be chosen in a way that only *domain experts* are able to participate, e.g. physicians [41] or architects [50]. In addition to these hard restrictions, there are soft criteria that are frequently based on the self-assessment of participants. Such constraints often aim to acquire participants with expertise in specific areas such as marketing, programming or data analysis [55]. We refer to this characteristic as *(semi-) professionals*. The last characteristic refers to hackathons, which have no restriction of participation apart from a basic interest in the topic [51], thus, they target the *general public*.

Resources. The last dimension differentiates whether resources are *provided* to the hackathon participants or *not*. Likewise, only some resources can be made available, which we characterize as *partially provided*. In our context, provided resources can be considered as an input, which is made available to the participants before or during the hackathon. The provided resources may be hardware, software or data sets as well as existing ideas, concepts or prototypes, which should be evolved [56]. Furthermore, human resources such as mentors or experts from practice can serve as an input for the participants [57]. Depending on the setting, the usage of resources can be voluntary or mandatory (cf. solution space). The question of whether or not resources will be provided may be related to single SDD dimensions. For example, existing ideas or concepts must be available as input for the participants if a hackathon aim to idea conversion or diffusion.

5 Discussion

OI has been around for several years now and scholars from different professions had already discussed many tools, especially in the context of web 2.0 and social software [26]. Hackathons combine elements of such OI tools with elements from the areas of open source and agile software development [49]. Thus, the dimensions and characteristics of our taxonomy of hackathons is not disconnected from other OI tools and practices, but features several similarities. Hackathons have event character and resemble innovations contests in the dimensions solution space, duration, degree of elaboration, venue and target audience [34]. Furthermore, the dimensions OI integration and solution space correspond to the typology of the customer co-creation by Piller et al. [36]. However, the taxonomy contains dimensions that cannot be found in other classifications and dimensions that have completely different characteristics. For instance, challenge design describes the IT-related aspects of hackathons, while incentives show that hackathons can be both competitive and collaborative. Our taxonomy also shows that hackathons are very diverse in their practical manifestation, which contradicts several restrictive definition approaches from literature on hackathons. Hackathons are frequently characterized as competitive, short-term events in which software is developed [e.g. 9, 25]. Our analysis showed that hackathons could be considered as OI tools with a wide range of applications, rather than being limited to competitions, short periods or software development projects.

Since hackathons must be incorporated into BPM, our taxonomy highlights many dimensions, such as resources or process participants to be considered [1]. Our approach transfers the established method of taxonomy development to the immature field of hackathons and thus, contribute to the knowledge base by exaptation [58]. Since organizations need assistance in managing innovation processes in the age of digitalization [7], our taxonomy of hackathons is intended to enable organizations to utilize hackathons for successful innovating. In this context, where serval uncertainties exist a central challenge poses the management of creativity-intense processes [6]. Our taxonomy can support organizations in planning creative processes in hackathons by constraining them, which in turn helps to manage uncertainties regarding (1) results, (2) processes and (3) resources [59]. Concerning the uncertainties of the (1) results, organizations can make detailed specifications regarding the solution space as well as the degree of elaboration in order to channel the creativity of the participants in a desired direction. In addition, uncertainties are generally more pronounced in the early stages of the innovation process than in the later ones, which is reflected by the dimension OI integration. The dimensions challenge design and the solution space have an influence on the (2) process uncertainties, which determine the form and substance of a hackathon. As mentioned above in Subsect. 4.1, all ODD dimensions also have a direct influence on the hackathon processes and their degree of uncertainty. For example, hackathons that have a short duration and take place at a physical location might be easier to predetermine beforehand than those that take place over long periods and include both physical and virtual forms of collaboration. In terms of (3) resource uncertainties, organizations can regulate e.g. the duration and, can provide resources for the participants. In addition, the availability of intangible resources such as expertise or skills can be influenced by the appropriate selection of a target audience.

Another aspect to be discussed is the categorization of SDD and ODD in our taxonomy of hackathons. We consider this a first step to gain a better understanding of how the strategic goals of organizations are linked to the design of hackathon processes. The taxonomy shows application scenarios (SDD) and operational design options (ODD), which can lead to a better strategic alignment, which is considered as a core element of BPM [60]. However, in this article our research approach focused on the design of the taxonomy rather than on the investigation of linkages between strategic and operational elements. In Sect. 6 we will discuss how we intend to achieve this in the future.

6 Conclusion

In this paper, we examine hackathons as a novel phenomenon at the crossroads of digital innovation and OI. We used the method of Nickerson et al. [12] combined with a systematic literature review to develop a taxonomy of hackathon. The result contributes to a better understanding of the opportunities and characteristics of hackathons and is therefore a first step towards a better integration of hackathons into organizational innovation processes. Our results not only give directions which kind of innovation challenges can be addressed, but also provide companies with initial recommendations on how to proceed when using this new resource in the BPM context. From a research perspective, the results contributes by expanding the knowledge base in the spectrum of OI tools and practices as well as in the field of collaborative work in the digital age.

The taxonomy can be considered as generally valid since it was derived from a comprehensive number of primary sources. However, our research is still in an early stage and some limitations exist. The taxonomy is currently based only on findings we have derived from a retrospective review of the literature. Thus, the significance of our results is limited due to the restrictions in the review strategy (restriction to certain databases and keywords). Although we have figured out which dimensions and objectives are discussed in the literature, we need further evidence to show that those aspects are actually relevant from a practical point of view. We aim to compensate for this shortcoming by conducting case studies and in-depth interviews examining the roles of the different actors in real-world hackathons in more detail. In this direction, our next step for further research is to study the relationships between individual dimensions or characteristics. In particular, we want to show the interplay of SDD and ODD dimensions in more detail and further develop the taxonomy into an ontology.

References

1. Smith, H., Fingar, P.: Business Process Management: The Third Wave. Meghan-Kiffer Press, Tampa (2003)
2. Chesbrough, H.W., Appleyard, M.M.: Open innovation and strategy. Calif. Manag. Rev. **50**, 57–76 (2007)
3. Chesbrough, H.W.: Open Innovation: The New Imperative for Creating and Profiting from Technology (2003)
4. Steen, M., Manschot, M., De Koning, N.: Benefits of co-design in service design projects marc. Int. J. Des. **5**, 53–60 (2011)
5. Davenport, T.H.: Analytics 3.0. Harv. Bus. Rev. **12**, 65–72 (2013)
6. Schmiedel, T., vom Brocke, J.: Business process management: potentials and challenges of driving innovation. In: vom Brocke, J., Schmiedel, T. (eds.) BPM - Driving Innovation in a Digital World. MP, pp. 3–15. Springer, Cham (2015)
7. Nambisan, S., Lyytinen, K., Majchrzak, A., Song, M.: Digital innovation management: reinventing innovation management research in a digital world. MIS Q. **41**, 223–238 (2017)
8. Pe-Than, E.P.P., Nolte, A., Filippova, A., Bird, C., Scallen, S., Herbsleb, J.D.: Designing corporate hackathons with a purpose: the future of software development. IEEE Softw. **36**, 15–22 (2019)

9. Rosell, B., Kumar, S., Shepherd, J.: Unleashing innovation through internal hackathons. In: Digest of Technical Papers - InnoTek 2014: 2014 IEEE Innovations in Technology Conference (2014)
10. Aloini, D., Lazzarotti, V., Manzini, R., Pellegrini, L.: Implementing open innovation: technological, organizational and managerial tools. Bus. Process Manag. J. **23**, 1086–1093 (2017)
11. Komssi, M., Pichlis, D., Raatikainen, M., Kindstrom, K., Jarvinen, J.: What are hackathons for? IEEE Softw. **32**, 60–67 (2015)
12. Nickerson, R.C., Varshney, U., Muntermann, J.: A method for taxonomy development and its application in information systems. Eur. J. Inf. Syst. **22**, 336–359 (2013)
13. Bailey, K.D.: Typologies and Taxonomies an Introduction to Classification Techniques. Sage Publications, Thousand Oaks (1994)
14. Glass, R.L., Vessey, I.: Contemporary application-domain taxonomies. IEEE Softw. **12**, 63–76 (1995)
15. Gassmann, O., Enkel, E., Chesbrough, H.: The future of open innovation. R D Manag. **40**, 213–221 (2010)
16. Seidel, S.: Toward a theory of managing creativity-intensive processes: a creative industries study. Inf. Syst. E-bus. Manag. **9**, 407–446 (2011)
17. Eveleens, C.: Innovation management; a literature review of innovation process models and their implications (2010). http://www.academia.edu/download/33190893/Innovation-management-literature-review-.pdf
18. Hansen, M.T., Birkinshaw, J.: The innovation value chain. Harv. Bus. Rev. **85** (2007)
19. Lazzarotti, V., Manzini, R.: Different modes of open innovation: a theoretical framework and an empirical study. Int. J. Innov. Manag. **13**, 615–636 (2009)
20. Gassmann, O., Enkel, E.: Towards a theory of open innovation: three core process archetypes. In: Proceedings of the R&D Management Conference (RADMA), Lisbon, Portugal (2004)
21. West, J., Bogers, M.: Leveraging external sources of innovation: a review of research on open innovation. J. Prod. Innov. Manag. **31**, 814–831 (2014)
22. Battistella, C., De Toni, A.F., Pessot, E.: Practising open innovation: a framework of reference. Bus. Process Manag. J. **23**, 1311–1336 (2017)
23. Möslein, K.M., Bansemir, B.: Strategic open innovation: basics, actors, tools and tensions. In: Michael, H., Pfeffermann, N. (eds.) Strategies and Communications for Innovations: An Integrative Management View for Companies and Networks, pp. 11–23. Springer, Berlin (2011)
24. Edvardsson, B., Kristensson, P., Magnusson, P., Sundström, E.: Customer integration within service development - a review of methods and an analysis of insitu and exsitu contributions. Technovation. **32**, 419–429 (2012)
25. Briscoe, G., Mulligan, C.: Digital innovation: the hackathon phenomenon (2014)
26. Robinson, P.J., Johnson, P.A.: Civic hackathons: new terrain for local government-citizen interaction? Urban Plan. **1**, 65–74 (2016)
27. Ciaghi, A., et al.: Hacking for Southern Africa: collaborative development of hyperlocal services for marginalised communities. In: 2016 IST-Africa Conference, IST-Africa 2016 (2016)
28. Choi, M.: Organizing open digital innovation: evidence from hackathons. In: International Conference on Information Systems (ICIS), Dublin, Ireland, pp. 1–11 (2016)
29. Nickerson, R.C., Varshney, U., Muntermann, J., Isaac, H.: Taxonomy development in information systems: developing a taxonomy of mobile applications. In: Proceedings of the European Conference on Information Systems (ECIS), Verona, Italy, p. 388 (2009)

30. Geiger, D., Seedorf, S., Schulze, T., Nickerson, R., Schader, M.: Managing the crowd: towards a taxanomy of crowdsourcing processes. In: AMCIS 2011 Proceedings (2011)

31. Berger, S., Denner, M.-S., Röglinger, M.: The nature of digital technologies – development of a mulit-layer taxonomy. In: 26th European Conference on Information Systems (ECIS 2018), pp. 1–18 (2018)

32. Hevner, A.R., March, S.T., Park, J., Ram, S.: Design science in information systems research. MIS Q. **28**, 75–105 (2004)

33. Wolfswinkel, J.F., Furtmueller, E., Wilderom, C.P.M.: Using grounded theory as a method for rigorously reviewing literature. Eur. J. Inf. Syst. **22**, 45–55 (2013)

34. Bullinger, A.C., Möslein, K.: Innovation contests – where are we? In: AMCIS 2010 Proceedings, pp. 1–9 (2010)

35. Dinter, B., Kollwitz, C., Fritzsche, A.: Teaching data driven innovation – facing a challenge for higher education. In: AMCIS 2017 - America's Conference on Information Systems: A Tradition of Innovation (2017)

36. Piller, F.T., Ihl, C., Vossen, A.: A typology of customer co-creation in the innovation process. In: New Forms of Collaborative Innovation and Production on the Internet: An Interdisciplinary Perspective. Universitätsverlag Göttingen, Göttingen (2011)

37. Cooper, H.M.: Organizing knowledge syntheses: a taxonomy of literature reviews. Knowl. Soc. **1**, 104–126 (1988)

38. vom Brocke, J., Simons, A., Niehaves, B., Reimer, K., Plattfaut, R., Cleven, A.: Reconstructing the giant: on the importance of rigour in documenting the literature search process. In: Proceedings of the European Conference on Information Systems (EICS 2009), Verona, p. 161 (2009)

39. Webster, J., Watson, R.T.: Analyzing the past to prepare for the future: writing a literature review. MIS Q. **26**, 13–23 (2002)

40. Vanauer, M., Bohle, C., Hellingrath, B.: Guiding the introduction of big data in organizations: a methodology with business- and data-driven ideation and enterprise architecture management-based implementation. In: Proceedings of the Annual Hawaii International Conference on System Sciences (HICSS), Kauai, pp. 908–917 (2015)

41. Wyngaard, J., Lynch, H., Nabrzyski, J., Pope, A., Jha, S.: Hacking at the divide between polar science and HPC: using hackathons as training tools. In: Proceedings - 2017 IEEE 31st International Parallel and Distributed Processing Symposium Workshops, IPDPSW 2017, pp. 352–359 (2017)

42. Alba, M., Avalos, M., Guzmán, C., Larios, V.M.: Synergy between smart cities' hackathons and living labs as a vehicle for accelerating tangible innovations on cities. In: IEEE 2nd International Smart Cities Conference: Improving the Citizens Quality of Life, ISC2 2016 - Proceedings (2016)

43. Kendrew, S., Deen, C., Radziwill, N., Crawford, S., Gilbert, J.: The first SPIE software hack day. In: Proceedings of SPIE, Montreal (2014)

44. Saravi, S., et al.: A systems engineering hackathon - a methodology involving multiple stakeholders to progress conceptual design of a complex engineered product. IEEE Access **6**, 38399–38410 (2018)

45. Charvat, K., Bye, B.L., Mildorf, T., Berre, A.-J., Jedlicka, K.: Open data, VGI and citizen observatories INSPIRE hackathon. Int. J. Spat. Data Infrastruct. Res. **13**, 109–130 (2018)

46. Pathanasethpong, A., et al.: Tackling regional public health issues using mobile health technology: event report of an mHealth hackathon in Thailand. JMIR mHealth uHealth **5**, e155 (2017)

47. Bernardo, F., Grierson, M., Fiebrink, R.: User-centred design actions for lightweight evaluation of an interactive machine learning toolkit. J. Sci. Technol. Arts. **10**, 25–38 (2018)

48. Lau, K., Lei, B.J.: IMS2017 hackathon: 30-minute circuits. IEEE Microw. Mag. **18**, 84 (2017)
49. Ahalt, S., et al.: Water science software institute: agile and open source scientific software development. Comput. Sci. Eng. **16**, 18–26 (2014)
50. Thomas, R.S.: Using design slam to foster lifelong learning solutions. Comput. (Long Beach Calif.) **50**, 32–33 (2017)
51. Concilio, G., Molinari, F., Morelli, N.: Empowering citizens with open data by urban hackathons. In: Proceedings of the 7th International Conference for e-Democracy and Open Government, CeDEM 2017, pp. 125–134 (2017)
52. Avalos, M., Larios, V.M., Salazar, P., Maciel, R.: Hackathons, semesterathons, and summerathons as vehicles to develop smart city local talent that via their innovations promote synergy between industry, academia, government and citizens. In: 2017 International Smart Cities Conference ISC2 2017 (2017)
53. Brenner, W., et al.: User, use & utility research: the digital user as new design perspective in business and information systems engineering. Bus. Inf. Syst. Eng. **6**, 55–61 (2014)
54. Decker, A., Eiselt, K., Voll, K.: Understanding and improving the culture of hackathons: think global hack local. In: Frontiers in Education Conference (2015)
55. Alekseenko, A., Sanchez-medina, J.: Lane departure prediction with naturalistic driving data (2017)
56. Tsukada, M., et al.: Software defined media: virtualization of audio-visual services. In: IEEE International Conference on Communications, pp. 1–7. IEEE (2017)
57. Madelska, S.: News from the field: coders and the creative unite to design and build apps for surface haptics. IEEE Trans. Haptics **8**, 128–129 (2015)
58. Gregor, S., Hevner, A.R.: Positioning and presenting design science research for maximum impact. MIS Q. **37**, 337–355 (2013)
59. Seidel, S., Mueller-Wienbergen, F., Rosemann, M.: Pockets of creativity in business processes. Commun. Assoc. Inf. Syst. **27**, 415–436 (2010)
60. Rosemann, M., vom Brocke, J.: The six core elements of business process management. In: vom Brocke, J., Rosemann, M. (eds.) Handbook on Business Process Management 1. IHIS, pp. 105–122. Springer, Heidelberg (2015)

Design Patterns for Business Process Individualization

Bastian Wurm[1][✉], Kanika Goel[2], Wasana Bandara[2], and Michael Rosemann[2]

[1] Vienna University of Economics and Business, Vienna, Austria
bastian.wurm@wu.ac.at
[2] Queensland University of Technology, Brisbane, Australia
{k.goel,w.bandara,m.rosemann}@qut.edu.au

Abstract. Competition is forcing organizations to constantly innovate and identify ways to deliver high quality services and products. The Business Process Management (BPM) discipline has contributed by providing a rich set of analysis and re-design techniques. However, BPM methods and guidelines are often driven by process standardization and economies of scale, while emerging digital technologies (e.g. advanced manufacturing, sophisticated data analytics) increasingly facilitate process individualization. In this paper we contribute to an extended BPM body of knowledge by presenting design patterns for process individualization. We argue that (1) technological developments have made scalable process variant management viable and that (2) these technologies enable new forms of process individualization altogether. In our research, we identified and analyzed design patterns that make use of rapid digitalization to obtain individualized products and services. A conceptual model supported by literature and case examples is presented. This model forms theory on design and action of business process individualization in the digital age. Companies can deploy the design patterns developed in this paper as guidelines in their quest for process individualization.

Keywords: Process individualization · Design patterns · Process design · Digital technologies

1 Introduction

An increasingly competitive environment and differentiated customer demands have shifted the focus from mass production to individualization of products and services over the last decades [57]. However, individualization entails increased complexity costs, as it requires different business process variants to be designed, implemented, managed and maintained. The more diverse the customer needs a company wants to address, the more process variants are required [51], leading to higher costs-to-serve. This creates a dilemma between revenue-sensitive process individualization and cost-sensitive process standardization, which can be observed in a number of industries (e.g. see detailed elaboration for the car manufacturing industry in [25]).

© Springer Nature Switzerland AG 2019
T. Hildebrandt et al. (Eds.): BPM 2019, LNCS 11675, pp. 370–385, 2019.
https://doi.org/10.1007/978-3-030-26619-6_24

Established Business Process Management (BPM) methods and process-oriented improvement programs such as Six Sigma, Total Quality Management, Lean Management, and popular process management life-cycle models (e.g. [16]), tend to focus on process standardization over individualization. These methods are driven by measures such as processing time, cost-per-outcome unit or minimal variation (Six Sigma), but rarely give guidance in terms of how to individualize processes leading to higher variety of services and products [17,41]. Ignoring individualization will no longer be viable for organizations [57], creating an increased demand for insights on how to approach it.

The rapid developments in the digital age, especially in the form of advanced manufacturing, robotic workflow management and data analytics brings tremendous potential to make process individualization cost-effective. These new affordances materialize in a higher variety of process outcomes and a reduced time to individualize. Thus, we argue that digital technologies have broadened the design space of business processes, providing the means for firms to individualize their products and services. However, the existing BPM method set does not provide sufficient support for capitalizing on this emerging affordance. We contribute towards addressing this gap by developing a defined set of design patterns for process individualization. In this way, we address the following research question: *What are design patterns for process individualization?*

This paper presents a conceptual model that explains how business processes can be individualized in the digital age. In particular, we derive four different design patterns for business process individualization. These patterns cover the essential constructs making up a business process. Contemporary case examples are provided in support of each design pattern as a means of illustrative evidence. The resulting framework contributes towards theory building by presenting a forming typology of process individualization with actionable design options. Thereby, we contribute towards forming theory of analyzing (Type I) and theory of design and action (Type V), as described in [21].

This paper is structured as follows. First, we outline the research background. Second, we introduce the design method that explains how we derived our theoretical model of process individualization patterns. Third, we present the conceptual model and explain the different design patterns for process individualization. We conclude the paper by summarizing its key contribution, and pointing to limitations and future work.

2 Research Background

Creating diverse process variants in an efficient way is a major barrier to the individualization of products and services. The developments in the digital age, especially robotic workflow management, sophisticated data analytics and advanced manufacturing (e.g. 3D printing) provide an entire new level of cost effective capabilities and make previously impossible forms of scalable process individualization accessible. In this section we summarize the contextual background to the key concepts underlying this study.

2.1   Stages of Individualization

Individualization refers to the degree to which products, services, and processes are configured to meet explicit as well as latent customer needs [57]. We distinguish between three stages of individualization (see Fig. 1).

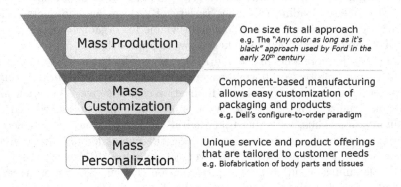

Fig. 1. Stages of individualization

The first stage consists of only standard products with no or very little individualization. Products and services that fall into this category are off-the-shelf products that follow a "one size fits all" approach. These products and services are uniform, as variation is either technically or economically not feasible, or there is no market for these offerings. On this stage of product and service individualization the customer does not play a role other than deciding and buying one of the products available in the market [31]. An example is Ford's "any color as long as it's black" approach in the early 20th century. By eliminating variation in the product, Ford was able to scale production in a way that was unprecedented. Nowadays, this level of individualization is predominant for daily products, where the costs of individualization outweigh the potential mark-up in price.

The second stage encompasses mass customized products or services that exhibit a certain level of individualization by offering different variants of the same product or service. As outlined by [19], there are different strategies that can be employed. Mass customization heavily relies on component-based manufacturing that enables companies to offer limited variation while still realizing returns of scale. In mass customization, the role of the customer is to choose from a variety of different modules that are produced and resembled by the manufacturer on large scale [31]. For example, Dell and many other computer manufactures allow customers to configure their device based on a pre-selection of components. In this stage, individualization is characterized by the plethora of options that are provided to the customer and the sophistication of product configuration and pricing engines that guide the user through the process.

The third and last stage reflects the highest level of individualization. Here, products and services are bespoke to an individual customer or purpose. Mass personalization combines the following four key properties as according to [57]. (1) As these products and services are tailored to specific customer needs, they are one of a kind. This is also referred to as the market-of-one. (2) Mass personalization needs to be paired with mass efficiency in order to be economically viable. (3) Companies need to employ customer co-creation to integrate the customer in all phases of the product life-cycle. (4) With an increasing level of product and service individualization, it becomes more important to detect and understand explicit as well as latent customer needs [34]. Modern technology enables this level of individualization. For example, hospitals can produce body parts by use of additive manufacturing (colloquially know as 3D printing), considering a patient's unique physical characteristics [33].

2.2 Business Process Variant Management

Process variants are created to configure processes to diverse contexts due to varying environmental and market conditions [10]. To respond to customer needs in different markets, products and services are adapted. In turn, underlying processes often need to be altered in order to reflect these changes [51].

To allow for the generation and management of different process variants, research has investigated configurable process models [20], software product lines [39], and assembly system design [26], to name only but a few. These approaches have in common that they exclusively focus on the sequence of activities and their causal relationship to create variation, but do not consider other components of business processes. Thus, the more customized products and services a firm wants to offer, the more diverse its business processes need to be leading to inefficiency and increased complexity in the management of the business process portfolio [51]. This is, why many companies refrain from competing via business process individualization, but aim at standardizing their business processes instead [53].

Furthermore, process variants operate on the level of mass customization, i.e. they result in a set of product options the customer can choose from. However, process variants are limited in that they cannot (and do not aim to) provide a unique customer experience and tailoring of the process.

2.3 Business Process Improvement and Redesign Patterns

Prior research provides a rich set of process improvement and process re-design methods and patterns. These patterns "target the resolution or mitigation of problems" [18, p. 8] to increase efficiency and improve other metrics of the devil's quadrangle [18] by addressing the "mechanics of the process" [42, p. 283]. Yet, how to provide companies with a set of design guidelines to differentiate their processes and customer touch points from competitors has so far been neglected.

We address these limitations by developing design patterns for process individualization. The patterns contribute to the body of knowledge in BPM by explaining and demonstrating how different components of business processes can be manipulated to individualize business processes and broaden their design space.

3   Design Method

In this section we explain how we derived design patterns for process individualization. We first introduce the key elements forming a business process, as all of these can potentially be manipulated to increase process variation. Second, we introduce the notion of design patterns [4] and describe how we utilized this concept for our research.

3.1   Conceptual Framework

Business processes are a sequence of activities leading to an output that generates value to an internal or external customer of an organization [16] by transforming inputs to outputs [32]. Figure 2 visualizes the different components of business processes and their interplay. A business process is composed of (1) process activities and buffers together with their respective sequence. Activities and steps of the process are carried out by (2) resources that are either capital assets or labor. Further, (3) the information and data associated with the process help to make process decisions and trigger process activities or sub-processes [32]. (4) The flow unit is a transient entity "that proceeds through various activities and finally exits the process as finished output" [32, p. 19].

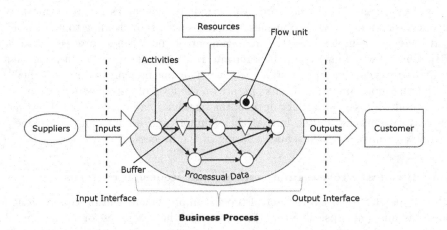

Fig. 2. Business process meta-model (adapted from [32])

Traditionally, companies focused on creating changes to the output of the process by using different inputs or adapting process activities and the sequence of the process. However, this increases complexity and costs. How business processes can be individualized by changes to other components such as resources, data, and the flow unit of the business process has received limited attention.

In the remainder of this paper, we address business process individualization and how digital technologies can contribute to resolving the dilemma of increased complexity costs versus satisfying external demands for individualized services. First, variation to a process cannot only be achieved by creating diverse process sequences and activities, but also by manipulation of resources, data, and the flow unit of the business process. Second, technological developments enable lower costs of providing process variation. Especially, ready access to and sophisticated analyses of vast amounts of data can increase the cost effective feasibility of process variations and change the organizing logic [54] of process design.

3.2 Synthesis of Design Patterns

The approach we employ in this study is based on the notion of design patterns introduced by Alexander [3]. With the term pattern, Alexander describes the description of an artefact endowed with a guideline that can be used for creating the artefact [4]. Further, "the term pattern appeals to the replicated similarity in a design, and in particular to similarity that makes room for variability and customization in each of the elements" [15, p. 1]. Thus, design patterns serve as general solutions to reoccurring problems, while leaving room for creative freedom [3]. In BPM, patterns have been discussed, amongst others, in the context of process models [49], control flow [2], and data flow [45].

To derive the design patterns we employed *heuristic theorizing* as outlined by Gregory and Muntermann [22]. This approach is suitable, since design patterns are a form of heuristics that help to reduce the search for a satisfactory solution [22, p. 642]. First, we *entered the heuristic search process and defined the problem at hand*, i.e. the generation of design patterns for business process individualization. Since we soon realized that process individualization can be approached from different angles, we *decomposed the problem* into simpler problems that could be approached individually. That is, we reformulated the problem to derive patterns for individualization for each of a business process' components, as defined above [32]. Next, we reviewed literature from real-life and published sources pertaining to case examples and the theoretical analysis of individualization. This extraction of prescriptive design knowledge from existing artifacts is also referred to as *design archaeology* [12]. Based on this information, we started *generating the design patterns*, followed by multiple rounds of *heuristic synthesis* and what Sein and associates call 'reflection and learning' [48]. When our patterns became stable, i.e. new cases did not change the derived design components, we *finalized the design patterns* and *exited the heuristic search process*. This *abductive* line of reasoning is common in design synthesis [30] and similar to the line of argument by Reijers et al. [42], who derive redesign patterns based on principles observed in practice and described in literature.

4   Design Patterns for Process Individualization

Based on the cases and literature analyzed, we derived four design patterns: (1) process sequence and activity individualization, (2) flow unit individualization, (3), resource individualization, and (4) data individualization. These patterns are distinct as each of them addresses a different facet of a business process. Thus, each design pattern can be used individually as well as in combination with one or more of the other design patterns. We capture this distinctive, yet interacting behavior of the patterns in Fig. 3, which depicts the resulting conceptual model.

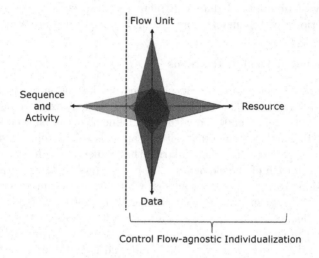

Fig. 3. Design patterns for business process individualization

Process sequence and activity individualization captures how technological developments can be used to more efficiently and effectively adjust the orchestration of tasks/steps and their sequence to provide an individualized outcome. The other three design patterns (flow unit, resource and data individualization) are *control flow-agnostic*, i.e. they do not change the control flow. We define control flow-agnostic individualization as: *Individualization that is characterized by the manipulation of data, resources, and/or the flow unit of a business process in order to tailor process outcomes to a specific customer or purpose, while at the same time, sequence and activities of the respective business process remain unaltered.*

Each design pattern is clustered in opportunity-driven and demand-driven strategies of business process individualization. Demand-driven individualization addresses explicit as well as implicit customer needs. This allows organizations to cope with increasingly differentiated customer demands [57]. In contrast, opportunity-driven individualization covers new ways that companies can use to individualize their processes by capitalizing on the rich pool of their internal resources. By aligning the business process with its context [10], effectiveness and efficiency can be further increased. In the following sections, we explain each design pattern in detail and provide evidence from practice how they can be utilized.

4.1 Sequence and Activity Individualization

Description. Sequence and activity individualization refers to the adaptation of process sequence and/or activities without changing the actual product or service. Accordingly, process sequence and execution of activities are bespoke to a particular customer, situation or condition.

Demand-Driven Sequence and Activity Individualization. First, process sequence and activity individualization can serve as a means to respond to customer needs. For example, consider the hotel brand Ritz-Carlton. Even though every guest receives the same service, i.e. an overnight stay at a hotel, the way different activities are executed is very much tailored to each individual customer [24]. Wilder, Collier and Barnes [52] discuss in detail how frontline employees can be supported in providing an adaptive service experience to customers. Beyond the question of how activities are carried out, Artificial Intelligence can provide support in choosing the next most suitable activity, i.e. answering the question what activity should be carried out. For example, IBM Watson for oncology can recommend the best next treatment option for cancer patients based on patient information and historical treatment data [27].

Opportunity-Driven Sequence and Activity Individualization. Second, companies can use process-related characteristics and information, such as process logs, to increase early individualization of their business processes. Based on historic and run-time information about the business process, more (precise) business rules and conditions can be formulated to trigger alternative process sequences. Pattern recognition can be used to derive detailed business rules given prior process instances and help configuring more individualized, robotic workflows that would not have been possible with human resources. Using current information including information about the flow unit (e.g. customer history), run-time adjustments to the process can be made. For example, banks use a combination of various attributes to calculate the loan default risk employing neural networks. These attributes can be re-incorporated into the process. Depending on the characteristics of a loan applicant, the extent of the process varies. Thus, applicants with high default risk run through a comprehensive screening, while for wealthy individuals with negligible default risk this process is shortened.

Third, environmental events or conditions can affect the execution of business processes. For example, Rosemann et al. [44] describe the claims handling process at an Australian insurance provider, which is highly context-sensitive. As some of Australia's regions are prone to storms in summer, there are considerable more claims requests in summer compared to winter. Due to the large variance in numbers of cases (more than double), the insurance provider operates two season-dependent variants of the claims handling process. While in winter there is a full registration of the claim, in summer (when there is storm season) the claims handling process is shortened to include a rapid lodgment of the claim.

Additionally, staff from other departments is re-deployed and casual staff are hired. This way, the insurance provider can offer a similar processing time, irrespective of the season. For a more detailed description of this case see [44]. The availability of micro-data has made such process individualization even more specific. For example, context-specific data about the situation of a customer (e.g. location of a car) can be used to trigger specific processes (e.g. automated remote speed-control).

Technical Realization. This type of individualization makes use of available environmental, processual, and customer related information. As processes become increasingly branched and individualized early, Artificial Intelligence can help route the respective flow units through the process. AI-algorithms can determine patterns in the data and create new process variants as the process is being executed. New variants can be compared to the existing process 'in the shadow' without impacting customers or process workers [46]. This allows not only for the formulation of more decision points, but also more complex business logic. For example, multiple attributes can be combined in order to make a decision. We can imagine that this eventually causes a shift from ex-ante process design to ongoing and even run-time and predictive process design. At the same time, declarative process modelling [38] can serve as an important tool to specify constraints in which the process has to be executed.

4.2   Flow Unit Individualization

Description. Flow unit individualization refers to the manipulation of the flow unit of a business process to deliver a unique outcome. This is the first of the three control flow-agnostic forms of individualization we present here. The sequence and activities of the process remains the same, but the flow unit is manipulated and exits the process as final individualized output.

Demand-Driven Flow Unit Individualization. Unique demands of customers can be met using flow unit individualization. For example, in the medical industry, biofabrication enables to print cell fibers, bones and even organs [33]. In case of an emergency, doctors and paramedics might soon be able to collect the details related to the injury of the patient and print the required body part. Therefore, a fiber, bone, or any other body part can be produced based on patient (customer) needs. The asset sharing platform launched by Healx is another example of demand driven flow unit individualization. It uses a machine learning algorithm based on patient's biological information to match drugs to disease symptoms and also reveal the level of effectiveness for that particular patient [29].

Koren et al. [31] discuss how the development of so-called open products allows for the re-configuration of products even after production. This product class is characterized by its customizability that allows adding physical components once the product has been purchased by the customer. Further, where the physical and the digital meet, products become re-programmable [55]. This allows producers as well as third party providers to constantly add new features to an existing physical device. Any smart device that allows for the installation of apps, such as smartphones, smartwatches, smartspeakers, etc., falls under this category. This is referred to as 'late individualization' as it only occurs when the customer is using the product over time, e.g. a standard smart phone at the point of purchase becomes a highly individualized product due to customers' downloads and settings.

Opportunity-Driven Flow Unit Individualization. Opportunity-driven individualization is initiated by internal needs of the organization. Internal needs cover various factors such as past knowledge, dearth or scads of resources or immediate need of a resource. The aerospace industry is utilizing the potential of 3D printing, as it provides unparalleled freedom in component design and fabrication [28]. Rolls-Royce is leveraging the potential of 3D printers to design and manufacture power systems for aircraft. The technology provides various advantages including design flexibility, quick iteration, and part consolidation [8]. 3D printing can also be used to produce spare parts and to repair machinery. This is of particular advantage, when idle time of capital assets result in large costs, as it is the case for trains [23], aircraft [5], different types of water-craft [40] as well as machines that are critical for production.

Flow unit individualization provides various advantages to consumers as well as businesses. Being able to produce a product based on unique consumer needs, increases customer satisfaction and trust [37]. Whereas, using available technology and resources to satisfy the internal needs of the organizations, results in reduced cost and time for businesses.

Technical Realization. Using technologies such as additive manufacturing and making use of open products and re-programmability, flow unit individualization can assist in producing a variety of products and services catered to individual consumer needs in an affordable manner. Flow unit individualization makes use of sophisticated technology to produce products based on internal needs, or cater for specific customer needs.

4.3 Resource Individualization

Description. Resource individualization determines the most appropriate resource for the activities a flow unit runs through. Because activities and process sequence remain unaltered, this type of individualization is control flow-agnostic. While resource specialization has undoubtedly led to a high level of efficiency in regards to activity execution, we argue that resources can also be used as a means to broaden the design space of business processes. Whether it is selecting an Uber driver with unique language skills for your ride to the airport, finding the right nanny for your child, or getting advice from someone with the same medical issue as yourself on patientslikeme.com, this type of individualization matches customer specific characteristics and requirements with available resources, while leaving sequence and activities of the process unchanged.

Demand-Driven Resource Individualization. Demand-driven resource individualization allows companies to respond to characteristics and likings of the customer by selecting a resource that matches these specifications. Applied correctly, resource individualization helps to increase customer satisfaction by tailoring services to customer needs. For this type of individualization, resources' personal traits and characteristics that match with customers' desires are of particular relevance. While complete business models of many start-ups and apps rely on matching resources, there are only few com-panies that use this from of resource individualization in their regular end-to-end business processes.

Platforms like Patientslikeme [36], Tinder [50], and CareGuide [11] allow customers to find patients with similar medical symptoms, a potential partner of their liking, or a perfect nanny to take care of their child. These companies provide a platform to choose resources as per one's own requirements, making the customers feel privileged and taken care of. By providing a platform, these applications essentially connect people with a predefined set of characteristics.

Opportunity-Driven Resource Individualization. Opportunity-driven resource individualization makes use of the diversity that the company internal resource-pool provides. Companies can incorporate screening processes into their regular business processes to check for and optimize current resources' utilization. When new process instances arrive, they can be routed to the most appropriate resource based on a set of predefined constraints. For example, an airline may route customer inquiries depending on the language proficiency of the customer calling. I.e. a Mandarin speaking customer will be matched with an agent that is familiar with Mandarin.

Resource individualization can also be used to ease critical process steps. This is the case when particular process activities determine the process outcome to a large extent. Often these parts of the process are non-routine and knowledge-intensive. By using specialized resources, companies are able to increase customer satisfaction, increase profitability, and guarantee that safety critical, legal or health related process aspects are executed correctly. In comparison to customer-oriented resource individualization, resources employed in process critical steps need to be highly specialized and have expert knowledge.

Insurance companies, for example, use resource individualization as part of a two-step procedure for their claims handling process. Customers calling to report on a claim, first report on some general information to an artificial call agent. The artificial call agent screens the information for inconsistencies and conspicuous patterns. If the algorithm detects any anomalies, the customer will be routed to an experienced, human call center agent. In a second step, the customer will be asked to provide more detailed information on the claimed case. A very experienced call agent can work on hard cases where fraud seems likely, while a new employee can work on easy cases that demonstrated low fraud potential in the first step of the process. As this case shows, resource individualization is most powerful, if combined with the analysis of customer information collected prior to or during process execution.

Technical Realization. From a technological perspective, resource individualization is enabled by data analytics and the information availability on customer characteristics and requirements as well as resource specific characteristics and features. With this information, companies can use classification algorithms to detect similarities and matches between customers and resources.

For demand-driven resource individualization, employing or buying all this different types of resources is not an economically viable strategy as this will cause high expenditures and yield low resource utilization. For this reason, companies can make use of crowdsourcing [9] and source tasks to individuals. For example, companies can use 99 Designs to commission different types of designs [1]. In many cases the outsourcing of tasks and sub-processes will require companies to build a community that they can default and delegate to.

For process critical steps, resource individualization helps to match already available resources with tasks that require their level of expertise. As these tasks often mark critical points of the process, require a high level of skills, experience, and trust, they cannot simply be sourced out. Also, there are only small incentives for highly experienced knowledge workers to participate in crowdsourcing.

4.4 Data Individualization

Description. With big data at the forefront, data serves as a valuable resource to make decisions [43]. Firms have access to vast amounts of customer, processual, and environmental data that provides innovation opportunities [35]. Amongst others, data can be used in a more integrated manner, to enable more agile, more accurate decision-making, and modify digital products.

Demand-Driven Data Individualization. Data can be individualized to meet the unique demands of the customer. Products and services that do not have a physical representation (anymore) such as music and movie streaming, but also insurances can make use of data individualization. For example, YouI car insurance adapts insurance premia of policy takers depending on how they use their car [56].

With the use of smart contracts on blockchain [14] or any other decentralized ledger, contracts can be automatically enforced. Insurance provider AXA offers a flight insurance against delayed flights [7] based on customer related data saved on an Ethereum blockchain. As the underlying smart contract is connected to a global air traffic database, policy holders are automatically reimbursed, once their flight is delayed. This principle can be used to adjust insurance payments to biological information, as available from fitbits or any smartwatch. This enables the tailoring of health insurances to individual characteristics and behavior of the customer. From an economic perspective, this tailoring can contribute to resolving information asymmetry, adverse selection, and moral hazard leading to more fair insurance premia.

Opportunity-Driven Data Individualization. Data individualization can also be used to enhance the decision-making process, contributing to the effectiveness of process outcomes. E.g. the Australian Taxation Office uses information from a range of social media sources to ensure relevant information is provided. Third-party sources include government bodies, employers, online selling platforms, stock exchanges, amongst others [6]. Social media and other personal data may be reviewed further, to make the right decision, when reviewing tax applications. Therefore, individual data can be used to make enhanced decisions, enabling organizations to achieve their goals in an effective manner.

Technical Realization. Data individualization is enabled by capturing, storing, and analyzing large volumes of data. Data analytics in form of Machine Learning and Artificial Intelligence provide the means to do so. To reap the benefits associated with this pattern, a strong foundation in data management is obligatory. For instance, to transform to a data driven insurer, AXA required cooperation of the data analytics, data management office and data engineering units [47]. The 3Vs, respectively 4Vs feature of big data [13] summarize the key challenges. First, companies need to be able to integrate and process data of different types and from various sources. Second, the volume of data is constantly increasing. Third, new data is continuously created (e.g. by sensors and equipment) and streamed to assigned data bases.

5   Summary and Conclusion

This paper presented a conceptual framework of four distinct design patterns for process individualization, namely: (1) sequence and activity individualization, (2) flow unit individualization, (3) resource individualization, and (4) data individualization. Drawing upon design patterns theory [3,4], the framework is built to extrapolate how different components of a process can be manipulated to derive individualization options that broaden the design space of business processes. The suggested design patterns also guide organizations on how to best apply digitalization to efficiently obtain individualized products and services at lower costs.

The resulting framework is the first to theorize about process individualization. First, by presenting a classification of process individualization options, we contribute towards theory of analyzing (Type 1), as explained by Gregor [21]. We identify and describe what different process individualization options are. We provide various examples that demonstrate how the patterns (can) materialize. Secondly, the actionable design options provide guidance on how to usefully deploy the design patterns. Presenting each design pattern in the form of sub-patterns, technical realizations and illustrative examples contributes towards theory of design and action (Type 5) [21] on process individualization.

The framework acts as a useful reference and guide for different stakeholders. For example, process owners/process change champions can use the framework to identify new opportunities to enhance their business processes with individualized products and services. Process architects can use the framework when (re-) designing a single process or a portfolio of processes; it can be applied to individualize existing processes or to design new individualized processes. It is also applicable for those engaged in product and service innovations, where a single or few of these patterns may be considered to create innovative customer experiences.

While there are many benefits, this work is still in its genesis and calls for further research. The empirical support for the design patterns were based on literature and (limited) case examples from practice. Detailed empirical validation, i.e. through in-depth case studies of existing individualization practices or

Action Design research where these patterns are newly executed, is warranted to further validate the patterns. The design patterns also need further specification in order to enhance their utility; in terms of its contextual applicability (i.e. how the patterns may be differently applicable based on process, organization and external-environmental contexts), and having detailed and validated procedure guidelines on how to implement the design patterns. Also, given the reliance of data across all patterns, data management considerations need to be carefully thought through and managed in order to maintain customer trust.

Acknowledgements. The work of Bastian Wurm has received funding from the EU H2020 program under the MSCA-RISE agreement 645751 (RISE_BPM).

References

1. 99 Designs: Design makes anything possible. https://99designs.com.au/
2. van der Aalst, W.M.P., ter Hofstede, A., Kiepuszewski, B., Barros, A.P.: Workflow patterns. Distrib. Parallel Databases **14**(1), 5–51 (2003)
3. Alexander, C.: Notes on the Synthesis of Form. Harvard University Press, Cambridge (1964)
4. Alexander, C.: The Timless Way of Building. Oxford University Press, New York (1979)
5. Alhart, T.: Brothers in arms: these robots put a new twist on 3D printing (2017). https://www.ge.com/reports/brothers-arms-robots-put-new-twist-3d-printing/
6. Australian Taxation Office: ATO Privacy Policy (2018). https://www.ato.gov.au/About-ATO/Commitments-and-reporting/In-detail/Privacy-and-information-gathering/Privacy-policy/
7. AXA: AXA goes blockchain with fizzy (2017). https://www.axa.com/en/newsroom/news/axa-goes-blockchain-with-fizzy
8. Boissonneault, T.: Rolls-Royce moves ahead with 3D printed Advance3 aircraft demonstrator engine (2018). https://www.3dprintingmedia.network/rolls-royce-advance3-engine/
9. Brabham, D.C.: Crowdsourcing as a model for problem solving. Int. J. Res. New Media Technol. **14**(1), 75–90 (2008)
10. vom Brocke, J., Zelt, S., Schmiedel, T.: On the role of context in business process management. Int. J. Inf. Manag. **36**(3), 486–495 (2016)
11. Careguide: Hire a Nanny or Find a Nanny Share. https://careguide.com/
12. Chandra Kruse, L., Seidel, S., vom Brocke, J.: Design archaeology: generating design knowledge from real-world artifact design. In: Tulu, B., Djamasbi, S., Leroy, G. (eds.) DESRIST 2019. LNCS, vol. 11491, pp. 32–45. Springer, Cham (2019). https://doi.org/10.1007/978-3-030-19504-5_3
13. Chen, M., Mao, S., Liu, Y.: Big data: a survey. Mob. Netw. Appl. **19**(2), 171–209 (2014)
14. Christidis, K., Devetsikiotis, M.: Blockchains and smart contracts for the internet of things. IEEE Access **4**, 2292–2303 (2016)
15. Coplien, J.O.: Software design patterns: common questions and answers. In: The Patterns Handbook: Techniques, Strategies, and Applications, pp. 311–320 (1998)
16. Dumas, M., La Rosa, M., Mendling, J., Reijers, H.A.: Fundamentals of Business Process Management, 2nd edn. Springer, Heidelberg (2018). https://doi.org/10.1007/978-3-662-56509-4

17. Estrada-Torres, B., del-Río-Ortega, A., Resinas, M., Ruiz-Cortés, A.: Identifying variability in process performance indicators. In: La Rosa, M., Loos, P., Pastor, O. (eds.) BPM 2016. LNBIP, vol. 260, pp. 91–107. Springer, Cham (2016). https://doi.org/10.1007/978-3-319-45468-9_6

18. Falk, T., Griesberger, P., Johannsen, F., Leist, S.: Patterns for business process improvement - a first approach. In: ECIS 2013 (2013)

19. Gilmore, J.H., Pine, B.J.: The four faces of mass customization. Harv. Bus. Rev. **75**(1), 91–101 (1997)

20. Gottschalk, F., Wagemakers, T.A., Jansen-Vullers, M.H., van der Aalst, W.M., La Rosa, M.: Configurable process models: a municipality case study. In: CAiSE 2009 (2009)

21. Gregor, S.: The nature of theory in information systems. MIS Q. **30**(3), 611–642 (2006)

22. Gregory, R.W., Muntermann, J.: Heuristic theorizing: proactively generating design theories. Inf. Syst. Res. **25**(3), 639–653 (2014)

23. Hafner, B.: Ersatzteile selber machen: 3D-Drucker machen's möglich (2018). https://blog.railcargo.com/ersatzteile-selber-machen-3d-drucker-machens-moegli ch/

24. Hall, J.M., Johnson, E.M.: When should a process be art, not science? Harv. Bus. Rev. **87**(3), 58–65 (2009)

25. Heese, H.S., Swaminathan, J.M.: Product line design with component commonality and cost-reduction effort. Manuf. Serv. Oper. Manag. **8**(2), 206–219 (2006)

26. Hu, S.J., et al.: Assembly system design and operations for product variety. CIRP Ann. - Manuf. Technol. **60**(2), 715–733 (2011)

27. IBM: IBM Watson for Oncology. https://www.ibm.com/us-en/marketplace/ibm-watson-for-oncology

28. Joshi, S.C., Sheikh, A.A.: 3D printing in aerospace and its long-term sustainability. Virtual Phys. Prototyp. **10**(4), 175–185 (2015)

29. Kavadias, S., Ladas, K., Loch, C.: The transformative business model. Harv. Bus. Rev. **94**, 91–98 (2016)

30. Kolko, J.: Abductive thinking and sensemaking: the drivers of design synthesis. MIT's Des. Issues **26**(1), 15–28 (2010)

31. Koren, Y., Shpitalni, M., Gu, P., Hu, S.J.: Product design for mass-individualization. Procedia CIRP **36**, 64–71 (2015)

32. Laguna, M., Marklund, J.: Business Process Modeling, Simulation and Design. CRC Press, Boca Raton (2013)

33. Mironov, V., Kasyanov, V., Markwald, R.R.: Organ printing: from bioprinter to organ biofabrication line. Curr. Opin. Biotechnol. **22**(5), 667–673 (2011)

34. Montgomery, A.L., Smith, M.D.: Prospects for personalization on the internet. J. Interact. Market. **23**(2), 130–137 (2009)

35. Parmar, R., Mackenzie, I., Cohn, D., Gann, D.: The new patterns of innovation: how to use data to drive growth. Harv. Bus. Rev. **92**(Jan–Feb), 86–95 (2014)

36. Patientslikeme: Living better starts here. https://www.patientslikeme.com/

37. Piccoli, G., Lui, T.W., Grün, B.: The impact of IT-enabled customer service systems on service personalization, customer service perceptions, and hotel performance. Tour. Manag. **59**, 349–362 (2017)

38. Pichler, P., Weber, B., Zugal, S., Pinggera, J., Mendling, J., Reijers, H.A.: Imperative versus declarative process modeling languages: an empirical investigation. In: Daniel, F., Barkaoui, K., Dustdar, S. (eds.) BPM 2011. LNBIP, vol. 99, pp. 383–394. Springer, Heidelberg (2012). https://doi.org/10.1007/978-3-642-28108-2_37

39. Pohl, K., Böckle, G., van Der Linden, F.J.: Software Product Line Engineering: Foundations, Principles and Techniques. Springer, Heidelberg (2005). https://doi.org/10.1007/3-540-28901-1
40. Pomerantz, D.: Ship shapes: new 3D printing research aims to rejuvenate navy gear (2018). https://www.ge.com/reports/ship-shapes-new-3d-printing-research-aims-rejuvenate-navy-gear/
41. Reichert, M., Hallerbach, A., Bauer, T.: Lifecycle management of business process variants. In: vom Brocke, J., Rosemann, M. (eds.) Handbook on Business Process Management 1. IHIS, pp. 251–278. Springer, Heidelberg (2015). https://doi.org/10.1007/978-3-642-45100-3_11
42. Reijers, H.A., Liman Mansar, S.: Best practices in business process redesign: an overview and qualitative evaluation of successful redesign heuristics. Omega **33**(4), 283–306 (2005)
43. Repenning, N.P., Kieffer, D., Repenning, J.: A new approach to designing work. Harv. Bus. Rev. **59**(2), 29–38 (2018)
44. Rosemann, M., Recker, J., Flender, C.: Contextualization of business processes. Int. J. Bus. Process Integr. Manag. **3**(1), 47–60 (2008)
45. Russell, N., ter Hofstede, A.H., Edmond, D., van der Aalst, W.M.P.: Workflow data patterns. Technical report FIT-TR-2004-01, Queensland University of Technology (2004)
46. Satyal, S., Weber, I., Paik, H., Di Ciccio, C., Mendling, J.: Shadow testing for business process improvement. In: Panetto, H., Debruyne, C., Proper, H., Ardagna, C., Roman, D., Meersman, R. (eds.) OTM 2018. LNCS, vol. 11229, pp. 153–171. Springer, Cham (2018). https://doi.org/10.1007/978-3-030-02610-3_9
47. Scheffler, A., Wirths, C.P.: Data innovation @ AXA Germany: journey towards a data-driven insurer. In: Urbach, N., Roeglinger, M. (eds.) Digitalization Cases: How Organizations Rethink their Business for the Digital Age, pp. 363–378 (2019)
48. Sein, M.K., Henfridsson, O., Purao, S., Rossi, M., Lindgren, R.: Action design research. MIS Q. **35**(1), 37–57 (2011). https://doi.org/10.2307/23043488
49. Smirnov, S., Weidlich, M., Mendling, J., Weske, M.: Action patterns in business process models. Comput. Ind. **63**(2), 98–111 (2012)
50. Tinder: Match. Date. Chat. https://tinder.com/?lang=en
51. Tregear, R.: Business process standardization. In: vom Brocke, J., Rosemann, M. (eds.) Handbook on Business Process Management 2. INFOSYS, pp. 307–327. Springer, Berlin Heidelberg (2010). https://doi.org/10.1007/978-3-642-01982-1_15
52. Wilder, K.M., Collier, J.E., Barnes, D.C.: Tailoring to customers' needs: understanding how to promote an adaptive service experience with frontline employees. J. Serv. Res. **17**(4), 446–459 (2014)
53. Wurm, B., Schmiedel, T., Mendling, J., Fleig, C.: Development of a measurement scale for business process standardization. In: ECIS 2018 (2018)
54. Yoo, Y., Boland, R.J., Lyytinen, K., Majchrzak, A.: Organizing for innovation in the digitized world. Organ. Sci. **23**(5), 1398–1408 (2012)
55. Yoo, Y., Lyytinen, K., Boland, R., Berente, N., Gaskin, J., Schutz, D.: The next wave of digital innovation: opportunities and challenges. Research workshop: "digital challenges in innovation research", pp. 1–37 (2010)
56. YouI Car Insurance: A different kind of car insurance. https://www.youi.com.au/car-insurance
57. Zhou, F., Ji, Y., Jiao, R.J.: Affective and cognitive design for mass personalization: status and prospect. J. Intell. Manuf. **24**(5), 1047–1069 (2013)

Understanding the Alignment
of Employee Appraisals and Rewards
with Business Processes

Aygun Shafagatova[✉]🆔 and Amy Van Looy🆔

Faculty of Economics and Business Administration,
Department of Business Informatics and Operations Management,
Ghent University, Tweekerkenstraat 2, 9000 Ghent, Belgium
{Aygun.Shafagatova, Amy.VanLooy}@UGent.be

Abstract. A successful implementation and adoption of Business Process
Management (BPM) requires an alignment with other management areas in an
organization, and specifically with practices related to Human Resource Management (HRM). While the BPM literature highlights the importance of aligning
HRM appraisals and rewards to business processes, little is known about how
organizations actually align these two areas in practice, and how they face the
challenges of this alignment. For this purpose, we conducted ten explorative
case studies to acquire empirical evidence and gain better insights on this issue.
We uncovered four patterns of BPM-HRM alignment and determined their
important components. This work discusses the critical factors that are important
for a successful BPM-HRM alignment and provides recommendations for this
alignment by differentiating between lower and higher levels of BPM maturity.

Keywords: Business Process Management · Process orientation · Alignment ·
Process-oriented appraisals · Process-oriented rewards · Case study

1 Introduction

In response to changing competitive environmental pressures, organizations are
undergoing fundamental transformations in their structures and management systems
[1]. The move to a horizontal process orientation is essential for organizations that are
interested in breaking down barriers within the vertical structures, improving end-to-
end communication for problem solving and increasing customer value [2]. In this
regard, Business Process Management (BPM) has been emerged as a response to these
calls to help organizations become more process-oriented.

While the technological aspects of BPM have drawn much attention, relatively
limited work has been delivered regarding the people factor of BPM [3]. However,
change in technology, processes, and structures is unlikely to yield long-term benefits
without altering human knowledge, skills and behaviors [4]. In this respect, a better
alignment between BPM and HRM practices is crucial if organizations intend to reap
the full benefits of a process orientation in the long run. More specifically, employee
appraisals and reward practices play an important strategic role to potentially influence

© Springer Nature Switzerland AG 2019
T. Hildebrandt et al. (Eds.): BPM 2019, LNCS 11675, pp. 386–401, 2019.
https://doi.org/10.1007/978-3-030-26619-6_25

employee behavior and performance. Therefore, BPM should be integrated into those HRM practices since linking appraisals and rewards to business processes will create a better line of sight for employees to focus on behavior and performance that ultimately serve to process success. Otherwise, employees will not be interested in process goals if they are merely evaluated and rewarded for functional/individual goals, and process success will be sub-optimized in this way.

However, today's holistic understanding of BPM as a management approach [3] doesn't go further than merely recognizing the importance of aligning people and HRM aspects with business processes, without a deeper examination. In particular, the strategic issue of aligning employee appraisals and rewards is still an under-researched area without profound empirical evidence from practice. To fill this gap, our research question sounds:

RQ. How do organizations align employee appraisals and rewards with their business processes?

This research contributes to a holistic approach to BPM by gaining a better understanding and deeper insight into how organizations actually align their appraisals and rewards to process needs. To this end, we report on multiple explorative case studies to offer first-hand empirical evidence and provide details about our pattern-matching exercise that identified the most important components related to the alignment of appraisals and rewards with a process orientation.

The remainder is structured as follows. Section 2 discusses relevant concepts and related works from both the BPM and HRM literature. Section 3 specifies our research method. Next, the findings are presented (Sect. 4) and discussed (Sect. 5). Section 6 ends up with concluding thoughts.

2 Theoretical Background

2.1 HRM

Employee performance appraisal is "*a variety of activities through which organizations seek to assess employees and develop their competence, enhance performance and distribute rewards*" [5] [p. 473]. Performance evaluation is based on what people achieve and how they achieve it. Consequently, the HRM literature identifies the following dimensions of employee evaluation: (1) goals and objectives, and (2) competencies [6–8] (Fig. 1). Aligning employees with the organization's strategic goals and values has become increasingly important as organizations struggle to gain or sustain a competitive advantage [9].

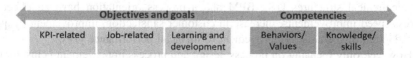

Fig. 1. Employee performance appraisal dimensions [23–25].

A reward system can be described as any conscious intervention within an organization aimed at encouraging or reinforcing required behaviors, or which compensates people for taking particular actions [4]. Typically, the reward strategies of organizations consist of two reward types: (1) financial (transactional) rewards and (2) non-financial (relational) rewards. [8, 10] (Fig. 2).

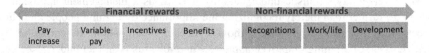

Fig. 2. Reward types [25, 27].

Employee appraisals and reward practices are grounded upon fundamental theories that shed light on divergent aspects such as motivation, goal-setting and self-determination [11–13]. Appraising and rewarding certain behaviors (and not others) has clear implications for performance. Thus, decisions about what is to be rewarded need to be made carefully and with attention to the overall business strategy [14].

The HRM literature recognizes the challenge that the existing traditional appraisals and reward systems do not fit within the context and needs of an organization that is downsized, delayered, dynamic, and diverse [1]. As a result, many organizations are rethinking their appraisals and reward strategies to better align them with the new business realities. Various studies have highlighted "reward and recognition" systems as one of HRM's major critical success elements [4].

In this regard, the recent focus on strategic HRM (SHRM) emphasizes its important role in defining and achieving the strategic goals of an organization [15]. According to the contingency debate within SHRM, there should be a fit between HRM practices and an organization's context and strategy in order to be successful and to contribute to organizational performance [16]. In this regard, however, no study was found that specifically covers this HRM fit with a business process context. Therefore, research on generic HRM appraisals, performance management and rewards (i.e. with its limited 'one-size-fits-all' approach) provides only a starting point to truly understand process-oriented appraisals and rewards.

2.2 BPM/BPO

BPM refers to a holistic management approach which focuses on the capabilities required to optimize process management practices within the organization [17]. Additionally, a Business Process Orientation (BPO) means focusing on business processes ranging from customer to customer, instead of placing emphasis on functional and hierarchical structures [18]. BPM and a process orientation have an effect on process speed improvements, increase in customer satisfaction, improvement of quality, reduction of costs, and improvement of financial performance [19].

However, only focusing on process design and process improvement is insufficient to ensure those benefits. If a redesigned process is embedded back into an existing functional organizational structure without other changes (e.g. no change in rewards and evaluations), the prevailing managerial emphasis on functional concerns will continue, and process performance will eventually suffer [20]. The horizontal processes will pull employees in one direction, while the traditional vertical (appraisals and rewards) management systems will pull them in another, resulting in confusion, conflict of interests, and eventually undermining performance [21]. Therefore, an alignment with other management systems, and especially with HRM appraisals and rewards, is essential to eliminate confusion and conflicts, and to reinforce employees to work towards process success.

While the recent focus of BPM and BPO as a holistic management discipline encourages research in a broader manner, aligning HRM appraisals and rewards to business processes remains an under-researched area. The literature agrees on the fact that if organizations want to successfully embrace BPM and BPO, their way of appraising and rewarding employees should become more process-oriented [18, 22, 23]. [24] identified HRM appraisals and rewards as one of the sub-capabilities of a process-oriented culture. [25] studied the value dimension of culture by presenting CERT (customer focus, excellence, responsibility and teamwork) as main values supporting BPM, without covering other HRM aspects. To our knowledge, no academic research exists that investigates how these aspects are aligned. Previous BPO research highlighted the people aspects of a process orientation in broad terms, such as linking employee management to a process orientation [26], exploring competencies of BPM professionals [27], roles of chief process officers [28] and process owners [29], or individual process orientation aspects [30], most of which assume an alignment between employee goals and process goals. A small number of academic publications has addressed appraisals and rewards in the context of total quality management (TQM) [31], which is less specific for BPM.

Likewise, few authors from industry have discussed the importance of making changes in performance evaluations and rewards to avoid conflicts between business processes and functions [32, 33]. While [33] implicitly covered feedback (i.e. appraisals) and consequences of performance (i.e. rewards), it does not encompass all components and facets of how process-oriented appraisals and rewards should be. Several BPM Maturity models [34–38] also mention appraisals and rewards, albeit with high-level statements. In sum, given the increasing attention for BPM/BPO and for further contextualizing employee performance, an opportunity exists to establish research that combines the HRM and BPM disciplines with regard to appraisals and rewards.

3 Methodology

Given the study's explorative character, a qualitative research approach was employed. A detailed understanding is needed since little knowledge exists [39]. Moreover, the case study research method is particularly useful in information systems (IS) research when interest has shifted to organizational rather than technical issues [40]. [41] defines a case study as *"an empirical inquiry that investigates a contemporary phenomenon (the case) in depth and within its real world context"* [p. 5]. According to [42], case study research allows to answer 'how' and 'why' questions by learning the state-of-the-art in practice to generate theory, and thus allowing insights into an emerging topic.

We conducted multiple case studies with different organizations in order to gain empirical evidence of how appraisals and rewards are actually being aligned with BPM/BPO. We employed 'maximal purposeful sampling' [40, 42] to select the case organizations in order to explore best practices. To this end, we contacted 27 potential candidate organizations via LinkedIn (of which ten positively responded) by searching for process-related management profiles (i.e. a Chief Process Officer, BPM manager or process owner), assuming that those organizations would have a higher process focus.

Table 1. Profile of the case organization and its representatives.

Coding companies	BPO maturity score	Sector	Size	Coding participants	Participant's experience in company	Participants position level	Participants expertise
Company A	3	Production-pharma	>10000	repA1	3–5 years	Low Level Management	BPM
				repA2	<1 year	Mid Level Management	HRM
Company B	2,6	Retailwholesale	>10000	repB1	5–10 years	Mid Level Management	BPM
				repB2	15–20 years	Mid Level Management	HRM
Company C	4,5	ICT Services	5001–10000	repC1	10–15 years	Top Level Management	BPM
				repC2	10–15 years	Top Level Management	HRM
Company D	2,9	Banking	>10000	repD1	1–3 years	Mid Level Management	BPM
				repD2	1–3 years	Mid Level Management	HRM
Company E	3.9	Production-pharma	>10000	repE	3–5 years	Mid Level Management	BPM
Company F	3.4	ICT Services	>10000	repF	1–3 years	Mid Level Management	IT/BPM
Company G	2.9	Banking	>10000	repG	5–10 years	Top Level Management	BPM
Company H	2.5	Human health	501–1000	repH	1–3 years	Mid Level Management	BPM
Company I	3.6	Banking	>10000	repI	>20 years	Top Level Management	IT/HRM
Company J	3.4	Production-beverages	>10000	repJ	5–10 years	Mid Level Management	IT/BPM

Data collection was conducted in two iteration rounds, resulting in 14 interviews across ten organizations in total. The first round covered four organizations with both the BPM and HRM managers as interview respondents, while the second round included six organizations with only BPM-related managers as respondents. After the first round, we felt that data from the HRM side was saturated, since the generic HRM practices that were used were all similar and confirming the HRM literature on practices, and we were specifically interested in more nuances about the process orientation side. More details about the case organizations are given in Table 1. The organizations and representatives are anonymized and coded with letters, while the rest of the data is real.

Most organizations are large in size and representatives are mostly from the top-level or mid-level management. The cases represent different sectors, such as banking (3), pharma (2), retail (1), ICT production and service (2), non-for-profit (1) and beverage production (1). Their BPM maturity varies between 2.4 and 4.5, on a 5-point Likert scale (i.e. in line with McCormack's [43] maturity assessment). This instrument has been repeatedly used in different studies and is a simple and effective way of measuring BPM maturity. The least mature case belongs to a non-for-profit healthcare organization, while the most mature case is an ICT production and service company.

3.1 Data Collection and Analysis

We used multiple sources of information [41]: semi-structured interviews, internal documents and online resources. Based on the BPM/HRM literature study, we developed semi-structured interview questions. An interview protocol was designed to guide the interview. The combination of both dimensions enabled us to depict the whole situation. For the BPM representatives, the interview questions focused more on process-oriented appraisals and rewards, while the HRM representatives were asked about generic performance management and reward practices. Nonetheless, both interviews were similarly structured: (1) general questions about the case organization and (2) the respondent, (3) BPO maturity assessment questions, followed by (4) semi-structured questions on appraisals and rewards (e.g. "Does a performance appraisal include process-related dimensions?", "Is an employee evaluated for the end-to-end Process KPIs that he/she executes? If yes, how? If no, Why not?") and (5) for BPM managers also open questions on how they align appraisals and rewards with business processes. Our explorative character enabled us to regularly refine and adjust the questions with newly acquired concepts. The interview duration was 45–60 min. Each interview was conducted face-to-face or via Skype and each respondent was inter-viewed once, with additional inquiries via email correspondence when needed. The respondents were also asked to provide relevant internal documents. In total, 129 pages of interview transcribes and 306 pages of internal and online documents were analyzed for the study. Thus, data triangulation was employed to gain a more nuanced under-standing and to enhance reliability and validity [42]. The collected internal documents were related to HRM policies, the company strategy, together with online content. All data were analyzed for further examination.

Coding, pattern-matching and content analysis techniques [40] were used to ana-lyze the data and to gain meaningful information [39, 42]. Coding was employed to categorize data (i.e. around concepts, key ideas or themes) by assigning labels (e.g. 'process owner appraisal', 'process improvement related') as units of meaning to data pieces. Since a qualitative data analysis is highly analytical and interpretive [42], we applied the NVivo coding tool. More specifically, we employed 'relational content analysis' [42, 44] since we were interested in the presence of certain concepts and in examining how those (pre-defined or emergent) concepts are related to each other within the data [39], as well as presence of certain patterns across the cases. In total, 63 nodes were made to code the data in NVivo based on 14 interviews and 28 internal and online source documents.

3.2 Research Rigor

To ensure the rigor of our qualitative study, five strategies [39] were employed: (1) triangulation of data sources and of analysis methods to increase construct validity, (2) rich analytical descriptions through summary figures to ensure transferability and validity, (3) protocols (i.e. a case study protocol and interview protocol) to enhance reliability, (4) member checking with participants to validate the accuracy and credibility of the results, and (5) interview tapes and transcripts for further reliability. Thus, we followed a rigorous approach for data collection, data analysis and reporting to ensure accuracy [39]. Yin's [41] principles of data collection were also taken into account: (1) using multiple sources of evidence (triangulation), (2) creating a case study database, (3) and maintaining a chain of evidence (for reliability). The presence of a co-author also ensured accuracy via cross-analysis and reviewing the findings [40]. Finally, an analytical generalization through theory and analysis was done in the form of best practices, namely for understanding the case's complexity [39].

4   Results

We observed a subtle gradation in how far the case organizations have aligned their appraisals and rewards to their business process needs and BPM context, indicated in Fig. 3 by means of four patterns across three gradations.

The first gradation refers to an "implicit alignment", which means embedding process-related goals and objectives in the appraisals indirectly, and only for certain departmental or functional processes. This is especially done for joint process owner roles (i.e. a functional manager who also takes a process ownership role) and for employees who execute functional processes.

The second gradation category is "limited explicit alignment", which means explicitly aligning appraisals and rewards for a limited number of end-to-end processes. In this category, two roles are remarkable: a separate (or distinct) process owner role and the process improvement teams (i.e. teams that are responsible to improve processes).

The third category is "explicit alignment", meaning explicitly applying process-oriented appraisals and rewards across the company for process owners, process improvement teams and process executing employees (i.e. employees who perform a process).

Based on pattern-matching, we differentiated four patterns or groups among the case organizations (i.e. symbolized with geometrical figures in Fig. 3). The first group has only an implicit alignment for process owners or managers, while the second group has both an implicit alignment (i.e. on the process executing employee level) and a limited explicit alignment (i.e. on the process owner and process improvement team level). The third group of cases showed a limited explicit alignment on the level of

Organizations	Comp H	Comp A	Comp B	Comp D	Comp J	Comp I	Comp E	Comp G	Comp F	Comp C
BPO Maturity score	2.4	3	2,6	2,9	3.3	3.5	3.8	2.9	3.5	4,5
Implicitly aligned (embedded and within certain department)	PO	PO	PO	PE	PE	PE	PE			
Limited explicitly aligned (certain e2e processes or units only)			PO; PIT	PO; PIT	PO; PIT	PO; PIT	PO; PIT	PO; PIT; PE; PET	PE; PIT; PET; PO	
Explicitly aligned across company										PO; PE; PIT

PO - process owner; **PE**- process executer; **PIT** - process improvement team; **PET** - process executing team

Fig. 3. Identified patterns among case organizations with regard to the appraisal and reward alignment.

process owners, process executing employees and process executing teams (i.e. teams that perform the process). Finally, the fourth group covers a single case as being a best-in-class example which has explicit alignment across the entire company for process executing employees, process owners and process improvement teams. Figure 3 also shows that BPM maturity plays a role, ranging from lower (group 1) over lower-medium (group 2, group 3) to higher BPM maturity (group 4).

4.1 Process-Oriented Appraisals and Performance Dimensions

According to the cases, crucial components for obtaining process-oriented appraisals and rewards are: (1) level and role (i.e. for whom the appraisals and evaluations is done), (2) performance dimensions (i.e. what kind of process-related performance and behavior components are included in their evaluation), and (3) reward types (i.e. which rewards they get for the process results and their contribution). As shown in Fig. 4, we identified two main components and five sub-components that can be aligned with business processes. The "objectives and goals" component has three process-related sub-components, related to: (1) process KPIs, (2) process improvements, and (3) learning and development. The "competence and behavior" component has two sub-components: (1) process-supportive behaviors and values, and (2) process-related knowledge and skills. Figure 4 summarizes the process-related evaluation dimensions per case group.

The first group of cases includes some high-level process KPIs in appraisals, but mainly for a joint process owner role. Appraisals are only within the functional, departmental boundaries. In some situations, organizations belonging to this group can have process-related objectives, or some process-supportive behavioral competencies (e.g. continuous improvement initiatives) can also be an evaluation dimension.

The second group of cases displays more BPM-HRM alignment. It concerns an explicit alignment for process owners and process improvement teams. Most of the organizations in this group already have a separate process owner position (i.e. someone who is explicitly appraised for end-to-end process performance and improvement efforts, as defined in a job description). Cross-functional process improvement teams (e.g. agile, lean, six sigma, supply chain teams) are usually responsible for process improvement projects, and are evaluated for reaching their improvement targets. Team-based appraisals in a process improvement context mostly happen informally as a project-based reflection that includes an evaluation of process KPIs or targets (e.g. in the six sigma control phase, or agile tribe and squad meetings (Case ID: i, j, d), in a post-implementation survey or in quarterly reviews of team KPIs (Case ID: e)).

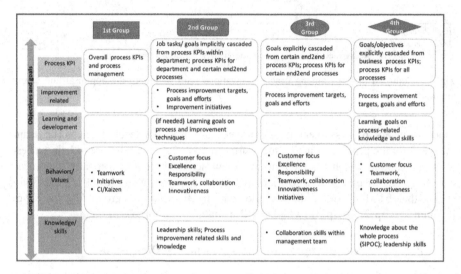

Fig. 4. Mapping of performance dimensions related to the process context of the case groups.

The appraisals of process executing employees are generally implicitly aligned, and largely depend on the department (i.e. managers decide whether to include process KPIs in evaluations or not). If included, process KPIs are mostly bounded to a department and thus internally embedded. All roles can have learning objectives regarding processes and process improvement skills. They can also be evaluated for process-supportive behaviors (e.g. customer focus, teamwork, excellence). For (Case ID: d, b), management decides whether or not to include process-related knowledge.

The third group of cases has a more explicit alignment of performance dimensions. Appraisals of employees executing certain end-to-end processes tend to include cascaded process goals. Process owners have more empowerment and are also strongly encouraged to collaborate with other process managers. Employee evaluations also contain process-supportive behavioral competencies. These organizations also have appraisals for certain end-to-end process executing teams (e.g. in monitoring and performance meetings). Process improvement teams are similar to the second group.

Finally, the fourth group has the highest BPM maturity, which also explains the highest BPM-HRM alignment across the company. Process executing employees have cascaded process KPIs, and are evaluated for SIPOC knowledge which is part of core competencies for each employee. SIPOC (i.e. supplier, input, process, output and customer) is aimed to rise process-awareness among employees. The observed issues and problems in process performance are translated into opportunities (e.g. improvement opportunities in process performance, and development opportunities for employees). Informal feedback meetings are held regularly to discuss and evaluate team performance. BPM-supportive CERT values [25] are present in appraisals, such as accountability, continuous improvement/excellence, team work, and a customer focus.

Thus, throughout the different groups, the process-oriented components eventually become part of the overall employee appraisals and evaluations which can result in rewards like yearly pay increase or bonuses (Sect. 4.2).

4.2 Process-Oriented Rewards

Similar to the performance appraisals of Sect. 4.1, rewards can also be given through different reward and recognition programs. Figure 5 represents the observed process-oriented rewards. Respectively, reward practices in organizations can be aligned on two dimensions: financial (i.e. pay increase, bonuses and incentives linked to process performance and improvement) and non-financial rewards (i.e. recognitions, celebrations, praise, positive feedback for process success). We bundled the observed reward possibilities along with the identified case groups.

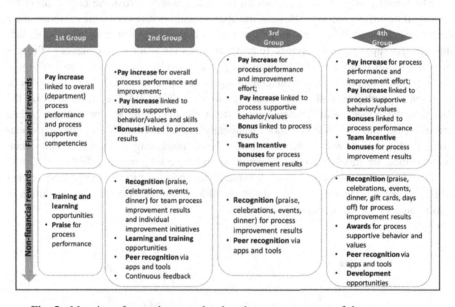

Fig. 5. Mapping of reward types related to the process context of the case groups.

The first group of organizations has the least aligned rewards. Joint process owners can get an annual pay increase as a result of yearly appraisals, which can also include process-related goals and competencies. Furthermore, process owners can get development opportunities related to process skills and praise for a good process operation.

Since most process owners are a separate role in the second group, they get explicitly rewarded with annual pay increase or bonuses, as well as recognitions for process performance and improvement efforts. Process improvement teams in this group rather get non-financial recognitions in the form of celebrations, praise and events, but mainly without financial rewards. They also get opportunities to develop their process-related skills. Process executing employees are indirectly rewarded with pay increase as a result of their overall assessment, namely if their appraisals include process-related goal achievement, process-supportive competence or a behavior evaluation (i.e. rather embedded within departments). Peer recognition via apps and tools are also used to acknowledge a contribution to common goals. Some organizations (Case ID: b, d) have initiative programs that reinforce bottom-up improvement ideas, and recognize them once they are implemented.

The third group of cases displays a more explicit reward alignment. All above-mentioned financial and non-financial rewards can be given to process owners, process improvement teams and process executing employees, with a more direct link to processes. Employees have clear process-related goals and objectives, but limited to certain end-to-end processes and certain units. They can get a pay increase and bonuses, as well as non-financial recognitions for achieving their goals. Process improvement teams usually get short-term incentive bonuses and recognitions if their improvement targets are met.

The fourth group of cases applies all possible rewards across the organization for almost all business processes. Besides the above-mentioned rewards, they also organize corporate-wide award and recognition programs to reinforce company values, including process-supportive behaviors (e.g. teamwork, innovation, excellence). Process owners can get more frequent bonuses for process results and improvement efforts.

In general, mostly middle management takes decisions on what type of rewards can be given to employees and teams. Case organizations (Case ID: d, c, b, i) recognize the fact that if feedback and informal evaluations are becoming the new normal, then rewarding should also become more frequently and aligned with continuous evaluations. In this regard, non-financial and team-based rewarding will get more important because they are flexible, foster cooperation, and have longer-term effects.

Based on our observations, Fig. 6 summarizes the evolution of the process-related employee roles depending on the scope of BPM-HRM alignment. This evolution is also related to the BPM maturity levels.

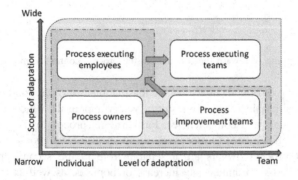

Fig. 6. Alignment scope linked to process-related roles.

Figure 6 shows that, when the scope of adaptation is narrow, only the process owners' appraisals and rewards are aligned with processes. It can grow to include process improvement teams to move from an individual level to a team level. When the scope of adaptation becomes wider, organizations also start aligning their process executing employees' appraisals and rewards to business processes (i.e. together with the two previously mentioned roles and levels). Ultimately, the scope of adaptation is at its widest point when appraisals and rewards exist on the level of process executing teams (i.e. together with the three previously mentioned roles of process owners, process improvement teams, and process executing teams).

5 Discussion

We summarized our findings on how the case organizations are aligning their appraisals and rewards with business processes in Figs. 4, 5 and 6. These figures are in line with generic HRM frameworks, while also elaborating on different process contexts. The literature of BPM maturity already positioned appraisals and rewards as a sub-capability of a process-oriented culture, which is now further enriched by the refinements of this study on process-oriented appraisals and rewards.

5.1 Critical Success Factors

The case interviews pointed us towards challenges and factors important for the success of aligning process-oriented appraisals and rewards. The respondents specifically mentioned the following five success factors.

(1) The level of BPM maturity in an organization matters a lot. The basics of BPM should be in place before organizations might consider process-oriented appraisals and rewards. Examples of preconditions are that business processes should be defined, full-time process owners should be appointed, and a process performance measurement system should be in place (Case ID: a, h). According to (Case ID: b, a, d), having a joint process owner position is not effective: while it costs less for the organization, those managers do not fully gain the required process thinking nor fully engage with the process due to a lack of time. Mostly, those process owners also lack empowerment to influence other people.

(2) An organization's culture can make or break the intended alignment. For instance, an individual mindset makes it more difficult to have team-based appraisals and rewards (Case ID: e), whereas a value-based mindset conflicts with evaluating process KPIs because behavior and values become more important in this case (Case ID: b). Resistance to change is another challenge, for which change management should be in place to facilitate a successful BPM-HRM alignment. Silo-thinking (Case ID: h, e, f) conveys an "it's not my problem" mentality in every department, which endangers cross-departmental collaboration and cooperation for process success.

(3) Top management commitment and managerial support are crucial (Case ID: d, e, b, j, c). Most respondents agree on the fact that changing behavior is easier when

it is driven top-down. For instance, in (Case ID: c), top managers were a key driver to progress that far. Leaders as a team should drive collaboration across their areas of responsibility, leading to change in the employee's attitudes and behaviors and in the way people work (Case ID: g). Furthermore, the existence of a Chief Process officer (CPO) role is equally important to drive changes (Case ID: g, c). In most cases, also the role of middle management was decisive for defining appraisals and reward procedures. Therefore, training middle managers on process thinking is crucial.

(4) All process participants should be engaged and involved in process design, process improvement and KPI definitions. Process goals/targets should be communicated to all employees involved, and the KPIs should be cascaded to lower levels to create a process awareness and increase commitment from employees (Case ID: b, d). It is also important to achieve a mind shift to give/get horizontal feedback on process executions (Case ID: b).

(5) For large and complex organizations (e.g. active across different countries and with complex legal systems), it can be hard to achieve standardization companywide and in all countries (Case ID: d, g, j, i, e). What in one country works well, does not necessarily work out in another country. Managers should acknowledge that the required BPM-HRM alignment can be achieved for certain units and employees, but not necessarily for everybody. Cascading process KPIs to the executing employee level in an effective way, seems very challenging for many cases (Case ID: d, b, e, f). A single employee does not have control over the entire business process, which can be demotivating if it is incorrectly imposed.

5.2 Recommendations Across BPM Maturity Levels

We now present recommendations for process-oriented employee appraisals and across lower and higher levels of BPM maturity (Fig. 7).

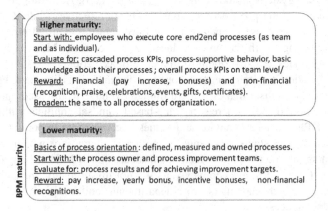

Fig. 7. Recommendations for aligning appraisals and rewards to lower and higher levels of BPM maturity.

If BPM maturity is low to medium, an organization should first make sure that the basics of BPM are in place, namely that its business processes are defined, measured and owned. In this case, the process owners and process improvement teams can be a starting point. These roles can be evaluated for process results and for achieving improvement targets. The evaluation of managers who are involved in cross-functional processes can include process-related goals and objectives, as well as behavioral competencies that support a process orientation (e.g. collaboration, change management). If an overall appraisal is tied to rewards, managers and process owners can get a pay increase or yearly bonus, as well as non-financial recognitions. Improvement teams can be rewarded with incentive bonuses (if possible) or with non-financial recognition (e.g. praise, celebration, dinner or gift cards).

In case of higher BPM maturity, organizations can go further in their alignment efforts by including process-related goals and objectives (i.e. mostly cascaded from end-to-end processes) within the evaluations of all employees who execute the core end-to-end processes. Furthermore, employees can be evaluated and rewarded for their process-supportive behavior, such as teamwork, customer focus, and continuous improvement initiatives. Process KPIs can also be defined on team level for the process executing teams, and they can be rewarded for achieving a better process performance. Continuous feedback and recognition on process performance can be given to those process teams. Afterwards, all business processes can be included in this BPM-HRM alignment. Basic knowledge about an organization's processes can be included in every employee's evaluation as being a core competence. Financial rewards (e.g. pay increase, bonuses) and non-financial rewards (e.g. days off, praise, celebrations, events, gifts, certificates) can be given to process executing employees and teams.

6 Conclusion

This exploratory case study approach has offered empirical evidence of how organizations align their employee appraisals and rewards to their particular business process context. We observed four patterns that organizations can use to ensure the required BPM-HRM alignment. We also presented an overview of the observed dimensions for process-oriented appraisals and rewards. Furthermore, we made suggestions for lower and higher levels of BPM maturity to improve the success of future alignment efforts.

Since this study intends to provide initial empirical insights, we acknowledge some limitations. The findings are based on a limited though reasonable number of cases and thus represent the experience of those organizations, albeit across different varieties of BPM maturity. Our study elaborates on the human aspects associated to the BPM discipline, and calls for a more extensive investigation with possibly a larger case sample. In future research, we will broaden our approach to end up with a comprehensive overview of possible types for process-oriented appraisals and rewards in the form of a managerial decision tool. Future research avenues can include linking and analyzing different HRM theories to an organization's BPM maturity level or to BPM practices specifically, as well as theorizing the findings with more quantitative methods and by also considering the individual employee perspective. Despite these limitations, the current work is relevant for practitioners who face challenges of misfit and conflicting messages between their organization's process orientation and their traditional way of appraising and rewarding.

References

1. Agarwal, N.C.: Reward systems: emerging trends and issues. Can. Psychol. **39**, 60–70 (1995)
2. Nadarajah, D., Syed, A., Kadir, S.L.: Measuring business process management using business process orientation and process improvement initiatives. Bus. Process Manag. J. **22**, 1069–1078 (2016)
3. vom Brocke, J., Rosemann, M.: Handbook on Business Process Management 1. Springer, Heidelberg (2015). https://doi.org/10.1007/978-3-642-45100-3
4. Zairi, M., Jarrar, Y.F., Aspinwall, E., Practices, B.: A reward, recognition, and appraisal system for future competitiveness: a UK survey of best practices, pp. 1–19 (2010)
5. Fletcher, C.: Performance appraisal and management: the developing research agenda. J. Occup. Organ. Psychol. **74**, 473–487 (2001)
6. Armstrong, M.: A Handbook of Human Resource Management Practice. Kogan Page, London (2014)
7. Aguinis, H.: Performance Management. Pearson Education Limited, Harlow (2019)
8. Noe, R., Hollenbeck, J., Gerhart, B., Wright, P.: Human Resource Management: Gaining a Competitive Advantage. McGraw-Hill, New York (2014)
9. Boswell, W.R., Boudreau, J.W.: Employee line of sight to the organization's strategic objectives – what it is, how it can be enhanced, and what it makes happen. In: CAHRS Working Paper Series, p. 69 (2001)
10. Armstrong, M.: Reward Management Practice: Improving Performance Through Reward. Kogan Page, London (2010)
11. Herzberg, F.: Pinpointing what ails the organization. J. Appl. Psychol. **55**, 73–789 (1974)
12. Ryan, R., Deci, E.: Self-determination theory and the facilitation of intrinsic motivation, social development, and well-being. Am. Psychol. **55**, 68–78 (2000)
13. Latham, G., Locke, E.: Goal-setting: a motivational technique that works. Organ. Dyn. **8**, 68–80 (1979)
14. Lawler, E.E.: Creating a new employment deal: total rewards and the new workforce. Organ. Dyn. **40**, 302–309 (2011)
15. Delery, J.E., Doty, D.: Modes of theorizing in strategic human resource management: test of universalistic, contingency and configurational performance predictions. Acad. Manag. J. **39**, 802–835 (1996)
16. Wood, S.: Human resource management and performance. Int. J. Manag. Rev. **1**, 367–413 (1999)
17. De Bruin, T., Rosemann, M.: Towards a business process management maturity model. In: Bartmann, D., Rajola, F., Kallinikos, J., Avison, D., Winter, R., Ein-Dor, P., et al. (eds.) ECIS 2005 Proceedings of the Thirteenth European Conference on Information Systems, Germany, 26–28 May 2005 (2005)
18. Willaert, P., Van den Bergh, J., Willems, J., Deschoolmeester, D.: The process-oriented organization: a holistic view. Data Knowl. Eng. **64**, 1–2 (2009)
19. Kohlbacher, M.: The effects of process orientation: a literature review. Bus. Process Manag. J. **16**, 135–152 (2010)
20. vom Brocke, J., Rosemann, M.: Handbook on Business Process Management 2. Springer, Heidelberg (2015). https://doi.org/10.1007/978-3-642-45103-4

21. Hammer, M.: The process audit. Harv. Bus Rev. **85**(4), 111–123 (2007)
22. Kohlbacher, M., Gruenwald, S.: Process orientation: conceptualization and measurement. Bus. Process Manag, J. **17**, 267–283 (2011)
23. Hammer, M., Stanton, S.: How process enterprises really work. Harv. Bus Rev. **77**(6), 108–118 (1999)
24. Van Looy, A., De Backer, M., Poels, G.: A conceptual framework and classification of capability areas for business process maturity. Enterp. Inf. Syst. **8**, 188–224 (2014)
25. Schmiedel, T., vom Brocke, J., Recker, J.: Which cultural values matter to business process management? Bus. Process Manag. J. **19**, 292–317 (2013)
26. Babic-Hodovic, V., Arslangic-Kalajdzic, M.: The influence of quality practices on BH companies' business performance. J. Manag. Cases Spec. Issue **14**(1), 305–307 (2015)
27. Müller, O., Schmiedel, T., Gorbacheva, E., vom Brocke, J.: Towards a typology of business process management professionals: identifying patterns of competences through latent semantic analysis. Enterp. Inf. Syst. **10**, 50–80 (2016)
28. Kratzer, S., Lohmann, P., Roeglinger, M., Rupprecht, L., zur Muehlen, M.: The role of the chief process officer in organizations. Bus. Process Manag. J. **25**, 688–706 (2018)
29. Danilova, K.B.: Process owners in business process management: a systematic literature review. Bus. Process Manag. J. (2018)
30. Leyer, M., Wollersheim, J.: How to learn process-oriented thinking: an experimental investigation of the effectiveness of different learning modes. Schmalenbach Bus. Rev. **65**, 454–474 (2013)
31. Waldman, D.A.: Designing performance management systems for total quality implementation. J. Organ. Change Manag. **7**, 31–44 (1994)
32. Harmon, P.: Business Process Change. Morgan Kaufmann Publishers, Burlington (2007)
33. Rummler, G., Brache, A.: Improving Performance: How to Manage the White Space on the Orgnization Chart. Jossey-Bass, San Francisco (2013)
34. OMG: Business Process Maturity Model (BPMM) (2008)
35. SEI: CMMI for Services, Version 1.3 (2010)
36. Rohloff, M.: An approach to assess the implementation of business process management in enterprises
37. Fisher, D.M.: The business process maturity model a practical approach for identifying opportunities for optimization, pp. 1–7 (2004)
38. Harmon, P.: Evaluating an organization's business process maturity executive (2004)
39. Creswell, J.W.: Qualitative Inquiry and Research Design: Choosing Among Five Approaches. Sage, Thousand Oaks (2007)
40. Myers, M., Avison, D.: An introduction to qualitative research in information systems. Qual. Res. Inf. Syst. **326**, 3–13 (2002)
41. Yin, R.K.: Case Study Research: Design and Methods. Sage Publishing, Los Angeles (2013)
42. Recker, J.: Scientific research in information systems: a beginner's guide (2013)
43. McCormack, K.P.: Business process orientation: do you have it? Qual. Prog. **34**, 51–58 (2001)
44. Krippendorff, K.: Content Analysis: An Introduction to Its Methodology. Sage Publications, Thousand Oaks (2004)

Business Process Improvement Activities: Differences in Organizational Size, Culture, and Resources

Iris Beerepoot[1,2(✉)], Inge van de Weerd[2], and Hajo A. Reijers[2,3]

[1] ICTZ B.V., Hoorn, The Netherlands
[2] Utrecht University, Utrecht, The Netherlands
{i.m.beerepoot,i.vande.weerd,h.a.reijers}@uu.nl
[3] Eindhoven University of Technology, Eindhoven, The Netherlands

Abstract. Although there are many business process improvement (BPI) methods, organizations are struggling to apply them effectively. We answer to the call to focus more on the organizational context in BPI projects. We use workarounds – deviations from the prescribed way of using an information system – as a specific angle to approach BPI. In five healthcare organizations of different contextual types, we study workarounds and make recommendations for process improvements. Based on this explorative multiple-case study, we propose a set of contextual activities for each stage of a BPI project. Thereby, we shed light on the differences in tackling process improvements in organizations that differ in size, culture, and the availability of resources for BPI projects. We evaluate the completeness and expected adoption of the proposed contextual BPI activities by organizing two focus groups and conducting a survey.

Keywords: Business process improvement · Context-awareness · Workarounds

1 Introduction

Business Process Improvement (BPI) is on the agenda of many organizations since it has the potential to improve performance, including stakeholder satisfaction and process cost and time [1, 2]. Many methods for process improvement exist, albeit under different titles: process reengineering, improvement, and process innovation [3]. Despite the availability of many methods, actually improving a business process is not an easy endeavor. A problem that may be at the heart of this is that many BPI projects follow a "cookbook approach" that does not adapt to organizational context [4]. Vom Brocke et al. [4] join Benner and Tuschman [5] in claiming that the lack of *context-awareness* is the reason that many of such projects fail. A study by Denner et al. [6] shows that only one in three Business Process Management (BPM) methods takes organizational dimensions into account, which underlines this viewpoint. A number of methods do take account of size and cultural differences – specifically, whether or not the organizations are supportive of BPM – but this is yet a limited view on the range of

© Springer Nature Switzerland AG 2019
T. Hildebrandt et al. (Eds.): BPM 2019, LNCS 11675, pp. 402–418, 2019.
https://doi.org/10.1007/978-3-030-26619-6_26

contextual factors that may be relevant. Additionally, none of the methods provide guidelines for both ends of the spectrum within these factors: e.g. for small start-ups and large multinationals [6].

We attempt to answer the call of multiple scholars [3, 7, 8] for more focus on context-awareness in BPM research and methods. We do so by focusing specifically on how to adapt BPI methods to the organizational context of the projects in which they are applied. Through our own work on the development and application of a specific BPI method, centered around "workarounds", we had the opportunity to carry out five improvement projects. These projects have all taken place within the same domain, i.e. healthcare, which ensured that we could apply our improvement method in a very similar way across the cases. By identifying and addressing workarounds, we also gained an in-depth understanding of the processes in question and closely engaged with various stakeholders. At the same time, the organizational contexts of these projects differed to such an extent that we could study and identify relevant contextual factors. On the basis of the experiences we collected in these projects, we provide an answer to the following question: *depending on an organization's context, which activities are essential in process improvement projects?* We identified the organizational contexts that are worthwhile to distinguish from each other and derived a set of essential improvement activities for each of these contexts. Throughout the paper, we will refer to these as *contextual BPI activities.*

The contribution of this work lies in our proposal of a list of contextual activities for each stage of an improvement project. These insights can help both researchers and practitioners to fine-tune their BPI method of choice. This may be beneficial to improve the success rate of the projects in which such a BPI method is applied. To ensure that our insights can indeed be transferred to and made specific for a wide range of BPI methods, we adopted the Stage-Activity framework by Kettinger et al. [9], which was recently extended by Gross et al. [3]. The framework identifies broadly recognizable stages in a BPI projects, as well as the typical activities that are carried out in these.

The structure of this paper is as follows. The next section contains an overview of the relevant literature. In Sect. 3, we describe our study's research methods. We present our proposed contextual BPI activities in Sect. 4. In the evaluation section, Sect. 5, we reflect on the completeness of our proposal and investigate its expected adoption in practice. We end our paper with a discussion of the related work on contextual factors and improvement activities in the context of our study and present ideas for future work.

2   Related Research

2.1   Context-Aware Business Process Management

Schilit and Theimer first coined the idea of context-awareness in relation to computing [10], to describe software that adapts to the location in which it is used, as well as to the objects nearby. The concept was later adopted in the BPM area and used in the sense of modeling context-aware processes [e.g. 7, 11] and context-aware process mining [12]. Vom Brocke et al. [4] designated context-awareness as the first of ten principles of good BPM. They argued that awareness of contextual factors plays a major role in the success of a BPI project and should be taken into account in relation to BPM methods. We attempt to answer the call of multiple authors [3, 7, 8] for more focus on context-awareness in BPM research and methods. The organizational factors from the framework by Vom Brocke et al. [8] and the activity framework by Gross et al. [3] form the basis for our proposal. From the extant literature, Vom Brocke et al. derive a set of contextual factors relevant for BPM. They distinguish four dimensions: goals, processes, organizations, and environments. As we are especially interested in the differences in types of organizations, we focus on the organization dimension. The organization dimension includes the factors scope, industry, size, culture, and resources.

Gross et al. [3] built on the Stage-Activity framework by Kettinger et al. [9]. Kettinger et al. distinguished six stages in Business Process Reengineering projects: (1) envision, (2) initiate, (3) diagnose, (4) redesign, (5) reconstruct, and (6) evaluate. They proposed a set of activities to be executed during each stage. Gross et al. [3] extended this framework with several more contemporary activities. In this study, we highlight from Gross et al.'s BPI activities the essential ones for each stage, depending on the contextual factors of an organization.

2.2 Workarounds as a Source for Business Process Improvement

In BPM literature, workarounds are often discussed in the context of users of process modeling languages, such as BPMN, inventing alternative ways of modeling processes [13–16]. Studies in other research domains discuss workarounds enacted by end users of ISs in general, or specific types of ISs such as Health Information Systems (HISs). They are often described as a form of appropriation [20] and a response to blockages [16], rigid constraints [17], or a misalignment between design and practice [18]. Fortunately, there is a positive side to workarounds. By acknowledging them, instead of ignoring them, organizations can perform corrective actions and improve their work systems [17, 18]. In earlier work, we developed the *Workaround Snapshot Approach* for identifying, analyzing and addressing workarounds in organizations, in order to achieve work system improvement [19]. We use this approach as a context for studying the role of organizational dimensions in improvement projects and to derive a set of contextual activities.

3 Methods

In this study, we explore how process improvement is to be tackled within different organizational contexts. We followed an explorative multiple-case study approach to identify contextual factors that influence the choice of activities in process improvement projects. The multiple-case study approach enabled us to investigate a contemporary phenomenon in its real-world context [20]. Furthermore, it allowed us to recognize general patterns in different settings [21] and to increase the external validity of our insights [20]. We assessed the completeness of these contextual factors and activities by engaging with two focus groups. Finally, we carried out a questionnaire to evaluate the adoption of the contextual activities in future process improvement projects.

3.1   Case Selection

We investigated five different organizations. Because the goal of our study is to replicate findings across cases [20], we chose our cases from one sector: healthcare. Focusing on organizations in one sector made it easier to compare the cases, as several variables (industry, scope) remained constant. In the healthcare sector, optimal process support is particularly important since care processes transcend departments [22] and are less predictable than industrial processes [23]. Table 1 presents an overview of the five case organizations we studied. All organizations use the same HIS, which is used for managing information related to patient records, patient logistics, and other administrative data. Although all organizations are from the same sector, they have several distinctive characteristics in terms of organization type, size, culture, etc.

Table 1. Overview of case organizations and their characteristics.

Case	Type	Department	Size	Culture	Resources
A	General hospital	Orthopedics and surgery	Medium	Flat	Average
B	District hospital	Urology and cardiology	Large	Hierarchical	Many
C	District hospital	Urology and pulmonary	Large	Hierarchical	Many
D	Specialized center	Rehabilitation	Small	Flat	Few
E	Specialized center	Rehabilitation	Small	Flat	Few

3.2   Data Collection

Data collection was performed by the first author of this paper and took place between April 2017 and August 2018. As presented in Table 2, data were collected via observations of caregivers, unstructured interviews with the observed caregivers, and semi-structured interviews with team leads, IT managers, and HIS experts. By using these multiple sources of data we enhanced the reliability of our analysis [21].

Table 2. Overview of data collection techniques and informants.

Type	Amount	Informants	Collection
Observations and unstructured interviews	16 (106 h)	Caregivers: physicians, nurses, office secretaries, clinical secretary, physician assistant, team lead, therapists	Field notes
Semi-structured interviews	22 (24 h)	Team leads, information architect, HIS experts, IT managers and coordinators, care administration employee	Recorded and transcribed

3.3   Data Analysis

We analyzed our data in several iterations. First, we conducted a *within-case analysis* of each of our case organizations. We reduced and made sense of the collected data by structuring our interview transcripts and field notes in 51 workaround snapshots. These snapshots capture a description of the workaround, the roles involved, a process model, an illustration of the impact on the existing process, the motivation of the user to enact the workaround, and an advice on how to use the snapshot as a basis for BPI in the organization [19]. This advice was based on the interviews with caregivers and HIS experts.

In our *across-case analysis*, we compared our workaround snapshots with the activity framework of Gross et al. [3]. Furthermore, we analyzed for each case organization the corresponding contextual factors from the framework by Vom Brocke et al. [8]. As the scope and industry of our cases were all equal – intra-organizational and healthcare sector – we focused on the differing contextual factors in size, culture, and resources. We collected information about those three contextual factors (presented in Table 1) from the caregivers and experts. Finally, for each type of context, we prioritized the most important activity for change. Figure 1 illustrates the methodological framework of our case study by showing how our within-case analysis and across-case analysis are connected. The result of our case analysis was a matrix containing activities for BPI linked to contextual factors.

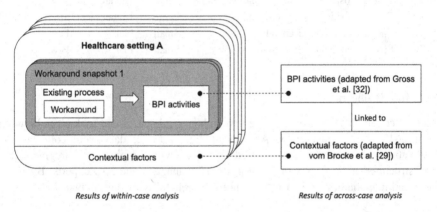

Fig. 1. Methodological framework of the multiple-case study.

3.4   Evaluation

We evaluated the case study results through two focus groups and a questionnaire. The participants in these evaluations were all employees of the company that implemented the HISs in the five case organizations. In addition to their current role as HIS consultant or developer, most of the participants also had an extensive background in the healthcare industry (e.g. as nurse or IT manager in a hospital). Table 3 provides an overview of the participants involved in the evaluation.

The goal of the *focus groups* was to test the *completeness* of the found BPI activities and their linked contextual factors. We organized two focus groups of six and two participants; HIS experts with extensive experience in healthcare organizations. We presented our BPI activities and contextual factors to the participants and asked them to evaluate these. We encouraged them to propose different contextual factors or activities if they did not fully agree.

The goal of the *questionnaire* was to discover whether possible end users intended to follow our proposed prioritization of BPI activities in their role as process change agents in new encounters. We developed a questionnaire based on Moody's method evaluation model [24] to evaluate our proposed set of activities on ease of use, usefulness, and intent to use. The questionnaire was administered to three HIS consultants. We first explained our proposal of factors and activities in detail and then let them answer the questions.

Table 3. Evaluation participants (BC, FC, TC = Business, Functional, Technical Consultant).

Evaluation part	Occupation	Previous occupation(s)	Years in healthcare
Focus group 1	Manager Business Improvement	IC nurse & head of IT (in hospital)	33
Focus group 1	Senior BC	IT developer (in hospital)	15
Focus group 1	Business Developer	Account manager	9
Focus group 1	Team Lead TCs	Senior TC	7
Focus group 1	Account Manager	N.a.	4
Focus group 1	CISO & Service Delivery Manager	N.a.	4
Focus group 2	Team Lead FCs	Senior FC	12
Focus group 2	Product Owner & Senior FC	N.a.	3
Questionnaire	Team Lead BCs and Senior BC	Nurse & Senior IT Advisor (in hospital)	29
Questionnaire	Senior BC	Nurse & Manager IT (in hospital)	30
Questionnaire	Junior BC	N.a.	1

4   Contextual BPI Activities

Based on our interviews and observations with HIS users and experts in five organizations that differ in context, we derived a set of contextual BPI activities and discuss these in detail in the following sections.

4.1   Envision

What is evident from our observations and interviews is that the identification of workarounds and the development of snapshots needs to be preceded by a set of preparation activities. For all types of organizations, it is essential to identify the process stakeholders and boundaries. What distinguishes the different contexts is the culture factor, specifically in terms of hierarchy. For hierarchical settings, it appeared to be especially important to establish management commitment and adhere to their vision. In case C, not all managers were sufficiently included in the pre-stages of the project. As a result, the improvement project was discontinued. On the other hand, in non-hierarchical settings such as case A, D and E, it appeared much more important to evaluate the existing culture when starting a BPI project. In such organizations, although change procedures are often undocumented, there are implicit procedures in place. When these procedures are not adhered to, resistance from staff can be expected. Table 4 presents the contextual BPI activities for the first stage.

Table 4. Contextual BPI activities in the envision stage.

Dominant factor	Values	Activities
Culture	Hierarchical	Establish and adhere to management commitment and vision
	Flat	Evaluate existing culture and implicit procedures
	All	Identify process stakeholders and identify process boundaries

4.2   Initiate

The findings presented in the envision stage highlight the importance of gaining commitment from staff – either through establishing commitment from management or through adhering to implicit procedures. In the initiation stage, gaining commitment from all those involved only becomes more important. If the staff is not committed, the diagnosis stage will be unsuccessful. Different types of organizations can be distinguished in this stage by their size. In large organizations we experienced the importance of defining ownership: during our research in case B, we discovered that another group within the organization felt they were assigned the task of improving the process in question. This could have been prevented by establishing ownership in the initiation stage of the improvement project. In smaller organizations it is less likely that two groups are working on the same task without them knowing about each other. In such organizations, it has turned out to be much more important to inform stakeholders of the initiation of the improvement project, giving them a chance to express their interest in the project and their willingness to contribute. Furthermore, in these organizations it is much more manageable to include the larger part of the stakeholders involved than in larger organizations. Table 5 shows the contextual activities related to this stage.

Table 5. Contextual BPI activities in the initiate stage.

Dominant factor	Values	Activities
Size	Large	Define ownership
	Small	Inform stakeholders
	All	Gain staff commitment

4.3 Diagnose

In the diagnosis stage, we again use size to distinguish different contexts, as presented in Table 6. Larger organizations allow for comparison of processes and workarounds over different departments within the same organization. A team lead described a specific workaround used in the urology department in case C and recalled the use of a similar workaround in the cardiology department. Such settings allow for bench-marking comparable processes in different departments of the same organization. In smaller organizations such as medical rehabilitation centers, there are seldom similar processes to compare with. What is more common in such organizations is to organize discussion meetings with similar organizations that encounter the same obstacles. A solution found by one can sometimes be directly implemented by another. For example, medical rehabilitation center D used an open source tool developed for autistic children to create daily schedules for rehabilitants with neurological damage. In medical rehabilitation center E, they used Microsoft Word to make such schedules. One of the recommended actions captured in the snapshot was for organization E to use the same tool as it was much more efficient. What appears to be important for all types of organizations is to obtain quantitative data on processes using techniques such as process mining. Diagnosis is currently most often done qualitatively, using a small sample. Analysis of a larger data set would allow for a more complete diagnosis of inefficient processes.

Table 6. Contextual BPI activities in the diagnose stage.

Dominant factor	Values	Activities
Size	Large	Benchmark process from within company
	Small	Benchmark process from competitors
	All	Obtain quantitative process data, e.g. via process mining

4.4 Redesign

During the redesign stage, we found that it is important for all organizations to estimate the required resources and organizational change needed. Only when this is done, it can be decided whether to move forward with the redesign. Not making a thorough esti-mation of the required resources and organizational change can endanger the continuity of the improvement process and can result in the loss of staff commitment. High-resource organizations making a significant investment in process improvement will also need to develop an elaborate improvement plan on top of this estimation in order to make the most of their investment. Organizations with a smaller budget will benefit from utilizing their stakeholders' knowledge of the process in coming up with improvement ideas in order to save resources. Moreover, having the stakeholders contribute improvement ideas often raises their engagement with the improvement project. Table 7 shows the contextual activities related to this stage.

Table 7. Contextual BPI activities in the redesign stage.

Dominant factor	Values	Activities
Resources	Many	Develop detailed improvement plan
	Few	Collect improvement ideas from stakeholders
	All	Estimate required resources and organizational change needed

4.5 Reconstruct

In Table 8, we present the contextual activities related to the reconstruct stage. We noticed in our case organizations the many consequences process changes can have on other processes. In smaller organizations, these consequences can be easily overseen. However, in larger organizations, the potential impact of changes on other processes need to be analyzed in order to prevent harmful consequences. We also experienced a certain 'change fatigue' in these larger organizations. Participants were frequently confronted with new change programs, receiving many communications on what was happening and what they needed to change in their work practices. In smaller organizations, stakeholders constantly reminded the interviewer that they wanted to be involved in any process changes. We therefore recommend smaller organizations to emphasize the communication of any information related to the improvement project, whereas we recommend larger organizations to hold back on heavy communication. For both types we see the importance of integrating process changes into existing processes. If not, keeping up with process changes will become unmanageable for process stakeholders.

Table 8. Contextual BPI activities in the reconstruct stage.

Dominant factor	Values	Activities
Size	Large	Analyze potential impact for other processes
	Small	Communicate process changes
	All	Integrate process

4.6 Evaluate

Building on the previous stage, we again make the distinction between different sizes, as described in Table 9. As larger organizations often have other improvement programs running, we suggest they should look for opportunities to link individual process improvement activities to existing programs. Doing so will hopefully decrease the change fatigue that participants are experiencing in these organizations. As mentioned in the previous stage, we found that participants in smaller organizations would like to be more involved and would like to hear about any outcomes of process changes. We therefore recommend smaller organizations to emphasize the communication of these outcomes to stakeholders. The importance of monitoring the changing environment and processes applies for all types of organizations. Processes and workarounds are always in flux and need to be monitored over time.

Table 9. Contextual BPI activities in the evaluate stage.

Dominant factor	Values	Activities
Size	Large	Link to continuous improvement programs
	Small	Report key process change outcomes
	All	Monitor environment for future needs to change

5   Evaluation

To evaluate the completeness of the contextual activities and the expected adoption of our proposal in practice, we organized two focus groups and distributed a questionnaire among potential end users of the method.

5.1   Completeness of the Contextual Factors

During one of the focus groups, an interesting discussion on the organizational factors of healthcare organizations arose. One of the critical notes was that, in the future, the amount of beds in hospitals would not be a valuable indicator of size, since healthcare is moving more and more towards home care. Looking at revenue and number of employees would give a more realistic view of the size of these organizations.

Another proposal made in the focus group was to add the contextual factor of maturity. Some organizations are more mature than others, for example by having procedures in place to address problems and knowledge present to bring HIS projects to successful completion. It was mentioned that in mature organizations, it would be possible to focus more on quality and patient satisfaction. In contrast, immature organizations need to focus on solving problems and getting their processes in order in the first place. However, participants in the focus groups acknowledged that it would be difficult to categorize organizations into a scale of maturity and the organizations themselves might be inclined to make misjudgments as to how they fare on the ladder. Moreover, many examples were given of small organizations that are in some aspects very mature and big organizations being surprisingly immature on some levels. This shows that it would be difficult to define simplified profiles, such as big, mature organizations and small, immature organizations. Doing so, we would exclude many organizations. The other three factors – size, culture and resources – are often interdependent. Most big organizations are hierarchical and have more resources than the more flat and smaller organizations, with some exceptions. In Table 10 we summarize the focus group's evaluation of the proposed context factors.

Table 10. Summary of the evaluation of contextual factors.

Opposed	Confirmed	Proposed additions
Operationalization of size: number of beds	Culture: flat or hierarchical	Operationalization of size: revenue and number of employees
	Resources: many or few	Maturity: mature or immature

5.2   Completeness of the Contextual Activities

Focusing on the activities of the method, some possibly missing ones were noted. First, the importance of the activities 'realize need for change' in the envision stage and 'outline key measurement variables' in the improvement stage were stressed by the focus group participants. This would apply for all types of organizations. The key measurement variables would then need to be evaluated in the evaluate stage. Such an activity is not included in the list of Gross et al. [3], although the activity 'evaluate process performance' comes close. Another activity considered important for all types of organizations in the evaluate stage is also not in the list of activities, namely 'solicit feedback'. This activity is listed in the improvement stage but is considered even more important in the evaluate stage according to the participants.

The participants also mentioned that – apart from the distinction in *which* activities to perform depending on context, which they mostly agreed on – a distinction can be made in *how* to perform certain activities. For example, when performing the activity 'analyze existing process' during the diagnosis stage, the way the data is collected differs depending on the type of organization. In a small medical rehabilitation center with only two secretaries at the front desk, the means of data collection and communication of process changes would differ considerably from a big hospital with sixty to seventy secretaries at multiple front desks.

What was evident both from our experience in looking at workarounds in the five cases and from the participants' experience in other healthcare organizations, many users of HISs experience a significant level of change fatigue. Especially caregivers in bigger organizations have participated in several reorganizations and process improvement programs. It is therefore important to prioritize process changes; to not only gain their commitment but also to retain their commitment, by soliciting feedback when necessary and by feeding back the results they helped achieve. In Table 11 we summarize the focus group's evaluation of the contextual BPI activities.

Table 11.   Summary of the evaluation of activities.

Opposed	Confirmed	Proposed additions
None	All	Realize need for change (stage: envision)
		Outline key measurement variables (stage: redesign)
		Evaluate process performance (stage: evaluate)
		Solicit feedback (stage: evaluate)

5.3   Expected Adoption of Our Proposal in Practice

The questionnaire on the ease of use, usefulness and intent to use of our proposed set of contextual BPI activities was completed by two senior business consultants (one of whom was also the team lead of the business consultancy team) and one junior business consultant. We scored the answers from 1 to 5 (e.g. for statement #1: strongly disagree = 1 and strongly agree = 5). Note that the scores on the negatively worded statements #4, #7, and #9 need to be inversed for a correct interpretation.

Our proposal is considered easy to understand and use (average of statements #1 through #4 = 3.75), although for those spending little time in the concerning organizations it may be difficult to apply in practice. Moreover, it is considered useful (statements #5 through #8 = 3.75 on average) but does not necessarily make it easier to perform BPI projects than other methods. The intention to use the ideas we proposed is high (statements #7 and #8 = 4.0 on average). The full results are depicted in Table 12.

Table 12. Results from the questionnaire on ease of use, usefulness and intent to use.

#	Statement	Strongly disagree (1)	Dis-agree (2)	Neutral (3)	Agree (4)	Strongly agree (5)
1	In general, the method seems to be well-applicable	0	0	0	3	0
2	It seems easy to learn the method	0	0	0	2	1
3	I find the stages and activities of the method clear and easy to understand	0	0	0	3	0
4	I am not confident I can apply the method in practice	0	1	1	0	1
5	I believe that this method can improve the work practices of HIS users	0	0	1	1	1
6	This method makes it easier for me to tackle improvement projects in healthcare organizations	0	0	2	1	0
7	I find other improvement methods more useful than this method	0	1	2	0	0
8	In general, I find this method useful	0	0	0	2	1
9	I would definitely not use this method to improve the use of HISs in healthcare organizations	1	2	0	0	0
10	I intend to use this method in future projects	0	0	1	2	0

6 Discussion

In this study, we argued that the essential BPI activities differ for organizations of varying size, culture, and resources. For each stage in a BPI project, we pointed out the dominant factor to distinguish organizations and suggested the corresponding contextual activities. In the following, we discuss related work on contextual factors and BPI activities and their relation to our study.

In four of the six stages of BPI projects, we found size to be the dominant factor in determining BPI activities for an organization. The importance of organizational size has been noted in several other studies. For example, a large firm size appeared to be the largest contributor to Total Quality Management success after industry type [25]. Similarly, Shah and Ward [26] studied the role of organizational context in lean manufacturing and concluded that plant size was the largest influencer in the likelihood of implementing lean practices. In IT innovation studies, organizational size also has been considered an important predictor of IT innovation adoption [27]. Our study complements these findings by suggesting that size is also an important factor in another way, namely in distinguishing which activities should be carried out during BPI projects.

The second contextual factor we studied was culture. As Schmiedel et al. [28] state: "bluntly put, BPM initiatives often fail for cultural reasons". Culture has been argued to be an important factor in BPM. BPM is often more successful when cultural values are high [29]. Moreover, the success of BPM methodologies depends on the culture of an organization. Thiemich and Puhlmann [30] for example, argued that an organization open for change benefits from the use of agile methodologies, while a continuity-valuing organization might benefit more from using traditional methods [8]. The difference in suitable management styles in organizations varying in culture has also been noted by Donaldson [31]. The latter also mentioned that size and culture are linked in this respect. Bureaucracy and hierarchy are often more suitable in bigger organizations than in smaller ones. Our results confirm these insights: we found the hierarchical culture of an organization an important factor in determining the pivotal activities in BPI projects.

The third contextual factor that we looked into was resources. This factor has received less attention in BPM studies than size and culture, but our study suggests that it is nonetheless an important aspect to consider in BPI projects. In the context of open process innovation, Niehaves [32] studied the role of personnel resource scarcity. He found that BPM outcomes are affected by personnel scarcity as it decreases customer involvement. Several authors have mentioned the importance of stakeholder involvement for improving processes, also in the context of workarounds. Wheeler et al. [33], for instance, state: "in the case of workarounds, organizations could capitalize on the mindfulness of employees by encouraging employees to share their workarounds in order to improve task design". It is believed that insights from users can guide system design [34, 35] and decrease resistance towards the system [36, 37]. In other words, even though previous studies have touched on this topic, our study puts the resources factor firmly on the map as an important contextual factor.

In the evaluation of our proposal, another contextual factor was raised: maturity. In the BPM literature, several studies have distinguished the difference between mature and immature organizations. For example, Reijers et al. [38] argued that "BPM projects are performed in a more systematic manner in larger and more mature organizations". Similarly, according to Burlton [39], "the more mature the organization is with regard to BPM, the more·sophisticated their process governance framework and their commitment to it". Ravesteyn and Jansen [40] went a step further and proposed a situational BPMS implementation method that uses an organization's maturity level to configure the activities that should be executed. In our study's evaluation it was mentioned that immature organizations need focus on improving existing processes – called *exploitation* [41] – while more mature organizations can move beyond their existing processes and focus on *exploration*. However, we recognize that most current organizations focus on exploitation and are not yet ready to move towards exploration [3]. Additionally, we found that it was difficult to assess the healthcare organizations of our study as either mature or immature. BPM maturity models such as the one by Rosemann [42] might be of help to operationalize the contextual factor maturity.

Until now, we discussed the different contextual factors separately. However, the factors size, culture, and resources are tightly linked. Most larger organizations have a hierarchical structure and more resources than the smaller and flatter organizations, with some exceptions. This finding of interdependency of contextual factors supports statements by several others [8, 26, 43, 44].

Our study does have limitations. The data collection was performed by one researcher only. However, we did collect data in multiple ways and have performed different methods of evaluation (including a quantitative survey) in order to make sure subjective views did not cloud the findings too much. Moreover, we proposed contextual BPI activities based on an intensive case study of five organizations, all of which in the healthcare sector, which provided a meaningful set for comparison. The small number of cases and the sole industry makes generalization difficult. Therefore, we extensively evaluated the proposed activities, leading to a number of clues for where our proposal might fall short in generalizability. Future studies may reveal whether our proposal would be applicable in other industries.

7 Conclusion and Future Work

In this study, we attempted to identify which activities are essential in improvement projects depending on organizational size, culture, and resources. We used a multiple-case study approach to discover how improvement is to be tackled in organizations of different contexts. We focused specifically on organizations in the healthcare sector, although findings may be generalizable to other sectors as well. We proposed a set of contextual activities for each stage in process improvement projects and evaluated our proposal on multiple levels. The evaluation revealed several points of departure for further refining our proposal. (1) In addition to size, culture, and resources, the maturity of an organization may be an important factor in tackling improvement projects. (2) The contextual factors size and maturity need to be further operationalized. For example, in the future, distinguishing healthcare organizations using number of beds will become irrelevant, as most of the care will be brought to the home. (3) In addition to defining the essential activities for each organizational context, we might also make a distinction in the way in which an activity is performed. (4) The stakeholders in improvement projects may experience a high level of change fatigue, which will need to be taken into account when tackling improvement projects in organizations.

In general, our proposal for the identification of contextual factors is considered relatively useful and easy to understand, although it may not be easy to apply for all. The intention to use the ideas is high among the three participants we involved in the questionnaire. Future work may look into the role of an organization's maturity in identifying contextual improvement activities. It may also focus on evaluating our proposal for sectors other than healthcare.

References

1. Altinkemer, K., Ozcelik, Y., Ozdemir, Z.D.: Productivity and performance effects of business process reengineering: a firm-level analysis. J. Manag. Inf. Syst. **27**, 129–162 (2011)
2. Vanwersch, R.J.B., et al.: A critical evaluation and framework of business process improvement methods. Bus. Inf. Syst. Eng. **58**, 43–53 (2016)
3. Gross, S., Malinova, M., Mendling, J.: Navigating through the maze of business process change methods. In: Proceedings of the 52nd Hawaii International Conference on System Sciences (2019)
4. Vom Brocke, J., Schmiedel, T., Recker, J., Trkman, P., Mertens, W., Viaene, S.: Ten principles of good business process management. Bus. Process Manag. J. **20**, 530–548 (2014)
5. Benner, M.J., Tushman, M.L.: Exploitation, exploration, and process management: the productivity dilemma revisited. Acad. Manag. Rev. **28**, 238–256 (2003)
6. Denner, M.-S., Röglinger, M., Schmiedel, T., Stelzl, K., Wehking, C.: How context-aware are extant BPM methods? - development of an assessment scheme. In: Weske, M., Montali, M., Weber, I., vom Brocke, J. (eds.) BPM 2018. LNCS, vol. 11080, pp. 480–495. Springer, Cham (2018). https://doi.org/10.1007/978-3-319-98648-7_28
7. Rosemann, M., Recker, J.C., Flender, C.: Contextualisation of business processes. Int. J. Bus. Process Integr. Manag. **3**, 47–60 (2008)
8. vom Brocke, J., Zelt, S., Schmiedel, T.: On the role of context in business process management. Int. J. Inf. Manag. **36**, 486–495 (2016)
9. Kettinger, W.J., Teng, J.T.C., Guha, S.: Business process change: a study of methodologies, techniques, and tools. MIS Q. **21**, 55–80 (1997)
10. Schilit, B.N., Theimer, M.M.: Disseminating active map information to mobile hosts. IEEE Netw. **8**, 22–32 (1994)
11. Ploesser, K., Recker, J.C.: Context-aware methods for process modeling. In: Business Process Modeling: Software Engineering, Analysis and Applications, pp. 117–134. Nova Publishers (2011)
12. Günther, C.W., Rinderle-Ma, S., Reichert, M., Van Der Aalst, W.M.P., Recker, J.: Using process mining to learn from process changes in evolutionary systems. Int. J. Bus. Process Integr. Manag. Spec. Issue Bus. Process Flex. **3**, 61–78 (2008)
13. Recker, J.: Opportunities and constraints: the current struggle with BPMN. Bus. Process Manag. J. **16**, 181–201 (2010)

14. Hahn, C., Recker, J., Mendling, J.: An exploratory study of IT-enabled collaborative process modeling. In: zur Muehlen, M., Su, J. (eds.) BPM 2010. LNBIP, vol. 66, pp. 61–72. Springer, Heidelberg (2011). https://doi.org/10.1007/978-3-642-20511-8_6

15. Puhlmann, F., Weske, M.: Investigations on soundness regarding lazy activities. In: Dustdar, S., Fiadeiro, J.L., Sheth, Amit P. (eds.) BPM 2006. LNCS, vol. 4102, pp. 145–160. Springer, Heidelberg (2006). https://doi.org/10.1007/11841760_11

16. Weber, I., Haller, J., Mulle, J.A.: Automated derivation of executable business processes from choreographies in virtual organisations. Int. J. Bus. Process Integr. Manag. **3**, 85 (2008)

17. Lalley, C., Malloch, K.: Workarounds: the hidden pathway to excellence. Nurse Lead. **8**, 29–32 (2010)

18. Safadi, H., Faraj, S.: The role of workarounds during an opensource electronic medical record system implementation. In: ICIS 2010 Proceedings, St. Louis (2010)

19. Beerepoot, I., Van De Weerd, I.: Prevent, redesign, adopt or ignore: improving healthcare using knowledge of workarounds. In: ECIS 2018 (2018)

20. Yin, R.K.: Case Study Research and Applications: Design and Methods. Sage Publications, Thousand Oaks (2017)

21. Eisenhardt, K.M.: Building theories from case study research. Acad. Manag. Rev. **14**, 532–550 (1989)

22. Lenz, R., Reichert, M.: IT support for healthcare processes. In: van der Aalst, W.M.P., Benatallah, B., Casati, F., Curbera, F. (eds.) BPM 2005. LNCS, vol. 3649, pp. 354–363. Springer, Heidelberg (2005). https://doi.org/10.1007/11538394_24

23. Reijers, H.A., Russell, N., van der Geer, S., Krekels, G.A.M.: Workflow for healthcare: a methodology for realizing flexible medical treatment processes. In: Rinderle-Ma, S., Sadiq, S., Leymann, F. (eds.) BPM 2009. LNBIP, vol. 43, pp. 593–604. Springer, Heidelberg (2010). https://doi.org/10.1007/978-3-642-12186-9_57

24. Moody, D.L.: The method evaluation model: a theoretical model for validating information systems design methods. In: ECIS 2003 Proceedings, p. 79 (2003)

25. Jayaram, J., Ahire, S.L., Dreyfus, P.: Contingency relationships of firm size, TQM duration, unionization, and industry context on TQM implementation: a focus on total effects. J. Oper. Manag. **28**, 345–356 (2010)

26. Shah, R., Ward, P.T.: Lean manufacturing: context, practice bundles, and performance. J. Oper. Manag. **21**, 129–149 (2003)

27. Lee, G., Xia, W.: Organizational size and IT innovation adoption: a meta-analysis. Inf. Manag. **43**, 975–985 (2006)

28. Schmiedel, T., vom Brocke, J., Recker, J.: Culture in business process management: how cultural values determine BPM success. In: vom Brocke, J., Rosemann, M. (eds.) Handbook on Business Process Management 2. IHIS, pp. 649–663. Springer, Heidelberg (2015). https://doi.org/10.1007/978-3-642-45103-4_27

29. Schmiedel, T., vom Brocke, J., Recker, J.: Which cultural values matter to business process management? Results from a global Delphi study. Bus. Process Manag. J. **19**, 292–317 (2013)

30. Thiemich, C., Puhlmann, F.: An agile BPM project methodology. In: Daniel, F., Wang, J., Weber, B. (eds.) BPM 2013. LNCS, vol. 8094, pp. 291–306. Springer, Heidelberg (2013). https://doi.org/10.1007/978-3-642-40176-3_25

31. Donaldson, L.: The Contingency Theory of Organizations. Sage, Thousand Oaks (2001)

32. Niehaves, B.: Open process innovation: the impact of personnel resource scarcity on the involvement of customers and consultants in public sector BPM. Bus. Process Manag. J. **16**, 377–393 (2010)

33. Wheeler, A.R., Halbesleben, J.R.B., Harris, K.J.: How job-level HRM effectiveness influences employee intent to turnover and workarounds in hospitals. J. Bus. Res. **65**, 547–554 (2012)
34. Blandford, A., Furniss, D., Vincent, C.: Patient safety and interactive medical devices: realigning work as imagined and work as done. Clin. Risk **20**, 107–110 (2014)
35. Park, S.Y., Chen, Y.: Adaptation as design: learning from an EMR deployment study. In: Proceedings of the Conference on Human Factors in Computing Systems, Austin, TX, pp. 2097–2106 (2012)
36. Barrett, A.K., Stephens, K.K.: Making electronic health records (EHRs) work: informal talk and workarounds in healthcare organizations. Health Commun. **32**, 1004–1013 (2017)
37. Malaurent, J., Avison, D.: From an apparent failure to a success story: ERP in China - post implementation. Int. J. Inf. Manag. **35**, 643–646 (2015)
38. Reijers, H.A., van Wijk, S., Mutschler, B., Leurs, M.: BPM in practice: who is doing what? In: Hull, R., Mendling, J., Tai, S. (eds.) BPM 2010. LNCS, vol. 6336, pp. 45–60. Springer, Heidelberg (2010). https://doi.org/10.1007/978-3-642-15618-2_6
39. Burlton, R.: BPM critical success factors lessons learned from successful BPM organizations. Bus. Rules J. **12**, 1–6 (2011)
40. Ravesteyn, P., Jansen, S.: A situational implementation method for business process management systems. In: AMCIS 2009 Proceedings, p. 632 (2009)
41. Rosemann, M.: Proposals for future BPM research directions. In: Ouyang, C., Jung, J.-Y. (eds.) AP-BPM 2014. LNBIP, vol. 181, pp. 1–15. Springer, Cham (2014). https://doi.org/10.1007/978-3-319-08222-6_1
42. Rosemann, M., de Bruin, T.: Towards a business process management maturity model. In: ECIS 2005 Proceedings, p. 37 (2005)
43. Malhotra, R., Temponi, C.: Critical decisions for ERP integration: small business issues. Int. J. Inf. Manag. **30**, 28–37 (2010)
44. Germain, R., Spears, N.: Quality management and its relationship with organizational context and design. Int. J. Qual. Reliab. Manag. **16**, 371–392 (1999)

Regulatory Instability, Business Process Management Technology, and BPM Skill Configurations

Patrick Lohmann$^{(\boxtimes)}$ and Michael zur Muehlen$^{(\boxtimes)}$

Stevens Institute of Technology, Castle Point on Hudson, Hoboken 07030, USA
{patrick.lohmann,michael.zurmuehlen}@stevens.edu

Abstract. This paper investigates how firms configure their business process management efforts in different industries. We generate a business process management (BPM) skills taxonomy through the computational linguistic analysis of job ads from Monster.com. We apply the taxonomy to LinkedIn.com resumes of professionals employed at retailer Walmart, pharmaceutical company Pfizer, and investment bank Goldman Sachs. We find that Walmart and Pfizer distribute change- and operations-related BPM skills among the same roles whereas Goldman Sachs distributes both kinds of skills among more separate roles. This separation reflects a trilateral configuration where line managers and analysts focus on operational BPM tasks related to running processes while change-related tasks are covered by project managers. At Walmart and Pfizer the tasks of the BPM project manager are shared among managers and analysts, reflecting a bilateral configuration. Comparing each firm's regulatory environments and BPM technology capabilities, we conjecture that the organizational configuration pattern is influenced by a firm's ability to reliably automate business processes, since this affects how much attention line managers and analysts have to spend on monitoring processes and on reconciling issues and exceptions. This attention could otherwise be spent on regulatory-imposed process change efforts. This configural logic suggests a reconfiguration of BPM professionals towards a bilateral configuration when an organization transforms its business with digital technology, because the focus of such efforts includes process and decision automation.

Keywords: BPM skills · BPM taxonomy · BPM professionals · BPM function

1 Introduction

Regulatory interventions are a frequent source of organizational change in industries such as Pharmaceuticals or Financial Services, whereas other industries such as Retail or Transportation are subject to more measured changes of the regulatory regime. By regulation we mean authoritative operating rules accompanied by some formal governance mechanisms that promote rule compliance and sanction non-compliance and misconduct [2]. Governments typically impose regulation on organizations to increase market stability and transparency by permitting, directing, constraining their operations. When regulations change, organizations need to adapt their policies and

© Springer Nature Switzerland AG 2019
T. Hildebrandt et al. (Eds.): BPM 2019, LNCS 11675, pp. 419–435, 2019.
https://doi.org/10.1007/978-3-030-26619-6_27

procedures, and hence they require business process management (BPM) professionals and a BPM function that can absorb the regulatory instability of their regulatory regime, akin to Ashby's [1] law of requisite variety. Which actions organizations take to match the complexity of their BPM function to that of their regulatory regime is thus an important question for regulators and those affected by regulation alike.

A regulatory regime is unstable when it comprises multiple supervisory authorities that collectively impose rules that are complex and frequently changing. A stable regulatory regime can be characterized by a limited number of authorities and a continuance of rules over time. The instability is different from a regulatory shock, i.e., sudden and extensive changes in the operating constraints [12]. *Regulatory shocks* are typically less predictable and more harmful to the business practices of affected organizations, either because they occur unanticipated (e.g., the imposition of tariffs in a trade conflict) or organizations delay the implementation of substantial rule changes (e.g., new privacy laws). In contrast, *regulatory instability* is a second-order measure of the delta in month-over-month, year-over-year changes in the rule book imposed by the regulatory regime that directs and constrains how business processes can be performed, making it a more predictable variable to which organizations can adapt and attend to.

Individuals are cognitively bounded with regard to how much information they can process at a time, and hence organizations need to configure their professionals to distribute their attention to salient issues and their solutions [22]. When organizations face a regulatory shock such as the introduction of the U.S. Sarbanes-Oxley Act, they often increase and/or complement their business and technology staff through new hires and audit and consulting engagements to ensure regulatory adaptation, and invest in regulatory technology to automate compliance monitoring and control [14, 16]. Unlike a shock, however, an unstable regulatory regime should require continual attention, and it stands to question whether affected organizations simply require more professionals than those operating under a stable regime or whether these organizations make more permanent changes to the configuration of their BPM function to reflect the different tasks performed by different professionals on a daily basis.

The skills of the professionals involved in BPM and their configurations can serve as a suitable proxy for the BPM function overall because organizations frequently practice BPM as a method to analyze, design, implement, monitor, and control their operations, treating processes as the socio-technical change objects [4]. When organizations practice BPM, they assume that processes have an ostensive and a performative aspect [9]. The ostensive aspect describes the process as a model and executable script that specifies the logical workflow design and implementation. The performative aspect relates to the actions performed by human and algorithmic system participants. The skills of BPM professionals constrain the change-related (ostensive) and operations-related (performative) BPM tasks they could possibly perform [21], and their collective configuration provides an upper bound of the ordinary and dynamic capabilities of what the BPM function can achieve in the context of an organization [18, 24].

In this paper, we ask *how the BPM function can be affected by regulatory instability, how such demands translate into different configurations of BPM professionals, and whether BPM technology can mediate between regulatory instability and these configurations.* By *BPM technology* we mean algorithms and computer systems that automate operational tasks and processes, substituting human performance without causing exceptions that require human attention [26]. First, we empirically generate a skills taxonomy from job ads. Second, we apply the taxonomy to public resumes of professionals employed at three organizations from differently regulated industries. Specifically, we look at the BPM skills configurations at retailer Walmart, pharmaceutical company Pfizer, and investment bank Goldman Sachs, exposing the skill configurations of their BPM functions. We interpret the configurations considering the relative differences in the stability of each company's regulatory regime and BPM technology capability.

We find that while the fundamental skills within the BPM functions of Walmart, Pfizer, and Goldman Sachs are similar, their configurations differ. Change- and operations-related BPM skills are distributed among line managers and analysts at unstable-regulated Pfizer. The configuration mirrors that of stable-regulated Walmart, reflecting a bilateral BPM configuration where both roles possess the necessary skills to collectively operate and adapt processes. The skills to operate and adapt processes are more distributed at Goldman Sachs which relies on project managers to complement its line managers and analysts in process change efforts. Goldman Sachs allows its line managers and analysts to attend more to operating business processes, reflecting a trilateral BPM configuration. Comparing the BPM technologies of Pfizer and Goldman Sachs, we conjecture that the BPM configuration also depends on the capacity to automate processes affected by unstable regulation. A sophisticated BPM technology capability can allow line managers and analysts to shift their attention to change-related BPM tasks rather than compliance and escalation-related operational tasks, rendering the project manager redundant when performative process exceptions are caught and resolved by BPM technology as specified in ostensive models and scripts.

2   Regulatory Instability and BPM Professionals

Regulation affects an organization's processes and systems. Organizations that produce similar products or services are historically assigned to the same industry [8], and hence are regulated by the same regulatory regime. Although the designs of their processes often differ, regulation manifests as controls that must be implemented within existing processes (e.g., margin requirements of an investment bank's client borrowing liquidity to trade securities), or that formulate new processes (e.g., which party reports a trade), or that must not be performed (e.g., the trading desk must not engage in proprietary trading). Not all regulation permits and limits the product and service portfolio of organizations, but it may affect internal operating policies and procedures. The stability of the regulatory regime therefore not only varies between organizations from different industries but also between processes and units within the same organization.

As for the United States, the amount of regulation published over time through the Office of the Federal Register can serve as a suitable proxy of an industry's regulatory stability.[1] The number of regulators and rules which organizations must monitor,

---

[1] A list of publications released can be provided by the authors on request.

comply with, and adapt to depend on the size of their product and service portfolio and on their operational footprint because regions and countries can have their own authorities and standards. As for the European Union, it is safe to say that the stability of regulatory regimes is comparable to their U.S. peers. In relative terms, organizations in Consumer Goods and Financial Services are regulated by a more unstable regime, while organization in Retail experience a more stable regime.

Like other individuals, BPM professionals have a finite absorptive capacity to attend to all information. According to the attention-based view, organizations need to specify roles assumed by individuals and their reporting relationships to distribute time and effort to issues that require attention [22]. By *attention* we mean the noticing, enticing, and focusing of time and effort on issues (i.e., problems, threats, and opportunities) and their solutions facing the organization [22]. An unstable regulatory regime is a significant concern for affected organizations, and their challenge is to configure skills into roles so that everyone can effectively perform a finite set of tasks, attending to the subset of information relevant to their tasks. Collectively, the configuration should maintain the capacity to monitor and ensure day-to-day operational compliance and at the same time ensure a timely response to rule volatility imposed by the unstable regime.

The skills required of individuals to perform BPM tasks relevant to their role are commonly outlined in job descriptions [20]. To maintain a BPM capability, organizations need to articulate the skills they deem desirable using some formal or technical language and assign them to roles. BPM roles require operational knowledge and thus sit at middle and lower managerial ranks. We therefore expect organizations independent of their industry to also publicly hire to fill vacancies.

3   Method

We select a method to computationally explore and extract skills from job descriptions that does not rely on a pre-specified classification schema. The categories of such a taxonomy (in our case skills) are unknown because we cannot specify ex-ante which skills organizations seek in the context of their BPM practice and what words they use to articulate their needs. We acknowledge that O*Net provides a generic taxonomy for skills across different professions, but we found that this taxonomy would not allow us to discriminate between managerial and technical professional roles that are characteristic of BPM [17].

3.1   Datasets

Job Ads. We obtained job descriptions from job ads because they describe the perceived deficiencies of organizations in their staffing to maintain specific capabilities [23]. We downloaded the complete set of job ads that contained *business process, BPM, process improvement, process innovation,* or *process change* from Monster.com, resulting in 45,484 job ads published in the U.S. and U.K. between January 2015 and 2016. We removed 20,121 ads related to non-permanent and heavy-industry production occupations, leaving 25,363 job ads. We focused on both countries because they share a similar regulatory regime and language. We randomly sampled 1,000 job ads from Retail (NAICS: 44), Consumer Goods (31), and Financial Services (52), respectively, in order to normalize the amount of text representing any particular sector. Without this step, sectors with more job ads could have biased the generated skills taxonomy. We sampled job ads published by organizations for which we could confirm their industry affiliation through Dun & Bradstreet.

Resumes. Job ads provide a partial window into organizations because they do not expose the skills and roles which they already have. We used resumes to obtain a more complete understanding of the BPM professionals at three theoretically sampled organizations. From LinkedIn.com we downloaded resumes of individuals who self-declared (as of September 2017) to work at retailer Walmart, pharma Pfizer, or investment bank Goldman Sachs. We only included those who used *business process*, *BPM*, *process improvement*, *process innovation*, or *process change* to describe their current full-time occupation. Again, we randomly sampled 1,000 resumes for each organization.

The three organizations are all large-scale in their employee size and among the most professionally-managed ones in their respective industry. From interviews with senior managers of each company, we learned that Goldman Sachs' process automation capability was constrained by that of their counterparties. Pfizer did not experience this degree of interdependence, being less dependent on external parties to complete a business process. Unlike Pfizer, Walmart and Goldman are service organizations but due to the nature of their transaction-like business operations, they have quasi-manufacturing processes.

3.2 Procedure

We generate a BPM skills taxonomy and map the skills of the professionals at Walmart, Pfizer, and Goldman Sachs into the taxonomy. First, we explore latent topics (in our case skills) across all job descriptions. Latent topics are word groups associated with a semantic context. In job ads, the semantic context can be thought of as skills, assuming that organizations can use different words to advertise the same skill. Second, we infer a skill set over each resume and cluster the skill sets for each firm, thereby exposing BPM configurations.

Modeling Skills. We use a topic model widely accepted in the computational linguistics literature [15], which is Latent Dirichlet Allocation (LDA) [5]. LDA is a generative model for classifying documents into multiple topics that are latent in their structure. A topic is a probability distribution over a lexicon. Topics are shared by all documents and the lexicon is shared among all topics. Words that have a high probability within a topic tend to co-occur across documents. LDA infers the classification scheme in form of word-topic and topic-document distributions.

The number of topics expected in the documents must be specified prior to model inference, and the optimal number can be identified by comparing their validity. We use mean topic coherence as an indicator of internal validity, which measures how accurately high-probability words of a topic do co-occur across documents [6]. Perplexity measures external validity, the capacity of the inferred word-topic distributions to capture word co-occurrences in previously unseen documents [5]. We run three-fold cross-validation to train and test each model, obtaining a more robust score. Both mean topic coherence and perplexity are technical scores and their interpretation should not go beyond model comparison.

Mapping Skills and Roles. We infer a topic-document distribution over an imaginary document composed of a resume's current job title, description, and skills using the topic model which we identify as optimal in the previous step. To explore variation in the skill configurations, we group the topic-document distributions and run separate cluster analyses for each firm. We cluster skill sets based on their pairwise Hellinger distances using a bottom-up algorithm (the Ward method) that aims to minimize the total within-cluster variance at each level. The emerging clusters can be thought of as distinct roles, i.e., skill sets. To interpret the clusters in a particular layer, we look at the most-representative resumes which we define as those whose topic-document distributions are closest to the mean distribution, i.e., the topic-role distribution, of all resumes assigned to a particular cluster. In other words, we look at the cluster centroids.

3.3   Analysis

We performed a number of text reduction steps to the job ads [15]. The outcome was a lexicon and sentence vectors counting the frequency with which each word occurred in a sentence. Not all information provided in job ads refer to the job description [23], and hence we cleansed them.

Removing Duplicate Job Ads. We removed duplicates based on the cosine distance of their aggregated sentence vectors. The .10-threshold yielded the best F-measure (.90) in detecting duplicates as classified by two researchers (Cohen's $\kappa = .78$). The threshold was conservative, given that the average job ad contained 93 distinct words (s.d. = 46). We identified 7,860 job ads as being duplicates, leaving 17,503.

Removing Noise Sentences. We applied LDA over the sentences to remove those that obviously did not address skills but contextual information. The idea was to interpret each sentence as a distribution of domain topics and noise topics, and to remove sentences from a job ad that exhibit a high probability of being associated with a noise topic. The 40-topic model provided the best balance between internal and external validity, separating distinct themes into different topics. We treated a topic as noise when it addressed a theme that was obviously not domain-related ($\kappa = .93$). A .50-threshold yielded the best F-measure (.82, $\kappa = .74$) in detecting noise sentences, resulting into a removal of 77,700 sentences (19.6%).

Modeling Skills. We aggregated the remaining sentence vectors for each job ad and reran LDA. The 24-topics model generated substantive topics and provided the best balance between internal and external validity. Two researchers independently labeled each topic and synthesized final labels with a third researcher.[2]

Mapping Skills and Roles. We selected the 24-topic model to infer a topic-document distribution over each resume's relevant sections which we identified by their proper HTML tags. We grouped the resumes for each firm and evaluated the cluster solutions. The best solution was identified by a distinct bent when being plotted and validated using the gap statistic which measures the goodness of a solution relative to a randomly sampled solution of the same number of clusters [25]. Both indicators suggested the five-cluster solution for Walmart and the six-cluster solution for Pfizer and Goldman Sachs, which produced simple models that exposed the fundamental structural differences between their respective BPM skill configurations. Two researchers independently inferred cluster labels from the skill configurations and job titles of the representative resumes and synthesized them with a third researcher.

4   Findings

We interpret the BPM skills as being related to either change- or operations-related tasks. Change-related BPM skills help to intentionally change the design, models, organizational structures, and software code of a business process (i.e., ostensive aspects [9]) and to translate such changes into operations (i.e., performative aspects). Operations-related BPM skills support individuals to align the actual operations of the process with its intended design to stabilize and standardize them. Together, both types of skills provide the basis for adapting and operating processes and systems.

Figures 1, 2, and 3 illustrate the skill configurations at Walmart, Pfizer, and Goldman Sachs. The dark crosses and circles represent the change- and operations-related skills ($\kappa = .94$). Their relative positioning on the map reflects the similarity of their underlying word-topic distributions generated by our LDA. To compare differences in the configurations, the opaqueness of a curve that links a skill with a cluster center is a function of whether the skill receives a cluster relevance that is within the 90th, 80th, 70th, or 60th percentile of skill attentions across all clusters.

4.1   BPM Professionals at Walmart

The professionals within Walmart's BPM function suggest a configuration into three line manager and two analyst roles (see Fig. 1). The *front-office manager* aggregates professionals skilled to perform and administer customer-facing functions such as marketing and sales. The *back-office manager* bundles those who work in enterprise- and partner-facing functions, e.g., finance and accounting. The *operations manager* comprises supply chain and logistics professionals. All three manager roles possess skills related with operations-related BPM, however, some change-related skills appear to be boundary-spanning in the sense that they integrate the roles: *business strategy, product development, business transformation,* and *change management* are shared

---

[2] A list of high-probability words per topic can be provided by the authors on request.

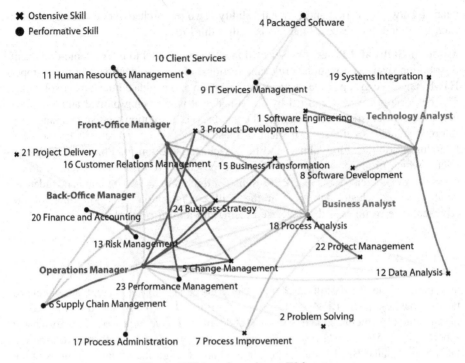

✖ Ostensive Skill
● Performative Skill

4 Packaged Software

10 Client Services

11 Human Resources Management ●

19 Systems Integration ✖

9 IT Services Management

Front-Office Manager

1 Software Engineering   Technology Analyst
✖ 3 Product Development

✖ 21 Project Delivery

16 Customer Relations Management   15 Business Transformation

8 Software Development

Back-Office Manager

Business Analyst

20 Finance and Accounting

24 Business Strategy

18 Process Analysis

13 Risk Management

22 Project Management

Operations Manager   5 Change Management

12 Data Analysis ✖

23 Performance Management

● 6 Supply Chain Management

2 Problem Solving ✖

17 Process Administration   7 Process Improvement

Fig. 1. BPM configuration at Walmart

change-related skills. These managers are typically responsible for the bottom-up championing and the top-down implementation of strategic programs, and hence they need the people skills necessary to execute and deliver operational changes, reflected in the *performance management* skill of *front-office* and *operations managers*. Walmart's back-office operations are highly-automated with their SAP systems, and hence performance management is less of a concern for *back-office managers*.

The *business analyst* role links to typical process project-related skills such as *project management*, *process analysis*, and *software engineering*, whereas professionals aggregated under the *technology analyst* role are skilled in *software development* and *systems integration* but also *data analysis*. Both roles link mostly to change-related BPM skills with the *business analyst* occupying a central position within the BPM configuration as an interface between business and technology. This configuration mirrors the common understanding of analyst role in the literature as a boundary spanner and knowledge broker. This role appears to be more assigned to a process on a project basis in order for its optimization or change.

The skills of *technology analysts* reflect Walmart's IT strategy to have a commercial ERP system for the standardization of non-differentiating processes, while engineering merchandizing and supply chain systems more on their own as a measure to better integrate e-commerce and department-store operations. The responsibilities for new software developments reside in Walmart's digital business unit Global

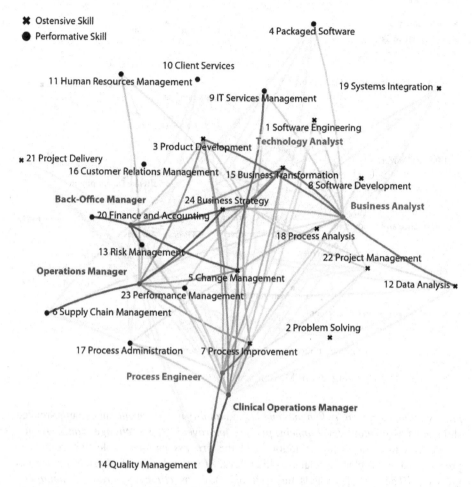

Fig. 2. BPM configuration at Pfizer

eCommerce, and hence it is plausible that Walmart's *technology analysts* are mostly skilled in the integration of backbone application systems.

4.2 BPM Professionals at Pfizer

The professionals within Pfizer's BPM function are grouped into three manager and three analyst roles (see Fig. 2). The *back-office manager* and *operations manager* comprise professionals with skills similar to their peers at Walmart which makes sense due to the similarity of their business models of selling physical products. Pfizer sells its products to commercial businesses rather than end consumers, which can explain the missing *front-office manager* role because out-bound processes are under the auspices of operations managers. Instead, a *clinical operations manager* role bundles the professionals skilled to monitor and control the new drug and medicine development processes. Professionals in this role possess operations-related BPM skills related to

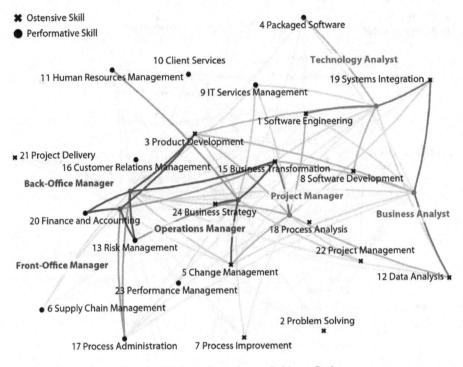

Fig. 3. BPM configuration at Goldman Sachs

process administration, risk management, and *quality management*, and change-related skills such as *product development, process improvement*, and *change management*.

Pfizer's manufacturing operations add the *process engineer* role that comprises professionals with change-related skills relevant for the design of physical production processes. These professionals have similar skills as *clinical operations managers*, however, *process engineers* are those who can engineer reliable manufacturing processes, according to their resumes. *Process engineers* are skilled to analyze, design, and improve the high-volume processes whose performances are highly automated within the firm. The *clinical operations manager* monitors and controls processes such as clinical trials which involve different actors from within and outside of the firm and which are less standardizable in their performance. The *business analyst* role summarizes skills akin to its peer at Walmart. Pfizer's *technology analysts* are more strategic-oriented towards change, as reflected in the links to *business strategy, product development, business transformation*, and *change management*. Neither the *business analyst* nor the *technology analyst* exposes software development and engineering skills, suggesting a skills chasm between the firm's BPM and IT function.

4.3 BPM Professionals at Goldman Sachs

The professionals within Goldman Sachs' BPM function are grouped into four manager and two analyst roles (see Fig. 3). The *front-office* and *back-office managers* comprise professionals with skills mostly related to operations-related BPM such as *risk management, process administration*, and *finance and accounting*, however, the development of new innovative financial products is also part of their skill sets. This suggest that these professionals see their role more focused on identifying, monitoring and controlling (new ways of) revenue-generating client interactions and transactions in alignment with the firm's risk appetite. The *operations manager* bundles the professionals skilled in change-related BPM, according to the links to *business strategy, product development, business transformation*, and *change management*. *Risk management* and *IT services management* being operations-related skills seem to be also their concern.

The emphasis of skills of Goldman Sachs' managers on emphasizing risk, compliance, and administration compared with a relatively technical orientation of their *business analysts* arguably necessitates the existence of the *project manager* role that comprises professionals with design and change skills to coordinate between business and technology. These professionals possess a skill set comparable to Walmart's business analysts.

5 Discussion

We asked how organizations configure their BPM professionals to attend to the changes caused by regulation. Our three cases suggest that organizations whose processes are regulated by an unstable regime separate change- from operations-related BPM tasks if the processes require extensive manual monitoring and control by managers and analysts. If operations-related BPM tasks are automated by BPM technology, less manual operational attention is needed. A higher BPM technology capability could allow end-to-end workflow automation with minimum exceptions, substituting human by algorithmic attention. Eliminating humans from a process can reduce variation between intended and actual process operations because processes are executed as specified by the model and executable script. This allows managers and analysts to attend more to change-related BPM tasks and regulatory adaptation. This configuration is reflected in the BPM professionals of an organization that is regulated by a stable regime. We thus distinguish between a *bilateral* and a *trilateral BPM configuration* and conjecture that the configuration of an organization operating under an unstable regulatory regime also depends on its BPM technology capability.

5.1 Bilateral and Trilateral BPM Configuration

The intended (ostensive) and actual (performative) operation of a process are in constant friction. That means the performative process can become the ostensive process when being performed repeatedly in deviation from its intended design, and the ostensive process may change even though this change does not materialize in the actual performance of the process [9]. Regulation affects an organization's ostensive processes, followed by the performative processes. That said, regulatory compliance is assessed against the performative processes, not the ostensive ones.

The *ostensive misfit* between external regulatory requirements and internal ostensive processes and the *performative misfit* between ostensive and performative processes impose pressures on an organization and demand attention. Both ostensive and performative misfits represent "exceptions," and BPM professionals have finite attention to address and solve all exceptions given finite time. Depending on the frequency of regulatory changes triggering ostensive misfits and the provenance of performative misfits, we propose that organizations rely either on a bilateral or trilateral configuration of their BPM professionals to maintain the necessary absorptive capacity to attend to these exceptions and their resolution (see Fig. 4).

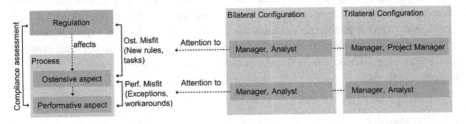

Fig. 4. Bilateral and trilateral BPM configuration

If the regulatory regime is stable, then exceptions are mostly caused by performative misfits. A bilateral BPM configuration allows to align the performance of processes to their intended designs, and to execute and implement intended changes because professionals combine the necessary BPM skills for design and execution. Performative misfits are either caused by individuals or technology performing process activities. Managers can coordinate and solve human misalignments whereas algorithmic misalignments are solved by analysts. Managers monitor and control everyday process operations to maintain performative fit, applying methods such as Lean Management to alter ostensive processes and Six Sigma to translate such changes into measurable performative improvements. These managers have the skills to identify performance problems and their root causes, and take action for their resolution. Business and technology analysts address algorithmic misalignments, and resolving such misfits is an ostensive rather than performative problem because it requires changes to executable scripts. The bilateral interactions between the professionals required to change ostensive and performative processes are characteristic of the bilateral BPM configuration.

Regulation is published as a complex web of textual non-machine-readable documents and are often written with a significant amount of ambiguity. Implementing new regulations is not a straight-forward task. It imposes significant amounts of sense-making time on human individuals. This sense-making involves understanding the documents and their relations to others, assessing implications on processes, and searching for an optimal way to implement requirements and change policies and procedures. This adaptation demands special attention [26].

Martinez-Moyano et al. [19] explain how agency problems in investment banks such as Goldman Sachs cause profit maximization pressures that run against compliance, increasing rule violations that in the absence of intervention derail the business. Pfizer faces similar tensions between maximizing output and ensuring regulatory compliance of its production processes. Its higher BPM technology capability though requires managers and analysts to spend less of their time with monitoring and control the compliancy of their operations, reflecting a bilateral BPM configuration. These processes have a higher straight-through processing rate to benefit from scale economies, allowing managers and analysts focus more on engineering rather than administration. It is therefore not surprising that these professionals are more engineers than classical analysts, indicating the comprehensive tasks performed by these professionals.

If the regulatory regime is unstable *and* processes *can* be reliably automated by BPM technology to cause minimum performative misfit that requires human intervention, ostensive misfits caused by differences between an organization's regulatory requirements and ostensive processes become the major source requiring attention. Under such a condition, managers and analysts can focus on regulatory realignment because BPM systems control and perform processes and activities. Ostensive changes to executable scripts directly translate into their automated performance.

Unlike Pharmaceutics, Financial Services is a heavily vertically-disintegrated industry with by many specialized firms buying and selling financial products both electronically and over the counter. Goldman Sachs processed more than one million trades per day with a straight-through processing rate of about 96% at the time of our data collection, with a significant amount of time of their operations managers and analysts being consumed by reconciling errors and interruptions. While Pfizer has more control of its unstably-regulated processes because it can buffer them from upstream and downstream partners, the capability of financial services providers to perform with minimal exceptions also depends on the technology capability of their counterparties because financial services production and delivery processes are heavily inter-organizational. The capability algorithmically buffer internal operations from, and reconcile, counterparty-caused exceptions depends on a firm's ability to develop automatable ostensive scripts that can algorithmically catch and handle such issues. The complexity in market interactions makes such engineering efforts inherently difficult.

If the regulatory regime is unstable *and* performative processes *cannot* be reliably automated because BPM technology has a lower capability, the organization simultaneously faces pressures from ostensive and performative misfits. Under such a condition, we propose that the organization relies on a trilateral BPM configuration because managers and analysts are more concerned with reconciling and resolving performative misfits to ensure that processes achieve their desired outcome. Therefore, a project manager addresses ostensive misfits, being in charge of redesign and adaptation. The trilateral interactions between the professionals required to change ostensive and performative processes allow an organization to maintain the requisite absorptive capacity to cope with an unstable regulatory regime when operational attention cannot be shifted to BPM technology.

Not all processes of an unstable-regulated organization experience regulatory instability. For example, regulatory requirements of typical support processes such as human resources and payroll are often stable. Different unstable-regulated processes typically also have a different BPM technology capability. We conjecture that organizations change such processes by applying a bilateral approach, coordinated by analysts rather than project managers because such processes require less attention to ostensive misfits. The bilateral and trilateral BPM configurations are not necessarily mutually-exclusive but can coexist within the same organization. Rather, these organizations situationally switch between a bilateral and trilateral approach to process management within their trilateral BPM configuration. We find support for this conjecture in Goldman Sachs' *analyst* and *project manager* clusters, which absorb process engineers in their periphery. These engineers have skills akin to Pfizer's process engineers – for digital rather than physical processes.

5.2 Implications

While our analysis is motivated by the bottom-up clustering and aggregation of skills of human individuals into collective skill configurations at three industry-leading firms, in practice it is more plausible that these organizations take a decompositional approach by assessing their regulatory regime and BPM technology capability first, and by specifying the roles and their required skills accordingly. Regardless of whether such specifications are based on macro-to-micro decomposition principles or micro-to-macro aggregation principles, or a mix of both, our cross-sectional analysis cuts levels of organizational analysis. We show how macro-level effects about regulatory instability and technology can relate with micro-level skill configurations of an organization's BPM practice. These configurations represent a human resources-based perspective on the microfoundations of an organization's ambidextrous process management capability that addresses the ostensive and performative issues that require attention [20]. Arguably because of a shortage of analysis techniques and datasets, the linkage between microfoundations (individual, skills) and macrofoundations (organization, capability) is mostly a theoretical debate [3, 10]. Our contributions here are methodwise, and our approach to uncover skills and configurations can help other academics better understand the linkages between individual and organizational aspects affecting human resources and organizational performance both within and outside of BPM [7].

On the practical side, our discovered configurations can serve as a basis for professionals in charge of a BPM practice better assess their current BPM target operating model, linking roles, skills, and capability. Digital and information technologies reduce vertical layers of management hierarchy [11, 13]. However, BPM technology may also alter the horizontal structuring of managers when processes become digitized and their operations automated. BPM technology capability creates options for Chief Process Officers to rethink the skill sets required of their staff to better enable and support the digital transformation of their organization over time. As organizations continue to automate their routine and non-routine tasks with artificial intelligence and machine learning, robotic process automation, cognitive agents, and distributed ledger technology, among other technologies, these digital transformations turn operations-related BPM tasks inherently into engineering problems. Chief Process Officers should keep an eye on their BPM technology capability and put in place plans for the enterprise-wide education and reskilling professionals involved in the operational management and administration of processes to allow for a shift from a potential trilateral configuration to a bilateral one. We speculate that digitally-transformed organizations can allow their managers and analysts to attend more to the innovation of minimum viable products and services. However, our analysis does not consider performance measures of both configurations, and hence future research should try to link both configurations with organizational performance implications.

5.3   Limitations

While our study provides important insights into the skills and configurations of BPM professionals, our findings are subject to a limitation that relates to the nature of job ads and self-reported resumes as a research dataset. For example, an organization may announce a presumed vacancy less with the motivation to fill this role but to be recognized as a legitimate business partner for (potential) customers. Unstable-regulated industries may be more likely to write about governance, risk, and compliance in their job ads than organizations operating under a more stable regulatory regime, ultimately paying less attention to other skills and tasks relevant to the role.

We tried to mitigate this concern by generating a common skills taxonomy across the Retail, Consumer Goods, and Financial Services industries rather than an industry-specific skills taxonomy, and by mapping the resumes into the common taxonomy. Similar concerns may exist for the skills and job descriptions reported in resumes. Professionals certainly use LinkedIn.com to connect and advertise themselves to increase their visibility and attractiveness for other employers, and hence they will likely select words in their resumes that add to their employability. We addressed this potential self-reporting bias methodologically by selecting a randomly-sampled and sufficiently large amount of resumes, and by averaging the skills reported in each research, looking at the cluster centroids rather than peripheries. The findings provide insights into the *means* and not ends of the BPM configurations of three theoretically-sampled organizations. Future research should test the BPM configurations and conjectures to a broader set of organizations, industries, and aim to establish a link between BPM skill configurations and performance implications of these organizations.

6   Conclusion

An organization's BPM technology can play an important mediating function between its regulatory regime and the configuration of its BPM professionals. Investment bank Goldman Sachs is an example of how a lower process automation capability can be associated with a trilateral BPM configuration that is used to maintain absorptive capacity to attend to the ostensive and performative misfits caused by regulation and operation. Pfizer is an organization that manages to maintain a higher automation capability within an unstable regulatory context and appears to be able to transfer performative BPM tasks from its professionals to the technology, reflecting a bilateral BPM configuration. This configuration mirrors that of an organization that operates under a stable regulatory regime, exemplified by our analysis of Walmart.

References

1. Ashby, W.R.: An Introduction to Cybernetics. Chapman & Hall, London (1956)
2. Baldwin, R., Scott, C., Hood, C.: A Reader on Regulation. Oxford University Press, Oxford (1998)
3. Barney, J., Felin, T.: What are microfoundations? Acad. Manag. Perspect. **27**, 138–155 (2013)
4. Benner, M.J., Tuschman, M.L.: Exploitation, exploration, and process management: the productivity dilemma revisited. Acad. Manag. Rev. **29**, 238–256 (2003)
5. Blei, D.M., Ng, A.Y., Jordan, M.I.: Latent Dirichlet allocation. J. Mach. Learn. **3**, 993–1022 (2003)
6. Boyd-Graber, J.L., Mimno, D., Newman, D.: Care and feeding of topic models: problems, diagnostics, and improvements. In: Handbook of Mixed Membership Models and their Applications. CRC Press (2014)
7. vom Brocke, J., Zelt, S., Schmiedel, T.: On the Role of Context in Business Process Management. Int. J. Inf. Manag. **36**, 486–495 (2016)
8. Executive Office of the President: National Industry Classification System (2017)
9. Feldman, M.S., Pentland, B.T.: Reconceptualizing organizational routines as a source of flexibility and change. Adm. Sci. Q. **48**, 94–118 (2003)
10. Felin, T., Foss, N.J., Heimeriks, K.H., Madsen, T.L.: Microfoundations of routines and capabilities: individuals, processes, and structure. J. Manag. Stud. **49**, 1351–1374 (2012)
11. Frey, C.B., Osborne, M.A.: The future of employment: how susceptible are jobs to computerization. University of Oxford (2013)
12. Haveman, H.A., Russo, M.V., Meyer, A.D.: Organizational environments in flux: the impact of regulatory punctuations on organizational domains. Organ. Sci. **12**, 253–273 (2001)
13. Hickson, D.J., Pugh, D.S., Pheysey, D.C.: Operations technology and organization structure: an empirical reappraisal. Adm. Sci. Q. **14**, 378–397 (1969)
14. Iliev, P.: The effect of SOX Section 404: costs, earnings quality, and stock prices. J. Finance **65**, 1163–1196 (2010)
15. Jurafsky, D., Martin, J.H.: Speech and Language Processing: An Introduction to Natural Language Processing. Prentice Hall, Upper Saddle River (2009)
16. Krishnan, J., Rama, D., Zhang, Y.: Costs to comply with SOX Section 404. Audit. J. Pract. Theory **27**, 169–186 (2008)
17. Lohmann, P., zur Muehlen, M.: Business process management skills and roles: an investigation of the demand and supply side of BPM professionals. In: 13th International Conference on Business Process Management (2015)
18. Martin, J.A.: Dynamic managerial capabilities. Organ. Sci. **22**, 118–140 (2011)
19. Martinez-Moyano, I.J., McCaffrey, D.P., Oliva, R.: Drift and adjustment in organizational rule compliance: explaining the "regulatory pendulum" in financial markets. Organ. Sci. **25**, 321–338 (2017)
20. Molloy, J.C., Barney, J.B.: Who captures the value created with human capital? A market-based view. Acad. Manag. Perspect. **29**, 309–325 (2015)
21. Nelson, R.R., Winter, S.G.: An Evolutionary Theory of Economic Change. Harvard University Press, Cambridge (1982)
22. Ocasio, W.: Towards an attention-based view of the firm. Strateg. Manag. J. **18**, 187–206 (1997)
23. Rafaeli, A., Oliver, A.L.: Employment ads: a configurational research agenda. J. Manag. Inq. **7**, 342–358 (1998)

24. Röglinger, M., Schwindenhammer, L., Stelzl, K.: How to put organizational ambidexterity into practice – towards a maturity model. In: Weske, M., Montali, M., Weber, I., vom Brocke, J. (eds.) BPM 2018. LNBIP, vol. 329, pp. 194–210. Springer, Cham (2018). https://doi.org/10.1007/978-3-319-98651-7_12

25. Tibshirani, R., Walther, G., Hastie, T.: Estimating the number of clusters in a data set via the gap statistic. J. Roy. Stat. Soc. B **63**, 411–423 (2001)

26. Woodward, R.E.: Task complexity: definition of the construct. Organ. Behav. Hum. Decis. Process. **37**, 60–82 (1986)

Author Index